Defect

Detect

DUmps Binaries Logs INternals

School of Security

Linux

Core Dump Analysis

Accelerated

Fourth Edition

Dmitry Vostokov
Software Diagnostics Services

Accelerated Linux Core Dump Analysis: Training Course Transcript with GDB and WinDbg Practice Exercises, Fourth Edition

Published by OpenTask, Republic of Ireland

OpenTask books and magazines are available through booksellers and distributors worldwide. For further information or comments, send requests to press@opentask.com.

A CIP catalog record for this book is available from the British Library.

ISBN-13: 978-1-912636-49-5 (Paperback)

Revision 4.01 (January 2025)

Contents

About the Author

Dmitry Vostokov is an internationally recognized expert, speaker, educator, scientist, inventor, and author. He founded the pattern-oriented software diagnostics, forensics, and prognostics discipline (Systematic Software Diagnostics) and Software Diagnostics Institute (DA+TA: DumpAnalysis.org + TraceAnalysis.org). Vostokov has also authored over 50 books on software diagnostics, anomaly detection and analysis, software and memory forensics, root cause analysis and problem solving, memory dump analysis, debugging, software trace and log analysis, reverse engineering, and malware analysis. He has over 30 years of experience in software architecture, design, development, and maintenance in various industries, including leadership, technical, and people management roles. Dmitry founded OpenTask Iterative and Incremental Publishing (OpenTask.com) and Software Diagnostics Technology and Services (former Memory Dump Analysis Services) PatternDiagnostics.com. In his spare time, he explores Software Narratology and Quantum Software Diagnostics. His interest areas are theoretical software diagnostics and its mathematical and computer science foundations, application of formal logic, semiotics, artificial intelligence, machine learning, and data mining to diagnostics and anomaly detection, software diagnostics engineering and diagnostics-driven development, diagnostics workflow and interaction. Recent interest areas also include functional programming, cloud native computing, monitoring, observability, visualization, security, automation, applications of category theory to software diagnostics, development and big data, and diagnostics of artificial intelligence.

Presentation Slides and Transcript

Hello, everyone, my name is Dmitry Vostokov, and I teach this training course.

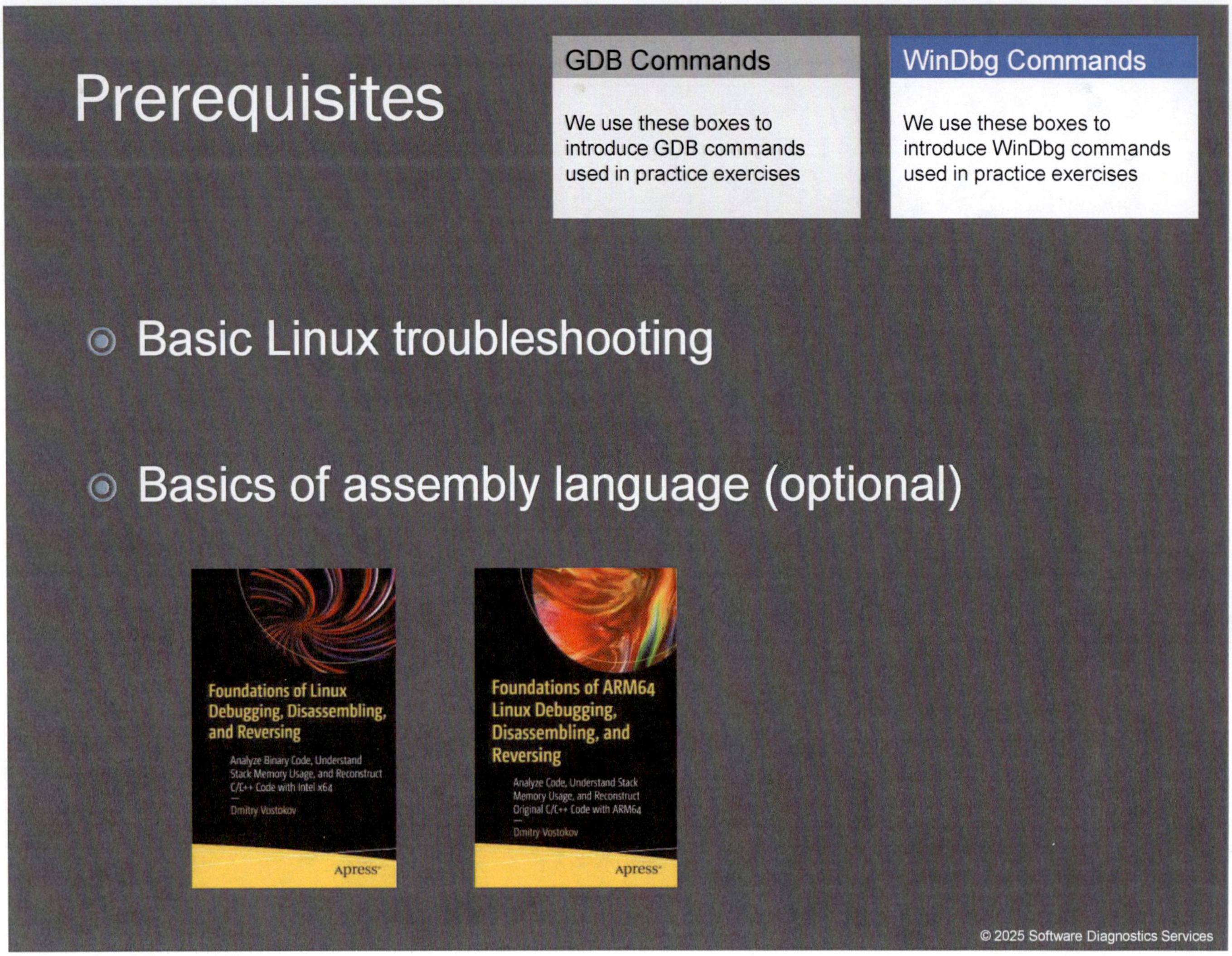

The prerequisites are hard to define. Some of you have software development experience, and some do not. However, one thing is certain: to get most of this training, you are expected to have basic troubleshooting experience. Another thing I expect you to be familiar with is hexadecimal notation and that you have seen or can read programming source code in some language. The ability to read assembly language has some advantages but is not really necessary for this training. Windows memory dump analysis experience may help ease the transition but is not absolutely necessary. If you have read either **Accelerated macOS Core Dump Analysis** or **Accelerated Windows Memory Dump Analysis** book or both, you may find a similar approach here. You may also find the additional Linux assembly language books useful:

Foundations of Linux Debugging, Disassembling, and Reversing
https://link.springer.com/book/10.1007/978-1-4842-9153-5

Foundations of ARM64 Linux Debugging, Disassembling, and Reversing
https://link.springer.com/book/10.1007/978-1-4842-9082-8

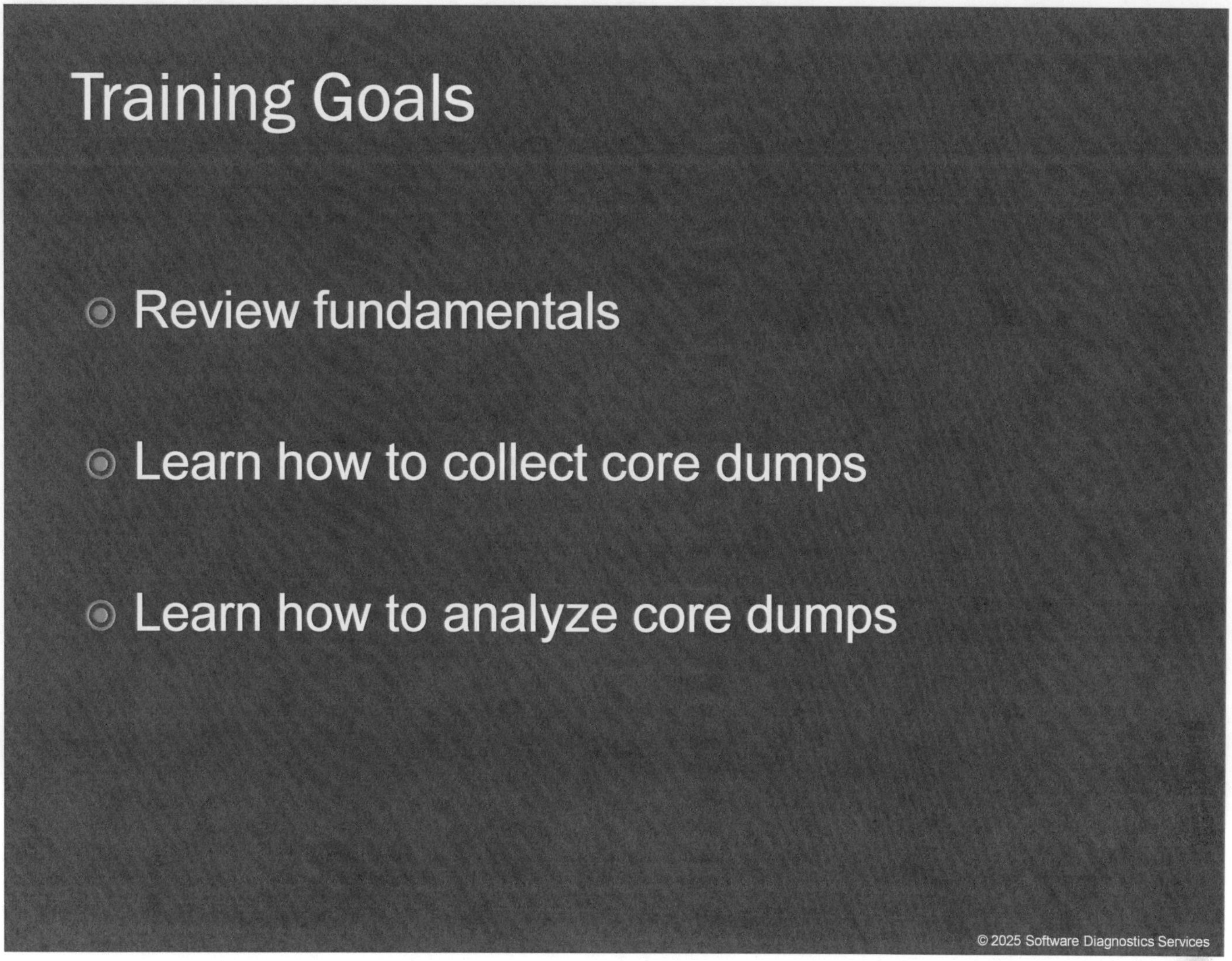

Our primary goal is to learn core dump analysis in an accelerated fashion. So first, we review absolutely essential fundamentals necessary for core dump analysis. Also, this training is mostly about user process core dump analysis with an accelerated transition to kernel core dump analysis, a topic fully explored in the follow-up course and book **Advanced Linux Core Dump Analysis with Data Structures**. An additional goal is to leverage Windows or macOS debugging and memory dump analysis experience you may have.

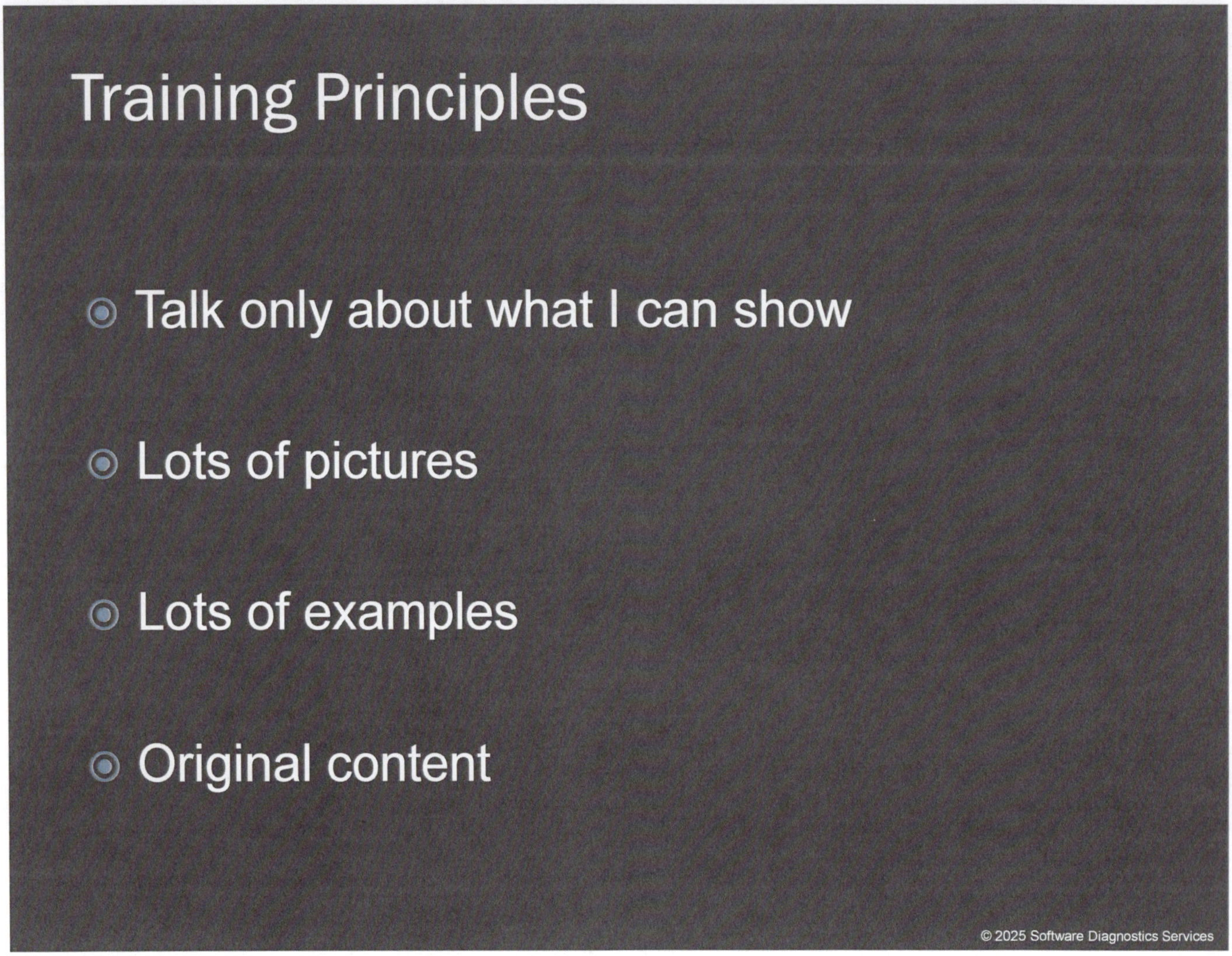

For me, there were many training formats to consider, and I decided that the best way is to concentrate on hands-on exercises. Specifically, for this training, I developed more than 50 of them, and they utilize the same pattern-oriented approach I used in **Accelerated Windows Memory Dump Analysis** and **Accelerated macOS Core Dump Analysis** training.

Schedule Overview

- Analysis fundamentals (x64 and ARM64)
- Process core dump collection
- Basic x64 assembly language review (GDB)
- Basic ARM64 assembly language review
- Process GDB core dump analysis (x64 and ARM64)
- Basic x64 assembly language review (WinDbg)
- Process WinDbg core dump analysis (x64 and ARM64)
- Kernel core dump collection
- Kernel core dump analysis (Crash tool, x64 and ARM64)
- Kernel core dump analysis (WinDbg)
- New analysis patterns
- Mechanisms

This slide shows a roughly planned schedule subject to changes as we go. Changes from the previous edition are also highlighted.

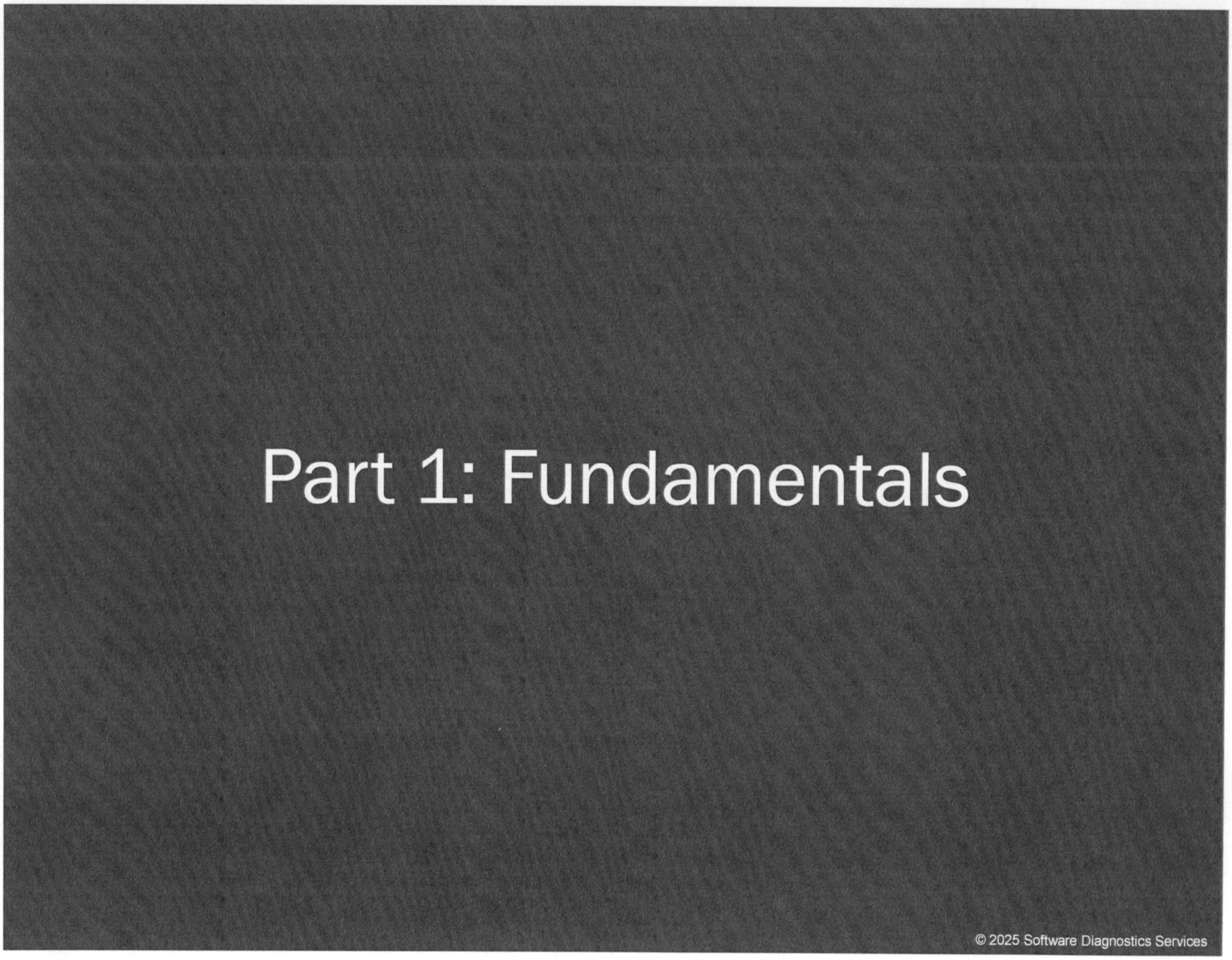

Now, I show you some pictures. I use 64-bit examples. Most of the time, fundamentals do not change when we move to 32-bit Linux, and the analysis process is mostly the same.

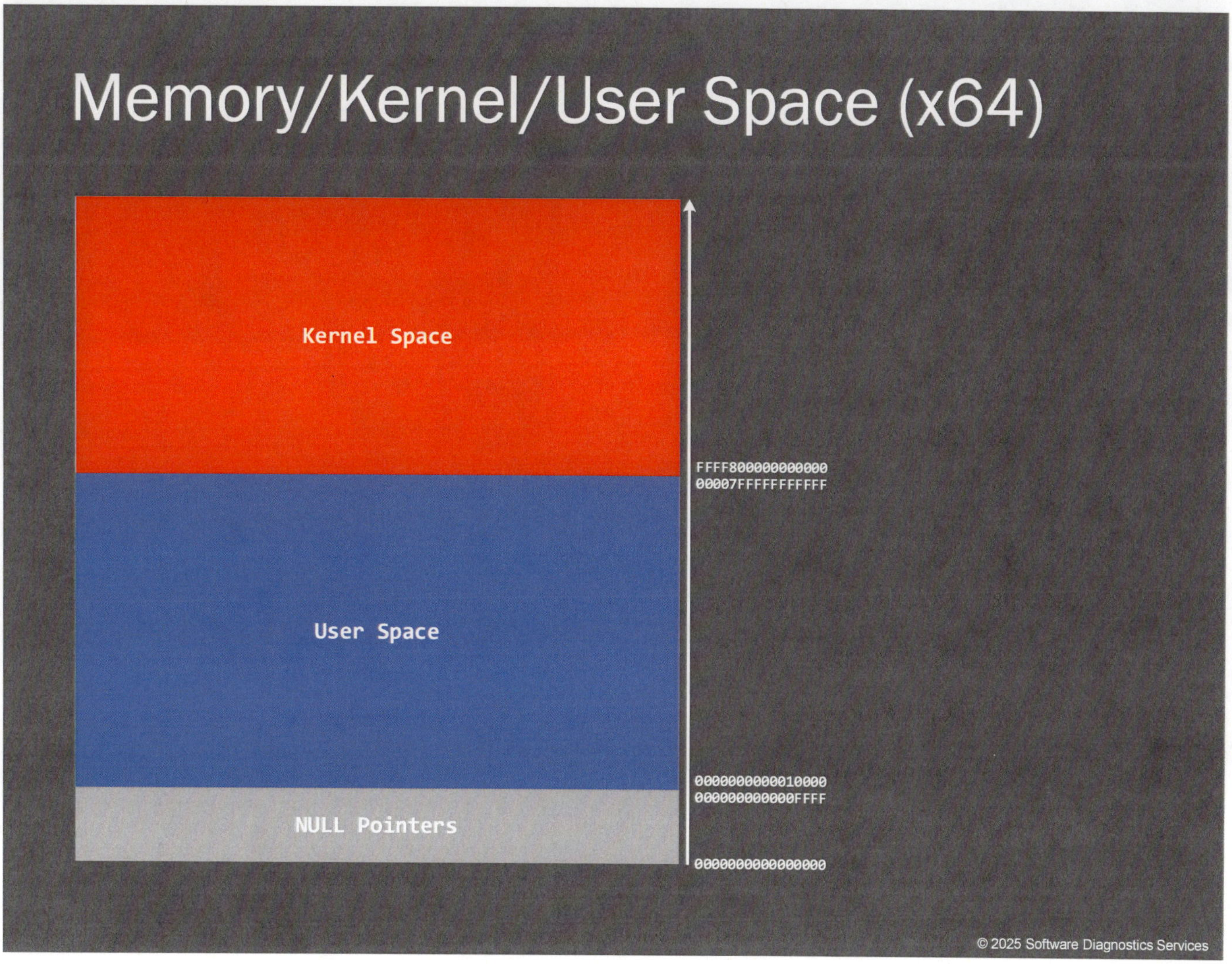

If you come from Windows or macOS background, you find fundamentals almost the same. For every process, the Linux memory range is divided into the kernel and user space parts and an inaccessible part for catching null pointers[1]. This non-accessible region is different from macOS, where it is 1 GB. I follow the long tradition of using red for the kernel and blue for the user part. Please note that there is a difference between space and mode. The mode is the execution privilege attribute; for example, code running in kernel space has a higher execution privilege than code running in user space. However, kernel code can access user space and access data there. We say that such code is running in kernel mode. On the contrary, the application code from user space is running in user mode, and because of its lower privilege, it cannot access kernel space. This division prevents accidental kernel modifications. Otherwise, you could easily crash your system. I put the addresses on the right. This uniform memory space is called virtual process space because it is an abstraction that allows us to analyze core dumps without thinking about how it is all organized in physical memory. When we look at process dumps, we are concerned with virtual space only. This diagram is for x64 Linux. I show changes for the ARM64 platform on the next slide.

[1] On my x64 Debian system it is 0xFFFF, as seen from /proc/sys/vm/mmap_min_addr value.

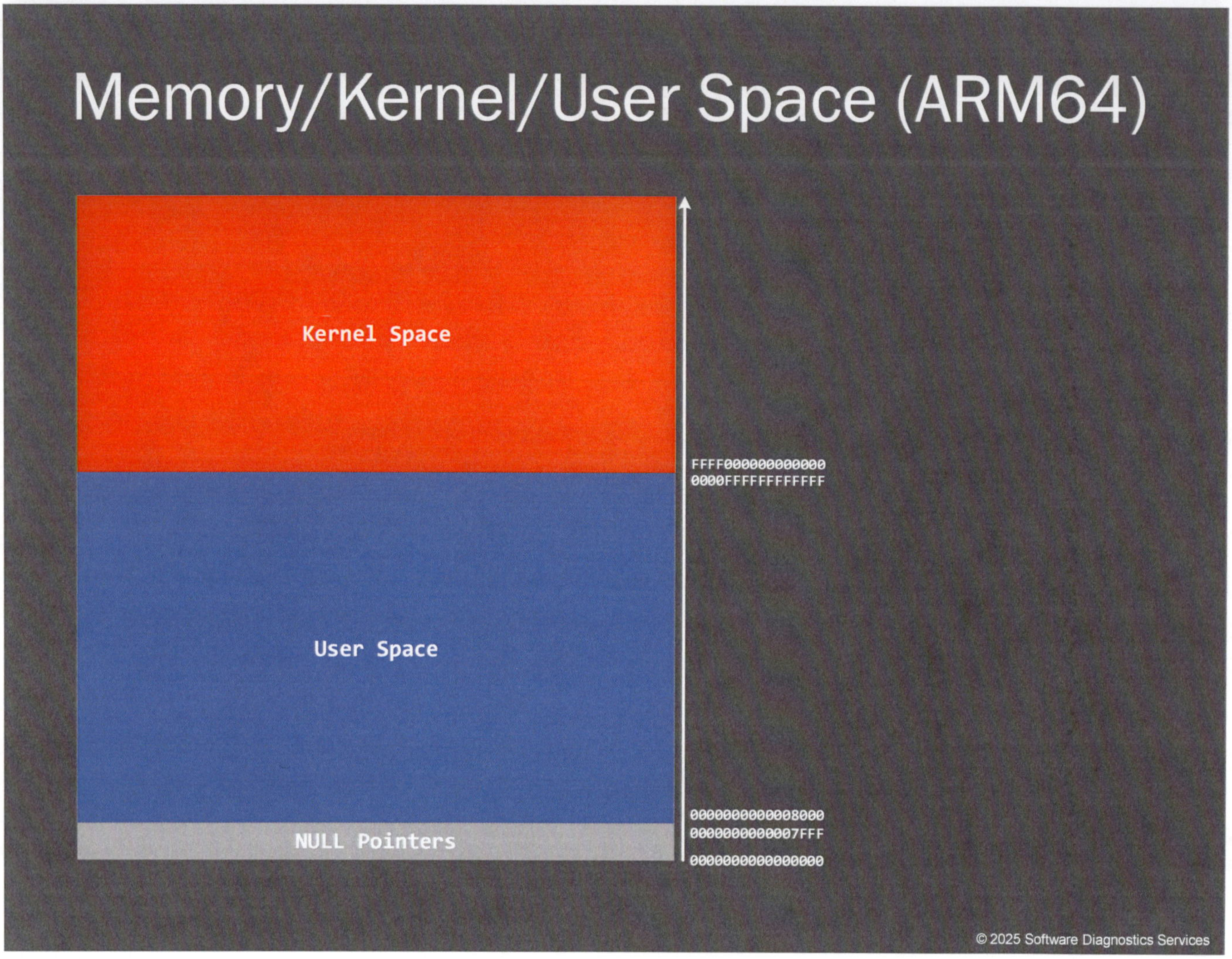

On ARM64 Linux, the address ranges are slightly different, including the default inaccessible part for catching null pointers[2]. The following slides assume an x64 Linux system.

---

[2] On my ARM64 Ubuntu system it is 0x7FFF, as seen from /proc/sys/vm/mmap_min_addr value.

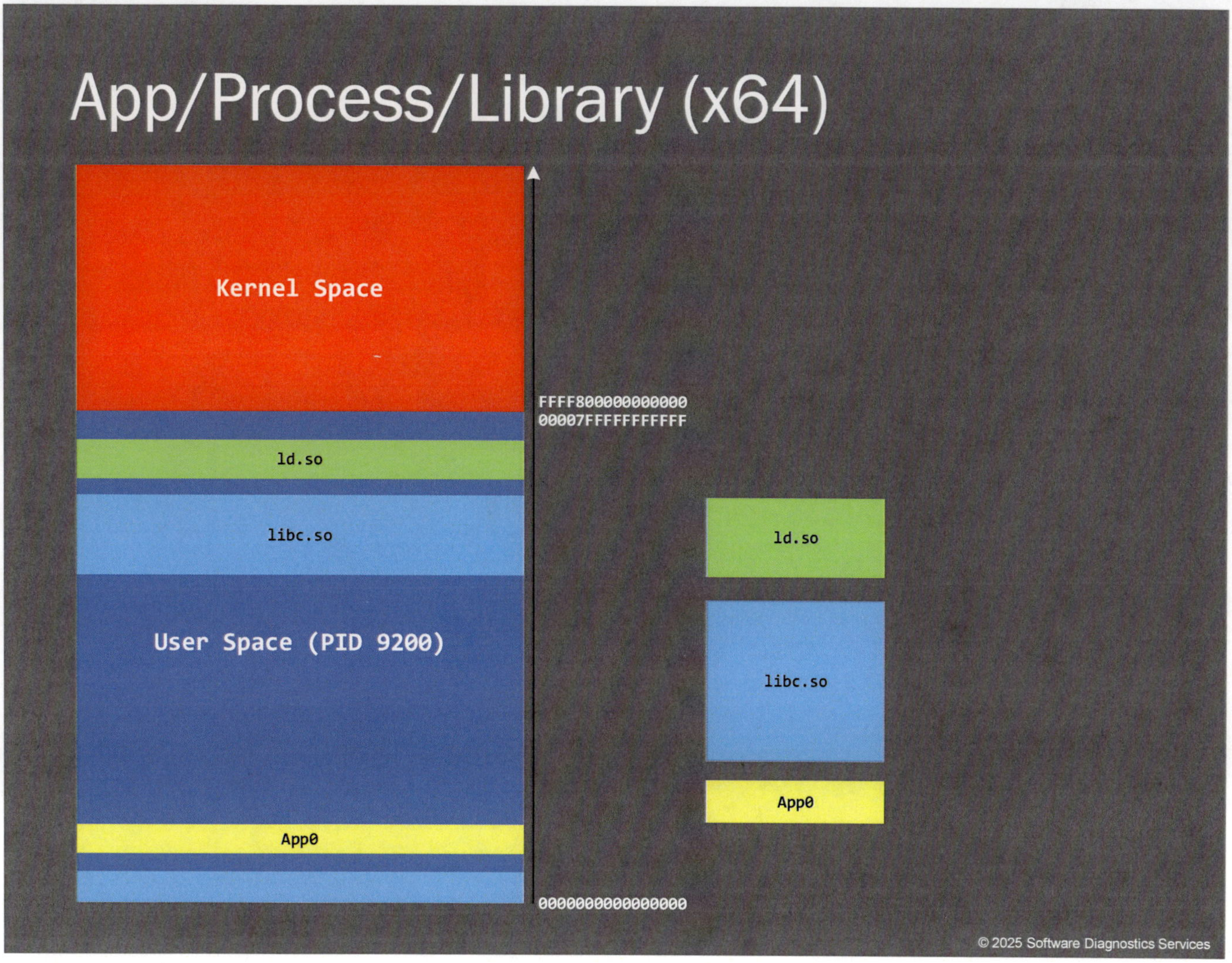

When an app is loaded, all its referenced dynamic libraries are mapped to virtual memory space. Different sections of the same file (like code and data) may be mapped into a different portion of memory. In contrast, modules in Windows are organized sequentially in virtual memory space. A process is then set up for running, and a process ID is assigned to it. If you run another such app, it has a different virtual memory space.

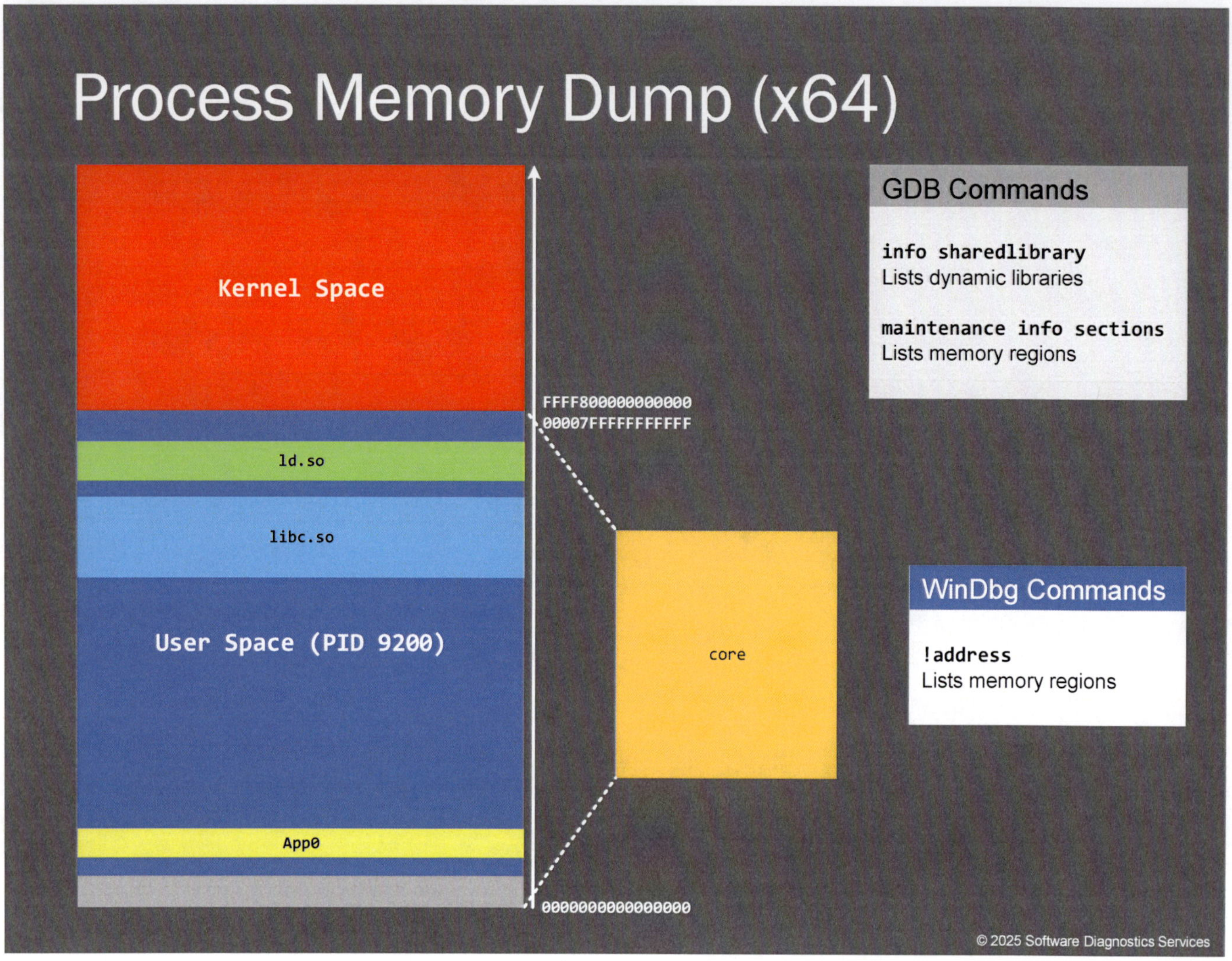

When we save a process core memory dump, a user space portion of the process space is saved without any kernel space stuff. However, we never see such large core dumps unless we have memory leaks. This is because process space has gaps unfilled with code and data. These unallocated parts are not saved in a core dump. However, if some parts were paged out and reside in a page file, they are usually brought back before saving a core dump.

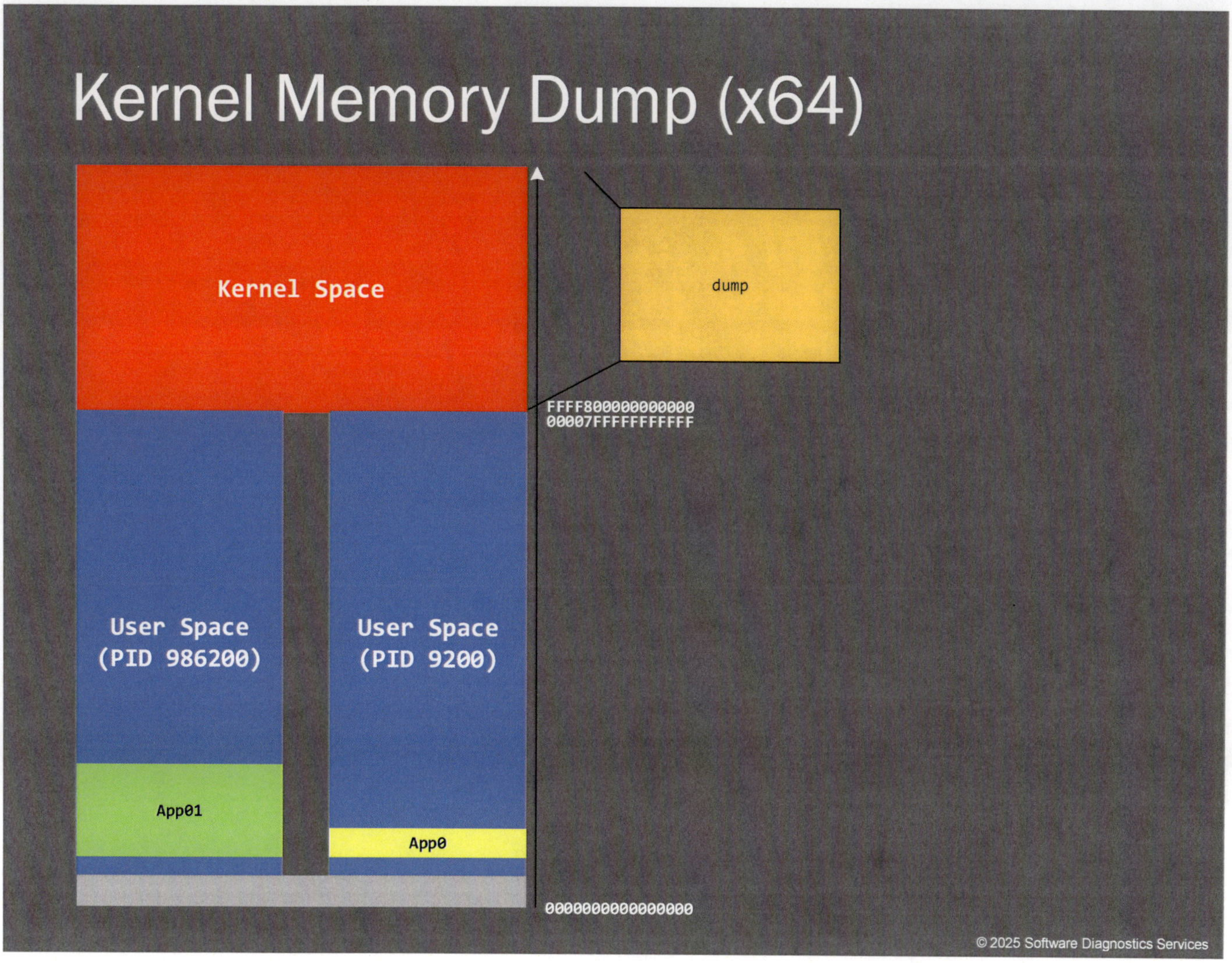

In case of a kernel panic, a kernel memory dump is saved if the appropriate mechanism is configured (mostly by default for recent distributions, such as Ubuntu). Virtual memories of running processes are not saved, however. For that, you need various physical memory acquisition methods and tools that are outside the scope of this course.

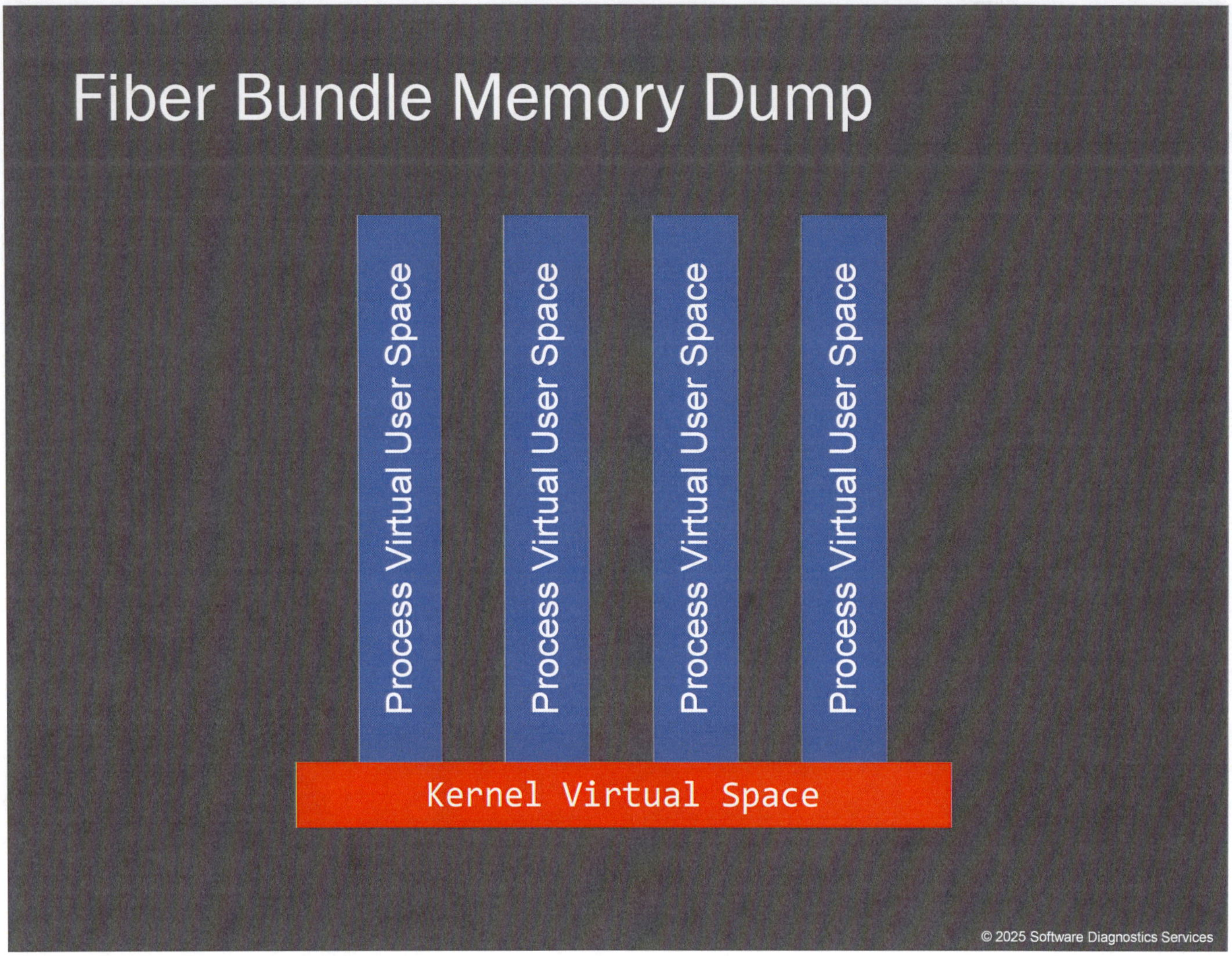

The lack of complete memory dumps may be circumvented by dumping individual processes and then forcing a kernel memory dump to analyze together. We call the resulting dump type **Fiber Bundle**.

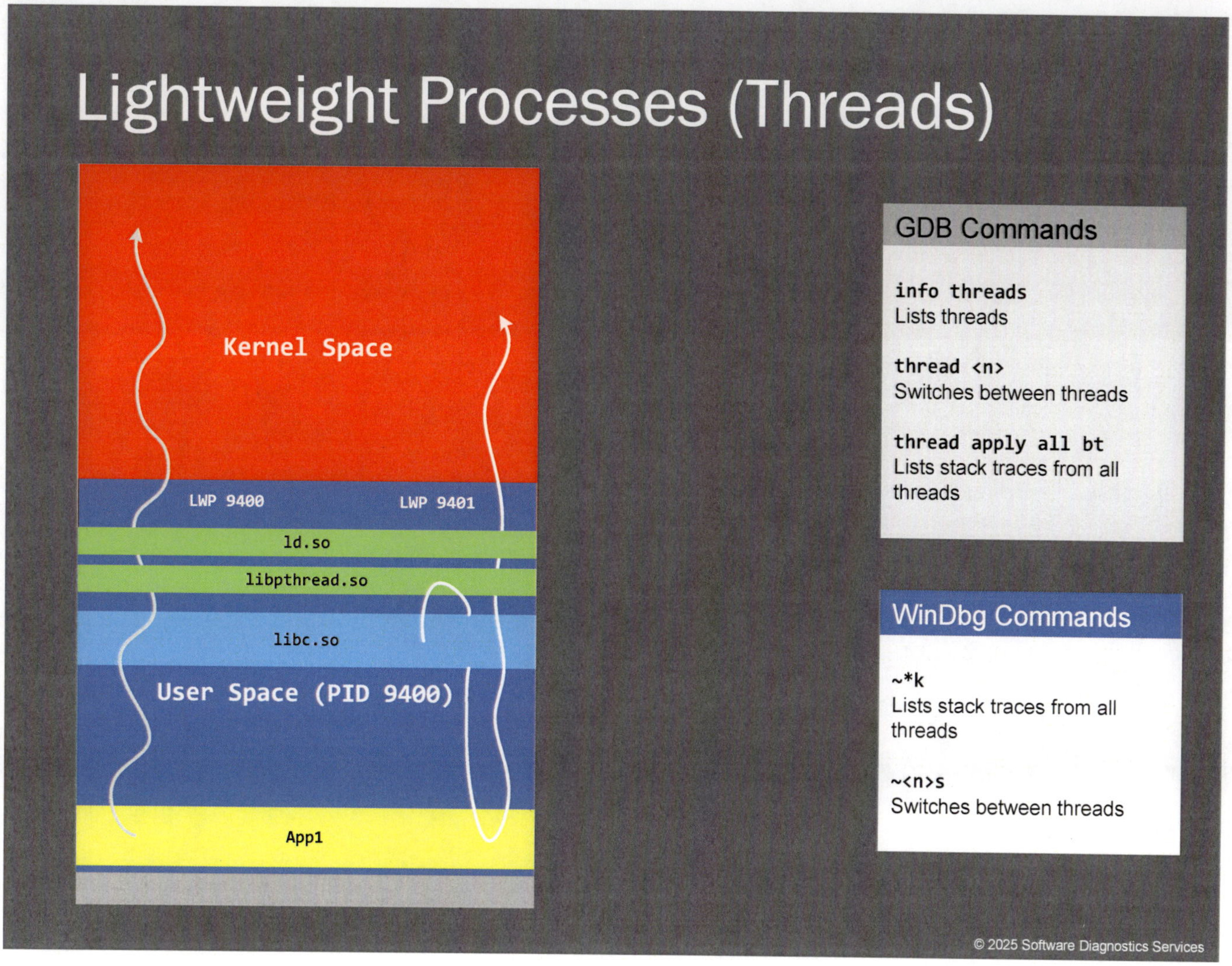

Now, we come to another important fundamental concept in Linux core dump analysis: a thread or lightweight process (LWP). It is basically a unit of execution, and there can be many threads (LWPs) for a given process (all of them share the same process space). Every thread just executes some code and performs various tasks. Every thread has its ID (LWP ID). In this training, we also learn how to navigate between process threads. Note that threads transition to kernel space via the *libc* dynamic library similar to *ntdll* on Windows and *libsystem_kernel* in macOS. Threads additional to the main thread (POSIX threads) originate from the *libc* and *libpthread* dynamic libraries similar to *libsystem_c* in macOS.

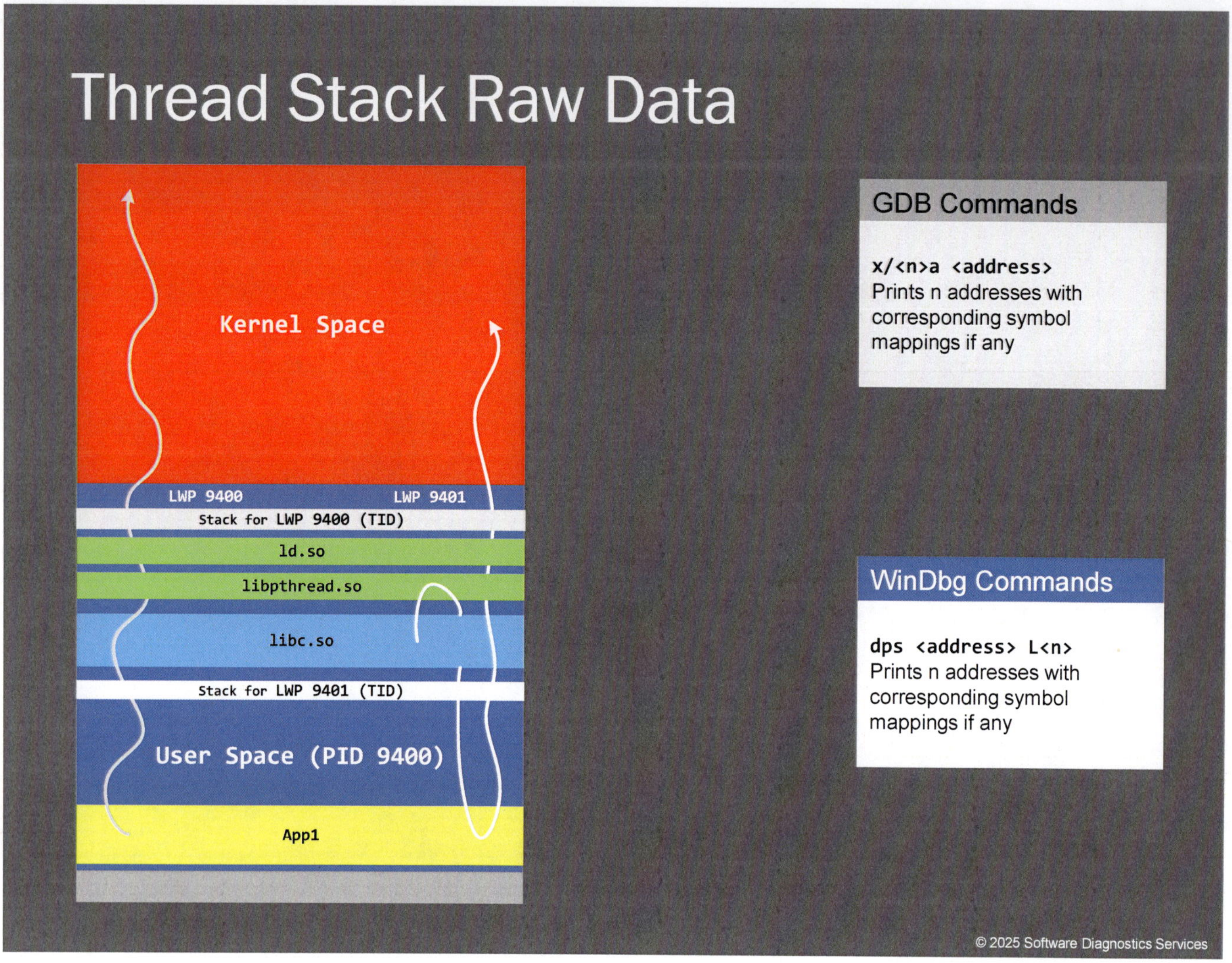

Every thread needs a temporary memory region to store its execution history and temporary data. This region is called a thread stack. Please note that the stack region is just any other memory region, and you can use any GDB data dumping commands there. We also learn how to get the address range of a thread stack region. Examining raw stack data can hint at the past process and kernel behavior: the so-called **Execution Residue** pattern.

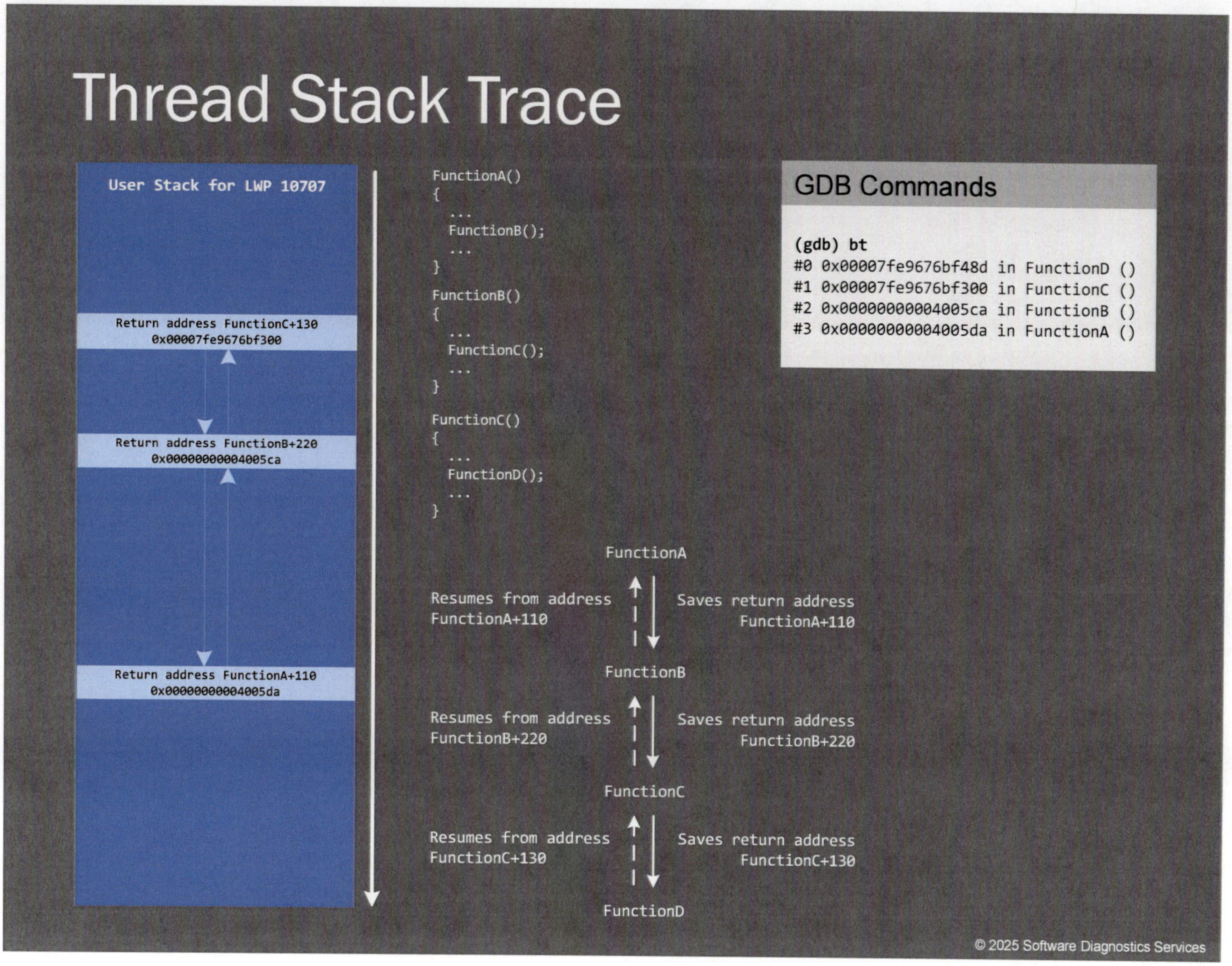

Now, we explain thread stack traces. Suppose we have source code where *FunctionA* calls *FunctionB* at some point, *FunctionB* calls *FunctionC*, and so on. This sequence is called a thread of execution. If *FunctionA* calls *FunctionB*, you expect the execution thread to return to the same place where it left, and to resume from there. This goal is achieved by saving a return address in the thread stack region. So every return address is saved and then restored during the course of thread execution. Although the memory addresses grow from top to bottom in this picture, return addresses are saved from bottom to top: the stack grows from higher to lower addresses. This picture might seem counter-intuitive to all previous pictures, but this is how you see the output from GDB commands. What GDB does when you instruct it to dump a backtrace from a given thread is to analyze the thread raw stack data and figure out return addresses, map them to a symbolic form according to symbol files and show them from top to bottom. Note that *FunctionD* is not present in the raw stack data on the left because it is a currently executing function called from *FunctionC*. However, *FunctionC* called *FunctionD*, and the return address of *FunctionC* was saved. In the box on the right, we see the result of the GDB **bt** command.

GDB vs. WinDbg vs. LLDB

GDB Commands

```
(gdb) bt
#0 0x00007fe9676bf48d in FunctionD ()
#1 0x00007fe9676bf300 in FunctionC ()
#2 0x00000000004005ca in FunctionB ()
#3 0x00000000004005da in FunctionA ()
```

WinDbg Commands

```
0:000> k
00 00007fe9676bf300 Module!FunctionD+offset
01 00000000004005ca Module!FunctionC+130
02 00000000004005da AppA!FunctionB+220
03 0000000000000000 AppA!FunctionA+110
```

LLDB Commands

```
(lldb) bt
frame #0: 0x000000020328982a Module`FunctionD + offset
frame #1: 0x00000002032889c Module`FunctionC + 130
frame #2: 0x0000000104da3ea9 AppA`FunctionB + 220
frame #3: 0x0000000104da3edb AppA`FunctionA + 110
```


The difference from WinDbg (from Debugging Tools for Windows) here is that the return address is on the same line for the function to return (except for *FunctionD*, where the address is the next instruction to execute), whereas, in WinDbg, it is for the function on the next line.

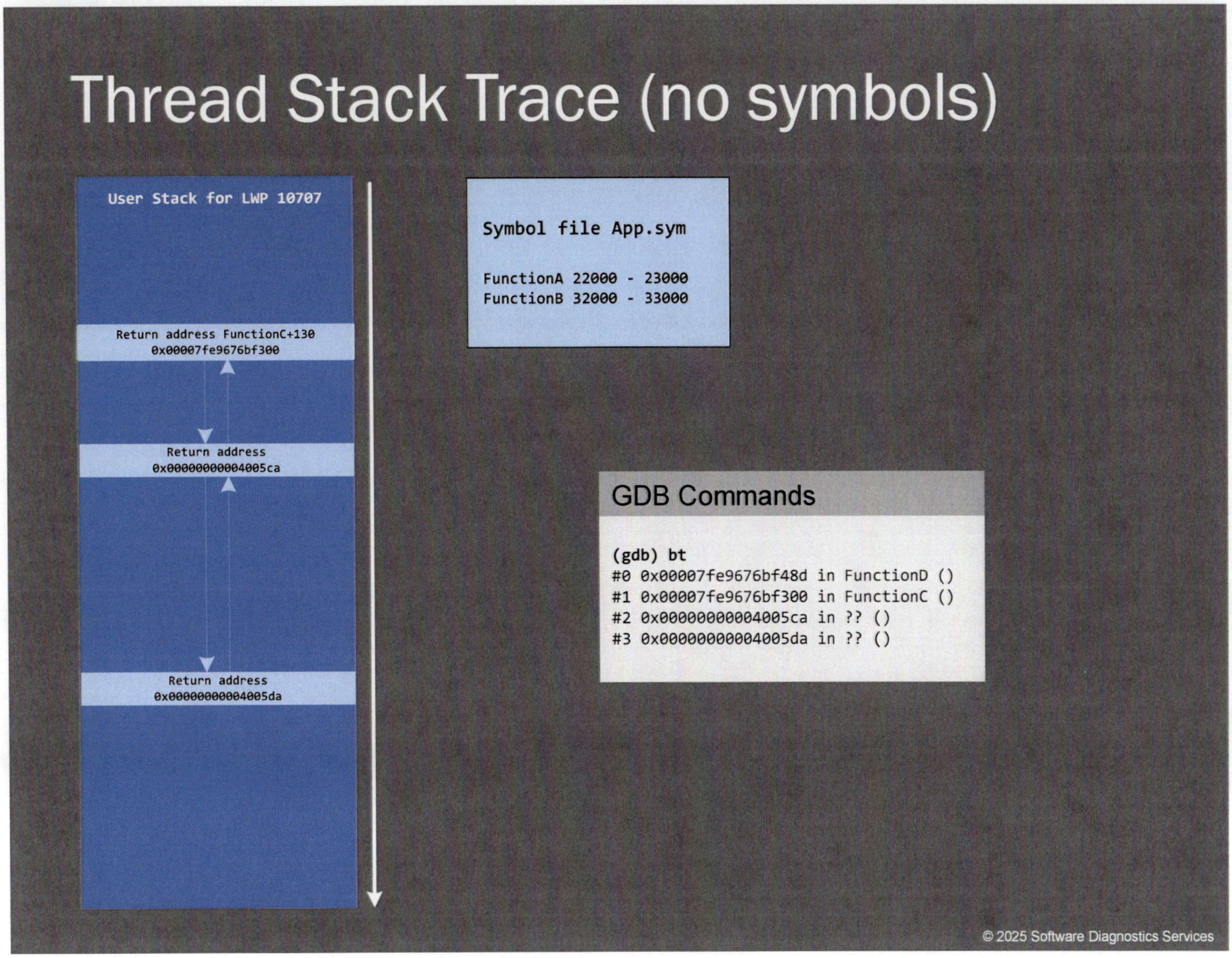

Here, I'd like to show you why symbol files are important and what stack traces you get without them. Symbol files provide mappings between memory address ranges and associated symbol names, like the table of contents in a book. So, without symbols, we are left with bare addresses saved in a dump. For example, without the App symbols, we have the output shown in the box on the right.

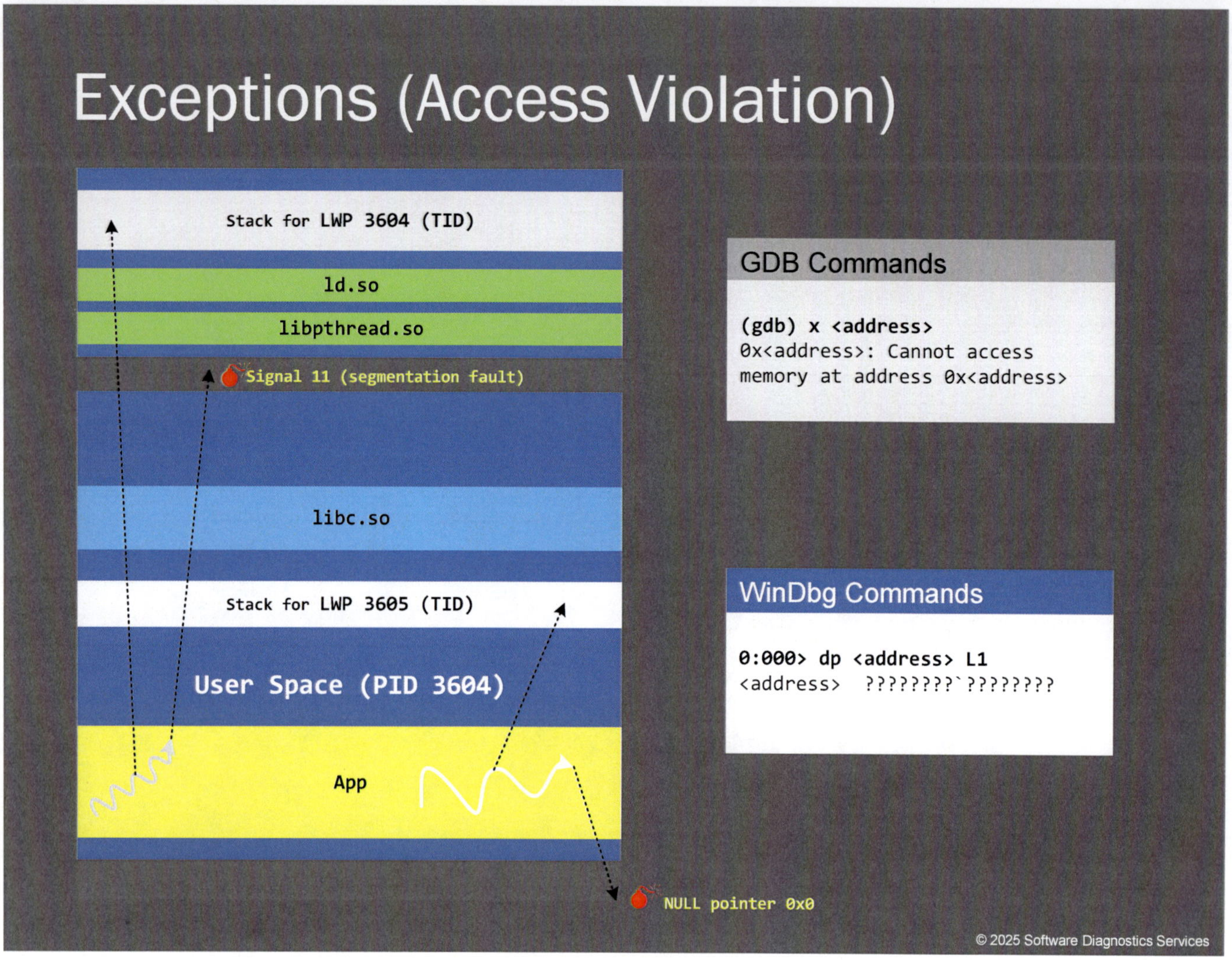

Now, we talk about access violation exceptions. During the thread execution, it accesses various memory addresses doing reads and writes. Sometimes, memory is not present due to gaps in virtual address space or different protection levels like read-only or no-execute memory regions. If a thread tries to violate that, we get an exception translated to a traditional UNIX signal. Certain regions are forbidden to read and write, such as the first 64KB in x64 Linux. If we have such an access violation there, then it is called NULL pointer access. Note that any thread can have an exception (a victim thread in macOS). It is also sometimes the case that code can catch these exceptions, preventing a user from seeing error messages. Such exceptions can contribute to corruption, and we call them hidden.

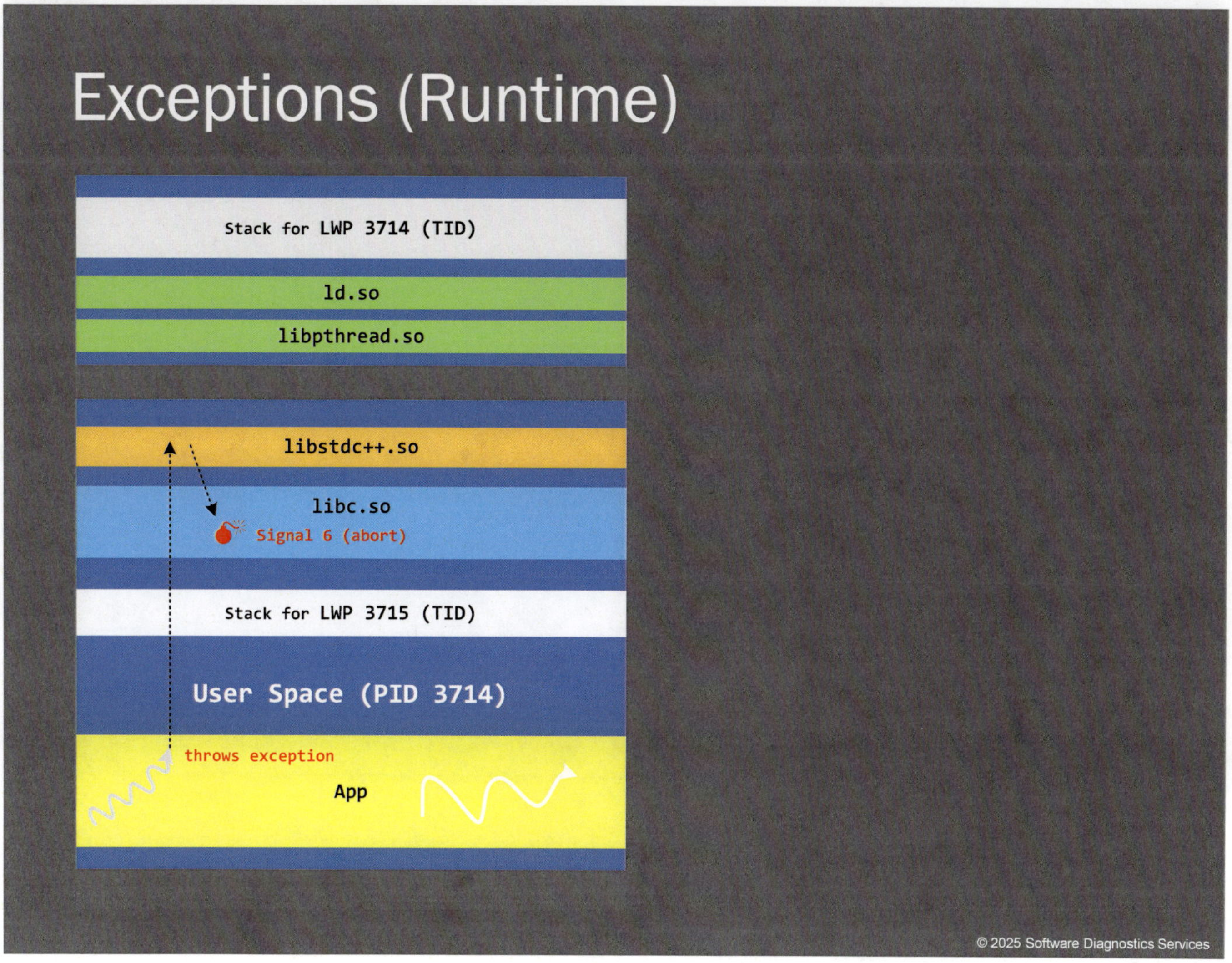

However, not all exceptions happen from invalid access. Many exceptions are generated by the code itself when it checks for some condition and it is not satisfied, for example, when the code checks a buffer or an array to verify whether it is full before trying to add more data. If it finds it is already full, the code throws an exception translated to SIGABRT. We would see that in one of our practice examples when C++ code throws a C++ exception. Such exceptions are usually called runtime exceptions.

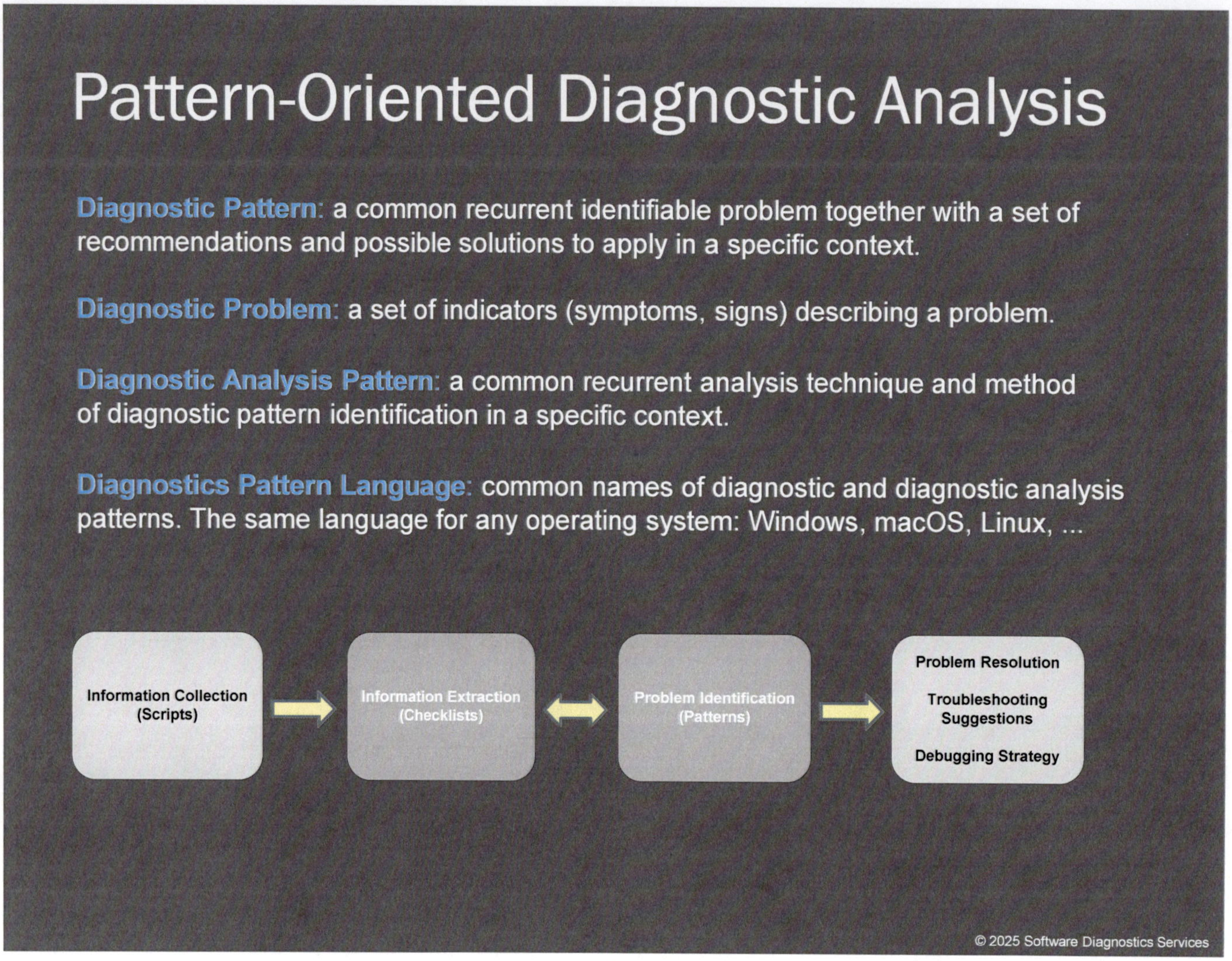

A few words about logs, checklists, and patterns: core memory dump analysis is usually an analysis of a text for the presence of diagnostic patterns. We run commands, they output text, and then we look at that textual output, and when we find suspicious diagnostic indicators, we execute more commands. Here, the pattern and command checklists can be very useful.

Core Dump Collection

Part 2: Core Dump Collection

Here, I'd like to show you how to collect core dumps because this option is switched off on Linux by default.

Enabling Collection (Processes)

- Temporary for the current user

```
$ ulimit -c unlimited
```

- Permanent for every user except root

Edit the file: `/etc/security/limits.conf`

Add or uncomment the line:

```
*      soft   core   unlimited
```

To limit root to 1GB, add or uncomment this line:

```
*      hard   core   1000000
```


On some systems, a process core dump is stored in the process's working directory. On other systems, you need to verify what is a configured path. We see that in the following slides.

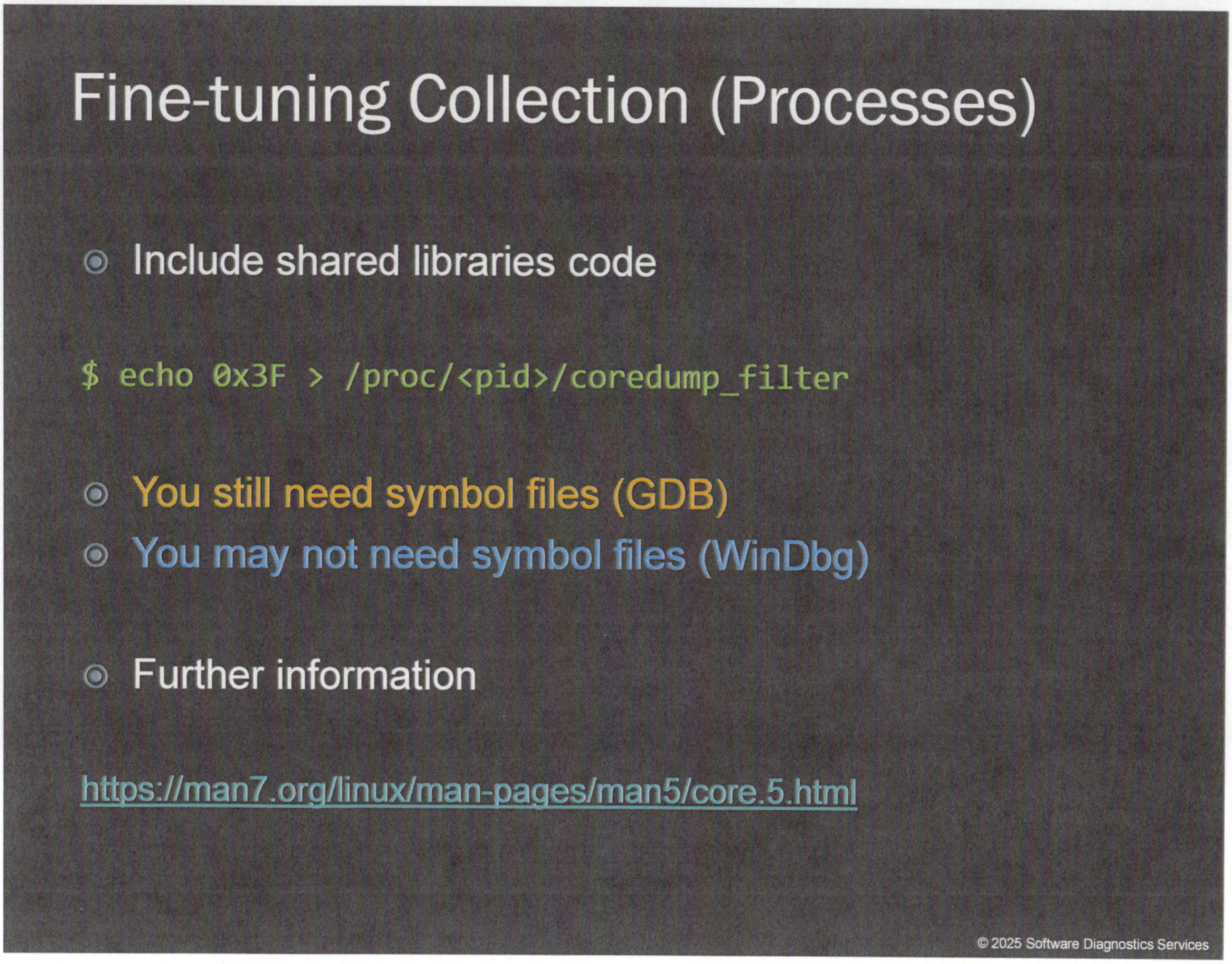

Shared libraries' code may not be saved in core dumps. If you configue to save them, you may still need symbol files, depending on the type of symbols you need or your choice of a debugger, as we see in some exercises.

Core man page
https://man7.org/linux/man-pages/man5/core.5.html

Generation Methods (Processes)

- kill (requires ulimit)

```
$ kill -s SIGQUIT PID
$ kill -s SIGABRT PID
```

- gcore

```
$ gcore [-o filename] PID
```

- procdump

https://github.com/Sysinternals/ProcDump-for-Linux

Procdump
https://github.com/Sysinternals/ProcDump-for-Linux

Finding Core Dumps (Processes)

- Check the current core dump directory and naming pattern

```
$ cat /proc/sys/kernel/core_pattern
```

- Search

```
$ sudo find / -name core.*
```

- Further information

https://man7.org/linux/man-pages/man5/core.5.html

Core man page

https://man7.org/linux/man-pages/man5/core.5.html

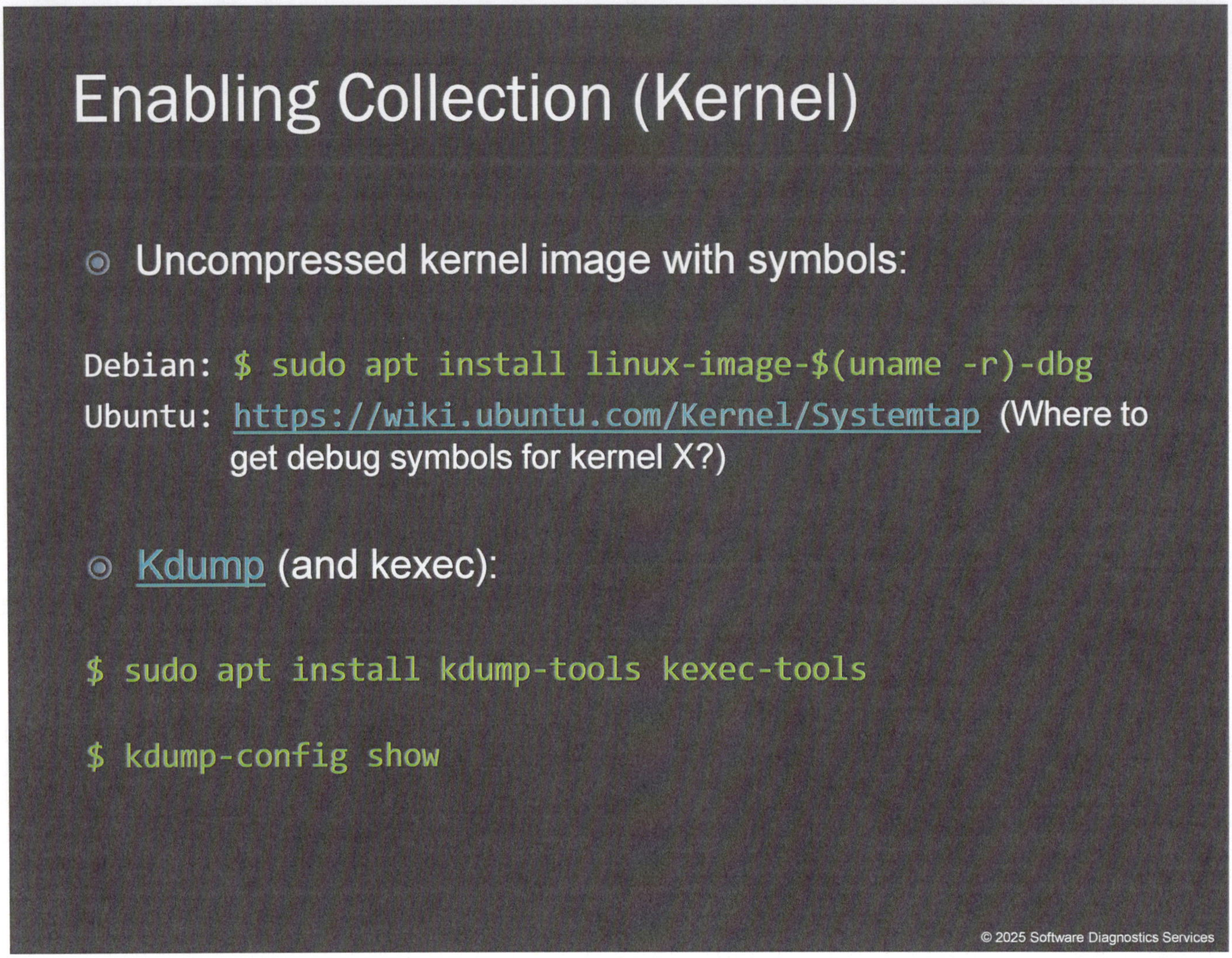

Ubuntu
https://wiki.ubuntu.com/Kernel/Systemtap

Kdump
https://www.kernel.org/doc/Documentation/kdump/kdump.txt

Configuring Collection (Kernel)

- General:

```
$ sudo nano /etc/default/kdump-tools

$ man makedumpfile
```

- Preprocessing (for WinDbg):

```
makedumpfile -c ... (ZLIB compression)

$ sudo makedumpfile -R date.kdump < dump.date
```

Generation Methods (Kernel)

- Manual (you may need to be root, not sudo)

```
$ sudo passwd root
$ su root
# echo 1 > /proc/sys/kernel/sysrq
# echo c > /proc/sysrq-trigger
```

- Kernel modules

Finding Core Dumps (Kernel)

- Core dumps

```
/var/crash
```

- `vmlinux`

```
/usr/lib/debug
```

Enabling Analysis (Kernel)

- Install crash tool (depends on distribution)

```
$ sudo apt install crash
```

- Compile crash tool from source

```
$ git clone https://github.com/crash-utility/crash.git
$ sudo apt install build-essential wget libgmp-dev
  libmpfr-dev libmpc-dev flex bison texinfo zlib1g-dev
  libncurses-dev
$ cd crash
$ make
$ sudo make install
```


Crash tool

https://github.com/crash-utility/crash.git

x64 Disassembly (AT&T GDB Flavor)

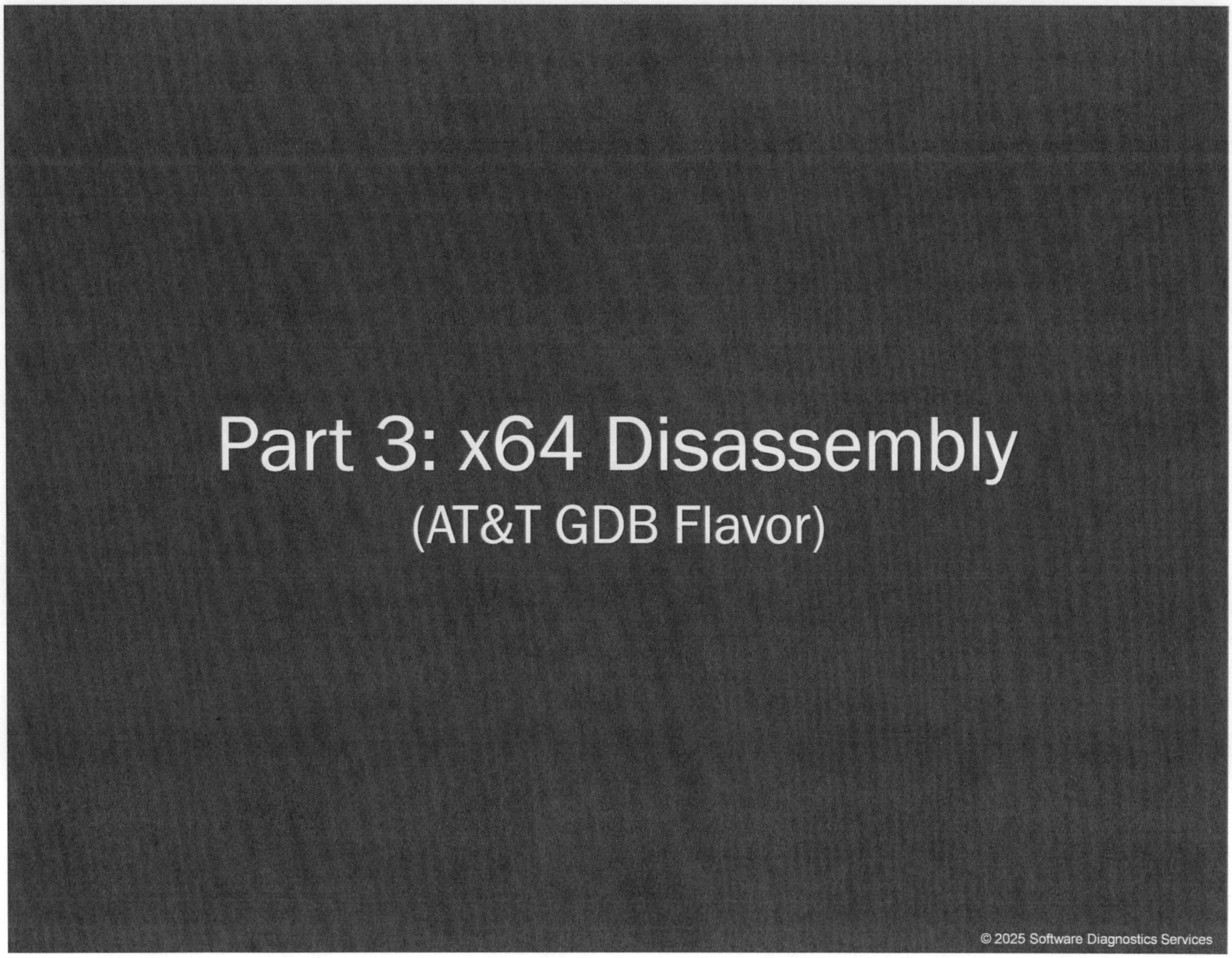

Now, we have come to a brief overview of the relevant x64 GDB disassembly. We only cover what we would see in the exercises.

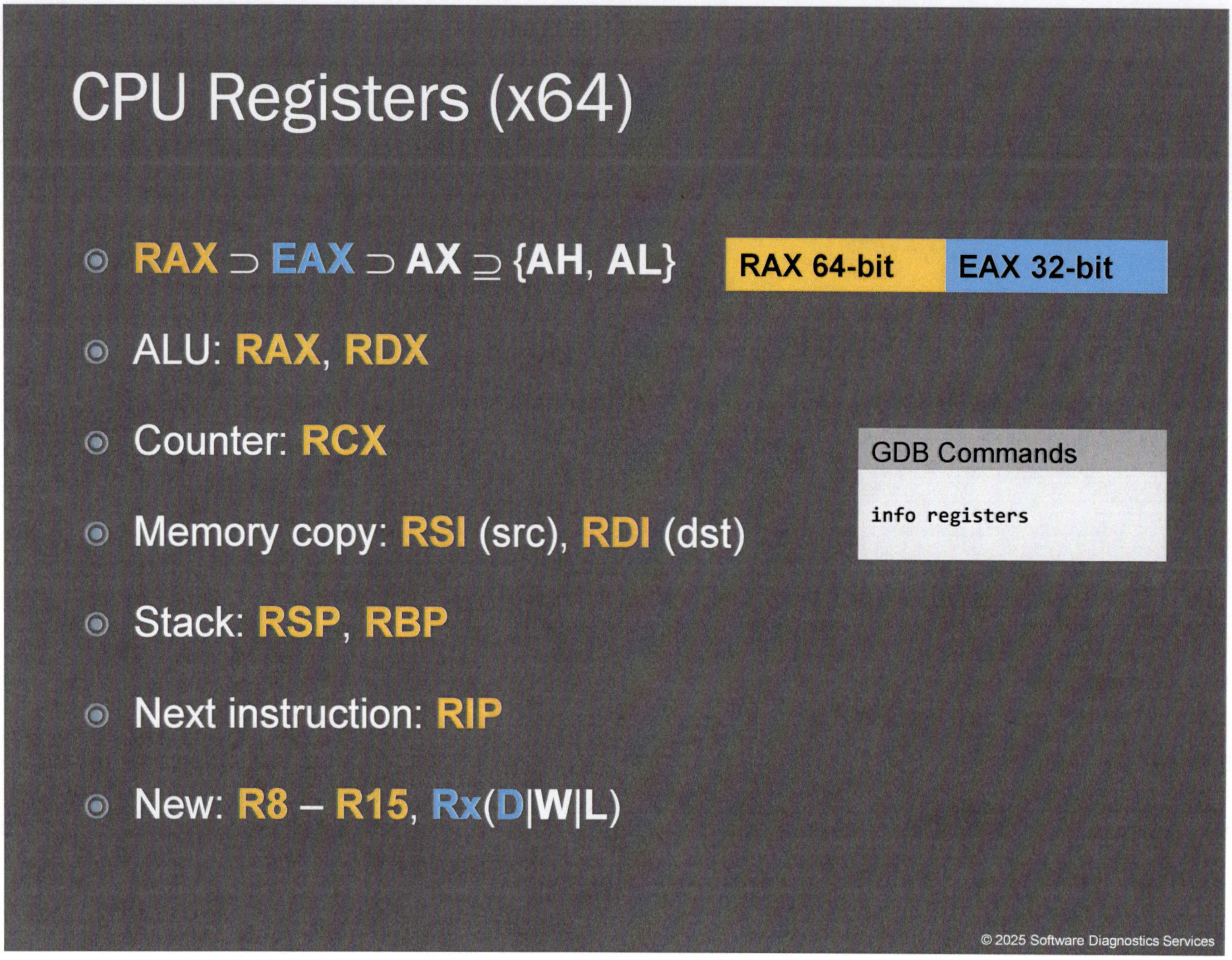

There are usual 32-bit CPU register names, such as **EAX,** that are extended to 64-bit names, such as **RAX**. Most of them are traditionally specialized, such as ALU, counter, and memory copy registers. Although now they all can be used as general-purpose registers. There is, of course, a stack pointer, **RSP**, and, additionally, a frame pointer, **RBP**, that is used to address local variables and saved parameters. It can be used for backtrace reconstruction. In some compiler code generation implementations, **RBP** is also used as a general-purpose register, with **RSP** taking the role of a frame pointer. An instruction pointer **RIP** is saved in the stack memory region with every function call, then restored on return from the called function. In addition, the x64 platform features another eight general-purpose registers, from **R8** to **R15**.

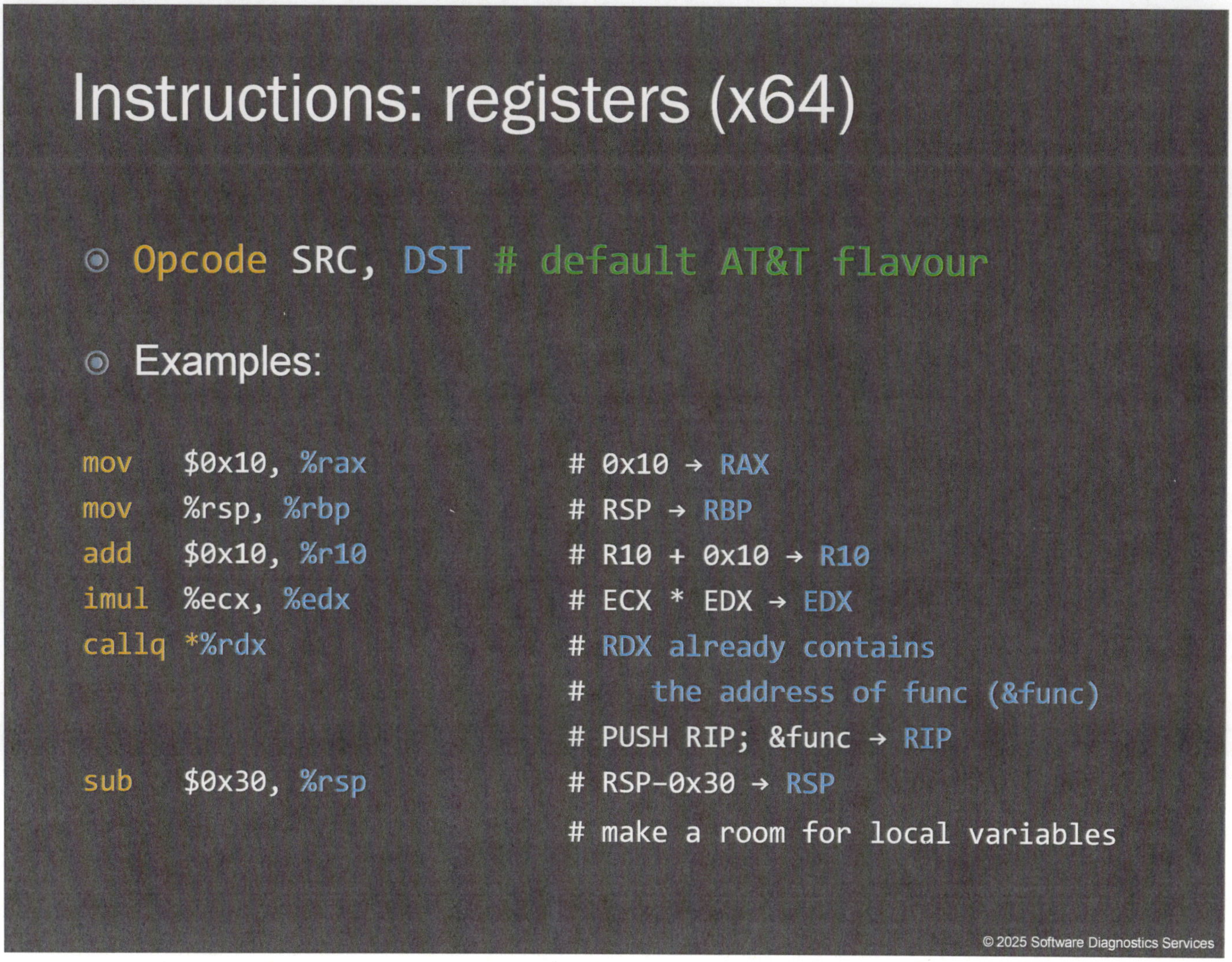

This slide shows a few examples of CPU instructions involving operations with registers, such as moving a value and doing arithmetic. The direction of operands is opposite to the Intel x64 disassembly flavor if you are accustomed to WinDbg on Windows. It is possible to use the Intel disassembly flavor in GDB, but I opted for the default AT&T disassembly flavor in line with my book **Foundations of Linux Debugging, Disassembly, and Reversing**.

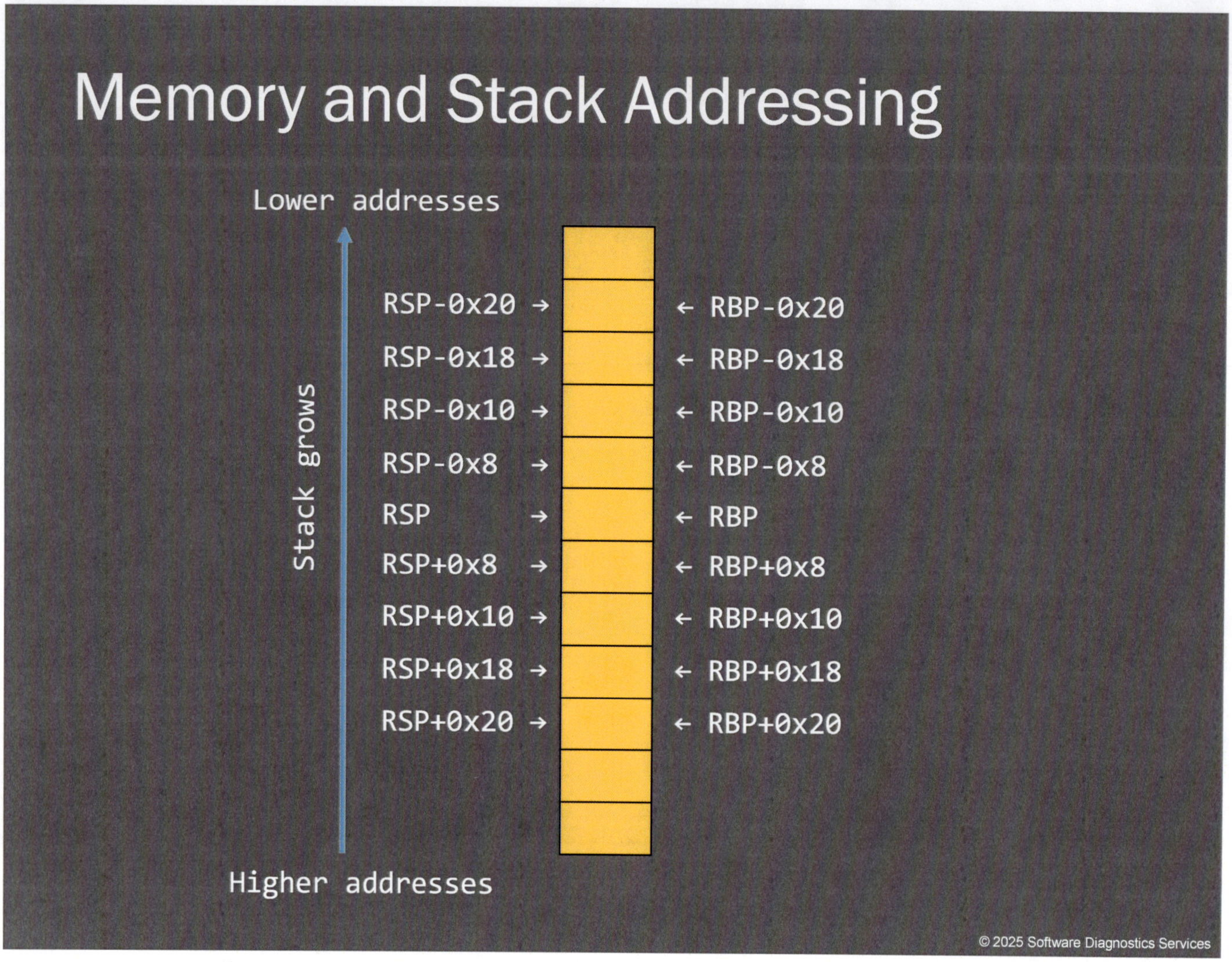

Before we look at operations with memory, let's look at a graphical representation of memory addressing. A thread stack is just any other memory region, so instead of **RSP** and **RBP,** any other register can be used. Please note that the stack grows towards lower addresses, so to access the previously pushed values, you need to use positive offsets from **RSP**.

Instructions: memory load (x64)

- Opcode Offset(SRC), DST
- Opcode DST
- Examples:

```
mov   0x10(%rsp), %rax        # value at address RSP+0x10 → RAX
mov   -0x10(%rbp), %rcx       # value at address RBP-0x10 → RCX
add   (%rax), %rdx            # RDX + value at address RAX → RDX
pop   %rdi                    # value at address RSP → RDI
                              # RSP + 8 → RSP
lea   0x20(%rbp), %r8         # address RBP+0x20 → R8
```


Constants are encoded in instructions, but if we need arbitrary values, we must get them from memory. Round brackets show memory access relative to an address stored in some register.

Instructions: memory store (x64)

- Opcode SRC, Offset(DST)
- Opcode SRC|DST
- Examples:

```
mov   %rcx, -0x20(%rbp)     # RCX → value at address RBP-0x20
addl  $1, (%rax)            # 1 + 32-bit value at address RAX →
                            #     32-bit value at address RAX
push  %rsi                  # RSP - 8 → RSP
                            # RSI → value at address RSP
inc   (%rcx)                # 1 + value at address RCX →
                            #     value at address RCX
```


Storing is similar to loading.

Instructions: indexing (x64)

- Opcode Offset(SRC_{base}, SRC_{index}, Scale), DST
- Opcode SRC, Offset(DST_{base}, DST_{index}, Scale)
- Examples:

```
mov   (%rdx, %rax, 1), %rax  # value at address RDX+RAX*1 → RAX
movq  $0x0, (%rdx, %rax, 8)  # 0 → value at address RDX+RAX*8
lea   0x0(, %rax, 8), %rdx   # address RAX*8+0 → RDX
```

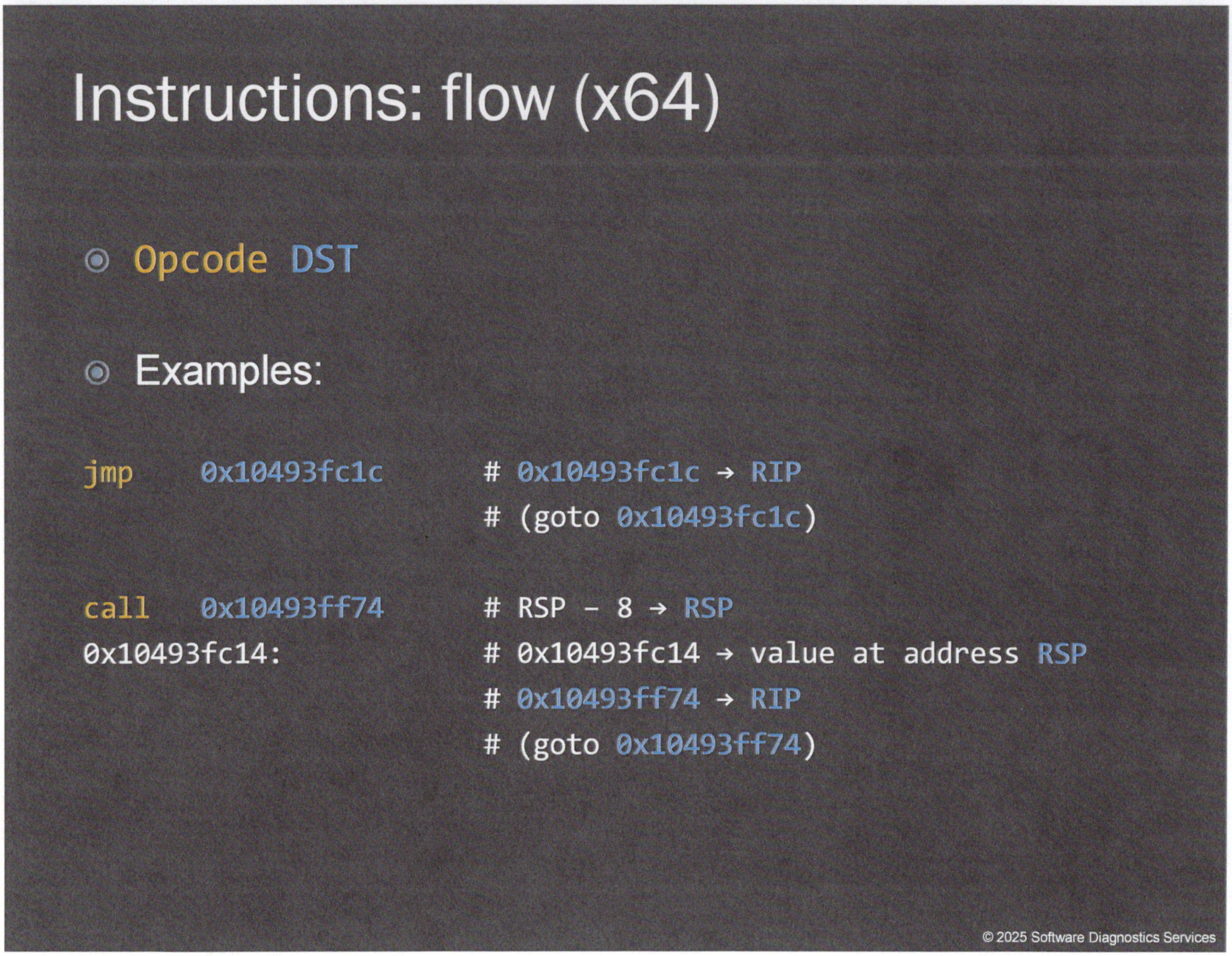

Goto (an unconditional jump) is implemented via the **JMP** instruction. Function calls are implemented via **CALL** instruction. For conditional branches, please look at the official Intel documentation. We don't use these instructions in our exercises.

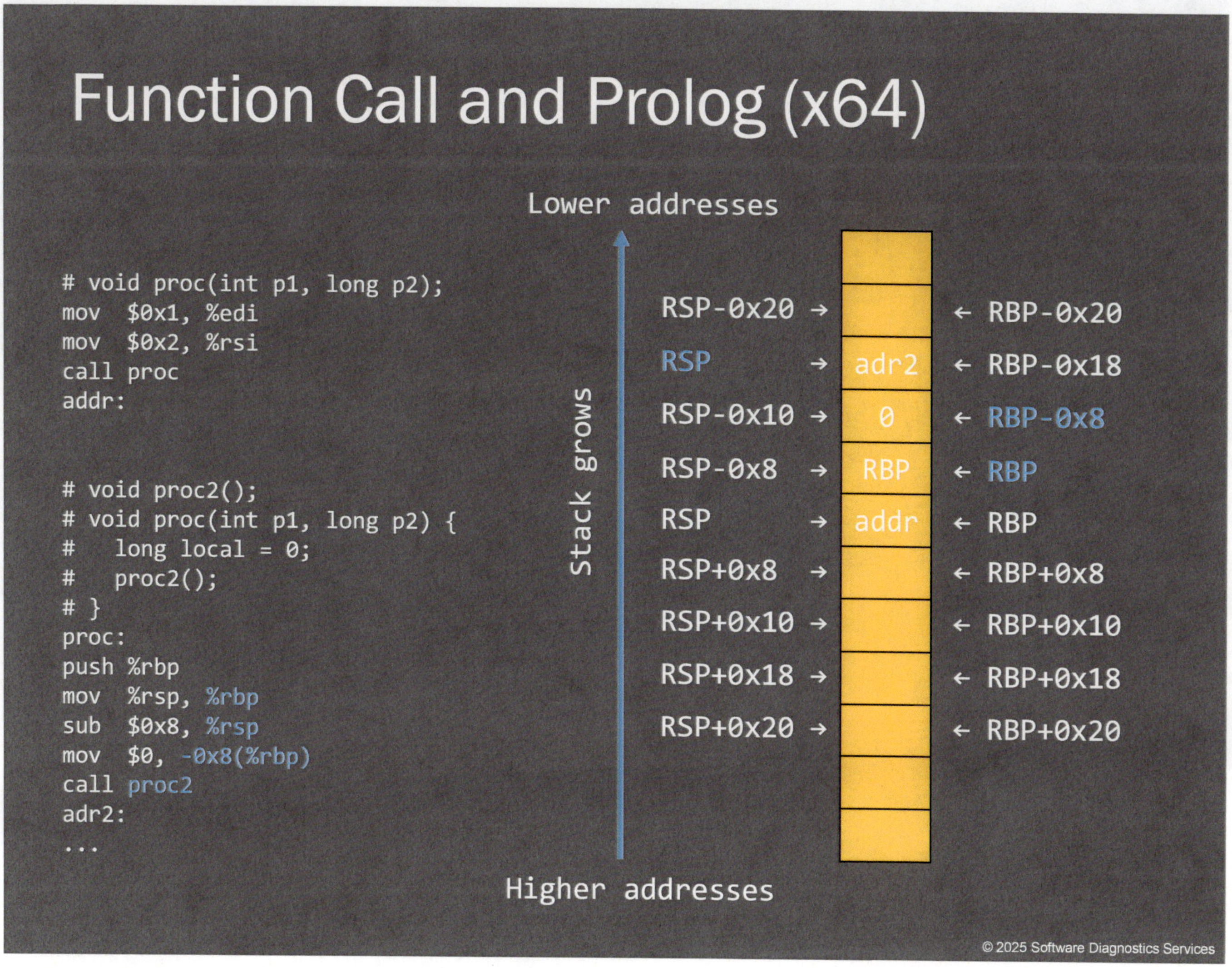

When a function is called from the caller, a callee needs to do certain operations to make room for local variables on the thread stack. There are different ways to do that, and the assembly language code on the left is one of them. I use a different color in the diagram on the right to highlight the updated **RSP** and **RBP** values before *proc2* is called. For simplicity of illustration, I only use 64-bit values.

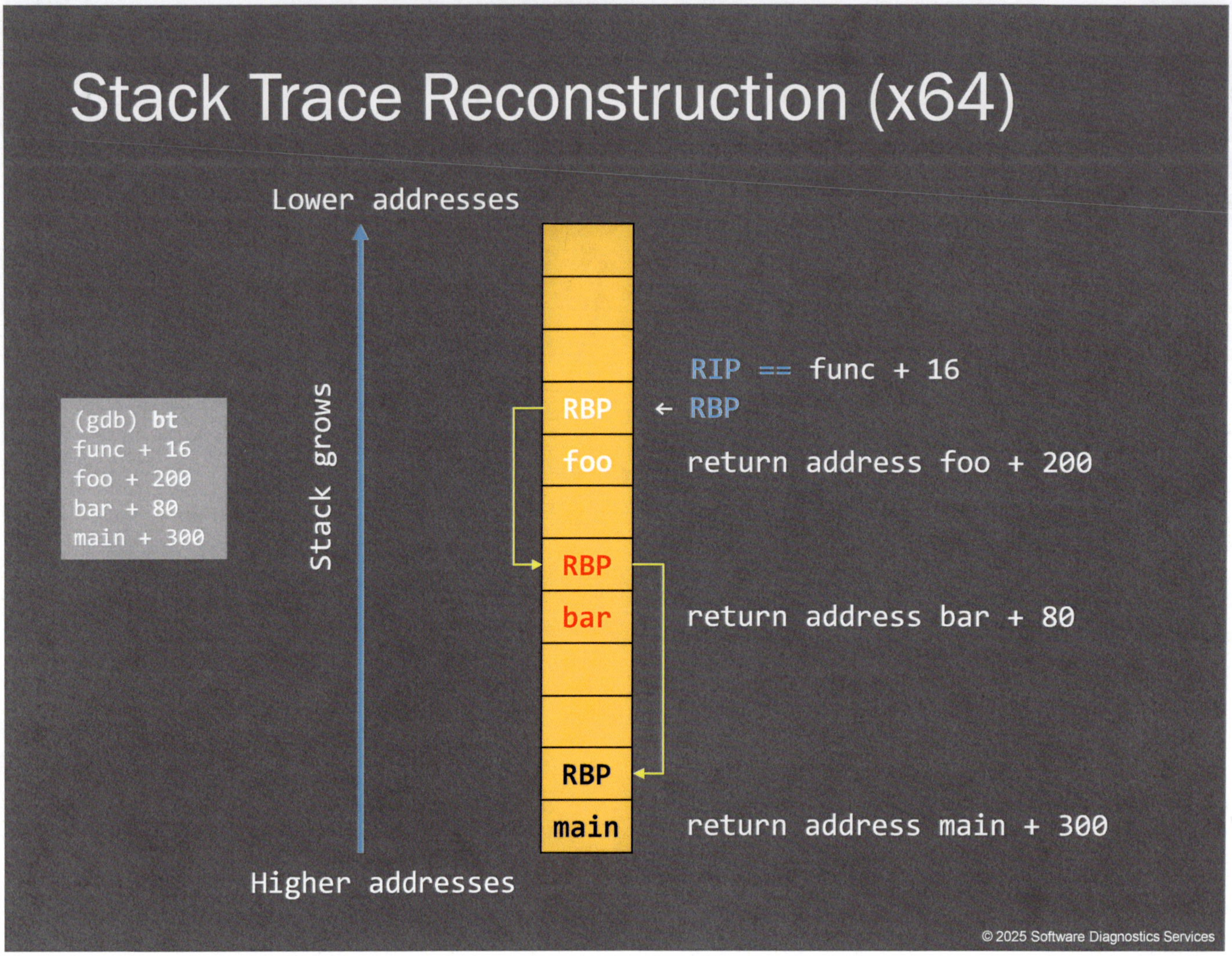

You may have noticed on the previous diagram that the new **RBP** points to the **RBP** of the caller, and below the previous **RBP** is the return address of the caller. So, if you know the **RBP** value, you can reconstruct the stack trace if the compiler follows the preceding function prolog convention.

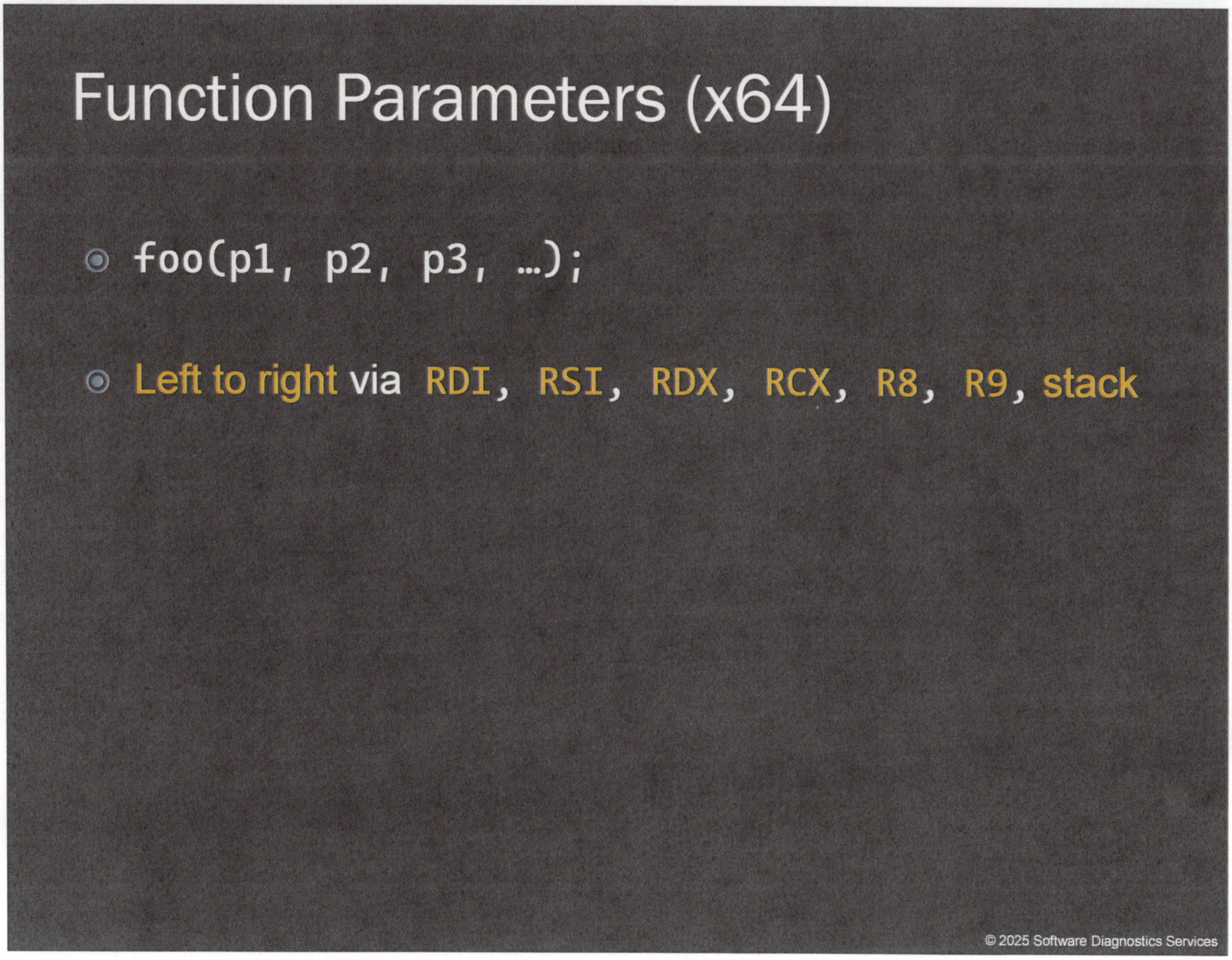

On the x64 Linux platform, the first six C and C++ function parameters from left to right are moved to CPU registers, and the rest are passed via stack locations.

ARM64 Disassembly

Part 4: ARM64 Disassembly

Now, we have come to a brief overview of the relevant ARM64 disassembly. We only cover what we would see in the exercises.

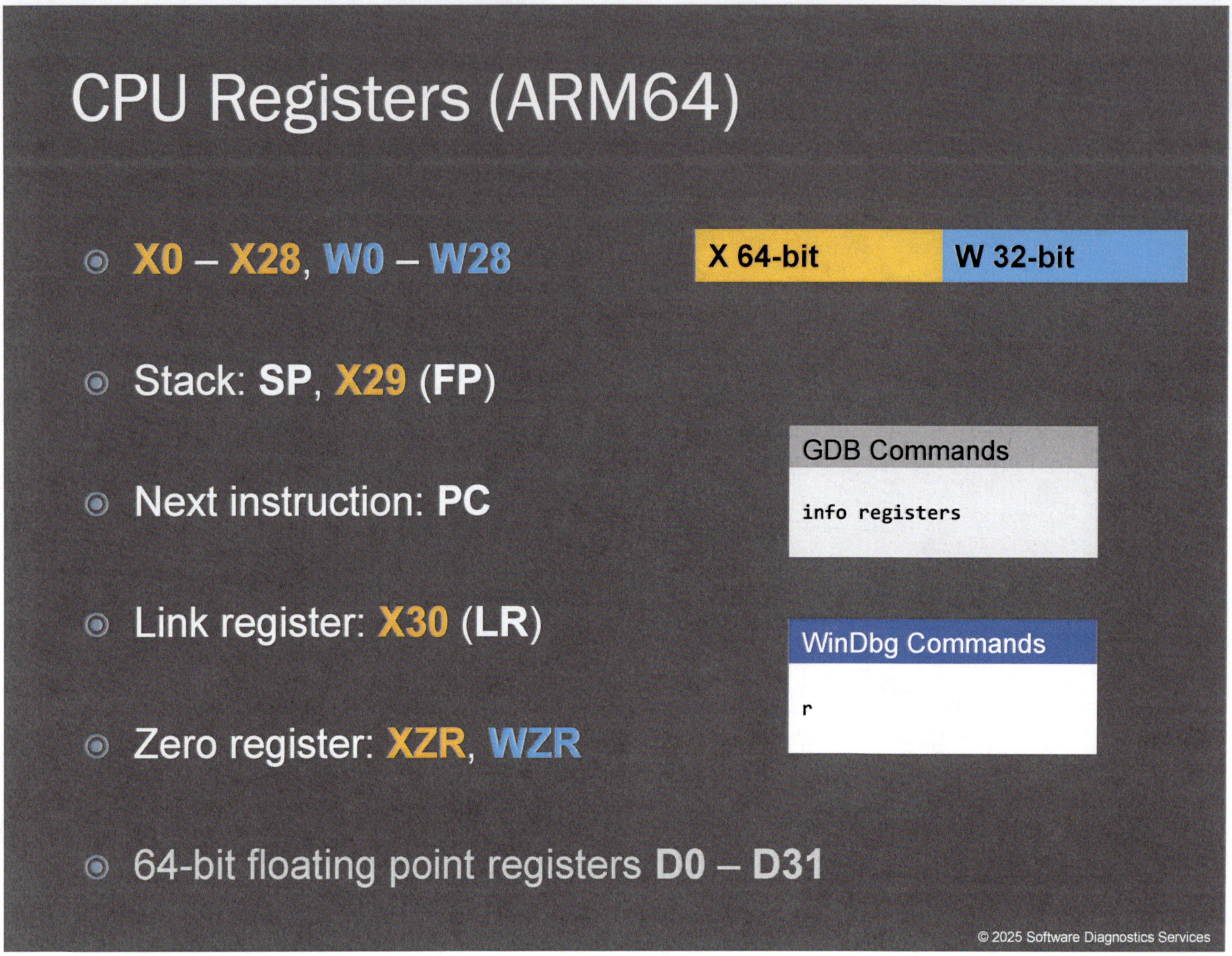

There are 31 general registers from **X0** and **X30**, with some delegated to specific tasks such as addressing stack frames (Frame Pointer, **FP**, **X29**) and return addresses, the so-called Link Register (**LR**, **X30**). When you call a function, the return address of a caller is saved in **LR**, not on the stack as in Intel/AMD x64. The return instruction in a callee uses the address in **LR** to assign it to **PC** and resume execution. But if a callee calls other functions, the current **LR** needs to be manually saved somewhere, usually on the stack. There's Stack Pointer, **SP**, of course. To get zero values, there's the so-called Zero Register, **XZR**. All **X** registers are 64-bit, and 32-bit lower parts are addressed via the **W** prefix. The References slide provides links to the ARM64 instruction set architecture. Next, we briefly look at some aspects related to our exercises.

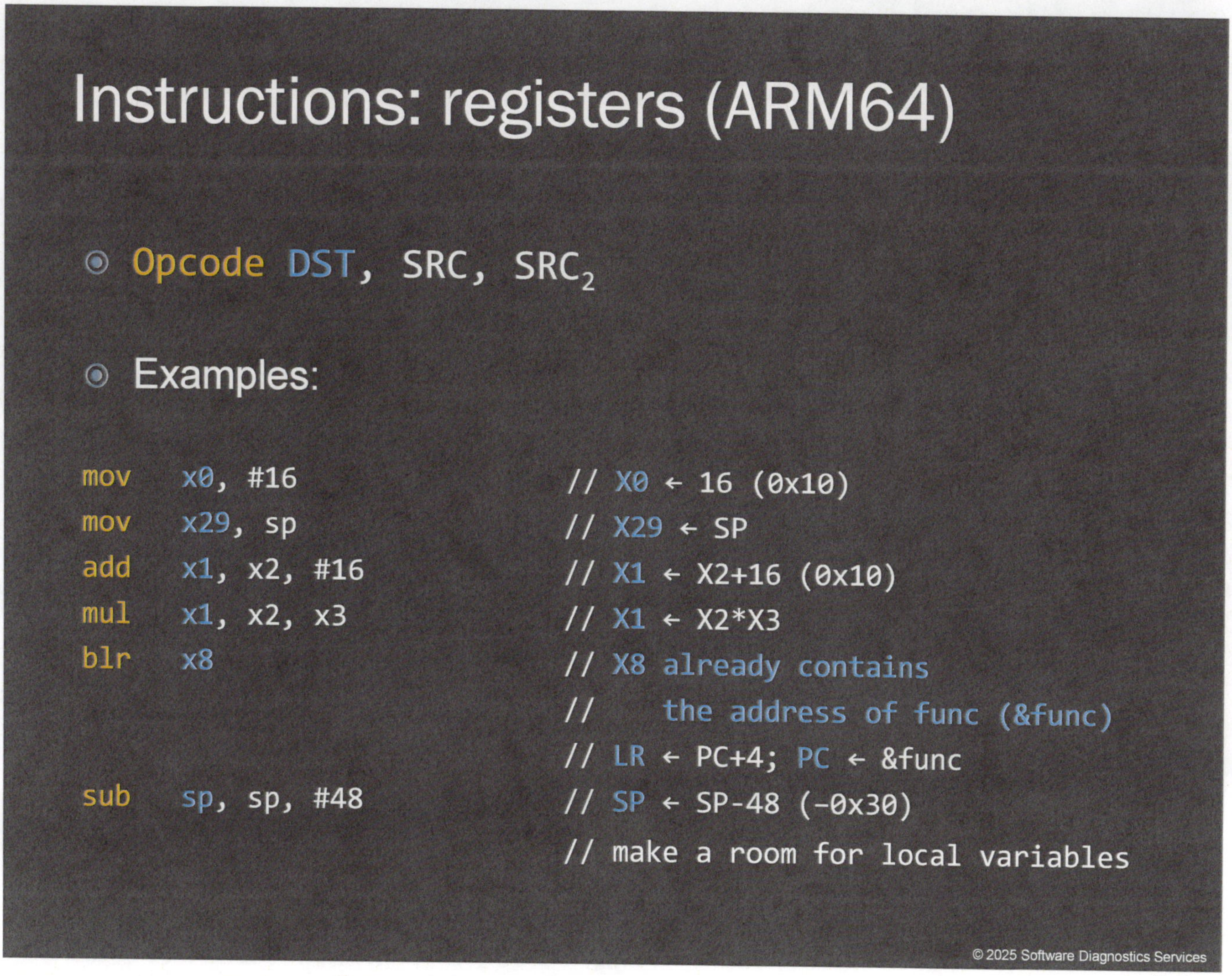

This slide shows a few examples of CPU instructions that involve operations with registers, for example, moving a value and doing arithmetic. The direction of operands is the same as in the Intel x64 disassembly flavor if you are accustomed to WinDbg on Windows. It is equivalent to an assignment. **BLR** is a call of some function whose address is in the register. **BL** means Branch and Link.

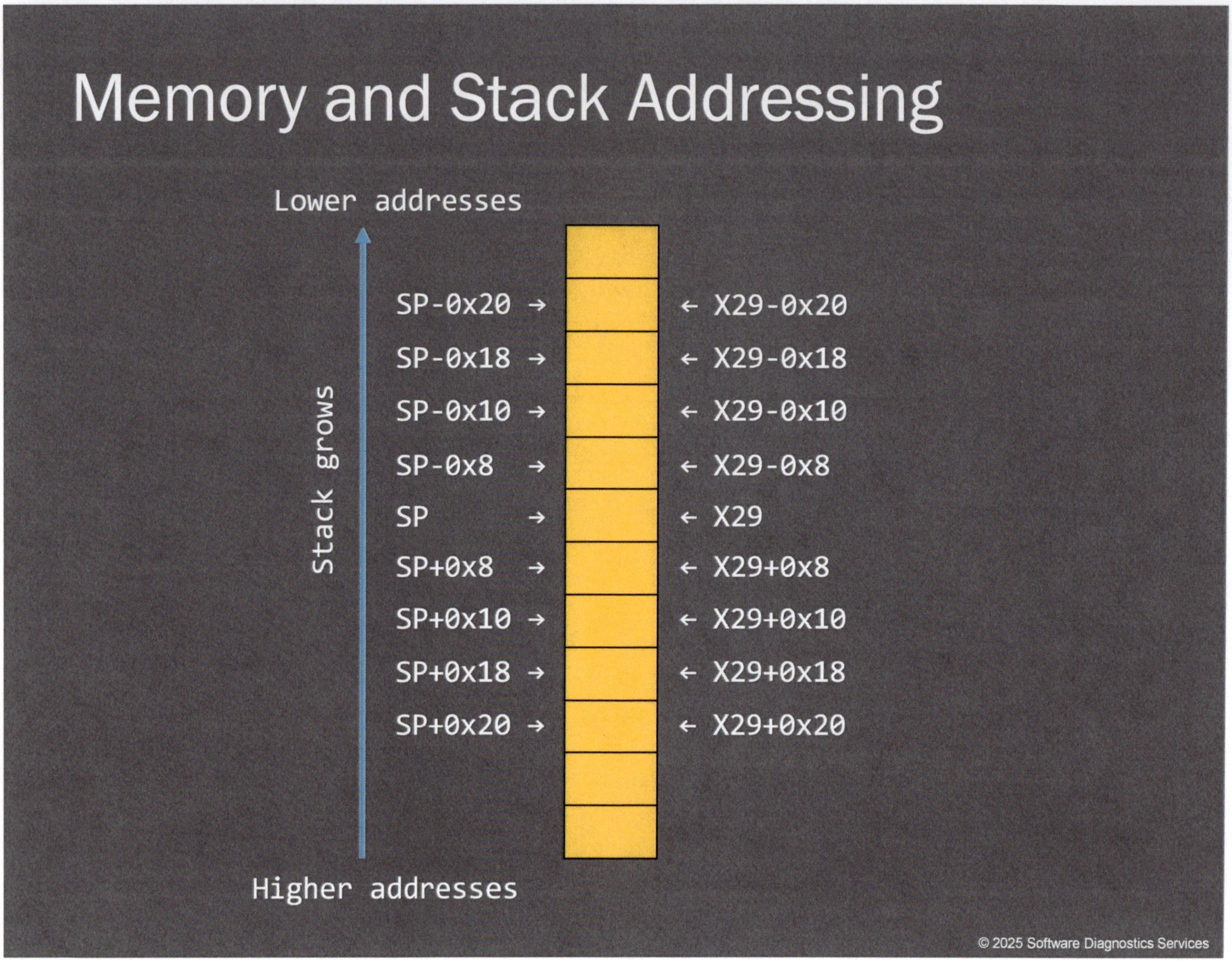

Before we look at operations with memory, let's look at a graphical representation of memory addressing. A thread stack is just any other memory region, so instead of **SP** and **X29** (**FP**), any other register can be used. Please note that the stack grows towards lower addresses, so to access the previously pushed values, you need to use positive offsets from **SP**.

Instructions: memory load (ARM64)

- Opcode DST, DST_2, [SRC, Offset]
- Opcode DST, DST_2, [SRC], Offset // Postincrement
- Examples:

```
ldr   x0, [sp]                  // X0 ← value at address SP+0
ldr   x0, [x29, #-8]            // X0 ← value at address X29-0x8
ldp   x29, x30, [sp, #32]       // X29 ← value at address SP+32 (0x20)
                                // X30 ← value at address SP+40 (0x28)
ldp   x29, x30, [sp], #16       // X29 ← value at address SP+0
                                // X30 ← value at address SP+8
                                // SP ← SP+16 (0x10)
```


Constants are encoded in instructions, but if we need arbitrary values, we must get them from memory. Square brackets show memory access relative to an address stored in some register. There's also an option to adjust the value of the register after load, the so-called **Postincrement**, which can be negative. As we see later, loading pairs of registers can be useful.

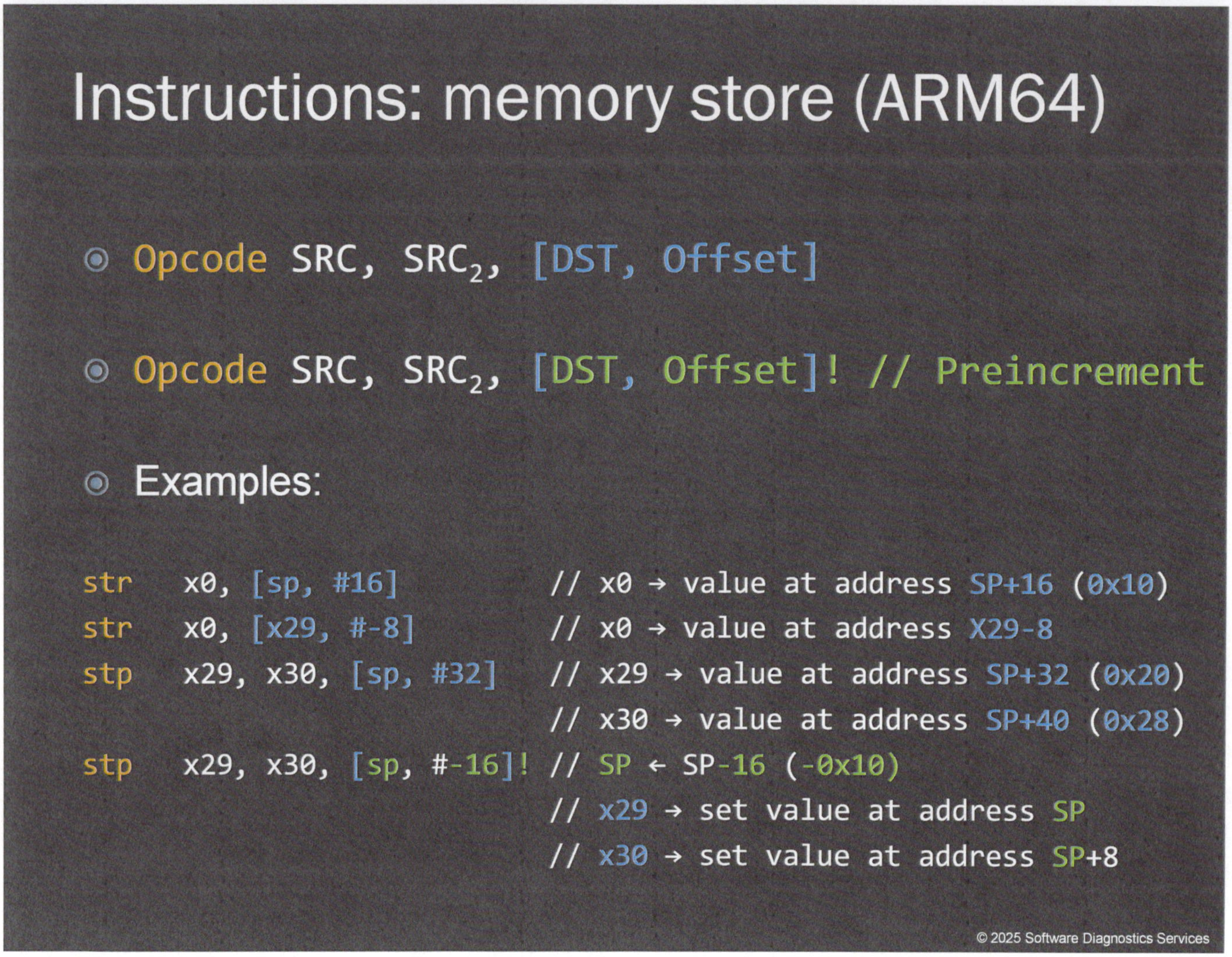

Storing operand order goes in the other direction compared to other instructions. There's a possibility to **Preincrement** the destination register before storing values.

Instructions: indexing (ARM64)

- Opcode DST, [SRC, SRC$_{offset}$, Shift]
- Opcode SRC, [DST, DST$_{Offset}$, Shift]
- Example:

```
ldr      x0, [x0, x1, lsl #3]    // X0 ← value at address X0+X1<<3
                                 //          (X0+X1*8)
```

Instructions: flow (ARM64)

- Opcode DST, SRC
- Examples:

```
adrp  x0, 0x420000        // x0 ← 0x420000

b     0x10493fc1c         // PC ← 0x10493fc1c
                          // (goto 0x10493fc1c)
br    x17                 // PC ← the value of X17

0x10493fc14:              // PC == 0x10493fc14
bl    0x10493ff74         // LR ← PC+4 (0x10493fc18)
                          // PC ← 0x10493ff74
                          // (goto 0x10493ff74)
```


Because the size of every instruction is 4 bytes (32 bits), it is only possible to encode a part of a large 4GB address range, either as a relative offset to the current **PC** or via **ADRP** instruction. Goto (an unconditional branch) is implemented via the **B** instruction. Function calls are implemented via the **BL** (Branch and Link) instruction. For conditional branches, please look at the official documentation provided on the References slide. We don't use these instructions in our exercises.

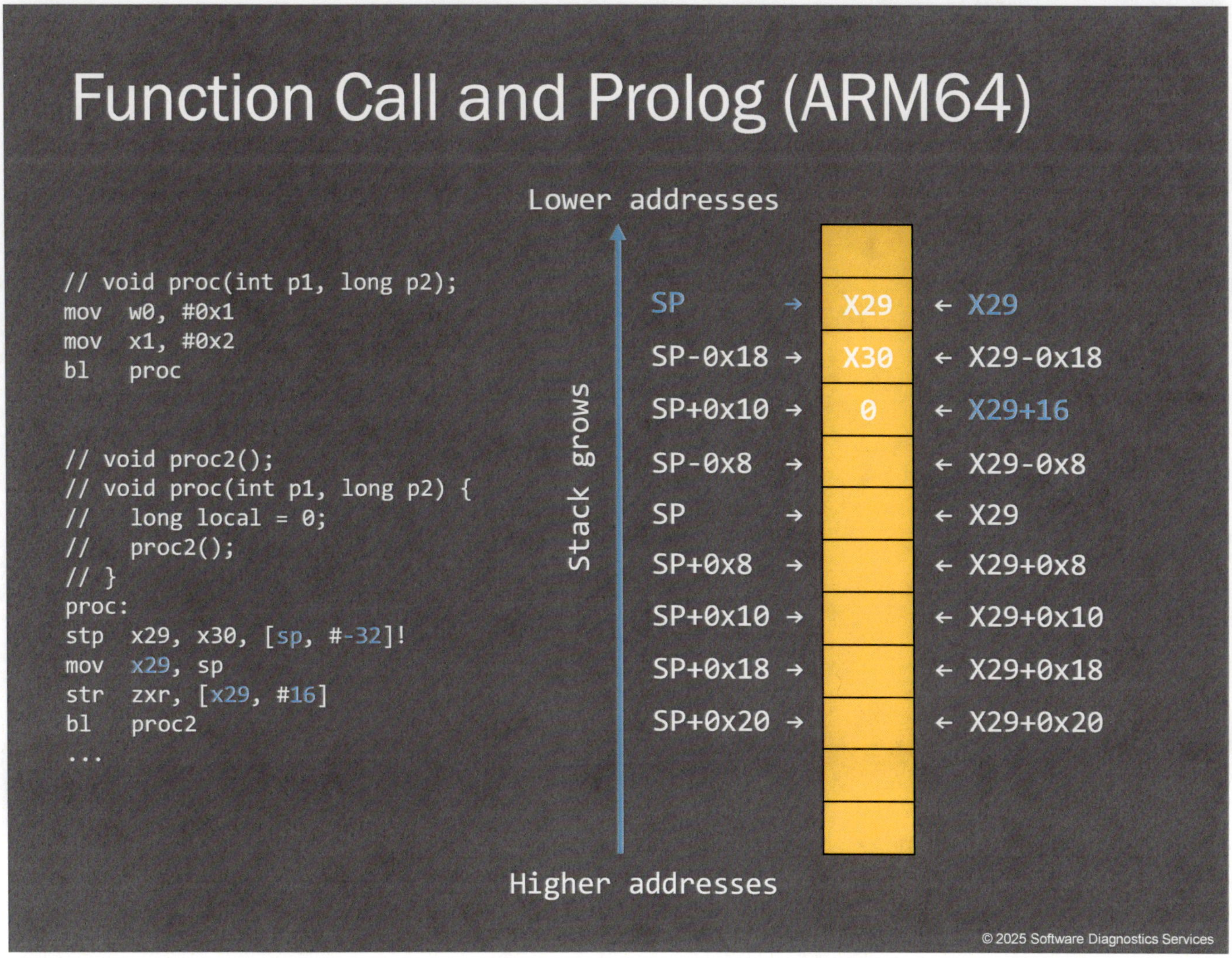

When a function is called from the caller, a callee needs to do certain operations to make room for local variables on the thread stack and save **LR** if there are further calls in the function body. There are different ways to do that, and the assembly language code on the left is one of them. I use a different color in the diagram on the right to highlight the updated **SP** and **X29** (**FP**) values before *proc2* is called. Please also note an example of zero register usage. For simplicity of illustration, I only use 64-bit values.

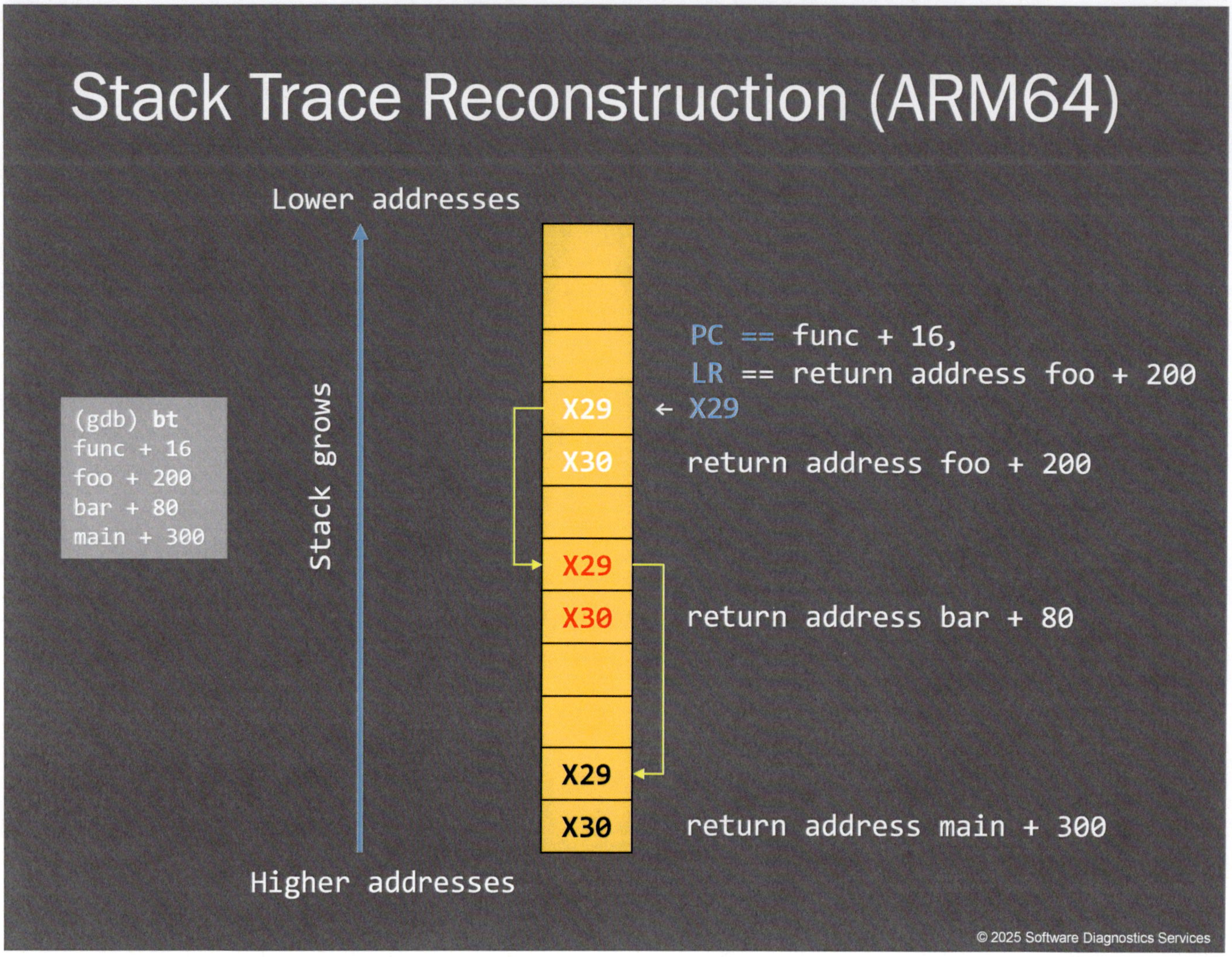

You may have noticed on the previous diagram that the new **X29** (**FP**) points to the **X29** of the caller, and below the previous **X29** is the return address of the caller. So, if you know either the return address in **LR** or **X29**, you can reconstruct the stack trace if the compiler follows the preceding function prolog convention.

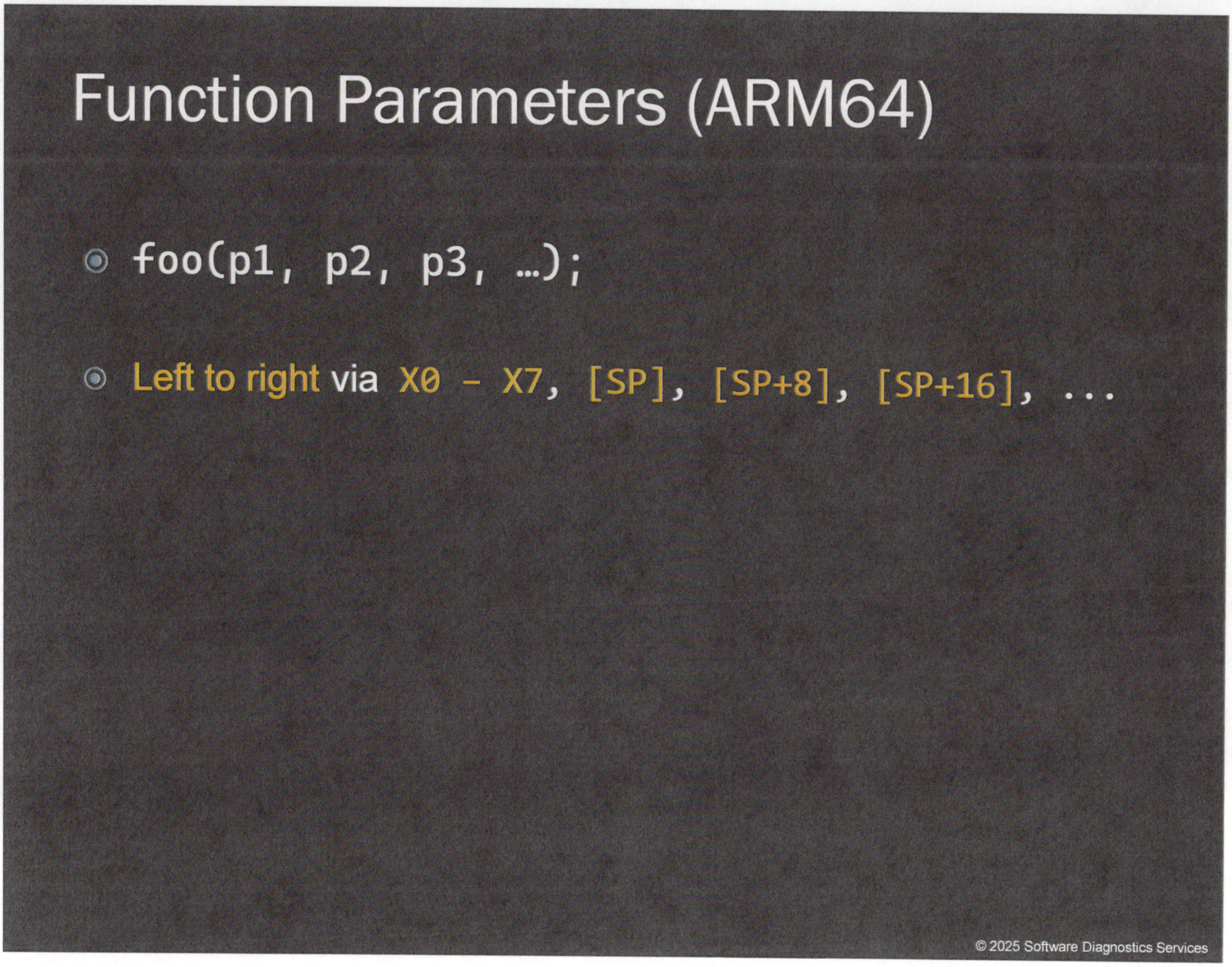

On the ARM64 Linux platform, the first eight parameters are passed via registers from left to right and the rest – via the stack locations.

x64 Disassembly (Intel WinDbg Flavor)

Part 5: x64 Disassembly

(Intel WinDbg Flavor)

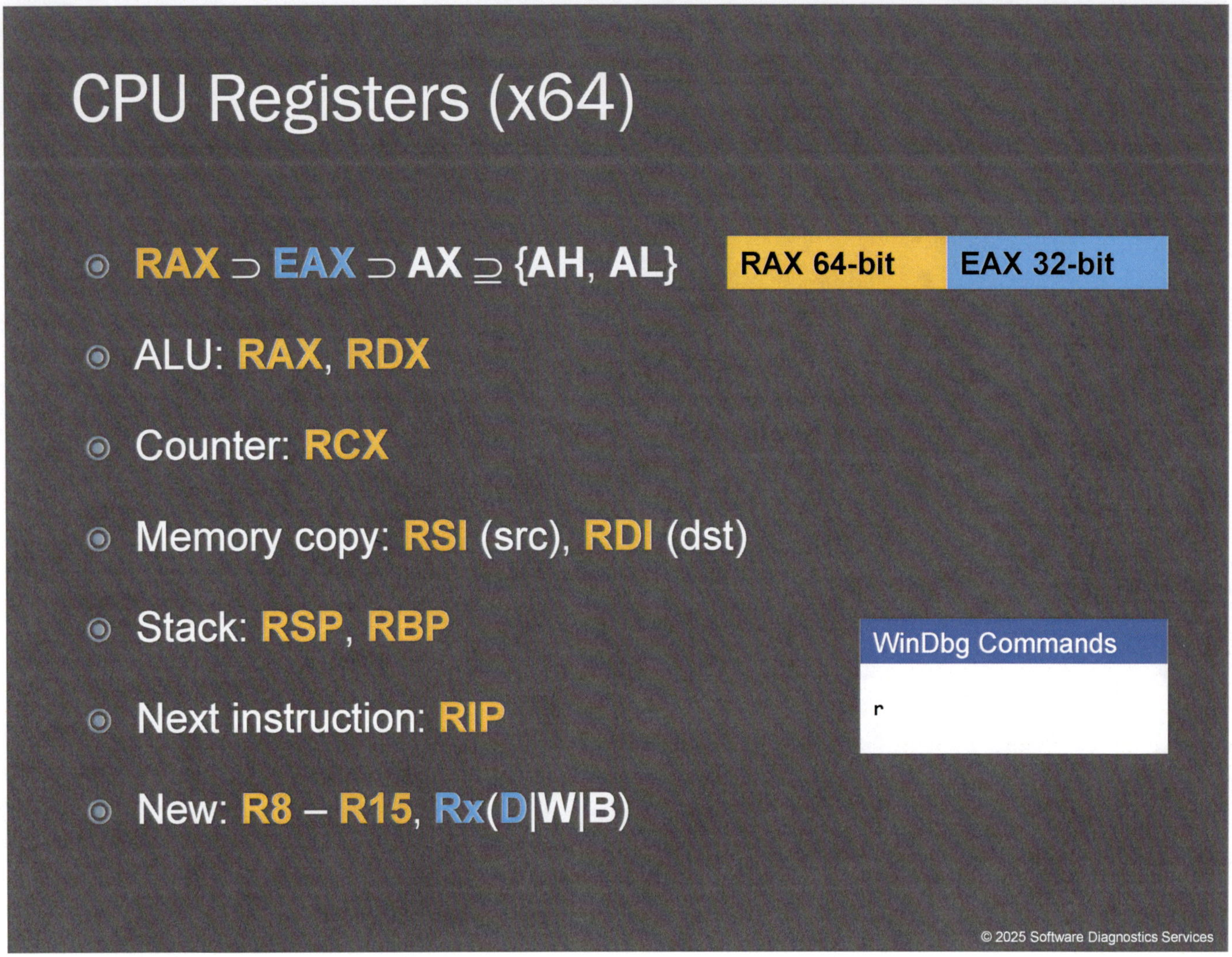

There are familiar 32-bit CPU register names, such as **EAX,** that are extended to 64-bit names, such as **RAX**. Most of them are traditionally specialized, such as ALU, counter, and memory copy registers. Although now they all can be used as general-purpose registers. There is, of course, a stack pointer, **RSP**, and it also takes the role of a frame pointer, which is also used to address local variables and saved parameters. In some compiler code generation implementations, **RBP** is also used as a general-purpose register, with **RSP** taking the role of a frame pointer. Together, they can be used for stack reconstruction. An instruction pointer **RIP** is saved in the stack memory region with every function call, then restored on return from the called function. In addition, the x64 platform features another eight general-purpose registers, from **R8** to **R15**.

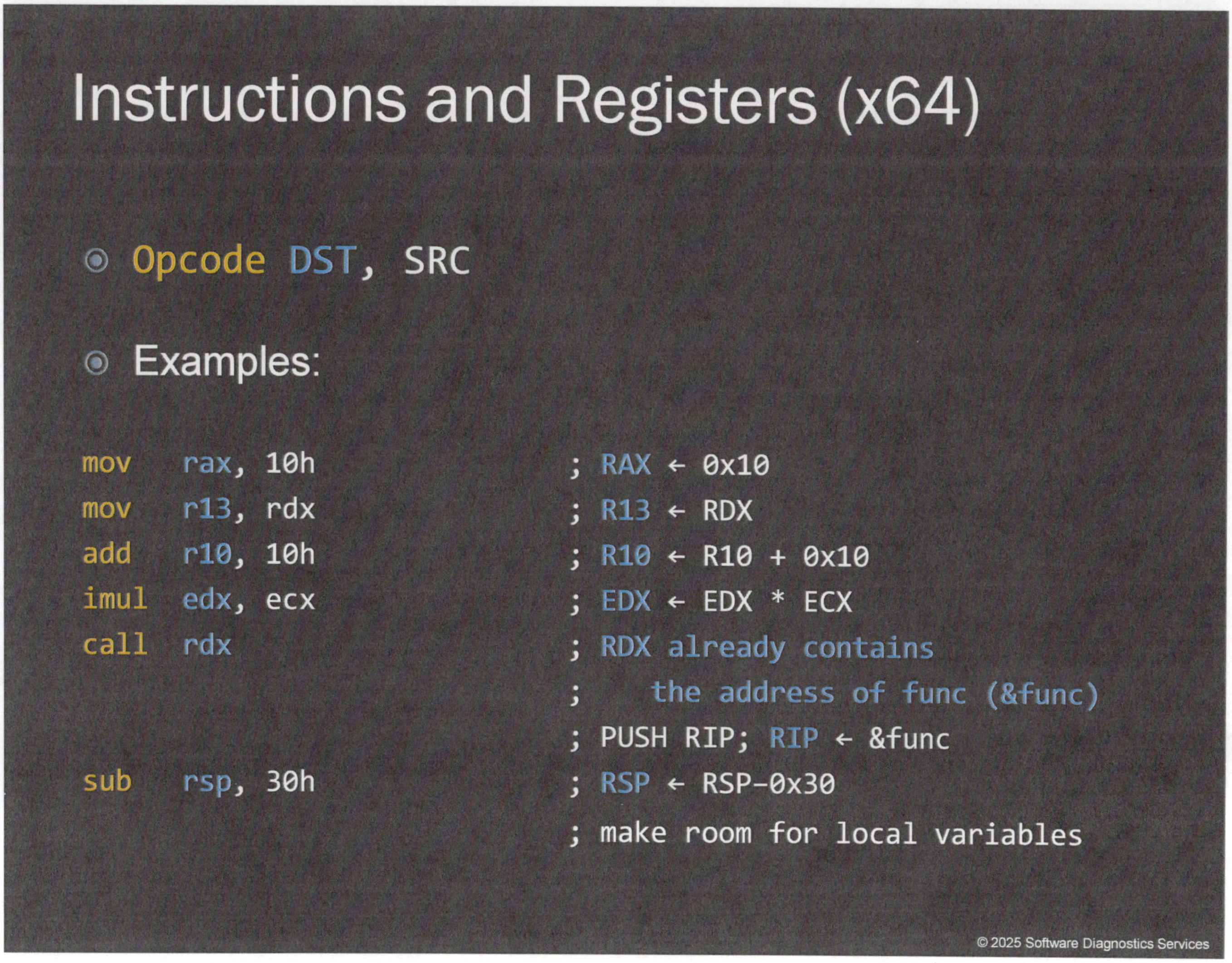

This slide shows a few examples of CPU instructions involving operations with registers, such as moving a value and doing arithmetic. The direction of operands is opposite to the AT&T x64 disassembly flavor if you are accustomed to default GDB disassembly on Linux.

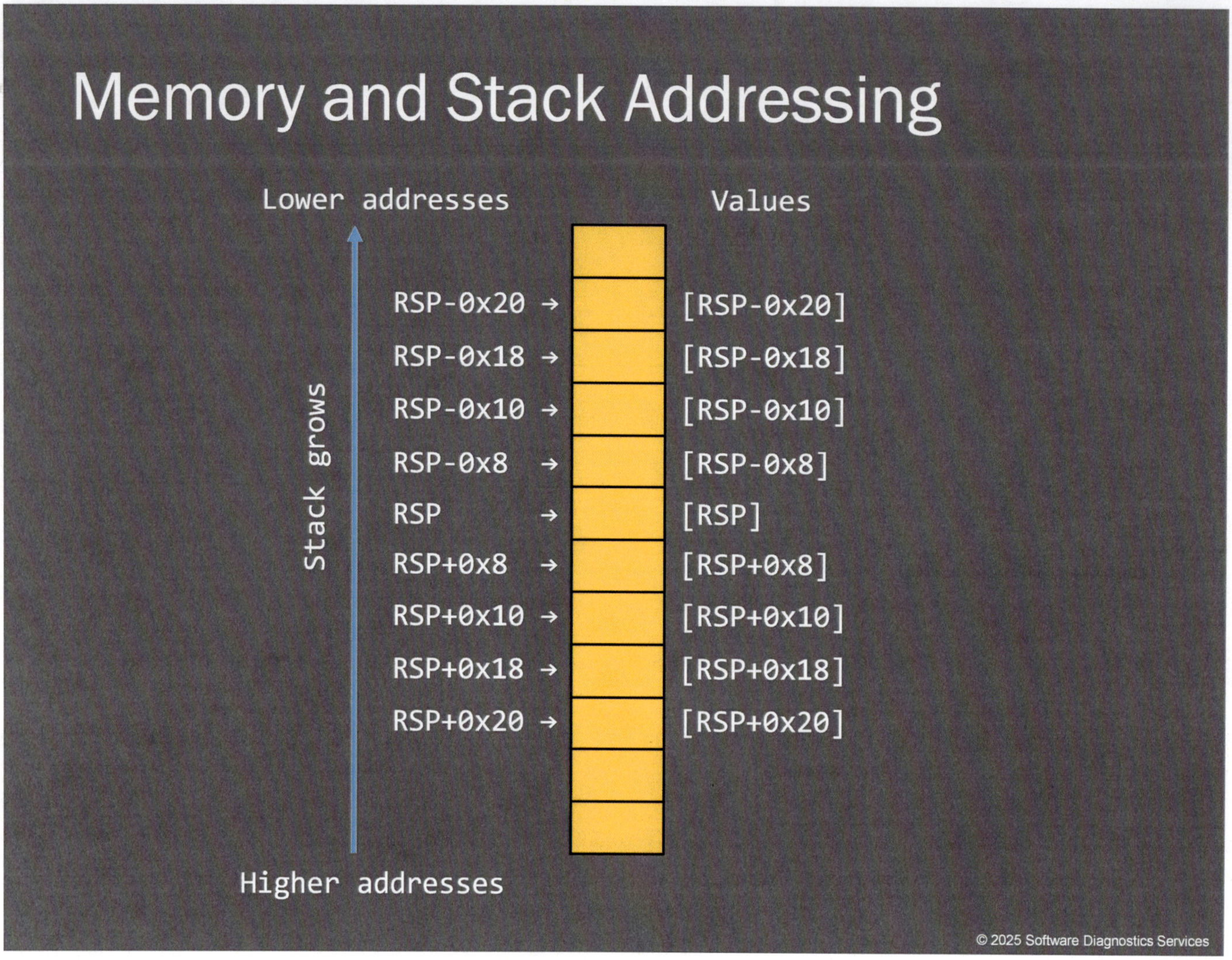

Before we look at operations with memory, let's look at a graphical representation of memory addressing where for simplicity, I use 64-bit (or 8-byte) memory cells. A thread stack is just any other memory region, so instead of **RSP,** any other register can be used. Please note that the stack grows towards lower addresses, so to access the previously pushed values, you need to use positive offsets from **RSP**.

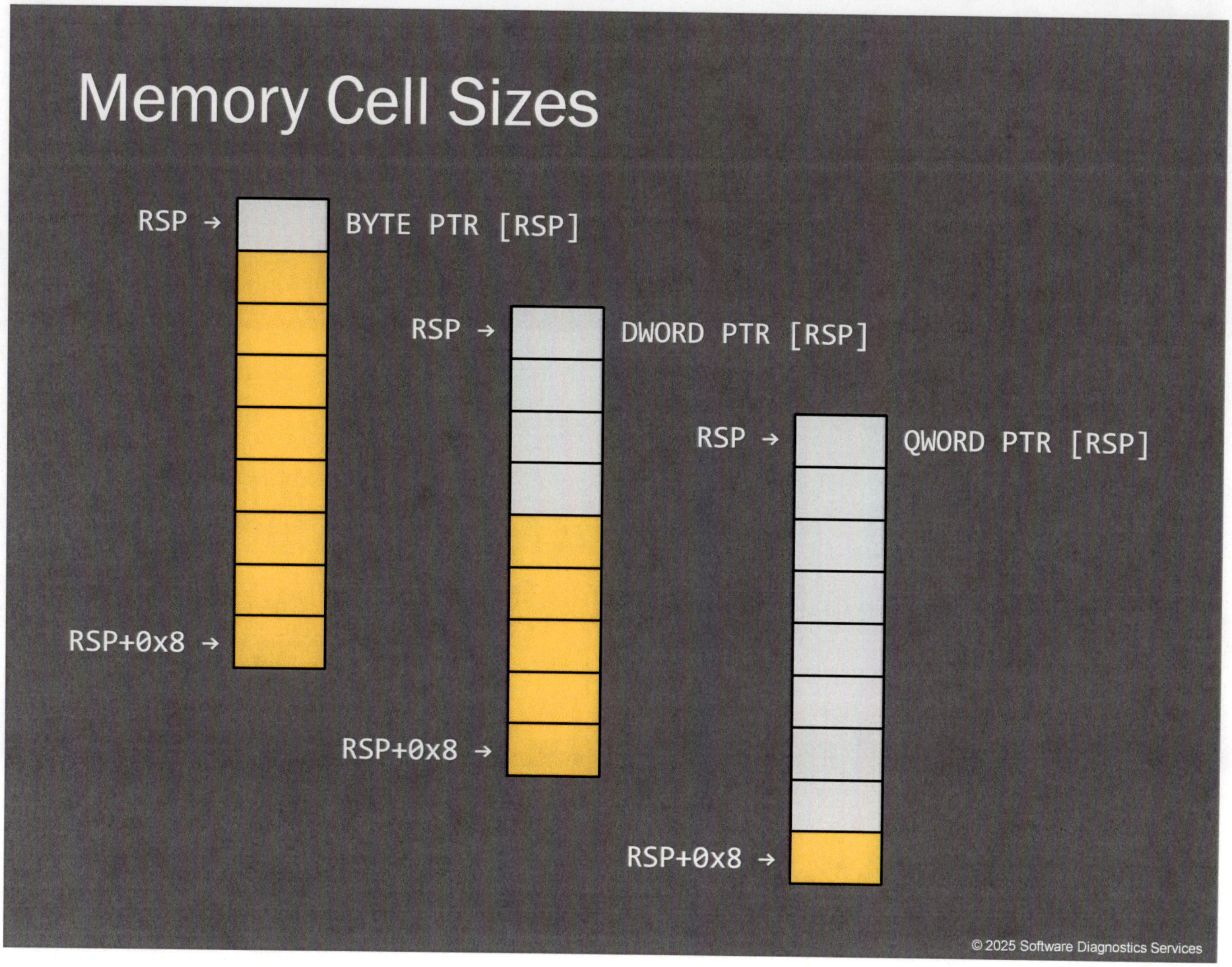

Here, each memory cell is 8-bit (or one byte). When we have a register pointing to memory, and we want to work with the value at that address, we need to specify the size of memory cells to work with, for example, **BYTE PTR** if we want to work with a byte, **DWORD PTR** if we want to work with 32-bit double words, and **QWORD PTR** if we want to work with 64-bit quad words. There's also **WORD PTR** for 16-bit values. This notation is different from Linux GDB, where we have bytes, half-words, words, and double words.

Memory Load Instructions (x64)

- Opcode DST, PTR [SRC+Offset]
- Opcode DST
- Examples:

```
mov   rax, qword ptr [rsp+10h] ; RAX ←
                               ; 64-bit value at address RSP+0x10
mov   ecx, dword ptr [20]      ; ECX ←
                               ; 32-bit value at address 0x20
pop   rdi                      ; RDI ← value at address RSP
                               ; RSP ← RSP + 8
lea   r8, [rsp+20h]            ; R8 ← address RSP+0x20
```


Constants are encoded in instructions, but if we need arbitrary values, we must get them from memory. Square brackets show memory access relative to an address stored in a register.

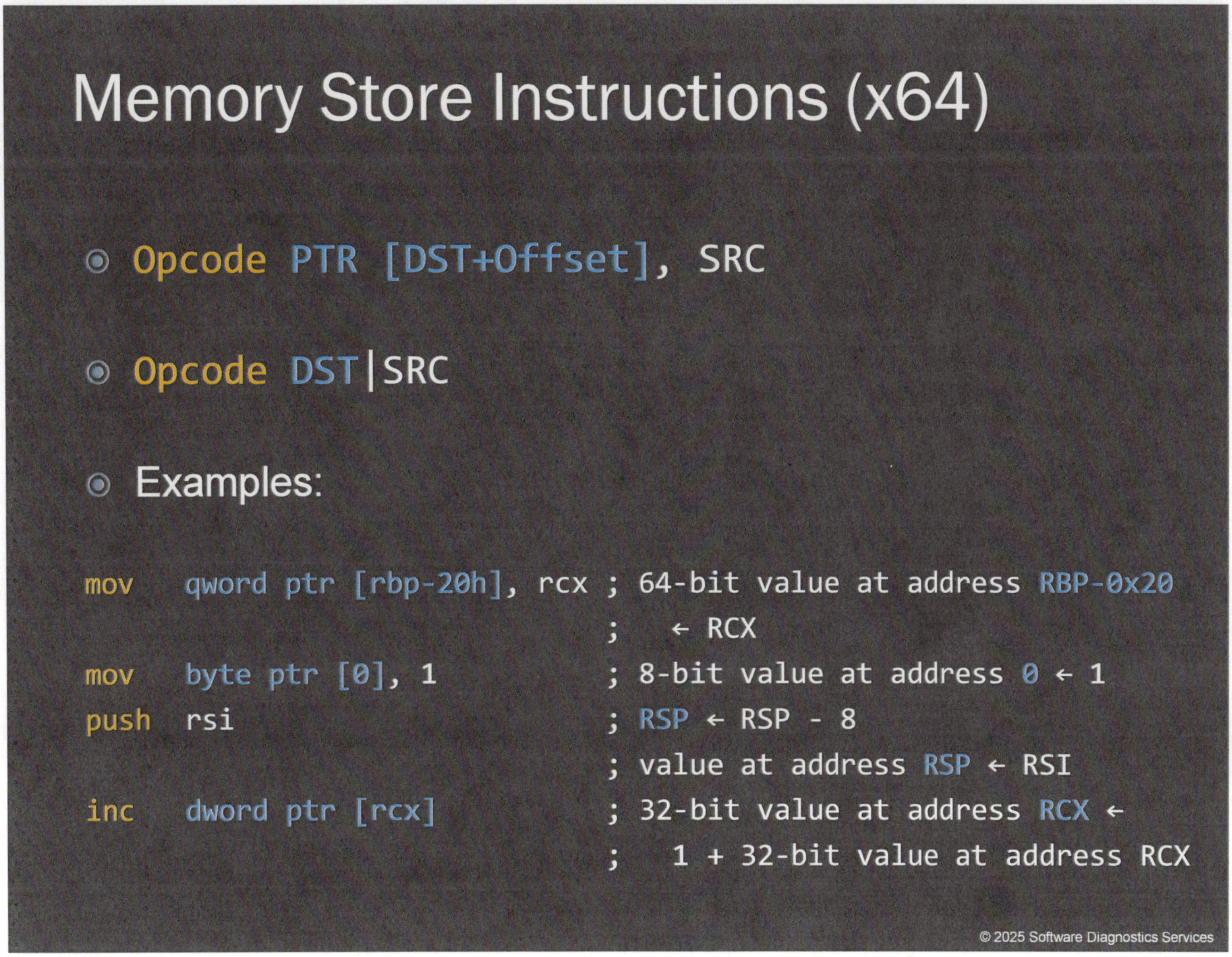

Storing is similar to loading.

Instructions: indexing (x64)

- Opcode DST, PTR [SRC$_{base}$ + SRC$_{index}$*Scale + Offset]
- Opcode PTR [DST$_{base}$ + DST$_{index}$*Scale + Offset], SRC
- Examples:

```
mov   rax, qword ptr [rdx+rax]   # RAX ← value at address RDX+RAX*1
mov   qword ptr [rdx+rax*8], 0   # value at address RDX+RAX*8 ← 0
lea   rdx, [rax*8]               # RDX ← address RAX*8
```

Flow Instructions (x64)

- Opcode DST
- Opcode PTR [DST]
- Examples:

```
jmp   00007ff6`9ef2f008    ; RIP ← 0x7ff69ef2f008
                           ; (goto 0x7ff69ef2f008)
jmp   qword ptr [rax+10h] ; RIP ← value at address RAX+0x10
call  00007ff6`9ef21400    ; RSP ← RSP - 8
00007ff6`9ef21057:         ; value at address RSP ← 0x7ff69ef21057
                           ; RIP ← 0x7ff69ef21400
                           ; (goto 0x7ff69ef21400)
```


Goto (an unconditional jump) is implemented via the **JMP** instruction. Function calls are implemented via **CALL** instruction. For conditional branches, please look at the official Intel documentation. We don't use these instructions in our exercises.

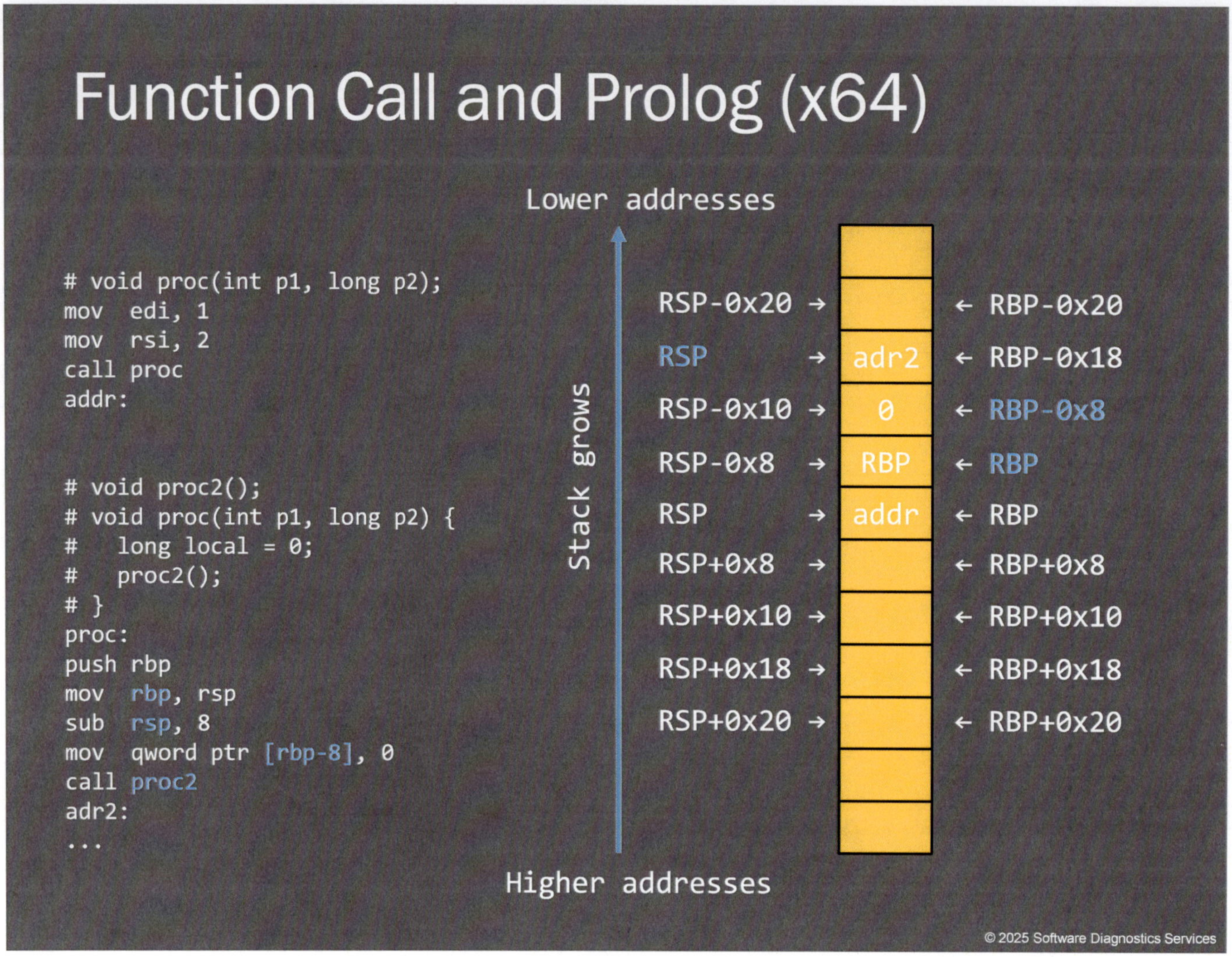

When a function is called from the caller, a callee needs to do certain operations to make room for local variables on the thread stack. There are different ways to do that, and the assembly language code on the left is one of them. I use different colors in the diagram on the right to highlight the updated **RSP** and **RBP** values from the start of the *proc* function up to the moment when the *proc2* function is called. For simplicity of illustration, I only use 64-bit values.

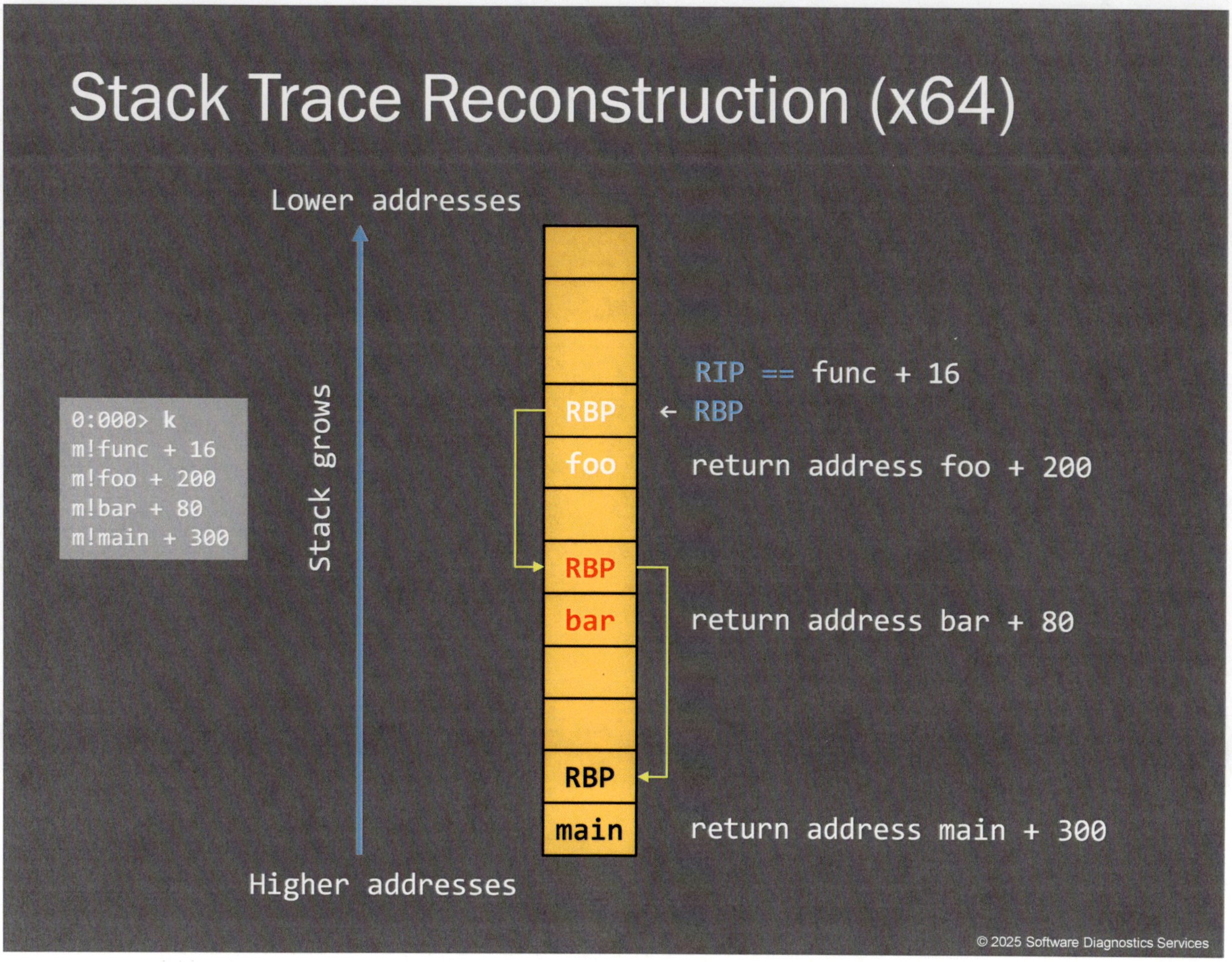

Stack Trace Reconstruction (x64)
Lower addresses
Stack grows
Higher addresses
0:000> k
m!func + 16
m!foo + 200
m!bar + 80
m!main + 300
RBP
foo
RBP
bar
RBP
main
RIP == func + 16
← RBP
return address foo + 200
return address bar + 80
return address main + 300
© 2025 Software Diagnostics Services

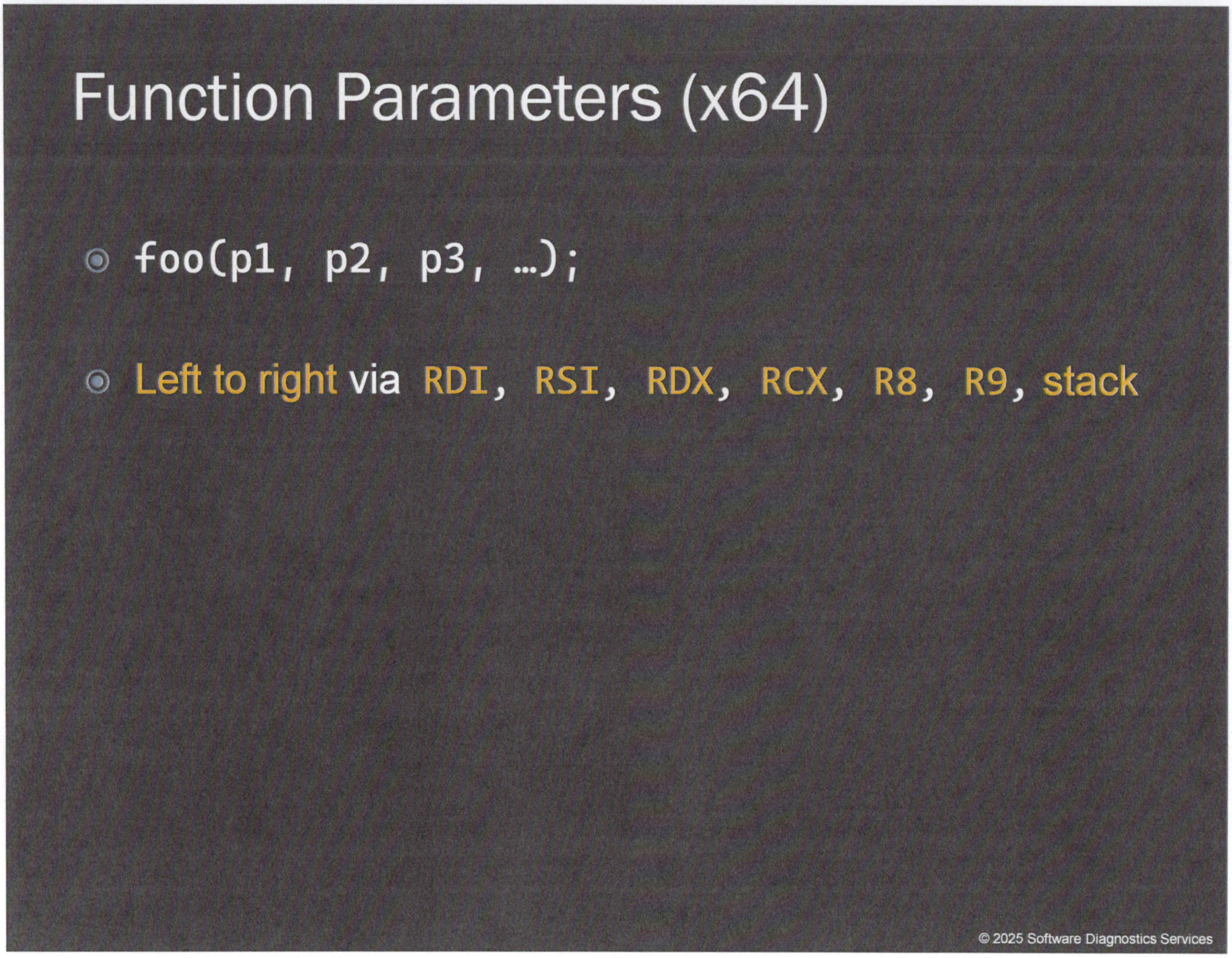

On the x64 Linux platform, the first six C and C++ function parameters from left to right are moved to CPU registers, and the rest are passed via stack locations.

Practice Exercises

Part 6: Practice Exercises

Now we come to practice. The goal is to show you important commands and how their output helps recognize patterns of abnormal software behavior.

Links

- Memory Dumps:

Included in Exercise 0

- Exercise Transcripts:

Included in this book

Exercise 0

- **Goal:** Install GDB and check if GDB loads a core dump correctly
- **Goal:** Install WinDbg or Debugging Tools for Windows or pull Docker image, and check that symbols are set up correctly
- **Patterns:** Stack Trace; Incorrect Stack Trace
- \ALCDA-Dumps\Exercise-A0-x64-GDB.pdf
- \ALCDA-Dumps\Exercise-A0-A64-GDB.pdf
- \ALCDA-Dumps\Exercise-A0-A64-x64-WinDbg.pdf

We have four similar exercise sets: x64 Linux core dumps/GDB, ARM64 Linux core dumps/GDB, ARM64 Linux core dumps/WinDbg, and (new for this edition) x64 Linux core dumps/WinDbg.

Exercise 0 (x64, GDB)

Goal: Install GDB and check if GDB loads a core dump correctly.

Patterns: Stack Trace; Incorrect Stack Trace.

1. Download core dump files if you haven't done that already and unpack the archives:

https://www.patterndiagnostics.com/Training/ALCDA/ALCDA-V2-Dumps.tar.gz
https://www.patterndiagnostics.com/Training/ALCDA/ALCDA-V4-Dumps2.zip
https://www.patterndiagnostics.com/Training/ALCDA/ALCDA-V4-Dumps3.zip
https://www.patterndiagnostics.com/Training/ALCDA/ALCDA-V4-Dumps4.zip
https://www.patterndiagnostics.com/Training/ALCDA/ALCDA-V4-Dumps5.zip
https://www.patterndiagnostics.com/Training/ALCDA/ALCDA-V4-Dumps6.zip

2. Download and install the latest version of GDB. For WSL2 Debian, we used the following commands:

```
$ sudo apt install build-essential
$ sudo apt install gdb
```

On our RHEL-type system, we installed the tools and GDB via:

```
$ sudo yum group install "Development Tools"
$ sudo yum install gdb
```

3. Verify that GDB is accessible and then exit it (**q** command):

```
$ gdb
GNU gdb (Debian 8.2.1-2+b3) 8.2.1
Copyright (C) 2018 Free Software Foundation, Inc.
License GPLv3+: GNU GPL version 3 or later <http://gnu.org/licenses/gpl.html>
This is free software: you are free to change and redistribute it.
There is NO WARRANTY, to the extent permitted by law.
Type "show copying" and "show warranty" for details.
This GDB was configured as "x86_64-linux-gnu".
Type "show configuration" for configuration details.
For bug reporting instructions, please see:
<http://www.gnu.org/software/gdb/bugs/>.
Find the GDB manual and other documentation resources online at:
    <http://www.gnu.org/software/gdb/documentation/>.

For help, type "help".
Type "apropos word" to search for commands related to "word".

(gdb) q
$
```

4. Load *core.App0* dump file and *App0* executable from the x64/App0 directory:

```
$ cd ALCDA2/x64/App0
```

```
~/ALCDA2/x64/App0$ gdb -c core.App0 -se App0
```

```
GNU gdb (Debian 8.2.1-2+b3) 8.2.1
Copyright (C) 2018 Free Software Foundation, Inc.
License GPLv3+: GNU GPL version 3 or later <http://gnu.org/licenses/gpl.html>
This is free software: you are free to change and redistribute it.
There is NO WARRANTY, to the extent permitted by law.
Type "show copying" and "show warranty" for details.
This GDB was configured as "x86_64-linux-gnu".
Type "show configuration" for configuration details.
For bug reporting instructions, please see:
<http://www.gnu.org/software/gdb/bugs/>.
Find the GDB manual and other documentation resources online at:
    <http://www.gnu.org/software/gdb/documentation/>.

For help, type "help".
Type "apropos word" to search for commands related to "word"...
Reading symbols from App0...(no debugging symbols found)...done.
[New LWP 4561]
Core was generated by `./App0'.
Program terminated with signal SIGABRT, Aborted.
#0  0x00000000004075cb in raise ()
```

5. Verify that the stack trace (back trace) is shown correctly with symbols:

```
(gdb) bt
#0  0x00000000004075cb in raise ()
#1  0x0000000000401205 in abort ()
#2  0x0000000000401b56 in bar ()
#3  0x0000000000401b64 in foo ()
#4  0x0000000000401b80 in main ()
```

6. We exit GDB.

```
(gdb) q
```

```
~/ALCDA2/x64/App0$
```

Exercise 0 (A64, GDB, GDB-Multiarch)

Goal: Install GDB and check if GDB loads a core dump correctly.

Patterns: Stack Trace; Incorrect Stack Trace.

1. Download core dump files if you haven't done that already and unpack the archives:

https://www.patterndiagnostics.com/Training/ALCDA/ALCDA-V2-Dumps.zip
https://www.patterndiagnostics.com/Training/ALCDA/ALCDA-V3-Dumps.tar.gz
https://www.patterndiagnostics.com/Training/ALCDA/ALCDA-V4-Dumps2.zip
https://www.patterndiagnostics.com/Training/ALCDA/ALCDA-V4-Dumps3.zip
https://www.patterndiagnostics.com/Training/ALCDA/ALCDA-V4-Dumps4.zip
https://www.patterndiagnostics.com/Training/ALCDA/ALCDA-V4-Dumps5.zip
https://www.patterndiagnostics.com/Training/ALCDA/ALCDA-V4-Dumps6.zip

2. Download and install the latest version of GDB. For Ubuntu, we used the following commands:

```
$ sudo apt install build-essential
$ sudo apt install gdb
```

3. Verify that GDB is accessible and then exit it (**q** command):

```
$ gdb
GNU gdb (Ubuntu 12.1-0ubuntu1~22.04) 12.1
Copyright (C) 2022 Free Software Foundation, Inc.
License GPLv3+: GNU GPL version 3 or later <http://gnu.org/licenses/gpl.html>
This is free software: you are free to change and redistribute it.
There is NO WARRANTY, to the extent permitted by law.
Type "show copying" and "show warranty" for details.
This GDB was configured as "aarch64-linux-gnu".
Type "show configuration" for configuration details.
For bug reporting instructions, please see:
<https://www.gnu.org/software/gdb/bugs/>.
Find the GDB manual and other documentation resources online at:
    <http://www.gnu.org/software/gdb/documentation/>.

For help, type "help".
Type "apropos word" to search for commands related to "word".
(gdb)

(gdb) q
$
```

4. Load *core.31918* dump file and *App0* executable from the A64/App0 directory:

```
$ cd ALCDA2/A64/App0
```

```
~/ALCDA2/A64/App0$ gdb -c core.31918 -se App0
GNU gdb (Ubuntu 12.1-0ubuntu1~22.04) 12.1
Copyright (C) 2022 Free Software Foundation, Inc.
License GPLv3+: GNU GPL version 3 or later <http://gnu.org/licenses/gpl.html>
This is free software: you are free to change and redistribute it.
There is NO WARRANTY, to the extent permitted by law.
Type "show copying" and "show warranty" for details.
This GDB was configured as "aarch64-linux-gnu".
Type "show configuration" for configuration details.
For bug reporting instructions, please see:
<https://www.gnu.org/software/gdb/bugs/>.
Find the GDB manual and other documentation resources online at:
    <http://www.gnu.org/software/gdb/documentation/>.

For help, type "help".
Type "apropos word" to search for commands related to "word"...
Reading symbols from App0...
(No debugging symbols found in App0)

warning: Can't open file /home/opc/ALCDA2/App0/App0 during file-backed mapping note processing
[New LWP 31918]
Core was generated by `./App0'.
Program terminated with signal SIGABRT, Aborted.
#0  0x0000000000415000 in raise ()
```

5. Verify that the stack trace (back trace) is shown correctly with symbols:

```
(gdb) bt
#0  0x0000000000415000 in raise ()
#1  0x0000000000402808 in abort ()
#2  0x0000000000401d24 in bar ()
#3  0x0000000000401d30 in foo ()
#4  0x0000000000401d4c in main ()
```

6. We exit GDB.

```
(gdb) q
```

```
~/ALCDA2/A64/App0$
```

7. It is also possible to analyze A64 core dumps on x64 platforms using GDB-Multiarch. For Debian, we used the following commands:

```
$ sudo apt install gdb-multiarch
```

8. Load *core.31918* dump file and *App0* executable from the A64/App0 directory:

```
$ cd ALCDA2/A64/App0
```

```
~/ALCDA2/A64/App0$ gdb-multiarch -c core.31918 -se App0
GNU gdb (Debian 8.2.1-2+b3) 8.2.1
Copyright (C) 2018 Free Software Foundation, Inc.
License GPLv3+: GNU GPL version 3 or later <http://gnu.org/licenses/gpl.html>
This is free software: you are free to change and redistribute it.
There is NO WARRANTY, to the extent permitted by law.
Type "show copying" and "show warranty" for details.
This GDB was configured as "x86_64-linux-gnu".
Type "show configuration" for configuration details.
For bug reporting instructions, please see:
<http://www.gnu.org/software/gdb/bugs/>.
Find the GDB manual and other documentation resources online at:
    <http://www.gnu.org/software/gdb/documentation/>.

For help, type "help".
Type "apropos word" to search for commands related to "word"...
Reading symbols from App0...(no debugging symbols found)...done.
[New LWP 31918]
Core was generated by `./App0'.
Program terminated with signal SIGABRT, Aborted.
#0  0x0000000000415000 in raise ()
```

9. Verify that the stack trace (back trace) is shown correctly with symbols:

```
(gdb) bt
#0  0x0000000000415000 in raise ()
#1  0x0000000000402808 in abort ()
#2  0x0000000000401d24 in bar ()
#3  0x0000000000401d30 in foo ()
#4  0x0000000000401d4c in main ()
```

10. We exit GDB-Multiarch.

```
(gdb) q

~/ALCDA2/A64/App0$
```

Exercise 0 (A64/x64, WinDbg, Classic WinDbg, Docker)

Goal: Install WinDbg or Debugging Tools for Windows or pull Docker image, and check that symbols are set up correctly.

Patterns: Stack Trace; Incorrect Stack Trace.

1. Download memory dump files if you haven't done that already and unpack the archives:

https://www.patterndiagnostics.com/Training/ALCDA/ALCDA-V2-Dumps.tar.gz
https://www.patterndiagnostics.com/Training/ALCDA/ALCDA-V2-Dumps.zip
https://www.patterndiagnostics.com/Training/ALCDA/ALCDA-V3-Dumps.tar.gz
https://www.patterndiagnostics.com/Training/ALCDA/ALCDA-V4-Dumps.zip
https://www.patterndiagnostics.com/Training/ALCDA/ALCDA-V4-Dumps2.zip
https://www.patterndiagnostics.com/Training/ALCDA/ALCDA-V4-Dumps3.zip
https://www.patterndiagnostics.com/Training/ALCDA/ALCDA-V4-Dumps4.zip
https://www.patterndiagnostics.com/Training/ALCDA/ALCDA-V4-Dumps5.zip
https://www.patterndiagnostics.com/Training/ALCDA/ALCDA-V4-Dumps6.zip

2. Install WinDbg (or upgrade existing WinDbg Preview) from https://learn.microsoft.com/en-gb/windows-hardware/drivers/debugger. Run WinDbg.

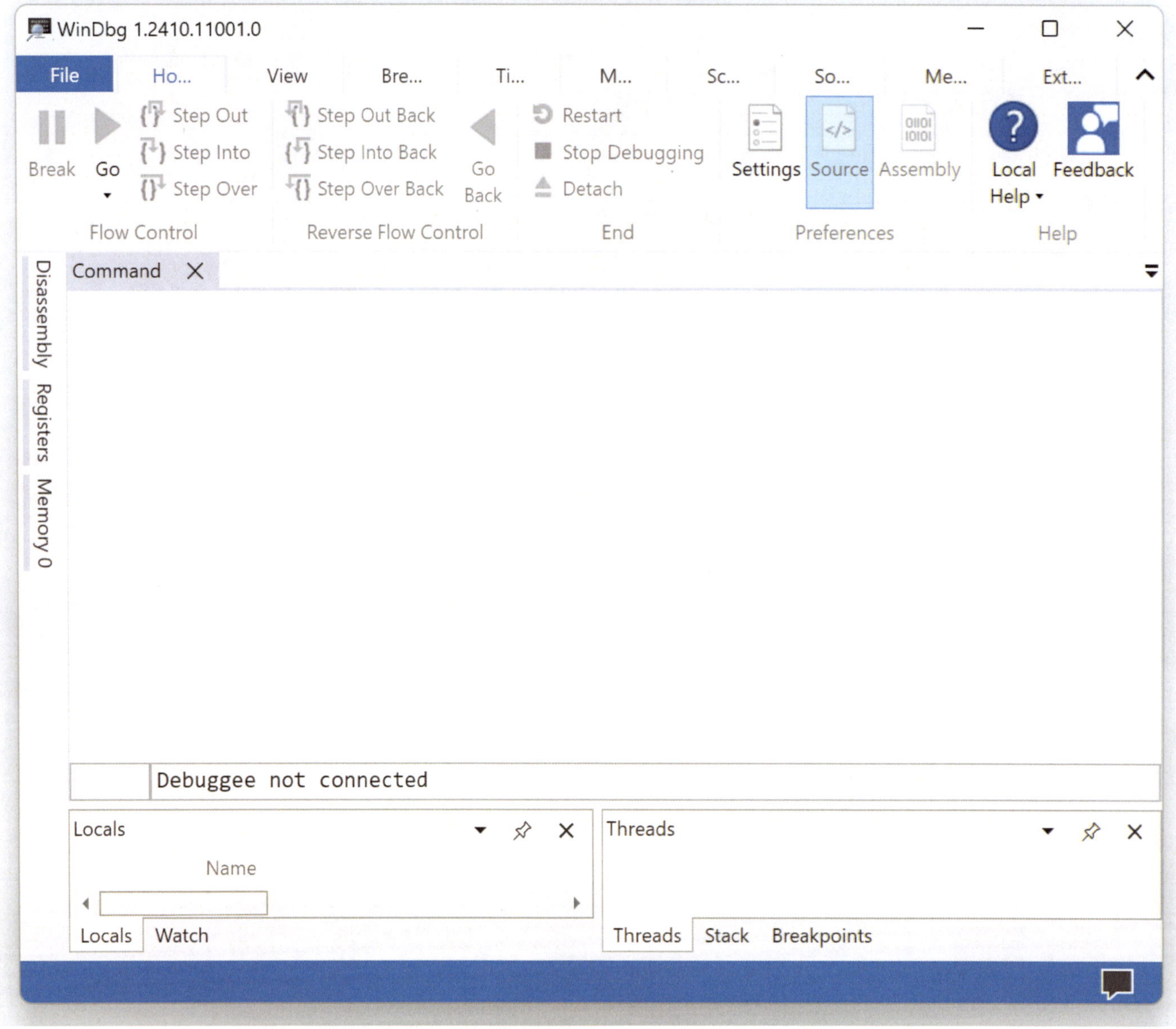

3. Open *\ALCDA2\A64\App0\core.31918*:

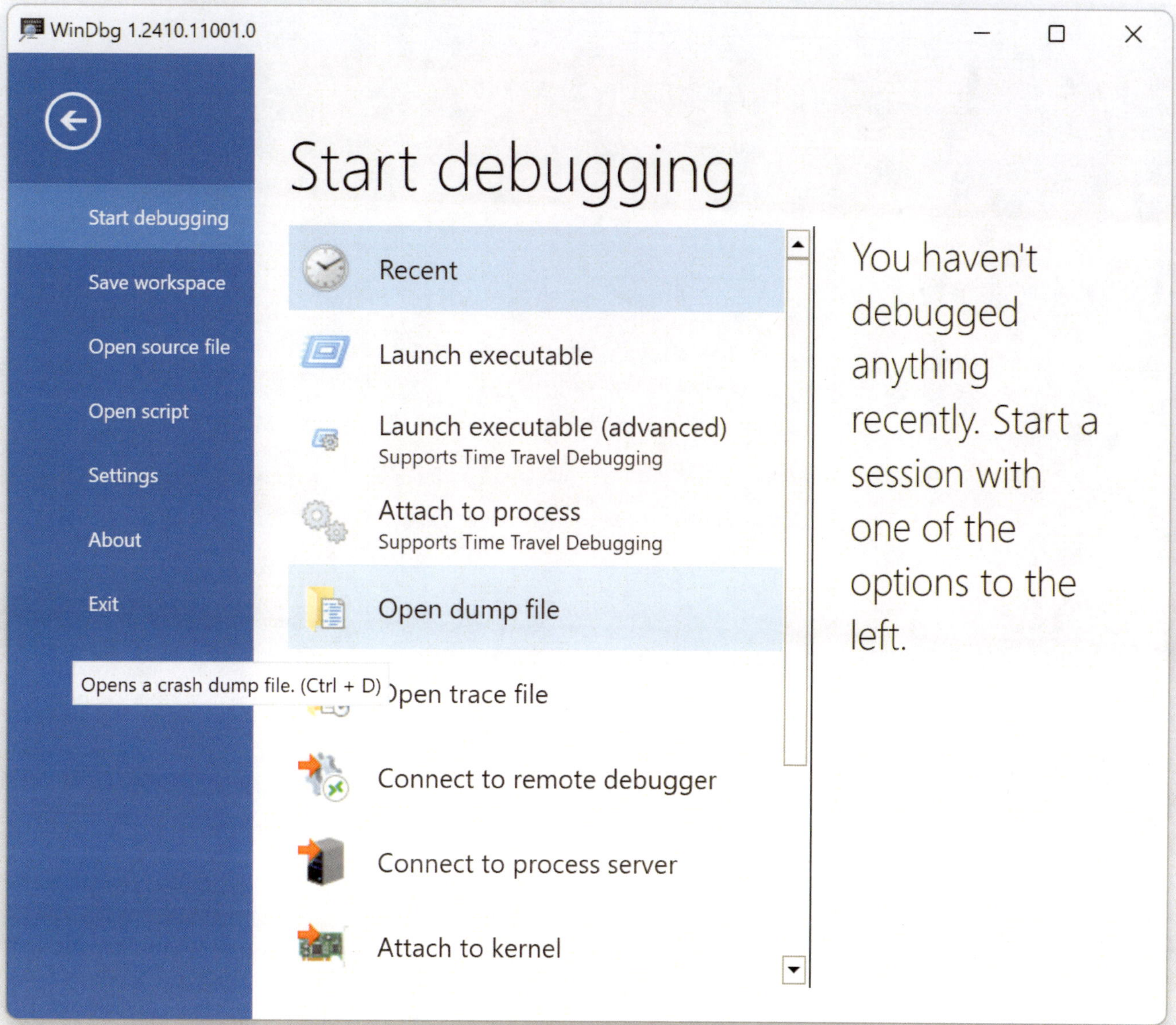

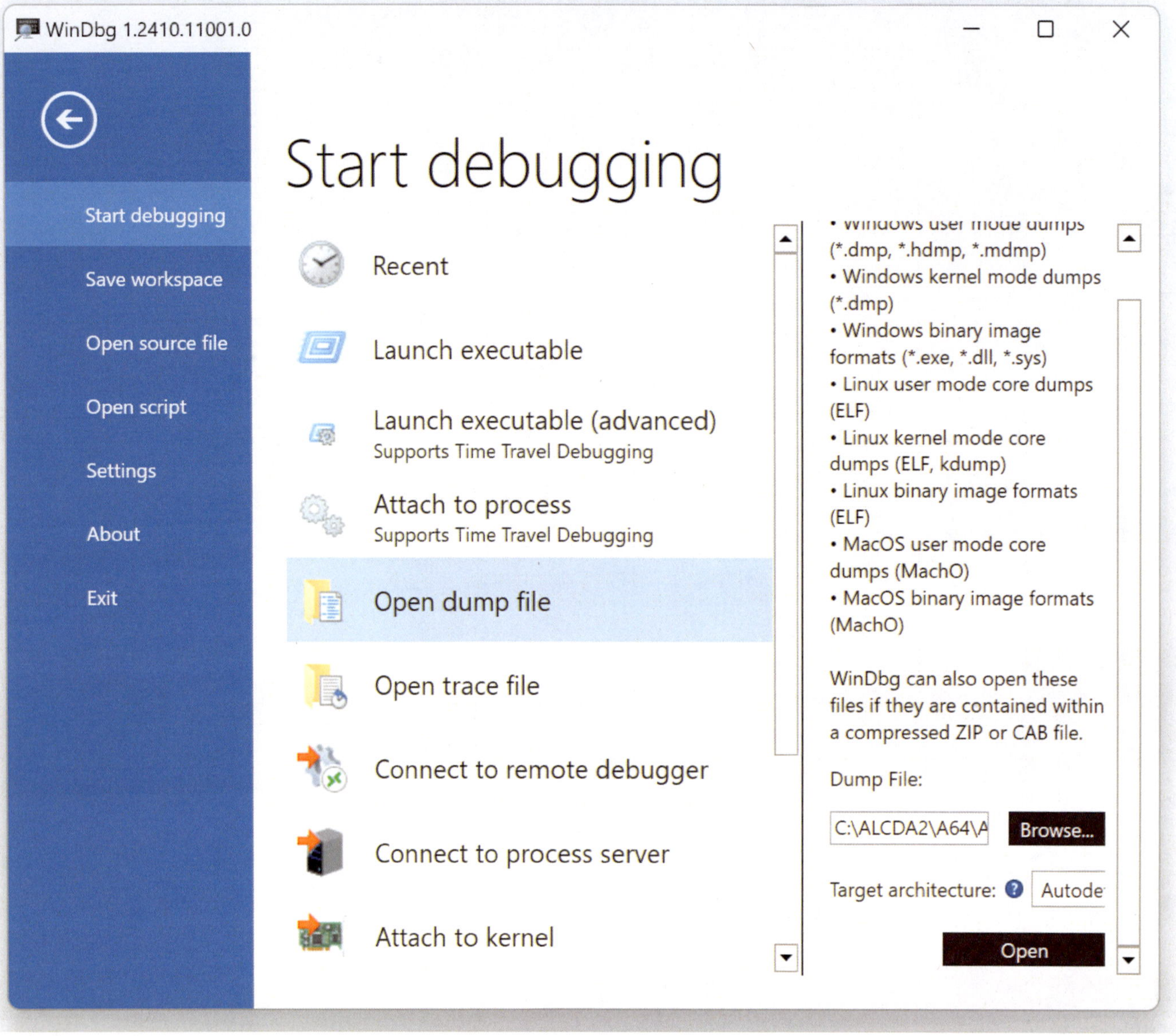
WinDbg 1.2410.11001.0
Start debugging
Start debugging
Save workspace
Open source file
Open script
Settings
About
Exit
Recent
Launch executable
Launch executable (advanced)
Supports Time Travel Debugging
Attach to process
Supports Time Travel Debugging
Open dump file
Open trace file
Connect to remote debugger
Connect to process server
Attach to kernel
(*.dmp, *.hdmp, *.mdmp)
• Windows kernel mode dumps (*.dmp)
• Windows binary image formats (*.exe, *.dll, *.sys)
• Linux user mode core dumps (ELF)
• Linux kernel mode core dumps (ELF, kdump)
• Linux binary image formats (ELF)
• MacOS user mode core dumps (MachO)
• MacOS binary image formats (MachO)
WinDbg can also open these files if they are contained within a compressed ZIP or CAB file.
Dump File:
C:\ALCDA2\A64\A
Browse...
Target architecture:
Autode
Open

4. We get the dump file loaded:

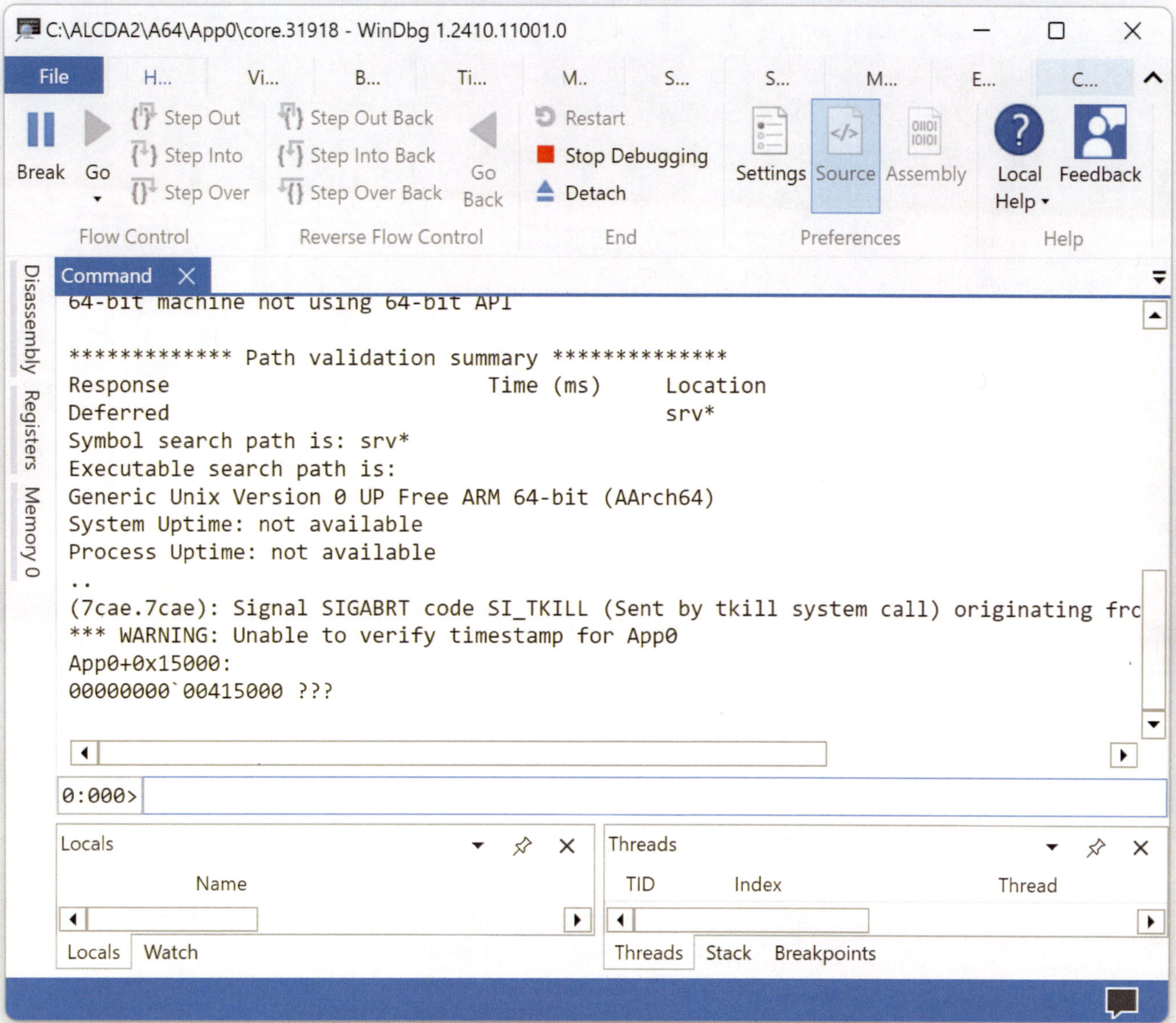

5. Type the **.sympath+** <path> command to set the symbol path:

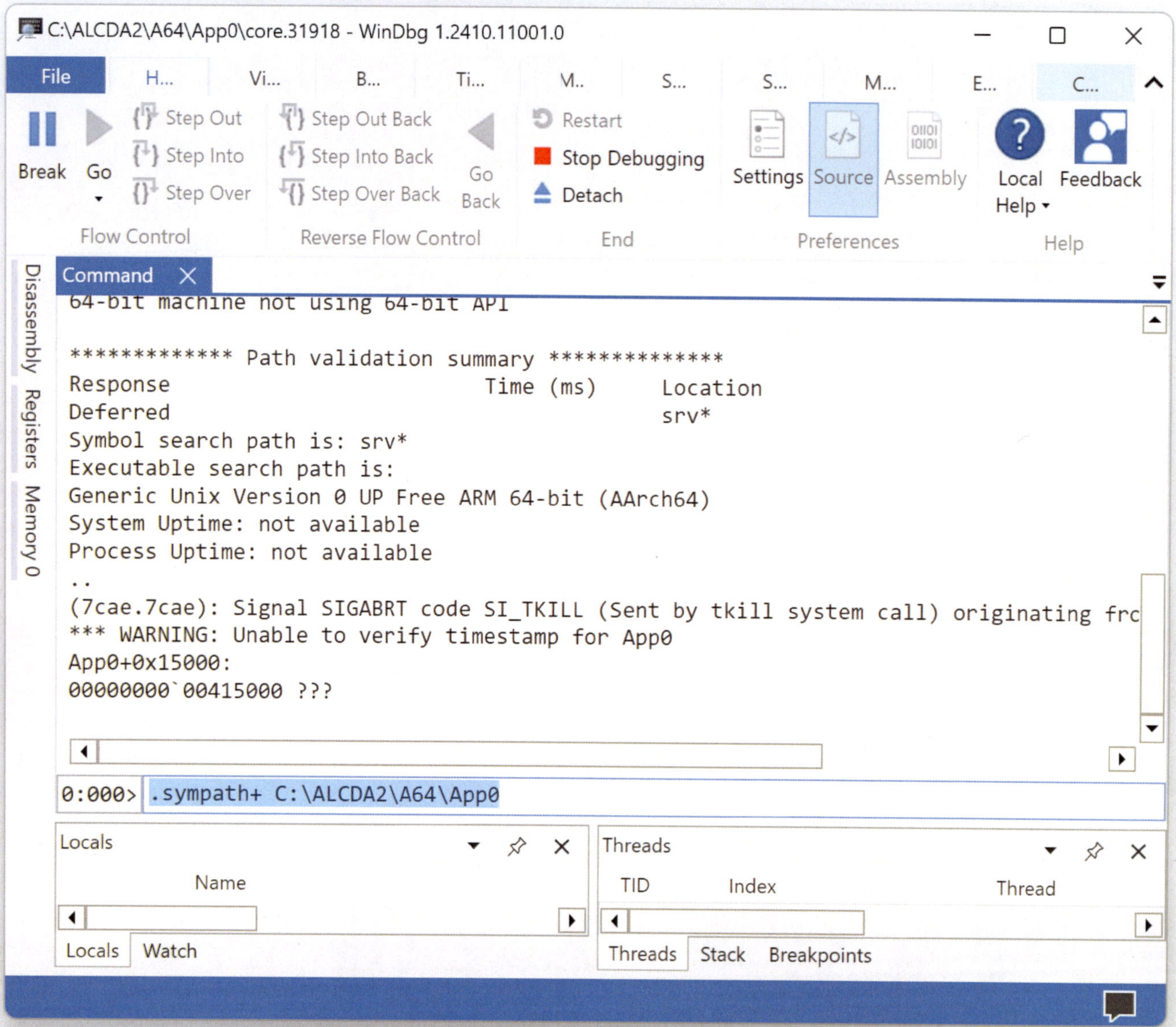

6. Type the **.reload** command to reload symbols:

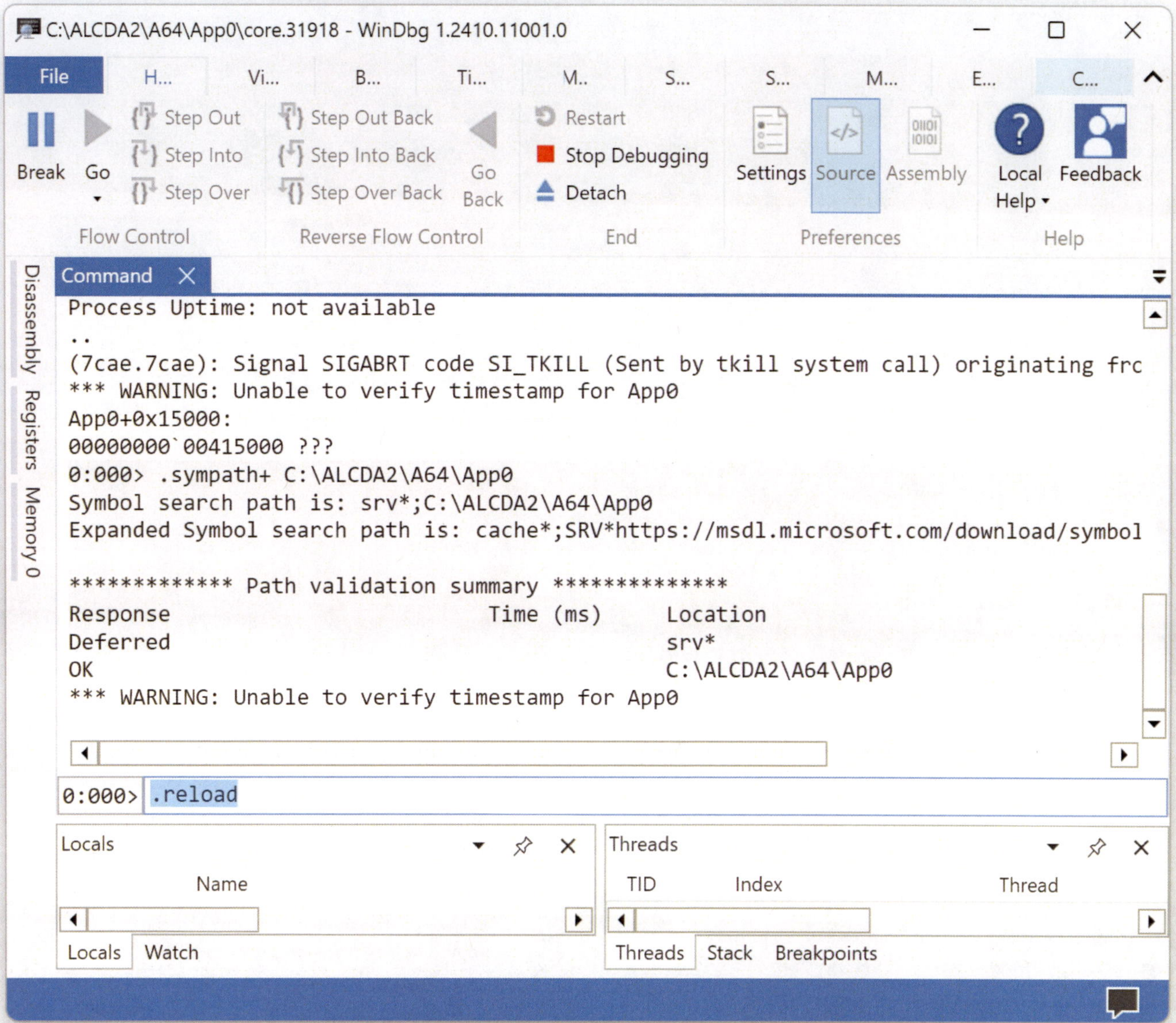

7. Type the **k** command to verify the correctness of the stack trace:

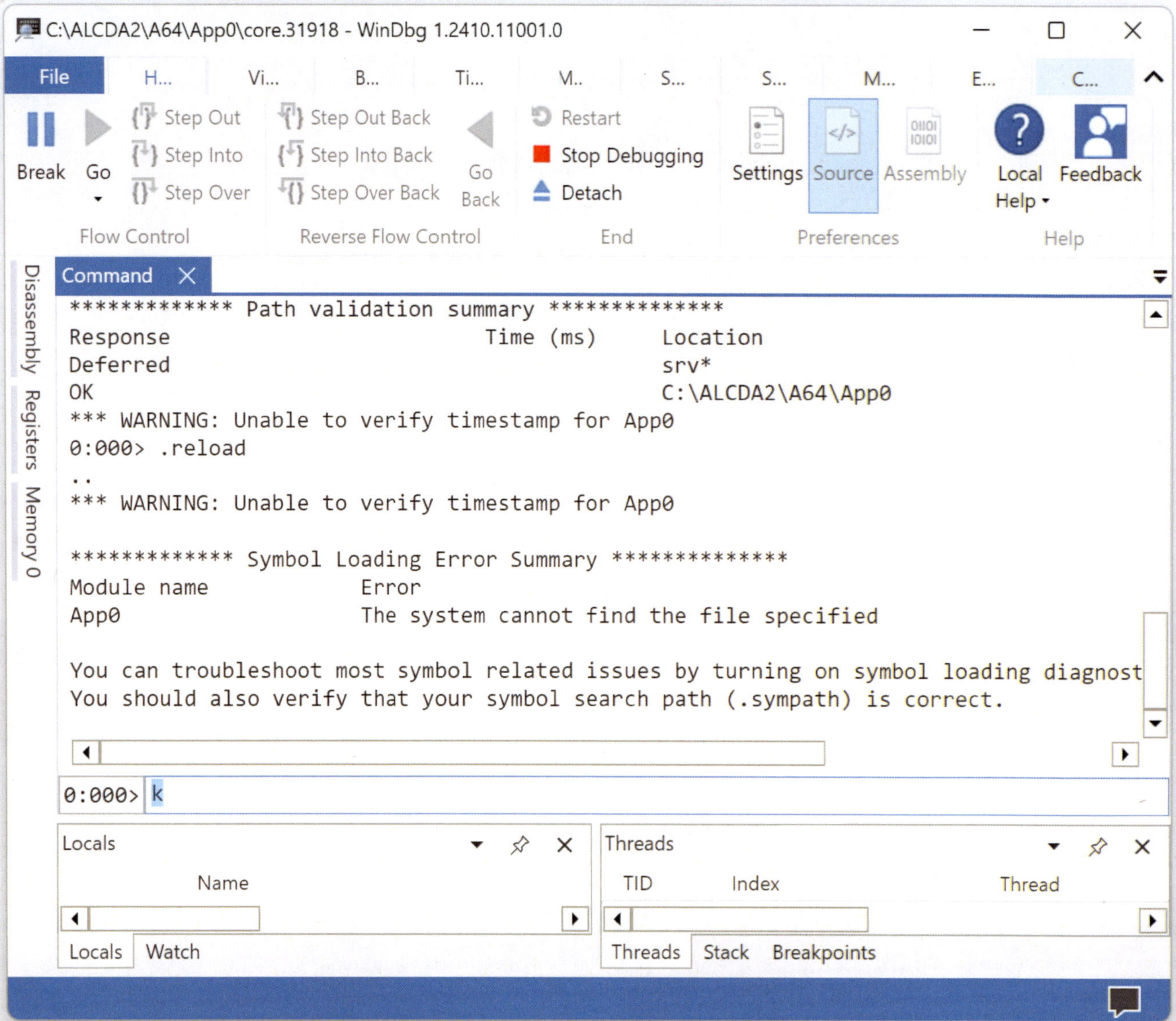

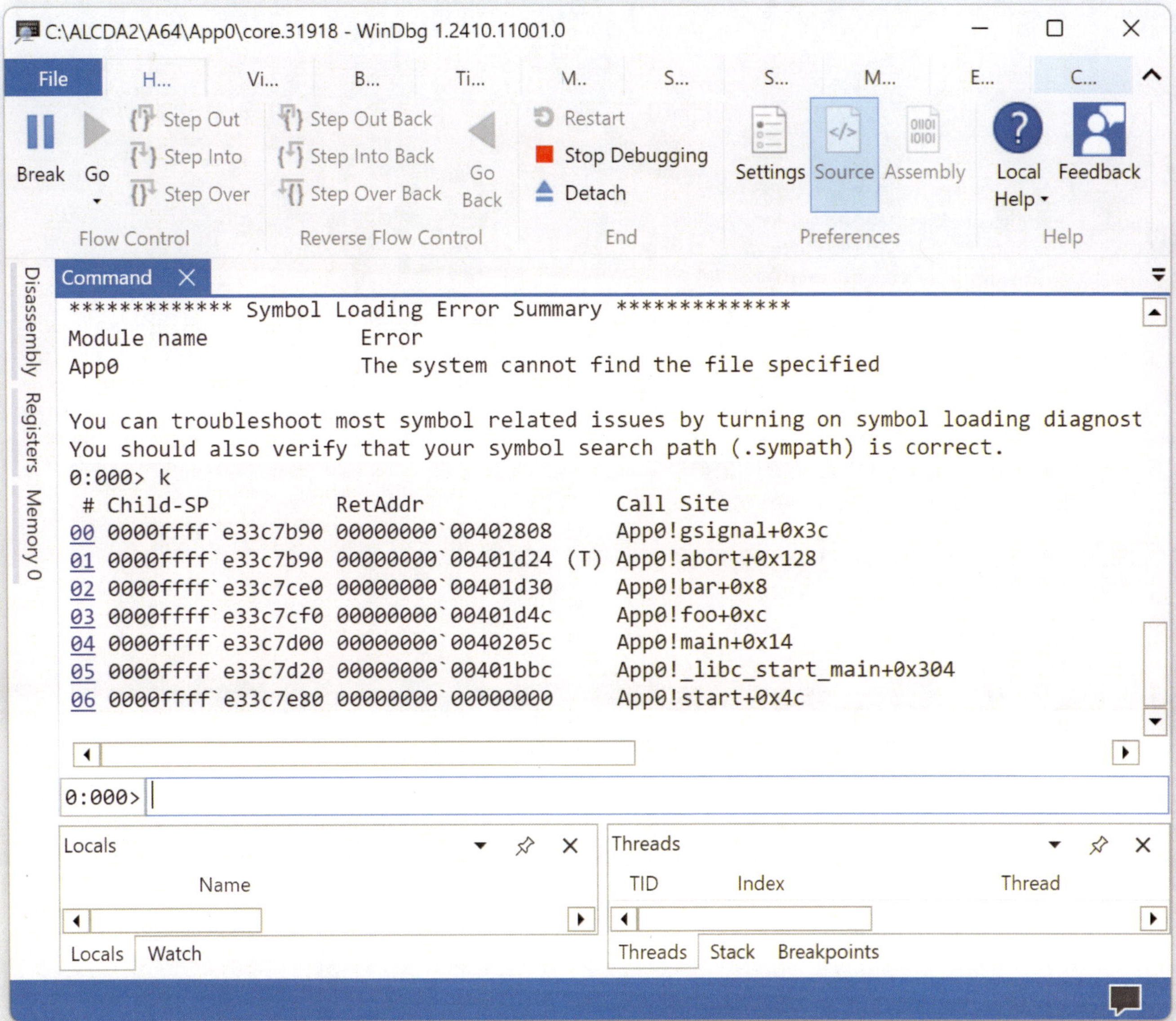

8. The output of the command should be this:

```
0:000> k
 # Child-SP          RetAddr               Call Site
00 0000ffff`e33c7b90 00000000`00402808     App0!gsignal+0x3c
01 0000ffff`e33c7b90 00000000`00401d24 (T) App0!abort+0x128
02 0000ffff`e33c7ce0 00000000`00401d30     App0!bar+0x8
03 0000ffff`e33c7cf0 00000000`00401d4c     App0!foo+0xc
04 0000ffff`e33c7d00 00000000`0040205c     App0!main+0x14
05 0000ffff`e33c7d20 00000000`00401bbc     App0!_libc_start_main+0x304
06 0000ffff`e33c7e80 00000000`00000000     App0!start+0x4c
```

If it has this form below with large offsets, then your symbol files were not set up correctly - **Incorrect Stack Trace** pattern:

```
0:000> k
# Child-SP          RetAddr               Call Site
00 0000ffff`e33c7b90 00000000`00401d24     App0+0x15000
01 0000ffff`e33c7ba0 00000000`00401d30     App0+0x1d24
02 0000ffff`e33c7cf0 00000000`00401d4c     App0+0x1d30
03 0000ffff`e33c7d00 00000000`0040205c     App0+0x1d4c
04 0000ffff`e33c7d10 00000000`00000000     App0+0x205c
```

9. Now, quit the current session (the **q** command), open *\ALCDA2\x64\App0\core.App0*, and repeat the same commands (we use the **.symfix** command to clear the previous symbol paths):

```
windbg> q
NatVis script unloaded from 'C:\Program
Files\WindowsApps\Microsoft.WinDbg_1.2410.11001.0_x64__8wekyb3d8bbwe\amd64\Visualizers\gstl.nat
vis'

Microsoft (R) Windows Debugger Version 10.0.27725.1000 AMD64
Copyright (c) Microsoft Corporation. All rights reserved.


Loading Dump File [C:\ALCDA2\x64\App0\core.App0]
64-bit machine not using 64-bit API

************* Path validation summary **************
Response                         Time (ms)     Location
Deferred                                       srv*
OK                                             C:\ALCDA2\A64\App0
Symbol search path is: srv*;C:\ALCDA2\A64\App0
Executable search path is:
Generic Unix Version 0 UP Free x64
System Uptime: not available
Process Uptime: not available
..
(11d1.11d1): Signal SIGABRT code SI_TKILL (Sent by tkill system call) originating from PID 11d1
*** WARNING: Unable to verify timestamp for App0
App0+0x75cb:
00000000`004075cb ???

0:000> .symfix
*** WARNING: Unable to verify timestamp for App0

0:000> .sympath+ C:\ALCDA2\x64\App0
Symbol search path is: srv*;C:\ALCDA2\x64\App0
Expanded Symbol search path is:
cache*;SRV*https://msdl.microsoft.com/download/symbols;c:\alcda2\x64\app0

************* Path validation summary **************
Response                         Time (ms)     Location
Deferred                                       srv*
OK                                             C:\ALCDA2\x64\App0
*** WARNING: Unable to verify timestamp for App0
```

```
0:000> .reload
..
*** WARNING: Unable to verify timestamp for App0

************* Symbol Loading Error Summary **************
Module name            Error
App0                   The system cannot find the file specified

You can troubleshoot most symbol related issues by turning on symbol loading diagnostics (!sym
noisy) and repeating the command that caused symbols to be loaded.
You should also verify that your symbol search path (.sympath) is correct.

0:000> k
 # Child-SP          RetAddr               Call Site
00 00007ffe`70adecd0 00000000`00401205     App0!gsignal+0x10b
01 00007ffe`70adedf0 00000000`00401b56 (T) App0!abort+0x121
02 00007ffe`70adef20 00000000`00401b64     App0!bar+0x4
03 00007ffe`70adef30 00000000`00401b80     App0!foo+0xe
04 00007ffe`70adef40 00000000`004021c1     App0!main+0x19
05 00007ffe`70adef60 00000000`00401a5a     App0!_libc_start_main+0x3d1
06 00007ffe`70adf060 ffffffff`ffffffff     App0!start+0x2a
07 00007ffe`70adf068 00000000`00000000     0xffffffff`ffffffff
```

10. [Optional] Download and install the recommended version of Debugging Tools for Windows (See windbg.org for quick links, WinDbg Quick Links \ Download Debugging Tools for Windows). For this part, we use WinDbg 10.0.26100.1 from Windows SDK 10.0.26100 for Windows 11, version 24H2.

11. Launch WinDbg from Windows Kits \ WinDbg (X64).

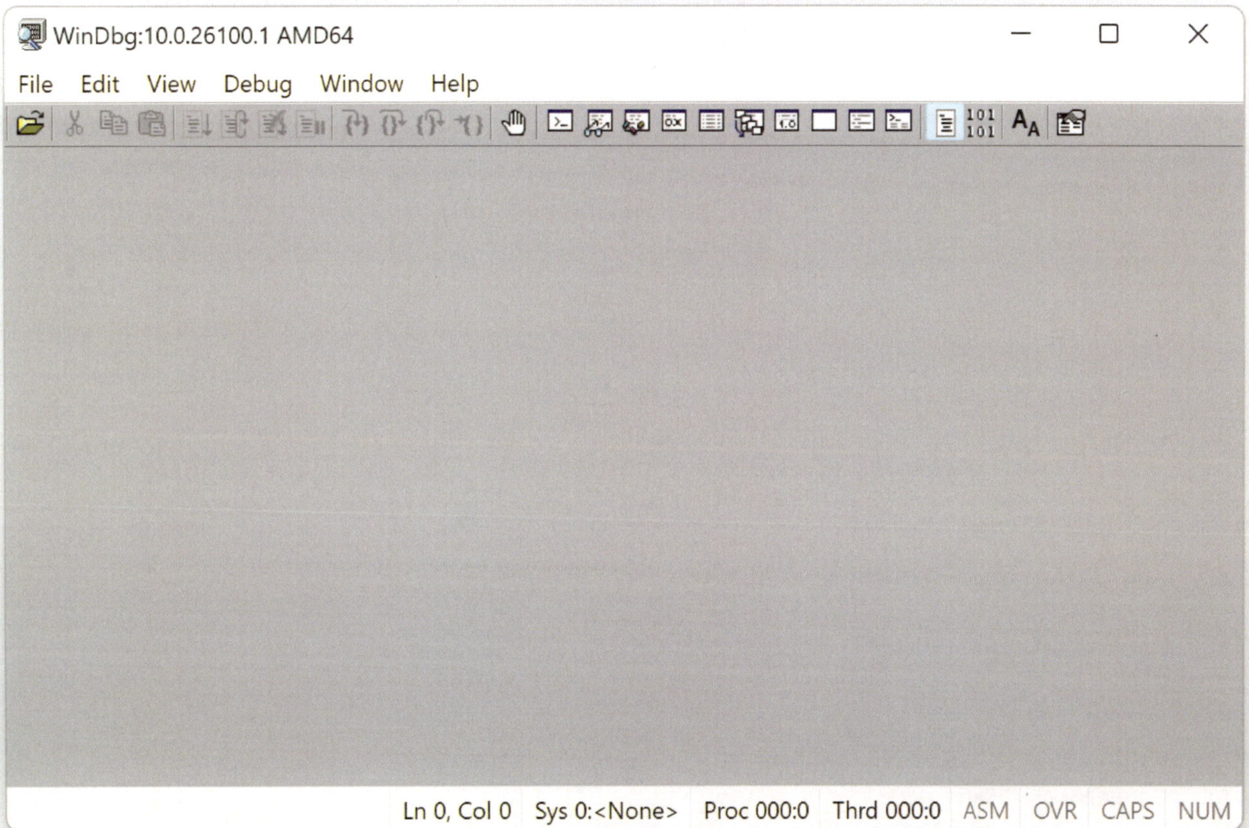

12. Open *\ALCDA2\A64\App0\core.31918*:

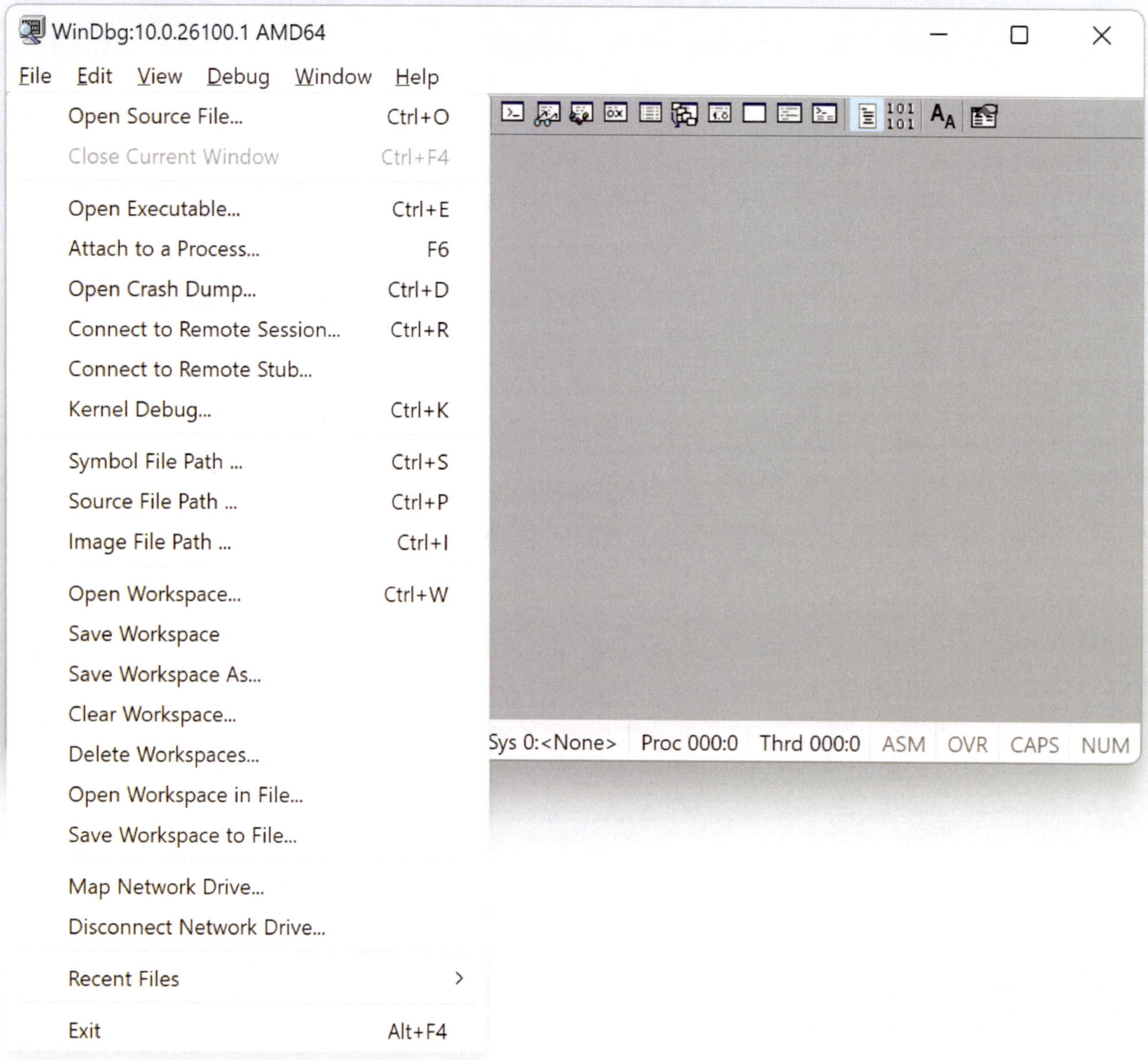

13. We get the dump file loaded:

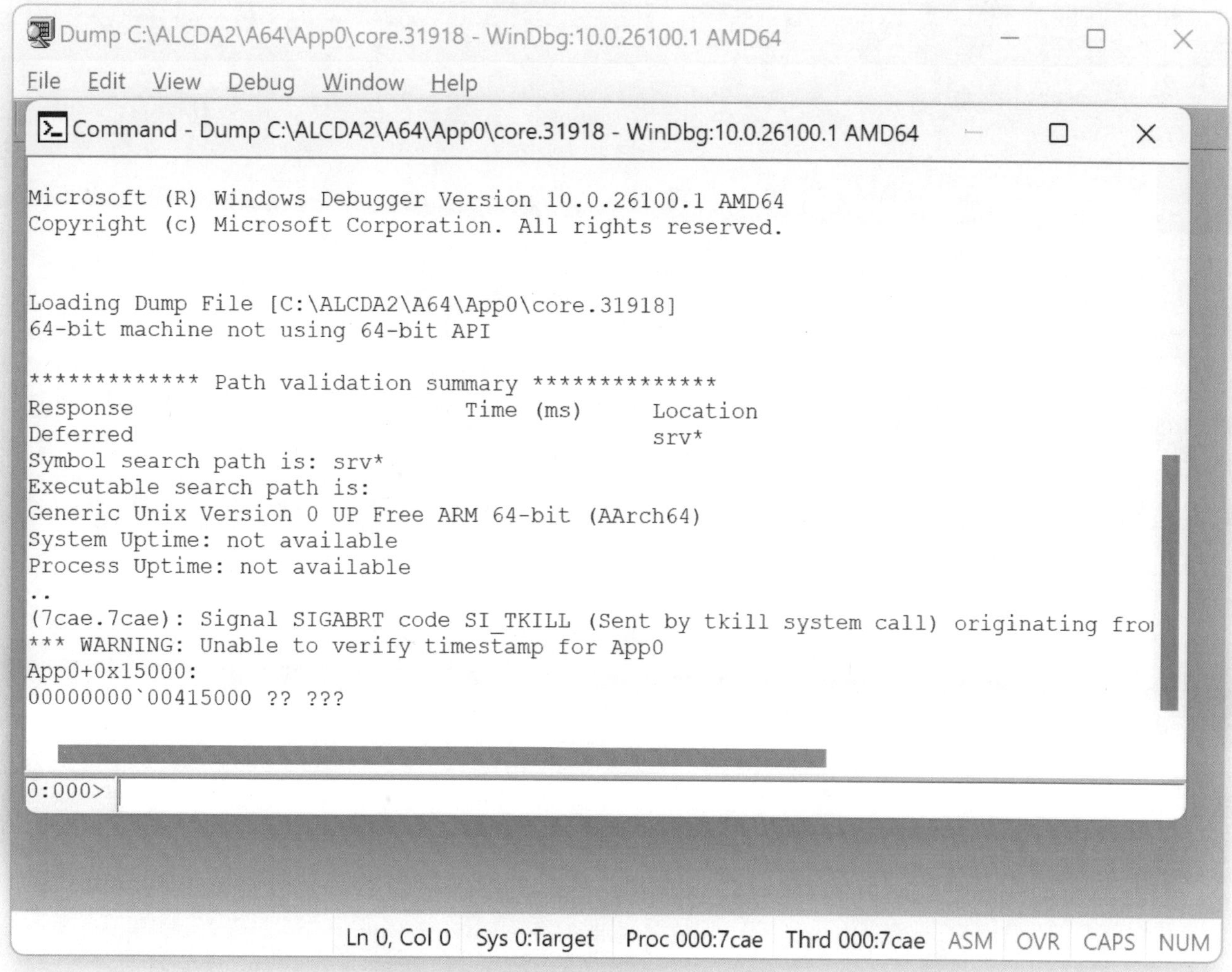

14. Type the **.sympath+** <path> command to set the symbol path:

```
Command - Dump C:\ALCDA2\A64\App0\core.31918 - WinDbg:10.0.26100.1 AMD64

Microsoft (R) Windows Debugger Version 10.0.26100.1 AMD64
Copyright (c) Microsoft Corporation. All rights reserved.


Loading Dump File [C:\ALCDA2\A64\App0\core.31918]
64-bit machine not using 64-bit API

************* Path validation summary **************
Response                         Time (ms)     Location
Deferred                                       srv*
Symbol search path is: srv*
Executable search path is:
Generic Unix Version 0 UP Free ARM 64-bit (AArch64)
System Uptime: not available
Process Uptime: not available
..
(7cae.7cae): Signal SIGABRT code SI_TKILL (Sent by tkill system call) originating fro
*** WARNING: Unable to verify timestamp for App0
App0+0x15000:
00000000`00415000 ?? ???

0:000> .sympath C:\ALCDA2\A64\App0
```

15. Type the **.reload** command to reload symbols:

```
Command - Dump C:\ALCDA2\A64\App0\core.31918 - WinDbg:10.0.26100.1 AMD64
************* Path validation summary **************
Response                         Time (ms)     Location
Deferred                                       srv*
Symbol search path is: srv*
Executable search path is:
Generic Unix Version 0 UP Free ARM 64-bit (AArch64)
System Uptime: not available
Process Uptime: not available
..
(7cae.7cae): Signal SIGABRT code SI_TKILL (Sent by tkill system call) originating fro
*** WARNING: Unable to verify timestamp for App0
App0+0x15000:
00000000`00415000 ?? ???
0:000> .sympath C:\ALCDA2\A64\App0
Symbol search path is: C:\ALCDA2\A64\App0
Expanded Symbol search path is: c:\alcda2\a64\app0

************* Path validation summary **************
Response                         Time (ms)     Location
OK                                             C:\ALCDA2\A64\App0
*** WARNING: Unable to verify timestamp for App0

0:000> .reload
```

16. Type **k** command to verify the correctness of the stack trace:

```
Command - Dump C:\ALCDA2\A64\App0\core.31918 - WinDbg:10.0.26100.1 AMD64
*** WARNING: Unable to verify timestamp for App0
App0+0x15000:
00000000`00415000 ?? ???
0:000> .sympath C:\ALCDA2\A64\App0
Symbol search path is: C:\ALCDA2\A64\App0
Expanded Symbol search path is: c:\alcda2\a64\app0

************* Path validation summary **************
Response                         Time (ms)     Location
OK                                             C:\ALCDA2\A64\App0
*** WARNING: Unable to verify timestamp for App0
0:000> .reload
..
*** WARNING: Unable to verify timestamp for App0

************* Symbol Loading Error Summary **************
Module name            Error
App0                   The system cannot find the file specified

You can troubleshoot most symbol related issues by turning on symbol loading diagnost
You should also verify that your symbol search path (.sympath) is correct.

0:000> k
```

```
Command - Dump C:\ALCDA2\A64\App0\core.31918 - WinDbg:10.0.26100.1 AMD64
OK                                             C:\ALCDA2\A64\App0
*** WARNING: Unable to verify timestamp for App0
0:000> .reload
..
*** WARNING: Unable to verify timestamp for App0

************* Symbol Loading Error Summary **************
Module name            Error
App0                   The system cannot find the file specified

You can troubleshoot most symbol related issues by turning on symbol loading diagnost
You should also verify that your symbol search path (.sympath) is correct.
0:000> k
 # Child-SP          RetAddr               Call Site
00 0000ffff`e33c7b90 00000000`00402808     App0!gsignal+0x3c
01 0000ffff`e33c7b90 00000000`00401d24 (T) App0!abort+0x128
02 0000ffff`e33c7ce0 00000000`00401d30     App0!bar+0x8
03 0000ffff`e33c7cf0 00000000`00401d4c     App0!foo+0xc
04 0000ffff`e33c7d00 00000000`0040205c     App0!main+0x14
05 0000ffff`e33c7d20 00000000`00401bbc     App0!_libc_start_main+0x304
06 0000ffff`e33c7e80 00000000`00000000     App0!start+0x4c

0:000>
```

17. [Optional] If you prefer using the Docker image with WinDbg and symbol files included, follow these steps below.

```
c:\ALCDA2>docker pull patterndiagnostics/windbg:10.0.26100.1-wsl
10.0.26100.1-wsl: Pulling from patterndiagnostics/windbg
7c76e5cf7755: Pull complete
dcd649075383: Pull complete
f7ad5fcf8308: Pull complete
9cbbb2624929: Pull complete
6d647f57d9a4: Pull complete
1bc4f383d696: Pull complete
Digest: sha256:7df2b05920f56d8ba5a39ae3f65fc323d70bcbffa3c7674adb19818a36319e9b
Status: Downloaded newer image for patterndiagnostics/windbg:10.0.26100.1-wsl
docker.io/patterndiagnostics/windbg:10.0.26100.1-wsl

c:\ALCDA2>docker run -it -v C:\ALCDA2:C:\ALCDA2 patterndiagnostics/windbg:10.0.26100.1-wsl
Microsoft Windows [Version 10.0.20348.2655]
(c) Microsoft Corporation. All rights reserved.

C:\WinDbg>windbg.bat C:\ALCDA2\A64\App0\core.31918

Microsoft (R) Windows Debugger Version 10.0.26100.1 AMD64
Copyright (c) Microsoft Corporation. All rights reserved.


Loading Dump File [C:\ALCDA2\A64\App0\core.31918]
64-bit machine not using 64-bit API

************* Path validation summary **************
Response                         Time (ms)     Location
OK                                             .
Symbol search path is: .
Executable search path is:
Generic Unix Version 0 UP Free ARM 64-bit (AArch64)
System Uptime: not available
Process Uptime: not available
..
(7cae.7cae): Signal SIGABRT code SI_TKILL (Sent by tkill system call) originating from PID 7cae
*** WARNING: Unable to verify timestamp for App0
App0+0x15000:
00000000`00415000 ?? ???

0:000> .sympath+ C:\ALCDA2\A64\App0
Symbol search path is: .;C:\ALCDA2\A64\App0
Expanded Symbol search path is: .;c:\alcda2\a64\app0

************* Path validation summary **************
Response                         Time (ms)     Location
OK                                             .
OK                                             C:\ALCDA2\A64\App0

0:000> .reload
..
*** WARNING: Unable to verify timestamp for App0

************* Symbol Loading Error Summary **************
Module name            Error
App0                   The system cannot find the file specified

You can troubleshoot most symbol related issues by turning on symbol loading diagnostics (!sym noisy) and
repeating the command that caused symbols to be loaded.
You should also verify that your symbol search path (.sympath) is correct.
```

```
0:000> k
Child-SP          RetAddr               Call Site
0000ffff`e33c7b90 00000000`00402808     App0!gsignal+0x3c
0000ffff`e33c7b90 00000000`00401d24 (T) App0!abort+0x128
0000ffff`e33c7ce0 00000000`00401d30     App0!bar+0x8
0000ffff`e33c7cf0 00000000`00401d4c     App0!foo+0xc
0000ffff`e33c7d00 00000000`0040205c     App0!main+0x14
0000ffff`e33c7d20 00000000`00401bbc     App0!_libc_start_main+0x304
0000ffff`e33c7e80 00000000`00000000     App0!start+0x4c

0:000> q
quit:
NatVis script unloaded from 'C:\Program Files\Windows Kits\10\Debuggers\x64\Visualizers\gstl.natvis'

C:\WinDbg>exit

c:\ALCDA2>
```

Process Core Dumps

Exercises A1 – A12

All exercises were modeled on real-life examples using specially constructed applications. We learn how to recognize and use more than 50 analysis patterns.

Exercise A1

- **Goal:** Learn how to list stack traces, disassemble functions, check their correctness, dump data, get environment

- **Patterns:** Manual Dump (Process); Stack Trace; Incorrect Stack Trace; Unrecognizable Symbolic Information; Truncated Stack Trace; Stack Trace Collection; Annotated Disassembly; Paratext; Not My Version; Environment Hint

- \ALCDA-Dumps\Exercise-A1-x64-GDB.pdf
- \ALCDA-Dumps\Exercise-A1-A64-GDB.pdf

- \ALCDA-Dumps\Exercise-A1-A64-WinDbg.pdf
- \ALCDA-Dumps\Exercise-A1-x64-WinDbg.pdf

Exercise A1 (x64, GDB)

Goal: Learn how to list stack traces, disassemble functions, check their correctness, dump data, get environment.

Patterns: Manual Dump (Process); Stack Trace; Incorrect Stack Trace; Unrecognizable Symbolic Information; Stack Trace Collection; Annotated Disassembly; Paratext; Not My Version; Environment Hint.

1. Load the core dump *App1.core.253* and *App1* executable from the x64/App1 directory:

```
~/ALCDA2/x64/App1$ gdb -c App1.core.253 -se App1
GNU gdb (Debian 8.2.1-2+b3) 8.2.1
Copyright (C) 2018 Free Software Foundation, Inc.
License GPLv3+: GNU GPL version 3 or later <http://gnu.org/licenses/gpl.html>
This is free software: you are free to change and redistribute it.
There is NO WARRANTY, to the extent permitted by law.
Type "show copying" and "show warranty" for details.
This GDB was configured as "x86_64-linux-gnu".
Type "show configuration" for configuration details.
For bug reporting instructions, please see:
<http://www.gnu.org/software/gdb/bugs/>.
Find the GDB manual and other documentation resources online at:
    <http://www.gnu.org/software/gdb/documentation/>.

For help, type "help".
Type "apropos word" to search for commands related to "word"...
Reading symbols from App1...done.
[New LWP 253]
[New LWP 254]
[New LWP 255]
[New LWP 256]
[New LWP 257]
[New LWP 258]
[Thread debugging using libthread_db enabled]
Using host libthread_db library "/lib/x86_64-linux-gnu/libthread_db.so.1".
Core was generated by `./App1'.
#0  0x0000000000441a10 in nanosleep ()
[Current thread is 1 (Thread 0x21b3880 (LWP 253))]
```

2. Set logging to a file in case of lengthy output from some commands:

```
(gdb) set logging on App1.log
Copying output to App1.log.
```

3. List all threads:

```
(gdb) info threads
  Id   Target Id                          Frame
* 1    Thread 0x21b3880 (LWP 253)         0x0000000000441a10 in nanosleep ()
  2    Thread 0x7f0fc16fb700 (LWP 254) 0x0000000000441a10 in nanosleep ()
  3    Thread 0x7f0fc0efa700 (LWP 255) 0x0000000000441a10 in nanosleep ()
  4    Thread 0x7f0fc06f9700 (LWP 256) 0x0000000000441a10 in nanosleep ()
  5    Thread 0x7f0fbfef8700 (LWP 257) 0x0000000000441a10 in nanosleep ()
  6    Thread 0x7f0fbf6f7700 (LWP 258) 0x0000000000441a10 in nanosleep ()
```

4. Get the current thread stack trace:

```
(gdb) bt
#0  0x0000000000441a10 in nanosleep ()
#1  0x000000000044199a in sleep ()
#2  0x0000000000401d92 in main () at pthread_create.c:688
```

5. Get all thread stack traces:

```
(gdb) thread apply all bt

Thread 6 (Thread 0x7f0fbf6f7700 (LWP 258)):
#0  0x0000000000441a10 in nanosleep ()
#1  0x000000000044199a in sleep ()
#2  0x0000000000401cb7 in bar_five ()
#3  0x0000000000401cc8 in foo_five ()
#4  0x0000000000401ce1 in thread_five ()
#5  0x00000000004030d3 in start_thread (arg=<optimized out>) at pthread_create.c:486
#6  0x000000000044426f in clone ()

Thread 5 (Thread 0x7f0fbfef8700 (LWP 257)):
#0  0x0000000000441a10 in nanosleep ()
#1  0x000000000044199a in sleep ()
#2  0x0000000000401c78 in bar_four () at pthread_create.c:688
#3  0x0000000000401c89 in foo_four () at pthread_create.c:688
#4  0x0000000000401ca2 in thread_four () at pthread_create.c:688
#5  0x00000000004030d3 in start_thread (arg=<optimized out>) at pthread_create.c:486
#6  0x000000000044426f in clone ()

Thread 4 (Thread 0x7f0fc06f9700 (LWP 256)):
#0  0x0000000000441a10 in nanosleep ()
#1  0x000000000044199a in sleep ()
#2  0x0000000000401c39 in bar_three () at pthread_create.c:688
#3  0x0000000000401c4a in foo_three () at pthread_create.c:688
#4  0x0000000000401c63 in thread_three () at pthread_create.c:688
#5  0x00000000004030d3 in start_thread (arg=<optimized out>) at pthread_create.c:486
#6  0x000000000044426f in clone ()

Thread 3 (Thread 0x7f0fc0efa700 (LWP 255)):
#0  0x0000000000441a10 in nanosleep ()
#1  0x000000000044199a in sleep ()
#2  0x0000000000401bfa in bar_two () at pthread_create.c:688
#3  0x0000000000401c0b in foo_two () at pthread_create.c:688
#4  0x0000000000401c24 in thread_two () at pthread_create.c:688
#5  0x00000000004030d3 in start_thread (arg=<optimized out>) at pthread_create.c:486
#6  0x000000000044426f in clone ()

Thread 2 (Thread 0x7f0fc16fb700 (LWP 254)):
#0  0x0000000000441a10 in nanosleep ()
#1  0x000000000044199a in sleep ()
#2  0x0000000000401bbb in bar_one () at pthread_create.c:688
#3  0x0000000000401bcc in foo_one () at pthread_create.c:688
#4  0x0000000000401be5 in thread_one () at pthread_create.c:688
#5  0x00000000004030d3 in start_thread (arg=<optimized out>) at pthread_create.c:486
#6  0x000000000044426f in clone ()

Thread 1 (Thread 0x21b3880 (LWP 253)):
#0  0x0000000000441a10 in nanosleep ()
#1  0x000000000044199a in sleep ()
#2  0x0000000000401d92 in main () at pthread_create.c:688
```

6. Switch to thread #2 and get its stack trace:

```
(gdb) thread 2
[Switching to thread 2 (Thread 0x7f0fc16fb700 (LWP 254))]
#0  0x0000000000441a10 in nanosleep ()

(gdb) bt
#0  0x0000000000441a10 in nanosleep ()
#1  0x000000000044199a in sleep ()
#2  0x0000000000401bbb in bar_one () at pthread_create.c:688
#3  0x0000000000401bcc in foo_one () at pthread_create.c:688
#4  0x0000000000401be5 in thread_one () at pthread_create.c:688
#5  0x00000000004030d3 in start_thread (arg=<optimized out>) at pthread_create.c:486
#6  0x000000000044426f in clone ()

(gdb) info threads
  Id   Target Id                          Frame
  1    Thread 0x21b3880 (LWP 253)         0x0000000000441a10 in nanosleep ()
* 2    Thread 0x7f0fc16fb700 (LWP 254) 0x0000000000441a10 in nanosleep ()
  3    Thread 0x7f0fc0efa700 (LWP 255) 0x0000000000441a10 in nanosleep ()
  4    Thread 0x7f0fc06f9700 (LWP 256) 0x0000000000441a10 in nanosleep ()
  5    Thread 0x7f0fbfef8700 (LWP 257) 0x0000000000441a10 in nanosleep ()
  6    Thread 0x7f0fbf6f7700 (LWP 258) 0x0000000000441a10 in nanosleep ()
```

7. Check that *bar_one* called the *sleep* function by comparing the return address on the call stack from the disassembly output:

```
(gdb) disassemble bar_one
Dump of assembler code for function bar_one:
   0x0000000000401bad <+0>:     push   %rbp
   0x0000000000401bae <+1>:     mov    %rsp,%rbp
   0x0000000000401bb1 <+4>:     mov    $0xffffffff,%edi
   0x0000000000401bb6 <+9>:     callq  0x441960 <sleep>
   0x0000000000401bbb <+14>:    nop
   0x0000000000401bbc <+15>:    pop    %rbp
   0x0000000000401bbd <+16>:    retq
End of assembler dump.
```

We see that the address in the stack trace for the *bar_one* function is the address to return to after calling the *sleep* function.

8. Compare with Intel disassembly flavor:

```
(gdb) set disassembly-flavor intel

(gdb) disassemble bar_two
Dump of assembler code for function bar_one:
   0x0000000000401bad <+0>:     push   rbp
   0x0000000000401bae <+1>:     mov    rbp,rsp
   0x0000000000401bb1 <+4>:     mov    edi,0xffffffff
   0x0000000000401bb6 <+9>:     call   0x441960 <sleep>
   0x0000000000401bbb <+14>:    nop
   0x0000000000401bbc <+15>:    pop    rbp
   0x0000000000401bbd <+16>:    ret
End of assembler dump.

(gdb) set disassembly-flavor att
```

9. Get *App1* data section from the output of pmap (*App1.pmap.253*):

```
(gdb) ^Z
[2]+  Stopped                 gdb -c App1.core.253 -se App1

~/ALCDA2/x64/App1$ cat App1.pmap.253
253:   ./App1
0000000000400000      4K r---- App1
0000000000401000    588K r-x-- App1
0000000000494000    156K r---- App1
00000000004bc000     24K rw--- App1
00000000004c2000     24K rw---   [ anon ]
00000000021b3000    140K rw---   [ anon ]
00007f0fbeef7000      4K -----   [ anon ]
00007f0fbeef8000   8192K rw---   [ anon ]
00007f0fbf6f8000      4K -----   [ anon ]
00007f0fbf6f9000   8192K rw---   [ anon ]
00007f0fbfef9000      4K -----   [ anon ]
00007f0fbfefa000   8192K rw---   [ anon ]
00007f0fc06fa000      4K -----   [ anon ]
00007f0fc06fb000   8192K rw---   [ anon ]
00007f0fc0efb000      4K -----   [ anon ]
00007f0fc0efc000   8192K rw---   [ anon ]
00007ffdf4545000    132K rw---   [ stack ]
00007ffdf45c6000     16K r----   [ anon ]
00007ffdf45ca000      4K r-x--   [ anon ]
 total            42068K

~/ALCDA2/x64/App1$ fg
gdb -c App1.core.253 -se App1


(gdb)
```

10. Compare with the section information in the core dump:

```
(gdb) maintenance info sections
Exec file:
    `/home/coredump/ALCDA2/x64/App1/App1', file type elf64-x86-64.
 [0]      0x00400200->0x00400220 at 0x00000200: .note.ABI-tag ALLOC LOAD READONLY DATA HAS_CONTENTS
 [1]      0x00400220->0x00400244 at 0x00000220: .note.gnu.build-id ALLOC LOAD READONLY DATA HAS_CONTENTS
 [2]      0x00400248->0x004004d0 at 0x00000248: .rela.plt ALLOC LOAD READONLY DATA HAS_CONTENTS
 [3]      0x00401000->0x00401017 at 0x00001000: .init ALLOC LOAD READONLY CODE HAS_CONTENTS
 [4]      0x00401018->0x004010f0 at 0x00001018: .plt ALLOC LOAD READONLY CODE HAS_CONTENTS
 [5]      0x004010f0->0x004933d0 at 0x000010f0: .text ALLOC LOAD READONLY CODE HAS_CONTENTS
 [6]      0x004933d0->0x00493f77 at 0x000933d0: __libc_freeres_fn ALLOC LOAD READONLY CODE HAS_CONTENTS
 [7]      0x00493f78->0x00493f81 at 0x00093f78: .fini ALLOC LOAD READONLY CODE HAS_CONTENTS
 [8]      0x00494000->0x004ae73c at 0x00094000: .rodata ALLOC LOAD READONLY DATA HAS_CONTENTS
 [9]      0x004ae740->0x004bab50 at 0x000ae740: .eh_frame ALLOC LOAD READONLY DATA HAS_CONTENTS
 [10]     0x004bab50->0x004babfc at 0x000bab50: .gcc_except_table ALLOC LOAD READONLY DATA HAS_CONTENTS
 [11]     0x004bc0b0->0x004bc0d8 at 0x000bb0b0: .tdata ALLOC LOAD DATA HAS_CONTENTS
 [12]     0x004bc0d8->0x004bc120 at 0x000bb0d8: .tbss ALLOC
 [13]     0x004bc0d8->0x004bc0e0 at 0x000bb0d8: .preinit_array ALLOC LOAD DATA HAS_CONTENTS
 [14]     0x004bc0e0->0x004bc0f0 at 0x000bb0e0: .init_array ALLOC LOAD DATA HAS_CONTENTS
 [15]     0x004bc0f0->0x004bc100 at 0x000bb0f0: .fini_array ALLOC LOAD DATA HAS_CONTENTS
 [16]     0x004bc100->0x004beef4 at 0x000bb100: .data.rel.ro ALLOC LOAD DATA HAS_CONTENTS
 [17]     0x004beef8->0x004bf000 at 0x000bdef8: .got ALLOC LOAD DATA HAS_CONTENTS
 [18]     0x004bf000->0x004bf0f0 at 0x000be000: .got.plt ALLOC LOAD DATA HAS_CONTENTS
 [19]     0x004bf100->0x004c0c30 at 0x000be100: .data ALLOC LOAD DATA HAS_CONTENTS
 [20]     0x004c0c30->0x004c0c90 at 0x000bfc30: __libc_subfreeres ALLOC LOAD DATA HAS_CONTENTS
 [21]     0x004c0ca0->0x004c1408 at 0x000bfca0: __libc_IO_vtables ALLOC LOAD DATA HAS_CONTENTS
 [22]     0x004c1408->0x004c1410 at 0x000c0408: __libc_atexit ALLOC LOAD DATA HAS_CONTENTS
 [23]     0x004c1420->0x004c7528 at 0x000c0410: .bss ALLOC
```

```
 [24]      0x004c7528->0x004c7558 at 0x000c0410: __libc_freeres_ptrs ALLOC
 [25]      0x00000000->0x00000038 at 0x000c0410: .comment READONLY HAS_CONTENTS
 [26]      0x00000000->0x00000420 at 0x000c0450: .debug_aranges READONLY HAS_CONTENTS
 [27]      0x00000000->0x000372ad at 0x000c0870: .debug_info READONLY HAS_CONTENTS
 [28]      0x00000000->0x000057e8 at 0x000f7b1d: .debug_abbrev READONLY HAS_CONTENTS
 [29]      0x00000000->0x0000aa2b at 0x000fd305: .debug_line READONLY HAS_CONTENTS
 [30]      0x00000000->0x00004d08 at 0x00107d30: .debug_str READONLY HAS_CONTENTS
 [31]      0x00000000->0x0000d4b8 at 0x0010ca38: .debug_loc READONLY HAS_CONTENTS
 [32]      0x00000000->0x000024c0 at 0x00119ef0: .debug_ranges READONLY HAS_CONTENTS
Core file:
    `/home/coredump/ALCDA2/x64/App1/App1.core.253', file type elf64-x86-64.
 [0]      0x00000000->0x00002ec4 at 0x000003f8: note0 READONLY HAS_CONTENTS
 [1]      0x00000000->0x000000d8 at 0x00000518: .reg/253 HAS_CONTENTS
 [2]      0x00000000->0x000000d8 at 0x00000518: .reg HAS_CONTENTS
 [3]      0x00000000->0x00000200 at 0x0000060c: .reg2/253 HAS_CONTENTS
 [4]      0x00000000->0x00000200 at 0x0000060c: .reg2 HAS_CONTENTS
 [5]      0x00000000->0x00000340 at 0x00000820: .reg-xstate/253 HAS_CONTENTS
 [6]      0x00000000->0x00000340 at 0x00000820: .reg-xstate HAS_CONTENTS
 [7]      0x00000000->0x00000080 at 0x00000b74: .note.linuxcore.siginfo/253 HAS_CONTENTS
 [8]      0x00000000->0x00000080 at 0x00000b74: .note.linuxcore.siginfo HAS_CONTENTS
 [9]      0x00000000->0x000000d8 at 0x00000c78: .reg/254 HAS_CONTENTS
 [10]      0x00000000->0x00000200 at 0x00000d6c: .reg2/254 HAS_CONTENTS
 [11]      0x00000000->0x00000340 at 0x00000f80: .reg-xstate/254 HAS_CONTENTS
 [12]      0x00000000->0x00000080 at 0x000012d4: .note.linuxcore.siginfo/254 HAS_CONTENTS
 [13]      0x00000000->0x000000d8 at 0x000013d8: .reg/255 HAS_CONTENTS
 [14]      0x00000000->0x00000200 at 0x000014cc: .reg2/255 HAS_CONTENTS
 [15]      0x00000000->0x00000340 at 0x000016e0: .reg-xstate/255 HAS_CONTENTS
 [16]      0x00000000->0x00000080 at 0x00001a34: .note.linuxcore.siginfo/255 HAS_CONTENTS
 [17]      0x00000000->0x000000d8 at 0x00001b38: .reg/256 HAS_CONTENTS
 [18]      0x00000000->0x00000200 at 0x00001c2c: .reg2/256 HAS_CONTENTS
 [19]      0x00000000->0x00000340 at 0x00001e40: .reg-xstate/256 HAS_CONTENTS
--Type <RET> for more, q to quit, c to continue without paging--
 [20]      0x00000000->0x00000080 at 0x00002194: .note.linuxcore.siginfo/256 HAS_CONTENTS
 [21]      0x00000000->0x000000d8 at 0x00002298: .reg/257 HAS_CONTENTS
 [22]      0x00000000->0x00000200 at 0x0000238c: .reg2/257 HAS_CONTENTS
 [23]      0x00000000->0x00000340 at 0x000025a0: .reg-xstate/257 HAS_CONTENTS
 [24]      0x00000000->0x00000080 at 0x000028f4: .note.linuxcore.siginfo/257 HAS_CONTENTS
 [25]      0x00000000->0x000000d8 at 0x000029f8: .reg/258 HAS_CONTENTS
 [26]      0x00000000->0x00000200 at 0x00002aec: .reg2/258 HAS_CONTENTS
 [27]      0x00000000->0x00000340 at 0x00002d00: .reg-xstate/258 HAS_CONTENTS
 [28]      0x00000000->0x00000080 at 0x00003054: .note.linuxcore.siginfo/258 HAS_CONTENTS
 [29]      0x00000000->0x00000140 at 0x000030e8: .auxv HAS_CONTENTS
 [30]      0x00000000->0x0000007e at 0x0000323c: .note.linuxcore.file/258 HAS_CONTENTS
 [31]      0x00000000->0x0000007e at 0x0000323c: .note.linuxcore.file HAS_CONTENTS
 [32]      0x00401000->0x00494000 at 0x000032bc: load1 ALLOC LOAD READONLY CODE HAS_CONTENTS
 [33]      0x004bc000->0x004c2000 at 0x000962bc: load2 ALLOC LOAD HAS_CONTENTS
 [34]      0x004c2000->0x004c8000 at 0x0009c2bc: load3 ALLOC LOAD HAS_CONTENTS
 [35]      0x021b3000->0x021d6000 at 0x000a22bc: load4 ALLOC LOAD HAS_CONTENTS
 [36]      0x7f0fbeef7000->0x7f0fbeef8000 at 0x000c52bc: load5 ALLOC LOAD READONLY HAS_CONTENTS
 [37]      0x7f0fbeef8000->0x7f0fbf6f8000 at 0x000c62bc: load6 ALLOC LOAD HAS_CONTENTS
 [38]      0x7f0fbf6f8000->0x7f0fbf6f9000 at 0x008c62bc: load7 ALLOC LOAD READONLY HAS_CONTENTS
 [39]      0x7f0fbf6f9000->0x7f0fbfef9000 at 0x008c72bc: load8 ALLOC LOAD HAS_CONTENTS
 [40]      0x7f0fbfef9000->0x7f0fbfefa000 at 0x010c72bc: load9 ALLOC LOAD READONLY HAS_CONTENTS
 [41]      0x7f0fbfefa000->0x7f0fc06fa000 at 0x010c82bc: load10 ALLOC LOAD HAS_CONTENTS
 [42]      0x7f0fc06fa000->0x7f0fc06fb000 at 0x018c82bc: load11 ALLOC LOAD READONLY HAS_CONTENTS
 [43]      0x7f0fc06fb000->0x7f0fc0efb000 at 0x018c92bc: load12 ALLOC LOAD HAS_CONTENTS
 [44]      0x7f0fc0efb000->0x7f0fc0efc000 at 0x020c92bc: load13 ALLOC LOAD READONLY HAS_CONTENTS
 [45]      0x7f0fc0efc000->0x7f0fc16fc000 at 0x020ca2bc: load14 ALLOC LOAD HAS_CONTENTS
 [46]      0x7ffdf4545000->0x7ffdf4566000 at 0x028ca2bc: load15 ALLOC LOAD HAS_CONTENTS
 [47]      0x7ffdf45ca000->0x7ffdf45cb000 at 0x028eb2bc: load16 ALLOC LOAD READONLY CODE HAS_CONTENTS
```

11. Dump the **.data** section with possible symbolic information:

```
(gdb) x/256a 0x004bf100
0x4bf100:       0x0     0x0
0x4bf110 <__nptl_nthreads>:     0x6     0x0
0x4bf120 <stack_used>:  0x7f0fbf6f79c0  0x7f0fc16fb9c0
0x4bf130 <stack_cache>: 0x4bf130 <stack_cache>  0x4bf130 <stack_cache>
0x4bf140 <__sched_fifo_max_prio>:       0xffffffffffffffff      0x0
0x4bf150 <__elision_aconf>:     0x300000003     0x300000000
0x4bf160 <_dl_tls_static_size>: 0x1180  0x494a88 <_nl_default_default_domain>
0x4bf170 <__exit_funcs>:        0x4c5a80 <initial>      0x493040 <__gcc_personality_v0>
0x4bf180 <_IO_list_all>:        0x4bf1a0 <_IO_2_1_stderr_>      0x0
0x4bf190:       0x0     0x0
0x4bf1a0 <_IO_2_1_stderr_>:     0xfbad2086      0x0
0x4bf1b0 <_IO_2_1_stderr_+16>:  0x0     0x0
0x4bf1c0 <_IO_2_1_stderr_+32>:  0x0     0x0
0x4bf1d0 <_IO_2_1_stderr_+48>:  0x0     0x0
0x4bf1e0 <_IO_2_1_stderr_+64>:  0x0     0x0
0x4bf1f0 <_IO_2_1_stderr_+80>:  0x0     0x0
0x4bf200 <_IO_2_1_stderr_+96>:  0x0     0x4bf3c0 <_IO_2_1_stdout_>
0x4bf210 <_IO_2_1_stderr_+112>: 0x8000000002    0xffffffffffffffff
0x4bf220 <_IO_2_1_stderr_+128>: 0x0     0x4c5ec0 <_IO_stdfile_2_lock>
0x4bf230 <_IO_2_1_stderr_+144>: 0xffffffffffffffff      0x0
0x4bf240 <_IO_2_1_stderr_+160>: 0x4bf280 <_IO_wide_data_2>      0x0
0x4bf250 <_IO_2_1_stderr_+176>: 0x0     0x0
0x4bf260 <_IO_2_1_stderr_+192>: 0x0     0x0
0x4bf270 <_IO_2_1_stderr_+208>: 0x0     0x4c1060 <_IO_file_jumps>
0x4bf280 <_IO_wide_data_2>:     0x0     0x0
0x4bf290 <_IO_wide_data_2+16>:  0x0     0x0
0x4bf2a0 <_IO_wide_data_2+32>:  0x0     0x0
0x4bf2b0 <_IO_wide_data_2+48>:  0x0     0x0
0x4bf2c0 <_IO_wide_data_2+64>:  0x0     0x0
0x4bf2d0 <_IO_wide_data_2+80>:  0x0     0x0
0x4bf2e0 <_IO_wide_data_2+96>:  0x0     0x0
0x4bf2f0 <_IO_wide_data_2+112>: 0x0     0x0
0x4bf300 <_IO_wide_data_2+128>: 0x0     0x0
0x4bf310 <_IO_wide_data_2+144>: 0x0     0x0
0x4bf320 <_IO_wide_data_2+160>: 0x0     0x0
0x4bf330 <_IO_wide_data_2+176>: 0x0     0x0
0x4bf340 <_IO_wide_data_2+192>: 0x0     0x0
0x4bf350 <_IO_wide_data_2+208>: 0x0     0x0
0x4bf360 <_IO_wide_data_2+224>: 0x0     0x0
0x4bf370 <_IO_wide_data_2+240>: 0x0     0x0
0x4bf380 <_IO_wide_data_2+256>: 0x0     0x0
0x4bf390 <_IO_wide_data_2+272>: 0x0     0x0
0x4bf3a0 <_IO_wide_data_2+288>: 0x0     0x0
0x4bf3b0 <_IO_wide_data_2+304>: 0x4c0e20 <_IO_wfile_jumps>      0x0
0x4bf3c0 <_IO_2_1_stdout_>:     0xfbad2084      0x0
0x4bf3d0 <_IO_2_1_stdout_+16>:  0x0     0x0
0x4bf3e0 <_IO_2_1_stdout_+32>:  0x0     0x0
0x4bf3f0 <_IO_2_1_stdout_+48>:  0x0     0x0
0x4bf400 <_IO_2_1_stdout_+64>:  0x0     0x0
0x4bf410 <_IO_2_1_stdout_+80>:  0x0     0x0
0x4bf420 <_IO_2_1_stdout_+96>:  0x0     0x4bf5e0 <_IO_2_1_stdin_>
0x4bf430 <_IO_2_1_stdout_+112>: 0x8000000001    0xffffffffffffffff
0x4bf440 <_IO_2_1_stdout_+128>: 0x0     0x4c5ed0 <_IO_stdfile_1_lock>
0x4bf450 <_IO_2_1_stdout_+144>: 0xffffffffffffffff      0x0
0x4bf460 <_IO_2_1_stdout_+160>: 0x4bf4a0 <_IO_wide_data_1>      0x0
0x4bf470 <_IO_2_1_stdout_+176>: 0x0     0x0
0x4bf480 <_IO_2_1_stdout_+192>: 0x0     0x0
```

```
--Type <RET> for more, q to quit, c to continue without paging--
0x4bf490 <_IO_2_1_stdout_+208>: 0x0     0x4c1060 <_IO_file_jumps>
0x4bf4a0 <_IO_wide_data_1>:     0x0     0x0
0x4bf4b0 <_IO_wide_data_1+16>:  0x0     0x0
0x4bf4c0 <_IO_wide_data_1+32>:  0x0     0x0
0x4bf4d0 <_IO_wide_data_1+48>:  0x0     0x0
0x4bf4e0 <_IO_wide_data_1+64>:  0x0     0x0
0x4bf4f0 <_IO_wide_data_1+80>:  0x0     0x0
0x4bf500 <_IO_wide_data_1+96>:  0x0     0x0
0x4bf510 <_IO_wide_data_1+112>: 0x0     0x0
0x4bf520 <_IO_wide_data_1+128>: 0x0     0x0
0x4bf530 <_IO_wide_data_1+144>: 0x0     0x0
0x4bf540 <_IO_wide_data_1+160>: 0x0     0x0
0x4bf550 <_IO_wide_data_1+176>: 0x0     0x0
0x4bf560 <_IO_wide_data_1+192>: 0x0     0x0
0x4bf570 <_IO_wide_data_1+208>: 0x0     0x0
0x4bf580 <_IO_wide_data_1+224>: 0x0     0x0
0x4bf590 <_IO_wide_data_1+240>: 0x0     0x0
0x4bf5a0 <_IO_wide_data_1+256>: 0x0     0x0
0x4bf5b0 <_IO_wide_data_1+272>: 0x0     0x0
0x4bf5c0 <_IO_wide_data_1+288>: 0x0     0x0
0x4bf5d0 <_IO_wide_data_1+304>: 0x4c0e20 <_IO_wfile_jumps>      0x0
0x4bf5e0 <_IO_2_1_stdin_>:      0xfbad2088      0x0
0x4bf5f0 <_IO_2_1_stdin_+16>:   0x0     0x0
0x4bf600 <_IO_2_1_stdin_+32>:   0x0     0x0
0x4bf610 <_IO_2_1_stdin_+48>:   0x0     0x0
0x4bf620 <_IO_2_1_stdin_+64>:   0x0     0x0
0x4bf630 <_IO_2_1_stdin_+80>:   0x0     0x0
0x4bf640 <_IO_2_1_stdin_+96>:   0x0     0x0
0x4bf650 <_IO_2_1_stdin_+112>:  0x8000000000    0xffffffffffffffff
0x4bf660 <_IO_2_1_stdin_+128>:  0x0     0x4c5ee0 <_IO_stdfile_0_lock>
0x4bf670 <_IO_2_1_stdin_+144>:  0xffffffffffffffff      0x0
0x4bf680 <_IO_2_1_stdin_+160>:  0x4bf6c0 <_IO_wide_data_0>      0x0
0x4bf690 <_IO_2_1_stdin_+176>:  0x0     0x0
0x4bf6a0 <_IO_2_1_stdin_+192>:  0x0     0x0
0x4bf6b0 <_IO_2_1_stdin_+208>:  0x0     0x4c1060 <_IO_file_jumps>
0x4bf6c0 <_IO_wide_data_0>:     0x0     0x0
0x4bf6d0 <_IO_wide_data_0+16>:  0x0     0x0
0x4bf6e0 <_IO_wide_data_0+32>:  0x0     0x0
0x4bf6f0 <_IO_wide_data_0+48>:  0x0     0x0
0x4bf700 <_IO_wide_data_0+64>:  0x0     0x0
0x4bf710 <_IO_wide_data_0+80>:  0x0     0x0
0x4bf720 <_IO_wide_data_0+96>:  0x0     0x0
0x4bf730 <_IO_wide_data_0+112>: 0x0     0x0
0x4bf740 <_IO_wide_data_0+128>: 0x0     0x0
0x4bf750 <_IO_wide_data_0+144>: 0x0     0x0
0x4bf760 <_IO_wide_data_0+160>: 0x0     0x0
0x4bf770 <_IO_wide_data_0+176>: 0x0     0x0
0x4bf780 <_IO_wide_data_0+192>: 0x0     0x0
0x4bf790 <_IO_wide_data_0+208>: 0x0     0x0
0x4bf7a0 <_IO_wide_data_0+224>: 0x0     0x0
0x4bf7b0 <_IO_wide_data_0+240>: 0x0     0x0
0x4bf7c0 <_IO_wide_data_0+256>: 0x0     0x0
0x4bf7d0 <_IO_wide_data_0+272>: 0x0     0x0
0x4bf7e0 <_IO_wide_data_0+288>: 0x0     0x0
0x4bf7f0 <_IO_wide_data_0+304>: 0x4c0e20 <_IO_wfile_jumps>      0x4bf1a0 <_IO_2_1_stderr_>
0x4bf800 <stdout>:      0x4bf3c0 <_IO_2_1_stdout_>      0x4bf5e0 <_IO_2_1_stdin_>
0x4bf810:       0x0     0x0
--Type <RET> for more, q to quit, c to continue without paging--
0x4bf820 <may_shrink_heap.11591>:       0x1ffffffff     0x1
```

```
0x4bf830:       0x0     0x0
0x4bf840 <mp_>: 0x20000 0x20000
0x4bf850 <mp_+16>:      0x20000 0x8
0x4bf860 <mp_+32>:      0x0     0x1000000000000
0x4bf870 <mp_+48>:      0x0     0x0
0x4bf880 <mp_+64>:      0x0     0x21b41c0
0x4bf890 <mp_+80>:      0x40    0x408
0x4bf8a0 <mp_+96>:      0x7     0x0
0x4bf8b0:       0x0     0x0
0x4bf8c0 <__memalign_hook>:     0x41aad0 <memalign_hook_ini>    0x41b0e0 <realloc_hook_ini>
0x4bf8d0 <__malloc_hook>:       0x0     0x0
0x4bf8e0 <main_arena>:  0x0     0x0
0x4bf8f0 <main_arena+16>:       0x0     0x0
```

The output is in the following format:

```
address:     value1    value2
```

Because the size of each value is 8 bytes, the next address is +16 bytes or $+10_{hex}$. The addresses can have associated symbolic names:

```
address <name>:  value1  value2
```

For example, from the output above:

```
0x4bf110 <__nptl_nthreads>:     0x6     0x0
```

Each value may also have an associated symbolic value:

```
address <name>:  value1 <name1>    value2
```

For example, from the output above:

```
0x4bf8c0 <__memalign_hook>:     0x41aad0 <memalign_hook_ini>    0x41b0e0 <realloc_hook_ini>
```

12. Explore the contents of memory pointed to by *__nptl_nthreads*, *_nl_default_default_domain*, and *__memalign_hook* addresses (**/x** is for hex, **/d** is for decimals, **/u** is for unsigned decimals, **/g** is for 64-bit values, **/w** is for 32-bit values, **/h** is for 16-bit values, **/b** is for byte values, **/a** is for addresses, **/c** and **/s** are for chars and strings):

```
(gdb) x/d 0x4bf110
0x4bf110 <__nptl_nthreads>:     6

(gdb) x/u &__nptl_nthreads
0x4bf110 <__nptl_nthreads>:     6

(gdb) x/wx 0x4bf110
0x4bf110 <__nptl_nthreads>:     0x00000006

(gdb) x/gx 0x4bf110
0x4bf110 <__nptl_nthreads>:     0x0000000000000006

(gdb) x/hx 0x4bf110
0x4bf110 <__nptl_nthreads>:     0x0006

(gdb) x/bx 0x4bf110
0x4bf110 <__nptl_nthreads>:     0x06
```

```
(gdb) x/2a 0x4bf160
0x4bf160 <_dl_tls_static_size>: 0x1180  0x494a88 <_nl_default_default_domain>
```

Note: Some symbols and addresses (for example, `0x494a88`) belong to read-only sections of executable image. If GDB refuses to read them you may need to run this command:

```
(gdb) set trust-readonly-sections on
```

```
(gdb) x/a &_nl_default_default_domain
0x494a88 <_nl_default_default_domain>:  0x736567617373656d
```

```
(gdb) x/a 0x494a88
0x494a88 <_nl_default_default_domain>:  0x736567617373656d
```

```
(gdb) x/s 0x494a88
0x494a88 <_nl_default_default_domain>:  "messages"
```

```
(gdb) x/10a 0x494a88
0x494a88 <_nl_default_default_domain>:  0x736567617373656d      0x6c006f6c00756c00
0x494a98:       0x786c00586c0069        0x7273752f00656372
0x494aa8:       0x6c2f65726168732f      0x656c61636f
0x494ab8 <aliasfile.10131>:     0x2e656c61636f6c2f      0x7361696c61
0x494ac8:       0x0     0x0
```

```
(gdb) x/8c 0x494a88
0x494a88 <_nl_default_default_domain>:  109 'm' 101 'e' 115 's' 115 's' 97 'a'  103 'g' 101 'e'
115 's'
```

```
(gdb) x/10s 0x494a88
0x494a88 <_nl_default_default_domain>:  "messages"
0x494a91:       "lu"
0x494a94:       "lo"
0x494a97:       "li"
0x494a9a:       "lX"
0x494a9d:       "lx"
0x494aa0:       "rce"
0x494aa4:       "/usr/share/locale"
0x494ab6:       ""
0x494ab7:       ""
```

Note: We see that a hook function is installed for *memalign* but not *malloc*. Please find the following documentation for hook functions here:

https://www.gnu.org/software/libc/manual/html_node/Hooks-for-Malloc.html

13. Explore the contents of memory pointed to by the *environ* variable address:

```
(gdb) x/a &environ
0x4c5f48 <environ>:     0x7ffdf45637f8
```

```
(gdb) x/10a 0x7ffdf45637f8
0x7ffdf45637f8: 0x7ffdf4565756  0x7ffdf4565766
0x7ffdf4563808: 0x7ffdf456577d  0x7ffdf4565794
0x7ffdf4563818: 0x7ffdf45657a9  0x7ffdf45657c7
0x7ffdf4563828: 0x7ffdf45657d8  0x7ffdf45657f3
0x7ffdf4563838: 0x7ffdf45657fe  0x7ffdf4565812
```

```
(gdb) x/10s 0x7ffdf4565756
0x7ffdf4565756: "SHELL=/bin/bash"
0x7ffdf4565766: "HISTCONTROL=ignoreboth"
0x7ffdf456577d: "WSL_DISTRO_NAME=Debian"
0x7ffdf4565794: "NAME=DESKTOP-IS6V2L0"
0x7ffdf45657a9: "PWD=/home/coredump/ALCDA/App1"
0x7ffdf45657c7: "LOGNAME=coredump"
0x7ffdf45657d8: "MC_TMPDIR=/tmp/mc-coredump"
0x7ffdf45657f3: "MC_SID=192"
0x7ffdf45657fe: "HOME=/home/coredump"
0x7ffdf4565812: "LANG=en_US.UTF-8"
```

Note: The last command interprets `0x7ffdf4565756` as an address of the sequence of 10 null-terminated strings.

14. Now, we look at how to perform a memory search. It is not possible to search in the entire virtual memory, only in the valid regions (WinDbg debugger is able).

```
(gdb) find /g 0x004bc000, 0x004d2000, 6
0x4bd5f8 <_nl_C_LC_NUMERIC+56>
0x4be880 <tunable_list+928>
0x4bea40 <dyn_temp.10655+32>
0x4bf110 <__nptl_nthreads>
warning: Unable to access 16000 bytes of target memory at 0x4c6e18, halting search.
4 patterns found.
```

```
(gdb) x/gd 0x4bf110
0x4bf110 <__nptl_nthreads>:     6
```

```
(gdb) x/s 0x7ffdf4565756
0x7ffdf4565756: "SHELL=/bin/bash"
```

```
(gdb) find 0x7ffdf4565756, +100, "bash"
0x7ffdf4565761
1 pattern found.
```

Note: "bash" is considered a null-terminated array of characters for the search. To search for a string sequence without a null terminator, use a sequence of characters:

```
(gdb) find 0x7ffdf4565756, +100, "bin"
Pattern not found.
```

```
(gdb) find 0x7ffdf4565756, +100, 'b', 'i', 'n'
0x7ffdf456575d
1 pattern found.
```

15. Get the list of loaded modules:

```
(gdb) info sharedlibrary
No shared libraries loaded at this time.
```

Note: We don't see any shared libraries because they were statically linked. We also created the version of a dynamically linked *App1.shared* executable. If we load its core dump *App1.shared.core.275*, we see the list of shared libraries:

```
~/ALCDA2/x64/App1$ gdb -c App1.shared.core.275 -se App1.shared
GNU gdb (Debian 8.2.1-2+b3) 8.2.1
Copyright (C) 2018 Free Software Foundation, Inc.
License GPLv3+: GNU GPL version 3 or later <http://gnu.org/licenses/gpl.html>
```

```
This is free software: you are free to change and redistribute it.
There is NO WARRANTY, to the extent permitted by law.
Type "show copying" and "show warranty" for details.
This GDB was configured as "x86_64-linux-gnu".
Type "show configuration" for configuration details.
For bug reporting instructions, please see:
<http://www.gnu.org/software/gdb/bugs/>.
Find the GDB manual and other documentation resources online at:
    <http://www.gnu.org/software/gdb/documentation/>.

For help, type "help".
Type "apropos word" to search for commands related to "word"...
Reading symbols from App1.shared...(no debugging symbols found)...done.
[New LWP 275]
[New LWP 276]
[New LWP 277]
[New LWP 278]
[New LWP 279]
[New LWP 280]
[Thread debugging using libthread_db enabled]
Using host libthread_db library "/lib/x86_64-linux-gnu/libthread_db.so.1".
Core was generated by `./App1.shared'.
#0  0x00007f1ae471e720 in __GI___nanosleep (requested_time=requested_time@entry=0x7ffc74957a90,
remaining=remaining@entry=0x7ffc74957a90) at ../sysdeps/unix/sysv/linux/nanosleep.c:28
28      ../sysdeps/unix/sysv/linux/nanosleep.c: No such file or directory.
[Current thread is 1 (Thread 0x7f1ae4655740 (LWP 275))]
```

```
(gdb) info sharedlibrary
From                To                  Syms Read   Shared Object Library
0x00007f1ae481f5b0  0x00007f1ae482d641  Yes         /lib/x86_64-linux-gnu/libpthread.so.0
0x00007f1ae467a320  0x00007f1ae47c039b  Yes         /lib/x86_64-linux-gnu/libc.so.6
0x00007f1ae4848090  0x00007f1ae4865b20  Yes         /lib64/ld-linux-x86-64.so.2
```

16. Disassemble the *bar_one* function and follow the indirect *sleep* function call:

```
(gdb) disassemble bar_one
Dump of assembler code for function bar_one:
   0x0000557e17348145 <+0>:     push   %rbp
   0x0000557e17348146 <+1>:     mov    %rsp,%rbp
   0x0000557e17348149 <+4>:     mov    $0xffffffff,%edi
   0x0000557e1734814e <+9>:     callq  0x557e17348040 <sleep@plt>
   0x0000557e17348153 <+14>:    nop
   0x0000557e17348154 <+15>:    pop    %rbp
   0x0000557e17348155 <+16>:    retq
End of assembler dump.
```

```
(gdb) disassemble 0x557e17348040
Dump of assembler code for function sleep@plt:
   0x0000557e17348040 <+0>:     jmpq   *0x2fda(%rip)        # 0x557e1734b020 <sleep@got.plt>
   0x0000557e17348046 <+6>:     pushq  $0x1
   0x0000557e1734804b <+11>:    jmpq   0x557e17348020
End of assembler dump.
```

17. Dump the annotated value as a memory address, interpreting its contents as a symbol:

```
(gdb) p/x 0x0000557e17348046+0x2fda
$1 = 0x557e1734b020
```

```
(gdb) x/a 0x557e1734b020
0x557e1734b020 <sleep@got.plt>: 0x7f1ae471e5f0 <__sleep>
```

Note: Since GDB gets shared library images from your analysis system that do not correspond to shared libraries from the crash system, most likely you get some random symbolic information (and also an invalid backtrace from the **bt** command):

```
(gdb) x/a 0x557e1734b020
0x557e1734b020 <sleep@got.plt>:  0x7f1ae471e5f0 <__getpwnam_r+288>
```

```
(gdb) bt
#0  __getpwnam_r (name=<optimized out>, resbuf=0x7ffc74957bf0, buffer=<optimized out>,
buflen=94000043556960, result=<optimized out>)
    at ../nss/getXXbyYY_r.c:416
#1  0x00007f1ae3652700 in ?? ()
#2  0x00007f1ae3e53700 in ?? ()
#3  0x00007f1ae4654700 in ?? ()
#4  0x0000557e17348340 in ?? ()
#5  0x00007f1ae467c09b in _IO_acquire_lock_fct (p=<optimized out>) at libioP.h:759
#6  _IO_getc (fp=0x557e1734832a <main+170>) at getc.c:39
#7  0x00007ffc74957bf8 in ?? ()
#8  0x0000000100040000 in ?? ()
#9  0x0000557e17348280 in thread_five ()
#10 0x0000000000000000 in ?? ()
```

Note: You need the original shared library images and debug symbol files from the problem system. To get the right results for this exercise, you can recreate the *App1.shared* core dump (see *main.c* for build instructions if necessary). There is also the ARM64 A1 exercise with shared libraries from the problem system.

18. *App1.shared.pmap.275* also shows library memory regions:

```
(gdb) q
```

```
~/ALCDA2/x64/App1$ cat App1.shared.pmap.275
275:   ./App1.shared
0000557e17347000      4K r---- App1.shared
0000557e17348000      4K r-x-- App1.shared
0000557e17349000      4K r---- App1.shared
0000557e1734a000      4K r---- App1.shared
0000557e1734b000      4K rw--- App1.shared
0000557e179ca000    132K rw---   [ anon ]
00007f1ae1e50000      4K -----   [ anon ]
00007f1ae1e51000   8192K rw---   [ anon ]
00007f1ae2651000      4K -----   [ anon ]
00007f1ae2652000   8192K rw---   [ anon ]
00007f1ae2e52000      4K -----   [ anon ]
00007f1ae2e53000   8192K rw---   [ anon ]
00007f1ae3653000      4K -----   [ anon ]
00007f1ae3654000   8192K rw---   [ anon ]
00007f1ae3e54000      4K -----   [ anon ]
00007f1ae3e55000   8204K rw---   [ anon ]
00007f1ae4658000    136K r---- libc-2.28.so
00007f1ae467a000   1312K r-x-- libc-2.28.so
00007f1ae47c2000    304K r---- libc-2.28.so
00007f1ae480e000      4K ----- libc-2.28.so
00007f1ae480f000     16K r---- libc-2.28.so
00007f1ae4813000      8K rw--- libc-2.28.so
00007f1ae4815000     16K rw---   [ anon ]
00007f1ae4819000     24K r---- libpthread-2.28.so
00007f1ae481f000     60K r-x-- libpthread-2.28.so
00007f1ae482e000     24K r---- libpthread-2.28.so
```

```
00007f1ae4834000      4K r---- libpthread-2.28.so
00007f1ae4835000      4K rw--- libpthread-2.28.so
00007f1ae4836000     24K rw---   [ anon ]
00007f1ae4847000      4K r---- ld-2.28.so
00007f1ae4848000    120K r-x-- ld-2.28.so
00007f1ae4866000     32K r---- ld-2.28.so
00007f1ae486e000      4K r---- ld-2.28.so
00007f1ae486f000      4K rw--- ld-2.28.so
00007f1ae4870000      4K rw---   [ anon ]
00007ffc74939000    132K rw---   [ stack ]
00007ffc749ac000     16K r----   [ anon ]
00007ffc749b0000      4K r-x--   [ anon ]
 total           43400K
```

Exercise A1 (A64, GDB)

Goal: Learn how to list stack traces, disassemble functions, check their correctness, dump data, get environment.

Patterns: Manual Dump (Process); Stack Trace; Incorrect Stack Trace; Truncated Stack Trace; Unrecognizable Symbolic Information; Stack Trace Collection; Annotated Disassembly; Paratext; Not My Version; Environment Hint.

1. Load the core dump *App1.core.21174* and *App1* executable from the A64/App1 directory. We use **gdb-multiarch** on x64 Debian:

```
~/ALCDA2/A64/App1$ gdb-multiarch -c App1.core.21174 -se App1
GNU gdb (Debian 8.2.1-2+b3) 8.2.1
Copyright (C) 2018 Free Software Foundation, Inc.
License GPLv3+: GNU GPL version 3 or later <http://gnu.org/licenses/gpl.html>
This is free software: you are free to change and redistribute it.
There is NO WARRANTY, to the extent permitted by law.
Type "show copying" and "show warranty" for details.
This GDB was configured as "x86_64-linux-gnu".
Type "show configuration" for configuration details.
For bug reporting instructions, please see:
<http://www.gnu.org/software/gdb/bugs/>.
Find the GDB manual and other documentation resources online at:
    <http://www.gnu.org/software/gdb/documentation/>.

For help, type "help".
Type "apropos word" to search for commands related to "word"...
Reading symbols from App1...(no debugging symbols found)...done.
[New LWP 21175]
[New LWP 21176]
[New LWP 21177]
[New LWP 21178]
[New LWP 21179]
[New LWP 21174]
Core was generated by `./App1'.
#0  0x000000000040c9b4 in nanosleep ()
[Current thread is 1 (LWP 21175)]
```

2. Set logging to a file in case of lengthy output from some commands:

```
(gdb) set logging on App1.log
Copying output to App1.log.
```

Note: If you use the newer GDB 12.x on an ARM64 Ubuntu instance instead, you need to use different logging commands, and you may also want to set color highlighting off:

```
(gdb) set logging file App1.log
```

```
(gdb) set logging enabled on
Copying output to App1.log.
Copying debug output to App1.log.
```

```
(gdb) set style enabled off
```

3. List all threads:

```
(gdb) info threads
  Id   Target Id         Frame
* 1    LWP 21175         0x000000000040c9b4 in nanosleep ()
  2    LWP 21176         0x000000000040c9b4 in nanosleep ()
  3    LWP 21177         0x000000000040c9b4 in nanosleep ()
  4    LWP 21178         0x000000000040c9b4 in nanosleep ()
  5    LWP 21179         0x000000000040c9b4 in nanosleep ()
  6    LWP 21174         0x000000000040c9b4 in nanosleep ()
```

4. Get the current thread stack trace:

```
(gdb) bt
#0  0x000000000040c9b4 in nanosleep ()
#1  0x0000000000424cb4 in sleep ()
#2  0x00000000004031f8 in bar_one ()
#3  0x000000000040320c in foo_one ()
#4  0x0000000000403224 in thread_one ()
#5  0x0000000000404c34 in start_thread ()
#6  0x0000000000429b60 in thread_start ()
```

5. Get all thread stack traces:

```
(gdb) thread apply all bt

Thread 6 (LWP 21174):
#0  0x000000000040c9b4 in nanosleep ()
#1  0x0000000000424cb4 in sleep ()
#2  0x00000000004033e0 in main ()

Thread 5 (LWP 21179):
#0  0x000000000040c9b4 in nanosleep ()
#1  0x0000000000424cb4 in sleep ()
#2  0x0000000000403318 in bar_five ()
#3  0x000000000040332c in foo_five ()
#4  0x0000000000403344 in thread_five ()
#5  0x0000000000404c34 in start_thread ()
#6  0x0000000000429b60 in thread_start ()

Thread 4 (LWP 21178):
#0  0x000000000040c9b4 in nanosleep ()
#1  0x0000000000424cb4 in sleep ()
#2  0x00000000004032d0 in bar_four ()
#3  0x00000000004032e4 in foo_four ()
#4  0x00000000004032fc in thread_four ()
#5  0x0000000000404c34 in start_thread ()
#6  0x0000000000429b60 in thread_start ()

Thread 3 (LWP 21177):
#0  0x000000000040c9b4 in nanosleep ()
#1  0x0000000000424cb4 in sleep ()
#2  0x0000000000403288 in bar_three ()
#3  0x000000000040329c in foo_three ()
#4  0x00000000004032b4 in thread_three ()
#5  0x0000000000404c34 in start_thread ()
#6  0x0000000000429b60 in thread_start ()

Thread 2 (LWP 21176):
#0  0x000000000040c9b4 in nanosleep ()
```

```
#1  0x0000000000424cb4 in sleep ()
#2  0x0000000000403240 in bar_two ()
#3  0x0000000000403254 in foo_two ()
#4  0x000000000040326c in thread_two ()
#5  0x0000000000404c34 in start_thread ()
#6  0x0000000000429b60 in thread_start ()

Thread 1 (LWP 21175):
#0  0x000000000040c9b4 in nanosleep ()
#1  0x0000000000424cb4 in sleep ()
#2  0x00000000004031f8 in bar_one ()
#3  0x000000000040320c in foo_one ()
#4  0x0000000000403224 in thread_one ()
#5  0x0000000000404c34 in start_thread ()
#6  0x0000000000429b60 in thread_start ()
```

6. Switch to thread #2 and get its stack trace:

```
(gdb) thread 2
[Switching to thread 2 (LWP 21176)]
#0  0x000000000040c9b4 in nanosleep ()

(gdb) bt
#0  0x000000000040c9b4 in nanosleep ()
#1  0x0000000000424cb4 in sleep ()
#2  0x0000000000403240 in bar_two ()
#3  0x0000000000403254 in foo_two ()
#4  0x000000000040326c in thread_two ()
#5  0x0000000000404c34 in start_thread ()
#6  0x0000000000429b60 in thread_start ()

(gdb) info threads
  Id   Target Id         Frame
  1    LWP 21175         0x000000000040c9b4 in nanosleep ()
* 2    LWP 21176         0x000000000040c9b4 in nanosleep ()
  3    LWP 21177         0x000000000040c9b4 in nanosleep ()
  4    LWP 21178         0x000000000040c9b4 in nanosleep ()
  5    LWP 21179         0x000000000040c9b4 in nanosleep ()
  6    LWP 21174         0x000000000040c9b4 in nanosleep ()
```

7. Check that *bar_two* called the *sleep* function by comparing the return address on the call stack from the disassembly output:

```
(gdb) disassemble bar_two
Dump of assembler code for function bar_two:
   0x0000000000403230 <+0>:     stp     x29, x30, [sp, #-16]!
   0x0000000000403234 <+4>:     mov     x29, sp
   0x0000000000403238 <+8>:     mov     w0, #0xffffffff                 // #-1
   0x000000000040323c <+12>:    bl      0x424ba4 <sleep>
   0x0000000000403240 <+16>:    ldp     x29, x30, [sp], #16
   0x0000000000403244 <+20>:    ret
End of assembler dump.
```

We see that the address in the stack trace for the *bar_two* function is the address to return to after calling the *sleep* function.

8. Get the *App1* data section from the output of pmap (*App1.pmap.21174*):

```
(gdb) ^Z
[1]+  Stopped                 gdb -c App1.core.21174 -se App1

~/ALCDA2/A64/App1$ cat App1.pmap.21174
21174:   ./App1
0000000000400000    768K r-x-- App1
00000000004c0000    128K rw--- App1
0000000001fa0000    256K rw---   [ anon ]
0000fffccab40000     64K -----   [ anon ]
0000fffccab50000   8192K rw---   [ anon ]
0000fffccb350000     64K -----   [ anon ]
0000fffccb360000   8192K rw---   [ anon ]
0000fffccbb60000     64K -----   [ anon ]
0000fffccbb70000   8192K rw---   [ anon ]
0000fffccc370000     64K -----   [ anon ]
0000fffccc380000   8192K rw---   [ anon ]
0000fffcccb80000     64K -----   [ anon ]
0000fffcccb90000   8192K rw---   [ anon ]
0000fffccd390000     64K r----   [ anon ]
0000fffccd3a0000     64K r-x--   [ anon ]
0000ffffd3090000    192K rw---   [ stack ]
 total            42752K

~/ALCDA2/A64/App1$ fg
gdb -c App1.core.21174 -se App1


(gdb)
```

9. Compare with the section information in the core dump:

```
(gdb) p/x 0x00000000004c0000+128*1024
$1 = 0x4e0000

(gdb) maintenance info sections
Exec file: `/home/ubuntu/ALCDA2/A64/App1/App1', file type elf64-littleaarch64.
 [0]      0x00400190->0x004001b0 at 0x00000190: .note.ABI-tag ALLOC LOAD READONLY DATA HAS_CONTENTS
 [1]      0x004001b0->0x004001d4 at 0x000001b0: .note.gnu.build-id ALLOC LOAD READONLY DATA HAS_CONTENTS
 [2]      0x004001d8->0x00400250 at 0x000001d8: .rela.plt ALLOC LOAD READONLY DATA HAS_CONTENTS
 [3]      0x00400250->0x00400264 at 0x00000250: .init ALLOC LOAD READONLY CODE HAS_CONTENTS
 [4]      0x00400270->0x004002c0 at 0x00000270: .plt ALLOC LOAD READONLY CODE HAS_CONTENTS
 [5]      0x004002c0->0x00487098 at 0x000002c0: .text ALLOC LOAD READONLY CODE HAS_CONTENTS
 [6]      0x00487098->0x00488d68 at 0x00087098: __libc_freeres_fn ALLOC LOAD READONLY CODE HAS_CONTENTS
 [7]      0x00488d68->0x004891b8 at 0x00088d68: __libc_thread_freeres_fn ALLOC LOAD READONLY CODE
HAS_CONTENTS
 [8]      0x004891b8->0x004891c8 at 0x000891b8: .fini ALLOC LOAD READONLY CODE HAS_CONTENTS
 [9]      0x004891d0->0x004a16ad at 0x000891d0: .rodata ALLOC LOAD READONLY DATA HAS_CONTENTS
 [10]     0x004a16ad->0x004a16ae at 0x000a16ad: .stapsdt.base ALLOC LOAD READONLY DATA HAS_CONTENTS
 [11]     0x004a16b0->0x004a1de8 at 0x000a16b0: __libc_IO_vtables ALLOC LOAD READONLY DATA HAS_CONTENTS
 [12]     0x004a1de8->0x004a1e50 at 0x000a1de8: __libc_subfreeres ALLOC LOAD READONLY DATA HAS_CONTENTS
 [13]     0x004a1e50->0x004a1e58 at 0x000a1e50: __libc_atexit ALLOC LOAD READONLY DATA HAS_CONTENTS
 [14]     0x004a1e58->0x004a1e68 at 0x000a1e58: __libc_thread_subfreeres ALLOC LOAD READONLY DATA
HAS_CONTENTS
 [15]     0x004a1e68->0x004b047c at 0x000a1e68: .eh_frame ALLOC LOAD READONLY DATA HAS_CONTENTS
 [16]     0x004b047c->0x004b0639 at 0x000b047c: .gcc_except_table ALLOC LOAD READONLY DATA HAS_CONTENTS
 [17]     0x004cfb20->0x004cfb48 at 0x000bfb20: .tdata ALLOC LOAD DATA HAS_CONTENTS
 [18]     0x004cfb48->0x004cfb98 at 0x000bfb48: .tbss ALLOC
 [19]     0x004cfb48->0x004cfb50 at 0x000bfb48: .init_array ALLOC LOAD DATA HAS_CONTENTS
 [20]     0x004cfb50->0x004cfb60 at 0x000bfb50: .fini_array ALLOC LOAD DATA HAS_CONTENTS
 [21]     0x004cfb60->0x004cfb68 at 0x000bfb60: .jcr ALLOC LOAD DATA HAS_CONTENTS
 [22]     0x004cfb68->0x004cff24 at 0x000bfb68: .data.rel.ro ALLOC LOAD DATA HAS_CONTENTS
```

```
 [23]      0x004cff28->0x004cffe8 at 0x000bff28: .got ALLOC LOAD DATA HAS_CONTENTS
 [24]      0x004cffe8->0x004d0028 at 0x000bffe8: .got.plt ALLOC LOAD DATA HAS_CONTENTS
 [25]      0x004d0030->0x004d1580 at 0x000c0030: .data ALLOC LOAD DATA HAS_CONTENTS
 [26]      0x004d1580->0x004d8050 at 0x000c1580: .bss ALLOC
 [27]      0x004d8050->0x004d8088 at 0x000c1580: __libc_freeres_ptrs ALLOC
 [28]      0x00000000->0x00000031 at 0x000c1580: .comment READONLY HAS_CONTENTS
 [29]      0x00000000->0x00001cb0 at 0x000c15b4: .note.stapsdt READONLY HAS_CONTENTS
Core file: `/home/ubuntu/ALCDA2/A64/App1/App1.core.21174', file type elf64-littleaarch64.
 [0]       0x00000000->0x00001c94 at 0x000003c0: note0 READONLY HAS_CONTENTS
 [1]       0x00000000->0x00000110 at 0x000004e0: .reg/21175 HAS_CONTENTS
 [2]       0x00000000->0x00000110 at 0x000004e0: .reg HAS_CONTENTS
 [3]       0x00000000->0x00000210 at 0x0000060c: .reg2/21175 HAS_CONTENTS
 [4]       0x00000000->0x00000210 at 0x0000060c: .reg2 HAS_CONTENTS
 [5]       0x00000000->0x00000080 at 0x00000830: .note.linuxcore.siginfo/21175 HAS_CONTENTS
 [6]       0x00000000->0x00000080 at 0x00000830: .note.linuxcore.siginfo HAS_CONTENTS
 [7]       0x00000000->0x00000110 at 0x00000934: .reg/21176 HAS_CONTENTS
 [8]       0x00000000->0x00000210 at 0x00000a60: .reg2/21176 HAS_CONTENTS
 [9]       0x00000000->0x00000080 at 0x00000c84: .note.linuxcore.siginfo/21176 HAS_CONTENTS
 [10]      0x00000000->0x00000110 at 0x00000d88: .reg/21177 HAS_CONTENTS
 [11]      0x00000000->0x00000210 at 0x00000eb4: .reg2/21177 HAS_CONTENTS
 [12]      0x00000000->0x00000080 at 0x000010d8: .note.linuxcore.siginfo/21177 HAS_CONTENTS
 [13]      0x00000000->0x00000110 at 0x000011dc: .reg/21178 HAS_CONTENTS
 [14]      0x00000000->0x00000210 at 0x00001308: .reg2/21178 HAS_CONTENTS
 [15]      0x00000000->0x00000080 at 0x0000152c: .note.linuxcore.siginfo/21178 HAS_CONTENTS
 [16]      0x00000000->0x00000110 at 0x00001630: .reg/21179 HAS_CONTENTS
 [17]      0x00000000->0x00000210 at 0x0000175c: .reg2/21179 HAS_CONTENTS
--Type <RET> for more, q to quit, c to continue without paging--
 [18]      0x00000000->0x00000080 at 0x00001980: .note.linuxcore.siginfo/21179 HAS_CONTENTS
 [19]      0x00000000->0x00000110 at 0x00001a84: .reg/21174 HAS_CONTENTS
 [20]      0x00000000->0x00000210 at 0x00001bb0: .reg2/21174 HAS_CONTENTS
 [21]      0x00000000->0x00000080 at 0x00001dd4: .note.linuxcore.siginfo/21174 HAS_CONTENTS
 [22]      0x00000000->0x00000160 at 0x00001e68: .auxv HAS_CONTENTS
 [23]      0x00000000->0x00000076 at 0x00001fdc: .note.linuxcore.file/21174 HAS_CONTENTS
 [24]      0x00000000->0x00000076 at 0x00001fdc: .note.linuxcore.file HAS_CONTENTS
 [25]      0x00400000->0x004c0000 at 0x00002054: load1 ALLOC LOAD READONLY CODE HAS_CONTENTS
 [26]      0x004c0000->0x004e0000 at 0x000c2054: load2 ALLOC LOAD HAS_CONTENTS
 [27]      0x01fa0000->0x01fe0000 at 0x000e2054: load3 ALLOC LOAD HAS_CONTENTS
 [28]      0xfffccab40000->0xfffccab50000 at 0x00122054: load4 ALLOC LOAD READONLY HAS_CONTENTS
 [29]      0xfffccab50000->0xfffccb350000 at 0x00132054: load5 ALLOC LOAD HAS_CONTENTS
 [30]      0xfffccb350000->0xfffccb360000 at 0x00932054: load6 ALLOC LOAD READONLY HAS_CONTENTS
 [31]      0xfffccb360000->0xfffccbb60000 at 0x00942054: load7 ALLOC LOAD HAS_CONTENTS
 [32]      0xfffccbb60000->0xfffccbb70000 at 0x01142054: load8 ALLOC LOAD READONLY HAS_CONTENTS
 [33]      0xfffccbb70000->0xfffccc370000 at 0x01152054: load9 ALLOC LOAD HAS_CONTENTS
 [34]      0xfffccc370000->0xfffccc380000 at 0x01952054: load10 ALLOC LOAD READONLY HAS_CONTENTS
 [35]      0xfffccc380000->0xfffcccb80000 at 0x01962054: load11 ALLOC LOAD HAS_CONTENTS
 [36]      0xfffcccb80000->0xfffcccb90000 at 0x02162054: load12 ALLOC LOAD READONLY HAS_CONTENTS
 [37]      0xfffcccb90000->0xfffccd390000 at 0x02172054: load13 ALLOC LOAD HAS_CONTENTS
 [38]      0xfffccd3a0000->0xfffccd3b0000 at 0x02972054: load14 ALLOC LOAD READONLY CODE HAS_CONTENTS
 [39]      0xffffd3090000->0xffffd30c0000 at 0x02982054: load15 ALLOC LOAD HAS_CONTENTS
```

10. Dump the first 600 addresses from the **.data** section with possible symbolic information:

```
(gdb) x/600a 0x004d0030
0x4d0030:       0x0     0x4d0038 <stack_cache>
0x4d0040 <stack_cache+8>:       0x4d0038 <stack_cache>  0x6
0x4d0050 <stack_used>:  0xfffccb34f140  0xfffccd38f140
0x4d0060 <__sched_fifo_max_prio>:       0xffffffffffffffff      0x890
0x4d0070 <__exit_funcs>:        0x4d5eb0 <initial>      0x486b88 <__gcc_personality_v0>
0x4d0080 <_IO_list_all>:        0x4d0088 <_IO_2_1_stderr_>      0xfbad2086
0x4d0090 <_IO_2_1_stderr_+8>:   0x0     0x0
0x4d00a0 <_IO_2_1_stderr_+24>:  0x0     0x0
0x4d00b0 <_IO_2_1_stderr_+40>:  0x0     0x0
0x4d00c0 <_IO_2_1_stderr_+56>:  0x0     0x0
0x4d00d0 <_IO_2_1_stderr_+72>:  0x0     0x0
0x4d00e0 <_IO_2_1_stderr_+88>:  0x0     0x0
```

```
0x4d00f0 <_IO_2_1_stderr_+104>: 0x4d02b0 <_IO_2_1_stdout_>      0x2
0x4d0100 <_IO_2_1_stderr_+120>: 0xffffffffffffffff      0x0
0x4d0110 <_IO_2_1_stderr_+136>: 0x4d6428 <_IO_stdfile_2_lock>   0xffffffffffffffff
0x4d0120 <_IO_2_1_stderr_+152>: 0x0     0x4d0168 <_IO_wide_data_2>
0x4d0130 <_IO_2_1_stderr_+168>: 0x0     0x0
0x4d0140 <_IO_2_1_stderr_+184>: 0x0     0x0
0x4d0150 <_IO_2_1_stderr_+200>: 0x0     0x0
0x4d0160 <_IO_2_1_stderr_+216>: 0x4a1950 <_IO_file_jumps>       0x0
0x4d0170 <_IO_wide_data_2+8>:   0x0     0x0
0x4d0180 <_IO_wide_data_2+24>:  0x0     0x0
0x4d0190 <_IO_wide_data_2+40>:  0x0     0x0
0x4d01a0 <_IO_wide_data_2+56>:  0x0     0x0
0x4d01b0 <_IO_wide_data_2+72>:  0x0     0x0
0x4d01c0 <_IO_wide_data_2+88>:  0x0     0x0
0x4d01d0 <_IO_wide_data_2+104>: 0x0     0x0
0x4d01e0 <_IO_wide_data_2+120>: 0x0     0x0
0x4d01f0 <_IO_wide_data_2+136>: 0x0     0x0
0x4d0200 <_IO_wide_data_2+152>: 0x0     0x0
0x4d0210 <_IO_wide_data_2+168>: 0x0     0x0
0x4d0220 <_IO_wide_data_2+184>: 0x0     0x0
0x4d0230 <_IO_wide_data_2+200>: 0x0     0x0
0x4d0240 <_IO_wide_data_2+216>: 0x0     0x0
0x4d0250 <_IO_wide_data_2+232>: 0x0     0x0
0x4d0260 <_IO_wide_data_2+248>: 0x0     0x0
0x4d0270 <_IO_wide_data_2+264>: 0x0     0x0
0x4d0280 <_IO_wide_data_2+280>: 0x0     0x0
0x4d0290 <_IO_wide_data_2+296>: 0x0     0x0
0x4d02a0 <_IO_wide_data_2+312>: 0x0     0x4a1800 <_IO_wfile_jumps>
0x4d02b0 <_IO_2_1_stdout_>:     0xfbad2084      0x0
0x4d02c0 <_IO_2_1_stdout_+16>:  0x0     0x0
0x4d02d0 <_IO_2_1_stdout_+32>:  0x0     0x0
0x4d02e0 <_IO_2_1_stdout_+48>:  0x0     0x0
0x4d02f0 <_IO_2_1_stdout_+64>:  0x0     0x0
0x4d0300 <_IO_2_1_stdout_+80>:  0x0     0x0
0x4d0310 <_IO_2_1_stdout_+96>:  0x0     0x4d04d8 <_IO_2_1_stdin_>
0x4d0320 <_IO_2_1_stdout_+112>: 0x1     0xffffffffffffffff
0x4d0330 <_IO_2_1_stdout_+128>: 0x0     0x4d6438 <_IO_stdfile_1_lock>
0x4d0340 <_IO_2_1_stdout_+144>: 0xffffffffffffffff      0x0
--Type <RET> for more, q to quit, c to continue without paging--
0x4d0350 <_IO_2_1_stdout_+160>: 0x4d0390 <_IO_wide_data_1>      0x0
0x4d0360 <_IO_2_1_stdout_+176>: 0x0     0x0
0x4d0370 <_IO_2_1_stdout_+192>: 0x0     0x0
0x4d0380 <_IO_2_1_stdout_+208>: 0x0     0x4a1950 <_IO_file_jumps>
0x4d0390 <_IO_wide_data_1>:     0x0     0x0
0x4d03a0 <_IO_wide_data_1+16>:  0x0     0x0
0x4d03b0 <_IO_wide_data_1+32>:  0x0     0x0
0x4d03c0 <_IO_wide_data_1+48>:  0x0     0x0
0x4d03d0 <_IO_wide_data_1+64>:  0x0     0x0
0x4d03e0 <_IO_wide_data_1+80>:  0x0     0x0
0x4d03f0 <_IO_wide_data_1+96>:  0x0     0x0
0x4d0400 <_IO_wide_data_1+112>: 0x0     0x0
0x4d0410 <_IO_wide_data_1+128>: 0x0     0x0
0x4d0420 <_IO_wide_data_1+144>: 0x0     0x0
0x4d0430 <_IO_wide_data_1+160>: 0x0     0x0
0x4d0440 <_IO_wide_data_1+176>: 0x0     0x0
0x4d0450 <_IO_wide_data_1+192>: 0x0     0x0
0x4d0460 <_IO_wide_data_1+208>: 0x0     0x0
0x4d0470 <_IO_wide_data_1+224>: 0x0     0x0
0x4d0480 <_IO_wide_data_1+240>: 0x0     0x0
0x4d0490 <_IO_wide_data_1+256>: 0x0     0x0
```

```
0x4d04a0 <_IO_wide_data_1+272>: 0x0      0x0
0x4d04b0 <_IO_wide_data_1+288>: 0x0      0x0
0x4d04c0 <_IO_wide_data_1+304>: 0x0      0x0
0x4d04d0 <_IO_wide_data_1+320>: 0x4a1800 <_IO_wfile_jumps>      0xfbad2088
0x4d04e0 <_IO_2_1_stdin_+8>:    0x0      0x0
0x4d04f0 <_IO_2_1_stdin_+24>:   0x0      0x0
0x4d0500 <_IO_2_1_stdin_+40>:   0x0      0x0
0x4d0510 <_IO_2_1_stdin_+56>:   0x0      0x0
0x4d0520 <_IO_2_1_stdin_+72>:   0x0      0x0
0x4d0530 <_IO_2_1_stdin_+88>:   0x0      0x0
0x4d0540 <_IO_2_1_stdin_+104>:  0x0      0x0
0x4d0550 <_IO_2_1_stdin_+120>:  0xffffffffffffffff      0x0
0x4d0560 <_IO_2_1_stdin_+136>:  0x4d6448 <_IO_stdfile_0_lock>   0xffffffffffffffff
0x4d0570 <_IO_2_1_stdin_+152>:  0x0      0x4d05b8 <_IO_wide_data_0>
0x4d0580 <_IO_2_1_stdin_+168>:  0x0      0x0
0x4d0590 <_IO_2_1_stdin_+184>:  0x0      0x0
0x4d05a0 <_IO_2_1_stdin_+200>:  0x0      0x0
0x4d05b0 <_IO_2_1_stdin_+216>:  0x4a1950 <_IO_file_jumps>       0x0
0x4d05c0 <_IO_wide_data_0+8>:   0x0      0x0
0x4d05d0 <_IO_wide_data_0+24>:  0x0      0x0
0x4d05e0 <_IO_wide_data_0+40>:  0x0      0x0
0x4d05f0 <_IO_wide_data_0+56>:  0x0      0x0
0x4d0600 <_IO_wide_data_0+72>:  0x0      0x0
0x4d0610 <_IO_wide_data_0+88>:  0x0      0x0
0x4d0620 <_IO_wide_data_0+104>: 0x0      0x0
0x4d0630 <_IO_wide_data_0+120>: 0x0      0x0
0x4d0640 <_IO_wide_data_0+136>: 0x0      0x0
0x4d0650 <_IO_wide_data_0+152>: 0x0      0x0
0x4d0660 <_IO_wide_data_0+168>: 0x0      0x0
--Type <RET> for more, q to quit, c to continue without paging--
0x4d0670 <_IO_wide_data_0+184>: 0x0      0x0
0x4d0680 <_IO_wide_data_0+200>: 0x0      0x0
0x4d0690 <_IO_wide_data_0+216>: 0x0      0x0
0x4d06a0 <_IO_wide_data_0+232>: 0x0      0x0
0x4d06b0 <_IO_wide_data_0+248>: 0x0      0x0
0x4d06c0 <_IO_wide_data_0+264>: 0x0      0x0
0x4d06d0 <_IO_wide_data_0+280>: 0x0      0x0
0x4d06e0 <_IO_wide_data_0+296>: 0x0      0x0
0x4d06f0 <_IO_wide_data_0+312>: 0x0      0x4a1800 <_IO_wfile_jumps>
0x4d0700 <stderr>:      0x4d0088 <_IO_2_1_stderr_>      0x4d02b0 <_IO_2_1_stdout_>
0x4d0710 <stdin>:       0x4d04d8 <_IO_2_1_stdin_>       0x20000
0x4d0720 <mp_+8>:       0x20000 0x20000
0x4d0730 <mp_+24>:      0x8     0x0
0x4d0740 <mp_+40>:      0x1000000000000 0x0
0x4d0750 <mp_+56>:      0x0     0x0
0x4d0760 <mp_+72>:      0x1fa0f88       0x40
0x4d0770 <mp_+88>:      0x408   0x7
0x4d0780 <mp_+104>:     0x0     0x0
0x4d0790 <main_arena+8>:        0x0      0x0
0x4d07a0 <main_arena+24>:       0x0      0x0
0x4d07b0 <main_arena+40>:       0x0      0x0
0x4d07c0 <main_arena+56>:       0x0      0x0
0x4d07d0 <main_arena+72>:       0x0      0x0
0x4d07e0 <main_arena+88>:       0x0      0x1fa28a0
0x4d07f0 <main_arena+104>:      0x0      0x4d07e8 <main_arena+96>
0x4d0800 <main_arena+120>:      0x4d07e8 <main_arena+96>        0x4d07f8 <main_arena+112>
0x4d0810 <main_arena+136>:      0x4d07f8 <main_arena+112>       0x4d0808 <main_arena+128>
0x4d0820 <main_arena+152>:      0x4d0808 <main_arena+128>       0x4d0818 <main_arena+144>
0x4d0830 <main_arena+168>:      0x4d0818 <main_arena+144>       0x4d0828 <main_arena+160>
0x4d0840 <main_arena+184>:      0x4d0828 <main_arena+160>       0x4d0838 <main_arena+176>
```

```
0x4d0850 <main_arena+200>:     0x4d0838 <main_arena+176>     0x4d0848 <main_arena+192>
0x4d0860 <main_arena+216>:     0x4d0848 <main_arena+192>     0x4d0858 <main_arena+208>
0x4d0870 <main_arena+232>:     0x4d0858 <main_arena+208>     0x4d0868 <main_arena+224>
0x4d0880 <main_arena+248>:     0x4d0868 <main_arena+224>     0x4d0878 <main_arena+240>
0x4d0890 <main_arena+264>:     0x4d0878 <main_arena+240>     0x4d0888 <main_arena+256>
0x4d08a0 <main_arena+280>:     0x4d0888 <main_arena+256>     0x4d0898 <main_arena+272>
0x4d08b0 <main_arena+296>:     0x4d0898 <main_arena+272>     0x4d08a8 <main_arena+288>
0x4d08c0 <main_arena+312>:     0x4d08a8 <main_arena+288>     0x4d08b8 <main_arena+304>
0x4d08d0 <main_arena+328>:     0x4d08b8 <main_arena+304>     0x4d08c8 <main_arena+320>
0x4d08e0 <main_arena+344>:     0x4d08c8 <main_arena+320>     0x4d08d8 <main_arena+336>
0x4d08f0 <main_arena+360>:     0x4d08d8 <main_arena+336>     0x4d08e8 <main_arena+352>
0x4d0900 <main_arena+376>:     0x4d08e8 <main_arena+352>     0x4d08f8 <main_arena+368>
0x4d0910 <main_arena+392>:     0x4d08f8 <main_arena+368>     0x4d0908 <main_arena+384>
0x4d0920 <main_arena+408>:     0x4d0908 <main_arena+384>     0x4d0918 <main_arena+400>
0x4d0930 <main_arena+424>:     0x4d0918 <main_arena+400>     0x4d0928 <main_arena+416>
0x4d0940 <main_arena+440>:     0x4d0928 <main_arena+416>     0x4d0938 <main_arena+432>
0x4d0950 <main_arena+456>:     0x4d0938 <main_arena+432>     0x4d0948 <main_arena+448>
0x4d0960 <main_arena+472>:     0x4d0948 <main_arena+448>     0x4d0958 <main_arena+464>
0x4d0970 <main_arena+488>:     0x4d0958 <main_arena+464>     0x4d0968 <main_arena+480>
0x4d0980 <main_arena+504>:     0x4d0968 <main_arena+480>     0x4d0978 <main_arena+496>
--Type <RET> for more, q to quit, c to continue without paging--
0x4d0990 <main_arena+520>:     0x4d0978 <main_arena+496>     0x4d0988 <main_arena+512>
0x4d09a0 <main_arena+536>:     0x4d0988 <main_arena+512>     0x4d0998 <main_arena+528>
0x4d09b0 <main_arena+552>:     0x4d0998 <main_arena+528>     0x4d09a8 <main_arena+544>
0x4d09c0 <main_arena+568>:     0x4d09a8 <main_arena+544>     0x4d09b8 <main_arena+560>
0x4d09d0 <main_arena+584>:     0x4d09b8 <main_arena+560>     0x4d09c8 <main_arena+576>
0x4d09e0 <main_arena+600>:     0x4d09c8 <main_arena+576>     0x4d09d8 <main_arena+592>
0x4d09f0 <main_arena+616>:     0x4d09d8 <main_arena+592>     0x4d09e8 <main_arena+608>
0x4d0a00 <main_arena+632>:     0x4d09e8 <main_arena+608>     0x4d09f8 <main_arena+624>
0x4d0a10 <main_arena+648>:     0x4d09f8 <main_arena+624>     0x4d0a08 <main_arena+640>
0x4d0a20 <main_arena+664>:     0x4d0a08 <main_arena+640>     0x4d0a18 <main_arena+656>
0x4d0a30 <main_arena+680>:     0x4d0a18 <main_arena+656>     0x4d0a28 <main_arena+672>
0x4d0a40 <main_arena+696>:     0x4d0a28 <main_arena+672>     0x4d0a38 <main_arena+688>
0x4d0a50 <main_arena+712>:     0x4d0a38 <main_arena+688>     0x4d0a48 <main_arena+704>
0x4d0a60 <main_arena+728>:     0x4d0a48 <main_arena+704>     0x4d0a58 <main_arena+720>
0x4d0a70 <main_arena+744>:     0x4d0a58 <main_arena+720>     0x4d0a68 <main_arena+736>
0x4d0a80 <main_arena+760>:     0x4d0a68 <main_arena+736>     0x4d0a78 <main_arena+752>
0x4d0a90 <main_arena+776>:     0x4d0a78 <main_arena+752>     0x4d0a88 <main_arena+768>
0x4d0aa0 <main_arena+792>:     0x4d0a88 <main_arena+768>     0x4d0a98 <main_arena+784>
0x4d0ab0 <main_arena+808>:     0x4d0a98 <main_arena+784>     0x4d0aa8 <main_arena+800>
0x4d0ac0 <main_arena+824>:     0x4d0aa8 <main_arena+800>     0x4d0ab8 <main_arena+816>
0x4d0ad0 <main_arena+840>:     0x4d0ab8 <main_arena+816>     0x4d0ac8 <main_arena+832>
0x4d0ae0 <main_arena+856>:     0x4d0ac8 <main_arena+832>     0x4d0ad8 <main_arena+848>
0x4d0af0 <main_arena+872>:     0x4d0ad8 <main_arena+848>     0x4d0ae8 <main_arena+864>
0x4d0b00 <main_arena+888>:     0x4d0ae8 <main_arena+864>     0x4d0af8 <main_arena+880>
0x4d0b10 <main_arena+904>:     0x4d0af8 <main_arena+880>     0x4d0b08 <main_arena+896>
0x4d0b20 <main_arena+920>:     0x4d0b08 <main_arena+896>     0x4d0b18 <main_arena+912>
0x4d0b30 <main_arena+936>:     0x4d0b18 <main_arena+912>     0x4d0b28 <main_arena+928>
0x4d0b40 <main_arena+952>:     0x4d0b28 <main_arena+928>     0x4d0b38 <main_arena+944>
0x4d0b50 <main_arena+968>:     0x4d0b38 <main_arena+944>     0x4d0b48 <main_arena+960>
0x4d0b60 <main_arena+984>:     0x4d0b48 <main_arena+960>     0x4d0b58 <main_arena+976>
0x4d0b70 <main_arena+1000>:    0x4d0b58 <main_arena+976>     0x4d0b68 <main_arena+992>
0x4d0b80 <main_arena+1016>:    0x4d0b68 <main_arena+992>     0x4d0b78 <main_arena+1008>
0x4d0b90 <main_arena+1032>:    0x4d0b78 <main_arena+1008>    0x4d0b88 <main_arena+1024>
0x4d0ba0 <main_arena+1048>:    0x4d0b88 <main_arena+1024>    0x4d0b98 <main_arena+1040>
0x4d0bb0 <main_arena+1064>:    0x4d0b98 <main_arena+1040>    0x4d0ba8 <main_arena+1056>
0x4d0bc0 <main_arena+1080>:    0x4d0ba8 <main_arena+1056>    0x4d0bb8 <main_arena+1072>
0x4d0bd0 <main_arena+1096>:    0x4d0bb8 <main_arena+1072>    0x4d0bc8 <main_arena+1088>
0x4d0be0 <main_arena+1112>:    0x4d0bc8 <main_arena+1088>    0x4d0bd8 <main_arena+1104>
0x4d0bf0 <main_arena+1128>:    0x4d0bd8 <main_arena+1104>    0x4d0be8 <main_arena+1120>
```

```
0x4d0c00 <main_arena+1144>:	0x4d0be8 <main_arena+1120>	0x4d0bf8 <main_arena+1136>
0x4d0c10 <main_arena+1160>:	0x4d0bf8 <main_arena+1136>	0x4d0c08 <main_arena+1152>
0x4d0c20 <main_arena+1176>:	0x4d0c08 <main_arena+1152>	0x4d0c18 <main_arena+1168>
0x4d0c30 <main_arena+1192>:	0x4d0c18 <main_arena+1168>	0x4d0c28 <main_arena+1184>
0x4d0c40 <main_arena+1208>:	0x4d0c28 <main_arena+1184>	0x4d0c38 <main_arena+1200>
0x4d0c50 <main_arena+1224>:	0x4d0c38 <main_arena+1200>	0x4d0c48 <main_arena+1216>
0x4d0c60 <main_arena+1240>:	0x4d0c48 <main_arena+1216>	0x4d0c58 <main_arena+1232>
0x4d0c70 <main_arena+1256>:	0x4d0c58 <main_arena+1232>	0x4d0c68 <main_arena+1248>
0x4d0c80 <main_arena+1272>:	0x4d0c68 <main_arena+1248>	0x4d0c78 <main_arena+1264>
0x4d0c90 <main_arena+1288>:	0x4d0c78 <main_arena+1264>	0x4d0c88 <main_arena+1280>
0x4d0ca0 <main_arena+1304>:	0x4d0c88 <main_arena+1280>	0x4d0c98 <main_arena+1296>
--Type <RET> for more, q to quit, c to continue without paging--
0x4d0cb0 <main_arena+1320>:	0x4d0c98 <main_arena+1296>	0x4d0ca8 <main_arena+1312>
0x4d0cc0 <main_arena+1336>:	0x4d0ca8 <main_arena+1312>	0x4d0cb8 <main_arena+1328>
0x4d0cd0 <main_arena+1352>:	0x4d0cb8 <main_arena+1328>	0x4d0cc8 <main_arena+1344>
0x4d0ce0 <main_arena+1368>:	0x4d0cc8 <main_arena+1344>	0x4d0cd8 <main_arena+1360>
0x4d0cf0 <main_arena+1384>:	0x4d0cd8 <main_arena+1360>	0x4d0ce8 <main_arena+1376>
0x4d0d00 <main_arena+1400>:	0x4d0ce8 <main_arena+1376>	0x4d0cf8 <main_arena+1392>
0x4d0d10 <main_arena+1416>:	0x4d0cf8 <main_arena+1392>	0x4d0d08 <main_arena+1408>
0x4d0d20 <main_arena+1432>:	0x4d0d08 <main_arena+1408>	0x4d0d18 <main_arena+1424>
0x4d0d30 <main_arena+1448>:	0x4d0d18 <main_arena+1424>	0x4d0d28 <main_arena+1440>
0x4d0d40 <main_arena+1464>:	0x4d0d28 <main_arena+1440>	0x4d0d38 <main_arena+1456>
0x4d0d50 <main_arena+1480>:	0x4d0d38 <main_arena+1456>	0x4d0d48 <main_arena+1472>
0x4d0d60 <main_arena+1496>:	0x4d0d48 <main_arena+1472>	0x4d0d58 <main_arena+1488>
0x4d0d70 <main_arena+1512>:	0x4d0d58 <main_arena+1488>	0x4d0d68 <main_arena+1504>
0x4d0d80 <main_arena+1528>:	0x4d0d68 <main_arena+1504>	0x4d0d78 <main_arena+1520>
0x4d0d90 <main_arena+1544>:	0x4d0d78 <main_arena+1520>	0x4d0d88 <main_arena+1536>
0x4d0da0 <main_arena+1560>:	0x4d0d88 <main_arena+1536>	0x4d0d98 <main_arena+1552>
0x4d0db0 <main_arena+1576>:	0x4d0d98 <main_arena+1552>	0x4d0da8 <main_arena+1568>
0x4d0dc0 <main_arena+1592>:	0x4d0da8 <main_arena+1568>	0x4d0db8 <main_arena+1584>
0x4d0dd0 <main_arena+1608>:	0x4d0db8 <main_arena+1584>	0x4d0dc8 <main_arena+1600>
0x4d0de0 <main_arena+1624>:	0x4d0dc8 <main_arena+1600>	0x4d0dd8 <main_arena+1616>
0x4d0df0 <main_arena+1640>:	0x4d0dd8 <main_arena+1616>	0x4d0de8 <main_arena+1632>
0x4d0e00 <main_arena+1656>:	0x4d0de8 <main_arena+1632>	0x4d0df8 <main_arena+1648>
0x4d0e10 <main_arena+1672>:	0x4d0df8 <main_arena+1648>	0x4d0e08 <main_arena+1664>
0x4d0e20 <main_arena+1688>:	0x4d0e08 <main_arena+1664>	0x4d0e18 <main_arena+1680>
0x4d0e30 <main_arena+1704>:	0x4d0e18 <main_arena+1680>	0x4d0e28 <main_arena+1696>
0x4d0e40 <main_arena+1720>:	0x4d0e28 <main_arena+1696>	0x4d0e38 <main_arena+1712>
0x4d0e50 <main_arena+1736>:	0x4d0e38 <main_arena+1712>	0x4d0e48 <main_arena+1728>
0x4d0e60 <main_arena+1752>:	0x4d0e48 <main_arena+1728>	0x4d0e58 <main_arena+1744>
0x4d0e70 <main_arena+1768>:	0x4d0e58 <main_arena+1744>	0x4d0e68 <main_arena+1760>
0x4d0e80 <main_arena+1784>:	0x4d0e68 <main_arena+1760>	0x4d0e78 <main_arena+1776>
0x4d0e90 <main_arena+1800>:	0x4d0e78 <main_arena+1776>	0x4d0e88 <main_arena+1792>
0x4d0ea0 <main_arena+1816>:	0x4d0e88 <main_arena+1792>	0x4d0e98 <main_arena+1808>
0x4d0eb0 <main_arena+1832>:	0x4d0e98 <main_arena+1808>	0x4d0ea8 <main_arena+1824>
0x4d0ec0 <main_arena+1848>:	0x4d0ea8 <main_arena+1824>	0x4d0eb8 <main_arena+1840>
0x4d0ed0 <main_arena+1864>:	0x4d0eb8 <main_arena+1840>	0x4d0ec8 <main_arena+1856>
0x4d0ee0 <main_arena+1880>:	0x4d0ec8 <main_arena+1856>	0x4d0ed8 <main_arena+1872>
0x4d0ef0 <main_arena+1896>:	0x4d0ed8 <main_arena+1872>	0x4d0ee8 <main_arena+1888>
0x4d0f00 <main_arena+1912>:	0x4d0ee8 <main_arena+1888>	0x4d0ef8 <main_arena+1904>
0x4d0f10 <main_arena+1928>:	0x4d0ef8 <main_arena+1904>	0x4d0f08 <main_arena+1920>
0x4d0f20 <main_arena+1944>:	0x4d0f08 <main_arena+1920>	0x4d0f18 <main_arena+1936>
0x4d0f30 <main_arena+1960>:	0x4d0f18 <main_arena+1936>	0x4d0f28 <main_arena+1952>
0x4d0f40 <main_arena+1976>:	0x4d0f28 <main_arena+1952>	0x4d0f38 <main_arena+1968>
0x4d0f50 <main_arena+1992>:	0x4d0f38 <main_arena+1968>	0x4d0f48 <main_arena+1984>
0x4d0f60 <main_arena+2008>:	0x4d0f48 <main_arena+1984>	0x4d0f58 <main_arena+2000>
0x4d0f70 <main_arena+2024>:	0x4d0f58 <main_arena+2000>	0x4d0f68 <main_arena+2016>
0x4d0f80 <main_arena+2040>:	0x4d0f68 <main_arena+2016>	0x4d0f78 <main_arena+2032>
0x4d0f90 <main_arena+2056>:	0x4d0f78 <main_arena+2032>	0x4d0f88 <main_arena+2048>
0x4d0fa0 <main_arena+2072>:	0x4d0f88 <main_arena+2048>	0x4d0f98 <main_arena+2064>
```

```
0x4d0fb0 <main_arena+2088>:     0x4d0f98 <main_arena+2064>      0x4d0fa8 <main_arena+2080>
0x4d0fc0 <main_arena+2104>:     0x4d0fa8 <main_arena+2080>      0x4d0fb8 <main_arena+2096>
--Type <RET> for more, q to quit, c to continue without paging--
0x4d0fd0 <main_arena+2120>:     0x4d0fb8 <main_arena+2096>      0x4d0fc8 <main_arena+2112>
0x4d0fe0 <main_arena+2136>:     0x4d0fc8 <main_arena+2112>      0x0
0x4d0ff0 <main_arena+2152>:     0x0     0x4d0788 <main_arena>
0x4d1000 <main_arena+2168>:     0x0     0x1
0x4d1010 <main_arena+2184>:     0x3f078 0x3f078
0x4d1020 <__morecore>:  0x421c08 <__default_morecore>   0x1
0x4d1030 <__libc_malloc_initialized>:   0xffffffff00000001      0x41cc00 <memalign_hook_ini>
0x4d1040 <__realloc_hook>:      0x41d688 <realloc_hook_ini>     0x0
0x4d1050 <LogFacility>: 0xffffffff00000008      0xff00000002
0x4d1060 <cached_result.10628>: 0xffffffff      0xffffd30bf6dd
0x4d1070 <program_invocation_name>:     0xffffd30bf6db  0x10000
0x4d1080 <_dl_stack_flags>:     0x6     0x0
0x4d1090 <_dl_load_write_lock+8>:       0x0     0x1
0x4d10a0 <_dl_load_write_lock+24>:      0x0     0x0
0x4d10b0 <_dl_load_write_lock+40>:      0x0     0x0
0x4d10c0 <_dl_load_lock+8>:     0x0     0x1
0x4d10d0 <_dl_load_lock+24>:    0x0     0x0
0x4d10e0 <_dl_load_lock+40>:    0x0     0x42c6a0 <_dl_make_stack_executable>
0x4d10f0 <_dl_correct_cache_id>:        0x200000a03     0x4045a8 <__pthread_init_static_tls>
0x4d1100 <_dl_starting_up>:     0x1     0xfffffffffffffffe
0x4d1110 <_dl_argv>:    0x4d1068 <program_invocation_short_name>        0x0
0x4d1120 <builtin_modules>:     0x48ad20        0x48ac30
0x4d1130 <builtin_modules+16>:  0x7fffffff00000001      0x48ac40
0x4d1140 <builtin_modules+32>:  0x0     0x0
0x4d1150 <builtin_modules+48>:  0x0     0x48ac30
0x4d1160 <builtin_modules+64>:  0x48ad20        0x7fffffff00000001
0x4d1170 <builtin_modules+80>:  0x48ac50        0x0
0x4d1180 <builtin_modules+96>:  0x0     0x0
0x4d1190 <builtin_modules+112>: 0x48ad20        0x48ac60
0x4d11a0 <builtin_modules+128>: 0x7fffffff00000001      0x48ac70
0x4d11b0 <builtin_modules+144>: 0x0     0x0
0x4d11c0 <builtin_modules+160>: 0x0     0x48ac60
0x4d11d0 <builtin_modules+176>: 0x48ad20        0x7fffffff00000001
0x4d11e0 <builtin_modules+192>: 0x48ac88        0x0
0x4d11f0 <builtin_modules+208>: 0x0     0x0
0x4d1200 <builtin_modules+224>: 0x48ad20        0x48aca0
0x4d1210 <builtin_modules+240>: 0x7fffffff00000001      0x48acb0
0x4d1220 <builtin_modules+256>: 0x0     0x0
0x4d1230 <builtin_modules+272>: 0x0     0x48aca0
0x4d1240 <builtin_modules+288>: 0x48ad20        0x7fffffff00000001
0x4d1250 <builtin_modules+304>: 0x48acc0        0x0
0x4d1260 <builtin_modules+320>: 0x0     0x0
0x4d1270 <builtin_modules+336>: 0x48acd0        0x48ad20
0x4d1280 <builtin_modules+352>: 0x7fffffff00000001      0x48ace0
0x4d1290 <builtin_modules+368>: 0x0     0x0
0x4d12a0 <builtin_modules+384>: 0x0     0x48ad20
0x4d12b0 <builtin_modules+400>: 0x48acd0        0x7fffffff00000001
0x4d12c0 <builtin_modules+416>: 0x48acf0        0x0
0x4d12d0 <builtin_modules+432>: 0x0     0x0
0x4d12e0 <builtin_modules+448>: 0x48ad00        0x48ad20
```

The output is in the following format:

```
address:     value1     value2
```

Because the size of each value is 8 bytes, the next address is +16 bytes or $+10_{hex}$. The addresses can have associated symbolic names:

```
address <name>:  value1  value2
```

Each value may also have an associated symbolic value:

```
address <name>:  value1 <name1>    value2
```

For example, from the output above:

```
0x4d1110 <_dl_argv>:     0x4d1068 <program_invocation_short_name>        0x0
```

11. Explore the contents of memory pointed to by *__nptl_nthreads*, *program_invocation_short_name*, and *__realloc_hook* addresses (**/x** is for hex, **/d** is for decimals, **/u** is for unsigned decimals, **/g** is for 64-bit values, **/w** is for 32-bit values, **/h** is for 16-bit values, **/b** is for byte values, **/a** is for addresses, **/c** and **/s** are for chars and strings):

```
(gdb) x/d &__nptl_nthreads
0x4d0048 <__nptl_nthreads>:     6

(gdb) x/u 0x4d0048
0x4d0048 <__nptl_nthreads>:     6

(gdb) x/wx 0x4d0048
0x4d0048 <__nptl_nthreads>:     0x00000006

(gdb) x/gx 0x4d0048
0x4d0048 <__nptl_nthreads>:     0x0000000000000006

(gdb) x/hx 0x4d0048
0x4d0048 <__nptl_nthreads>:     0x0006

(gdb) x/bx 0x4d0048
0x4d0048 <__nptl_nthreads>:     0x06

(gdb) x/a 0x4d1068
0x4d1068 <program_invocation_short_name>:      0xffffd30bf6dd

(gdb) x/a 0xffffd30bf6dd
0xffffd30bf6dd: 0x4744580031707041

(gdb) x/s 0xffffd30bf6dd
0xffffd30bf6dd: "App1"

(gdb) x/8c 0xffffd30bf6dd
0xffffd30bf6dd: 65 'A'  112 'p' 112 'p' 49 '1'  0 '\000'       88 'X'  68 'D'  71 'G'

(gdb) x/10s 0xffffd30bf6dd
0xffffd30bf6dd: "App1"
0xffffd30bf6e2: "XDG_SESSION_ID=6850"
0xffffd30bf6f6: "HOSTNAME=instance-20211109-2004"
0xffffd30bf716: "SELINUX_ROLE_REQUESTED="
0xffffd30bf72e: "TERM=xterm-256color"
0xffffd30bf742: "SHELL=/bin/bash"
0xffffd30bf752: "HISTSIZE=1000"
0xffffd30bf760: "SSH_CLIENT=37.228.238.120 61099 22"
0xffffd30bf783: "SELINUX_USE_CURRENT_RANGE="
0xffffd30bf79e: "SSH_TTY=/dev/pts/1"

(gdb) x/a &__realloc_hook
0x4d1040 <__realloc_hook>:     0x41d688 <realloc_hook_ini>
```

```
(gdb) x/10i 0x41d688
   0x41d688 <realloc_hook_ini>: stp     x29, x30, [sp, #-112]!
   0x41d68c <realloc_hook_ini+4>:       mov     x29, sp
   0x41d690 <realloc_hook_ini+8>:       stp     x25, x26, [sp, #64]
   0x41d694 <realloc_hook_ini+12>:      adrp    x25, 0x4d0000
   0x41d698 <realloc_hook_ini+16>:      add     x2, x25, #0x718
   0x41d69c <realloc_hook_ini+20>:      stp     x21, x22, [sp, #32]
   0x41d6a0 <realloc_hook_ini+24>:      ldr     w3, [x2, #2328]
   0x41d6a4 <realloc_hook_ini+28>:      ldr     x21, 0x41da48
   0x41d6a8 <realloc_hook_ini+32>:      ldr     x2, 0x41da40
   0x41d6ac <realloc_hook_ini+36>:      stp     x19, x20, [sp, #16]
```

Note: We see that a hook function is installed for *realloc*. Please find the following documentation for hook functions here:

https://www.gnu.org/software/libc/manual/html_node/Hooks-for-Malloc.html

12. Explore the contents of memory pointed to by the *environ* variable address:

```
(gdb) x/a &environ
0x4d64c8 <environ>:     0xffffd30b8888

(gdb) x/10a 0xffffd30b8888
0xffffd30b8888: 0xffffd30bf6e2  0xffffd30bf6f6
0xffffd30b8898: 0xffffd30bf716  0xffffd30bf72e
0xffffd30b88a8: 0xffffd30bf742  0xffffd30bf752
0xffffd30b88b8: 0xffffd30bf760  0xffffd30bf783
0xffffd30b88c8: 0xffffd30bf79e  0xffffd30bf7b1

(gdb) x/10s 0xffffd30bf6e2
0xffffd30bf6e2: "XDG_SESSION_ID=6850"
0xffffd30bf6f6: "HOSTNAME=instance-20211109-2004"
0xffffd30bf716: "SELINUX_ROLE_REQUESTED="
0xffffd30bf72e: "TERM=xterm-256color"
0xffffd30bf742: "SHELL=/bin/bash"
0xffffd30bf752: "HISTSIZE=1000"
0xffffd30bf760: "SSH_CLIENT=37.228.238.120 61099 22"
0xffffd30bf783: "SELINUX_USE_CURRENT_RANGE="
0xffffd30bf79e: "SSH_TTY=/dev/pts/1"
0xffffd30bf7b1: "USER=opc"
```

13. Now, we look at how to perform a memory search. It is not possible to search in the entire virtual memory, only in the valid regions.

```
(gdb) find /g 0x004d0030, 0x005d0030, 6
0x4d0048 <__nptl_nthreads>
0x4d1080 <_dl_stack_flags>
0x4d7e00 <_dl_phnum>
warning: Unable to access 16000 bytes of target memory at 0x4dfb08, halting search.
3 patterns found.

(gdb) x/gd 0x4d0048
0x4d0048 <__nptl_nthreads>:     6

(gdb) find 0xffffd30bf6e2, +1000, "bash"
0xffffd30bf74d
1 pattern found.
```

```
(gdb) x/s 0xffffd30bf74d-11
0xffffd30bf742: "SHELL=/bin/bash"
```

Note: "bash" is considered a null-terminated array of characters for the search. To search for a string sequence without a null terminator, use a sequence of characters:

```
(gdb) find 0xffffd30bf6e2, +1000, "bin"
Pattern not found.
```

```
(gdb) find 0xffffd30bf6e2, +1000, 'b', 'i', 'n'
0xffffd30bf749
1 pattern found.
```

14. Get the list of loaded modules:

```
(gdb) info sharedlibrary
No shared libraries loaded at this time.
```

Note: We don't see any shared libraries because they were statically linked. We also created the version of a dynamically linked *App1.shared* executable. If we load its core dump *App1.shared.core.184724* from the App1S directory, we see the list of shared libraries:

```
~/ALCDA2/A64/App1S$ gdb-multiarch -c App1.shared.core.184724 -se App1.shared
GNU gdb (Debian 8.2.1-2+b3) 8.2.1
Copyright (C) 2018 Free Software Foundation, Inc.
License GPLv3+: GNU GPL version 3 or later <http://gnu.org/licenses/gpl.html>
This is free software: you are free to change and redistribute it.
There is NO WARRANTY, to the extent permitted by law.
Type "show copying" and "show warranty" for details.
This GDB was configured as "x86_64-linux-gnu".
Type "show configuration" for configuration details.
For bug reporting instructions, please see:
<http://www.gnu.org/software/gdb/bugs/>.
Find the GDB manual and other documentation resources online at:
    <http://www.gnu.org/software/gdb/documentation/>.

For help, type "help".
Type "apropos word" to search for commands related to "word"...
Reading symbols from App1.shared...(no debugging symbols found)...done.
[New LWP 184724]
[New LWP 184725]
[New LWP 184726]
[New LWP 184727]
[New LWP 184728]
[New LWP 184729]

warning: Could not load shared library symbols for 2 libraries, e.g. /lib/aarch64-linux-
gnu/libc.so.6.
Use the "info sharedlibrary" command to see the complete listing.
Do you need "set solib-search-path" or "set sysroot"?
Core was generated by `./App1.shared'.
#0  0x0000ffff81451924 in ?? ()
[Current thread is 1 (LWP 184724)]
```

Note: Since GDB needs shared libraries from the crash system and we don't have them, most likely you get some random symbolic information (and, also, an invalid backtrace from the **bt** command):

```
(gdb) bt
#0  0x0000ffff81451924 in ?? ()
#1  0x0000ffff81586640 in ?? ()
Backtrace stopped: previous frame inner to this frame (corrupt stack?)
```

```
(gdb) info sharedlibrary
From                To                  Syms Read   Shared Object Library
                                        No          /lib/aarch64-linux-gnu/libc.so.6
                                        No          /lib/ld-linux-aarch64.so.1
```

15. Since we have saved shared libraries, we set the search path for them:

```
(gdb) set solib-search-path .
Reading symbols from /home/coredump/ALCDA2/A64/App1S/libc.so.6...(no debugging symbols
found)...done.
Reading symbols from /home/coredump/ALCDA2/A64/App1S/ld-linux-aarch64.so.1...(no debugging
symbols found)...done.
```

```
(gdb) bt
#0  0x0000ffff81451924 in clock_nanosleep () from /home/coredump/ALCDA2/A64/App1S/libc.so.6
#1  0x0000ffff81456aec in nanosleep () from /home/coredump/ALCDA2/A64/App1S/libc.so.6
#2  0x0000ffff814569b8 in sleep () from /home/coredump/ALCDA2/A64/App1S/libc.so.6
#3  0x0000aaaad0be0ab4 in main ()
```

16. Disassemble the *bar_one* function and follow the indirect *sleep* function call:

```
(gdb) disassemble bar_one
Dump of assembler code for function bar_one:
   0x0000aaaad0be0894 <+0>:     stp     x29, x30, [sp, #-16]!
   0x0000aaaad0be0898 <+4>:     mov     x29, sp
   0x0000aaaad0be089c <+8>:     mov     w0, #0xffffffff                 // #-1
   0x0000aaaad0be08a0 <+12>:    bl      0xaaaad0be0710 <sleep@plt>
   0x0000aaaad0be08a4 <+16>:    ldp     x29, x30, [sp], #16
   0x0000aaaad0be08a8 <+20>:    ret
End of assembler dump.
```

```
(gdb) disassemble 0xaaaad0be0710
Dump of assembler code for function sleep@plt:
   0x0000aaaad0be0710 <+0>:     adrp    x16, 0xaaaad0bf1000
   0x0000aaaad0be0714 <+4>:     ldr     x17, [x16, #4000]
   0x0000aaaad0be0718 <+8>:     add     x16, x16, #0xfa0
   0x0000aaaad0be071c <+12>:    br      x17
End of assembler dump.
```

```
(gdb) x/a 0xaaaad0bf1000+4000
0xaaaad0bf1fa0 <sleep@got.plt>: 0xffff81456970 <__sleep>
```

17. *App1.shared.pmap.184724* also shows library memory regions:

```
(gdb) q
```

```
~/ALCDA2/A64/App1S$ cat App1.shared.pmap.184724
184724:   ./App1.shared
0000aaaad0be0000      4K r-x-- App1.shared
0000aaaad0bf1000      4K r---- App1.shared
0000aaaad0bf2000      4K rw--- App1.shared
0000aaaafe503000    132K rw---   [ anon ]
0000ffff7eb50000     64K -----   [ anon ]
0000ffff7eb60000   8192K rw---   [ anon ]
```

```
0000ffff7f360000     64K -----   [ anon ]
0000ffff7f370000   8192K rw---   [ anon ]
0000ffff7fb70000     64K -----   [ anon ]
0000ffff7fb80000   8192K rw---   [ anon ]
0000ffff80380000     64K -----   [ anon ]
0000ffff80390000   8192K rw---   [ anon ]
0000ffff80b90000     64K -----   [ anon ]
0000ffff80ba0000   8192K rw---   [ anon ]
0000ffff813a0000   1572K r-x-- libc.so.6
0000ffff81529000     60K ----- libc.so.6
0000ffff81538000     16K r---- libc.so.6
0000ffff8153c000      8K rw--- libc.so.6
0000ffff8153e000     48K rw---   [ anon ]
0000ffff81550000    172K r-x-- ld-linux-aarch64.so.1
0000ffff81585000      8K rw---   [ anon ]
0000ffff81587000      8K r----   [ anon ]
0000ffff81589000      4K r-x--   [ anon ]
0000ffff8158a000      8K r---- ld-linux-aarch64.so.1
0000ffff8158c000      8K rw--- ld-linux-aarch64.so.1
0000ffffc23c8000    132K rw---   [ stack ]
 total            43468K
```

Exercise A1 (x64, WinDbg)

Goal: Learn how to list stack traces, disassemble functions, check their correctness, dump data, get environment.

Patterns: Manual Dump; Stack Trace; Incorrect Stack Trace; Unrecognizable Symbolic Information; Stack Trace Collection; Annotated Disassembly; Paratext; Not My Version; Environment Hint.

1. Launch WinDbg.

2. Load the core dump *App1.core.253* from the x64\App1 folder:

```
Microsoft (R) Windows Debugger Version 10.0.27725.1000 AMD64
Copyright (c) Microsoft Corporation. All rights reserved.


Loading Dump File [C:\ALCDA2\x64\App1\App1.core.253]
64-bit machine not using 64-bit API

************* Path validation summary **************
Response                         Time (ms)     Location
Deferred                                       srv*
Symbol search path is: srv*
Executable search path is:
Generic Unix Version 0 UP Free x64
System Uptime: not available
Process Uptime: not available
..
*** WARNING: Unable to verify timestamp for App1
App1+0x41a10:
00000000`00441a10 cmp     rax,0FFFFFFFFFFFFF000h
```

3. Set logging to a file in case of lengthy output from some commands:

```
0:000> .logopen C:\ALCDA2\x64\App1\App1-WinDbg.log
Opened log file 'C:\ALCDA2\x64\App1\App1-WinDbg.log'
```

4. Specify the dump folder as the symbol path and reload symbols:

```
0:000> .symfix; .sympath+ C:\ALCDA2\x64\App1\
Symbol search path is: srv*;C:\ALCDA2\x64\App1\
Expanded Symbol search path is:
cache*;SRV*https://msdl.microsoft.com/download/symbols;c:\alcda2\x64\app1\

************* Path validation summary **************
Response                         Time (ms)     Location
Deferred                                       srv*
OK                                             C:\ALCDA2\x64\App1\
*** WARNING: Unable to verify timestamp for App1

0:000> .reload
..
*** WARNING: Unable to verify timestamp for App1

************* Symbol Loading Error Summary **************
Module name            Error
App1                   The system cannot find the file specified
```

```
You can troubleshoot most symbol related issues by turning on symbol loading diagnostics (!sym
noisy) and repeating the command that caused symbols to be loaded.
You should also verify that your symbol search path (.sympath) is correct.
```

Note: We ignore warnings and errors as they are not relevant for now.

5. List all threads:

```
0:000> ~
Unable to get thread data for thread 0
.  0  Id: fd.fd Suspend: 0 Teb: 00000000`00000000 Unfrozen
Unable to get thread data for thread 1
   1  Id: fd.fe Suspend: 0 Teb: 00000000`00000000 Unfrozen
Unable to get thread data for thread 2
   2  Id: fd.ff Suspend: 0 Teb: 00000000`00000000 Unfrozen
Unable to get thread data for thread 3
   3  Id: fd.100 Suspend: 0 Teb: 00000000`00000000 Unfrozen
Unable to get thread data for thread 4
   4  Id: fd.101 Suspend: 0 Teb: 00000000`00000000 Unfrozen
Unable to get thread data for thread 5
   5  Id: fd.102 Suspend: 0 Teb: 00000000`00000000 Unfrozen
```

Note: WinDbg uses the same output format as for Windows memory dumps. Therefore, some data is either reported as errors or shows 0 or NULL pointer values. However, we see process and thread IDs in the format PID.TID:

```
0:000> .formats fd
Evaluate expression:
  Hex:     00000000`000000fd
  Decimal: 253
  Decimal (unsigned) : 253
  Octal:   0000000000000000000375
  Binary:  00000000 00000000 00000000 00000000 00000000 00000000 00000000 11111101
  Chars:   ........
  Time:    Thu Jan  1 00:04:13 1970
  Float:   low 3.54529e-043 high 0
  Double:  1.24999e-321

0:000> ? fd
Evaluate expression: 253 = 00000000`000000fd
```

6. Get the current thread stack trace:

```
0:000> k
# Child-SP          RetAddr               Call Site
00 00007ffd`f4563610 00000000`00000000     App1+0x41a10
```

Note: We see the truncated stack trace because WinDbg couldn't get symbols for some reason. We direct it to try again:

```
0:000> .symopt+ 0x40
Symbol options are 0x30377:
  0x00000001 - SYMOPT_CASE_INSENSITIVE
  0x00000002 - SYMOPT_UNDNAME
  0x00000004 - SYMOPT_DEFERRED_LOADS
  0x00000010 - SYMOPT_LOAD_LINES
  0x00000020 - SYMOPT_OMAP_FIND_NEAREST
  0x00000040 - SYMOPT_LOAD_ANYTHING
```

```
  0x00000100 - SYMOPT_NO_UNQUALIFIED_LOADS
  0x00000200 - SYMOPT_FAIL_CRITICAL_ERRORS
  0x00010000 - SYMOPT_AUTO_PUBLICS
  0x00020000 - SYMOPT_NO_IMAGE_SEARCH
*** WARNING: Unable to verify timestamp for App1

0:000> .reload
..
*** WARNING: Unable to verify timestamp for App1

************* Symbol Loading Error Summary **************
Module name            Error
App1                   The system cannot find the file specified

You can troubleshoot most symbol related issues by turning on symbol loading diagnostics (!sym
noisy) and repeating the command that caused symbols to be loaded.
You should also verify that your symbol search path (.sympath) is correct.

0:000> k
 # Child-SP          RetAddr               Call Site
00 00007ffd`f4563610 00000000`0044199a     App1!nanosleep+0x40
01 00007ffd`f4563640 00000000`00401d92     App1!sleep+0x3a
02 00007ffd`f4563680 00000000`00407581     App1!main+0xaa
03 00007ffd`f45636d0 00000000`00401aba     App1!_libc_start_main+0x3d1
04 00007ffd`f45637d0 ffffffff`ffffffff     App1!start+0x2a
05 00007ffd`f45637d8 00000000`00000000     0xffffffff`ffffffff
```

7. Get all thread stack traces without source code references (**L**):

```
0:000> ~*kL

Unable to get thread data for thread 0
.  0  Id: fd.fd Suspend: 0 Teb: 00000000`00000000 Unfrozen
 # Child-SP          RetAddr               Call Site
00 00007ffd`f4563610 00000000`0044199a     App1!nanosleep+0x40
01 00007ffd`f4563640 00000000`00401d92     App1!sleep+0x3a
02 00007ffd`f4563680 00000000`00407581     App1!main+0xaa
03 00007ffd`f45636d0 00000000`00401aba     App1!_libc_start_main+0x3d1
04 00007ffd`f45637d0 ffffffff`ffffffff     App1!start+0x2a
05 00007ffd`f45637d8 00000000`00000000     0xffffffff`ffffffff

Unable to get thread data for thread 1
   1  Id: fd.fe Suspend: 0 Teb: 00000000`00000000 Unfrozen
 # Child-SP          RetAddr               Call Site
00 00007f0f`c16fad10 00000000`0044199a     App1!nanosleep+0x40
01 00007f0f`c16fad40 00000000`00401bbb     App1!sleep+0x3a
02 00007f0f`c16fad80 00000000`00401bcc     App1!bar_one+0xe
03 00007f0f`c16fad90 00000000`00401be5     App1!foo_one+0xe
04 00007f0f`c16fada0 00000000`004030d3     App1!thread_one+0x16
05 00007f0f`c16fadc0 00000000`0044426f     App1!start_thread+0xf3
06 00007f0f`c16fae80 ffffffff`ffffffff     App1!_clone+0x3f
07 00007f0f`c16fae88 00000000`00000000     0xffffffff`ffffffff

Unable to get thread data for thread 2
   2  Id: fd.ff Suspend: 0 Teb: 00000000`00000000 Unfrozen
 # Child-SP          RetAddr               Call Site
00 00007f0f`c0ef9d10 00000000`0044199a     App1!nanosleep+0x40
01 00007f0f`c0ef9d40 00000000`00401bfa     App1!sleep+0x3a
02 00007f0f`c0ef9d80 00000000`00401c0b     App1!bar_two+0xe
03 00007f0f`c0ef9d90 00000000`00401c24     App1!foo_two+0xe
```

```
04 00007f0f`c0ef9da0 00000000`004030d3      App1!thread_two+0x16
05 00007f0f`c0ef9dc0 00000000`0044426f      App1!start_thread+0xf3
06 00007f0f`c0ef9e80 ffffffff`ffffffff      App1!_clone+0x3f
07 00007f0f`c0ef9e88 00000000`00000000      0xffffffff`ffffffff

Unable to get thread data for thread 3
   3  Id: fd.100 Suspend: 0 Teb: 00000000`00000000 Unfrozen
 # Child-SP          RetAddr                Call Site
00 00007f0f`c06f8d10 00000000`0044199a      App1!nanosleep+0x40
01 00007f0f`c06f8d40 00000000`00401c39      App1!sleep+0x3a
02 00007f0f`c06f8d80 00000000`00401c4a      App1!bar_three+0xe
03 00007f0f`c06f8d90 00000000`00401c63      App1!foo_three+0xe
04 00007f0f`c06f8da0 00000000`004030d3      App1!thread_three+0x16
05 00007f0f`c06f8dc0 00000000`0044426f      App1!start_thread+0xf3
06 00007f0f`c06f8e80 ffffffff`ffffffff      App1!_clone+0x3f
07 00007f0f`c06f8e88 00000000`00000000      0xffffffff`ffffffff

Unable to get thread data for thread 4
   4  Id: fd.101 Suspend: 0 Teb: 00000000`00000000 Unfrozen
 # Child-SP          RetAddr                Call Site
00 00007f0f`bfef7d10 00000000`0044199a      App1!nanosleep+0x40
01 00007f0f`bfef7d40 00000000`00401c78      App1!sleep+0x3a
02 00007f0f`bfef7d80 00000000`00401c89      App1!bar_four+0xe
03 00007f0f`bfef7d90 00000000`00401ca2      App1!foo_four+0xe
04 00007f0f`bfef7da0 00000000`004030d3      App1!thread_four+0x16
05 00007f0f`bfef7dc0 00000000`0044426f      App1!start_thread+0xf3
06 00007f0f`bfef7e80 ffffffff`ffffffff      App1!_clone+0x3f
07 00007f0f`bfef7e88 00000000`00000000      0xffffffff`ffffffff

Unable to get thread data for thread 5
   5  Id: fd.102 Suspend: 0 Teb: 00000000`00000000 Unfrozen
 # Child-SP          RetAddr                Call Site
00 00007f0f`bf6f6d10 00000000`0044199a      App1!nanosleep+0x40
01 00007f0f`bf6f6d40 00000000`00401cb7      App1!sleep+0x3a
02 00007f0f`bf6f6d80 00000000`00401cc8      App1!bar_five+0xe
03 00007f0f`bf6f6d90 00000000`00401ce1      App1!foo_five+0xe
04 00007f0f`bf6f6da0 00000000`004030d3      App1!thread_five+0x16
05 00007f0f`bf6f6dc0 00000000`0044426f      App1!start_thread+0xf3
06 00007f0f`bf6f6e80 ffffffff`ffffffff      App1!_clone+0x3f
07 00007f0f`bf6f6e88 00000000`00000000      0xffffffff`ffffffff
```

8. Switch to thread #1 (threads are numbered from 0) and get its stack trace:

```
0:000> ~1s
App1!nanosleep+0x40:
00000000`00441a10 cmp     rax,0FFFFFFFFFFFFF000h

0:001> kL
# Child-SP          RetAddr                Call Site
00 00007f0f`c16fad10 00000000`0044199a      App1!nanosleep+0x40
01 00007f0f`c16fad40 00000000`00401bbb      App1!sleep+0x3a
02 00007f0f`c16fad80 00000000`00401bcc      App1!bar_one+0xe
03 00007f0f`c16fad90 00000000`00401be5      App1!foo_one+0xe
04 00007f0f`c16fada0 00000000`004030d3      App1!thread_one+0x16
05 00007f0f`c16fadc0 00000000`0044426f      App1!start_thread+0xf3
06 00007f0f`c16fae80 ffffffff`ffffffff      App1!_clone+0x3f
07 00007f0f`c16fae88 00000000`00000000      0xffffffff`ffffffff
```

9. Check that *bar_one* called the *sleep* function by comparing the return address on the call stack from the disassembly output:

```
0:001> uf bar_one
App1!bar_one:
00000000`00401bad push    rbp
00000000`00401bae mov     rbp,rsp
00000000`00401bb1 mov     edi,0FFFFFFFFh
00000000`00401bb6 call    App1!sleep (00000000`00441960)
00000000`00401bbb nop
00000000`00401bbc pop     rbp
00000000`00401bbd ret
```

Another way to do that is to disassemble backward the return address and check if the last instruction is CALL:

```
0:001> ub 00000000`00401bbb
App1!frame_dummy+0x1d:
00000000`00401b9d pop     rbp
00000000`00401b9e jmp     App1!register_tm_clones (00000000`00401b00)
00000000`00401ba3 nop     dword ptr [rax+rax]
00000000`00401ba8 jmp     App1!register_tm_clones (00000000`00401b00)
App1!bar_one:
00000000`00401bad push    rbp
00000000`00401bae mov     rbp,rsp
00000000`00401bb1 mov     edi,0FFFFFFFFh
00000000`00401bb6 call    App1!sleep (00000000`00441960)
```

10. Get *App1* data section from the contents of pmap (*App1.pmap.253*):

```
253:   ./App1
0000000000400000      4K r---- App1
0000000000401000    588K r-x-- App1
0000000000494000    156K r---- App1
00000000004bc000     24K rw--- App1
00000000004c2000     24K rw---   [ anon ]
00000000021b3000    140K rw---   [ anon ]
00007f0fbeef7000      4K -----   [ anon ]
00007f0fbeef8000   8192K rw---   [ anon ]
00007f0fbf6f8000      4K -----   [ anon ]
00007f0fbf6f9000   8192K rw---   [ anon ]
00007f0fbfef9000      4K -----   [ anon ]
00007f0fbfefa000   8192K rw---   [ anon ]
00007f0fc06fa000      4K -----   [ anon ]
00007f0fc06fb000   8192K rw---   [ anon ]
00007f0fc0efb000      4K -----   [ anon ]
00007f0fc0efc000   8192K rw---   [ anon ]
00007ffdf4545000    132K rw---   [ stack ]
00007ffdf45c6000     16K r----   [ anon ]
00007ffdf45ca000      4K r-x--   [ anon ]
 total            42068K
```

11. Compare with the region information in the core dump:

```
0:001> !address

Mapping file section regions...
Mapping module regions...
Mapping heap regions...

        BaseAddress      EndAddress+1        RegionSize     Type       State                 Protect             Usage
--------------------------------------------------------------------------------------------------------------------------
+        0`00000000       0`00400000        0`00400000                                                             <unknown>
+        0`00400000       0`00401000        0`00001000 MEM_PRIVATE MEM_COMMIT  PAGE_EXECUTE_READ                   Image      [App1; "/home/coredump/ALCDA/App1/App1"]
+        0`00401000       0`00494000        0`00093000 MEM_PRIVATE MEM_COMMIT  PAGE_EXECUTE_READ                   Image      [App1; "/home/coredump/ALCDA/App1/App1"]
+        0`00494000       0`004bc000        0`00028000                                                             Image      [App1; "/home/coredump/ALCDA/App1/App1"]
+        0`004bc000       0`004c2000        0`00006000 MEM_PRIVATE MEM_COMMIT  PAGE_READWRITE                      Image      [App1; "/home/coredump/ALCDA/App1/App1"]
+        0`004c2000       0`004c8000        0`00006000 MEM_PRIVATE MEM_COMMIT  PAGE_READWRITE                      <unknown>  [................]
+        0`004c8000       0`021b3000        0`01ceb000                                                             <unknown>
+        0`021b3000       0`021d6000        0`00023000 MEM_PRIVATE MEM_COMMIT  PAGE_READWRITE                      <unknown>  [................]
```

```
+       0`021d6000     7f0f`beef7000     7f0f`bcd21000                                                             <unknown>
+    7f0f`beef7000     7f0f`beef8000        0`00001000 MEM_PRIVATE MEM_COMMIT  PAGE_READONLY                       <unknown>  [................]
+    7f0f`beef8000     7f0f`bf6f8000        0`00800000 MEM_PRIVATE MEM_COMMIT  PAGE_READWRITE                      <unknown>  [................]
+    7f0f`bf6f8000     7f0f`bf6f9000        0`00001000 MEM_PRIVATE MEM_COMMIT  PAGE_READONLY                       <unknown>  [................]
+    7f0f`bf6f9000     7f0f`bfef9000        0`00800000 MEM_PRIVATE MEM_COMMIT  PAGE_READWRITE                      <unknown>  [................]
+    7f0f`bfef9000     7f0f`bfefa000        0`00001000 MEM_PRIVATE MEM_COMMIT  PAGE_READONLY                       <unknown>  [................]
+    7f0f`bfefa000     7f0f`c06fa000        0`00800000 MEM_PRIVATE MEM_COMMIT  PAGE_READWRITE                      <unknown>  [................]
+    7f0f`c06fa000     7f0f`c06fb000        0`00001000 MEM_PRIVATE MEM_COMMIT  PAGE_READONLY                       <unknown>  [................]
+    7f0f`c06fb000     7f0f`c0efb000        0`00800000 MEM_PRIVATE MEM_COMMIT  PAGE_READWRITE                      <unknown>  [................]
+    7f0f`c0efb000     7f0f`c0efc000        0`00001000 MEM_PRIVATE MEM_COMMIT  PAGE_READONLY                       <unknown>  [................]
+    7f0f`c0efc000     7f0f`c16fc000        0`00800000 MEM_PRIVATE MEM_COMMIT  PAGE_READWRITE                      <unknown>  [................]
+    7f0f`c16fc000     7ffd`f4545000       ee`32e49000                                                             <unknown>
+    7ffd`f4545000     7ffd`f4566000        0`00021000 MEM_PRIVATE MEM_COMMIT  PAGE_READWRITE                      <unknown>  [................]
+    7ffd`f4566000     7ffd`f45ca000        0`00064000                                                             <unknown>
+    7ffd`f45ca000     7ffd`f45cb000        0`00001000 MEM_PRIVATE MEM_COMMIT  PAGE_EXECUTE_READ                   Image      [linux_vdso_so; "linux-vdso.so.1"]
```

12. Dump the data region with possible symbolic information (we truncated the output):

```
0:001> dps 0`004bc000 0`004c2000
[...]
00000000`004bea88  00000000`00000000
00000000`004bea90  00000000`00000000
00000000`004bea98  00000000`00000000
00000000`004beaa0  00007ffd`f4563a09
00000000`004beaa8  00000000`004c01c8 App1!_progname
00000000`004beab0  00007ffd`f45637d8
00000000`004beab8  00000000`00000000
[...]
00000000`004bf868  00010000`00000000
00000000`004bf870  00000000`00000000
00000000`004bf878  00000000`00000000
00000000`004bf880  00000000`00000000
00000000`004bf888  00000000`021b41c0
00000000`004bf890  00000000`00000040
00000000`004bf898  00000000`00000408
00000000`004bf8a0  00000000`00000007
00000000`004bf8a8  00000000`00000000
00000000`004bf8b0  00000000`00000000
00000000`004bf8b8  00000000`00000000
00000000`004bf8c0  00000000`0041aad0 App1!memalign_hook_ini
00000000`004bf8c8  00000000`0041b0e0 App1!realloc_hook_ini
00000000`004bf8d0  00000000`00000000
00000000`004bf8d8  00000000`00000000
00000000`004bf8e0  00000000`00000000
00000000`004bf8e8  00000000`00000000
00000000`004bf8f0  00000000`00000000
00000000`004bf8f8  00000000`00000000
00000000`004bf900  00000000`00000000
00000000`004bf908  00000000`00000000
[...]
```

The output is in the following format:

```
address   value
```

Some values may have associated symbols in the format module!name+offset:

```
address   value   symbol
```

For example, from the output above:

```
00000000`004d1110  00000000`004d1068 App1!_progname
```

To list all values with symbols, we can use the **dpS** command (it doesn't show the value addresses):

```
0:001> dpS 0`004bc000 0`004c2000
 00000000`004c65a0 App1!res
 00000000`004c0aa0 App1!nl_global_locale
 00000000`004c0aa0 App1!nl_global_locale
 00000000`004c0ac0 App1!nl_global_locale+0x20
 00000000`004c0aa8 App1!nl_global_locale+0x8
[...]
 00007ffd`f45ca168 linux_vdso_so!LINUX_2.6+0x168
 00000000`004c01c8 App1!_progname
 00000000`00498f28 App1!_PRETTY_FUNCTION__.9662+0x58
[...]
 00000000`0044fbc0 App1!_gconv_transform_internal_ucs2reverse
 00000000`004530c0 App1!nl_postload_ctype
 00000000`004bc1c0 App1!nl_C_LC_CTYPE
 00000000`004bd5c0 App1!nl_C_LC_NUMERIC
 00000000`004bd640 App1!nl_C_LC_TIME
 00000000`004bdec0 App1!nl_C_LC_COLLATE
 00000000`004bd400 App1!nl_C_LC_MONETARY
 00000000`004bd380 App1!nl_C_LC_MESSAGES
 00000000`004bdb80 App1!nl_C_LC_PAPER
 00000000`004bdbe0 App1!nl_C_LC_NAME
 00000000`004bdc60 App1!nl_C_LC_ADDRESS
 00000000`004bdd20 App1!nl_C_LC_TELEPHONE
 00000000`004bdda0 App1!nl_C_LC_MEASUREMENT
 00000000`004bde00 App1!nl_C_LC_IDENTIFICATION
 00000000`004bc1c0 App1!nl_C_LC_CTYPE
 00000000`004bd5c0 App1!nl_C_LC_NUMERIC
 00000000`004bd640 App1!nl_C_LC_TIME
 00000000`004bdec0 App1!nl_C_LC_COLLATE
 00000000`004bd400 App1!nl_C_LC_MONETARY
 00000000`004bd380 App1!nl_C_LC_MESSAGES
 00000000`004bdb80 App1!nl_C_LC_PAPER
 00000000`004bdbe0 App1!nl_C_LC_NAME
 00000000`004bdc60 App1!nl_C_LC_ADDRESS
 00000000`004bdd20 App1!nl_C_LC_TELEPHONE
 00000000`004bdda0 App1!nl_C_LC_MEASUREMENT
 00000000`004bde00 App1!nl_C_LC_IDENTIFICATION
 00000000`0049bc00 App1!nl_C_LC_CTYPE_class+0x100
 00000000`0049ad00 App1!nl_C_LC_CTYPE_tolower+0x200
 00000000`0049b300 App1!nl_C_LC_CTYPE_toupper+0x200
 00000000`00498c88 App1!nl_C_name
 00000000`00498c88 App1!nl_C_name
[...]
 00000000`004c0e20 App1!IO_wfile_jumps
 00000000`004bf1a0 App1!IO_2_1_stderr_
 00000000`004bf3c0 App1!IO_2_1_stdout_
 00000000`004bf5e0 App1!IO_2_1_stdin_
 00000000`0041aad0 App1!memalign_hook_ini
 00000000`0041b0e0 App1!realloc_hook_ini
 00000000`004bf940 App1!main_arena+0x60
 00000000`004bf940 App1!main_arena+0x60
 00000000`004bf950 App1!main_arena+0x70
 00000000`004bf950 App1!main_arena+0x70
[...]
 00000000`00414ef0 App1!IO_default_imbue
 00000000`004145a0 App1!IO_cleanup
 00000000`004ae798 App1!_EH_FRAME_BEGIN__
```

13. Explore the contents of memory pointed to by *App1!memalign_hook_ini* and *App1!_progname* addresses:

```
0:001> u 00000000`0041aad0
App1!memalign_hook_ini:
00000000`0041aad0 sub     rsp,18h
00000000`0041aad4 mov     eax,dword ptr [App1!_libc_malloc_initialized (00000000`004bf824)]
00000000`0041aada mov     qword ptr [App1!_memalign_hook (00000000`004bf8c0)],0
00000000`0041aae5 test    eax,eax
00000000`0041aae7 jns     App1!memalign_hook_ini+0x30 (00000000`0041ab00)
00000000`0041aae9 mov     qword ptr [rsp+8],rsi
00000000`0041aaee mov     qword ptr [rsp],rdi
00000000`0041aaf2 call    App1!ptmalloc_init.part.0 (00000000`00416570)

0:001> dp App1!_progname
00000000`004c01c8  00007ffd`f4565751 00007ffd`f456574f
00000000`004c01d8  00000000`00000000 00000000`00000000
00000000`004c01e8  00000000`00000000 00000000`00000001
00000000`004c01f8  00000000`00000000 00000000`00000000
00000000`004c0208  00000000`00000000 00000000`00000000
00000000`004c0218  00000000`00000000 00000000`00000000
00000000`004c0228  00000000`00000000 00000000`00000001
00000000`004c0238  00000000`00000000 00000000`00000000

0:001> dc 00007ffd`f4565751
00007ffd`f4565751  31707041 45485300 2f3d4c4c 2f6e6962  App1.SHELL=/bin/
00007ffd`f4565761  68736162 53494800 4e4f4354 4c4f5254  bash.HISTCONTROL
00007ffd`f4565771  6e67693d 6265726f 0068746f 5f4c5357  =ignoreboth.WSL_
00007ffd`f4565781  54534944 4e5f4f52 3d454d41 69626544  DISTRO_NAME=Debi
00007ffd`f4565791  4e006e61 3d454d41 4b534544 2d504f54  an.NAME=DESKTOP-
00007ffd`f45657a1  56365349 00304c32 3d445750 6d6f682f  IS6V2L0.PWD=/hom
00007ffd`f45657b1  6f632f65 75646572 412f706d 4144434c  e/coredump/ALCDA
00007ffd`f45657c1  7070412f 4f4c0031 4d414e47 6f633d45  /App1.LOGNAME=co

0:001> da 00007ffd`f4565751
00007ffd`f4565751  "App1"

0:001> db 00007ffd`f4565751
00007ffd`f4565751  41 70 70 31 00 53 48 45-4c 4c 3d 2f 62 69 6e 2f  App1.SHELL=/bin/
00007ffd`f4565761  62 61 73 68 00 48 49 53-54 43 4f 4e 54 52 4f 4c  bash.HISTCONTROL
00007ffd`f4565771  3d 69 67 6e 6f 72 65 62-6f 74 68 00 57 53 4c 5f  =ignoreboth.WSL_
00007ffd`f4565781  44 49 53 54 52 4f 5f 4e-41 4d 45 3d 44 65 62 69  DISTRO_NAME=Debi
00007ffd`f4565791  61 6e 00 4e 41 4d 45 3d-44 45 53 4b 54 4f 50 2d  an.NAME=DESKTOP-
00007ffd`f45657a1  49 53 36 56 32 4c 30 00-50 57 44 3d 2f 68 6f 6d  IS6V2L0.PWD=/hom
00007ffd`f45657b1  65 2f 63 6f 72 65 64 75-6d 70 2f 41 4c 43 44 41  e/coredump/ALCDA
00007ffd`f45657c1  2f 41 70 70 31 00 4c 4f-47 4e 41 4d 45 3d 63 6f  /App1.LOGNAME=co
```

Note: We see that a hook function is installed for *memalign* and *realloc*. Please find the following documentation for hook functions here:

https://www.gnu.org/software/libc/manual/html_node/Hooks-for-Malloc.html

14. Explore the contents of memory pointed to by the *environ* variable:

```
0:001> dp environ
00000000`004c5f48  00007ffd`f45637f8 00000000`00000000
00000000`004c5f58  00000000`00000000 00000001`00000000
00000000`004c5f68  00000000`00000000 00000000`00000000
00000000`004c5f78  00000000`00000000 00000000`00000001
00000000`004c5f88  00000000`00000030 00000000`004c5f98
```

```
00000000`004c5f98  00000000`00000000 00000000`00000000
00000000`004c5fa8  00000000`00402590 00000000`00000000
00000000`004c5fb8  00000000`00000000 00000000`00000000
```

```
0:001> dp 00007ffd`f45637f8
00007ffd`f45637f8  00007ffd`f4565756 00007ffd`f4565766
00007ffd`f4563808  00007ffd`f456577d 00007ffd`f4565794
00007ffd`f4563818  00007ffd`f45657a9 00007ffd`f45657c7
00007ffd`f4563828  00007ffd`f45657d8 00007ffd`f45657f3
00007ffd`f4563838  00007ffd`f45657fe 00007ffd`f4565812
00007ffd`f4563848  00007ffd`f4565823 00007ffd`f4565844
00007ffd`f4563858  00007ffd`f4565e26 00007ffd`f4565e40
00007ffd`f4563868  00007ffd`f4565e54 00007ffd`f4565e62
```

```
0:001> da 00007ffd`f4565756
00007ffd`f4565756  "SHELL=/bin/bash"
```

```
0:001> dpa 00007ffd`f45637f8
00007ffd`f45637f8  00007ffd`f4565756 "SHELL=/bin/bash"
00007ffd`f4563800  00007ffd`f4565766 "HISTCONTROL=ignoreboth"
00007ffd`f4563808  00007ffd`f456577d "WSL_DISTRO_NAME=Debian"
00007ffd`f4563810  00007ffd`f4565794 "NAME=DESKTOP-IS6V2L0"
00007ffd`f4563818  00007ffd`f45657a9 "PWD=/home/coredump/ALCDA/App1"
00007ffd`f4563820  00007ffd`f45657c7 "LOGNAME=coredump"
00007ffd`f4563828  00007ffd`f45657d8 "MC_TMPDIR=/tmp/mc-coredump"
00007ffd`f4563830  00007ffd`f45657f3 "MC_SID=192"
00007ffd`f4563838  00007ffd`f45657fe "HOME=/home/coredump"
00007ffd`f4563840  00007ffd`f4565812 "LANG=en_US.UTF-8"
00007ffd`f4563848  00007ffd`f4565823 "WSL_INTEROP=/run/WSL/117_interop"
00007ffd`f4563850  00007ffd`f4565844 "LS_COLORS=rs=0:di=01;34:ln=01;36:mh=00:pi=40;33:so=01;3"
00007ffd`f4563858  00007ffd`f4565e26 "WAYLAND_DISPLAY=wayland-0"
00007ffd`f4563860  00007ffd`f4565e40 "TERM=xterm-256color"
00007ffd`f4563868  00007ffd`f4565e54 "USER=coredump"
00007ffd`f4563870  00007ffd`f4565e62 "DISPLAY=:0"
```

18. Now we look at how to perform a memory search.

```
0:001> s 0`004bc000 0`004fc000 6
00000000`004bcc31  06 46 00 00 00 00 00 56-06 46 00 00 00 00 00 4b  .F.....V.F.....K
00000000`004bcc39  06 46 00 00 00 00 00 4b-06 46 00 00 00 00 00 40  .F.....K.F.....@
00000000`004bcc41  06 46 00 00 00 00 00 40-06 46 00 00 00 00 00 f8  .F.....@.F......
00000000`004bcc49  06 46 00 00 00 00 00 f8-03 46 00 00 00 00 00 a8  .F.......F......
00000000`004bd5f8  06 00 00 00 00 00 00 00-d9 7d 49 00 00 00 00 00  .........}I.....
00000000`004bde40  06 86 4a 00 00 00 00 00-70 86 4a 00 00 00 00 00  ..J.....p.J.....
00000000`004be880  06 00 00 00 00 00 00 00-00 00 00 00 00 00 00 00  ................
00000000`004bea40  06 00 00 00 00 00 00 00-b8 a1 5c f4 fd 7f 00 00  ..........\.....
00000000`004beb5b  06 00 00 00 00 96 8f 49-00 00 00 00 00 c0 da 44  .......I.......D
00000000`004beb79  06 04 04 00 00 00 00 b6-8f 49 00 00 00 00 00 f0  .........I......
00000000`004bf110  06 00 00 00 00 00 00 00-00 00 00 00 00 00 00 00  ................
00000000`004c0248  06 00 00 00 7f 03 00 00-03 03 00 00 02 00 00 00  ................
00000000`004c02d1  06 4c 00 00 00 00 00 00-00 00 00 00 00 00 00 00  .L..............
00000000`004c06c1  06 4c 00 00 00 00 00 00-00 00 00 00 00 00 00 00  .L..............
00000000`004c06e9  06 4c 00 00 00 00 00 20-06 4c 00 00 00 00 00 00  .L..... .L......
00000000`004c06f1  06 4c 00 00 00 00 00 00-00 00 00 00 00 00 00 00  .L..............
00000000`004c6829  06 08 00 00 08 08 05 23-32 da fe ff fb 8b 1f 00  .......#2.......
00000000`004c6858  06 00 00 00 8e 00 00 00-80 03 00 00 00 00 00 00  ................
```

Note: It is possible to search through non-accessible regions as well; they are ignored:

```
0:001> s-q 0 Lffffff 6
00000000`0049a308  00000000`00000006 00000000`0000009f
00000000`0049a7c8  00000000`00000006 00000018`00000001
00000000`0049a8e8  00000000`00000006 00000018`00000001
00000000`0049a9a8  00000000`00000006 00000018`00000001
00000000`004a8d08  00000000`00000006 00000000`00000002
00000000`004b17e8  00000000`00000006 00003088`00000010
00000000`004bd5f8  00000000`00000006 00000000`00497dd9
00000000`004be880  00000000`00000006 00000000`00000000
00000000`004bea40  00000000`00000006 00007ffd`f45ca1b8
00000000`004bf110  00000000`00000006 00000000`00000000
```

```
0:001> s-a 00007ffd`f45637f8 L100000 "bin"
00007ffd`f456575d  62 69 6e 2f 62 61 73 68-00 48 49 53 54 43 4f 4e  bin/bash.HISTCON
00007ffd`f4565e9d  62 69 6e 2d 68 61 64 6f-6f 70 32 2e 37 00 58 44  bin-hadoop2.7.XD
00007ffd`f4565ef4  62 69 6e 3a 2f 75 73 72-2f 6c 6f 63 61 6c 2f 62  bin:/usr/local/b
00007ffd`f4565f03  62 69 6e 3a 2f 75 73 72-2f 62 69 6e 3a 2f 62 69  bin:/usr/bin:/bi
00007ffd`f4565f0c  62 69 6e 3a 2f 62 69 6e-3a 2f 75 73 72 2f 6c 6f  bin:/bin:/usr/lo
00007ffd`f4565f11  62 69 6e 3a 2f 75 73 72-2f 6c 6f 63 61 6c 2f 67  bin:/usr/local/g
00007ffd`f4565f4e  62 69 6e 2d 68 61 64 6f-6f 70 32 2e 37 2f 62 69  bin-hadoop2.7/bi
00007ffd`f4565f5c  62 69 6e 3a 2f 75 73 72-2f 73 68 61 72 65 2f 73  bin:/usr/share/s
00007ffd`f4565f7d  62 69 6e 2d 68 61 64 6f-6f 70 32 2e 37 2f 62 69  bin-hadoop2.7/bi
00007ffd`f4565f8b  62 69 6e 00 48 4f 53 54-54 59 50 45 3d 78 38 36  bin.HOSTTYPE=x86
```

Note: It is also possible to show all possible string fragments if any:

```
0:001> s-sa 0 Lfffffff
00000000`00400001  "ELF"
00000000`0040020c  "GNU"
00000000`0040022c  "GNU"
00000000`00400236  "Y_I"
00000000`004011f4  "uAH"
00000000`0040121f  "=,H"
[...]
00000000`0049750f  "../sysdeps/x86/cacheinfo.c"
00000000`0049752a  "! "cannot happen""
00000000`0049753c  "offset == 2"
00000000`00497840  "handle_amd"
00000000`00497850  "intel_check_word"
00000000`00497861  "ANSI_X3.4-1968//TRANSLIT"
00000000`0049787a  "mbsrtowcs_l.c"
00000000`00497888  "result > 0"
00000000`00497893  "__mbsinit (data.__statep)"
00000000`004978b0  "((wchar_t *) data.__outbuf)[-1] "
00000000`004978d0  "== L'\0'"
00000000`004978e0  "status == __GCONV_OK || status ="
00000000`00497900  "= __GCONV_EMPTY_INPUT || status "
00000000`00497920  "== __GCONV_ILLEGAL_INPUT || stat"
00000000`00497940  "us == __GCONV_INCOMPLETE_INPUT |"
00000000`00497960  "| status == __GCONV_FULL_OUTPUT"
00000000`00497980  "__mbsrtowcs_l"
00000000`0049798e  "/usr/lib/getconf"
00000000`0049799f  "GETCONF_DIR"
00000000`004979ab  "/proc/sys/kernel/ngroups_max"
00000000`004979c8  "ILP32_OFF32"
00000000`004979d4  "ILP32_OFFBIG"
00000000`004979e1  "/proc/sys/kernel/rtsig-max"
[...]
```

```
00000000`021b4420  "/home/coredump/ALCDA/App1"
00000000`021b4900  "linux-vdso.so.1"
00000000`021b49a0  "tls//x86_64/tls/x86_64/"
00000000`021b4a08  " uJ"
00000000`021b4a58  "7uJ"
00000000`021b4aa8  "RuJ"
00000000`021b4af8  "XuJ"
```

15. To get process uid/gid and other useful data use this WinDbg extension command:

```
0:000> !ntprpsinfo
NT_PRPSINFO (process info):
    state: 0, sname: t, zomb: 0, nice: 0, flag: 0x4040400000000000
    uid: 1000, gid: 1000, pid: 253, ppid: 192, pgrp: 253, sid: 192
    fname: App1
    psargs: ./App1
```

16. Get the list of loaded modules:

```
0:001> lm
start             end                 module name
00000000`00400000 00000000`004c2000   App1     T (service symbols: DWARF Private Symbols)
c:\alcda2\x64\app1\App1
00007ffd`f45ca000 00007ffd`f45cb000   linux_vdso_so T (service symbols: ELF In Memory Symbols)

0:001> lmv
start             end                 module name
00000000`00400000 00000000`004c2000   App1     T (service symbols: DWARF Private Symbols)
c:\alcda2\x64\app1\App1
    Loaded symbol image file: App1
    Image path: /home/coredump/ALCDA/App1/App1
    Image name: App1
    Browse all global symbols  functions  data  Symbol Reload
    Timestamp:        unavailable (FFFFFFFE)
    CheckSum:         missing
    ImageSize:        000C2000
    Details:
00007ffd`f45ca000 00007ffd`f45cb000   linux_vdso_so T (service symbols: ELF In Memory Symbols)
    Loaded symbol image file: linux-vdso.so.1
    Image path: linux-vdso.so.1
    Image name: linux-vdso.so.1
    Browse all global symbols  functions  data  Symbol Reload
    Timestamp:        unavailable (FFFFFFFE)
    CheckSum:         missing
    ImageSize:        00001000
    Index Key:        (Build Id) 8dd3bd6bb4492768a24ad26802eb38105a15ffe7
    Details:
```

Note: We don't see shared libraries except *vdso* (https://man7.org/linux/man-pages/man7/vdso.7.html) because they were statically linked. We also created the version of a dynamically linked *App1.shared* executable. If we load its core dump *App1.shared.core.275* in the new instance of WinDbg, we see the list of shared libraries:

```
Microsoft (R) Windows Debugger Version 10.0.27725.1000 AMD64
Copyright (c) Microsoft Corporation. All rights reserved.


Loading Dump File [C:\ALCDA2\x64\App1\App1.shared.core.275]
64-bit machine not using 64-bit API
```

```
************* Path validation summary **************
Response                         Time (ms)     Location
Deferred                                       srv*
Symbol search path is: srv*
Executable search path is:
Generic Unix Version 0 UP Free x64
System Uptime: not available
Process Uptime: not available
.....
*** WARNING: Unable to verify timestamp for libc-2.28.so
libc_2_28+0xc5720:
00007f1a`e471e720 ???
```

```
0:000> .logappend C:\ALCDA2\x64\App1\App1-WinDbg.log
Opened log file 'C:\ALCDA2\x64\App1\App1-WinDbg.log'
```

```
0:000> lm
start             end                 module name
0000557e`17348000 0000557e`1734c000   App1       (deferred)
00007f1a`e4659000 00007f1a`e4815000   libc_2_28 T (no symbols)
00007f1a`e481a000 00007f1a`e4836000   libpthread_2_28   (deferred)
00007f1a`e4847000 00007f1a`e4870000   ld_2_28    (deferred)
00007ffc`749b0000 00007ffc`749b1000   linux_vdso_so    (deferred)
```

17. Let's set symbols to get the correct stack trace:

```
0:000> k
 # Child-SP          RetAddr               Call Site
00 00007ffc`74957a60 00000000`00000000     libc_2_28+0xc5720
```

```
0:000> uf bar_one
Couldn't resolve error at 'bar_one'
```

```
0:000> .sympath+ C:\ALCDA2\x64\App1
Symbol search path is: srv*;C:\ALCDA2\x64\App1
Expanded Symbol search path is:
cache*;SRV*https://msdl.microsoft.com/download/symbols;c:\alcda2\x64\app1

************* Path validation summary **************
Response                         Time (ms)     Location
Deferred                                       srv*
OK                                             C:\ALCDA2\x64\App1
*** WARNING: Unable to verify timestamp for libc-2.28.so
```

```
0:000> .reload
.....
*** WARNING: Unable to verify timestamp for libc-2.28.so

************* Symbol Loading Error Summary **************
Module name            Error
libc-2.28              The system cannot find the file specified

You can troubleshoot most symbol related issues by turning on symbol loading diagnostics (!sym
noisy) and repeating the command that caused symbols to be loaded.
You should also verify that your symbol search path (.sympath) is correct.
```

```
0:000> .symopt+ 0x40
Symbol options are 0x30377:
  0x00000001 - SYMOPT_CASE_INSENSITIVE
  0x00000002 - SYMOPT_UNDNAME
  0x00000004 - SYMOPT_DEFERRED_LOADS
  0x00000010 - SYMOPT_LOAD_LINES
  0x00000020 - SYMOPT_OMAP_FIND_NEAREST
  0x00000040 - SYMOPT_LOAD_ANYTHING
  0x00000100 - SYMOPT_NO_UNQUALIFIED_LOADS
  0x00000200 - SYMOPT_FAIL_CRITICAL_ERRORS
  0x00010000 - SYMOPT_AUTO_PUBLICS
  0x00020000 - SYMOPT_NO_IMAGE_SEARCH
*** WARNING: Unable to verify timestamp for libc-2.28.so
```

```
0:000> k
 # Child-SP          RetAddr               Call Site
00 00007ffc`74957a60 00000000`00000000     libc_2_28+0xc5720
```

```
0:000> uf bar_one
Couldn't resolve error at 'bar_one'
```

Note: We see WinDbg is not able to get the symbols even for the App1 module, probably due to the way the core dump was saved. We created another core dump, this time saved with the 0x3F option:

```
~/ALCDA2/x64/App1$ ./App1.shared &
[1] 28
```

```
~/ALCDA2/x64/App1$ echo 0x3F > /proc/28/coredump_filter
```

```
~/ALCDA2/x64/App1$ gcore -o App1.shared.core 28
```

Now, we load the core dump *App1.shared.core.28* in the new instance of WinDbg:

```
Microsoft (R) Windows Debugger Version 10.0.27725.1000 AMD64
Copyright (c) Microsoft Corporation. All rights reserved.


Loading Dump File [C:\ALCDA2\x64\App1\App1.shared.core.28]
64-bit machine not using 64-bit API

************* Path validation summary **************
Response                         Time (ms)     Location
Deferred                                       srv*
Symbol search path is: srv*
Executable search path is:
Generic Unix Version 0 UP Free x64
System Uptime: not available
Process Uptime: not available
.....
*** WARNING: Unable to verify timestamp for libc-2.28.so
*** WARNING: Unable to verify timestamp for App1.shared
libc_2_28!nanosleep+0x40:
00007ff6`429dc5c0 cmp     rax,0FFFFFFFFFFFFF000h
```

```
0:000> .logappend C:\ALCDA2\x64\App1\App1-WinDbg.log
Opened log file 'C:\ALCDA2\x64\App1\App1-WinDbg.log'
```

```
0:000> lm
start             end                 module name
000055b1`b4e04000 000055b1`b4e09000   App1      T (service symbols: ELF In Memory Symbols)
00007ff6`42916000 00007ff6`42ad2000   libc_2_28 T (service symbols: ELF In Memory Symbols)
00007ff6`42ad6000 00007ff6`42af3000   libpthread_2_28   (deferred)
00007ff6`42b04000 00007ff6`42b2d000   ld_2_28    (deferred)
00007fff`cc76d000 00007fff`cc76e000   linux_vdso_so    (deferred)
```

```
0:000> k
 # Child-SP          RetAddr               Call Site
00 00007fff`cc685f70 00007ff6`429dc4ca     libc_2_28!nanosleep+0x40
01 00007fff`cc685fa0 000055b1`b4e0532a     libc_2_28!sleep+0x3a
02 00007fff`cc685fe0 00007ff6`4293a09b     App1!pthread_create+0x132a
03 00007fff`cc686030 000055b1`b4e0508a     libc_2_28!_libc_start_main+0xeb
04 00007fff`cc6860f0 ffffffff`ffffffff     App1!pthread_create+0x108a
05 00007fff`cc6860f8 00000000`00000000     0xffffffff`ffffffff
```

```
0:000> uf bar_one
Couldn't resolve error at 'bar_one'
```

Note: Although the stack trace looks better, we need to specify the App1 symbols:

```
0:000> .sympath+ C:\ALCDA2\x64\App1
*** WARNING: Unable to verify timestamp for libc-2.28.so
Symbol search path is: srv*;C:\ALCDA2\x64\App1
Expanded Symbol search path is:
cache*;SRV*https://msdl.microsoft.com/download/symbols;c:\alcda2\x64\app1

************* Path validation summary **************
Response                         Time (ms)     Location
Deferred                                       srv*
OK                                             C:\ALCDA2\x64\App1
*** WARNING: Unable to verify timestamp for App1.shared
```

```
0:000> .reload
...*** WARNING: Unable to verify timestamp for libc-2.28.so
..
*** WARNING: Unable to verify timestamp for App1.shared

************* Symbol Loading Error Summary **************
Module name            Error
App1                   The system cannot find the file specified
libc-2.28              The system cannot find the file specified

You can troubleshoot most symbol related issues by turning on symbol loading diagnostics (!sym
noisy) and repeating the command that caused symbols to be loaded.
You should also verify that your symbol search path (.sympath) is correct.
```

```
0:000> k
 # Child-SP          RetAddr               Call Site
00 00007fff`cc685f70 00007ff6`429dc4ca     libc_2_28!nanosleep+0x40
01 00007fff`cc685fa0 000055b1`b4e0532a     libc_2_28!sleep+0x3a
02 00007fff`cc685fe0 00007ff6`4293a09b     App1!main+0xaa
03 00007fff`cc686030 000055b1`b4e0508a     libc_2_28!_libc_start_main+0xeb
04 00007fff`cc6860f0 ffffffff`ffffffff     App1!start+0x2a
05 00007fff`cc6860f8 00000000`00000000     0xffffffff`ffffffff
```

```
0:000> uf bar_one
App1!bar_one:
000055b1`b4e05145 push    rbp
000055b1`b4e05146 mov     rbp,rsp
000055b1`b4e05149 mov     edi,0FFFFFFFFh
000055b1`b4e0514e call    App1!sleep$plt (000055b1`b4e05040)
000055b1`b4e05153 nop
000055b1`b4e05154 pop     rbp
000055b1`b4e05155 ret
```

```
0:000> u 000055b1`b4e05040
App1!sleep$plt:
000055b1`b4e05040 jmp     qword ptr [App1!GLOBAL_OFFSET_TABLE_+0x20 (000055b1`b4e08020)]
000055b1`b4e05046 push    1
000055b1`b4e0504b jmp     App1+0x1020 (000055b1`b4e05020)
App1!:
000055b1`b4e05050 jmp     qword ptr [App1!+0x20 (000055b1`b4e07ff8)]
000055b1`b4e05056 nop
000055b1`b4e05058 add     byte ptr [rax],al
000055b1`b4e0505a add     byte ptr [rax],al
000055b1`b4e0505c add     byte ptr [rax],al
```

```
0:000> dps 000055b1`b4e08020 L1
000055b1`b4e08020  00007ff6`429dc490 libc_2_28!sleep
```

18. *App1.shared.pmap.28* also shows library memory regions:

```
28:   ./App1.shared
000055b1b4e04000      4K r---- App1.shared
000055b1b4e05000      4K r-x-- App1.shared
000055b1b4e06000      4K r---- App1.shared
000055b1b4e07000      4K r---- App1.shared
000055b1b4e08000      4K rw--- App1.shared
000055b1b92e4000    132K rw---   [ anon ]
00007ff64010e000      4K -----   [ anon ]
00007ff64010f000   8192K rw---   [ anon ]
00007ff64090f000      4K -----   [ anon ]
00007ff640910000   8192K rw---   [ anon ]
00007ff641110000      4K -----   [ anon ]
00007ff641111000   8192K rw---   [ anon ]
00007ff641911000      4K -----   [ anon ]
00007ff641912000   8192K rw---   [ anon ]
00007ff642112000      4K -----   [ anon ]
00007ff642113000   8204K rw---   [ anon ]
00007ff642916000    136K r---- libc-2.28.so
00007ff642938000   1308K r-x-- libc-2.28.so
00007ff642a7f000    304K r---- libc-2.28.so
00007ff642acb000      4K ----- libc-2.28.so
00007ff642acc000     16K r---- libc-2.28.so
00007ff642ad0000      8K rw--- libc-2.28.so
00007ff642ad2000     16K rw---   [ anon ]
00007ff642ad6000     24K r---- libpthread-2.28.so
00007ff642adc000     60K r-x-- libpthread-2.28.so
00007ff642aeb000     24K r---- libpthread-2.28.so
00007ff642af1000      4K r---- libpthread-2.28.so
00007ff642af2000      4K rw--- libpthread-2.28.so
00007ff642af3000     24K rw---   [ anon ]
00007ff642b04000      4K r---- ld-2.28.so
00007ff642b05000    120K r-x-- ld-2.28.so
00007ff642b23000     32K r---- ld-2.28.so
```

```
00007ff642b2b000      4K r---- ld-2.28.so
00007ff642b2c000      4K rw--- ld-2.28.so
00007ff642b2d000      4K rw---   [ anon ]
00007fffcc667000    132K rw---   [ stack ]
00007fffcc769000     16K r----   [ anon ]
00007fffcc76d000      8K r-x--   [ anon ]
 total           43400K
```

Note: We can also see shared library mappings in the output of the **!address** command:

```
0:000> !address

Mapping file section regions...
Mapping module regions...
Mapping heap regions...

        BaseAddress      EndAddress+1        RegionSize     Type       State                 Protect             Usage
--------------------------------------------------------------------------------------------------------------------------
+        0`00000000     55b1`b4e04000     55b1`b4e04000                                                          <unknown>
+     55b1`b4e04000     55b1`b4e05000        0`00001000 MEM_PRIVATE MEM_COMMIT  PAGE_READONLY                      Image      [App1; "/home/coredump/ALCDA2/x64/App1/App1.shared"]
+     55b1`b4e05000     55b1`b4e06000        0`00001000 MEM_PRIVATE MEM_COMMIT  PAGE_EXECUTE_READ                  Image      [App1; "/home/coredump/ALCDA2/x64/App1/App1.shared"]
+     55b1`b4e06000     55b1`b4e07000        0`00001000 MEM_PRIVATE MEM_COMMIT  PAGE_READONLY                      Image      [App1; "/home/coredump/ALCDA2/x64/App1/App1.shared"]
+     55b1`b4e07000     55b1`b4e08000        0`00001000 MEM_PRIVATE MEM_COMMIT  PAGE_READONLY                      Image      [App1; "/home/coredump/ALCDA2/x64/App1/App1.shared"]
+     55b1`b4e08000     55b1`b4e09000        0`00001000 MEM_PRIVATE MEM_COMMIT  PAGE_READWRITE                     Image      [App1; "/home/coredump/ALCDA2/x64/App1/App1.shared"]
+     55b1`b4e09000     55b1`b92e4000        0`044db000                                                          <unknown>
+     55b1`b92e4000     55b1`b9305000        0`00021000 MEM_PRIVATE MEM_COMMIT  PAGE_READWRITE                     <unknown>  [........Q.......]
+     55b1`b9305000     7ff6`4010e000     2a44`86e09000                                                          <unknown>
+     7ff6`4010e000     7ff6`4010f000        0`00001000 MEM_PRIVATE MEM_COMMIT  PAGE_READONLY                      <unknown>  [................]
+     7ff6`4010f000     7ff6`4090f000        0`00800000 MEM_PRIVATE MEM_COMMIT  PAGE_READWRITE                     <unknown>  [................]
+     7ff6`4090f000     7ff6`40910000        0`00001000 MEM_PRIVATE MEM_COMMIT  PAGE_READONLY                      <unknown>  [................]
+     7ff6`40910000     7ff6`41110000        0`00800000 MEM_PRIVATE MEM_COMMIT  PAGE_READWRITE                     <unknown>  [................]
+     7ff6`41110000     7ff6`41111000        0`00001000 MEM_PRIVATE MEM_COMMIT  PAGE_READONLY                      <unknown>  [................]
+     7ff6`41111000     7ff6`41911000        0`00800000 MEM_PRIVATE MEM_COMMIT  PAGE_READWRITE                     <unknown>  [................]
+     7ff6`41911000     7ff6`41912000        0`00001000 MEM_PRIVATE MEM_COMMIT  PAGE_READONLY                      <unknown>  [................]
+     7ff6`41912000     7ff6`42112000        0`00800000 MEM_PRIVATE MEM_COMMIT  PAGE_READWRITE                     <unknown>  [................]
+     7ff6`42112000     7ff6`42113000        0`00001000 MEM_PRIVATE MEM_COMMIT  PAGE_READONLY                      <unknown>  [................]
+     7ff6`42113000     7ff6`42916000        0`00803000 MEM_PRIVATE MEM_COMMIT  PAGE_READWRITE                     <unknown>  [................]
+     7ff6`42916000     7ff6`42938000        0`00022000 MEM_PRIVATE MEM_COMMIT  PAGE_READONLY                      Image      [libc_2_28; "/lib/x86_64-linux-gnu/libc-2.28.so"]
+     7ff6`42938000     7ff6`42a7f000        0`00147000 MEM_PRIVATE MEM_COMMIT  PAGE_EXECUTE_READ                  Image      [libc_2_28; "/lib/x86_64-linux-gnu/libc-2.28.so"]
+     7ff6`42a7f000     7ff6`42acb000        0`0004c000 MEM_PRIVATE MEM_COMMIT  PAGE_READONLY                      Image      [libc_2_28; "/lib/x86_64-linux-gnu/libc-2.28.so"]
+     7ff6`42acb000     7ff6`42acc000        0`00001000 MEM_PRIVATE MEM_COMMIT  PAGE_READONLY                      Image      [libc_2_28; "/lib/x86_64-linux-gnu/libc-2.28.so"]
+     7ff6`42acc000     7ff6`42ad0000        0`00004000 MEM_PRIVATE MEM_COMMIT  PAGE_READONLY                      Image      [libc_2_28; "/lib/x86_64-linux-gnu/libc-2.28.so"]
+     7ff6`42ad0000     7ff6`42ad2000        0`00002000 MEM_PRIVATE MEM_COMMIT  PAGE_READWRITE                     Image      [libc_2_28; "/lib/x86_64-linux-gnu/libc-2.28.so"]
+     7ff6`42ad2000     7ff6`42ad6000        0`00004000 MEM_PRIVATE MEM_COMMIT  PAGE_READWRITE                     <unknown>  [................]
+     7ff6`42ad6000     7ff6`42adc000        0`00006000 MEM_PRIVATE MEM_COMMIT  PAGE_READONLY                      Image      [libpthread_2_28; "/lib/x86_64-linux-gnu/libpthread-2.28.so"]
+     7ff6`42adc000     7ff6`42aeb000        0`0000f000 MEM_PRIVATE MEM_COMMIT  PAGE_EXECUTE_READ                  Image      [libpthread_2_28; "/lib/x86_64-linux-gnu/libpthread-2.28.so"]
+     7ff6`42aeb000     7ff6`42af1000        0`00006000 MEM_PRIVATE MEM_COMMIT  PAGE_READONLY                      Image      [libpthread_2_28; "/lib/x86_64-linux-gnu/libpthread-2.28.so"]
+     7ff6`42af1000     7ff6`42af2000        0`00001000 MEM_PRIVATE MEM_COMMIT  PAGE_READONLY                      Image      [libpthread_2_28; "/lib/x86_64-linux-gnu/libpthread-2.28.so"]
+     7ff6`42af2000     7ff6`42af3000        0`00001000 MEM_PRIVATE MEM_COMMIT  PAGE_READWRITE                     Image      [libpthread_2_28; "/lib/x86_64-linux-gnu/libpthread-2.28.so"]
+     7ff6`42af3000     7ff6`42af9000        0`00006000 MEM_PRIVATE MEM_COMMIT  PAGE_READWRITE                     <unknown>  [................]
+     7ff6`42af9000     7ff6`42b04000        0`0000b000                                                          <unknown>
+     7ff6`42b04000     7ff6`42b05000        0`00001000 MEM_PRIVATE MEM_COMMIT  PAGE_READONLY                      Image      [ld_2_28; "/lib/x86_64-linux-gnu/ld-2.28.so"]
+     7ff6`42b05000     7ff6`42b23000        0`0001e000 MEM_PRIVATE MEM_COMMIT  PAGE_EXECUTE_READ                  Image      [ld_2_28; "/lib/x86_64-linux-gnu/ld-2.28.so"]
+     7ff6`42b23000     7ff6`42b2b000        0`00008000 MEM_PRIVATE MEM_COMMIT  PAGE_READONLY                      Image      [ld_2_28; "/lib/x86_64-linux-gnu/ld-2.28.so"]
+     7ff6`42b2b000     7ff6`42b2c000        0`00001000 MEM_PRIVATE MEM_COMMIT  PAGE_READONLY                      Image      [ld_2_28; "/lib/x86_64-linux-gnu/ld-2.28.so"]
+     7ff6`42b2c000     7ff6`42b2d000        0`00001000 MEM_PRIVATE MEM_COMMIT  PAGE_READWRITE                     Image      [ld_2_28; "/lib/x86_64-linux-gnu/ld-2.28.so"]
+     7ff6`42b2d000     7ff6`42b2e000        0`00001000 MEM_PRIVATE MEM_COMMIT  PAGE_READWRITE                     <unknown>  [AI.B............]
+     7ff6`42b2e000     7fff`cc667000        9`89b39000                                                          <unknown>
+     7fff`cc667000     7fff`cc688000        0`00021000 MEM_PRIVATE MEM_COMMIT  PAGE_READWRITE                     <unknown>  [................]
+     7fff`cc688000     7fff`cc76d000        0`000e5000                                                          <unknown>
+     7fff`cc76d000     7fff`cc76e000        0`00001000 MEM_PRIVATE MEM_COMMIT  PAGE_EXECUTE_READ                  Image      [linux_vdso_so; "linux-vdso.so.1"]
      7fff`cc76e000     7fff`cc76f000        0`00001000 MEM_PRIVATE MEM_COMMIT  PAGE_EXECUTE_READ                  <unknown>  [................]
```

19. We close logging before exiting WinDbg sessions:

```
0:000> .logclose
Closing open log file 'C:\ALCDA2\x64\App1\App1-WinDbg.log'
```

We recommend exiting WinDbg after each exercise.

Exercise A1 (A64, WinDbg)

Goal: Learn how to list stack traces, disassemble functions, check their correctness, dump data, get environment.

Patterns: Manual Dump; Stack Trace; Incorrect Stack Trace; Stack Trace Collection; Annotated Disassembly; Paratext; Not My Version; Environment Hint.

1. Launch WinDbg.

2. Load the core dump *App1.core.21174* from the A64\App1 folder:

```
Microsoft (R) Windows Debugger Version 10.0.27725.1000 AMD64
Copyright (c) Microsoft Corporation. All rights reserved.


Loading Dump File [C:\ALCDA2\A64\App1\App1.core.21174]
64-bit machine not using 64-bit API

************* Path validation summary **************
Response                         Time (ms)     Location
Deferred                                       srv*
Symbol search path is: srv*
Executable search path is:
Generic Unix Version 0 UP Free ARM 64-bit (AArch64)
System Uptime: not available
Process Uptime: not available
..
*** WARNING: Unable to verify timestamp for App1
App1+0xc9b4:
00000000`0040c9b4 svc         #0
```

3. Set logging to a file in case of lengthy output from some commands:

```
0:000> .logopen C:\ALCDA2\A64\App1\App1-WinDbg.log
Opened log file 'C:\ALCDA2\A64\App1\App1-WinDbg.log'
```

4. Specify the dump folder as the symbol path and reload symbols:

```
0:000> .symfix; .sympath+ C:\ALCDA2\A64\App1\
Symbol search path is: srv*;C:\ALCDA2\A64\App1\
Expanded Symbol search path is:
cache*;SRV*https://msdl.microsoft.com/download/symbols;c:\alcda2\a64\app1\

************* Path validation summary **************
Response                         Time (ms)     Location
Deferred                                       srv*
OK                                             C:\ALCDA2\A64\App1\
*** WARNING: Unable to verify timestamp for App1
```

```
0:000> .reload
..
*** WARNING: Unable to verify timestamp for App1

************* Symbol Loading Error Summary **************
Module name            Error
App1                   The system cannot find the file specified

You can troubleshoot most symbol related issues by turning on symbol loading diagnostics (!sym
noisy) and repeating the command that caused symbols to be loaded.
You should also verify that your symbol search path (.sympath) is correct.
```

Note: We ignore warnings and errors as they are not relevant for now.

5. List all threads:

```
0:000> ~
Unable to get thread data for thread 0
.  0  Id: 52b6.52b7 Suspend: 0 Teb: 00000000`00000000 Unfrozen
Unable to get thread data for thread 1
   1  Id: 52b6.52b8 Suspend: 0 Teb: 00000000`00000000 Unfrozen
Unable to get thread data for thread 2
   2  Id: 52b6.52b9 Suspend: 0 Teb: 00000000`00000000 Unfrozen
Unable to get thread data for thread 3
   3  Id: 52b6.52ba Suspend: 0 Teb: 00000000`00000000 Unfrozen
Unable to get thread data for thread 4
   4  Id: 52b6.52bb Suspend: 0 Teb: 00000000`00000000 Unfrozen
Unable to get thread data for thread 5
   5  Id: 52b6.52b6 Suspend: 0 Teb: 00000000`00000000 Unfrozen
```

Note: WinDbg uses the same output format as for Windows memory dumps. Therefore, some data is either reported as errors or shows 0 or NULL pointer values. However, we see process and thread IDs in the format PID.TID:

```
0:000> .formats 52b6
Evaluate expression:
  Hex:     00000000`000052b6
  Decimal: 21174
  Octal:   0000000000000000051266
  Binary:  00000000 00000000 00000000 00000000 00000000 00000000 01010010 10110110
  Chars:   ......R.
  Time:    Thu Jan  1 05:52:54 1970
  Float:   low 2.96711e-041 high 0
  Double:  1.04613e-319

0:000> ? 52b6
Evaluate expression: 21174 = 00000000`000052b6
```

6. Get the current thread stack trace:

```
0:000> k
 # Child-SP          RetAddr           Call Site
00 0000fffc`cd38e5f0 00000000`00424cb4 App1!_libc_nanosleep+0x24
01 0000fffc`cd38e630 00000000`004031f8 App1!sleep+0x110
02 0000fffc`cd38e820 00000000`0040320c App1!bar_one+0x10
03 0000fffc`cd38e830 00000000`00403224 App1!foo_one+0xc
04 0000fffc`cd38e840 00000000`00404c34 App1!thread_one+0x10
05 0000fffc`cd38e860 00000000`00429b60 App1!start_thread+0xb4
06 0000fffc`cd38e990 ffffffff`ffffffff App1!thread_start+0x30
07 0000fffc`cd38e990 00000000`00000000 0xffffffff`ffffffff
```

7. Get all thread stack traces:

```
0:000> ~*k

Unable to get thread data for thread 0
.  0  Id: 52b6.52b7 Suspend: 0 Teb: 00000000`00000000 Unfrozen
 # Child-SP          RetAddr               Call Site
00 0000fffc`cd38e5f0 00000000`00424cb4     App1!_libc_nanosleep+0x24
01 0000fffc`cd38e630 00000000`004031f8     App1!sleep+0x110
02 0000fffc`cd38e820 00000000`0040320c     App1!bar_one+0x10
03 0000fffc`cd38e830 00000000`00403224     App1!foo_one+0xc
04 0000fffc`cd38e840 00000000`00404c34     App1!thread_one+0x10
05 0000fffc`cd38e860 00000000`00429b60     App1!start_thread+0xb4
06 0000fffc`cd38e990 ffffffff`ffffffff     App1!thread_start+0x30
07 0000fffc`cd38e990 00000000`00000000     0xffffffff`ffffffff

Unable to get thread data for thread 1
   1  Id: 52b6.52b8 Suspend: 0 Teb: 00000000`00000000 Unfrozen
 # Child-SP          RetAddr               Call Site
00 0000fffc`ccb7e5f0 00000000`00424cb4     App1!_libc_nanosleep+0x24
01 0000fffc`ccb7e630 00000000`00403240     App1!sleep+0x110
02 0000fffc`ccb7e820 00000000`00403254     App1!bar_two+0x10
03 0000fffc`ccb7e830 00000000`0040326c     App1!foo_two+0xc
04 0000fffc`ccb7e840 00000000`00404c34     App1!thread_two+0x10
05 0000fffc`ccb7e860 00000000`00429b60     App1!start_thread+0xb4
06 0000fffc`ccb7e990 ffffffff`ffffffff     App1!thread_start+0x30
07 0000fffc`ccb7e990 00000000`00000000     0xffffffff`ffffffff

Unable to get thread data for thread 2
   2  Id: 52b6.52b9 Suspend: 0 Teb: 00000000`00000000 Unfrozen
 # Child-SP          RetAddr               Call Site
00 0000fffc`cc36e5f0 00000000`00424cb4     App1!_libc_nanosleep+0x24
01 0000fffc`cc36e630 00000000`00403288     App1!sleep+0x110
02 0000fffc`cc36e820 00000000`0040329c     App1!bar_three+0x10
03 0000fffc`cc36e830 00000000`004032b4     App1!foo_three+0xc
04 0000fffc`cc36e840 00000000`00404c34     App1!thread_three+0x10
05 0000fffc`cc36e860 00000000`00429b60     App1!start_thread+0xb4
06 0000fffc`cc36e990 ffffffff`ffffffff     App1!thread_start+0x30
07 0000fffc`cc36e990 00000000`00000000     0xffffffff`ffffffff

Unable to get thread data for thread 3
   3  Id: 52b6.52ba Suspend: 0 Teb: 00000000`00000000 Unfrozen
 # Child-SP          RetAddr               Call Site
00 0000fffc`cbb5e5f0 00000000`00424cb4     App1!_libc_nanosleep+0x24
01 0000fffc`cbb5e630 00000000`004032d0     App1!sleep+0x110
02 0000fffc`cbb5e820 00000000`004032e4     App1!bar_four+0x10
03 0000fffc`cbb5e830 00000000`004032fc     App1!foo_four+0xc
04 0000fffc`cbb5e840 00000000`00404c34     App1!thread_four+0x10
05 0000fffc`cbb5e860 00000000`00429b60     App1!start_thread+0xb4
06 0000fffc`cbb5e990 ffffffff`ffffffff     App1!thread_start+0x30
07 0000fffc`cbb5e990 00000000`00000000     0xffffffff`ffffffff

Unable to get thread data for thread 4
   4  Id: 52b6.52bb Suspend: 0 Teb: 00000000`00000000 Unfrozen
 # Child-SP          RetAddr               Call Site
00 0000fffc`cb34e5f0 00000000`00424cb4     App1!_libc_nanosleep+0x24
01 0000fffc`cb34e630 00000000`00403318     App1!sleep+0x110
02 0000fffc`cb34e820 00000000`0040332c     App1!bar_five+0x10
03 0000fffc`cb34e830 00000000`00403344     App1!foo_five+0xc
04 0000fffc`cb34e840 00000000`00404c34     App1!thread_five+0x10
```

```
05 0000fffc`cb34e860 00000000`00429b60     App1!start_thread+0xb4
06 0000fffc`cb34e990 ffffffff`ffffffff     App1!thread_start+0x30
07 0000fffc`cb34e990 00000000`00000000     0xffffffff`ffffffff

Unable to get thread data for thread 5
   5  Id: 52b6.52b6 Suspend: 0 Teb: 00000000`00000000 Unfrozen
 # Child-SP          RetAddr               Call Site
00 0000ffff`d30b8490 00000000`00424cb4     App1!_libc_nanosleep+0x24
01 0000ffff`d30b84d0 00000000`004033e0     App1!sleep+0x110
02 0000ffff`d30b86c0 00000000`0040ec4c     App1!main+0x90
03 0000ffff`d30b8710 00000000`00403090     App1!_libc_start_main+0x304
04 0000ffff`d30b8870 00000000`00000000     App1!start+0x4c
```

8. Switch to thread #1 (threads are numbered from 0) and get its stack trace:

```
0:000> ~1s
App1!_libc_nanosleep+0x24:
00000000`0040c9b4 d4000001 svc          #0

0:001> k
 # Child-SP          RetAddr               Call Site
00 0000fffc`ccb7e5f0 00000000`00424cb4     App1!_libc_nanosleep+0x24
01 0000fffc`ccb7e630 00000000`00403240     App1!sleep+0x110
02 0000fffc`ccb7e820 00000000`00403254     App1!bar_two+0x10
03 0000fffc`ccb7e830 00000000`0040326c     App1!foo_two+0xc
04 0000fffc`ccb7e840 00000000`00404c34     App1!thread_two+0x10
05 0000fffc`ccb7e860 00000000`00429b60     App1!start_thread+0xb4
06 0000fffc`ccb7e990 ffffffff`ffffffff     App1!thread_start+0x30
07 0000fffc`ccb7e990 00000000`00000000     0xffffffff`ffffffff
```

9. Check that *bar_two* called the *sleep* function by comparing the return address on the call stack from the disassembly output:

```
0:001> uf bar_two
App1!bar_two:
00000000`00403230 a9bf7bfd stp      fp,lr,[sp,#-0x10]!
00000000`00403234 910003fd mov      fp,sp
00000000`00403238 12800000 mov      w0,#-1
00000000`0040323c 9400865a bl       App1!sleep (00000000`00424ba4)
00000000`00403240 a8c17bfd ldp      fp,lr,[sp],#0x10
00000000`00403244 d65f03c0 ret
```

Another way to do that is to disassemble backward the return address and check if the last instruction is BL:

```
0:001> ub 00000000`00403240
App1!thread_one+0xc:
00000000`00403220 97fffff8 bl       App1!foo_one (00000000`00403200)
00000000`00403224 d2800000 mov      x0,#0
00000000`00403228 a8c27bfd ldp      fp,lr,[sp],#0x20
00000000`0040322c d65f03c0 ret
App1!bar_two:
00000000`00403230 a9bf7bfd stp      fp,lr,[sp,#-0x10]!
00000000`00403234 910003fd mov      fp,sp
00000000`00403238 12800000 mov      w0,#-1
00000000`0040323c 9400865a bl       App1!sleep (00000000`00424ba4)
```

10. Get the *App1* data section from the contents of pmap (*App1.pmap.21174*):

```
21174:   ./App1
0000000000400000    768K r-x-- App1
00000000004c0000    128K rw--- App1
0000000001fa0000    256K rw---   [ anon ]
0000fffccab40000     64K -----  [ anon ]
0000fffccab50000   8192K rw---  [ anon ]
0000fffccb350000     64K -----  [ anon ]
0000fffccb360000   8192K rw---  [ anon ]
0000fffccbb60000     64K -----  [ anon ]
0000fffccbb70000   8192K rw---  [ anon ]
0000fffccc370000     64K -----  [ anon ]
0000fffccc380000   8192K rw---  [ anon ]
0000fffcccb80000     64K -----  [ anon ]
0000fffcccb90000   8192K rw---  [ anon ]
0000fffccd390000     64K r----  [ anon ]
0000fffccd3a0000     64K r-x--  [ anon ]
0000ffffd3090000    192K rw---  [ stack ]
 total            42752K
```

11. Compare with the region information in the core dump:

```
0:001> !address

Mapping file section regions...
Mapping module regions...

        BaseAddress      EndAddress+1        RegionSize     Type       State                 Protect             Usage
--------------------------------------------------------------------------------------------------------------------------
+        0`00000000        0`00400000        0`00400000                                                         <unknown>
+        0`00400000        0`004c0000        0`000c0000 MEM_PRIVATE MEM_COMMIT  PAGE_EXECUTE_READ                  Image      [App1; "/home/opc/ALCDA2/App1/App1"]
+        0`004c0000        0`004e0000        0`00020000 MEM_PRIVATE MEM_COMMIT  PAGE_READWRITE                     Image      [App1; "/home/opc/ALCDA2/App1/App1"]
+        0`004e0000        0`01fa0000        0`01ac0000                                                         <unknown>
+        0`01fa0000        0`01fe0000        0`00040000 MEM_PRIVATE MEM_COMMIT  PAGE_READWRITE                     <unknown>  [................]
+        0`01fe0000     fffc`cab40000     fffc`c8b60000                                                         <unknown>
+     fffc`cab40000     fffc`cab50000        0`00010000 MEM_PRIVATE MEM_COMMIT  PAGE_READONLY                      <unknown>  [................]
+     fffc`cab50000     fffc`cb350000        0`00800000 MEM_PRIVATE MEM_COMMIT  PAGE_READWRITE                     <unknown>  [................]
+     fffc`cb350000     fffc`cb360000        0`00010000 MEM_PRIVATE MEM_COMMIT  PAGE_READONLY                      <unknown>  [................]
+     fffc`cb360000     fffc`cbb60000        0`00800000 MEM_PRIVATE MEM_COMMIT  PAGE_READWRITE                     <unknown>  [................]
+     fffc`cbb60000     fffc`cbb70000        0`00010000 MEM_PRIVATE MEM_COMMIT  PAGE_READONLY                      <unknown>  [................]
+     fffc`cbb70000     fffc`cc370000        0`00800000 MEM_PRIVATE MEM_COMMIT  PAGE_READWRITE                     <unknown>  [................]
+     fffc`cc370000     fffc`cc380000        0`00010000 MEM_PRIVATE MEM_COMMIT  PAGE_READONLY                      <unknown>  [................]
+     fffc`cc380000     fffc`ccb80000        0`00800000 MEM_PRIVATE MEM_COMMIT  PAGE_READWRITE                     <unknown>  [................]
+     fffc`ccb80000     fffc`ccb90000        0`00010000 MEM_PRIVATE MEM_COMMIT  PAGE_READONLY                      <unknown>  [................]
+     fffc`ccb90000     fffc`cd390000        0`00800000 MEM_PRIVATE MEM_COMMIT  PAGE_READWRITE                     <unknown>  [................]
+     fffc`cd390000     fffc`cd3a0000        0`00010000                                                         <unknown>
+     fffc`cd3a0000     fffc`cd3b0000        0`00010000 MEM_PRIVATE MEM_COMMIT  PAGE_EXECUTE_READ                  Image      [linux_vdso_so; "linux-vdso.so.1"]
+     fffc`cd3b0000     ffff`d3090000        3`05ce0000                                                         <unknown>
+     ffff`d3090000     ffff`d30c0000        0`00030000 MEM_PRIVATE MEM_COMMIT  PAGE_READWRITE                     <unknown>  [................]
```

12. Dump the data region with possible symbolic information (we truncated the output):

```
0:001> dps 0`004c0000 0`004e0000
[...]
00000000`004d0fe8  00000000`00000000
00000000`004d0ff0  00000000`00000000
00000000`004d0ff8  00000000`004d0788 App1!main_arena
00000000`004d1000  00000000`00000000
00000000`004d1008  00000000`00000001
00000000`004d1010  00000000`0003f078
00000000`004d1018  00000000`0003f078
00000000`004d1020  00000000`00421c08 App1!_default_morecore
00000000`004d1028  00000000`00000001
00000000`004d1030  ffffffff`00000001
00000000`004d1038  00000000`0041cc00 App1!memalign_hook_ini
00000000`004d1040  00000000`0041d688 App1!realloc_hook_ini
00000000`004d1048  00000000`00000000
00000000`004d1050  ffffffff`00000008
00000000`004d1058  000000ff`00000002
00000000`004d1060  00000000`ffffffff
```

```
00000000`004d1068  0000ffff`d30bf6dd
00000000`004d1070  0000ffff`d30bf6db
00000000`004d1078  00000000`00010000
00000000`004d1080  00000000`00000006
00000000`004d1088  00000000`00000000
00000000`004d1090  00000000`00000000
00000000`004d1098  00000000`00000001
00000000`004d10a0  00000000`00000000
00000000`004d10a8  00000000`00000000
00000000`004d10b0  00000000`00000000
00000000`004d10b8  00000000`00000000
00000000`004d10c0  00000000`00000000
00000000`004d10c8  00000000`00000001
00000000`004d10d0  00000000`00000000
00000000`004d10d8  00000000`00000000
00000000`004d10e0  00000000`00000000
00000000`004d10e8  00000000`0042c6a0 App1!dl_make_stack_executable
00000000`004d10f0  00000002`00000a03
00000000`004d10f8  00000000`004045a8 App1!_pthread_init_static_tls
00000000`004d1100  00000000`00000001
00000000`004d1108  ffffffff`fffffffe
00000000`004d1110  00000000`004d1068 App1!_progname
00000000`004d1118  00000000`00000000
00000000`004d1120  00000000`0048ad20 App1!$d+0xe0
00000000`004d1128  00000000`0048ac30 App1!$d+0x38
00000000`004d1130  7fffffff`00000001
00000000`004d1138  00000000`0048ac40 App1!$d
00000000`004d1140  00000000`00000000
00000000`004d1148  00000000`00000000
00000000`004d1150  00000000`00000000
[...]
```

The output is in the following format:

```
address   value
```

Some values may have associated symbols in the format module!name+offset:

```
address   value   symbol
```

For example, from the output above:

```
00000000`004d1110  00000000`004d1068 App1!_progname
```

To list all values with symbols, we can use the **dpS** command (it doesn't show the value addresses):

```
0:001> dpS 0`004c0000 0`004e0000
 00000000`004d6e70 App1!res
 00000000`004d13c0 App1!nl_global_locale
 00000000`004d13c0 App1!nl_global_locale
 00000000`004d13e0 App1!nl_global_locale+0x20
 00000000`004d13c8 App1!nl_global_locale+0x8
 00000000`00403190 App1!frame_dummy
 00000000`00403140 App1!_do_global_dtors_aux
 00000000`00402ffc App1!fini
 00000000`0048a2d0 App1!$d+0x20
 00000000`0048a2f0 App1!$d+0x40
 00000000`0048a308 App1!$d+0x58
 00000000`0048a320 App1!$d+0x70
 00000000`0048a330 App1!$d+0x80
```

```
00000000`0048a348 App1!$d+0x98
00000000`0048a358 App1!$d+0xa8
00000000`0048a368 App1!$d+0xb8
00000000`0048a380 App1!$d+0xd0
00000000`0048a398 App1!$d+0xe8
00000000`0048a3c0 App1!$d+0x110
00000000`0048a3d8 App1!$d+0x128
00000000`0048a3e8 App1!$d+0x138
00000000`0048a400 App1!$d+0x150
00000000`0048a418 App1!$d+0x168
00000000`0048a438 App1!$d+0x188
00000000`0048a450 App1!$d+0x1a0
00000000`0048a470 App1!$d+0x1c0
00000000`0048a488 App1!$d+0x1d8
00000000`0048a4a0 App1!$d+0x1f0
00000000`0048a4b8 App1!$d+0x208
00000000`0048a4d0 App1!$d+0x220
00000000`00409a50 App1!_pthread_key_create
00000000`004231c0 App1!_memmove_generic
00000000`004231d0 App1!_memcpy_generic
00000000`00423fc0 App1!_memset_generic
00000000`00424480 App1!_strlen_generic
00000000`00424480 App1!_strlen_generic
00000000`004d0038 App1!stack_cache
00000000`004d0038 App1!stack_cache
00000000`004d5eb0 App1!initial
00000000`00486b88 App1!_gcc_personality_v0
00000000`004d0088 App1!IO_2_1_stderr_
00000000`004d02b0 App1!IO_2_1_stdout_
00000000`004d6428 App1!IO_stdfile_2_lock
00000000`004d0168 App1!IO_wide_data_2
00000000`004a1950 App1!IO_file_jumps
00000000`004a1800 App1!IO_wfile_jumps
00000000`004d04d8 App1!IO_2_1_stdin_
00000000`004d6438 App1!IO_stdfile_1_lock
00000000`004d0390 App1!IO_wide_data_1
00000000`004a1950 App1!IO_file_jumps
00000000`004a1800 App1!IO_wfile_jumps
00000000`004d6448 App1!IO_stdfile_0_lock
00000000`004d05b8 App1!IO_wide_data_0
00000000`004a1950 App1!IO_file_jumps
00000000`004a1800 App1!IO_wfile_jumps
00000000`004d0088 App1!IO_2_1_stderr_
00000000`004d02b0 App1!IO_2_1_stdout_
00000000`004d04d8 App1!IO_2_1_stdin_
00000000`004d07e8 App1!main_arena+0x60
00000000`004d07e8 App1!main_arena+0x60
00000000`004d07f8 App1!main_arena+0x70
00000000`004d07f8 App1!main_arena+0x70
00000000`004d0808 App1!main_arena+0x80
00000000`004d0808 App1!main_arena+0x80
00000000`004d0818 App1!main_arena+0x90
00000000`004d0818 App1!main_arena+0x90
00000000`004d0828 App1!main_arena+0xa0
00000000`004d0828 App1!main_arena+0xa0
00000000`004d0838 App1!main_arena+0xb0
00000000`004d0838 App1!main_arena+0xb0
00000000`004d0848 App1!main_arena+0xc0
00000000`004d0848 App1!main_arena+0xc0
00000000`004d0858 App1!main_arena+0xd0
```

```
00000000`004d0858 App1!main_arena+0xd0
00000000`004d0868 App1!main_arena+0xe0
00000000`004d0868 App1!main_arena+0xe0
00000000`004d0878 App1!main_arena+0xf0
00000000`004d0878 App1!main_arena+0xf0
00000000`004d0888 App1!main_arena+0x100
00000000`004d0888 App1!main_arena+0x100
00000000`004d0898 App1!main_arena+0x110
[...]
00000000`004d0fc8 App1!main_arena+0x840
00000000`004d0788 App1!main_arena
00000000`00421c08 App1!_default_morecore
00000000`0041cc00 App1!memalign_hook_ini
00000000`0041d688 App1!realloc_hook_ini
00000000`0042c6a0 App1!dl_make_stack_executable
00000000`004045a8 App1!_pthread_init_static_tls
00000000`004d1068 App1!_progname
00000000`0048ad20 App1!$d+0xe0
00000000`0048ac30 App1!$d+0x38
00000000`0048ac40 App1!$d
00000000`0048ac30 App1!$d+0x38
00000000`0048ad20 App1!$d+0xe0
00000000`0048ac50 App1!$d+0x10
00000000`0048ad20 App1!$d+0xe0
00000000`0048ac60 App1!$d+0x20
00000000`0048ac70 App1!$d+0x30
00000000`0048ac60 App1!$d+0x20
00000000`0048ad20 App1!$d+0xe0
00000000`0048ac88 App1!$d+0x48
00000000`0048ad20 App1!$d+0xe0
00000000`0048aca0 App1!$d+0x60
00000000`0048acb0 App1!$d+0x70
00000000`0048aca0 App1!$d+0x60
00000000`0048ad20 App1!$d+0xe0
00000000`0048acc0 App1!$d+0x80
00000000`0048acd0 App1!$d+0x90
00000000`0048ad20 App1!$d+0xe0
00000000`0048ace0 App1!$d+0xa0
00000000`0048ad20 App1!$d+0xe0
00000000`0048acd0 App1!$d+0x90
00000000`0048acf0 App1!$d+0xb0
00000000`0048ad00 App1!$d+0xc0
00000000`0048ad20 App1!$d+0xe0
00000000`0048ad18 App1!$d+0xd8
00000000`0048ad20 App1!$d+0xe0
00000000`0048ad00 App1!$d+0xc0
00000000`0048ad30 App1!$d+0xf0
00000000`0048ad48 App1!$d+0x108
00000000`0048ad20 App1!$d+0xe0
00000000`0048ad58 App1!$d+0x118
00000000`0048ad20 App1!$d+0xe0
00000000`0048ad48 App1!$d+0x108
00000000`0048ad70 App1!$d+0x130
00000000`0048b888 App1!nl_C_LC_CTYPE
00000000`00499f18 App1!nl_C_LC_NUMERIC
00000000`00499f88 App1!nl_C_LC_TIME
00000000`0049aec0 App1!nl_C_LC_COLLATE
00000000`00499d58 App1!nl_C_LC_MONETARY
00000000`00499ce0 App1!nl_C_LC_MESSAGES
00000000`0049a9e0 App1!nl_C_LC_PAPER
```

```
00000000`0049aa38 App1!nl_C_LC_NAME
00000000`0049aac0 App1!nl_C_LC_ADDRESS
00000000`0049ab98 App1!nl_C_LC_TELEPHONE
00000000`0049ac10 App1!nl_C_LC_MEASUREMENT
00000000`0049ad08 App1!nl_C_LC_IDENTIFICATION
00000000`0048d1c0 App1!nl_C_LC_CTYPE_class+0x100
00000000`0048c2c0 App1!nl_C_LC_CTYPE_tolower+0x200
00000000`0048c8c0 App1!nl_C_LC_CTYPE_toupper+0x200
00000000`00497450 App1!nl_C_name
00000000`00497450 App1!nl_C_name
00000000`00497450 App1!nl_C_name
00000000`00497450 App1!nl_C_name
00000000`00497450 App1!nl_C_name
00000000`00497450 App1!nl_C_name
00000000`00497450 App1!nl_C_name
00000000`00497450 App1!nl_C_name
00000000`00497450 App1!nl_C_name
00000000`00497450 App1!nl_C_name
00000000`00497450 App1!nl_C_name
00000000`00497450 App1!nl_C_name
00000000`00497450 App1!nl_C_name
00000000`004975d0 App1!nl_C_locobj+0x158
00000000`00498850 App1!$d+0x30
00000000`00498850 App1!$d+0x30
00000000`00465268 App1!_libc_dlopen_mode
00000000`004651ec App1!_libc_dlsym
00000000`0046517c App1!_libc_dlclose
00000000`00465460 App1!dl_initial_error_catch_tsd
00000000`0049b540 App1!nl_default_default_domain
00000000`0047e9e8 App1!_dlopen
00000000`0047ea3c App1!_dlclose
00000000`0047ea98 App1!_dlsym
00000000`0047eb4c App1!_dlvsym
00000000`00470f60 App1!_dlerror
00000000`00471324 App1!_dladdr
00000000`00471330 App1!_dladdr1
00000000`00471470 App1!_dlinfo
00000000`00471528 App1!_dlmopen
00000000`004d1078 App1!dl_pagesize
00000000`004a1e68 App1!_EH_FRAME_BEGIN__
00000000`004cfb20 App1!
00000000`004d5618 App1!static_map
00000000`00403f44 App1!_reclaim_stacks
00000000`004d1588 App1!object.6205
00000000`004d7d40 App1!_libc_multiple_threads
00000000`004d5a78 App1!static_slotinfo
00000000`004d78e0 App1!_fork_generation
00000000`004d6570 App1!fork_handler_pool+0x8
00000000`0048a618 App1!unsecure_envvars.10865+0x118
00000000`004046f0 App1!_wait_lookup_done
00000000`00400040 App1+0x40
????????`????????
```

13. Explore the contents of memory pointed to by *App1!memalign_hook_ini* and *App1!_progname* addresses:

```
0:001> u 00000000`0041cc00
App1!memalign_hook_ini:
00000000`0041cc00 a9b97bfd stp          fp,lr,[sp,#-0x70]!
00000000`0041cc04 910003fd mov          fp,sp
00000000`0041cc08 a9025bf5 stp          x21,x22,[sp,#0x20]
00000000`0041cc0c 900005b6 adrp         x22,App1!+0x18 (00000000`004d0000)
00000000`0041cc10 58004815 ldr          x21,App1!$d (00000000`0041d510)
00000000`0041cc14 911c62c2 add          x2,x22,#0x718
00000000`0041cc18 a90153f3 stp          x19,x20,[sp,#0x10]
00000000`0041cc1c a90363f7 stp          x23,x24,[sp,#0x30]
```

```
0:001> dp App1!_progname
00000000`004d1068  0000ffff`d30bf6dd 0000ffff`d30bf6db
00000000`004d1078  00000000`00010000 00000000`00000006
00000000`004d1088  00000000`00000000 00000000`00000000
00000000`004d1098  00000000`00000001 00000000`00000000
00000000`004d10a8  00000000`00000000 00000000`00000000
00000000`004d10b8  00000000`00000000 00000000`00000000
00000000`004d10c8  00000000`00000001 00000000`00000000
00000000`004d10d8  00000000`00000000 00000000`00000000
```

```
0:001> dc 0000ffff`d30bf6dd
0000ffff`d30bf6dd  31707041 47445800 5345535f 4e4f4953  App1.XDG_SESSION
0000ffff`d30bf6ed  3d44495f 30353836 534f4800 4d414e54  _ID=6850.HOSTNAM
0000ffff`d30bf6fd  6e693d45 6e617473 322d6563 31313230  E=instance-20211
0000ffff`d30bf70d  2d393031 34303032 4c455300 58554e49  109-2004.SELINUX
0000ffff`d30bf71d  4c4f525f 45525f45 53455551 3d444554  _ROLE_REQUESTED=
0000ffff`d30bf72d  52455400 74783d4d 2d6d7265 63363532  .TERM=xterm-256c
0000ffff`d30bf73d  726f6c6f 45485300 2f3d4c4c 2f6e6962  olor.SHELL=/bin/
0000ffff`d30bf74d  68736162 53494800 5a495354 30313d45  bash.HISTSIZE=10
```

```
0:001> da 0000ffff`d30bf6dd
0000ffff`d30bf6dd  "App1"
```

```
0:001> db 0000ffff`d30bf6dd
0000ffff`d30bf6dd  41 70 70 31 00 58 44 47-5f 53 45 53 53 49 4f 4e  App1.XDG_SESSION
0000ffff`d30bf6ed  5f 49 44 3d 36 38 35 30-00 48 4f 53 54 4e 41 4d  _ID=6850.HOSTNAM
0000ffff`d30bf6fd  45 3d 69 6e 73 74 61 6e-63 65 2d 32 30 32 31 31  E=instance-20211
0000ffff`d30bf70d  31 30 39 2d 32 30 30 34-00 53 45 4c 49 4e 55 58  109-2004.SELINUX
0000ffff`d30bf71d  5f 52 4f 4c 45 5f 52 45-51 55 45 53 54 45 44 3d  _ROLE_REQUESTED=
0000ffff`d30bf72d  00 54 45 52 4d 3d 78 74-65 72 6d 2d 32 35 36 63  .TERM=xterm-256c
0000ffff`d30bf73d  6f 6c 6f 72 00 53 48 45-4c 4c 3d 2f 62 69 6e 2f  olor.SHELL=/bin/
0000ffff`d30bf74d  62 61 73 68 00 48 49 53-54 53 49 5a 45 3d 31 30  bash.HISTSIZE=10
```

Note: We see that a hook function is installed for *memalign* and *realloc*. Please find the following documentation for hook functions here:

https://www.gnu.org/software/libc/manual/html_node/Hooks-for-Malloc.html

14. Explore the contents of memory pointed to by the *environ* variable:

```
0:001> dp environ
00000000`004d64c8  0000ffff`d30b8888 00000000`00000000
00000000`004d64d8  00000000`00000000 00000000`00000000
00000000`004d64e8  00000000`00000000 00000000`00000000
00000000`004d64f8  00000000`00000000 00000000`00000000
00000000`004d6508  00000000`00000000 00000000`00000000
```

```
00000000`004d6518  00000000`00000000 00000000`00000000
00000000`004d6528  00000000`00000000 00000000`00000000
00000000`004d6538  00000000`00000000 00000000`00000000

0:001> dp 0000ffff`d30b8888
0000ffff`d30b8888  0000ffff`d30bf6e2 0000ffff`d30bf6f6
0000ffff`d30b8898  0000ffff`d30bf716 0000ffff`d30bf72e
0000ffff`d30b88a8  0000ffff`d30bf742 0000ffff`d30bf752
0000ffff`d30b88b8  0000ffff`d30bf760 0000ffff`d30bf783
0000ffff`d30b88c8  0000ffff`d30bf79e 0000ffff`d30bf7b1
0000ffff`d30b88d8  0000ffff`d30bf7ba 0000ffff`d30bfe72
0000ffff`d30b88e8  0000ffff`d30bfe8b 0000ffff`d30bfee5
0000ffff`d30b88f8  0000ffff`d30bfeff 0000ffff`d30bff10

0:001> da 0000ffff`d30bf6e2
0000ffff`d30bf6e2  "XDG_SESSION_ID=6850"

0:001> dpa 0000ffff`d30b8888
0000ffff`d30b8888  0000ffff`d30bf6e2 "XDG_SESSION_ID=6850"
0000ffff`d30b8890  0000ffff`d30bf6f6 "HOSTNAME=instance-20211109-2004"
0000ffff`d30b8898  0000ffff`d30bf716 "SELINUX_ROLE_REQUESTED="
0000ffff`d30b88a0  0000ffff`d30bf72e "TERM=xterm-256color"
0000ffff`d30b88a8  0000ffff`d30bf742 "SHELL=/bin/bash"
0000ffff`d30b88b0  0000ffff`d30bf752 "HISTSIZE=1000"
0000ffff`d30b88b8  0000ffff`d30bf760 "SSH_CLIENT=37.228.238.120 61099 22"
0000ffff`d30b88c0  0000ffff`d30bf783 "SELINUX_USE_CURRENT_RANGE="
0000ffff`d30b88c8  0000ffff`d30bf79e "SSH_TTY=/dev/pts/1"
0000ffff`d30b88d0  0000ffff`d30bf7b1 "USER=opc"
0000ffff`d30b88d8  0000ffff`d30bf7ba "LS_COLORS=rs=0:di=38;5;27:ln=38;5;51:mh=44;38;5;15:pi=4"
0000ffff`d30b88e0  0000ffff`d30bfe72 "MAIL=/var/spool/mail/opc"
0000ffff`d30b88e8  0000ffff`d30bfe8b "PATH=/usr/local/bin:/usr/bin:/usr/local/sbin:/usr/sbin:"
0000ffff`d30b88f0  0000ffff`d30bfee5 "PWD=/home/opc/ALCDA2/App1"
0000ffff`d30b88f8  0000ffff`d30bfeff "LANG=en_US.UTF-8"
0000ffff`d30b8900  0000ffff`d30bff10 "SELINUX_LEVEL_REQUESTED="
```

19. Now we look at how to perform a memory search.

```
0:001> s 0`004c0000 0`004f0000 6
00000000`004c002a  06 9a 05 9b 04 9c 03 02-49 0a de dd dc db da d9  ........I.......
00000000`004c007e  06 9a 05 45 95 0a 96 09-46 9b 04 9c 03 6c 0a de  ...E....F....l..
00000000`004c012d  06 00 00 00 41 0e a0 01-9d 14 9e 13 41 0d 1d 46  ....A.......A..F
00000000`004c018d  06 9e 05 41 0d 1d 41 93-04 94 03 5b 0a de dd d4  ...A..A....[....
00000000`004c020d  06 9e 05 41 0d 1d 41 93-04 94 03 5b 0a de dd d4  ...A..A....[....
00000000`004c0285  06 9e 05 41 0d 1d 42 93-04 94 03 95 02 96 01 75  ...A..B........u
00000000`004c04fe  06 04 00 00 80 07 88 01-90 0b 00 b0 08 04 00 00  ................
00000000`004cfe78  06 00 00 00 00 00 00 00-50 01 3a cd fc ff 00 00  ........P.:.....
00000000`004d0048  06 00 00 00 00 00 00 00-40 f1 34 cb fc ff 00 00  ........@.4.....
00000000`004d1080  06 00 00 00 00 00 00 00-00 00 00 00 00 00 00 00  ................
00000000`004d7e00  06 00 00 00 00 00 00 00-00 00 00 00 00 00 00 00  ................
```

Note: It is possible to search through non-accessible regions as well; they are ignored:

```
0:001> s-q 0 Lffffff 6
00000000`0048b208  00000000`00000006 00000000`0000006f
00000000`0048be40  00000000`00000006 00000018`00000001
00000000`0048bf28  00000000`00000006 00000018`00000001
00000000`0048bfc0  00000000`00000006 00000018`00000001
00000000`00499f50  00000000`00000006 00000000`00498240
00000000`0049b728  00000000`00000006 00000000`00000002
00000000`004cfe78  00000000`00000006 0000fffc`cd3a0150
```

```
00000000`004d0048  00000000`00000006 0000fffc`cb34f140
00000000`004d1080  00000000`00000006 00000000`00000000
00000000`004d7e00  00000000`00000006 00000000`00000000
[...]
```

```
0:001> s-a 0000ffff`d30b88a8 L100000 "bin"
0000ffff`d30bf749  62 69 6e 2f 62 61 73 68-00 48 49 53 54 53 49 5a  bin/bash.HISTSIZ
0000ffff`d30bfe9b  62 69 6e 3a 2f 75 73 72-2f 62 69 6e 3a 2f 75 73  bin:/usr/bin:/us
0000ffff`d30bfea4  62 69 6e 3a 2f 75 73 72-2f 6c 6f 63 61 6c 2f 73  bin:/usr/local/s
0000ffff`d30bfeb4  62 69 6e 3a 2f 75 73 72-2f 73 62 69 6e 3a 2f 68  bin:/usr/sbin:/h
0000ffff`d30bfebe  62 69 6e 3a 2f 68 6f 6d-65 2f 6f 70 63 2f 2e 6c  bin:/home/opc/.l
0000ffff`d30bfed3  62 69 6e 3a 2f 68 6f 6d-65 2f 6f 70 63 2f 62 69  bin:/home/opc/bi
0000ffff`d30bfee1  62 69 6e 00 50 57 44 3d-2f 68 6f 6d 65 2f 6f 70  bin.PWD=/home/op
0000ffff`d30bffa5  62 69 6e 2f 6c 65 73 73-70 69 70 65 2e 73 68 20  bin/lesspipe.sh
```

Note: It is also possible to show all possible string fragments if any:

```
0:001> s-sa 0 Lfffffff
00000000`00400001  "ELF"
00000000`00400018  "D0@"
00000000`0040019c  "GNU"
00000000`004001bc  "GNU"
00000000`004001d1  "48y"
[...]
00000000`004a12b0  "weak version `"
00000000`004a12c0  "' not found (required by "
00000000`004a12e0  "version `"
00000000`004a12f0  "version lookup error"
00000000`004a1308  "cannot allocate version referenc"
00000000`004a1328  "e table"
00000000`004a1330  " of Verneed record"
00000000`004a1348  "RTLD_NEXT used in code not dynam"
00000000`004a1368  "ically loaded"
[...]
00000000`004d6588  "D?@"
00000000`004d7880  "@}M"
00000000`004d7d08  "xZM"
00000000`004d7d38  "peM"
00000000`01fa0700  "pnM"
00000000`01fa1680  "linux-vdso.so.1"
00000000`01fa16e0  "tls/atomics/"
```

15. To get process uid/gid and other useful data, use this WinDbg extension command:

```
0:000> !ntprpsinfo
NT_PRPSINFO (process info):
    state: 0, sname: t, zomb: 0, nice: 0, flag: 0x40400000
    uid: 1000, gid: 1000, pid: 21174, ppid: 20730, pgrp: 21174, sid: 20730
    fname: App1
    psargs: ./App1
```

16. Get the list of loaded modules:

```
0:001> lm
start             end                 module name
00000000`00400000 00000000`004e0000   App1       T (service symbols: ELF Export Symbols)
c:\alcda2\a64\app1\App1
```

```
0:001> lmv
start             end                 module name
00000000`00400000 00000000`004e0000   App1     T (service symbols: ELF Export Symbols)
c:\alcda2\a64\app1\App1
    Loaded symbol image file: App1
    Image path: /home/opc/ALCDA2/App1/App1
    Image name: App1
    Browse all global symbols  functions  data
    Timestamp:        unavailable (FFFFFFFE)
    CheckSum:         missing
    ImageSize:        000E0000
    Details:
0000fffc`cd3a0000 0000fffc`cd3b0000   linux_vdso_so T (service symbols: ELF In Memory Symbols)
    Loaded symbol image file: linux-vdso.so.1
    Image path: linux-vdso.so.1
    Image name: linux-vdso.so.1
    Browse all global symbols  functions  data
    Timestamp:        unavailable (FFFFFFFE)
    CheckSum:         missing
    ImageSize:        00010000
    Details:
```

Note: We don't see shared libraries except *vdso* (https://man7.org/linux/man-pages/man7/vdso.7.html) because they were statically linked. We also created the version of a dynamically linked *App1.shared* executable. If we load its core dump *App1.shared.core.22442* in the new instance of WinDbg, we see the list of shared libraries:

```
Microsoft (R) Windows Debugger Version 10.0.27725.1000 AMD64
Copyright (c) Microsoft Corporation. All rights reserved.


Loading Dump File [C:\ALCDA2\A64\App1\App1.shared.core.22442]
64-bit machine not using 64-bit API

************* Path validation summary **************
Response                         Time (ms)     Location
Deferred                                       srv*
Symbol search path is: srv*
Executable search path is:
Generic Unix Version 0 UP Free ARM 64-bit (AArch64)
System Uptime: not available
Process Uptime: not available
.....
*** WARNING: Unable to verify timestamp for libc-2.17.so
*** WARNING: Unable to verify timestamp for App1.shared
libc_2_17!nanosleep+0x24:
0000ffff`0496dd64 svc         #0

0:000> .logappend C:\ALCDA2\A64\App1\App1-WinDbg.log
Opened log file 'C:\ALCDA2\A64\App1\App1-WinDbg.log'

0:000> .sympath+ C:\ALCDA2\A64\App1
*** WARNING: Unable to verify timestamp for libc-2.17.so
Symbol search path is: srv*;C:\ALCDA2\A64\App1
Expanded Symbol search path is:
cache*;SRV*https://msdl.microsoft.com/download/symbols;c:\alcda2\a64\app1

************* Path validation summary **************
Response                         Time (ms)     Location
Deferred                                       srv*
```

```
OK                                              C:\ALCDA2\A64\App1

0:000> .reload
....*** WARNING: Unable to verify timestamp for libc-2.17.so
.
*** WARNING: Unable to verify timestamp for App1.shared

************* Symbol Loading Error Summary **************
Module name            Error
App1                   The system cannot find the file specified
libc-2.17              The system cannot find the file specified

You can troubleshoot most symbol related issues by turning on symbol loading diagnostics (!sym
noisy) and repeating the command that caused symbols to be loaded.
You should also verify that your symbol search path (.sympath) is correct.

0:000> lm
start             end                 module name
00000000`00400000 00000000`00430000   App1     T (service symbols: ELF Export Symbols)
c:\alcda2\a64\app1\App1.shared
0000ffff`048c0000 0000ffff`04a50000   libc_2_17 T (service symbols: ELF In Memory Symbols)
0000ffff`04a50000 0000ffff`04a90000   libpthread_2_17 T (service symbols: ELF In Memory
Symbols)
0000ffff`04ab0000 0000ffff`04ac0000   linux_vdso_so   (deferred)
0000ffff`04ac0000 0000ffff`04af1168   ld_2_17     (deferred)
```

17. Disassemble the *bar_one* function and follow the indirect *sleep* function call:

```
0:000> k
 # Child-SP          RetAddr               Call Site
00 0000ffff`048be750 0000ffff`0496da20     libc_2_17!nanosleep+0x24
01 0000ffff`048be790 00000000`00400738     libc_2_17!sleep+0x11c
02 0000ffff`048be990 00000000`0040074c     App1!bar_one+0x10
03 0000ffff`048be9a0 00000000`00400764     App1!foo_one+0xc
04 0000ffff`048be9b0 0000ffff`04a57d40     App1!thread_one+0x10
05 0000ffff`048be9d0 0000ffff`049a2d00     libpthread_2_17!_pthread_get_minstack+0x1394
06 0000ffff`048beb00 ffffffff`ffffffff     libc_2_17!clone+0x80
07 0000ffff`048beb00 00000000`00000000     0xffffffff`ffffffff

0:000> uf bar_one
App1!bar_one:
00000000`00400728 a9bf7bfd stp         fp,lr,[sp,#-0x10]!
00000000`0040072c 910003fd mov         fp,sp
00000000`00400730 12800000 mov         w0,#-1
00000000`00400734 97ffff93 bl          App1!$x+0x30 (00000000`00400580)
00000000`00400738 a8c17bfd ldp         fp,lr,[sp],#0x10
00000000`0040073c d65f03c0 ret

0:000> u 00000000`00400580
App1!$x+0x30:
00000000`00400580 90000110 adrp        xip0,App1!+0x18 (00000000`00420000)
00000000`00400584 f9400611 ldr         xip1,[xip0,#8]
00000000`00400588 91002210 add         xip0,xip0,#8
00000000`0040058c d61f0220 br          xip1
00000000`00400590 90000110 adrp        xip0,App1!+0x18 (00000000`00420000)
00000000`00400594 f9400a11 ldr         xip1,[xip0,#0x10]
00000000`00400598 91004210 add         xip0,xip0,#0x10
00000000`0040059c d61f0220 br          xip1
```

Note: XIP0/XIP1 are mnemonics for X16/X17 registers used for inter-procedure-call.

```
0:000> dp 00000000`00420000 + 8
00000000`00420008  0000ffff`0496d904 0000ffff`04a57fd0
00000000`00420018  00000000`00400550 00000000`00400550
00000000`00420028  00000000`00000000 00000000`00000000
00000000`00420038  00000000`00000000 00000000`00000000
00000000`00420048  00000000`00000000 00000000`00000000
00000000`00420058  00000000`00000000 00000000`00000000
00000000`00420068  00000000`00000000 00000000`00000000
00000000`00420078  00000000`00000000 00000000`00000000

0:000> u 0000ffff`0496d904
libc_2_17!sleep:
0000ffff`0496d904 d106c3ff sub      sp,sp,#0x1B0
0000ffff`0496d908 a9bb7bfd stp      fp,lr,[sp,#-0x50]!
0000ffff`0496d90c 910003fd mov      fp,sp
0000ffff`0496d910 a90153f3 stp      x19,x20,[sp,#0x10]
0000ffff`0496d914 a9025bf5 stp      x21,x22,[sp,#0x20]
0000ffff`0496d918 a90363f7 stp      x23,x24,[sp,#0x30]
0000ffff`0496d91c f90023f9 str      x25,[sp,#0x40]
0000ffff`0496d920 34000e40 cbz      w0,libc_2_17!sleep+0x1e4 (0000ffff`0496dae8)

0:000> ln 0000ffff`0496d904
Browse module
Set bu breakpoint

(0000ffff`0496d904)   libc_2_17!sleep
Exact matches:
    libc_2_17!sleep = <no type information>

0:000> dps 00000000`00420000 + 8
00000000`00420008  0000ffff`0496d904 libc_2_17!sleep
00000000`00420010  0000ffff`04a57fd0 libpthread_2_17!pthread_create
00000000`00420018  00000000`00400550 App1!$x
00000000`00420020  00000000`00400550 App1!$x
00000000`00420028  00000000`00000000
00000000`00420030  00000000`00000000
00000000`00420038  00000000`00000000
00000000`00420040  00000000`00000000
00000000`00420048  00000000`00000000
00000000`00420050  00000000`00000000
00000000`00420058  00000000`00000000
00000000`00420060  00000000`00000000
00000000`00420068  00000000`00000000
00000000`00420070  00000000`00000000
```

18. *App1.shared.pmap.22442* also shows library memory regions:

```
22442:   ./App1.shared
0000000000400000     64K r-x-- App1.shared
0000000000410000     64K r---- App1.shared
0000000000420000     64K rw--- App1.shared
0000000036a80000    192K rw---   [ anon ]
0000ffff02070000     64K -----   [ anon ]
0000ffff02080000   8192K rw---   [ anon ]
0000ffff02880000     64K -----   [ anon ]
0000ffff02890000   8192K rw---   [ anon ]
0000ffff03090000     64K -----   [ anon ]
0000ffff030a0000   8192K rw---   [ anon ]
```

```
0000ffff038a0000     64K -----    [ anon ]
0000ffff038b0000   8192K rw---    [ anon ]
0000ffff040b0000     64K -----    [ anon ]
0000ffff040c0000   8192K rw---    [ anon ]
0000ffff048c0000   1472K r-x-- libc-2.17.so
0000ffff04a30000     64K r---- libc-2.17.so
0000ffff04a40000     64K rw--- libc-2.17.so
0000ffff04a50000    128K r-x-- libpthread-2.17.so
0000ffff04a70000     64K r---- libpthread-2.17.so
0000ffff04a80000     64K rw--- libpthread-2.17.so
0000ffff04aa0000     64K r----    [ anon ]
0000ffff04ab0000     64K r-x--    [ anon ]
0000ffff04ac0000    128K r-x-- ld-2.17.so
0000ffff04ae0000     64K r---- ld-2.17.so
0000ffff04af0000     64K rw--- ld-2.17.so
0000ffffe2fc0000    192K rw---    [ stack ]
 total            44096K
```

Note: We can also see shared library mappings in the output of the **!address** command:

```
0:000> !address

Mapping file section regions...
Mapping module regions...

        BaseAddress      EndAddress+1        RegionSize     Type       State                 Protect             Usage
--------------------------------------------------------------------------------------------------------------------------
+        0`00000000        0`00400000        0`00400000                                                          <unknown>
+        0`00400000        0`00410000        0`00010000 MEM_PRIVATE MEM_COMMIT  PAGE_EXECUTE_READ                Image      [App1;
"/home/opc/ALCDA2/App1/App1.shared"]
+        0`00410000        0`00420000        0`00010000 MEM_PRIVATE MEM_COMMIT  PAGE_READONLY                    Image      [App1;
"/home/opc/ALCDA2/App1/App1.shared"]
+        0`00420000        0`00430000        0`00010000 MEM_PRIVATE MEM_COMMIT  PAGE_READWRITE                   Image      [App1;
"/home/opc/ALCDA2/App1/App1.shared"]
+        0`00430000        0`36a80000        0`36650000                                                          <unknown>
+        0`36a80000        0`36ab0000        0`00030000 MEM_PRIVATE MEM_COMMIT  PAGE_READWRITE                   <unknown>  [........Q.......]
+        0`36ab0000     ffff`02070000     fffe`cb5c0000                                                          <unknown>
+     ffff`02070000     ffff`02080000        0`00010000 MEM_PRIVATE MEM_COMMIT  PAGE_READONLY                    <unknown>  [................]
+     ffff`02080000     ffff`02880000        0`00800000 MEM_PRIVATE MEM_COMMIT  PAGE_READWRITE                   <unknown>  [................]
+     ffff`02880000     ffff`02890000        0`00010000 MEM_PRIVATE MEM_COMMIT  PAGE_READONLY                    <unknown>  [................]
+     ffff`02890000     ffff`03090000        0`00800000 MEM_PRIVATE MEM_COMMIT  PAGE_READWRITE                   <unknown>  [................]
+     ffff`03090000     ffff`030a0000        0`00010000 MEM_PRIVATE MEM_COMMIT  PAGE_READONLY                    <unknown>  [................]
+     ffff`030a0000     ffff`038a0000        0`00800000 MEM_PRIVATE MEM_COMMIT  PAGE_READWRITE                   <unknown>  [................]
+     ffff`038a0000     ffff`038b0000        0`00010000 MEM_PRIVATE MEM_COMMIT  PAGE_READONLY                    <unknown>  [................]
+     ffff`038b0000     ffff`040b0000        0`00800000 MEM_PRIVATE MEM_COMMIT  PAGE_READWRITE                   <unknown>  [................]
+     ffff`040b0000     ffff`040c0000        0`00010000 MEM_PRIVATE MEM_COMMIT  PAGE_READONLY                    <unknown>  [................]
+     ffff`040c0000     ffff`048c0000        0`00800000 MEM_PRIVATE MEM_COMMIT  PAGE_READWRITE                   <unknown>  [................]
+     ffff`048c0000     ffff`04a30000        0`00170000 MEM_PRIVATE MEM_COMMIT  PAGE_EXECUTE_READ                Image      [libc_2_17; "/usr/lib64/libc-
2.17.so"]
+     ffff`04a30000     ffff`04a40000        0`00010000 MEM_PRIVATE MEM_COMMIT  PAGE_READONLY                    Image      [libc_2_17; "/usr/lib64/libc-
2.17.so"]
+     ffff`04a40000     ffff`04a50000        0`00010000 MEM_PRIVATE MEM_COMMIT  PAGE_READWRITE                   Image      [libc_2_17; "/usr/lib64/libc-
2.17.so"]
+     ffff`04a50000     ffff`04a70000        0`00020000 MEM_PRIVATE MEM_COMMIT  PAGE_EXECUTE_READ                Image      [libpthread_2_17;
"/usr/lib64/libpthread-2.17.so"]
+     ffff`04a70000     ffff`04a80000        0`00010000 MEM_PRIVATE MEM_COMMIT  PAGE_READONLY                    Image      [libpthread_2_17;
"/usr/lib64/libpthread-2.17.so"]
+     ffff`04a80000     ffff`04a90000        0`00010000 MEM_PRIVATE MEM_COMMIT  PAGE_READWRITE                   Image      [libpthread_2_17;
"/usr/lib64/libpthread-2.17.so"]
+     ffff`04a90000     ffff`04ab0000        0`00020000                                                          <unknown>
+     ffff`04ab0000     ffff`04ac0000        0`00010000 MEM_PRIVATE MEM_COMMIT  PAGE_EXECUTE_READ                Image      [linux_vdso_so; "linux-
vdso.so.1"]
+     ffff`04ac0000     ffff`04ae0000        0`00020000 MEM_PRIVATE MEM_COMMIT  PAGE_EXECUTE_READ                Image      [ld_2_17; "/usr/lib64/ld-
2.17.so"]
+     ffff`04ae0000     ffff`04af0000        0`00010000 MEM_PRIVATE MEM_COMMIT  PAGE_READONLY                    Image      [ld_2_17; "/usr/lib64/ld-
2.17.so"]
+     ffff`04af0000     ffff`04b00000        0`00010000 MEM_PRIVATE MEM_COMMIT  PAGE_READWRITE                   Image      [ld_2_17; "/usr/lib64/ld-
2.17.so"]
+     ffff`04b00000     ffff`e2fc0000        0`de4c0000                                                          <unknown>
+     ffff`e2fc0000     ffff`e2ff0000        0`00030000 MEM_PRIVATE MEM_COMMIT  PAGE_READWRITE                   <unknown>  [................]
```

19. We close logging before exiting WinDbg sessions:

```
0:000> .logclose
Closing open log file 'C:\ALCDA2\A64\App1\App1-WinDbg.log'
```

We recommend exiting WinDbg after each exercise.

Exercise A2D

- **Goal:** Learn how to identify exceptions, find problem threads and CPU instructions
- **Patterns:** Crash Signature; NULL Pointer (Data); Active Thread (x64, GDB)
- \ALCDA-Dumps\Exercise-A2D-x64-GDB.pdf
- \ALCDA-Dumps\Exercise-A2D-A64-GDB.pdf
- \ALCDA-Dumps\Exercise-A2D-A64-WinDbg.pdf
- \ALCDA-Dumps\Exercise-A2D-x64-WinDbg.pdf

Exercise A2D (x64, GDB)

Goal: Learn how to identify exceptions, find problem threads and CPU instructions.

Patterns: Crash Signature; NULL Pointer (Data); Active Thread.

1. Load the *core.App2D* dump file and *App2D* executable from the x64/App2D directory:

```
~/ALCDA2/x64/App2D$ gdb -c core.App2D -se App2D
GNU gdb (Debian 8.2.1-2+b3) 8.2.1
Copyright (C) 2018 Free Software Foundation, Inc.
License GPLv3+: GNU GPL version 3 or later <http://gnu.org/licenses/gpl.html>
This is free software: you are free to change and redistribute it.
There is NO WARRANTY, to the extent permitted by law.
Type "show copying" and "show warranty" for details.
This GDB was configured as "x86_64-linux-gnu".
Type "show configuration" for configuration details.
For bug reporting instructions, please see:
<http://www.gnu.org/software/gdb/bugs/>.
Find the GDB manual and other documentation resources online at:
    <http://www.gnu.org/software/gdb/documentation/>.

For help, type "help".
Type "apropos word" to search for commands related to "word"...
Reading symbols from App2D...done.
[New LWP 3577]
[New LWP 3575]
[New LWP 3576]
[New LWP 3579]
[New LWP 3578]
[Thread debugging using libthread_db enabled]
Using host libthread_db library "/lib/x86_64-linux-gnu/libthread_db.so.1".
Core was generated by `./App2D'.
Program terminated with signal SIGSEGV, Segmentation fault.
#0  0x0000000000401bbd in procA ()
[Current thread is 1 (Thread 0x7faf71659700 (LWP 3577))]
```

2. Set logging to a file in case of lengthy output from some commands:

```
(gdb) set logging on App2D.log
Copying output to App2D.log.
```

3. List all threads:

```
(gdb) info threads
  Id   Target Id                          Frame
* 1    Thread 0x7faf71659700 (LWP 3577) 0x0000000000401bbd in procA ()
  2    Thread 0xb97880 (LWP 3575)       0x00000000004442a1 in clone ()
  3    Thread 0x7faf71e5a700 (LWP 3576) 0x0000000000441a50 in nanosleep ()
  4    Thread 0x7faf70657700 (LWP 3579) 0x00000000004442a1 in clone ()
  5    Thread 0x7faf70e58700 (LWP 3578) 0x0000000000441a50 in nanosleep ()
```

4. The problem thread seems to be the current thread:

```
(gdb) thread 1
[Switching to thread 1 (Thread 0x7faf71659700 (LWP 3577))]
#0  0x0000000000401bbd in procA ()
```

```
(gdb) bt
#0  0x0000000000401bbd in procA ()
#1  0x0000000000401c3b in bar_two ()
#2  0x0000000000401c4c in foo_two ()
#3  0x0000000000401c65 in thread_two ()
#4  0x0000000000403113 in start_thread (arg=<optimized out>) at pthread_create.c:486
#5  0x00000000004442af in clone ()
```

5. Disassemble the problem instruction and check CPU register(s) details (NULL data pointer):

```
(gdb) x/i 0x0000000000401bbd
=> 0x401bbd <procA+16>: movl   $0x1,(%rax)
```

```
(gdb) info r $rax
rax            0x0  0
```

```
(gdb) x $rax
   0x0: Cannot access memory at address 0x0
```

6. List all thread stack traces and identify other anomalies, such as non-waiting active threads:

```
(gdb) thread apply all bt

Thread 5 (Thread 0x7faf70e58700 (LWP 3578)):
#0  0x0000000000441a50 in nanosleep ()
#1  0x00000000004419da in sleep ()
#2  0x0000000000401c7a in bar_three () at pthread_create.c:688
#3  0x0000000000401c8b in foo_three () at pthread_create.c:688
#4  0x0000000000401ca4 in thread_three () at pthread_create.c:688
#5  0x0000000000403113 in start_thread (arg=<optimized out>) at pthread_create.c:486
#6  0x00000000004442af in clone ()

Thread 4 (Thread 0x7faf70657700 (LWP 3579)):
#0  0x00000000004442a1 in clone ()
#1  0x0000000000403020 in ?? () at pthread_create.c:362
#2  0x00007faf70657700 in ?? ()
#3  0x0000000000000000 in ?? ()

Thread 3 (Thread 0x7faf71e5a700 (LWP 3576)):
#0  0x0000000000441a50 in nanosleep ()
#1  0x00000000004419da in sleep ()
#2  0x0000000000401bfc in bar_one () at pthread_create.c:688
#3  0x0000000000401c0d in foo_one () at pthread_create.c:688
#4  0x0000000000401c26 in thread_one () at pthread_create.c:688
#5  0x0000000000403113 in start_thread (arg=<optimized out>) at pthread_create.c:486
#6  0x00000000004442af in clone ()

Thread 2 (Thread 0xb97880 (LWP 3575)):
#0  0x00000000004442a1 in clone ()
#1  0x0000000000401f4f in create_thread (pd=pd@entry=0x7faf70657700,
attr=attr@entry=0x7fffc8d6bcf0, stopped_start=stopped_start@entry=0x7fffc8d6bcee,
stackaddr=stackaddr@entry=0x7faf70656e80,
    thread_ran=thread_ran@entry=0x7fffc8d6bcef) at
../sysdeps/unix/sysv/linux/createthread.c:101
#2  0x0000000000403986 in __pthread_create_2_1 (newthread=<optimized out>, attr=<optimized
out>, start_routine=<optimized out>, arg=<optimized out>) at pthread_create.c:826
#3  0x0000000000401dac in main () at pthread_create.c:688
```

```
Thread 1 (Thread 0x7faf71659700 (LWP 3577)):
#0  0x0000000000401bbd in procA () at pthread_create.c:688
#1  0x0000000000401c3b in bar_two () at pthread_create.c:688
#2  0x0000000000401c4c in foo_two () at pthread_create.c:688
#3  0x0000000000401c65 in thread_two () at pthread_create.c:688
#4  0x0000000000403113 in start_thread (arg=<optimized out>) at pthread_create.c:486
#5  0x00000000004442af in clone ()
```

7. Check the CPU instruction and the stack pointer of thread #4 for any signs of stack overflow (unaccessible stack addresses below the current stack pointer):

```
(gdb) thread 4
[Switching to thread 4 (Thread 0x7faf70657700 (LWP 3579))]
#0  0x00000000004442a1 in clone ()

(gdb) bt
#0  0x00000000004442a1 in clone ()
#1  0x0000000000403020 in ?? () at pthread_create.c:362
#2  0x00007faf70657700 in ?? ()
#3  0x0000000000000000 in ?? ()

(gdb) x/i 0x00000000004442a1
=> 0x4442a1 <clone+49>: test   %rax,%rax

(gdb) x/gx $rsp
0x7faf70656e70: 0x0000000000403020

(gdb) x/gx $rsp-8
0x7faf70656e68: 0x0000000000000000

(gdb) x/gx $rsp-0x10
0x7faf70656e60: 0x0000000000000000
```

8. Switch to thread #2 and verify that the *main* function was being engaged in thread creation (this may correlate with the last thread #4 caught in being created):

```
(gdb) thread 2
[Switching to thread 2 (Thread 0xb97880 (LWP 3575))]
#0  0x00000000004442a1 in clone ()

(gdb) bt
#0  0x00000000004442a1 in clone ()
#1  0x0000000000401f4f in create_thread (pd=pd@entry=0x7faf70657700,
attr=attr@entry=0x7fffc8d6bcf0, stopped_start=stopped_start@entry=0x7fffc8d6bcee,
stackaddr=stackaddr@entry=0x7faf70656e80,
    thread_ran=thread_ran@entry=0x7fffc8d6bcef) at
../sysdeps/unix/sysv/linux/createthread.c:101
#2  0x0000000000403986 in __pthread_create_2_1 (newthread=<optimized out>, attr=<optimized
out>, start_routine=<optimized out>, arg=<optimized out>) at pthread_create.c:826
#3  0x0000000000401dac in main () at pthread_create.c:688

(gdb) disassemble main
Dump of assembler code for function main:
   0x0000000000401d29 <+0>:     push   %rbp
   0x0000000000401d2a <+1>:     mov    %rsp,%rbp
   0x0000000000401d2d <+4>:     sub    $0x40,%rsp
   0x0000000000401d31 <+8>:     mov    %edi,-0x34(%rbp)
   0x0000000000401d34 <+11>:    mov    %rsi,-0x40(%rbp)
   0x0000000000401d38 <+15>:    lea    -0x8(%rbp),%rax
```

```
   0x0000000000401d3c <+19>:    mov    $0x0,%ecx
   0x0000000000401d41 <+24>:    lea    -0x138(%rip),%rdx        # 0x401c10 <thread_one>
   0x0000000000401d48 <+31>:    mov    $0x0,%esi
   0x0000000000401d4d <+36>:    mov    %rax,%rdi
   0x0000000000401d50 <+39>:    callq  0x403400 <__pthread_create_2_1>
   0x0000000000401d55 <+44>:    lea    -0x10(%rbp),%rax
   0x0000000000401d59 <+48>:    mov    $0x0,%ecx
   0x0000000000401d5e <+53>:    lea    -0x116(%rip),%rdx        # 0x401c4f <thread_two>
   0x0000000000401d65 <+60>:    mov    $0x0,%esi
   0x0000000000401d6a <+65>:    mov    %rax,%rdi
   0x0000000000401d6d <+68>:    callq  0x403400 <__pthread_create_2_1>
   0x0000000000401d72 <+73>:    lea    -0x18(%rbp),%rax
   0x0000000000401d76 <+77>:    mov    $0x0,%ecx
   0x0000000000401d7b <+82>:    lea    -0xf4(%rip),%rdx        # 0x401c8e <thread_three>
   0x0000000000401d82 <+89>:    mov    $0x0,%esi
   0x0000000000401d87 <+94>:    mov    %rax,%rdi
   0x0000000000401d8a <+97>:    callq  0x403400 <__pthread_create_2_1>
   0x0000000000401d8f <+102>:   lea    -0x20(%rbp),%rax
   0x0000000000401d93 <+106>:   mov    $0x0,%ecx
   0x0000000000401d98 <+111>:   lea    -0xd2(%rip),%rdx        # 0x401ccd <thread_four>
   0x0000000000401d9f <+118>:   mov    $0x0,%esi
   0x0000000000401da4 <+123>:   mov    %rax,%rdi
   0x0000000000401da7 <+126>:   callq  0x403400 <__pthread_create_2_1>
   0x0000000000401dac <+131>:   lea    -0x28(%rbp),%rax
   0x0000000000401db0 <+135>:   mov    $0x0,%ecx
   0x0000000000401db5 <+140>:   lea    -0xb0(%rip),%rdx        # 0x401d0c <thread_five>
   0x0000000000401dbc <+147>:   mov    $0x0,%esi
   0x0000000000401dc1 <+152>:   mov    %rax,%rdi
   0x0000000000401dc4 <+155>:   callq  0x403400 <__pthread_create_2_1>
   0x0000000000401dc9 <+160>:   mov    $0x3,%edi
   0x0000000000401dce <+165>:   callq  0x4419a0 <sleep>
   0x0000000000401dd3 <+170>:   mov    $0x0,%eax
   0x0000000000401dd8 <+175>:   leaveq
   0x0000000000401dd9 <+176>:   retq
End of assembler dump.
```

Exercise A2D (A64, GDB)

Goal: Learn how to identify exceptions, find problem threads and CPU instructions.

Patterns: Crash Signature; NULL Pointer (Data).

1. Load the *core.14554* dump file and *App2D* executable from the A64/App2D directory:

```
~/ALCDA2/A64/App2D$ gdb-multiarch -c core.14554 -se App2D
GNU gdb (Debian 8.2.1-2+b3) 8.2.1
Copyright (C) 2018 Free Software Foundation, Inc.
License GPLv3+: GNU GPL version 3 or later <http://gnu.org/licenses/gpl.html>
This is free software: you are free to change and redistribute it.
There is NO WARRANTY, to the extent permitted by law.
Type "show copying" and "show warranty" for details.
This GDB was configured as "x86_64-linux-gnu".
Type "show configuration" for configuration details.
For bug reporting instructions, please see:
<http://www.gnu.org/software/gdb/bugs/>.
Find the GDB manual and other documentation resources online at:
    <http://www.gnu.org/software/gdb/documentation/>.

For help, type "help".
Type "apropos word" to search for commands related to "word"...
Reading symbols from App2D...(no debugging symbols found)...done.
[New LWP 14556]
[New LWP 14554]
[New LWP 14559]
[New LWP 14557]
[New LWP 14555]
[New LWP 14558]
Core was generated by `./App2D'.
Program terminated with signal SIGSEGV, Segmentation fault.
#0  0x00000000004031f8 in procA ()
[Current thread is 1 (LWP 14556)]
```

2. Set logging to a file in case of lengthy output from some commands:

```
(gdb) set logging on App2D.log
Copying output to App2D.log.
```

3. List all threads:

```
(gdb) info threads
  Id   Target Id         Frame
* 1    LWP 14556         0x00000000004031f8 in procA ()
  2    LWP 14554         0x000000000040c9f4 in nanosleep ()
  3    LWP 14559         0x000000000040c9f4 in nanosleep ()
  4    LWP 14557         0x000000000040c9f4 in nanosleep ()
  5    LWP 14555         0x000000000040c9f4 in nanosleep ()
  6    LWP 14558         0x000000000040c9f4 in nanosleep ()
```

4. The problem thread seems to be the current thread:

```
(gdb) thread 1
[Switching to thread 1 (LWP 14556)]
#0  0x00000000004031f8 in procA ()
```

```
(gdb) bt
#0  0x00000000004031f8 in procA ()
#1  0x000000000040327c in bar_two ()
#2  0x0000000000403290 in foo_two ()
#3  0x00000000004032a8 in thread_two ()
#4  0x0000000000404c74 in start_thread ()
#5  0x0000000000429ba0 in thread_start ()
```

5. Disassemble the problem instruction and check CPU register(s) details (NULL data pointer):

```
(gdb) x/i 0x00000000004031f8
=> 0x4031f8 <procA+16>: str     w1, [x0]
```

```
(gdb) info r x0
x0             0x0                 0
```

```
(gdb) x $x0
   0x0: Cannot access memory at address 0x0
```

6. List all thread stack traces to see any other possible anomalies, such as non-waiting active threads:

```
(gdb) thread apply all bt

Thread 6 (LWP 14558):
#0  0x000000000040c9f4 in nanosleep ()
#1  0x0000000000424cf4 in sleep ()
#2  0x0000000000403214 in proc ()
#3  0x0000000000403308 in bar_four ()
#4  0x000000000040331c in foo_four ()
#5  0x0000000000403334 in thread_four ()
#6  0x0000000000404c74 in start_thread ()
#7  0x0000000000429ba0 in thread_start ()

Thread 5 (LWP 14555):
#0  0x000000000040c9f4 in nanosleep ()
#1  0x0000000000424cf4 in sleep ()
#2  0x0000000000403238 in bar_one ()
#3  0x000000000040324c in foo_one ()
#4  0x0000000000403264 in thread_one ()
#5  0x0000000000404c74 in start_thread ()
#6  0x0000000000429ba0 in thread_start ()

Thread 4 (LWP 14557):
#0  0x000000000040c9f4 in nanosleep ()
#1  0x0000000000424cf4 in sleep ()
#2  0x00000000004032c4 in bar_three ()
#3  0x00000000004032d8 in foo_three ()
#4  0x00000000004032f0 in thread_three ()
#5  0x0000000000404c74 in start_thread ()
#6  0x0000000000429ba0 in thread_start ()

Thread 3 (LWP 14559):
#0  0x000000000040c9f4 in nanosleep ()
#1  0x0000000000424cf4 in sleep ()
#2  0x0000000000403350 in bar_five ()
#3  0x0000000000403364 in foo_five ()
#4  0x000000000040337c in thread_five ()
#5  0x0000000000404c74 in start_thread ()
#6  0x0000000000429ba0 in thread_start ()
```

```
Thread 2 (LWP 14554):
#0  0x000000000040c9f4 in nanosleep ()
#1  0x0000000000424cf4 in sleep ()
#2  0x0000000000403418 in main ()

Thread 1 (LWP 14556):
#0  0x00000000004031f8 in procA ()
#1  0x000000000040327c in bar_two ()
#2  0x0000000000403290 in foo_two ()
#3  0x00000000004032a8 in thread_two ()
#4  0x0000000000404c74 in start_thread ()
#5  0x0000000000429ba0 in thread_start ()
```

Exercise A2D (x64, WinDbg)

Goal: Learn how to identify exceptions, find problem threads and CPU instructions.

Patterns: Crash Signature; NULL Pointer (Data).

1. Launch WinDbg.

2. Load the *core.App2D* dump file from the x64\App2D folder:

```
Microsoft (R) Windows Debugger Version 10.0.27725.1000 AMD64
Copyright (c) Microsoft Corporation. All rights reserved.


Loading Dump File [C:\ALCDA2\x64\App2D\core.App2D]
64-bit machine not using 64-bit API

************* Path validation summary **************
Response                         Time (ms)     Location
Deferred                                       srv*
Symbol search path is: srv*
Executable search path is:
Generic Unix Version 0 UP Free x64
System Uptime: not available
Process Uptime: not available
..
(df7.df9): Signal SIGSEGV (Segmentation fault) code SEGV_MAPERR (Address not mapped to object)
at 0x0
*** WARNING: Unable to verify timestamp for App2D
App2D+0x1bbd:
00000000`00401bbd ???
```

3. Set logging to a file in case of lengthy output from some commands:

```
0:000> .logopen C:\ALCDA2\x64\App2D\App2D-WinDbg.log
Opened log file 'C:\ALCDA2\x64\App2D\App2D-WinDbg.log'
```

4. Specify the dump folder as the symbol path and reload symbols:

```
0:000> .symfix; .sympath+ C:\ALCDA2\x64\App2D\
Symbol search path is: srv*;C:\ALCDA2\x64\App2D\
Expanded Symbol search path is:
cache*;SRV*https://msdl.microsoft.com/download/symbols;c:\alcda2\x64\app2d\

************* Path validation summary **************
Response                         Time (ms)     Location
Deferred                                       srv*
OK                                             C:\ALCDA2\x64\App2D\
*** WARNING: Unable to verify timestamp for App2D

0:000> .reload
..
*** WARNING: Unable to verify timestamp for App2D

************* Symbol Loading Error Summary **************
Module name            Error
```

```
App2D                    The system cannot find the file specified

You can troubleshoot most symbol related issues by turning on symbol loading diagnostics (!sym
noisy) and repeating the command that caused symbols to be loaded.
You should also verify that your symbol search path (.sympath) is correct.
```

Note: We ignore warnings and errors as they are not relevant for now.

5. The problem thread seems to be the current thread:

```
0:000> kL
 # Child-SP          RetAddr           Call Site
00 00007faf`71658d78 00000000`00401c3b App2D!procA+0x10
01 00007faf`71658d88 00000000`00401c4c App2D!bar_two+0xe
02 00007faf`71658d98 00000000`00401c65 App2D!foo_two+0xe
03 00007faf`71658da8 00000000`00403113 App2D!thread_two+0x16
04 00007faf`71658dc0 00000000`004442af App2D!start_thread+0xf3
05 00007faf`71658e80 ffffffff`ffffffff App2D!_clone+0x3f
06 00007faf`71658e88 00000000`00000000 0xffffffff`ffffffff
```

6. Check the problem instruction and CPU register(s) details (NULL data pointer):

```
0:000> r
rax=0000000000000000 rbx=0000000000000000 rcx=00007faf71659700
rdx=d15304f943177aab rsi=0000000000000000 rdi=0000000000000000
rip=0000000000401bbd rsp=00007faf71658d78 rbp=00007faf71658d78
 r8=00007faf71659700  r9=00007faf71659700 r10=00007faf716599d0
r11=0000000000000202 r12=00007fffc8d6bcee r13=00007fffc8d6bcef
r14=00007faf71659700 r15=0000000000000000
iopl=0         nv up ei pl nz ac pe nc
cs=0033  ss=002b  ds=0000  es=0000  fs=0000  gs=0000             efl=00010212
App2D!procA+0x10:
00000000`00401bbd mov     dword ptr [rax],1      ds:00000000`00000000=????????
```

7. List all thread stack traces and check if there are other anomalies, such as non-waiting active threads:

```
0:000> ~*kL

Unable to get thread data for thread 0
.  0  Id: df7.df9 Suspend: 0 Teb: 00000000`00000000 Unfrozen
 # Child-SP          RetAddr           Call Site
00 00007faf`71658d78 00000000`00401c3b App2D!procA+0x10
01 00007faf`71658d88 00000000`00401c4c App2D!bar_two+0xe
02 00007faf`71658d98 00000000`00401c65 App2D!foo_two+0xe
03 00007faf`71658da8 00000000`00403113 App2D!thread_two+0x16
04 00007faf`71658dc0 00000000`004442af App2D!start_thread+0xf3
05 00007faf`71658e80 ffffffff`ffffffff App2D!_clone+0x3f
06 00007faf`71658e88 00000000`00000000 0xffffffff`ffffffff

Unable to get thread data for thread 1
   1  Id: df7.df7 Suspend: 0 Teb: 00000000`00000000 Unfrozen
 # Child-SP          RetAddr           Call Site
00 00007fff`c8d6bc48 00000000`00401f4f App2D!_clone+0x31
01 00007fff`c8d6bc50 00000000`00403986 App2D!create_thread+0x6f
02 00007fff`c8d6bc90 00000000`00401dac App2D!__pthread_create_2_1+0x400586
03 00007fff`c8d6bd70 00000000`004075c1 App2D!main+0x83
04 00007fff`c8d6bdc0 00000000`00401aba App2D!_libc_start_main+0x3d1
05 00007fff`c8d6bec0 ffffffff`ffffffff App2D!start+0x2a
06 00007fff`c8d6bec8 00000000`00000000 0xffffffff`ffffffff
```

```
Unable to get thread data for thread 2
   2  Id: df7.df8 Suspend: 0 Teb: 00000000`00000000 Unfrozen
 # Child-SP          RetAddr               Call Site
00 00007faf`71e59d10 00000000`004419da     App2D!nanosleep+0x40
01 00007faf`71e59d40 00000000`00401bfc     App2D!sleep+0x3a
02 00007faf`71e59d80 00000000`00401c0d     App2D!bar_one+0xe
03 00007faf`71e59d90 00000000`00401c26     App2D!foo_one+0xe
04 00007faf`71e59da0 00000000`00403113     App2D!thread_one+0x16
05 00007faf`71e59dc0 00000000`004442af     App2D!start_thread+0xf3
06 00007faf`71e59e80 ffffffff`ffffffff     App2D!_clone+0x3f
07 00007faf`71e59e88 00000000`00000000     0xffffffff`ffffffff

Unable to get thread data for thread 3
   3  Id: df7.dfb Suspend: 0 Teb: 00000000`00000000 Unfrozen
 # Child-SP          RetAddr               Call Site
00 00007faf`70656e70 00000000`00403020     App2D!_clone+0x31
01 00007faf`70656e78 00000000`00000000     App2D!start_thread

Unable to get thread data for thread 4
   4  Id: df7.dfa Suspend: 0 Teb: 00000000`00000000 Unfrozen
 # Child-SP          RetAddr               Call Site
00 00007faf`70e57d10 00000000`004419da     App2D!nanosleep+0x40
01 00007faf`70e57d40 00000000`00401c7a     App2D!sleep+0x3a
02 00007faf`70e57d80 00000000`00401c8b     App2D!bar_three+0xe
03 00007faf`70e57d90 00000000`00401ca4     App2D!foo_three+0xe
04 00007faf`70e57da0 00000000`00403113     App2D!thread_three+0x16
05 00007faf`70e57dc0 00000000`004442af     App2D!start_thread+0xf3
06 00007faf`70e57e80 ffffffff`ffffffff     App2D!_clone+0x3f
07 00007faf`70e57e88 00000000`00000000     0xffffffff`ffffffff
```

Note: There are two other active threads, #1 and #3.

9. Let's look at thread #1 and check the current CPU instruction and the stack pointer for any signs of stack overflow (unaccessible stack addresses below the current stack pointer):

```
0:000> ~1s
App2D!_clone+0x31:
00000000`004442a1 test    rax,rax

0:001> kL
 # Child-SP          RetAddr               Call Site
00 00007fff`c8d6bc48 00000000`00401f4f     App2D!_clone+0x31
01 00007fff`c8d6bc50 00000000`00403986     App2D!create_thread+0x6f
02 00007fff`c8d6bc90 00000000`00401dac     App2D!__pthread_create_2_1+0x400586
03 00007fff`c8d6bd70 00000000`004075c1     App2D!main+0x83
04 00007fff`c8d6bdc0 00000000`00401aba     App2D!_libc_start_main+0x3d1
05 00007fff`c8d6bec0 ffffffff`ffffffff     App2D!start+0x2a
06 00007fff`c8d6bec8 00000000`00000000     0xffffffff`ffffffff

0:001> r
rax=0000000000000dfb rbx=00007faf70657700 rcx=00000000004442a1
rdx=00007faf706579d0 rsi=00007faf70656e70 rdi=00000000003d0f00
rip=00000000004442a1 rsp=00007fffc8d6bc48 rbp=00007fffc8d6bcf0
 r8=00007faf70657700  r9=00007faf70657700 r10=00007faf706579d0
r11=0000000000000202 r12=00007fffc8d6bcee r13=00007fffc8d6bcef
r14=00007faf70657700 r15=0000000000000000
iopl=0         nv up ei pl nz na pe nc
cs=0033  ss=002b  ds=0000  es=0000  fs=0000  gs=0000             efl=00000202
```

```
App2D!_clone+0x31:
00000000`004442a1 test    rax,rax

0:001> dp @rsp-20
00007fff`c8d6bc28  00000000`0041b51a 00000000`00498999
00007fff`c8d6bc38  00000000`004463cb 00000000`00b98eb0
00007fff`c8d6bc48  00000000`00401f4f 00007faf`706579d0
00007fff`c8d6bc58  00007faf`70657700 00007fff`c8d6bd60
00007fff`c8d6bc68  00007faf`70657700 00007fff`c8d6bd60
00007fff`c8d6bc78  00007faf`70656e80 00007fff`c8d6bcf0
00007fff`c8d6bc88  00000000`00403986 00000000`00000170
00007fff`c8d6bc98  00007faf`706579c0 00000035`00000000
```

8. Similar results are for thread #3:

```
0:001> ~3s
App2D!_clone+0x31:
00000000`004442a1 test    rax,rax

0:003> kL
 # Child-SP          RetAddr           Call Site
00 00007faf`70656e70 00000000`00403020 App2D!_clone+0x31
01 00007faf`70656e78 00000000`00000000 App2D!start_thread

0:003> r
rax=0000000000000000 rbx=00007faf70657700 rcx=00000000004442a1
rdx=00007faf706579d0 rsi=00007faf70656e70 rdi=00000000003d0f00
rip=00000000004442a1 rsp=00007faf70656e70 rbp=00007fffc8d6bcf0
 r8=00007faf70657700  r9=00007faf70657700 r10=00007faf706579d0
r11=0000000000000202 r12=00007fffc8d6bcee r13=00007fffc8d6bcef
r14=00007faf70657700 r15=0000000000000000
iopl=0         nv up ei pl nz na pe nc
cs=0033  ss=002b  ds=0000  es=0000  fs=0000  gs=0000             efl=00000202
App2D!_clone+0x31:
00000000`004442a1 test    rax,rax

0:003> dp @rsp-20
00007faf`70656e50  00000000`00000000 00000000`00000000
00007faf`70656e60  00000000`00000000 00000000`00000000
00007faf`70656e70  00000000`00403020 00007faf`70657700
00007faf`70656e80  00000000`00000000 00000000`00000000
00007faf`70656e90  00000000`00000000 00000000`00000000
00007faf`70656ea0  00000000`00000000 00000000`00000000
00007faf`70656eb0  00000000`00000000 00000000`00000000
00007faf`70656ec0  00000000`00000000 00000000`00000000
```

9. We close logging before exiting WinDbg:

```
0:000> .logclose
Closing open log file 'C:\ALCDA2\x64\App2D\App2D-WinDbg.log'
```

Exercise A2D (A64, WinDbg)

Goal: Learn how to identify exceptions, find problem threads and CPU instructions.

Patterns: Crash Signature; NULL Pointer (Data).

1. Launch WinDbg.

2. Load the *core.14554* dump file from the A64\App2D folder:

```
Microsoft (R) Windows Debugger Version 10.0.27725.1000 AMD64
Copyright (c) Microsoft Corporation. All rights reserved.


Loading Dump File [C:\ALCDA2\A64\App2D\core.14554]
64-bit machine not using 64-bit API

************* Path validation summary **************
Response                         Time (ms)     Location
Deferred                                       srv*
Symbol search path is: srv*
Executable search path is:
Generic Unix Version 0 UP Free ARM 64-bit (AArch64)
System Uptime: not available
Process Uptime: not available
..
(38da.38dc): Signal SIGSEGV (Segmentation fault) code SEGV_MAPERR (Address not mapped to
object) at 0x0
*** WARNING: Unable to verify timestamp for App2D
App2D+0x31f8:
00000000`004031f8 str         w1,[x0]
```

3. Set logging to a file in case of lengthy output from some commands:

```
0:000> .logopen C:\ALCDA2\A64\App2D\App2D-WinDbg.log
Opened log file 'C:\ALCDA2\A64\App2D\App2D-WinDbg.log'
```

4. Specify the dump folder as the symbol path and reload symbols:

```
0:000> .symfix; .sympath+ C:\ALCDA2\A64\App2D\
Symbol search path is: srv*;C:\ALCDA2\A64\App2D\
Expanded Symbol search path is:
cache*;SRV*https://msdl.microsoft.com/download/symbols;c:\alcda2\a64\app2d\

************* Path validation summary **************
Response                         Time (ms)     Location
Deferred                                       srv*
OK                                             C:\ALCDA2\A64\App2D\
*** WARNING: Unable to verify timestamp for App2D

0:000> .reload
..
*** WARNING: Unable to verify timestamp for App2D

************* Symbol Loading Error Summary **************
Module name            Error
```

```
App2D                       The system cannot find the file specified

You can troubleshoot most symbol related issues by turning on symbol loading diagnostics (!sym
noisy) and repeating the command that caused symbols to be loaded.
You should also verify that your symbol search path (.sympath) is correct.
```

Note: We ignore warnings and errors as they are not relevant for now.

5. The problem thread seems to be the current thread:

```
0:000> k
 # Child-SP          RetAddr               Call Site
00 0000fffe`1eeee810 00000000`0040327c     App2D!procA+0x10
01 0000fffe`1eeee820 00000000`00403290     App2D!bar_two+0xc
02 0000fffe`1eeee830 00000000`004032a8     App2D!foo_two+0xc
03 0000fffe`1eeee840 00000000`00404c74     App2D!thread_two+0x10
04 0000fffe`1eeee860 00000000`00429ba0     App2D!start_thread+0xb4
05 0000fffe`1eeee990 ffffffff`ffffffff     App2D!thread_start+0x30
06 0000fffe`1eeee990 00000000`00000000     0xffffffff`ffffffff
```

6. Check the problem instruction and CPU register(s) details (NULL data pointer):

```
0:000> r
 x0=0000000000000000   x1=0000000000000001   x2=0000fffe1eeef080   x3=3a2398bf2f00aa18
 x4=0000fffe1eeee860   x5=3a23674131ee4278   x6=0000fffe1eeef150   x7=0000000000000000
 x8=0000000000000063   x9=0000000000800000  x10=0000000000404bc0  x11=00000000003d0f00
x12=0000fffe1eeef080  x13=0000000000000000  x14=0000000000000000  x15=0000000000000000
x16=00000000004d0010  x17=0000000000424000  x18=0000000000000110  x19=0000fffe1eeef080
x20=0000000000000000  x21=00000000004d0000  x22=0000000000403298  x23=0000000000000000
x24=0000fffe1eeef770  x25=00000000301b06f0  x26=00000000004d7890  x27=0000000000010000
x28=0000000000810000   fp=0000fffe1eeee820   lr=000000000040327c   sp=0000fffe1eeee810
 pc=00000000004031f8  psr=20001000 --C- EL0
App2D!procA+0x10:
00000000`004031f8 b9000001 str         w1,[x0]
```

7. List all thread stack traces and check if there are other anomalies, such as non-waiting active threads:

```
0:000> ~*k

Unable to get thread data for thread 0
.  0  Id: 38da.38dc Suspend: 0 Teb: 00000000`00000000 Unfrozen
 # Child-SP          RetAddr               Call Site
00 0000fffe`1eeee810 00000000`0040327c     App2D!procA+0x10
01 0000fffe`1eeee820 00000000`00403290     App2D!bar_two+0xc
02 0000fffe`1eeee830 00000000`004032a8     App2D!foo_two+0xc
03 0000fffe`1eeee840 00000000`00404c74     App2D!thread_two+0x10
04 0000fffe`1eeee860 00000000`00429ba0     App2D!start_thread+0xb4
05 0000fffe`1eeee990 ffffffff`ffffffff     App2D!thread_start+0x30
06 0000fffe`1eeee990 00000000`00000000     0xffffffff`ffffffff

Unable to get thread data for thread 1
   1  Id: 38da.38da Suspend: 0 Teb: 00000000`00000000 Unfrozen
 # Child-SP          RetAddr               Call Site
00 0000ffff`dbdf3ec0 00000000`00424cf4     App2D!_libc_nanosleep+0x24
01 0000ffff`dbdf3f00 00000000`00403418     App2D!sleep+0x110
02 0000ffff`dbdf40f0 00000000`0040ec8c     App2D!main+0x90
03 0000ffff`dbdf4140 00000000`00403090     App2D!_libc_start_main+0x304
04 0000ffff`dbdf42a0 00000000`00000000     App2D!start+0x4c
```

```
Unable to get thread data for thread 2
   2  Id: 38da.38df Suspend: 0 Teb: 00000000`00000000 Unfrozen
 # Child-SP          RetAddr               Call Site
00 0000fffe`1d6be5f0 00000000`00424cf4     App2D!_libc_nanosleep+0x24
01 0000fffe`1d6be630 00000000`00403350     App2D!sleep+0x110
02 0000fffe`1d6be820 00000000`00403364     App2D!bar_five+0x10
03 0000fffe`1d6be830 00000000`0040337c     App2D!foo_five+0xc
04 0000fffe`1d6be840 00000000`00404c74     App2D!thread_five+0x10
05 0000fffe`1d6be860 00000000`00429ba0     App2D!start_thread+0xb4
06 0000fffe`1d6be990 ffffffff`ffffffff     App2D!thread_start+0x30
07 0000fffe`1d6be990 00000000`00000000     0xffffffff`ffffffff

Unable to get thread data for thread 3
   3  Id: 38da.38dd Suspend: 0 Teb: 00000000`00000000 Unfrozen
 # Child-SP          RetAddr               Call Site
00 0000fffe`1e6de5f0 00000000`00424cf4     App2D!_libc_nanosleep+0x24
01 0000fffe`1e6de630 00000000`004032c4     App2D!sleep+0x110
02 0000fffe`1e6de820 00000000`004032d8     App2D!bar_three+0x10
03 0000fffe`1e6de830 00000000`004032f0     App2D!foo_three+0xc
04 0000fffe`1e6de840 00000000`00404c74     App2D!thread_three+0x10
05 0000fffe`1e6de860 00000000`00429ba0     App2D!start_thread+0xb4
06 0000fffe`1e6de990 ffffffff`ffffffff     App2D!thread_start+0x30
07 0000fffe`1e6de990 00000000`00000000     0xffffffff`ffffffff

Unable to get thread data for thread 4
   4  Id: 38da.38db Suspend: 0 Teb: 00000000`00000000 Unfrozen
 # Child-SP          RetAddr               Call Site
00 0000fffe`1f6fe5f0 00000000`00424cf4     App2D!_libc_nanosleep+0x24
01 0000fffe`1f6fe630 00000000`00403238     App2D!sleep+0x110
02 0000fffe`1f6fe820 00000000`0040324c     App2D!bar_one+0x10
03 0000fffe`1f6fe830 00000000`00403264     App2D!foo_one+0xc
04 0000fffe`1f6fe840 00000000`00404c74     App2D!thread_one+0x10
05 0000fffe`1f6fe860 00000000`00429ba0     App2D!start_thread+0xb4
06 0000fffe`1f6fe990 ffffffff`ffffffff     App2D!thread_start+0x30
07 0000fffe`1f6fe990 00000000`00000000     0xffffffff`ffffffff

Unable to get thread data for thread 5
   5  Id: 38da.38de Suspend: 0 Teb: 00000000`00000000 Unfrozen
 # Child-SP          RetAddr               Call Site
00 0000fffe`1dece5d0 00000000`00424cf4     App2D!_libc_nanosleep+0x24
01 0000fffe`1dece610 00000000`00403214     App2D!sleep+0x110
02 0000fffe`1dece800 00000000`00403308     App2D!procB+0x10
03 0000fffe`1dece820 00000000`0040331c     App2D!bar_four+0xc
04 0000fffe`1dece830 00000000`00403334     App2D!foo_four+0xc
05 0000fffe`1dece840 00000000`00404c74     App2D!thread_four+0x10
06 0000fffe`1dece860 00000000`00429ba0     App2D!start_thread+0xb4
07 0000fffe`1dece990 ffffffff`ffffffff     App2D!thread_start+0x30
08 0000fffe`1dece990 00000000`00000000     0xffffffff`ffffffff
```

Note: There are no other active threads.

8. We close logging before exiting WinDbg:

```
0:000> .logclose
Closing open log file 'C:\ALCDA2\A64\App2D\App2D-WinDbg.log'
```

Exercise A2C

- **Goal:** Learn how to identify exceptions, find problem threads and CPU instructions

- **Patterns:** NULL Pointer (Code); Disassembly Ambiguity (WinDbg)

- \ALCDA-Dumps\Exercise-A2C-x64-GDB.pdf
- \ALCDA-Dumps\Exercise-A2C-A64-GDB.pdf

- \ALCDA-Dumps\Exercise-A2C-A64-WinDbg.pdf
- \ALCDA-Dumps\Exercise-A2C-x64-WinDbg.pdf

Exercise A2C (x64, GDB)

Goal: Learn how to identify exceptions, find problem threads and CPU instructions.

Patterns: NULL Pointer (Code).

1. Load the *core.App2C* dump file and *App2C* executable from the x64/App2C directory:

```
~/ALCDA2/x64/App2C$ gdb -c core.App2C -se App2C
GNU gdb (Debian 8.2.1-2+b3) 8.2.1
Copyright (C) 2018 Free Software Foundation, Inc.
License GPLv3+: GNU GPL version 3 or later <http://gnu.org/licenses/gpl.html>
This is free software: you are free to change and redistribute it.
There is NO WARRANTY, to the extent permitted by law.
Type "show copying" and "show warranty" for details.
This GDB was configured as "x86_64-linux-gnu".
Type "show configuration" for configuration details.
For bug reporting instructions, please see:
<http://www.gnu.org/software/gdb/bugs/>.
Find the GDB manual and other documentation resources online at:
    <http://www.gnu.org/software/gdb/documentation/>.

For help, type "help".
Type "apropos word" to search for commands related to "word"...
Reading symbols from App2C...done.
[New LWP 3651]
[New LWP 3647]
[New LWP 3648]
[New LWP 3650]
[New LWP 3649]
[New LWP 3652]
[Thread debugging using libthread_db enabled]
Using host libthread_db library "/lib/x86_64-linux-gnu/libthread_db.so.1".
Core was generated by `./App2C'.
Program terminated with signal SIGSEGV, Segmentation fault.
#0  0x0000000000000000 in ?? ()
[Current thread is 1 (Thread 0x7f7d259c4700 (LWP 3651))]
```

2. Set logging to a file in case of lengthy output from some commands:

```
(gdb) set logging on App2C.log
Copying output to App2C.log.
```

3. List all threads:

```
(gdb) info threads
  Id   Target Id                            Frame
* 1    Thread 0x7f7d259c4700 (LWP 3651) 0x0000000000000000 in ?? ()
  2    Thread 0x1bd4880 (LWP 3647)      0x0000000000441a60 in nanosleep ()
  3    Thread 0x7f7d271c7700 (LWP 3648) 0x0000000000441a60 in nanosleep ()
  4    Thread 0x7f7d261c5700 (LWP 3650) 0x0000000000441a60 in nanosleep ()
  5    Thread 0x7f7d269c6700 (LWP 3649) 0x0000000000441a60 in nanosleep ()
  6    Thread 0x7f7d251c3700 (LWP 3652) 0x0000000000441a60 in nanosleep ()
```

4. The problem thread seems to be the current thread:

```
(gdb) bt
#0  0x0000000000000000 in ?? ()
#1  0x0000000000401bf9 in proc ()
#2  0x0000000000401cc7 in bar_four ()
#3  0x0000000000401cd8 in foo_four ()
#4  0x0000000000401cf1 in thread_four ()
#5  0x0000000000403123 in start_thread (arg=<optimized out>) at pthread_create.c:486
#6  0x00000000004442bf in clone ()
```

Note: It looks like our GDB version prints the non-existent *proc* function instead of *procB*.

```
(gdb) disassemble proc
No symbol "proc" in current context.
```

5. Check the CPU instruction and a dereferenced pointer for any signs of a NULL pointer:

```
(gdb) disassemble procB
Dump of assembler code for function procB:
   0x0000000000401bd4 <+0>:     push   %rbp
   0x0000000000401bd5 <+1>:     mov    %rsp,%rbp
   0x0000000000401bd8 <+4>:     sub    $0x10,%rsp
   0x0000000000401bdc <+8>:     mov    $0x1,%edi
   0x0000000000401be1 <+13>:    callq  0x4419b0 <sleep>
   0x0000000000401be6 <+18>:    movq   $0x0,-0x8(%rbp)
   0x0000000000401bee <+26>:    mov    -0x8(%rbp),%rdx
   0x0000000000401bf2 <+30>:    mov    $0x0,%eax
   0x0000000000401bf7 <+35>:    callq  *%rdx
   0x0000000000401bf9 <+37>:    nop
   0x0000000000401bfa <+38>:    leaveq
   0x0000000000401bfb <+39>:    retq
End of assembler dump.

(gdb) info r rdx
rdx            0x0  0
```

6. List all thread stack traces to check for other anomalies, such as non-waiting active threads:

```
(gdb) thread apply all bt

Thread 6 (Thread 0x7f7d251c3700 (LWP 3652)):
#0  0x0000000000441a60 in nanosleep ()
#1  0x00000000004419ea in sleep ()
#2  0x0000000000401d06 in bar_five () at pthread_create.c:688
#3  0x0000000000401d17 in foo_five () at pthread_create.c:688
#4  0x0000000000401d30 in thread_five () at pthread_create.c:688
#5  0x0000000000403123 in start_thread (arg=<optimized out>) at pthread_create.c:486
#6  0x00000000004442bf in clone ()

Thread 5 (Thread 0x7f7d269c6700 (LWP 3649)):
#0  0x0000000000441a60 in nanosleep ()
#1  0x00000000004419ea in sleep ()
#2  0x0000000000401bbf in procA () at pthread_create.c:688
#3  0x0000000000401c49 in bar_two () at pthread_create.c:688
#4  0x0000000000401c5a in foo_two () at pthread_create.c:688
#5  0x0000000000401c73 in thread_two () at pthread_create.c:688
#6  0x0000000000403123 in start_thread (arg=<optimized out>) at pthread_create.c:486
#7  0x00000000004442bf in clone ()
```

```
Thread 4 (Thread 0x7f7d261c5700 (LWP 3650)):
#0  0x0000000000441a60 in nanosleep ()
#1  0x00000000004419ea in sleep ()
#2  0x0000000000401c88 in bar_three () at pthread_create.c:688
#3  0x0000000000401c99 in foo_three () at pthread_create.c:688
#4  0x0000000000401cb2 in thread_three () at pthread_create.c:688
#5  0x0000000000403123 in start_thread (arg=<optimized out>) at pthread_create.c:486
#6  0x00000000004442bf in clone ()

Thread 3 (Thread 0x7f7d271c7700 (LWP 3648)):
#0  0x0000000000441a60 in nanosleep ()
#1  0x00000000004419ea in sleep ()
#2  0x0000000000401c0a in bar_one () at pthread_create.c:688
#3  0x0000000000401c1b in foo_one () at pthread_create.c:688
#4  0x0000000000401c34 in thread_one () at pthread_create.c:688
#5  0x0000000000403123 in start_thread (arg=<optimized out>) at pthread_create.c:486
#6  0x00000000004442bf in clone ()

Thread 2 (Thread 0x1bd4880 (LWP 3647)):
#0  0x0000000000441a60 in nanosleep ()
#1  0x00000000004419ea in sleep ()
#2  0x0000000000401de1 in main () at pthread_create.c:688

Thread 1 (Thread 0x7f7d259c4700 (LWP 3651)):
#0  0x0000000000000000 in ?? ()
#1  0x0000000000401bf9 in proc () at pthread_create.c:688
#2  0x0000000000401cc7 in bar_four () at pthread_create.c:688
#3  0x0000000000401cd8 in foo_four () at pthread_create.c:688
#4  0x0000000000401cf1 in thread_four () at pthread_create.c:688
#5  0x0000000000403123 in start_thread (arg=<optimized out>) at pthread_create.c:486
#6  0x00000000004442bf in clone ()
```

Exercise A2C (A64, GDB)

Goal: Learn how to identify exceptions, find problem threads and CPU instructions.

Patterns: NULL Pointer (Code).

1. Load the *core.24559* dump file and *App2C* executable from the A64/App2C directory:

```
~/ALCDA2/A64/App2C$ gdb-multiarch -c core.24559 -se App2C
GNU gdb (Debian 8.2.1-2+b3) 8.2.1
Copyright (C) 2018 Free Software Foundation, Inc.
License GPLv3+: GNU GPL version 3 or later <http://gnu.org/licenses/gpl.html>
This is free software: you are free to change and redistribute it.
There is NO WARRANTY, to the extent permitted by law.
Type "show copying" and "show warranty" for details.
This GDB was configured as "x86_64-linux-gnu".
Type "show configuration" for configuration details.
For bug reporting instructions, please see:
<http://www.gnu.org/software/gdb/bugs/>.
Find the GDB manual and other documentation resources online at:
    <http://www.gnu.org/software/gdb/documentation/>.

For help, type "help".
Type "apropos word" to search for commands related to "word"...
Reading symbols from App2C...(no debugging symbols found)...done.
[New LWP 24563]
[New LWP 24559]
[New LWP 24560]
[New LWP 24561]
[New LWP 24564]
[New LWP 24562]
Core was generated by `./App2C'.
Program terminated with signal SIGSEGV, Segmentation fault.
#0  0x0000000000000000 in ?? ()
[Current thread is 1 (LWP 24563)]
```

2. Set logging to a file in case of lengthy output from some commands:

```
(gdb) set logging on App2C.log
Copying output to App2C.log.
```

3. List all threads:

```
(gdb) info threads
  Id   Target Id         Frame
* 1    LWP 24563         0x0000000000000000 in ?? ()
  2    LWP 24559         0x000000000040c9f4 in nanosleep ()
  3    LWP 24560         0x000000000040c9f4 in nanosleep ()
  4    LWP 24561         0x000000000040c9f4 in nanosleep ()
  5    LWP 24564         0x000000000040c9f4 in nanosleep ()
  6    LWP 24562         0x000000000040c9f4 in nanosleep ()
```

4. The problem thread seems to be the current thread:

```
(gdb) bt
#0  0x0000000000000000 in ?? ()
#1  0x000000000040322c in proc ()
#2  0x0000000000403314 in bar_four ()
#3  0x0000000000403328 in foo_four ()
#4  0x0000000000403340 in thread_four ()
#5  0x0000000000404c74 in start_thread ()
#6  0x0000000000429ba0 in thread_start ()
```

Note: It looks like our GDB version prints the non-existent *proc* function instead of *procB*.

```
(gdb) disassemble proc
No symbol table is loaded.  Use the "file" command.
```

5. Check the CPU instruction and a dereferenced pointer for any signs of a NULL pointer:

```
(gdb) disassemble procB
Dump of assembler code for function procB:
   0x0000000000403210 <+0>:     stp     x29, x30, [sp, #-32]!
   0x0000000000403214 <+4>:     mov     x29, sp
   0x0000000000403218 <+8>:     mov     w0, #0x1                          // #1
   0x000000000040321c <+12>:    bl      0x424be4 <sleep>
   0x0000000000403220 <+16>:    str     xzr, [x29, #24]
   0x0000000000403224 <+20>:    ldr     x0, [x29, #24]
   0x0000000000403228 <+24>:    blr     x0
   0x000000000040322c <+28>:    ldp     x29, x30, [sp], #32
   0x0000000000403230 <+32>:    ret
End of assembler dump.
```

```
(gdb) info r x0
x0             0x0   0
```

6. List all thread stack traces to check for other anomalies, such as non-waiting active threads:

```
(gdb) thread apply all bt

Thread 6 (LWP 24562):
#0  0x000000000040c9f4 in nanosleep ()
#1  0x0000000000424cf4 in sleep ()
#2  0x00000000004032d0 in bar_three ()
#3  0x00000000004032e4 in foo_three ()
#4  0x00000000004032fc in thread_three ()
#5  0x0000000000404c74 in start_thread ()
#6  0x0000000000429ba0 in thread_start ()

Thread 5 (LWP 24564):
#0  0x000000000040c9f4 in nanosleep ()
#1  0x0000000000424cf4 in sleep ()
#2  0x000000000040335c in bar_five ()
#3  0x0000000000403370 in foo_five ()
#4  0x0000000000403388 in thread_five ()
#5  0x0000000000404c74 in start_thread ()
#6  0x0000000000429ba0 in thread_start ()

Thread 4 (LWP 24561):
#0  0x000000000040c9f4 in nanosleep ()
#1  0x0000000000424cf4 in sleep ()
#2  0x00000000004031f8 in procA ()
```

```
#3  0x0000000000403288 in bar_two ()
#4  0x000000000040329c in foo_two ()
#5  0x00000000004032b4 in thread_two ()
#6  0x0000000000404c74 in start_thread ()
#7  0x0000000000429ba0 in thread_start ()

Thread 3 (LWP 24560):
#0  0x000000000040c9f4 in nanosleep ()
#1  0x0000000000424cf4 in sleep ()
#2  0x0000000000403244 in bar_one ()
#3  0x0000000000403258 in foo_one ()
#4  0x0000000000403270 in thread_one ()
#5  0x0000000000404c74 in start_thread ()
#6  0x0000000000429ba0 in thread_start ()

Thread 2 (LWP 24559):
#0  0x000000000040c9f4 in nanosleep ()
#1  0x0000000000424cf4 in sleep ()
#2  0x0000000000403424 in main ()

Thread 1 (LWP 24563):
#0  0x0000000000000000 in ?? ()
#1  0x000000000040322c in proc ()
#2  0x0000000000403314 in bar_four ()
#3  0x0000000000403328 in foo_four ()
#4  0x0000000000403340 in thread_four ()
#5  0x0000000000404c74 in start_thread ()
#6  0x0000000000429ba0 in thread_start ()
```

Exercise A2C (x64, WinDbg)

Goal: Learn how to identify exceptions, find problem threads and CPU instructions.

Patterns: NULL Pointer (Code); Disassembly Ambiguity.

1. Launch WinDbg.

2. Load the *core.App2C* dump file from the x64/App2C folder:

```
Microsoft (R) Windows Debugger Version 10.0.27725.1000 AMD64
Copyright (c) Microsoft Corporation. All rights reserved.


Loading Dump File [C:\ALCDA2\x64\App2C\core.App2C]
64-bit machine not using 64-bit API

************* Path validation summary **************
Response                         Time (ms)     Location
Deferred                                       srv*
Symbol search path is: srv*
Executable search path is:
Generic Unix Version 0 UP Free x64
System Uptime: not available
Process Uptime: not available
..
(e3f.e43): Signal SIGSEGV (Segmentation fault) code SEGV_MAPERR (Address not mapped to object)
at 0x0
*** WARNING: Unable to verify timestamp for App2C
00000000`00000000 ???
```

3. Set logging to a file in case of lengthy output from some commands:

```
0:000> .logopen C:\ALCDA2\x64\App2C\App2C-WinDbg.log
Opened log file 'C:\ALCDA2\x64\App2C\App2C-WinDbg.log'
```

4. Specify the dump folder as the symbol path and reload symbols:

```
0:000> .symfix; .sympath+ C:\ALCDA2\x64\App2C\
Symbol search path is: srv*;C:\ALCDA2\x64\App2C\
Expanded Symbol search path is:
cache*;SRV*https://msdl.microsoft.com/download/symbols;c:\alcda2\x64\app2c\

************* Path validation summary **************
Response                         Time (ms)     Location
Deferred                                       srv*
OK                                             C:\ALCDA2\x64\App2C\
*** WARNING: Unable to verify timestamp for App2C

0:000> .reload
..
*** WARNING: Unable to verify timestamp for App2C

************* Symbol Loading Error Summary **************
Module name            Error
App2C                  The system cannot find the file specified
```

```
You can troubleshoot most symbol related issues by turning on symbol loading diagnostics (!sym
noisy) and repeating the command that caused symbols to be loaded.
You should also verify that your symbol search path (.sympath) is correct.
```

Note: We ignore warnings and errors as they are not relevant for now.

5. The problem thread seems to be the current thread:

```
0:000> kL
 # Child-SP          RetAddr           Call Site
00 00007f7d`259c3d58 00000000`00401bf9 0x0
01 00007f7d`259c3d60 00000000`00401cc7 App2C!procB+0x25
02 00007f7d`259c3d80 00000000`00401cd8 App2C!bar_four+0xe
03 00007f7d`259c3d90 00000000`00401cf1 App2C!foo_four+0xe
04 00007f7d`259c3da0 00000000`00403123 App2C!thread_four+0x16
05 00007f7d`259c3dc0 00000000`004442bf App2C!start_thread+0xf3
06 00007f7d`259c3e80 ffffffff`ffffffff App2C!_clone+0x3f
07 00007f7d`259c3e88 00000000`00000000 0xffffffff`ffffffff
```

6. Disassemble the return address backward:

```
0:000> ub 00000000`00401bf9
App2C!procB+0xe:
00000000`00401be2 retf    3FDh
00000000`00401be5 add     byte ptr [rax-39h],cl
00000000`00401be8 clc
00000000`00401bea add     byte ptr [rax],al
00000000`00401bec add     byte ptr [rax],al
00000000`00401bee mov     rdx,qword ptr [rbp-8]
00000000`00401bf2 mov     eax,0
00000000`00401bf7 call    rdx

0:000> r rdx
rdx=0000000000000000
```

Note: We see that the value of the RDX register was loaded from a stack location, but we don't see what the value was stored at that location, and we also have some impossible code before. We need to either disassemble the whole function or specify the length unless we get the code right:

```
0:000> uf App2C!procB
00000000`00401bd4 push    rbp
00000000`00401bd5 mov     rbp,rsp
00000000`00401bd8 sub     rsp,10h
00000000`00401bdc mov     edi,1
00000000`00401be1 call    App2C!sleep (00000000`004419b0)
00000000`00401be6 mov     qword ptr [rbp-8],0
00000000`00401bee mov     rdx,qword ptr [rbp-8]
00000000`00401bf2 mov     eax,0
00000000`00401bf7 call    rdx
00000000`00401bf9 nop
00000000`00401bfa leave
00000000`00401bfb ret
```

```
0:000> ub 00000000`00401bf9 L8
App2C!procB+0xe:
00000000`00401be2 retf    3FDh
00000000`00401be5 add     byte ptr [rax-39h],cl
00000000`00401be8 clc
00000000`00401bea add     byte ptr [rax],al
00000000`00401bec add     byte ptr [rax],al
00000000`00401bee mov     rdx,qword ptr [rbp-8]
00000000`00401bf2 mov     eax,0
00000000`00401bf7 call    rdx
```

```
0:000> ub 00000000`00401bf9  L9
App2C!procB:
00000000`00401bd4 push    rbp
00000000`00401bd5 mov     rbp,rsp
00000000`00401bd8 sub     rsp,10h
00000000`00401bdc mov     edi,1
00000000`00401be1 call    App2C!sleep (00000000`004419b0)
00000000`00401be6 mov     qword ptr [rbp-8],0
00000000`00401bee mov     rdx,qword ptr [rbp-8]
00000000`00401bf2 mov     eax,0
00000000`00401bf7 call    rdx
```

7. List all thread stack traces to check for other anomalies, such as non-waiting active threads:

```
0:000> ~*kL

Unable to get thread data for thread 0
.  0  Id: e3f.e43 Suspend: 0 Teb: 00000000`00000000 Unfrozen
 # Child-SP          RetAddr           Call Site
00 00007f7d`259c3d58 00000000`00401bf9 0x0
01 00007f7d`259c3d60 00000000`00401cc7 App2C!procB+0x25
02 00007f7d`259c3d80 00000000`00401cd8 App2C!bar_four+0xe
03 00007f7d`259c3d90 00000000`00401cf1 App2C!foo_four+0xe
04 00007f7d`259c3da0 00000000`00403123 App2C!thread_four+0x16
05 00007f7d`259c3dc0 00000000`004442bf App2C!start_thread+0xf3
06 00007f7d`259c3e80 ffffffff`ffffffff App2C!_clone+0x3f
07 00007f7d`259c3e88 00000000`00000000 0xffffffff`ffffffff

Unable to get thread data for thread 1
   1  Id: e3f.e3f Suspend: 0 Teb: 00000000`00000000 Unfrozen
 # Child-SP          RetAddr           Call Site
00 00007ffd`57ca50c0 00000000`004419ea App2C!nanosleep+0x40
01 00007ffd`57ca50f0 00000000`00401de1 App2C!sleep+0x3a
02 00007ffd`57ca5130 00000000`004075d1 App2C!main+0xaa
03 00007ffd`57ca5180 00000000`00401aba App2C!_libc_start_main+0x3d1
04 00007ffd`57ca5280 ffffffff`ffffffff App2C!start+0x2a
05 00007ffd`57ca5288 00000000`00000000 0xffffffff`ffffffff

Unable to get thread data for thread 2
   2  Id: e3f.e40 Suspend: 0 Teb: 00000000`00000000 Unfrozen
 # Child-SP          RetAddr           Call Site
00 00007f7d`271c6d10 00000000`004419ea App2C!nanosleep+0x40
01 00007f7d`271c6d40 00000000`00401c0a App2C!sleep+0x3a
02 00007f7d`271c6d80 00000000`00401c1b App2C!bar_one+0xe
03 00007f7d`271c6d90 00000000`00401c34 App2C!foo_one+0xe
04 00007f7d`271c6da0 00000000`00403123 App2C!thread_one+0x16
05 00007f7d`271c6dc0 00000000`004442bf App2C!start_thread+0xf3
06 00007f7d`271c6e80 ffffffff`ffffffff App2C!_clone+0x3f
07 00007f7d`271c6e88 00000000`00000000 0xffffffff`ffffffff
```

```
Unable to get thread data for thread 3
   3  Id: e3f.e42 Suspend: 0 Teb: 00000000`00000000 Unfrozen
 # Child-SP          RetAddr               Call Site
00 00007f7d`261c4d10 00000000`004419ea     App2C!nanosleep+0x40
01 00007f7d`261c4d40 00000000`00401c88     App2C!sleep+0x3a
02 00007f7d`261c4d80 00000000`00401c99     App2C!bar_three+0xe
03 00007f7d`261c4d90 00000000`00401cb2     App2C!foo_three+0xe
04 00007f7d`261c4da0 00000000`00403123     App2C!thread_three+0x16
05 00007f7d`261c4dc0 00000000`004442bf     App2C!start_thread+0xf3
06 00007f7d`261c4e80 ffffffff`ffffffff     App2C!_clone+0x3f
07 00007f7d`261c4e88 00000000`00000000     0xffffffff`ffffffff

Unable to get thread data for thread 4
   4  Id: e3f.e41 Suspend: 0 Teb: 00000000`00000000 Unfrozen
 # Child-SP          RetAddr               Call Site
00 00007f7d`269c5cf0 00000000`004419ea     App2C!nanosleep+0x40
01 00007f7d`269c5d20 00000000`00401bbf     App2C!sleep+0x3a
02 00007f7d`269c5d60 00000000`00401c49     App2C!procA+0x12
03 00007f7d`269c5d80 00000000`00401c5a     App2C!bar_two+0xe
04 00007f7d`269c5d90 00000000`00401c73     App2C!foo_two+0xe
05 00007f7d`269c5da0 00000000`00403123     App2C!thread_two+0x16
06 00007f7d`269c5dc0 00000000`004442bf     App2C!start_thread+0xf3
07 00007f7d`269c5e80 ffffffff`ffffffff     App2C!_clone+0x3f
08 00007f7d`269c5e88 00000000`00000000     0xffffffff`ffffffff

Unable to get thread data for thread 5
   5  Id: e3f.e44 Suspend: 0 Teb: 00000000`00000000 Unfrozen
 # Child-SP          RetAddr               Call Site
00 00007f7d`251c2d10 00000000`004419ea     App2C!nanosleep+0x40
01 00007f7d`251c2d40 00000000`00401d06     App2C!sleep+0x3a
02 00007f7d`251c2d80 00000000`00401d17     App2C!bar_five+0xe
03 00007f7d`251c2d90 00000000`00401d30     App2C!foo_five+0xe
04 00007f7d`251c2da0 00000000`00403123     App2C!thread_five+0x16
05 00007f7d`251c2dc0 00000000`004442bf     App2C!start_thread+0xf3
06 00007f7d`251c2e80 ffffffff`ffffffff     App2C!_clone+0x3f
07 00007f7d`251c2e88 00000000`00000000     0xffffffff`ffffffff
```

9. We close logging before exiting WinDbg:

```
0:000> .logclose
Closing open log file 'C:\ALCDA2\x64\App2C\App2C-WinDbg.log'
```

Exercise A2C (A64, WinDbg)

Goal: Learn how to identify exceptions, find problem threads and CPU instructions.

Patterns: NULL Pointer (Code).

1. Launch WinDbg.

2. Load the *core.24559* dump file from the A64\App2C folder:

```
Microsoft (R) Windows Debugger Version 10.0.27725.1000 AMD64
Copyright (c) Microsoft Corporation. All rights reserved.


Loading Dump File [C:\ALCDA2\A64\App2C\core.24559]
64-bit machine not using 64-bit API

************* Path validation summary **************
Response                         Time (ms)     Location
Deferred                                       srv*
Symbol search path is: srv*
Executable search path is:
Generic Unix Version 0 UP Free ARM 64-bit (AArch64)
System Uptime: not available
Process Uptime: not available
..
(5fef.5ff3): Signal SIGSEGV (Segmentation fault) code SEGV_MAPERR (Address not mapped to
object) at 0x0
*** WARNING: Unable to verify timestamp for App2C
00000000`00000000 ???
```

3. Set logging to a file in case of lengthy output from some commands:

```
0:000> .logopen C:\ALCDA2\A64\App2C\App2C-WinDbg.log
Opened log file 'C:\ALCDA2\A64\App2C\App2C-WinDbg.log'
```

4. Specify the dump folder as the symbol path and reload symbols:

```
0:000> .sympath+ C:\ALCDA2\A64\App2C\
Symbol search path is: srv*;C:\ALCDA2\A64\App2C\
Expanded Symbol search path is:
cache*;SRV*https://msdl.microsoft.com/download/symbols;c:\alcda2\a64\app2c\

************* Path validation summary **************
Response                         Time (ms)     Location
Deferred                                       srv*
OK                                             C:\ALCDA2\A64\App2C\
*** WARNING: Unable to verify timestamp for App2C

0:000> .reload
..
*** WARNING: Unable to verify timestamp for App2C

************* Symbol Loading Error Summary **************
Module name            Error
App2C                  The system cannot find the file specified
```

```
You can troubleshoot most symbol related issues by turning on symbol loading diagnostics (!sym
noisy) and repeating the command that caused symbols to be loaded.
You should also verify that your symbol search path (.sympath) is correct.
```

Note: We ignore warnings and errors as they are not relevant for now.

5. The problem thread seems to be the current thread:

```
0:000> k
 # Child-SP          RetAddr               Call Site
00 0000fffc`694ce800 00000000`0040322c     0x0
01 0000fffc`694ce800 00000000`00403314     App2C!procB+0x1c
02 0000fffc`694ce820 00000000`00403328     App2C!bar_four+0xc
03 0000fffc`694ce830 00000000`00403340     App2C!foo_four+0xc
04 0000fffc`694ce840 00000000`00404c74     App2C!thread_four+0x10
05 0000fffc`694ce860 00000000`00429ba0     App2C!start_thread+0xb4
06 0000fffc`694ce990 ffffffff`ffffffff     App2C!thread_start+0x30
07 0000fffc`694ce990 00000000`00000000     0xffffffff`ffffffff
```

6. Disassemble the return address backward:

```
0:000> ub 00000000`0040322c
App2C!procA+0x24:
00000000`0040320c d65f03c0 ret
App2C!procB:
00000000`00403210 a9be7bfd stp          fp,lr,[sp,#-0x20]!
00000000`00403214 910003fd mov          fp,sp
00000000`00403218 52800020 mov          w0,#1
00000000`0040321c 94008672 bl           App2C!sleep (00000000`00424be4)
00000000`00403220 f9000fbf str          xzr,[fp,#0x18]
00000000`00403224 f9400fa0 ldr          x0,[fp,#0x18]
00000000`00403228 d63f0000 blr          x0
```

```
0:000> r x0
x0=0000000000000000
```

Note: We see that 0 (the value of the xzr register) was stored in a stack location and then loaded into the x0 register. The fp register is an alias to the x29 register.

7. List all thread stack traces to check for other anomalies, such as non-waiting active threads:

```
0:000> ~*k

Unable to get thread data for thread 0
.  0  Id: 5fef.5ff3 Suspend: 0 Teb: 00000000`00000000 Unfrozen
 # Child-SP          RetAddr               Call Site
00 0000fffc`694ce800 00000000`00403314     0x0
01 0000fffc`694ce810 00000000`00403328     App2C!bar_four+0xc
02 0000fffc`694ce830 00000000`00403340     App2C!foo_four+0xc
03 0000fffc`694ce840 00000000`00404c74     App2C!thread_four+0x10
04 0000fffc`694ce860 00000000`00429ba0     App2C!start_thread+0xb4
05 0000fffc`694ce990 ffffffff`ffffffff     App2C!thread_start+0x30
06 0000fffc`694ce990 00000000`00000000     0xffffffff`ffffffff
```

```
Unable to get thread data for thread 1
   1  Id: 5fef.5fef Suspend: 0 Teb: 00000000`00000000 Unfrozen
 # Child-SP          RetAddr               Call Site
00 0000ffff`c86b1620 00000000`00424cf4     App2C!_libc_nanosleep+0x24
01 0000ffff`c86b1660 00000000`00403424     App2C!sleep+0x110
02 0000ffff`c86b1850 00000000`0040ec8c     App2C!main+0x90
03 0000ffff`c86b18a0 00000000`00403090     App2C!_libc_start_main+0x304
04 0000ffff`c86b1a00 00000000`00000000     App2C!start+0x4c

Unable to get thread data for thread 2
   2  Id: 5fef.5ff0 Suspend: 0 Teb: 00000000`00000000 Unfrozen
 # Child-SP          RetAddr               Call Site
00 0000fffc`6acfe5f0 00000000`00424cf4     App2C!_libc_nanosleep+0x24
01 0000fffc`6acfe630 00000000`00403244     App2C!sleep+0x110
02 0000fffc`6acfe820 00000000`00403258     App2C!bar_one+0x10
03 0000fffc`6acfe830 00000000`00403270     App2C!foo_one+0xc
04 0000fffc`6acfe840 00000000`00404c74     App2C!thread_one+0x10
05 0000fffc`6acfe860 00000000`00429ba0     App2C!start_thread+0xb4
06 0000fffc`6acfe990 ffffffff`ffffffff     App2C!thread_start+0x30
07 0000fffc`6acfe990 00000000`00000000     0xffffffff`ffffffff

Unable to get thread data for thread 3
   3  Id: 5fef.5ff1 Suspend: 0 Teb: 00000000`00000000 Unfrozen
 # Child-SP          RetAddr               Call Site
00 0000fffc`6a4ee5d0 00000000`00424cf4     App2C!_libc_nanosleep+0x24
01 0000fffc`6a4ee610 00000000`004031f8     App2C!sleep+0x110
02 0000fffc`6a4ee800 00000000`00403288     App2C!procA+0x10
03 0000fffc`6a4ee820 00000000`0040329c     App2C!bar_two+0xc
04 0000fffc`6a4ee830 00000000`004032b4     App2C!foo_two+0xc
05 0000fffc`6a4ee840 00000000`00404c74     App2C!thread_two+0x10
06 0000fffc`6a4ee860 00000000`00429ba0     App2C!start_thread+0xb4
07 0000fffc`6a4ee990 ffffffff`ffffffff     App2C!thread_start+0x30
08 0000fffc`6a4ee990 00000000`00000000     0xffffffff`ffffffff

Unable to get thread data for thread 4
   4  Id: 5fef.5ff4 Suspend: 0 Teb: 00000000`00000000 Unfrozen
 # Child-SP          RetAddr               Call Site
00 0000fffc`68cbe5f0 00000000`00424cf4     App2C!_libc_nanosleep+0x24
01 0000fffc`68cbe630 00000000`0040335c     App2C!sleep+0x110
02 0000fffc`68cbe820 00000000`00403370     App2C!bar_five+0x10
03 0000fffc`68cbe830 00000000`00403388     App2C!foo_five+0xc
04 0000fffc`68cbe840 00000000`00404c74     App2C!thread_five+0x10
05 0000fffc`68cbe860 00000000`00429ba0     App2C!start_thread+0xb4
06 0000fffc`68cbe990 ffffffff`ffffffff     App2C!thread_start+0x30
07 0000fffc`68cbe990 00000000`00000000     0xffffffff`ffffffff

Unable to get thread data for thread 5
   5  Id: 5fef.5ff2 Suspend: 0 Teb: 00000000`00000000 Unfrozen
 # Child-SP          RetAddr               Call Site
00 0000fffc`69cde5f0 00000000`00424cf4     App2C!_libc_nanosleep+0x24
01 0000fffc`69cde630 00000000`004032d0     App2C!sleep+0x110
02 0000fffc`69cde820 00000000`004032e4     App2C!bar_three+0x10
03 0000fffc`69cde830 00000000`004032fc     App2C!foo_three+0xc
04 0000fffc`69cde840 00000000`00404c74     App2C!thread_three+0x10
05 0000fffc`69cde860 00000000`00429ba0     App2C!start_thread+0xb4
06 0000fffc`69cde990 ffffffff`ffffffff     App2C!thread_start+0x30
07 0000fffc`69cde990 00000000`00000000     0xffffffff`ffffffff
```

10. We close logging before exiting WinDbg:

```
0:000> .logclose
Closing open log file 'C:\ALCDA2\A64\App2C\App2C-WinDbg.log'
```

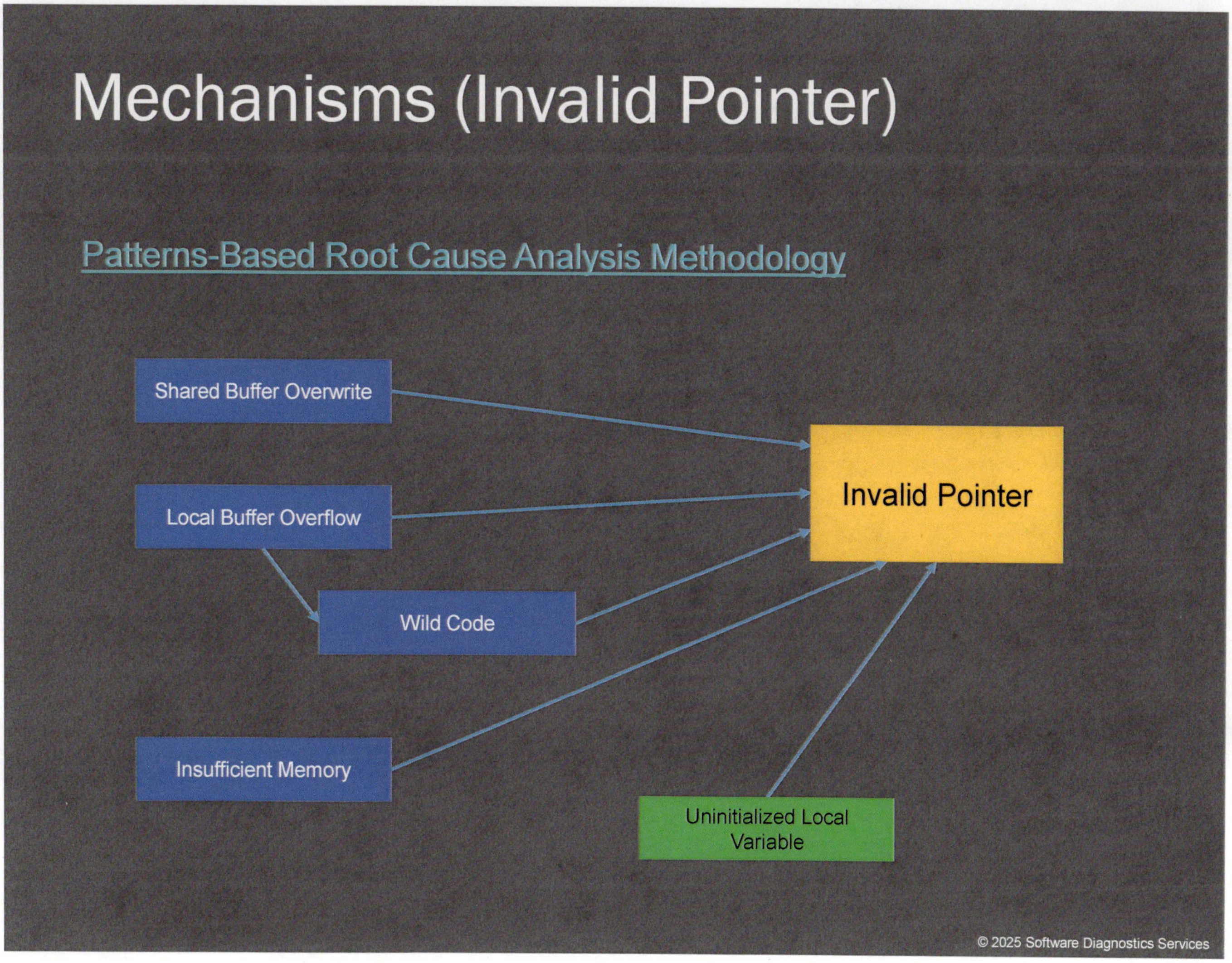

Patterns-Based Root Cause Analysis Methodology
https://www.dumpanalysis.org/pattern-oriented-root-cause-analysis

Exercise A2S

- **Goal:** Learn how to use external debugging information

- \ALCDA-Dumps\Exercise-A2S-x64-GDB.pdf
- \ALCDA-Dumps\Exercise-A2S-A64-GDB.pdf

- \ALCDA-Dumps\Exercise-A2S-A64-WinDbg.pdf
- \ALCDA-Dumps\Exercise-A2S-x64-WinDbg.pdf

Exercise A2S (x64, GDB)

Goal: Learn how to use external debugging information.

1. Load the *core.App2S* dump file and *App2S* executable from the x64/App2S directory:

```
~/ALCDA2/x64/App2S$ gdb -c core.App2S -se App2S
GNU gdb (Debian 8.2.1-2+b3) 8.2.1
Copyright (C) 2018 Free Software Foundation, Inc.
License GPLv3+: GNU GPL version 3 or later <http://gnu.org/licenses/gpl.html>
This is free software: you are free to change and redistribute it.
There is NO WARRANTY, to the extent permitted by law.
Type "show copying" and "show warranty" for details.
This GDB was configured as "x86_64-linux-gnu".
Type "show configuration" for configuration details.
For bug reporting instructions, please see:
<http://www.gnu.org/software/gdb/bugs/>.
Find the GDB manual and other documentation resources online at:
    <http://www.gnu.org/software/gdb/documentation/>.

For help, type "help".
Type "apropos word" to search for commands related to "word"...
Reading symbols from App2S...(no debugging symbols found)...done.
[New LWP 3736]
[New LWP 3738]
[New LWP 3735]
[New LWP 3734]
[New LWP 3737]
[New LWP 3739]
[Thread debugging using libthread_db enabled]
Using host libthread_db library "/lib/x86_64-linux-gnu/libthread_db.so.1".
Core was generated by `./App2S'.
Program terminated with signal SIGSEGV, Segmentation fault.
#0  0x0000000000401bcb in procA ()
[Current thread is 1 (Thread 0x7f30da538700 (LWP 3736))]
```

2. Set logging to a file in case of lengthy output from some commands:

```
(gdb) set logging on App2S.log
Copying output to App2S.log.
```

3. We check the current stack trace:

```
(gdb) bt
#0  0x0000000000401bcb in procA ()
#1  0x0000000000401c49 in bar_two ()
#2  0x0000000000401c5a in foo_two ()
#3  0x0000000000401c73 in thread_two ()
#4  0x0000000000403123 in start_thread ()
#5  0x00000000004442bf in clone ()
```

Note: We see that the problem happened in *procA,* but we want to locate it in the source code. The executable *App2S* was stripped from debugging symbols before its distribution to customers. Fortunately, the executable with debugging information was saved in a separate *App2S.debug* file.

4. We load the *App2S.debug* file with debugging symbols:

```
(gdb) symbol-file App2S.debug
Reading symbols from App2S.debug...done.
```

5. Now we get the stack trace with file numbers:

```
(gdb) bt
#0  0x0000000000401bcb in procA () at main.c:26
#1  0x0000000000401c49 in bar_two () at main.c:56
#2  0x0000000000401c5a in foo_two () at main.c:56
#3  0x0000000000401c73 in thread_two (arg=0x0) at main.c:56
#4  0x0000000000403123 in start_thread (arg=<optimized out>) at pthread_create.c:486
#5  0x00000000004442bf in clone ()
```

6. If we have the source file, we can list the exact location:

```
(gdb) list main.c:26
21      {
22          sleep(1);
23
24          int *p = NULL;
25
26          *p = 1;
27      }
28
29      void procB()
30      {
```

7. Alternatively, we can load the executable with debugging symbols from the start:

```
~/ALCDA2/x64/App2S$ gdb -c core.App2S -se App2S.debug
GNU gdb (Debian 8.2.1-2+b3) 8.2.1
Copyright (C) 2018 Free Software Foundation, Inc.
License GPLv3+: GNU GPL version 3 or later <http://gnu.org/licenses/gpl.html>
This is free software: you are free to change and redistribute it.
There is NO WARRANTY, to the extent permitted by law.
Type "show copying" and "show warranty" for details.
This GDB was configured as "x86_64-linux-gnu".
Type "show configuration" for configuration details.
For bug reporting instructions, please see:
<http://www.gnu.org/software/gdb/bugs/>.
Find the GDB manual and other documentation resources online at:
    <http://www.gnu.org/software/gdb/documentation/>.

For help, type "help".
Type "apropos word" to search for commands related to "word"...
Reading symbols from App2S.debug...done.

warning: core file may not match specified executable file.
[New LWP 3736]
[New LWP 3738]
[New LWP 3735]
[New LWP 3734]
[New LWP 3737]
[New LWP 3739]
[Thread debugging using libthread_db enabled]
Using host libthread_db library "/lib/x86_64-linux-gnu/libthread_db.so.1".
Core was generated by `./App2S'.
```

```
Program terminated with signal SIGSEGV, Segmentation fault.
#0  0x0000000000401bcb in procA () at main.c:26

warning: Source file is more recent than executable.
26          *p = 1;
[Current thread is 1 (Thread 0x7f30da538700 (LWP 3736))]

(gdb) bt
#0  0x0000000000401bcb in procA () at main.c:26
#1  0x0000000000401c49 in bar_two () at main.c:56
#2  0x0000000000401c5a in foo_two () at main.c:56
#3  0x0000000000401c73 in thread_two (arg=0x0) at main.c:56
#4  0x0000000000403123 in start_thread (arg=<optimized out>) at pthread_create.c:486
#5  0x00000000004442bf in clone ()
```

Note: We also see the warning that the source code is more recent (we modified some comments after compilation).

Exercise A2S (A64, GDB)

Goal: Learn how to use external debugging information.

1. Load the *core._home_ubuntu_ALCDA2_A64_App2S_App2S.1001.3d452460-e216-4918-b09f-304672052efe.202652.172563749* dump file and *App2S* executable from the A64/App2S directory:

```
~/ALCDA2/A64/App2S$ gdb-multiarch -c core._home_ubuntu_ALCDA2_A64_App2S_App2S.1001.3d452460-
e216-4918-b09f-304672052efe.202652.172563749 -se App2S
GNU gdb (Debian 8.2.1-2+b3) 8.2.1
Copyright (C) 2018 Free Software Foundation, Inc.
License GPLv3+: GNU GPL version 3 or later <http://gnu.org/licenses/gpl.html>
This is free software: you are free to change and redistribute it.
There is NO WARRANTY, to the extent permitted by law.
Type "show copying" and "show warranty" for details.
This GDB was configured as "x86_64-linux-gnu".
Type "show configuration" for configuration details.
For bug reporting instructions, please see:
<http://www.gnu.org/software/gdb/bugs/>.
Find the GDB manual and other documentation resources online at:
    <http://www.gnu.org/software/gdb/documentation/>.

For help, type "help".
Type "apropos word" to search for commands related to "word"...
Reading symbols from App2S...(no debugging symbols found)...done.
[New LWP 202654]
[New LWP 202657]
[New LWP 202652]
[New LWP 202653]
[New LWP 202655]
[New LWP 202656]
Core was generated by `./App2S'.
Program terminated with signal SIGSEGV, Segmentation fault.
#0  0x00000000004006f0 in procA ()
[Current thread is 1 (LWP 202654)]
```

2. Set logging to a file in case of lengthy output from some commands:

```
(gdb) set logging on App2S.log
Copying output to App2S.log.
```

3. We check the current stack trace:

```
(gdb) bt
#0  0x00000000004006f0 in procA ()
#1  0x000000000040077c in bar_two ()
#2  0x0000000000400790 in foo_two ()
#3  0x00000000004007a8 in thread_two ()
#4  0x000000000040eca4 in start_thread ()
#5  0x000000000044365c in thread_start ()
```

Note: We see that the problem happened in *procA,* but we want to locate it in the source code. The executable *App2S* was stripped from debugging symbols before its distribution to customers. Fortunately, the executable with debugging information was saved in a separate *App2S.debug* file.

4. We load the *App2S.debug* file with debugging symbols:

```
(gdb) symbol-file App2S.debug
Reading symbols from App2S.debug...
```

5. Now we get the stack trace with file numbers:

```
(gdb) bt
#0  0x00000000004006f0 in procA () at main.c:26
#1  0x000000000040077c in bar_two () at main.c:56
#2  0x0000000000400790 in foo_two () at main.c:56
#3  0x00000000004007a8 in thread_two (arg=0x0) at main.c:56
#4  0x000000000040eca4 in start_thread ()
#5  0x000000000044365c in thread_start ()
```

6. If we have the source file, we can list the exact location:

```
(gdb) list main.c:26
21      {
22          sleep(1);
23
24          int *p = NULL;
25
26          *p = 1;
27      }
28
29      void procB()
30      {
```

7. Alternatively, we can load the executable with debugging symbols from the start:

```
~/ALCDA2/A64/App2S$ gdb-multiarch -c core._home_ubuntu_ALCDA2_A64_App2S_App2S.1001.3d452460-
e216-4918-b09f-304672052efe.202652.172563749 -se App2S.debug
GNU gdb (Debian 8.2.1-2+b3) 8.2.1
Copyright (C) 2018 Free Software Foundation, Inc.
License GPLv3+: GNU GPL version 3 or later <http://gnu.org/licenses/gpl.html>
This is free software: you are free to change and redistribute it.
There is NO WARRANTY, to the extent permitted by law.
Type "show copying" and "show warranty" for details.
This GDB was configured as "x86_64-linux-gnu".
Type "show configuration" for configuration details.
For bug reporting instructions, please see:
<http://www.gnu.org/software/gdb/bugs/>.
Find the GDB manual and other documentation resources online at:
    <http://www.gnu.org/software/gdb/documentation/>.

For help, type "help".
Type "apropos word" to search for commands related to "word"...
Reading symbols from App2S.debug...done.

warning: core file may not match specified executable file.
[New LWP 202654]
[New LWP 202657]
[New LWP 202652]
[New LWP 202653]
[New LWP 202655]
[New LWP 202656]
Core was generated by `./App2S'.
Program terminated with signal SIGSEGV, Segmentation fault.
```

```
#0  0x00000000004006f0 in procA () at main.c:26
26          *p = 1;
[Current thread is 1 (LWP 202654)]

(gdb) bt
#0  0x00000000004006f0 in procA () at main.c:26
#1  0x000000000040077c in bar_two () at main.c:56
#2  0x0000000000400790 in foo_two () at main.c:56
#3  0x00000000004007a8 in thread_two (arg=0x0) at main.c:56
#4  0x000000000040eca4 in start_thread ()
#5  0x000000000044365c in thread_start ()
```

Exercise A2S (x64, WinDbg)

Goal: Learn how to use external debugging information.

1. Launch WinDbg.

2. Load the *core.App2S* dump file from the x64/App2S folder:

```
Microsoft (R) Windows Debugger Version 10.0.27725.1000 AMD64
Copyright (c) Microsoft Corporation. All rights reserved.


Loading Dump File [C:\ALCDA2\x64\App2S\core.App2S]
64-bit machine not using 64-bit API

************* Path validation summary **************
Response                         Time (ms)     Location
Deferred                                       srv*
Symbol search path is: srv*
Executable search path is:
Generic Unix Version 0 UP Free x64
System Uptime: not available
Process Uptime: not available
..
(e96.e98): Signal SIGSEGV (Segmentation fault) code SEGV_MAPERR (Address not mapped to object)
at 0x0
*** WARNING: Unable to verify timestamp for App2S
App2S+0x1bcb:
00000000`00401bcb ???
```

3. Set logging to a file in case of lengthy output from some commands:

```
0:000> .logopen C:\ALCDA2\x64\App2S\App2S-WinDbg.log
Opened log file 'C:\ALCDA2\x64\App2S\App2S-WinDbg.log'
```

4. Specify the dump folder as the symbol path and reload symbols:

```
0:000> .symfix; .sympath+ C:\ALCDA2\x64\App2S\
Symbol search path is: srv*;C:\ALCDA2\x64\App2S\
Expanded Symbol search path is:
cache*;SRV*https://msdl.microsoft.com/download/symbols;c:\alcda2\x64\app2s\

************* Path validation summary **************
Response                         Time (ms)     Location
Deferred                                       srv*
OK                                             C:\ALCDA2\x64\App2S\
*** WARNING: Unable to verify timestamp for App2S

0:000> .reload
..
*** WARNING: Unable to verify timestamp for App2S

************* Symbol Loading Error Summary **************
Module name            Error
App2S                  The system cannot find the file specified
```

```
You can troubleshoot most symbol related issues by turning on symbol loading diagnostics (!sym
noisy) and repeating the command that caused symbols to be loaded.
You should also verify that your symbol search path (.sympath) is correct.
```

```
0:000> k
 # Child-SP          RetAddr               Call Site
00 00007f30`da537d60 00000000`00401c49     App2S!procA+0x1e
01 00007f30`da537d80 00000000`00401c5a     App2S!bar_two+0xe
02 00007f30`da537d90 00000000`00401c73     App2S!foo_two+0xe
03 00007f30`da537da0 00000000`00403123     App2S!thread_two+0x16
04 00007f30`da537dc0 00000000`004442bf     App2S!start_thread+0xf3
05 00007f30`da537e80 ffffffff`ffffffff     App2S!_clone+0x3f
06 00007f30`da537e88 00000000`00000000     0xffffffff`ffffffff
```

Note: We see that the problem happened in *procA,* but we want to locate it in the source code. The executable *App2S* was stripped from debugging symbols before its distribution to customers. Fortunately, the executable with debugging information was saved in a separate *App2S.debug* file. We quit our debugging session (**q**), rename the *AppS* executable file to *AppS.nosymbols*, and rename *AppS.debug* to *AppS*.

5. Load *core.App2S* dump file from the x64/App2S folder again:

```
Microsoft (R) Windows Debugger Version 10.0.27725.1000 AMD64
Copyright (c) Microsoft Corporation. All rights reserved.


Loading Dump File [C:\ALCDA2\x64\App2S\core.App2S]
64-bit machine not using 64-bit API

************* Path validation summary **************
Response                         Time (ms)     Location
Deferred                                       srv*
Symbol search path is: srv*
Executable search path is:
Generic Unix Version 0 UP Free x64
System Uptime: not available
Process Uptime: not available
..
(e96.e98): Signal SIGSEGV (Segmentation fault) code SEGV_MAPERR (Address not mapped to object)
at 0x0
*** WARNING: Unable to verify timestamp for App2S
App2S+0x1bcb:
00000000`00401bcb ???
```

6. Append logging to the existing file in case of lengthy output from some commands:

```
0:000> .logappend C:\ALCDA2\x64\App2S\App2S-WinDbg.log
Opened log file 'C:\ALCDA2\x64\App2S\App2S-WinDbg.log'
```

7. Specify the dump folder as the symbol path and reload symbols:

```
0:000> .symfix; .sympath+ C:\ALCDA2\x64\App2S\
Symbol search path is: srv*;C:\ALCDA2\x64\App2S\
Expanded Symbol search path is:
cache*;SRV*https://msdl.microsoft.com/download/symbols;c:\alcda2\x64\app2s\

************* Path validation summary **************
Response                         Time (ms)     Location
```

```
Deferred                                       srv*
OK                                             C:\ALCDA2\x64\App2S\
*** WARNING: Unable to verify timestamp for App2S

0:000> .reload
..
*** WARNING: Unable to verify timestamp for App2S

************* Symbol Loading Error Summary **************
Module name            Error
App2S                  The system cannot find the file specified

You can troubleshoot most symbol related issues by turning on symbol loading diagnostics (!sym
noisy) and repeating the command that caused symbols to be loaded.
You should also verify that your symbol search path (.sympath) is correct.

0:000> k
 # Child-SP          RetAddr               Call Site
00 00007f30`da537d60 00000000`00401c49     App2S!procA+0x1e [/home/coredump/ALCDA2/x64/App2S/main.c @ 26]
01 00007f30`da537d80 00000000`00401c5a     App2S!bar_two+0xe [/home/coredump/ALCDA2/x64/App2S/main.c @ 56]
02 00007f30`da537d90 00000000`00401c73     App2S!foo_two+0xe [/home/coredump/ALCDA2/x64/App2S/main.c @ 56]
03 00007f30`da537da0 00000000`00403123     App2S!thread_two+0x16 [/home/coredump/ALCDA2/x64/App2S/main.c @ 56]
04 00007f30`da537dc0 00000000`004442bf     App2S!start_thread+0xf3 [/build/glibc-vjB4T1/glibc-2.28/nptl/pthread_create.c @ 487]
05 00007f30`da537e80 ffffffff`ffffffff     App2S!_clone+0x3f
06 00007f30`da537e88 00000000`00000000     0xffffffff`ffffffff
```

8. If we set the source code folder, we should see the problem source code location directly:

```
0:000> .srcpath C:\ALCDA2\x64\App2S\
Symbol search path is: srv*;C:\ALCDA2\x64\App2S\
Expanded Symbol search path is:
cache*;SRV*https://msdl.microsoft.com/download/symbols;c:\alcda2\x64\app2s\
```

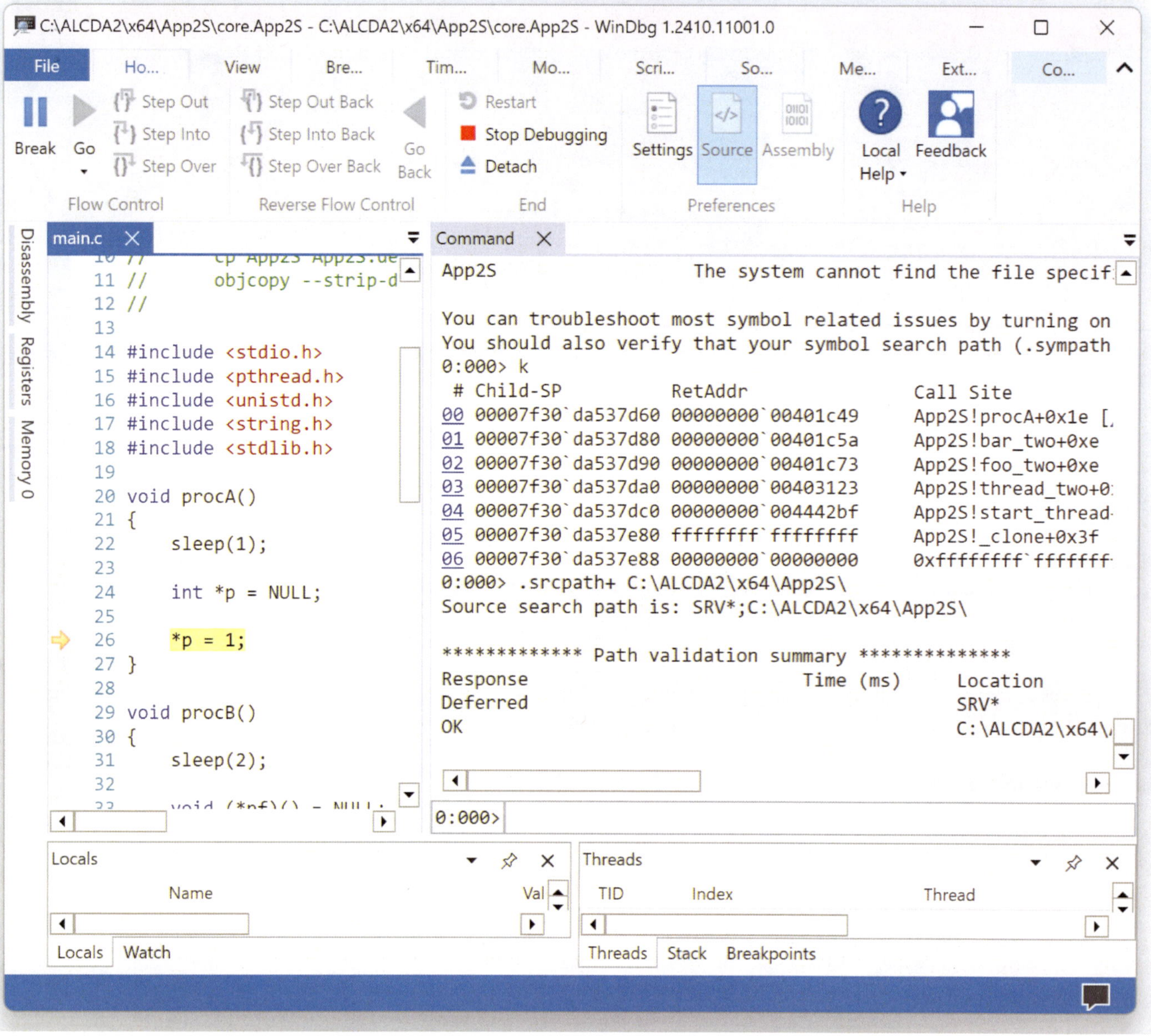

9. We close logging before exiting WinDbg:

```
0:000> .logclose
Closing open log file 'C:\ALCDA2\x64\App2S\App2S-WinDbg.log'
```

Exercise A2S (A64, WinDbg)

Goal: Learn how to use external debugging information.

1. Launch WinDbg.

2. Load the *core._home_ubuntu_ALCDA2_A64_App2S_App2S.1001.3d452460-e216-4918-b09f-304672052efe.202652.172563749* dump file from the A64/App2S folder:

```
Microsoft (R) Windows Debugger Version 10.0.27725.1000 AMD64
Copyright (c) Microsoft Corporation. All rights reserved.


Loading Dump File [C:\ALCDA2\A64\App2S\core._home_ubuntu_ALCDA2_A64_App2S_App2S.1001.3d452460-
e216-4918-b09f-304672052efe.202652.172563749]
64-bit machine not using 64-bit API

************* Path validation summary **************
Response                         Time (ms)     Location
Deferred                                       srv*
Symbol search path is: srv*
Executable search path is:
Generic Unix Version 0 UP Free ARM 64-bit (AArch64)
System Uptime: not available
Process Uptime: not available
..
(3179c.3179e): Signal SIGSEGV (Segmentation fault) code SEGV_MAPERR (Address not mapped to
object) at 0x0
*** WARNING: Unable to verify timestamp for App2S
App2S+0x6f0:
00000000`004006f0 str         w1,[x0]
```

3. Set logging to a file in case of lengthy output from some commands:

```
0:000> .logopen C:\ALCDA2\A64\App2S\App2S-WinDbg.log
Opened log file 'C:\ALCDA2\A64\App2S\App2S-WinDbg.log'
```

4. Specify the dump folder as the symbol path and reload symbols:

```
0:000> .symfix; .sympath+ C:\ALCDA2\A64\App2S\
Symbol search path is: srv*;C:\ALCDA2\A64\App2S\
Expanded Symbol search path is:
cache*;SRV*https://msdl.microsoft.com/download/symbols;c:\alcda2\a64\app2s\

************* Path validation summary **************
Response                         Time (ms)     Location
Deferred                                       srv*
OK                                             C:\ALCDA2\A64\App2S\
*** WARNING: Unable to verify timestamp for App2S

0:000> .reload
..
*** WARNING: Unable to verify timestamp for App2S

************* Symbol Loading Error Summary **************
Module name            Error
```

```
App2S                 The system cannot find the file specified

You can troubleshoot most symbol related issues by turning on symbol loading diagnostics (!sym
noisy) and repeating the command that caused symbols to be loaded.
You should also verify that your symbol search path (.sympath) is correct.
```

```
0:000> k
 # Child-SP          RetAddr               Call Site
00 0000ffff`8a239b40 00000000`0040077c     App2S!procA+0x1c
01 0000ffff`8a239b60 00000000`00400790     App2S!bar_two+0xc
02 0000ffff`8a239b70 00000000`004007a8     App2S!foo_two+0xc
03 0000ffff`8a239b80 00000000`0040eca4     App2S!thread_two+0x10
04 0000ffff`8a239ba0 00000000`0044365c     App2S!start_thread+0x2e4
05 0000ffff`8a239cc0 ffffffff`ffffffff     App2S!thread_start+0xc
06 0000ffff`8a239cc0 00000000`00000000     0xffffffff`ffffffff
```

Note: We see that the problem happened in *procA,* but we want to locate it in the source code. The executable *App2S* was stripped from debugging symbols before its distribution to customers. Fortunately, the executable with debugging information was saved in a separate *App2S.debug* file. We quit our debugging session (**q**), rename the *AppS* executable file to *AppS.nosymbols*, and rename *AppS.debug* to *AppS*.

5. Load the *core._home_ubuntu_ALCDA2_A64_App2S_App2S.1001.3d452460-e216-4918-b09f-304672052efe.202652.172563749* dump file from the x64/App2S folder again:

```
Microsoft (R) Windows Debugger Version 10.0.27725.1000 AMD64
Copyright (c) Microsoft Corporation. All rights reserved.


Loading Dump File [C:\ALCDA2\x64\App2S\core.App2S]
64-bit machine not using 64-bit API

************* Path validation summary **************
Response                         Time (ms)     Location
Deferred                                       srv*
Symbol search path is: srv*
Executable search path is:
Generic Unix Version 0 UP Free x64
System Uptime: not available
Process Uptime: not available
..
(e96.e98): Signal SIGSEGV (Segmentation fault) code SEGV_MAPERR (Address not mapped to object)
at 0x0
*** WARNING: Unable to verify timestamp for App2S
App2S+0x1bcb:
00000000`00401bcb ???
```

6. Append logging to the existing file in case of lengthy output from some commands:

```
0:000> .logappend C:\ALCDA2\A64\App2S\App2S-WinDbg.log
Opened log file 'C:\ALCDA2\A64\App2S\App2S-WinDbg.log'
```

7. Specify the dump folder as the symbol path and reload symbols:

```
0:000> .symfix; .sympath+ C:\ALCDA2\A64\App2S\
Symbol search path is: srv*;C:\ALCDA2\A64\App2S\
Expanded Symbol search path is:
cache*;SRV*https://msdl.microsoft.com/download/symbols;c:\alcda2\a64\app2s\

************* Path validation summary **************
Response                         Time (ms)     Location
Deferred                                       srv*
OK                                             C:\ALCDA2\A64\App2S\
*** WARNING: Unable to verify timestamp for App2S

0:000> .reload
..
*** WARNING: Unable to verify timestamp for App2S

************* Symbol Loading Error Summary **************
Module name            Error
App2S                  The system cannot find the file specified

You can troubleshoot most symbol related issues by turning on symbol loading diagnostics (!sym
noisy) and repeating the command that caused symbols to be loaded.
You should also verify that your symbol search path (.sympath) is correct.

0:000> k
 # Child-SP          RetAddr               Call Site
00 0000ffff`8a239b40 00000000`0040077c     App2S!procA+0x1c [/home/ubuntu/ALCDA2/A64/App2S/main.c @ 26]
01 0000ffff`8a239b60 00000000`00400790     App2S!bar_two+0xc [/home/ubuntu/ALCDA2/A64/App2S/main.c @ 56]
02 0000ffff`8a239b70 00000000`004007a8     App2S!foo_two+0xc [/home/ubuntu/ALCDA2/A64/App2S/main.c @ 56]
03 0000ffff`8a239b80 00000000`0040eca4     App2S!thread_two+0x10 [/home/ubuntu/ALCDA2/A64/App2S/main.c @ 56]
04 0000ffff`8a239ba0 00000000`0044365c     App2S!start_thread+0x2e4
05 0000ffff`8a239cc0 ffffffff`ffffffff     App2S!thread_start+0xc
06 0000ffff`8a239cc0 00000000`00000000     0xffffffff`ffffffff
```

8. If we set the source code folder, we should see the problem source code location directly:

```
0:000> .srcpath C:\ALCDA2\A64\App2S\
Symbol search path is: srv*;C:\ALCDA2\A64\App2S\
Expanded Symbol search path is:
cache*;SRV*https://msdl.microsoft.com/download/symbols;c:\alcda2\a64\app2s\
```

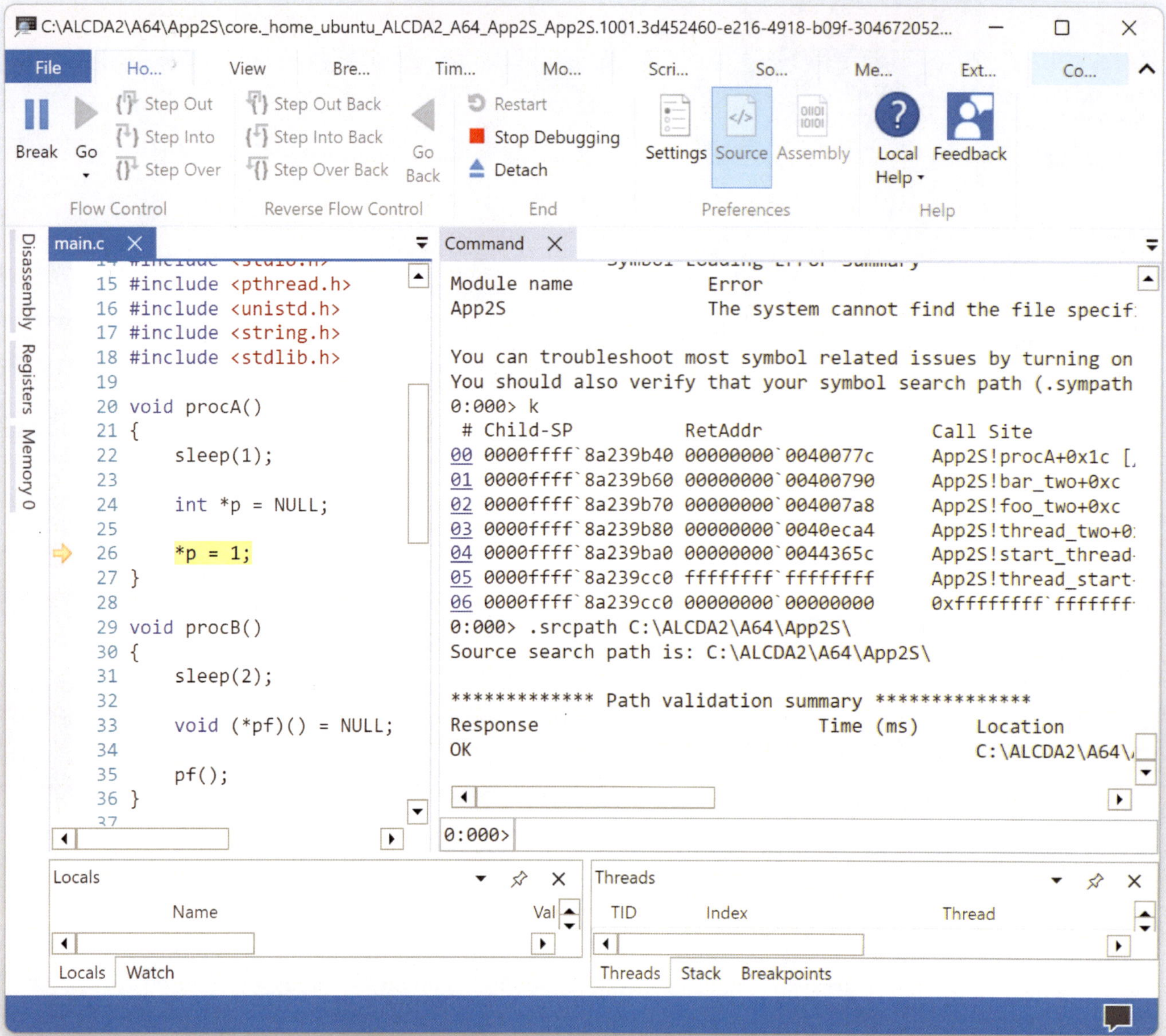

9. We close logging before exiting WinDbg:

```
0:000> .logclose
Closing open log file 'C:\ALCDA2\A64\App2S\App2S-WinDbg.log'
```

Exercise A3

- **Goal:** Learn how to identify spiking threads
- **Patterns:** Active Thread; Spiking Thread; Well-Tested Function
- \ALCDA-Dumps\Exercise-A3-x64-GDB.pdf
- \ALCDA-Dumps\Exercise-A3-A64-GDB.pdf
- \ALCDA-Dumps\Exercise-A2C-A64-WinDbg.pdf
- \ALCDA-Dumps\Exercise-A2C-x64-WinDbg.pdf

Exercise A3 (x64, GDB)

Goal: Learn how to identify spiking threads.

Patterns: Active Thread; Spiking Thread; Well-Tested Function.

1. The application **App3** was consuming 100% CPU (from the **top** command output):

```
$ top
top - 13:19:10 up 23:14,  0 users,  load average: 0.74, 0.25, 0.09
Tasks:  10 total,   1 running,   9 sleeping,   0 stopped,   0 zombie
%Cpu(s): 12.5 us,  0.0 sy,  0.0 ni, 87.5 id,  0.0 wa,  0.0 hi,  0.0 si,  0.0 st
MiB Mem :   7912.4 total,   5556.1 free,    270.2 used,   2086.1 buff/cache
MiB Swap:   2048.0 total,   2048.0 free,      0.0 used.   7386.6 avail Mem

  PID USER      PR  NI    VIRT    RES    SHR S  %CPU  %MEM     TIME+ COMMAND
 3975 coredump  20   0   42068      4      0 S 100.0   0.0   1:20.69 App3
    1 root      20   0    1744   1080   1016 S   0.0   0.0   0:00.00 init
  117 root      20   0    1764     84      0 S   0.0   0.0   0:06.16 init
 3121 coredump  20   0   42068    112    104 S   0.0   0.0   0:00.02 App1
 3343 root      20   0    1764     68      0 S   0.0   0.0   0:00.00 init
 3344 root      20   0    1764     84      0 S   0.0   0.0   0:03.54 init
 3345 coredump  20   0    6992   3852   3248 S   0.0   0.0   0:00.02 bash
 3349 coredump  20   0   26124   9476   6988 S   0.0   0.1   0:07.67 mc
 3351 coredump  20   0    7124   3872   3212 S   0.0   0.0   0:00.87 bash
 3940 coredump  20   0   10968   3524   3040 R   0.0   0.0   0:00.00 top
```

Its core dump was saved using **gcore**:

```
~/ALCDA2/x64/App3$ gcore -o App3.core 3975
[New LWP 3976]
[New LWP 3977]
[New LWP 3978]
[New LWP 3979]
[New LWP 3980]
[Thread debugging using libthread_db enabled]
Using host libthread_db library "/lib/x86_64-linux-gnu/libthread_db.so.1".
0x0000000000441a80 in nanosleep ()
Saved corefile App3.core.3975
[Inferior 1 (process 3975) detached]
```

2. Load the *App3.core.3975* dump file and *App3* executable from the x64/App3 directory:

```
~/ALCDA2/x64/App3$ gdb -c App3.core.3975 -se App3
GNU gdb (Debian 8.2.1-2+b3) 8.2.1
Copyright (C) 2018 Free Software Foundation, Inc.
License GPLv3+: GNU GPL version 3 or later <http://gnu.org/licenses/gpl.html>
This is free software: you are free to change and redistribute it.
There is NO WARRANTY, to the extent permitted by law.
Type "show copying" and "show warranty" for details.
This GDB was configured as "x86_64-linux-gnu".
Type "show configuration" for configuration details.
For bug reporting instructions, please see:
<http://www.gnu.org/software/gdb/bugs/>.
Find the GDB manual and other documentation resources online at:
    <http://www.gnu.org/software/gdb/documentation/>.
```

```
For help, type "help".
Type "apropos word" to search for commands related to "word"...
Reading symbols from App3...done.
[New LWP 3975]
[New LWP 3976]
[New LWP 3977]
[New LWP 3978]
[New LWP 3979]
[New LWP 3980]
[Thread debugging using libthread_db enabled]
Using host libthread_db library "/lib/x86_64-linux-gnu/libthread_db.so.1".
Core was generated by `./App3'.
#0  0x0000000000441a80 in nanosleep ()
[Current thread is 1 (Thread 0xbfc880 (LWP 3975))]
```

3. Set logging to a file in case of lengthy output from some commands:

```
(gdb) set logging on App3.log
Copying output to App3.log.
```

4. List all threads:

```
(gdb) info threads
  Id   Target Id                          Frame
* 1    Thread 0xbfc880 (LWP 3975)         0x0000000000441a80 in nanosleep ()
  2    Thread 0x7fc68ca9f700 (LWP 3976) 0x0000000000441a80 in nanosleep ()
  3    Thread 0x7fc68c29e700 (LWP 3977) 0x0000000000441a80 in nanosleep ()
  4    Thread 0x7fc68ba9d700 (LWP 3978) 0x0000000000441a80 in nanosleep ()
  5    Thread 0x7fc68b29c700 (LWP 3979) 0x0000000000441a80 in nanosleep ()
  6    Thread 0x7fc68aa9b700 (LWP 3980) 0x0000000000401e04 in __sqrt_finite ()
```

5. Switch to the active thread #6:

```
(gdb) thread 6
[Switching to thread 6 (Thread 0x7fc68aa9b700 (LWP 3980))]
#0  0x0000000000401e04 in __sqrt_finite ()

(gdb) bt
#0  0x0000000000401e04 in __sqrt_finite ()
#1  0x0000000000401bdc in proc ()
#2  0x0000000000401cf1 in bar_five ()
#3  0x0000000000401d02 in foo_five ()
#4  0x0000000000401d1b in thread_five ()
#5  0x0000000000403143 in start_thread (arg=<optimized out>) at pthread_create.c:486
#6  0x00000000004442df in clone ()
```

6. Disassemble the current instruction and check if it is normal:

```
(gdb) x/i 0x0000000000401e04
   0x401e04 <__sqrt_finite+4>:   retq

(gdb) disassemble __sqrt_finite
Dump of assembler code for function __sqrt_finite:
   0x0000000000401e00 <+0>:     sqrtsd %xmm0,%xmm0
   0x0000000000401e04 <+4>:     retq
End of assembler dump.
```

Note: The library functions are usually well-tested, so most likely the problem originated in their callers.

7. Disassemble the return address for the *proc* function (this GDB version shows proc instead of *procB* from the source code) to see an infinite loop:

```
(gdb) disassemble 0x0000000000401bdc
Dump of assembler code for function procB:
   0x0000000000401bbd <+0>:     push   %rbp
   0x0000000000401bbe <+1>:     mov    %rsp,%rbp
   0x0000000000401bc1 <+4>:     sub    $0x10,%rsp
   0x0000000000401bc5 <+8>:     movsd  0x9243b(%rip),%xmm0        # 0x494008
   0x0000000000401bcd <+16>:    movsd  %xmm0,-0x8(%rbp)
   0x0000000000401bd2 <+21>:    movsd  -0x8(%rbp),%xmm0
   0x0000000000401bd7 <+26>:    callq  0x401de0 <sqrtf64>
   0x0000000000401bdc <+31>:    movq   %xmm0,%rax
   0x0000000000401be1 <+36>:    mov    %rax,-0x8(%rbp)
   0x0000000000401be5 <+40>:    jmp    0x401bd2 <procB+21>
End of assembler dump.
```

Exercise A3 (A64, GDB)

Goal: Learn how to identify spiking threads.

Patterns: Active Thread; Spiking Thread; Well-Tested Function.

1. The application App3 was consuming 100% CPU (from the **top** command output):

```
$ top
top - 19:59:39 up 31 days, 19:09,  1 user,  load average: 1.00, 0.72, 0.34
Tasks: 184 total,   1 running, 128 sleeping,   0 stopped,   0 zombie
%Cpu(s): 25.1 us,  0.0 sy,  0.0 ni, 74.8 id,  0.0 wa,  0.1 hi,  0.0 si,  0.0 st
KiB Mem : 23799872 total, 19518400 free,   816064 used,  3465408 buff/cache
KiB Swap:  8388544 total,  8388544 free,        0 used. 19342592 avail Mem

  PID USER      PR  NI    VIRT    RES    SHR S  %CPU %MEM     TIME+ COMMAND
21335 opc       20   0   42752     64      0 S  99.7  0.0   6:08.44 App3
21348 opc       20   0  119360   8000   3776 R   0.3  0.0   0:00.37 top
    1 root      20   0  165888  14976   7488 S   0.0  0.1   5:44.10 systemd
    2 root      20   0       0      0      0 S   0.0  0.0   0:02.24 kthreadd
    3 root       0 -20       0      0      0 I   0.0  0.0   0:00.00 rcu_gp
    4 root       0 -20       0      0      0 I   0.0  0.0   0:00.00 rcu_par_gp
    6 root       0 -20       0      0      0 I   0.0  0.0   0:00.00 kworker/0:0H-kb
    8 root       0 -20       0      0      0 I   0.0  0.0   0:00.04 mm_percpu_wq
    9 root      20   0       0      0      0 S   0.0  0.0   0:27.66 ksoftirqd/0
   10 root      20   0       0      0      0 I   0.0  0.0   9:59.60 rcu_sched
   11 root      rt   0       0      0      0 S   0.0  0.0   0:31.70 migration/0
   13 root      20   0       0      0      0 S   0.0  0.0   0:00.00 cpuhp/0
   14 root      20   0       0      0      0 S   0.0  0.0   0:00.00 cpuhp/1
   15 root      rt   0       0      0      0 S   0.0  0.0   0:34.69 migration/1
   16 root      20   0       0      0      0 S   0.0  0.0   0:23.54 ksoftirqd/1
   18 root       0 -20       0      0      0 I   0.0  0.0   0:31.65 kworker/1:0H-kb
   19 root       0 -20       0      0      0 I   0.0  0.0   0:00.00 kworker/1:1H
   20 root      20   0       0      0      0 S   0.0  0.0   0:00.00 cpuhp/2
   21 root      rt   0       0      0      0 S   0.0  0.0   0:31.60 migration/2
   22 root      20   0       0      0      0 S   0.0  0.0   0:23.26 ksoftirqd/2
   24 root       0 -20       0      0      0 I   0.0  0.0   0:25.78 kworker/2:0H-kb
   25 root      20   0       0      0      0 S   0.0  0.0   0:00.00 cpuhp/3
```

Its core dump was saved using **gcore**:

```
~/ALCDA2/A64/App3$ gcore -o App3.core 21335
[New LWP 21340]
[New LWP 21339]
[New LWP 21338]
[New LWP 21337]
[New LWP 21336]
[Thread debugging using libthread_db enabled]
Using host libthread_db library "/lib64/libthread_db.so.1".
0x0000000000414364 in nanosleep ()
Saved corefile App3.core.21335
[Inferior 1 (process 21335) detached]
```

2. Load the *App3.core.21335* dump file and *App3* executable from the A64/App3 directory:

```
~/ALCDA2/A64/App3$ gdb-multiarch -c App3.core.21335 -se App3
GNU gdb (Debian 8.2.1-2+b3) 8.2.1
Copyright (C) 2018 Free Software Foundation, Inc.
License GPLv3+: GNU GPL version 3 or later <http://gnu.org/licenses/gpl.html>
This is free software: you are free to change and redistribute it.
There is NO WARRANTY, to the extent permitted by law.
Type "show copying" and "show warranty" for details.
This GDB was configured as "x86_64-linux-gnu".
Type "show configuration" for configuration details.
For bug reporting instructions, please see:
<http://www.gnu.org/software/gdb/bugs/>.
Find the GDB manual and other documentation resources online at:
    <http://www.gnu.org/software/gdb/documentation/>.

For help, type "help".
Type "apropos word" to search for commands related to "word"...
Reading symbols from App3...(no debugging symbols found)...done.
[New LWP 21336]
[New LWP 21337]
[New LWP 21338]
[New LWP 21339]
[New LWP 21340]
[New LWP 21335]
Core was generated by `./App3'.
#0  0x0000000000414364 in nanosleep ()
[Current thread is 1 (LWP 21336)]
```

3. Set logging to a file in case of lengthy output from some commands:

```
(gdb) set logging on App3.log
Copying output to App3.log.
```

4. List all threads:

```
(gdb) info threads
  Id   Target Id         Frame
* 1    LWP 21336         0x0000000000414364 in nanosleep ()
  2    LWP 21337         0x0000000000414364 in nanosleep ()
  3    LWP 21338         0x0000000000414364 in nanosleep ()
  4    LWP 21339         0x0000000000414364 in nanosleep ()
  5    LWP 21340         0x0000000000408400 in __sqrt_finite ()
  6    LWP 21335         0x0000000000414364 in nanosleep ()
```

5. Switch to the active thread #5:

```
(gdb) thread 5
[Switching to thread 5 (LWP 21340)]
#0  0x0000000000408400 in __sqrt_finite ()

(gdb) bt
#0  0x0000000000408400 in __sqrt_finite ()
#1  0x0000000000403214 in proc ()
#2  0x0000000000403350 in bar_five ()
#3  0x0000000000403364 in foo_five ()
#4  0x000000000040337c in thread_five ()
#5  0x000000000040c5e4 in start_thread ()
#6  0x0000000000431920 in thread_start ()
```

6. Disassemble the current instruction and check if it is normal:

```
(gdb) x/i 0x0000000000408400
=> 0x408400 <__sqrt_finite+328>:        fcmpe   d1, d0

(gdb) disassemble __sqrt_finite
Dump of assembler code for function __sqrt_finite:
   0x00000000004082b8 <+0>:      fmov    x1, d0
   0x00000000004082bc <+4>:      asr     x0, x1, #32
   0x00000000004082c0 <+8>:      and     w2, w0, #0x1fffff
   0x00000000004082c4 <+12>:     orr     w3, w2, #0x3fe00000
   0x00000000004082c8 <+16>:     stp     x29, x30, [sp, #-16]!
   0x00000000004082cc <+20>:     sub     w4, w0, #0x100, lsl #12
   0x00000000004082d0 <+24>:     bfi     x1, x3, #32, #32
   0x00000000004082d4 <+28>:     mov     w3, #0x7fdfffff                 // #2145386495
   0x00000000004082d8 <+32>:     cmp     w4, w3
   0x00000000004082dc <+36>:     mov     x29, sp
   0x00000000004082e0 <+40>:     adrp    x4, 0x490000 <arena_thread_freeres+72>
   0x00000000004082e4 <+44>:     asr     w2, w2, #14
   0x00000000004082e8 <+48>:     add     x4, x4, #0xce0
   0x00000000004082ec <+52>:     mov     x3, #0x0                        // #0
   0x00000000004082f0 <+56>:     ldr     d2, [x4, w2, sxtw #3]
   0x00000000004082f4 <+60>:     fmov    d3, x1
   0x00000000004082f8 <+64>:     b.hi    0x40841c <__sqrt_finite+356>  // b.pmore
   0x00000000004082fc <+68>:     fmul    d0, d2, d3
   0x0000000000408300 <+72>:     fmul    d0, d0, d2
   0x0000000000408304 <+76>:     fmov    d1, #1.000000000000000000e+00
   0x0000000000408308 <+80>:     fsub    d0, d1, d0
   0x000000000040830c <+84>:     ldr     d1, 0x408498
   0x0000000000408310 <+88>:     ldr     d4, 0x4084a0
   0x0000000000408314 <+92>:     fmul    d1, d0, d1
   0x0000000000408318 <+96>:     fadd    d1, d1, d4
   0x000000000040831c <+100>:    ldr     d4, 0x4084a8
   0x0000000000408320 <+104>:    fmul    d1, d1, d0
   0x0000000000408324 <+108>:    fadd    d1, d1, d4
   0x0000000000408328 <+112>:    fmul    d0, d1, d0
   0x000000000040832c <+116>:    ldr     d1, 0x4084b0
   0x0000000000408330 <+120>:    and     w0, w0, #0x7fe00000
   0x0000000000408334 <+124>:    fadd    d0, d0, d1
   0x0000000000408338 <+128>:    fmul    d0, d0, d2
   0x000000000040833c <+132>:    ldr     d1, 0x4084b8
   0x0000000000408340 <+136>:    fmul    d2, d0, d3
   0x0000000000408344 <+140>:    fadd    d4, d2, d1
   0x0000000000408348 <+144>:    fsub    d4, d4, d1
   0x000000000040834c <+148>:    fsub    d5, d2, d4
   0x0000000000408350 <+152>:    fmul    d1, d4, d4
   0x0000000000408354 <+156>:    fadd    d4, d2, d4
   0x0000000000408358 <+160>:    fsub    d1, d3, d1
   0x000000000040835c <+164>:    fmul    d4, d5, d4
   0x0000000000408360 <+168>:    fmov    d5, #5.000000000000000000e-01
   0x0000000000408364 <+172>:    fmul    d0, d0, d5
   0x0000000000408368 <+176>:    fsub    d4, d1, d4
   0x000000000040836c <+180>:    fmul    d4, d0, d4
   0x0000000000408370 <+184>:    fadd    d1, d2, d4
   0x0000000000408374 <+188>:    fsub    d2, d2, d1
   0x0000000000408378 <+192>:    ldr     d0, 0x4084c0
--Type <RET> for more, q to quit, c to continue without paging--
   0x000000000040837c <+196>:    fadd    d4, d2, d4
   0x0000000000408380 <+200>:    fmul    d0, d4, d0
```

```
   0x0000000000408384 <+204>:   fadd    d0, d0, d1
   0x0000000000408388 <+208>:   mov     w1, #0x20000000                 // #536870912
   0x000000000040838c <+212>:   add     w0, w1, w0, lsr #1
   0x0000000000408390 <+216>:   fcmp    d0, d1
   0x0000000000408394 <+220>:   bfi     x3, x0, #32, #32
   0x0000000000408398 <+224>:   b.eq    0x40845c <__sqrt_finite+420>  // b.none
   0x000000000040839c <+228>:   fmov    d0, #1.50000000000000000000e+00
   0x00000000004083a0 <+232>:   ldr     d2, 0x4084c8
   0x00000000004083a4 <+236>:   fmul    d4, d4, d0
   0x00000000004083a8 <+240>:   fadd    d0, d4, d1
   0x00000000004083ac <+244>:   fmul    d4, d1, d2
   0x00000000004083b0 <+248>:   fmul    d2, d0, d2
   0x00000000004083b4 <+252>:   fsub    d6, d1, d4
   0x00000000004083b8 <+256>:   fsub    d5, d0, d2
   0x00000000004083bc <+260>:   fadd    d4, d6, d4
   0x00000000004083c0 <+264>:   fadd    d2, d5, d2
   0x00000000004083c4 <+268>:   fsub    d6, d0, d2
   0x00000000004083c8 <+272>:   fmul    d16, d4, d2
   0x00000000004083cc <+276>:   fmul    d5, d1, d0
   0x00000000004083d0 <+280>:   fsub    d7, d1, d4
   0x00000000004083d4 <+284>:   fsub    d16, d16, d5
   0x00000000004083d8 <+288>:   fmul    d4, d4, d6
   0x00000000004083dc <+292>:   fmul    d2, d7, d2
   0x00000000004083e0 <+296>:   fadd    d4, d16, d4
   0x00000000004083e4 <+300>:   fadd    d2, d4, d2
   0x00000000004083e8 <+304>:   fmul    d7, d7, d6
   0x00000000004083ec <+308>:   fsub    d3, d5, d3
   0x00000000004083f0 <+312>:   fadd    d6, d2, d7
   0x00000000004083f4 <+316>:   fadd    d3, d3, d6
   0x00000000004083f8 <+320>:   fcmpe   d3, #0.0
   0x00000000004083fc <+324>:   b.mi    0x408484 <__sqrt_finite+460>  // b.first
=> 0x0000000000408400 <+328>:   fcmpe   d1, d0
   0x0000000000408404 <+332>:   b.gt    0x40840c <__sqrt_finite+340>
   0x0000000000408408 <+336>:   fmov    d0, d1
   0x000000000040840c <+340>:   fmov    d1, x3
   0x0000000000408410 <+344>:   fmul    d0, d0, d1
   0x0000000000408414 <+348>:   ldp     x29, x30, [sp], #16
   0x0000000000408418 <+352>:   ret
   0x000000000040841c <+356>:   and     w2, w0, #0x7ff00000
   0x0000000000408420 <+360>:   mov     w1, #0x7ff00000                 // #2146435072
   0x0000000000408424 <+364>:   cmp     w2, w1
   0x0000000000408428 <+368>:   b.eq    0x40846c <__sqrt_finite+436>  // b.none
   0x000000000040842c <+372>:   fcmp    d0, #0.0
   0x0000000000408430 <+376>:   b.eq    0x408414 <__sqrt_finite+348>  // b.none
   0x0000000000408434 <+380>:   tbnz    w0, #31, 0x408478 <__sqrt_finite+448>
   0x0000000000408438 <+384>:   adrp    x0, 0x491000 <inroot+800>
   0x000000000040843c <+388>:   ldr     d1, [x0, #224]
   0x0000000000408440 <+392>:   fmul    d0, d0, d1
--Type <RET> for more, q to quit, c to continue without paging--
   0x0000000000408444 <+396>:   bl      0x4082b8 <__sqrt_finite>
   0x0000000000408448 <+400>:   adrp    x0, 0x491000 <inroot+800>
   0x000000000040844c <+404>:   ldr     d1, [x0, #232]
   0x0000000000408450 <+408>:   ldp     x29, x30, [sp], #16
   0x0000000000408454 <+412>:   fmul    d0, d1, d0
   0x0000000000408458 <+416>:   ret
   0x000000000040845c <+420>:   fmov    d2, x3
   0x0000000000408460 <+424>:   fmul    d0, d1, d2
   0x0000000000408464 <+428>:   ldp     x29, x30, [sp], #16
   0x0000000000408468 <+432>:   ret
   0x000000000040846c <+436>:   fmul    d1, d0, d0
```

```
   0x0000000000408470 <+440>:   fadd    d0, d1, d0
   0x0000000000408474 <+444>:   b       0x408414 <__sqrt_finite+348>
   0x0000000000408478 <+448>:   fsub    d0, d0, d0
   0x000000000040847c <+452>:   fdiv    d0, d0, d0
   0x0000000000408480 <+456>:   b       0x408414 <__sqrt_finite+348>
   0x0000000000408484 <+460>:   fcmpe   d1, d0
   0x0000000000408488 <+464>:   b.mi    0x40840c <__sqrt_finite+340>  // b.first
   0x000000000040848c <+468>:   fmov    d0, d1
   0x0000000000408490 <+472>:   b       0x40840c <__sqrt_finite+340>
End of assembler dump.
```

Note: The function is quite large compared to the x64 version, where there is a dedicated instruction. But the library functions are usually well-tested, so most likely, the problem originated in their callers.

7. Disassemble the return address for the *proc* function (this GDB version shows *proc* instead of *procB* from the source code) to see an infinite loop:

```
(gdb) disassemble 0x0000000000403214
Dump of assembler code for function procB:
   0x00000000004031fc <+0>:     stp     x29, x30, [sp, #-32]!
   0x0000000000403200 <+4>:     mov     x29, sp
   0x0000000000403204 <+8>:     ldr     x0, 0x403220
   0x0000000000403208 <+12>:    str     x0, [x29, #24]
   0x000000000040320c <+16>:    ldr     d0, [x29, #24]
   0x0000000000403210 <+20>:    bl      0x403424 <sqrt>
   0x0000000000403214 <+24>:    str     d0, [x29, #24]
   0x0000000000403218 <+28>:    b       0x40320c <procB+16>
End of assembler dump.
```

Exercise A3 (x64, WinDbg)

Goal: Learn how to identify spiking threads.

Patterns: Active Thread; Spiking Thread; Well-Tested Function.

1. The application **App3** was consuming 100% CPU (from the **top** command output):

```
$ top
top - 13:19:10 up 23:14,  0 users,  load average: 0.74, 0.25, 0.09
Tasks:  10 total,   1 running,   9 sleeping,   0 stopped,   0 zombie
%Cpu(s): 12.5 us,  0.0 sy,  0.0 ni, 87.5 id,  0.0 wa,  0.0 hi,  0.0 si,  0.0 st
MiB Mem :   7912.4 total,   5556.1 free,    270.2 used,   2086.1 buff/cache
MiB Swap:   2048.0 total,   2048.0 free,      0.0 used.   7386.6 avail Mem

  PID USER      PR  NI    VIRT    RES    SHR S  %CPU  %MEM     TIME+ COMMAND
 3975 coredump  20   0   42068      4      0 S 100.0   0.0   1:20.69 App3
    1 root      20   0    1744   1080   1016 S   0.0   0.0   0:00.00 init
  117 root      20   0    1764     84      0 S   0.0   0.0   0:06.16 init
 3121 coredump  20   0   42068    112    104 S   0.0   0.0   0:00.02 App1
 3343 root      20   0    1764     68      0 S   0.0   0.0   0:00.00 init
 3344 root      20   0    1764     84      0 S   0.0   0.0   0:03.54 init
 3345 coredump  20   0    6992   3852   3248 S   0.0   0.0   0:00.02 bash
 3349 coredump  20   0   26124   9476   6988 S   0.0   0.1   0:07.67 mc
 3351 coredump  20   0    7124   3872   3212 S   0.0   0.0   0:00.87 bash
 3940 coredump  20   0   10968   3524   3040 R   0.0   0.0   0:00.00 to
```

Its core dump was saved using **gcore**:

```
~/ALCDA2/A64/App3$ gcore -o App3.core 21335
[New LWP 3976]
[New LWP 3977]
[New LWP 3978]
[New LWP 3979]
[New LWP 3980]
[Thread debugging using libthread_db enabled]
Using host libthread_db library "/lib/x86_64-linux-gnu/libthread_db.so.1".
0x0000000000441a80 in nanosleep ()
Saved corefile App3.core.3975
[Inferior 1 (process 3975) detached]
```

2. Launch WinDbg.

3. Load the *App3.core.3975* dump file from the x64\App3 folder:

```
Microsoft (R) Windows Debugger Version 10.0.27725.1000 AMD64
Copyright (c) Microsoft Corporation. All rights reserved.


Loading Dump File [C:\ALCDA2\x64\App3\App3.core.3975]
64-bit machine not using 64-bit API

************* Path validation summary **************
Response                         Time (ms)     Location
Deferred                                       srv*
Symbol search path is: srv*
```

```
Executable search path is:
Generic Unix Version 0 UP Free x64
System Uptime: not available
Process Uptime: not available
..
*** WARNING: Unable to verify timestamp for App3
App3+0x41a80:
00000000`00441a80 cmp     rax,0FFFFFFFFFFFFF000h
```

4. Set logging to a file in case of lengthy output from some commands:

```
0:000> .logopen C:\ALCDA2\x64\App3\App3-WinDbg.log
Opened log file 'C:\ALCDA2\x64\App3\App3-WinDbg.log'
```

5. Specify the dump folder as the symbol path and reload symbols:

```
0:000> .symfix; .sympath+ C:\ALCDA2\x64\App3\
Symbol search path is: srv*;C:\ALCDA2\x64\App3\
Expanded Symbol search path is:
cache*;SRV*https://msdl.microsoft.com/download/symbols;c:\alcda2\x64\app3\

************* Path validation summary **************
Response                         Time (ms)     Location
Deferred                                       srv*
OK                                             C:\ALCDA2\x64\App3\
*** WARNING: Unable to verify timestamp for App3

0:000> .reload
..
*** WARNING: Unable to verify timestamp for App3

************* Symbol Loading Error Summary **************
Module name            Error
App3                   The system cannot find the file specified

You can troubleshoot most symbol related issues by turning on symbol loading diagnostics (!sym
noisy) and repeating the command that caused symbols to be loaded.
You should also verify that your symbol search path (.sympath) is correct.
```

Note: We ignore warnings and errors as they are not relevant for now.

6. List all thread stack traces to identify active threads:

```
0:000> ~*k

Unable to get thread data for thread 0
.  0  Id: f87.f87 Suspend: 0 Teb: 00000000`00000000 Unfrozen
 # Child-SP          RetAddr               Call Site
00 00007ffc`1e122a70 00000000`00000000     App3+0x41a80

Unable to get thread data for thread 1
   1  Id: f87.f88 Suspend: 0 Teb: 00000000`00000000 Unfrozen
 # Child-SP          RetAddr               Call Site
00 00007fc6`8ca9ed10 00000000`00000000     App3+0x41a80

Unable to get thread data for thread 2
   2  Id: f87.f89 Suspend: 0 Teb: 00000000`00000000 Unfrozen
 # Child-SP          RetAddr               Call Site
```

```
00 00007fc6`8c29dd10 00000000`00000000     App3+0x41a80

Unable to get thread data for thread 3
   3  Id: f87.f8a Suspend: 0 Teb: 00000000`00000000 Unfrozen
 # Child-SP          RetAddr               Call Site
00 00007fc6`8ba9cd00 00000000`00000000     App3+0x41a80

Unable to get thread data for thread 4
   4  Id: f87.f8b Suspend: 0 Teb: 00000000`00000000 Unfrozen
 # Child-SP          RetAddr               Call Site
00 00007fc6`8b29bd10 00000000`00000000     App3+0x41a80

Unable to get thread data for thread 5
   5  Id: f87.f8c Suspend: 0 Teb: 00000000`00000000 Unfrozen
 # Child-SP          RetAddr               Call Site
00 00007fc6`8aa9ad58 00000000`00401cf1     App3+0x1e04
01 00007fc6`8aa9ad80 00000000`00401d02     App3+0x1cf1
02 00007fc6`8aa9ad90 00000000`00401d1b     App3+0x1d02
03 00007fc6`8aa9ada0 00000000`00000000     App3+0x1d1b
```

Note: We still have incorrect traces, so we apply some symbol options:

```
0:000> .symopt+ 0x40
Symbol options are 0x30377:
  0x00000001 - SYMOPT_CASE_INSENSITIVE
  0x00000002 - SYMOPT_UNDNAME
  0x00000004 - SYMOPT_DEFERRED_LOADS
  0x00000010 - SYMOPT_LOAD_LINES
  0x00000020 - SYMOPT_OMAP_FIND_NEAREST
  0x00000040 - SYMOPT_LOAD_ANYTHING
  0x00000100 - SYMOPT_NO_UNQUALIFIED_LOADS
  0x00000200 - SYMOPT_FAIL_CRITICAL_ERRORS
  0x00010000 - SYMOPT_AUTO_PUBLICS
  0x00020000 - SYMOPT_NO_IMAGE_SEARCH
*** WARNING: Unable to verify timestamp for App3

0:000> ~*kL

Unable to get thread data for thread 0
.  0  Id: f87.f87 Suspend: 0 Teb: 00000000`00000000 Unfrozen
 # Child-SP          RetAddr               Call Site
00 00007ffc`1e122a70 00000000`00441a0a     App3!nanosleep+0x40
01 00007ffc`1e122aa0 00000000`00401dcc     App3!sleep+0x3a
02 00007ffc`1e122ae0 00000000`004075f1     App3!main+0xaa
03 00007ffc`1e122b30 00000000`00401aba     App3!_libc_start_main+0x3d1
04 00007ffc`1e122c30 ffffffff`ffffffff     App3!start+0x2a
05 00007ffc`1e122c38 00000000`00000000     0xffffffff`ffffffff

Unable to get thread data for thread 1
   1  Id: f87.f88 Suspend: 0 Teb: 00000000`00000000 Unfrozen
 # Child-SP          RetAddr               Call Site
00 00007fc6`8ca9ed10 00000000`00441a0a     App3!nanosleep+0x40
01 00007fc6`8ca9ed40 00000000`00401bf5     App3!sleep+0x3a
02 00007fc6`8ca9ed80 00000000`00401c06     App3!bar_one+0xe
03 00007fc6`8ca9ed90 00000000`00401c1f     App3!foo_one+0xe
04 00007fc6`8ca9eda0 00000000`00403143     App3!thread_one+0x16
05 00007fc6`8ca9edc0 00000000`004442df     App3!start_thread+0xf3
06 00007fc6`8ca9ee80 ffffffff`ffffffff     App3!_clone+0x3f
07 00007fc6`8ca9ee88 00000000`00000000     0xffffffff`ffffffff
```

```
Unable to get thread data for thread 2
   2  Id: f87.f89 Suspend: 0 Teb: 00000000`00000000 Unfrozen
 # Child-SP          RetAddr               Call Site
00 00007fc6`8c29dd10 00000000`00441a0a     App3!nanosleep+0x40
01 00007fc6`8c29dd40 00000000`00401c34     App3!sleep+0x3a
02 00007fc6`8c29dd80 00000000`00401c45     App3!bar_two+0xe
03 00007fc6`8c29dd90 00000000`00401c5e     App3!foo_two+0xe
04 00007fc6`8c29dda0 00000000`00403143     App3!thread_two+0x16
05 00007fc6`8c29ddc0 00000000`004442df     App3!start_thread+0xf3
06 00007fc6`8c29de80 ffffffff`ffffffff     App3!_clone+0x3f
07 00007fc6`8c29de88 00000000`00000000     0xffffffff`ffffffff

Unable to get thread data for thread 3
   3  Id: f87.f8a Suspend: 0 Teb: 00000000`00000000 Unfrozen
 # Child-SP          RetAddr               Call Site
00 00007fc6`8ba9cd00 00000000`00441a0a     App3!nanosleep+0x40
01 00007fc6`8ba9cd30 00000000`00401bbb     App3!sleep+0x3a
02 00007fc6`8ba9cd70 00000000`00401c73     App3!procA+0xe
03 00007fc6`8ba9cd80 00000000`00401c84     App3!bar_three+0xe
04 00007fc6`8ba9cd90 00000000`00401c9d     App3!foo_three+0xe
05 00007fc6`8ba9cda0 00000000`00403143     App3!thread_three+0x16
06 00007fc6`8ba9cdc0 00000000`004442df     App3!start_thread+0xf3
07 00007fc6`8ba9ce80 ffffffff`ffffffff     App3!_clone+0x3f
08 00007fc6`8ba9ce88 00000000`00000000     0xffffffff`ffffffff

Unable to get thread data for thread 4
   4  Id: f87.f8b Suspend: 0 Teb: 00000000`00000000 Unfrozen
 # Child-SP          RetAddr               Call Site
00 00007fc6`8b29bd10 00000000`00441a0a     App3!nanosleep+0x40
01 00007fc6`8b29bd40 00000000`00401cb2     App3!sleep+0x3a
02 00007fc6`8b29bd80 00000000`00401cc3     App3!bar_four+0xe
03 00007fc6`8b29bd90 00000000`00401cdc     App3!foo_four+0xe
04 00007fc6`8b29bda0 00000000`00403143     App3!thread_four+0x16
05 00007fc6`8b29bdc0 00000000`004442df     App3!start_thread+0xf3
06 00007fc6`8b29be80 ffffffff`ffffffff     App3!_clone+0x3f
07 00007fc6`8b29be88 00000000`00000000     0xffffffff`ffffffff

Unable to get thread data for thread 5
   5  Id: f87.f8c Suspend: 0 Teb: 00000000`00000000 Unfrozen
 # Child-SP          RetAddr               Call Site
00 00007fc6`8aa9ad58 00000000`00401bdc     App3!_sqrt_finite+0x4
01 00007fc6`8aa9ad60 00000000`00401cf1     App3!procB+0x1f
02 00007fc6`8aa9ad80 00000000`00401d02     App3!bar_five+0xe
03 00007fc6`8aa9ad90 00000000`00401d1b     App3!foo_five+0xe
04 00007fc6`8aa9ada0 00000000`00403143     App3!thread_five+0x16
05 00007fc6`8aa9adc0 00000000`004442df     App3!start_thread+0xf3
06 00007fc6`8aa9ae80 ffffffff`ffffffff     App3!_clone+0x3f
07 00007fc6`8aa9ae88 00000000`00000000     0xffffffff`ffffffff
```

7. Switch to the active thread #4:

```
0:000> ~5s
App3!_sqrt_finite+0x4:
00000000`00401e04 ret
```

```
0:005> kL
 # Child-SP          RetAddr               Call Site
00 00007fc6`8aa9ad58 00000000`00401bdc     App3!_sqrt_finite+0x4
01 00007fc6`8aa9ad60 00000000`00401cf1     App3!procB+0x1f
02 00007fc6`8aa9ad80 00000000`00401d02     App3!bar_five+0xe
03 00007fc6`8aa9ad90 00000000`00401d1b     App3!foo_five+0xe
04 00007fc6`8aa9ada0 00000000`00403143     App3!thread_five+0x16
05 00007fc6`8aa9adc0 00000000`004442df     App3!start_thread+0xf3
06 00007fc6`8aa9ae80 ffffffff`ffffffff     App3!_clone+0x3f
07 00007fc6`8aa9ae88 00000000`00000000     0xffffffff`ffffffff
```

Note: We see that the current instruction is normal, related to floating-point operations. The library functions are usually well-tested, so most likely, the problem originated in their callers.

8. Disassemble the return address for the *procB* function to see an infinite loop:

```
0:005> uf 00000000`00401bdc
pp3!procB+0x15:
00000000`00401bd2 movsd    xmm0,mmword ptr [rbp-8]
00000000`00401bd7 call     App3!sqrt (00000000`00401de0)

App3!procB+0x1f:
00000000`00401bdc movq     rax,xmm0
00000000`00401be1 mov      qword ptr [rbp-8],rax
00000000`00401be5 jmp      App3!procB+0x15 (00000000`00401bd2)  Branch
```

9. We close logging before exiting WinDbg:

```
0:005> .logclose
Closing open log file 'C:\ALCDA2\x64\App3\App3-WinDbg.log'
```

Exercise A3 (A64, WinDbg)

Goal: Learn how to identify spiking threads.

Patterns: Active Thread; Spiking Thread; Well-Tested Function.

1. The application **App3** was consuming 100% CPU (from the **top** command output):

```
$ top
top - 19:59:39 up 31 days, 19:09,  1 user,  load average: 1.00, 0.72, 0.34
Tasks: 184 total,   1 running, 128 sleeping,   0 stopped,   0 zombie
%Cpu(s): 25.1 us,  0.0 sy,  0.0 ni, 74.8 id,  0.0 wa,  0.1 hi,  0.0 si,  0.0 st
KiB Mem : 23799872 total, 19518400 free,   816064 used,  3465408 buff/cache
KiB Swap:  8388544 total,  8388544 free,        0 used. 19342592 avail Mem

  PID USER      PR  NI    VIRT    RES    SHR S  %CPU %MEM     TIME+ COMMAND
21335 opc       20   0   42752     64      0 S  99.7  0.0   6:08.44 App3
21348 opc       20   0  119360   8000   3776 R   0.3  0.0   0:00.37 top
    1 root      20   0  165888  14976   7488 S   0.0  0.1   5:44.10 systemd
    2 root      20   0       0      0      0 S   0.0  0.0   0:02.24 kthreadd
    3 root       0 -20       0      0      0 I   0.0  0.0   0:00.00 rcu_gp
    4 root       0 -20       0      0      0 I   0.0  0.0   0:00.00 rcu_par_gp
    6 root       0 -20       0      0      0 I   0.0  0.0   0:00.00 kworker/0:0H-kb
    8 root       0 -20       0      0      0 I   0.0  0.0   0:00.04 mm_percpu_wq
    9 root      20   0       0      0      0 S   0.0  0.0   0:27.66 ksoftirqd/0
   10 root      20   0       0      0      0 I   0.0  0.0   9:59.60 rcu_sched
   11 root      rt   0       0      0      0 S   0.0  0.0   0:31.70 migration/0
   13 root      20   0       0      0      0 S   0.0  0.0   0:00.00 cpuhp/0
   14 root      20   0       0      0      0 S   0.0  0.0   0:00.00 cpuhp/1
   15 root      rt   0       0      0      0 S   0.0  0.0   0:34.69 migration/1
   16 root      20   0       0      0      0 S   0.0  0.0   0:23.54 ksoftirqd/1
   18 root       0 -20       0      0      0 I   0.0  0.0   0:31.65 kworker/1:0H-kb
   19 root       0 -20       0      0      0 I   0.0  0.0   0:00.00 kworker/1:1H
   20 root      20   0       0      0      0 S   0.0  0.0   0:00.00 cpuhp/2
   21 root      rt   0       0      0      0 S   0.0  0.0   0:31.60 migration/2
   22 root      20   0       0      0      0 S   0.0  0.0   0:23.26 ksoftirqd/2
   24 root       0 -20       0      0      0 I   0.0  0.0   0:25.78 kworker/2:0H-kb
   25 root      20   0       0      0      0 S   0.0  0.0   0:00.00 cpuhp/3
```

Its core dump was saved using **gcore**:

```
~/ALCDA2/A64/App3$ gcore -o App3.core 21335
[New LWP 21340]
[New LWP 21339]
[New LWP 21338]
[New LWP 21337]
[New LWP 21336]
[Thread debugging using libthread_db enabled]
Using host libthread_db library "/lib64/libthread_db.so.1".
0x0000000000414364 in nanosleep ()
Saved corefile App3.core.21335
[Inferior 1 (process 21335) detached]
```

2. Launch WinDbg.

3. Load the *App3.core.21335* dump file from the A64\App3 folder:

```
Microsoft (R) Windows Debugger Version 10.0.27725.1000 AMD64
Copyright (c) Microsoft Corporation. All rights reserved.


Loading Dump File [C:\ALCDA2\A64\App3\App3.core.21335]
64-bit machine not using 64-bit API

************* Path validation summary **************
Response                         Time (ms)     Location
Deferred                                       srv*
Symbol search path is: srv*
Executable search path is:
Generic Unix Version 0 UP Free ARM 64-bit (AArch64)
System Uptime: not available
Process Uptime: not available
..
*** WARNING: Unable to verify timestamp for App3
App3+0x14364:
00000000`00414364 svc         #0
```

4. Set logging to a file in case of lengthy output from some commands:

```
0:000> .logopen C:\ALCDA2\A64\App3\App3-WinDbg.log
Opened log file 'C:\ALCDA2\A64\App3\App3-WinDbg.log'
```

5. Specify the dump folder as the symbol path and reload symbols:

```
0:000> .symfix; .sympath+ C:\ALCDA2\A64\App3\
Symbol search path is: srv*;C:\ALCDA2\A64\App3\
Expanded Symbol search path is:
cache*;SRV*https://msdl.microsoft.com/download/symbols;c:\alcda2\a64\app3\

************* Path validation summary **************
Response                         Time (ms)     Location
Deferred                                       srv*
OK                                             C:\ALCDA2\A64\App3\
*** WARNING: Unable to verify timestamp for App3

0:000> .reload
..
*** WARNING: Unable to verify timestamp for App3

************* Symbol Loading Error Summary **************
Module name            Error
App3                   The system cannot find the file specified

You can troubleshoot most symbol related issues by turning on symbol loading diagnostics (!sym
noisy) and repeating the command that caused symbols to be loaded.
You should also verify that your symbol search path (.sympath) is correct.
```

Note: We ignore warnings and errors as they are not relevant for now.

6. List all thread stack traces to identify active threads:

```
0:000> ~*k

Unable to get thread data for thread 0
.  0  Id: 5357.5358 Suspend: 0 Teb: 00000000`00000000 Unfrozen
 # Child-SP          RetAddr               Call Site
00 0000fffc`8dbde5f0 00000000`0042ca74     App3!_libc_nanosleep+0x24
01 0000fffc`8dbde630 00000000`00403238     App3!sleep+0x110
02 0000fffc`8dbde820 00000000`0040324c     App3!bar_one+0x10
03 0000fffc`8dbde830 00000000`00403264     App3!foo_one+0xc
04 0000fffc`8dbde840 00000000`0040c5e4     App3!thread_one+0x10
05 0000fffc`8dbde860 00000000`00431920     App3!start_thread+0xb4
06 0000fffc`8dbde990 ffffffff`ffffffff     App3!thread_start+0x30
07 0000fffc`8dbde990 00000000`00000000     0xffffffff`ffffffff

Unable to get thread data for thread 1
   1  Id: 5357.5359 Suspend: 0 Teb: 00000000`00000000 Unfrozen
 # Child-SP          RetAddr               Call Site
00 0000fffc`8d3ce5f0 00000000`0042ca74     App3!_libc_nanosleep+0x24
01 0000fffc`8d3ce630 00000000`00403280     App3!sleep+0x110
02 0000fffc`8d3ce820 00000000`00403294     App3!bar_two+0x10
03 0000fffc`8d3ce830 00000000`004032ac     App3!foo_two+0xc
04 0000fffc`8d3ce840 00000000`0040c5e4     App3!thread_two+0x10
05 0000fffc`8d3ce860 00000000`00431920     App3!start_thread+0xb4
06 0000fffc`8d3ce990 ffffffff`ffffffff     App3!thread_start+0x30
07 0000fffc`8d3ce990 00000000`00000000     0xffffffff`ffffffff

Unable to get thread data for thread 2
   2  Id: 5357.535a Suspend: 0 Teb: 00000000`00000000 Unfrozen
 # Child-SP          RetAddr               Call Site
00 0000fffc`8cbbe5e0 00000000`0042ca74     App3!_libc_nanosleep+0x24
01 0000fffc`8cbbe620 00000000`004031f8     App3!sleep+0x110
02 0000fffc`8cbbe810 00000000`004032c4     App3!procA+0x10
03 0000fffc`8cbbe820 00000000`004032d8     App3!bar_three+0xc
04 0000fffc`8cbbe830 00000000`004032f0     App3!foo_three+0xc
05 0000fffc`8cbbe840 00000000`0040c5e4     App3!thread_three+0x10
06 0000fffc`8cbbe860 00000000`00431920     App3!start_thread+0xb4
07 0000fffc`8cbbe990 ffffffff`ffffffff     App3!thread_start+0x30
08 0000fffc`8cbbe990 00000000`00000000     0xffffffff`ffffffff

Unable to get thread data for thread 3
   3  Id: 5357.535b Suspend: 0 Teb: 00000000`00000000 Unfrozen
 # Child-SP          RetAddr               Call Site
00 0000fffc`8c3ae5f0 00000000`0042ca74     App3!_libc_nanosleep+0x24
01 0000fffc`8c3ae630 00000000`0040330c     App3!sleep+0x110
02 0000fffc`8c3ae820 00000000`00403320     App3!bar_four+0x10
03 0000fffc`8c3ae830 00000000`00403338     App3!foo_four+0xc
04 0000fffc`8c3ae840 00000000`0040c5e4     App3!thread_four+0x10
05 0000fffc`8c3ae860 00000000`00431920     App3!start_thread+0xb4
06 0000fffc`8c3ae990 ffffffff`ffffffff     App3!thread_start+0x30
07 0000fffc`8c3ae990 00000000`00000000     0xffffffff`ffffffff

Unable to get thread data for thread 4
   4  Id: 5357.535c Suspend: 0 Teb: 00000000`00000000 Unfrozen
 # Child-SP          RetAddr               Call Site
00 0000fffc`8bb9e7f0 00000000`00403214     App3!_sqrt_finite+0x148
01 0000fffc`8bb9e800 00000000`00403350     App3!procB+0x18
02 0000fffc`8bb9e820 00000000`00403364     App3!bar_five+0xc
03 0000fffc`8bb9e830 00000000`0040337c     App3!foo_five+0xc
```

```
04 0000fffc`8bb9e840 00000000`0040c5e4     App3!thread_five+0x10
05 0000fffc`8bb9e860 00000000`00431920     App3!start_thread+0xb4
06 0000fffc`8bb9e990 ffffffff`ffffffff     App3!thread_start+0x30
07 0000fffc`8bb9e990 00000000`00000000     0xffffffff`ffffffff

Unable to get thread data for thread 5
   5  Id: 5357.5357 Suspend: 0 Teb: 00000000`00000000 Unfrozen
 # Child-SP          RetAddr               Call Site
00 0000ffff`d4ed8dd0 00000000`0042ca74     App3!_libc_nanosleep+0x24
01 0000ffff`d4ed8e10 00000000`00403418     App3!sleep+0x110
02 0000ffff`d4ed9000 00000000`004165fc     App3!main+0x90
03 0000ffff`d4ed9050 00000000`00403090     App3!_libc_start_main+0x304
04 0000ffff`d4ed91b0 00000000`00000000     App3!start+0x4c
```

7. Switch to the active thread #4:

```
0:000> ~4s
App3!_sqrt_finite+0x148:
00000000`00408400 1e602030 fcmpe       d1,d0

0:004> k
 # Child-SP          RetAddr               Call Site
00 0000fffc`8bb9e7f0 00000000`00403214     App3!_sqrt_finite+0x148
01 0000fffc`8bb9e800 00000000`00403350     App3!procB+0x18
02 0000fffc`8bb9e820 00000000`00403364     App3!bar_five+0xc
03 0000fffc`8bb9e830 00000000`0040337c     App3!foo_five+0xc
04 0000fffc`8bb9e840 00000000`0040c5e4     App3!thread_five+0x10
05 0000fffc`8bb9e860 00000000`00431920     App3!start_thread+0xb4
06 0000fffc`8bb9e990 ffffffff`ffffffff     App3!thread_start+0x30
07 0000fffc`8bb9e990 00000000`00000000     0xffffffff`ffffffff
```

Note: We see that the current instruction is normal, related to floating-point operations. The library functions are usually well-tested, so most likely, the problem originated in their callers.

8. Disassemble the return address for the *procB* function to see an infinite loop:

```
0:004> uf 00000000`00403214
App3!procB+0x10:
00000000`0040320c fd400fa0 ldr         d0,[fp,#0x18]
00000000`00403210 94000085 bl          App3!sqrt (00000000`00403424)

App3!procB+0x18:
00000000`00403214 fd000fa0 str         d0,[fp,#0x18]
00000000`00403218 17fffffd b           App3!procB+0x10 (00000000`0040320c)   Branch
```

9. We close logging before exiting WinDbg:

```
0:004> .logclose
Closing open log file 'C:\ALCDA2\A64\App3\App3-WinDbg.log'
```

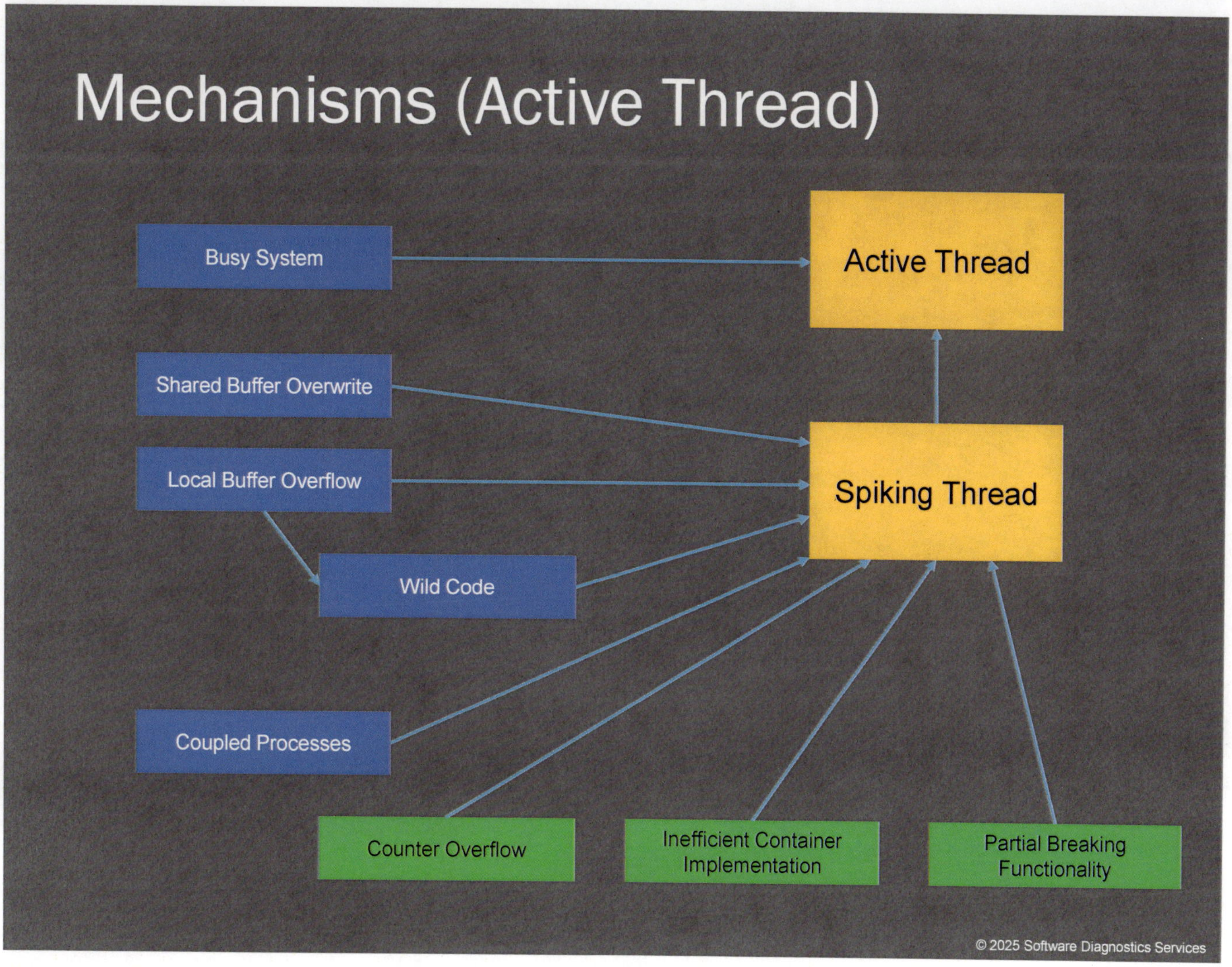

Defect Mechanism Patterns (DMP), Part 1
https://dumpanalysis.org/defect-mechanism-patterns-part1

Exercise A4

- **Goal:** Learn how to identify heap regions and heap corruption

- **Patterns:** Dynamic Memory Corruption (Process Heap); Regular Data; Wild Pointer

- \ALCDA-Dumps\Exercise-A4-x64-GDB.pdf
- \ALCDA-Dumps\Exercise-A4-A64-GDB.pdf

- \ALCDA-Dumps\Exercise-A4-A64-WinDbg.pdf
- \ALCDA-Dumps\Exercise-A4-x64-WinDbg.pdf

Exercise A4 (x64, GDB)

Goal: Learn how to identify heap regions and heap corruption.

Patterns: Dynamic Memory Corruption (Process Heap); Regular Data; Wild Pointer.

1. Load the *core.App4* dump file and *App4* executable from the x64/App4 directory:

```
~/ALCDA2/x64/App4$ gdb -c core.App4 -se App4
GNU gdb (Debian 8.2.1-2+b3) 8.2.1
Copyright (C) 2018 Free Software Foundation, Inc.
License GPLv3+: GNU GPL version 3 or later <http://gnu.org/licenses/gpl.html>
This is free software: you are free to change and redistribute it.
There is NO WARRANTY, to the extent permitted by law.
Type "show copying" and "show warranty" for details.
This GDB was configured as "x86_64-linux-gnu".
Type "show configuration" for configuration details.
For bug reporting instructions, please see:
<http://www.gnu.org/software/gdb/bugs/>.
Find the GDB manual and other documentation resources online at:
    <http://www.gnu.org/software/gdb/documentation/>.

For help, type "help".
Type "apropos word" to search for commands related to "word"...
Reading symbols from App4...done.
[New LWP 4304]
[New LWP 4303]
[New LWP 4302]
[New LWP 4301]
[New LWP 4305]
[New LWP 4306]
[Thread debugging using libthread_db enabled]
Using host libthread_db library "/lib/x86_64-linux-gnu/libthread_db.so.1".
Core was generated by `./App4'.
Program terminated with signal SIGSEGV, Segmentation fault.
#0  0x000000000041a906 in malloc ()
[Current thread is 1 (Thread 0x7f8d66b3a700 (LWP 4304))]
```

2. Set logging to a file in case of lengthy output from some commands:

```
(gdb) set logging on App4.log
Copying output to App4.log.
```

3. List threads:

```
(gdb) info threads
* 1    Thread 0x7f8d66b3a700 (LWP 4304) 0x000000000041a906 in malloc ()
  2    Thread 0x7f8d6733b700 (LWP 4303) 0x0000000000441d00 in nanosleep ()
  3    Thread 0x7f8d67b3c700 (LWP 4302) 0x0000000000441d00 in nanosleep ()
  4    Thread 0x124f880 (LWP 4301)      0x0000000000441d00 in nanosleep ()
  5    Thread 0x7f8d66339700 (LWP 4305) 0x0000000000441d00 in nanosleep ()
  6    Thread 0x7f8d65b38700 (LWP 4306) 0x0000000000441d00 in nanosleep ()
```

4. The identified problem thread #1 is the current thread. List its stack trace:

```
(gdb) bt
#0  0x000000000041a906 in malloc ()
#1  0x0000000000401e24 in proc ()
#2  0x0000000000401f2d in bar_three ()
#3  0x0000000000401f3e in foo_three ()
#4  0x0000000000401f57 in thread_three ()
#5  0x00000000004033c3 in start_thread (arg=<optimized out>) at pthread_create.c:486
#6  0x000000000044455f in clone ()
```

5. We see that the segmentation fault happened internally in the *malloc* function when *proc* was allocating heap memory. Disassemble the *proc* function:

```
(gdb) disassemble proc
Dump of assembler code for function proc:
   0x0000000000401bad <+0>:     push   %rbp
   0x0000000000401bae <+1>:     mov    %rsp,%rbp
   0x0000000000401bb1 <+4>:     sub    $0x40,%rsp
   0x0000000000401bb5 <+8>:     mov    $0x1,%edi
   0x0000000000401bba <+13>:    callq  0x441c50 <sleep>
   0x0000000000401bbf <+18>:    mov    $0x100,%edi
   0x0000000000401bc4 <+23>:    callq  0x41a7c0 <malloc>
   0x0000000000401bc9 <+28>:    mov    %rax,-0x8(%rbp)
   0x0000000000401bcd <+32>:    mov    $0x100,%edi
   0x0000000000401bd2 <+37>:    callq  0x41a7c0 <malloc>
   0x0000000000401bd7 <+42>:    mov    %rax,-0x10(%rbp)
   0x0000000000401bdb <+46>:    mov    $0x100,%edi
   0x0000000000401be0 <+51>:    callq  0x41a7c0 <malloc>
   0x0000000000401be5 <+56>:    mov    %rax,-0x18(%rbp)
   0x0000000000401be9 <+60>:    mov    $0x100,%edi
   0x0000000000401bee <+65>:    callq  0x41a7c0 <malloc>
   0x0000000000401bf3 <+70>:    mov    %rax,-0x20(%rbp)
   0x0000000000401bf7 <+74>:    mov    $0x100,%edi
   0x0000000000401bfc <+79>:    callq  0x41a7c0 <malloc>
   0x0000000000401c01 <+84>:    mov    %rax,-0x28(%rbp)
   0x0000000000401c05 <+88>:    mov    $0x100,%edi
   0x0000000000401c0a <+93>:    callq  0x41a7c0 <malloc>
   0x0000000000401c0f <+98>:    mov    %rax,-0x30(%rbp)
   0x0000000000401c13 <+102>:   mov    $0x100,%edi
   0x0000000000401c18 <+107>:   callq  0x41a7c0 <malloc>
   0x0000000000401c1d <+112>:   mov    %rax,-0x38(%rbp)
   0x0000000000401c21 <+116>:   mov    -0x30(%rbp),%rax
   0x0000000000401c25 <+120>:   mov    %rax,%rdi
   0x0000000000401c28 <+123>:   callq  0x41ae00 <free>
   0x0000000000401c2d <+128>:   mov    -0x20(%rbp),%rax
   0x0000000000401c31 <+132>:   mov    %rax,%rdi
   0x0000000000401c34 <+135>:   callq  0x41ae00 <free>
   0x0000000000401c39 <+140>:   mov    -0x10(%rbp),%rax
   0x0000000000401c3d <+144>:   mov    %rax,%rdi
   0x0000000000401c40 <+147>:   callq  0x41ae00 <free>
   0x0000000000401c45 <+152>:   mov    -0x10(%rbp),%rax
   0x0000000000401c49 <+156>:   movabs $0x7243206f6c6c6548,%rdx
   0x0000000000401c53 <+166>:   movabs $0x6548202132687361,%rcx
   0x0000000000401c5d <+176>:   mov    %rdx,(%rax)
   0x0000000000401c60 <+179>:   mov    %rcx,0x8(%rax)
   0x0000000000401c64 <+183>:   movabs $0x73617243206f6c6c,%rsi
   0x0000000000401c6e <+193>:   movabs $0x6c6c654820213268,%rdi
   0x0000000000401c78 <+203>:   mov    %rsi,0x10(%rax)
   0x0000000000401c7c <+207>:   mov    %rdi,0x18(%rax)
```

```
   0x0000000000401c80 <+211>:   movabs $0x326873617243206f,%rdx
   0x0000000000401c8a <+221>:   movabs $0x206f6c6c65482021,%rcx
   0x0000000000401c94 <+231>:   mov    %rdx,0x20(%rax)
   0x0000000000401c98 <+235>:   mov    %rcx,0x28(%rax)
   0x0000000000401c9c <+239>:   movabs $0x202132687361724,%rsi
   0x0000000000401ca6 <+249>:   movabs $0x7243206f6c6c6548,%rdi
   0x0000000000401cb0 <+259>:   mov    %rsi,0x30(%rax)
   0x0000000000401cb4 <+263>:   mov    %rdi,0x38(%rax)
   0x0000000000401cb8 <+267>:   movl   $0x32687361,0x40(%rax)
   0x0000000000401cbf <+274>:   movw   $0x21,0x44(%rax)
   0x0000000000401cc5 <+280>:   mov    -0x20(%rbp),%rax
   0x0000000000401cc9 <+284>:   movabs $0x7243206f6c6c6548,%rdx
--Type <RET> for more, q to quit, c to continue without paging--
   0x0000000000401cd3 <+294>:   movabs $0x6548202134687361,%rcx
   0x0000000000401cdd <+304>:   mov    %rdx,(%rax)
   0x0000000000401ce0 <+307>:   mov    %rcx,0x8(%rax)
   0x0000000000401ce4 <+311>:   movabs $0x73617243206f6c6c,%rsi
   0x0000000000401cee <+321>:   movabs $0x6c6c654820213468,%rdi
   0x0000000000401cf8 <+331>:   mov    %rsi,0x10(%rax)
   0x0000000000401cfc <+335>:   mov    %rdi,0x18(%rax)
   0x0000000000401d00 <+339>:   movabs $0x346873617243206f,%rdx
   0x0000000000401d0a <+349>:   movabs $0x206f6c6c65482021,%rcx
   0x0000000000401d14 <+359>:   mov    %rdx,0x20(%rax)
   0x0000000000401d18 <+363>:   mov    %rcx,0x28(%rax)
   0x0000000000401d1c <+367>:   movabs $0x2021346873617243,%rsi
   0x0000000000401d26 <+377>:   movabs $0x7243206f6c6c6548,%rdi
   0x0000000000401d30 <+387>:   mov    %rsi,0x30(%rax)
   0x0000000000401d34 <+391>:   mov    %rdi,0x38(%rax)
   0x0000000000401d38 <+395>:   movabs $0x6548202134687361,%rdx
   0x0000000000401d42 <+405>:   movabs $0x73617243206f6c6c,%rcx
   0x0000000000401d4c <+415>:   mov    %rdx,0x40(%rax)
   0x0000000000401d50 <+419>:   mov    %rcx,0x48(%rax)
   0x0000000000401d54 <+423>:   movl   $0x213468,0x50(%rax)
   0x0000000000401d5b <+430>:   mov    -0x30(%rbp),%rax
   0x0000000000401d5f <+434>:   movabs $0x7243206f6c6c6548,%rsi
   0x0000000000401d69 <+444>:   movabs $0x6548202136687361,%rdi
   0x0000000000401d73 <+454>:   mov    %rsi,(%rax)
   0x0000000000401d76 <+457>:   mov    %rdi,0x8(%rax)
   0x0000000000401d7a <+461>:   movabs $0x73617243206f6c6c,%rdx
   0x0000000000401d84 <+471>:   movabs $0x6c6c654820213668,%rcx
   0x0000000000401d8e <+481>:   mov    %rdx,0x10(%rax)
   0x0000000000401d92 <+485>:   mov    %rcx,0x18(%rax)
   0x0000000000401d96 <+489>:   movabs $0x366873617243206f,%rsi
   0x0000000000401da0 <+499>:   movabs $0x206f6c6c65482021,%rdi
   0x0000000000401daa <+509>:   mov    %rsi,0x20(%rax)
   0x0000000000401dae <+513>:   mov    %rdi,0x28(%rax)
   0x0000000000401db2 <+517>:   movabs $0x2021366873617243,%rdx
   0x0000000000401dbc <+527>:   movabs $0x7243206f6c6c6548,%rcx
   0x0000000000401dc6 <+537>:   mov    %rdx,0x30(%rax)
   0x0000000000401dca <+541>:   mov    %rcx,0x38(%rax)
   0x0000000000401dce <+545>:   movabs $0x6548202136687361,%rsi
   0x0000000000401dd8 <+555>:   movabs $0x73617243206f6c6c,%rdi
   0x0000000000401de2 <+565>:   mov    %rsi,0x40(%rax)
   0x0000000000401de6 <+569>:   mov    %rdi,0x48(%rax)
   0x0000000000401dea <+573>:   movabs $0x6c6c654820213668,%rdx
   0x0000000000401df4 <+583>:   movabs $0x366873617243206f,%rcx
   0x0000000000401dfe <+593>:   mov    %rdx,0x50(%rax)
   0x0000000000401e02 <+597>:   mov    %rcx,0x58(%rax)
   0x0000000000401e06 <+601>:   movw   $0x21,0x60(%rax)
   0x0000000000401e0c <+607>:   mov    $0x100,%edi
```

```
   0x0000000000401e11 <+612>:    callq  0x41a7c0 <malloc>
   0x0000000000401e16 <+617>:    mov    %rax,-0x10(%rbp)
   0x0000000000401e1a <+621>:    mov    $0x100,%edi
   0x0000000000401e1f <+626>:    callq  0x41a7c0 <malloc>
   0x0000000000401e24 <+631>:    mov    %rax,-0x20(%rbp)
   0x0000000000401e28 <+635>:    mov    $0x100,%edi
   0x0000000000401e2d <+640>:    callq  0x41a7c0 <malloc>
   0x0000000000401e32 <+645>:    mov    %rax,-0x30(%rbp)
   0x0000000000401e36 <+649>:    mov    $0x12c,%edi
   0x0000000000401e3b <+654>:    callq  0x441c50 <sleep>
--Type <RET> for more, q to quit, c to continue without paging--
   0x0000000000401e40 <+659>:    mov    -0x38(%rbp),%rax
   0x0000000000401e44 <+663>:    mov    %rax,%rdi
   0x0000000000401e47 <+666>:    callq  0x41ae00 <free>
   0x0000000000401e4c <+671>:    mov    -0x30(%rbp),%rax
   0x0000000000401e50 <+675>:    mov    %rax,%rdi
   0x0000000000401e53 <+678>:    callq  0x41ae00 <free>
   0x0000000000401e58 <+683>:    mov    -0x28(%rbp),%rax
   0x0000000000401e5c <+687>:    mov    %rax,%rdi
   0x0000000000401e5f <+690>:    callq  0x41ae00 <free>
   0x0000000000401e64 <+695>:    mov    -0x20(%rbp),%rax
   0x0000000000401e68 <+699>:    mov    %rax,%rdi
   0x0000000000401e6b <+702>:    callq  0x41ae00 <free>
   0x0000000000401e70 <+707>:    mov    -0x18(%rbp),%rax
   0x0000000000401e74 <+711>:    mov    %rax,%rdi
   0x0000000000401e77 <+714>:    callq  0x41ae00 <free>
   0x0000000000401e7c <+719>:    mov    -0x10(%rbp),%rax
   0x0000000000401e80 <+723>:    mov    %rax,%rdi
   0x0000000000401e83 <+726>:    callq  0x41ae00 <free>
   0x0000000000401e88 <+731>:    mov    -0x8(%rbp),%rax
   0x0000000000401e8c <+735>:    mov    %rax,%rdi
   0x0000000000401e8f <+738>:    callq  0x41ae00 <free>
   0x0000000000401e94 <+743>:    mov    $0xffffffff,%edi
   0x0000000000401e99 <+748>:    callq  0x441c50 <sleep>
   0x0000000000401e9e <+753>:    nop
   0x0000000000401e9f <+754>:    leaveq
   0x0000000000401ea0 <+755>:    retq
End of assembler dump.
```

Note: We see that before the problem *malloc* call, there were three buffer writes to memory addresses pointed to by values located at the following addresses: rbp-0x10, rbp-0x20, and rbp-0x30 (highlighted in red in disassembly). However, before buffer writes, there were *free* function calls with values located at the same addresses: rbp-0x30, rbp-0x20, and rbp-0x10 (highlighted in blue in disassembly). Therefore, we see "write after free" behavior.

6. We have the standard function prolog (highlighted in green in disassembly). Switch to stack frame #1 to check the addresses, their values, and memory contents they point to:

```
(gdb) frame 1
#1  0x0000000000401e24 in proc () at pthread_create.c:688
688     in pthread_create.c

(gdb) x/gx $rbp-0x10
0x7f8d66b39d60: 0x00007f8d60000c30

(gdb) x/s 0x00007f8d60000c30
0x7f8d60000c30: "Hello Cr"

(gdb) x/gx $rbp-0x20
0x7f8d66b39d50: 0x00007f8d60000e50
```

```
(gdb) x/s 0x00007f8d60000e50
0x7f8d60000e50: "Hello Crash4! Hello Crash4! Hello Crash4! Hello Crash4! Hello Crash4! Hello
Crash4!"
```

7. We know the addresses passed to heap management functions, for example, 0x00007f8d60000xxx. Find the heap region in the section list:

```
(gdb) maintenance info sections
Exec file:
    `/home/coredump/ALCDA2/x64/App4/App4', file type elf64-x86-64.
 [0]      0x00400200->0x00400220 at 0x00000200: .note.ABI-tag ALLOC LOAD READONLY DATA HAS_CONTENTS
 [1]      0x00400220->0x00400244 at 0x00000220: .note.gnu.build-id ALLOC LOAD READONLY DATA HAS_CONTENTS
 [2]      0x00400248->0x004004d0 at 0x00000248: .rela.plt ALLOC LOAD READONLY DATA HAS_CONTENTS
 [3]      0x00401000->0x00401017 at 0x00001000: .init ALLOC LOAD READONLY CODE HAS_CONTENTS
 [4]      0x00401018->0x004010f0 at 0x00001018: .plt ALLOC LOAD READONLY CODE HAS_CONTENTS
 [5]      0x004010f0->0x004936c0 at 0x000010f0: .text ALLOC LOAD READONLY CODE HAS_CONTENTS
 [6]      0x004936c0->0x00494267 at 0x000936c0: __libc_freeres_fn ALLOC LOAD READONLY CODE HAS_CONTENTS
 [7]      0x00494268->0x00494271 at 0x00094268: .fini ALLOC LOAD READONLY CODE HAS_CONTENTS
 [8]      0x00495000->0x004af73c at 0x00095000: .rodata ALLOC LOAD READONLY DATA HAS_CONTENTS
 [9]      0x004af740->0x004bbb70 at 0x000af740: .eh_frame ALLOC LOAD READONLY DATA HAS_CONTENTS
 [10]      0x004bbb70->0x004bbc1c at 0x000bbb70: .gcc_except_table ALLOC LOAD READONLY DATA HAS_CONTENTS
 [11]      0x004bd0b0->0x004bd0d8 at 0x000bc0b0: .tdata ALLOC LOAD DATA HAS_CONTENTS
 [12]      0x004bd0d8->0x004bd120 at 0x000bc0d8: .tbss ALLOC
 [13]      0x004bd0d8->0x004bd0e0 at 0x000bc0d8: .preinit_array ALLOC LOAD DATA HAS_CONTENTS
 [14]      0x004bd0e0->0x004bd0f0 at 0x000bc0e0: .init_array ALLOC LOAD DATA HAS_CONTENTS
 [15]      0x004bd0f0->0x004bd100 at 0x000bc0f0: .fini_array ALLOC LOAD DATA HAS_CONTENTS
 [16]      0x004bd100->0x004bfef4 at 0x000bc100: .data.rel.ro ALLOC LOAD DATA HAS_CONTENTS
 [17]      0x004bfef8->0x004c0000 at 0x000beef8: .got ALLOC LOAD DATA HAS_CONTENTS
 [18]      0x004c0000->0x004c00f0 at 0x000bf000: .got.plt ALLOC LOAD DATA HAS_CONTENTS
 [19]      0x004c0100->0x004c1c30 at 0x000bf100: .data ALLOC LOAD DATA HAS_CONTENTS
 [20]      0x004c1c30->0x004c1c90 at 0x000c0c30: __libc_subfreeres ALLOC LOAD DATA HAS_CONTENTS
 [21]      0x004c1ca0->0x004c2408 at 0x000c0ca0: __libc_IO_vtables ALLOC LOAD DATA HAS_CONTENTS
 [22]      0x004c2408->0x004c2410 at 0x000c1408: __libc_atexit ALLOC LOAD DATA HAS_CONTENTS
 [23]      0x004c2420->0x004c8528 at 0x000c1410: .bss ALLOC
 [24]      0x004c8528->0x004c8558 at 0x000c1410: __libc_freeres_ptrs ALLOC
 [25]      0x00000000->0x00000038 at 0x000c1410: .comment READONLY HAS_CONTENTS
 [26]      0x00000000->0x00000420 at 0x000c1450: .debug_aranges READONLY HAS_CONTENTS
 [27]      0x00000000->0x000372ad at 0x000c1870: .debug_info READONLY HAS_CONTENTS
 [28]      0x00000000->0x000057e8 at 0x000f8b1d: .debug_abbrev READONLY HAS_CONTENTS
 [29]      0x00000000->0x0000aa2b at 0x000fe305: .debug_line READONLY HAS_CONTENTS
 [30]      0x00000000->0x00004d08 at 0x00108d30: .debug_str READONLY HAS_CONTENTS
 [31]      0x00000000->0x0000d4b8 at 0x0010da38: .debug_loc READONLY HAS_CONTENTS
 [32]      0x00000000->0x000024c0 at 0x0011aef0: .debug_ranges READONLY HAS_CONTENTS
Core file:
    `/home/coredump/ALCDA2/x64/App4/core.App4', file type elf64-x86-64.
 [0]      0x00000000->0x00002c60 at 0x00000510: note0 READONLY HAS_CONTENTS
 [1]      0x00000000->0x000000d8 at 0x00000594: .reg/4304 HAS_CONTENTS
 [2]      0x00000000->0x000000d8 at 0x00000594: .reg HAS_CONTENTS
 [3]      0x00000000->0x00000080 at 0x00000724: .note.linuxcore.siginfo/4304 HAS_CONTENTS
 [4]      0x00000000->0x00000080 at 0x00000724: .note.linuxcore.siginfo HAS_CONTENTS
 [5]      0x00000000->0x00000140 at 0x000007b8: .auxv HAS_CONTENTS
 [6]      0x00000000->0x00000100 at 0x0000090c: .note.linuxcore.file/4304 HAS_CONTENTS
 [7]      0x00000000->0x00000100 at 0x0000090c: .note.linuxcore.file HAS_CONTENTS
 [8]      0x00000000->0x00000200 at 0x00000a20: .reg2/4304 HAS_CONTENTS
 [9]      0x00000000->0x00000200 at 0x00000a20: .reg2 HAS_CONTENTS
 [10]      0x00000000->0x00000340 at 0x00000c34: .reg-xstate/4304 HAS_CONTENTS
 [11]      0x00000000->0x00000340 at 0x00000c34: .reg-xstate HAS_CONTENTS
 [12]      0x00000000->0x000000d8 at 0x00000ff8: .reg/4303 HAS_CONTENTS
 [13]      0x00000000->0x00000200 at 0x000010ec: .reg2/4303 HAS_CONTENTS
 [14]      0x00000000->0x00000340 at 0x00001300: .reg-xstate/4303 HAS_CONTENTS
 [15]      0x00000000->0x000000d8 at 0x000016c4: .reg/4302 HAS_CONTENTS
 [16]      0x00000000->0x00000200 at 0x000017b8: .reg2/4302 HAS_CONTENTS
 [17]      0x00000000->0x00000340 at 0x000019cc: .reg-xstate/4302 HAS_CONTENTS
 [18]      0x00000000->0x000000d8 at 0x00001d90: .reg/4301 HAS_CONTENTS
 [19]      0x00000000->0x00000200 at 0x00001e84: .reg2/4301 HAS_CONTENTS
--Type <RET> for more, q to quit, c to continue without paging--
```

```
[20]     0x00000000->0x00000340 at 0x00002098: .reg-xstate/4301 HAS_CONTENTS
[21]     0x00000000->0x000000d8 at 0x0000245c: .reg/4305 HAS_CONTENTS
[22]     0x00000000->0x00000200 at 0x00002550: .reg2/4305 HAS_CONTENTS
[23]     0x00000000->0x00000340 at 0x00002764: .reg-xstate/4305 HAS_CONTENTS
[24]     0x00000000->0x000000d8 at 0x00002b28: .reg/4306 HAS_CONTENTS
[25]     0x00000000->0x00000200 at 0x00002c1c: .reg2/4306 HAS_CONTENTS
[26]     0x00000000->0x00000340 at 0x00002e30: .reg-xstate/4306 HAS_CONTENTS
[27]     0x00400000->0x00401000 at 0x00004000: load1 ALLOC LOAD READONLY HAS_CONTENTS
[28]     0x00401000->0x00401000 at 0x00005000: load2 ALLOC READONLY CODE
[29]     0x00495000->0x00495000 at 0x00005000: load3 ALLOC READONLY
[30]     0x004bd000->0x004c3000 at 0x00005000: load4 ALLOC LOAD HAS_CONTENTS
[31]     0x004c3000->0x004c9000 at 0x0000b000: load5 ALLOC LOAD HAS_CONTENTS
[32]     0x0124f000->0x01272000 at 0x00011000: load6 ALLOC LOAD HAS_CONTENTS
[33]     0x7f8d60000000->0x7f8d60021000 at 0x00034000: load7 ALLOC LOAD HAS_CONTENTS
[34]     0x7f8d60021000->0x7f8d60021000 at 0x00055000: load8 ALLOC READONLY
[35]     0x7f8d65338000->0x7f8d65338000 at 0x00055000: load9 ALLOC READONLY
[36]     0x7f8d65339000->0x7f8d65b39000 at 0x00055000: load10 ALLOC LOAD HAS_CONTENTS
[37]     0x7f8d65b39000->0x7f8d65b39000 at 0x00855000: load11 ALLOC READONLY
[38]     0x7f8d65b3a000->0x7f8d6633a000 at 0x00855000: load12 ALLOC LOAD HAS_CONTENTS
[39]     0x7f8d6633a000->0x7f8d6633a000 at 0x01055000: load13 ALLOC READONLY
[40]     0x7f8d6633b000->0x7f8d66b3b000 at 0x01055000: load14 ALLOC LOAD HAS_CONTENTS
[41]     0x7f8d66b3b000->0x7f8d66b3b000 at 0x01855000: load15 ALLOC READONLY
[42]     0x7f8d66b3c000->0x7f8d6733c000 at 0x01855000: load16 ALLOC LOAD HAS_CONTENTS
[43]     0x7f8d6733c000->0x7f8d6733c000 at 0x02055000: load17 ALLOC READONLY
[44]     0x7f8d6733d000->0x7f8d67b3d000 at 0x02055000: load18 ALLOC LOAD HAS_CONTENTS
[45]     0x7ffc80658000->0x7ffc80679000 at 0x02855000: load19 ALLOC LOAD HAS_CONTENTS
[46]     0x7ffc806ff000->0x7ffc80703000 at 0x02876000: load20 ALLOC LOAD READONLY HAS_CONTENTS
[47]     0x7ffc80703000->0x7ffc80704000 at 0x0287a000: load21 ALLOC LOAD READONLY CODE HAS_CONTENTS
```

8. Check the faulting instruction and the problem memory address:

```
(gdb) bt
#0  0x000000000041a906 in malloc ()
#1  0x0000000000401e24 in proc () at pthread_create.c:688
#2  0x0000000000401f2d in bar_three () at pthread_create.c:688
#3  0x0000000000401f3e in foo_three () at pthread_create.c:688
#4  0x0000000000401f57 in thread_three () at pthread_create.c:688
#5  0x00000000004033c3 in start_thread (arg=<optimized out>) at pthread_create.c:486
#6  0x000000000044455f in clone ()

(gdb) frame 0
#0  0x000000000041a906 in malloc ()

(gdb) x/i $rip
=> 0x41a906 <malloc+326>:       mov    (%rdx),%rsi

(gdb) x $rdx
   0x7243206f6c6c6548:  Cannot access memory at address 0x7243206f6c6c6548

(gdb) p (char[8])0x7243206f6c6c6548
$1 = "Hello Cr"
```

Note: We see that the “Hello Cr” fragment correlates with the “Hello Cr” buffer overwrite that we saw previously in step #5.

Exercise A4 (A64, GDB)

Goal: Learn how to identify heap regions and heap corruption.

Patterns: Dynamic Memory Corruption (Process Heap); Regular Data; Wild Pointer.

1. Load the *core.8800* dump file and *App4* executable from the A64/App4 directory:

```
~/ALCDA2/A64/App4$ gdb-multiarch -c core.8800 -se App4
GNU gdb (Debian 8.2.1-2+b3) 8.2.1
Copyright (C) 2018 Free Software Foundation, Inc.
License GPLv3+: GNU GPL version 3 or later <http://gnu.org/licenses/gpl.html>
This is free software: you are free to change and redistribute it.
There is NO WARRANTY, to the extent permitted by law.
Type "show copying" and "show warranty" for details.
This GDB was configured as "x86_64-linux-gnu".
Type "show configuration" for configuration details.
For bug reporting instructions, please see:
<http://www.gnu.org/software/gdb/bugs/>.
Find the GDB manual and other documentation resources online at:
    <http://www.gnu.org/software/gdb/documentation/>.

For help, type "help".
Type "apropos word" to search for commands related to "word"...
Reading symbols from App4...(no debugging symbols found)...done.
[New LWP 8803]
[New LWP 8801]
[New LWP 8800]
[New LWP 8802]
[New LWP 8804]
[New LWP 8805]
Core was generated by `./App4'.
Program terminated with signal SIGSEGV, Segmentation fault.
#0  0x000000000041cbec in malloc ()
[Current thread is 1 (LWP 8803)]
```

2. Set logging to a file in case of lengthy output from some commands:

```
(gdb) set logging on App4.log
Copying output to App4.log.
```

3. List threads:

```
(gdb) info threads
* 1    LWP 8803          0x000000000041cbec in malloc ()
  2    LWP 8801          0x000000000040cb34 in nanosleep ()
  3    LWP 8800          0x000000000040cb34 in nanosleep ()
  4    LWP 8802          0x000000000040cb34 in nanosleep ()
  5    LWP 8804          0x000000000040cb34 in nanosleep ()
  6    LWP 8805          0x000000000040cb34 in nanosleep ()
```

4. The identified problem thread #1 is the current thread. List its stack trace:

```
(gdb) bt
#0  0x000000000041cbec in malloc ()
#1  0x0000000000403304 in proc ()
#2  0x0000000000403400 in bar_three ()
```

```
#3  0x0000000000403414 in foo_three ()
#4  0x000000000040342c in thread_three ()
#5  0x0000000000404db4 in start_thread ()
#6  0x0000000000429ce0 in thread_start ()
```

5. We see that the segmentation fault happened internally in the *malloc* function when *proc* was allocating heap memory. Disassemble the *proc* function:

```
(gdb) disassemble proc
Dump of assembler code for function proc:
   0x00000000004031e8 <+0>:     stp     x29, x30, [sp, #-80]!
   0x00000000004031ec <+4>:     mov     x29, sp
   0x00000000004031f0 <+8>:     mov     w0, #0x1                        // #1
   0x00000000004031f4 <+12>:    bl      0x424d24 <sleep>
   0x00000000004031f8 <+16>:    mov     x0, #0x100                      // #256
   0x00000000004031fc <+20>:    bl      0x41cb60 <malloc>
   0x0000000000403200 <+24>:    str     x0, [x29, #72]
   0x0000000000403204 <+28>:    mov     x0, #0x100                      // #256
   0x0000000000403208 <+32>:    bl      0x41cb60 <malloc>
   0x000000000040320c <+36>:    str     x0, [x29, #64]
   0x0000000000403210 <+40>:    mov     x0, #0x100                      // #256
   0x0000000000403214 <+44>:    bl      0x41cb60 <malloc>
   0x0000000000403218 <+48>:    str     x0, [x29, #56]
   0x000000000040321c <+52>:    mov     x0, #0x100                      // #256
   0x0000000000403220 <+56>:    bl      0x41cb60 <malloc>
   0x0000000000403224 <+60>:    str     x0, [x29, #48]
   0x0000000000403228 <+64>:    mov     x0, #0x100                      // #256
   0x000000000040322c <+68>:    bl      0x41cb60 <malloc>
   0x0000000000403230 <+72>:    str     x0, [x29, #40]
   0x0000000000403234 <+76>:    mov     x0, #0x100                      // #256
   0x0000000000403238 <+80>:    bl      0x41cb60 <malloc>
   0x000000000040323c <+84>:    str     x0, [x29, #32]
   0x0000000000403240 <+88>:    mov     x0, #0x100                      // #256
   0x0000000000403244 <+92>:    bl      0x41cb60 <malloc>
   0x0000000000403248 <+96>:    str     x0, [x29, #24]
   0x000000000040324c <+100>:   ldr     x0, [x29, #32]
   0x0000000000403250 <+104>:   bl      0x41d698 <free>
   0x0000000000403254 <+108>:   ldr     x0, [x29, #48]
   0x0000000000403258 <+112>:   bl      0x41d698 <free>
   0x000000000040325c <+116>:   ldr     x0, [x29, #64]
   0x0000000000403260 <+120>:   bl      0x41d698 <free>
   0x0000000000403264 <+124>:   ldr     x0, [x29, #64]
   0x0000000000403268 <+128>:   adrp    x1, 0x489000 <arena_thread_freeres+280>
   0x000000000040326c <+132>:   add     x1, x1, #0x360
   0x0000000000403270 <+136>:   ldp     x2, x3, [x1]
   0x0000000000403274 <+140>:   stp     x2, x3, [x0]
   0x0000000000403278 <+144>:   ldp     x2, x3, [x1, #16]
   0x000000000040327c <+148>:   stp     x2, x3, [x0, #16]
   0x0000000000403280 <+152>:   ldp     x2, x3, [x1, #32]
   0x0000000000403284 <+156>:   stp     x2, x3, [x0, #32]
   0x0000000000403288 <+160>:   ldp     x2, x3, [x1, #48]
   0x000000000040328c <+164>:   stp     x2, x3, [x0, #48]
   0x0000000000403290 <+168>:   ldr     w2, [x1, #64]
   0x0000000000403294 <+172>:   str     w2, [x0, #64]
   0x0000000000403298 <+176>:   ldrh    w1, [x1, #68]
   0x000000000040329c <+180>:   strh    w1, [x0, #68]
   0x00000000004032a0 <+184>:   ldr     x0, [x29, #48]
   0x00000000004032a4 <+188>:   adrp    x1, 0x489000 <arena_thread_freeres+280>
   0x00000000004032a8 <+192>:   add     x1, x1, #0x3a8
--Type <RET> for more, q to quit, c to continue without paging--
```

```
   0x00000000004032ac <+196>:   ldp     x2, x3, [x1]
   0x00000000004032b0 <+200>:   stp     x2, x3, [x0]
   0x00000000004032b4 <+204>:   ldp     x2, x3, [x1, #16]
   0x00000000004032b8 <+208>:   stp     x2, x3, [x0, #16]
   0x00000000004032bc <+212>:   ldp     x2, x3, [x1, #32]
   0x00000000004032c0 <+216>:   stp     x2, x3, [x0, #32]
   0x00000000004032c4 <+220>:   ldp     x2, x3, [x1, #48]
   0x00000000004032c8 <+224>:   stp     x2, x3, [x0, #48]
   0x00000000004032cc <+228>:   ldp     x2, x3, [x1, #64]
   0x00000000004032d0 <+232>:   stp     x2, x3, [x0, #64]
   0x00000000004032d4 <+236>:   ldr     w1, [x1, #80]
   0x00000000004032d8 <+240>:   str     w1, [x0, #80]
   0x00000000004032dc <+244>:   ldr     x0, [x29, #32]
   0x00000000004032e0 <+248>:   adrp    x1, 0x489000 <arena_thread_freeres+280>
   0x00000000004032e4 <+252>:   add     x1, x1, #0x400
   0x00000000004032e8 <+256>:   mov     x2, #0x62                    // #98
   0x00000000004032ec <+260>:   bl      0x400280
   0x00000000004032f0 <+264>:   mov     x0, #0x100                   // #256
   0x00000000004032f4 <+268>:   bl      0x41cb60 <malloc>
   0x00000000004032f8 <+272>:   str     x0, [x29, #64]
   0x00000000004032fc <+276>:   mov     x0, #0x100                   // #256
   0x0000000000403300 <+280>:   bl      0x41cb60 <malloc>
   0x0000000000403304 <+284>:   str     x0, [x29, #48]
   0x0000000000403308 <+288>:   mov     x0, #0x100                   // #256
   0x000000000040330c <+292>:   bl      0x41cb60 <malloc>
   0x0000000000403310 <+296>:   str     x0, [x29, #32]
   0x0000000000403314 <+300>:   mov     w0, #0x12c                   // #300
   0x0000000000403318 <+304>:   bl      0x424d24 <sleep>
   0x000000000040331c <+308>:   ldr     x0, [x29, #24]
   0x0000000000403320 <+312>:   bl      0x41d698 <free>
   0x0000000000403324 <+316>:   ldr     x0, [x29, #32]
   0x0000000000403328 <+320>:   bl      0x41d698 <free>
   0x000000000040332c <+324>:   ldr     x0, [x29, #40]
   0x0000000000403330 <+328>:   bl      0x41d698 <free>
   0x0000000000403334 <+332>:   ldr     x0, [x29, #48]
   0x0000000000403338 <+336>:   bl      0x41d698 <free>
   0x000000000040333c <+340>:   ldr     x0, [x29, #56]
   0x0000000000403340 <+344>:   bl      0x41d698 <free>
   0x0000000000403344 <+348>:   ldr     x0, [x29, #64]
   0x0000000000403348 <+352>:   bl      0x41d698 <free>
   0x000000000040334c <+356>:   ldr     x0, [x29, #72]
   0x0000000000403350 <+360>:   bl      0x41d698 <free>
   0x0000000000403354 <+364>:   mov     w0, #0xffffffff              // #-1
   0x0000000000403358 <+368>:   bl      0x424d24 <sleep>
   0x000000000040335c <+372>:   ldp     x29, x30, [sp], #80
   0x0000000000403360 <+376>:   ret
End of assembler dump.
```

Note: We see that before the problem *malloc* call, there were three buffer writes to memory addresses pointed to by values located at the following addresses: x29+64, x29+48, and x29+32 (highlighted in red in disassembly). However, before buffer writes, there were *free* function calls with values located at the same addresses: x29+64, x29+48, and x29+32 (highlighted in blue in disassembly). Therefore, we see "write after free" behavior.

6. We have the standard function prolog (highlighted in green in disassembly). Switch to stack frame #1 to check the addresses, their values, and memory contents they point to:

```
(gdb) frame 1
#1  0x0000000000403304 in proc ()
```

```
(gdb) x/gx $x29+32
0xfffc03e5e7f0: 0x0000fffbfc001070
```

```
(gdb) x/s 0x0000fffbfc001070
0xfffbfc001070: "Hello Crash6! Hello Crash6! Hello Crash6! Hello Crash6! Hello Crash6! Hello
Crash6! Hello Crash6!"
```

```
(gdb) x/gx $x29+48
0xfffc03e5e800: 0x0000fffbfc000e50
```

```
(gdb) x/s 0x0000fffbfc000e50
0xfffbfc000e50: "Hello Crash4! Hello Crash4! Hello Crash4! Hello Crash4! Hello Crash4! Hello
Crash4!"
```

7. We know the addresses passed to heap management functions, for example, 0x0000fffbfc000xxx. Find the heap region in the section list:

```
(gdb) maintenance info sections
Exec file: `/home/ubuntu/ALCDA2/A64/App4/App4', file type elf64-littleaarch64.
 [0]      0x00400190->0x004001b0 at 0x00000190: .note.ABI-tag ALLOC LOAD READONLY DATA HAS_CONTENTS
 [1]      0x004001b0->0x004001d4 at 0x000001b0: .note.gnu.build-id ALLOC LOAD READONLY DATA HAS_CONTENTS
 [2]      0x004001d8->0x00400250 at 0x000001d8: .rela.plt ALLOC LOAD READONLY DATA HAS_CONTENTS
 [3]      0x00400250->0x00400264 at 0x00000250: .init ALLOC LOAD READONLY CODE HAS_CONTENTS
 [4]      0x00400270->0x004002c0 at 0x00000270: .plt ALLOC LOAD READONLY CODE HAS_CONTENTS
 [5]      0x004002c0->0x00487218 at 0x000002c0: .text ALLOC LOAD READONLY CODE HAS_CONTENTS
 [6]      0x00487218->0x00488ee8 at 0x00087218: __libc_freeres_fn ALLOC LOAD READONLY CODE HAS_CONTENTS
 [7]      0x00488ee8->0x00489338 at 0x00088ee8: __libc_thread_freeres_fn ALLOC LOAD READONLY CODE HAS_CONTENTS
 [8]      0x00489338->0x00489348 at 0x00089338: .fini ALLOC LOAD READONLY CODE HAS_CONTENTS
 [9]      0x00489350->0x004a193d at 0x00089350: .rodata ALLOC LOAD READONLY DATA HAS_CONTENTS
 [10]     0x004a193d->0x004a193e at 0x000a193d: .stapsdt.base ALLOC LOAD READONLY DATA HAS_CONTENTS
 [11]     0x004a1940->0x004a2078 at 0x000a1940: __libc_IO_vtables ALLOC LOAD READONLY DATA HAS_CONTENTS
 [12]     0x004a2078->0x004a20e0 at 0x000a2078: __libc_subfreeres ALLOC LOAD READONLY DATA HAS_CONTENTS
 [13]     0x004a20e0->0x004a20e8 at 0x000a20e0: __libc_atexit ALLOC LOAD READONLY DATA HAS_CONTENTS
 [14]     0x004a20e8->0x004a20f8 at 0x000a20e8: __libc_thread_subfreeres ALLOC LOAD READONLY DATA HAS_CONTENTS
 [15]     0x004a20f8->0x004b0734 at 0x000a20f8: .eh_frame ALLOC LOAD READONLY DATA HAS_CONTENTS
 [16]     0x004b0734->0x004b08f1 at 0x000b0734: .gcc_except_table ALLOC LOAD READONLY DATA HAS_CONTENTS
 [17]     0x004cfb20->0x004cfb48 at 0x000bfb20: .tdata ALLOC LOAD DATA HAS_CONTENTS
 [18]     0x004cfb48->0x004cfb98 at 0x000bfb48: .tbss ALLOC
 [19]     0x004cfb48->0x004cfb50 at 0x000bfb48: .init_array ALLOC LOAD DATA HAS_CONTENTS
 [20]     0x004cfb50->0x004cfb60 at 0x000bfb50: .fini_array ALLOC LOAD DATA HAS_CONTENTS
 [21]     0x004cfb60->0x004cfb68 at 0x000bfb60: .jcr ALLOC LOAD DATA HAS_CONTENTS
 [22]     0x004cfb68->0x004cff24 at 0x000bfb68: .data.rel.ro ALLOC LOAD DATA HAS_CONTENTS
 [23]     0x004cff28->0x004cffe8 at 0x000bff28: .got ALLOC LOAD DATA HAS_CONTENTS
 [24]     0x004cffe8->0x004d0028 at 0x000bffe8: .got.plt ALLOC LOAD DATA HAS_CONTENTS
 [25]     0x004d0030->0x004d1580 at 0x000c0030: .data ALLOC LOAD DATA HAS_CONTENTS
 [26]     0x004d1580->0x004d8050 at 0x000c1580: .bss ALLOC
 [27]     0x004d8050->0x004d8088 at 0x000c1580: __libc_freeres_ptrs ALLOC
 [28]     0x00000000->0x00000031 at 0x000c1580: .comment READONLY HAS_CONTENTS
 [29]     0x00000000->0x00001cb0 at 0x000c15b4: .note.stapsdt READONLY HAS_CONTENTS
Core file: `/home/ubuntu/ALCDA2/A64/App4/core.8800', file type elf64-littleaarch64.
 [0]      0x00000000->0x00002838 at 0x00000468: note0 READONLY HAS_CONTENTS
 [1]      0x00000000->0x00000110 at 0x000004ec: .reg/8803 HAS_CONTENTS
 [2]      0x00000000->0x00000110 at 0x000004ec: .reg HAS_CONTENTS
 [3]      0x00000000->0x00000080 at 0x000006b4: .note.linuxcore.siginfo/8803 HAS_CONTENTS
 [4]      0x00000000->0x00000080 at 0x000006b4: .note.linuxcore.siginfo HAS_CONTENTS
 [5]      0x00000000->0x00000160 at 0x00000748: .auxv HAS_CONTENTS
 [6]      0x00000000->0x00000076 at 0x000008bc: .note.linuxcore.file/8803 HAS_CONTENTS
 [7]      0x00000000->0x00000076 at 0x000008bc: .note.linuxcore.file HAS_CONTENTS
 [8]      0x00000000->0x00000210 at 0x00000948: .reg2/8803 HAS_CONTENTS
 [9]      0x00000000->0x00000210 at 0x00000948: .reg2 HAS_CONTENTS
 [10]     0x00000000->0x00000008 at 0x00000b6c: .reg-aarch-tls/8803 HAS_CONTENTS
 [11]     0x00000000->0x00000008 at 0x00000b6c: .reg-aarch-tls HAS_CONTENTS
 [12]     0x00000000->0x00000108 at 0x00000b88: .reg-aarch-hw-break/8803 HAS_CONTENTS
 [13]     0x00000000->0x00000108 at 0x00000b88: .reg-aarch-hw-break HAS_CONTENTS
 [14]     0x00000000->0x00000108 at 0x00000ca4: .reg-aarch-hw-watch/8803 HAS_CONTENTS
 [15]     0x00000000->0x00000108 at 0x00000ca4: .reg-aarch-hw-watch HAS_CONTENTS
 [16]     0x00000000->0x00000110 at 0x00000e48: .reg/8801 HAS_CONTENTS
 [17]     0x00000000->0x00000210 at 0x00000f74: .reg2/8801 HAS_CONTENTS
--Type <RET> for more, q to quit, c to continue without paging--
 [18]     0x00000000->0x00000008 at 0x00001198: .reg-aarch-tls/8801 HAS_CONTENTS
```

```
[19]      0x00000000->0x00000108 at 0x000011b4: .reg-aarch-hw-break/8801 HAS_CONTENTS
[20]      0x00000000->0x00000108 at 0x000012d0: .reg-aarch-hw-watch/8801 HAS_CONTENTS
[21]      0x00000000->0x00000110 at 0x00001474: .reg/8800 HAS_CONTENTS
[22]      0x00000000->0x00000210 at 0x000015a0: .reg2/8800 HAS_CONTENTS
[23]      0x00000000->0x00000008 at 0x000017c4: .reg-aarch-tls/8800 HAS_CONTENTS
[24]      0x00000000->0x00000108 at 0x000017e0: .reg-aarch-hw-break/8800 HAS_CONTENTS
[25]      0x00000000->0x00000108 at 0x000018fc: .reg-aarch-hw-watch/8800 HAS_CONTENTS
[26]      0x00000000->0x00000110 at 0x00001aa0: .reg/8802 HAS_CONTENTS
[27]      0x00000000->0x00000210 at 0x00001bcc: .reg2/8802 HAS_CONTENTS
[28]      0x00000000->0x00000008 at 0x00001df0: .reg-aarch-tls/8802 HAS_CONTENTS
[29]      0x00000000->0x00000108 at 0x00001e0c: .reg-aarch-hw-break/8802 HAS_CONTENTS
[30]      0x00000000->0x00000108 at 0x00001f28: .reg-aarch-hw-watch/8802 HAS_CONTENTS
[31]      0x00000000->0x00000110 at 0x000020cc: .reg/8804 HAS_CONTENTS
[32]      0x00000000->0x00000210 at 0x000021f8: .reg2/8804 HAS_CONTENTS
[33]      0x00000000->0x00000008 at 0x0000241c: .reg-aarch-tls/8804 HAS_CONTENTS
[34]      0x00000000->0x00000108 at 0x00002438: .reg-aarch-hw-break/8804 HAS_CONTENTS
[35]      0x00000000->0x00000108 at 0x00002554: .reg-aarch-hw-watch/8804 HAS_CONTENTS
[36]      0x00000000->0x00000110 at 0x000026f8: .reg/8805 HAS_CONTENTS
[37]      0x00000000->0x00000210 at 0x00002824: .reg2/8805 HAS_CONTENTS
[38]      0x00000000->0x00000008 at 0x00002a48: .reg-aarch-tls/8805 HAS_CONTENTS
[39]      0x00000000->0x00000108 at 0x00002a64: .reg-aarch-hw-break/8805 HAS_CONTENTS
[40]      0x00000000->0x00000108 at 0x00002b80: .reg-aarch-hw-watch/8805 HAS_CONTENTS
[41]      0x00400000->0x00410000 at 0x00010000: load1a ALLOC LOAD READONLY CODE HAS_CONTENTS
[42]      0x00410000->0x004c0000 at 0x00020000: load1b ALLOC READONLY CODE
[43]      0x004c0000->0x004e0000 at 0x00020000: load2 ALLOC LOAD HAS_CONTENTS
[44]      0x31db0000->0x31df0000 at 0x00040000: load3 ALLOC LOAD HAS_CONTENTS
[45]      0xfffbfc000000->0xfffbfc030000 at 0x00080000: load4 ALLOC LOAD HAS_CONTENTS
[46]      0xfffbfc030000->0xfffc00000000 at 0x000b0000: load5 ALLOC READONLY
[47]      0xfffc02630000->0xfffc02640000 at 0x000b0000: load6 ALLOC LOAD READONLY HAS_CONTENTS
[48]      0xfffc02640000->0xfffc02e40000 at 0x000c0000: load7 ALLOC LOAD HAS_CONTENTS
[49]      0xfffc02e40000->0xfffc02e50000 at 0x008c0000: load8 ALLOC LOAD READONLY HAS_CONTENTS
[50]      0xfffc02e50000->0xfffc03650000 at 0x008d0000: load9 ALLOC LOAD HAS_CONTENTS
[51]      0xfffc03650000->0xfffc03660000 at 0x010d0000: load10 ALLOC LOAD READONLY HAS_CONTENTS
[52]      0xfffc03660000->0xfffc03e60000 at 0x010e0000: load11 ALLOC LOAD HAS_CONTENTS
[53]      0xfffc03e60000->0xfffc03e70000 at 0x018e0000: load12 ALLOC LOAD READONLY HAS_CONTENTS
[54]      0xfffc03e70000->0xfffc04670000 at 0x018f0000: load13 ALLOC LOAD HAS_CONTENTS
[55]      0xfffc04670000->0xfffc04680000 at 0x020f0000: load14 ALLOC LOAD READONLY HAS_CONTENTS
[56]      0xfffc04680000->0xfffc04e80000 at 0x02100000: load15 ALLOC LOAD HAS_CONTENTS
[57]      0xfffc04e80000->0xfffc04e90000 at 0x02900000: load16 ALLOC LOAD READONLY HAS_CONTENTS
[58]      0xfffc04e90000->0xfffc04ea0000 at 0x02910000: load17 ALLOC LOAD READONLY CODE HAS_CONTENTS
[59]      0xffffd31d0000->0xffffd3200000 at 0x02920000: load18 ALLOC LOAD HAS_CONTENTS
```

8. Check the faulting instruction and the problem memory address:

```
(gdb) bt
#0  0x000000000041cbec in malloc ()
#1  0x0000000000403304 in proc ()
#2  0x0000000000403400 in bar_three ()
#3  0x0000000000403414 in foo_three ()
#4  0x000000000040342c in thread_three ()
#5  0x0000000000404db4 in start_thread ()
#6  0x0000000000429ce0 in thread_start ()

(gdb) frame 0
#0  0x000000000041cbec in malloc ()

(gdb) x/i $pc
=> 0x41cbec <malloc+140>:       ldr     x1, [x4]

(gdb) x $x4
   0x7243206f6c6c6548:  Cannot access memory at address 0x7243206f6c6c6548

(gdb) p (char[8])0x7243206f6c6c6548
$1 = "Hello Cr"
```

Note: We see that the "Hello Cr" fragment correlates with the "Hello Cr" buffer overwrite that we saw previously in step #6.

Exercise A4 (x64, WinDbg)

Goal: Learn how to identify heap regions and heap corruption.

Patterns: Dynamic Memory Corruption (Process Heap); Regular Data; Wild Pointer.

1. Launch WinDbg.

2. Load the *core.App4* dump file from the x64\App4 folder:

```
Microsoft (R) Windows Debugger Version 10.0.27725.1000 AMD64
Copyright (c) Microsoft Corporation. All rights reserved.


Loading Dump File [C:\ALCDA2\x64\App4\core.App4]
64-bit machine not using 64-bit API

************* Path validation summary **************
Response                         Time (ms)     Location
Deferred                                       srv*
Symbol search path is: srv*
Executable search path is:
Generic Unix Version 0 UP Free x64
System Uptime: not available
Process Uptime: not available
..
(10cd.10d0): Signal SIGSEGV (Segmentation fault) code 128 at 0x0
*** WARNING: Unable to verify timestamp for App4
App4+0x1a906:
00000000`0041a906 ???
```

3. Set logging to a file in case of lengthy output from some commands:

```
0:000> .logopen C:\ALCDA2\x64\App4\App4-WinDbg.log
Opened log file 'C:\ALCDA2\x64\App4\App4-WinDbg.log'
```

4. Specify the dump folder as the symbol path and reload symbols:

```
0:000> .symfix; .sympath+ C:\ALCDA2\x64\App4\
Symbol search path is: srv*;C:\ALCDA2\x64\App4\
Expanded Symbol search path is:
cache*;SRV*https://msdl.microsoft.com/download/symbols;c:\alcda2\x64\app4\

************* Path validation summary **************
Response                         Time (ms)     Location
Deferred                                       srv*
OK                                             C:\ALCDA2\x64\App4\
*** WARNING: Unable to verify timestamp for App4

0:000> .reload
..
*** WARNING: Unable to verify timestamp for App4

************* Symbol Loading Error Summary **************
Module name            Error
App4                   The system cannot find the file specified
```

```
You can troubleshoot most symbol related issues by turning on symbol loading diagnostics (!sym
noisy) and repeating the command that caused symbols to be loaded.
You should also verify that your symbol search path (.sympath) is correct.
```

Note: We ignore warnings and errors as they are not relevant for now.

5. List all threads and their first frame:

```
0:000> ~*k 1

Unable to get thread data for thread 0
.  0  Id: 10cd.10d0 Suspend: 0 Teb: 00000000`00000000 Unfrozen
 # Child-SP          RetAddr               Call Site
00 00007f8d`66b39d10 00000000`00401e24     App4!malloc+0x146

Unable to get thread data for thread 1
   1  Id: 10cd.10cf Suspend: 0 Teb: 00000000`00000000 Unfrozen
 # Child-SP          RetAddr               Call Site
00 00007f8d`6733ad10 00000000`00441c8a     App4!nanosleep+0x40

Unable to get thread data for thread 2
   2  Id: 10cd.10ce Suspend: 0 Teb: 00000000`00000000 Unfrozen
 # Child-SP          RetAddr               Call Site
00 00007f8d`67b3bd10 00000000`00441c8a     App4!nanosleep+0x40

Unable to get thread data for thread 3
   3  Id: 10cd.10cd Suspend: 0 Teb: 00000000`00000000 Unfrozen
 # Child-SP          RetAddr               Call Site
00 00007ffc`80678200 00000000`00441c8a     App4!nanosleep+0x40

Unable to get thread data for thread 4
   4  Id: 10cd.10d1 Suspend: 0 Teb: 00000000`00000000 Unfrozen
 # Child-SP          RetAddr               Call Site
00 00007f8d`66338d10 00000000`00441c8a     App4!nanosleep+0x40

Unable to get thread data for thread 5
   5  Id: 10cd.10d2 Suspend: 0 Teb: 00000000`00000000 Unfrozen
 # Child-SP          RetAddr               Call Site
00 00007f8d`65b37d10 00000000`00441c8a     App4!nanosleep+0x40
```

6. List the current thread stack trace:

```
0:000> kL
 # Child-SP          RetAddr               Call Site
00 00007f8d`66b39d10 00000000`00401e24     App4!malloc+0x146
01 00007f8d`66b39d30 00000000`00401f2d     App4!proc+0x277
02 00007f8d`66b39d80 00000000`00401f3e     App4!bar_three+0xe
03 00007f8d`66b39d90 00000000`00401f57     App4!foo_three+0xe
04 00007f8d`66b39da0 00000000`004033c3     App4!thread_three+0x16
05 00007f8d`66b39dc0 00000000`0044455f     App4!start_thread+0xf3
06 00007f8d`66b39e80 ffffffff`ffffffff     App4!_clone+0x3f
07 00007f8d`66b39e88 00000000`00000000     0xffffffff`ffffffff
```

7. We see that the segmentation fault happened internally in the *malloc* function when *proc* was allocating heap memory. Disassemble the *proc* function:

```
0:000> uf proc
App4!proc:
00000000`00401bad push    rbp
00000000`00401bae mov     rbp,rsp
00000000`00401bb1 sub     rsp,40h
00000000`00401bb5 mov     edi,1
00000000`00401bba call    App4!sleep (00000000`00441c50)
00000000`00401bbf mov     edi,100h
00000000`00401bc4 call    App4!malloc (00000000`0041a7c0)
00000000`00401bc9 mov     qword ptr [rbp-8],rax
00000000`00401bcd mov     edi,100h
00000000`00401bd2 call    App4!malloc (00000000`0041a7c0)
00000000`00401bd7 mov     qword ptr [rbp-10h],rax
00000000`00401bdb mov     edi,100h
00000000`00401be0 call    App4!malloc (00000000`0041a7c0)
00000000`00401be5 mov     qword ptr [rbp-18h],rax
00000000`00401be9 mov     edi,100h
00000000`00401bee call    App4!malloc (00000000`0041a7c0)
00000000`00401bf3 mov     qword ptr [rbp-20h],rax
00000000`00401bf7 mov     edi,100h
00000000`00401bfc call    App4!malloc (00000000`0041a7c0)
00000000`00401c01 mov     qword ptr [rbp-28h],rax
00000000`00401c05 mov     edi,100h
00000000`00401c0a call    App4!malloc (00000000`0041a7c0)
00000000`00401c0f mov     qword ptr [rbp-30h],rax
00000000`00401c13 mov     edi,100h
00000000`00401c18 call    App4!malloc (00000000`0041a7c0)
00000000`00401c1d mov     qword ptr [rbp-38h],rax
00000000`00401c21 mov     rax,qword ptr [rbp-30h]
00000000`00401c25 mov     rdi,rax
00000000`00401c28 call    App4!_free (00000000`0041ae00)
00000000`00401c2d mov     rax,qword ptr [rbp-20h]
00000000`00401c31 mov     rdi,rax
00000000`00401c34 call    App4!_free (00000000`0041ae00)
00000000`00401c39 mov     rax,qword ptr [rbp-10h]
00000000`00401c3d mov     rdi,rax
00000000`00401c40 call    App4!_free (00000000`0041ae00)
00000000`00401c45 mov     rax,qword ptr [rbp-10h]
00000000`00401c49 mov     rdx,7243206F6C6C6548h
00000000`00401c53 mov     rcx,6548202132687361h
00000000`00401c5d mov     qword ptr [rax],rdx
00000000`00401c60 mov     qword ptr [rax+8],rcx
00000000`00401c64 mov     rsi,73617243206F6C6Ch
00000000`00401c6e mov     rdi,6C6C654820213268h
00000000`00401c78 mov     qword ptr [rax+10h],rsi
00000000`00401c7c mov     qword ptr [rax+18h],rdi
00000000`00401c80 mov     rdx,326873617243206Fh
00000000`00401c8a mov     rcx,206F6C6C65482021h
00000000`00401c94 mov     qword ptr [rax+20h],rdx
00000000`00401c98 mov     qword ptr [rax+28h],rcx
00000000`00401c9c mov     rsi,2021326873617243h
00000000`00401ca6 mov     rdi,7243206F6C6C6548h
00000000`00401cb0 mov     qword ptr [rax+30h],rsi
00000000`00401cb4 mov     qword ptr [rax+38h],rdi
00000000`00401cb8 mov     dword ptr [rax+40h],32687361h
00000000`00401cbf mov     word ptr [rax+44h],21h
```

```
00000000`00401cc5 mov     rax,qword ptr [rbp-20h]
00000000`00401cc9 mov     rdx,7243206F6C6C6548h
00000000`00401cd3 mov     rcx,6548202134687361h
00000000`00401cdd mov     qword ptr [rax],rdx
00000000`00401ce0 mov     qword ptr [rax+8],rcx
00000000`00401ce4 mov     rsi,73617243206F6C6Ch
00000000`00401cee mov     rdi,6C6C654820213468h
00000000`00401cf8 mov     qword ptr [rax+10h],rsi
00000000`00401cfc mov     qword ptr [rax+18h],rdi
00000000`00401d00 mov     rdx,346873617243206Fh
00000000`00401d0a mov     rcx,206F6C6C65482021h
00000000`00401d14 mov     qword ptr [rax+20h],rdx
00000000`00401d18 mov     qword ptr [rax+28h],rcx
00000000`00401d1c mov     rsi,2021346873617243h
00000000`00401d26 mov     rdi,7243206F6C6C6548h
00000000`00401d30 mov     qword ptr [rax+30h],rsi
00000000`00401d34 mov     qword ptr [rax+38h],rdi
00000000`00401d38 mov     rdx,6548202134687361h
00000000`00401d42 mov     rcx,73617243206F6C6Ch
00000000`00401d4c mov     qword ptr [rax+40h],rdx
00000000`00401d50 mov     qword ptr [rax+48h],rcx
00000000`00401d54 mov     dword ptr [rax+50h],213468h
00000000`00401d5b mov     rax,qword ptr [rbp-30h]
00000000`00401d5f mov     rsi,7243206F6C6C6548h
00000000`00401d69 mov     rdi,6548202136687361h
00000000`00401d73 mov     qword ptr [rax],rsi
00000000`00401d76 mov     qword ptr [rax+8],rdi
00000000`00401d7a mov     rdx,73617243206F6C6Ch
00000000`00401d84 mov     rcx,6C6C654820213668h
00000000`00401d8e mov     qword ptr [rax+10h],rdx
00000000`00401d92 mov     qword ptr [rax+18h],rcx
00000000`00401d96 mov     rsi,366873617243206Fh
00000000`00401da0 mov     rdi,206F6C6C65482021h
00000000`00401daa mov     qword ptr [rax+20h],rsi
00000000`00401dae mov     qword ptr [rax+28h],rdi
00000000`00401db2 mov     rdx,2021366873617243h
00000000`00401dbc mov     rcx,7243206F6C6C6548h
00000000`00401dc6 mov     qword ptr [rax+30h],rdx
00000000`00401dca mov     qword ptr [rax+38h],rcx
00000000`00401dce mov     rsi,6548202136687361h
00000000`00401dd8 mov     rdi,73617243206F6C6Ch
00000000`00401de2 mov     qword ptr [rax+40h],rsi
00000000`00401de6 mov     qword ptr [rax+48h],rdi
00000000`00401dea mov     rdx,6C6C654820213668h
00000000`00401df4 mov     rcx,366873617243206Fh
00000000`00401dfe mov     qword ptr [rax+50h],rdx
00000000`00401e02 mov     qword ptr [rax+58h],rcx
00000000`00401e06 mov     word ptr [rax+60h],21h
00000000`00401e0c mov     edi,100h
00000000`00401e11 call    App4!malloc (00000000`0041a7c0)
00000000`00401e16 mov     qword ptr [rbp-10h],rax
00000000`00401e1a mov     edi,100h
00000000`00401e1f call    App4!malloc (00000000`0041a7c0)
00000000`00401e24 mov     qword ptr [rbp-20h],rax
00000000`00401e28 mov     edi,100h
00000000`00401e2d call    App4!malloc (00000000`0041a7c0)
00000000`00401e32 mov     qword ptr [rbp-30h],rax
00000000`00401e36 mov     edi,12Ch
00000000`00401e3b call    App4!sleep (00000000`00441c50)
00000000`00401e40 mov     rax,qword ptr [rbp-38h]
```

```
00000000`00401e44 mov     rdi,rax
00000000`00401e47 call    App4!_free (00000000`0041ae00)
00000000`00401e4c mov     rax,qword ptr [rbp-30h]
00000000`00401e50 mov     rdi,rax
00000000`00401e53 call    App4!_free (00000000`0041ae00)
00000000`00401e58 mov     rax,qword ptr [rbp-28h]
00000000`00401e5c mov     rdi,rax
00000000`00401e5f call    App4!_free (00000000`0041ae00)
00000000`00401e64 mov     rax,qword ptr [rbp-20h]
00000000`00401e68 mov     rdi,rax
00000000`00401e6b call    App4!_free (00000000`0041ae00)
00000000`00401e70 mov     rax,qword ptr [rbp-18h]
00000000`00401e74 mov     rdi,rax
00000000`00401e77 call    App4!_free (00000000`0041ae00)
00000000`00401e7c mov     rax,qword ptr [rbp-10h]
00000000`00401e80 mov     rdi,rax
00000000`00401e83 call    App4!_free (00000000`0041ae00)
00000000`00401e88 mov     rax,qword ptr [rbp-8]
00000000`00401e8c mov     rdi,rax
00000000`00401e8f call    App4!_free (00000000`0041ae00)
00000000`00401e94 mov     edi,0FFFFFFFFh
00000000`00401e99 call    App4!sleep (00000000`00441c50)
00000000`00401e9e nop
00000000`00401e9f leave
00000000`00401ea0 ret
```

Note: We see that before the problem *malloc* call, there were three buffer writes to memory addresses pointed to by values located at the following addresses: rbp-0x10, rbp-0x20, and rbp-0x30 (highlighted in red in disassembly). However, before buffer writes, there were *free* function calls with values located at the same addresses: rbp-0x30, rbp-0x20, and rbp-0x10 (highlighted in blue in disassembly). Therefore, we see "write after free" behavior.

8. We have the standard function prolog (highlighted in green in disassembly). Switch to stack frame #1 to check the addresses, their values, and memory contents they point to:

```
0:000> .frame /c /r 1
01 00007f8d`66b39d30 00000000`00401f2d     App4!proc+0x277
rax=00007f8d600008d0 rbx=0000000000000000 rcx=00007f8d60000948
rdx=7243206f6c6c6548 rsi=7243206f6c6c6548 rdi=0000000000000100
rip=0000000000401e24 rsp=00007f8d66b39d30 rbp=00007f8d66b39d70
 r8=00000000000000ff  r9=00007f8d60000c30 r10=0000000000000002
r11=00007f8d600008d0 r12=00007ffc806781ee r13=00007ffc806781ef
r14=00007f8d66b3a700 r15=0000000000000000
iopl=0         nv up ei ng nz na po cy
cs=0033  ss=002b  ds=0000  es=0000  fs=0000  gs=0000             efl=00010287
App4!proc+0x277:
00000000`00401e24 mov     qword ptr [rbp-20h],rax ss:00007f8d`66b39d50=00007f8d60000e50

0:000> dp rbp-20 L1
00007f8d`66b39d50  00007f8d`60000e50

0:000> dp 00007f8d`60000e50
00007f8d`60000e50  7243206f`6c6c6548 65482021`34687361
00007f8d`60000e60  73617243`206f6c6c 6c6c6548`20213468
00007f8d`60000e70  34687361`7243206f 206f6c6c`65482021
00007f8d`60000e80  20213468`73617243 7243206f`6c6c6548
00007f8d`60000e90  65482021`34687361 73617243`206f6c6c
00007f8d`60000ea0  00000000`00213468 00000000`00000000
00007f8d`60000eb0  00000000`00000000 00000000`00000000
00007f8d`60000ec0  00000000`00000000 00000000`00000000
```

```
0:000> da 00007f8d`60000e50
00007f8d`60000e50  "Hello Crash4! Hello Crash4! Hell"
00007f8d`60000e70  "o Crash4! Hello Crash4! Hello Cr"
00007f8d`60000e90  "ash4! Hello Crash4!"
```

```
0:000> dpa rbp-20 L1
00007f8d`66b39d50  00007f8d`60000e50 "Hello Crash4! Hello Crash4! Hello Crash4! Hello Crash4!"
```

9. We know the addresses passed to heap management functions, for example, 00007f8d`66b39xxx. Find the heap region in the section and module region list:

```
0:000> !address

Mapping file section regions...
Mapping module regions...
Mapping heap regions...

        BaseAddress      EndAddress+1        RegionSize     Type       State                 Protect             Usage
--------------------------------------------------------------------------------------------------------------------------
+        0`00000000        0`00400000        0`00400000                                                          <unknown>
+        0`00400000        0`00401000        0`00001000 MEM_PRIVATE MEM_COMMIT  PAGE_READONLY                   Image      [App4;
"/home/coredump/ALCDA2/x64/App4/App4"]
+        0`00401000        0`004bd000        0`000bc000                                                          Image      [App4;
"/home/coredump/ALCDA2/x64/App4/App4"]
+        0`004bd000        0`004c3000        0`00006000 MEM_PRIVATE MEM_COMMIT  PAGE_READWRITE                  Image      [App4;
"/home/coredump/ALCDA2/x64/App4/App4"]
+        0`004c3000        0`004c9000        0`00006000 MEM_PRIVATE MEM_COMMIT  PAGE_READWRITE                  <unknown>  [................]
+        0`004c9000        0`0124f000        0`00d86000                                                          <unknown>
+        0`0124f000        0`01272000        0`00023000 MEM_PRIVATE MEM_COMMIT  PAGE_READWRITE                  <unknown>  [................]
+        0`01272000     7f8d`60000000     7f8d`5ed8e000                                                          <unknown>
+     7f8d`60000000     7f8d`60021000        0`00021000 MEM_PRIVATE MEM_COMMIT  PAGE_READWRITE                  <unknown>  [................]
+     7f8d`60021000     7f8d`65339000        0`05318000                                                          <unknown>
+     7f8d`65339000     7f8d`65b39000        0`00800000 MEM_PRIVATE MEM_COMMIT  PAGE_READWRITE                  <unknown>  [................]
+     7f8d`65b39000     7f8d`65b3a000        0`00001000                                                          <unknown>
+     7f8d`65b3a000     7f8d`6633a000        0`00800000 MEM_PRIVATE MEM_COMMIT  PAGE_READWRITE                  <unknown>  [................]
+     7f8d`6633a000     7f8d`6633b000        0`00001000                                                          <unknown>
+     7f8d`6633b000     7f8d`66b3b000        0`00800000 MEM_PRIVATE MEM_COMMIT  PAGE_READWRITE                  <unknown>  [................]
+     7f8d`66b3b000     7f8d`66b3c000        0`00001000                                                          <unknown>
+     7f8d`66b3c000     7f8d`6733c000        0`00800000 MEM_PRIVATE MEM_COMMIT  PAGE_READWRITE                  <unknown>  [................]
+     7f8d`6733c000     7f8d`6733d000        0`00001000                                                          <unknown>
+     7f8d`6733d000     7f8d`67b3d000        0`00800000 MEM_PRIVATE MEM_COMMIT  PAGE_READWRITE                  <unknown>  [................]
+     7f8d`67b3d000     7ffc`80658000       6f`18b1b000                                                          <unknown>
+     7ffc`80658000     7ffc`80679000        0`00021000 MEM_PRIVATE MEM_COMMIT  PAGE_READWRITE                  <unknown>  [................]
+     7ffc`80679000     7ffc`806ff000        0`00086000                                                          <unknown>
+     7ffc`806ff000     7ffc`80703000        0`00004000 MEM_PRIVATE MEM_COMMIT  PAGE_READONLY                   <unknown>  [................]
+     7ffc`80703000     7ffc`80704000        0`00001000 MEM_PRIVATE MEM_COMMIT  PAGE_EXECUTE_READ               Image      [linux_vdso_so; "linux-
vdso.so.1"]
```

10. Check the faulting instruction and the problem memory address:

```
0:000> .cxr
Resetting default scope
```

```
0:000> r
rax=00007f8d600008d0 rbx=00000000000000ff rcx=00007f8d60000948
rdx=7243206f6c6c6548 rsi=7243206f6c6c6548 rdi=0000000000000100
rip=000000000041a906 rsp=00007f8d66b39d10 rbp=0000000000000100
 r8=00000000000000ff  r9=00007f8d60000c30 r10=0000000000000002
r11=00007f8d600008d0 r12=000000000000000f r13=00007ffc806781ef
r14=00007f8d66b3a700 r15=0000000000000000
iopl=0         nv up ei ng nz na po cy
cs=0033  ss=002b  ds=0000  es=0000  fs=0000  gs=0000             efl=00010287
App4!malloc+0x146:
00000000`0041a906 mov     rsi,qword ptr [rdx] ds:7243206f`6c6c6548=????????????????
```

```
0:000> dp rdx
7243206f`6c6c6548  ????????`???????? ????????`????????
7243206f`6c6c6558  ????????`???????? ????????`????????
7243206f`6c6c6568  ????????`???????? ????????`????????
7243206f`6c6c6578  ????????`???????? ????????`????????
7243206f`6c6c6588  ????????`???????? ????????`????????
7243206f`6c6c6598  ????????`???????? ????????`????????
```

```
7243206f`6c6c65a8  ????????`???????? ????????`????????
7243206f`6c6c65b8  ????????`???????? ????????`????????
```

```
0:000> .formats 7243206f`6c6c6548
Evaluate expression:
  Hex:     7243206f`6c6c6548
  Decimal: 8233460206695900488
  Octal:   0711031006755433062510
  Binary:  01110010 01000011 00100000 01101111 01101100 01101100 01100101 01001000
  Chars:   rC olleH
  Time:    Thu Oct 18 19:57:49.590 27691 (UTC + 0:00)
  Float:   low 1.14314e+027 high 3.86488e+030
  Double:  2.55074e+242
```

Note: We see that the "rC olleH" ("Hello Cr" in little-endian interpretation) fragment correlates with the "Hello Cr" buffer overwrite that we saw previously in step #8.

10. We close logging before exiting WinDbg:

```
0:000> .logclose
Closing open log file 'C:\ALCDA2\x64\App4\App4-WinDbg.log'
```

Exercise A4 (A64, WinDbg)

Goal: Learn how to identify heap regions and heap corruption.

Patterns: Dynamic Memory Corruption (Process Heap); Regular Data; Wild Pointer.

1. Launch WinDbg.

2. Load the *core.8800* dump file from the A64\App4 folder:

```
Microsoft (R) Windows Debugger Version 10.0.27725.1000 AMD64
Copyright (c) Microsoft Corporation. All rights reserved.


Loading Dump File [C:\ALCDA2\A64\App4\core.8800]
64-bit machine not using 64-bit API

************* Path validation summary **************
Response                         Time (ms)     Location
Deferred                                       srv*
Symbol search path is: srv*
Executable search path is:
Generic Unix Version 0 UP Free ARM 64-bit (AArch64)
System Uptime: not available
Process Uptime: not available
..
(2260.2263): Signal SIGSEGV (Segmentation fault) code SEGV_MAPERR (Address not mapped to
object) at 0x43206f6c6c6548
*** WARNING: Unable to verify timestamp for App4
App4+0x1cbec:
00000000`0041cbec ???
```

3. Set logging to a file in case of lengthy output from some commands:

```
0:000> .logopen C:\ALCDA2\A64\App4\App4-WinDbg.log
Opened log file 'C:\ALCDA2\A64\App4\App4-WinDbg.log'
```

4. Specify the dump folder as the symbol path and reload symbols:

```
0:000> .symfix; .sympath+ C:\ALCDA2\A64\App4\
Symbol search path is: srv*;C:\ALCDA2\A64\App4\
Expanded Symbol search path is:
cache*;SRV*https://msdl.microsoft.com/download/symbols;c:\alcda2\a64\app4\

************* Path validation summary **************
Response                         Time (ms)     Location
Deferred                                       srv*
OK                                             C:\ALCDA2\A64\App4\
*** WARNING: Unable to verify timestamp for App4
```

```
0:000> .reload
..
*** WARNING: Unable to verify timestamp for App4

************* Symbol Loading Error Summary **************
Module name            Error
```

```
App4                      The system cannot find the file specified

You can troubleshoot most symbol related issues by turning on symbol loading diagnostics (!sym
noisy) and repeating the command that caused symbols to be loaded.
You should also verify that your symbol search path (.sympath) is correct.
```

Note: We ignore warnings and errors as they are not relevant for now.

5. List all threads and their first frame:

```
0:000> ~*k 1

Unable to get thread data for thread 0
.  0  Id: 2260.2263 Suspend: 0 Teb: 00000000`00000000 Unfrozen
 # Child-SP          RetAddr               Call Site
00 0000fffc`03e5e790 00000000`00403304     App4!malloc+0x8c

Unable to get thread data for thread 1
   1  Id: 2260.2261 Suspend: 0 Teb: 00000000`00000000 Unfrozen
 # Child-SP          RetAddr               Call Site
00 0000fffc`04e7e5f0 00000000`00424e34     App4!_libc_nanosleep+0x24

Unable to get thread data for thread 2
   2  Id: 2260.2260 Suspend: 0 Teb: 00000000`00000000 Unfrozen
 # Child-SP          RetAddr               Call Site
00 0000ffff`d31fe360 00000000`00424e34     App4!_libc_nanosleep+0x24

Unable to get thread data for thread 3
   3  Id: 2260.2262 Suspend: 0 Teb: 00000000`00000000 Unfrozen
 # Child-SP          RetAddr               Call Site
00 0000fffc`0466e5f0 00000000`00424e34     App4!_libc_nanosleep+0x24

Unable to get thread data for thread 4
   4  Id: 2260.2264 Suspend: 0 Teb: 00000000`00000000 Unfrozen
 # Child-SP          RetAddr               Call Site
00 0000fffc`0364e5f0 00000000`00424e34     App4!_libc_nanosleep+0x24

Unable to get thread data for thread 5
   5  Id: 2260.2265 Suspend: 0 Teb: 00000000`00000000 Unfrozen
 # Child-SP          RetAddr               Call Site
00 0000fffc`02e3e5f0 00000000`00424e34     App4!_libc_nanosleep+0x24
```

6. List the current thread stack trace:

```
0:000> k
 # Child-SP          RetAddr               Call Site
00 0000fffc`03e5e790 00000000`00403304     App4!malloc+0x8c
01 0000fffc`03e5e7d0 00000000`00403400     App4!proc+0x11c
02 0000fffc`03e5e820 00000000`00403414     App4!bar_three+0xc
03 0000fffc`03e5e830 00000000`0040342c     App4!foo_three+0xc
04 0000fffc`03e5e840 00000000`00404db4     App4!thread_three+0x10
05 0000fffc`03e5e860 00000000`00429ce0     App4!start_thread+0xb4
06 0000fffc`03e5e990 ffffffff`ffffffff     App4!thread_start+0x30
07 0000fffc`03e5e990 00000000`00000000     0xffffffff`ffffffff
```

7. We see that the segmentation fault happened internally in the *malloc* function when *proc* was allocating heap memory. Disassemble the *proc* function:

```
0:000> uf proc
App4!proc:
00000000`004031e8 a9bb7bfd stp         fp,lr,[sp,#-0x50]!
00000000`004031ec 910003fd mov         fp,sp
00000000`004031f0 52800020 mov         w0,#1
00000000`004031f4 940086cc bl          App4!sleep (00000000`00424d24)
00000000`004031f8 d2802000 mov         x0,#0x100
00000000`004031fc 94006659 bl          App4!malloc (00000000`0041cb60)
00000000`00403200 f90027a0 str         x0,[fp,#0x48]
00000000`00403204 d2802000 mov         x0,#0x100
00000000`00403208 94006656 bl          App4!malloc (00000000`0041cb60)
00000000`0040320c f90023a0 str         x0,[fp,#0x40]
00000000`00403210 d2802000 mov         x0,#0x100
00000000`00403214 94006653 bl          App4!malloc (00000000`0041cb60)
00000000`00403218 f9001fa0 str         x0,[fp,#0x38]
00000000`0040321c d2802000 mov         x0,#0x100
00000000`00403220 94006650 bl          App4!malloc (00000000`0041cb60)
00000000`00403224 f9001ba0 str         x0,[fp,#0x30]
00000000`00403228 d2802000 mov         x0,#0x100
00000000`0040322c 9400664d bl          App4!malloc (00000000`0041cb60)
00000000`00403230 f90017a0 str         x0,[fp,#0x28]
00000000`00403234 d2802000 mov         x0,#0x100
00000000`00403238 9400664a bl          App4!malloc (00000000`0041cb60)
00000000`0040323c f90013a0 str         x0,[fp,#0x20]
00000000`00403240 d2802000 mov         x0,#0x100
00000000`00403244 94006647 bl          App4!malloc (00000000`0041cb60)
00000000`00403248 f9000fa0 str         x0,[fp,#0x18]
00000000`0040324c f94013a0 ldr         x0,[fp,#0x20]
00000000`00403250 94006912 bl          App4!_cfree (00000000`0041d698)
00000000`00403254 f9401ba0 ldr         x0,[fp,#0x30]
00000000`00403258 94006910 bl          App4!_cfree (00000000`0041d698)
00000000`0040325c f94023a0 ldr         x0,[fp,#0x40]
00000000`00403260 9400690e bl          App4!_cfree (00000000`0041d698)
00000000`00403264 f94023a0 ldr         x0,[fp,#0x40]
00000000`00403268 d0000421 adrp        x1,App4!arena_thread_freeres+0x118 (00000000`00489000)
00000000`0040326c 910d8021 add         x1,x1,#0x360
00000000`00403270 a9400c22 ldp         x2,x3,[x1]
00000000`00403274 a9000c02 stp         x2,x3,[x0]
00000000`00403278 a9410c22 ldp         x2,x3,[x1,#0x10]
00000000`0040327c a9010c02 stp         x2,x3,[x0,#0x10]
00000000`00403280 a9420c22 ldp         x2,x3,[x1,#0x20]
00000000`00403284 a9020c02 stp         x2,x3,[x0,#0x20]
00000000`00403288 a9430c22 ldp         x2,x3,[x1,#0x30]
00000000`0040328c a9030c02 stp         x2,x3,[x0,#0x30]
00000000`00403290 b9404022 ldr         w2,[x1,#0x40]
00000000`00403294 b9004002 str         w2,[x0,#0x40]
00000000`00403298 79408821 ldrh        w1,[x1,#0x44]
00000000`0040329c 79008801 strh        w1,[x0,#0x44]
00000000`004032a0 f9401ba0 ldr         x0,[fp,#0x30]
00000000`004032a4 d0000421 adrp        x1,App4!arena_thread_freeres+0x118 (00000000`00489000)
00000000`004032a8 910ea021 add         x1,x1,#0x3A8
00000000`004032ac a9400c22 ldp         x2,x3,[x1]
00000000`004032b0 a9000c02 stp         x2,x3,[x0]
00000000`004032b4 a9410c22 ldp         x2,x3,[x1,#0x10]
00000000`004032b8 a9010c02 stp         x2,x3,[x0,#0x10]
00000000`004032bc a9420c22 ldp         x2,x3,[x1,#0x20]
```

```
00000000`004032c0 a9020c02 stp          x2,x3,[x0,#0x20]
00000000`004032c4 a9430c22 ldp          x2,x3,[x1,#0x30]
00000000`004032c8 a9030c02 stp          x2,x3,[x0,#0x30]
00000000`004032cc a9440c22 ldp          x2,x3,[x1,#0x40]
00000000`004032d0 a9040c02 stp          x2,x3,[x0,#0x40]
00000000`004032d4 b9405021 ldr          w1,[x1,#0x50]
00000000`004032d8 b9005001 str          w1,[x0,#0x50]
00000000`004032dc f94013a0 ldr          x0,[fp,#0x20]
00000000`004032e0 d0000421 adrp         x1,App4!arena_thread_freeres+0x118 (00000000`00489000)
00000000`004032e4 91100021 add          x1,x1,#0x400
00000000`004032e8 d2800c42 mov          x2,#0x62
00000000`004032ec 97fff3e5 bl           App4!+0x10 (00000000`00400280)
00000000`004032f0 d2802000 mov          x0,#0x100
00000000`004032f4 9400661b bl           App4!malloc (00000000`0041cb60)
00000000`004032f8 f90023a0 str          x0,[fp,#0x40]
00000000`004032fc d2802000 mov          x0,#0x100
00000000`00403300 94006618 bl           App4!malloc (00000000`0041cb60)
00000000`00403304 f9001ba0 str          x0,[fp,#0x30]
00000000`00403308 d2802000 mov          x0,#0x100
00000000`0040330c 94006615 bl           App4!malloc (00000000`0041cb60)
00000000`00403310 f90013a0 str          x0,[fp,#0x20]
00000000`00403314 52802580 mov          w0,#0x12C
00000000`00403318 94008683 bl           App4!sleep (00000000`00424d24)
00000000`0040331c f9400fa0 ldr          x0,[fp,#0x18]
00000000`00403320 940068de bl           App4!_cfree (00000000`0041d698)
00000000`00403324 f94013a0 ldr          x0,[fp,#0x20]
00000000`00403328 940068dc bl           App4!_cfree (00000000`0041d698)
00000000`0040332c f94017a0 ldr          x0,[fp,#0x28]
00000000`00403330 940068da bl           App4!_cfree (00000000`0041d698)
00000000`00403334 f9401ba0 ldr          x0,[fp,#0x30]
00000000`00403338 940068d8 bl           App4!_cfree (00000000`0041d698)
00000000`0040333c f9401fa0 ldr          x0,[fp,#0x38]
00000000`00403340 940068d6 bl           App4!_cfree (00000000`0041d698)
00000000`00403344 f94023a0 ldr          x0,[fp,#0x40]
00000000`00403348 940068d4 bl           App4!_cfree (00000000`0041d698)
00000000`0040334c f94027a0 ldr          x0,[fp,#0x48]
00000000`00403350 940068d2 bl           App4!_cfree (00000000`0041d698)
00000000`00403354 12800000 mov          w0,#-1
00000000`00403358 94008673 bl           App4!sleep (00000000`00424d24)
00000000`0040335c a8c57bfd ldp          fp,lr,[sp],#0x50
00000000`00403360 d65f03c0 ret
```

Note: We see that before the problem *malloc* call, there were three buffer writes to memory addresses pointed to by values located at the following addresses: fp+0x40, fp+0x30, and fp+0x20 (highlighted in red in disassembly). However, before buffer writes, there were *free* function calls with values located at the same addresses: fp+0x20, fp+0x30, and fp+0x40 (highlighted in blue in disassembly). Therefore, we see "write after free" behavior.

8. We have the standard function prolog (highlighted in green in disassembly). Switch to stack frame #1 to check the addresses, their values, and memory contents they point to:

```
0:000> .frame /c /r 1
01 0000fffc`03e5e7d0 00000000`00403400     App4!proc+0x11c
 x0=0000fffb00000000   x1=00000000004d0000   x2=0000fffbfc000948   x3=0000fffbfc001070
 x4=7243206f6c6c6548   x5=0000fffbfc0010d2   x6=6548202136687361   x7=73617243206f6c6c
 x8=6c6c654820213668   x9=366873617243206f  x10=206f6c6c65482021  x11=0021366873617243
x12=6548202136687361  x13=73617243206f6c6c  x14=0000000000000000  x15=0000000000000000
x16=00000000004d0008  x17=0000000000423350  x18=0000000000000078  x19=0000fffc03e5f080
x20=0000000000000000  x21=00000000004d0000  x22=000000000040341c  x23=0000000000000000
x24=0000fffc03e5f770  x25=0000000031db06f0  x26=00000000004d7890  x27=0000000000010000
```

```
x28=0000000000810000   fp=0000fffc03e5e7d0   lr=0000000000403304   sp=0000fffc03e5e7d0
 pc=0000000000403304  psr=80001000 N--- EL0
App4!proc+0x11c:
00000000`00403304 f9001ba0 str        x0,[fp,#0x30]
```

```
0:000> dp fp+0x30 L1
0000fffc`03e5e800  0000fffb`fc000e50
```

```
0:000> dp 0000fffb`fc000e50
0000fffb`fc000e50  7243206f`6c6c6548 65482021`34687361
0000fffb`fc000e60  73617243`206f6c6c 6c6c6548`20213468
0000fffb`fc000e70  34687361`7243206f 206f6c6c`65482021
0000fffb`fc000e80  20213468`73617243 7243206f`6c6c6548
0000fffb`fc000e90  65482021`34687361 73617243`206f6c6c
0000fffb`fc000ea0  00000000`00213468 00000000`00000000
0000fffb`fc000eb0  00000000`00000000 00000000`00000000
0000fffb`fc000ec0  00000000`00000000 00000000`00000000
```

```
0:000> da 0000fffb`fc000e50
0000fffb`fc000e50  "Hello Crash4! Hello Crash4! Hell"
0000fffb`fc000e70  "o Crash4! Hello Crash4! Hello Cr"
0000fffb`fc000e90  "ash4! Hello Crash4!"
```

```
0:000> dpa fp+0x30 L1
0000fffc`03e5e800  0000fffb`fc000e50 "Hello Crash4! Hello Crash4! Hello Crash4! Hello Crash4!"
```

9. We know the addresses passed to heap management functions, for example, 0000fffb`fc000xxx. Find the heap region in the section and module region list:

```
0:000> !address

Mapping file section regions...
Mapping module regions...

        BaseAddress      EndAddress+1        RegionSize     Type       State                 Protect             Usage
--------------------------------------------------------------------------------------------------------------------------
+        0`00000000       0`00400000        0`00400000                                                       <unknown>
+        0`00400000       0`00410000        0`00010000 MEM_PRIVATE MEM_COMMIT  PAGE_EXECUTE_READ             Image      [App4;
"/home/opc/ALCDA2/App4/App4"]
+        0`00410000       0`004c0000        0`000b0000                                                       Image      [App4;
"/home/opc/ALCDA2/App4/App4"]
+        0`004c0000       0`004e0000        0`00020000 MEM_PRIVATE MEM_COMMIT  PAGE_READWRITE                Image      [App4;
"/home/opc/ALCDA2/App4/App4"]
+        0`004e0000       0`31db0000        0`318d0000                                                       <unknown>
+        0`31db0000       0`31df0000        0`00040000 MEM_PRIVATE MEM_COMMIT  PAGE_READWRITE                <unknown>  [................]
+        0`31df0000    fffb`fc000000     fffb`ca210000                                                       <unknown>
+     fffb`fc000000    fffb`fc030000        0`00030000 MEM_PRIVATE MEM_COMMIT  PAGE_READWRITE                <unknown>  [................]
+     fffb`fc030000    fffc`02630000        0`06600000                                                       <unknown>
+     fffc`02630000    fffc`02640000        0`00010000 MEM_PRIVATE MEM_COMMIT                                <unknown>  [................]
+     fffc`02640000    fffc`02e40000        0`00800000 MEM_PRIVATE MEM_COMMIT  PAGE_READWRITE                <unknown>  [................]
+     fffc`02e40000    fffc`02e50000        0`00010000 MEM_PRIVATE MEM_COMMIT                                <unknown>  [................]
+     fffc`02e50000    fffc`03650000        0`00800000 MEM_PRIVATE MEM_COMMIT  PAGE_READWRITE                <unknown>  [................]
+     fffc`03650000    fffc`03660000        0`00010000 MEM_PRIVATE MEM_COMMIT                                <unknown>  [................]
+     fffc`03660000    fffc`03e60000        0`00800000 MEM_PRIVATE MEM_COMMIT  PAGE_READWRITE                <unknown>  [................]
+     fffc`03e60000    fffc`03e70000        0`00010000 MEM_PRIVATE MEM_COMMIT                                <unknown>  [................]
+     fffc`03e70000    fffc`04670000        0`00800000 MEM_PRIVATE MEM_COMMIT  PAGE_READWRITE                <unknown>  [................]
+     fffc`04670000    fffc`04680000        0`00010000 MEM_PRIVATE MEM_COMMIT                                <unknown>  [................]
+     fffc`04680000    fffc`04e80000        0`00800000 MEM_PRIVATE MEM_COMMIT  PAGE_READWRITE                <unknown>  [................]
+     fffc`04e80000    fffc`04e90000        0`00010000 MEM_PRIVATE MEM_COMMIT  PAGE_READONLY                 <unknown>  [..0.......rB....]
+     fffc`04e90000    fffc`04ea0000        0`00010000 MEM_PRIVATE MEM_COMMIT  PAGE_EXECUTE_READ             Image      [linux_vdso_so; "linux-
vdso.so.1"]
+     fffc`04ea0000    ffff`d31d0000        3`ce330000                                                       <unknown>
+     ffff`d31d0000    ffff`d3200000        0`00030000 MEM_PRIVATE MEM_COMMIT  PAGE_READWRITE                <unknown>  [................]
```

10. Check the faulting instruction and the problem memory address:

```
0:000> .cxr
Resetting default scope
```

```
0:000> r
 x0=0000fffb00000000   x1=00000000004d0000  x2=0000fffbfc000948   x3=0000fffbfc001070
 x4=7243206f6c6c6548   x5=0000fffbfc0010d2  x6=6548202136687361   x7=73617243206f6c6c
 x8=6c6c654820213668   x9=366873617243206f x10=206f6c6c65482021 x11=0021366873617243
x12=6548202136687361  x13=73617243206f6c6c x14=0000000000000000 x15=0000000000000000
x16=00000000004d0008  x17=0000000000423350 x18=0000000000000078 x19=0000000000000100
x20=000000000000000f  x21=0000fffc03e5f770 x22=000000000040341c x23=0000000000000000
x24=0000fffc03e5f770  x25=0000000031db06f0 x26=00000000004d7890 x27=0000000000010000
x28=0000000000810000   fp=0000fffc03e5e790  lr=0000000000403304  sp=0000fffc03e5e790
 pc=000000000041cbec  psr=80001000 N--- EL0
App4!malloc+0x8c:
00000000`0041cbec f9400081 ldr         x1,[x4]

0:000> dp x4
7243206f`6c6c6548  ????????`???????? ????????`????????
7243206f`6c6c6558  ????????`???????? ????????`????????
7243206f`6c6c6568  ????????`???????? ????????`????????
7243206f`6c6c6578  ????????`???????? ????????`????????
7243206f`6c6c6588  ????????`???????? ????????`????????
7243206f`6c6c6598  ????????`???????? ????????`????????
7243206f`6c6c65a8  ????????`???????? ????????`????????
7243206f`6c6c65b8  ????????`???????? ????????`????????

0:000> .formats 7243206f`6c6c6548
Evaluate expression:
  Hex:     7243206f`6c6c6548
  Decimal: 8233460206695900488
  Octal:   0711031006755433062510
  Binary:  01110010 01000011 00100000 01101111 01101100 01101100 01100101 01001000
  Chars:   rC olleH
  Time:    Thu Oct 18 19:57:49.590 27691 (UTC + 0:00)
  Float:   low 1.14314e+027 high 3.86488e+030
  Double:  2.55074e+242
```

Note: We see that the "rC olleH" ("Hello Cr" in little-endian interpretation) fragment correlates with the "Hello Cr" buffer overwrite that we saw previously in step #8.

11. We close logging before exiting WinDbg:

```
0:000> .logclose
Closing open log file 'C:\ALCDA2\A64\App4\App4-WinDbg.log'
```

Mechanisms (Heap Corruption)

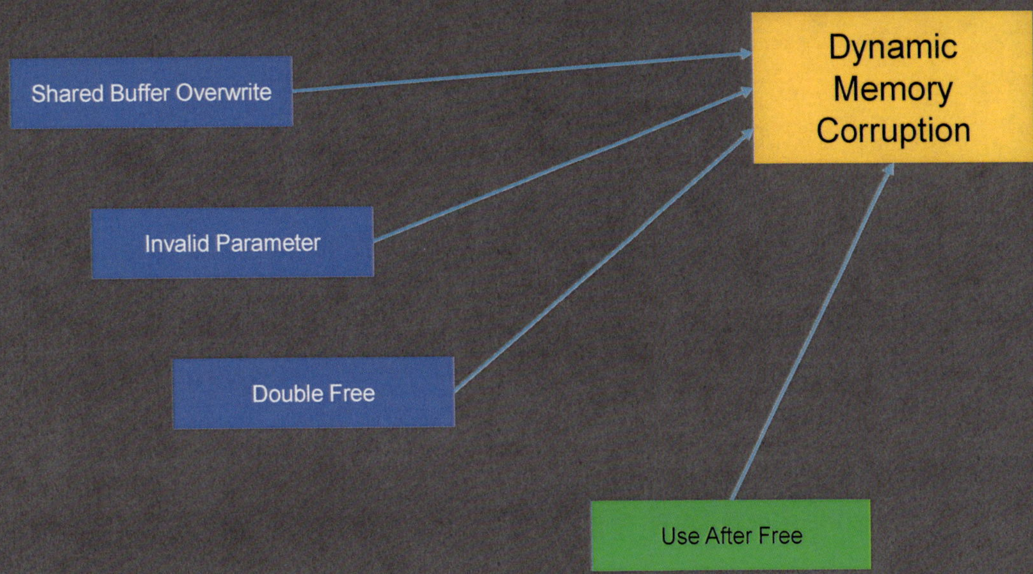

Exercise A5

- **Goal:** Learn how to identify stack corruption
- **Patterns:** Local Buffer Overflow (User Space); Execution Residue (User Space); Past Stack Trace
- \ALCDA-Dumps\Exercise-A5-x64-GDB.pdf
- \ALCDA-Dumps\Exercise-A5-A64-GDB.pdf
- \ALCDA-Dumps\Exercise-A5-A64-WinDbg.pdf
- \ALCDA-Dumps\Exercise-A5-x64-WinDbg.pdf

Exercise A5 (x64, GDB)

Goal: Learn how to identify stack corruption.

Patterns: Local Buffer Overflow (User Space); Execution Residue (User Space); Past Stack Trace.

1. Load the *core.App5* dump file and *App5* executable from the x64/App5 directory:

```
~/ALCDA2/x64/App5$ gdb -c core.App5 -se App5
GNU gdb (Debian 8.2.1-2+b3) 8.2.1
Copyright (C) 2018 Free Software Foundation, Inc.
License GPLv3+: GNU GPL version 3 or later <http://gnu.org/licenses/gpl.html>
This is free software: you are free to change and redistribute it.
There is NO WARRANTY, to the extent permitted by law.
Type "show copying" and "show warranty" for details.
This GDB was configured as "x86_64-linux-gnu".
Type "show configuration" for configuration details.
For bug reporting instructions, please see:
<http://www.gnu.org/software/gdb/bugs/>.
Find the GDB manual and other documentation resources online at:
    <http://www.gnu.org/software/gdb/documentation/>.

For help, type "help".
Type "apropos word" to search for commands related to "word"...
Reading symbols from App5...done.
[New LWP 4604]
[New LWP 4603]
[New LWP 4605]
[New LWP 4606]
[New LWP 4607]
[New LWP 4608]
[Thread debugging using libthread_db enabled]
Using host libthread_db library "/lib/x86_64-linux-gnu/libthread_db.so.1".
Core was generated by `./App5'.
Program terminated with signal SIGSEGV, Segmentation fault.
#0  0x0000000000007265 in ?? ()
[Current thread is 1 (Thread 0x7fb71bd94700 (LWP 4604))]
```

2. Set logging to a file in case of lengthy output from some commands:

```
(gdb) set logging on App5.log
Copying output to App5.log.
```

3. List threads and show stack trace of the problem thread:

```
(gdb) info threads
  Id   Target Id                          Frame
* 1    Thread 0x7fb71bd94700 (LWP 4604) 0x0000000000007265 in ?? ()
  2    Thread 0x1a56880 (LWP 4603)      0x0000000000441b30 in nanosleep ()
  3    Thread 0x7fb71b593700 (LWP 4605) 0x0000000000441b30 in nanosleep ()
  4    Thread 0x7fb71ad92700 (LWP 4606) 0x0000000000441b30 in nanosleep ()
  5    Thread 0x7fb71a591700 (LWP 4607) 0x0000000000441b30 in nanosleep ()
  6    Thread 0x7fb719d90700 (LWP 4608) 0x0000000000441b30 in nanosleep ()

(gdb) bt
#0  0x0000000000007265 in ?? ()
#1  0x0000000000000000 in ?? ()
```

4. We don't see expected stack trace frames as in a normal thread stack trace:

```
(gdb) thread apply 3 bt

Thread 3 (Thread 0x7fb71b593700 (LWP 4605)):
#0  0x0000000000441b30 in nanosleep ()
#1  0x0000000000441aba in sleep ()
#2  0x0000000000401d1a in bar_two ()
#3  0x0000000000401d2b in foo_two ()
#4  0x0000000000401d44 in thread_two ()
#5  0x00000000004031f3 in start_thread (arg=<optimized out>) at pthread_create.c:486
#6  0x000000000044438f in clone ()
```

5. We are still in thread #1. Dump raw stack data around the current stack pointer and find an ASCII buffer around a return address:

```
(gdb) info registers rsp
sp             0x7fb71bd93d80      0x7fb71bd93d80

(gdb) x/100a $rsp-0x100
0x7fb71bd93c80: 0x0     0x441aba <sleep+58>
0x7fb71bd93c90: 0x1     0x0
0x7fb71bd93ca0: 0x0     0x35216b7a748f2c00
0x7fb71bd93cb0: 0x0     0x0
0x7fb71bd93cc0: 0x7fb71bd93d50  0x401bc3 <procB+22>            ; rbp, retaddr
0x7fb71bd93cd0: 0x0     0x7fb71bd93d66
0x7fb71bd93ce0: 0x422077654e20794d      0x7542207265676769
0x7fb71bd93cf0: 0x72656666      0x0
0x7fb71bd93d00: 0x0     0x0
0x7fb71bd93d10: 0x0     0x0
0x7fb71bd93d20: 0x0     0x0
0x7fb71bd93d30: 0x0     0x0
0x7fb71bd93d40: 0x0     0x0
0x7fb71bd93d50: 0x7fb71bd93d70  0x401cca <procA+40>            ; rbp, retaddr
0x7fb71bd93d60: 0x794d000000000000      0x6769422077654e20
0x7fb71bd93d70: 0x6666754220726567      0x7265                 ; rbp, retaddr
0x7fb71bd93d80: 0x0     0x0
0x7fb71bd93d90: 0x0     0x0
0x7fb71bd93da0: 0x0     0x0
0x7fb71bd93db0: 0x0     0x0
0x7fb71bd93dc0: 0x0     0x7fb71bd90000
0x7fb71bd93dd0: 0x7fb71bd94700  0x6ca0e0818989a649
0x7fb71bd93de0: 0x7ffc1803c31e  0x7ffc1803c31f
0x7fb71bd93df0: 0x7fb71bd94700  0x0
0x7fb71bd93e00: 0x93ced733f209a649      0x6ca0e001eabba649
0x7fb71bd93e10: 0x0     0x0
0x7fb71bd93e20: 0x0     0x0
0x7fb71bd93e30: 0x0     0x0
0x7fb71bd93e40: 0x0     0x0
0x7fb71bd93e50: 0x0     0x35216b7a748f2c00
0x7fb71bd93e60: 0x0     0x7fb71bd94700
0x7fb71bd93e70: 0x7fb71bd94700  0x44438f <clone+63>
0x7fb71bd93e80: 0x0     0x0
0x7fb71bd93e90: 0x0     0x0
0x7fb71bd93ea0: 0x0     0x0
0x7fb71bd93eb0: 0x0     0x0
0x7fb71bd93ec0: 0x0     0x0
0x7fb71bd93ed0: 0x0     0x0
0x7fb71bd93ee0: 0x0     0x0
0x7fb71bd93ef0: 0x0     0x0
```

```
0x7fb71bd93f00: 0x0      0x0
0x7fb71bd93f10: 0x0      0x0
0x7fb71bd93f20: 0x0      0x0
0x7fb71bd93f30: 0x0      0x0
0x7fb71bd93f40: 0x0      0x0
0x7fb71bd93f50: 0x0      0x0
0x7fb71bd93f60: 0x0      0x0
0x7fb71bd93f70: 0x0      0x0
0x7fb71bd93f80: 0x0      0x0
0x7fb71bd93f90: 0x0      0x0
```

```
(gdb) x/s 0x7fb71bd93d60+8
0x7fb71bd93d68: " New Bigger Buffer"
```

Note: We also reconstructed the possible past stack trace before the crash through the linkage of saved RBP values:

```
procB+22
procA+40
```

Exercise A5 (A64, GDB)

Goal: Learn how to identify stack corruption.

Patterns: Local Buffer Overflow (User Space); Execution Residue (User Space); Past Stack Trace.

1. Load the *core.11157* dump file and *App5* executable from the A64/App5 directory:

```
~/ALCDA2/A64/App5$ gdb-multiarch -c core.11157 -se App5
GNU gdb (Debian 8.2.1-2+b3) 8.2.1
Copyright (C) 2018 Free Software Foundation, Inc.
License GPLv3+: GNU GPL version 3 or later <http://gnu.org/licenses/gpl.html>
This is free software: you are free to change and redistribute it.
There is NO WARRANTY, to the extent permitted by law.
Type "show copying" and "show warranty" for details.
This GDB was configured as "x86_64-linux-gnu".
Type "show configuration" for configuration details.
For bug reporting instructions, please see:
<http://www.gnu.org/software/gdb/bugs/>.
Find the GDB manual and other documentation resources online at:
    <http://www.gnu.org/software/gdb/documentation/>.

For help, type "help".
Type "apropos word" to search for commands related to "word"...
Reading symbols from App5...(no debugging symbols found)...done.
[New LWP 11158]
[New LWP 11160]
[New LWP 11162]
[New LWP 11157]
[New LWP 11159]
[New LWP 11161]
Core was generated by `./App5'.
Program terminated with signal SIGSEGV, Segmentation fault.
#0  0x0000000000000000 in ?? ()
[Current thread is 1 (LWP 11158)]
```

2. Set logging to a file in case of lengthy output from some commands:

```
(gdb) set logging on App5.log
Copying output to App5.log.
```

3. List threads and show stack trace of the problem thread:

```
(gdb) info threads
  Id   Target Id         Frame
* 1    LWP 11158         0x0000000000000000 in ?? ()
  2    LWP 11160         0x000000000040ca54 in nanosleep ()
  3    LWP 11162         0x000000000040ca54 in nanosleep ()
  4    LWP 11157         0x000000000040ca54 in nanosleep ()
  5    LWP 11159         0x000000000040ca54 in nanosleep ()
  6    LWP 11161         0x000000000040ca54 in nanosleep ()
```

```
(gdb) bt
#0  0x0000000000000000 in ?? ()
Backtrace stopped: previous frame identical to this frame (corrupt stack?)
```

4. We don't see expected stack trace frames as in a normal thread stack trace:

```
(gdb) thread apply 3 bt

Thread 3 (LWP 11162):
#0  0x000000000040ca54 in nanosleep ()
#1  0x0000000000424d74 in sleep ()
#2  0x00000000004033bc in bar_five ()
#3  0x00000000004033d0 in foo_five ()
#4  0x00000000004033e8 in thread_five ()
#5  0x0000000000404cd4 in start_thread ()
#6  0x0000000000429c20 in thread_start ()
```

5. We are still in thread #1. Dump raw stack data around the current stack pointer and find an ASCII buffer around a return address:

```
(gdb) info registers sp
sp             0xfffcbdfee830      0xfffcbdfee830

(gdb) x/100a $sp-0x100
0xfffcbdfee730: 0x0     0x0
0xfffcbdfee740: 0x0     0x0
0xfffcbdfee750: 0x0     0x0
0xfffcbdfee760: 0x0     0x0
0xfffcbdfee770: 0xfffcbdfee800  0x403288 <procA+44>         ; x29, lr
0xfffcbdfee780: 0x0     0xfffcbdfee810
0xfffcbdfee790: 0x0     0x422077654e20794d
0xfffcbdfee7a0: 0x7542207265676769      0x72656666
0xfffcbdfee7b0: 0x0     0x0
0xfffcbdfee7c0: 0x0     0x0
0xfffcbdfee7d0: 0x0     0x0
0xfffcbdfee7e0: 0x0     0x0
0xfffcbdfee7f0: 0x0     0x0
0xfffcbdfee800: 0xfffcbdfee820  0x40329c <bar_one+12>       ; x29, lr
0xfffcbdfee810: 0x422077654e20794d      0x7542207265676769
0xfffcbdfee820: 0x72656666      0x0                          ; x29, lr
0xfffcbdfee830: 0x0     0x0
0xfffcbdfee840: 0x0     0x0
0xfffcbdfee850: 0x0     0x0
0xfffcbdfee860: 0x0     0x0
0xfffcbdfee870: 0xfffc00000000  0x4d7890 <__default_pthread_attr>
0xfffcbdfee880: 0x4d0000        0x0
0xfffcbdfee890: 0xfffcbdfef49c  0xfffcbdfef080
0xfffcbdfee8a0: 0x0     0x0
0xfffcbdfee8b0: 0xfffcbdfef080  0x4d7890 <__default_pthread_attr>
0xfffcbdfee8c0: 0x4d0000        0x4032b8 <thread_one>
0xfffcbdfee8d0: 0x0     0xfffcbdfef770
0xfffcbdfee8e0: 0x3ea606f0      0x4d7890 <__default_pthread_attr>
0xfffcbdfee8f0: 0x10000 0x810000
0xfffcbdfee900: 0xfffcbdfee860  0xa8d4758adeef427
0xfffcbdfee910: 0x0     0xa8db8a4105050e7
0xfffcbdfee920: 0x0     0x0
0xfffcbdfee930: 0x0     0x0
0xfffcbdfee940: 0x0     0x0
0xfffcbdfee950: 0x0     0x0
0xfffcbdfee960: 0x0     0x0
0xfffcbdfee970: 0x0     0x0
0xfffcbdfee980: 0x0     0x0
0xfffcbdfee990: 0x0     0x0
0xfffcbdfee9a0: 0x0     0x0
```

```
0xfffcbdfee9b0: 0x0      0x0
0xfffcbdfee9c0: 0x0      0x0
0xfffcbdfee9d0: 0x0      0x0
0xfffcbdfee9e0: 0x0      0x0
0xfffcbdfee9f0: 0x0      0x0
0xfffcbdfeea00: 0x0      0x0
0xfffcbdfeea10: 0x0      0x0
0xfffcbdfeea20: 0x0      0x0
0xfffcbdfeea30: 0x0      0x0
0xfffcbdfeea40: 0x0      0x0
```

```
(gdb) x/s 0xfffcbdfee820
0xfffcbdfee820: "ffer"
```

```
(gdb) x/s 0xfffcbdfee810
0xfffcbdfee810: "My New Bigger Buffer"
```

Note: We also reconstructed the possible past stack trace before the crash through the linkage of saved X29 values:

```
procA+44
bar_one+12
```

Exercise A5 (x64, WinDbg)

Goal: Learn how to identify stack corruption.

Patterns: Local Buffer Overflow (User Space); Execution Residue (User Space); Past Stack Trace.

1. Launch WinDbg.

2. Load the *core.App5* dump file from the x64\App5 folder:

```
Microsoft (R) Windows Debugger Version 10.0.27725.1000 AMD64
Copyright (c) Microsoft Corporation. All rights reserved.


Loading Dump File [C:\ALCDA2\x64\App5\core.App5]
64-bit machine not using 64-bit API

************* Path validation summary **************
Response                         Time (ms)     Location
Deferred                                       srv*
Symbol search path is: srv*
Executable search path is:
Generic Unix Version 0 UP Free x64
System Uptime: not available
Process Uptime: not available
..
(11fb.11fc): Signal SIGSEGV (Segmentation fault) code SEGV_MAPERR (Address not mapped to
object) at 0x7265
00000000`00007265 ???
```

3. Set logging to a file in case of lengthy output from some commands:

```
0:000> .logopen C:\ALCDA2\x64\App5\App5-WinDbg.log
Opened log file 'C:\ALCDA2\x64\App5\App5-WinDbg.log'
```

4. Specify the dump folder as the symbol path and reload symbols:

```
0:000> .symfix; .sympath+ C:\ALCDA2\x64\App5\
Symbol search path is: srv*;C:\ALCDA2\x64\App5\
Expanded Symbol search path is:
cache*;SRV*https://msdl.microsoft.com/download/symbols;c:\alcda2\x64\app5\

************* Path validation summary **************
Response                         Time (ms)     Location
Deferred                                       srv*
OK                                             C:\ALCDA2\x64\App5\

0:000> .reload
..
```

5. List threads and show stack trace of the problem thread:

```
0:000> ~*k 1

Unable to get thread data for thread 0
.  0  Id: 11fb.11fc Suspend: 0 Teb: 00000000`00000000 Unfrozen
 # Child-SP          RetAddr               Call Site
00 00007fb7`1bd93d80 00000000`00000000     0x7265

Unable to get thread data for thread 1
   1  Id: 11fb.11fb Suspend: 0 Teb: 00000000`00000000 Unfrozen
*** WARNING: Unable to verify timestamp for App5
 # Child-SP          RetAddr               Call Site
00 00007ffc`1803c330 00000000`00441aba     App5!nanosleep+0x40

Unable to get thread data for thread 2
   2  Id: 11fb.11fd Suspend: 0 Teb: 00000000`00000000 Unfrozen
 # Child-SP          RetAddr               Call Site
00 00007fb7`1b592d10 00000000`00441aba     App5!nanosleep+0x40

Unable to get thread data for thread 3
   3  Id: 11fb.11fe Suspend: 0 Teb: 00000000`00000000 Unfrozen
 # Child-SP          RetAddr               Call Site
00 00007fb7`1ad91d10 00000000`00441aba     App5!nanosleep+0x40

Unable to get thread data for thread 4
   4  Id: 11fb.11ff Suspend: 0 Teb: 00000000`00000000 Unfrozen
 # Child-SP          RetAddr               Call Site
00 00007fb7`1a590d10 00000000`00441aba     App5!nanosleep+0x40

Unable to get thread data for thread 5
   5  Id: 11fb.1200 Suspend: 0 Teb: 00000000`00000000 Unfrozen
 # Child-SP          RetAddr               Call Site
00 00007fb7`19d8fd10 00000000`00441aba     App5!nanosleep+0x40

0:000> k
 # Child-SP          RetAddr               Call Site
00 00007fb7`1bd93d80 00000000`00000000     0x7265
```

6. We don't see expected stack trace frames as in a normal thread stack trace:

```
0:000> ~3kL
 # Child-SP          RetAddr               Call Site
00 00007fb7`1ad91d10 00000000`00441aba     App5!nanosleep+0x40
01 00007fb7`1ad91d40 00000000`00401d59     App5!sleep+0x3a
02 00007fb7`1ad91d80 00000000`00401d6a     App5!bar_three+0xe
03 00007fb7`1ad91d90 00000000`00401d83     App5!foo_three+0xe
04 00007fb7`1ad91da0 00000000`004031f3     App5!thread_three+0x16
05 00007fb7`1ad91dc0 00000000`0044438f     App5!start_thread+0xf3
06 00007fb7`1ad91e80 ffffffff`ffffffff     App5!_clone+0x3f
07 00007fb7`1ad91e88 00000000`00000000     0xffffffff`ffffffff
```

7. We are still in thread #0. Dump raw stack data around the current stack pointer and find an ASCII buffer around a return address:

```
0:000> r rsp
rsp=00007fb71bd93d80
```

```
0:000> r rip
rip=0000000000007265

0:000> dps rsp-100 rsp+100
00007fb7`1bd93c80  00000000`00000000
00007fb7`1bd93c88  00000000`00441aba App5!sleep+0x3a
00007fb7`1bd93c90  00000000`00000001
00007fb7`1bd93c98  00000000`00000000
00007fb7`1bd93ca0  00000000`00000000
00007fb7`1bd93ca8  35216b7a`748f2c00
00007fb7`1bd93cb0  00000000`00000000
00007fb7`1bd93cb8  00000000`00000000
00007fb7`1bd93cc0  00007fb7`1bd93d50                         ; rbp
00007fb7`1bd93cc8  00000000`00401bc3 App5!procB+0x16         ; retaddr
00007fb7`1bd93cd0  00000000`00000000
00007fb7`1bd93cd8  00007fb7`1bd93d66
00007fb7`1bd93ce0  42207765`4e20794d
00007fb7`1bd93ce8  75422072`65676769
00007fb7`1bd93cf0  00000000`72656666
00007fb7`1bd93cf8  00000000`00000000
00007fb7`1bd93d00  00000000`00000000
00007fb7`1bd93d08  00000000`00000000
00007fb7`1bd93d10  00000000`00000000
00007fb7`1bd93d18  00000000`00000000
00007fb7`1bd93d20  00000000`00000000
00007fb7`1bd93d28  00000000`00000000
00007fb7`1bd93d30  00000000`00000000
00007fb7`1bd93d38  00000000`00000000
00007fb7`1bd93d40  00000000`00000000
00007fb7`1bd93d48  00000000`00000000
00007fb7`1bd93d50  00007fb7`1bd93d70                         ; rbp
00007fb7`1bd93d58  00000000`00401cca App5!procA+0x28         ; retaddr
00007fb7`1bd93d60  794d0000`00000000
00007fb7`1bd93d68  67694220`77654e20
00007fb7`1bd93d70  66667542`20726567                         ; rbp
00007fb7`1bd93d78  00000000`00007265                         ; retaddr
00007fb7`1bd93d80  00000000`00000000
00007fb7`1bd93d88  00000000`00000000
00007fb7`1bd93d90  00000000`00000000
00007fb7`1bd93d98  00000000`00000000
00007fb7`1bd93da0  00000000`00000000
00007fb7`1bd93da8  00000000`00000000
00007fb7`1bd93db0  00000000`00000000
00007fb7`1bd93db8  00000000`00000000
00007fb7`1bd93dc0  00000000`00000000
00007fb7`1bd93dc8  00007fb7`1bd90000
00007fb7`1bd93dd0  00007fb7`1bd94700
00007fb7`1bd93dd8  6ca0e081`8989a649
00007fb7`1bd93de0  00007ffc`1803c31e
00007fb7`1bd93de8  00007ffc`1803c31f
00007fb7`1bd93df0  00007fb7`1bd94700
00007fb7`1bd93df8  00000000`00000000
00007fb7`1bd93e00  93ced733`f209a649
00007fb7`1bd93e08  6ca0e001`eabba649
00007fb7`1bd93e10  00000000`00000000
00007fb7`1bd93e18  00000000`00000000
00007fb7`1bd93e20  00000000`00000000
00007fb7`1bd93e28  00000000`00000000
00007fb7`1bd93e30  00000000`00000000
00007fb7`1bd93e38  00000000`00000000
```

```
00007fb7`1bd93e40  00000000`00000000
00007fb7`1bd93e48  00000000`00000000
00007fb7`1bd93e50  00000000`00000000
00007fb7`1bd93e58  35216b7a`748f2c00
00007fb7`1bd93e60  00000000`00000000
00007fb7`1bd93e68  00007fb7`1bd94700
00007fb7`1bd93e70  00007fb7`1bd94700
00007fb7`1bd93e78  00000000`0044438f App5!_clone+0x3f
00007fb7`1bd93e80  00000000`00000000
```

```
0:000> da 00007fb7`1bd93d68
00007fb7`1bd93d68  " New Bigger Buffer"
```

Note: We are also able to reconstruct the past stack trace through the linkage of saved RBP values:

```
00007fb7`1bd93cc8  00000000`00401bc3 App5!procB+0x16        ; retaddr
00007fb7`1bd93d58  00000000`00401cca App5!procA+0x28        ; retaddr
```

8. We close logging before exiting WinDbg:

```
0:000> .logclose
Closing open log file 'C:\ALCDA2\x64\App5\App5-WinDbg.log'
```

Exercise A5 (A64, WinDbg)

Goal: Learn how to identify stack corruption.

Patterns: Local Buffer Overflow (User Space); Execution Residue (User Space); Past Stack Trace.

1. Launch WinDbg.

2. Load the *core.11157* dump file from the A64\App5 folder:

```
Microsoft (R) Windows Debugger Version 10.0.27725.1000 AMD64
Copyright (c) Microsoft Corporation. All rights reserved.


Loading Dump File [C:\ALCDA2\A64\App5\core.11157]
64-bit machine not using 64-bit API

************* Path validation summary **************
Response                         Time (ms)     Location
Deferred                                       srv*
Symbol search path is: srv*
Executable search path is:
Generic Unix Version 0 UP Free ARM 64-bit (AArch64)
System Uptime: not available
Process Uptime: not available
..
(2b95.2b96): Signal SIGSEGV (Segmentation fault) code SEGV_MAPERR (Address not mapped to
object) at 0x0
00000000`00000000 ???
```

3. Set logging to a file in case of lengthy output from some commands:

```
0:000> .logopen C:\ALCDA2\A64\App5\App5-WinDbg.log
Opened log file 'C:\ALCDA2\A64\App5\App5-WinDbg.log'
```

4. Specify the dump folder as the symbol path and reload symbols:

```
0:000> .symfix; .sympath+ C:\ALCDA2\A64\App5\
Symbol search path is: srv*;C:\ALCDA2\A64\App5\
Expanded Symbol search path is:
cache*;SRV*https://msdl.microsoft.com/download/symbols;c:\alcda2\a64\app5\

************* Path validation summary **************
Response                         Time (ms)     Location
Deferred                                       srv*
OK                                             C:\ALCDA2\A64\App5\

0:000> .reload
..
```

5. List threads and show stack trace of the problem thread:

```
0:000> ~*k 1

Unable to get thread data for thread 0
.  0  Id: 2b95.2b96 Suspend: 0 Teb: 00000000`00000000 Unfrozen
 # Child-SP          RetAddr               Call Site
00 0000fffc`bdfee830 00000000`00000000     0x0

Unable to get thread data for thread 1
   1  Id: 2b95.2b98 Suspend: 0 Teb: 00000000`00000000 Unfrozen
Unable to load image /home/opc/ALCDA2/App5/App5, Win32 error 0n2
*** WARNING: Unable to verify timestamp for App5
 # Child-SP          RetAddr               Call Site
00 0000fffc`bcfce5f0 00000000`00424d74     App5!_libc_nanosleep+0x24

Unable to get thread data for thread 2
   2  Id: 2b95.2b9a Suspend: 0 Teb: 00000000`00000000 Unfrozen
 # Child-SP          RetAddr               Call Site
00 0000fffc`bbfae5f0 00000000`00424d74     App5!_libc_nanosleep+0x24

Unable to get thread data for thread 3
   3  Id: 2b95.2b95 Suspend: 0 Teb: 00000000`00000000 Unfrozen
 # Child-SP          RetAddr               Call Site
00 0000ffff`ca3bae40 00000000`00424d74     App5!_libc_nanosleep+0x24

Unable to get thread data for thread 4
   4  Id: 2b95.2b97 Suspend: 0 Teb: 00000000`00000000 Unfrozen
 # Child-SP          RetAddr               Call Site
00 0000fffc`bd7de5f0 00000000`00424d74     App5!_libc_nanosleep+0x24

Unable to get thread data for thread 5
   5  Id: 2b95.2b99 Suspend: 0 Teb: 00000000`00000000 Unfrozen
 # Child-SP          RetAddr               Call Site
00 0000fffc`bc7be5f0 00000000`00424d74     App5!_libc_nanosleep+0x24

0:000> k
 # Child-SP          RetAddr               Call Site
00 0000fffc`bdfee830 00000000`00000000     0x0
```

6. We don't see expected stack trace frames as in a normal thread stack trace:

```
0:000> ~3k
 # Child-SP          RetAddr               Call Site
00 0000ffff`ca3bae40 00000000`00424d74     App5!_libc_nanosleep+0x24
01 0000ffff`ca3bae80 00000000`00403484     App5!sleep+0x110
02 0000ffff`ca3bb070 00000000`0040ecec     App5!main+0x90
03 0000ffff`ca3bb0c0 00000000`00403090     App5!_libc_start_main+0x304
04 0000ffff`ca3bb220 00000000`00000000     App5!start+0x4c
```

7. We are still in thread #0. Dump raw stack data around the current stack pointer and find an ASCII buffer around a return address:

```
0:000> r sp
sp=0000fffcbdfee830

0:000> r lr
lr=0000000000000000
```

```
0:000> dps sp-100 sp+100
0000fffc`bdfee730  00000000`00000000
0000fffc`bdfee738  00000000`00000000
0000fffc`bdfee740  00000000`00000000
0000fffc`bdfee748  00000000`00000000
0000fffc`bdfee750  00000000`00000000
0000fffc`bdfee758  00000000`00000000
0000fffc`bdfee760  00000000`00000000
0000fffc`bdfee768  00000000`00000000
0000fffc`bdfee770  0000fffc`bdfee800                          ; fp
0000fffc`bdfee778  00000000`00403288 App5!procA+0x2c          ; lr
0000fffc`bdfee780  00000000`00000000
0000fffc`bdfee788  0000fffc`bdfee810
0000fffc`bdfee790  00000000`00000000
0000fffc`bdfee798  42207765`4e20794d
0000fffc`bdfee7a0  75422072`65676769
0000fffc`bdfee7a8  00000000`72656666
0000fffc`bdfee7b0  00000000`00000000
0000fffc`bdfee7b8  00000000`00000000
0000fffc`bdfee7c0  00000000`00000000
0000fffc`bdfee7c8  00000000`00000000
0000fffc`bdfee7d0  00000000`00000000
0000fffc`bdfee7d8  00000000`00000000
0000fffc`bdfee7e0  00000000`00000000
0000fffc`bdfee7e8  00000000`00000000
0000fffc`bdfee7f0  00000000`00000000
0000fffc`bdfee7f8  00000000`00000000
0000fffc`bdfee800  0000fffc`bdfee820                          ; fp
0000fffc`bdfee808  00000000`0040329c App5!bar_one+0xc         ; lr
0000fffc`bdfee810  42207765`4e20794d
0000fffc`bdfee818  75422072`65676769
0000fffc`bdfee820  00000000`72656666                          ; fp
0000fffc`bdfee828  00000000`00000000                          ; lr
0000fffc`bdfee830  00000000`00000000
0000fffc`bdfee838  00000000`00000000
0000fffc`bdfee840  00000000`00000000
0000fffc`bdfee848  00000000`00000000
0000fffc`bdfee850  00000000`00000000
0000fffc`bdfee858  00000000`00000000
0000fffc`bdfee860  00000000`00000000
0000fffc`bdfee868  00000000`00000000
0000fffc`bdfee870  0000fffc`00000000
0000fffc`bdfee878  00000000`004d7890 App5!_default_pthread_attr
0000fffc`bdfee880  00000000`004d0000 App5!+0x18
0000fffc`bdfee888  00000000`00000000
0000fffc`bdfee890  0000fffc`bdfef49c
0000fffc`bdfee898  0000fffc`bdfef080
0000fffc`bdfee8a0  00000000`00000000
0000fffc`bdfee8a8  00000000`00000000
0000fffc`bdfee8b0  0000fffc`bdfef080
0000fffc`bdfee8b8  00000000`004d7890 App5!_default_pthread_attr
0000fffc`bdfee8c0  00000000`004d0000 App5!+0x18
0000fffc`bdfee8c8  00000000`004032b8 App5!thread_one
0000fffc`bdfee8d0  00000000`00000000
0000fffc`bdfee8d8  0000fffc`bdfef770
0000fffc`bdfee8e0  00000000`3ea606f0
0000fffc`bdfee8e8  00000000`004d7890 App5!_default_pthread_attr
0000fffc`bdfee8f0  00000000`00010000
0000fffc`bdfee8f8  00000000`00810000
0000fffc`bdfee900  0000fffc`bdfee860
```

```
0000fffc`bdfee908  0a8d4758`adeef427
0000fffc`bdfee910  00000000`00000000
0000fffc`bdfee918  0a8db8a4`105050e7
0000fffc`bdfee920  00000000`00000000
0000fffc`bdfee928  00000000`00000000
0000fffc`bdfee930  00000000`00000000
```

```
0:000> da 0000fffc`bdfee810
0000fffc`bdfee810  "My New Bigger Buffer"
```

Note: We are also able to reconstruct the past stack trace through the linkage of LR values:

```
0000fffc`bdfee778  00000000`00403288 App5!procA+0x2c        ; lr
0000fffc`bdfee808  00000000`0040329c App5!bar_one+0xc       ; lr
```

8. We close logging before exiting WinDbg:

```
0:000> .logclose
Closing open log file 'C:\ALCDA2\A64\App5\App5-WinDbg.log'
```

Mechanisms (Stack Corruption)

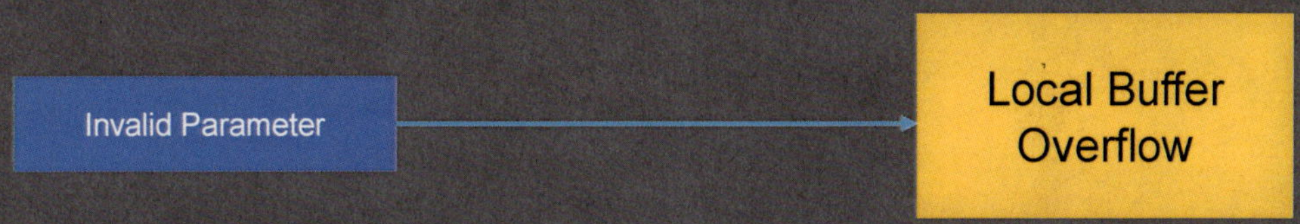

Exercise A6

- **Goal:** Learn how to identify stack overflow, stack boundaries, reconstruct stack trace

- **Patterns:** Stack Overflow (User Mode)

- \ALCDA-Dumps\Exercise-A6-x64-GDB.pdf
- \ALCDA-Dumps\Exercise-A6-A64-GDB.pdf

- \ALCDA-Dumps\Exercise-A6-A64-WinDbg.pdf
- \ALCDA-Dumps\Exercise-A6-x64-WinDbg.pdf

Exercise A6 (x64, GDB)

Goal: Learn how to identify stack overflow, stack boundaries, reconstruct stack trace.

Patterns: Stack Overflow (User Mode).

1. Load the *core.App6* dump file and *App6* executable from the x64/App6 directory:

```
~/ALCDA2/x64/App6$ gdb -c core.App6 -se App6
GNU gdb (Debian 8.2.1-2+b3) 8.2.1
Copyright (C) 2018 Free Software Foundation, Inc.
License GPLv3+: GNU GPL version 3 or later <http://gnu.org/licenses/gpl.html>
This is free software: you are free to change and redistribute it.
There is NO WARRANTY, to the extent permitted by law.
Type "show copying" and "show warranty" for details.
This GDB was configured as "x86_64-linux-gnu".
Type "show configuration" for configuration details.
For bug reporting instructions, please see:
<http://www.gnu.org/software/gdb/bugs/>.
Find the GDB manual and other documentation resources online at:
    <http://www.gnu.org/software/gdb/documentation/>.

For help, type "help".
Type "apropos word" to search for commands related to "word"...
Reading symbols from App6...done.
[New LWP 4704]
[New LWP 4707]
[New LWP 4705]
[New LWP 4703]
[New LWP 4706]
[New LWP 4708]
[Thread debugging using libthread_db enabled]
Using host libthread_db library "/lib/x86_64-linux-gnu/libthread_db.so.1".
Core was generated by `./App6'.
Program terminated with signal SIGSEGV, Segmentation fault.
#0  0x0000000000401bb8 in procF ()
[Current thread is 1 (Thread 0x7f91e6de8700 (LWP 4704))]
```

2. Set logging to a file in case of lengthy output from some commands:

```
(gdb) set logging on App6.log
Copying output to App6.log.
```

3. List threads:

```
(gdb) info threads
  Id   Target Id                          Frame
* 1    Thread 0x7f91e6de8700 (LWP 4704) 0x0000000000401bb8 in procF ()
  2    Thread 0x7f91e55e5700 (LWP 4707) 0x0000000000441ab0 in nanosleep ()
  3    Thread 0x7f91e65e7700 (LWP 4705) 0x0000000000441ab0 in nanosleep ()
  4    Thread 0xec2880 (LWP 4703)        0x0000000000441ab0 in nanosleep ()
  5    Thread 0x7f91e5de6700 (LWP 4706) 0x0000000000441ab0 in nanosleep ()
  6    Thread 0x7f91e4de4700 (LWP 4708) 0x0000000000441ab0 in nanosleep ()
```

4. If we try to print the problem stack trace, we get an endless number of frames, so we quit:

```
(gdb) bt
#0  0x0000000000401bb8 in procF ()
#1  0x0000000000401c05 in procF ()
#2  0x0000000000401c05 in procF ()
#3  0x0000000000401c05 in procF ()
#4  0x0000000000401c05 in procF ()
#5  0x0000000000401c05 in procF ()
#6  0x0000000000401c05 in procF ()
#7  0x0000000000401c05 in procF ()
#8  0x0000000000401c05 in procF ()
#9  0x0000000000401c05 in procF ()
#10 0x0000000000401c05 in procF ()
#11 0x0000000000401c05 in procF ()
#12 0x0000000000401c05 in procF ()
#13 0x0000000000401c05 in procF ()
#14 0x0000000000401c05 in procF ()
#15 0x0000000000401c05 in procF ()
#16 0x0000000000401c05 in procF ()
#17 0x0000000000401c05 in procF ()
#18 0x0000000000401c05 in procF ()
#19 0x0000000000401c05 in procF ()
#20 0x0000000000401c05 in procF ()
#21 0x0000000000401c05 in procF ()
#22 0x0000000000401c05 in procF ()
#23 0x0000000000401c05 in procF ()
#24 0x0000000000401c05 in procF ()
#25 0x0000000000401c05 in procF ()
#26 0x0000000000401c05 in procF ()
#27 0x0000000000401c05 in procF ()
#28 0x0000000000401c05 in procF ()
#29 0x0000000000401c05 in procF ()
#30 0x0000000000401c05 in procF ()
#31 0x0000000000401c05 in procF ()
#32 0x0000000000401c05 in procF ()
#33 0x0000000000401c05 in procF ()
#34 0x0000000000401c05 in procF ()
#35 0x0000000000401c05 in procF ()
#36 0x0000000000401c05 in procF ()
#37 0x0000000000401c05 in procF ()
#38 0x0000000000401c05 in procF ()
#39 0x0000000000401c05 in procF ()
#40 0x0000000000401c05 in procF ()
#41 0x0000000000401c05 in procF ()
#42 0x0000000000401c05 in procF ()
#43 0x0000000000401c05 in procF ()
#44 0x0000000000401c05 in procF ()
#45 0x0000000000401c05 in procF ()
#46 0x0000000000401c05 in procF ()
#47 0x0000000000401c05 in procF ()
#48 0x0000000000401c05 in procF ()
#49 0x0000000000401c05 in procF ()
#50 0x0000000000401c05 in procF ()
#51 0x0000000000401c05 in procF ()
#52 0x0000000000401c05 in procF ()
#53 0x0000000000401c05 in procF ()
#54 0x0000000000401c05 in procF ()
#55 0x0000000000401c05 in procF ()
#56 0x0000000000401c05 in procF ()
```

```
--Type <RET> for more, q to quit, c to continue without paging--
#57 0x0000000000401c05 in procF ()
#58 0x0000000000401c05 in procF ()
#59 0x0000000000401c05 in procF ()
#60 0x0000000000401c05 in procF ()
#61 0x0000000000401c05 in procF ()
#62 0x0000000000401c05 in procF ()
#63 0x0000000000401c05 in procF ()
#64 0x0000000000401c05 in procF ()
#65 0x0000000000401c05 in procF ()
#66 0x0000000000401c05 in procF ()
#67 0x0000000000401c05 in procF ()
#68 0x0000000000401c05 in procF ()
#69 0x0000000000401c05 in procF ()
#70 0x0000000000401c05 in procF ()
#71 0x0000000000401c05 in procF ()
#72 0x0000000000401c05 in procF ()
#73 0x0000000000401c05 in procF ()
#74 0x0000000000401c05 in procF ()
#75 0x0000000000401c05 in procF ()
#76 0x0000000000401c05 in procF ()
#77 0x0000000000401c05 in procF ()
#78 0x0000000000401c05 in procF ()
#79 0x0000000000401c05 in procF ()
#80 0x0000000000401c05 in procF ()
#81 0x0000000000401c05 in procF ()
#82 0x0000000000401c05 in procF ()
#83 0x0000000000401c05 in procF ()
#84 0x0000000000401c05 in procF ()
#85 0x0000000000401c05 in procF ()
#86 0x0000000000401c05 in procF ()
#87 0x0000000000401c05 in procF ()
#88 0x0000000000401c05 in procF ()
#89 0x0000000000401c05 in procF ()
#90 0x0000000000401c05 in procF ()
#91 0x0000000000401c05 in procF ()
#92 0x0000000000401c05 in procF ()
#93 0x0000000000401c05 in procF ()
#94 0x0000000000401c05 in procF ()
#95 0x0000000000401c05 in procF ()
#96 0x0000000000401c05 in procF ()
#97 0x0000000000401c05 in procF ()
#98 0x0000000000401c05 in procF ()
#99 0x0000000000401c05 in procF ()
#100 0x0000000000401c05 in procF ()
#101 0x0000000000401c05 in procF ()
#102 0x0000000000401c05 in procF ()
#103 0x0000000000401c05 in procF ()
#104 0x0000000000401c05 in procF ()
#105 0x0000000000401c05 in procF ()
#106 0x0000000000401c05 in procF ()
#107 0x0000000000401c05 in procF ()
#108 0x0000000000401c05 in procF ()
#109 0x0000000000401c05 in procF ()
#110 0x0000000000401c05 in procF ()
#111 0x0000000000401c05 in procF ()
#112 0x0000000000401c05 in procF ()
#113 0x0000000000401c05 in procF ()
--Type <RET> for more, q to quit, c to continue without paging--q
Quit
```

Note: It looks like a stack overflow.

5. Check if this is a stack overflow indeed. The stack region can be identified from *App6.pmap.4703* from the thread number. Since the problem thread has LWP 4704, it should be located just below the main stack region:

```
4703:   ./App6
0000000000400000      4K r---- App6
0000000000401000    592K r-x-- App6
0000000000495000    156K r---- App6
00000000004bd000     24K rw--- App6
00000000004c3000     24K rw---   [ anon ]
0000000000ec2000    140K rw---   [ anon ]
00007f91e45e4000      4K -----   [ anon ]
00007f91e45e5000   8192K rw---   [ anon ]
00007f91e4de5000      4K -----   [ anon ]
00007f91e4de6000   8192K rw---   [ anon ]
00007f91e55e6000      4K -----   [ anon ]
00007f91e55e7000   8192K rw---   [ anon ]
00007f91e5de7000      4K -----   [ anon ]
00007f91e5de8000   8192K rw---   [ anon ]
00007f91e65e8000      4K -----   [ anon ]
00007f91e65e9000   8192K rw---   [ anon ]
00007ffcec95d000    132K rw---   [ stack ]
00007ffcec9a9000     16K r----   [ anon ]
00007ffcec9ad000      4K r-x--   [ anon ]
 total            42072K
```

6. Check that manually based on the stack pointer value and section boundary addresses:

```
(gdb) x $rsp
0x7f91e65e8ef0: Cannot access memory at address 0x7f91e65e8ef0

(gdb) frame 1
#1  0x0000000000401c05 in procF ()

(gdb) x $rsp
0x7f91e65e9110: 0x00000000

(gdb) frame 2
#2  0x0000000000401c05 in procF ()

(gdb) x $rsp
0x7f91e65e9330: 0x00000000

(gdb) maintenance info sections
```

```
Exec file:
    `/home/coredump/ALCDA2/x64/App6/App6', file type elf64-x86-64.
 [0]      0x00400200->0x00400220 at 0x00000200: .note.ABI-tag ALLOC LOAD READONLY DATA HAS_CONTENTS
 [1]      0x00400220->0x00400244 at 0x00000220: .note.gnu.build-id ALLOC LOAD READONLY DATA HAS_CONTENTS
 [2]      0x00400248->0x004004d0 at 0x00000248: .rela.plt ALLOC LOAD READONLY DATA HAS_CONTENTS
 [3]      0x00401000->0x00401017 at 0x00001000: .init ALLOC LOAD READONLY CODE HAS_CONTENTS
 [4]      0x00401018->0x004010f0 at 0x00001018: .plt ALLOC LOAD READONLY CODE HAS_CONTENTS
 [5]      0x004010f0->0x00493470 at 0x000010f0: .text ALLOC LOAD READONLY CODE HAS_CONTENTS
 [6]      0x00493470->0x00494017 at 0x00093470: __libc_freeres_fn ALLOC LOAD READONLY CODE HAS_CONTENTS
 [7]      0x00494018->0x00494021 at 0x00094018: .fini ALLOC LOAD READONLY CODE HAS_CONTENTS
 [8]      0x00495000->0x004af73c at 0x00095000: .rodata ALLOC LOAD READONLY DATA HAS_CONTENTS
 [9]      0x004af740->0x004bbb90 at 0x000af740: .eh_frame ALLOC LOAD READONLY DATA HAS_CONTENTS
 [10]      0x004bbb90->0x004bbc3c at 0x000bbb90: .gcc_except_table ALLOC LOAD READONLY DATA HAS_CONTENTS
 [11]      0x004bd0b0->0x004bd0d8 at 0x000bc0b0: .tdata ALLOC LOAD DATA HAS_CONTENTS
```

```
 [12]     0x004bd0d8->0x004bd120 at 0x000bc0d8: .tbss ALLOC
 [13]     0x004bd0d8->0x004bd0e0 at 0x000bc0d8: .preinit_array ALLOC LOAD DATA HAS_CONTENTS
 [14]     0x004bd0e0->0x004bd0f0 at 0x000bc0e0: .init_array ALLOC LOAD DATA HAS_CONTENTS
 [15]     0x004bd0f0->0x004bd100 at 0x000bc0f0: .fini_array ALLOC LOAD DATA HAS_CONTENTS
 [16]     0x004bd100->0x004bfef4 at 0x000bc100: .data.rel.ro ALLOC LOAD DATA HAS_CONTENTS
 [17]     0x004bfef8->0x004c0000 at 0x000beef8: .got ALLOC LOAD DATA HAS_CONTENTS
 [18]     0x004c0000->0x004c00f0 at 0x000bf000: .got.plt ALLOC LOAD DATA HAS_CONTENTS
 [19]     0x004c0100->0x004c1c30 at 0x000bf100: .data ALLOC LOAD DATA HAS_CONTENTS
 [20]     0x004c1c30->0x004c1c90 at 0x000c0c30: __libc_subfreeres ALLOC LOAD DATA HAS_CONTENTS
 [21]     0x004c1ca0->0x004c2408 at 0x000c0ca0: __libc_IO_vtables ALLOC LOAD DATA HAS_CONTENTS
 [22]     0x004c2408->0x004c2410 at 0x000c1408: __libc_atexit ALLOC LOAD DATA HAS_CONTENTS
 [23]     0x004c2420->0x004c8528 at 0x000c1410: .bss ALLOC
 [24]     0x004c8528->0x004c8558 at 0x000c1410: __libc_freeres_ptrs ALLOC
 [25]     0x00000000->0x00000038 at 0x000c1410: .comment READONLY HAS_CONTENTS
 [26]     0x00000000->0x00000420 at 0x000c1450: .debug_aranges READONLY HAS_CONTENTS
 [27]     0x00000000->0x000372ad at 0x000c1870: .debug_info READONLY HAS_CONTENTS
 [28]     0x00000000->0x000057e8 at 0x000f8b1d: .debug_abbrev READONLY HAS_CONTENTS
 [29]     0x00000000->0x0000aa2b at 0x000fe305: .debug_line READONLY HAS_CONTENTS
 [30]     0x00000000->0x00004d08 at 0x00108d30: .debug_str READONLY HAS_CONTENTS
 [31]     0x00000000->0x0000d4b8 at 0x0010da38: .debug_loc READONLY HAS_CONTENTS
 [32]     0x00000000->0x000024c0 at 0x0011aef0: .debug_ranges READONLY HAS_CONTENTS
Core file:
     `/home/coredump/ALCDA2/x64/App6/core.App6', file type elf64-x86-64.
 [0]     0x00000000->0x00002c60 at 0x000004a0: note0 READONLY HAS_CONTENTS
 [1]     0x00000000->0x000000d8 at 0x00000524: .reg/4704 HAS_CONTENTS
 [2]     0x00000000->0x000000d8 at 0x00000524: .reg HAS_CONTENTS
 [3]     0x00000000->0x00000080 at 0x000006b4: .note.linuxcore.siginfo/4704 HAS_CONTENTS
 [4]     0x00000000->0x00000080 at 0x000006b4: .note.linuxcore.siginfo HAS_CONTENTS
 [5]     0x00000000->0x00000140 at 0x00000748: .auxv HAS_CONTENTS
 [6]     0x00000000->0x00000100 at 0x0000089c: .note.linuxcore.file/4704 HAS_CONTENTS
 [7]     0x00000000->0x00000100 at 0x0000089c: .note.linuxcore.file HAS_CONTENTS
 [8]     0x00000000->0x00000200 at 0x000009b0: .reg2/4704 HAS_CONTENTS
 [9]     0x00000000->0x00000200 at 0x000009b0: .reg2 HAS_CONTENTS
 [10]     0x00000000->0x00000340 at 0x00000bc4: .reg-xstate/4704 HAS_CONTENTS
 [11]     0x00000000->0x00000340 at 0x00000bc4: .reg-xstate HAS_CONTENTS
 [12]     0x00000000->0x000000d8 at 0x00000f88: .reg/4707 HAS_CONTENTS
 [13]     0x00000000->0x00000200 at 0x0000107c: .reg2/4707 HAS_CONTENTS
 [14]     0x00000000->0x00000340 at 0x00001290: .reg-xstate/4707 HAS_CONTENTS
 [15]     0x00000000->0x000000d8 at 0x00001654: .reg/4705 HAS_CONTENTS
 [16]     0x00000000->0x00000200 at 0x00001748: .reg2/4705 HAS_CONTENTS
 [17]     0x00000000->0x00000340 at 0x0000195c: .reg-xstate/4705 HAS_CONTENTS
 [18]     0x00000000->0x000000d8 at 0x00001d20: .reg/4703 HAS_CONTENTS
 [19]     0x00000000->0x00000200 at 0x00001e14: .reg2/4703 HAS_CONTENTS
--Type <RET> for more, q to quit, c to continue without paging--
 [20]     0x00000000->0x00000340 at 0x00002028: .reg-xstate/4703 HAS_CONTENTS
 [21]     0x00000000->0x000000d8 at 0x000023ec: .reg/4706 HAS_CONTENTS
 [22]     0x00000000->0x00000200 at 0x000024e0: .reg2/4706 HAS_CONTENTS
 [23]     0x00000000->0x00000340 at 0x000026f4: .reg-xstate/4706 HAS_CONTENTS
 [24]     0x00000000->0x000000d8 at 0x00002ab8: .reg/4708 HAS_CONTENTS
 [25]     0x00000000->0x00000200 at 0x00002bac: .reg2/4708 HAS_CONTENTS
 [26]     0x00000000->0x00000340 at 0x00002dc0: .reg-xstate/4708 HAS_CONTENTS
 [27]     0x00400000->0x00401000 at 0x00004000: load1 ALLOC LOAD READONLY HAS_CONTENTS
 [28]     0x00401000->0x00401000 at 0x00005000: load2 ALLOC READONLY CODE
 [29]     0x00495000->0x00495000 at 0x00005000: load3 ALLOC READONLY
 [30]     0x004bd000->0x004c3000 at 0x00005000: load4 ALLOC LOAD HAS_CONTENTS
 [31]     0x004c3000->0x004c9000 at 0x0000b000: load5 ALLOC LOAD HAS_CONTENTS
 [32]     0x00ec2000->0x00ee5000 at 0x00011000: load6 ALLOC LOAD HAS_CONTENTS
 [33]     0x7f91e45e4000->0x7f91e45e4000 at 0x00034000: load7 ALLOC READONLY
 [34]     0x7f91e45e5000->0x7f91e4de5000 at 0x00034000: load8 ALLOC LOAD HAS_CONTENTS
 [35]     0x7f91e4de5000->0x7f91e4de5000 at 0x00834000: load9 ALLOC READONLY
 [36]     0x7f91e4de6000->0x7f91e55e6000 at 0x00834000: load10 ALLOC LOAD HAS_CONTENTS
 [37]     0x7f91e55e6000->0x7f91e55e6000 at 0x01034000: load11 ALLOC READONLY
 [38]     0x7f91e55e7000->0x7f91e5de7000 at 0x01034000: load12 ALLOC LOAD HAS_CONTENTS
 [39]     0x7f91e5de7000->0x7f91e5de7000 at 0x01834000: load13 ALLOC READONLY
 [40]     0x7f91e5de8000->0x7f91e65e8000 at 0x01834000: load14 ALLOC LOAD HAS_CONTENTS
 [41]     0x7f91e65e8000->0x7f91e65e8000 at 0x02034000: load15 ALLOC READONLY
 [42]     0x7f91e65e9000->0x7f91e6de9000 at 0x02034000: load16 ALLOC LOAD HAS_CONTENTS
```

```
[43]      0x7ffcec95d000->0x7ffcec97e000 at 0x02834000: load17 ALLOC LOAD HAS_CONTENTS
[44]      0x7ffcec9a9000->0x7ffcec9ad000 at 0x02855000: load18 ALLOC LOAD READONLY HAS_CONTENTS
[45]      0x7ffcec9ad000->0x7ffcec9ae000 at 0x02859000: load19 ALLOC LOAD READONLY CODE HAS_CONTENTS
```

7. Dump the bottom of the raw stack to see execution residue, such as thread startup:

```
(gdb) x/1024a 0x7f91e6de9000-0x2000
0x7f91e6de7000: 0x0     0x0
0x7f91e6de7010: 0x0     0x0
0x7f91e6de7020: 0x0     0x0
0x7f91e6de7030: 0x0     0x0
0x7f91e6de7040: 0x0     0x0
0x7f91e6de7050: 0x0     0x0
0x7f91e6de7060: 0x0     0x0
0x7f91e6de7070: 0x0     0x0
0x7f91e6de7080: 0x0     0x0
0x7f91e6de7090: 0x0     0x0
0x7f91e6de70a0: 0x7f91e6de72c0  0x401c05 <procF+88>
0x7f91e6de70b0: 0x0     0x600000000
0x7f91e6de70c0: 0xffffffff      0x7
0x7f91e6de70d0: 0xffffffff      0x0
0x7f91e6de70e0: 0x0     0x0
0x7f91e6de70f0: 0x0     0x0
0x7f91e6de7100: 0x0     0x0
0x7f91e6de7110: 0x0     0x0
0x7f91e6de7120: 0x0     0x0
0x7f91e6de7130: 0x0     0x0
0x7f91e6de7140: 0x0     0x0
0x7f91e6de7150: 0x0     0x0
0x7f91e6de7160: 0x0     0x0
0x7f91e6de7170: 0x0     0x0
0x7f91e6de7180: 0x0     0x0
0x7f91e6de7190: 0x0     0x0
0x7f91e6de71a0: 0x0     0x0
0x7f91e6de71b0: 0x0     0x0
0x7f91e6de71c0: 0x0     0x0
0x7f91e6de71d0: 0x0     0x0
0x7f91e6de71e0: 0x0     0x0
0x7f91e6de71f0: 0x0     0x0
0x7f91e6de7200: 0x0     0x0
0x7f91e6de7210: 0x0     0x0
0x7f91e6de7220: 0x0     0x0
0x7f91e6de7230: 0x0     0x0
0x7f91e6de7240: 0x0     0x0
0x7f91e6de7250: 0x0     0x0
0x7f91e6de7260: 0x0     0x0
0x7f91e6de7270: 0x0     0x0
0x7f91e6de7280: 0x0     0x0
0x7f91e6de7290: 0x0     0x0
0x7f91e6de72a0: 0x0     0x0
0x7f91e6de72b0: 0x0     0x0
0x7f91e6de72c0: 0x7f91e6de74e0  0x401c05 <procF+88>
0x7f91e6de72d0: 0x0     0x500000000
0x7f91e6de72e0: 0xffffffff      0x6
0x7f91e6de72f0: 0xffffffff      0x0
0x7f91e6de7300: 0x0     0x0
0x7f91e6de7310: 0x0     0x0
0x7f91e6de7320: 0x0     0x0
0x7f91e6de7330: 0x0     0x0
0x7f91e6de7340: 0x0     0x0
```

```
0x7f91e6de7350: 0x0     0x0
0x7f91e6de7360: 0x0     0x0
0x7f91e6de7370: 0x0     0x0
0x7f91e6de7380: 0x0     0x0
--Type <RET> for more, q to quit, c to continue without paging--
0x7f91e6de7390: 0x0     0x0
0x7f91e6de73a0: 0x0     0x0
0x7f91e6de73b0: 0x0     0x0
0x7f91e6de73c0: 0x0     0x0
0x7f91e6de73d0: 0x0     0x0
0x7f91e6de73e0: 0x0     0x0
0x7f91e6de73f0: 0x0     0x0
0x7f91e6de7400: 0x0     0x0
0x7f91e6de7410: 0x0     0x0
0x7f91e6de7420: 0x0     0x0
0x7f91e6de7430: 0x0     0x0
0x7f91e6de7440: 0x0     0x0
0x7f91e6de7450: 0x0     0x0
0x7f91e6de7460: 0x0     0x0
0x7f91e6de7470: 0x0     0x0
0x7f91e6de7480: 0x0     0x0
0x7f91e6de7490: 0x0     0x0
0x7f91e6de74a0: 0x0     0x0
0x7f91e6de74b0: 0x0     0x0
0x7f91e6de74c0: 0x0     0x0
0x7f91e6de74d0: 0x0     0x0
0x7f91e6de74e0: 0x7f91e6de7700  0x401c05 <procF+88>
0x7f91e6de74f0: 0x0     0x400000000
0x7f91e6de7500: 0xffffffff      0x5
0x7f91e6de7510: 0xffffffff      0x0
0x7f91e6de7520: 0x0     0x0
0x7f91e6de7530: 0x0     0x0
0x7f91e6de7540: 0x0     0x0
0x7f91e6de7550: 0x0     0x0
0x7f91e6de7560: 0x0     0x0
0x7f91e6de7570: 0x0     0x0
0x7f91e6de7580: 0x0     0x0
0x7f91e6de7590: 0x0     0x0
0x7f91e6de75a0: 0x0     0x0
0x7f91e6de75b0: 0x0     0x0
0x7f91e6de75c0: 0x0     0x0
0x7f91e6de75d0: 0x0     0x0
0x7f91e6de75e0: 0x0     0x0
0x7f91e6de75f0: 0x0     0x0
0x7f91e6de7600: 0x0     0x0
0x7f91e6de7610: 0x0     0x0
0x7f91e6de7620: 0x0     0x0
0x7f91e6de7630: 0x0     0x0
0x7f91e6de7640: 0x0     0x0
0x7f91e6de7650: 0x0     0x0
0x7f91e6de7660: 0x0     0x0
0x7f91e6de7670: 0x0     0x0
0x7f91e6de7680: 0x0     0x0
0x7f91e6de7690: 0x0     0x0
0x7f91e6de76a0: 0x0     0x0
0x7f91e6de76b0: 0x0     0x0
0x7f91e6de76c0: 0x0     0x0
0x7f91e6de76d0: 0x0     0x0
0x7f91e6de76e0: 0x0     0x0
0x7f91e6de76f0: 0x0     0x0
```

```
0x7f91e6de7700: 0x7f91e6de7920  0x401c05 <procF+88>
0x7f91e6de7710: 0x0     0x300000000
--Type <RET> for more, q to quit, c to continue without paging--
0x7f91e6de7720: 0xffffffff      0x4
0x7f91e6de7730: 0xffffffff      0x0
0x7f91e6de7740: 0x0     0x0
0x7f91e6de7750: 0x0     0x0
0x7f91e6de7760: 0x0     0x0
0x7f91e6de7770: 0x0     0x0
0x7f91e6de7780: 0x0     0x0
0x7f91e6de7790: 0x0     0x0
0x7f91e6de77a0: 0x0     0x0
0x7f91e6de77b0: 0x0     0x0
0x7f91e6de77c0: 0x0     0x0
0x7f91e6de77d0: 0x0     0x0
0x7f91e6de77e0: 0x0     0x0
0x7f91e6de77f0: 0x0     0x0
0x7f91e6de7800: 0x0     0x0
0x7f91e6de7810: 0x0     0x0
0x7f91e6de7820: 0x0     0x0
0x7f91e6de7830: 0x0     0x0
0x7f91e6de7840: 0x0     0x0
0x7f91e6de7850: 0x0     0x0
0x7f91e6de7860: 0x0     0x0
0x7f91e6de7870: 0x0     0x0
0x7f91e6de7880: 0x0     0x0
0x7f91e6de7890: 0x0     0x0
0x7f91e6de78a0: 0x0     0x0
0x7f91e6de78b0: 0x0     0x0
0x7f91e6de78c0: 0x0     0x0
0x7f91e6de78d0: 0x0     0x0
0x7f91e6de78e0: 0x0     0x0
0x7f91e6de78f0: 0x0     0x0
0x7f91e6de7900: 0x0     0x0
0x7f91e6de7910: 0x0     0x0
0x7f91e6de7920: 0x7f91e6de7b40  0x401c05 <procF+88>
0x7f91e6de7930: 0x0     0x200000000
0x7f91e6de7940: 0xffffffff      0x3
0x7f91e6de7950: 0xffffffff      0x0
0x7f91e6de7960: 0x0     0x0
0x7f91e6de7970: 0x0     0x0
0x7f91e6de7980: 0x0     0x0
0x7f91e6de7990: 0x0     0x0
0x7f91e6de79a0: 0x0     0x0
0x7f91e6de79b0: 0x0     0x0
0x7f91e6de79c0: 0x0     0x0
0x7f91e6de79d0: 0x0     0x0
0x7f91e6de79e0: 0x0     0x0
0x7f91e6de79f0: 0x0     0x0
0x7f91e6de7a00: 0x0     0x0
0x7f91e6de7a10: 0x0     0x0
0x7f91e6de7a20: 0x0     0x0
0x7f91e6de7a30: 0x0     0x0
0x7f91e6de7a40: 0x0     0x0
0x7f91e6de7a50: 0x0     0x0
0x7f91e6de7a60: 0x0     0x0
0x7f91e6de7a70: 0x0     0x0
0x7f91e6de7a80: 0x0     0x0
0x7f91e6de7a90: 0x0     0x0
0x7f91e6de7aa0: 0x0     0x0
```

```
--Type <RET> for more, q to quit, c to continue without paging--
0x7f91e6de7ab0: 0x0     0x0
0x7f91e6de7ac0: 0x0     0x0
0x7f91e6de7ad0: 0x0     0x0
0x7f91e6de7ae0: 0x0     0x0
0x7f91e6de7af0: 0x0     0x0
0x7f91e6de7b00: 0x0     0x0
0x7f91e6de7b10: 0x0     0x0
0x7f91e6de7b20: 0x0     0x0
0x7f91e6de7b30: 0x0     0x0
0x7f91e6de7b40: 0x7f91e6de7d60  0x401c05 <procF+88>
0x7f91e6de7b50: 0x0     0x100000000
0x7f91e6de7b60: 0xffffffff      0x2
0x7f91e6de7b70: 0xffffffff      0x0
0x7f91e6de7b80: 0x0     0x0
0x7f91e6de7b90: 0x0     0x0
0x7f91e6de7ba0: 0x0     0x0
0x7f91e6de7bb0: 0x0     0x0
0x7f91e6de7bc0: 0x0     0x0
0x7f91e6de7bd0: 0x0     0x0
0x7f91e6de7be0: 0x0     0x0
0x7f91e6de7bf0: 0x0     0x0
0x7f91e6de7c00: 0x0     0x0
0x7f91e6de7c10: 0x0     0x0
0x7f91e6de7c20: 0x0     0x0
0x7f91e6de7c30: 0x0     0x0
0x7f91e6de7c40: 0x0     0x0
0x7f91e6de7c50: 0x0     0x0
0x7f91e6de7c60: 0x0     0x0
0x7f91e6de7c70: 0x0     0x0
0x7f91e6de7c80: 0x0     0x0
0x7f91e6de7c90: 0x0     0x0
0x7f91e6de7ca0: 0x0     0x0
0x7f91e6de7cb0: 0x0     0x0
0x7f91e6de7cc0: 0x0     0x0
0x7f91e6de7cd0: 0x0     0x0
0x7f91e6de7ce0: 0x0     0x0
0x7f91e6de7cf0: 0x0     0x0
0x7f91e6de7d00: 0x0     0x0
0x7f91e6de7d10: 0x0     0x0
0x7f91e6de7d20: 0x0     0x0
0x7f91e6de7d30: 0x0     0x0
0x7f91e6de7d40: 0x0     0x0
0x7f91e6de7d50: 0x0     0x0
0x7f91e6de7d60: 0x7f91e6de7d70  0x401c16 <procE+14>
0x7f91e6de7d70: 0x7f91e6de7d80  0x401c31 <bar_one+24>
0x7f91e6de7d80: 0x7f91e6de7d90  0x401c42 <foo_one+14>
0x7f91e6de7d90: 0x7f91e6de7db0  0x401c5b <thread_one+22>
0x7f91e6de7da0: 0x0     0x0
0x7f91e6de7db0: 0x0     0x403173 <start_thread+243>
0x7f91e6de7dc0: 0x0     0x7f91e6de8700
0x7f91e6de7dd0: 0x7f91e6de8700  0x83fb3fb8616de639
0x7f91e6de7de0: 0x7ffcec97d22e  0x7ffcec97d22f
0x7f91e6de7df0: 0x7f91e6de8700  0x0
0x7f91e6de7e00: 0x7cd8f2049aede639      0x83fb3f38035fe639
0x7f91e6de7e10: 0x0     0x0
0x7f91e6de7e20: 0x0     0x0
0x7f91e6de7e30: 0x0     0x0
--Type <RET> for more, q to quit, c to continue without paging--
0x7f91e6de7e40: 0x0     0x0
```

```
0x7f91e6de7e50: 0x0     0x40061a1f48adcb00
0x7f91e6de7e60: 0x0     0x7f91e6de8700
0x7f91e6de7e70: 0x7f91e6de8700  0x44430f <clone+63>
0x7f91e6de7e80: 0x0     0x0
0x7f91e6de7e90: 0x0     0x0
0x7f91e6de7ea0: 0x0     0x0
0x7f91e6de7eb0: 0x0     0x0
0x7f91e6de7ec0: 0x0     0x0
0x7f91e6de7ed0: 0x0     0x0
0x7f91e6de7ee0: 0x0     0x0
0x7f91e6de7ef0: 0x0     0x0
0x7f91e6de7f00: 0x0     0x0
0x7f91e6de7f10: 0x0     0x0
0x7f91e6de7f20: 0x0     0x0
0x7f91e6de7f30: 0x0     0x0
0x7f91e6de7f40: 0x0     0x0
0x7f91e6de7f50: 0x0     0x0
0x7f91e6de7f60: 0x0     0x0
0x7f91e6de7f70: 0x0     0x0
0x7f91e6de7f80: 0x0     0x0
0x7f91e6de7f90: 0x0     0x0
0x7f91e6de7fa0: 0x0     0x0
0x7f91e6de7fb0: 0x0     0x0
0x7f91e6de7fc0: 0x0     0x0
0x7f91e6de7fd0: 0x0     0x0
0x7f91e6de7fe0: 0x0     0x0
0x7f91e6de7ff0: 0x0     0x0
0x7f91e6de8000: 0x0     0x0
0x7f91e6de8010: 0x0     0x0
0x7f91e6de8020: 0x0     0x0
0x7f91e6de8030: 0x0     0x0
0x7f91e6de8040: 0x0     0x0
0x7f91e6de8050: 0x0     0x0
0x7f91e6de8060: 0x0     0x0
0x7f91e6de8070: 0x0     0x0
0x7f91e6de8080: 0x0     0x0
0x7f91e6de8090: 0x0     0x0
0x7f91e6de80a0: 0x0     0x0
0x7f91e6de80b0: 0x0     0x0
0x7f91e6de80c0: 0x0     0x0
0x7f91e6de80d0: 0x0     0x0
0x7f91e6de80e0: 0x0     0x0
0x7f91e6de80f0: 0x0     0x0
0x7f91e6de8100: 0x0     0x0
0x7f91e6de8110: 0x0     0x0
0x7f91e6de8120: 0x0     0x0
0x7f91e6de8130: 0x0     0x0
0x7f91e6de8140: 0x0     0x0
0x7f91e6de8150: 0x0     0x0
0x7f91e6de8160: 0x0     0x0
0x7f91e6de8170: 0x0     0x0
0x7f91e6de8180: 0x0     0x0
0x7f91e6de8190: 0x0     0x0
0x7f91e6de81a0: 0x0     0x0
0x7f91e6de81b0: 0x0     0x0
0x7f91e6de81c0: 0x0     0x0
--Type <RET> for more, q to quit, c to continue without paging--
0x7f91e6de81d0: 0x0     0x0
0x7f91e6de81e0: 0x0     0x0
0x7f91e6de81f0: 0x0     0x0
```

```
0x7f91e6de8200: 0x0     0x0
0x7f91e6de8210: 0x0     0x0
0x7f91e6de8220: 0x0     0x0
0x7f91e6de8230: 0x0     0x0
0x7f91e6de8240: 0x0     0x0
0x7f91e6de8250: 0x0     0x0
0x7f91e6de8260: 0x0     0x0
0x7f91e6de8270: 0x0     0x0
0x7f91e6de8280: 0x0     0x0
0x7f91e6de8290: 0x0     0x0
0x7f91e6de82a0: 0x0     0x0
0x7f91e6de82b0: 0x0     0x0
0x7f91e6de82c0: 0x0     0x0
0x7f91e6de82d0: 0x0     0x0
0x7f91e6de82e0: 0x0     0x0
0x7f91e6de82f0: 0x0     0x0
0x7f91e6de8300: 0x0     0x0
0x7f91e6de8310: 0x0     0x0
0x7f91e6de8320: 0x0     0x0
0x7f91e6de8330: 0x0     0x0
0x7f91e6de8340: 0x0     0x0
0x7f91e6de8350: 0x0     0x0
0x7f91e6de8360: 0x0     0x0
0x7f91e6de8370: 0x0     0x0
0x7f91e6de8380: 0x0     0x0
0x7f91e6de8390: 0x0     0x0
0x7f91e6de83a0: 0x0     0x0
0x7f91e6de83b0: 0x0     0x0
0x7f91e6de83c0: 0x0     0x0
0x7f91e6de83d0: 0x0     0x0
0x7f91e6de83e0: 0x0     0x0
0x7f91e6de83f0: 0x0     0x0
0x7f91e6de8400: 0x0     0x0
0x7f91e6de8410: 0x0     0x0
0x7f91e6de8420: 0x0     0x0
0x7f91e6de8430: 0x0     0x0
0x7f91e6de8440: 0x0     0x0
0x7f91e6de8450: 0x0     0x0
0x7f91e6de8460: 0x0     0x0
0x7f91e6de8470: 0x0     0x0
0x7f91e6de8480: 0x0     0x0
0x7f91e6de8490: 0x0     0x0
0x7f91e6de84a0: 0x0     0x0
0x7f91e6de84b0: 0x0     0x0
0x7f91e6de84c0: 0x0     0x0
0x7f91e6de84d0: 0x0     0x0
0x7f91e6de84e0: 0x0     0x0
0x7f91e6de84f0: 0x0     0x0
0x7f91e6de8500: 0x0     0x0
0x7f91e6de8510: 0x0     0x0
0x7f91e6de8520: 0x0     0x0
0x7f91e6de8530: 0x0     0x0
0x7f91e6de8540: 0x0     0x0
0x7f91e6de8550: 0x0     0x0
--Type <RET> for more, q to quit, c to continue without paging--
0x7f91e6de8560: 0x0     0x0
0x7f91e6de8570: 0x0     0x0
0x7f91e6de8580: 0x0     0x0
0x7f91e6de8590: 0x0     0x0
0x7f91e6de85a0: 0x0     0x0
```

```
0x7f91e6de85b0: 0x0     0x0
0x7f91e6de85c0: 0x0     0x0
0x7f91e6de85d0: 0x0     0x0
0x7f91e6de85e0: 0x0     0x0
0x7f91e6de85f0: 0x0     0x0
0x7f91e6de8600: 0x0     0x0
0x7f91e6de8610: 0x0     0x0
0x7f91e6de8620: 0x0     0x0
0x7f91e6de8630: 0x0     0x0
0x7f91e6de8640: 0x0     0x0
0x7f91e6de8650: 0x0     0x0
0x7f91e6de8660: 0x0     0x0
0x7f91e6de8670: 0x0     0x0
0x7f91e6de8680: 0x0     0x0
0x7f91e6de8690: 0x7f91e6de8db8  0x4c1aa0 <_nl_global_locale>
0x7f91e6de86a0: 0x4c1aa0 <_nl_global_locale>    0x4c1ac0 <_nl_global_locale+32>
0x7f91e6de86b0: 0x4c1aa8 <_nl_global_locale+8>  0x0
0x7f91e6de86c0: 0x49bd00 <_nl_C_LC_CTYPE_tolower+512>   0x49c300 <_nl_C_LC_CTYPE_toupper+512>
0x7f91e6de86d0: 0x49cc00 <_nl_C_LC_CTYPE_class+256>     0x0
0x7f91e6de86e0: 0x0     0x0
0x7f91e6de86f0: 0x0     0x0
0x7f91e6de8700: 0x7f91e6de8700  0xec3b50
0x7f91e6de8710: 0x7f91e6de8700  0x1
0x7f91e6de8720: 0x0     0x40061a1f48adcb00
0x7f91e6de8730: 0xf31cc1fd9fdc30b6      0x0
0x7f91e6de8740: 0x0     0x0
0x7f91e6de8750: 0x0     0x0
0x7f91e6de8760: 0x0     0x0
0x7f91e6de8770: 0x0     0x0
0x7f91e6de8780: 0x0     0x0
0x7f91e6de8790: 0x0     0x0
0x7f91e6de87a0: 0x0     0x0
0x7f91e6de87b0: 0x0     0x0
0x7f91e6de87c0: 0x0     0x0
0x7f91e6de87d0: 0x0     0x0
0x7f91e6de87e0: 0x0     0x0
0x7f91e6de87f0: 0x0     0x0
0x7f91e6de8800: 0x0     0x0
0x7f91e6de8810: 0x0     0x0
0x7f91e6de8820: 0x0     0x0
0x7f91e6de8830: 0x0     0x0
0x7f91e6de8840: 0x0     0x0
0x7f91e6de8850: 0x0     0x0
0x7f91e6de8860: 0x0     0x0
0x7f91e6de8870: 0x0     0x0
0x7f91e6de8880: 0x0     0x0
0x7f91e6de8890: 0x0     0x0
0x7f91e6de88a0: 0x0     0x0
0x7f91e6de88b0: 0x0     0x0
0x7f91e6de88c0: 0x0     0x0
0x7f91e6de88d0: 0x0     0x0
0x7f91e6de88e0: 0x0     0x0
--Type <RET> for more, q to quit, c to continue without paging--
0x7f91e6de88f0: 0x0     0x0
0x7f91e6de8900: 0x0     0x0
0x7f91e6de8910: 0x0     0x0
0x7f91e6de8920: 0x0     0x0
0x7f91e6de8930: 0x0     0x0
0x7f91e6de8940: 0x0     0x0
0x7f91e6de8950: 0x0     0x0
```

```
0x7f91e6de8960: 0x0     0x0
0x7f91e6de8970: 0x0     0x0
0x7f91e6de8980: 0x0     0x0
0x7f91e6de8990: 0x0     0x0
0x7f91e6de89a0: 0x0     0x0
0x7f91e6de89b0: 0x0     0x0
0x7f91e6de89c0: 0x4c0120 <stack_used>   0x7f91e65e79c0
0x7f91e6de89d0: 0x1260  0x7f91e6de89e0
0x7f91e6de89e0: 0x7f91e6de89e0  0xffffffffffffffe0
0x7f91e6de89f0: 0x0     0x0
0x7f91e6de8a00: 0x7f91e6de7dd0  0x0
0x7f91e6de8a10: 0x0     0x0
0x7f91e6de8a20: 0x0     0x0
0x7f91e6de8a30: 0x0     0x0
0x7f91e6de8a40: 0x0     0x0
0x7f91e6de8a50: 0x0     0x0
0x7f91e6de8a60: 0x0     0x0
0x7f91e6de8a70: 0x0     0x0
0x7f91e6de8a80: 0x0     0x0
0x7f91e6de8a90: 0x0     0x0
0x7f91e6de8aa0: 0x0     0x0
0x7f91e6de8ab0: 0x0     0x0
0x7f91e6de8ac0: 0x0     0x0
0x7f91e6de8ad0: 0x0     0x0
0x7f91e6de8ae0: 0x0     0x0
0x7f91e6de8af0: 0x0     0x0
0x7f91e6de8b00: 0x0     0x0
0x7f91e6de8b10: 0x0     0x0
0x7f91e6de8b20: 0x0     0x0
0x7f91e6de8b30: 0x0     0x0
0x7f91e6de8b40: 0x0     0x0
0x7f91e6de8b50: 0x0     0x0
0x7f91e6de8b60: 0x0     0x0
0x7f91e6de8b70: 0x0     0x0
0x7f91e6de8b80: 0x0     0x0
0x7f91e6de8b90: 0x0     0x0
0x7f91e6de8ba0: 0x0     0x0
0x7f91e6de8bb0: 0x0     0x0
0x7f91e6de8bc0: 0x0     0x0
0x7f91e6de8bd0: 0x0     0x0
0x7f91e6de8be0: 0x0     0x0
0x7f91e6de8bf0: 0x0     0x0
0x7f91e6de8c00: 0x0     0x0
0x7f91e6de8c10: 0x7f91e6de8a10  0x0
0x7f91e6de8c20: 0x0     0x0
0x7f91e6de8c30: 0x0     0x0
0x7f91e6de8c40: 0x0     0x0
0x7f91e6de8c50: 0x0     0x0
0x7f91e6de8c60: 0x0     0x0
0x7f91e6de8c70: 0x0     0x0
--Type <RET> for more, q to quit, c to continue without paging--
0x7f91e6de8c80: 0x0     0x0
0x7f91e6de8c90: 0x0     0x0
0x7f91e6de8ca0: 0x0     0x0
0x7f91e6de8cb0: 0x0     0x0
0x7f91e6de8cc0: 0x0     0x0
0x7f91e6de8cd0: 0x0     0x0
0x7f91e6de8ce0: 0x0     0x0
0x7f91e6de8cf0: 0x0     0x0
0x7f91e6de8d00: 0x0     0x0
```

```
0x7f91e6de8d10: 0x0      0x0
0x7f91e6de8d20: 0x16eaf938be3c7 0x0
0x7f91e6de8d30: 0x0      0x0
0x7f91e6de8d40: 0x401c45 <thread_one>    0x0
0x7f91e6de8d50: 0x0      0x0
0x7f91e6de8d60: 0x0      0x0
0x7f91e6de8d70: 0x0      0x0
0x7f91e6de8d80: 0x0      0x0
0x7f91e6de8d90: 0x7f91e65e8000  0x801000
0x7f91e6de8da0: 0x1000   0x1000
0x7f91e6de8db0: 0x0      0x0
0x7f91e6de8dc0: 0x0      0x0
0x7f91e6de8dd0: 0x0      0x0
0x7f91e6de8de0: 0x0      0x0
0x7f91e6de8df0: 0x0      0x0
0x7f91e6de8e00: 0x0      0x0
0x7f91e6de8e10: 0x0      0x0
0x7f91e6de8e20: 0x0      0x0
0x7f91e6de8e30: 0x0      0x0
0x7f91e6de8e40: 0x0      0x0
0x7f91e6de8e50: 0x0      0x0
0x7f91e6de8e60: 0x0      0x0
0x7f91e6de8e70: 0x0      0x0
0x7f91e6de8e80: 0x0      0x0
0x7f91e6de8e90: 0x0      0x0
0x7f91e6de8ea0: 0x0      0x0
0x7f91e6de8eb0: 0x0      0x0
0x7f91e6de8ec0: 0x0      0x0
0x7f91e6de8ed0: 0x0      0x0
0x7f91e6de8ee0: 0x0      0x0
0x7f91e6de8ef0: 0x0      0x0
0x7f91e6de8f00: 0x0      0x0
0x7f91e6de8f10: 0x0      0x0
0x7f91e6de8f20: 0x0      0x0
0x7f91e6de8f30: 0x0      0x0
0x7f91e6de8f40: 0x0      0x0
0x7f91e6de8f50: 0x0      0x0
0x7f91e6de8f60: 0x0      0x0
0x7f91e6de8f70: 0x0      0x0
0x7f91e6de8f80: 0x0      0x0
0x7f91e6de8f90: 0x0      0x0
0x7f91e6de8fa0: 0x0      0x0
0x7f91e6de8fb0: 0x0      0x0
0x7f91e6de8fc0: 0x0      0x0
0x7f91e6de8fd0: 0x0      0x0
0x7f91e6de8fe0: 0x0      0x0
0x7f91e6de8ff0: 0x0      0x0
```

8. See that the reconstruction of the stack trace is possible because of the standard function prologue and epilogue:

```
[...]
0x7f91e6de70a0: 0x7f91e6de72c0  0x401c05 <procF+88>
0x7f91e6de72c0: 0x7f91e6de74e0  0x401c05 <procF+88>
0x7f91e6de74e0: 0x7f91e6de7700  0x401c05 <procF+88>
0x7f91e6de7700: 0x7f91e6de7920  0x401c05 <procF+88>
0x7f91e6de7920: 0x7f91e6de7b40  0x401c05 <procF+88>
0x7f91e6de7b40: 0x7f91e6de7d60  0x401c05 <procF+88>
0x7f91e6de7d60: 0x7f91e6de7d70  0x401c16 <procE+14>
0x7f91e6de7d70: 0x7f91e6de7d80  0x401c31 <bar_one+24>
```

```
0x7f91e6de7d80: 0x7f91e6de7d90  0x401c42 <foo_one+14>
0x7f91e6de7d90: 0x7f91e6de7db0  0x401c5b <thread_one+22>
0x7f91e6de7db0: 0x0     0x403173 <start_thread+243>
```

```
(gdb) disass procF
Dump of assembler code for function procF:
   0x0000000000401bad <+0>:     push   %rbp
   0x0000000000401bae <+1>:     mov    %rsp,%rbp
   0x0000000000401bb1 <+4>:     sub    $0x210,%rsp
   0x0000000000401bb8 <+11>:    mov    %edi,-0x204(%rbp)
   0x0000000000401bbe <+17>:    lea    -0x200(%rbp),%rdx
   0x0000000000401bc5 <+24>:    mov    $0x0,%eax
   0x0000000000401bca <+29>:    mov    $0x40,%ecx
   0x0000000000401bcf <+34>:    mov    %rdx,%rdi
   0x0000000000401bd2 <+37>:    rep stos %rax,%es:(%rdi)
   0x0000000000401bd5 <+40>:    movl   $0xffffffff,-0x200(%rbp)
   0x0000000000401bdf <+50>:    mov    -0x204(%rbp),%eax
   0x0000000000401be5 <+56>:    add    $0x1,%eax
   0x0000000000401be8 <+59>:    mov    %eax,-0x1f8(%rbp)
   0x0000000000401bee <+65>:    movl   $0xffffffff,-0x1f0(%rbp)
   0x0000000000401bf8 <+75>:    mov    -0x1f8(%rbp),%eax
   0x0000000000401bfe <+81>:    mov    %eax,%edi
   0x0000000000401c00 <+83>:    callq  0x401bad <procF>
=> 0x0000000000401c05 <+88>:    nop
   0x0000000000401c06 <+89>:    leaveq
   0x0000000000401c07 <+90>:    retq
End of assembler dump.
```

Note: The *leaveq* CPU instruction in the epilog reverses the effect of the two prolog instructions, *push* and *mov*.

9. Use the backtrace command variant to get to the bottom of the stack trace:

```
(gdb) bt -20
#15398 0x0000000000401c05 in procF () at pthread_create.c:688
#15399 0x0000000000401c05 in procF () at pthread_create.c:688
#15400 0x0000000000401c05 in procF () at pthread_create.c:688
#15401 0x0000000000401c05 in procF () at pthread_create.c:688
#15402 0x0000000000401c05 in procF () at pthread_create.c:688
#15403 0x0000000000401c05 in procF () at pthread_create.c:688
#15404 0x0000000000401c05 in procF () at pthread_create.c:688
#15405 0x0000000000401c05 in procF () at pthread_create.c:688
#15406 0x0000000000401c05 in procF () at pthread_create.c:688
#15407 0x0000000000401c05 in procF () at pthread_create.c:688
#15408 0x0000000000401c05 in procF () at pthread_create.c:688
#15409 0x0000000000401c05 in procF () at pthread_create.c:688
#15410 0x0000000000401c05 in procF () at pthread_create.c:688
#15411 0x0000000000401c05 in procF () at pthread_create.c:688
#15412 0x0000000000401c16 in procE () at pthread_create.c:688
#15413 0x0000000000401c31 in bar_one () at pthread_create.c:688
#15414 0x0000000000401c42 in foo_one () at pthread_create.c:688
#15415 0x0000000000401c5b in thread_one () at pthread_create.c:688
#15416 0x0000000000403173 in start_thread (arg=<optimized out>) at pthread_create.c:486
#15417 0x000000000044430f in clone ()
```

Exercise A6 (A64, GDB)

Goal: Learn how to identify stack overflow, stack boundaries, reconstruct stack trace.

Patterns: Stack Overflow (User Mode).

1. Load the *core.19393* dump file and *App6* executable from the A64/App6 directory:

```
~/ALCDA2/A64/App6$ gdb-multiarch -c core.19393 -se App6
GNU gdb (Debian 8.2.1-2+b3) 8.2.1
Copyright (C) 2018 Free Software Foundation, Inc.
License GPLv3+: GNU GPL version 3 or later <http://gnu.org/licenses/gpl.html>
This is free software: you are free to change and redistribute it.
There is NO WARRANTY, to the extent permitted by law.
Type "show copying" and "show warranty" for details.
This GDB was configured as "x86_64-linux-gnu".
Type "show configuration" for configuration details.
For bug reporting instructions, please see:
<http://www.gnu.org/software/gdb/bugs/>.
Find the GDB manual and other documentation resources online at:
    <http://www.gnu.org/software/gdb/documentation/>.

For help, type "help".
Type "apropos word" to search for commands related to "word"...
Reading symbols from App6...(no debugging symbols found)...done.
[New LWP 19394]
[New LWP 19393]
[New LWP 19398]
[New LWP 19397]
[New LWP 19396]
[New LWP 19395]
Core was generated by `./App6'.
Program terminated with signal SIGSEGV, Segmentation fault.
#0  0x00000000004031ec in procF ()
[Current thread is 1 (LWP 19394)]
```

2. Set logging to a file in case of lengthy output from some commands:

```
(gdb) set logging on App6.log
Copying output to App6.log.
```

3. List threads:

```
(gdb) info threads
  Id   Target Id         Frame
* 1    LWP 19394         0x00000000004031ec in procF ()
  2    LWP 19393         0x000000000040ca54 in nanosleep ()
  3    LWP 19398         0x000000000040ca54 in nanosleep ()
  4    LWP 19397         0x000000000040ca54 in nanosleep ()
  5    LWP 19396         0x000000000040ca58 in nanosleep ()
  6    LWP 19395         0x000000000040ca54 in nanosleep ()
```

4. If we try to print the problem stack trace, we get an endless number of frames, so we quit:

```
(gdb) bt
#0  0x00000000004031ec in procF ()
#1  0x0000000000403244 in procF ()
#2  0x0000000000403244 in procF ()
#3  0x0000000000403244 in procF ()
#4  0x0000000000403244 in procF ()
#5  0x0000000000403244 in procF ()
#6  0x0000000000403244 in procF ()
#7  0x0000000000403244 in procF ()
#8  0x0000000000403244 in procF ()
#9  0x0000000000403244 in procF ()
#10 0x0000000000403244 in procF ()
#11 0x0000000000403244 in procF ()
#12 0x0000000000403244 in procF ()
#13 0x0000000000403244 in procF ()
#14 0x0000000000403244 in procF ()
#15 0x0000000000403244 in procF ()
#16 0x0000000000403244 in procF ()
#17 0x0000000000403244 in procF ()
#18 0x0000000000403244 in procF ()
#19 0x0000000000403244 in procF ()
#20 0x0000000000403244 in procF ()
#21 0x0000000000403244 in procF ()
#22 0x0000000000403244 in procF ()
#23 0x0000000000403244 in procF ()
#24 0x0000000000403244 in procF ()
#25 0x0000000000403244 in procF ()
#26 0x0000000000403244 in procF ()
#27 0x0000000000403244 in procF ()
#28 0x0000000000403244 in procF ()
#29 0x0000000000403244 in procF ()
#30 0x0000000000403244 in procF ()
#31 0x0000000000403244 in procF ()
#32 0x0000000000403244 in procF ()
#33 0x0000000000403244 in procF ()
#34 0x0000000000403244 in procF ()
#35 0x0000000000403244 in procF ()
#36 0x0000000000403244 in procF ()
#37 0x0000000000403244 in procF ()
#38 0x0000000000403244 in procF ()
#39 0x0000000000403244 in procF ()
#40 0x0000000000403244 in procF ()
#41 0x0000000000403244 in procF ()
#42 0x0000000000403244 in procF ()
#43 0x0000000000403244 in procF ()
#44 0x0000000000403244 in procF ()
#45 0x0000000000403244 in procF ()
#46 0x0000000000403244 in procF ()
#47 0x0000000000403244 in procF ()
#48 0x0000000000403244 in procF ()
--Type <RET> for more, q to quit, c to continue without paging--
#49 0x0000000000403244 in procF ()
#50 0x0000000000403244 in procF ()
#51 0x0000000000403244 in procF ()
#52 0x0000000000403244 in procF ()
#53 0x0000000000403244 in procF ()
#54 0x0000000000403244 in procF ()
#55 0x0000000000403244 in procF ()
```

```
#56 0x0000000000403244 in procF ()
#57 0x0000000000403244 in procF ()
#58 0x0000000000403244 in procF ()
#59 0x0000000000403244 in procF ()
#60 0x0000000000403244 in procF ()
#61 0x0000000000403244 in procF ()
#62 0x0000000000403244 in procF ()
#63 0x0000000000403244 in procF ()
#64 0x0000000000403244 in procF ()
#65 0x0000000000403244 in procF ()
#66 0x0000000000403244 in procF ()
#67 0x0000000000403244 in procF ()
#68 0x0000000000403244 in procF ()
#69 0x0000000000403244 in procF ()
#70 0x0000000000403244 in procF ()
#71 0x0000000000403244 in procF ()
#72 0x0000000000403244 in procF ()
#73 0x0000000000403244 in procF ()
#74 0x0000000000403244 in procF ()
#75 0x0000000000403244 in procF ()
#76 0x0000000000403244 in procF ()
#77 0x0000000000403244 in procF ()
#78 0x0000000000403244 in procF ()
#79 0x0000000000403244 in procF ()
#80 0x0000000000403244 in procF ()
#81 0x0000000000403244 in procF ()
#82 0x0000000000403244 in procF ()
#83 0x0000000000403244 in procF ()
#84 0x0000000000403244 in procF ()
#85 0x0000000000403244 in procF ()
#86 0x0000000000403244 in procF ()
#87 0x0000000000403244 in procF ()
#88 0x0000000000403244 in procF ()
#89 0x0000000000403244 in procF ()
#90 0x0000000000403244 in procF ()
#91 0x0000000000403244 in procF ()
#92 0x0000000000403244 in procF ()
#93 0x0000000000403244 in procF ()
#94 0x0000000000403244 in procF ()
#95 0x0000000000403244 in procF ()
#96 0x0000000000403244 in procF ()
#97 0x0000000000403244 in procF ()
--Type <RET> for more, q to quit, c to continue without paging--
#98 0x0000000000403244 in procF ()
#99 0x0000000000403244 in procF ()
#100 0x0000000000403244 in procF ()
#101 0x0000000000403244 in procF ()
#102 0x0000000000403244 in procF ()
#103 0x0000000000403244 in procF ()
#104 0x0000000000403244 in procF ()
#105 0x0000000000403244 in procF ()
#106 0x0000000000403244 in procF ()
#107 0x0000000000403244 in procF ()
#108 0x0000000000403244 in procF ()
#109 0x0000000000403244 in procF ()
#110 0x0000000000403244 in procF ()
#111 0x0000000000403244 in procF ()
#112 0x0000000000403244 in procF ()
#113 0x0000000000403244 in procF ()
#114 0x0000000000403244 in procF ()
```

```
#115 0x0000000000403244 in procF ()
#116 0x0000000000403244 in procF ()
#117 0x0000000000403244 in procF ()
#118 0x0000000000403244 in procF ()
#119 0x0000000000403244 in procF ()
#120 0x0000000000403244 in procF ()
#121 0x0000000000403244 in procF ()
#122 0x0000000000403244 in procF ()
#123 0x0000000000403244 in procF ()
#124 0x0000000000403244 in procF ()
#125 0x0000000000403244 in procF ()
#126 0x0000000000403244 in procF ()
#127 0x0000000000403244 in procF ()
#128 0x0000000000403244 in procF ()
#129 0x0000000000403244 in procF ()
#130 0x0000000000403244 in procF ()
#131 0x0000000000403244 in procF ()
#132 0x0000000000403244 in procF ()
#133 0x0000000000403244 in procF ()
#134 0x0000000000403244 in procF ()
#135 0x0000000000403244 in procF ()
#136 0x0000000000403244 in procF ()
#137 0x0000000000403244 in procF ()
#138 0x0000000000403244 in procF ()
#139 0x0000000000403244 in procF ()
#140 0x0000000000403244 in procF ()
#141 0x0000000000403244 in procF ()
#142 0x0000000000403244 in procF ()
#143 0x0000000000403244 in procF ()
#144 0x0000000000403244 in procF ()
#145 0x0000000000403244 in procF ()
#146 0x0000000000403244 in procF ()
--Type <RET> for more, q to quit, c to continue without paging--q
Quit
```

Note: It looks like a stack overflow.

5. Check if this is a stack overflow indeed. The stack region can be identified from *App6.pmap.19393* from the thread number. Since the problem thread has LWP 19394, it should be located just below the main stack region:

```
19393:   ./App6
0000000000400000     768K r-x-- App6
00000000004c0000     128K rw--- App6
0000000030aa0000     256K rw---   [ anon ]
0000ffff685c0000      64K -----   [ anon ]
0000ffff685d0000    8192K rw---   [ anon ]
0000ffff68dd0000      64K -----   [ anon ]
0000ffff68de0000    8192K rw---   [ anon ]
0000ffff695e0000      64K -----   [ anon ]
0000ffff695f0000    8192K rw---   [ anon ]
0000ffff69df0000      64K -----   [ anon ]
0000ffff69e00000    8192K rw---   [ anon ]
0000ffff6a600000      64K -----   [ anon ]
0000ffff6a610000    8192K rw---   [ anon ]
0000ffff6ae10000      64K r----   [ anon ]
0000ffff6ae20000      64K r-x--   [ anon ]
0000ffffe3b20000     192K rw---   [ stack ]
 total             42752K
```

6. Check that manually based on the stack pointer value and section boundary addresses:

```
(gdb) x $sp
0xffff6a610000: 0x00000000

(gdb) x $sp-10
0xffff6a60fff6: 0x00000000

(gdb) frame 1
#1  0x0000000000403244 in procF ()

(gdb) x $sp
0xffff6a610210: 0x6a610430

(gdb) frame 2
#2  0x0000000000403244 in procF ()

(gdb) x $sp
0xffff6a610430: 0x6a610650

(gdb) maintenance info sections
Exec file: `/home/ubuntu/ALCDA2/A64/App6/App6', file type elf64-littleaarch64.
 [0]      0x00400190->0x004001b0 at 0x00000190: .note.ABI-tag ALLOC LOAD READONLY DATA HAS_CONTENTS
 [1]      0x004001b0->0x004001d4 at 0x000001b0: .note.gnu.build-id ALLOC LOAD READONLY DATA HAS_CONTENTS
 [2]      0x004001d8->0x00400250 at 0x000001d8: .rela.plt ALLOC LOAD READONLY DATA HAS_CONTENTS
 [3]      0x00400250->0x00400264 at 0x00000250: .init ALLOC LOAD READONLY CODE HAS_CONTENTS
 [4]      0x00400270->0x004002c0 at 0x00000270: .plt ALLOC LOAD READONLY CODE HAS_CONTENTS
 [5]      0x004002c0->0x00487158 at 0x000002c0: .text ALLOC LOAD READONLY CODE HAS_CONTENTS
 [6]      0x00487158->0x00488e28 at 0x00087158: __libc_freeres_fn ALLOC LOAD READONLY CODE HAS_CONTENTS
 [7]      0x00488e28->0x00489278 at 0x00088e28: __libc_thread_freeres_fn ALLOC LOAD READONLY CODE HAS_CONTENTS
 [8]      0x00489278->0x00489288 at 0x00089278: .fini ALLOC LOAD READONLY CODE HAS_CONTENTS
 [9]      0x00489290->0x004a176d at 0x00089290: .rodata ALLOC LOAD READONLY DATA HAS_CONTENTS
 [10]     0x004a176d->0x004a176e at 0x000a176d: .stapsdt.base ALLOC LOAD READONLY DATA HAS_CONTENTS
 [11]     0x004a1770->0x004a1ea8 at 0x000a1770: __libc_IO_vtables ALLOC LOAD READONLY DATA HAS_CONTENTS
 [12]     0x004a1ea8->0x004a1f10 at 0x000a1ea8: __libc_subfreeres ALLOC LOAD READONLY DATA HAS_CONTENTS
 [13]     0x004a1f10->0x004a1f18 at 0x000a1f10: __libc_atexit ALLOC LOAD READONLY DATA HAS_CONTENTS
 [14]     0x004a1f18->0x004a1f28 at 0x000a1f18: __libc_thread_subfreeres ALLOC LOAD READONLY DATA HAS_CONTENTS
 [15]     0x004a1f28->0x004b0594 at 0x000a1f28: .eh_frame ALLOC LOAD READONLY DATA HAS_CONTENTS
 [16]     0x004b0594->0x004b0751 at 0x000b0594: .gcc_except_table ALLOC LOAD READONLY DATA HAS_CONTENTS
 [17]     0x004cfb20->0x004cfb48 at 0x000bfb20: .tdata ALLOC LOAD DATA HAS_CONTENTS
 [18]     0x004cfb48->0x004cfb98 at 0x000bfb48: .tbss ALLOC
 [19]     0x004cfb48->0x004cfb50 at 0x000bfb48: .init_array ALLOC LOAD DATA HAS_CONTENTS
 [20]     0x004cfb50->0x004cfb60 at 0x000bfb50: .fini_array ALLOC LOAD DATA HAS_CONTENTS
 [21]     0x004cfb60->0x004cfb68 at 0x000bfb60: .jcr ALLOC LOAD DATA HAS_CONTENTS
 [22]     0x004cfb68->0x004cff24 at 0x000bfb68: .data.rel.ro ALLOC LOAD DATA HAS_CONTENTS
 [23]     0x004cff28->0x004cffe8 at 0x000bff28: .got ALLOC LOAD DATA HAS_CONTENTS
 [24]     0x004cffe8->0x004d0028 at 0x000bffe8: .got.plt ALLOC LOAD DATA HAS_CONTENTS
 [25]     0x004d0030->0x004d1580 at 0x000c0030: .data ALLOC LOAD DATA HAS_CONTENTS
 [26]     0x004d1580->0x004d8050 at 0x000c1580: .bss ALLOC
 [27]     0x004d8050->0x004d8088 at 0x000c1580: __libc_freeres_ptrs ALLOC
 [28]     0x00000000->0x00000031 at 0x000c1580: .comment READONLY HAS_CONTENTS
 [29]     0x00000000->0x00001cb0 at 0x000c15b4: .note.stapsdt READONLY HAS_CONTENTS
Core file: `/home/ubuntu/ALCDA2/A64/App6/core.19393', file type elf64-littleaarch64.
 [0]      0x00000000->0x00002838 at 0x000003f8: note0 READONLY HAS_CONTENTS
 [1]      0x00000000->0x00000110 at 0x0000047c: .reg/19394 HAS_CONTENTS
 [2]      0x00000000->0x00000110 at 0x0000047c: .reg HAS_CONTENTS
 [3]      0x00000000->0x00000080 at 0x00000644: .note.linuxcore.siginfo/19394 HAS_CONTENTS
 [4]      0x00000000->0x00000080 at 0x00000644: .note.linuxcore.siginfo HAS_CONTENTS
 [5]      0x00000000->0x00000160 at 0x000006d8: .auxv HAS_CONTENTS
 [6]      0x00000000->0x00000076 at 0x0000084c: .note.linuxcore.file/19394 HAS_CONTENTS
 [7]      0x00000000->0x00000076 at 0x0000084c: .note.linuxcore.file HAS_CONTENTS
 [8]      0x00000000->0x00000210 at 0x000008d8: .reg2/19394 HAS_CONTENTS
 [9]      0x00000000->0x00000210 at 0x000008d8: .reg2 HAS_CONTENTS
 [10]     0x00000000->0x00000008 at 0x00000afc: .reg-aarch-tls/19394 HAS_CONTENTS
 [11]     0x00000000->0x00000008 at 0x00000afc: .reg-aarch-tls HAS_CONTENTS
 [12]     0x00000000->0x00000108 at 0x00000b18: .reg-aarch-hw-break/19394 HAS_CONTENTS
 [13]     0x00000000->0x00000108 at 0x00000b18: .reg-aarch-hw-break HAS_CONTENTS
 [14]     0x00000000->0x00000108 at 0x00000c34: .reg-aarch-hw-watch/19394 HAS_CONTENTS
 [15]     0x00000000->0x00000108 at 0x00000c34: .reg-aarch-hw-watch HAS_CONTENTS
 [16]     0x00000000->0x00000110 at 0x00000dd8: .reg/19393 HAS_CONTENTS
```

```
--Type <RET> for more, q to quit, c to continue without paging--
 [17]     0x00000000->0x00000210 at 0x00000f04: .reg2/19393 HAS_CONTENTS
 [18]     0x00000000->0x00000008 at 0x00001128: .reg-aarch-tls/19393 HAS_CONTENTS
 [19]     0x00000000->0x00000108 at 0x00001144: .reg-aarch-hw-break/19393 HAS_CONTENTS
 [20]     0x00000000->0x00000108 at 0x00001260: .reg-aarch-hw-watch/19393 HAS_CONTENTS
 [21]     0x00000000->0x00000110 at 0x00001404: .reg/19398 HAS_CONTENTS
 [22]     0x00000000->0x00000210 at 0x00001530: .reg2/19398 HAS_CONTENTS
 [23]     0x00000000->0x00000008 at 0x00001754: .reg-aarch-tls/19398 HAS_CONTENTS
 [24]     0x00000000->0x00000108 at 0x00001770: .reg-aarch-hw-break/19398 HAS_CONTENTS
 [25]     0x00000000->0x00000108 at 0x0000188c: .reg-aarch-hw-watch/19398 HAS_CONTENTS
 [26]     0x00000000->0x00000110 at 0x00001a30: .reg/19397 HAS_CONTENTS
 [27]     0x00000000->0x00000210 at 0x00001b5c: .reg2/19397 HAS_CONTENTS
 [28]     0x00000000->0x00000008 at 0x00001d80: .reg-aarch-tls/19397 HAS_CONTENTS
 [29]     0x00000000->0x00000108 at 0x00001d9c: .reg-aarch-hw-break/19397 HAS_CONTENTS
 [30]     0x00000000->0x00000108 at 0x00001eb8: .reg-aarch-hw-watch/19397 HAS_CONTENTS
 [31]     0x00000000->0x00000110 at 0x0000205c: .reg/19396 HAS_CONTENTS
 [32]     0x00000000->0x00000210 at 0x00002188: .reg2/19396 HAS_CONTENTS
 [33]     0x00000000->0x00000008 at 0x000023ac: .reg-aarch-tls/19396 HAS_CONTENTS
 [34]     0x00000000->0x00000108 at 0x000023c8: .reg-aarch-hw-break/19396 HAS_CONTENTS
 [35]     0x00000000->0x00000108 at 0x000024e4: .reg-aarch-hw-watch/19396 HAS_CONTENTS
 [36]     0x00000000->0x00000110 at 0x00002688: .reg/19395 HAS_CONTENTS
 [37]     0x00000000->0x00000210 at 0x000027b4: .reg2/19395 HAS_CONTENTS
 [38]     0x00000000->0x00000008 at 0x000029d8: .reg-aarch-tls/19395 HAS_CONTENTS
 [39]     0x00000000->0x00000108 at 0x000029f4: .reg-aarch-hw-break/19395 HAS_CONTENTS
 [40]     0x00000000->0x00000108 at 0x00002b10: .reg-aarch-hw-watch/19395 HAS_CONTENTS
 [41]     0x00400000->0x00410000 at 0x00010000: load1a ALLOC LOAD READONLY CODE HAS_CONTENTS
 [42]     0x00410000->0x004c0000 at 0x00020000: load1b ALLOC READONLY CODE
 [43]     0x004c0000->0x004e0000 at 0x00020000: load2 ALLOC LOAD HAS_CONTENTS
 [44]     0x30aa0000->0x30ae0000 at 0x00040000: load3 ALLOC LOAD HAS_CONTENTS
 [45]     0xffff685c0000->0xffff685d0000 at 0x00080000: load4 ALLOC LOAD READONLY HAS_CONTENTS
 [46]     0xffff685d0000->0xffff68dd0000 at 0x00090000: load5 ALLOC LOAD HAS_CONTENTS
 [47]     0xffff68dd0000->0xffff68de0000 at 0x00890000: load6 ALLOC LOAD READONLY HAS_CONTENTS
 [48]     0xffff68de0000->0xffff695e0000 at 0x008a0000: load7 ALLOC LOAD HAS_CONTENTS
 [49]     0xffff695e0000->0xffff695f0000 at 0x010a0000: load8 ALLOC LOAD READONLY HAS_CONTENTS
 [50]     0xffff695f0000->0xffff69df0000 at 0x010b0000: load9 ALLOC LOAD HAS_CONTENTS
 [51]     0xffff69df0000->0xffff69e00000 at 0x018b0000: load10 ALLOC LOAD READONLY HAS_CONTENTS
 [52]     0xffff69e00000->0xffff6a600000 at 0x018c0000: load11 ALLOC LOAD HAS_CONTENTS
 [53]     0xffff6a600000->0xffff6a610000 at 0x020c0000: load12 ALLOC LOAD READONLY HAS_CONTENTS
 [54]     0xffff6a610000->0xffff6ae10000 at 0x020d0000: load13 ALLOC LOAD HAS_CONTENTS
 [55]     0xffff6ae10000->0xffff6ae20000 at 0x028d0000: load14 ALLOC LOAD READONLY HAS_CONTENTS
 [56]     0xffff6ae20000->0xffff6ae30000 at 0x028e0000: load15 ALLOC LOAD READONLY CODE HAS_CONTENTS
 [57]     0xffffe3b20000->0xffffe3b50000 at 0x028f0000: load16 ALLOC LOAD HAS_CONTENTS
```

Note: The stack pointer points to the start of the stack region. The addresses below it should be inaccessible at runtime. However, the committed pages were included in the crash dump, and we see zeroes since GDB can read them.

7. Dump the bottom of the raw stack to see execution residue, such as thread startup:

```
(gdb) x/1024a 0xffff6ae10000-0x2000
0xffff6ae0e000: 0x0     0x0
0xffff6ae0e010: 0x0     0x0
0xffff6ae0e020: 0x0     0x0
0xffff6ae0e030: 0x0     0x0
0xffff6ae0e040: 0x0     0x0
0xffff6ae0e050: 0x0     0x0
0xffff6ae0e060: 0x0     0x0
0xffff6ae0e070: 0x0     0x0
0xffff6ae0e080: 0x0     0x0
0xffff6ae0e090: 0x0     0x0
0xffff6ae0e0a0: 0x0     0x0
0xffff6ae0e0b0: 0x0     0x0
0xffff6ae0e0c0: 0x0     0x0
0xffff6ae0e0d0: 0x0     0x0
0xffff6ae0e0e0: 0x0     0x0
0xffff6ae0e0f0: 0x0     0x0
0xffff6ae0e100: 0x0     0x0
```

```
0xffff6ae0e110: 0x0     0x0
0xffff6ae0e120: 0x0     0x0
0xffff6ae0e130: 0x0     0x0
0xffff6ae0e140: 0x0     0x0
0xffff6ae0e150: 0x0     0x0
0xffff6ae0e160: 0x0     0x0
0xffff6ae0e170: 0x0     0x0
0xffff6ae0e180: 0x0     0x0
0xffff6ae0e190: 0x0     0x0
0xffff6ae0e1a0: 0x0     0x0
0xffff6ae0e1b0: 0xffff6ae0e3d0  0x403244 <procF+92>
0xffff6ae0e1c0: 0x0     0x300000000
0xffff6ae0e1d0: 0xffffffff      0x4
0xffff6ae0e1e0: 0xffffffff      0x0
0xffff6ae0e1f0: 0x0     0x0
0xffff6ae0e200: 0x0     0x0
0xffff6ae0e210: 0x0     0x0
0xffff6ae0e220: 0x0     0x0
0xffff6ae0e230: 0x0     0x0
0xffff6ae0e240: 0x0     0x0
0xffff6ae0e250: 0x0     0x0
0xffff6ae0e260: 0x0     0x0
0xffff6ae0e270: 0x0     0x0
0xffff6ae0e280: 0x0     0x0
0xffff6ae0e290: 0x0     0x0
0xffff6ae0e2a0: 0x0     0x0
0xffff6ae0e2b0: 0x0     0x0
0xffff6ae0e2c0: 0x0     0x0
0xffff6ae0e2d0: 0x0     0x0
0xffff6ae0e2e0: 0x0     0x0
0xffff6ae0e2f0: 0x0     0x0
0xffff6ae0e300: 0x0     0x0
--Type <RET> for more, q to quit, c to continue without paging--
0xffff6ae0e310: 0x0     0x0
0xffff6ae0e320: 0x0     0x0
0xffff6ae0e330: 0x0     0x0
0xffff6ae0e340: 0x0     0x0
0xffff6ae0e350: 0x0     0x0
0xffff6ae0e360: 0x0     0x0
0xffff6ae0e370: 0x0     0x0
0xffff6ae0e380: 0x0     0x0
0xffff6ae0e390: 0x0     0x0
0xffff6ae0e3a0: 0x0     0x0
0xffff6ae0e3b0: 0x0     0x0
0xffff6ae0e3c0: 0x0     0x0
0xffff6ae0e3d0: 0xffff6ae0e5f0  0x403244 <procF+92>
0xffff6ae0e3e0: 0x0     0x200000000
0xffff6ae0e3f0: 0xffffffff      0x3
0xffff6ae0e400: 0xffffffff      0x0
0xffff6ae0e410: 0x0     0x0
0xffff6ae0e420: 0x0     0x0
0xffff6ae0e430: 0x0     0x0
0xffff6ae0e440: 0x0     0x0
0xffff6ae0e450: 0x0     0x0
0xffff6ae0e460: 0x0     0x0
0xffff6ae0e470: 0x0     0x0
0xffff6ae0e480: 0x0     0x0
0xffff6ae0e490: 0x0     0x0
0xffff6ae0e4a0: 0x0     0x0
0xffff6ae0e4b0: 0x0     0x0
```

```
0xffff6ae0e4c0: 0x0     0x0
0xffff6ae0e4d0: 0x0     0x0
0xffff6ae0e4e0: 0x0     0x0
0xffff6ae0e4f0: 0x0     0x0
0xffff6ae0e500: 0x0     0x0
0xffff6ae0e510: 0x0     0x0
0xffff6ae0e520: 0x0     0x0
0xffff6ae0e530: 0x0     0x0
0xffff6ae0e540: 0x0     0x0
0xffff6ae0e550: 0x0     0x0
0xffff6ae0e560: 0x0     0x0
0xffff6ae0e570: 0x0     0x0
0xffff6ae0e580: 0x0     0x0
0xffff6ae0e590: 0x0     0x0
0xffff6ae0e5a0: 0x0     0x0
0xffff6ae0e5b0: 0x0     0x0
0xffff6ae0e5c0: 0x0     0x0
0xffff6ae0e5d0: 0x0     0x0
0xffff6ae0e5e0: 0x0     0x0
0xffff6ae0e5f0: 0xffff6ae0e810  0x403260 <procE+16>
0xffff6ae0e600: 0xffff6ae0e670  0x100000000
0xffff6ae0e610: 0xffffffff      0x2
--Type <RET> for more, q to quit, c to continue without paging--
0xffff6ae0e620: 0xffffffff      0x0
0xffff6ae0e630: 0x0     0x0
0xffff6ae0e640: 0x0     0x0
0xffff6ae0e650: 0x0     0x0
0xffff6ae0e660: 0x0     0x0
0xffff6ae0e670: 0x0     0x0
0xffff6ae0e680: 0x0     0x0
0xffff6ae0e690: 0x0     0x0
0xffff6ae0e6a0: 0x0     0x0
0xffff6ae0e6b0: 0x0     0x0
0xffff6ae0e6c0: 0x0     0x0
0xffff6ae0e6d0: 0x0     0x0
0xffff6ae0e6e0: 0x0     0x0
0xffff6ae0e6f0: 0x0     0x0
0xffff6ae0e700: 0x0     0x0
0xffff6ae0e710: 0x0     0x0
0xffff6ae0e720: 0x0     0x0
0xffff6ae0e730: 0x0     0x0
0xffff6ae0e740: 0x0     0x0
0xffff6ae0e750: 0x0     0x0
0xffff6ae0e760: 0x0     0x0
0xffff6ae0e770: 0x0     0x0
0xffff6ae0e780: 0x0     0x0
0xffff6ae0e790: 0x0     0x0
0xffff6ae0e7a0: 0x0     0x0
0xffff6ae0e7b0: 0x0     0x0
0xffff6ae0e7c0: 0x0     0x0
0xffff6ae0e7d0: 0x0     0x0
0xffff6ae0e7e0: 0x0     0x0
0xffff6ae0e7f0: 0x0     0x0
0xffff6ae0e800: 0x0     0x0
0xffff6ae0e810: 0xffff6ae0e820  0x40327c <bar_one+20>
0xffff6ae0e820: 0xffff6ae0e830  0x403290 <foo_one+12>
0xffff6ae0e830: 0xffff6ae0e840  0x4032a8 <thread_one+16>
0xffff6ae0e840: 0xffff6ae0e860  0x404cd4 <start_thread+180>
0xffff6ae0e850: 0xffff6ae0f080  0x0
0xffff6ae0e860: 0x0     0x429c20 <thread_start+48>
```

```
0xffff6ae0e870: 0xffff6ae0f080  0x4d7890 <__default_pthread_attr>
0xffff6ae0e880: 0x4d0000        0x0
0xffff6ae0e890: 0xffff6ae0f49c  0xffff6ae0f080
0xffff6ae0e8a0: 0x0     0x0
0xffff6ae0e8b0: 0xffff6ae0f080  0x4d7890 <__default_pthread_attr>
0xffff6ae0e8c0: 0x4d0000        0x403298 <thread_one>
0xffff6ae0e8d0: 0x0     0xffff6ae0f770
0xffff6ae0e8e0: 0x30aa06f0      0x4d7890 <__default_pthread_attr>
0xffff6ae0e8f0: 0x10000 0x810000
0xffff6ae0e900: 0xffff6ae0e860  0x5afbedf415cdf4fb
0xffff6ae0e910: 0x0     0x5afb120b7f6d503b
0xffff6ae0e920: 0x0     0x0
--Type <RET> for more, q to quit, c to continue without paging--
0xffff6ae0e930: 0x0     0x0
0xffff6ae0e940: 0x0     0x0
0xffff6ae0e950: 0x0     0x0
0xffff6ae0e960: 0x0     0x0
0xffff6ae0e970: 0x0     0x0
0xffff6ae0e980: 0x0     0x0
0xffff6ae0e990: 0x0     0x0
0xffff6ae0e9a0: 0x0     0x0
0xffff6ae0e9b0: 0x0     0x0
0xffff6ae0e9c0: 0x0     0x0
0xffff6ae0e9d0: 0x0     0x0
0xffff6ae0e9e0: 0x0     0x0
0xffff6ae0e9f0: 0x0     0x0
0xffff6ae0ea00: 0x0     0x0
0xffff6ae0ea10: 0x0     0x0
0xffff6ae0ea20: 0x0     0x0
0xffff6ae0ea30: 0x0     0x0
0xffff6ae0ea40: 0x0     0x0
0xffff6ae0ea50: 0x0     0x0
0xffff6ae0ea60: 0x0     0x0
0xffff6ae0ea70: 0x0     0x0
0xffff6ae0ea80: 0x0     0x0
0xffff6ae0ea90: 0x0     0x0
0xffff6ae0eaa0: 0x0     0x0
0xffff6ae0eab0: 0x0     0x0
0xffff6ae0eac0: 0x0     0x0
0xffff6ae0ead0: 0x0     0x0
0xffff6ae0eae0: 0x0     0x0
0xffff6ae0eaf0: 0x0     0x0
0xffff6ae0eb00: 0x0     0x0
0xffff6ae0eb10: 0x0     0x0
0xffff6ae0eb20: 0x0     0x0
0xffff6ae0eb30: 0x0     0x0
0xffff6ae0eb40: 0x0     0x0
0xffff6ae0eb50: 0x0     0x0
0xffff6ae0eb60: 0x0     0x0
0xffff6ae0eb70: 0x0     0x0
0xffff6ae0eb80: 0x0     0x0
0xffff6ae0eb90: 0x0     0x0
0xffff6ae0eba0: 0x0     0x0
0xffff6ae0ebb0: 0x0     0x0
0xffff6ae0ebc0: 0x0     0x0
0xffff6ae0ebd0: 0x0     0x0
0xffff6ae0ebe0: 0x0     0x0
0xffff6ae0ebf0: 0x0     0x0
0xffff6ae0ec00: 0x0     0x0
0xffff6ae0ec10: 0x0     0x0
```

```
0xffff6ae0ec20: 0x0     0x0
0xffff6ae0ec30: 0x0     0x0
--Type <RET> for more, q to quit, c to continue without paging--
0xffff6ae0ec40: 0x0     0x0
0xffff6ae0ec50: 0x0     0x0
0xffff6ae0ec60: 0x0     0x0
0xffff6ae0ec70: 0x0     0x0
0xffff6ae0ec80: 0x0     0x0
0xffff6ae0ec90: 0x0     0x0
0xffff6ae0eca0: 0x0     0x0
0xffff6ae0ecb0: 0x0     0x0
0xffff6ae0ecc0: 0x0     0x0
0xffff6ae0ecd0: 0x0     0x0
0xffff6ae0ece0: 0x0     0x0
0xffff6ae0ecf0: 0x0     0x0
0xffff6ae0ed00: 0x0     0x0
0xffff6ae0ed10: 0x0     0x0
0xffff6ae0ed20: 0x0     0x0
0xffff6ae0ed30: 0x0     0x0
0xffff6ae0ed40: 0x0     0x0
0xffff6ae0ed50: 0x0     0x0
0xffff6ae0ed60: 0x0     0x0
0xffff6ae0ed70: 0x0     0x0
0xffff6ae0ed80: 0x0     0x0
0xffff6ae0ed90: 0x0     0x0
0xffff6ae0eda0: 0x0     0x0
0xffff6ae0edb0: 0x0     0x0
0xffff6ae0edc0: 0x0     0x0
0xffff6ae0edd0: 0x0     0x0
0xffff6ae0ede0: 0x0     0x0
0xffff6ae0edf0: 0x0     0x0
0xffff6ae0ee00: 0x0     0x0
0xffff6ae0ee10: 0x0     0x0
0xffff6ae0ee20: 0x0     0x0
0xffff6ae0ee30: 0x0     0x0
0xffff6ae0ee40: 0x0     0x0
0xffff6ae0ee50: 0x0     0x0
0xffff6ae0ee60: 0x0     0x0
0xffff6ae0ee70: 0x0     0x0
0xffff6ae0ee80: 0x0     0x0
0xffff6ae0ee90: 0x0     0x0
0xffff6ae0eea0: 0x0     0x0
0xffff6ae0eeb0: 0x0     0x0
0xffff6ae0eec0: 0x0     0x0
0xffff6ae0eed0: 0x0     0x0
0xffff6ae0eee0: 0x0     0x0
0xffff6ae0eef0: 0x0     0x0
0xffff6ae0ef00: 0x0     0x0
0xffff6ae0ef10: 0x0     0x0
0xffff6ae0ef20: 0x0     0x0
0xffff6ae0ef30: 0x0     0x0
0xffff6ae0ef40: 0x0     0x0
--Type <RET> for more, q to quit, c to continue without paging--
0xffff6ae0ef50: 0x0     0x0
0xffff6ae0ef60: 0x0     0x0
0xffff6ae0ef70: 0x0     0x0
0xffff6ae0ef80: 0x0     0x0
0xffff6ae0ef90: 0x0     0x0
0xffff6ae0efa0: 0x0     0x0
0xffff6ae0efb0: 0x0     0x0
```

```
0xffff6ae0efc0: 0x0     0x0
0xffff6ae0efd0: 0x0     0x0
0xffff6ae0efe0: 0x0     0x0
0xffff6ae0eff0: 0x0     0x0
0xffff6ae0f000: 0x0     0x0
0xffff6ae0f010: 0x0     0x0
0xffff6ae0f020: 0x0     0x0
0xffff6ae0f030: 0x0     0x0
0xffff6ae0f040: 0x0     0x0
0xffff6ae0f050: 0x0     0x0
0xffff6ae0f060: 0x0     0x0
0xffff6ae0f070: 0x0     0x0
0xffff6ae0f080: 0x1     0x0
0xffff6ae0f090: 0x0     0x0
0xffff6ae0f0a0: 0x0     0x0
0xffff6ae0f0b0: 0x0     0x0
0xffff6ae0f0c0: 0x0     0x0
0xffff6ae0f0d0: 0x0     0x0
0xffff6ae0f0e0: 0x0     0x0
0xffff6ae0f0f0: 0x0     0x0
0xffff6ae0f100: 0x0     0x0
0xffff6ae0f110: 0x0     0x0
0xffff6ae0f120: 0x0     0x0
0xffff6ae0f130: 0x0     0x0
0xffff6ae0f140: 0x4d0050 <stack_used>   0xffff6a5ff140
0xffff6ae0f150: 0x4bc100004bc2  0xffff6ae0f160
0xffff6ae0f160: 0xffff6ae0f160  0xffffffffffffffe0
0xffff6ae0f170: 0x0     0x0
0xffff6ae0f180: 0xffff6ae0e8b0  0x0
0xffff6ae0f190: 0x0     0x0
0xffff6ae0f1a0: 0x0     0x0
0xffff6ae0f1b0: 0x0     0x0
0xffff6ae0f1c0: 0x0     0x0
0xffff6ae0f1d0: 0x0     0x0
0xffff6ae0f1e0: 0x0     0x0
0xffff6ae0f1f0: 0x0     0x0
0xffff6ae0f200: 0x0     0x0
0xffff6ae0f210: 0x0     0x0
0xffff6ae0f220: 0x0     0x0
0xffff6ae0f230: 0x0     0x0
0xffff6ae0f240: 0x0     0x0
0xffff6ae0f250: 0x0     0x0
--Type <RET> for more, q to quit, c to continue without paging--
0xffff6ae0f260: 0x0     0x0
0xffff6ae0f270: 0x0     0x0
0xffff6ae0f280: 0x0     0x0
0xffff6ae0f290: 0x0     0x0
0xffff6ae0f2a0: 0x0     0x0
0xffff6ae0f2b0: 0x0     0x0
0xffff6ae0f2c0: 0x0     0x0
0xffff6ae0f2d0: 0x0     0x0
0xffff6ae0f2e0: 0x0     0x0
0xffff6ae0f2f0: 0x0     0x0
0xffff6ae0f300: 0x0     0x0
0xffff6ae0f310: 0x0     0x0
0xffff6ae0f320: 0x0     0x0
0xffff6ae0f330: 0x0     0x0
0xffff6ae0f340: 0x0     0x0
0xffff6ae0f350: 0x0     0x0
0xffff6ae0f360: 0x0     0x0
```

```
0xffff6ae0f370: 0x0     0x0
0xffff6ae0f380: 0x0     0x0
0xffff6ae0f390: 0xffff6ae0f190  0x0
0xffff6ae0f3a0: 0x0     0x0
0xffff6ae0f3b0: 0x0     0x0
0xffff6ae0f3c0: 0x0     0x0
0xffff6ae0f3d0: 0x0     0x0
0xffff6ae0f3e0: 0x0     0x0
0xffff6ae0f3f0: 0x0     0x0
0xffff6ae0f400: 0x0     0x0
0xffff6ae0f410: 0x0     0x0
0xffff6ae0f420: 0x0     0x0
0xffff6ae0f430: 0x0     0x0
0xffff6ae0f440: 0x0     0x0
0xffff6ae0f450: 0x0     0x0
0xffff6ae0f460: 0x0     0x0
0xffff6ae0f470: 0x0     0x0
0xffff6ae0f480: 0x0     0x0
0xffff6ae0f490: 0x0     0x0
0xffff6ae0f4a0: 0x0     0x0
0xffff6ae0f4b0: 0x0     0x403298 <thread_one>
0xffff6ae0f4c0: 0x0     0x0
0xffff6ae0f4d0: 0x0     0x0
0xffff6ae0f4e0: 0x0     0x0
0xffff6ae0f4f0: 0x0     0x0
0xffff6ae0f500: 0x0     0x0
0xffff6ae0f510: 0xffff6a600000  0x810000
0xffff6ae0f520: 0x10000 0x10000
0xffff6ae0f530: 0x0     0x0
0xffff6ae0f540: 0x0     0x0
0xffff6ae0f550: 0x0     0x0
0xffff6ae0f560: 0x0     0x0
--Type <RET> for more, q to quit, c to continue without paging--
0xffff6ae0f570: 0x0     0x0
0xffff6ae0f580: 0x0     0x0
0xffff6ae0f590: 0x0     0x0
0xffff6ae0f5a0: 0x0     0x0
0xffff6ae0f5b0: 0x0     0x0
0xffff6ae0f5c0: 0x0     0x0
0xffff6ae0f5d0: 0x0     0x0
0xffff6ae0f5e0: 0x0     0x0
0xffff6ae0f5f0: 0x0     0x0
0xffff6ae0f600: 0x0     0x0
0xffff6ae0f610: 0x0     0x0
0xffff6ae0f620: 0x0     0x0
0xffff6ae0f630: 0x0     0x0
0xffff6ae0f640: 0x0     0x0
0xffff6ae0f650: 0x0     0x0
0xffff6ae0f660: 0x0     0x0
0xffff6ae0f670: 0x0     0x0
0xffff6ae0f680: 0x0     0x0
0xffff6ae0f690: 0x0     0x0
0xffff6ae0f6a0: 0x0     0x0
0xffff6ae0f6b0: 0x0     0x0
0xffff6ae0f6c0: 0x0     0x0
0xffff6ae0f6d0: 0x0     0x0
0xffff6ae0f6e0: 0x0     0x0
0xffff6ae0f6f0: 0x0     0x0
0xffff6ae0f700: 0x0     0x0
0xffff6ae0f710: 0x0     0x0
```

```
0xffff6ae0f720: 0x0     0x0
0xffff6ae0f730: 0x0     0x0
0xffff6ae0f740: 0x0     0x0
0xffff6ae0f750: 0x0     0x0
0xffff6ae0f760: 0x0     0x0
0xffff6ae0f770: 0x30aa1d80      0x0
0xffff6ae0f780: 0xffff6ae0f538  0x4d13c0 <_nl_global_locale>
0xffff6ae0f790: 0x4d13c0 <_nl_global_locale>    0x4d13e0 <_nl_global_locale+32>
0xffff6ae0f7a0: 0x4d13c8 <_nl_global_locale+8>  0x0
0xffff6ae0f7b0: 0x48d280 <_nl_C_LC_CTYPE_class+256>     0x48c980 <_nl_C_LC_CTYPE_toupper+512>
0xffff6ae0f7c0: 0x48c380 <_nl_C_LC_CTYPE_tolower+512>   0x0
0xffff6ae0f7d0: 0x0     0x0
0xffff6ae0f7e0: 0x0     0x0
0xffff6ae0f7f0: 0x0     0x0
0xffff6ae0f800: 0x0     0x0
0xffff6ae0f810: 0x0     0x0
0xffff6ae0f820: 0x0     0x0
0xffff6ae0f830: 0x0     0x0
0xffff6ae0f840: 0x0     0x0
0xffff6ae0f850: 0x0     0x0
0xffff6ae0f860: 0x0     0x0
0xffff6ae0f870: 0x0     0x0
--Type <RET> for more, q to quit, c to continue without paging--
0xffff6ae0f880: 0x0     0x0
0xffff6ae0f890: 0x0     0x0
0xffff6ae0f8a0: 0x0     0x0
0xffff6ae0f8b0: 0x0     0x0
0xffff6ae0f8c0: 0x0     0x0
0xffff6ae0f8d0: 0x0     0x0
0xffff6ae0f8e0: 0x0     0x0
0xffff6ae0f8f0: 0x0     0x0
0xffff6ae0f900: 0x0     0x0
0xffff6ae0f910: 0x0     0x0
0xffff6ae0f920: 0x0     0x0
0xffff6ae0f930: 0x0     0x0
0xffff6ae0f940: 0x0     0x0
0xffff6ae0f950: 0x0     0x0
0xffff6ae0f960: 0x0     0x0
0xffff6ae0f970: 0x0     0x0
0xffff6ae0f980: 0x0     0x0
0xffff6ae0f990: 0x0     0x0
0xffff6ae0f9a0: 0x0     0x0
0xffff6ae0f9b0: 0x0     0x0
0xffff6ae0f9c0: 0x0     0x0
0xffff6ae0f9d0: 0x0     0x0
0xffff6ae0f9e0: 0x0     0x0
0xffff6ae0f9f0: 0x0     0x0
0xffff6ae0fa00: 0x0     0x0
0xffff6ae0fa10: 0x0     0x0
0xffff6ae0fa20: 0x0     0x0
0xffff6ae0fa30: 0x0     0x0
0xffff6ae0fa40: 0x0     0x0
0xffff6ae0fa50: 0x0     0x0
0xffff6ae0fa60: 0x0     0x0
0xffff6ae0fa70: 0x0     0x0
0xffff6ae0fa80: 0x0     0x0
0xffff6ae0fa90: 0x0     0x0
0xffff6ae0faa0: 0x0     0x0
0xffff6ae0fab0: 0x0     0x0
0xffff6ae0fac0: 0x0     0x0
```

```
0xffff6ae0fad0: 0x0     0x0
0xffff6ae0fae0: 0x0     0x0
0xffff6ae0faf0: 0x0     0x0
0xffff6ae0fb00: 0x0     0x0
0xffff6ae0fb10: 0x0     0x0
0xffff6ae0fb20: 0x0     0x0
0xffff6ae0fb30: 0x0     0x0
0xffff6ae0fb40: 0x0     0x0
0xffff6ae0fb50: 0x0     0x0
0xffff6ae0fb60: 0x0     0x0
0xffff6ae0fb70: 0x0     0x0
0xffff6ae0fb80: 0x0     0x0
--Type <RET> for more, q to quit, c to continue without paging--
0xffff6ae0fb90: 0x0     0x0
0xffff6ae0fba0: 0x0     0x0
0xffff6ae0fbb0: 0x0     0x0
0xffff6ae0fbc0: 0x0     0x0
0xffff6ae0fbd0: 0x0     0x0
0xffff6ae0fbe0: 0x0     0x0
0xffff6ae0fbf0: 0x0     0x0
0xffff6ae0fc00: 0x0     0x0
0xffff6ae0fc10: 0x0     0x0
0xffff6ae0fc20: 0x0     0x0
0xffff6ae0fc30: 0x0     0x0
0xffff6ae0fc40: 0x0     0x0
0xffff6ae0fc50: 0x0     0x0
0xffff6ae0fc60: 0x0     0x0
0xffff6ae0fc70: 0x0     0x0
0xffff6ae0fc80: 0x0     0x0
0xffff6ae0fc90: 0x0     0x0
0xffff6ae0fca0: 0x0     0x0
0xffff6ae0fcb0: 0x0     0x0
0xffff6ae0fcc0: 0x0     0x0
0xffff6ae0fcd0: 0x0     0x0
0xffff6ae0fce0: 0x0     0x0
0xffff6ae0fcf0: 0x0     0x0
0xffff6ae0fd00: 0x0     0x0
0xffff6ae0fd10: 0x0     0x0
0xffff6ae0fd20: 0x0     0x0
0xffff6ae0fd30: 0x0     0x0
0xffff6ae0fd40: 0x0     0x0
0xffff6ae0fd50: 0x0     0x0
0xffff6ae0fd60: 0x0     0x0
0xffff6ae0fd70: 0x0     0x0
0xffff6ae0fd80: 0x0     0x0
0xffff6ae0fd90: 0x0     0x0
0xffff6ae0fda0: 0x0     0x0
0xffff6ae0fdb0: 0x0     0x0
0xffff6ae0fdc0: 0x0     0x0
0xffff6ae0fdd0: 0x0     0x0
0xffff6ae0fde0: 0x0     0x0
0xffff6ae0fdf0: 0x0     0x0
0xffff6ae0fe00: 0x0     0x0
0xffff6ae0fe10: 0x0     0x0
0xffff6ae0fe20: 0x0     0x0
0xffff6ae0fe30: 0x0     0x0
0xffff6ae0fe40: 0x0     0x0
0xffff6ae0fe50: 0x0     0x0
0xffff6ae0fe60: 0x0     0x0
0xffff6ae0fe70: 0x0     0x0
```

```
0xffff6ae0fe80: 0x0     0x0
0xffff6ae0fe90: 0x0     0x0
--Type <RET> for more, q to quit, c to continue without paging--
0xffff6ae0fea0: 0x0     0x0
0xffff6ae0feb0: 0x0     0x0
0xffff6ae0fec0: 0x0     0x0
0xffff6ae0fed0: 0x0     0x0
0xffff6ae0fee0: 0x0     0x0
0xffff6ae0fef0: 0x0     0x0
0xffff6ae0ff00: 0x0     0x0
0xffff6ae0ff10: 0x0     0x0
0xffff6ae0ff20: 0x0     0x0
0xffff6ae0ff30: 0x0     0x0
0xffff6ae0ff40: 0x0     0x0
0xffff6ae0ff50: 0x0     0x0
0xffff6ae0ff60: 0x0     0x0
0xffff6ae0ff70: 0x0     0x0
0xffff6ae0ff80: 0x0     0x0
0xffff6ae0ff90: 0x0     0x0
0xffff6ae0ffa0: 0x0     0x0
0xffff6ae0ffb0: 0x0     0x0
0xffff6ae0ffc0: 0x0     0x0
0xffff6ae0ffd0: 0x0     0x0
0xffff6ae0ffe0: 0x0     0x0
0xffff6ae0fff0: 0x0     0x0
```

8. See that the reconstruction of the stack trace is possible because of the standard function prologue and epilogue:

```
[...]
0xffff6ae0e1b0: 0xffff6ae0e3d0  0x403244 <procF+92>
0xffff6ae0e3d0: 0xffff6ae0e5f0  0x403244 <procF+92>
0xffff6ae0e5f0: 0xffff6ae0e810  0x403260 <procE+16>
0xffff6ae0e810: 0xffff6ae0e820  0x40327c <bar_one+20>
0xffff6ae0e820: 0xffff6ae0e830  0x403290 <foo_one+12>
0xffff6ae0e830: 0xffff6ae0e840  0x4032a8 <thread_one+16>
0xffff6ae0e840: 0xffff6ae0e860  0x404cd4 <start_thread+180>
```

```
(gdb) disass procF
Dump of assembler code for function procF:
   0x00000000004031e8 <+0>:     sub     sp, sp, #0x210
   0x00000000004031ec <+4>:     stp     x29, x30, [sp, #-16]!
   0x00000000004031f0 <+8>:     mov     x29, sp
   0x00000000004031f4 <+12>:    add     x1, x29, #0x1c
   0x00000000004031f8 <+16>:    str     w0, [x1]
   0x00000000004031fc <+20>:    add     x0, x29, #0x20
   0x0000000000403200 <+24>:    mov     x2, #0x200                  // #512
   0x0000000000403204 <+28>:    mov     w1, #0x0                    // #0
   0x0000000000403208 <+32>:    bl      0x400290
   0x000000000040320c <+36>:    add     x0, x29, #0x20
   0x0000000000403210 <+40>:    mov     w1, #0xffffffff             // #-1
   0x0000000000403214 <+44>:    str     w1, [x0]
   0x0000000000403218 <+48>:    add     x0, x29, #0x1c
   0x000000000040321c <+52>:    ldr     w0, [x0]
   0x0000000000403220 <+56>:    add     w1, w0, #0x1
   0x0000000000403224 <+60>:    add     x0, x29, #0x20
   0x0000000000403228 <+64>:    str     w1, [x0, #8]
   0x000000000040322c <+68>:    add     x0, x29, #0x20
   0x0000000000403230 <+72>:    mov     w1, #0xffffffff             // #-1
   0x0000000000403234 <+76>:    str     w1, [x0, #16]
```

```
   0x0000000000403238 <+80>:    add     x0, x29, #0x20
   0x000000000040323c <+84>:    ldr     w0, [x0, #8]
   0x0000000000403240 <+88>:    bl      0x4031e8 <procF>
=> 0x0000000000403244 <+92>:    ldp     x29, x30, [sp], #16
   0x0000000000403248 <+96>:    add     sp, sp, #0x210
   0x000000000040324c <+100>:   ret
End of assembler dump.
```

9. Use the back trace command variant to get to the bottom of the stack trace:

```
(gdb) bt -20
#15395 0x0000000000403244 in procF ()
#15396 0x0000000000403244 in procF ()
#15397 0x0000000000403244 in procF ()
#15398 0x0000000000403244 in procF ()
#15399 0x0000000000403244 in procF ()
#15400 0x0000000000403244 in procF ()
#15401 0x0000000000403244 in procF ()
#15402 0x0000000000403244 in procF ()
#15403 0x0000000000403244 in procF ()
#15404 0x0000000000403244 in procF ()
#15405 0x0000000000403244 in procF ()
#15406 0x0000000000403244 in procF ()
#15407 0x0000000000403244 in procF ()
#15408 0x0000000000403244 in procF ()
#15409 0x0000000000403260 in procE ()
#15410 0x000000000040327c in bar_one ()
#15411 0x0000000000403290 in foo_one ()
#15412 0x00000000004032a8 in thread_one ()
#15413 0x0000000000404cd4 in start_thread ()
#15414 0x0000000000429c20 in thread_start ()
```

Exercise A6 (x64, WinDbg)

Goal: Learn how to identify stack overflow, stack boundaries, reconstruct stack trace.

Patterns: Stack Overflow (User Mode).

1. Launch WinDbg.

2. Load the *core.App6* dump file from the x64\App6 folder:

```
Microsoft (R) Windows Debugger Version 10.0.27725.1000 AMD64
Copyright (c) Microsoft Corporation. All rights reserved.


Loading Dump File [C:\ALCDA2\x64\App6\core.App6]
64-bit machine not using 64-bit API

************* Path validation summary **************
Response                         Time (ms)     Location
Deferred                                       srv*
Symbol search path is: srv*
Executable search path is:
Generic Unix Version 0 UP Free x64
System Uptime: not available
Process Uptime: not available
..
(125f.1260): Signal SIGSEGV (Segmentation fault) code SEGV_ACCERR (Invalid permissions for
mapped object) at 0x7f91e65e8efc
*** WARNING: Unable to verify timestamp for App6
App6+0x1bb8:
00000000`00401bb8 ???
```

3. Set logging to a file in case of lengthy output from some commands:

```
0:000> .logopen C:\ALCDA2\x64\App6\App6-WinDbg.log
Opened log file 'C:\ALCDA2\x64\App6\App6-WinDbg.log'
```

4. Specify the dump folder as the symbol path and reload symbols:

```
0:000> .symfix; .sympath+ C:\ALCDA2\x64\App6\
Symbol search path is: srv*;C:\ALCDA2\x64\App6\
Expanded Symbol search path is:
cache*;SRV*https://msdl.microsoft.com/download/symbols;c:\alcda2\x64\app6\

************* Path validation summary **************
Response                         Time (ms)     Location
Deferred                                       srv*
OK                                             C:\ALCDA2\x64\App6\
*** WARNING: Unable to verify timestamp for App6
```

```
0:000> .reload
..
*** WARNING: Unable to verify timestamp for App6

************* Symbol Loading Error Summary **************
Module name            Error
App6                   The system cannot find the file specified

You can troubleshoot most symbol related issues by turning on symbol loading diagnostics (!sym
noisy) and repeating the command that caused symbols to be loaded.
You should also verify that your symbol search path (.sympath) is correct.
```

Note: We ignore warnings and errors as they are not relevant for now.

5. List threads:

```
0:000> ~*k 1

Unable to get thread data for thread 0
.  0  Id: 125f.1260 Suspend: 0 Teb: 00000000`00000000 Unfrozen
 # Child-SP          RetAddr               Call Site
00 00007f91`e65e8ef0 00000000`00401c05     App6!procF+0xb

Unable to get thread data for thread 1
   1  Id: 125f.1263 Suspend: 0 Teb: 00000000`00000000 Unfrozen
 # Child-SP          RetAddr               Call Site
00 00007f91`e55e4d10 00000000`00441a3a     App6!nanosleep+0x40

Unable to get thread data for thread 2
   2  Id: 125f.1261 Suspend: 0 Teb: 00000000`00000000 Unfrozen
 # Child-SP          RetAddr               Call Site
00 00007f91`e65e6d10 00000000`00441a3a     App6!nanosleep+0x40

Unable to get thread data for thread 3
   3  Id: 125f.125f Suspend: 0 Teb: 00000000`00000000 Unfrozen
 # Child-SP          RetAddr               Call Site
00 00007ffc`ec97d240 00000000`00441a3a     App6!nanosleep+0x40

Unable to get thread data for thread 4
   4  Id: 125f.1262 Suspend: 0 Teb: 00000000`00000000 Unfrozen
 # Child-SP          RetAddr               Call Site
00 00007f91`e5de5d10 00000000`00441a3a     App6!nanosleep+0x40

Unable to get thread data for thread 5
   5  Id: 125f.1264 Suspend: 0 Teb: 00000000`00000000 Unfrozen
 # Child-SP          RetAddr               Call Site
00 00007f91`e4de3d10 00000000`00441a3a     App6!nanosleep+0x40
```

6. If we try to print the problem stack trace, we get 256 frames before stopping:

```
0:000> .kframes ff
Default stack trace depth is 0n255 frames

0:000> k
 # Child-SP          RetAddr               Call Site
00 00007f91`e65e8ef0 00000000`00401c05     App6!procF+0xb
01 00007f91`e65e9110 00000000`00401c05     App6!procF+0x58
02 00007f91`e65e9330 00000000`00401c05     App6!procF+0x58
03 00007f91`e65e9550 00000000`00401c05     App6!procF+0x58
```

```
...
...
...
f3 00007f91`e6609350 00000000`00401c05      App6!procF+0x58
f4 00007f91`e6609570 00000000`00401c05      App6!procF+0x58
f5 00007f91`e6609790 00000000`00401c05      App6!procF+0x58
f6 00007f91`e66099b0 00000000`00401c05      App6!procF+0x58
f7 00007f91`e6609bd0 00000000`00401c05      App6!procF+0x58
f8 00007f91`e6609df0 00000000`00401c05      App6!procF+0x58
f9 00007f91`e660a010 00000000`00401c05      App6!procF+0x58
fa 00007f91`e660a230 00000000`00401c05      App6!procF+0x58
fb 00007f91`e660a450 00000000`00401c05      App6!procF+0x58
fc 00007f91`e660a670 00000000`00401c05      App6!procF+0x58
fd 00007f91`e660a890 00000000`00401c05      App6!procF+0x58
fe 00007f91`e660aab0 00000000`00401c05      App6!procF+0x58
```

Note: We don't see that start frames, and it looks like a stack overflow.

7. Check if this is a stack overflow indeed. The stack region can be identified from *App6.pmap.4703* from the thread number. Since the problem thread has TID=PID+1 (Id: 125f.1260), it should be located just below the main stack region:

```
4703:   ./App6
0000000000400000       4K r---- App6
0000000000401000     592K r-x-- App6
0000000000495000     156K r---- App6
00000000004bd000      24K rw--- App6
00000000004c3000      24K rw---   [ anon ]
0000000000ec2000     140K rw---   [ anon ]
00007f91e45e4000       4K -----   [ anon ]
00007f91e45e5000    8192K rw---   [ anon ]
00007f91e4de5000       4K -----   [ anon ]
00007f91e4de6000    8192K rw---   [ anon ]
00007f91e55e6000       4K -----   [ anon ]
00007f91e55e7000    8192K rw---   [ anon ]
00007f91e5de7000       4K -----   [ anon ]
00007f91e5de8000    8192K rw---   [ anon ]
00007f91e65e8000       4K -----   [ anon ]
00007f91e65e9000    8192K rw---   [ anon ]
00007ffcec95d000     132K rw---   [ stack ]
00007ffcec9a9000      16K r----   [ anon ]
00007ffcec9ad000       4K r-x--   [ anon ]
 total             42072K
```

8. Check that manually based on the stack pointer value and section boundary addresses:

```
0:000> r rsp
rsp=00007f91e65e8ef0

0:000> dp rsp
00007f91`e65e8ef0  ????????`???????? ????????`????????
00007f91`e65e8f00  ????????`???????? ????????`????????
00007f91`e65e8f10  ????????`???????? ????????`????????
00007f91`e65e8f20  ????????`???????? ????????`????????
00007f91`e65e8f30  ????????`???????? ????????`????????
00007f91`e65e8f40  ????????`???????? ????????`????????
00007f91`e65e8f50  ????????`???????? ????????`????????
00007f91`e65e8f60  ????????`???????? ????????`????????
```

```
0:000> .frame /c 1
01 00007f91`e65e9110 00000000`00401c05     App6!procF+0x58
rax=0000000000003c34 rbx=0000000000000000 rcx=0000000000000000
rdx=00007f91e65e9120 rsi=00007f91e6de7d40 rdi=0000000000003c34
rip=0000000000401c05 rsp=00007f91e65e9110 rbp=00007f91e65e9320
 r8=00007f91e6de8700  r9=00007f91e6de8700 r10=00007f91e6de89d0
r11=0000000000000000 r12=00007ffcec97d22e r13=00007ffcec97d22f
r14=00007f91e6de8700 r15=0000000000000000
iopl=0         nv up ei pl nz na po nc
cs=0033  ss=002b  ds=0000  es=0000  fs=0000  gs=0000             efl=00010206
App6!procF+0x58:
00000000`00401c05 nop
```

```
0:000> r rsp
Last set context:
rsp=00007f91e65e9110
```

```
0:000> dp rsp
00007f91`e65e9110  00000000`00000000 00003c33`00000000
00007f91`e65e9120  00000000`ffffffff 00000000`00003c34
00007f91`e65e9130  00000000`ffffffff 00000000`00000000
00007f91`e65e9140  00000000`00000000 00000000`00000000
00007f91`e65e9150  00000000`00000000 00000000`00000000
00007f91`e65e9160  00000000`00000000 00000000`00000000
00007f91`e65e9170  00000000`00000000 00000000`00000000
00007f91`e65e9180  00000000`00000000 00000000`00000000
```

```
0:000> !address

Mapping file section regions...
Mapping module regions...
Mapping heap regions...

        BaseAddress      EndAddress+1        RegionSize     Type       State                 Protect             Usage
--------------------------------------------------------------------------------------------------------------------------
+        0`00000000        0`00400000        0`00400000                                                      <unknown>
+        0`00400000        0`00401000        0`00001000 MEM_PRIVATE MEM_COMMIT  PAGE_READONLY                Image      [App6; "/home/coredump/ALCDA2/x64/App6/App6"]
+        0`00401000        0`004bd000        0`000bc000                                                      Image      [App6; "/home/coredump/ALCDA2/x64/App6/App6"]
+        0`004bd000        0`004c3000        0`00006000 MEM_PRIVATE MEM_COMMIT  PAGE_READWRITE               Image      [App6; "/home/coredump/ALCDA2/x64/App6/App6"]
+        0`004c3000        0`004c9000        0`00006000 MEM_PRIVATE MEM_COMMIT  PAGE_READWRITE               <unknown>  [................]
+        0`004c9000        0`00ec2000        0`009f9000                                                      <unknown>
+        0`00ec2000        0`00ee5000        0`00023000 MEM_PRIVATE MEM_COMMIT  PAGE_READWRITE               <unknown>  [................]
+        0`00ee5000     7f91`e45e5000     7f91`e3700000                                                      <unknown>
+     7f91`e45e5000     7f91`e4de5000        0`00800000 MEM_PRIVATE MEM_COMMIT  PAGE_READWRITE               <unknown>  [................]
+     7f91`e4de5000     7f91`e4de6000        0`00001000                                                      <unknown>
+     7f91`e4de6000     7f91`e55e6000        0`00800000 MEM_PRIVATE MEM_COMMIT  PAGE_READWRITE               <unknown>  [................]
+     7f91`e55e6000     7f91`e55e7000        0`00001000                                                      <unknown>
+     7f91`e55e7000     7f91`e5de7000        0`00800000 MEM_PRIVATE MEM_COMMIT  PAGE_READWRITE               <unknown>  [................]
+     7f91`e5de7000     7f91`e5de8000        0`00001000                                                      <unknown>
+     7f91`e5de8000     7f91`e65e8000        0`00800000 MEM_PRIVATE MEM_COMMIT  PAGE_READWRITE               <unknown>  [................]
+     7f91`e65e8000     7f91`e65e9000        0`00001000                                                      <unknown>
+     7f91`e65e9000     7f91`e6de9000        0`00800000 MEM_PRIVATE MEM_COMMIT  PAGE_READWRITE               <unknown>  [................]
+     7f91`e6de9000     7ffc`ec95d000       6b`05b74000                                                      <unknown>
+     7ffc`ec95d000     7ffc`ec97e000        0`00021000 MEM_PRIVATE MEM_COMMIT  PAGE_READWRITE               <unknown>  [................]
+     7ffc`ec97e000     7ffc`ec9a9000        0`0002b000                                                      <unknown>
+     7ffc`ec9a9000     7ffc`ec9ad000        0`00004000 MEM_PRIVATE MEM_COMMIT  PAGE_READONLY                <unknown>  [................]
+     7ffc`ec9ad000     7ffc`ec9ae000        0`00001000 MEM_PRIVATE MEM_COMMIT  PAGE_EXECUTE_READ            Image      [linux_vdso_so; "linux-vdso.so.1"]
```

9. Dump the bottom of the raw stack with symbols to see execution residue, such as thread startup:

```
0:000> dps 7f91`e6de9000-2000 7f91`e6de9000
00007f91`e6de7000  00000000`00000000
00007f91`e6de7008  00000000`00000000
00007f91`e6de7010  00000000`00000000
00007f91`e6de7018  00000000`00000000
00007f91`e6de7020  00000000`00000000
00007f91`e6de7028  00000000`00000000
00007f91`e6de7030  00000000`00000000
00007f91`e6de7038  00000000`00000000
00007f91`e6de7040  00000000`00000000
00007f91`e6de7048  00000000`00000000
00007f91`e6de7050  00000000`00000000
```

```
00007f91`e6de7058  00000000`00000000
00007f91`e6de7060  00000000`00000000
00007f91`e6de7068  00000000`00000000
00007f91`e6de7070  00000000`00000000
00007f91`e6de7078  00000000`00000000
00007f91`e6de7080  00000000`00000000
00007f91`e6de7088  00000000`00000000
00007f91`e6de7090  00000000`00000000
00007f91`e6de7098  00000000`00000000
00007f91`e6de70a0  00007f91`e6de72c0
00007f91`e6de70a8  00000000`00401c05 App6!procF+0x58
00007f91`e6de70b0  00000000`00000000
00007f91`e6de70b8  00000006`00000000
00007f91`e6de70c0  00000000`ffffffff
00007f91`e6de70c8  00000000`00000007
00007f91`e6de70d0  00000000`ffffffff
00007f91`e6de70d8  00000000`00000000
00007f91`e6de70e0  00000000`00000000
00007f91`e6de70e8  00000000`00000000
00007f91`e6de70f0  00000000`00000000
00007f91`e6de70f8  00000000`00000000
00007f91`e6de7100  00000000`00000000
00007f91`e6de7108  00000000`00000000
00007f91`e6de7110  00000000`00000000
00007f91`e6de7118  00000000`00000000
00007f91`e6de7120  00000000`00000000
00007f91`e6de7128  00000000`00000000
00007f91`e6de7130  00000000`00000000
00007f91`e6de7138  00000000`00000000
00007f91`e6de7140  00000000`00000000
00007f91`e6de7148  00000000`00000000
00007f91`e6de7150  00000000`00000000
00007f91`e6de7158  00000000`00000000
00007f91`e6de7160  00000000`00000000
00007f91`e6de7168  00000000`00000000
00007f91`e6de7170  00000000`00000000
00007f91`e6de7178  00000000`00000000
00007f91`e6de7180  00000000`00000000
00007f91`e6de7188  00000000`00000000
00007f91`e6de7190  00000000`00000000
00007f91`e6de7198  00000000`00000000
00007f91`e6de71a0  00000000`00000000
00007f91`e6de71a8  00000000`00000000
00007f91`e6de71b0  00000000`00000000
00007f91`e6de71b8  00000000`00000000
00007f91`e6de71c0  00000000`00000000
00007f91`e6de71c8  00000000`00000000
00007f91`e6de71d0  00000000`00000000
00007f91`e6de71d8  00000000`00000000
00007f91`e6de71e0  00000000`00000000
00007f91`e6de71e8  00000000`00000000
00007f91`e6de71f0  00000000`00000000
00007f91`e6de71f8  00000000`00000000
00007f91`e6de7200  00000000`00000000
00007f91`e6de7208  00000000`00000000
00007f91`e6de7210  00000000`00000000
00007f91`e6de7218  00000000`00000000
00007f91`e6de7220  00000000`00000000
00007f91`e6de7228  00000000`00000000
00007f91`e6de7230  00000000`00000000
```

```
00007f91`e6de7238  00000000`00000000
00007f91`e6de7240  00000000`00000000
00007f91`e6de7248  00000000`00000000
00007f91`e6de7250  00000000`00000000
00007f91`e6de7258  00000000`00000000
00007f91`e6de7260  00000000`00000000
00007f91`e6de7268  00000000`00000000
00007f91`e6de7270  00000000`00000000
00007f91`e6de7278  00000000`00000000
00007f91`e6de7280  00000000`00000000
00007f91`e6de7288  00000000`00000000
00007f91`e6de7290  00000000`00000000
00007f91`e6de7298  00000000`00000000
00007f91`e6de72a0  00000000`00000000
00007f91`e6de72a8  00000000`00000000
00007f91`e6de72b0  00000000`00000000
00007f91`e6de72b8  00000000`00000000
00007f91`e6de72c0  00007f91`e6de74e0
00007f91`e6de72c8  00000000`00401c05 App6!procF+0x58
00007f91`e6de72d0  00000000`00000000
00007f91`e6de72d8  00000005`00000000
00007f91`e6de72e0  00000000`ffffffff
00007f91`e6de72e8  00000000`00000006
00007f91`e6de72f0  00000000`ffffffff
00007f91`e6de72f8  00000000`00000000
00007f91`e6de7300  00000000`00000000
00007f91`e6de7308  00000000`00000000
00007f91`e6de7310  00000000`00000000
00007f91`e6de7318  00000000`00000000
00007f91`e6de7320  00000000`00000000
00007f91`e6de7328  00000000`00000000
00007f91`e6de7330  00000000`00000000
00007f91`e6de7338  00000000`00000000
00007f91`e6de7340  00000000`00000000
00007f91`e6de7348  00000000`00000000
00007f91`e6de7350  00000000`00000000
00007f91`e6de7358  00000000`00000000
00007f91`e6de7360  00000000`00000000
00007f91`e6de7368  00000000`00000000
00007f91`e6de7370  00000000`00000000
00007f91`e6de7378  00000000`00000000
00007f91`e6de7380  00000000`00000000
00007f91`e6de7388  00000000`00000000
00007f91`e6de7390  00000000`00000000
00007f91`e6de7398  00000000`00000000
00007f91`e6de73a0  00000000`00000000
00007f91`e6de73a8  00000000`00000000
00007f91`e6de73b0  00000000`00000000
00007f91`e6de73b8  00000000`00000000
00007f91`e6de73c0  00000000`00000000
00007f91`e6de73c8  00000000`00000000
00007f91`e6de73d0  00000000`00000000
00007f91`e6de73d8  00000000`00000000
00007f91`e6de73e0  00000000`00000000
00007f91`e6de73e8  00000000`00000000
00007f91`e6de73f0  00000000`00000000
00007f91`e6de73f8  00000000`00000000
00007f91`e6de7400  00000000`00000000
00007f91`e6de7408  00000000`00000000
00007f91`e6de7410  00000000`00000000
```

```
00007f91`e6de7418  00000000`00000000
00007f91`e6de7420  00000000`00000000
00007f91`e6de7428  00000000`00000000
00007f91`e6de7430  00000000`00000000
00007f91`e6de7438  00000000`00000000
00007f91`e6de7440  00000000`00000000
00007f91`e6de7448  00000000`00000000
00007f91`e6de7450  00000000`00000000
00007f91`e6de7458  00000000`00000000
00007f91`e6de7460  00000000`00000000
00007f91`e6de7468  00000000`00000000
00007f91`e6de7470  00000000`00000000
00007f91`e6de7478  00000000`00000000
00007f91`e6de7480  00000000`00000000
00007f91`e6de7488  00000000`00000000
00007f91`e6de7490  00000000`00000000
00007f91`e6de7498  00000000`00000000
00007f91`e6de74a0  00000000`00000000
00007f91`e6de74a8  00000000`00000000
00007f91`e6de74b0  00000000`00000000
00007f91`e6de74b8  00000000`00000000
00007f91`e6de74c0  00000000`00000000
00007f91`e6de74c8  00000000`00000000
00007f91`e6de74d0  00000000`00000000
00007f91`e6de74d8  00000000`00000000
00007f91`e6de74e0  00007f91`e6de7700
00007f91`e6de74e8  00000000`00401c05 App6!procF+0x58
00007f91`e6de74f0  00000000`00000000
00007f91`e6de74f8  00000004`00000000
00007f91`e6de7500  00000000`ffffffff
00007f91`e6de7508  00000000`00000005
00007f91`e6de7510  00000000`ffffffff
00007f91`e6de7518  00000000`00000000
00007f91`e6de7520  00000000`00000000
00007f91`e6de7528  00000000`00000000
00007f91`e6de7530  00000000`00000000
00007f91`e6de7538  00000000`00000000
00007f91`e6de7540  00000000`00000000
00007f91`e6de7548  00000000`00000000
00007f91`e6de7550  00000000`00000000
00007f91`e6de7558  00000000`00000000
00007f91`e6de7560  00000000`00000000
00007f91`e6de7568  00000000`00000000
00007f91`e6de7570  00000000`00000000
00007f91`e6de7578  00000000`00000000
00007f91`e6de7580  00000000`00000000
00007f91`e6de7588  00000000`00000000
00007f91`e6de7590  00000000`00000000
00007f91`e6de7598  00000000`00000000
00007f91`e6de75a0  00000000`00000000
00007f91`e6de75a8  00000000`00000000
00007f91`e6de75b0  00000000`00000000
00007f91`e6de75b8  00000000`00000000
00007f91`e6de75c0  00000000`00000000
00007f91`e6de75c8  00000000`00000000
00007f91`e6de75d0  00000000`00000000
00007f91`e6de75d8  00000000`00000000
00007f91`e6de75e0  00000000`00000000
00007f91`e6de75e8  00000000`00000000
00007f91`e6de75f0  00000000`00000000
```

```
00007f91`e6de75f8  00000000`00000000
00007f91`e6de7600  00000000`00000000
00007f91`e6de7608  00000000`00000000
00007f91`e6de7610  00000000`00000000
00007f91`e6de7618  00000000`00000000
00007f91`e6de7620  00000000`00000000
00007f91`e6de7628  00000000`00000000
00007f91`e6de7630  00000000`00000000
00007f91`e6de7638  00000000`00000000
00007f91`e6de7640  00000000`00000000
00007f91`e6de7648  00000000`00000000
00007f91`e6de7650  00000000`00000000
00007f91`e6de7658  00000000`00000000
00007f91`e6de7660  00000000`00000000
00007f91`e6de7668  00000000`00000000
00007f91`e6de7670  00000000`00000000
00007f91`e6de7678  00000000`00000000
00007f91`e6de7680  00000000`00000000
00007f91`e6de7688  00000000`00000000
00007f91`e6de7690  00000000`00000000
00007f91`e6de7698  00000000`00000000
00007f91`e6de76a0  00000000`00000000
00007f91`e6de76a8  00000000`00000000
00007f91`e6de76b0  00000000`00000000
00007f91`e6de76b8  00000000`00000000
00007f91`e6de76c0  00000000`00000000
00007f91`e6de76c8  00000000`00000000
00007f91`e6de76d0  00000000`00000000
00007f91`e6de76d8  00000000`00000000
00007f91`e6de76e0  00000000`00000000
00007f91`e6de76e8  00000000`00000000
00007f91`e6de76f0  00000000`00000000
00007f91`e6de76f8  00000000`00000000
00007f91`e6de7700  00007f91`e6de7920
00007f91`e6de7708  00000000`00401c05 App6!procF+0x58
00007f91`e6de7710  00000000`00000000
00007f91`e6de7718  00000003`00000000
00007f91`e6de7720  00000000`ffffffff
00007f91`e6de7728  00000000`00000004
00007f91`e6de7730  00000000`ffffffff
00007f91`e6de7738  00000000`00000000
00007f91`e6de7740  00000000`00000000
00007f91`e6de7748  00000000`00000000
00007f91`e6de7750  00000000`00000000
00007f91`e6de7758  00000000`00000000
00007f91`e6de7760  00000000`00000000
00007f91`e6de7768  00000000`00000000
00007f91`e6de7770  00000000`00000000
00007f91`e6de7778  00000000`00000000
00007f91`e6de7780  00000000`00000000
00007f91`e6de7788  00000000`00000000
00007f91`e6de7790  00000000`00000000
00007f91`e6de7798  00000000`00000000
00007f91`e6de77a0  00000000`00000000
00007f91`e6de77a8  00000000`00000000
00007f91`e6de77b0  00000000`00000000
00007f91`e6de77b8  00000000`00000000
00007f91`e6de77c0  00000000`00000000
00007f91`e6de77c8  00000000`00000000
00007f91`e6de77d0  00000000`00000000
```

```
00007f91`e6de77d8  00000000`00000000
00007f91`e6de77e0  00000000`00000000
00007f91`e6de77e8  00000000`00000000
00007f91`e6de77f0  00000000`00000000
00007f91`e6de77f8  00000000`00000000
00007f91`e6de7800  00000000`00000000
00007f91`e6de7808  00000000`00000000
00007f91`e6de7810  00000000`00000000
00007f91`e6de7818  00000000`00000000
00007f91`e6de7820  00000000`00000000
00007f91`e6de7828  00000000`00000000
00007f91`e6de7830  00000000`00000000
00007f91`e6de7838  00000000`00000000
00007f91`e6de7840  00000000`00000000
00007f91`e6de7848  00000000`00000000
00007f91`e6de7850  00000000`00000000
00007f91`e6de7858  00000000`00000000
00007f91`e6de7860  00000000`00000000
00007f91`e6de7868  00000000`00000000
00007f91`e6de7870  00000000`00000000
00007f91`e6de7878  00000000`00000000
00007f91`e6de7880  00000000`00000000
00007f91`e6de7888  00000000`00000000
00007f91`e6de7890  00000000`00000000
00007f91`e6de7898  00000000`00000000
00007f91`e6de78a0  00000000`00000000
00007f91`e6de78a8  00000000`00000000
00007f91`e6de78b0  00000000`00000000
00007f91`e6de78b8  00000000`00000000
00007f91`e6de78c0  00000000`00000000
00007f91`e6de78c8  00000000`00000000
00007f91`e6de78d0  00000000`00000000
00007f91`e6de78d8  00000000`00000000
00007f91`e6de78e0  00000000`00000000
00007f91`e6de78e8  00000000`00000000
00007f91`e6de78f0  00000000`00000000
00007f91`e6de78f8  00000000`00000000
00007f91`e6de7900  00000000`00000000
00007f91`e6de7908  00000000`00000000
00007f91`e6de7910  00000000`00000000
00007f91`e6de7918  00000000`00000000
00007f91`e6de7920  00007f91`e6de7b40
00007f91`e6de7928  00000000`00401c05 App6!procF+0x58
00007f91`e6de7930  00000000`00000000
00007f91`e6de7938  00000002`00000000
00007f91`e6de7940  00000000`ffffffff
00007f91`e6de7948  00000000`00000003
00007f91`e6de7950  00000000`ffffffff
00007f91`e6de7958  00000000`00000000
00007f91`e6de7960  00000000`00000000
00007f91`e6de7968  00000000`00000000
00007f91`e6de7970  00000000`00000000
00007f91`e6de7978  00000000`00000000
00007f91`e6de7980  00000000`00000000
00007f91`e6de7988  00000000`00000000
00007f91`e6de7990  00000000`00000000
00007f91`e6de7998  00000000`00000000
00007f91`e6de79a0  00000000`00000000
00007f91`e6de79a8  00000000`00000000
00007f91`e6de79b0  00000000`00000000
```

```
00007f91`e6de79b8  00000000`00000000
00007f91`e6de79c0  00000000`00000000
00007f91`e6de79c8  00000000`00000000
00007f91`e6de79d0  00000000`00000000
00007f91`e6de79d8  00000000`00000000
00007f91`e6de79e0  00000000`00000000
00007f91`e6de79e8  00000000`00000000
00007f91`e6de79f0  00000000`00000000
00007f91`e6de79f8  00000000`00000000
00007f91`e6de7a00  00000000`00000000
00007f91`e6de7a08  00000000`00000000
00007f91`e6de7a10  00000000`00000000
00007f91`e6de7a18  00000000`00000000
00007f91`e6de7a20  00000000`00000000
00007f91`e6de7a28  00000000`00000000
00007f91`e6de7a30  00000000`00000000
00007f91`e6de7a38  00000000`00000000
00007f91`e6de7a40  00000000`00000000
00007f91`e6de7a48  00000000`00000000
00007f91`e6de7a50  00000000`00000000
00007f91`e6de7a58  00000000`00000000
00007f91`e6de7a60  00000000`00000000
00007f91`e6de7a68  00000000`00000000
00007f91`e6de7a70  00000000`00000000
00007f91`e6de7a78  00000000`00000000
00007f91`e6de7a80  00000000`00000000
00007f91`e6de7a88  00000000`00000000
00007f91`e6de7a90  00000000`00000000
00007f91`e6de7a98  00000000`00000000
00007f91`e6de7aa0  00000000`00000000
00007f91`e6de7aa8  00000000`00000000
00007f91`e6de7ab0  00000000`00000000
00007f91`e6de7ab8  00000000`00000000
00007f91`e6de7ac0  00000000`00000000
00007f91`e6de7ac8  00000000`00000000
00007f91`e6de7ad0  00000000`00000000
00007f91`e6de7ad8  00000000`00000000
00007f91`e6de7ae0  00000000`00000000
00007f91`e6de7ae8  00000000`00000000
00007f91`e6de7af0  00000000`00000000
00007f91`e6de7af8  00000000`00000000
00007f91`e6de7b00  00000000`00000000
00007f91`e6de7b08  00000000`00000000
00007f91`e6de7b10  00000000`00000000
00007f91`e6de7b18  00000000`00000000
00007f91`e6de7b20  00000000`00000000
00007f91`e6de7b28  00000000`00000000
00007f91`e6de7b30  00000000`00000000
00007f91`e6de7b38  00000000`00000000
00007f91`e6de7b40  00007f91`e6de7d60
00007f91`e6de7b48  00000000`00401c05 App6!procF+0x58
00007f91`e6de7b50  00000000`00000000
00007f91`e6de7b58  00000001`00000000
00007f91`e6de7b60  00000000`ffffffff
00007f91`e6de7b68  00000000`00000002
00007f91`e6de7b70  00000000`ffffffff
00007f91`e6de7b78  00000000`00000000
00007f91`e6de7b80  00000000`00000000
00007f91`e6de7b88  00000000`00000000
00007f91`e6de7b90  00000000`00000000
```

```
00007f91`e6de7b98  00000000`00000000
00007f91`e6de7ba0  00000000`00000000
00007f91`e6de7ba8  00000000`00000000
00007f91`e6de7bb0  00000000`00000000
00007f91`e6de7bb8  00000000`00000000
00007f91`e6de7bc0  00000000`00000000
00007f91`e6de7bc8  00000000`00000000
00007f91`e6de7bd0  00000000`00000000
00007f91`e6de7bd8  00000000`00000000
00007f91`e6de7be0  00000000`00000000
00007f91`e6de7be8  00000000`00000000
00007f91`e6de7bf0  00000000`00000000
00007f91`e6de7bf8  00000000`00000000
00007f91`e6de7c00  00000000`00000000
00007f91`e6de7c08  00000000`00000000
00007f91`e6de7c10  00000000`00000000
00007f91`e6de7c18  00000000`00000000
00007f91`e6de7c20  00000000`00000000
00007f91`e6de7c28  00000000`00000000
00007f91`e6de7c30  00000000`00000000
00007f91`e6de7c38  00000000`00000000
00007f91`e6de7c40  00000000`00000000
00007f91`e6de7c48  00000000`00000000
00007f91`e6de7c50  00000000`00000000
00007f91`e6de7c58  00000000`00000000
00007f91`e6de7c60  00000000`00000000
00007f91`e6de7c68  00000000`00000000
00007f91`e6de7c70  00000000`00000000
00007f91`e6de7c78  00000000`00000000
00007f91`e6de7c80  00000000`00000000
00007f91`e6de7c88  00000000`00000000
00007f91`e6de7c90  00000000`00000000
00007f91`e6de7c98  00000000`00000000
00007f91`e6de7ca0  00000000`00000000
00007f91`e6de7ca8  00000000`00000000
00007f91`e6de7cb0  00000000`00000000
00007f91`e6de7cb8  00000000`00000000
00007f91`e6de7cc0  00000000`00000000
00007f91`e6de7cc8  00000000`00000000
00007f91`e6de7cd0  00000000`00000000
00007f91`e6de7cd8  00000000`00000000
00007f91`e6de7ce0  00000000`00000000
00007f91`e6de7ce8  00000000`00000000
00007f91`e6de7cf0  00000000`00000000
00007f91`e6de7cf8  00000000`00000000
00007f91`e6de7d00  00000000`00000000
00007f91`e6de7d08  00000000`00000000
00007f91`e6de7d10  00000000`00000000
00007f91`e6de7d18  00000000`00000000
00007f91`e6de7d20  00000000`00000000
00007f91`e6de7d28  00000000`00000000
00007f91`e6de7d30  00000000`00000000
00007f91`e6de7d38  00000000`00000000
00007f91`e6de7d40  00000000`00000000
00007f91`e6de7d48  00000000`00000000
00007f91`e6de7d50  00000000`00000000
00007f91`e6de7d58  00000000`00000000
00007f91`e6de7d60  00007f91`e6de7d70
00007f91`e6de7d68  00000000`00401c16 App6!procE+0xe
00007f91`e6de7d70  00007f91`e6de7d80
```

```
00007f91`e6de7d78  00000000`00401c31 App6!bar_one+0x18
00007f91`e6de7d80  00007f91`e6de7d90
00007f91`e6de7d88  00000000`00401c42 App6!foo_one+0xe
00007f91`e6de7d90  00007f91`e6de7db0
00007f91`e6de7d98  00000000`00401c5b App6!thread_one+0x16
00007f91`e6de7da0  00000000`00000000
00007f91`e6de7da8  00000000`00000000
00007f91`e6de7db0  00000000`00000000
00007f91`e6de7db8  00000000`00403173 App6!start_thread+0xf3 [/build/glibc-vjB4T1/glibc-
2.28/nptl/pthread_create.c @ 487]
00007f91`e6de7dc0  00000000`00000000
...
...
...
00007f91`e6de8ff8  00000000`00000000
00007f91`e6de9000  ????????`????????
```

10. See that the reconstruction of the stack trace is possible because of the standard function prologue and epilogue:

```
[...]
00007f91`e6de7920  00007f91`e6de7b40
00007f91`e6de7928  00000000`00401c05 App6!procF+0x58
00007f91`e6de7b40  00007f91`e6de7d60
00007f91`e6de7b48  00000000`00401c05 App6!procF+0x58
00007f91`e6de7d60  00007f91`e6de7d70
00007f91`e6de7d68  00000000`00401c16 App6!procE+0xe
00007f91`e6de7d70  00007f91`e6de7d80
00007f91`e6de7d78  00000000`00401c31 App6!bar_one+0x18
00007f91`e6de7d80  00007f91`e6de7d90
00007f91`e6de7d88  00000000`00401c42 App6!foo_one+0xe
00007f91`e6de7d90  00007f91`e6de7db0
00007f91`e6de7d98  00000000`00401c5b App6!thread_one+0x16
00007f91`e6de7da0  00000000`00000000
00007f91`e6de7da8  00000000`00000000
00007f91`e6de7db0  00000000`00000000
00007f91`e6de7db8  00000000`00403173 App6!start_thread+0xf3

0:000> uf procF
App6!procF:
00000000`00401bad push    rbp
00000000`00401bae mov     rbp,rsp
00000000`00401bb1 sub     rsp,210h
00000000`00401bb8 mov     dword ptr [rbp-204h],edi
00000000`00401bbe lea     rdx,[rbp-200h]
00000000`00401bc5 mov     eax,0
00000000`00401bca mov     ecx,40h
00000000`00401bcf mov     rdi,rdx
00000000`00401bd2 rep stos qword ptr [rdi]
00000000`00401bd5 mov     dword ptr [rbp-200h],0FFFFFFFFh
00000000`00401bdf mov     eax,dword ptr [rbp-204h]
00000000`00401be5 add     eax,1
00000000`00401be8 mov     dword ptr [rbp-1F8h],eax
00000000`00401bee mov     dword ptr [rbp-1F0h],0FFFFFFFFh
00000000`00401bf8 mov     eax,dword ptr [rbp-1F8h]
00000000`00401bfe mov     edi,eax
00000000`00401c00 call    App6!procF (00000000`00401bad)
00000000`00401c05 nop
00000000`00401c06 leave
00000000`00401c07 ret
```

Note: The *leaveq* CPU instruction in the epilog reverses the effect of the two prolog instructions, *push* and *mov*.

11. To see the bottom of the stack trace, we can increase the default number of frames:

```
0:000> .kframes 0xffff
Default stack trace depth is 0n65535 frames

0:000> kL
  *** Stack trace for last set context - .thread/.cxr resets it
 # Child-SP          RetAddr               Call Site
01 00007f91`e65e9110 00000000`00401c05     App6!procF+0x58
02 00007f91`e65e9330 00000000`00401c05     App6!procF+0x58
03 00007f91`e65e9550 00000000`00401c05     App6!procF+0x58
04 00007f91`e65e9770 00000000`00401c05     App6!procF+0x58
05 00007f91`e65e9990 00000000`00401c05     App6!procF+0x58
06 00007f91`e65e9bb0 00000000`00401c05     App6!procF+0x58
07 00007f91`e65e9dd0 00000000`00401c05     App6!procF+0x58
08 00007f91`e65e9ff0 00000000`00401c05     App6!procF+0x58
09 00007f91`e65ea210 00000000`00401c05     App6!procF+0x58
0a 00007f91`e65ea430 00000000`00401c05     App6!procF+0x58
0b 00007f91`e65ea650 00000000`00401c05     App6!procF+0x58
0c 00007f91`e65ea870 00000000`00401c05     App6!procF+0x58
0d 00007f91`e65eaa90 00000000`00401c05     App6!procF+0x58
0e 00007f91`e65eacb0 00000000`00401c05     App6!procF+0x58
0f 00007f91`e65eaed0 00000000`00401c05     App6!procF+0x58
10 00007f91`e65eb0f0 00000000`00401c05     App6!procF+0x58
[...]
3c25 00007f91`e6de5d90 00000000`00401c05     App6!procF+0x58
3c26 00007f91`e6de5fb0 00000000`00401c05     App6!procF+0x58
3c27 00007f91`e6de61d0 00000000`00401c05     App6!procF+0x58
3c28 00007f91`e6de63f0 00000000`00401c05     App6!procF+0x58
3c29 00007f91`e6de6610 00000000`00401c05     App6!procF+0x58
3c2a 00007f91`e6de6830 00000000`00401c05     App6!procF+0x58
3c2b 00007f91`e6de6a50 00000000`00401c05     App6!procF+0x58
3c2c 00007f91`e6de6c70 00000000`00401c05     App6!procF+0x58
3c2d 00007f91`e6de6e90 00000000`00401c05     App6!procF+0x58
3c2e 00007f91`e6de70b0 00000000`00401c05     App6!procF+0x58
3c2f 00007f91`e6de72d0 00000000`00401c05     App6!procF+0x58
3c30 00007f91`e6de74f0 00000000`00401c05     App6!procF+0x58
3c31 00007f91`e6de7710 00000000`00401c05     App6!procF+0x58
3c32 00007f91`e6de7930 00000000`00401c05     App6!procF+0x58
3c33 00007f91`e6de7b50 00000000`00401c16     App6!procF+0x58
3c34 00007f91`e6de7d70 00000000`00401c31     App6!procE+0xe
3c35 00007f91`e6de7d80 00000000`00401c42     App6!bar_one+0x18
3c36 00007f91`e6de7d90 00000000`00401c5b     App6!foo_one+0xe
3c37 00007f91`e6de7da0 00000000`00403173     App6!thread_one+0x16
3c38 00007f91`e6de7dc0 00000000`0044430f     App6!start_thread+0xf3
3c39 00007f91`e6de7e80 ffffffff`ffffffff     App6!_clone+0x3f
3c3a 00007f91`e6de7e88 00000000`00000000     0xffffffff`ffffffff
```

9. We close logging before exiting WinDbg:

```
0:000> .logclose
Closing open log file 'C:\ALCDA2\x64\App6\App6-WinDbg.log'
```

Exercise A6 (A64, WinDbg)

Goal: Learn how to identify stack overflow, stack boundaries, reconstruct stack trace.

Patterns: Stack Overflow (User Mode).

1. Launch WinDbg Preview.

2. Load the *core.19393* dump file from the A64\App6 folder:

```
Microsoft (R) Windows Debugger Version 10.0.27725.1000 AMD64
Copyright (c) Microsoft Corporation. All rights reserved.


Loading Dump File [C:\ALCDA2\A64\App6\core.19393]
64-bit machine not using 64-bit API

************* Path validation summary **************
Response                         Time (ms)     Location
Deferred                                       srv*
Symbol search path is: srv*
Executable search path is:
Generic Unix Version 0 UP Free ARM 64-bit (AArch64)
System Uptime: not available
Process Uptime: not available
..
(4bc1.4bc2): Signal SIGSEGV (Segmentation fault) code SEGV_ACCERR (Invalid permissions for
mapped object) at 0xffff6a60fff0
*** WARNING: Unable to verify timestamp for App6
App6+0x31ec:
00000000`004031ec stp         fp,lr,[sp,#-0x10]!
```

3. Set logging to a file in case of lengthy output from some commands:

```
0:000> .logopen C:\ALCDA2\A64\App6\App6-WinDbg.log
Opened log file 'C:\ALCDA2\A64\App6\App6-WinDbg.log'
```

4. Specify the dump folder as the symbol path and reload symbols:

```
0:000> .symfix; .sympath+ C:\ALCDA2\A64\App6\
Symbol search path is: srv*;C:\ALCDA2\A64\App6\
Expanded Symbol search path is:
cache*;SRV*https://msdl.microsoft.com/download/symbols;c:\alcda2\a64\app6\

************* Path validation summary **************
Response                         Time (ms)     Location
Deferred                                       srv*
OK                                             C:\ALCDA2\A64\App6\
*** WARNING: Unable to verify timestamp for App6
```

```
0:000> .reload
..
*** WARNING: Unable to verify timestamp for App6

************* Symbol Loading Error Summary **************
Module name            Error
App6                   The system cannot find the file specified

You can troubleshoot most symbol related issues by turning on symbol loading diagnostics (!sym
noisy) and repeating the command that caused symbols to be loaded.
You should also verify that your symbol search path (.sympath) is correct.
```

Note: We ignore warnings and errors as they are not relevant for now.

5. List threads:

```
0:000> ~*k 1

Unable to get thread data for thread 0
.  0  Id: 4bc1.4bc2 Suspend: 0 Teb: 00000000`00000000 Unfrozen
 # Child-SP          RetAddr               Call Site
00 0000ffff`6a610000 00000000`00403244     App6!procF+0x4

Unable to get thread data for thread 1
   1  Id: 4bc1.4bc1 Suspend: 0 Teb: 00000000`00000000 Unfrozen
 # Child-SP          RetAddr               Call Site
00 0000ffff`e3b450f0 00000000`00424d74     App6!_libc_nanosleep+0x24

Unable to get thread data for thread 2
   2  Id: 4bc1.4bc6 Suspend: 0 Teb: 00000000`00000000 Unfrozen
 # Child-SP          RetAddr               Call Site
00 0000ffff`68dce5f0 00000000`00424d74     App6!_libc_nanosleep+0x24

Unable to get thread data for thread 3
   3  Id: 4bc1.4bc5 Suspend: 0 Teb: 00000000`00000000 Unfrozen
 # Child-SP          RetAddr               Call Site
00 0000ffff`695de5f0 00000000`00424d74     App6!_libc_nanosleep+0x24

Unable to get thread data for thread 4
   4  Id: 4bc1.4bc4 Suspend: 0 Teb: 00000000`00000000 Unfrozen
 # Child-SP          RetAddr               Call Site
00 0000ffff`69dee5f0 00000000`00424d74     App6!_libc_nanosleep+0x28

Unable to get thread data for thread 5
   5  Id: 4bc1.4bc3 Suspend: 0 Teb: 00000000`00000000 Unfrozen
 # Child-SP          RetAddr               Call Site
00 0000ffff`6a5fe5f0 00000000`00424d74     App6!_libc_nanosleep+0x24
```

6. If we try to print the problem stack trace, we get 256 frames before stopping:

```
0:000> .kframes ff
Default stack trace depth is 0n255 frames

0:000> k
 # Child-SP          RetAddr               Call Site
00 0000ffff`6a610000 00000000`00403244     App6!procF+0x4
01 0000ffff`6a610210 00000000`00403244     App6!procF+0x5c
02 0000ffff`6a610430 00000000`00403244     App6!procF+0x5c
03 0000ffff`6a610650 00000000`00403244     App6!procF+0x5c
```

```
...
...
...
fc 0000ffff`6a631770 00000000`00403244      App6!procF+0x5c
fd 0000ffff`6a631990 00000000`00403244      App6!procF+0x5c
fe 0000ffff`6a631bb0 00000000`00403244      App6!procF+0x5c
ff 0000ffff`6a631dd0 00000000`00403244      App6!procF+0x5c
```

Note: We don't see that start frames, and it looks like a stack overflow.

7. Check if this is a stack overflow indeed. The stack region can be identified from *App6.pmap.19393* from the thread number. Since the problem thread has TID=PID+1 (Id: 4bc1.4bc2), it should be located just below the main stack region:

```
19393:   ./App6
0000000000400000     768K r-x-- App6
00000000004c0000     128K rw--- App6
0000000030aa0000     256K rw---   [ anon ]
0000ffff685c0000      64K -----   [ anon ]
0000ffff685d0000    8192K rw---   [ anon ]
0000ffff68dd0000      64K -----   [ anon ]
0000ffff68de0000    8192K rw---   [ anon ]
0000ffff695e0000      64K -----   [ anon ]
0000ffff695f0000    8192K rw---   [ anon ]
0000ffff69df0000      64K -----   [ anon ]
0000ffff69e00000    8192K rw---   [ anon ]
0000ffff6a600000      64K -----   [ anon ]
0000ffff6a610000    8192K rw---   [ anon ]
0000ffff6ae10000      64K r----   [ anon ]
0000ffff6ae20000      64K r-x--   [ anon ]
0000ffffe3b20000     192K rw---   [ stack ]
 total             42752K
```

8. Check that manually based on the stack pointer value and section boundary addresses:

```
0:000> r sp
sp=0000ffff6a610000

0:000> dp sp - 10
0000ffff`6a60fff0  00000000`00000000 00000000`00000000
0000ffff`6a610000  00000000`00000000 00000000`00000000
0000ffff`6a610010  00000000`00000000 00000000`00000000
0000ffff`6a610020  00000000`00000000 00000000`00000000
0000ffff`6a610030  00000000`00000000 00000000`00000000
0000ffff`6a610040  00000000`00000000 00000000`00000000
0000ffff`6a610050  00000000`00000000 00000000`00000000
0000ffff`6a610060  00000000`00000000 00000000`00000000
```

Note: The stack pointer points to the start of the stack region. The addresses below it should be inaccessible at runtime. However, the committed pages were included in the crash dump, and we see zeroes since WinDbg can read it.

```
0:000> !address

Mapping file section regions...
Mapping module regions...

        BaseAddress      EndAddress+1        RegionSize     Type       State                 Protect             Usage
--------------------------------------------------------------------------------------------------------------------------
+        0`00000000        0`00400000        0`00400000                                                  <unknown>
+        0`00400000        0`00410000        0`00010000 MEM_PRIVATE MEM_COMMIT  PAGE_EXECUTE_READ        Image      [App6; "/home/opc/ALCDA2/App6/App6"]
+        0`00410000        0`004c0000        0`000b0000                                                  Image      [App6; "/home/opc/ALCDA2/App6/App6"]
+        0`004c0000        0`004e0000        0`00020000 MEM_PRIVATE MEM_COMMIT  PAGE_READWRITE           Image      [App6; "/home/opc/ALCDA2/App6/App6"]
+        0`004e0000        0`30aa0000        0`305c0000                                                  <unknown>
+        0`30aa0000        0`30ae0000        0`00040000 MEM_PRIVATE MEM_COMMIT  PAGE_READWRITE           <unknown>  [................]
+        0`30ae0000     ffff`685c0000     ffff`37ae0000                                                  <unknown>
+     ffff`685c0000     ffff`685d0000        0`00010000 MEM_PRIVATE MEM_COMMIT                           <unknown>  [................]
+     ffff`685d0000     ffff`68dd0000        0`00800000 MEM_PRIVATE MEM_COMMIT  PAGE_READWRITE           <unknown>  [................]
+     ffff`68dd0000     ffff`68de0000        0`00010000 MEM_PRIVATE MEM_COMMIT                           <unknown>  [................]
+     ffff`68de0000     ffff`695e0000        0`00800000 MEM_PRIVATE MEM_COMMIT  PAGE_READWRITE           <unknown>  [................]
+     ffff`695e0000     ffff`695f0000        0`00010000 MEM_PRIVATE MEM_COMMIT                           <unknown>  [................]
+     ffff`695f0000     ffff`69df0000        0`00800000 MEM_PRIVATE MEM_COMMIT  PAGE_READWRITE           <unknown>  [................]
+     ffff`69df0000     ffff`69e00000        0`00010000 MEM_PRIVATE MEM_COMMIT                           <unknown>  [................]
+     ffff`69e00000     ffff`6a600000        0`00800000 MEM_PRIVATE MEM_COMMIT  PAGE_READWRITE           <unknown>  [................]
+     ffff`6a600000     ffff`6a610000        0`00010000 MEM_PRIVATE MEM_COMMIT                           <unknown>  [................]
+     ffff`6a610000     ffff`6ae10000        0`00800000 MEM_PRIVATE MEM_COMMIT  PAGE_READWRITE           <unknown>  [................]
+     ffff`6ae10000     ffff`6ae20000        0`00010000 MEM_PRIVATE MEM_COMMIT  PAGE_READONLY            <unknown>  [.S......FH..z...]
+     ffff`6ae20000     ffff`6ae30000        0`00010000 MEM_PRIVATE MEM_COMMIT  PAGE_EXECUTE_READ        Image      [linux_vdso_so; "linux-vdso.so.1"]
+     ffff`6ae30000     ffff`e3b20000        0`78cf0000                                                  <unknown>
+     ffff`e3b20000     ffff`e3b50000        0`00030000 MEM_PRIVATE MEM_COMMIT  PAGE_READWRITE           <unknown>  [................]
```

9. Dump the bottom of the raw stack with symbols to see execution residue, such as thread startup:

```
0:000> dps ffff`6ae10000-2000 ffff`6ae10000
0000ffff`6ae0e000  00000000`00000000
0000ffff`6ae0e008  00000000`00000000
0000ffff`6ae0e010  00000000`00000000
0000ffff`6ae0e018  00000000`00000000
0000ffff`6ae0e020  00000000`00000000
0000ffff`6ae0e028  00000000`00000000
0000ffff`6ae0e030  00000000`00000000
0000ffff`6ae0e038  00000000`00000000
0000ffff`6ae0e040  00000000`00000000
0000ffff`6ae0e048  00000000`00000000
0000ffff`6ae0e050  00000000`00000000
0000ffff`6ae0e058  00000000`00000000
0000ffff`6ae0e060  00000000`00000000
0000ffff`6ae0e068  00000000`00000000
0000ffff`6ae0e070  00000000`00000000
0000ffff`6ae0e078  00000000`00000000
0000ffff`6ae0e080  00000000`00000000
0000ffff`6ae0e088  00000000`00000000
0000ffff`6ae0e090  00000000`00000000
0000ffff`6ae0e098  00000000`00000000
0000ffff`6ae0e0a0  00000000`00000000
0000ffff`6ae0e0a8  00000000`00000000
0000ffff`6ae0e0b0  00000000`00000000
0000ffff`6ae0e0b8  00000000`00000000
0000ffff`6ae0e0c0  00000000`00000000
0000ffff`6ae0e0c8  00000000`00000000
0000ffff`6ae0e0d0  00000000`00000000
0000ffff`6ae0e0d8  00000000`00000000
0000ffff`6ae0e0e0  00000000`00000000
0000ffff`6ae0e0e8  00000000`00000000
0000ffff`6ae0e0f0  00000000`00000000
0000ffff`6ae0e0f8  00000000`00000000
0000ffff`6ae0e100  00000000`00000000
0000ffff`6ae0e108  00000000`00000000
0000ffff`6ae0e110  00000000`00000000
0000ffff`6ae0e118  00000000`00000000
0000ffff`6ae0e120  00000000`00000000
0000ffff`6ae0e128  00000000`00000000
0000ffff`6ae0e130  00000000`00000000
```

```
0000ffff`6ae0e138  00000000`00000000
0000ffff`6ae0e140  00000000`00000000
0000ffff`6ae0e148  00000000`00000000
0000ffff`6ae0e150  00000000`00000000
0000ffff`6ae0e158  00000000`00000000
0000ffff`6ae0e160  00000000`00000000
0000ffff`6ae0e168  00000000`00000000
0000ffff`6ae0e170  00000000`00000000
0000ffff`6ae0e178  00000000`00000000
0000ffff`6ae0e180  00000000`00000000
0000ffff`6ae0e188  00000000`00000000
0000ffff`6ae0e190  00000000`00000000
0000ffff`6ae0e198  00000000`00000000
0000ffff`6ae0e1a0  00000000`00000000
0000ffff`6ae0e1a8  00000000`00000000
0000ffff`6ae0e1b0  0000ffff`6ae0e3d0
0000ffff`6ae0e1b8  00000000`00403244 App6!procF+0x5c
0000ffff`6ae0e1c0  00000000`00000000
0000ffff`6ae0e1c8  00000003`00000000
0000ffff`6ae0e1d0  00000000`ffffffff
0000ffff`6ae0e1d8  00000000`00000004
0000ffff`6ae0e1e0  00000000`ffffffff
0000ffff`6ae0e1e8  00000000`00000000
0000ffff`6ae0e1f0  00000000`00000000
0000ffff`6ae0e1f8  00000000`00000000
0000ffff`6ae0e200  00000000`00000000
0000ffff`6ae0e208  00000000`00000000
0000ffff`6ae0e210  00000000`00000000
0000ffff`6ae0e218  00000000`00000000
0000ffff`6ae0e220  00000000`00000000
0000ffff`6ae0e228  00000000`00000000
0000ffff`6ae0e230  00000000`00000000
0000ffff`6ae0e238  00000000`00000000
0000ffff`6ae0e240  00000000`00000000
0000ffff`6ae0e248  00000000`00000000
0000ffff`6ae0e250  00000000`00000000
0000ffff`6ae0e258  00000000`00000000
0000ffff`6ae0e260  00000000`00000000
0000ffff`6ae0e268  00000000`00000000
0000ffff`6ae0e270  00000000`00000000
0000ffff`6ae0e278  00000000`00000000
0000ffff`6ae0e280  00000000`00000000
0000ffff`6ae0e288  00000000`00000000
0000ffff`6ae0e290  00000000`00000000
0000ffff`6ae0e298  00000000`00000000
0000ffff`6ae0e2a0  00000000`00000000
0000ffff`6ae0e2a8  00000000`00000000
0000ffff`6ae0e2b0  00000000`00000000
0000ffff`6ae0e2b8  00000000`00000000
0000ffff`6ae0e2c0  00000000`00000000
0000ffff`6ae0e2c8  00000000`00000000
0000ffff`6ae0e2d0  00000000`00000000
0000ffff`6ae0e2d8  00000000`00000000
0000ffff`6ae0e2e0  00000000`00000000
0000ffff`6ae0e2e8  00000000`00000000
0000ffff`6ae0e2f0  00000000`00000000
0000ffff`6ae0e2f8  00000000`00000000
0000ffff`6ae0e300  00000000`00000000
0000ffff`6ae0e308  00000000`00000000
0000ffff`6ae0e310  00000000`00000000
```

```
0000ffff`6ae0e318  00000000`00000000
0000ffff`6ae0e320  00000000`00000000
0000ffff`6ae0e328  00000000`00000000
0000ffff`6ae0e330  00000000`00000000
0000ffff`6ae0e338  00000000`00000000
0000ffff`6ae0e340  00000000`00000000
0000ffff`6ae0e348  00000000`00000000
0000ffff`6ae0e350  00000000`00000000
0000ffff`6ae0e358  00000000`00000000
0000ffff`6ae0e360  00000000`00000000
0000ffff`6ae0e368  00000000`00000000
0000ffff`6ae0e370  00000000`00000000
0000ffff`6ae0e378  00000000`00000000
0000ffff`6ae0e380  00000000`00000000
0000ffff`6ae0e388  00000000`00000000
0000ffff`6ae0e390  00000000`00000000
0000ffff`6ae0e398  00000000`00000000
0000ffff`6ae0e3a0  00000000`00000000
0000ffff`6ae0e3a8  00000000`00000000
0000ffff`6ae0e3b0  00000000`00000000
0000ffff`6ae0e3b8  00000000`00000000
0000ffff`6ae0e3c0  00000000`00000000
0000ffff`6ae0e3c8  00000000`00000000
0000ffff`6ae0e3d0  0000ffff`6ae0e5f0
0000ffff`6ae0e3d8  00000000`00403244 App6!procF+0x5c
0000ffff`6ae0e3e0  00000000`00000000
0000ffff`6ae0e3e8  00000002`00000000
0000ffff`6ae0e3f0  00000000`ffffffff
0000ffff`6ae0e3f8  00000000`00000003
0000ffff`6ae0e400  00000000`ffffffff
0000ffff`6ae0e408  00000000`00000000
0000ffff`6ae0e410  00000000`00000000
0000ffff`6ae0e418  00000000`00000000
0000ffff`6ae0e420  00000000`00000000
0000ffff`6ae0e428  00000000`00000000
0000ffff`6ae0e430  00000000`00000000
0000ffff`6ae0e438  00000000`00000000
0000ffff`6ae0e440  00000000`00000000
0000ffff`6ae0e448  00000000`00000000
0000ffff`6ae0e450  00000000`00000000
0000ffff`6ae0e458  00000000`00000000
0000ffff`6ae0e460  00000000`00000000
0000ffff`6ae0e468  00000000`00000000
0000ffff`6ae0e470  00000000`00000000
0000ffff`6ae0e478  00000000`00000000
0000ffff`6ae0e480  00000000`00000000
0000ffff`6ae0e488  00000000`00000000
0000ffff`6ae0e490  00000000`00000000
0000ffff`6ae0e498  00000000`00000000
0000ffff`6ae0e4a0  00000000`00000000
0000ffff`6ae0e4a8  00000000`00000000
0000ffff`6ae0e4b0  00000000`00000000
0000ffff`6ae0e4b8  00000000`00000000
0000ffff`6ae0e4c0  00000000`00000000
0000ffff`6ae0e4c8  00000000`00000000
0000ffff`6ae0e4d0  00000000`00000000
0000ffff`6ae0e4d8  00000000`00000000
0000ffff`6ae0e4e0  00000000`00000000
0000ffff`6ae0e4e8  00000000`00000000
0000ffff`6ae0e4f0  00000000`00000000
```

```
0000ffff`6ae0e4f8  00000000`00000000
0000ffff`6ae0e500  00000000`00000000
0000ffff`6ae0e508  00000000`00000000
0000ffff`6ae0e510  00000000`00000000
0000ffff`6ae0e518  00000000`00000000
0000ffff`6ae0e520  00000000`00000000
0000ffff`6ae0e528  00000000`00000000
0000ffff`6ae0e530  00000000`00000000
0000ffff`6ae0e538  00000000`00000000
0000ffff`6ae0e540  00000000`00000000
0000ffff`6ae0e548  00000000`00000000
0000ffff`6ae0e550  00000000`00000000
0000ffff`6ae0e558  00000000`00000000
0000ffff`6ae0e560  00000000`00000000
0000ffff`6ae0e568  00000000`00000000
0000ffff`6ae0e570  00000000`00000000
0000ffff`6ae0e578  00000000`00000000
0000ffff`6ae0e580  00000000`00000000
0000ffff`6ae0e588  00000000`00000000
0000ffff`6ae0e590  00000000`00000000
0000ffff`6ae0e598  00000000`00000000
0000ffff`6ae0e5a0  00000000`00000000
0000ffff`6ae0e5a8  00000000`00000000
0000ffff`6ae0e5b0  00000000`00000000
0000ffff`6ae0e5b8  00000000`00000000
0000ffff`6ae0e5c0  00000000`00000000
0000ffff`6ae0e5c8  00000000`00000000
0000ffff`6ae0e5d0  00000000`00000000
0000ffff`6ae0e5d8  00000000`00000000
0000ffff`6ae0e5e0  00000000`00000000
0000ffff`6ae0e5e8  00000000`00000000
0000ffff`6ae0e5f0  0000ffff`6ae0e810
0000ffff`6ae0e5f8  00000000`00403260 App6!procE+0x10
0000ffff`6ae0e600  0000ffff`6ae0e670
0000ffff`6ae0e608  00000001`00000000
0000ffff`6ae0e610  00000000`ffffffff
0000ffff`6ae0e618  00000000`00000002
0000ffff`6ae0e620  00000000`ffffffff
0000ffff`6ae0e628  00000000`00000000
0000ffff`6ae0e630  00000000`00000000
0000ffff`6ae0e638  00000000`00000000
0000ffff`6ae0e640  00000000`00000000
0000ffff`6ae0e648  00000000`00000000
0000ffff`6ae0e650  00000000`00000000
0000ffff`6ae0e658  00000000`00000000
0000ffff`6ae0e660  00000000`00000000
0000ffff`6ae0e668  00000000`00000000
0000ffff`6ae0e670  00000000`00000000
0000ffff`6ae0e678  00000000`00000000
0000ffff`6ae0e680  00000000`00000000
0000ffff`6ae0e688  00000000`00000000
0000ffff`6ae0e690  00000000`00000000
0000ffff`6ae0e698  00000000`00000000
0000ffff`6ae0e6a0  00000000`00000000
0000ffff`6ae0e6a8  00000000`00000000
0000ffff`6ae0e6b0  00000000`00000000
0000ffff`6ae0e6b8  00000000`00000000
0000ffff`6ae0e6c0  00000000`00000000
0000ffff`6ae0e6c8  00000000`00000000
0000ffff`6ae0e6d0  00000000`00000000
```

```
0000ffff`6ae0e6d8  00000000`00000000
0000ffff`6ae0e6e0  00000000`00000000
0000ffff`6ae0e6e8  00000000`00000000
0000ffff`6ae0e6f0  00000000`00000000
0000ffff`6ae0e6f8  00000000`00000000
0000ffff`6ae0e700  00000000`00000000
0000ffff`6ae0e708  00000000`00000000
0000ffff`6ae0e710  00000000`00000000
0000ffff`6ae0e718  00000000`00000000
0000ffff`6ae0e720  00000000`00000000
0000ffff`6ae0e728  00000000`00000000
0000ffff`6ae0e730  00000000`00000000
0000ffff`6ae0e738  00000000`00000000
0000ffff`6ae0e740  00000000`00000000
0000ffff`6ae0e748  00000000`00000000
0000ffff`6ae0e750  00000000`00000000
0000ffff`6ae0e758  00000000`00000000
0000ffff`6ae0e760  00000000`00000000
0000ffff`6ae0e768  00000000`00000000
0000ffff`6ae0e770  00000000`00000000
0000ffff`6ae0e778  00000000`00000000
0000ffff`6ae0e780  00000000`00000000
0000ffff`6ae0e788  00000000`00000000
0000ffff`6ae0e790  00000000`00000000
0000ffff`6ae0e798  00000000`00000000
0000ffff`6ae0e7a0  00000000`00000000
0000ffff`6ae0e7a8  00000000`00000000
0000ffff`6ae0e7b0  00000000`00000000
0000ffff`6ae0e7b8  00000000`00000000
0000ffff`6ae0e7c0  00000000`00000000
0000ffff`6ae0e7c8  00000000`00000000
0000ffff`6ae0e7d0  00000000`00000000
0000ffff`6ae0e7d8  00000000`00000000
0000ffff`6ae0e7e0  00000000`00000000
0000ffff`6ae0e7e8  00000000`00000000
0000ffff`6ae0e7f0  00000000`00000000
0000ffff`6ae0e7f8  00000000`00000000
0000ffff`6ae0e800  00000000`00000000
0000ffff`6ae0e808  00000000`00000000
0000ffff`6ae0e810  0000ffff`6ae0e820
0000ffff`6ae0e818  00000000`0040327c App6!bar_one+0x14
0000ffff`6ae0e820  0000ffff`6ae0e830
0000ffff`6ae0e828  00000000`00403290 App6!foo_one+0xc
0000ffff`6ae0e830  0000ffff`6ae0e840
0000ffff`6ae0e838  00000000`004032a8 App6!thread_one+0x10
0000ffff`6ae0e840  0000ffff`6ae0e860
0000ffff`6ae0e848  00000000`00404cd4 App6!start_thread+0xb4
0000ffff`6ae0e850  0000ffff`6ae0f080
0000ffff`6ae0e858  00000000`00000000
0000ffff`6ae0e860  00000000`00000000
0000ffff`6ae0e868  00000000`00429c20 App6!thread_start+0x30
0000ffff`6ae0e870  0000ffff`6ae0f080
0000ffff`6ae0e878  00000000`004d7890 App6!_default_pthread_attr
0000ffff`6ae0e880  00000000`004d0000 App6!+0x18
...
...
...
0000ffff`6ae0fff8  00000000`00000000
0000ffff`6ae10000  00000002`0eca5306
```

10. See that the reconstruction of the stack trace is possible because of the standard function prologue and epilogue:

```
[...]
0000ffff`6ae0e1b0  0000ffff`6ae0e3d0
0000ffff`6ae0e1b8  00000000`00403244 App6!procF+0x5c
0000ffff`6ae0e3d0  0000ffff`6ae0e5f0
0000ffff`6ae0e3d8  00000000`00403244 App6!procF+0x5c
0000ffff`6ae0e5f0  0000ffff`6ae0e810
0000ffff`6ae0e5f8  00000000`00403260 App6!procE+0x10
0000ffff`6ae0e810  0000ffff`6ae0e820
0000ffff`6ae0e818  00000000`0040327c App6!bar_one+0x14
0000ffff`6ae0e820  0000ffff`6ae0e830
0000ffff`6ae0e828  00000000`00403290 App6!foo_one+0xc
0000ffff`6ae0e830  0000ffff`6ae0e840
0000ffff`6ae0e838  00000000`004032a8 App6!thread_one+0x10
0000ffff`6ae0e840  0000ffff`6ae0e860
0000ffff`6ae0e848  00000000`00404cd4 App6!start_thread+0xb4
0000ffff`6ae0e850  0000ffff`6ae0f080
0000ffff`6ae0e858  00000000`00000000
0000ffff`6ae0e860  00000000`00000000
0000ffff`6ae0e868  00000000`00429c20 App6!thread_start+0x30
```

```
0:000> uf procF
App6!procF:
00000000`004031e8 d10843ff sub          sp,sp,#0x210
00000000`004031ec a9bf7bfd stp          fp,lr,[sp,#-0x10]!
00000000`004031f0 910003fd mov          fp,sp
00000000`004031f4 910073a1 add          x1,fp,#0x1C
00000000`004031f8 b9000020 str          w0,[x1]
00000000`004031fc 910083a0 add          x0,fp,#0x20
00000000`00403200 d2804002 mov          x2,#0x200
00000000`00403204 52800001 mov          w1,#0
00000000`00403208 97fff422 bl           App6!+0x20 (00000000`00400290)
00000000`0040320c 910083a0 add          x0,fp,#0x20
00000000`00403210 12800001 mov          w1,#-1
00000000`00403214 b9000001 str          w1,[x0]
00000000`00403218 910073a0 add          x0,fp,#0x1C
00000000`0040321c b9400000 ldr          w0,[x0]
00000000`00403220 11000401 add          w1,w0,#1
00000000`00403224 910083a0 add          x0,fp,#0x20
00000000`00403228 b9000801 str          w1,[x0,#8]
00000000`0040322c 910083a0 add          x0,fp,#0x20
00000000`00403230 12800001 mov          w1,#-1
00000000`00403234 b9001001 str          w1,[x0,#0x10]
00000000`00403238 910083a0 add          x0,fp,#0x20
00000000`0040323c b9400800 ldr          w0,[x0,#8]
00000000`00403240 97ffffea bl           App6!procF (00000000`004031e8)
00000000`00403244 a8c17bfd ldp          fp,lr,[sp],#0x10
00000000`00403248 910843ff add          sp,sp,#0x210
00000000`0040324c d65f03c0 ret
```

11. To see the bottom of the stack trace, we can increase the default number of frames:

```
0:000> .kframes 0xffff
Default stack trace depth is 0n65535 frames
```

```
0:000> k
 # Child-SP          RetAddr           Call Site
00 0000ffff`6a610000 00000000`00403244 App6!procF+0x4
01 0000ffff`6a610210 00000000`00403244 App6!procF+0x5c
02 0000ffff`6a610430 00000000`00403244 App6!procF+0x5c
03 0000ffff`6a610650 00000000`00403244 App6!procF+0x5c
04 0000ffff`6a610870 00000000`00403244 App6!procF+0x5c
05 0000ffff`6a610a90 00000000`00403244 App6!procF+0x5c
06 0000ffff`6a610cb0 00000000`00403244 App6!procF+0x5c
07 0000ffff`6a610ed0 00000000`00403244 App6!procF+0x5c
08 0000ffff`6a6110f0 00000000`00403244 App6!procF+0x5c
09 0000ffff`6a611310 00000000`00403244 App6!procF+0x5c
0a 0000ffff`6a611530 00000000`00403244 App6!procF+0x5c
[...]
3c2e 0000ffff`6ae0e1b0 00000000`00403244  App6!procF+0x5c
3c2f 0000ffff`6ae0e3d0 00000000`00403244  App6!procF+0x5c
3c30 0000ffff`6ae0e5f0 00000000`00403260  App6!procF+0x5c
3c31 0000ffff`6ae0e810 00000000`0040327c  App6!procE+0x10
3c32 0000ffff`6ae0e820 00000000`00403290  App6!bar_one+0x14
3c33 0000ffff`6ae0e830 00000000`004032a8  App6!foo_one+0xc
3c34 0000ffff`6ae0e840 00000000`00404cd4  App6!thread_one+0x10
3c35 0000ffff`6ae0e860 00000000`00429c20  App6!start_thread+0xb4
3c36 0000ffff`6ae0e990 ffffffff`ffffffff  App6!thread_start+0x30
3c37 0000ffff`6ae0e990 00000000`00000000  0xffffffff`ffffffff
```

10. We close logging before exiting WinDbg:

```
0:000> .logclose
Closing open log file 'C:\ALCDA2\A64\App6\App6-WinDbg.log'
```

Mechanisms (Stack Overflow)

Exercise A7

- **Goal:** Learn how to identify active threads
- **Patterns:** Divide by Zero (User Mode, x64); Invalid Pointer (General); Multiple Exceptions (User Mode); Near Exception
- \ALCDA-Dumps\Exercise-A7-x64-GDB.pdf
- \ALCDA-Dumps\Exercise-A7-x64-WinDbg.pdf

Exercise A7 (x64, GDB)

Goal: Learn how to identify active threads.

Patterns: Divide by Zero (User Mode, x64); Invalid Pointer (General); Multiple Exceptions (User Mode); Near Exception.

1. Load the *core.App7* dump file and *App7* executable from the x64/App7 directory:

```
~/ALCDA2/x64/App7$ gdb -c core.App7 -se App7
GNU gdb (Debian 8.2.1-2+b3) 8.2.1
Copyright (C) 2018 Free Software Foundation, Inc.
License GPLv3+: GNU GPL version 3 or later <http://gnu.org/licenses/gpl.html>
This is free software: you are free to change and redistribute it.
There is NO WARRANTY, to the extent permitted by law.
Type "show copying" and "show warranty" for details.
This GDB was configured as "x86_64-linux-gnu".
Type "show configuration" for configuration details.
For bug reporting instructions, please see:
<http://www.gnu.org/software/gdb/bugs/>.
Find the GDB manual and other documentation resources online at:
    <http://www.gnu.org/software/gdb/documentation/>.

For help, type "help".
Type "apropos word" to search for commands related to "word"...
Reading symbols from App7...done.
[New LWP 71]
[New LWP 68]
[New LWP 69]
[New LWP 70]
[New LWP 73]
[New LWP 72]
[Thread debugging using libthread_db enabled]
Using host libthread_db library "/lib/x86_64-linux-gnu/libthread_db.so.1".
Core was generated by `./App7'.
Program terminated with signal SIGFPE, Arithmetic exception.
#0  0x0000000000401c27 in procD ()
[Current thread is 1 (Thread 0x7f64c3075700 (LWP 71))]
```

2. Set logging to a file in case of lengthy output from some commands:

```
(gdb) set logging on App7.log
Copying output to App7.log.
```

3. List and identify the possible problem threads:

```
(gdb) info threads
  Id   Target Id                            Frame
* 1    Thread 0x7f64c3075700 (LWP 71) 0x0000000000401c27 in procD ()
  2    Thread 0x1d10880 (LWP 68)      0x0000000000441bf0 in nanosleep ()
  3    Thread 0x7f64c4077700 (LWP 69) 0x0000000000007265 in ?? ()
  4    Thread 0x7f64c3876700 (LWP 70) 0x0000000000441bf0 in nanosleep ()
  5    Thread 0x7f64c2073700 (LWP 73) 0x0000000000401bb8 in procF ()
  6    Thread 0x7f64c2874700 (LWP 72) 0x0000000000441bf0 in nanosleep ()
```

4. We see there is an arithmetic exception in the current thread. Let's list the stack trace for the current problem thread #1 and identify the problem instruction:

```
(gdb) bt
#0  0x0000000000401c27 in procD ()
#1  0x0000000000401c3f in procC ()
#2  0x0000000000401dfd in bar_three ()
#3  0x0000000000401e0e in foo_three ()
#4  0x0000000000401e27 in thread_three ()
#5  0x00000000004032b3 in start_thread (arg=<optimized out>) at pthread_create.c:486
#6  0x000000000044444f in clone ()
```

```
(gdb) x/i $rip
=> 0x401c27 <procD+14>: idivl  -0x8(%rbp)
```

```
(gdb) info r $rax
rax            0x1                 1
```

```
(gdb) x/w $rbp-0x8
0x7f64c3074d58: 0x00000000
```

5. We also see something abnormal on thread 3. Switch to it and check the currently executing instruction:

```
(gdb) thread 3
[Switching to thread 3 (Thread 0x7f64c4077700 (LWP 69))]
#0  0x0000000000007265 in ?? ()
```

```
(gdb) x/i $rip
=> 0x7265:       Cannot access memory at address 0x7265
```

Note: We see that the current instruction pointer points to an invalid memory address. It can also be considered NULL Pointer (Code) since the address belongs to an inaccessible part of memory to catch NULL pointers. We also see that there can be exceptions on different threads simultaneously.

6. Thread #5 looks active, and we compare the stack pointer with the stack region boundaries since we suspect stack overflow:

```
(gdb) thread 5
[Switching to thread 5 (Thread 0x7f64c2073700 (LWP 73))]
#0  0x0000000000401bb8 in procF () at pthread_create.c:688
688     pthread_create.c: No such file or directory.
```

```
(gdb) bt
#0  0x0000000000401bb8 in procF () at pthread_create.c:688
#1  0x0000000000401c05 in procF () at pthread_create.c:688
#2  0x0000000000401c05 in procF () at pthread_create.c:688
#3  0x0000000000401c05 in procF () at pthread_create.c:688
#4  0x0000000000401c05 in procF () at pthread_create.c:688
#5  0x0000000000401c05 in procF () at pthread_create.c:688
#6  0x0000000000401c05 in procF () at pthread_create.c:688
#7  0x0000000000401c05 in procF () at pthread_create.c:688
#8  0x0000000000401c05 in procF () at pthread_create.c:688
#9  0x0000000000401c05 in procF () at pthread_create.c:688
#10 0x0000000000401c05 in procF () at pthread_create.c:688
#11 0x0000000000401c05 in procF () at pthread_create.c:688
#12 0x0000000000401c05 in procF () at pthread_create.c:688
#13 0x0000000000401c05 in procF () at pthread_create.c:688
#14 0x0000000000401c05 in procF () at pthread_create.c:688
```

```
#15 0x0000000000401c05 in procF () at pthread_create.c:688
#16 0x0000000000401c05 in procF () at pthread_create.c:688
#17 0x0000000000401c05 in procF () at pthread_create.c:688
#18 0x0000000000401c05 in procF () at pthread_create.c:688
#19 0x0000000000401c05 in procF () at pthread_create.c:688
#20 0x0000000000401c05 in procF () at pthread_create.c:688
#21 0x0000000000401c05 in procF () at pthread_create.c:688
#22 0x0000000000401c05 in procF () at pthread_create.c:688
#23 0x0000000000401c05 in procF () at pthread_create.c:688
#24 0x0000000000401c05 in procF () at pthread_create.c:688
#25 0x0000000000401c05 in procF () at pthread_create.c:688
#26 0x0000000000401c05 in procF () at pthread_create.c:688
#27 0x0000000000401c05 in procF () at pthread_create.c:688
#28 0x0000000000401c16 in procE () at pthread_create.c:688
#29 0x0000000000401e8f in bar_five () at pthread_create.c:688
#30 0x0000000000401ea0 in foo_five () at pthread_create.c:688
#31 0x0000000000401eb9 in thread_five () at pthread_create.c:688
#32 0x00000000004032b3 in start_thread (arg=<optimized out>) at pthread_create.c:486
#33 0x000000000044444f in clone ()

(gdb) x/i $rip
=> 0x401bb8 <procF+11>: mov    %edi,-0x1004(%rbp)

(gdb) x/a $rbp-0x1004
0x7f64c20569fc: 0x0

(gdb) disassemble $rip
Dump of assembler code for function procF:
   0x0000000000401bad <+0>:     push   %rbp
   0x0000000000401bae <+1>:     mov    %rsp,%rbp
   0x0000000000401bb1 <+4>:     sub    $0x1010,%rsp
=> 0x0000000000401bb8 <+11>:    mov    %edi,-0x1004(%rbp)
   0x0000000000401bbe <+17>:    lea    -0x1000(%rbp),%rdx
   0x0000000000401bc5 <+24>:    mov    $0x0,%eax
   0x0000000000401bca <+29>:    mov    $0x200,%ecx
   0x0000000000401bcf <+34>:    mov    %rdx,%rdi
   0x0000000000401bd2 <+37>:    rep stos %rax,%es:(%rdi)
   0x0000000000401bd5 <+40>:    movl   $0xffffffff,-0x1000(%rbp)
   0x0000000000401bdf <+50>:    mov    -0x1004(%rbp),%eax
   0x0000000000401be5 <+56>:    add    $0x1,%eax
   0x0000000000401be8 <+59>:    mov    %eax,-0xff8(%rbp)
   0x0000000000401bee <+65>:    movl   $0xffffffff,-0xff0(%rbp)
   0x0000000000401bf8 <+75>:    mov    -0xff8(%rbp),%eax
   0x0000000000401bfe <+81>:    mov    %eax,%edi
   0x0000000000401c00 <+83>:    callq  0x401bad <procF>
   0x0000000000401c05 <+88>:    nop
   0x0000000000401c06 <+89>:    leaveq
   0x0000000000401c07 <+90>:    retq
End of assembler dump.

(gdb) info r $rsp
rsp            0x7f64c20569f0      0x7f64c20569f0

(gdb) maintenance info sections
Exec file:
    `/home/coredump/ALCDA2/x64/App7/App7', file type elf64-x86-64.
 [0]      0x00400200->0x00400220 at 0x00000200: .note.ABI-tag ALLOC LOAD READONLY DATA HAS_CONTENTS
 [1]      0x00400220->0x00400244 at 0x00000220: .note.gnu.build-id ALLOC LOAD READONLY DATA HAS_CONTENTS
 [2]      0x00400248->0x004004d0 at 0x00000248: .rela.plt ALLOC LOAD READONLY DATA HAS_CONTENTS
 [3]      0x00401000->0x00401017 at 0x00001000: .init ALLOC LOAD READONLY CODE HAS_CONTENTS
 [4]      0x00401018->0x004010f0 at 0x00001018: .plt ALLOC LOAD READONLY CODE HAS_CONTENTS
```

```
 [5]      0x004010f0->0x004935b0 at 0x000010f0: .text ALLOC LOAD READONLY CODE HAS_CONTENTS
 [6]      0x004935b0->0x00494157 at 0x000935b0: __libc_freeres_fn ALLOC LOAD READONLY CODE HAS_CONTENTS
 [7]      0x00494158->0x00494161 at 0x00094158: .fini ALLOC LOAD READONLY CODE HAS_CONTENTS
 [8]      0x00495000->0x004af73c at 0x00095000: .rodata ALLOC LOAD READONLY DATA HAS_CONTENTS
 [9]      0x004af740->0x004bbc10 at 0x000af740: .eh_frame ALLOC LOAD READONLY DATA HAS_CONTENTS
 [10]      0x004bbc10->0x004bbcbc at 0x000bbc10: .gcc_except_table ALLOC LOAD READONLY DATA HAS_CONTENTS
 [11]      0x004bd0b0->0x004bd0d8 at 0x000bc0b0: .tdata ALLOC LOAD DATA HAS_CONTENTS
 [12]      0x004bd0d8->0x004bd120 at 0x000bc0d8: .tbss ALLOC
 [13]      0x004bd0d8->0x004bd0e0 at 0x000bc0d8: .preinit_array ALLOC LOAD DATA HAS_CONTENTS
 [14]      0x004bd0e0->0x004bd0f0 at 0x000bc0e0: .init_array ALLOC LOAD DATA HAS_CONTENTS
 [15]      0x004bd0f0->0x004bd100 at 0x000bc0f0: .fini_array ALLOC LOAD DATA HAS_CONTENTS
 [16]      0x004bd100->0x004bfef4 at 0x000bc100: .data.rel.ro ALLOC LOAD DATA HAS_CONTENTS
 [17]      0x004bfef8->0x004c0000 at 0x000beef8: .got ALLOC LOAD DATA HAS_CONTENTS
 [18]      0x004c0000->0x004c00f0 at 0x000bf000: .got.plt ALLOC LOAD DATA HAS_CONTENTS
 [19]      0x004c0100->0x004c1c30 at 0x000bf100: .data ALLOC LOAD DATA HAS_CONTENTS
 [20]      0x004c1c30->0x004c1c90 at 0x000c0c30: __libc_subfreeres ALLOC LOAD DATA HAS_CONTENTS
 [21]      0x004c1ca0->0x004c2408 at 0x000c0ca0: __libc_IO_vtables ALLOC LOAD DATA HAS_CONTENTS
 [22]      0x004c2408->0x004c2410 at 0x000c1408: __libc_atexit ALLOC LOAD DATA HAS_CONTENTS
 [23]      0x004c2420->0x004c8528 at 0x000c1410: .bss ALLOC
 [24]      0x004c8528->0x004c8558 at 0x000c1410: __libc_freeres_ptrs ALLOC
 [25]      0x00000000->0x00000038 at 0x000c1410: .comment READONLY HAS_CONTENTS
 [26]      0x00000000->0x00000420 at 0x000c1450: .debug_aranges READONLY HAS_CONTENTS
 [27]      0x00000000->0x000372ad at 0x000c1870: .debug_info READONLY HAS_CONTENTS
 [28]      0x00000000->0x000057e8 at 0x000f8b1d: .debug_abbrev READONLY HAS_CONTENTS
 [29]      0x00000000->0x0000aa2b at 0x000fe305: .debug_line READONLY HAS_CONTENTS
 [30]      0x00000000->0x00004d08 at 0x00108d30: .debug_str READONLY HAS_CONTENTS
 [31]      0x00000000->0x0000d4b8 at 0x0010da38: .debug_loc READONLY HAS_CONTENTS
 [32]      0x00000000->0x000024c0 at 0x0011aef0: .debug_ranges READONLY HAS_CONTENTS
Core file:
    `/home/coredump/ALCDA2/x64/App7/core.App7', file type elf64-x86-64.
 [0]      0x00000000->0x00002c24 at 0x000004a0: note0 READONLY HAS_CONTENTS
 [1]      0x00000000->0x000000d8 at 0x00000524: .reg/71 HAS_CONTENTS
 [2]      0x00000000->0x000000d8 at 0x00000524: .reg HAS_CONTENTS
 [3]      0x00000000->0x00000080 at 0x000006b4: .note.linuxcore.siginfo/71 HAS_CONTENTS
 [4]      0x00000000->0x00000080 at 0x000006b4: .note.linuxcore.siginfo HAS_CONTENTS
 [5]      0x00000000->0x00000140 at 0x00000748: .auxv HAS_CONTENTS
 [6]      0x00000000->0x000000c4 at 0x0000089c: .note.linuxcore.file/71 HAS_CONTENTS
 [7]      0x00000000->0x000000c4 at 0x0000089c: .note.linuxcore.file HAS_CONTENTS
 [8]      0x00000000->0x00000200 at 0x00000974: .reg2/71 HAS_CONTENTS
 [9]      0x00000000->0x00000200 at 0x00000974: .reg2 HAS_CONTENTS
 [10]      0x00000000->0x00000340 at 0x00000b88: .reg-xstate/71 HAS_CONTENTS
 [11]      0x00000000->0x00000340 at 0x00000b88: .reg-xstate HAS_CONTENTS
 [12]      0x00000000->0x000000d8 at 0x00000f4c: .reg/68 HAS_CONTENTS
 [13]      0x00000000->0x00000200 at 0x00001040: .reg2/68 HAS_CONTENTS
 [14]      0x00000000->0x00000340 at 0x00001254: .reg-xstate/68 HAS_CONTENTS
 [15]      0x00000000->0x000000d8 at 0x00001618: .reg/69 HAS_CONTENTS
 [16]      0x00000000->0x00000200 at 0x0000170c: .reg2/69 HAS_CONTENTS
 [17]      0x00000000->0x00000340 at 0x00001920: .reg-xstate/69 HAS_CONTENTS
 [18]      0x00000000->0x000000d8 at 0x00001ce4: .reg/70 HAS_CONTENTS
 [19]      0x00000000->0x00000200 at 0x00001dd8: .reg2/70 HAS_CONTENTS
--Type <RET> for more, q to quit, c to continue without paging--
 [20]      0x00000000->0x00000340 at 0x00001fec: .reg-xstate/70 HAS_CONTENTS
 [21]      0x00000000->0x000000d8 at 0x000023b0: .reg/73 HAS_CONTENTS
 [22]      0x00000000->0x00000200 at 0x000024a4: .reg2/73 HAS_CONTENTS
 [23]      0x00000000->0x00000340 at 0x000026b8: .reg-xstate/73 HAS_CONTENTS
 [24]      0x00000000->0x000000d8 at 0x00002a7c: .reg/72 HAS_CONTENTS
 [25]      0x00000000->0x00000200 at 0x00002b70: .reg2/72 HAS_CONTENTS
 [26]      0x00000000->0x00000340 at 0x00002d84: .reg-xstate/72 HAS_CONTENTS
 [27]      0x00400000->0x00401000 at 0x00004000: load1 ALLOC LOAD READONLY HAS_CONTENTS
 [28]      0x00401000->0x00401000 at 0x00005000: load2 ALLOC READONLY CODE
 [29]      0x00495000->0x00495000 at 0x00005000: load3 ALLOC READONLY
 [30]      0x004bd000->0x004c3000 at 0x00005000: load4 ALLOC LOAD HAS_CONTENTS
 [31]      0x004c3000->0x004c9000 at 0x0000b000: load5 ALLOC LOAD HAS_CONTENTS
 [32]      0x01d10000->0x01d33000 at 0x00011000: load6 ALLOC LOAD HAS_CONTENTS
 [33]      0x7f64c1873000->0x7f64c1873000 at 0x00034000: load7 ALLOC READONLY
 [34]      0x7f64c1874000->0x7f64c2074000 at 0x00034000: load8 ALLOC LOAD HAS_CONTENTS
 [35]      0x7f64c2074000->0x7f64c2074000 at 0x00834000: load9 ALLOC READONLY
```

```
[36]    0x7f64c2075000->0x7f64c2875000 at 0x00834000: load10 ALLOC LOAD HAS_CONTENTS
[37]    0x7f64c2875000->0x7f64c2875000 at 0x01034000: load11 ALLOC READONLY
[38]    0x7f64c2876000->0x7f64c3076000 at 0x01034000: load12 ALLOC LOAD HAS_CONTENTS
[39]    0x7f64c3076000->0x7f64c3076000 at 0x01834000: load13 ALLOC READONLY
[40]    0x7f64c3077000->0x7f64c3877000 at 0x01834000: load14 ALLOC LOAD HAS_CONTENTS
[41]    0x7f64c3877000->0x7f64c3877000 at 0x02034000: load15 ALLOC READONLY
[42]    0x7f64c3878000->0x7f64c4078000 at 0x02034000: load16 ALLOC LOAD HAS_CONTENTS
[43]    0x7ffdfcdd0000->0x7ffdfcdf1000 at 0x02834000: load17 ALLOC LOAD HAS_CONTENTS
[44]    0x7ffdfcdf5000->0x7ffdfcdf9000 at 0x02855000: load18 ALLOC LOAD READONLY HAS_CONTENTS
[45]    0x7ffdfcdf9000->0x7ffdfcdfa000 at 0x02859000: load19 ALLOC LOAD READONLY CODE HAS_CONTENTS
```

Note: We see that the stack pointer value **0x7f64c2056**9f0 is inside the stack region address range **0x7f64c187**4000 - **0x7f64c207**4000.

Exercise A7 (x64, WinDbg)

Goal: Learn how to identify active threads.

Patterns: Divide by Zero (User Mode, x64); Invalid Pointer (General); Multiple Exceptions (User Mode); Near Exception.

1. Launch WinDbg.

2. Load the *core.App7* dump file from the x64\App7 folder:

```
Microsoft (R) Windows Debugger Version 10.0.27725.1000 AMD64
Copyright (c) Microsoft Corporation. All rights reserved.


Loading Dump File [C:\ALCDA2\x64\App7\core.App7]
64-bit machine not using 64-bit API

************* Path validation summary **************
Response                         Time (ms)     Location
Deferred                                       srv*
Symbol search path is: srv*
Executable search path is:
Generic Unix Version 0 UP Free x64
System Uptime: not available
Process Uptime: not available
..
(44.47): Signal SIGFPE (Floating point exception) code FPE_INTDIV (Integer divide by zero) at
0x401c27
*** WARNING: Unable to verify timestamp for App7
App7+0x1c27:
00000000`00401c27 ???
```

3. Set logging to a file in case of lengthy output from some commands:

```
0:000> .logopen C:\ALCDA2\x64\App7\App7-WinDbg.log
Opened log file 'C:\ALCDA2\x64\App7\App7-WinDbg.log'
```

4. Specify the dump folder as the symbol path and reload symbols:

```
0:000> .symfix; .sympath+ C:\ALCDA2\x64\App7\
Symbol search path is: srv*;C:\ALCDA2\x64\App7\
Expanded Symbol search path is:
cache*;SRV*https://msdl.microsoft.com/download/symbols;c:\alcda2\x64\app7\

************* Path validation summary **************
Response                         Time (ms)     Location
Deferred                                       srv*
OK                                             C:\ALCDA2\x64\App7\
*** WARNING: Unable to verify timestamp for App7
```

```
0:000> .reload
..
*** WARNING: Unable to verify timestamp for App7

************* Symbol Loading Error Summary **************
Module name            Error
App7                   The system cannot find the file specified

You can troubleshoot most symbol related issues by turning on symbol loading diagnostics (!sym
noisy) and repeating the command that caused symbols to be loaded.
You should also verify that your symbol search path (.sympath) is correct.
```

Note: We ignore warnings and errors as they are not relevant for now.

5. List and identify the possible problem threads:

```
0:000> ~*k 1

Unable to get thread data for thread 0
.  0  Id: 44.47 Suspend: 0 Teb: 00000000`00000000 Unfrozen
 # Child-SP          RetAddr           Call Site
00 00007f64`c3074d60 00000000`00401c3f App7!procD+0xe

Unable to get thread data for thread 1
   1  Id: 44.44 Suspend: 0 Teb: 00000000`00000000 Unfrozen
 # Child-SP          RetAddr           Call Site
00 00007ffd`fcdee880 00000000`00441b7a App7!nanosleep+0x40

Unable to get thread data for thread 2
   2  Id: 44.45 Suspend: 0 Teb: 00000000`00000000 Unfrozen
 # Child-SP          RetAddr           Call Site
00 00007f64`c4076d80 00000000`00000000 0x7265

Unable to get thread data for thread 3
   3  Id: 44.46 Suspend: 0 Teb: 00000000`00000000 Unfrozen
 # Child-SP          RetAddr           Call Site
00 00007f64`c3875d10 00000000`00441b7a App7!nanosleep+0x40

Unable to get thread data for thread 4
   4  Id: 44.49 Suspend: 0 Teb: 00000000`00000000 Unfrozen
 # Child-SP          RetAddr           Call Site
00 00007f64`c20569f0 00000000`00401c05 App7!procF+0xb

Unable to get thread data for thread 5
   5  Id: 44.48 Suspend: 0 Teb: 00000000`00000000 Unfrozen
 # Child-SP          RetAddr           Call Site
00 00007f64`c2873d10 00000000`00441b7a App7!nanosleep+0x40
```

6. We see there is an arithmetic exception in the current thread. Let's list the stack trace for the current problem thread #1 and identify the problem instruction:

```
0:000> kL
 # Child-SP          RetAddr           Call Site
00 00007f64`c3074d60 00000000`00401c3f App7!procD+0xe
01 00007f64`c3074d70 00000000`00401dfd App7!procC+0x13
02 00007f64`c3074d80 00000000`00401e0e App7!bar_three+0x18
03 00007f64`c3074d90 00000000`00401e27 App7!foo_three+0xe
04 00007f64`c3074da0 00000000`004032b3 App7!thread_three+0x16
05 00007f64`c3074dc0 00000000`0044444f App7!start_thread+0xf3
```

```
06 00007f64`c3074e80 ffffffff`ffffffff     App7!_clone+0x3f
07 00007f64`c3074e88 00000000`00000000     0xffffffff`ffffffff
```

```
0:000> r
rax=0000000000000001 rbx=0000000000000000 rcx=0000000000441bf0
rdx=0000000000000000 rsi=0000000000000000 rdi=0000000000000001
rip=0000000000401c27 rsp=00007f64c3074d60 rbp=00007f64c3074d60
 r8=00007f64c3075700  r9=00007f64c3075700 r10=00007f64c30759d0
r11=0000000000000000 r12=00007ffdfcdee86e r13=00007ffdfcdee86f
r14=00007f64c3075700 r15=0000000000000000
iopl=0         nv up ei pl nz na pe nc
cs=0033  ss=002b  ds=0000  es=0000  fs=0000  gs=0000             efl=00010202
App7!procD+0xe:
00000000`00401c27 idiv    eax,dword ptr [rbp-8]   ss:00007f64`c3074d58=00000000
```

```
0:000> dd rbp-8 L1
00007f64`c3074d58  00000000
```

7. We also see something abnormal on thread #2. Switch to it and check the currently executing instruction::

```
0:000> ~2s
00000000`00007265 ???
```

```
0:002> r
rax=00007f64c4076d66 rbx=0000000000000000 rcx=0000000000000000
rdx=0000000000000000 rsi=00007f64c4076d40 rdi=00007f64c4076d66
rip=0000000000007265 rsp=00007f64c4076d80 rbp=6666754220726567
 r8=00007f64c4077700  r9=00007f64c4077700 r10=00007f64c40779d0
r11=0000000000000000 r12=00007ffdfcdee86e r13=00007ffdfcdee86f
r14=00007f64c4077700 r15=0000000000000000
iopl=0         nv up ei pl nz na po nc
cs=0033  ss=002b  ds=0000  es=0000  fs=0000  gs=0000             efl=00010206
00000000`00007265 ???
```

```
0:002> dp rip L1
00000000`00007265  ????????`????????
```

Note: We see that the current instruction pointer points to an invalid memory address. It can also be considered NULL Pointer (Code) since the address belongs to an inaccessible part of memory to catch NULL pointers. We also see that there can be exceptions on different threads simultaneously.

8. Thread #4 looks active, and we compare the stack pointer with the stack region boundaries since we suspect stack overflow:

```
0:002> ~4s
App7!procF+0xb:
00000000`00401bb8 mov     dword ptr [rbp-1004h],edi ss:00007f64`c20569fc=00000000
```

```
0:004> kL
 # Child-SP          RetAddr           Call Site
00 00007f64`c20569f0 00000000`00401c05     App7!procF+0xb
01 00007f64`c2057a10 00000000`00401c05     App7!procF+0x58
02 00007f64`c2058a30 00000000`00401c05     App7!procF+0x58
03 00007f64`c2059a50 00000000`00401c05     App7!procF+0x58
04 00007f64`c205aa70 00000000`00401c05     App7!procF+0x58
05 00007f64`c205ba90 00000000`00401c05     App7!procF+0x58
06 00007f64`c205cab0 00000000`00401c05     App7!procF+0x58
07 00007f64`c205dad0 00000000`00401c05     App7!procF+0x58
```

```
08 00007f64`c205eaf0 00000000`00401c05     App7!procF+0x58
09 00007f64`c205fb10 00000000`00401c05     App7!procF+0x58
0a 00007f64`c2060b30 00000000`00401c05     App7!procF+0x58
0b 00007f64`c2061b50 00000000`00401c05     App7!procF+0x58
0c 00007f64`c2062b70 00000000`00401c05     App7!procF+0x58
0d 00007f64`c2063b90 00000000`00401c05     App7!procF+0x58
0e 00007f64`c2064bb0 00000000`00401c05     App7!procF+0x58
0f 00007f64`c2065bd0 00000000`00401c05     App7!procF+0x58
10 00007f64`c2066bf0 00000000`00401c05     App7!procF+0x58
11 00007f64`c2067c10 00000000`00401c05     App7!procF+0x58
12 00007f64`c2068c30 00000000`00401c05     App7!procF+0x58
13 00007f64`c2069c50 00000000`00401c05     App7!procF+0x58
14 00007f64`c206ac70 00000000`00401c05     App7!procF+0x58
15 00007f64`c206bc90 00000000`00401c05     App7!procF+0x58
16 00007f64`c206ccb0 00000000`00401c05     App7!procF+0x58
17 00007f64`c206dcd0 00000000`00401c05     App7!procF+0x58
18 00007f64`c206ecf0 00000000`00401c05     App7!procF+0x58
19 00007f64`c206fd10 00000000`00401c05     App7!procF+0x58
1a 00007f64`c2070d30 00000000`00401c05     App7!procF+0x58
1b 00007f64`c2071d50 00000000`00401c16     App7!procF+0x58
1c 00007f64`c2072d70 00000000`00401e8f     App7!procE+0xe
1d 00007f64`c2072d80 00000000`00401ea0     App7!bar_five+0x18
1e 00007f64`c2072d90 00000000`00401eb9     App7!foo_five+0xe
1f 00007f64`c2072da0 00000000`004032b3     App7!thread_five+0x16
20 00007f64`c2072dc0 00000000`0044444f     App7!start_thread+0xf3
21 00007f64`c2072e80 ffffffff`ffffffff     App7!_clone+0x3f
22 00007f64`c2072e88 00000000`00000000     0xffffffff`ffffffff

0:004> dd rbp-1004h L1
00007f64`c20569fc  00000000

0:004> uf rip
App7!procF+0xb:
00000000`00401bb8 mov     dword ptr [rbp-1004h],edi
00000000`00401bbe lea     rdx,[rbp-1000h]
00000000`00401bc5 mov     eax,0
00000000`00401bca mov     ecx,200h
00000000`00401bcf mov     rdi,rdx
00000000`00401bd2 rep stos qword ptr [rdi]
00000000`00401bd5 mov     dword ptr [rbp-1000h],0FFFFFFFFh
00000000`00401bdf mov     eax,dword ptr [rbp-1004h]
00000000`00401be5 add     eax,1
00000000`00401be8 mov     dword ptr [rbp-0FF8h],eax
00000000`00401bee mov     dword ptr [rbp-0FF0h],0FFFFFFFFh
00000000`00401bf8 mov     eax,dword ptr [rbp-0FF8h]
00000000`00401bfe mov     edi,eax
00000000`00401c00 call    App7!procF (00000000`00401bad)
00000000`00401c05 nop
00000000`00401c06 leave
00000000`00401c07 ret

0:004> r rsp
rsp=00007f64c20569f0
```

```
0:004> !address

Mapping file section regions...
Mapping module regions...
Mapping heap regions...

        BaseAddress      EndAddress+1        RegionSize     Type       State                 Protect             Usage
--------------------------------------------------------------------------------------------------------------------------
+        0`00000000        0`00400000        0`00400000                                                           <unknown>
+        0`00400000        0`00401000        0`00001000 MEM_PRIVATE MEM_COMMIT  PAGE_READONLY                      Image          [App7; "/mnt/wslg/dumps/App7"]
+        0`00401000        0`004bd000        0`000bc000                                                           Image          [App7; "/mnt/wslg/dumps/App7"]
+        0`004bd000        0`004c3000        0`00006000 MEM_PRIVATE MEM_COMMIT  PAGE_READWRITE                     Image          [App7; "/mnt/wslg/dumps/App7"]
+        0`004c3000        0`004c9000        0`00006000 MEM_PRIVATE MEM_COMMIT  PAGE_READWRITE                     <unknown>  [................]
+        0`004c9000        0`01d10000        0`01847000                                                           <unknown>
+        0`01d10000        0`01d33000        0`00023000 MEM_PRIVATE MEM_COMMIT  PAGE_READWRITE                     <unknown>  [................]
+        0`01d33000     7f64`c1874000     7f64`bfb41000                                                           <unknown>
+     7f64`c1874000     7f64`c2074000        0`00800000 MEM_PRIVATE MEM_COMMIT  PAGE_READWRITE                     <unknown>  [................]
+     7f64`c2074000     7f64`c2075000        0`00001000                                                           <unknown>
+     7f64`c2075000     7f64`c2875000        0`00800000 MEM_PRIVATE MEM_COMMIT  PAGE_READWRITE                     <unknown>  [................]
+     7f64`c2875000     7f64`c2876000        0`00001000                                                           <unknown>
+     7f64`c2876000     7f64`c3076000        0`00800000 MEM_PRIVATE MEM_COMMIT  PAGE_READWRITE                     <unknown>  [................]
+     7f64`c3076000     7f64`c3077000        0`00001000                                                           <unknown>
+     7f64`c3077000     7f64`c3877000        0`00800000 MEM_PRIVATE MEM_COMMIT  PAGE_READWRITE                     <unknown>  [................]
+     7f64`c3877000     7f64`c3878000        0`00001000                                                           <unknown>
+     7f64`c3878000     7f64`c4078000        0`00800000 MEM_PRIVATE MEM_COMMIT  PAGE_READWRITE                     <unknown>  [................]
+     7f64`c4078000     7ffd`fcdd0000       99`38d58000                                                           <unknown>
+     7ffd`fcdd0000     7ffd`fcdf1000        0`00021000 MEM_PRIVATE MEM_COMMIT  PAGE_READWRITE                     <unknown>  [................]
+     7ffd`fcdf1000     7ffd`fcdf5000        0`00004000                                                           <unknown>
+     7ffd`fcdf5000     7ffd`fcdf9000        0`00004000 MEM_PRIVATE MEM_COMMIT  PAGE_READONLY                      <unknown>  [................]
+     7ffd`fcdf9000     7ffd`fcdfa000        0`00001000 MEM_PRIVATE MEM_COMMIT  PAGE_EXECUTE_READ                  Image      [linux_vdso_so; "linux-vdso.so.1"]
```

Note: We see that the stack pointer value 0x7f64c20569f0 is inside the stack region address range 7f64`c1874000 7f64`c2074000.

11. We close logging before exiting WinDbg:

```
0:000> .logclose
Closing open log file 'C:\ALCDA2\x64\App7\App7-WinDbg.log'
```

Exercise A8

- **Goal:** Learn how to identify runtime exceptions, past execution residue and stack traces, identify handled exceptions
- **Patterns:** C++ Exception; Coincidental Symbolic Information; Handled Exception (User Space)
- \ALCDA-Dumps\Exercise-A8-x64-GDB.pdf
- \ALCDA-Dumps\Exercise-A8-A64-GDB.pdf
- \ALCDA-Dumps\Exercise-A8-A64-WinDbg.pdf
- \ALCDA-Dumps\Exercise-A8-x64-WinDbg.pdf

Exercise A8 (x64, GDB)

Goal: Learn how to identify runtime exceptions, past execution residue and stack traces, identify handled exceptions.

Patterns: C++ Exception; Coincidental Symbolic Information; Handled Exception (User Space).

1. Load the *core.App8* dump file and *App8* executable from the x64/App8 directory:

```
~/ALCDA2/x64/App8$ gdb -c core.App8 -se App8
GNU gdb (Debian 8.2.1-2+b3) 8.2.1
Copyright (C) 2018 Free Software Foundation, Inc.
License GPLv3+: GNU GPL version 3 or later <http://gnu.org/licenses/gpl.html>
This is free software: you are free to change and redistribute it.
There is NO WARRANTY, to the extent permitted by law.
Type "show copying" and "show warranty" for details.
This GDB was configured as "x86_64-linux-gnu".
Type "show configuration" for configuration details.
For bug reporting instructions, please see:
<http://www.gnu.org/software/gdb/bugs/>.
Find the GDB manual and other documentation resources online at:
    <http://www.gnu.org/software/gdb/documentation/>.

For help, type "help".
Type "apropos word" to search for commands related to "word"...
Reading symbols from App8...done.
[New LWP 162]
[New LWP 164]
[New LWP 165]
[New LWP 163]
[New LWP 161]
[New LWP 166]
[Thread debugging using libthread_db enabled]
Using host libthread_db library "/lib/x86_64-linux-gnu/libthread_db.so.1".
Core was generated by `./App8'.
Program terminated with signal SIGABRT, Aborted.
#0  0x0000000000424fdb in raise ()
[Current thread is 1 (Thread 0x7f4d60082700 (LWP 162))]
```

1. Set logging to a file in case of lengthy output from some commands:

```
(gdb) set logging on App8.log
Copying output to App8.log.
```

2. List all thread stack traces:

```
(gdb) thread apply all bt

Thread 6 (Thread 0x7f4d5e07e700 (LWP 166)):
#0  0x000000000045aa70 in nanosleep ()
#1  0x000000000045a9fa in sleep ()
#2  0x00000000004023b6 in procNE() ()
#3  0x0000000000402482 in bar_five() ()
#4  0x000000000040248e in foo_five() ()
#5  0x00000000004024a2 in thread_five(void*) ()
#6  0x000000000041b483 in start_thread (arg=<optimized out>) at pthread_create.c:486
#7  0x000000000045d22f in clone ()
```

```
Thread 5 (Thread 0x19ad880 (LWP 161)):
#0  0x000000000045aa70 in nanosleep ()
#1  0x000000000045a9fa in sleep ()
#2  0x0000000000402553 in main () at pthread_create.c:688

Thread 4 (Thread 0x7f4d5f881700 (LWP 163)):
#0  0x000000000045aa70 in nanosleep ()
#1  0x000000000045a9fa in sleep ()
#2  0x00000000004023b6 in procNE() () at pthread_create.c:688
#3  0x00000000004023f2 in bar_two() () at pthread_create.c:688
#4  0x00000000004023fe in foo_two() () at pthread_create.c:688
#5  0x0000000000402412 in thread_two(void*) () at pthread_create.c:688
#6  0x000000000041b483 in start_thread (arg=<optimized out>) at pthread_create.c:486
#7  0x000000000045d22f in clone ()

Thread 3 (Thread 0x7f4d5e87f700 (LWP 165)):
#0  0x000000000045aa70 in nanosleep ()
#1  0x000000000045a9fa in sleep ()
#2  0x00000000004023b6 in procNE() () at pthread_create.c:688
#3  0x0000000000402452 in bar_four() () at pthread_create.c:688
#4  0x000000000040245e in foo_four() () at pthread_create.c:688
#5  0x0000000000402472 in thread_four(void*) () at pthread_create.c:688
#6  0x000000000041b483 in start_thread (arg=<optimized out>) at pthread_create.c:486
#7  0x000000000045d22f in clone ()

Thread 2 (Thread 0x7f4d5f080700 (LWP 164)):
#0  0x000000000045aa70 in nanosleep ()
#1  0x000000000045a9fa in sleep ()
#2  0x000000000040236c in procH() () at pthread_create.c:688
#3  0x0000000000402422 in bar_three() () at pthread_create.c:688
#4  0x000000000040242e in foo_three() () at pthread_create.c:688
#5  0x0000000000402442 in thread_three(void*) () at pthread_create.c:688
#6  0x000000000041b483 in start_thread (arg=<optimized out>) at pthread_create.c:486
#7  0x000000000045d22f in clone ()

Thread 1 (Thread 0x7f4d60082700 (LWP 162)):
#0  0x0000000000424fdb in raise ()
#1  0x00000000004017d3 in abort () at pthread_create.c:688
#2  0x0000000000401553 in __gnu_cxx::__verbose_terminate_handler() [clone .cold.1] ()
#3  0x0000000000402b46 in __cxxabiv1::__terminate(void (*)()) () at pthread_create.c:688
#4  0x0000000000402b81 in std::terminate() () at pthread_create.c:688
#5  0x0000000000402ac4 in __cxa_throw () at pthread_create.c:688
#6  0x00000000004022de in procB() () at pthread_create.c:688
#7  0x000000000040233b in procA() () at pthread_create.c:688
#8  0x00000000004023a0 in procNH() () at pthread_create.c:688
#9  0x00000000004023c2 in bar_one() () at pthread_create.c:688
--Type <RET> for more, q to quit, c to continue without paging--
#10 0x00000000004023ce in foo_one() () at pthread_create.c:688
#11 0x00000000004023e2 in thread_one(void*) () at pthread_create.c:688
#12 0x000000000041b483 in start_thread (arg=<optimized out>) at pthread_create.c:486
#13 0x000000000045d22f in clone ()
```

Note: We have C++ exception processing in thread #1.

3. Go to thread #4, identify the execution residue of *work* functions, check their correctness, and reconstruct the past stack trace:

```
(gdb) thread 4
[Switching to thread 4 (Thread 0x7f4d5f881700 (LWP 163))]
#0  0x000000000045aa70 in nanosleep ()

(gdb) bt
#0  0x000000000045aa70 in nanosleep ()
#1  0x000000000045a9fa in sleep ()
#2  0x00000000004023b6 in procNE() () at pthread_create.c:688
#3  0x00000000004023f2 in bar_two() () at pthread_create.c:688
#4  0x00000000004023fe in foo_two() () at pthread_create.c:688
#5  0x0000000000402412 in thread_two(void*) () at pthread_create.c:688
#6  0x000000000041b483 in start_thread (arg=<optimized out>) at pthread_create.c:486
#7  0x000000000045d22f in clone ()

(gdb) x/512a $rsp-2000
0x7f4d5f880530: 0x0     0x0
0x7f4d5f880540: 0x0     0x0
0x7f4d5f880550: 0x0     0x0
0x7f4d5f880560: 0x0     0x0
0x7f4d5f880570: 0x0     0x0
0x7f4d5f880580: 0x0     0x0
0x7f4d5f880590: 0x0     0x0
0x7f4d5f8805a0: 0x0     0x0
0x7f4d5f8805b0: 0x0     0x0
0x7f4d5f8805c0: 0x0     0x0
0x7f4d5f8805d0: 0x0     0x0
0x7f4d5f8805e0: 0x0     0x0
0x7f4d5f8805f0: 0x0     0x0
0x7f4d5f880600: 0x0     0x0
0x7f4d5f880610: 0x0     0x0
0x7f4d5f880620: 0x0     0x0
0x7f4d5f880630: 0x0     0x0
0x7f4d5f880640: 0x0     0x0
0x7f4d5f880650: 0x0     0x0
0x7f4d5f880660: 0x0     0x0
0x7f4d5f880670: 0x0     0x0
0x7f4d5f880680: 0x0     0x0
0x7f4d5f880690: 0x0     0x0
0x7f4d5f8806a0: 0x0     0x0
0x7f4d5f8806b0: 0x0     0x0
0x7f4d5f8806c0: 0x0     0x0
0x7f4d5f8806d0: 0x0     0x0
0x7f4d5f8806e0: 0x0     0x0
0x7f4d5f8806f0: 0x0     0x0
0x7f4d5f880700: 0x0     0x0
0x7f4d5f880710: 0x0     0x0
0x7f4d5f880720: 0x0     0x0
0x7f4d5f880730: 0x0     0x0
0x7f4d5f880740: 0x0     0x0
0x7f4d5f880750: 0x0     0x0
0x7f4d5f880760: 0x0     0x0
0x7f4d5f880770: 0x0     0x0
0x7f4d5f880780: 0x0     0x0
0x7f4d5f880790: 0x0     0x0
0x7f4d5f8807a0: 0x0     0x0
0x7f4d5f8807b0: 0x0     0x0
0x7f4d5f8807c0: 0x0     0x0
```

```
0x7f4d5f8807d0: 0x0     0x0
0x7f4d5f8807e0: 0x0     0x0
0x7f4d5f8807f0: 0x0     0x0
0x7f4d5f880800: 0x0     0x0
0x7f4d5f880810: 0x0     0x0
0x7f4d5f880820: 0x0     0x0
0x7f4d5f880830: 0x0     0x0
0x7f4d5f880840: 0x0     0x0
0x7f4d5f880850: 0x0     0x0
0x7f4d5f880860: 0x0     0x0
0x7f4d5f880870: 0x0     0x0
0x7f4d5f880880: 0x0     0x0
0x7f4d5f880890: 0x0     0x0
0x7f4d5f8808a0: 0x0     0x0
0x7f4d5f8808b0: 0x7f4d5f8808c0  0x4021dd <_Z6work_8v+9>
--Type <RET> for more, q to quit, c to continue without paging--
0x7f4d5f8808c0: 0x7f4d5f8808d0  0x4021e9 <_Z6work_7v+9>
0x7f4d5f8808d0: 0x7f4d5f8808e0  0x4021f5 <_Z6work_6v+9>
0x7f4d5f8808e0: 0x7f4d5f8808f0  0x402201 <_Z6work_5v+9>
0x7f4d5f8808f0: 0x7f4d5f880900  0x40220d <_Z6work_4v+9>
0x7f4d5f880900: 0x7f4d5f880910  0x402219 <_Z6work_3v+9>
0x7f4d5f880910: 0x7f4d5f880920  0x402225 <_Z6work_2v+9>
0x7f4d5f880920: 0x7f4d5f880930  0x402231 <_Z6work_1v+9>
0x7f4d5f880930: 0x7f4d5f880d40  0x402244 <_Z4workv+16>
0x7f4d5f880940: 0x0     0x0
0x7f4d5f880950: 0x0     0x0
0x7f4d5f880960: 0x0     0x0
0x7f4d5f880970: 0x0     0x0
0x7f4d5f880980: 0x0     0x0
0x7f4d5f880990: 0x0     0x0
...
...
...

(gdb) disassemble 0x402219
Dump of assembler code for function _Z6work_3v:
   0x0000000000402210 <+0>:     push   %rbp
   0x0000000000402211 <+1>:     mov    %rsp,%rbp
   0x0000000000402214 <+4>:     callq  0x402204 <_Z6work_4v>
   0x0000000000402219 <+9>:     nop
   0x000000000040221a <+10>:    pop    %rbp
   0x000000000040221b <+11>:    retq
End of assembler dump.
```

Note: Since the saved %rbp register value points to the next line, we can easily reconstruct the fragment of the past stack trace:

```
0x7f4d5f8808b0: 0x7f4d5f8808c0  0x4021dd <_Z6work_8v+9>
0x7f4d5f8808c0: 0x7f4d5f8808d0  0x4021e9 <_Z6work_7v+9>
0x7f4d5f8808d0: 0x7f4d5f8808e0  0x4021f5 <_Z6work_6v+9>
0x7f4d5f8808e0: 0x7f4d5f8808f0  0x402201 <_Z6work_5v+9>
0x7f4d5f8808f0: 0x7f4d5f880900  0x40220d <_Z6work_4v+9>
0x7f4d5f880900: 0x7f4d5f880910  0x402219 <_Z6work_3v+9>
0x7f4d5f880910: 0x7f4d5f880920  0x402225 <_Z6work_2v+9>
0x7f4d5f880920: 0x7f4d5f880930  0x402231 <_Z6work_1v+9>
0x7f4d5f880930: 0x7f4d5f880d40  0x402244 <_Z4workv+16>
```

4. Go to thread #2, identify the handled exception processing code, and check its validity:

```
(gdb) thread 2
[Switching to thread 2 (Thread 0x7f4d5f080700 (LWP 164))]
#0  0x000000000045aa70 in nanosleep ()

(gdb) bt
#0  0x000000000045aa70 in nanosleep ()
#1  0x000000000045a9fa in sleep ()
#2  0x000000000040236c in procH() () at pthread_create.c:688
#3  0x0000000000402422 in bar_three() () at pthread_create.c:688
#4  0x000000000040242e in foo_three() () at pthread_create.c:688
#5  0x0000000000402442 in thread_three(void*) () at pthread_create.c:688
#6  0x000000000041b483 in start_thread (arg=<optimized out>) at pthread_create.c:486
#7  0x000000000045d22f in clone ()

(gdb) x/512a $rsp-2000
0x7f4d5f07f520: 0x418950 <fde_single_encoding_compare>  0x418600 <frame_downheap+112>
0x7f4d5f07f530: 0x7f4d58002520  0x4df460 <object.6779>
0x7f4d5f07f540: 0x7f4d580044c0  0xe3
0x7f4d5f07f550: 0x1130000038c   0x0
0x7f4d5f07f560: 0x7f4d580044b0  0x4df460 <object.6779>
0x7f4d5f07f570: 0x1cb70 0x6cb
0x7f4d5f07f580: 0x7f4d580044a0  0x4186e1 <frame_heapsort+145>
0x7f4d5f07f590: 0x38b8  0x3e6ca15e6c37ea00
0x7f4d5f07f5a0: 0x401b72 <read_encoded_value_with_base.cold.0>  0x418950
<fde_single_encoding_compare>
0x7f4d5f07f5b0: 0x4df460 <object.6779>  0x49
0x7f4d5f07f5c0: 0x7f4d58000be0  0x417d0d <_Unwind_RaiseException+61>
0x7f4d5f07f5d0: 0x4d4dd8        0x4197e6 <search_object+854>
0x7f4d5f07f5e0: 0x0     0x7f4d5f07f628
0x7f4d5f07f5f0: 0x7f4d5f07f630  0x7f4d0000001b
0x7f4d5f07f600: 0x0     0x7f4d0000000b
0x7f4d5f07f610: 0x7f4d5f07fc88  0x7f4d5f07fc90
0x7f4d5f07f620: 0x0     0x40234a <_Z5procHv>
0x7f4d5f07f630: 0x43    0x0
0x7f4d5f07f640: 0x7f4d5f07fd40  0x4df460 <object.6779>
0x7f4d5f07f650: 0x7f4d5f07f760  0x7f4d5f07fab8
0x7f4d5f07f660: 0x41db80 <__pthread_key_create> 0x4030b8 <__gxx_personality_v0+184>
0x7f4d5f07f670: 0x402357 <_Z5procHv+13> 0x7f4d58000b80
0x7f4d5f07f680: 0x60140234a     0x0
0x7f4d5f07f690: 0x4d60c0        0x7f4d5f07f601
0x7f4d5f07f6a0: 0x7f4d5f07fd50  0x40233b <_Z5procAv+9>
0x7f4d5f07f6b0: 0x0     0x4c43d9
0x7f4d5f07f6c0: 0x4c43d9        0x5f07fa10
0x7f4d5f07f6d0: 0x0     0x1b
0x7f4d5f07f6e0: 0x7f4d5f07f760  0x4165d0 <uw_frame_state_for+800>
0x7f4d5f07f6f0: 0x0     0x9b00000000
0x7f4d5f07f700: 0x4c4339        0x7f4d5f07f718
0x7f4d5f07f710: 0x7f4d5f07f760  0x4d60c0
0x7f4d5f07f720: 0x7f4d5f07f760  0x7f4d5f07fa10
0x7f4d5f07f730: 0x4     0x7f4d58000b80
0x7f4d5f07f740: 0x7f4d5f07f760  0x4
0x7f4d5f07f750: 0x7f4d5f07fb00  0x4176fb <_Unwind_RaiseException_Phase2+75>
0x7f4d5f07f760: 0x0     0x0
0x7f4d5f07f770: 0x0     0x0
0x7f4d5f07f780: 0x0     0x0
0x7f4d5f07f790: 0xffffffffffffffe8      0x1
0x7f4d5f07f7a0: 0x0     0x0
```

```
0x7f4d5f07f7b0: 0x0      0x0
0x7f4d5f07f7c0: 0xfffffffffffffff0      0x1
0x7f4d5f07f7d0: 0x0      0x0
0x7f4d5f07f7e0: 0x0      0x0
0x7f4d5f07f7f0: 0x0      0x0
0x7f4d5f07f800: 0x0      0x0
0x7f4d5f07f810: 0x0      0x0
0x7f4d5f07f820: 0x0      0x0
0x7f4d5f07f830: 0x0      0x0
0x7f4d5f07f840: 0x0      0x0
0x7f4d5f07f850: 0x0      0x0
0x7f4d5f07f860: 0xfffffffffffffff8      0x1
0x7f4d5f07f870: 0x0      0x0
0x7f4d5f07f880: 0x0      0x10
0x7f4d5f07f890: 0x6      0x0
0x7f4d5f07f8a0: 0x1      0x40238c <_Z5procHv+66>
--Type <RET> for more, q to quit, c to continue without paging--
0x7f4d5f07f8b0: 0x403000 <__gxx_personality_v0> 0xfffffffffffffff8
0x7f4d5f07f8c0: 0x1      0x10
0x7f4d5f07f8d0: 0x11b1b 0x0
0x7f4d5f07f8e0: 0x7f4d58000b80  0x7f4d5f07fa10
0x7f4d5f07f8f0: 0x7f4d5f07fcc0  0x7f4d5f07fb00
0x7f4d5f07f900: 0x7f4d58000b80  0x7f4d5f07fd60
0x7f4d5f07f910: 0x0      0x417faa <_Unwind_RaiseException+730>
0x7f4d5f07f920: 0x7f4d5f07fc88  0x7f4d5f07fc90
0x7f4d5f07f930: 0x0      0x7f4d5f07fc98
0x7f4d5f07f940: 0x0      0x0
0x7f4d5f07f950: 0x7f4d5f07fcc0  0x0
0x7f4d5f07f960: 0x0      0x0
0x7f4d5f07f970: 0x0      0x0
0x7f4d5f07f980: 0x7f4d5f07fca0  0x7f4d5f07fca8
0x7f4d5f07f990: 0x7f4d5f07fcb0  0x7f4d5f07fcb8
0x7f4d5f07f9a0: 0x7f4d5f07fcc8  0x0
0x7f4d5f07f9b0: 0x7f4d5f07fcd0  0x402ab7 <__cxa_throw+55>
0x7f4d5f07f9c0: 0x0      0x0
0x7f4d5f07f9d0: 0x0      0x417cd0 <_Unwind_RaiseException>
0x7f4d5f07f9e0: 0x4000000000000000      0x0
0x7f4d5f07f9f0: 0x0      0x0
0x7f4d5f07fa00: 0x0      0x0
0x7f4d5f07fa10: 0x7f4d5f07fc88  0x7f4d5f07fc90
0x7f4d5f07fa20: 0x0      0x7f4d5f07fd28
0x7f4d5f07fa30: 0x0      0x0
0x7f4d5f07fa40: 0x7f4d5f07fd50  0x7f4d5f07f908
0x7f4d5f07fa50: 0x0      0x0
0x7f4d5f07fa60: 0x0      0x0
...
...
...

(gdb) disassemble 0x417faa
Dump of assembler code for function _Unwind_RaiseException:
   0x0000000000417cd0 <+0>:     push   %rbp
   0x0000000000417cd1 <+1>:     mov    %rsp,%rbp
   0x0000000000417cd4 <+4>:     push   %r15
   0x0000000000417cd6 <+6>:     push   %r14
   0x0000000000417cd8 <+8>:     lea    -0x3a0(%rbp),%r14
   0x0000000000417cdf <+15>:    lea    0x10(%rbp),%rsi
   0x0000000000417ce3 <+19>:    push   %r13
   0x0000000000417ce5 <+21>:    mov    %rdi,%r13
   0x0000000000417ce8 <+24>:    mov    %r14,%rdi
```

```
   0x0000000000417ceb <+27>:    push   %r12
   0x0000000000417ced <+29>:    lea    -0x1c0(%rbp),%r12
   0x0000000000417cf4 <+36>:    push   %rbx
   0x0000000000417cf5 <+37>:    lea    -0x2b0(%rbp),%rbx
   0x0000000000417cfc <+44>:    push   %rdx
   0x0000000000417cfd <+45>:    push   %rax
   0x0000000000417cfe <+46>:    sub    $0x368,%rsp
   0x0000000000417d05 <+53>:    mov    0x8(%rbp),%rdx
   0x0000000000417d09 <+57>:    callq  0x4174a0 <uw_init_context_1>
   0x0000000000417d0e <+62>:    movdqa -0x3a0(%rbp),%xmm0
   0x0000000000417d16 <+70>:    movdqa -0x390(%rbp),%xmm1
   0x0000000000417d1e <+78>:    movdqa -0x380(%rbp),%xmm2
   0x0000000000417d26 <+86>:    movdqa -0x370(%rbp),%xmm3
   0x0000000000417d2e <+94>:    movdqa -0x360(%rbp),%xmm4
   0x0000000000417d36 <+102>:   movdqa -0x350(%rbp),%xmm5
   0x0000000000417d3e <+110>:   movaps %xmm0,-0x2b0(%rbp)
   0x0000000000417d45 <+117>:   movdqa -0x340(%rbp),%xmm6
   0x0000000000417d4d <+125>:   movaps %xmm1,-0x2a0(%rbp)
   0x0000000000417d54 <+132>:   movdqa -0x330(%rbp),%xmm7
   0x0000000000417d5c <+140>:   movaps %xmm2,-0x290(%rbp)
   0x0000000000417d63 <+147>:   movdqa -0x320(%rbp),%xmm0
   0x0000000000417d6b <+155>:   movdqa -0x310(%rbp),%xmm1
   0x0000000000417d73 <+163>:   movaps %xmm3,-0x280(%rbp)
   0x0000000000417d7a <+170>:   movdqa -0x300(%rbp),%xmm2
   0x0000000000417d82 <+178>:   movdqa -0x2f0(%rbp),%xmm3
   0x0000000000417d8a <+186>:   movaps %xmm4,-0x270(%rbp)
   0x0000000000417d91 <+193>:   movdqa -0x2e0(%rbp),%xmm4
   0x0000000000417d99 <+201>:   movaps %xmm5,-0x260(%rbp)
   0x0000000000417da0 <+208>:   movdqa -0x2d0(%rbp),%xmm5
   0x0000000000417da8 <+216>:   movaps %xmm6,-0x250(%rbp)
   0x0000000000417daf <+223>:   movdqa -0x2c0(%rbp),%xmm6
   0x0000000000417db7 <+231>:   movaps %xmm7,-0x240(%rbp)
   0x0000000000417dbe <+238>:   movaps %xmm0,-0x230(%rbp)
   0x0000000000417dc5 <+245>:   movaps %xmm1,-0x220(%rbp)
   0x0000000000417dcc <+252>:   movaps %xmm2,-0x210(%rbp)
   0x0000000000417dd3 <+259>:   movaps %xmm3,-0x200(%rbp)
   0x0000000000417dda <+266>:   movaps %xmm4,-0x1f0(%rbp)
   0x0000000000417de1 <+273>:   movaps %xmm5,-0x1e0(%rbp)
   0x0000000000417de8 <+280>:   movaps %xmm6,-0x1d0(%rbp)
   0x0000000000417def <+287>:   jmp    0x417e30 <_Unwind_RaiseException+352>
   0x0000000000417df1 <+289>:   nopl   0x0(%rax)
   0x0000000000417df8 <+296>:   test   %eax,%eax
   0x0000000000417dfa <+298>:   jne    0x417e60 <_Unwind_RaiseException+400>
   0x0000000000417dfc <+300>:   mov    -0x70(%rbp),%rax
   0x0000000000417e00 <+304>:   test   %rax,%rax
   0x0000000000417e03 <+307>:   je     0x417e25 <_Unwind_RaiseException+341>
   0x0000000000417e05 <+309>:   mov    %rbx,%r8
--Type <RET> for more, q to quit, c to continue without paging--
   0x0000000000417e08 <+312>:   mov    %r13,%rcx
   0x0000000000417e0b <+315>:   mov    0x0(%r13),%rdx
   0x0000000000417e0f <+319>:   mov    $0x1,%esi
   0x0000000000417e14 <+324>:   mov    $0x1,%edi
   0x0000000000417e19 <+329>:   callq  *%rax
   0x0000000000417e1b <+331>:   cmp    $0x6,%eax
   0x0000000000417e1e <+334>:   je     0x417e70 <_Unwind_RaiseException+416>
   0x0000000000417e20 <+336>:   cmp    $0x8,%eax
   0x0000000000417e23 <+339>:   jne    0x417e60 <_Unwind_RaiseException+400>
   0x0000000000417e25 <+341>:   mov    %r12,%rsi
   0x0000000000417e28 <+344>:   mov    %rbx,%rdi
   0x0000000000417e2b <+347>:   callq  0x417620 <uw_update_context>
```

```
   0x0000000000417e30 <+352>:   mov    %r12,%rsi
   0x0000000000417e33 <+355>:   mov    %rbx,%rdi
   0x0000000000417e36 <+358>:   callq  0x4162b0 <uw_frame_state_for>
   0x0000000000417e3b <+363>:   cmp    $0x5,%eax
   0x0000000000417e3e <+366>:   jne    0x417df8 <_Unwind_RaiseException+296>
   0x0000000000417e40 <+368>:   mov    -0x28(%rbp),%rbx
   0x0000000000417e44 <+372>:   mov    -0x20(%rbp),%r12
   0x0000000000417e48 <+376>:   mov    -0x18(%rbp),%r13
   0x0000000000417e4c <+380>:   mov    -0x10(%rbp),%r14
   0x0000000000417e50 <+384>:   mov    -0x8(%rbp),%r15
   0x0000000000417e54 <+388>:   leaveq
   0x0000000000417e55 <+389>:   retq
   0x0000000000417e56 <+390>:   nopw   %cs:0x0(%rax,%rax,1)
   0x0000000000417e60 <+400>:   mov    $0x3,%eax
   0x0000000000417e65 <+405>:   jmp    0x417e40 <_Unwind_RaiseException+368>
   0x0000000000417e67 <+407>:   nopw   0x0(%rax,%rax,1)
   0x0000000000417e70 <+416>:   movdqa -0x3a0(%rbp),%xmm7
   0x0000000000417e78 <+424>:   mov    -0x1f0(%rbp),%rax
   0x0000000000417e7f <+431>:   movq   $0x0,0x10(%r13)
   0x0000000000417e87 <+439>:   mov    %r12,%rdx
   0x0000000000417e8a <+442>:   movdqa -0x350(%rbp),%xmm0
   0x0000000000417e92 <+450>:   mov    -0x220(%rbp),%rcx
   0x0000000000417e99 <+457>:   mov    %rbx,%rsi
   0x0000000000417e9c <+460>:   mov    %r13,%rdi
   0x0000000000417e9f <+463>:   movaps %xmm7,-0x2b0(%rbp)
   0x0000000000417ea6 <+470>:   movdqa -0x390(%rbp),%xmm7
   0x0000000000417eae <+478>:   shr    $0x3f,%rax
   0x0000000000417eb2 <+482>:   movdqa -0x340(%rbp),%xmm1
   0x0000000000417eba <+490>:   movaps %xmm0,-0x260(%rbp)
   0x0000000000417ec1 <+497>:   movdqa -0x330(%rbp),%xmm2
   0x0000000000417ec9 <+505>:   movdqa -0x320(%rbp),%xmm3
   0x0000000000417ed1 <+513>:   sub    %rax,%rcx
   0x0000000000417ed4 <+516>:   movaps %xmm7,-0x2a0(%rbp)
   0x0000000000417edb <+523>:   movdqa -0x380(%rbp),%xmm7
   0x0000000000417ee3 <+531>:   movdqa -0x310(%rbp),%xmm4
   0x0000000000417eeb <+539>:   movdqa -0x300(%rbp),%xmm5
   0x0000000000417ef3 <+547>:   movdqa -0x2f0(%rbp),%xmm6
   0x0000000000417efb <+555>:   mov    %rcx,0x18(%r13)
   0x0000000000417eff <+559>:   movaps %xmm7,-0x290(%rbp)
   0x0000000000417f06 <+566>:   movdqa -0x370(%rbp),%xmm7
   0x0000000000417f0e <+574>:   movdqa -0x2d0(%rbp),%xmm0
   0x0000000000417f16 <+582>:   movaps %xmm1,-0x250(%rbp)
   0x0000000000417f1d <+589>:   movaps %xmm7,-0x280(%rbp)
   0x0000000000417f24 <+596>:   movdqa -0x360(%rbp),%xmm7
   0x0000000000417f2c <+604>:   movaps %xmm2,-0x240(%rbp)
--Type <RET> for more, q to quit, c to continue without paging--
   0x0000000000417f33 <+611>:   movaps %xmm7,-0x270(%rbp)
   0x0000000000417f3a <+618>:   movdqa -0x2e0(%rbp),%xmm7
   0x0000000000417f42 <+626>:   movaps %xmm3,-0x230(%rbp)
   0x0000000000417f49 <+633>:   movaps %xmm4,-0x220(%rbp)
   0x0000000000417f50 <+640>:   movaps %xmm5,-0x210(%rbp)
   0x0000000000417f57 <+647>:   movaps %xmm6,-0x200(%rbp)
   0x0000000000417f5e <+654>:   movaps %xmm7,-0x1f0(%rbp)
   0x0000000000417f65 <+661>:   movaps %xmm0,-0x1e0(%rbp)
   0x0000000000417f6c <+668>:   movdqa -0x2c0(%rbp),%xmm1
   0x0000000000417f74 <+676>:   movaps %xmm1,-0x1d0(%rbp)
   0x0000000000417f7b <+683>:   callq  0x4176b0 <_Unwind_RaiseException_Phase2>
   0x0000000000417f80 <+688>:   cmp    $0x7,%eax
   0x0000000000417f83 <+691>:   jne    0x417e40 <_Unwind_RaiseException+368>
   0x0000000000417f89 <+697>:   mov    %rbx,%rsi
```

```
   0x0000000000417f8c <+700>:   mov    %r14,%rdi
   0x0000000000417f8f <+703>:   callq  0x417890 <uw_install_context_1>
   0x0000000000417f94 <+708>:   mov    -0x218(%rbp),%r8
   0x0000000000417f9b <+715>:   mov    -0x220(%rbp),%rdi
   0x0000000000417fa2 <+722>:   mov    %r8,%rsi
   0x0000000000417fa5 <+725>:   callq  0x417cc0 <_Unwind_DebugHook>
   0x0000000000417faa <+730>:   mov    %rax,%rcx
   0x0000000000417fad <+733>:   mov    %r8,0x8(%rbp,%rax,1)
   0x0000000000417fb2 <+738>:   mov    -0x38(%rbp),%rax
   0x0000000000417fb6 <+742>:   lea    0x8(%rbp,%rcx,1),%rcx
   0x0000000000417fbb <+747>:   mov    -0x30(%rbp),%rdx
   0x0000000000417fbf <+751>:   mov    -0x28(%rbp),%rbx
   0x0000000000417fc3 <+755>:   mov    -0x20(%rbp),%r12
   0x0000000000417fc7 <+759>:   mov    -0x18(%rbp),%r13
   0x0000000000417fcb <+763>:   mov    -0x10(%rbp),%r14
   0x0000000000417fcf <+767>:   mov    -0x8(%rbp),%r15
   0x0000000000417fd3 <+771>:   mov    0x0(%rbp),%rbp
   0x0000000000417fd7 <+775>:   mov    %rcx,%rsp
   0x0000000000417fda <+778>:   retq
End of assembler dump.
```

Exercise A8 (A64, GDB)

Goal: Learn how to identify runtime exceptions, past execution residue and stack traces, identify handled exceptions.

Patterns: C++ Exception; Coincidental Symbolic Information; Handled Exception (User Space).

1. Load the *core.25889* dump file and *App8* executable from the A64/App8 directory:

```
~/ALCDA2/A64/App8$ gdb-multiarch -c core.25889 -se App8
GNU gdb (Debian 8.2.1-2+b3) 8.2.1
Copyright (C) 2018 Free Software Foundation, Inc.
License GPLv3+: GNU GPL version 3 or later <http://gnu.org/licenses/gpl.html>
This is free software: you are free to change and redistribute it.
There is NO WARRANTY, to the extent permitted by law.
Type "show copying" and "show warranty" for details.
This GDB was configured as "x86_64-linux-gnu".
Type "show configuration" for configuration details.
For bug reporting instructions, please see:
<http://www.gnu.org/software/gdb/bugs/>.
Find the GDB manual and other documentation resources online at:
    <http://www.gnu.org/software/gdb/documentation/>.

For help, type "help".
Type "apropos word" to search for commands related to "word"...
Reading symbols from App8...(no debugging symbols found)...done.
[New LWP 25890]
[New LWP 25892]
[New LWP 25889]
[New LWP 25891]
[New LWP 25894]
[New LWP 25893]
Core was generated by `./App8'.
Program terminated with signal SIGABRT, Aborted.
#0  0x0000000000420cfc in raise ()
[Current thread is 1 (LWP 25890)]
```

2. Set logging to a file in case of lengthy output from some commands:

```
(gdb) set logging on App8.log
Copying output to App8.log.
```

3. List all thread stack traces:

```
(gdb) thread apply all bt

Thread 6 (LWP 25893):
#0  0x0000000000420174 in nanosleep ()
#1  0x0000000000438e34 in sleep ()
#2  0x0000000000403520 in procNE() ()
#3  0x0000000000403600 in bar_four() ()
#4  0x0000000000403614 in foo_four() ()
#5  0x000000000040362c in thread_four(void*) ()
#6  0x00000000004183f4 in start_thread ()
#7  0x000000000043dd20 in thread_start ()
```

```
Thread 5 (LWP 25894):
#0  0x0000000000420174 in nanosleep ()
#1  0x0000000000438e34 in sleep ()
#2  0x0000000000403520 in procNE() ()
#3  0x0000000000403644 in bar_five() ()
#4  0x0000000000403658 in foo_five() ()
#5  0x0000000000403670 in thread_five(void*) ()
#6  0x00000000004183f4 in start_thread ()
#7  0x000000000043dd20 in thread_start ()

Thread 4 (LWP 25891):
#0  0x0000000000420174 in nanosleep ()
#1  0x0000000000438e34 in sleep ()
#2  0x0000000000403520 in procNE() ()
#3  0x0000000000403578 in bar_two() ()
#4  0x000000000040358c in foo_two() ()
#5  0x00000000004035a4 in thread_two(void*) ()
#6  0x00000000004183f4 in start_thread ()
#7  0x000000000043dd20 in thread_start ()

Thread 3 (LWP 25889):
#0  0x0000000000420174 in nanosleep ()
#1  0x0000000000438e34 in sleep ()
#2  0x000000000040370c in main ()

Thread 2 (LWP 25892):
#0  0x0000000000420174 in nanosleep ()
#1  0x0000000000438e34 in sleep ()
#2  0x00000000004034cc in procH() ()
#3  0x00000000004035bc in bar_three() ()
#4  0x00000000004035d0 in foo_three() ()
#5  0x00000000004035e8 in thread_three(void*) ()
#6  0x00000000004183f4 in start_thread ()
#7  0x000000000043dd20 in thread_start ()

Thread 1 (LWP 25890):
#0  0x0000000000420cfc in raise ()
#1  0x0000000000422d38 in abort ()
--Type <RET> for more, q to quit, c to continue without paging--
#2  0x00000000004086f0 in __gnu_cxx::__verbose_terminate_handler() ()
#3  0x0000000000404c0c in __cxxabiv1::__terminate(void (*)()) ()
#4  0x0000000000404c30 in std::terminate() ()
#5  0x0000000000404d88 in __cxa_throw ()
#6  0x0000000000403424 in procB() ()
#7  0x0000000000403490 in procA() ()
#8  0x0000000000403504 in procNH() ()
#9  0x0000000000403534 in bar_one() ()
#10 0x0000000000403548 in foo_one() ()
#11 0x0000000000403560 in thread_one(void*) ()
#12 0x00000000004183f4 in start_thread ()
#13 0x000000000043dd20 in thread_start ()
```

Note: We have C++ exception processing in thread #1.

4. Go to thread #4, identify the execution residue of *work* functions, check their correctness, and reconstruct the past stack trace:

```
(gdb) thread 4
[Switching to thread 4 (LWP 25891)]
#0  0x0000000000420174 in nanosleep ()

(gdb) bt
#0  0x0000000000420174 in nanosleep ()
#1  0x0000000000438e34 in sleep ()
#2  0x0000000000403520 in procNE() ()
#3  0x0000000000403578 in bar_two() ()
#4  0x000000000040358c in foo_two() ()
#5  0x00000000004035a4 in thread_two(void*) ()
#6  0x00000000004183f4 in start_thread ()
#7  0x000000000043dd20 in thread_start ()

(gdb) x/512a $sp-2000
0xfffe79bbde00: 0x0     0x0
0xfffe79bbde10: 0x0     0x0
0xfffe79bbde20: 0x0     0x0
0xfffe79bbde30: 0x0     0x0
0xfffe79bbde40: 0x0     0x0
0xfffe79bbde50: 0x0     0x0
0xfffe79bbde60: 0x0     0x0
0xfffe79bbde70: 0x0     0x0
0xfffe79bbde80: 0x0     0x0
0xfffe79bbde90: 0x0     0x0
0xfffe79bbdea0: 0x0     0x0
0xfffe79bbdeb0: 0x0     0x0
0xfffe79bbdec0: 0x0     0x0
0xfffe79bbded0: 0x0     0x0
0xfffe79bbdee0: 0x0     0x0
0xfffe79bbdef0: 0x0     0x0
0xfffe79bbdf00: 0x0     0x0
0xfffe79bbdf10: 0x0     0x0
0xfffe79bbdf20: 0x0     0x0
0xfffe79bbdf30: 0x0     0x0
0xfffe79bbdf40: 0x0     0x0
0xfffe79bbdf50: 0x0     0x0
0xfffe79bbdf60: 0x0     0x0
0xfffe79bbdf70: 0x0     0x0
0xfffe79bbdf80: 0x0     0x0
0xfffe79bbdf90: 0x0     0x0
0xfffe79bbdfa0: 0x0     0x0
0xfffe79bbdfb0: 0x0     0x0
0xfffe79bbdfc0: 0x0     0x0
0xfffe79bbdfd0: 0x0     0x0
0xfffe79bbdfe0: 0x0     0x0
0xfffe79bbdff0: 0x0     0x0
0xfffe79bbe000: 0x0     0x0
0xfffe79bbe010: 0x0     0x0
0xfffe79bbe020: 0x0     0x0
0xfffe79bbe030: 0x0     0x0
0xfffe79bbe040: 0x0     0x0
0xfffe79bbe050: 0x0     0x0
0xfffe79bbe060: 0x0     0x0
0xfffe79bbe070: 0x0     0x0
0xfffe79bbe080: 0x0     0x0
0xfffe79bbe090: 0x0     0x0
```

```
0xfffe79bbe0a0: 0x0     0x0
0xfffe79bbe0b0: 0x0     0x0
0xfffe79bbe0c0: 0x0     0x0
0xfffe79bbe0d0: 0x0     0x0
0xfffe79bbe0e0: 0x0     0x0
0xfffe79bbe0f0: 0x0     0x0
0xfffe79bbe100: 0x0     0x0
--Type <RET> for more, q to quit, c to continue without paging--
0xfffe79bbe110: 0x0     0x0
0xfffe79bbe120: 0x0     0x0
0xfffe79bbe130: 0x0     0x0
0xfffe79bbe140: 0x0     0x0
0xfffe79bbe150: 0x0     0x0
0xfffe79bbe160: 0x0     0x0
0xfffe79bbe170: 0x0     0x0
0xfffe79bbe180: 0x0     0x0
0xfffe79bbe190: 0x0     0x0
0xfffe79bbe1a0: 0x0     0x0
0xfffe79bbe1b0: 0x0     0x0
0xfffe79bbe1c0: 0x0     0x0
0xfffe79bbe1d0: 0x0     0x0
0xfffe79bbe1e0: 0x0     0x0
0xfffe79bbe1f0: 0x0     0x0
0xfffe79bbe200: 0x0     0x0
0xfffe79bbe210: 0x0     0x0
0xfffe79bbe220: 0x0     0x0
0xfffe79bbe230: 0x0     0x0
0xfffe79bbe240: 0x0     0x0
0xfffe79bbe250: 0x0     0x0
0xfffe79bbe260: 0x0     0x0
0xfffe79bbe270: 0x0     0x0
0xfffe79bbe280: 0x0     0x0
0xfffe79bbe290: 0x0     0x0
0xfffe79bbe2a0: 0x0     0x0
0xfffe79bbe2b0: 0x0     0x0
0xfffe79bbe2c0: 0x0     0x0
0xfffe79bbe2d0: 0x0     0x0
0xfffe79bbe2e0: 0x0     0x0
0xfffe79bbe2f0: 0x0     0x0
0xfffe79bbe300: 0x0     0x0
0xfffe79bbe310: 0x0     0x0
0xfffe79bbe320: 0x0     0x0
0xfffe79bbe330: 0x0     0x0
0xfffe79bbe340: 0x0     0x0
0xfffe79bbe350: 0xfffe79bbe360  0x403304 <_Z6work_7v+12>
0xfffe79bbe360: 0xfffe79bbe370  0x403318 <_Z6work_6v+12>
0xfffe79bbe370: 0xfffe79bbe380  0x40332c <_Z6work_5v+12>
0xfffe79bbe380: 0xfffe79bbe390  0x403340 <_Z6work_4v+12>
0xfffe79bbe390: 0xfffe79bbe3a0  0x403354 <_Z6work_3v+12>
0xfffe79bbe3a0: 0xfffe79bbe3b0  0x403368 <_Z6work_2v+12>
0xfffe79bbe3b0: 0xfffe79bbe3c0  0x40337c <_Z6work_1v+12>
0xfffe79bbe3c0: 0xfffe79bbe3d0  0x403394 <_Z4workv+16>
0xfffe79bbe3d0: 0xfffe79bbe7e0  0x40347c <_Z6procNBv+12>
0xfffe79bbe3e0: 0x0     0x0
0xfffe79bbe3f0: 0x0     0x0
0xfffe79bbe400: 0x0     0x0
...
...
...
```

```
(gdb) disassemble 0x403354
Dump of assembler code for function _Z6work_3v:
   0x0000000000403348 <+0>:     stp     x29, x30, [sp, #-16]!
   0x000000000040334c <+4>:     mov     x29, sp
   0x0000000000403350 <+8>:     bl      0x403334 <_Z6work_4v>
   0x0000000000403354 <+12>:    ldp     x29, x30, [sp], #16
   0x0000000000403358 <+16>:    ret
End of assembler dump.
```

Note: Since the saved X29 register value points to the next line, we can easily reconstruct the fragment of the past stack trace:

```
0xfffe79bbe350: 0xfffe79bbe360  0x403304 <_Z6work_7v+12>
0xfffe79bbe360: 0xfffe79bbe370  0x403318 <_Z6work_6v+12>
0xfffe79bbe370: 0xfffe79bbe380  0x40332c <_Z6work_5v+12>
0xfffe79bbe380: 0xfffe79bbe390  0x403340 <_Z6work_4v+12>
0xfffe79bbe390: 0xfffe79bbe3a0  0x403354 <_Z6work_3v+12>
0xfffe79bbe3a0: 0xfffe79bbe3b0  0x403368 <_Z6work_2v+12>
0xfffe79bbe3b0: 0xfffe79bbe3c0  0x40337c <_Z6work_1v+12>
0xfffe79bbe3c0: 0xfffe79bbe3d0  0x403394 <_Z4workv+16>
0xfffe79bbe3d0: 0xfffe79bbe7e0  0x40347c <_Z6procNBv+12>
```

5. Go to thread #2, identify the handled exception processing code, and check its validity:

```
(gdb) thread 2
[Switching to thread 2 (LWP 25892)]
#0  0x0000000000420174 in nanosleep ()

(gdb) bt
#0  0x0000000000420174 in nanosleep ()
#1  0x0000000000438e34 in sleep ()
#2  0x00000000004034cc in procH() ()
#3  0x00000000004035bc in bar_three() ()
#4  0x00000000004035d0 in foo_three() ()
#5  0x00000000004035e8 in thread_three(void*) ()
#6  0x00000000004183f4 in start_thread ()
#7  0x000000000043dd20 in thread_start ()

(gdb) x/1024a $sp-8000
0xfffe793ac680: 0x0     0x0
0xfffe793ac690: 0x0     0x0
...
...
...
0xfffe793ad0e0: 0xfffe793ad0f0  0x404754 <__gxx_personality_v0+240>
0xfffe793ad0f0: 0xfffe793ad1e0  0x4145ac <_Unwind_RaiseException_Phase2+112>
0xfffe793ad100: 0xfffe793add30  0xfffe793ad220
0xfffe793ad110: 0x4     0xfffe74000b80
0xfffe793ad120: 0x4     0xfffe793af760
0xfffe793ad130: 0x32b706f0      0x4f9540 <__default_pthread_attr>
0xfffe793ad140: 0x10000 0x810000
0xfffe793ad150: 0xfffe793ad1e0  0x414570 <_Unwind_RaiseException_Phase2+52>
0xfffe793ad160: 0xfffe793add30  0x4c57d8
0xfffe793ad170: 0x0     0xfffe74000b80
0xfffe793ad180: 0x4     0x0
0xfffe793ad190: 0x32b706f0      0x4f9540 <__default_pthread_attr>
0xfffe793ad1a0: 0x10000 0x810000
0xfffe793ad1b0: 0x0     0x0
```

```
0xfffe793ad1c0: 0xfffe793ad1e0  0x4145cc <_Unwind_RaiseException_Phase2+144>
0xfffe793ad1d0: 0xfffffffffffffff8      0x76a28b436af36f00
0xfffe793ad1e0: 0xfffe793ad8a0  0x414bf4 <_Unwind_RaiseException+324>
0xfffe793ad1f0: 0xfffe793add30  0xfffe793ae0f0
0xfffe793ad200: 0xfffe74000b80  0xfffe793ad970
0xfffe793ad210: 0x0     0xfffe793ae770
0xfffe793ad220: 0x0     0x0
0xfffe793ad230: 0x0     0x0
0xfffe793ad240: 0x0     0x0
0xfffe793ad250: 0x0     0x0
0xfffe793ad260: 0x0     0x0
0xfffe793ad270: 0x0     0x0
0xfffe793ad280: 0x0     0x0
0xfffe793ad290: 0x0     0x0
0xfffe793ad2a0: 0x0     0x0
0xfffe793ad2b0: 0x0     0x0
--Type <RET> for more, q to quit, c to continue without paging--
0xfffe793ad2c0: 0x0     0x0
0xfffe793ad2d0: 0x0     0x0
0xfffe793ad2e0: 0x0     0x0
0xfffe793ad2f0: 0x0     0x0
0xfffe793ad300: 0x0     0x0
0xfffe793ad310: 0x0     0x0
0xfffe793ad320: 0x0     0x0
0xfffe793ad330: 0x0     0x0
0xfffe793ad340: 0x0     0x0
0xfffe793ad350: 0xfffffffffffffff0      0x1
0xfffe793ad360: 0x0     0x0
0xfffe793ad370: 0x0     0x0
0xfffe793ad380: 0x0     0x0
0xfffe793ad390: 0x0     0x0
0xfffe793ad3a0: 0x0     0x0
0xfffe793ad3b0: 0x0     0x0
0xfffe793ad3c0: 0x0     0x0
0xfffe793ad3d0: 0x0     0x0
0xfffe793ad3e0: 0x0     0x0
0xfffe793ad3f0: 0xffffffffffffffe0      0x1
0xfffe793ad400: 0xffffffffffffffe8      0x1
0xfffe793ad410: 0x0     0x0
0xfffe793ad420: 0x0     0x0
0xfffe793ad430: 0x0     0x0
0xfffe793ad440: 0x0     0x0
0xfffe793ad450: 0x0     0x0
0xfffe793ad460: 0x0     0x0
0xfffe793ad470: 0x0     0x0
0xfffe793ad480: 0x0     0x0
0xfffe793ad490: 0x0     0x0
0xfffe793ad4a0: 0x0     0x0
0xfffe793ad4b0: 0x0     0x0
0xfffe793ad4c0: 0x0     0x0
0xfffe793ad4d0: 0x0     0x0
0xfffe793ad4e0: 0x0     0x0
0xfffe793ad4f0: 0x0     0x0
0xfffe793ad500: 0x0     0x0
0xfffe793ad510: 0x0     0x0
0xfffe793ad520: 0x0     0x0
0xfffe793ad530: 0x0     0x0
0xfffe793ad540: 0x0     0x0
0xfffe793ad550: 0x0     0x0
0xfffe793ad560: 0x0     0x0
```

```
0xfffe793ad570: 0x0     0x0
0xfffe793ad580: 0x0     0x0
0xfffe793ad590: 0x0     0x0
0xfffe793ad5a0: 0x0     0x0
0xfffe793ad5b0: 0x0     0x0
0xfffe793ad5c0: 0x0     0x0
0xfffe793ad5d0: 0x0     0x0
0xfffe793ad5e0: 0x0     0x0
0xfffe793ad5f0: 0x0     0x0
0xfffe793ad600: 0x0     0x0
0xfffe793ad610: 0x0     0x0
0xfffe793ad620: 0x0     0x0
0xfffe793ad630: 0x0     0x0
0xfffe793ad640: 0x0     0x0
0xfffe793ad650: 0x0     0x0
0xfffe793ad660: 0x0     0x0
0xfffe793ad670: 0x0     0x0
0xfffe793ad680: 0x0     0x0
0xfffe793ad690: 0x0     0x0
0xfffe793ad6a0: 0x0     0x0
0xfffe793ad6b0: 0x0     0x0
0xfffe793ad6c0: 0x0     0x0
0xfffe793ad6d0: 0x0     0x0
0xfffe793ad6e0: 0x0     0x0
0xfffe793ad6f0: 0x0     0x0
0xfffe793ad700: 0x0     0x0
0xfffe793ad710: 0x0     0x0
0xfffe793ad720: 0x0     0x0
0xfffe793ad730: 0x0     0x0
0xfffe793ad740: 0x0     0x0
0xfffe793ad750: 0x0     0x0
0xfffe793ad760: 0x0     0x0
0xfffe793ad770: 0x0     0x0
0xfffe793ad780: 0x0     0x0
0xfffe793ad790: 0x0     0x0
0xfffe793ad7a0: 0x0     0x0
0xfffe793ad7b0: 0x0     0x0
0xfffe793ad7c0: 0x0     0x0
0xfffe793ad7d0: 0x0     0x0
0xfffe793ad7e0: 0x0     0x0
0xfffe793ad7f0: 0x0     0x0
0xfffe793ad800: 0x0     0x0
0xfffe793ad810: 0x0     0x0
0xfffe793ad820: 0x0     0x0
0xfffe793ad830: 0x0     0x0
0xfffe793ad840: 0x0     0x20
0xfffe793ad850: 0xfffe793ad8a0  0x414c08 <_Unwind_RaiseException+344>
0xfffe793ad860: 0xfffe793add30  0xfffe793ae0f0
0xfffe793ad870: 0xfffe74000b80  0xfffe793ad970
0xfffe793ad880: 0x0     0x1e
0xfffe793ad890: 0x11b1b 0xfffe793ae7f0
0xfffe793ad8a0: 0xfffe793ae7f0  0x4034c0 <_Z5procHv+20>
0xfffe793ad8b0: 0xfffe74000b80  0x1
0xfffe793ad8c0: 0x0     0x1
0xfffe793ad8d0: 0xfffe793af070  0x0
0xfffe793ad8e0: 0x4e0000        0x4035d8 <_Z12thread_threePv>
0xfffe793ad8f0: 0x0     0xfffe793af760
0xfffe793ad900: 0x32b706f0      0x4f9540 <__default_pthread_attr>
0xfffe793ad910: 0x10000 0x810000
0xfffe793ad920: 0x0     0x0
```

```
0xfffe793ad930: 0x0     0x0
0xfffe793ad940: 0x0     0x0
0xfffe793ad950: 0x0     0x0
0xfffe793ad960: 0x0     0x80
0xfffe793ad970: 0xfffe793ad8b0  0xfffe793ad8b8
0xfffe793ad980: 0xfffe793ad8c0  0xfffe793ad8c8
0xfffe793ad990: 0x0     0x0
0xfffe793ad9a0: 0x0     0x0
0xfffe793ad9b0: 0x0     0x0
0xfffe793ad9c0: 0x0     0x0
0xfffe793ad9d0: 0x0     0x0
0xfffe793ad9e0: 0x0     0x0
0xfffe793ad9f0: 0x0     0x0
0xfffe793ada00: 0x0     0xfffe793ad8d0
0xfffe793ada10: 0xfffe793ad8d8  0xfffe793ad8e0
0xfffe793ada20: 0xfffe793ad8e8  0xfffe793ad8f0
0xfffe793ada30: 0xfffe793ad8f8  0xfffe793ad900
0xfffe793ada40: 0xfffe793ad908  0xfffe793ad910
0xfffe793ada50: 0xfffe793ad918  0xfffe793ad8a0
0xfffe793ada60: 0xfffe793ad8a8  0x0
0xfffe793ada70: 0x0     0x0
0xfffe793ada80: 0x0     0x0
0xfffe793ada90: 0x0     0x0
0xfffe793adaa0: 0x0     0x0
0xfffe793adab0: 0x0     0x0
0xfffe793adac0: 0x0     0x0
0xfffe793adad0: 0x0     0x0
0xfffe793adae0: 0x0     0x0
0xfffe793adaf0: 0x0     0x0
0xfffe793adb00: 0x0     0x0
0xfffe793adb10: 0x0     0x0
0xfffe793adb20: 0x0     0x0
0xfffe793adb30: 0x0     0x0
0xfffe793adb40: 0x0     0x0
0xfffe793adb50: 0x0     0x0
0xfffe793adb60: 0x0     0x0
0xfffe793adb70: 0x0     0x0
0xfffe793adb80: 0x0     0x0
0xfffe793adb90: 0x0     0x0
0xfffe793adba0: 0x0     0x0
0xfffe793adbb0: 0xfffe793ad920  0xfffe793ad928
0xfffe793adbc0: 0xfffe793ad930  0xfffe793ad938
0xfffe793adbd0: 0xfffe793ad940  0xfffe793ad948
0xfffe793adbe0: 0xfffe793ad950  0xfffe793ad958
0xfffe793adbf0: 0x0     0x0
0xfffe793adc00: 0x0     0x0
0xfffe793adc10: 0x0     0x0
0xfffe793adc20: 0x0     0x0
0xfffe793adc30: 0x0     0x0
0xfffe793adc40: 0x0     0x0
0xfffe793adc50: 0x0     0x0
0xfffe793adc60: 0x0     0x0
0xfffe793adc70: 0x0     0x0
0xfffe793adc80: 0xfffe793ae770  0x404d7c <__cxa_throw+144>
0xfffe793adc90: 0x0     0x0
0xfffe793adca0: 0x0     0x414ab0 <_Unwind_RaiseException>
...
...
...
```

```
(gdb) disassemble 0x414bf4
Dump of assembler code for function _Unwind_RaiseException:
   0x0000000000414ab0 <+0>:     sub     sp, sp, #0xe10
   0x0000000000414ab4 <+4>:     stp     x29, x30, [sp, #-192]!
   0x0000000000414ab8 <+8>:     mov     x29, sp
   0x0000000000414abc <+12>:    stp     x21, x22, [sp, #64]
   0x0000000000414ac0 <+16>:    add     x22, x29, #0xd0
   0x0000000000414ac4 <+20>:    stp     x0, x1, [sp, #16]
   0x0000000000414ac8 <+24>:    stp     x2, x3, [sp, #32]
   0x0000000000414acc <+28>:    add     x1, x29, #0xed0
   0x0000000000414ad0 <+32>:    mov     x2, x30
   0x0000000000414ad4 <+36>:    mov     x21, x0
   0x0000000000414ad8 <+40>:    mov     x0, x22
   0x0000000000414adc <+44>:    stp     x19, x20, [sp, #48]
   0x0000000000414ae0 <+48>:    stp     d8, d9, [sp, #128]
   0x0000000000414ae4 <+52>:    stp     d10, d11, [sp, #144]
   0x0000000000414ae8 <+56>:    stp     d12, d13, [sp, #160]
   0x0000000000414aec <+60>:    stp     d14, d15, [sp, #176]
   0x0000000000414af0 <+64>:    stp     x23, x24, [sp, #80]
   0x0000000000414af4 <+68>:    stp     x25, x26, [sp, #96]
   0x0000000000414af8 <+72>:    stp     x27, x28, [sp, #112]
   0x0000000000414afc <+76>:    add     x19, x29, #0x490
   0x0000000000414b00 <+80>:    bl      0x414268 <uw_init_context_1>
   0x0000000000414b04 <+84>:    mov     x0, x19
   0x0000000000414b08 <+88>:    mov     x1, x22
   0x0000000000414b0c <+92>:    mov     x2, #0x3c0                      // #960
   0x0000000000414b10 <+96>:    bl      0x400280
   0x0000000000414b14 <+100>:   add     x20, x29, #0x850
   0x0000000000414b18 <+104>:   b       0x414b4c <_Unwind_RaiseException+156>
   0x0000000000414b1c <+108>:   cbnz    w2, 0x414bbc <_Unwind_RaiseException+268>
   0x0000000000414b20 <+112>:   ldr     x5, [x20, #1616]
   0x0000000000414b24 <+116>:   cbz     x5, 0x414b40 <_Unwind_RaiseException+144>
   0x0000000000414b28 <+120>:   ldr     x2, [x21]
   0x0000000000414b2c <+124>:   blr     x5
   0x0000000000414b30 <+128>:   cmp     w0, #0x6
   0x0000000000414b34 <+132>:   b.eq    0x414bc4 <_Unwind_RaiseException+276>  // b.none
   0x0000000000414b38 <+136>:   cmp     w0, #0x8
   0x0000000000414b3c <+140>:   b.ne    0x414bbc <_Unwind_RaiseException+268>  // b.any
   0x0000000000414b40 <+144>:   mov     x0, x19
   0x0000000000414b44 <+148>:   mov     x1, x20
   0x0000000000414b48 <+152>:   bl      0x414490 <uw_update_context>
   0x0000000000414b4c <+156>:   mov     x1, x20
   0x0000000000414b50 <+160>:   mov     x0, x19
   0x0000000000414b54 <+164>:   bl      0x413100 <uw_frame_state_for>
   0x0000000000414b58 <+168>:   mov     w2, w0
   0x0000000000414b5c <+172>:   cmp     w2, #0x5
   0x0000000000414b60 <+176>:   mov     w0, #0x1                        // #1
   0x0000000000414b64 <+180>:   mov     x3, x21
   0x0000000000414b68 <+184>:   mov     x4, x19
   0x0000000000414b6c <+188>:   mov     w1, w0
--Type <RET> for more, q to quit, c to continue without paging--
   0x0000000000414b70 <+192>:   b.ne    0x414b1c <_Unwind_RaiseException+108>  // b.any
   0x0000000000414b74 <+196>:   mov     w0, w2
   0x0000000000414b78 <+200>:   mov     x4, #0x0                        // #0
   0x0000000000414b7c <+204>:   ldp     x2, x3, [sp, #32]
   0x0000000000414b80 <+208>:   ldp     x19, x20, [sp, #48]
   0x0000000000414b84 <+212>:   ldp     x21, x22, [sp, #64]
   0x0000000000414b88 <+216>:   ldp     x23, x24, [sp, #80]
   0x0000000000414b8c <+220>:   ldp     x25, x26, [sp, #96]
   0x0000000000414b90 <+224>:   ldp     x27, x28, [sp, #112]
```

```
   0x0000000000414b94 <+228>:   ldp     d8, d9, [sp, #128]
   0x0000000000414b98 <+232>:   ldp     d10, d11, [sp, #144]
   0x0000000000414b9c <+236>:   ldp     d12, d13, [sp, #160]
   0x0000000000414ba0 <+240>:   ldp     d14, d15, [sp, #176]
   0x0000000000414ba4 <+244>:   ldp     x0, x1, [sp, #16]
   0x0000000000414ba8 <+248>:   ldp     x29, x30, [sp], #192
   0x0000000000414bac <+252>:   mov     x16, sp
   0x0000000000414bb0 <+256>:   add     sp, sp, x4
   0x0000000000414bb4 <+260>:   add     sp, sp, #0xe10
   0x0000000000414bb8 <+264>:   ret
   0x0000000000414bbc <+268>:   mov     w0, #0x3                        // #3
   0x0000000000414bc0 <+272>:   b       0x414b78 <_Unwind_RaiseException+200>
   0x0000000000414bc4 <+276>:   ldr     x1, [x19, #784]
   0x0000000000414bc8 <+280>:   ldr     x0, [x19, #832]
   0x0000000000414bcc <+284>:   mov     x2, #0x3c0                      // #960
   0x0000000000414bd0 <+288>:   sub     x0, x1, x0, lsr #63
   0x0000000000414bd4 <+292>:   str     x0, [x21, #24]
   0x0000000000414bd8 <+296>:   mov     x1, x22
   0x0000000000414bdc <+300>:   str     xzr, [x21, #16]
   0x0000000000414be0 <+304>:   mov     x0, x19
   0x0000000000414be4 <+308>:   bl      0x400280
   0x0000000000414be8 <+312>:   mov     x0, x21
   0x0000000000414bec <+316>:   mov     x1, x19
   0x0000000000414bf0 <+320>:   bl      0x41453c <_Unwind_RaiseException_Phase2>
   0x0000000000414bf4 <+324>:   cmp     w0, #0x7
   0x0000000000414bf8 <+328>:   b.ne    0x414b78 <_Unwind_RaiseException+200>  // b.any
   0x0000000000414bfc <+332>:   mov     x1, x19
   0x0000000000414c00 <+336>:   mov     x0, x22
   0x0000000000414c04 <+340>:   bl      0x4146fc <uw_install_context_1>
   0x0000000000414c08 <+344>:   ldr     x1, [x22, #832]
   0x0000000000414c0c <+348>:   mov     x4, x0
   0x0000000000414c10 <+352>:   ldr     x20, [x19, #792]
   0x0000000000414c14 <+356>:   ldr     x0, [x22, #784]
   0x0000000000414c18 <+360>:   tbz     x1, #61, 0x414c2c <_Unwind_RaiseException+380>
   0x0000000000414c1c <+364>:   mov     x17, x20
   0x0000000000414c20 <+368>:   mov     x16, x0
   0x0000000000414c24 <+372>:   pacia1716
   0x0000000000414c28 <+376>:   mov     x20, x17
   0x0000000000414c2c <+380>:   ldr     x0, [x19, #784]
   0x0000000000414c30 <+384>:   mov     x1, x20
   0x0000000000414c34 <+388>:   str     x4, [x29, #200]
   0x0000000000414c38 <+392>:   bl      0x414aa8 <_Unwind_DebugHook>
   0x0000000000414c3c <+396>:   ldr     x4, [x29, #200]
   0x0000000000414c40 <+400>:   str     x20, [sp, #8]
   0x0000000000414c44 <+404>:   b       0x414b7c <_Unwind_RaiseException+204>
End of assembler dump.
```

Exercise A8 (x64, WinDbg)

Goal: Learn how to identify runtime exceptions, past execution residue and stack traces, identify handled exceptions.

Patterns: C++ Exception; Coincidental Symbolic Information; Handled Exception (User Space).

1. Launch WinDbg.

2. Load the *core.App8* dump file from the x64\App8 folder:

```
Microsoft (R) Windows Debugger Version 10.0.27725.1000 AMD64
Copyright (c) Microsoft Corporation. All rights reserved.


Loading Dump File [C:\ALCDA2\x64\App8\core.App8]
64-bit machine not using 64-bit API

************* Path validation summary **************
Response                         Time (ms)     Location
Deferred                                       srv*
Symbol search path is: srv*
Executable search path is:
Generic Unix Version 0 UP Free x64
System Uptime: not available
Process Uptime: not available
..
(a1.a2): Signal SIGABRT code SI_TKILL (Sent by tkill system call) originating from PID a1
*** WARNING: Unable to verify timestamp for App8
App8+0x24fdb:
00000000`00424fdb ???
```

3. Set logging to a file in case of lengthy output from some commands:

```
0:000> .logopen C:\ALCDA2\x64\App8\App8-WinDbg.log
Opened log file 'C:\ALCDA2\x64\App8\App8-WinDbg.log'
```

4. Specify the dump folder as the symbol path and reload symbols:

```
0:000> .symfix; .sympath+ C:\ALCDA2\x64\App8\
Symbol search path is: srv*;C:\ALCDA2\x64\App8\
Expanded Symbol search path is:
cache*;SRV*https://msdl.microsoft.com/download/symbols;c:\alcda2\x64\app8\

************* Path validation summary **************
Response                         Time (ms)     Location
Deferred                                       srv*
OK                                             C:\ALCDA2\x64\App8\
*** WARNING: Unable to verify timestamp for App8
```

```
0:000> .reload
..
*** WARNING: Unable to verify timestamp for App8

************* Symbol Loading Error Summary **************
Module name            Error
App8                   The system cannot find the file specified

You can troubleshoot most symbol related issues by turning on symbol loading diagnostics (!sym
noisy) and repeating the command that caused symbols to be loaded.
You should also verify that your symbol search path (.sympath) is correct.
```

Note: We ignore warnings and errors as they are not relevant for now.

5. List all thread stack traces:

```
0:000> ~*kL

Unable to get thread data for thread 0
.  0  Id: a1.a2 Suspend: 0 Teb: 00000000`00000000 Unfrozen
 # Child-SP          RetAddr               Call Site
00 00007f4d`60081a40 00000000`004017d3     App8!gsignal+0x10b
01 00007f4d`60081b60 00000000`00401553     App8!abort+0x121
02 00007f4d`60081c90 00000000`00402b46     App8!__gnu_cxx::__verbose_terminate_handler+0x59
03 00007f4d`60081cc0 00000000`00402b81 (T) App8!__cxxabiv1::__terminate+0x6
04 00007f4d`60081cd0 00000000`00402ac4 (T) App8!std::terminate+0xc
05 00007f4d`60081ce0 00000000`004022de     App8!_cxa_throw+0x3f
06 00007f4d`60081d00 00000000`0040233b     App8!procB+0x8d
07 00007f4d`60081d60 00000000`004023a0     App8!procA+0x9
08 00007f4d`60081d70 00000000`004023c2     App8!procNH+0x13
09 00007f4d`60081d80 00000000`004023ce     App8!bar_one+0x9
0a 00007f4d`60081d90 00000000`004023e2     App8!foo_one+0x9
0b 00007f4d`60081da0 00000000`0041b483     App8!thread_one+0x11
0c 00007f4d`60081dc0 00000000`0045d22f     App8!start_thread+0xf3
0d 00007f4d`60081e80 ffffffff`ffffffff     App8!_clone+0x3f
0e 00007f4d`60081e88 00000000`00000000     0xffffffff`ffffffff

Unable to get thread data for thread 1
   1  Id: a1.a4 Suspend: 0 Teb: 00000000`00000000 Unfrozen
 # Child-SP          RetAddr               Call Site
00 00007f4d`5f07fcf0 00000000`0045a9fa     App8!nanosleep+0x40
01 00007f4d`5f07fd20 00000000`0040236c     App8!sleep+0x3a
02 00007f4d`5f07fd60 00000000`00402422     App8!procH+0x22
03 00007f4d`5f07fd80 00000000`0040242e     App8!bar_three+0x9
04 00007f4d`5f07fd90 00000000`00402442     App8!foo_three+0x9
05 00007f4d`5f07fda0 00000000`0041b483     App8!thread_three+0x11
06 00007f4d`5f07fdc0 00000000`0045d22f     App8!start_thread+0xf3
07 00007f4d`5f07fe80 ffffffff`ffffffff     App8!_clone+0x3f
08 00007f4d`5f07fe88 00000000`00000000     0xffffffff`ffffffff

Unable to get thread data for thread 2
   2  Id: a1.a5 Suspend: 0 Teb: 00000000`00000000 Unfrozen
 # Child-SP          RetAddr               Call Site
00 00007f4d`5e87ed00 00000000`0045a9fa     App8!nanosleep+0x40
01 00007f4d`5e87ed30 00000000`004023b6     App8!sleep+0x3a
02 00007f4d`5e87ed70 00000000`00402452     App8!procNE+0x13
03 00007f4d`5e87ed80 00000000`0040245e     App8!bar_four+0x9
04 00007f4d`5e87ed90 00000000`00402472     App8!foo_four+0x9
05 00007f4d`5e87eda0 00000000`0041b483     App8!thread_four+0x11
```

```
06 00007f4d`5e87edc0 00000000`0045d22f      App8!start_thread+0xf3
07 00007f4d`5e87ee80 ffffffff`ffffffff      App8!_clone+0x3f
08 00007f4d`5e87ee88 00000000`00000000      0xffffffff`ffffffff

Unable to get thread data for thread 3
   3  Id: a1.a3 Suspend: 0 Teb: 00000000`00000000 Unfrozen
 # Child-SP          RetAddr               Call Site
00 00007f4d`5f880d00 00000000`0045a9fa      App8!nanosleep+0x40
01 00007f4d`5f880d30 00000000`004023b6      App8!sleep+0x3a
02 00007f4d`5f880d70 00000000`004023f2      App8!procNE+0x13
03 00007f4d`5f880d80 00000000`004023fe      App8!bar_two+0x9
04 00007f4d`5f880d90 00000000`00402412      App8!foo_two+0x9
05 00007f4d`5f880da0 00000000`0041b483      App8!thread_two+0x11
06 00007f4d`5f880dc0 00000000`0045d22f      App8!start_thread+0xf3
07 00007f4d`5f880e80 ffffffff`ffffffff      App8!_clone+0x3f
08 00007f4d`5f880e88 00000000`00000000      0xffffffff`ffffffff

Unable to get thread data for thread 4
   4  Id: a1.a1 Suspend: 0 Teb: 00000000`00000000 Unfrozen
 # Child-SP          RetAddr               Call Site
00 00007ffd`dda43c10 00000000`0045a9fa      App8!nanosleep+0x40
01 00007ffd`dda43c40 00000000`00402553      App8!sleep+0x3a
02 00007ffd`dda43c80 00000000`0041f9d1      App8!main+0xaa
03 00007ffd`dda43cd0 00000000`004020da      App8!_libc_start_main+0x3d1
04 00007ffd`dda43dd0 ffffffff`ffffffff      App8!start+0x2a
05 00007ffd`dda43dd8 00000000`00000000      0xffffffff`ffffffff

Unable to get thread data for thread 5
   5  Id: a1.a6 Suspend: 0 Teb: 00000000`00000000 Unfrozen
 # Child-SP          RetAddr               Call Site
00 00007f4d`5e07dd00 00000000`0045a9fa      App8!nanosleep+0x40
01 00007f4d`5e07dd30 00000000`004023b6      App8!sleep+0x3a
02 00007f4d`5e07dd70 00000000`00402482      App8!procNE+0x13
03 00007f4d`5e07dd80 00000000`0040248e      App8!bar_five+0x9
04 00007f4d`5e07dd90 00000000`004024a2      App8!foo_five+0x9
05 00007f4d`5e07dda0 00000000`0041b483      App8!thread_five+0x11
06 00007f4d`5e07ddc0 00000000`0045d22f      App8!start_thread+0xf3
07 00007f4d`5e07de80 ffffffff`ffffffff      App8!_clone+0x3f
08 00007f4d`5e07de88 00000000`00000000      0xffffffff`ffffffff
```

Note: We have C++ exception processing in the current thread #0.

6. Go to thread #3, identify the execution residue of *work* functions, check their correctness, and reconstruct the past stack trace:

```
0:000> ~3s
App8!nanosleep+0x40:
00000000`0045aa70 cmp     rax,0FFFFFFFFFFFFF000h

0:003> kL
 # Child-SP          RetAddr               Call Site
00 00007f4d`5f880d00 00000000`0045a9fa      App8!nanosleep+0x40
01 00007f4d`5f880d30 00000000`004023b6      App8!sleep+0x3a
02 00007f4d`5f880d70 00000000`004023f2      App8!procNE+0x13
03 00007f4d`5f880d80 00000000`004023fe      App8!bar_two+0x9
04 00007f4d`5f880d90 00000000`00402412      App8!foo_two+0x9
05 00007f4d`5f880da0 00000000`0041b483      App8!thread_two+0x11
06 00007f4d`5f880dc0 00000000`0045d22f      App8!start_thread+0xf3
07 00007f4d`5f880e80 ffffffff`ffffffff      App8!_clone+0x3f
```

```
08 00007f4d`5f880e88 00000000`00000000      0xffffffff`ffffffff
```

```
0:003> dps rsp-500 rsp
00007f4d`5f880800  00000000`00000000
00007f4d`5f880808  00000000`00000000
00007f4d`5f880810  00000000`00000000
00007f4d`5f880818  00000000`00000000
00007f4d`5f880820  00000000`00000000
00007f4d`5f880828  00000000`00000000
00007f4d`5f880830  00000000`00000000
00007f4d`5f880838  00000000`00000000
00007f4d`5f880840  00000000`00000000
00007f4d`5f880848  00000000`00000000
00007f4d`5f880850  00000000`00000000
00007f4d`5f880858  00000000`00000000
00007f4d`5f880860  00000000`00000000
00007f4d`5f880868  00000000`00000000
00007f4d`5f880870  00000000`00000000
00007f4d`5f880878  00000000`00000000
00007f4d`5f880880  00000000`00000000
00007f4d`5f880888  00000000`00000000
00007f4d`5f880890  00000000`00000000
00007f4d`5f880898  00000000`00000000
00007f4d`5f8808a0  00000000`00000000
00007f4d`5f8808a8  00000000`00000000
00007f4d`5f8808b0  00007f4d`5f8808c0
00007f4d`5f8808b8  00000000`004021dd App8!work_8+0x9
00007f4d`5f8808c0  00007f4d`5f8808d0
00007f4d`5f8808c8  00000000`004021e9 App8!work_7+0x9
00007f4d`5f8808d0  00007f4d`5f8808e0
00007f4d`5f8808d8  00000000`004021f5 App8!work_6+0x9
00007f4d`5f8808e0  00007f4d`5f8808f0
00007f4d`5f8808e8  00000000`00402201 App8!work_5+0x9
00007f4d`5f8808f0  00007f4d`5f880900
00007f4d`5f8808f8  00000000`0040220d App8!work_4+0x9
00007f4d`5f880900  00007f4d`5f880910
00007f4d`5f880908  00000000`00402219 App8!work_3+0x9
00007f4d`5f880910  00007f4d`5f880920
00007f4d`5f880918  00000000`00402225 App8!work_2+0x9
00007f4d`5f880920  00007f4d`5f880930
00007f4d`5f880928  00000000`00402231 App8!work_1+0x9
00007f4d`5f880930  00007f4d`5f880d40
00007f4d`5f880938  00000000`00402244 App8!work+0x10
00007f4d`5f880940  00000000`00000000
...
...
...
```

```
0:003> ub 00000000`00402219
App8!work_4+0x2:
00000000`00402206 mov     ebp,esp
00000000`00402208 call    App8!work_5 (00000000`004021f8)
00000000`0040220d nop
00000000`0040220e pop     rbp
00000000`0040220f ret
App8!work_3:
00000000`00402210 push    rbp
00000000`00402211 mov     rbp,rsp
00000000`00402214 call    App8!work_4 (00000000`00402204)
```

Note: Since the saved fp value points to the next line we can easily reconstract the fragment of the past stack trace:

```
00007f4d`5f8808b0  00007f4d`5f8808c0
00007f4d`5f8808b8  00000000`004021dd App8!work_8+0x9
00007f4d`5f8808c0  00007f4d`5f8808d0
00007f4d`5f8808c8  00000000`004021e9 App8!work_7+0x9
00007f4d`5f8808d0  00007f4d`5f8808e0
00007f4d`5f8808d8  00000000`004021f5 App8!work_6+0x9
00007f4d`5f8808e0  00007f4d`5f8808f0
00007f4d`5f8808e8  00000000`00402201 App8!work_5+0x9
00007f4d`5f8808f0  00007f4d`5f880900
00007f4d`5f8808f8  00000000`0040220d App8!work_4+0x9
00007f4d`5f880900  00007f4d`5f880910
00007f4d`5f880908  00000000`00402219 App8!work_3+0x9
00007f4d`5f880910  00007f4d`5f880920
00007f4d`5f880918  00000000`00402225 App8!work_2+0x9
00007f4d`5f880920  00007f4d`5f880930
00007f4d`5f880928  00000000`00402231 App8!work_1+0x9
00007f4d`5f880930  00007f4d`5f880d40
00007f4d`5f880938  00000000`00402244 App8!work+0x10
```

7. Go to thread #1, identify the handled exception processing code, and check its validity:

```
0:003> ~1s
App8!nanosleep+0x40:
00000000`0045aa70 cmp     rax,0FFFFFFFFFFFFF000h

0:001> kL
 # Child-SP          RetAddr           Call Site
00 00007f4d`5f07fcf0 00000000`0045a9fa App8!nanosleep+0x40
01 00007f4d`5f07fd20 00000000`0040236c App8!sleep+0x3a
02 00007f4d`5f07fd60 00000000`00402422 App8!procH+0x22
03 00007f4d`5f07fd80 00000000`0040242e App8!bar_three+0x9
04 00007f4d`5f07fd90 00000000`00402442 App8!foo_three+0x9
05 00007f4d`5f07fda0 00000000`0041b483 App8!thread_three+0x11
06 00007f4d`5f07fdc0 00000000`0045d22f App8!start_thread+0xf3
07 00007f4d`5f07fe80 ffffffff`ffffffff App8!_clone+0x3f
08 00007f4d`5f07fe88 00000000`00000000 0xffffffff`ffffffff

0:001> dps rsp-2000 rsp
00007f4d`5f07ecf0  00000000`00000000
00007f4d`5f07ecf8  00000000`00000000
...
...
...
00007f4d`5f07f740  00007f4d`5f07f760
00007f4d`5f07f748  00000000`00000004
00007f4d`5f07f750  00007f4d`5f07fb00
00007f4d`5f07f758  00000000`004176fb App8!Unwind_RaiseException_Phase2+0x4b
00007f4d`5f07f760  00000000`00000000
00007f4d`5f07f768  00000000`00000000
00007f4d`5f07f770  00000000`00000000
00007f4d`5f07f778  00000000`00000000
00007f4d`5f07f780  00000000`00000000
00007f4d`5f07f788  00000000`00000000
00007f4d`5f07f790  ffffffff`ffffffe8
00007f4d`5f07f798  00000000`00000001
00007f4d`5f07f7a0  00000000`00000000
00007f4d`5f07f7a8  00000000`00000000
00007f4d`5f07f7b0  00000000`00000000
```

```
00007f4d`5f07f7b8  00000000`00000000
00007f4d`5f07f7c0  ffffffff`fffffff0
00007f4d`5f07f7c8  00000000`00000001
00007f4d`5f07f7d0  00000000`00000000
00007f4d`5f07f7d8  00000000`00000000
00007f4d`5f07f7e0  00000000`00000000
00007f4d`5f07f7e8  00000000`00000000
00007f4d`5f07f7f0  00000000`00000000
00007f4d`5f07f7f8  00000000`00000000
00007f4d`5f07f800  00000000`00000000
00007f4d`5f07f808  00000000`00000000
00007f4d`5f07f810  00000000`00000000
00007f4d`5f07f818  00000000`00000000
00007f4d`5f07f820  00000000`00000000
00007f4d`5f07f828  00000000`00000000
00007f4d`5f07f830  00000000`00000000
00007f4d`5f07f838  00000000`00000000
00007f4d`5f07f840  00000000`00000000
00007f4d`5f07f848  00000000`00000000
00007f4d`5f07f850  00000000`00000000
00007f4d`5f07f858  00000000`00000000
00007f4d`5f07f860  ffffffff`fffffff8
00007f4d`5f07f868  00000000`00000001
00007f4d`5f07f870  00000000`00000000
00007f4d`5f07f878  00000000`00000000
00007f4d`5f07f880  00000000`00000000
00007f4d`5f07f888  00000000`00000010
00007f4d`5f07f890  00000000`00000006
00007f4d`5f07f898  00000000`00000000
00007f4d`5f07f8a0  00000000`00000001
00007f4d`5f07f8a8  00000000`0040238c App8!procH+0x42
00007f4d`5f07f8b0  00000000`00403000 App8!_gxx_personality_v0
00007f4d`5f07f8b8  ffffffff`fffffff8
00007f4d`5f07f8c0  00000000`00000001
00007f4d`5f07f8c8  00000000`00000010
00007f4d`5f07f8d0  00000000`00011b1b
00007f4d`5f07f8d8  00000000`00000000
00007f4d`5f07f8e0  00007f4d`58000b80
00007f4d`5f07f8e8  00007f4d`5f07fa10
00007f4d`5f07f8f0  00007f4d`5f07fcc0
00007f4d`5f07f8f8  00007f4d`5f07fb00
00007f4d`5f07f900  00007f4d`58000b80
00007f4d`5f07f908  00007f4d`5f07fd60
00007f4d`5f07f910  00000000`00000000
00007f4d`5f07f918  00000000`00417faa App8!Unwind_RaiseException+0x2da
00007f4d`5f07f920  00007f4d`5f07fc88
00007f4d`5f07f928  00007f4d`5f07fc90
00007f4d`5f07f930  00000000`00000000
00007f4d`5f07f938  00007f4d`5f07fc98
00007f4d`5f07f940  00000000`00000000
00007f4d`5f07f948  00000000`00000000
00007f4d`5f07f950  00007f4d`5f07fcc0
00007f4d`5f07f958  00000000`00000000
00007f4d`5f07f960  00000000`00000000
00007f4d`5f07f968  00000000`00000000
00007f4d`5f07f970  00000000`00000000
00007f4d`5f07f978  00000000`00000000
00007f4d`5f07f980  00007f4d`5f07fca0
00007f4d`5f07f988  00007f4d`5f07fca8
00007f4d`5f07f990  00007f4d`5f07fcb0
```

```
00007f4d`5f07f998  00007f4d`5f07fcb8
00007f4d`5f07f9a0  00007f4d`5f07fcc8
00007f4d`5f07f9a8  00000000`00000000
00007f4d`5f07f9b0  00007f4d`5f07fcd0
00007f4d`5f07f9b8  00000000`00402ab7 App8!_cxa_throw+0x37
00007f4d`5f07f9c0  00000000`00000000
00007f4d`5f07f9c8  00000000`00000000
00007f4d`5f07f9d0  00000000`00000000
00007f4d`5f07f9d8  00000000`00417cd0 App8!Unwind_RaiseException
00007f4d`5f07f9e0  40000000`00000000
00007f4d`5f07f9e8  00000000`00000000
00007f4d`5f07f9f0  00000000`00000000
...
...
...

0:001> ub 00000000`00417faa
App8!Unwind_RaiseException+0x2b4:
00000000`00417f84 test    dword ptr [rdi+48FFFFFEh],esi
00000000`00417f8a mov     esi,ebx
00000000`00417f8c mov     rdi,r14
00000000`00417f8f call    App8!uw_install_context_1 (00000000`00417890)
00000000`00417f94 mov     r8,qword ptr [rbp-218h]
00000000`00417f9b mov     rdi,qword ptr [rbp-220h]
00000000`00417fa2 mov     rsi,r8
00000000`00417fa5 call    App8!Unwind_DebugHook (00000000`00417cc0)
```

12. We close logging before exiting WinDbg:

```
0:001> .logclose
Closing open log file 'C:\ALCDA2\x64\App8\App8-WinDbg.log'
```

Exercise A8 (A64, WinDbg)

Goal: Learn how to identify runtime exceptions, past execution residue and stack traces, identify handled exceptions.

Patterns: C++ Exception; Coincidental Symbolic Information; Handled Exception (User Space).

1. Launch WinDbg.

2. Load the *core.25889* dump file from the A64\App8 folder:

```
Microsoft (R) Windows Debugger Version 10.0.27725.1000 AMD64
Copyright (c) Microsoft Corporation. All rights reserved.


Loading Dump File [C:\ALCDA2\A64\App8\core.25889]
64-bit machine not using 64-bit API

************* Path validation summary **************
Response                         Time (ms)     Location
Deferred                                       srv*
Symbol search path is: srv*
Executable search path is:
Generic Unix Version 0 UP Free ARM 64-bit (AArch64)
System Uptime: not available
Process Uptime: not available
..
(6521.6522): Signal SIGABRT code SI_TKILL (Sent by tkill system call) originating from PID 6521
*** WARNING: Unable to verify timestamp for App8
App8+0x20cfc:
00000000`00420cfc ???
```

3. Set logging to a file in case of lengthy output from some commands:

```
0:000> .logopen C:\ALCDA2\A64\App8\App8-WinDbg.log
Opened log file 'C:\ALCDA2\A64\App8\App8-WinDbg.log'
```

4. Specify the dump folder as the symbol path and reload symbols:

```
0:000> .symfix; .sympath+ C:\ALCDA2\A64\App8\
Symbol search path is: srv*;C:\ALCDA2\A64\App8\
Expanded Symbol search path is:
cache*;SRV*https://msdl.microsoft.com/download/symbols;c:\alcda2\a64\app8\

************* Path validation summary **************
Response                         Time (ms)     Location
Deferred                                       srv*
OK                                             C:\ALCDA2\A64\App8\
*** WARNING: Unable to verify timestamp for App8
```

```
0:000> .reload
..
*** WARNING: Unable to verify timestamp for App8

************* Symbol Loading Error Summary **************
Module name            Error
App8                   The system cannot find the file specified

You can troubleshoot most symbol related issues by turning on symbol loading diagnostics (!sym
noisy) and repeating the command that caused symbols to be loaded.
You should also verify that your symbol search path (.sympath) is correct.
```

Note: We ignore warnings and errors as they are not relevant for now.

5. List all thread stack traces:

```
0:000> ~*k

Unable to get thread data for thread 0
.  0  Id: 6521.6522 Suspend: 0 Teb: 00000000`00000000 Unfrozen
 # Child-SP          RetAddr               Call Site
00 0000fffe`7a3ce5c0 00000000`00422d38     App8!raise+0x2c
01 0000fffe`7a3ce5c0 00000000`004086f0     App8!abort+0x128
02 0000fffe`7a3ce710 00000000`00404c0c     App8!__gnu_cxx::__verbose_terminate_handler+0x16c
03 0000fffe`7a3ce760 00000000`00404c30 (T) App8!__cxxabiv1::__terminate+0xc
04 0000fffe`7a3ce770 00000000`00404d88 (T) App8!std::terminate+0x14
05 0000fffe`7a3ce780 00000000`00403424     App8!_cxa_throw+0x98
06 0000fffe`7a3ce7b0 00000000`00403490     App8!procB+0x7c
07 0000fffe`7a3ce7f0 00000000`00403504     App8!procA+0xc
08 0000fffe`7a3ce800 00000000`00403534     App8!procNH+0x14
09 0000fffe`7a3ce810 00000000`00403548     App8!bar_one+0xc
0a 0000fffe`7a3ce820 00000000`00403560     App8!foo_one+0xc
0b 0000fffe`7a3ce830 00000000`004183f4     App8!thread_one+0x10
0c 0000fffe`7a3ce850 00000000`0043dd20     App8!start_thread+0xb4
0d 0000fffe`7a3ce980 ffffffff`ffffffff     App8!thread_start+0x30
0e 0000fffe`7a3ce980 00000000`00000000     0xffffffff`ffffffff

Unable to get thread data for thread 1
   1  Id: 6521.6524 Suspend: 0 Teb: 00000000`00000000 Unfrozen
 # Child-SP          RetAddr               Call Site
00 0000fffe`793ae5c0 00000000`00438e34     App8!_libc_nanosleep+0x24
01 0000fffe`793ae600 00000000`004034cc     App8!sleep+0x110
02 0000fffe`793ae7f0 00000000`004035bc     App8!procH+0x20
03 0000fffe`793ae810 00000000`004035d0     App8!bar_three+0xc
04 0000fffe`793ae820 00000000`004035e8     App8!foo_three+0xc
05 0000fffe`793ae830 00000000`004183f4     App8!thread_three+0x10
06 0000fffe`793ae850 00000000`0043dd20     App8!start_thread+0xb4
07 0000fffe`793ae980 ffffffff`ffffffff     App8!thread_start+0x30
08 0000fffe`793ae980 00000000`00000000     0xffffffff`ffffffff

Unable to get thread data for thread 2
   2  Id: 6521.6521 Suspend: 0 Teb: 00000000`00000000 Unfrozen
 # Child-SP          RetAddr               Call Site
00 0000ffff`d79fcc20 00000000`00438e34     App8!_libc_nanosleep+0x24
01 0000ffff`d79fcc60 00000000`0040370c     App8!sleep+0x110
02 0000ffff`d79fce50 00000000`0042240c     App8!main+0x90
03 0000ffff`d79fcea0 00000000`00403188     App8!_libc_start_main+0x304
04 0000ffff`d79fd000 00000000`00000000     App8!start+0x4c
```

```
Unable to get thread data for thread 3
   3  Id: 6521.6523 Suspend: 0 Teb: 00000000`00000000 Unfrozen
 # Child-SP          RetAddr               Call Site
00 0000fffe`79bbe5d0 00000000`00438e34     App8!_libc_nanosleep+0x24
01 0000fffe`79bbe610 00000000`00403520     App8!sleep+0x110
02 0000fffe`79bbe800 00000000`00403578     App8!procNE+0x14
03 0000fffe`79bbe810 00000000`0040358c     App8!bar_two+0xc
04 0000fffe`79bbe820 00000000`004035a4     App8!foo_two+0xc
05 0000fffe`79bbe830 00000000`004183f4     App8!thread_two+0x10
06 0000fffe`79bbe850 00000000`0043dd20     App8!start_thread+0xb4
07 0000fffe`79bbe980 ffffffff`ffffffff     App8!thread_start+0x30
08 0000fffe`79bbe980 00000000`00000000     0xffffffff`ffffffff

Unable to get thread data for thread 4
   4  Id: 6521.6526 Suspend: 0 Teb: 00000000`00000000 Unfrozen
 # Child-SP          RetAddr               Call Site
00 0000fffe`73ffe5d0 00000000`00438e34     App8!_libc_nanosleep+0x24
01 0000fffe`73ffe610 00000000`00403520     App8!sleep+0x110
02 0000fffe`73ffe800 00000000`00403644     App8!procNE+0x14
03 0000fffe`73ffe810 00000000`00403658     App8!bar_five+0xc
04 0000fffe`73ffe820 00000000`00403670     App8!foo_five+0xc
05 0000fffe`73ffe830 00000000`004183f4     App8!thread_five+0x10
06 0000fffe`73ffe850 00000000`0043dd20     App8!start_thread+0xb4
07 0000fffe`73ffe980 ffffffff`ffffffff     App8!thread_start+0x30
08 0000fffe`73ffe980 00000000`00000000     0xffffffff`ffffffff

Unable to get thread data for thread 5
   5  Id: 6521.6525 Suspend: 0 Teb: 00000000`00000000 Unfrozen
 # Child-SP          RetAddr               Call Site
00 0000fffe`78b9e5d0 00000000`00438e34     App8!_libc_nanosleep+0x24
01 0000fffe`78b9e610 00000000`00403520     App8!sleep+0x110
02 0000fffe`78b9e800 00000000`00403600     App8!procNE+0x14
03 0000fffe`78b9e810 00000000`00403614     App8!bar_four+0xc
04 0000fffe`78b9e820 00000000`0040362c     App8!foo_four+0xc
05 0000fffe`78b9e830 00000000`004183f4     App8!thread_four+0x10
06 0000fffe`78b9e850 00000000`0043dd20     App8!start_thread+0xb4
07 0000fffe`78b9e980 ffffffff`ffffffff     App8!thread_start+0x30
08 0000fffe`78b9e980 00000000`00000000     0xffffffff`ffffffff
```

Note: We have C++ exception processing in the current thread #0.

8. Go to thread #3, identify the execution residue of *work* functions, check their correctness, and reconstruct the past stack trace:

```
0:000> ~3s
App8!_libc_nanosleep+0x24:
00000000`00420174 d4000001 svc          #0

0:003> k
 # Child-SP          RetAddr               Call Site
00 0000fffe`79bbe5d0 00000000`00438e34     App8!_libc_nanosleep+0x24
01 0000fffe`79bbe610 00000000`00403520     App8!sleep+0x110
02 0000fffe`79bbe800 00000000`00403578     App8!procNE+0x14
03 0000fffe`79bbe810 00000000`0040358c     App8!bar_two+0xc
04 0000fffe`79bbe820 00000000`004035a4     App8!foo_two+0xc
05 0000fffe`79bbe830 00000000`004183f4     App8!thread_two+0x10
06 0000fffe`79bbe850 00000000`0043dd20     App8!start_thread+0xb4
07 0000fffe`79bbe980 ffffffff`ffffffff     App8!thread_start+0x30
08 0000fffe`79bbe980 00000000`00000000     0xffffffff`ffffffff
```

```
0:003> dps sp-300 sp
0000fffe`79bbe2d0  00000000`00000000
0000fffe`79bbe2d8  00000000`00000000
0000fffe`79bbe2e0  00000000`00000000
0000fffe`79bbe2e8  00000000`00000000
0000fffe`79bbe2f0  00000000`00000000
0000fffe`79bbe2f8  00000000`00000000
0000fffe`79bbe300  00000000`00000000
0000fffe`79bbe308  00000000`00000000
0000fffe`79bbe310  00000000`00000000
0000fffe`79bbe318  00000000`00000000
0000fffe`79bbe320  00000000`00000000
0000fffe`79bbe328  00000000`00000000
0000fffe`79bbe330  00000000`00000000
0000fffe`79bbe338  00000000`00000000
0000fffe`79bbe340  00000000`00000000
0000fffe`79bbe348  00000000`00000000
0000fffe`79bbe350  0000fffe`79bbe360
0000fffe`79bbe358  00000000`00403304 App8!work_7+0xc
0000fffe`79bbe360  0000fffe`79bbe370
0000fffe`79bbe368  00000000`00403318 App8!work_6+0xc
0000fffe`79bbe370  0000fffe`79bbe380
0000fffe`79bbe378  00000000`0040332c App8!work_5+0xc
0000fffe`79bbe380  0000fffe`79bbe390
0000fffe`79bbe388  00000000`00403340 App8!work_4+0xc
0000fffe`79bbe390  0000fffe`79bbe3a0
0000fffe`79bbe398  00000000`00403354 App8!work_3+0xc
0000fffe`79bbe3a0  0000fffe`79bbe3b0
0000fffe`79bbe3a8  00000000`00403368 App8!work_2+0xc
0000fffe`79bbe3b0  0000fffe`79bbe3c0
0000fffe`79bbe3b8  00000000`0040337c App8!work_1+0xc
0000fffe`79bbe3c0  0000fffe`79bbe3d0
0000fffe`79bbe3c8  00000000`00403394 App8!work+0x10
0000fffe`79bbe3d0  0000fffe`79bbe7e0
0000fffe`79bbe3d8  00000000`0040347c App8!procNB+0xc
0000fffe`79bbe3e0  00000000`00000000
0000fffe`79bbe3e8  00000000`00000000
0000fffe`79bbe3f0  00000000`00000000
0000fffe`79bbe3f8  00000000`00000000
0000fffe`79bbe400  00000000`00000000
0000fffe`79bbe408  00000000`00000000
0000fffe`79bbe410  00000000`00000000
0000fffe`79bbe418  00000000`00000000
...
...
...

0:003> ub 00000000`00403354
App8!work_4:
00000000`00403334 a9bf7bfd stp         fp,lr,[sp,#-0x10]!
00000000`00403338 910003fd mov         fp,sp
00000000`0040333c 97fffff9 bl          App8!work_5 (00000000`00403320)
00000000`00403340 a8c17bfd ldp         fp,lr,[sp],#0x10
00000000`00403344 d65f03c0 ret
App8!work_3:
00000000`00403348 a9bf7bfd stp         fp,lr,[sp,#-0x10]!
00000000`0040334c 910003fd mov         fp,sp
00000000`00403350 97fffff9 bl          App8!work_4 (00000000`00403334)
```

Note: Since the saved fp value points to the next line we can easily reconstract the fragment of the past stack trace:

```
0000fffe`79bbe350  0000fffe`79bbe360
0000fffe`79bbe358  00000000`00403304 App8!work_7+0xc
0000fffe`79bbe360  0000fffe`79bbe370
0000fffe`79bbe368  00000000`00403318 App8!work_6+0xc
0000fffe`79bbe370  0000fffe`79bbe380
0000fffe`79bbe378  00000000`0040332c App8!work_5+0xc
0000fffe`79bbe380  0000fffe`79bbe390
0000fffe`79bbe388  00000000`00403340 App8!work_4+0xc
0000fffe`79bbe390  0000fffe`79bbe3a0
0000fffe`79bbe398  00000000`00403354 App8!work_3+0xc
0000fffe`79bbe3a0  0000fffe`79bbe3b0
0000fffe`79bbe3a8  00000000`00403368 App8!work_2+0xc
0000fffe`79bbe3b0  0000fffe`79bbe3c0
0000fffe`79bbe3b8  00000000`0040337c App8!work_1+0xc
0000fffe`79bbe3c0  0000fffe`79bbe3d0
0000fffe`79bbe3c8  00000000`00403394 App8!work+0x10
0000fffe`79bbe3d0  0000fffe`79bbe7e0
0000fffe`79bbe3d8  00000000`0040347c App8!procNB+0xc
```

9. Go to thread #1, identify the handled exception processing code, and check its validity:

```
0:003> ~1s
App8!_libc_nanosleep+0x24:
00000000`00420174 d4000001 svc         #0

0:001> k
 # Child-SP          RetAddr               Call Site
00 0000fffe`793ae5c0 00000000`00438e34     App8!_libc_nanosleep+0x24
01 0000fffe`793ae600 00000000`004034cc     App8!sleep+0x110
02 0000fffe`793ae7f0 00000000`004035bc     App8!procH+0x20
03 0000fffe`793ae810 00000000`004035d0     App8!bar_three+0xc
04 0000fffe`793ae820 00000000`004035e8     App8!foo_three+0xc
05 0000fffe`793ae830 00000000`004183f4     App8!thread_three+0x10
06 0000fffe`793ae850 00000000`0043dd20     App8!start_thread+0xb4
07 0000fffe`793ae980 ffffffff`ffffffff     App8!thread_start+0x30
08 0000fffe`793ae980 00000000`00000000     0xffffffff`ffffffff

0:001> dps sp-1000 sp
0000fffe`793ac5c0  00000000`00000000
0000fffe`793ac5c8  00000000`00000000
...
...
...
0000fffe`793ad0e0  0000fffe`793ad0f0
0000fffe`793ad0e8  00000000`00404754 App8!_gxx_personality_v0+0xf0
0000fffe`793ad0f0  0000fffe`793ad1e0
0000fffe`793ad0f8  00000000`004145ac App8!Unwind_RaiseException_Phase2+0x70
0000fffe`793ad100  0000fffe`793add30
0000fffe`793ad108  0000fffe`793ad220
0000fffe`793ad110  00000000`00000004
0000fffe`793ad118  0000fffe`74000b80
0000fffe`793ad120  00000000`00000004
0000fffe`793ad128  0000fffe`793af760
0000fffe`793ad130  00000000`32b706f0
0000fffe`793ad138  00000000`004f9540 App8!_default_pthread_attr
0000fffe`793ad140  00000000`00010000
0000fffe`793ad148  00000000`00810000
0000fffe`793ad150  0000fffe`793ad1e0
```

```
0000fffe`793ad158  00000000`00414570 App8!Unwind_RaiseException_Phase2+0x34
0000fffe`793ad160  0000fffe`793add30
0000fffe`793ad168  00000000`004c57d8 App8!$d+0x1
0000fffe`793ad170  00000000`00000000
0000fffe`793ad178  0000fffe`74000b80
0000fffe`793ad180  00000000`00000004
0000fffe`793ad188  00000000`00000000
0000fffe`793ad190  00000000`32b706f0
0000fffe`793ad198  00000000`004f9540 App8!_default_pthread_attr
0000fffe`793ad1a0  00000000`00010000
0000fffe`793ad1a8  00000000`00810000
0000fffe`793ad1b0  00000000`00000000
0000fffe`793ad1b8  00000000`00000000
0000fffe`793ad1c0  0000fffe`793ad1e0
0000fffe`793ad1c8  00000000`004145cc App8!Unwind_RaiseException_Phase2+0x90
0000fffe`793ad1d0  ffffffff`fffffff8
0000fffe`793ad1d8  76a28b43`6af36f00
0000fffe`793ad1e0  0000fffe`793ad8a0
0000fffe`793ad1e8  00000000`00414bf4 App8!Unwind_RaiseException+0x144
0000fffe`793ad1f0  0000fffe`793add30
0000fffe`793ad1f8  0000fffe`793ae0f0
0000fffe`793ad200  0000fffe`74000b80
0000fffe`793ad208  0000fffe`793ad970
0000fffe`793ad210  00000000`00000000
0000fffe`793ad218  0000fffe`793ae770
0000fffe`793ad220  00000000`00000000
0000fffe`793ad228  00000000`00000000
0000fffe`793ad230  00000000`00000000
0000fffe`793ad238  00000000`00000000
0000fffe`793ad240  00000000`00000000
0000fffe`793ad248  00000000`00000000
0000fffe`793ad250  00000000`00000000
0000fffe`793ad258  00000000`00000000
0000fffe`793ad260  00000000`00000000
0000fffe`793ad268  00000000`00000000
0000fffe`793ad270  00000000`00000000
0000fffe`793ad278  00000000`00000000
0000fffe`793ad280  00000000`00000000
0000fffe`793ad288  00000000`00000000
0000fffe`793ad290  00000000`00000000
0000fffe`793ad298  00000000`00000000
0000fffe`793ad2a0  00000000`00000000
0000fffe`793ad2a8  00000000`00000000
0000fffe`793ad2b0  00000000`00000000
0000fffe`793ad2b8  00000000`00000000
0000fffe`793ad2c0  00000000`00000000
0000fffe`793ad2c8  00000000`00000000
0000fffe`793ad2d0  00000000`00000000
0000fffe`793ad2d8  00000000`00000000
0000fffe`793ad2e0  00000000`00000000
0000fffe`793ad2e8  00000000`00000000
0000fffe`793ad2f0  00000000`00000000
0000fffe`793ad2f8  00000000`00000000
0000fffe`793ad300  00000000`00000000
0000fffe`793ad308  00000000`00000000
0000fffe`793ad310  00000000`00000000
0000fffe`793ad318  00000000`00000000
0000fffe`793ad320  00000000`00000000
0000fffe`793ad328  00000000`00000000
0000fffe`793ad330  00000000`00000000
```

```
0000fffe`793ad338  00000000`00000000
0000fffe`793ad340  00000000`00000000
0000fffe`793ad348  00000000`00000000
0000fffe`793ad350  ffffffff`fffffff0
0000fffe`793ad358  00000000`00000001
0000fffe`793ad360  00000000`00000000
0000fffe`793ad368  00000000`00000000
0000fffe`793ad370  00000000`00000000
0000fffe`793ad378  00000000`00000000
0000fffe`793ad380  00000000`00000000
0000fffe`793ad388  00000000`00000000
0000fffe`793ad390  00000000`00000000
0000fffe`793ad398  00000000`00000000
0000fffe`793ad3a0  00000000`00000000
0000fffe`793ad3a8  00000000`00000000
0000fffe`793ad3b0  00000000`00000000
0000fffe`793ad3b8  00000000`00000000
0000fffe`793ad3c0  00000000`00000000
0000fffe`793ad3c8  00000000`00000000
0000fffe`793ad3d0  00000000`00000000
0000fffe`793ad3d8  00000000`00000000
0000fffe`793ad3e0  00000000`00000000
0000fffe`793ad3e8  00000000`00000000
0000fffe`793ad3f0  ffffffff`ffffffe0
0000fffe`793ad3f8  00000000`00000001
0000fffe`793ad400  ffffffff`ffffffe8
0000fffe`793ad408  00000000`00000001
0000fffe`793ad410  00000000`00000000
0000fffe`793ad418  00000000`00000000
0000fffe`793ad420  00000000`00000000
0000fffe`793ad428  00000000`00000000
0000fffe`793ad430  00000000`00000000
0000fffe`793ad438  00000000`00000000
0000fffe`793ad440  00000000`00000000
0000fffe`793ad448  00000000`00000000
0000fffe`793ad450  00000000`00000000
0000fffe`793ad458  00000000`00000000
0000fffe`793ad460  00000000`00000000
0000fffe`793ad468  00000000`00000000
0000fffe`793ad470  00000000`00000000
0000fffe`793ad478  00000000`00000000
0000fffe`793ad480  00000000`00000000
0000fffe`793ad488  00000000`00000000
0000fffe`793ad490  00000000`00000000
0000fffe`793ad498  00000000`00000000
0000fffe`793ad4a0  00000000`00000000
0000fffe`793ad4a8  00000000`00000000
0000fffe`793ad4b0  00000000`00000000
0000fffe`793ad4b8  00000000`00000000
0000fffe`793ad4c0  00000000`00000000
0000fffe`793ad4c8  00000000`00000000
0000fffe`793ad4d0  00000000`00000000
0000fffe`793ad4d8  00000000`00000000
0000fffe`793ad4e0  00000000`00000000
0000fffe`793ad4e8  00000000`00000000
0000fffe`793ad4f0  00000000`00000000
0000fffe`793ad4f8  00000000`00000000
0000fffe`793ad500  00000000`00000000
0000fffe`793ad508  00000000`00000000
0000fffe`793ad510  00000000`00000000
```

```
0000fffe`793ad518  00000000`00000000
0000fffe`793ad520  00000000`00000000
0000fffe`793ad528  00000000`00000000
0000fffe`793ad530  00000000`00000000
0000fffe`793ad538  00000000`00000000
0000fffe`793ad540  00000000`00000000
0000fffe`793ad548  00000000`00000000
0000fffe`793ad550  00000000`00000000
0000fffe`793ad558  00000000`00000000
0000fffe`793ad560  00000000`00000000
0000fffe`793ad568  00000000`00000000
0000fffe`793ad570  00000000`00000000
0000fffe`793ad578  00000000`00000000
0000fffe`793ad580  00000000`00000000
0000fffe`793ad588  00000000`00000000
0000fffe`793ad590  00000000`00000000
0000fffe`793ad598  00000000`00000000
0000fffe`793ad5a0  00000000`00000000
0000fffe`793ad5a8  00000000`00000000
0000fffe`793ad5b0  00000000`00000000
0000fffe`793ad5b8  00000000`00000000
0000fffe`793ad5c0  00000000`00000000
0000fffe`793ad5c8  00000000`00000000
0000fffe`793ad5d0  00000000`00000000
0000fffe`793ad5d8  00000000`00000000
0000fffe`793ad5e0  00000000`00000000
0000fffe`793ad5e8  00000000`00000000
0000fffe`793ad5f0  00000000`00000000
0000fffe`793ad5f8  00000000`00000000
0000fffe`793ad600  00000000`00000000
0000fffe`793ad608  00000000`00000000
0000fffe`793ad610  00000000`00000000
0000fffe`793ad618  00000000`00000000
0000fffe`793ad620  00000000`00000000
0000fffe`793ad628  00000000`00000000
0000fffe`793ad630  00000000`00000000
0000fffe`793ad638  00000000`00000000
0000fffe`793ad640  00000000`00000000
0000fffe`793ad648  00000000`00000000
0000fffe`793ad650  00000000`00000000
0000fffe`793ad658  00000000`00000000
0000fffe`793ad660  00000000`00000000
0000fffe`793ad668  00000000`00000000
0000fffe`793ad670  00000000`00000000
0000fffe`793ad678  00000000`00000000
0000fffe`793ad680  00000000`00000000
0000fffe`793ad688  00000000`00000000
0000fffe`793ad690  00000000`00000000
0000fffe`793ad698  00000000`00000000
0000fffe`793ad6a0  00000000`00000000
0000fffe`793ad6a8  00000000`00000000
0000fffe`793ad6b0  00000000`00000000
0000fffe`793ad6b8  00000000`00000000
0000fffe`793ad6c0  00000000`00000000
0000fffe`793ad6c8  00000000`00000000
0000fffe`793ad6d0  00000000`00000000
0000fffe`793ad6d8  00000000`00000000
0000fffe`793ad6e0  00000000`00000000
0000fffe`793ad6e8  00000000`00000000
0000fffe`793ad6f0  00000000`00000000
```

```
0000fffe`793ad6f8  00000000`00000000
0000fffe`793ad700  00000000`00000000
0000fffe`793ad708  00000000`00000000
0000fffe`793ad710  00000000`00000000
0000fffe`793ad718  00000000`00000000
0000fffe`793ad720  00000000`00000000
0000fffe`793ad728  00000000`00000000
0000fffe`793ad730  00000000`00000000
0000fffe`793ad738  00000000`00000000
0000fffe`793ad740  00000000`00000000
0000fffe`793ad748  00000000`00000000
0000fffe`793ad750  00000000`00000000
0000fffe`793ad758  00000000`00000000
0000fffe`793ad760  00000000`00000000
0000fffe`793ad768  00000000`00000000
0000fffe`793ad770  00000000`00000000
0000fffe`793ad778  00000000`00000000
0000fffe`793ad780  00000000`00000000
0000fffe`793ad788  00000000`00000000
0000fffe`793ad790  00000000`00000000
0000fffe`793ad798  00000000`00000000
0000fffe`793ad7a0  00000000`00000000
0000fffe`793ad7a8  00000000`00000000
0000fffe`793ad7b0  00000000`00000000
0000fffe`793ad7b8  00000000`00000000
0000fffe`793ad7c0  00000000`00000000
0000fffe`793ad7c8  00000000`00000000
0000fffe`793ad7d0  00000000`00000000
0000fffe`793ad7d8  00000000`00000000
0000fffe`793ad7e0  00000000`00000000
0000fffe`793ad7e8  00000000`00000000
0000fffe`793ad7f0  00000000`00000000
0000fffe`793ad7f8  00000000`00000000
0000fffe`793ad800  00000000`00000000
0000fffe`793ad808  00000000`00000000
0000fffe`793ad810  00000000`00000000
0000fffe`793ad818  00000000`00000000
0000fffe`793ad820  00000000`00000000
0000fffe`793ad828  00000000`00000000
0000fffe`793ad830  00000000`00000000
0000fffe`793ad838  00000000`00000000
0000fffe`793ad840  00000000`00000000
0000fffe`793ad848  00000000`00000020
0000fffe`793ad850  0000fffe`793ad8a0
0000fffe`793ad858  00000000`00414c08 App8!Unwind_RaiseException+0x158
0000fffe`793ad860  0000fffe`793add30
0000fffe`793ad868  0000fffe`793ae0f0
0000fffe`793ad870  0000fffe`74000b80
0000fffe`793ad878  0000fffe`793ad970
0000fffe`793ad880  00000000`00000000
0000fffe`793ad888  00000000`0000001e
0000fffe`793ad890  00000000`00011b1b
0000fffe`793ad898  0000fffe`793ae7f0
0000fffe`793ad8a0  0000fffe`793ae7f0
0000fffe`793ad8a8  00000000`004034c0 App8!Z5procHv+0x14
0000fffe`793ad8b0  0000fffe`74000b80
0000fffe`793ad8b8  00000000`00000001
0000fffe`793ad8c0  00000000`00000000
0000fffe`793ad8c8  00000000`00000001
0000fffe`793ad8d0  0000fffe`793af070
```

```
0000fffe`793ad8d8  00000000`00000000
0000fffe`793ad8e0  00000000`004e0000 App8!+0x18
0000fffe`793ad8e8  00000000`004035d8 App8!Z12thread_threePv
0000fffe`793ad8f0  00000000`00000000
0000fffe`793ad8f8  0000fffe`793af760
0000fffe`793ad900  00000000`32b706f0
0000fffe`793ad908  00000000`004f9540 App8!_default_pthread_attr
0000fffe`793ad910  00000000`00010000
0000fffe`793ad918  00000000`00810000
0000fffe`793ad920  00000000`00000000
0000fffe`793ad928  00000000`00000000
0000fffe`793ad930  00000000`00000000
0000fffe`793ad938  00000000`00000000
0000fffe`793ad940  00000000`00000000
0000fffe`793ad948  00000000`00000000
0000fffe`793ad950  00000000`00000000
0000fffe`793ad958  00000000`00000000
0000fffe`793ad960  00000000`00000000
0000fffe`793ad968  00000000`00000080
0000fffe`793ad970  0000fffe`793ad8b0
0000fffe`793ad978  0000fffe`793ad8b8
0000fffe`793ad980  0000fffe`793ad8c0
0000fffe`793ad988  0000fffe`793ad8c8
0000fffe`793ad990  00000000`00000000
0000fffe`793ad998  00000000`00000000
0000fffe`793ad9a0  00000000`00000000
0000fffe`793ad9a8  00000000`00000000
0000fffe`793ad9b0  00000000`00000000
0000fffe`793ad9b8  00000000`00000000
0000fffe`793ad9c0  00000000`00000000
0000fffe`793ad9c8  00000000`00000000
0000fffe`793ad9d0  00000000`00000000
0000fffe`793ad9d8  00000000`00000000
0000fffe`793ad9e0  00000000`00000000
0000fffe`793ad9e8  00000000`00000000
0000fffe`793ad9f0  00000000`00000000
0000fffe`793ad9f8  00000000`00000000
0000fffe`793ada00  00000000`00000000
0000fffe`793ada08  0000fffe`793ad8d0
0000fffe`793ada10  0000fffe`793ad8d8
0000fffe`793ada18  0000fffe`793ad8e0
0000fffe`793ada20  0000fffe`793ad8e8
0000fffe`793ada28  0000fffe`793ad8f0
0000fffe`793ada30  0000fffe`793ad8f8
0000fffe`793ada38  0000fffe`793ad900
0000fffe`793ada40  0000fffe`793ad908
0000fffe`793ada48  0000fffe`793ad910
0000fffe`793ada50  0000fffe`793ad918
0000fffe`793ada58  0000fffe`793ad8a0
0000fffe`793ada60  0000fffe`793ad8a8
0000fffe`793ada68  00000000`00000000
0000fffe`793ada70  00000000`00000000
0000fffe`793ada78  00000000`00000000
0000fffe`793ada80  00000000`00000000
0000fffe`793ada88  00000000`00000000
0000fffe`793ada90  00000000`00000000
0000fffe`793ada98  00000000`00000000
0000fffe`793adaa0  00000000`00000000
0000fffe`793adaa8  00000000`00000000
0000fffe`793adab0  00000000`00000000
```

```
0000fffe`793adab8  00000000`00000000
0000fffe`793adac0  00000000`00000000
0000fffe`793adac8  00000000`00000000
0000fffe`793adad0  00000000`00000000
0000fffe`793adad8  00000000`00000000
0000fffe`793adae0  00000000`00000000
0000fffe`793adae8  00000000`00000000
0000fffe`793adaf0  00000000`00000000
0000fffe`793adaf8  00000000`00000000
0000fffe`793adb00  00000000`00000000
0000fffe`793adb08  00000000`00000000
0000fffe`793adb10  00000000`00000000
0000fffe`793adb18  00000000`00000000
0000fffe`793adb20  00000000`00000000
0000fffe`793adb28  00000000`00000000
0000fffe`793adb30  00000000`00000000
0000fffe`793adb38  00000000`00000000
0000fffe`793adb40  00000000`00000000
0000fffe`793adb48  00000000`00000000
0000fffe`793adb50  00000000`00000000
0000fffe`793adb58  00000000`00000000
0000fffe`793adb60  00000000`00000000
0000fffe`793adb68  00000000`00000000
0000fffe`793adb70  00000000`00000000
0000fffe`793adb78  00000000`00000000
0000fffe`793adb80  00000000`00000000
0000fffe`793adb88  00000000`00000000
0000fffe`793adb90  00000000`00000000
0000fffe`793adb98  00000000`00000000
0000fffe`793adba0  00000000`00000000
0000fffe`793adba8  00000000`00000000
0000fffe`793adbb0  0000fffe`793ad920
0000fffe`793adbb8  0000fffe`793ad928
0000fffe`793adbc0  0000fffe`793ad930
0000fffe`793adbc8  0000fffe`793ad938
0000fffe`793adbd0  0000fffe`793ad940
0000fffe`793adbd8  0000fffe`793ad948
0000fffe`793adbe0  0000fffe`793ad950
0000fffe`793adbe8  0000fffe`793ad958
0000fffe`793adbf0  00000000`00000000
0000fffe`793adbf8  00000000`00000000
0000fffe`793adc00  00000000`00000000
0000fffe`793adc08  00000000`00000000
0000fffe`793adc10  00000000`00000000
0000fffe`793adc18  00000000`00000000
0000fffe`793adc20  00000000`00000000
0000fffe`793adc28  00000000`00000000
0000fffe`793adc30  00000000`00000000
0000fffe`793adc38  00000000`00000000
0000fffe`793adc40  00000000`00000000
0000fffe`793adc48  00000000`00000000
0000fffe`793adc50  00000000`00000000
0000fffe`793adc58  00000000`00000000
0000fffe`793adc60  00000000`00000000
0000fffe`793adc68  00000000`00000000
0000fffe`793adc70  00000000`00000000
0000fffe`793adc78  00000000`00000000
0000fffe`793adc80  0000fffe`793ae770
0000fffe`793adc88  00000000`00404d7c App8!_cxa_throw+0x90
0000fffe`793adc90  00000000`00000000
```

```
0000fffe`793adc98  00000000`00000000
0000fffe`793adca0  00000000`00000000
0000fffe`793adca8  00000000`00414ab0 App8!Unwind_RaiseException
0000fffe`793adcb0  40000000`00000000
0000fffe`793adcb8  00000000`00000000
...
...
...
```

```
0:001> ub 00000000`004145cc
App8!Unwind_RaiseException_Phase2+0x70:
00000000`004145ac 71001c1f cmp      w0,#7
00000000`004145b0 54000120 beq      App8!Unwind_RaiseException_Phase2+0x98 (00000000`004145d4)
00000000`004145b4 7100201f cmp      w0,#8
00000000`004145b8 540000c1 bne      App8!Unwind_RaiseException_Phase2+0x94 (00000000`004145d0)
00000000`004145bc 35000195 cbnz     w21,App8!Unwind_RaiseException_Phase2+0xb0 (00000000`004145ec)
00000000`004145c0 aa1303e0 mov      x0,x19
00000000`004145c4 aa1403e1 mov      x1,x20
00000000`004145c8 97ffffb2 bl       App8!uw_update_context (00000000`00414490)
```

13. We close logging before exiting WinDbg:

```
0:001> .logclose
Closing open log file 'C:\ALCDA2\A64\App8\App8-WinDbg.log'
```

Exercise A9

- **Goal:** Learn how to identify heap leaks
- **Patterns:** Memory Leak (Process Heap); Module Hint; Historical Information
- \ALCDA-Dumps\Exercise-A9-x64-GDB.pdf
- \ALCDA-Dumps\Exercise-A9-A64-GDB.pdf
- \ALCDA-Dumps\Exercise-A9-A64-WinDbg.pdf
- \ALCDA-Dumps\Exercise-A9-x64-WinDbg.pdf

Exercise A9 (x64, GDB)

Goal: Learn how to identify heap leaks.

Patterns: Memory Leak (Process Heap); Module Hint; Historical Information.

1. The application *App9* was found to consume more and more memory. Several core memory dumps were saved at different times with corresponding *pmap* logs. Load the *App9.core.2.230* dump file and *App9* executable from the x64/App9 directory:

```
~/ALCDA2/x64/App9$ gdb -c App9.core.2.230 -se App9
GNU gdb (Debian 8.2.1-2+b3) 8.2.1
Copyright (C) 2018 Free Software Foundation, Inc.
License GPLv3+: GNU GPL version 3 or later <http://gnu.org/licenses/gpl.html>
This is free software: you are free to change and redistribute it.
There is NO WARRANTY, to the extent permitted by law.
Type "show copying" and "show warranty" for details.
This GDB was configured as "x86_64-linux-gnu".
Type "show configuration" for configuration details.
For bug reporting instructions, please see:
<http://www.gnu.org/software/gdb/bugs/>.
Find the GDB manual and other documentation resources online at:
    <http://www.gnu.org/software/gdb/documentation/>.

For help, type "help".
Type "apropos word" to search for commands related to "word"...
Reading symbols from App9...done.
[New LWP 230]
[New LWP 231]
[New LWP 232]
[New LWP 233]
[New LWP 234]
[New LWP 235]
[Thread debugging using libthread_db enabled]
Using host libthread_db library "/lib/x86_64-linux-gnu/libthread_db.so.1".
Core was generated by `./App9'.
#0  0x0000000000441ad0 in nanosleep ()
[Current thread is 1 (Thread 0x1778880 (LWP 230))]
```

2. Set logging to a file in case of lengthy output from some commands:

```
(gdb) set logging on App9.log
Copying output to App9.log.
```

3. Notice the size of the largest section and quit gdb:

```
(gdb) maintenance info sections
Exec file:
    `/home/coredump/ALCDA2/x64/App9/App9', file type elf64-x86-64.
 [0]      0x00400200->0x00400220 at 0x00000200: .note.ABI-tag ALLOC LOAD READONLY DATA HAS_CONTENTS
 [1]      0x00400220->0x00400244 at 0x00000220: .note.gnu.build-id ALLOC LOAD READONLY DATA HAS_CONTENTS
 [2]      0x00400248->0x004004d0 at 0x00000248: .rela.plt ALLOC LOAD READONLY DATA HAS_CONTENTS
 [3]      0x00401000->0x00401017 at 0x00001000: .init ALLOC LOAD READONLY CODE HAS_CONTENTS
 [4]      0x00401018->0x004010f0 at 0x00001018: .plt ALLOC LOAD READONLY CODE HAS_CONTENTS
 [5]      0x004010f0->0x00493490 at 0x000010f0: .text ALLOC LOAD READONLY CODE HAS_CONTENTS
 [6]      0x00493490->0x00494037 at 0x00093490: __libc_freeres_fn ALLOC LOAD READONLY CODE HAS_CONTENTS
 [7]      0x00494038->0x00494041 at 0x00094038: .fini ALLOC LOAD READONLY CODE HAS_CONTENTS
 [8]      0x00495000->0x004af73c at 0x00095000: .rodata ALLOC LOAD READONLY DATA HAS_CONTENTS
```

```
 [9]      0x004af740->0x004bbbd0 at 0x000af740: .eh_frame ALLOC LOAD READONLY DATA HAS_CONTENTS
 [10]     0x004bbbd0->0x004bbc7c at 0x000bbbd0: .gcc_except_table ALLOC LOAD READONLY DATA HAS_CONTENTS
 [11]     0x004bd0b0->0x004bd0d8 at 0x000bc0b0: .tdata ALLOC LOAD DATA HAS_CONTENTS
 [12]     0x004bd0d8->0x004bd120 at 0x000bc0d8: .tbss ALLOC
 [13]     0x004bd0d8->0x004bd0e0 at 0x000bc0d8: .preinit_array ALLOC LOAD DATA HAS_CONTENTS
 [14]     0x004bd0e0->0x004bd0f0 at 0x000bc0e0: .init_array ALLOC LOAD DATA HAS_CONTENTS
 [15]     0x004bd0f0->0x004bd100 at 0x000bc0f0: .fini_array ALLOC LOAD DATA HAS_CONTENTS
 [16]     0x004bd100->0x004bfef4 at 0x000bc100: .data.rel.ro ALLOC LOAD DATA HAS_CONTENTS
 [17]     0x004bfef8->0x004c0000 at 0x000beef8: .got ALLOC LOAD DATA HAS_CONTENTS
 [18]     0x004c0000->0x004c00f0 at 0x000bf000: .got.plt ALLOC LOAD DATA HAS_CONTENTS
 [19]     0x004c0100->0x004c1c30 at 0x000bf100: .data ALLOC LOAD DATA HAS_CONTENTS
 [20]     0x004c1c30->0x004c1c90 at 0x000c0c30: __libc_subfreeres ALLOC LOAD DATA HAS_CONTENTS
 [21]     0x004c1ca0->0x004c2408 at 0x000c0ca0: __libc_IO_vtables ALLOC LOAD DATA HAS_CONTENTS
 [22]     0x004c2408->0x004c2410 at 0x000c1408: __libc_atexit ALLOC LOAD DATA HAS_CONTENTS
 [23]     0x004c2420->0x004c8528 at 0x000c1410: .bss ALLOC
 [24]     0x004c8528->0x004c8558 at 0x000c1410: __libc_freeres_ptrs ALLOC
 [25]     0x00000000->0x00000038 at 0x000c1410: .comment READONLY HAS_CONTENTS
 [26]     0x00000000->0x00000420 at 0x000c1450: .debug_aranges READONLY HAS_CONTENTS
 [27]     0x00000000->0x000372ad at 0x000c1870: .debug_info READONLY HAS_CONTENTS
 [28]     0x00000000->0x000057e8 at 0x000f8b1d: .debug_abbrev READONLY HAS_CONTENTS
 [29]     0x00000000->0x0000aa2b at 0x000fe305: .debug_line READONLY HAS_CONTENTS
 [30]     0x00000000->0x00004d08 at 0x00108d30: .debug_str READONLY HAS_CONTENTS
 [31]     0x00000000->0x0000d4b8 at 0x0010da38: .debug_loc READONLY HAS_CONTENTS
 [32]     0x00000000->0x000024c0 at 0x0011aef0: .debug_ranges READONLY HAS_CONTENTS
Core file:
    `/home/coredump/ALCDA2/x64/App9/App9.core.2.230', file type elf64-x86-64.
 [0]      0x00000000->0x00002ecc at 0x000004a0: note0 READONLY HAS_CONTENTS
 [1]      0x00000000->0x000000d8 at 0x000005c0: .reg/230 HAS_CONTENTS
 [2]      0x00000000->0x000000d8 at 0x000005c0: .reg HAS_CONTENTS
 [3]      0x00000000->0x00000200 at 0x000006b4: .reg2/230 HAS_CONTENTS
 [4]      0x00000000->0x00000200 at 0x000006b4: .reg2 HAS_CONTENTS
 [5]      0x00000000->0x00000340 at 0x000008c8: .reg-xstate/230 HAS_CONTENTS
 [6]      0x00000000->0x00000340 at 0x000008c8: .reg-xstate HAS_CONTENTS
 [7]      0x00000000->0x00000080 at 0x00000c1c: .note.linuxcore.siginfo/230 HAS_CONTENTS
 [8]      0x00000000->0x00000080 at 0x00000c1c: .note.linuxcore.siginfo HAS_CONTENTS
 [9]      0x00000000->0x000000d8 at 0x00000d20: .reg/231 HAS_CONTENTS
 [10]     0x00000000->0x00000200 at 0x00000e14: .reg2/231 HAS_CONTENTS
 [11]     0x00000000->0x00000340 at 0x00001028: .reg-xstate/231 HAS_CONTENTS
 [12]     0x00000000->0x00000080 at 0x0000137c: .note.linuxcore.siginfo/231 HAS_CONTENTS
 [13]     0x00000000->0x000000d8 at 0x00001480: .reg/232 HAS_CONTENTS
 [14]     0x00000000->0x00000200 at 0x00001574: .reg2/232 HAS_CONTENTS
 [15]     0x00000000->0x00000340 at 0x00001788: .reg-xstate/232 HAS_CONTENTS
 [16]     0x00000000->0x00000080 at 0x00001adc: .note.linuxcore.siginfo/232 HAS_CONTENTS
 [17]     0x00000000->0x000000d8 at 0x00001be0: .reg/233 HAS_CONTENTS
 [18]     0x00000000->0x00000200 at 0x00001cd4: .reg2/233 HAS_CONTENTS
 [19]     0x00000000->0x00000340 at 0x00001ee8: .reg-xstate/233 HAS_CONTENTS
--Type <RET> for more, q to quit, c to continue without paging--
 [20]     0x00000000->0x00000080 at 0x0000223c: .note.linuxcore.siginfo/233 HAS_CONTENTS
 [21]     0x00000000->0x000000d8 at 0x00002340: .reg/234 HAS_CONTENTS
 [22]     0x00000000->0x00000200 at 0x00002434: .reg2/234 HAS_CONTENTS
 [23]     0x00000000->0x00000340 at 0x00002648: .reg-xstate/234 HAS_CONTENTS
 [24]     0x00000000->0x00000080 at 0x0000299c: .note.linuxcore.siginfo/234 HAS_CONTENTS
 [25]     0x00000000->0x000000d8 at 0x00002aa0: .reg/235 HAS_CONTENTS
 [26]     0x00000000->0x00000200 at 0x00002b94: .reg2/235 HAS_CONTENTS
 [27]     0x00000000->0x00000340 at 0x00002da8: .reg-xstate/235 HAS_CONTENTS
 [28]     0x00000000->0x00000080 at 0x000030fc: .note.linuxcore.siginfo/235 HAS_CONTENTS
 [29]     0x00000000->0x00000140 at 0x00003190: .auxv HAS_CONTENTS
 [30]     0x00000000->0x00000088 at 0x000032e4: .note.linuxcore.file/235 HAS_CONTENTS
 [31]     0x00000000->0x00000088 at 0x000032e4: .note.linuxcore.file HAS_CONTENTS
 [32]     0x00401000->0x00495000 at 0x0000336c: load1 ALLOC LOAD READONLY CODE HAS_CONTENTS
 [33]     0x004bd000->0x004c3000 at 0x0009736c: load2 ALLOC LOAD HAS_CONTENTS
 [34]     0x004c3000->0x004c9000 at 0x0009d36c: load3 ALLOC LOAD HAS_CONTENTS
 [35]     0x01778000->0x0179b000 at 0x000a336c: load4 ALLOC LOAD HAS_CONTENTS
 [36]     0x7f08dc000000->0x7f08dc227000 at 0x000c636c: load5 ALLOC LOAD HAS_CONTENTS
 [37]     0x7f08dc227000->0x7f08e0000000 at 0x002ed36c: load6 ALLOC LOAD READONLY HAS_CONTENTS
 [38]     0x7f08e4000000->0x7f08e8000000 at 0x040c636c: load7 ALLOC LOAD HAS_CONTENTS
 [39]     0x7f08eb528000->0x7f08eb529000 at 0x080c636c: load8 ALLOC LOAD READONLY HAS_CONTENTS
```

```
[40]    0x7f08eb529000->0x7f08ebd29000 at 0x080c736c: load9 ALLOC LOAD HAS_CONTENTS
[41]    0x7f08ebd29000->0x7f08ebd2a000 at 0x088c736c: load10 ALLOC LOAD READONLY HAS_CONTENTS
[42]    0x7f08ebd2a000->0x7f08ec52a000 at 0x088c836c: load11 ALLOC LOAD HAS_CONTENTS
[43]    0x7f08ec52a000->0x7f08ec52b000 at 0x090c836c: load12 ALLOC LOAD READONLY HAS_CONTENTS
[44]    0x7f08ec52b000->0x7f08ecd2b000 at 0x090c936c: load13 ALLOC LOAD HAS_CONTENTS
[45]    0x7f08ecd2b000->0x7f08ecd2c000 at 0x098c936c: load14 ALLOC LOAD READONLY HAS_CONTENTS
[46]    0x7f08ecd2c000->0x7f08ed52c000 at 0x098ca36c: load15 ALLOC LOAD HAS_CONTENTS
[47]    0x7f08ed52c000->0x7f08ed52d000 at 0x0a0ca36c: load16 ALLOC LOAD READONLY HAS_CONTENTS
[48]    0x7f08ed52d000->0x7f08edd2d000 at 0x0a0cb36c: load17 ALLOC LOAD HAS_CONTENTS
[49]    0x7ffe4333f000->0x7ffe43360000 at 0x0a8cb36c: load18 ALLOC LOAD HAS_CONTENTS
[50]    0x7ffe43385000->0x7ffe43386000 at 0x0a8ec36c: load19 ALLOC LOAD READONLY CODE HAS_CONTENTS

(gdb) q
```

4. Load the *App9.core.3.230* dump file and *App9* executable from x64/App9 directory:

```
~/ALCDA2/x64/App9$ gdb -c App9.core.3.230 -se App9
GNU gdb (Debian 8.2.1-2+b3) 8.2.1
Copyright (C) 2018 Free Software Foundation, Inc.
License GPLv3+: GNU GPL version 3 or later <http://gnu.org/licenses/gpl.html>
This is free software: you are free to change and redistribute it.
There is NO WARRANTY, to the extent permitted by law.
Type "show copying" and "show warranty" for details.
This GDB was configured as "x86_64-linux-gnu".
Type "show configuration" for configuration details.
For bug reporting instructions, please see:
<http://www.gnu.org/software/gdb/bugs/>.
Find the GDB manual and other documentation resources online at:
    <http://www.gnu.org/software/gdb/documentation/>.

For help, type "help".
Type "apropos word" to search for commands related to "word"...
Reading symbols from App9...done.
[New LWP 230]
[New LWP 231]
[New LWP 232]
[New LWP 233]
[New LWP 234]
[New LWP 235]
[Thread debugging using libthread_db enabled]
Using host libthread_db library "/lib/x86_64-linux-gnu/libthread_db.so.1".
Core was generated by `./App9'.
#0  0x0000000000441ad0 in nanosleep ()
[Current thread is 1 (Thread 0x1778880 (LWP 230))]
```

5. Set logging to a file in case of lengthy verbose output from some commands (GDB appends data):

```
(gdb) set logging on App9.log
Copying output to App9.log.

(gdb) show logging
Future logs will be written to gdb.txt.
Logs will be appended to the log file.
Output will be logged and displayed.
```

6. Notice that another large section appeared after some time.

```
(gdb) maintenance info sections
Exec file:
    `/home/coredump/ALCDA2/x64/App9/App9', file type elf64-x86-64.
 [0]      0x00400200->0x00400220 at 0x00000200: .note.ABI-tag ALLOC LOAD READONLY DATA HAS_CONTENTS
 [1]      0x00400220->0x00400244 at 0x00000220: .note.gnu.build-id ALLOC LOAD READONLY DATA HAS_CONTENTS
 [2]      0x00400248->0x004004d0 at 0x00000248: .rela.plt ALLOC LOAD READONLY DATA HAS_CONTENTS
 [3]      0x00401000->0x00401017 at 0x00001000: .init ALLOC LOAD READONLY CODE HAS_CONTENTS
 [4]      0x00401018->0x004010f0 at 0x00001018: .plt ALLOC LOAD READONLY CODE HAS_CONTENTS
 [5]      0x004010f0->0x00493490 at 0x000010f0: .text ALLOC LOAD READONLY CODE HAS_CONTENTS
 [6]      0x00493490->0x00494037 at 0x00093490: __libc_freeres_fn ALLOC LOAD READONLY CODE HAS_CONTENTS
 [7]      0x00494038->0x00494041 at 0x00094038: .fini ALLOC LOAD READONLY CODE HAS_CONTENTS
 [8]      0x00495000->0x004af73c at 0x00095000: .rodata ALLOC LOAD READONLY DATA HAS_CONTENTS
 [9]      0x004af740->0x004bbbd0 at 0x000af740: .eh_frame ALLOC LOAD READONLY DATA HAS_CONTENTS
 [10]      0x004bbbd0->0x004bbc7c at 0x000bbbd0: .gcc_except_table ALLOC LOAD READONLY DATA HAS_CONTENTS
 [11]      0x004bd0b0->0x004bd0d8 at 0x000bc0b0: .tdata ALLOC LOAD DATA HAS_CONTENTS
 [12]      0x004bd0d8->0x004bd120 at 0x000bc0d8: .tbss ALLOC
 [13]      0x004bd0d8->0x004bd0e0 at 0x000bc0d8: .preinit_array ALLOC LOAD DATA HAS_CONTENTS
 [14]      0x004bd0e0->0x004bd0f0 at 0x000bc0e0: .init_array ALLOC LOAD DATA HAS_CONTENTS
 [15]      0x004bd0f0->0x004bd100 at 0x000bc0f0: .fini_array ALLOC LOAD DATA HAS_CONTENTS
 [16]      0x004bd100->0x004bfef4 at 0x000bc100: .data.rel.ro ALLOC LOAD DATA HAS_CONTENTS
 [17]      0x004bfef8->0x004c0000 at 0x000beef8: .got ALLOC LOAD DATA HAS_CONTENTS
 [18]      0x004c0000->0x004c00f0 at 0x000bf000: .got.plt ALLOC LOAD DATA HAS_CONTENTS
 [19]      0x004c0100->0x004c1c30 at 0x000bf100: .data ALLOC LOAD DATA HAS_CONTENTS
 [20]      0x004c1c30->0x004c1c90 at 0x000c0c30: __libc_subfreeres ALLOC LOAD DATA HAS_CONTENTS
 [21]      0x004c1ca0->0x004c2408 at 0x000c0ca0: __libc_IO_vtables ALLOC LOAD DATA HAS_CONTENTS
 [22]      0x004c2408->0x004c2410 at 0x000c1408: __libc_atexit ALLOC LOAD DATA HAS_CONTENTS
 [23]      0x004c2420->0x004c8528 at 0x000c1410: .bss ALLOC
 [24]      0x004c8528->0x004c8558 at 0x000c1410: __libc_freeres_ptrs ALLOC
 [25]      0x00000000->0x00000038 at 0x000c1410: .comment READONLY HAS_CONTENTS
 [26]      0x00000000->0x00000420 at 0x000c1450: .debug_aranges READONLY HAS_CONTENTS
 [27]      0x00000000->0x000372ad at 0x000c1870: .debug_info READONLY HAS_CONTENTS
 [28]      0x00000000->0x000057e8 at 0x000f8b1d: .debug_abbrev READONLY HAS_CONTENTS
 [29]      0x00000000->0x0000aa2b at 0x000fe305: .debug_line READONLY HAS_CONTENTS
 [30]      0x00000000->0x00004d08 at 0x00108d30: .debug_str READONLY HAS_CONTENTS
 [31]      0x00000000->0x0000d4b8 at 0x0010da38: .debug_loc READONLY HAS_CONTENTS
 [32]      0x00000000->0x000024c0 at 0x0011aef0: .debug_ranges READONLY HAS_CONTENTS
Core file:
    `/home/coredump/ALCDA2/x64/App9/App9.core.3.230', file type elf64-x86-64.
 [0]      0x00000000->0x00002ecc at 0x000004a0: note0 READONLY HAS_CONTENTS
 [1]      0x00000000->0x000000d8 at 0x000005c0: .reg/230 HAS_CONTENTS
 [2]      0x00000000->0x000000d8 at 0x000005c0: .reg HAS_CONTENTS
 [3]      0x00000000->0x00000200 at 0x000006b4: .reg2/230 HAS_CONTENTS
 [4]      0x00000000->0x00000200 at 0x000006b4: .reg2 HAS_CONTENTS
 [5]      0x00000000->0x00000340 at 0x000008c8: .reg-xstate/230 HAS_CONTENTS
 [6]      0x00000000->0x00000340 at 0x000008c8: .reg-xstate HAS_CONTENTS
 [7]      0x00000000->0x00000080 at 0x00000c1c: .note.linuxcore.siginfo/230 HAS_CONTENTS
 [8]      0x00000000->0x00000080 at 0x00000c1c: .note.linuxcore.siginfo HAS_CONTENTS
 [9]      0x00000000->0x000000d8 at 0x00000d20: .reg/231 HAS_CONTENTS
 [10]      0x00000000->0x00000200 at 0x00000e14: .reg2/231 HAS_CONTENTS
 [11]      0x00000000->0x00000340 at 0x00001028: .reg-xstate/231 HAS_CONTENTS
 [12]      0x00000000->0x00000080 at 0x0000137c: .note.linuxcore.siginfo/231 HAS_CONTENTS
 [13]      0x00000000->0x000000d8 at 0x00001480: .reg/232 HAS_CONTENTS
 [14]      0x00000000->0x00000200 at 0x00001574: .reg2/232 HAS_CONTENTS
 [15]      0x00000000->0x00000340 at 0x00001788: .reg-xstate/232 HAS_CONTENTS
 [16]      0x00000000->0x00000080 at 0x00001adc: .note.linuxcore.siginfo/232 HAS_CONTENTS
 [17]      0x00000000->0x000000d8 at 0x00001be0: .reg/233 HAS_CONTENTS
 [18]      0x00000000->0x00000200 at 0x00001cd4: .reg2/233 HAS_CONTENTS
 [19]      0x00000000->0x00000340 at 0x00001ee8: .reg-xstate/233 HAS_CONTENTS
--Type <RET> for more, q to quit, c to continue without paging--
 [20]      0x00000000->0x00000080 at 0x0000223c: .note.linuxcore.siginfo/233 HAS_CONTENTS
 [21]      0x00000000->0x000000d8 at 0x00002340: .reg/234 HAS_CONTENTS
 [22]      0x00000000->0x00000200 at 0x00002434: .reg2/234 HAS_CONTENTS
 [23]      0x00000000->0x00000340 at 0x00002648: .reg-xstate/234 HAS_CONTENTS
 [24]      0x00000000->0x00000080 at 0x0000299c: .note.linuxcore.siginfo/234 HAS_CONTENTS
```

```
[25]      0x00000000->0x000000d8 at 0x00002aa0: .reg/235 HAS_CONTENTS
[26]      0x00000000->0x00000200 at 0x00002b94: .reg2/235 HAS_CONTENTS
[27]      0x00000000->0x00000340 at 0x00002da8: .reg-xstate/235 HAS_CONTENTS
[28]      0x00000000->0x00000080 at 0x000030fc: .note.linuxcore.siginfo/235 HAS_CONTENTS
[29]      0x00000000->0x00000140 at 0x00003190: .auxv HAS_CONTENTS
[30]      0x00000000->0x00000088 at 0x000032e4: .note.linuxcore.file/235 HAS_CONTENTS
[31]      0x00000000->0x00000088 at 0x000032e4: .note.linuxcore.file HAS_CONTENTS
[32]      0x00401000->0x00495000 at 0x0000336c: load1 ALLOC LOAD READONLY CODE HAS_CONTENTS
[33]      0x004bd000->0x004c3000 at 0x0009736c: load2 ALLOC LOAD HAS_CONTENTS
[34]      0x004c3000->0x004c9000 at 0x0009d36c: load3 ALLOC LOAD HAS_CONTENTS
[35]      0x01778000->0x0179b000 at 0x000a336c: load4 ALLOC LOAD HAS_CONTENTS
[36]      0x7f08dc000000->0x7f08e0300000 at 0x000c636c: load5 ALLOC LOAD HAS_CONTENTS
[37]      0x7f08e0300000->0x7f08e4000000 at 0x043c636c: load6 ALLOC LOAD READONLY HAS_CONTENTS
[38]      0x7f08e4000000->0x7f08e8000000 at 0x080c636c: load7 ALLOC LOAD HAS_CONTENTS
[39]      0x7f08eb528000->0x7f08eb529000 at 0x0c0c636c: load8 ALLOC LOAD READONLY HAS_CONTENTS
[40]      0x7f08eb529000->0x7f08ebd29000 at 0x0c0c736c: load9 ALLOC LOAD HAS_CONTENTS
[41]      0x7f08ebd29000->0x7f08ebd2a000 at 0x0c8c736c: load10 ALLOC LOAD READONLY HAS_CONTENTS
[42]      0x7f08ebd2a000->0x7f08ec52a000 at 0x0c8c836c: load11 ALLOC LOAD HAS_CONTENTS
[43]      0x7f08ec52a000->0x7f08ec52b000 at 0x0d0c836c: load12 ALLOC LOAD READONLY HAS_CONTENTS
[44]      0x7f08ec52b000->0x7f08ecd2b000 at 0x0d0c936c: load13 ALLOC LOAD HAS_CONTENTS
[45]      0x7f08ecd2b000->0x7f08ecd2c000 at 0x0d8c936c: load14 ALLOC LOAD READONLY HAS_CONTENTS
[46]      0x7f08ecd2c000->0x7f08ed52c000 at 0x0d8ca36c: load15 ALLOC LOAD HAS_CONTENTS
[47]      0x7f08ed52c000->0x7f08ed52d000 at 0x0e0ca36c: load16 ALLOC LOAD READONLY HAS_CONTENTS
[48]      0x7f08ed52d000->0x7f08edd2d000 at 0x0e0cb36c: load17 ALLOC LOAD HAS_CONTENTS
[49]      0x7ffe4333f000->0x7ffe43360000 at 0x0e8cb36c: load18 ALLOC LOAD HAS_CONTENTS
[50]      0x7ffe43385000->0x7ffe43386000 at 0x0e8ec36c: load19 ALLOC LOAD READONLY CODE HAS_CONTENTS
```

7. Examine segment contents for any execution residue and hints (we choose a smaller address range from the section address range):

```
(gdb) x/1000a 0x7f08dc000000
0x7f08dc000000: 0x7f08e4000020  0x7f08e4000000
0x7f08dc000010: 0x4000000       0x4000000
0x7f08dc000020: 0x0     0x115
0x7f08dc000030: 0x657461636f6c6c61      0x79726f6d656d2064
0x7f08dc000040: 0x0     0x0
0x7f08dc000050: 0x401bad <procD>        0x0
0x7f08dc000060: 0x0     0x0
0x7f08dc000070: 0x0     0x0
0x7f08dc000080: 0x0     0x0
0x7f08dc000090: 0x0     0x0
0x7f08dc0000a0: 0x0     0x0
0x7f08dc0000b0: 0x0     0x0
0x7f08dc0000c0: 0x0     0x0
0x7f08dc0000d0: 0x0     0x0
0x7f08dc0000e0: 0x0     0x0
0x7f08dc0000f0: 0x0     0x0
0x7f08dc000100: 0x0     0x0
0x7f08dc000110: 0x0     0x0
0x7f08dc000120: 0x0     0x0
0x7f08dc000130: 0x0     0x115
0x7f08dc000140: 0x657461636f6c6c61      0x79726f6d656d2064
0x7f08dc000150: 0x0     0x0
0x7f08dc000160: 0x401bad <procD>        0x0
0x7f08dc000170: 0x0     0x0
0x7f08dc000180: 0x0     0x0
0x7f08dc000190: 0x0     0x0
0x7f08dc0001a0: 0x0     0x0
0x7f08dc0001b0: 0x0     0x0
0x7f08dc0001c0: 0x0     0x0
0x7f08dc0001d0: 0x0     0x0
0x7f08dc0001e0: 0x0     0x0
```

```
0x7f08dc0001f0: 0x0     0x0
0x7f08dc000200: 0x0     0x0
0x7f08dc000210: 0x0     0x0
0x7f08dc000220: 0x0     0x0
0x7f08dc000230: 0x0     0x0
0x7f08dc000240: 0x0     0x115
[...]
0x7f08dc001df0: 0x657461636f6c6c61      0x79726f6d656d2064
0x7f08dc001e00: 0x0     0x0
0x7f08dc001e10: 0x401bad <procD>        0x0
0x7f08dc001e20: 0x0     0x0
0x7f08dc001e30: 0x0     0x0
0x7f08dc001e40: 0x0     0x0
0x7f08dc001e50: 0x0     0x0
0x7f08dc001e60: 0x0     0x0
0x7f08dc001e70: 0x0     0x0
0x7f08dc001e80: 0x0     0x0
0x7f08dc001e90: 0x0     0x0
0x7f08dc001ea0: 0x0     0x0
0x7f08dc001eb0: 0x0     0x0
0x7f08dc001ec0: 0x0     0x0
0x7f08dc001ed0: 0x0     0x0
0x7f08dc001ee0: 0x0     0x0
0x7f08dc001ef0: 0x0     0x115
0x7f08dc001f00: 0x657461636f6c6c61      0x79726f6d656d2064
0x7f08dc001f10: 0x0     0x0
0x7f08dc001f20: 0x401bad <procD>        0x0
0x7f08dc001f30: 0x0     0x0

(gdb) x/s 0x7f08dc001f00
0x7f08dc001f00: "allocated memory"
```

8. Compare pmap logs *App9.pmap.1.230*, *App9.pmap.2.230*, and *App9.pmap.3.230* (the first one was saved before the leak started, and the other two correspond to core dumps we looked at):

```
230:   ./App9
0000000000400000      4K r---- App9
0000000000401000    592K r-x-- App9
0000000000495000    156K r---- App9
00000000004bd000     24K rw--- App9
00000000004c3000     24K rw---   [ anon ]
0000000001778000    140K rw---   [ anon ]
00007f08e4000000   1332K rw---   [ anon ]
00007f08e414d000  64204K -----   [ anon ]
00007f08eb528000      4K -----   [ anon ]
00007f08eb529000   8192K rw---   [ anon ]
00007f08ebd29000      4K -----   [ anon ]
00007f08ebd2a000   8192K rw---   [ anon ]
00007f08ec52a000      4K -----   [ anon ]
00007f08ec52b000   8192K rw---   [ anon ]
00007f08ecd2b000      4K -----   [ anon ]
00007f08ecd2c000   8192K rw---   [ anon ]
00007f08ed52c000      4K -----   [ anon ]
00007f08ed52d000   8192K rw---   [ anon ]
00007ffe4333f000    132K rw---   [ stack ]
00007ffe43381000     16K r----   [ anon ]
00007ffe43385000      4K r-x--   [ anon ]
 total           107608K

230:   ./App9
```

```
0000000000400000      4K r---- App9
0000000000401000    592K r-x-- App9
0000000000495000    156K r---- App9
00000000004bd000     24K rw--- App9
00000000004c3000     24K rw---   [ anon ]
0000000001778000    140K rw---   [ anon ]
00007f08dc000000   2204K rw---   [ anon ]
00007f08dc227000  63332K -----   [ anon ]
00007f08e4000000  65536K rw---   [ anon ]
00007f08eb528000      4K -----   [ anon ]
00007f08eb529000   8192K rw---   [ anon ]
00007f08ebd29000      4K -----   [ anon ]
00007f08ebd2a000   8192K rw---   [ anon ]
00007f08ec52a000      4K -----   [ anon ]
00007f08ec52b000   8192K rw---   [ anon ]
00007f08ecd2b000      4K -----   [ anon ]
00007f08ecd2c000   8192K rw---   [ anon ]
00007f08ed52c000      4K -----   [ anon ]
00007f08ed52d000   8192K rw---   [ anon ]
00007ffe4333f000    132K rw---   [ stack ]
00007ffe43381000     16K r----   [ anon ]
00007ffe43385000      4K r-x--   [ anon ]
 total           173144K

230:   ./App9
0000000000400000      4K r---- App9
0000000000401000    592K r-x-- App9
0000000000495000    156K r---- App9
00000000004bd000     24K rw--- App9
00000000004c3000     24K rw---   [ anon ]
0000000001778000    140K rw---   [ anon ]
00007f08dc000000  68608K rw---   [ anon ]
00007f08e0300000  62464K -----   [ anon ]
00007f08e4000000  65536K rw---   [ anon ]
00007f08eb528000      4K -----   [ anon ]
00007f08eb529000   8192K rw---   [ anon ]
00007f08ebd29000      4K -----   [ anon ]
00007f08ebd2a000   8192K rw---   [ anon ]
00007f08ec52a000      4K -----   [ anon ]
00007f08ec52b000   8192K rw---   [ anon ]
00007f08ecd2b000      4K -----   [ anon ]
00007f08ecd2c000   8192K rw---   [ anon ]
00007f08ed52c000      4K -----   [ anon ]
00007f08ed52d000   8192K rw---   [ anon ]
00007ffe4333f000    132K rw---   [ stack ]
00007ffe43381000     16K r----   [ anon ]
00007ffe43385000      4K r-x--   [ anon ]
 total           238680K
```

Exercise A9 (A64, GDB)

Goal: Learn how to identify heap leaks.

Patterns: Memory Leak (Process Heap); Module Hint; Historical Information.

1. The application *App9* was found to consume more and more memory. Several core memory dumps were saved at different times with corresponding *pmap* logs. Load the *App9.core.2.12057* dump file and *App9* executable from the A64/App9 directory:

```
~/ALCDA2/A64/App9$ gdb-multiarch -c App9.core.2.12057 -se App9
GNU gdb (Debian 8.2.1-2+b3) 8.2.1
Copyright (C) 2018 Free Software Foundation, Inc.
License GPLv3+: GNU GPL version 3 or later <http://gnu.org/licenses/gpl.html>
This is free software: you are free to change and redistribute it.
There is NO WARRANTY, to the extent permitted by law.
Type "show copying" and "show warranty" for details.
This GDB was configured as "x86_64-linux-gnu".
Type "show configuration" for configuration details.
For bug reporting instructions, please see:
<http://www.gnu.org/software/gdb/bugs/>.
Find the GDB manual and other documentation resources online at:
    <http://www.gnu.org/software/gdb/documentation/>.

For help, type "help".
Type "apropos word" to search for commands related to "word"...
Reading symbols from App9...(no debugging symbols found)...done.
[New LWP 12058]
[New LWP 12059]
[New LWP 12060]
[New LWP 12061]
[New LWP 12062]
[New LWP 12057]
Core was generated by `./App9'.
#0  0x000000000040ca84 in nanosleep ()
[Current thread is 1 (LWP 12058)]
```

2. Set logging to a file in case of lengthy output from some commands:

```
(gdb) set logging on App9.log
Copying output to App9.log.
```

3. Notice the size of the largest section and quit GDB:

```
(gdb) maintenance info sections
Exec file: `/home/ubuntu/ALCDA2/A64/App9/App9', file type elf64-littleaarch64.
 [0]      0x00400190->0x004001b0 at 0x00000190: .note.ABI-tag ALLOC LOAD READONLY DATA HAS_CONTENTS
 [1]      0x004001b0->0x004001d4 at 0x000001b0: .note.gnu.build-id ALLOC LOAD READONLY DATA HAS_CONTENTS
 [2]      0x004001d8->0x00400250 at 0x000001d8: .rela.plt ALLOC LOAD READONLY DATA HAS_CONTENTS
 [3]      0x00400250->0x00400264 at 0x00000250: .init ALLOC LOAD READONLY CODE HAS_CONTENTS
 [4]      0x00400270->0x004002c0 at 0x00000270: .plt ALLOC LOAD READONLY CODE HAS_CONTENTS
 [5]      0x004002c0->0x00487158 at 0x000002c0: .text ALLOC LOAD READONLY CODE HAS_CONTENTS
 [6]      0x00487158->0x00488e28 at 0x00087158: __libc_freeres_fn ALLOC LOAD READONLY CODE HAS_CONTENTS
 [7]      0x00488e28->0x00489278 at 0x00088e28: __libc_thread_freeres_fn ALLOC LOAD READONLY CODE HAS_CONTENTS
 [8]      0x00489278->0x00489288 at 0x00089278: .fini ALLOC LOAD READONLY CODE HAS_CONTENTS
 [9]      0x00489290->0x004a178d at 0x00089290: .rodata ALLOC LOAD READONLY DATA HAS_CONTENTS
 [10]     0x004a178d->0x004a178e at 0x000a178d: .stapsdt.base ALLOC LOAD READONLY DATA HAS_CONTENTS
 [11]     0x004a1790->0x004a1ec8 at 0x000a1790: __libc_IO_vtables ALLOC LOAD READONLY DATA HAS_CONTENTS
 [12]     0x004a1ec8->0x004a1f30 at 0x000a1ec8: __libc_subfreeres ALLOC LOAD READONLY DATA HAS_CONTENTS
 [13]     0x004a1f30->0x004a1f38 at 0x000a1f30: __libc_atexit ALLOC LOAD READONLY DATA HAS_CONTENTS
```

```
 [14]      0x004a1f38->0x004a1f48 at 0x000a1f38: __libc_thread_subfreeres ALLOC LOAD READONLY DATA HAS_CONTENTS
 [15]      0x004a1f48->0x004b05ec at 0x000a1f48: .eh_frame ALLOC LOAD READONLY DATA HAS_CONTENTS
 [16]      0x004b05ec->0x004b07a9 at 0x000b05ec: .gcc_except_table ALLOC LOAD READONLY DATA HAS_CONTENTS
 [17]      0x004cfb20->0x004cfb48 at 0x000bfb20: .tdata ALLOC LOAD DATA HAS_CONTENTS
 [18]      0x004cfb48->0x004cfb98 at 0x000bfb48: .tbss ALLOC
 [19]      0x004cfb48->0x004cfb50 at 0x000bfb48: .init_array ALLOC LOAD DATA HAS_CONTENTS
 [20]      0x004cfb50->0x004cfb60 at 0x000bfb50: .fini_array ALLOC LOAD DATA HAS_CONTENTS
 [21]      0x004cfb60->0x004cfb68 at 0x000bfb60: .jcr ALLOC LOAD DATA HAS_CONTENTS
 [22]      0x004cfb68->0x004cff24 at 0x000bfb68: .data.rel.ro ALLOC LOAD DATA HAS_CONTENTS
 [23]      0x004cff28->0x004cffe8 at 0x000bff28: .got ALLOC LOAD DATA HAS_CONTENTS
 [24]      0x004cffe8->0x004d0028 at 0x000bffe8: .got.plt ALLOC LOAD DATA HAS_CONTENTS
 [25]      0x004d0030->0x004d1580 at 0x000c0030: .data ALLOC LOAD DATA HAS_CONTENTS
 [26]      0x004d1580->0x004d8050 at 0x000c1580: .bss ALLOC
 [27]      0x004d8050->0x004d8088 at 0x000c1580: __libc_freeres_ptrs ALLOC
 [28]      0x00000000->0x00000031 at 0x000c1580: .comment READONLY HAS_CONTENTS
 [29]      0x00000000->0x00001cb0 at 0x000c15b4: .note.stapsdt READONLY HAS_CONTENTS
Core file: `/home/ubuntu/ALCDA2/A64/App9/App9.core.2.12057', file type elf64-littleaarch64.
 [0]       0x00000000->0x00001c94 at 0x00000468: note0 READONLY HAS_CONTENTS
 [1]       0x00000000->0x00000110 at 0x00000588: .reg/12058 HAS_CONTENTS
 [2]       0x00000000->0x00000110 at 0x00000588: .reg HAS_CONTENTS
 [3]       0x00000000->0x00000210 at 0x000006b4: .reg2/12058 HAS_CONTENTS
 [4]       0x00000000->0x00000210 at 0x000006b4: .reg2 HAS_CONTENTS
 [5]       0x00000000->0x00000080 at 0x000008d8: .note.linuxcore.siginfo/12058 HAS_CONTENTS
 [6]       0x00000000->0x00000080 at 0x000008d8: .note.linuxcore.siginfo HAS_CONTENTS
 [7]       0x00000000->0x00000110 at 0x000009dc: .reg/12059 HAS_CONTENTS
 [8]       0x00000000->0x00000210 at 0x00000b08: .reg2/12059 HAS_CONTENTS
 [9]       0x00000000->0x00000080 at 0x00000d2c: .note.linuxcore.siginfo/12059 HAS_CONTENTS
 [10]      0x00000000->0x00000110 at 0x00000e30: .reg/12060 HAS_CONTENTS
 [11]      0x00000000->0x00000210 at 0x00000f5c: .reg2/12060 HAS_CONTENTS
 [12]      0x00000000->0x00000080 at 0x00001180: .note.linuxcore.siginfo/12060 HAS_CONTENTS
 [13]      0x00000000->0x00000110 at 0x00001284: .reg/12061 HAS_CONTENTS
 [14]      0x00000000->0x00000210 at 0x000013b0: .reg2/12061 HAS_CONTENTS
 [15]      0x00000000->0x00000080 at 0x000015d4: .note.linuxcore.siginfo/12061 HAS_CONTENTS
 [16]      0x00000000->0x00000110 at 0x000016d8: .reg/12062 HAS_CONTENTS
--Type <RET> for more, q to quit, c to continue without paging--
 [17]      0x00000000->0x00000210 at 0x00001804: .reg2/12062 HAS_CONTENTS
 [18]      0x00000000->0x00000080 at 0x00001a28: .note.linuxcore.siginfo/12062 HAS_CONTENTS
 [19]      0x00000000->0x00000110 at 0x00001b2c: .reg/12057 HAS_CONTENTS
 [20]      0x00000000->0x00000210 at 0x00001c58: .reg2/12057 HAS_CONTENTS
 [21]      0x00000000->0x00000080 at 0x00001e7c: .note.linuxcore.siginfo/12057 HAS_CONTENTS
 [22]      0x00000000->0x00000160 at 0x00001f10: .auxv HAS_CONTENTS
 [23]      0x00000000->0x00000076 at 0x00002084: .note.linuxcore.file/12057 HAS_CONTENTS
 [24]      0x00000000->0x00000076 at 0x00002084: .note.linuxcore.file HAS_CONTENTS
 [25]      0x00400000->0x004c0000 at 0x000020fc: load1 ALLOC LOAD READONLY CODE HAS_CONTENTS
 [26]      0x004c0000->0x004e0000 at 0x000c20fc: load2 ALLOC LOAD HAS_CONTENTS
 [27]      0x2f860000->0x2f8a0000 at 0x000e20fc: load3 ALLOC LOAD HAS_CONTENTS
 [28]      0xfffce8000000->0xfffce8230000 at 0x001220fc: load4 ALLOC LOAD HAS_CONTENTS
 [29]      0xfffce8230000->0xfffcec000000 at 0x003520fc: load5 ALLOC LOAD READONLY HAS_CONTENTS
 [30]      0xfffcf0000000->0xfffcf4000000 at 0x041220fc: load6 ALLOC LOAD HAS_CONTENTS
 [31]      0xfffcf7400000->0xfffcf7410000 at 0x081220fc: load7 ALLOC LOAD READONLY HAS_CONTENTS
 [32]      0xfffcf7410000->0xfffcf7c10000 at 0x081320fc: load8 ALLOC LOAD HAS_CONTENTS
 [33]      0xfffcf7c10000->0xfffcf7c20000 at 0x089320fc: load9 ALLOC LOAD READONLY HAS_CONTENTS
 [34]      0xfffcf7c20000->0xfffcf8420000 at 0x089420fc: load10 ALLOC LOAD HAS_CONTENTS
 [35]      0xfffcf8420000->0xfffcf8430000 at 0x091420fc: load11 ALLOC LOAD READONLY HAS_CONTENTS
 [36]      0xfffcf8430000->0xfffcf8c30000 at 0x091520fc: load12 ALLOC LOAD HAS_CONTENTS
 [37]      0xfffcf8c30000->0xfffcf8c40000 at 0x099520fc: load13 ALLOC LOAD READONLY HAS_CONTENTS
 [38]      0xfffcf8c40000->0xfffcf9440000 at 0x099620fc: load14 ALLOC LOAD HAS_CONTENTS
 [39]      0xfffcf9440000->0xfffcf9450000 at 0x0a1620fc: load15 ALLOC LOAD READONLY HAS_CONTENTS
 [40]      0xfffcf9450000->0xfffcf9c50000 at 0x0a1720fc: load16 ALLOC LOAD HAS_CONTENTS
 [41]      0xfffcf9c60000->0xfffcf9c70000 at 0x0a9720fc: load17 ALLOC LOAD READONLY CODE HAS_CONTENTS
 [42]      0xffffc2f60000->0xffffc2f90000 at 0x0a9820fc: load18 ALLOC LOAD HAS_CONTENTS

(gdb) q
```

4. Load the *App9.core.3.12057* dump file and *App9* executable from A64/App9 directory:

```
~/ALCDA2/A64/App9$ gdb -c App9.core.3.12057 -se App9
GNU gdb (Ubuntu 12.1-0ubuntu1~22.04) 12.1
Copyright (C) 2022 Free Software Foundation, Inc.
License GPLv3+: GNU GPL version 3 or later <http://gnu.org/licenses/gpl.html>
This is free software: you are free to change and redistribute it.
There is NO WARRANTY, to the extent permitted by law.
Type "show copying" and "show warranty" for details.
This GDB was configured as "aarch64-linux-gnu".
Type "show configuration" for configuration details.
For bug reporting instructions, please see:
<https://www.gnu.org/software/gdb/bugs/>.
Find the GDB manual and other documentation resources online at:
    <http://www.gnu.org/software/gdb/documentation/>.

For help, type "help".
Type "apropos word" to search for commands related to "word"...
Reading symbols from App9...
(No debugging symbols found in App9)

warning: Can't open file /home/opc/ALCDA2/App9/App9 during file-backed mapping note processing
[New LWP 12058]
[New LWP 12059]
[New LWP 12060]
[New LWP 12061]
[New LWP 12062]
[New LWP 12057]
Core was generated by `./App9'.
#0  0x000000000040ca84 in nanosleep ()
[Current thread is 1 (LWP 12058)]
```

5. Set logging to a file in case of lengthy verbose output from some commands (GDB appends data):

```
(gdb) set logging on App9.log
Copying output to App9.log.
```

```
(gdb) show logging
Future logs will be written to gdb.txt.
Logs will be appended to the log file.
Output will be logged and displayed.
```

6. Notice that another large section appeared after some time.

```
(gdb) maintenance info sections
Exec file: `/home/ubuntu/ALCDA2/A64/App9/App9', file type elf64-littleaarch64.
 [0]      0x00400190->0x004001b0 at 0x00000190: .note.ABI-tag ALLOC LOAD READONLY DATA HAS_CONTENTS
 [1]      0x004001b0->0x004001d4 at 0x000001b0: .note.gnu.build-id ALLOC LOAD READONLY DATA HAS_CONTENTS
 [2]      0x004001d8->0x00400250 at 0x000001d8: .rela.plt ALLOC LOAD READONLY DATA HAS_CONTENTS
 [3]      0x00400250->0x00400264 at 0x00000250: .init ALLOC LOAD READONLY CODE HAS_CONTENTS
 [4]      0x00400270->0x004002c0 at 0x00000270: .plt ALLOC LOAD READONLY CODE HAS_CONTENTS
 [5]      0x004002c0->0x00487158 at 0x000002c0: .text ALLOC LOAD READONLY CODE HAS_CONTENTS
 [6]      0x00487158->0x00488e28 at 0x00087158: __libc_freeres_fn ALLOC LOAD READONLY CODE HAS_CONTENTS
 [7]      0x00488e28->0x00489278 at 0x00088e28: __libc_thread_freeres_fn ALLOC LOAD READONLY CODE HAS_CONTENTS
 [8]      0x00489278->0x00489288 at 0x00089278: .fini ALLOC LOAD READONLY CODE HAS_CONTENTS
 [9]      0x00489290->0x004a178d at 0x00089290: .rodata ALLOC LOAD READONLY DATA HAS_CONTENTS
 [10]     0x004a178d->0x004a178e at 0x000a178d: .stapsdt.base ALLOC LOAD READONLY DATA HAS_CONTENTS
 [11]     0x004a1790->0x004a1ec8 at 0x000a1790: __libc_IO_vtables ALLOC LOAD READONLY DATA HAS_CONTENTS
 [12]     0x004a1ec8->0x004a1f30 at 0x000a1ec8: __libc_subfreeres ALLOC LOAD READONLY DATA HAS_CONTENTS
 [13]     0x004a1f30->0x004a1f38 at 0x000a1f30: __libc_atexit ALLOC LOAD READONLY DATA HAS_CONTENTS
 [14]     0x004a1f38->0x004a1f48 at 0x000a1f38: __libc_thread_subfreeres ALLOC LOAD READONLY DATA HAS_CONTENTS
 [15]     0x004a1f48->0x004b05ec at 0x000a1f48: .eh_frame ALLOC LOAD READONLY DATA HAS_CONTENTS
 [16]     0x004b05ec->0x004b07a9 at 0x000b05ec: .gcc_except_table ALLOC LOAD READONLY DATA HAS_CONTENTS
```

```
 [17]     0x004cfb20->0x004cfb48 at 0x000bfb20: .tdata ALLOC LOAD DATA HAS_CONTENTS
 [18]     0x004cfb48->0x004cfb98 at 0x000bfb48: .tbss ALLOC
 [19]     0x004cfb48->0x004cfb50 at 0x000bfb48: .init_array ALLOC LOAD DATA HAS_CONTENTS
 [20]     0x004cfb50->0x004cfb60 at 0x000bfb50: .fini_array ALLOC LOAD DATA HAS_CONTENTS
 [21]     0x004cfb60->0x004cfb68 at 0x000bfb60: .jcr ALLOC LOAD DATA HAS_CONTENTS
 [22]     0x004cfb68->0x004cff24 at 0x000bfb68: .data.rel.ro ALLOC LOAD DATA HAS_CONTENTS
 [23]     0x004cff28->0x004cffe8 at 0x000bff28: .got ALLOC LOAD DATA HAS_CONTENTS
 [24]     0x004cffe8->0x004d0028 at 0x000bffe8: .got.plt ALLOC LOAD DATA HAS_CONTENTS
 [25]     0x004d0030->0x004d1580 at 0x000c0030: .data ALLOC LOAD DATA HAS_CONTENTS
 [26]     0x004d1580->0x004d8050 at 0x000c1580: .bss ALLOC
 [27]     0x004d8050->0x004d8088 at 0x000c1580: __libc_freeres_ptrs ALLOC
 [28]     0x00000000->0x00000031 at 0x000c1580: .comment READONLY HAS_CONTENTS
 [29]     0x00000000->0x00001cb0 at 0x000c15b4: .note.stapsdt READONLY HAS_CONTENTS
Core file: `/home/ubuntu/ALCDA2/A64/App9/App9.core.3.12057', file type elf64-littleaarch64.
 [0]      0x00000000->0x00001c94 at 0x00000468: note0 READONLY HAS_CONTENTS
 [1]      0x00000000->0x00000110 at 0x00000588: .reg/12058 HAS_CONTENTS
 [2]      0x00000000->0x00000110 at 0x00000588: .reg HAS_CONTENTS
 [3]      0x00000000->0x00000210 at 0x000006b4: .reg2/12058 HAS_CONTENTS
 [4]      0x00000000->0x00000210 at 0x000006b4: .reg2 HAS_CONTENTS
 [5]      0x00000000->0x00000080 at 0x000008d8: .note.linuxcore.siginfo/12058 HAS_CONTENTS
 [6]      0x00000000->0x00000080 at 0x000008d8: .note.linuxcore.siginfo HAS_CONTENTS
 [7]      0x00000000->0x00000110 at 0x000009dc: .reg/12059 HAS_CONTENTS
 [8]      0x00000000->0x00000210 at 0x00000b08: .reg2/12059 HAS_CONTENTS
 [9]      0x00000000->0x00000080 at 0x00000d2c: .note.linuxcore.siginfo/12059 HAS_CONTENTS
 [10]     0x00000000->0x00000110 at 0x00000e30: .reg/12060 HAS_CONTENTS
 [11]     0x00000000->0x00000210 at 0x00000f5c: .reg2/12060 HAS_CONTENTS
 [12]     0x00000000->0x00000080 at 0x00001180: .note.linuxcore.siginfo/12060 HAS_CONTENTS
 [13]     0x00000000->0x00000110 at 0x00001284: .reg/12061 HAS_CONTENTS
 [14]     0x00000000->0x00000210 at 0x000013b0: .reg2/12061 HAS_CONTENTS
 [15]     0x00000000->0x00000080 at 0x000015d4: .note.linuxcore.siginfo/12061 HAS_CONTENTS
 [16]     0x00000000->0x00000110 at 0x000016d8: .reg/12062 HAS_CONTENTS
--Type <RET> for more, q to quit, c to continue without paging--
 [17]     0x00000000->0x00000210 at 0x00001804: .reg2/12062 HAS_CONTENTS
 [18]     0x00000000->0x00000080 at 0x00001a28: .note.linuxcore.siginfo/12062 HAS_CONTENTS
 [19]     0x00000000->0x00000110 at 0x00001b2c: .reg/12057 HAS_CONTENTS
 [20]     0x00000000->0x00000210 at 0x00001c58: .reg2/12057 HAS_CONTENTS
 [21]     0x00000000->0x00000080 at 0x00001e7c: .note.linuxcore.siginfo/12057 HAS_CONTENTS
 [22]     0x00000000->0x00000160 at 0x00001f10: .auxv HAS_CONTENTS
 [23]     0x00000000->0x00000076 at 0x00002084: .note.linuxcore.file/12057 HAS_CONTENTS
 [24]     0x00000000->0x00000076 at 0x00002084: .note.linuxcore.file HAS_CONTENTS
 [25]     0x00400000->0x004c0000 at 0x000020fc: load1 ALLOC LOAD READONLY CODE HAS_CONTENTS
 [26]     0x004c0000->0x004e0000 at 0x000c20fc: load2 ALLOC LOAD HAS_CONTENTS
 [27]     0x2f860000->0x2f8a0000 at 0x000e20fc: load3 ALLOC LOAD HAS_CONTENTS
 [28]     0xfffce8000000->0xfffcec300000 at 0x001220fc: load4 ALLOC LOAD HAS_CONTENTS
 [29]     0xfffcec300000->0xfffcf0000000 at 0x044220fc: load5 ALLOC LOAD READONLY HAS_CONTENTS
 [30]     0xfffcf0000000->0xfffcf4000000 at 0x081220fc: load6 ALLOC LOAD HAS_CONTENTS
 [31]     0xfffcf7400000->0xfffcf7410000 at 0x0c1220fc: load7 ALLOC LOAD READONLY HAS_CONTENTS
 [32]     0xfffcf7410000->0xfffcf7c10000 at 0x0c1320fc: load8 ALLOC LOAD HAS_CONTENTS
 [33]     0xfffcf7c10000->0xfffcf7c20000 at 0x0c9320fc: load9 ALLOC LOAD READONLY HAS_CONTENTS
 [34]     0xfffcf7c20000->0xfffcf8420000 at 0x0c9420fc: load10 ALLOC LOAD HAS_CONTENTS
 [35]     0xfffcf8420000->0xfffcf8430000 at 0x0d1420fc: load11 ALLOC LOAD READONLY HAS_CONTENTS
 [36]     0xfffcf8430000->0xfffcf8c30000 at 0x0d1520fc: load12 ALLOC LOAD HAS_CONTENTS
 [37]     0xfffcf8c30000->0xfffcf8c40000 at 0x0d9520fc: load13 ALLOC LOAD READONLY HAS_CONTENTS
 [38]     0xfffcf8c40000->0xfffcf9440000 at 0x0d9620fc: load14 ALLOC LOAD HAS_CONTENTS
 [39]     0xfffcf9440000->0xfffcf9450000 at 0x0e1620fc: load15 ALLOC LOAD READONLY HAS_CONTENTS
 [40]     0xfffcf9450000->0xfffcf9c50000 at 0x0e1720fc: load16 ALLOC LOAD HAS_CONTENTS
 [41]     0xfffcf9c60000->0xfffcf9c70000 at 0x0e9720fc: load17 ALLOC LOAD READONLY CODE HAS_CONTENTS
 [42]     0xffffc2f60000->0xffffc2f90000 at 0x0e9820fc: load18 ALLOC LOAD HAS_CONTENTS
```

7. Examine segment contents for any execution residue and hints (we choose some smaller address range from the section address range):

```
(gdb) x/1000a 0xfffce8000000
0xfffce8000000: 0xfffcf0000020  0xfffcf0000000
0xfffce8000010: 0x4000000       0x4000000
0xfffce8000020: 0x0     0x115
0xfffce8000030: 0x657461636f6c6c61      0x79726f6d656d2064
0xfffce8000040: 0x0     0x0
0xfffce8000050: 0x4031e8 <procD>        0x0
0xfffce8000060: 0x0     0x0
0xfffce8000070: 0x0     0x0
0xfffce8000080: 0x0     0x0
0xfffce8000090: 0x0     0x0
0xfffce80000a0: 0x0     0x0
0xfffce80000b0: 0x0     0x0
0xfffce80000c0: 0x0     0x0
0xfffce80000d0: 0x0     0x0
0xfffce80000e0: 0x0     0x0
0xfffce80000f0: 0x0     0x0
0xfffce8000100: 0x0     0x0
0xfffce8000110: 0x0     0x0
0xfffce8000120: 0x0     0x0
0xfffce8000130: 0x0     0x115
0xfffce8000140: 0x657461636f6c6c61      0x79726f6d656d2064
0xfffce8000150: 0x0     0x0
0xfffce8000160: 0x4031e8 <procD>        0x0
0xfffce8000170: 0x0     0x0
0xfffce8000180: 0x0     0x0
0xfffce8000190: 0x0     0x0
0xfffce80001a0: 0x0     0x0
0xfffce80001b0: 0x0     0x0
0xfffce80001c0: 0x0     0x0
0xfffce80001d0: 0x0     0x0
0xfffce80001e0: 0x0     0x0
0xfffce80001f0: 0x0     0x0
0xfffce8000200: 0x0     0x0
0xfffce8000210: 0x0     0x0
0xfffce8000220: 0x0     0x0
0xfffce8000230: 0x0     0x0
0xfffce8000240: 0x0     0x115
0xfffce8000250: 0x657461636f6c6c61      0x79726f6d656d2064
0xfffce8000260: 0x0     0x0
0xfffce8000270: 0x4031e8 <procD>        0x0
0xfffce8000280: 0x0     0x0
0xfffce8000290: 0x0     0x0
0xfffce80002a0: 0x0     0x0
0xfffce80002b0: 0x0     0x0
0xfffce80002c0: 0x0     0x0
0xfffce80002d0: 0x0     0x0
0xfffce80002e0: 0x0     0x0
0xfffce80002f0: 0x0     0x0
0xfffce8000300: 0x0     0x0
--Type <RET> for more, q to quit, c to continue without paging--
0xfffce8000310: 0x0     0x0
0xfffce8000320: 0x0     0x0
0xfffce8000330: 0x0     0x0
0xfffce8000340: 0x0     0x0
0xfffce8000350: 0x0     0x115
[...]
```

```
0xfffce8001ce0: 0x657461636f6c6c61      0x79726f6d656d2064
0xfffce8001cf0: 0x0     0x0
0xfffce8001d00: 0x4031e8 <procD>        0x0
0xfffce8001d10: 0x0     0x0
0xfffce8001d20: 0x0     0x0
0xfffce8001d30: 0x0     0x0
0xfffce8001d40: 0x0     0x0
0xfffce8001d50: 0x0     0x0
0xfffce8001d60: 0x0     0x0
0xfffce8001d70: 0x0     0x0
0xfffce8001d80: 0x0     0x0
0xfffce8001d90: 0x0     0x0
0xfffce8001da0: 0x0     0x0
0xfffce8001db0: 0x0     0x0
0xfffce8001dc0: 0x0     0x0
0xfffce8001dd0: 0x0     0x0
0xfffce8001de0: 0x0     0x115
0xfffce8001df0: 0x657461636f6c6c61      0x79726f6d656d2064
0xfffce8001e00: 0x0     0x0
0xfffce8001e10: 0x4031e8 <procD>        0x0
0xfffce8001e20: 0x0     0x0
0xfffce8001e30: 0x0     0x0
0xfffce8001e40: 0x0     0x0
0xfffce8001e50: 0x0     0x0
0xfffce8001e60: 0x0     0x0
0xfffce8001e70: 0x0     0x0
0xfffce8001e80: 0x0     0x0
0xfffce8001e90: 0x0     0x0
--Type <RET> for more, q to quit, c to continue without paging--
0xfffce8001ea0: 0x0     0x0
0xfffce8001eb0: 0x0     0x0
0xfffce8001ec0: 0x0     0x0
0xfffce8001ed0: 0x0     0x0
0xfffce8001ee0: 0x0     0x0
0xfffce8001ef0: 0x0     0x115
0xfffce8001f00: 0x657461636f6c6c61      0x79726f6d656d2064
0xfffce8001f10: 0x0     0x0
0xfffce8001f20: 0x4031e8 <procD>        0x0
0xfffce8001f30: 0x0     0x0

(gdb) x/s 0xfffce8001f00
0xfffce8001f00: "allocated memory"
```

8. Compare pmap logs *App9.pmap.1.12057*, *App9.pmap.2.12057*, and *App9.pmap.3.12057* (the first one was saved before the leak started, and the other two correspond to core dumps we looked at):

```
12057:   ./App9
0000000000400000    768K r-x-- App9
00000000004c0000    128K rw--- App9
000000002f860000    256K rw---   [ anon ]
0000fffcf0000000   1344K rw---   [ anon ]
0000fffcf0150000  64192K -----   [ anon ]
0000fffcf7400000     64K -----   [ anon ]
0000fffcf7410000   8192K rw---   [ anon ]
0000fffcf7c10000     64K -----   [ anon ]
0000fffcf7c20000   8192K rw---   [ anon ]
0000fffcf8420000     64K -----   [ anon ]
0000fffcf8430000   8192K rw---   [ anon ]
0000fffcf8c30000     64K -----   [ anon ]
0000fffcf8c40000   8192K rw---   [ anon ]
```

```
0000fffcf9440000      64K -----   [ anon ]
0000fffcf9450000    8192K rw---   [ anon ]
0000fffcf9c50000      64K r----   [ anon ]
0000fffcf9c60000      64K r-x--   [ anon ]
0000ffffc2f60000     192K rw---   [ stack ]
 total            108288K

12057:   ./App9
0000000000400000     768K r-x-- App9
00000000004c0000     128K rw--- App9
000000002f860000     256K rw---   [ anon ]
0000fffce8000000    2240K rw---   [ anon ]
0000fffce8230000   63296K -----   [ anon ]
0000fffcf0000000   65536K rw---   [ anon ]
0000fffcf7400000      64K -----   [ anon ]
0000fffcf7410000    8192K rw---   [ anon ]
0000fffcf7c10000      64K -----   [ anon ]
0000fffcf7c20000    8192K rw---   [ anon ]
0000fffcf8420000      64K -----   [ anon ]
0000fffcf8430000    8192K rw---   [ anon ]
0000fffcf8c30000      64K -----   [ anon ]
0000fffcf8c40000    8192K rw---   [ anon ]
0000fffcf9440000      64K -----   [ anon ]
0000fffcf9450000    8192K rw---   [ anon ]
0000fffcf9c50000      64K r----   [ anon ]
0000fffcf9c60000      64K r-x--   [ anon ]
0000ffffc2f60000     192K rw---   [ stack ]
 total            173824K

12057:   ./App9
0000000000400000     768K r-x-- App9
00000000004c0000     128K rw--- App9
000000002f860000     256K rw---   [ anon ]
0000fffce8000000   68608K rw---   [ anon ]
0000fffcec300000   62464K -----   [ anon ]
0000fffcf0000000   65536K rw---   [ anon ]
0000fffcf7400000      64K -----   [ anon ]
0000fffcf7410000    8192K rw---   [ anon ]
0000fffcf7c10000      64K -----   [ anon ]
0000fffcf7c20000    8192K rw---   [ anon ]
0000fffcf8420000      64K -----   [ anon ]
0000fffcf8430000    8192K rw---   [ anon ]
0000fffcf8c30000      64K -----   [ anon ]
0000fffcf8c40000    8192K rw---   [ anon ]
0000fffcf9440000      64K -----   [ anon ]
0000fffcf9450000    8192K rw---   [ anon ]
0000fffcf9c50000      64K r----   [ anon ]
0000fffcf9c60000      64K r-x--   [ anon ]
0000ffffc2f60000     192K rw---   [ stack ]
 total            239360K
```

Exercise A9 (x64, WinDbg)

Goal: Learn how to identify heap leaks.

Patterns: Memory Leak (Process Heap); Module Hint; Historical Information.

1. Launch WinDbg.

2. The application *App9* was found to consume more and more memory. Several core memory dumps were saved at different times with corresponding *pmap* logs. Load the *App9.core.2.230* dump file from the x64\App9 folder:

```
Microsoft (R) Windows Debugger Version 10.0.27725.1000 AMD64
Copyright (c) Microsoft Corporation. All rights reserved.


Loading Dump File [C:\ALCDA2\x64\App9\App9.core.2.230]
64-bit machine not using 64-bit API

************* Path validation summary **************
Response                         Time (ms)     Location
Deferred                                       srv*
Symbol search path is: srv*
Executable search path is:
Generic Unix Version 0 UP Free x64
System Uptime: not available
Process Uptime: not available
..
*** WARNING: Unable to verify timestamp for App9
App9+0x41ad0:
00000000`00441ad0 cmp     rax,0FFFFFFFFFFFFF000h
```

3. Set logging to a file in case of lengthy output from some commands:

```
0:000> .logopen C:\ALCDA2\x64\App9\App9-WinDbg.log
Opened log file 'C:\ALCDA2\x64\App9\App9-WinDBg.log'
```

4. Specify the dump folder as the symbol path and reload symbols:

```
0:000> .symfix; .sympath+ C:\ALCDA2\x64\App9\
Symbol search path is: srv*;C:\ALCDA2\x64\App9
Expanded Symbol search path is:
cache*;SRV*https://msdl.microsoft.com/download/symbols;c:\alcda2\x64\app9

************* Path validation summary **************
Response                         Time (ms)     Location
Deferred                                       srv*
OK                                             C:\ALCDA2\x64\App9
*** WARNING: Unable to verify timestamp for App9
```

```
0:000> .reload
..
*** WARNING: Unable to verify timestamp for App9

************* Symbol Loading Error Summary **************
Module name            Error
App9                   The system cannot find the file specified

You can troubleshoot most symbol related issues by turning on symbol loading diagnostics (!sym
noisy) and repeating the command that caused symbols to be loaded.
You should also verify that your symbol search path (.sympath) is correct.
```

Note: We ignore warnings and errors as they are not relevant for now.

5. Notice the size of the largest PAGE_READWRITE region, close logging, and quit WinDbg:

```
0:000> !address

Mapping file section regions...
Mapping module regions...
Mapping heap regions...

        BaseAddress      EndAddress+1        RegionSize     Type       State                 Protect             Usage
--------------------------------------------------------------------------------------------------------------------------
+        0`00000000        0`00400000        0`00400000                                                          <unknown>
+        0`00400000        0`00401000        0`00001000 MEM_PRIVATE MEM_COMMIT  PAGE_EXECUTE_READ                  Image      [App9; "/home/coredump/ALCDA2/x64/App9/App9"]
+        0`00401000        0`00495000        0`00094000 MEM_PRIVATE MEM_COMMIT  PAGE_EXECUTE_READ                  Image      [App9; "/home/coredump/ALCDA2/x64/App9/App9"]
+        0`00495000        0`004bd000        0`00028000                                                          Image      [App9; "/home/coredump/ALCDA2/x64/App9/App9"]
+        0`004bd000        0`004c3000        0`00006000 MEM_PRIVATE MEM_COMMIT  PAGE_READWRITE                     Image      [App9; "/home/coredump/ALCDA2/x64/App9/App9"]
+        0`004c3000        0`004c9000        0`00006000 MEM_PRIVATE MEM_COMMIT  PAGE_READWRITE                     <unknown>  [................]
+        0`004c9000        0`01778000        0`012af000                                                          <unknown>
+        0`01778000        0`0179b000        0`00023000 MEM_PRIVATE MEM_COMMIT  PAGE_READWRITE                     <unknown>  [................]
+        0`0179b000     7f08`dc000000     7f08`da865000                                                          <unknown>
+     7f08`dc000000     7f08`dc227000        0`00227000 MEM_PRIVATE MEM_COMMIT  PAGE_READWRITE                     <unknown>  [................]
+     7f08`dc227000     7f08`e0000000        0`03dd9000 MEM_PRIVATE MEM_COMMIT  PAGE_READONLY                      <unknown>  [................]
+     7f08`e0000000     7f08`e4000000        0`04000000                                                          <unknown>
+     7f08`e4000000     7f08`e8000000        0`04000000 MEM_PRIVATE MEM_COMMIT  PAGE_READWRITE                     <unknown>  [................]
+     7f08`e8000000     7f08`eb528000        0`03528000                                                          <unknown>
+     7f08`eb528000     7f08`eb529000        0`00001000 MEM_PRIVATE MEM_COMMIT  PAGE_READONLY                      <unknown>  [................]
+     7f08`eb529000     7f08`ebd29000        0`00800000 MEM_PRIVATE MEM_COMMIT  PAGE_READWRITE                     <unknown>  [................]
+     7f08`ebd29000     7f08`ebd2a000        0`00001000 MEM_PRIVATE MEM_COMMIT  PAGE_READONLY                      <unknown>  [................]
+     7f08`ebd2a000     7f08`ec52a000        0`00800000 MEM_PRIVATE MEM_COMMIT  PAGE_READWRITE                     <unknown>  [................]
+     7f08`ec52a000     7f08`ec52b000        0`00001000 MEM_PRIVATE MEM_COMMIT  PAGE_READONLY                      <unknown>  [................]
+     7f08`ec52b000     7f08`ecd2b000        0`00800000 MEM_PRIVATE MEM_COMMIT  PAGE_READWRITE                     <unknown>  [................]
+     7f08`ecd2b000     7f08`ecd2c000        0`00001000 MEM_PRIVATE MEM_COMMIT  PAGE_READONLY                      <unknown>  [................]
+     7f08`ecd2c000     7f08`ed52c000        0`00800000 MEM_PRIVATE MEM_COMMIT  PAGE_READWRITE                     <unknown>  [................]
+     7f08`ed52c000     7f08`ed52d000        0`00001000 MEM_PRIVATE MEM_COMMIT  PAGE_READONLY                      <unknown>  [................]
+     7f08`ed52d000     7f08`edd2d000        0`00800000 MEM_PRIVATE MEM_COMMIT  PAGE_READWRITE                     <unknown>  [................]
+     7f08`edd2d000     7ffe`4333f000       f5`55612000                                                          <unknown>
+     7ffe`4333f000     7ffe`43360000        0`00021000 MEM_PRIVATE MEM_COMMIT  PAGE_READWRITE                     <unknown>  [................]
+     7ffe`43360000     7ffe`43385000        0`00025000                                                          <unknown>
+     7ffe`43385000     7ffe`43386000        0`00001000 MEM_PRIVATE MEM_COMMIT  PAGE_EXECUTE_READ                  Image      [linux_vdso_so; "linux-vdso.so.1"]

0:000> .logclose
Closing open log file 'C:\ALCDA2\x64\App9\App9-WinDbg.log'
```

6. Open another instance of WinDbg and load the *App9.core.3.230* dump file from x64\App9 folder. Set up symbol path, reload symbols, and set append logging to the same log file as previously:

```
Microsoft (R) Windows Debugger Version 10.0.27725.1000 AMD64
Copyright (c) Microsoft Corporation. All rights reserved.


Loading Dump File [C:\ALCDA2\x64\App9\App9.core.3.230]
64-bit machine not using 64-bit API

************* Path validation summary **************
Response                         Time (ms)     Location
Deferred                                       srv*
Symbol search path is: srv*
Executable search path is:
Generic Unix Version 0 UP Free x64
System Uptime: not available
Process Uptime: not available
```

```
..
*** WARNING: Unable to verify timestamp for App9
App9+0x41ad0:
00000000`00441ad0 cmp     rax,0FFFFFFFFFFFFF000h

0:000> .symfix; .sympath+ C:\ALCDA2\x64\App9\
Symbol search path is: srv*;C:\ALCDA2\x64\App9
Expanded Symbol search path is:
cache*;SRV*https://msdl.microsoft.com/download/symbols;c:\alcda2\x64\app9

************* Path validation summary **************
Response                         Time (ms)     Location
Deferred                                       srv*
OK                                             C:\ALCDA2\x64\App9
*** WARNING: Unable to verify timestamp for App9

0:000> .reload
..
*** WARNING: Unable to verify timestamp for App9

************* Symbol Loading Error Summary **************
Module name            Error
App9                   The system cannot find the file specified

You can troubleshoot most symbol related issues by turning on symbol loading diagnostics (!sym
noisy) and repeating the command that caused symbols to be loaded.
You should also verify that your symbol search path (.sympath) is correct.

0:000> .logappend C:\ALCDA2\x64\App9\App9-WinDbg.log
Opened log file 'C:\ALCDA2\x64\App9\App9-WinDbg.log'
```

Note: We ignore warnings and errors as they are not relevant for now.

7. Notice that another PAGE_READWRITE large region appeared after some time.

```
0:000> !address

Mapping file section regions...
Mapping module regions...
Mapping heap regions...

        BaseAddress      EndAddress+1        RegionSize     Type       State                 Protect             Usage
-----------------------------------------------------------------------------------------------------------------------------
+        0`00000000        0`00400000        0`00400000                                                        <unknown>
+        0`00400000        0`00401000        0`00001000 MEM_PRIVATE MEM_COMMIT  PAGE_EXECUTE_READ               Image      [App9; "/home/coredump/ALCDA2/x64/App9/App9"]
+        0`00401000        0`00495000        0`00094000 MEM_PRIVATE MEM_COMMIT  PAGE_EXECUTE_READ               Image      [App9; "/home/coredump/ALCDA2/x64/App9/App9"]
+        0`00495000        0`004bd000        0`00028000                                                        Image      [App9; "/home/coredump/ALCDA2/x64/App9/App9"]
+        0`004bd000        0`004c3000        0`00006000 MEM_PRIVATE MEM_COMMIT  PAGE_READWRITE                  Image      [App9; "/home/coredump/ALCDA2/x64/App9/App9"]
+        0`004c3000        0`004c9000        0`00006000 MEM_PRIVATE MEM_COMMIT  PAGE_READWRITE                  <unknown>  [................]
+        0`004c9000        0`01778000        0`012af000                                                        <unknown>
+        0`01778000        0`0179b000        0`00023000 MEM_PRIVATE MEM_COMMIT  PAGE_READWRITE                  <unknown>  [................]
+        0`0179b000     7f08`dc000000     7f08`da865000                                                        <unknown>
+     7f08`dc000000     7f08`e0300000        0`04300000 MEM_PRIVATE MEM_COMMIT  PAGE_READWRITE                  <unknown>  [................]
+     7f08`e0300000     7f08`e4000000        0`03d00000 MEM_PRIVATE MEM_COMMIT  PAGE_READONLY                   <unknown>  [................]
+     7f08`e4000000     7f08`e8000000        0`04000000 MEM_PRIVATE MEM_COMMIT  PAGE_READWRITE                  <unknown>  [................]
+     7f08`e8000000     7f08`eb528000        0`03528000                                                        <unknown>
+     7f08`eb528000     7f08`eb529000        0`00001000 MEM_PRIVATE MEM_COMMIT  PAGE_READONLY                   <unknown>  [................]
+     7f08`eb529000     7f08`ebd29000        0`00800000 MEM_PRIVATE MEM_COMMIT  PAGE_READWRITE                  <unknown>  [................]
+     7f08`ebd29000     7f08`ebd2a000        0`00001000 MEM_PRIVATE MEM_COMMIT  PAGE_READONLY                   <unknown>  [................]
+     7f08`ebd2a000     7f08`ec52a000        0`00800000 MEM_PRIVATE MEM_COMMIT  PAGE_READWRITE                  <unknown>  [................]
+     7f08`ec52a000     7f08`ec52b000        0`00001000 MEM_PRIVATE MEM_COMMIT  PAGE_READONLY                   <unknown>  [................]
+     7f08`ec52b000     7f08`ecd2b000        0`00800000 MEM_PRIVATE MEM_COMMIT  PAGE_READWRITE                  <unknown>  [................]
+     7f08`ecd2b000     7f08`ecd2c000        0`00001000 MEM_PRIVATE MEM_COMMIT  PAGE_READONLY                   <unknown>  [................]
+     7f08`ecd2c000     7f08`ed52c000        0`00800000 MEM_PRIVATE MEM_COMMIT  PAGE_READWRITE                  <unknown>  [................]
+     7f08`ed52c000     7f08`ed52d000        0`00001000 MEM_PRIVATE MEM_COMMIT  PAGE_READONLY                   <unknown>  [................]
+     7f08`ed52d000     7f08`edd2d000        0`00800000 MEM_PRIVATE MEM_COMMIT  PAGE_READWRITE                  <unknown>  [................]
+     7f08`edd2d000     7ffe`4333f000       f5`55612000                                                        <unknown>
+     7ffe`4333f000     7ffe`43360000        0`00021000 MEM_PRIVATE MEM_COMMIT  PAGE_READWRITE                  <unknown>  [................]
+     7ffe`43360000     7ffe`43385000        0`00025000                                                        <unknown>
+     7ffe`43385000     7ffe`43386000        0`00001000 MEM_PRIVATE MEM_COMMIT  PAGE_EXECUTE_READ               Image      [linux_vdso_so; "linux-vdso.so.1"]
```

8. Examine region contents for any execution residue and hints (we choose a smaller address range from the section address range):

```
0:000> dps 7f08`dc000000 7f08`dc000000+1000
00007f08`dc000000  00007f08`e4000020
00007f08`dc000008  00007f08`e4000000
00007f08`dc000010  00000000`04000000
00007f08`dc000018  00000000`04000000
00007f08`dc000020  00000000`00000000
00007f08`dc000028  00000000`00000115
00007f08`dc000030  65746163`6f6c6c61
00007f08`dc000038  79726f6d`656d2064
00007f08`dc000040  00000000`00000000
00007f08`dc000048  00000000`00000000
00007f08`dc000050  00000000`00401bad App9+0x1bad
00007f08`dc000058  00000000`00000000
00007f08`dc000060  00000000`00000000
00007f08`dc000068  00000000`00000000
00007f08`dc000070  00000000`00000000
00007f08`dc000078  00000000`00000000
00007f08`dc000080  00000000`00000000
00007f08`dc000088  00000000`00000000
00007f08`dc000090  00000000`00000000
00007f08`dc000098  00000000`00000000
00007f08`dc0000a0  00000000`00000000
00007f08`dc0000a8  00000000`00000000
00007f08`dc0000b0  00000000`00000000
00007f08`dc0000b8  00000000`00000000
00007f08`dc0000c0  00000000`00000000
00007f08`dc0000c8  00000000`00000000
00007f08`dc0000d0  00000000`00000000
00007f08`dc0000d8  00000000`00000000
00007f08`dc0000e0  00000000`00000000
00007f08`dc0000e8  00000000`00000000
00007f08`dc0000f0  00000000`00000000
00007f08`dc0000f8  00000000`00000000
00007f08`dc000100  00000000`00000000
00007f08`dc000108  00000000`00000000
00007f08`dc000110  00000000`00000000
00007f08`dc000118  00000000`00000000
00007f08`dc000120  00000000`00000000
00007f08`dc000128  00000000`00000000
00007f08`dc000130  00000000`00000000
00007f08`dc000138  00000000`00000115
00007f08`dc000140  65746163`6f6c6c61
00007f08`dc000148  79726f6d`656d2064
00007f08`dc000150  00000000`00000000
00007f08`dc000158  00000000`00000000
00007f08`dc000160  00000000`00401bad App9+0x1bad
00007f08`dc000168  00000000`00000000
00007f08`dc000170  00000000`00000000
00007f08`dc000178  00000000`00000000
00007f08`dc000180  00000000`00000000
00007f08`dc000188  00000000`00000000
00007f08`dc000190  00000000`00000000
00007f08`dc000198  00000000`00000000
00007f08`dc0001a0  00000000`00000000
00007f08`dc0001a8  00000000`00000000
00007f08`dc0001b0  00000000`00000000
00007f08`dc0001b8  00000000`00000000
```

```
00007f08`dc0001c0  00000000`00000000
00007f08`dc0001c8  00000000`00000000
[...]
00007f08`dc000f10  65746163`6f6c6c61
00007f08`dc000f18  79726f6d`656d2064
00007f08`dc000f20  00000000`00000000
00007f08`dc000f28  00000000`00000000
00007f08`dc000f30  00000000`00401bad App9+0x1bad
00007f08`dc000f38  00000000`00000000
00007f08`dc000f40  00000000`00000000
00007f08`dc000f48  00000000`00000000
00007f08`dc000f50  00000000`00000000
00007f08`dc000f58  00000000`00000000
00007f08`dc000f60  00000000`00000000
00007f08`dc000f68  00000000`00000000
00007f08`dc000f70  00000000`00000000
00007f08`dc000f78  00000000`00000000
00007f08`dc000f80  00000000`00000000
00007f08`dc000f88  00000000`00000000
00007f08`dc000f90  00000000`00000000
00007f08`dc000f98  00000000`00000000
00007f08`dc000fa0  00000000`00000000
00007f08`dc000fa8  00000000`00000000
00007f08`dc000fb0  00000000`00000000
00007f08`dc000fb8  00000000`00000000
00007f08`dc000fc0  00000000`00000000
00007f08`dc000fc8  00000000`00000000
00007f08`dc000fd0  00000000`00000000
00007f08`dc000fd8  00000000`00000000
00007f08`dc000fe0  00000000`00000000
00007f08`dc000fe8  00000000`00000000
00007f08`dc000ff0  00000000`00000000
00007f08`dc000ff8  00000000`00000000
00007f08`dc001000  00000000`00000000

0:000> da 0000fffc`e8000f10
0000fffc`e8000f10  "allocated memory"
```

9. Compare pmap logs *App9.pmap.1.230*, *App9.pmap.2.230*, and *App9.pmap.3.230* (the first one was saved before the leak started, and the other two correspond to core dumps we looked at):

```
230:   ./App9
0000000000400000      4K r---- App9
0000000000401000    592K r-x-- App9
0000000000495000    156K r---- App9
00000000004bd000     24K rw--- App9
00000000004c3000     24K rw---   [ anon ]
0000000001778000    140K rw---   [ anon ]
00007f08e4000000   1332K rw---   [ anon ]
00007f08e414d000  64204K -----   [ anon ]
00007f08eb528000      4K -----   [ anon ]
00007f08eb529000   8192K rw---   [ anon ]
00007f08ebd29000      4K -----   [ anon ]
00007f08ebd2a000   8192K rw---   [ anon ]
00007f08ec52a000      4K -----   [ anon ]
00007f08ec52b000   8192K rw---   [ anon ]
00007f08ecd2b000      4K -----   [ anon ]
00007f08ecd2c000   8192K rw---   [ anon ]
00007f08ed52c000      4K -----   [ anon ]
00007f08ed52d000   8192K rw---   [ anon ]
```

```
00007ffe4333f000     132K rw---   [ stack ]
00007ffe43381000      16K r----   [ anon ]
00007ffe43385000       4K r-x--   [ anon ]
 total            107608K

230:   ./App9
0000000000400000       4K r---- App9
0000000000401000     592K r-x-- App9
0000000000495000     156K r---- App9
00000000004bd000      24K rw--- App9
00000000004c3000      24K rw---   [ anon ]
0000000001778000     140K rw---   [ anon ]
00007f08dc000000    2204K rw---   [ anon ]
00007f08dc227000   63332K -----   [ anon ]
00007f08e4000000   65536K rw---   [ anon ]
00007f08eb528000       4K -----   [ anon ]
00007f08eb529000    8192K rw---   [ anon ]
00007f08ebd29000       4K -----   [ anon ]
00007f08ebd2a000    8192K rw---   [ anon ]
00007f08ec52a000       4K -----   [ anon ]
00007f08ec52b000    8192K rw---   [ anon ]
00007f08ecd2b000       4K -----   [ anon ]
00007f08ecd2c000    8192K rw---   [ anon ]
00007f08ed52c000       4K -----   [ anon ]
00007f08ed52d000    8192K rw---   [ anon ]
00007ffe4333f000     132K rw---   [ stack ]
00007ffe43381000      16K r----   [ anon ]
00007ffe43385000       4K r-x--   [ anon ]
 total            173144K

230:   ./App9
0000000000400000       4K r---- App9
0000000000401000     592K r-x-- App9
0000000000495000     156K r---- App9
00000000004bd000      24K rw--- App9
00000000004c3000      24K rw---   [ anon ]
0000000001778000     140K rw---   [ anon ]
00007f08dc000000   68608K rw---   [ anon ]
00007f08e0300000   62464K -----   [ anon ]
00007f08e4000000   65536K rw---   [ anon ]
00007f08eb528000       4K -----   [ anon ]
00007f08eb529000    8192K rw---   [ anon ]
00007f08ebd29000       4K -----   [ anon ]
00007f08ebd2a000    8192K rw---   [ anon ]
00007f08ec52a000       4K -----   [ anon ]
00007f08ec52b000    8192K rw---   [ anon ]
00007f08ecd2b000       4K -----   [ anon ]
00007f08ecd2c000    8192K rw---   [ anon ]
00007f08ed52c000       4K -----   [ anon ]
00007f08ed52d000    8192K rw---   [ anon ]
00007ffe4333f000     132K rw---   [ stack ]
00007ffe43381000      16K r----   [ anon ]
00007ffe43385000       4K r-x--   [ anon ]
 total            238680K
```

10. We close logging before exiting WinDbg:

```
0:000> .logclose
Closing open log file 'C:\ALCDA2\x64\App9\App9-WinDbg.log
```

Exercise A9 (A64, WinDbg)

Goal: Learn how to identify heap leaks.

Patterns: Memory Leak (Process Heap); Module Hint; Historical Information.

1. Launch WinDbg.

2. The application *App9* was found to consume more and more memory. Several core memory dumps were saved at different times with corresponding *pmap* logs. Load the *App9.core.2.12057* dump file from the A64\App9 folder:

```
Microsoft (R) Windows Debugger Version 10.0.27725.1000 AMD64
Copyright (c) Microsoft Corporation. All rights reserved.


Loading Dump File [C:\ALCDA2\A64\App9\App9.core.2.12057]
64-bit machine not using 64-bit API

************* Path validation summary **************
Response                         Time (ms)     Location
Deferred                                       srv*
Symbol search path is: srv*
Executable search path is:
Generic Unix Version 0 UP Free ARM 64-bit (AArch64)
System Uptime: not available
Process Uptime: not available
..
*** WARNING: Unable to verify timestamp for App9
App9+0xca84:
00000000`0040ca84 svc          #0
```

3. Set logging to a file in case of lengthy output from some commands:

```
0:000> .logopen C:\ALCDA2\A64\App9\App9-WinDbg.log
Opened log file 'C:\ALCDA2\A64\App9\App9-WinDbg.log'
```

4. Specify the dump folder as the symbol path and reload symbols:

```
0:000> .symfix; .sympath+ C:\ALCDA2\A64\App9\
Symbol search path is: srv*;C:\ALCDA2\A64\App9\
Expanded Symbol search path is:
cache*;SRV*https://msdl.microsoft.com/download/symbols;c:\alcda2\a64\app9\

************* Path validation summary **************
Response                         Time (ms)     Location
Deferred                                       srv*
OK                                             C:\ALCDA2\A64\App9\
*** WARNING: Unable to verify timestamp for App9
```

```
0:000> .reload
..
*** WARNING: Unable to verify timestamp for App9

************* Symbol Loading Error Summary **************
Module name            Error
App9                   The system cannot find the file specified

You can troubleshoot most symbol related issues by turning on symbol loading diagnostics (!sym
noisy) and repeating the command that caused symbols to be loaded.
You should also verify that your symbol search path (.sympath) is correct.
```

Note: We ignore warnings and errors as they are not relevant for now.

5. Notice the size of the largest PAGE_READWRITE region, close logging, and quit WinDbg Preview:

```
0:000> !address

Mapping file section regions...
Mapping module regions...

        BaseAddress      EndAddress+1        RegionSize     Type       State                 Protect             Usage
-----------------------------------------------------------------------------------------------------------------------
+        0`00000000        0`00400000        0`00400000                                                          <unknown>
+        0`00400000        0`004c0000        0`000c0000 MEM_PRIVATE MEM_COMMIT  PAGE_EXECUTE_READ                Image      [App9;
"/home/opc/ALCDA2/App9/App9"]
+        0`004c0000        0`004e0000        0`00020000 MEM_PRIVATE MEM_COMMIT  PAGE_READWRITE                   Image      [App9;
"/home/opc/ALCDA2/App9/App9"]
+        0`004e0000        0`2f860000        0`2f380000                                                          <unknown>
+        0`2f860000        0`2f8a0000        0`00040000 MEM_PRIVATE MEM_COMMIT  PAGE_READWRITE                   <unknown>  [................]
+        0`2f8a0000     fffc`e8000000     fffc`b8760000                                                          <unknown>
+     fffc`e8000000     fffc`e8230000        0`00230000 MEM_PRIVATE MEM_COMMIT  PAGE_READWRITE                   <unknown>  [................]
+     fffc`e8230000     fffc`ec000000        0`03dd0000 MEM_PRIVATE MEM_COMMIT  PAGE_READONLY                    <unknown>  [................]
+     fffc`ec000000     fffc`f0000000        0`04000000                                                          <unknown>
+     fffc`f0000000     fffc`f4000000        0`04000000 MEM_PRIVATE MEM_COMMIT  PAGE_READWRITE                   <unknown>  [................]
+     fffc`f4000000     fffc`f7400000        0`03400000                                                          <unknown>
+     fffc`f7400000     fffc`f7410000        0`00010000 MEM_PRIVATE MEM_COMMIT  PAGE_READONLY                    <unknown>  [................]
+     fffc`f7410000     fffc`f7c10000        0`00800000 MEM_PRIVATE MEM_COMMIT  PAGE_READWRITE                   <unknown>  [................]
+     fffc`f7c10000     fffc`f7c20000        0`00010000 MEM_PRIVATE MEM_COMMIT  PAGE_READONLY                    <unknown>  [................]
+     fffc`f7c20000     fffc`f8420000        0`00800000 MEM_PRIVATE MEM_COMMIT  PAGE_READWRITE                   <unknown>  [................]
+     fffc`f8420000     fffc`f8430000        0`00010000 MEM_PRIVATE MEM_COMMIT  PAGE_READONLY                    <unknown>  [................]
+     fffc`f8430000     fffc`f8c30000        0`00800000 MEM_PRIVATE MEM_COMMIT  PAGE_READWRITE                   <unknown>  [................]
+     fffc`f8c30000     fffc`f8c40000        0`00010000 MEM_PRIVATE MEM_COMMIT  PAGE_READONLY                    <unknown>  [................]
+     fffc`f8c40000     fffc`f9440000        0`00800000 MEM_PRIVATE MEM_COMMIT  PAGE_READWRITE                   <unknown>  [................]
+     fffc`f9440000     fffc`f9450000        0`00010000 MEM_PRIVATE MEM_COMMIT  PAGE_READONLY                    <unknown>  [................]
+     fffc`f9450000     fffc`f9c50000        0`00800000 MEM_PRIVATE MEM_COMMIT  PAGE_READWRITE                   <unknown>  [................]
+     fffc`f9c50000     fffc`f9c60000        0`00010000                                                          <unknown>
+     fffc`f9c60000     fffc`f9c70000        0`00010000 MEM_PRIVATE MEM_COMMIT  PAGE_EXECUTE_READ                Image      [linux_vdso_so; "linux-
vdso.so.1"]
+     fffc`f9c70000     ffff`c2f60000        2`c92f0000                                                          <unknown>
+     ffff`c2f60000     ffff`c2f90000        0`00030000 MEM_PRIVATE MEM_COMMIT  PAGE_READWRITE                   <unknown>  [................]

0:000> .logclose
Closing open log file 'C:\ALCDA2\A64\App9\App9-WinDbg.log'
```

6. Open another instance of WinDbg Preview and load *App9.core.3.12057* dump file from A64\App9 folder. Set up symbol path, reload symbols, and set append logging to the same log file as previously:

```
Microsoft (R) Windows Debugger Version 10.0.27725.1000 AMD64
Copyright (c) Microsoft Corporation. All rights reserved.


Loading Dump File [C:\ALCDA2\A64\App9\App9.core.3.12057]
64-bit machine not using 64-bit API

************* Path validation summary **************
Response                         Time (ms)     Location
Deferred                                       srv*
Symbol search path is: srv*
Executable search path is:
Generic Unix Version 0 UP Free ARM 64-bit (AArch64)
System Uptime: not available
```

```
Process Uptime: not available
..
*** WARNING: Unable to verify timestamp for App9
App9+0xca84:
00000000`0040ca84 svc        #0
```

```
0:000> .symfix; .sympath+ C:\ALCDA2\A64\App9\
Symbol search path is: srv*;C:\ALCDA2\A64\App9\
Expanded Symbol search path is:
cache*;SRV*https://msdl.microsoft.com/download/symbols;c:\alcda2\a64\app9\

************* Path validation summary **************
Response                         Time (ms)     Location
Deferred                                       srv*
OK                                             C:\ALCDA2\A64\App9\
*** WARNING: Unable to verify timestamp for App9
```

```
0:000> .reload
..
*** WARNING: Unable to verify timestamp for App9

************* Symbol Loading Error Summary **************
Module name            Error
App9                   The system cannot find the file specified

You can troubleshoot most symbol related issues by turning on symbol loading diagnostics (!sym
noisy) and repeating the command that caused symbols to be loaded.
You should also verify that your symbol search path (.sympath) is correct.
```

```
0:000> .logappend C:\ALCDA2\A64\App9\App9-WinDbg.log
Opened log file 'C:\ALCDA2\A64\App9\App9-WinDbg.log'
```

Note: We ignore warnings and errors as they are not relevant for now.

7. Notice that another PAGE_READWRITE large region appeared after some time.

```
0:000> !address
Mapping file section regions...
Mapping module regions...

        BaseAddress      EndAddress+1        RegionSize     Type       State                 Protect             Usage
--------------------------------------------------------------------------------------------------------------------------
+        0`00000000        0`00400000        0`00400000                                                     <unknown>
+        0`00400000        0`004c0000        0`000c0000 MEM_PRIVATE MEM_COMMIT  PAGE_EXECUTE_READ           Image      [App9;
"/home/opc/ALCDA2/App9/App9"]
+        0`004c0000        0`004e0000        0`00020000 MEM_PRIVATE MEM_COMMIT  PAGE_READWRITE              Image      [App9;
"/home/opc/ALCDA2/App9/App9"]
+        0`004e0000        0`2f860000        0`2f380000                                                     <unknown>
+        0`2f860000        0`2f8a0000        0`00040000 MEM_PRIVATE MEM_COMMIT  PAGE_READWRITE              <unknown>  [................]
+        0`2f8a0000     fffc`e8000000     fffc`b8760000                                                     <unknown>
+     fffc`e8000000     fffc`ec300000        0`04300000 MEM_PRIVATE MEM_COMMIT  PAGE_READWRITE              <unknown>  [................]
+     fffc`ec300000     fffc`f0000000        0`03d00000 MEM_PRIVATE MEM_COMMIT  PAGE_READONLY               <unknown>  [................]
+     fffc`f0000000     fffc`f4000000        0`04000000 MEM_PRIVATE MEM_COMMIT  PAGE_READWRITE              <unknown>  [................]
+     fffc`f4000000     fffc`f7400000        0`03400000                                                     <unknown>
+     fffc`f7400000     fffc`f7410000        0`00010000 MEM_PRIVATE MEM_COMMIT  PAGE_READONLY               <unknown>  [................]
+     fffc`f7410000     fffc`f7c10000        0`00800000 MEM_PRIVATE MEM_COMMIT  PAGE_READWRITE              <unknown>  [................]
+     fffc`f7c10000     fffc`f7c20000        0`00010000 MEM_PRIVATE MEM_COMMIT  PAGE_READONLY               <unknown>  [................]
+     fffc`f7c20000     fffc`f8420000        0`00800000 MEM_PRIVATE MEM_COMMIT  PAGE_READWRITE              <unknown>  [................]
+     fffc`f8420000     fffc`f8430000        0`00010000 MEM_PRIVATE MEM_COMMIT  PAGE_READONLY               <unknown>  [................]
+     fffc`f8430000     fffc`f8c30000        0`00800000 MEM_PRIVATE MEM_COMMIT  PAGE_READWRITE              <unknown>  [................]
+     fffc`f8c30000     fffc`f8c40000        0`00010000 MEM_PRIVATE MEM_COMMIT  PAGE_READONLY               <unknown>  [................]
+     fffc`f8c40000     fffc`f9440000        0`00800000 MEM_PRIVATE MEM_COMMIT  PAGE_READWRITE              <unknown>  [................]
+     fffc`f9440000     fffc`f9450000        0`00010000 MEM_PRIVATE MEM_COMMIT  PAGE_READONLY               <unknown>  [................]
+     fffc`f9450000     fffc`f9c50000        0`00800000 MEM_PRIVATE MEM_COMMIT  PAGE_READWRITE              <unknown>  [................]
+     fffc`f9c50000     fffc`f9c60000        0`00010000                                                     <unknown>
+     fffc`f9c60000     fffc`f9c70000        0`00010000 MEM_PRIVATE MEM_COMMIT  PAGE_EXECUTE_READ           Image      [linux_vdso_so; "linux-
vdso.so.1"]
+     fffc`f9c70000     ffff`c2f60000        2`c92f0000                                                     <unknown>
+     ffff`c2f60000     ffff`c2f90000        0`00030000 MEM_PRIVATE MEM_COMMIT  PAGE_READWRITE              <unknown>  [................]
```

8. Examine region contents for any execution residue and hints (we choose some smaller address range from the section address range):

```
0:000> dps fffc`e8000000 fffc`e8000000+1000
0000fffc`e8000000  0000fffc`f0000020
0000fffc`e8000008  0000fffc`f0000000
0000fffc`e8000010  00000000`04000000
0000fffc`e8000018  00000000`04000000
0000fffc`e8000020  00000000`00000000
0000fffc`e8000028  00000000`00000115
0000fffc`e8000030  65746163`6f6c6c61
0000fffc`e8000038  79726f6d`656d2064
0000fffc`e8000040  00000000`00000000
0000fffc`e8000048  00000000`00000000
0000fffc`e8000050  00000000`004031e8 App9!procD
0000fffc`e8000058  00000000`00000000
0000fffc`e8000060  00000000`00000000
0000fffc`e8000068  00000000`00000000
0000fffc`e8000070  00000000`00000000
0000fffc`e8000078  00000000`00000000
0000fffc`e8000080  00000000`00000000
0000fffc`e8000088  00000000`00000000
0000fffc`e8000090  00000000`00000000
0000fffc`e8000098  00000000`00000000
0000fffc`e80000a0  00000000`00000000
0000fffc`e80000a8  00000000`00000000
0000fffc`e80000b0  00000000`00000000
0000fffc`e80000b8  00000000`00000000
0000fffc`e80000c0  00000000`00000000
0000fffc`e80000c8  00000000`00000000
0000fffc`e80000d0  00000000`00000000
0000fffc`e80000d8  00000000`00000000
0000fffc`e80000e0  00000000`00000000
0000fffc`e80000e8  00000000`00000000
0000fffc`e80000f0  00000000`00000000
0000fffc`e80000f8  00000000`00000000
0000fffc`e8000100  00000000`00000000
0000fffc`e8000108  00000000`00000000
0000fffc`e8000110  00000000`00000000
0000fffc`e8000118  00000000`00000000
0000fffc`e8000120  00000000`00000000
0000fffc`e8000128  00000000`00000000
0000fffc`e8000130  00000000`00000000
0000fffc`e8000138  00000000`00000115
0000fffc`e8000140  65746163`6f6c6c61
0000fffc`e8000148  79726f6d`656d2064
0000fffc`e8000150  00000000`00000000
0000fffc`e8000158  00000000`00000000
0000fffc`e8000160  00000000`004031e8 App9!procD
0000fffc`e8000168  00000000`00000000
0000fffc`e8000170  00000000`00000000
0000fffc`e8000178  00000000`00000000
0000fffc`e8000180  00000000`00000000
0000fffc`e8000188  00000000`00000000
0000fffc`e8000190  00000000`00000000
0000fffc`e8000198  00000000`00000000
0000fffc`e80001a0  00000000`00000000
0000fffc`e80001a8  00000000`00000000
0000fffc`e80001b0  00000000`00000000
[...]
```

```
0000fffc`e8000eb0  00000000`00000000
0000fffc`e8000eb8  00000000`00000000
0000fffc`e8000ec0  00000000`00000000
0000fffc`e8000ec8  00000000`00000000
0000fffc`e8000ed0  00000000`00000000
0000fffc`e8000ed8  00000000`00000000
0000fffc`e8000ee0  00000000`00000000
0000fffc`e8000ee8  00000000`00000000
0000fffc`e8000ef0  00000000`00000000
0000fffc`e8000ef8  00000000`00000000
0000fffc`e8000f00  00000000`00000000
0000fffc`e8000f08  00000000`00000115
0000fffc`e8000f10  65746163`6f6c6c61
0000fffc`e8000f18  79726f6d`656d2064
0000fffc`e8000f20  00000000`00000000
0000fffc`e8000f28  00000000`00000000
0000fffc`e8000f30  00000000`004031e8 App9!procD
0000fffc`e8000f38  00000000`00000000
0000fffc`e8000f40  00000000`00000000
0000fffc`e8000f48  00000000`00000000
0000fffc`e8000f50  00000000`00000000
0000fffc`e8000f58  00000000`00000000
0000fffc`e8000f60  00000000`00000000
0000fffc`e8000f68  00000000`00000000
0000fffc`e8000f70  00000000`00000000
0000fffc`e8000f78  00000000`00000000
0000fffc`e8000f80  00000000`00000000
0000fffc`e8000f88  00000000`00000000
0000fffc`e8000f90  00000000`00000000
0000fffc`e8000f98  00000000`00000000
0000fffc`e8000fa0  00000000`00000000
0000fffc`e8000fa8  00000000`00000000
0000fffc`e8000fb0  00000000`00000000
0000fffc`e8000fb8  00000000`00000000
0000fffc`e8000fc0  00000000`00000000
0000fffc`e8000fc8  00000000`00000000
0000fffc`e8000fd0  00000000`00000000
0000fffc`e8000fd8  00000000`00000000
0000fffc`e8000fe0  00000000`00000000
0000fffc`e8000fe8  00000000`00000000
0000fffc`e8000ff0  00000000`00000000
0000fffc`e8000ff8  00000000`00000000
0000fffc`e8001000  00000000`00000000

0:000> da 0000fffc`e8000f10
0000fffc`e8000f10  "allocated memory"
```

9. Compare pmap logs *App9.pmap.1.12057*, *App9.pmap.2.12057*, and *App9.pmap.3.12057* (the first one was saved before the leak started, and the other two correspond to core dumps we looked at):

```
12057:   ./App9
0000000000400000     768K r-x-- App9
00000000004c0000     128K rw--- App9
000000002f860000     256K rw---   [ anon ]
0000fffcf0000000    1344K rw---   [ anon ]
0000fffcf0150000   64192K -----   [ anon ]
0000fffcf7400000      64K -----   [ anon ]
0000fffcf7410000    8192K rw---   [ anon ]
0000fffcf7c10000      64K -----   [ anon ]
0000fffcf7c20000    8192K rw---   [ anon ]
```

```
0000fffcf8420000      64K -----    [ anon ]
0000fffcf8430000    8192K rw---    [ anon ]
0000fffcf8c30000      64K -----    [ anon ]
0000fffcf8c40000    8192K rw---    [ anon ]
0000fffcf9440000      64K -----    [ anon ]
0000fffcf9450000    8192K rw---    [ anon ]
0000fffcf9c50000      64K r----    [ anon ]
0000fffcf9c60000      64K r-x--    [ anon ]
0000ffffc2f60000     192K rw---    [ stack ]
 total            108288K

12057:   ./App9
0000000000400000     768K r-x-- App9
00000000004c0000     128K rw--- App9
000000002f860000     256K rw---    [ anon ]
0000fffce8000000    2240K rw---    [ anon ]
0000fffce8230000   63296K -----    [ anon ]
0000fffcf0000000   65536K rw---    [ anon ]
0000fffcf7400000      64K -----    [ anon ]
0000fffcf7410000    8192K rw---    [ anon ]
0000fffcf7c10000      64K -----    [ anon ]
0000fffcf7c20000    8192K rw---    [ anon ]
0000fffcf8420000      64K -----    [ anon ]
0000fffcf8430000    8192K rw---    [ anon ]
0000fffcf8c30000      64K -----    [ anon ]
0000fffcf8c40000    8192K rw---    [ anon ]
0000fffcf9440000      64K -----    [ anon ]
0000fffcf9450000    8192K rw---    [ anon ]
0000fffcf9c50000      64K r----    [ anon ]
0000fffcf9c60000      64K r-x--    [ anon ]
0000ffffc2f60000     192K rw---    [ stack ]
 total            173824K

12057:   ./App9
0000000000400000     768K r-x-- App9
00000000004c0000     128K rw--- App9
000000002f860000     256K rw---    [ anon ]
0000fffce8000000   68608K rw---    [ anon ]
0000fffcec300000   62464K -----    [ anon ]
0000fffcf0000000   65536K rw---    [ anon ]
0000fffcf7400000      64K -----    [ anon ]
0000fffcf7410000    8192K rw---    [ anon ]
0000fffcf7c10000      64K -----    [ anon ]
0000fffcf7c20000    8192K rw---    [ anon ]
0000fffcf8420000      64K -----    [ anon ]
0000fffcf8430000    8192K rw---    [ anon ]
0000fffcf8c30000      64K -----    [ anon ]
0000fffcf8c40000    8192K rw---    [ anon ]
0000fffcf9440000      64K -----    [ anon ]
0000fffcf9450000    8192K rw---    [ anon ]
0000fffcf9c50000      64K r----    [ anon ]
0000fffcf9c60000      64K r-x--    [ anon ]
0000ffffc2f60000     192K rw---    [ stack ]
 total            239360K
```

10. We close logging before exiting WinDbg:

```
0:000> .logclose
Closing open log file 'C:\ALCDA2\A64\App9\App9-WinDbg.log
```

Mechanisms (Memory Leak)

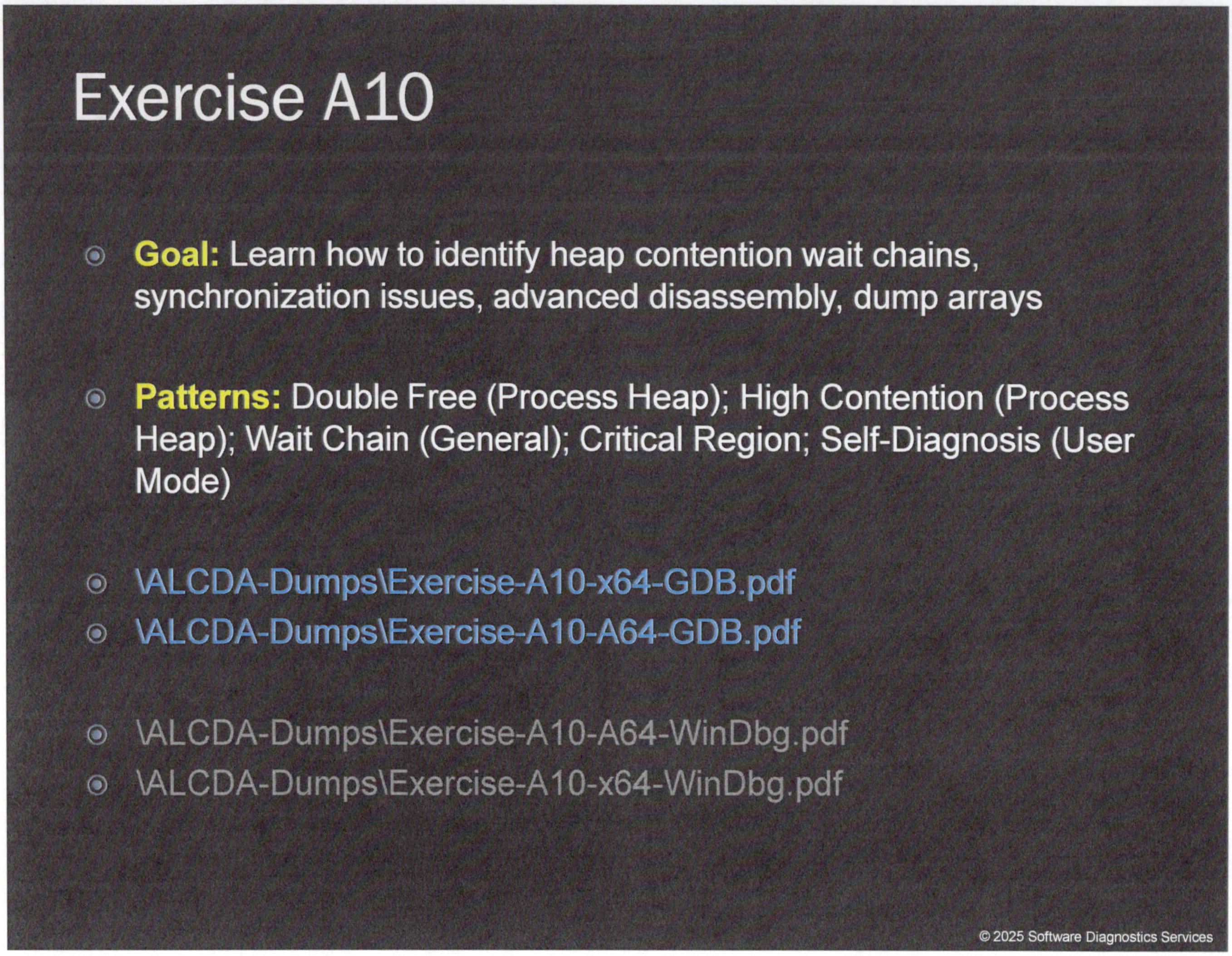
Exercise A10
Goal: Learn how to identify heap contention wait chains, synchronization issues, advanced disassembly, dump arrays
Patterns: Double Free (Process Heap); High Contention (Process Heap); Wait Chain (General); Critical Region; Self-Diagnosis (User Mode)
\ALCDA-Dumps\Exercise-A10-x64-GDB.pdf
\ALCDA-Dumps\Exercise-A10-A64-GDB.pdf
\ALCDA-Dumps\Exercise-A10-A64-WinDbg.pdf
\ALCDA-Dumps\Exercise-A10-x64-WinDbg.pdf
© 2025 Software Diagnostics Services

Exercise A10 (x64, GDB)

Goal: Learn how to identify heap contention wait chains, synchronization issues, advanced disassembly, dump arrays.

Patterns: Double Free (Process Heap); High Contention (Process Heap); Wait Chain (General); Critical Region; Self-Diagnosis (User Mode).

1. When we launched *App10,* we got this console output and a core dump was saved:

```
~/ALCDA2/x64/App10$ ./App10
double free or corruption (!prev)
Aborted (core dumped)
```

2. Load the *core.App10* dump file and *App10* executable from the x64/App10 directory:

```
~/ALCDA2/x64/App10$ gdb -c core.App10 -se App10
GNU gdb (Debian 8.2.1-2+b3) 8.2.1
Copyright (C) 2018 Free Software Foundation, Inc.
License GPLv3+: GNU GPL version 3 or later <http://gnu.org/licenses/gpl.html>
This is free software: you are free to change and redistribute it.
There is NO WARRANTY, to the extent permitted by law.
Type "show copying" and "show warranty" for details.
This GDB was configured as "x86_64-linux-gnu".
Type "show configuration" for configuration details.
For bug reporting instructions, please see:
<http://www.gnu.org/software/gdb/bugs/>.
Find the GDB manual and other documentation resources online at:
    <http://www.gnu.org/software/gdb/documentation/>.

For help, type "help".
Type "apropos word" to search for commands related to "word"...
Reading symbols from App10...done.
[New LWP 398]
[New LWP 396]
[New LWP 397]
[New LWP 401]
[New LWP 400]
[New LWP 399]
[Thread debugging using libthread_db enabled]
Using host libthread_db library "/lib/x86_64-linux-gnu/libthread_db.so.1".
Core was generated by `./App10'.
Program terminated with signal SIGABRT, Aborted.
#0  0x000000000040cc6b in raise ()
[Current thread is 1 (Thread 0x7ff7dbab4700 (LWP 398))]
```

3. Set logging to a file in case of lengthy output from some commands:

```
(gdb) set logging on App10.log
Copying output to App10.log.
```

4. Check all threads and identify problem top frames:

```
(gdb) info threads
  Id   Target Id                         Frame
* 1    Thread 0x7ff7dbab4700 (LWP 398) 0x000000000040cc6b in raise ()
  2    Thread 0xc56880 (LWP 396)       0x0000000000441b10 in nanosleep ()
  3    Thread 0x7ff7dc2b5700 (LWP 397) 0x00000000004431e7 in mprotect ()
  4    Thread 0x7ff7da2b1700 (LWP 401) __lll_lock_wait_private () at
../sysdeps/unix/sysv/linux/x86_64/lowlevellock.S:63
  5    Thread 0x7ff7daab2700 (LWP 400) __lll_lock_wait_private () at
../sysdeps/unix/sysv/linux/x86_64/lowlevellock.S:63
  6    Thread 0x7ff7db2b3700 (LWP 399) __lll_lock_wait_private () at
../sysdeps/unix/sysv/linux/x86_64/lowlevellock.S:63
```

5. Check thread #4 and find where it was being executed:

```
(gdb) thread 4
[Switching to thread 4 (Thread 0x7ff7da2b1700 (LWP 401))]
#0  __lll_lock_wait_private () at ../sysdeps/unix/sysv/linux/x86_64/lowlevellock.S:63
63      in ../sysdeps/unix/sysv/linux/x86_64/lowlevellock.S

(gdb) bt
#0  __lll_lock_wait_private () at ../sysdeps/unix/sysv/linux/x86_64/lowlevellock.S:63
#1  0x000000000041a7b0 in malloc ()
#2  0x0000000000401c79 in proc () at pthread_create.c:688
#3  0x0000000000401da3 in bar_five () at pthread_create.c:688
#4  0x0000000000401db4 in foo_five () at pthread_create.c:688
#5  0x0000000000401dcd in thread_five () at pthread_create.c:688
#6  0x00000000004031c3 in start_thread (arg=<optimized out>) at pthread_create.c:486
#7  0x000000000044436f in clone ()

(gdb) disassemble proc
Dump of assembler code for function proc:
   0x0000000000401bad <+0>:     push   %rbp
   0x0000000000401bae <+1>:     mov    %rsp,%rbp
   0x0000000000401bb1 <+4>:     sub    $0x10,%rsp
   0x0000000000401bb5 <+8>:     callq  0x40d8d0 <rand>
   0x0000000000401bba <+13>:    mov    %eax,%ecx
   0x0000000000401bbc <+15>:    mov    $0x68db8bad,%edx
   0x0000000000401bc1 <+20>:    mov    %ecx,%eax
   0x0000000000401bc3 <+22>:    imul   %edx
   0x0000000000401bc5 <+24>:    sar    $0xc,%edx
   0x0000000000401bc8 <+27>:    mov    %ecx,%eax
   0x0000000000401bca <+29>:    sar    $0x1f,%eax
   0x0000000000401bcd <+32>:    sub    %eax,%edx
   0x0000000000401bcf <+34>:    mov    %edx,%eax
   0x0000000000401bd1 <+36>:    mov    %eax,-0x4(%rbp)
   0x0000000000401bd4 <+39>:    mov    -0x4(%rbp),%eax
   0x0000000000401bd7 <+42>:    imul   $0x2710,%eax,%eax
   0x0000000000401bdd <+48>:    sub    %eax,%ecx
   0x0000000000401bdf <+50>:    mov    %ecx,%eax
   0x0000000000401be1 <+52>:    mov    %eax,-0x4(%rbp)
   0x0000000000401be4 <+55>:    callq  0x40d8d0 <rand>
   0x0000000000401be9 <+60>:    mov    %eax,%ecx
   0x0000000000401beb <+62>:    mov    $0x68db8bad,%edx
   0x0000000000401bf0 <+67>:    mov    %ecx,%eax
   0x0000000000401bf2 <+69>:    imul   %edx
   0x0000000000401bf4 <+71>:    sar    $0xc,%edx
   0x0000000000401bf7 <+74>:    mov    %ecx,%eax
   0x0000000000401bf9 <+76>:    sar    $0x1f,%eax
```

```
   0x0000000000401bfc <+79>:    sub    %eax,%edx
   0x0000000000401bfe <+81>:    mov    %edx,%eax
   0x0000000000401c00 <+83>:    mov    %eax,-0x8(%rbp)
   0x0000000000401c03 <+86>:    mov    -0x8(%rbp),%eax
   0x0000000000401c06 <+89>:    imul   $0x2710,%eax,%eax
   0x0000000000401c0c <+95>:    sub    %eax,%ecx
   0x0000000000401c0e <+97>:    mov    %ecx,%eax
   0x0000000000401c10 <+99>:    mov    %eax,-0x8(%rbp)
   0x0000000000401c13 <+102>:   mov    -0x4(%rbp),%eax
   0x0000000000401c16 <+105>:   cltq
   0x0000000000401c18 <+107>:   lea    0x0(,%rax,8),%rdx
   0x0000000000401c20 <+115>:   lea    0xc0919(%rip),%rax        # 0x4c2540 <pAllocBuf>
   0x0000000000401c27 <+122>:   mov    (%rdx,%rax,1),%rax
   0x0000000000401c2b <+126>:   test   %rax,%rax
   0x0000000000401c2e <+129>:   je     0x401c6c <proc+191>
   0x0000000000401c30 <+131>:   mov    -0x4(%rbp),%eax
   0x0000000000401c33 <+134>:   cltq
   0x0000000000401c35 <+136>:   lea    0x0(,%rax,8),%rdx
   0x0000000000401c3d <+144>:   lea    0xc08fc(%rip),%rax        # 0x4c2540 <pAllocBuf>
   0x0000000000401c44 <+151>:   mov    (%rdx,%rax,1),%rax
   0x0000000000401c48 <+155>:   mov    %rax,%rdi
   0x0000000000401c4b <+158>:   callq  0x41ac10 <free>
   0x0000000000401c50 <+163>:   mov    -0x4(%rbp),%eax
   0x0000000000401c53 <+166>:   cltq
   0x0000000000401c55 <+168>:   lea    0x0(,%rax,8),%rdx
   0x0000000000401c5d <+176>:   lea    0xc08dc(%rip),%rax        # 0x4c2540 <pAllocBuf>
   0x0000000000401c64 <+183>:   movq   $0x0,(%rdx,%rax,1)
   0x0000000000401c6c <+191>:   mov    -0x8(%rbp),%eax
   0x0000000000401c6f <+194>:   cltq
--Type <RET> for more, q to quit, c to continue without paging--
   0x0000000000401c71 <+196>:   mov    %rax,%rdi
   0x0000000000401c74 <+199>:   callq  0x41a5d0 <malloc>
   0x0000000000401c79 <+204>:   mov    %rax,%rcx
   0x0000000000401c7c <+207>:   mov    -0x4(%rbp),%eax
   0x0000000000401c7f <+210>:   cltq
   0x0000000000401c81 <+212>:   lea    0x0(,%rax,8),%rdx
   0x0000000000401c89 <+220>:   lea    0xc08b0(%rip),%rax        # 0x4c2540 <pAllocBuf>
   0x0000000000401c90 <+227>:   mov    %rcx,(%rdx,%rax,1)
   0x0000000000401c94 <+231>:   jmpq   0x401bb5 <proc+8>
End of assembler dump.
```

6. Check thread #5 and find where it was being executed:

```
(gdb) thread 5
[Switching to thread 5 (Thread 0x7ff7daab2700 (LWP 400))]
#0  __lll_lock_wait_private () at ../sysdeps/unix/sysv/linux/x86_64/lowlevellock.S:63
63      in ../sysdeps/unix/sysv/linux/x86_64/lowlevellock.S

(gdb) bt
#0  __lll_lock_wait_private () at ../sysdeps/unix/sysv/linux/x86_64/lowlevellock.S:63
#1  0x0000000000417a43 in _int_free ()
#2  0x0000000000401c50 in proc () at pthread_create.c:688
#3  0x0000000000401d64 in bar_four () at pthread_create.c:688
#4  0x0000000000401d75 in foo_four () at pthread_create.c:688
#5  0x0000000000401d8e in thread_four () at pthread_create.c:688
#6  0x00000000004031c3 in start_thread (arg=<optimized out>) at pthread_create.c:486
#7  0x000000000044436f in clone ()
```

```
(gdb) disassemble proc
Dump of assembler code for function proc:
   0x0000000000401bad <+0>:     push   %rbp
   0x0000000000401bae <+1>:     mov    %rsp,%rbp
   0x0000000000401bb1 <+4>:     sub    $0x10,%rsp
   0x0000000000401bb5 <+8>:     callq  0x40d8d0 <rand>
   0x0000000000401bba <+13>:    mov    %eax,%ecx
   0x0000000000401bbc <+15>:    mov    $0x68db8bad,%edx
   0x0000000000401bc1 <+20>:    mov    %ecx,%eax
   0x0000000000401bc3 <+22>:    imul   %edx
   0x0000000000401bc5 <+24>:    sar    $0xc,%edx
   0x0000000000401bc8 <+27>:    mov    %ecx,%eax
   0x0000000000401bca <+29>:    sar    $0x1f,%eax
   0x0000000000401bcd <+32>:    sub    %eax,%edx
   0x0000000000401bcf <+34>:    mov    %edx,%eax
   0x0000000000401bd1 <+36>:    mov    %eax,-0x4(%rbp)
   0x0000000000401bd4 <+39>:    mov    -0x4(%rbp),%eax
   0x0000000000401bd7 <+42>:    imul   $0x2710,%eax,%eax
   0x0000000000401bdd <+48>:    sub    %eax,%ecx
   0x0000000000401bdf <+50>:    mov    %ecx,%eax
   0x0000000000401be1 <+52>:    mov    %eax,-0x4(%rbp)
   0x0000000000401be4 <+55>:    callq  0x40d8d0 <rand>
   0x0000000000401be9 <+60>:    mov    %eax,%ecx
   0x0000000000401beb <+62>:    mov    $0x68db8bad,%edx
   0x0000000000401bf0 <+67>:    mov    %ecx,%eax
   0x0000000000401bf2 <+69>:    imul   %edx
   0x0000000000401bf4 <+71>:    sar    $0xc,%edx
   0x0000000000401bf7 <+74>:    mov    %ecx,%eax
   0x0000000000401bf9 <+76>:    sar    $0x1f,%eax
   0x0000000000401bfc <+79>:    sub    %eax,%edx
   0x0000000000401bfe <+81>:    mov    %edx,%eax
   0x0000000000401c00 <+83>:    mov    %eax,-0x8(%rbp)
   0x0000000000401c03 <+86>:    mov    -0x8(%rbp),%eax
   0x0000000000401c06 <+89>:    imul   $0x2710,%eax,%eax
   0x0000000000401c0c <+95>:    sub    %eax,%ecx
   0x0000000000401c0e <+97>:    mov    %ecx,%eax
   0x0000000000401c10 <+99>:    mov    %eax,-0x8(%rbp)
   0x0000000000401c13 <+102>:   mov    -0x4(%rbp),%eax
   0x0000000000401c16 <+105>:   cltq
   0x0000000000401c18 <+107>:   lea    0x0(,%rax,8),%rdx
   0x0000000000401c20 <+115>:   lea    0xc0919(%rip),%rax        # 0x4c2540 <pAllocBuf>
   0x0000000000401c27 <+122>:   mov    (%rdx,%rax,1),%rax
   0x0000000000401c2b <+126>:   test   %rax,%rax
   0x0000000000401c2e <+129>:   je     0x401c6c <proc+191>
   0x0000000000401c30 <+131>:   mov    -0x4(%rbp),%eax
   0x0000000000401c33 <+134>:   cltq
   0x0000000000401c35 <+136>:   lea    0x0(,%rax,8),%rdx
   0x0000000000401c3d <+144>:   lea    0xc08fc(%rip),%rax        # 0x4c2540 <pAllocBuf>
   0x0000000000401c44 <+151>:   mov    (%rdx,%rax,1),%rax
   0x0000000000401c48 <+155>:   mov    %rax,%rdi
   0x0000000000401c4b <+158>:   callq  0x41ac10 <free>
   0x0000000000401c50 <+163>:   mov    -0x4(%rbp),%eax
   0x0000000000401c53 <+166>:   cltq
   0x0000000000401c55 <+168>:   lea    0x0(,%rax,8),%rdx
   0x0000000000401c5d <+176>:   lea    0xc08dc(%rip),%rax        # 0x4c2540 <pAllocBuf>
   0x0000000000401c64 <+183>:   movq   $0x0,(%rdx,%rax,1)
   0x0000000000401c6c <+191>:   mov    -0x8(%rbp),%eax
   0x0000000000401c6f <+194>:   cltq
--Type <RET> for more, q to quit, c to continue without paging--
   0x0000000000401c71 <+196>:   mov    %rax,%rdi
```

```
   0x0000000000401c74 <+199>:   callq  0x41a5d0 <malloc>
   0x0000000000401c79 <+204>:   mov    %rax,%rcx
   0x0000000000401c7c <+207>:   mov    -0x4(%rbp),%eax
   0x0000000000401c7f <+210>:   cltq
   0x0000000000401c81 <+212>:   lea    0x0(,%rax,8),%rdx
   0x0000000000401c89 <+220>:   lea    0xc08b0(%rip),%rax        # 0x4c2540 <pAllocBuf>
   0x0000000000401c90 <+227>:   mov    %rcx,(%rdx,%rax,1)
   0x0000000000401c94 <+231>:   jmpq   0x401bb5 <proc+8>
End of assembler dump.
```

7. Check thread #6 and find where it was being executed:

```
(gdb) thread 6
[Switching to thread 6 (Thread 0x7ff7db2b3700 (LWP 399))]
#0  __lll_lock_wait_private () at ../sysdeps/unix/sysv/linux/x86_64/lowlevellock.S:63
63      in ../sysdeps/unix/sysv/linux/x86_64/lowlevellock.S
```

```
(gdb) bt
#0  __lll_lock_wait_private () at ../sysdeps/unix/sysv/linux/x86_64/lowlevellock.S:63
#1  0x0000000000417a43 in _int_free ()
#2  0x0000000000401c50 in proc () at pthread_create.c:688
#3  0x0000000000401d25 in bar_three () at pthread_create.c:688
#4  0x0000000000401d36 in foo_three () at pthread_create.c:688
#5  0x0000000000401d4f in thread_three () at pthread_create.c:688
#6  0x00000000004031c3 in start_thread (arg=<optimized out>) at pthread_create.c:486
#7  0x000000000044436f in clone ()
```

Note: Thread #6 is the same as thread #5. We disassemble *proc* again and put addresses there that we identified from threads #4 and #5:

```
(gdb) disassemble proc
Dump of assembler code for function proc:
   0x0000000000401bad <+0>:     push   %rbp
   0x0000000000401bae <+1>:     mov    %rsp,%rbp
   0x0000000000401bb1 <+4>:     sub    $0x10,%rsp
   0x0000000000401bb5 <+8>:     callq  0x40d8d0 <rand>
   0x0000000000401bba <+13>:    mov    %eax,%ecx
   0x0000000000401bbc <+15>:    mov    $0x68db8bad,%edx
   0x0000000000401bc1 <+20>:    mov    %ecx,%eax
   0x0000000000401bc3 <+22>:    imul   %edx
   0x0000000000401bc5 <+24>:    sar    $0xc,%edx
   0x0000000000401bc8 <+27>:    mov    %ecx,%eax
   0x0000000000401bca <+29>:    sar    $0x1f,%eax
   0x0000000000401bcd <+32>:    sub    %eax,%edx
   0x0000000000401bcf <+34>:    mov    %edx,%eax
   0x0000000000401bd1 <+36>:    mov    %eax,-0x4(%rbp)
   0x0000000000401bd4 <+39>:    mov    -0x4(%rbp),%eax
   0x0000000000401bd7 <+42>:    imul   $0x2710,%eax,%eax
   0x0000000000401bdd <+48>:    sub    %eax,%ecx
   0x0000000000401bdf <+50>:    mov    %ecx,%eax
   0x0000000000401be1 <+52>:    mov    %eax,-0x4(%rbp)
   0x0000000000401be4 <+55>:    callq  0x40d8d0 <rand>
   0x0000000000401be9 <+60>:    mov    %eax,%ecx
   0x0000000000401beb <+62>:    mov    $0x68db8bad,%edx
   0x0000000000401bf0 <+67>:    mov    %ecx,%eax
   0x0000000000401bf2 <+69>:    imul   %edx
   0x0000000000401bf4 <+71>:    sar    $0xc,%edx
   0x0000000000401bf7 <+74>:    mov    %ecx,%eax
   0x0000000000401bf9 <+76>:    sar    $0x1f,%eax
   0x0000000000401bfc <+79>:    sub    %eax,%edx
```

```
   0x0000000000401bfe <+81>:    mov    %edx,%eax
   0x0000000000401c00 <+83>:    mov    %eax,-0x8(%rbp)
   0x0000000000401c03 <+86>:    mov    -0x8(%rbp),%eax
   0x0000000000401c06 <+89>:    imul   $0x2710,%eax,%eax
   0x0000000000401c0c <+95>:    sub    %eax,%ecx
   0x0000000000401c0e <+97>:    mov    %ecx,%eax
   0x0000000000401c10 <+99>:    mov    %eax,-0x8(%rbp)
   0x0000000000401c13 <+102>:   mov    -0x4(%rbp),%eax
   0x0000000000401c16 <+105>:   cltq
   0x0000000000401c18 <+107>:   lea    0x0(,%rax,8),%rdx
   0x0000000000401c20 <+115>:   lea    0xc0919(%rip),%rax        # 0x4c2540 <pAllocBuf>
   0x0000000000401c27 <+122>:   mov    (%rdx,%rax,1),%rax
   0x0000000000401c2b <+126>:   test   %rax,%rax
   0x0000000000401c2e <+129>:   je     0x401c6c <proc+191>
   0x0000000000401c30 <+131>:   mov    -0x4(%rbp),%eax
   0x0000000000401c33 <+134>:   cltq
   0x0000000000401c35 <+136>:   lea    0x0(,%rax,8),%rdx
   0x0000000000401c3d <+144>:   lea    0xc08fc(%rip),%rax        # 0x4c2540 <pAllocBuf>
   0x0000000000401c44 <+151>:   mov    (%rdx,%rax,1),%rax
   0x0000000000401c48 <+155>:   mov    %rax,%rdi
   0x0000000000401c4b <+158>:   callq  0x41ac10 <free>
   0x0000000000401c50 <+163>:   mov    -0x4(%rbp),%eax
   0x0000000000401c53 <+166>:   cltq
   0x0000000000401c55 <+168>:   lea    0x0(,%rax,8),%rdx
   0x0000000000401c5d <+176>:   lea    0xc08dc(%rip),%rax        # 0x4c2540 <pAllocBuf>
   0x0000000000401c64 <+183>:   movq   $0x0,(%rdx,%rax,1)
   0x0000000000401c6c <+191>:   mov    -0x8(%rbp),%eax
   0x0000000000401c6f <+194>:   cltq
--Type <RET> for more, q to quit, c to continue without paging--
   0x0000000000401c71 <+196>:   mov    %rax,%rdi
   0x0000000000401c74 <+199>:   callq  0x41a5d0 <malloc>
   0x0000000000401c79 <+204>:   mov    %rax,%rcx
   0x0000000000401c7c <+207>:   mov    -0x4(%rbp),%eax
   0x0000000000401c7f <+210>:   cltq
   0x0000000000401c81 <+212>:   lea    0x0(,%rax,8),%rdx
   0x0000000000401c89 <+220>:   lea    0xc08b0(%rip),%rax        # 0x4c2540 <pAllocBuf>
   0x0000000000401c90 <+227>:   mov    %rcx,(%rdx,%rax,1)
   0x0000000000401c94 <+231>:   jmpq   0x401bb5 <proc+8>
End of assembler dump.
```

Note: We see some buffer **0x4c2540** "sandwiched" between *free* and *malloc* calls that internally call "lock" and "unlock" functions.

8. Check thread #3 and find where it was being executed:

```
(gdb) thread 3
[Switching to thread 3 (Thread 0x7ff7dc2b5700 (LWP 397))]
#0  0x00000000004431e7 in mprotect ()
```

```
(gdb) bt
#0  0x00000000004431e7 in mprotect ()
#1  0x000000000041834c in sysmalloc ()
#2  0x00000000004194e1 in _int_malloc ()
#3  0x000000000041a7c2 in malloc ()
#4  0x0000000000401c79 in proc () at pthread_create.c:688
#5  0x0000000000401ca7 in bar_one () at pthread_create.c:688
#6  0x0000000000401cb8 in foo_one () at pthread_create.c:688
#7  0x0000000000401cd1 in thread_one () at pthread_create.c:688
#8  0x00000000004031c3 in start_thread (arg=<optimized out>) at pthread_create.c:486
#9  0x000000000044436f in clone ()
```

Note: Thread #3 is the same as thread #4.

9. Check thread #1 and identify a diagnostic message:

```
(gdb) thread 1
[Switching to thread 1 (Thread 0x7ff7dbab4700 (LWP 398))]
#0  0x000000000040cc6b in raise ()

(gdb) bt
#0  0x000000000040cc6b in raise ()
#1  0x0000000000401241 in abort () at pthread_create.c:688
#2  0x0000000000410828 in __libc_message ()
#3  0x0000000000415fea in malloc_printerr ()
#4  0x00000000004179fc in _int_free ()
#5  0x0000000000401c50 in proc () at pthread_create.c:688
#6  0x0000000000401ce6 in bar_two () at pthread_create.c:688
#7  0x0000000000401cf7 in foo_two () at pthread_create.c:688
#8  0x0000000000401d10 in thread_two () at pthread_create.c:688
#9  0x00000000004031c3 in start_thread (arg=<optimized out>) at pthread_create.c:486
#10 0x000000000044436f in clone ()

(gdb) disassemble __libc_message
Dump of assembler code for function __libc_message:
   0x0000000000410560 <+0>:     push   %rbp
   0x0000000000410561 <+1>:     mov    %rsp,%rbp
   0x0000000000410564 <+4>:     push   %r15
   0x0000000000410566 <+6>:     push   %r14
   0x0000000000410568 <+8>:     push   %r13
   0x000000000041056a <+10>:    mov    %edi,%r13d
   0x000000000041056d <+13>:    push   %r12
   0x000000000041056f <+15>:    push   %rbx
   0x0000000000410570 <+16>:    mov    %rsi,%rbx
   0x0000000000410573 <+19>:    sub    $0x68,%rsp
   0x0000000000410577 <+23>:    mov    %rdx,-0x50(%rbp)
   0x000000000041057b <+27>:    mov    %rcx,-0x48(%rbp)
   0x000000000041057f <+31>:    mov    %r8,-0x40(%rbp)
   0x0000000000410583 <+35>:    mov    %r9,-0x38(%rbp)
   0x0000000000410587 <+39>:    mov    %fs:0x28,%rax
   0x0000000000410590 <+48>:    mov    %rax,-0x68(%rbp)
   0x0000000000410594 <+52>:    xor    %eax,%eax
   0x0000000000410596 <+54>:    lea    0x10(%rbp),%rax
   0x000000000041059a <+58>:    and    $0x2,%edi
   0x000000000041059d <+61>:    movl   $0x10,-0x80(%rbp)
   0x00000000004105a4 <+68>:    mov    %rax,-0x78(%rbp)
   0x00000000004105a8 <+72>:    lea    -0x60(%rbp),%rax
   0x00000000004105ac <+76>:    mov    %rax,-0x70(%rbp)
   0x00000000004105b0 <+80>:    jne    0x410761 <__libc_message+513>
   0x00000000004105b6 <+86>:    movl   $0x2,-0x84(%rbp)
   0x00000000004105c0 <+96>:    movzbl (%rbx),%r12d
   0x00000000004105c4 <+100>:   and    $0x1,%r13d
   0x00000000004105c8 <+104>:   xor    %r14d,%r14d
   0x00000000004105cb <+107>:   mov    $0x20,%r15d
   0x00000000004105d1 <+113>:   mov    %r13d,-0x88(%rbp)
   0x00000000004105d8 <+120>:   xor    %r13d,%r13d
   0x00000000004105db <+123>:   test   %r12b,%r12b
   0x00000000004105de <+126>:   je     0x410737 <__libc_message+471>
   0x00000000004105e4 <+132>:   nopl   0x0(%rax)
   0x00000000004105e8 <+136>:   mov    %r12d,%edx
   0x00000000004105eb <+139>:   mov    %rbx,%rax
   0x00000000004105ee <+142>:   jmp    0x410605 <__libc_message+165>
```

```
   0x00000000004105f0 <+144>:   lea    0x1(%rax),%rdi
   0x00000000004105f4 <+148>:   mov    $0x25,%esi
   0x00000000004105f9 <+153>:   callq  0x401060
   0x00000000004105fe <+158>:   movzbl (%rax),%edx
   0x0000000000410601 <+161>:   test   %dl,%dl
   0x0000000000410603 <+163>:   je     0x410610 <__libc_message+176>
   0x0000000000410605 <+165>:   cmp    $0x25,%dl
   0x0000000000410608 <+168>:   jne    0x4105f0 <__libc_message+144>
   0x000000000041060a <+170>:   cmpb   $0x73,0x1(%rax)
   0x000000000041060e <+174>:   jne    0x4105f0 <__libc_message+144>
   0x0000000000410610 <+176>:   cmp    $0x25,%r12b
   0x0000000000410614 <+180>:   je     0x410650 <__libc_message+240>
   0x0000000000410616 <+182>:   mov    %rax,%r9
   0x0000000000410619 <+185>:   mov    %rbx,%rsi
   0x000000000041061c <+188>:   sub    %rbx,%r9
   0x000000000041061f <+191>:   mov    %rax,%rbx
   0x0000000000410622 <+194>:   sub    %r15,%rsp
   0x0000000000410625 <+197>:   lea    0x1(%r14),%r8d
   0x0000000000410629 <+201>:   lea    0xf(%rsp),%rdx
--Type <RET> for more, q to quit, c to continue without paging--
   0x000000000041062e <+206>:   and    $0xfffffffffffffff0,%rdx
   0x0000000000410632 <+210>:   mov    %rsi,(%rdx)
   0x0000000000410635 <+213>:   mov    %r9,0x8(%rdx)
   0x0000000000410639 <+217>:   mov    %r13,0x10(%rdx)
   0x000000000041063d <+221>:   movzbl (%rbx),%r12d
   0x0000000000410641 <+225>:   test   %r12b,%r12b
   0x0000000000410644 <+228>:   je     0x410690 <__libc_message+304>
   0x0000000000410646 <+230>:   movslq %r8d,%r14
   0x0000000000410649 <+233>:   mov    %rdx,%r13
   0x000000000041064c <+236>:   jmp    0x4105e8 <__libc_message+136>
   0x000000000041064e <+238>:   xchg   %ax,%ax
   0x0000000000410650 <+240>:   cmpb   $0x73,0x1(%rbx)
   0x0000000000410654 <+244>:   jne    0x410616 <__libc_message+182>
   0x0000000000410656 <+246>:   mov    -0x80(%rbp),%eax
   0x0000000000410659 <+249>:   cmp    $0x2f,%eax
   0x000000000041065c <+252>:   ja     0x410750 <__libc_message+496>
   0x0000000000410662 <+258>:   mov    %eax,%edx
   0x0000000000410664 <+260>:   add    $0x8,%eax
   0x0000000000410667 <+263>:   add    -0x70(%rbp),%rdx
   0x000000000041066b <+267>:   mov    %eax,-0x80(%rbp)
   0x000000000041066e <+270>:   mov    (%rdx),%rsi
   0x0000000000410671 <+273>:   add    $0x2,%rbx
   0x0000000000410675 <+277>:   mov    %rsi,%rdi
   0x0000000000410678 <+280>:   mov    %rsi,-0x90(%rbp)
   0x000000000041067f <+287>:   callq  0x4010d8
   0x0000000000410684 <+292>:   mov    -0x90(%rbp),%rsi
   0x000000000041068b <+299>:   mov    %rax,%r9
   0x000000000041068e <+302>:   jmp    0x410622 <__libc_message+194>
   0x0000000000410690 <+304>:   movslq %r8d,%r8
   0x0000000000410693 <+307>:   shl    $0x4,%r14
   0x0000000000410697 <+311>:   xor    %edx,%edx
   0x0000000000410699 <+313>:   mov    %r8,%rax
   0x000000000041069c <+316>:   shl    $0x4,%rax
   0x00000000004106a0 <+320>:   add    $0x10,%rax
   0x00000000004106a4 <+324>:   sub    %rax,%rsp
   0x00000000004106a7 <+327>:   lea    0xf(%rsp),%rbx
   0x00000000004106ac <+332>:   and    $0xfffffffffffffff0,%rbx
   0x00000000004106b0 <+336>:   lea    (%rbx,%r14,1),%rax
   0x00000000004106b4 <+340>:   mov    %rbx,%r12
   0x00000000004106b7 <+343>:   mov    %rax,%rdi
```

```
   0x00000000004106ba <+346>:   sub    %r14,%rdi
   0x00000000004106bd <+349>:   jmp    0x4106d0 <__libc_message+368>
   0x00000000004106bf <+351>:   nop
   0x00000000004106c0 <+352>:   mov    0x0(%r13),%rsi
   0x00000000004106c4 <+356>:   mov    0x8(%r13),%r9
   0x00000000004106c8 <+360>:   sub    $0x10,%rax
   0x00000000004106cc <+364>:   mov    0x10(%r13),%r13
   0x00000000004106d0 <+368>:   mov    %r9,0x8(%rax)
   0x00000000004106d4 <+372>:   add    %rdx,%r9
   0x00000000004106d7 <+375>:   mov    %rsi,(%rax)
   0x00000000004106da <+378>:   mov    %r9,%rdx
   0x00000000004106dd <+381>:   cmp    %rax,%rdi
   0x00000000004106e0 <+384>:   jne    0x4106c0 <__libc_message+352>
   0x00000000004106e2 <+386>:   mov    $0x14,%r10d
   0x00000000004106e8 <+392>:   nopl   0x0(%rax,%rax,1)
   0x00000000004106f0 <+400>:   mov    %r8,%rdx
   0x00000000004106f3 <+403>:   mov    %rbx,%rsi
--Type <RET> for more, q to quit, c to continue without paging--
   0x00000000004106f6 <+406>:   mov    -0x84(%rbp),%edi
   0x00000000004106fc <+412>:   mov    %r10d,%eax
   0x00000000004106ff <+415>:   syscall
   0x0000000000410701 <+417>:   cmp    $0xfffffffffffffffc,%rax
   0x0000000000410705 <+421>:   je     0x4106f0 <__libc_message+400>
   0x0000000000410707 <+423>:   mov    -0x88(%rbp),%eax
   0x000000000041070d <+429>:   test   %eax,%eax
   0x000000000041070f <+431>:   jne    0x4107a2 <__libc_message+578>
   0x0000000000410715 <+437>:   mov    -0x68(%rbp),%rax
   0x0000000000410719 <+441>:   xor    %fs:0x28,%rax
   0x0000000000410722 <+450>:   jne    0x410828 <__libc_message+712>
   0x0000000000410728 <+456>:   lea    -0x28(%rbp),%rsp
   0x000000000041072c <+460>:   pop    %rbx
   0x000000000041072d <+461>:   pop    %r12
   0x000000000041072f <+463>:   pop    %r13
   0x0000000000410731 <+465>:   pop    %r14
   0x0000000000410733 <+467>:   pop    %r15
   0x0000000000410735 <+469>:   pop    %rbp
   0x0000000000410736 <+470>:   retq
   0x0000000000410737 <+471>:   mov    -0x88(%rbp),%edx
   0x000000000041073d <+477>:   test   %edx,%edx
   0x000000000041073f <+479>:   je     0x410715 <__libc_message+437>
   0x0000000000410741 <+481>:   jmpq   0x410823 <__libc_message+707>
   0x0000000000410746 <+486>:   nopw   %cs:0x0(%rax,%rax,1)
   0x0000000000410750 <+496>:   mov    -0x78(%rbp),%rdx
   0x0000000000410754 <+500>:   lea    0x8(%rdx),%rax
   0x0000000000410758 <+504>:   mov    %rax,-0x78(%rbp)
   0x000000000041075c <+508>:   jmpq   0x41066e <__libc_message+270>
   0x0000000000410761 <+513>:   lea    0x8585c(%rip),%rdi        # 0x495fc4
   0x0000000000410768 <+520>:   callq  0x453da0 <secure_getenv>
   0x000000000041076d <+525>:   test   %rax,%rax
   0x0000000000410770 <+528>:   je     0x41077b <__libc_message+539>
   0x0000000000410772 <+530>:   cmpb   $0x0,(%rax)
   0x0000000000410775 <+533>:   jne    0x4105b6 <__libc_message+86>
   0x000000000041077b <+539>:   mov    $0x902,%esi
   0x0000000000410780 <+544>:   lea    0x85850(%rip),%rdi        # 0x495fd7
   0x0000000000410787 <+551>:   xor    %eax,%eax
   0x0000000000410789 <+553>:   callq  0x442da0 <__open_nocancel>
   0x000000000041078e <+558>:   mov    %eax,-0x84(%rbp)
   0x0000000000410794 <+564>:   cmp    $0xffffffff,%eax
   0x0000000000410797 <+567>:   jne    0x4105c0 <__libc_message+96>
   0x000000000041079d <+573>:   jmpq   0x4105b6 <__libc_message+86>
```

```
   0x00000000004107a2 <+578>:   mov    0xb0aaf(%rip),%rax        # 0x4c1258 <_dl_pagesize>
   0x00000000004107a9 <+585>:   mov    $0xffffffff,%r8d
   0x00000000004107af <+591>:   mov    $0x3,%edx
   0x00000000004107b4 <+596>:   xor    %edi,%edi
   0x00000000004107b6 <+598>:   lea    (%r9,%rax,1),%rcx
   0x00000000004107ba <+602>:   neg    %rax
   0x00000000004107bd <+605>:   xor    %r9d,%r9d
   0x00000000004107c0 <+608>:   and    %rax,%rcx
   0x00000000004107c3 <+611>:   mov    %rcx,%r13
   0x00000000004107c6 <+614>:   mov    $0x22,%ecx
   0x00000000004107cb <+619>:   mov    %r13,%rsi
   0x00000000004107ce <+622>:   callq  0x4430d0 <mmap64>
   0x00000000004107d3 <+627>:   mov    %rax,%r15
   0x00000000004107d6 <+630>:   cmp    $0xffffffffffffffff,%rax
   0x00000000004107da <+634>:   je     0x410823 <__libc_message+707>
--Type <RET> for more, q to quit, c to continue without paging--
   0x00000000004107dc <+636>:   mov    %r13d,(%rax)
   0x00000000004107df <+639>:   lea    0x10(%rbx,%r14,1),%rbx
   0x00000000004107e4 <+644>:   lea    0x4(%rax),%rax
   0x00000000004107e8 <+648>:   nopl   0x0(%rax,%rax,1)
   0x00000000004107f0 <+656>:   mov    0x8(%r12),%rdx
   0x00000000004107f5 <+661>:   mov    (%r12),%rsi
   0x00000000004107f9 <+665>:   mov    %rax,%rdi
   0x00000000004107fc <+668>:   add    $0x10,%r12
   0x0000000000410800 <+672>:   callq  0x4010b8
   0x0000000000410805 <+677>:   cmp    %r12,%rbx
   0x0000000000410808 <+680>:   jne    0x4107f0 <__libc_message+656>
   0x000000000041080a <+682>:   movb   $0x0,(%rax)
   0x000000000041080d <+685>:   mov    %r15,%rdi
   0x0000000000410810 <+688>:   xchg   %rdi,0xc9b69(%rip)        # 0x4da380 <__abort_msg>
   0x0000000000410817 <+695>:   test   %rdi,%rdi
   0x000000000041081a <+698>:   je     0x410823 <__libc_message+707>
   0x000000000041081c <+700>:   mov    (%rdi),%esi
   0x000000000041081e <+702>:   callq  0x4431b0 <munmap>
   0x0000000000410823 <+707>:   callq  0x401120 <abort>
   0x0000000000410828 <+712>:   callq  0x4449a0 <__stack_chk_fail_local>
End of assembler dump.

(gdb) x/a 0x4da380
0x4da380 <__abort_msg>: 0x7ff7d9ab0000

(gdb) x/10s 0x7ff7d9ab0000
0x7ff7d9ab0000: ""
0x7ff7d9ab0001: "\020"
0x7ff7d9ab0003: ""
0x7ff7d9ab0004: "double free or corruption (!prev)\n"
0x7ff7d9ab0027: ""
0x7ff7d9ab0028: ""
0x7ff7d9ab0029: ""
0x7ff7d9ab002a: ""
0x7ff7d9ab002b: ""
0x7ff7d9ab002c: ""
```

10. Check the address that was being freed:

```
(gdb) bt
#0  0x000000000040cc6b in raise ()
#1  0x0000000000401241 in abort () at pthread_create.c:688
#2  0x0000000000410828 in __libc_message ()
#3  0x0000000000415fea in malloc_printerr ()
#4  0x00000000004179fc in _int_free ()
#5  0x0000000000401c50 in proc () at pthread_create.c:688
#6  0x0000000000401ce6 in bar_two () at pthread_create.c:688
#7  0x0000000000401cf7 in foo_two () at pthread_create.c:688
#8  0x0000000000401d10 in thread_two () at pthread_create.c:688
#9  0x00000000004031c3 in start_thread (arg=<optimized out>) at pthread_create.c:486
#10 0x000000000044436f in clone ()

(gdb) frame 5
#5  0x0000000000401c50 in proc () at pthread_create.c:688
688     pthread_create.c: No such file or directory.

(gdb) disassemble proc
Dump of assembler code for function proc:
   0x0000000000401bad <+0>:     push   %rbp
   0x0000000000401bae <+1>:     mov    %rsp,%rbp
   0x0000000000401bb1 <+4>:     sub    $0x10,%rsp
   0x0000000000401bb5 <+8>:     callq  0x40d8d0 <rand>
   0x0000000000401bba <+13>:    mov    %eax,%ecx
   0x0000000000401bbc <+15>:    mov    $0x68db8bad,%edx
   0x0000000000401bc1 <+20>:    mov    %ecx,%eax
   0x0000000000401bc3 <+22>:    imul   %edx
   0x0000000000401bc5 <+24>:    sar    $0xc,%edx
   0x0000000000401bc8 <+27>:    mov    %ecx,%eax
   0x0000000000401bca <+29>:    sar    $0x1f,%eax
   0x0000000000401bcd <+32>:    sub    %eax,%edx
   0x0000000000401bcf <+34>:    mov    %edx,%eax
   0x0000000000401bd1 <+36>:    mov    %eax,-0x4(%rbp)
   0x0000000000401bd4 <+39>:    mov    -0x4(%rbp),%eax
   0x0000000000401bd7 <+42>:    imul   $0x2710,%eax,%eax
   0x0000000000401bdd <+48>:    sub    %eax,%ecx
   0x0000000000401bdf <+50>:    mov    %ecx,%eax
   0x0000000000401be1 <+52>:    mov    %eax,-0x4(%rbp)
   0x0000000000401be4 <+55>:    callq  0x40d8d0 <rand>
   0x0000000000401be9 <+60>:    mov    %eax,%ecx
   0x0000000000401beb <+62>:    mov    $0x68db8bad,%edx
   0x0000000000401bf0 <+67>:    mov    %ecx,%eax
   0x0000000000401bf2 <+69>:    imul   %edx
   0x0000000000401bf4 <+71>:    sar    $0xc,%edx
   0x0000000000401bf7 <+74>:    mov    %ecx,%eax
   0x0000000000401bf9 <+76>:    sar    $0x1f,%eax
   0x0000000000401bfc <+79>:    sub    %eax,%edx
   0x0000000000401bfe <+81>:    mov    %edx,%eax
   0x0000000000401c00 <+83>:    mov    %eax,-0x8(%rbp)
   0x0000000000401c03 <+86>:    mov    -0x8(%rbp),%eax
   0x0000000000401c06 <+89>:    imul   $0x2710,%eax,%eax
   0x0000000000401c0c <+95>:    sub    %eax,%ecx
   0x0000000000401c0e <+97>:    mov    %ecx,%eax
   0x0000000000401c10 <+99>:    mov    %eax,-0x8(%rbp)
   0x0000000000401c13 <+102>:   mov    -0x4(%rbp),%eax
   0x0000000000401c16 <+105>:   cltq
   0x0000000000401c18 <+107>:   lea    0x0(,%rax,8),%rdx
   0x0000000000401c20 <+115>:   lea    0xc0919(%rip),%rax        # 0x4c2540 <pAllocBuf>
```

```
   0x0000000000401c27 <+122>:    mov    (%rdx,%rax,1),%rax
   0x0000000000401c2b <+126>:    test   %rax,%rax
   0x0000000000401c2e <+129>:    je     0x401c6c <proc+191>
   0x0000000000401c30 <+131>:    mov    -0x4(%rbp),%eax
   0x0000000000401c33 <+134>:    cltq
   0x0000000000401c35 <+136>:    lea    0x0(,%rax,8),%rdx
   0x0000000000401c3d <+144>:    lea    0xc08fc(%rip),%rax        # 0x4c2540 <pAllocBuf>
   0x0000000000401c44 <+151>:    mov    (%rdx,%rax,1),%rax
   0x0000000000401c48 <+155>:    mov    %rax,%rdi
   0x0000000000401c4b <+158>:    callq  0x41ac10 <free>
=> 0x0000000000401c50 <+163>:    mov    -0x4(%rbp),%eax
   0x0000000000401c53 <+166>:    cltq
   0x0000000000401c55 <+168>:    lea    0x0(,%rax,8),%rdx
   0x0000000000401c5d <+176>:    lea    0xc08dc(%rip),%rax        # 0x4c2540 <pAllocBuf>
   0x0000000000401c64 <+183>:    movq   $0x0,(%rdx,%rax,1)
   0x0000000000401c6c <+191>:    mov    -0x8(%rbp),%eax
   0x0000000000401c6f <+194>:    cltq
--Type <RET> for more, q to quit, c to continue without paging--
   0x0000000000401c71 <+196>:    mov    %rax,%rdi
   0x0000000000401c74 <+199>:    callq  0x41a5d0 <malloc>
   0x0000000000401c79 <+204>:    mov    %rax,%rcx
   0x0000000000401c7c <+207>:    mov    -0x4(%rbp),%eax
   0x0000000000401c7f <+210>:    cltq
   0x0000000000401c81 <+212>:    lea    0x0(,%rax,8),%rdx
   0x0000000000401c89 <+220>:    lea    0xc08b0(%rip),%rax        # 0x4c2540 <pAllocBuf>
   0x0000000000401c90 <+227>:    mov    %rcx,(%rdx,%rax,1)
   0x0000000000401c94 <+231>:    jmpq   0x401bb5 <proc+8>
End of assembler dump.
```

```
(gdb) x/gx 0x4c2540
0x4c2540 <pAllocBuf>:   0x00007ff7c8062b10
```

```
(gdb) x/wx $rbp-4
0x7ff7dbab3d6c: 0x00000254
```

```
(gdb) x/gx 0x254*8+0x4c2540*1
0x4c37e0 <pAllocBuf+4768>:      0x00007ff7c4108bc0
```

11. Scaled indexing instruction **mov (%rdx,%rax,1),%rax** suggests that we have an array. Dump the first 1000 elements of array *pAllocBuf* (0x4c2540) found in *proc* function disassembly (this can be done in two different ways):

```
(gdb) print/x *0x4c2540@1000
$0 = {0xc8062b10, 0x7ff7, 0x0 <repeats 14 times>, 0xc809fac0, 0x7ff7, 0x0, 0x0, 0x0, 0x0, 0x0,
0x0, 0xd001a3f0, 0x7ff7, 0x0, 0x0, 0x0, 0x0, 0x0, 0x0, 0x0, 0x0, 0xc410eb00, 0x7ff7,
  0x0 <repeats 20 times>, 0xd402ba20, 0x7ff7, 0x0, 0x0, 0x0, 0x0, 0x0, 0x0, 0x0, 0x0, 0x0, 0x0,
0xd4081a10, 0x7ff7, 0x0, 0x0, 0x0, 0x0, 0xc80dabe0, 0x7ff7, 0x0 <repeats 22 times>, 0xd0047d50,
  0x7ff7, 0x0 <repeats 62 times>, 0xc800bb40, 0x7ff7, 0x0, 0x0, 0xd403af80, 0x7ff7, 0x0
<repeats 20 times>, 0xc8136e10, 0x7ff7, 0x0, 0x0, 0x0, 0x0, 0xd4011980, 0x7ff7, 0x0 <repeats 32
times>,
  0xc4106b00, 0x7ff7, 0xc40eb100, 0x7ff7, 0x0 <repeats 16 times>, 0xd401f6e0, 0x7ff7, 0x0, 0x0,
0xc8029560, 0x7ff7, 0xd4043cf0, 0x7ff7, 0x0 <repeats 48 times>, 0xc80e2760, 0x7ff7, 0x0, 0x0,
  0xc8082fa0, 0x7ff7, 0x0 <repeats 18 times>, 0xc40d0f70, 0x7ff7, 0x0 <repeats 36 times>,
0xc80e0fc0, 0x7ff7, 0x0, 0x0, 0x0, 0x0, 0xc813fdc0, 0x7ff7, 0xc40ddf70, 0x7ff7, 0x0, 0x0, 0x0,
0x0, 0x0,
  0x0, 0x0, 0x0, 0xc8102800, 0x7ff7, 0x0, 0x0...}
```

```
(gdb) print/x *(long *)0x4c2540@1000
$1 = {0x7ff7c8062b10, 0x0, 0x0, 0x0, 0x0, 0x0, 0x0, 0x0, 0x7ff7c809fac0, 0x0, 0x0, 0x0,
0x7ff7d001a3f0, 0x0, 0x0, 0x0, 0x0, 0x7ff7c410eb00, 0x0, 0x0,
  0x0, 0x0, 0x0, 0x0, 0x0, 0x0, 0x0, 0x0, 0x7ff7d402ba20, 0x0, 0x0, 0x0, 0x0, 0x0,
0x7ff7d4081a10, 0x0, 0x0, 0x7ff7c80dabe0, 0x0 <repeats 11 times>,
  0x7ff7d0047d50, 0x0 <repeats 31 times>, 0x7ff7c800bb40, 0x0, 0x7ff7d403af80, 0x0, 0x0, 0x0,
0x0, 0x0, 0x0, 0x0, 0x0, 0x0, 0x0, 0x7ff7c8136e10, 0x0,
  0x0, 0x7ff7d4011980, 0x0 <repeats 16 times>, 0x7ff7c4106b00, 0x7ff7c40eb100, 0x0, 0x0, 0x0,
0x0, 0x0, 0x0, 0x0, 0x0, 0x7ff7d401f6e0, 0x0,
  0x7ff7c8029560, 0x7ff7d4043cf0, 0x0 <repeats 24 times>, 0x7ff7c80e2760, 0x0, 0x7ff7c8082fa0,
0x0, 0x0, 0x0, 0x0, 0x0, 0x0, 0x0, 0x0, 0x0,
  0x7ff7c40d0f70, 0x0 <repeats 18 times>, 0x7ff7c80e0fc0, 0x0, 0x0, 0x7ff7c813fdc0,
0x7ff7c40ddf70, 0x0, 0x0, 0x0, 0x0, 0x7ff7c8102800, 0x0, 0x0, 0x0,
  0x0, 0x7ff7c8008660, 0x0 <repeats 18 times>, 0x7ff7c40c4a40, 0x0 <repeats 36 times>,
0x7ff7c4059ca0, 0x0 <repeats 15 times>, 0x7ff7c8056260,
  0x7ff7cc0703a0, 0x0, 0x0, 0x0, 0x0, 0x0, 0x0, 0x0, 0x0, 0x7ff7c40cc3c0, 0x0 <repeats 14
times>...}
```

```
(gdb) x/1000gx 0x4c2540
0x4c2540 <pAllocBuf>:   0x00007ff7c8062b10      0x0000000000000000
0x4c2550 <pAllocBuf+16>:        0x0000000000000000      0x0000000000000000
0x4c2560 <pAllocBuf+32>:        0x0000000000000000      0x0000000000000000
0x4c2570 <pAllocBuf+48>:        0x0000000000000000      0x0000000000000000
0x4c2580 <pAllocBuf+64>:        0x00007ff7c809fac0      0x0000000000000000
0x4c2590 <pAllocBuf+80>:        0x0000000000000000      0x0000000000000000
0x4c25a0 <pAllocBuf+96>:        0x00007ff7d001a3f0      0x0000000000000000
0x4c25b0 <pAllocBuf+112>:       0x0000000000000000      0x0000000000000000
0x4c25c0 <pAllocBuf+128>:       0x0000000000000000      0x00007ff7c410eb00
0x4c25d0 <pAllocBuf+144>:       0x0000000000000000      0x0000000000000000
0x4c25e0 <pAllocBuf+160>:       0x0000000000000000      0x0000000000000000
0x4c25f0 <pAllocBuf+176>:       0x0000000000000000      0x0000000000000000
0x4c2600 <pAllocBuf+192>:       0x0000000000000000      0x0000000000000000
0x4c2610 <pAllocBuf+208>:       0x0000000000000000      0x0000000000000000
0x4c2620 <pAllocBuf+224>:       0x00007ff7d402ba20      0x0000000000000000
0x4c2630 <pAllocBuf+240>:       0x0000000000000000      0x0000000000000000
0x4c2640 <pAllocBuf+256>:       0x0000000000000000      0x0000000000000000
0x4c2650 <pAllocBuf+272>:       0x00007ff7d4081a10      0x0000000000000000
0x4c2660 <pAllocBuf+288>:       0x0000000000000000      0x00007ff7c80dabe0
0x4c2670 <pAllocBuf+304>:       0x0000000000000000      0x0000000000000000
0x4c2680 <pAllocBuf+320>:       0x0000000000000000      0x0000000000000000
0x4c2690 <pAllocBuf+336>:       0x0000000000000000      0x0000000000000000
0x4c26a0 <pAllocBuf+352>:       0x0000000000000000      0x0000000000000000
0x4c26b0 <pAllocBuf+368>:       0x0000000000000000      0x0000000000000000
0x4c26c0 <pAllocBuf+384>:       0x0000000000000000      0x00007ff7d0047d50
0x4c26d0 <pAllocBuf+400>:       0x0000000000000000      0x0000000000000000
0x4c26e0 <pAllocBuf+416>:       0x0000000000000000      0x0000000000000000
0x4c26f0 <pAllocBuf+432>:       0x0000000000000000      0x0000000000000000
0x4c2700 <pAllocBuf+448>:       0x0000000000000000      0x0000000000000000
0x4c2710 <pAllocBuf+464>:       0x0000000000000000      0x0000000000000000
0x4c2720 <pAllocBuf+480>:       0x0000000000000000      0x0000000000000000
0x4c2730 <pAllocBuf+496>:       0x0000000000000000      0x0000000000000000
0x4c2740 <pAllocBuf+512>:       0x0000000000000000      0x0000000000000000
0x4c2750 <pAllocBuf+528>:       0x0000000000000000      0x0000000000000000
0x4c2760 <pAllocBuf+544>:       0x0000000000000000      0x0000000000000000
0x4c2770 <pAllocBuf+560>:       0x0000000000000000      0x0000000000000000
0x4c2780 <pAllocBuf+576>:       0x0000000000000000      0x0000000000000000
[...]
```

Exercise A10 (A64, GDB)

Goal: Learn how to identify heap contention wait chains, synchronization issues, advanced disassembly, dump arrays.

Patterns: Double Free (Process Heap); High Contention (Process Heap); Wait Chain (General); Critical Region; Self-Diagnosis (User Mode).

1. Load the *core.10881* dump file and *App10* executable from the A64/App10 directory:

```
~/ALCDA2/A64/App10$ gdb-multiarch -c core.10881 -se App10
GNU gdb (Debian 8.2.1-2+b3) 8.2.1
Copyright (C) 2018 Free Software Foundation, Inc.
License GPLv3+: GNU GPL version 3 or later <http://gnu.org/licenses/gpl.html>
This is free software: you are free to change and redistribute it.
There is NO WARRANTY, to the extent permitted by law.
Type "show copying" and "show warranty" for details.
This GDB was configured as "x86_64-linux-gnu".
Type "show configuration" for configuration details.
For bug reporting instructions, please see:
<http://www.gnu.org/software/gdb/bugs/>.
Find the GDB manual and other documentation resources online at:
    <http://www.gnu.org/software/gdb/documentation/>.

For help, type "help".
Type "apropos word" to search for commands related to "word"...
Reading symbols from App10...(no debugging symbols found)...done.
[New LWP 10882]
[New LWP 10881]
[New LWP 10886]
[New LWP 10884]
[New LWP 10885]
[New LWP 10883]
Core was generated by `./App10'.
Program terminated with signal SIGSEGV, Segmentation fault.
#0  0x0000000000419a3c in _int_free ()
[Current thread is 1 (LWP 10882)]
```

2. Set logging to a file in case of lengthy output from some commands:

```
(gdb) set logging on App10.log
Copying output to App10.log.
```

3. Check all threads and identify problem top frames:

```
(gdb) info threads
  Id   Target Id         Frame
* 1    LWP 10882         0x0000000000419a3c in _int_free ()
  2    LWP 10881         0x000000000040ca44 in nanosleep ()
  3    LWP 10886         0x000000000040bcec in __lll_lock_wait_private ()
  4    LWP 10884         0x000000000040bcc0 in __lll_lock_wait_private ()
  5    LWP 10885         0x000000000040bcec in __lll_lock_wait_private ()
  6    LWP 10883         0x000000000040bcf0 in __lll_lock_wait_private ()
```

4. Check thread #3 and find where it was being executed:

```
(gdb) thread 3
[Switching to thread 3 (LWP 10886)]
#0  0x000000000040bcec in __lll_lock_wait_private ()

(gdb) bt
#0  0x000000000040bcec in __lll_lock_wait_private ()
#1  0x000000000041a02c in _int_free ()
#2  0x0000000000403254 in proc ()
#3  0x00000000004033a0 in bar_five ()
#4  0x00000000004033b4 in foo_five ()
#5  0x00000000004033cc in thread_five ()
#6  0x0000000000404cc4 in start_thread ()
#7  0x0000000000429c20 in thread_start ()

(gdb) disassemble proc
Dump of assembler code for function proc:
   0x00000000004031e8 <+0>:     stp     x29, x30, [sp, #-32]!
   0x00000000004031ec <+4>:     mov     x29, sp
   0x00000000004031f0 <+8>:     bl      0x40fadc <rand>
   0x00000000004031f4 <+12>:    mov     w1, #0x2710                     // #10000
   0x00000000004031f8 <+16>:    sdiv    w2, w0, w1
   0x00000000004031fc <+20>:    mov     w1, #0x2710                     // #10000
   0x0000000000403200 <+24>:    mul     w1, w2, w1
   0x0000000000403204 <+28>:    sub     w0, w0, w1
   0x0000000000403208 <+32>:    str     w0, [x29, #28]
   0x000000000040320c <+36>:    bl      0x40fadc <rand>
   0x0000000000403210 <+40>:    mov     w1, #0x2710                     // #10000
   0x0000000000403214 <+44>:    sdiv    w2, w0, w1
   0x0000000000403218 <+48>:    mov     w1, #0x2710                     // #10000
   0x000000000040321c <+52>:    mul     w1, w2, w1
   0x0000000000403220 <+56>:    sub     w0, w0, w1
   0x0000000000403224 <+60>:    str     w0, [x29, #24]
   0x0000000000403228 <+64>:    adrp    x0, 0x4d1000 <main_arena+2168>
   0x000000000040322c <+68>:    add     x0, x0, #0x668
   0x0000000000403230 <+72>:    ldrsw   x1, [x29, #28]
   0x0000000000403234 <+76>:    ldr     x0, [x0, x1, lsl #3]
   0x0000000000403238 <+80>:    cmp     x0, xzr
   0x000000000040323c <+84>:    b.eq    0x403264 <proc+124>  // b.none
   0x0000000000403240 <+88>:    adrp    x0, 0x4d1000 <main_arena+2168>
   0x0000000000403244 <+92>:    add     x0, x0, #0x668
   0x0000000000403248 <+96>:    ldrsw   x1, [x29, #28]
   0x000000000040324c <+100>:   ldr     x0, [x0, x1, lsl #3]
   0x0000000000403250 <+104>:   bl      0x41d5c8 <free>
   0x0000000000403254 <+108>:   adrp    x0, 0x4d1000 <main_arena+2168>
   0x0000000000403258 <+112>:   add     x0, x0, #0x668
   0x000000000040325c <+116>:   ldrsw   x1, [x29, #28]
   0x0000000000403260 <+120>:   str     xzr, [x0, x1, lsl #3]
   0x0000000000403264 <+124>:   ldrsw   x0, [x29, #24]
   0x0000000000403268 <+128>:   bl      0x41ca90 <malloc>
   0x000000000040326c <+132>:   mov     x2, x0
   0x0000000000403270 <+136>:   adrp    x0, 0x4d1000 <main_arena+2168>
   0x0000000000403274 <+140>:   add     x0, x0, #0x668
   0x0000000000403278 <+144>:   ldrsw   x1, [x29, #28]
   0x000000000040327c <+148>:   str     x2, [x0, x1, lsl #3]
   0x0000000000403280 <+152>:   b       0x4031f0 <proc+8>
End of assembler dump.
```

5. Check threads #4, #5, and #6, and find where it was being executed:

```
(gdb) thread 4
[Switching to thread 4 (LWP 10884)]
#0  0x000000000040bcc0 in __lll_lock_wait_private ()

(gdb) bt
#0  0x000000000040bcc0 in __lll_lock_wait_private ()
#1  0x000000000041a02c in _int_free ()
#2  0x0000000000403254 in proc ()
#3  0x0000000000403318 in bar_three ()
#4  0x000000000040332c in foo_three ()
#5  0x0000000000403344 in thread_three ()
#6  0x0000000000404cc4 in start_thread ()
#7  0x0000000000429c20 in thread_start ()

(gdb) thread 5
[Switching to thread 5 (LWP 10885)]
#0  0x000000000040bcec in __lll_lock_wait_private ()

(gdb) bt
#0  0x000000000040bcec in __lll_lock_wait_private ()
#1  0x000000000041a02c in _int_free ()
#2  0x0000000000403254 in proc ()
#3  0x000000000040335c in bar_four ()
#4  0x0000000000403370 in foo_four ()
#5  0x0000000000403388 in thread_four ()
#6  0x0000000000404cc4 in start_thread ()
#7  0x0000000000429c20 in thread_start ()

(gdb) thread 6
[Switching to thread 6 (LWP 10883)]
#0  0x000000000040bcf0 in __lll_lock_wait_private ()

(gdb) bt
#0  0x000000000040bcf0 in __lll_lock_wait_private ()
#1  0x000000000041a02c in _int_free ()
#2  0x0000000000403254 in proc ()
#3  0x00000000004032d4 in bar_two ()
#4  0x00000000004032e8 in foo_two ()
#5  0x0000000000403300 in thread_two ()
#6  0x0000000000404cc4 in start_thread ()
#7  0x0000000000429c20 in thread_start ()
```

Note: We see that all waiting threads are the same in their return addresses from *free*.

6. Check thread #1 and find where it was being executed:

```
(gdb) thread 1
[Switching to thread 1 (LWP 10882)]
#0  0x0000000000419a3c in _int_free ()

(gdb) bt
#0  0x0000000000419a3c in _int_free ()
#1  0x0000000000403254 in proc ()
#2  0x0000000000403290 in bar_one ()
#3  0x00000000004032a4 in foo_one ()
#4  0x00000000004032bc in thread_one ()
#5  0x0000000000404cc4 in start_thread ()
#6  0x0000000000429c20 in thread_start ()
```

Note: We see that it also has the same return addresses from *free*. It means all these threads are contending for the same free function. However, thread #1 got a segmentation fault signal. Since *free* calls were done from the same *proc* function location, we suspect a double free:

```
(gdb) x/i 0x0000000000419a3c
=> 0x419a3c <_int_free+268>:    ldr     x2, [x19, #8]

(gdb) x $x19+8
   0xfffffffffc12e28:  Cannot access memory at address 0xfffffffffc12e28
```

7. Check the address that was being freed:

```
(gdb) disassemble proc
Dump of assembler code for function proc:
   0x00000000004031e8 <+0>:     stp     x29, x30, [sp, #-32]!
   0x00000000004031ec <+4>:     mov     x29, sp
   0x00000000004031f0 <+8>:     bl      0x40fadc <rand>
   0x00000000004031f4 <+12>:    mov     w1, #0x2710                     // #10000
   0x00000000004031f8 <+16>:    sdiv    w2, w0, w1
   0x00000000004031fc <+20>:    mov     w1, #0x2710                     // #10000
   0x0000000000403200 <+24>:    mul     w1, w2, w1
   0x0000000000403204 <+28>:    sub     w0, w0, w1
   0x0000000000403208 <+32>:    str     w0, [x29, #28]
   0x000000000040320c <+36>:    bl      0x40fadc <rand>
   0x0000000000403210 <+40>:    mov     w1, #0x2710                     // #10000
   0x0000000000403214 <+44>:    sdiv    w2, w0, w1
   0x0000000000403218 <+48>:    mov     w1, #0x2710                     // #10000
   0x000000000040321c <+52>:    mul     w1, w2, w1
   0x0000000000403220 <+56>:    sub     w0, w0, w1
   0x0000000000403224 <+60>:    str     w0, [x29, #24]
   0x0000000000403228 <+64>:    adrp    x0, 0x4d1000 <main_arena+2168>
   0x000000000040322c <+68>:    add     x0, x0, #0x668
   0x0000000000403230 <+72>:    ldrsw   x1, [x29, #28]
   0x0000000000403234 <+76>:    ldr     x0, [x0, x1, lsl #3]
   0x0000000000403238 <+80>:    cmp     x0, xzr
   0x000000000040323c <+84>:    b.eq    0x403264 <proc+124>  // b.none
   0x0000000000403240 <+88>:    adrp    x0, 0x4d1000 <main_arena+2168>
   0x0000000000403244 <+92>:    add     x0, x0, #0x668
   0x0000000000403248 <+96>:    ldrsw   x1, [x29, #28]
   0x000000000040324c <+100>:   ldr     x0, [x0, x1, lsl #3]
   0x0000000000403250 <+104>:   bl      0x41d5c8 <free>
   0x0000000000403254 <+108>:   adrp    x0, 0x4d1000 <main_arena+2168>
   0x0000000000403258 <+112>:   add     x0, x0, #0x668
   0x000000000040325c <+116>:   ldrsw   x1, [x29, #28]
   0x0000000000403260 <+120>:   str     xzr, [x0, x1, lsl #3]
   0x0000000000403264 <+124>:   ldrsw   x0, [x29, #24]
   0x0000000000403268 <+128>:   bl      0x41ca90 <malloc>
   0x000000000040326c <+132>:   mov     x2, x0
   0x0000000000403270 <+136>:   adrp    x0, 0x4d1000 <main_arena+2168>
   0x0000000000403274 <+140>:   add     x0, x0, #0x668
   0x0000000000403278 <+144>:   ldrsw   x1, [x29, #28]
   0x000000000040327c <+148>:   str     x2, [x0, x1, lsl #3]
   0x0000000000403280 <+152>:   b       0x4031f0 <proc+8>
End of assembler dump.
```

Note: We see that we pass some location from the index array, which starts from the address 0x4d1000 + 0x668:

```
(gdb) x/gx 0x4d1000 + 0x668
0x4d1668 <pAllocBuf>:   0x0000fffba93b4e00

(gdb) frame 1
#1  0x0000000000403254 in proc ()

(gdb) x/wx $x29+28
0xfffbc684e81c: 0x0000264e

(gdb) p/x 0x0000264e << 3
$2 = 0x13270

(gdb) p/x 0x0000264e*8
$3 = 0x13270

(gdb) x/gx 0x4d1668 + 0x13270
0x4e48d8 <pAllocBuf+78448>:     0x0000fffba8b15610
```

8. Dump the first 100 elements of the identified array:

```
(gdb) print/x *0x4d1668@1000
$0 = {0xa93b4e00, 0xfffb, 0xa90c1af0, 0xfffb, 0xaa939280, 0xfffb, 0xaae8e2d0, 0xfffb,
0xa98aa350, 0xfffb, 0xa8fd48b0,
  0xfffb, 0xa912d220, 0xfffb, 0xaa420ad0, 0xfffb, 0xaae7f930, 0xfffb, 0xa87c2b20, 0xfffb,
0xa83d3e10, 0xfffb, 0x0, 0x0,
  0xaa65da80, 0xfffb, 0xaa869280, 0xfffb, 0xaa5c5f80, 0xfffb, 0xa8459f40, 0xfffb, 0xa81e4e30,
0xfffb, 0xa810f820, 0xfffb,
  0xa9e857a0, 0xfffb, 0xa9deacf0, 0xfffb, 0xa8933250, 0xfffb, 0xa8306260, 0xfffb, 0xaa9303e0,
0xfffb, 0xa85ef530, 0xfffb,
  0xaaefa020, 0xfffb, 0xa8b6f670, 0xfffb, 0xaadd5320, 0xfffb, 0xaaab54f0, 0xfffb, 0xa8ce7fc0,
0xfffb, 0xa8087370, 0xfffb,
  0xa823ab80, 0xfffb, 0xa8927f20, 0xfffb, 0xa9bc66d0, 0xfffb, 0xaa81d670, 0xfffb, 0xa8478270,
0xfffb, 0xa92edf60, 0xfffb,
  0xa8065330, 0xfffb, 0xa893faa0, 0xfffb, 0xaa0fe190, 0xfffb, 0xa8fc1450, 0xfffb, 0xa84c8f20,
0xfffb, 0xa8b79280, 0xfffb,
  0xaabe7040, 0xfffb, 0xa83d9110, 0xfffb, 0xa97dade0, 0xfffb, 0xa8fd0e80, 0xfffb, 0xaa20dc20,
0xfffb, 0xaa56f580, 0xfffb,
  0xa9724a30, 0xfffb, 0xaa241aa0, 0xfffb, 0xa8049e50, 0xfffb, 0xa82f3e40, 0xfffb, 0xa93b3cf0,
0xfffb, 0xaa9978d0, 0xfffb,
  0xa9223440, 0xfffb, 0x0, 0x0, 0xa9cffd00, 0xfffb, 0xa9e323a0, 0xfffb, 0xa9230070, 0xfffb,
0xa8cfc710, 0xfffb, 0xa9e48810,
  0xfffb, 0xa8474ea0, 0xfffb, 0xa9557cf0, 0xfffb, 0xa86617f0, 0xfffb, 0xa8737030, 0xfffb,
0xa92da510, 0xfffb, 0x0, 0x0,
  0xaa1977d0, 0xfffb, 0xa9287350, 0xfffb, 0xa8071640, 0xfffb, 0xa9d15240, 0xfffb, 0xa8ec3f00,
0xfffb, 0xa88273b0, 0xfffb,
  0xbc00d7b0, 0xfffb, 0x0, 0x0, 0xa8d41340, 0xfffb, 0xaa48f100, 0xfffb, 0xa8f9b680, 0xfffb,
0xa8badda0, 0xfffb, 0xa91d85e0,
  0xfffb, 0xa81f7730, 0xfffb, 0xa91ca3f0, 0xfffb, 0xa9688d40, 0xfffb, 0xaa760170, 0xfffb,
0xa878cbd0, 0xfffb, 0xa8edbc30,
  0xfffb, 0xa877fe70, 0xfffb, 0xa861ca80, 0xfffb, 0xa9003de0, 0xfffb, 0xa8cd3b50, 0xfffb,
0xaa310670, 0xfffb, 0xa91095f0,
  0xfffb, 0xa840f270, 0xfffb, 0xa8b094f0, 0xfffb, 0xa84334f0, 0xfffb, 0xaa272b90, 0xfffb,
0xa8e280e0, 0xfffb, 0xa8c32df0,
  0xfffb, 0xaa81b390, 0xfffb, 0xa888cb80, 0xfffb...}
```

```
(gdb) print/x *(long *)0x4d1668@1000
$1 = {0xfffba93b4e00, 0xfffba90c1af0, 0xfffbaa939280, 0xfffbaae8e2d0, 0xfffba98aa350,
0xfffba8fd48b0, 0xfffba912d220,
  0xfffbaa420ad0, 0xfffbaae7f930, 0xfffba87c2b20, 0xfffba83d3e10, 0x0, 0xfffbaa65da80,
0xfffbaa869280, 0xfffbaa5c5f80,
  0xfffba8459f40, 0xfffba81e4e30, 0xfffba810f820, 0xfffba9e857a0, 0xfffba9deacf0,
0xfffba8933250, 0xfffba8306260,
  0xfffbaa9303e0, 0xfffba85ef530, 0xfffbaaefa020, 0xfffba8b6f670, 0xfffbaadd5320,
0xfffbaaab54f0, 0xfffba8ce7fc0,
  0xfffba8087370, 0xfffba823ab80, 0xfffba8927f20, 0xfffba9bc66d0, 0xfffbaa81d670,
0xfffba8478270, 0xfffba92edf60,
  0xfffba8065330, 0xfffba893faa0, 0xfffbaa0fe190, 0xfffba8fc1450, 0xfffba84c8f20,
0xfffba8b79280, 0xfffbaabe7040,
  0xfffba83d9110, 0xfffba97dade0, 0xfffba8fd0e80, 0xfffbaa20dc20, 0xfffbaa56f580,
0xfffba9724a30, 0xfffbaa241aa0,
  0xfffba8049e50, 0xfffba82f3e40, 0xfffba93b3cf0, 0xfffbaa9978d0, 0xfffba9223440, 0x0,
0xfffba9cffd00, 0xfffba9e323a0,
  0xfffba9230070, 0xfffba8cfc710, 0xfffba9e48810, 0xfffba8474ea0, 0xfffba9557cf0,
0xfffba86617f0, 0xfffba8737030,
  0xfffba92da510, 0x0, 0xfffbaa1977d0, 0xfffba9287350, 0xfffba8071640, 0xfffba9d15240,
0xfffba8ec3f00, 0xfffba88273b0,
  0xfffbbc00d7b0, 0x0, 0xfffba8d41340, 0xfffbaa48f100, 0xfffba8f9b680, 0xfffba8badda0,
0xfffba91d85e0, 0xfffba81f7730,
  0xfffba91ca3f0, 0xfffba9688d40, 0xfffbaa760170, 0xfffba878cbd0, 0xfffba8edbc30,
0xfffba877fe70, 0xfffba861ca80,
  0xfffba9003de0, 0xfffba8cd3b50, 0xfffbaa310670, 0xfffba91095f0, 0xfffba840f270,
0xfffba8b094f0, 0xfffba84334f0,
  0xfffbaa272b90, 0xfffba8e280e0, 0xfffba8c32df0, 0xfffbaa81b390, 0xfffba888cb80, 0x0,
0xfffbaa5009a0, 0xfffba8d5aaf0,
  0xfffba895fa50, 0xfffba8726760, 0xfffbaa3bdf80, 0xfffba8088d40, 0xfffba8e63930,
0xfffba8726130, 0xfffbaad1af40,
  0xfffbaa300ed0, 0xfffba992f670, 0xfffbaa194090, 0xfffba9c5a300, 0xfffbaa5ea990,
0xfffba92ab6d0, 0xfffbaa2f3700,
  0xfffba83e0b30, 0xfffba8692620, 0xfffba90d8260, 0xfffbaa62d8a0, 0xfffba939e180,
0xfffba8596f00, 0xfffba9419c70,
  0xfffbaa59f5a0, 0xfffbaa01ffd0, 0xfffba85c1260, 0xfffbaa1a6250, 0xfffba8b66780,
0xfffbaaa696f0, 0xfffba86e3f60,
  0xfffba8bf7240, 0xfffbaa1e3ae0, 0xfffba91c0f30, 0xfffba9fc6b10, 0xfffbaa6e4700,
0xfffbaa660770, 0xfffba9a92e80,
  0xfffbaaac2fc0, 0xfffba8ba0340, 0xfffba9cf6240, 0xfffba8451290, 0xfffba88880c0,
0xfffba92517e0, 0xfffbaae65de0,
  0xfffba84ab520, 0xfffba84d0b70, 0xfffba8264490, 0xfffbaa4749b0, 0xfffba9546660,
0xfffba8a011c0, 0xfffba938f9e0,
  0xfffbaaebe240, 0xfffba9999440, 0xfffba9a72850, 0xfffbaab01a00, 0xfffbaa6795b0,
0xfffbaae9a180, 0xfffbaa39e590,
  0xfffbaa08c140, 0xfffba922c030, 0xfffba9cd6540, 0xfffba81cc7d0, 0xfffba816e2b0,
0xfffbaa8a2070, 0x0, 0xfffbaa2f7740,
  0xfffba98fa130, 0xfffba9811090, 0xfffba85ca940, 0xfffba94f0ed0, 0xfffba922a680,
0xfffba9a709d0, 0xfffba8dc52e0,
  0xfffba9e61de0, 0xfffba856afe0, 0xfffba823e260, 0xfffba896e350, 0xfffba96f19a0,
0xfffba902b650, 0xfffba8095120,
  0xfffba89cc910, 0xfffbaac57210, 0xfffbaa78a580, 0xfffba8bc4120, 0xfffba97b25d0,
0xfffbaa243c10, 0x0, 0xfffbaa7ba1a0,
  0xfffba8b94d90, 0xfffba84977b0, 0xfffba82c4910, 0xfffbaad189f0, 0xfffba8f72680,
0xfffba998bdc0, 0xfffba8219e10,
  0xfffba90c16c0, 0xfffba9535ab0, 0xfffba8a68630, 0xfffba87432d0...}
```

```
(gdb) x/1000gx 0x4d1668
0x4d1668 <pAllocBuf>:   0x0000fffba93b4e00      0x0000fffba90c1af0
0x4d1678 <pAllocBuf+16>:        0x0000fffbaa939280      0x0000fffbaae8e2d0
0x4d1688 <pAllocBuf+32>:        0x0000fffba98aa350      0x0000fffba8fd48b0
0x4d1698 <pAllocBuf+48>:        0x0000fffba912d220      0x0000fffbaa420ad0
0x4d16a8 <pAllocBuf+64>:        0x0000fffbaae7f930      0x0000fffba87c2b20
0x4d16b8 <pAllocBuf+80>:        0x0000fffba83d3e10      0x0000000000000000
0x4d16c8 <pAllocBuf+96>:        0x0000fffbaa65da80      0x0000fffbaa869280
0x4d16d8 <pAllocBuf+112>:       0x0000fffbaa5c5f80      0x0000fffba8459f40
0x4d16e8 <pAllocBuf+128>:       0x0000fffba81e4e30      0x0000fffba810f820
0x4d16f8 <pAllocBuf+144>:       0x0000fffba9e857a0      0x0000fffba9deacf0
0x4d1708 <pAllocBuf+160>:       0x0000fffba8933250      0x0000fffba8306260
0x4d1718 <pAllocBuf+176>:       0x0000fffbaa9303e0      0x0000fffba85ef530
0x4d1728 <pAllocBuf+192>:       0x0000fffbaaefa020      0x0000fffba8b6f670
0x4d1738 <pAllocBuf+208>:       0x0000fffbaadd5320      0x0000fffbaaab54f0
0x4d1748 <pAllocBuf+224>:       0x0000fffba8ce7fc0      0x0000fffba8087370
0x4d1758 <pAllocBuf+240>:       0x0000fffba823ab80      0x0000fffba8927f20
0x4d1768 <pAllocBuf+256>:       0x0000fffba9bc66d0      0x0000fffbaa81d670
0x4d1778 <pAllocBuf+272>:       0x0000fffba8478270      0x0000fffba92edf60
0x4d1788 <pAllocBuf+288>:       0x0000fffba8065330      0x0000fffba893faa0
0x4d1798 <pAllocBuf+304>:       0x0000fffbaa0fe190      0x0000fffba8fc1450
0x4d17a8 <pAllocBuf+320>:       0x0000fffba84c8f20      0x0000fffba8b79280
0x4d17b8 <pAllocBuf+336>:       0x0000fffbaabe7040      0x0000fffba83d9110
0x4d17c8 <pAllocBuf+352>:       0x0000fffba97dade0      0x0000fffba8fd0e80
0x4d17d8 <pAllocBuf+368>:       0x0000fffbaa20dc20      0x0000fffbaa56f580
0x4d17e8 <pAllocBuf+384>:       0x0000fffba9724a30      0x0000fffbaa241aa0
0x4d17f8 <pAllocBuf+400>:       0x0000fffba8049e50      0x0000fffba82f3e40
0x4d1808 <pAllocBuf+416>:       0x0000fffba93b3cf0      0x0000fffbaa9978d0
0x4d1818 <pAllocBuf+432>:       0x0000fffba9223440      0x0000000000000000
0x4d1828 <pAllocBuf+448>:       0x0000fffba9cffd00      0x0000fffba9e323a0
0x4d1838 <pAllocBuf+464>:       0x0000fffba9230070      0x0000fffba8cfc710
0x4d1848 <pAllocBuf+480>:       0x0000fffba9e48810      0x0000fffba8474ea0
0x4d1858 <pAllocBuf+496>:       0x0000fffba9557cf0      0x0000fffba86617f0
0x4d1868 <pAllocBuf+512>:       0x0000fffba8737030      0x0000fffba92da510
0x4d1878 <pAllocBuf+528>:       0x0000000000000000      0x0000fffbaa1977d0
0x4d1888 <pAllocBuf+544>:       0x0000fffba9287350      0x0000fffba8071640
0x4d1898 <pAllocBuf+560>:       0x0000fffba9d15240      0x0000fffba8ec3f00
0x4d18a8 <pAllocBuf+576>:       0x0000fffba88273b0      0x0000fffbbc00d7b0
0x4d18b8 <pAllocBuf+592>:       0x0000000000000000      0x0000fffba8d41340
0x4d18c8 <pAllocBuf+608>:       0x0000fffbaa48f100      0x0000fffba8f9b680
0x4d18d8 <pAllocBuf+624>:       0x0000fffba8badda0      0x0000fffba91d85e0
0x4d18e8 <pAllocBuf+640>:       0x0000fffba81f7730      0x0000fffba91ca3f0
0x4d18f8 <pAllocBuf+656>:       0x0000fffba9688d40      0x0000fffbaa760170
0x4d1908 <pAllocBuf+672>:       0x0000fffba878cbd0      0x0000fffba8edbc30
0x4d1918 <pAllocBuf+688>:       0x0000fffba877fe70      0x0000fffba861ca80
0x4d1928 <pAllocBuf+704>:       0x0000fffba9003de0      0x0000fffba8cd3b50
0x4d1938 <pAllocBuf+720>:       0x0000fffbaa310670      0x0000fffba91095f0
0x4d1948 <pAllocBuf+736>:       0x0000fffba840f270      0x0000fffba8b094f0
0x4d1958 <pAllocBuf+752>:       0x0000fffba84334f0      0x0000fffbaa272b90
0x4d1968 <pAllocBuf+768>:       0x0000fffba8e280e0      0x0000fffba8c32df0
--Type <RET> for more, q to quit, c to continue without paging--q
Quit
```

Exercise A10 (x64, WinDbg)

Goal: Learn how to identify heap contention wait chains, synchronization issues, advanced disassembly, dump arrays.

Patterns: Double Free (Process Heap); High Contention (Process Heap); Wait Chain (General); Critical Region; Self-Diagnosis (User Mode).

1. Launch WinDbg.

2. Load the *core.App10* dump file from the x64\App10 folder:

```
Microsoft (R) Windows Debugger Version 10.0.27725.1000 AMD64
Copyright (c) Microsoft Corporation. All rights reserved.


Loading Dump File [C:\ALCDA2\x64\App10\core.App10]
64-bit machine not using 64-bit API

************* Path validation summary **************
Response                         Time (ms)     Location
Deferred                                       srv*
Symbol search path is: srv*
Executable search path is:
Generic Unix Version 0 UP Free x64
System Uptime: not available
Process Uptime: not available
..
(18c.18e): Signal SIGABRT code SI_TKILL (Sent by tkill system call) originating from PID 18c
*** WARNING: Unable to verify timestamp for App10
App10+0xcc6b:
00000000`0040cc6b ???
```

3. Set logging to a file in case of lengthy output from some commands:

```
0:000> .logopen C:\ALCDA2\x64\App10\App10-WinDbg.log
Opened log file 'C:\ALCDA2\x64\App10\App10-WinDbg.log'
```

4. Specify the dump folder as the symbol path and reload symbols:

```
0:000> .symfix; .sympath+ C:\ALCDA2\x64\App10\
Symbol search path is: srv*;C:\ALCDA2\x64\App10\
Expanded Symbol search path is:
cache*;SRV*https://msdl.microsoft.com/download/symbols;c:\alcda2\x64\app10\

************* Path validation summary **************
Response                         Time (ms)     Location
Deferred                                       srv*
OK                                             C:\ALCDA2\x64\App10\
*** WARNING: Unable to verify timestamp for App10
```

```
0:000> .reload
..
*** WARNING: Unable to verify timestamp for App10

************* Symbol Loading Error Summary **************
Module name            Error
App10                  The system cannot find the file specified

You can troubleshoot most symbol related issues by turning on symbol loading diagnostics (!sym
noisy) and repeating the command that caused symbols to be loaded.
You should also verify that your symbol search path (.sympath) is correct.
```

Note: We ignore warnings and errors as they are not relevant for now.

5. Check all threads and identify problem top frames:

```
0:000> ~*kL 1

Unable to get thread data for thread 0
.  0  Id: 18c.18e Suspend: 0 Teb: 00000000`00000000 Unfrozen
 # Child-SP          RetAddr           Call Site
00 00007ff7`dbab3980 00000000`00401241     App10!gsignal+0x10b

Unable to get thread data for thread 1
   1  Id: 18c.18c Suspend: 0 Teb: 00000000`00000000 Unfrozen
 # Child-SP          RetAddr           Call Site
00 00007ffd`e35bfc10 00000000`00441a9a     App10!nanosleep+0x40

Unable to get thread data for thread 2
   2  Id: 18c.18d Suspend: 0 Teb: 00000000`00000000 Unfrozen
 # Child-SP          RetAddr           Call Site
00 00007ff7`dc2b4c08 00000000`0041834c     App10!_mprotect+0x7

Unable to get thread data for thread 3
   3  Id: 18c.191 Suspend: 0 Teb: 00000000`00000000 Unfrozen
 # Child-SP          RetAddr           Call Site
00 00007ff7`da2b0ca8 00000000`0041a7b0     App10!_lll_lock_wait_private+0x1b

Unable to get thread data for thread 4
   4  Id: 18c.190 Suspend: 0 Teb: 00000000`00000000 Unfrozen
 # Child-SP          RetAddr           Call Site
00 00007ff7`daab1c58 00000000`00417a43     App10!_lll_lock_wait_private+0x1b

Unable to get thread data for thread 5
   5  Id: 18c.18f Suspend: 0 Teb: 00000000`00000000 Unfrozen
 # Child-SP          RetAddr           Call Site
00 00007ff7`db2b2c58 00000000`00417a43     App10!_lll_lock_wait_private+0x1b
```

6. Check thread #3 and find where it was being executed:

```
0:000> ~3s
App10!_lll_lock_wait_private+0x1b:
00000000`00405e2b mov     eax,edx
```

```
0:002> k
 # Child-SP          RetAddr           Call Site
00 00007ff7`da2b0ca8 00000000`0041a7b0 App10!_lll_lock_wait_private+0x1b
01 00007ff7`da2b0cc0 00000000`00401c79 App10!malloc+0x1e0
02 00007ff7`da2b0d60 00000000`00401da3 App10!proc+0xcc
03 00007ff7`da2b0d80 00000000`00401db4 App10!bar_five+0xe
04 00007ff7`da2b0d90 00000000`00401dcd App10!foo_five+0xe
05 00007ff7`da2b0da0 00000000`004031c3 App10!thread_five+0x16
06 00007ff7`da2b0dc0 00000000`0044436f App10!start_thread+0xf3
07 00007ff7`da2b0e80 ffffffff`ffffffff App10!_clone+0x3f
08 00007ff7`da2b0e88 00000000`00000000 0xffffffff`ffffffff
```

```
0:003> ub 00000000`00401c79
App10!proc+0xa6:
00000000`00401c53 cdqe
00000000`00401c55 lea     rdx,[rax*8]
00000000`00401c5d lea     rax,[App10!pAllocBuf (00000000`004c2540)]
00000000`00401c64 mov     qword ptr [rdx+rax],0
00000000`00401c6c mov     eax,dword ptr [rbp-8]
00000000`00401c6f cdqe
00000000`00401c71 mov     rdi,rax
00000000`00401c74 call    App10!malloc (00000000`0041a5d0)
```

7. Check the remaining threads #4 and #5, and find where they were being executed:

```
0:003> ~4kL
 # Child-SP          RetAddr           Call Site
00 00007ff7`daab1c58 00000000`00417a43 App10!_lll_lock_wait_private+0x1b
01 00007ff7`daab1c70 00000000`00401c50 App10!int_free+0x6c3
02 00007ff7`daab1d60 00000000`00401d64 App10!proc+0xa3
03 00007ff7`daab1d80 00000000`00401d75 App10!bar_four+0xe
04 00007ff7`daab1d90 00000000`00401d8e App10!foo_four+0xe
05 00007ff7`daab1da0 00000000`004031c3 App10!thread_four+0x16
06 00007ff7`daab1dc0 00000000`0044436f App10!start_thread+0xf3
07 00007ff7`daab1e80 ffffffff`ffffffff App10!_clone+0x3f
08 00007ff7`daab1e88 00000000`00000000 0xffffffff`ffffffff
```

```
0:003> ~5kL
 # Child-SP          RetAddr           Call Site
00 00007ff7`db2b2c58 00000000`00417a43 App10!_lll_lock_wait_private+0x1b
01 00007ff7`db2b2c70 00000000`00401c50 App10!int_free+0x6c3
02 00007ff7`db2b2d60 00000000`00401d25 App10!proc+0xa3
03 00007ff7`db2b2d80 00000000`00401d36 App10!bar_three+0xe
04 00007ff7`db2b2d90 00000000`00401d4f App10!foo_three+0xe
05 00007ff7`db2b2da0 00000000`004031c3 App10!thread_three+0x16
06 00007ff7`db2b2dc0 00000000`0044436f App10!start_thread+0xf3
07 00007ff7`db2b2e80 ffffffff`ffffffff App10!_clone+0x3f
08 00007ff7`db2b2e88 00000000`00000000 0xffffffff`ffffffff
```

```
0:003> ub 00000000`00401c50
App10!proc+0x81:
00000000`00401c2e je      App10!proc+0xbf (00000000`00401c6c)
00000000`00401c30 mov     eax,dword ptr [rbp-4]
00000000`00401c33 cdqe
00000000`00401c35 lea     rdx,[rax*8]
00000000`00401c3d lea     rax,[App10!pAllocBuf (00000000`004c2540)]
00000000`00401c44 mov     rax,qword ptr [rdx+rax]
00000000`00401c48 mov     rdi,rax
00000000`00401c4b call    App10!_free (00000000`0041ac10)
```

```
0:003> uf proc
App10!proc:
00000000`00401bad push    rbp
00000000`00401bae mov     rbp,rsp
00000000`00401bb1 sub     rsp,10h

App10!proc+0x8:
00000000`00401bb5 call    App10!rand (00000000`0040d8d0)
00000000`00401bba mov     ecx,eax
00000000`00401bbc mov     edx,68DB8BADh
00000000`00401bc1 mov     eax,ecx
00000000`00401bc3 imul    edx
00000000`00401bc5 sar     edx,0Ch
00000000`00401bc8 mov     eax,ecx
00000000`00401bca sar     eax,1Fh
00000000`00401bcd sub     edx,eax
00000000`00401bcf mov     eax,edx
00000000`00401bd1 mov     dword ptr [rbp-4],eax
00000000`00401bd4 mov     eax,dword ptr [rbp-4]
00000000`00401bd7 imul    eax,eax,2710h
00000000`00401bdd sub     ecx,eax
00000000`00401bdf mov     eax,ecx
00000000`00401be1 mov     dword ptr [rbp-4],eax
00000000`00401be4 call    App10!rand (00000000`0040d8d0)
00000000`00401be9 mov     ecx,eax
00000000`00401beb mov     edx,68DB8BADh
00000000`00401bf0 mov     eax,ecx
00000000`00401bf2 imul    edx
00000000`00401bf4 sar     edx,0Ch
00000000`00401bf7 mov     eax,ecx
00000000`00401bf9 sar     eax,1Fh
00000000`00401bfc sub     edx,eax
00000000`00401bfe mov     eax,edx
00000000`00401c00 mov     dword ptr [rbp-8],eax
00000000`00401c03 mov     eax,dword ptr [rbp-8]
00000000`00401c06 imul    eax,eax,2710h
00000000`00401c0c sub     ecx,eax
00000000`00401c0e mov     eax,ecx
00000000`00401c10 mov     dword ptr [rbp-8],eax
00000000`00401c13 mov     eax,dword ptr [rbp-4]
00000000`00401c16 cdqe
00000000`00401c18 lea     rdx,[rax*8]
00000000`00401c20 lea     rax,[App10!pAllocBuf (00000000`004c2540)]
00000000`00401c27 mov     rax,qword ptr [rdx+rax]
00000000`00401c2b test    rax,rax
00000000`00401c2e je      App10!proc+0xbf (00000000`00401c6c)  Branch

App10!proc+0x83:
00000000`00401c30 mov     eax,dword ptr [rbp-4]
00000000`00401c33 cdqe
00000000`00401c35 lea     rdx,[rax*8]
00000000`00401c3d lea     rax,[App10!pAllocBuf (00000000`004c2540)]
00000000`00401c44 mov     rax,qword ptr [rdx+rax]
00000000`00401c48 mov     rdi,rax
00000000`00401c4b call    App10!_free (00000000`0041ac10)
00000000`00401c50 mov     eax,dword ptr [rbp-4]
00000000`00401c53 cdqe
00000000`00401c55 lea     rdx,[rax*8]
00000000`00401c5d lea     rax,[App10!pAllocBuf (00000000`004c2540)]
00000000`00401c64 mov     qword ptr [rdx+rax],0
```

```
App10!proc+0xbf:
00000000`00401c6c mov     eax,dword ptr [rbp-8]
00000000`00401c6f cdqe
00000000`00401c71 mov     rdi,rax
00000000`00401c74 call    App10!malloc (00000000`0041a5d0)
00000000`00401c79 mov     rcx,rax
00000000`00401c7c mov     eax,dword ptr [rbp-4]
00000000`00401c7f cdqe
00000000`00401c81 lea     rdx,[rax*8]
00000000`00401c89 lea     rax,[App10!pAllocBuf (00000000`004c2540)]
00000000`00401c90 mov     qword ptr [rdx+rax],rcx
00000000`00401c94 jmp     App10!proc+0x8 (00000000`00401bb5)  Branch
```

Note: We see some buffer **0x4c2540** "sandwiched" between *free* and *malloc* calls that internally call "lock" and "unlock" functions.

8. Check thread #2 and find where it was being executed:

```
0:003> ~2s
App10!_mprotect+0x7:
00000000`004431e7 cmp     rax,0FFFFFFFFFFFFF001h

0:002> kL
 # Child-SP          RetAddr               Call Site
00 00007ff7`dc2b4c08 00000000`0041834c     App10!_mprotect+0x7
01 00007ff7`dc2b4c10 00000000`004194e1     App10!sysmalloc+0x3bc
02 00007ff7`dc2b4c80 00000000`0041a7c2     App10!int_malloc+0xd31
03 00007ff7`dc2b4d40 00000000`00401c79     App10!malloc+0x1f2
04 00007ff7`dc2b4d60 00000000`00401ca7     App10!proc+0xcc
05 00007ff7`dc2b4d80 00000000`00401cb8     App10!bar_one+0xe
06 00007ff7`dc2b4d90 00000000`00401cd1     App10!foo_one+0xe
07 00007ff7`dc2b4da0 00000000`004031c3     App10!thread_one+0x16
08 00007ff7`dc2b4dc0 00000000`0044436f     App10!start_thread+0xf3
09 00007ff7`dc2b4e80 ffffffff`ffffffff     App10!_clone+0x3f
0a 00007ff7`dc2b4e88 00000000`00000000     0xffffffff`ffffffff
```

Note: Thread #2 is the same as thread #3.

9. Check thread #0 and identify a diagnostic message:

```
0:002> ~0s
App10!gsignal+0x10b:
00000000`0040cc6b mov     rcx,qword ptr [rsp+108h] ss:00007ff7`dbab3a88=9a814e1071ce6100

0:000> kL
 # Child-SP          RetAddr               Call Site
00 00007ff7`dbab3980 00000000`00401241     App10!gsignal+0x10b
01 00007ff7`dbab3aa0 00000000`00410828     App10!abort+0x121
02 00007ff7`dbab3bd0 00000000`00415fea (T) App10!_libc_message+0x2c8
03 00007ff7`dbab3ce0 00000000`004179fc     App10!malloc_printerr+0x15
04 00007ff7`dbab3cf0 00000000`00401c50     App10!int_free+0x67c
05 00007ff7`dbab3d60 00000000`00401ce6     App10!proc+0xa3
06 00007ff7`dbab3d80 00000000`00401cf7     App10!bar_two+0xe
07 00007ff7`dbab3d90 00000000`00401d10     App10!foo_two+0xe
08 00007ff7`dbab3da0 00000000`004031c3     App10!thread_two+0x16
09 00007ff7`dbab3dc0 00000000`0044436f     App10!start_thread+0xf3
0a 00007ff7`dbab3e80 ffffffff`ffffffff     App10!_clone+0x3f
0b 00007ff7`dbab3e88 00000000`00000000     0xffffffff`ffffffff
```

```
0:000> ub 00000000`00410828
App10!_libc_message+0x2ab:
00000000`0041080b add     byte ptr [rax],al
00000000`0041080d mov     rdi,r15
00000000`00410810 xchg    rdi,qword ptr [App10!_abort_msg (00000000`004da380)]
00000000`00410817 test    rdi,rdi
00000000`0041081a je      App10!_libc_message+0x2c3 (00000000`00410823)
00000000`0041081c mov     esi,dword ptr [rdi]
00000000`0041081e call    App10!munmap (00000000`004431b0)
00000000`00410823 call    App10!abort (00000000`00401120)

0:000> dp 00000000`004da380 L1
00000000`004da380  00007ff7`d9ab0000

0:000> dc 00007ff7`d9ab0000
00007ff7`d9ab0000  00001000 62756f64 6620656c 20656572  ....double free
00007ff7`d9ab0010  6320726f 7572726f 6f697470 2128206e  or corruption (!
00007ff7`d9ab0020  76657270 00000a29 00000000 00000000  prev)...........
00007ff7`d9ab0030  00000000 00000000 00000000 00000000  ................
00007ff7`d9ab0040  00000000 00000000 00000000 00000000  ................
00007ff7`d9ab0050  00000000 00000000 00000000 00000000  ................
00007ff7`d9ab0060  00000000 00000000 00000000 00000000  ................
00007ff7`d9ab0070  00000000 00000000 00000000 00000000  ................

0:000> da 00007ff7`d9ab0000+4
00007ff7`d9ab0004  "double free or corruption (!prev"
00007ff7`d9ab0024  ")."

0:000> da /c 90 00007ff7`d9ab0000+4
00007ff7`d9ab0004  "double free or corruption (!prev)."
```

10. Check the address that was being freed:

```
0:000> kL
 # Child-SP          RetAddr               Call Site
00 00007ff7`dbab3980 00000000`00401241     App10!gsignal+0x10b
01 00007ff7`dbab3aa0 00000000`00410828     App10!abort+0x121
02 00007ff7`dbab3bd0 00000000`00415fea (T) App10!_libc_message+0x2c8
03 00007ff7`dbab3ce0 00000000`004179fc     App10!malloc_printerr+0x15
04 00007ff7`dbab3cf0 00000000`00401c50     App10!int_free+0x67c
05 00007ff7`dbab3d60 00000000`00401ce6     App10!proc+0xa3
06 00007ff7`dbab3d80 00000000`00401cf7     App10!bar_two+0xe
07 00007ff7`dbab3d90 00000000`00401d10     App10!foo_two+0xe
08 00007ff7`dbab3da0 00000000`004031c3     App10!thread_two+0x16
09 00007ff7`dbab3dc0 00000000`0044436f     App10!start_thread+0xf3
0a 00007ff7`dbab3e80 ffffffff`ffffffff     App10!_clone+0x3f
0b 00007ff7`dbab3e88 00000000`00000000     0xffffffff`ffffffff

0:000> ub 00000000`00401c50
App10!proc+0x81:
00000000`00401c2e je      App10!proc+0xbf (00000000`00401c6c)
00000000`00401c30 mov     eax,dword ptr [rbp-4]
00000000`00401c33 cdqe
00000000`00401c35 lea     rdx,[rax*8]
00000000`00401c3d lea     rax,[App10!pAllocBuf (00000000`004c2540)]
00000000`00401c44 mov     rax,qword ptr [rdx+rax]
00000000`00401c48 mov     rdi,rax
00000000`00401c4b call    App10!_free (00000000`0041ac10)
```

```
0:000> .frame /c 5
05 00007ff7`dbab3d60 00000000`00401ce6     App10!proc+0xa3
rax=0000000000000000 rbx=0000000000000000 rcx=000000000040cc6b
rdx=0000000000000000 rsi=00007ff7dbab3980 rdi=0000000000000002
rip=0000000000401c50 rsp=00007ff7dbab3d60 rbp=00007ff7dbab3d70
 r8=0000000000000000  r9=00007ff7dbab3980 r10=0000000000000008
r11=0000000000000246 r12=00007ffde35bfbfe r13=00007ffde35bfbff
r14=00007ff7dbab4700 r15=0000000000000000
iopl=0         nv up ei pl zr na po nc
cs=0033  ss=002b  ds=0000  es=0000  fs=0000  gs=0000             efl=00000246
App10!proc+0xa3:
00000000`00401c50 mov     eax,dword ptr [rbp-4]   ss:00007ff7`dbab3d6c=00000254

0:000> dd rbp-4 L1
00007ff7`dbab3d6c  00000254

0:000> dp 254*8+00000000`004c2540 L1
00000000`004c37e0  00007ff7`c4108bc0
```

11. Scaled indexing instruction **mov rax,qword ptr [rdx+rax]** suggests that we have an array. Dump the first 100 elements of the identified array:

```
0:000> dp 00000000`004c2540 L100
00000000`004c2540  00007ff7`c8062b10 00000000`00000000
00000000`004c2550  00000000`00000000 00000000`00000000
00000000`004c2560  00000000`00000000 00000000`00000000
00000000`004c2570  00000000`00000000 00000000`00000000
00000000`004c2580  00007ff7`c809fac0 00000000`00000000
00000000`004c2590  00000000`00000000 00000000`00000000
00000000`004c25a0  00007ff7`d001a3f0 00000000`00000000
00000000`004c25b0  00000000`00000000 00000000`00000000
00000000`004c25c0  00000000`00000000 00007ff7`c410eb00
00000000`004c25d0  00000000`00000000 00000000`00000000
00000000`004c25e0  00000000`00000000 00000000`00000000
00000000`004c25f0  00000000`00000000 00000000`00000000
00000000`004c2600  00000000`00000000 00000000`00000000
00000000`004c2610  00000000`00000000 00000000`00000000
00000000`004c2620  00007ff7`d402ba20 00000000`00000000
00000000`004c2630  00000000`00000000 00000000`00000000
00000000`004c2640  00000000`00000000 00000000`00000000
00000000`004c2650  00007ff7`d4081a10 00000000`00000000
00000000`004c2660  00000000`00000000 00007ff7`c80dabe0
00000000`004c2670  00000000`00000000 00000000`00000000
00000000`004c2680  00000000`00000000 00000000`00000000
00000000`004c2690  00000000`00000000 00000000`00000000
00000000`004c26a0  00000000`00000000 00000000`00000000
00000000`004c26b0  00000000`00000000 00000000`00000000
00000000`004c26c0  00000000`00000000 00007ff7`d0047d50
00000000`004c26d0  00000000`00000000 00000000`00000000
00000000`004c26e0  00000000`00000000 00000000`00000000
00000000`004c26f0  00000000`00000000 00000000`00000000
00000000`004c2700  00000000`00000000 00000000`00000000
[...]
```

11. We close logging before exiting WinDbg:

```
0:000> .logclose
Closing open log file 'C:\ALCDA2\x64\App10\App10-WinDbg.log
```

Exercise A10 (A64, WinDbg)

Goal: Learn how to identify heap contention wait chains, synchronization issues, advanced disassembly, dump arrays.

Patterns: Double Free (Process Heap); High Contention (Process Heap); Wait Chain (General); Critical Region; Self-Diagnosis (User Mode).

1. Launch WinDbg.

2. Load the *core.10881* dump file from the A64\App10 folder:

```
Microsoft (R) Windows Debugger Version 10.0.27725.1000 AMD64
Copyright (c) Microsoft Corporation. All rights reserved.


Loading Dump File [C:\ALCDA2\A64\App10\core.10881]
64-bit machine not using 64-bit API

************* Path validation summary **************
Response                         Time (ms)     Location
Deferred                                       srv*
Symbol search path is: srv*
Executable search path is:
Generic Unix Version 0 UP Free ARM 64-bit (AArch64)
System Uptime: not available
Process Uptime: not available
..
(2a81.2a82): Signal SIGSEGV (Segmentation fault) code SEGV_MAPERR (Address not mapped to
object) at 0xfffffffffc12e28
*** WARNING: Unable to verify timestamp for App10
App10+0x19a3c:
00000000`00419a3c ???
```

3. Set logging to a file in case of lengthy output from some commands:

```
0:000> .logopen C:\ALCDA2\A64\App10\App10-WinDbg.log
Opened log file 'C:\ALCDA2\A64\App10\App10-WinDbg.log'
```

4. Specify the dump folder as the symbol path and reload symbols:

```
0:000> .symfix; .sympath+ C:\ALCDA2\A64\App10\
Symbol search path is: srv*;C:\ALCDA2\A64\App10\
Expanded Symbol search path is:
cache*;SRV*https://msdl.microsoft.com/download/symbols;c:\alcda2\a64\app10\

************* Path validation summary **************
Response                         Time (ms)     Location
Deferred                                       srv*
OK                                             C:\ALCDA2\A64\App10\
*** WARNING: Unable to verify timestamp for App10
```

```
0:000> .reload
..
*** WARNING: Unable to verify timestamp for App10

************* Symbol Loading Error Summary **************
Module name            Error
App10                  The system cannot find the file specified

You can troubleshoot most symbol related issues by turning on symbol loading diagnostics (!sym
noisy) and repeating the command that caused symbols to be loaded.
You should also verify that your symbol search path (.sympath) is correct.
```

Note: We ignore warnings and errors as they are not relevant for now.

5. Check all threads and identify problem top frames:

```
0:000> ~*k 1

Unable to get thread data for thread 0
.  0  Id: 2a81.2a82 Suspend: 0 Teb: 00000000`00000000 Unfrozen
 # Child-SP          RetAddr               Call Site
00 0000fffb`c684e780 00000000`00403254     App10!int_free+0x10c

Unable to get thread data for thread 1
   1  Id: 2a81.2a81 Suspend: 0 Teb: 00000000`00000000 Unfrozen
 # Child-SP          RetAddr               Call Site
00 0000ffff`c53dc670 00000000`00424d74     App10!_libc_nanosleep+0x24

Unable to get thread data for thread 2
   2  Id: 2a81.2a86 Suspend: 0 Teb: 00000000`00000000 Unfrozen
 # Child-SP          RetAddr               Call Site
00 0000fffb`c480e780 00000000`0041a02c     App10!_lll_lock_wait_private+0x5c

Unable to get thread data for thread 3
   3  Id: 2a81.2a84 Suspend: 0 Teb: 00000000`00000000 Unfrozen
 # Child-SP          RetAddr               Call Site
00 0000fffb`c582e780 00000000`0041a02c     App10!_lll_lock_wait_private+0x30

Unable to get thread data for thread 4
   4  Id: 2a81.2a85 Suspend: 0 Teb: 00000000`00000000 Unfrozen
 # Child-SP          RetAddr               Call Site
00 0000fffb`c501e780 00000000`0041a02c     App10!_lll_lock_wait_private+0x5c

Unable to get thread data for thread 5
   5  Id: 2a81.2a83 Suspend: 0 Teb: 00000000`00000000 Unfrozen
 # Child-SP          RetAddr               Call Site
00 0000fffb`c603e780 00000000`0041a02c     App10!_lll_lock_wait_private+0x60
```

6. Check thread #2 and find where it was being executed:

```
0:000> ~2s
App10!_lll_lock_wait_private+0x5c:
00000000`0040bcec d4000001 svc       #0
```

```
0:002> kL
 # Child-SP          RetAddr               Call Site
00 0000fffb`c480e780 00000000`0041a02c     App10!_lll_lock_wait_private+0x5c
01 0000fffb`c480e780 00000000`00403254     App10!int_free+0x6fc
02 0000fffb`c480e800 00000000`004033a0     App10!proc+0x6c
03 0000fffb`c480e820 00000000`004033b4     App10!bar_five+0xc
04 0000fffb`c480e830 00000000`004033cc     App10!foo_five+0xc
05 0000fffb`c480e840 00000000`00404cc4     App10!thread_five+0x10
06 0000fffb`c480e860 00000000`00429c20     App10!start_thread+0xb4
07 0000fffb`c480e990 ffffffff`ffffffff     App10!thread_start+0x30
08 0000fffb`c480e990 00000000`00000000     0xffffffff`ffffffff
```

```
0:002> ub 00000000`00403254
App10!proc+0x4c:
00000000`00403234 ldr          x0,[x0,x1 lsl #3]
00000000`00403238 cmp          x0,xzr
00000000`0040323c beq          App10!proc+0x7c (00000000`00403264)
00000000`00403240 adrp         x0,App10!main_arena+0x878 (00000000`004d1000)
00000000`00403244 add          x0,x0,#0x668
00000000`00403248 ldrsw        x1,[fp,#0x1C]
00000000`0040324c ldr          x0,[x0,x1 lsl #3]
00000000`00403250 bl           App10!_cfree (00000000`0041d5c8)
```

7. Check other remaining threads #3, #4, and #5, and find where they were being executed:

```
0:002> ~3k
 # Child-SP          RetAddr               Call Site
00 0000fffb`c582e780 00000000`0041a02c     App10!_lll_lock_wait_private+0x30
01 0000fffb`c582e780 00000000`00403254     App10!int_free+0x6fc
02 0000fffb`c582e800 00000000`00403318     App10!proc+0x6c
03 0000fffb`c582e820 00000000`0040332c     App10!bar_three+0xc
04 0000fffb`c582e830 00000000`00403344     App10!foo_three+0xc
05 0000fffb`c582e840 00000000`00404cc4     App10!thread_three+0x10
06 0000fffb`c582e860 00000000`00429c20     App10!start_thread+0xb4
07 0000fffb`c582e990 ffffffff`ffffffff     App10!thread_start+0x30
08 0000fffb`c582e990 00000000`00000000     0xffffffff`ffffffff
```

```
0:002> ~4k
 # Child-SP          RetAddr               Call Site
00 0000fffb`c501e780 00000000`0041a02c     App10!_lll_lock_wait_private+0x5c
01 0000fffb`c501e780 00000000`00403254     App10!int_free+0x6fc
02 0000fffb`c501e800 00000000`0040335c     App10!proc+0x6c
03 0000fffb`c501e820 00000000`00403370     App10!bar_four+0xc
04 0000fffb`c501e830 00000000`00403388     App10!foo_four+0xc
05 0000fffb`c501e840 00000000`00404cc4     App10!thread_four+0x10
06 0000fffb`c501e860 00000000`00429c20     App10!start_thread+0xb4
07 0000fffb`c501e990 ffffffff`ffffffff     App10!thread_start+0x30
08 0000fffb`c501e990 00000000`00000000     0xffffffff`ffffffff
```

```
0:002> ~5k
 # Child-SP          RetAddr               Call Site
00 0000fffb`c603e780 00000000`0041a02c     App10!_lll_lock_wait_private+0x60
01 0000fffb`c603e780 00000000`00403254     App10!int_free+0x6fc
02 0000fffb`c603e800 00000000`004032d4     App10!proc+0x6c
03 0000fffb`c603e820 00000000`004032e8     App10!bar_two+0xc
04 0000fffb`c603e830 00000000`00403300     App10!foo_two+0xc
05 0000fffb`c603e840 00000000`00404cc4     App10!thread_two+0x10
06 0000fffb`c603e860 00000000`00429c20     App10!start_thread+0xb4
07 0000fffb`c603e990 ffffffff`ffffffff     App10!thread_start+0x30
08 0000fffb`c603e990 00000000`00000000     0xffffffff`ffffffff
```

Note: We see that all waiting threads are the same in their return addresses from *free*.

8. Check thread #0 and find where it was being executed:

```
0:002> ~0s
App10!int_free+0x10c:
00000000`00419a3c f9400662 ldr          x2,[x19,#8]

0:000> k
 # Child-SP          RetAddr           Call Site
00 0000fffb`c684e780 00000000`00403254 App10!int_free+0x10c
01 0000fffb`c684e800 00000000`00403290 App10!proc+0x6c
02 0000fffb`c684e820 00000000`004032a4 App10!bar_one+0xc
03 0000fffb`c684e830 00000000`004032bc App10!foo_one+0xc
04 0000fffb`c684e840 00000000`00404cc4 App10!thread_one+0x10
05 0000fffb`c684e860 00000000`00429c20 App10!start_thread+0xb4
06 0000fffb`c684e990 ffffffff`ffffffff App10!thread_start+0x30
07 0000fffb`c684e990 00000000`00000000 0xffffffff`ffffffff
```

Note: We see that it also has the same return addresses from *free*. It means all these threads are contending for the same free function. However, thread #0 got a segmentation fault signal. Since *free* calls were done from the same *proc* function location, we suspect a double free:

```
0:000> r
 x0=0000fffb00000000  x1=0000000000000000  x2=0000000000000002  x3=0000000000000000
 x4=0000fffba8000020  x5=0000000000000002  x6=00000000004d1560  x7=000000003d64234e
 x8=0000000000000062  x9=0000fffbc0000690 x10=0000000000000068 x11=0000fffbc00008d0
x12=0000000000000007 x13=0000000000000000 x14=0000000000000004 x15=0000000000000000
x16=0000000000000001 x17=00000000004d0788 x18=0000000000000d18 x19=ffffffffffc12e20
x20=0000000000000e60 x21=0000fffba8000020 x22=0000fffba8903120 x23=0000000000000030
x24=0000fffbc684f770 x25=0000000000000000 x26=00000000004eb1c8 x27=00000000004e9000
x28=0000000000810000  fp=0000fffbc684e780  lr=000000000041a02c  sp=0000fffbc684e780
 pc=0000000000419a3c psr=80001000 N--- EL0
App10!int_free+0x10c:
00000000`00419a3c f9400662 ldr          x2,[x19,#8]

0:000> dp x19+8
ffffffff`ffc12e28  ????????`???????? ????????`????????
ffffffff`ffc12e38  ????????`???????? ????????`????????
ffffffff`ffc12e48  ????????`???????? ????????`????????
ffffffff`ffc12e58  ????????`???????? ????????`????????
ffffffff`ffc12e68  ????????`???????? ????????`????????
ffffffff`ffc12e78  ????????`???????? ????????`????????
ffffffff`ffc12e88  ????????`???????? ????????`????????
ffffffff`ffc12e98  ????????`???????? ????????`????????
```

9. Check the address that was being freed:

```
0:000> uf proc
App10!proc:
00000000`004031e8 a9be7bfd stp          fp,lr,[sp,#-0x20]!
00000000`004031ec 910003fd mov          fp,sp

App10!proc+0x8:
00000000`004031f0 9400323b bl           App10!rand (00000000`0040fadc)
00000000`004031f4 5284e201 mov          w1,#0x2710
00000000`004031f8 1ac10c02 sdiv         w2,w0,w1
```

```
00000000`004031fc 5284e201 mov          w1,#0x2710
00000000`00403200 1b017c41 mul          w1,w2,w1
00000000`00403204 4b010000 sub          w0,w0,w1
00000000`00403208 b9001fa0 str          w0,[fp,#0x1C]
00000000`0040320c 94003234 bl           App10!rand (00000000`0040fadc)
00000000`00403210 5284e201 mov          w1,#0x2710
00000000`00403214 1ac10c02 sdiv         w2,w0,w1
00000000`00403218 5284e201 mov          w1,#0x2710
00000000`0040321c 1b017c41 mul          w1,w2,w1
00000000`00403220 4b010000 sub          w0,w0,w1
00000000`00403224 b9001ba0 str          w0,[fp,#0x18]
00000000`00403228 d0000660 adrp         x0,App10!main_arena+0x878 (00000000`004d1000)
00000000`0040322c 9119a000 add          x0,x0,#0x668
00000000`00403230 b9801fa1 ldrsw        x1,[fp,#0x1C]
00000000`00403234 f8617800 ldr          x0,[x0,x1 lsl #3]
00000000`00403238 eb1f001f cmp          x0,xzr
00000000`0040323c 54000140 beq          App10!proc+0x7c (00000000`00403264)  Branch

App10!proc+0x58:
00000000`00403240 d0000660 adrp         x0,App10!main_arena+0x878 (00000000`004d1000)
00000000`00403244 9119a000 add          x0,x0,#0x668
00000000`00403248 b9801fa1 ldrsw        x1,[fp,#0x1C]
00000000`0040324c f8617800 ldr          x0,[x0,x1 lsl #3]
00000000`00403250 940068de bl           App10!_cfree (00000000`0041d5c8)
00000000`00403254 d0000660 adrp         x0,App10!main_arena+0x878 (00000000`004d1000)
00000000`00403258 9119a000 add          x0,x0,#0x668
00000000`0040325c b9801fa1 ldrsw        x1,[fp,#0x1C]
00000000`00403260 f821781f str          xzr,[x0,x1 lsl #3]

App10!proc+0x7c:
00000000`00403264 b9801ba0 ldrsw        x0,[fp,#0x18]
00000000`00403268 9400660a bl           App10!malloc (00000000`0041ca90)
00000000`0040326c aa0003e2 mov          x2,x0
00000000`00403270 d0000660 adrp         x0,App10!main_arena+0x878 (00000000`004d1000)
00000000`00403274 9119a000 add          x0,x0,#0x668
00000000`00403278 b9801fa1 ldrsw        x1,[fp,#0x1C]
00000000`0040327c f8217802 str          x2,[x0,x1 lsl #3]
00000000`00403280 17ffffdc b            App10!proc+0x8 (00000000`004031f0)  Branch
```

Note: We see that we pass some location from the index array, which starts from the address `00000000`004d1000 + 0x668`:

```
0:000> ? 00000000`004d1000 + 0x668
Evaluate expression: 5052008 = 00000000`004d1668
```

```
0:000> .frame /c 1
01 0000fffb`c684e800 00000000`00403290     App10!proc+0x6c
 x0=0000fffba8cef4a0   x1=0000000000000000   x2=0000000000000002   x3=0000000000000000
 x4=0000fffba8000020   x5=0000000000000002   x6=00000000004d1560   x7=000000003d64234e
 x8=0000000000000062   x9=0000fffbc0000690  x10=0000000000000068  x11=0000fffbc00008d0
x12=0000000000000007  x13=0000000000000000  x14=0000000000000004  x15=0000000000000000
x16=0000000000000001  x17=00000000004d0788  x18=0000000000000d18  x19=0000fffbc684f080
x20=0000000000000000  x21=00000000004d0000  x22=00000000004032ac  x23=0000000000000000
x24=0000fffbc684f770  x25=00000000341206f0  x26=00000000004eb1c8  x27=0000000000010000
x28=0000000000810000   fp=0000fffbc684e800   lr=0000000000403254   sp=0000fffbc684e800
 pc=0000000000403254  psr=80001000 N--- EL0
App10!proc+0x6c:
00000000`00403254 adrp        x0,App10!main_arena+0x878 (00000000`004d1000)
```

```
0:000> dd fp+1c L1
0000fffb`c684e81c  0000264e

0:000> dp (0000264e<<3)+00000000`004d1668 L1
00000000`004e48d8  0000fffb`a8b15610

0:000> dp 0000264e*8+00000000`004d1668 L1
00000000`004e48d8  0000fffb`a8b15610
```

10. Dump the first 100 elements of the identified array:

```
0:000> dp 00000000`004d1668 L100
00000000`004d1668  0000fffb`a93b4e00 0000fffb`a90c1af0
00000000`004d1678  0000fffb`aa939280 0000fffb`aae8e2d0
00000000`004d1688  0000fffb`a98aa350 0000fffb`a8fd48b0
00000000`004d1698  0000fffb`a912d220 0000fffb`aa420ad0
00000000`004d16a8  0000fffb`aae7f930 0000fffb`a87c2b20
00000000`004d16b8  0000fffb`a83d3e10 00000000`00000000
00000000`004d16c8  0000fffb`aa65da80 0000fffb`aa869280
00000000`004d16d8  0000fffb`aa5c5f80 0000fffb`a8459f40
00000000`004d16e8  0000fffb`a81e4e30 0000fffb`a810f820
00000000`004d16f8  0000fffb`a9e857a0 0000fffb`a9deacf0
00000000`004d1708  0000fffb`a8933250 0000fffb`a8306260
00000000`004d1718  0000fffb`aa9303e0 0000fffb`a85ef530
00000000`004d1728  0000fffb`aaefa020 0000fffb`a8b6f670
00000000`004d1738  0000fffb`aadd5320 0000fffb`aaab54f0
00000000`004d1748  0000fffb`a8ce7fc0 0000fffb`a8087370
00000000`004d1758  0000fffb`a823ab80 0000fffb`a8927f20
00000000`004d1768  0000fffb`a9bc66d0 0000fffb`aa81d670
00000000`004d1778  0000fffb`a8478270 0000fffb`a92edf60
00000000`004d1788  0000fffb`a8065330 0000fffb`a893faa0
00000000`004d1798  0000fffb`aa0fe190 0000fffb`a8fc1450
00000000`004d17a8  0000fffb`a84c8f20 0000fffb`a8b79280
00000000`004d17b8  0000fffb`aabe7040 0000fffb`a83d9110
00000000`004d17c8  0000fffb`a97dade0 0000fffb`a8fd0e80
00000000`004d17d8  0000fffb`aa20dc20 0000fffb`aa56f580
00000000`004d17e8  0000fffb`a9724a30 0000fffb`aa241aa0
00000000`004d17f8  0000fffb`a8049e50 0000fffb`a82f3e40
00000000`004d1808  0000fffb`a93b3cf0 0000fffb`aa9978d0
00000000`004d1818  0000fffb`a9223440 00000000`00000000
00000000`004d1828  0000fffb`a9cffd00 0000fffb`a9e323a0
00000000`004d1838  0000fffb`a9230070 0000fffb`a8cfc710
00000000`004d1848  0000fffb`a9e48810 0000fffb`a8474ea0
00000000`004d1858  0000fffb`a9557cf0 0000fffb`a86617f0
00000000`004d1868  0000fffb`a8737030 0000fffb`a92da510
00000000`004d1878  00000000`00000000 0000fffb`aa1977d0
00000000`004d1888  0000fffb`a9287350 0000fffb`a8071640
00000000`004d1898  0000fffb`a9d15240 0000fffb`a8ec3f00
00000000`004d18a8  0000fffb`a88273b0 0000fffb`bc00d7b0
[...]
```

12. We close logging before exiting WinDbg:

```
0:000> .logclose
Closing open log file 'C:\ALCDA2\A64\App10\App10-WinDbg.log
```

Exercise A11

- **Goal:** Learn how to identify synchronization wait chains, deadlocks, hidden and handled exceptions
- **Patterns:** Wait Chain (Mutex Objects); Deadlock (Mutex Objects, User Space); Disassembly Hole (WinDbg)
- \ALCDA-Dumps\Exercise-A11-x64-GDB.pdf
- \ALCDA-Dumps\Exercise-A11-A64-GDB.pdf
- \ALCDA-Dumps\Exercise-A11-A64-WinDbg.pdf
- \ALCDA-Dumps\Exercise-A11-x64-WinDbg.pdf

Exercise A11 (x64, GDB)

Goal: Learn how to identify synchronization wait chains, deadlocks, hidden and handled exceptions.

Patterns: Wait Chain (Mutex Objects); Deadlock (Mutex Objects).

1. Load the *App11.core.594* dump file and *App11* executable from the x64/App11 directory:

```
~/ALCDA2/x64/App11$ gdb -c App11.core.594 -se App11
GNU gdb (Debian 8.2.1-2+b3) 8.2.1
Copyright (C) 2018 Free Software Foundation, Inc.
License GPLv3+: GNU GPL version 3 or later <http://gnu.org/licenses/gpl.html>
This is free software: you are free to change and redistribute it.
There is NO WARRANTY, to the extent permitted by law.
Type "show copying" and "show warranty" for details.
This GDB was configured as "x86_64-linux-gnu".
Type "show configuration" for configuration details.
For bug reporting instructions, please see:
<http://www.gnu.org/software/gdb/bugs/>.
Find the GDB manual and other documentation resources online at:
    <http://www.gnu.org/software/gdb/documentation/>.

For help, type "help".
Type "apropos word" to search for commands related to "word"...
Reading symbols from App11...done.
[New LWP 594]
[New LWP 595]
[New LWP 596]
[New LWP 597]
[New LWP 598]
[New LWP 599]
[Thread debugging using libthread_db enabled]
Using host libthread_db library "/lib/x86_64-linux-gnu/libthread_db.so.1".
Core was generated by `./App11'.
#0  0x0000000000452970 in nanosleep ()
[Current thread is 1 (Thread 0x13b9880 (LWP 594))]
```

2. Set logging to a file in case of lengthy output from some commands:

```
(gdb) set logging on App11.log
Copying output to App11.log.
```

3. List all thread stack traces and identify possible wait chains and deadlock:

```
(gdb) thread apply all bt

Thread 6 (Thread 0x7fa8cb7fe700 (LWP 599)):
#0  0x0000000000452970 in nanosleep ()
#1  0x00000000004528fa in sleep ()
#2  0x0000000000402024 in bar_five() ()
#3  0x0000000000402030 in foo_five() ()
#4  0x0000000000402044 in thread_five(void*) ()
#5  0x00000000004137f3 in start_thread (arg=<optimized out>) at pthread_create.c:486
#6  0x000000000045512f in clone ()
```

```
Thread 5 (Thread 0x7fa8cbfff700 (LWP 598)):
#0  __lll_lock_wait () at ../sysdeps/unix/sysv/linux/x86_64/lowlevellock.S:103
#1  0x0000000000415294 in __pthread_mutex_lock (mutex=0x4d34a0 <mutexA>) at
../nptl/pthread_mutex_lock.c:80
#2  0x0000000000401f27 in procB() () at pthread_create.c:688
#3  0x0000000000401fef in bar_four() () at pthread_create.c:688
#4  0x0000000000401ffb in foo_four() () at pthread_create.c:688
#5  0x000000000040200f in thread_four(void*) () at pthread_create.c:688
#6  0x00000000004137f3 in start_thread (arg=<optimized out>) at pthread_create.c:486
#7  0x000000000045512f in clone ()

Thread 4 (Thread 0x7fa8d086d700 (LWP 597)):
#0  0x0000000000452970 in nanosleep ()
#1  0x00000000004528fa in sleep ()
#2  0x0000000000401fbf in bar_three() () at pthread_create.c:688
#3  0x0000000000401fcb in foo_three() () at pthread_create.c:688
#4  0x0000000000401fdf in thread_three(void*) () at pthread_create.c:688
#5  0x00000000004137f3 in start_thread (arg=<optimized out>) at pthread_create.c:486
#6  0x000000000045512f in clone ()

Thread 3 (Thread 0x7fa8d106e700 (LWP 596)):
#0  __lll_lock_wait () at ../sysdeps/unix/sysv/linux/x86_64/lowlevellock.S:103
#1  0x0000000000415294 in __pthread_mutex_lock (mutex=0x4d34e0 <mutex>) at
../nptl/pthread_mutex_lock.c:80
#2  0x0000000000401eec in procA() () at pthread_create.c:688
#3  0x0000000000401f8a in bar_two() () at pthread_create.c:688
#4  0x0000000000401f96 in foo_two() () at pthread_create.c:688
#5  0x0000000000401faa in thread_two(void*) () at pthread_create.c:688
#6  0x00000000004137f3 in start_thread (arg=<optimized out>) at pthread_create.c:486
#7  0x000000000045512f in clone ()

Thread 2 (Thread 0x7fa8d186f700 (LWP 595)):
#0  0x0000000000452970 in nanosleep ()
#1  0x00000000004528fa in sleep ()
#2  0x0000000000401f5a in bar_one() () at pthread_create.c:688
#3  0x0000000000401f66 in foo_one() () at pthread_create.c:688
#4  0x0000000000401f7a in thread_one(void*) () at pthread_create.c:688
#5  0x00000000004137f3 in start_thread (arg=<optimized out>) at pthread_create.c:486
#6  0x000000000045512f in clone ()

Thread 1 (Thread 0x13b9880 (LWP 594)):
#0  0x0000000000452970 in nanosleep ()
#1  0x00000000004528fa in sleep ()
#2  0x0000000000402121 in main () at pthread_create.c:688
```

4. Check **thread #5** and its waiting code:

```
(gdb) thread 5
[Switching to thread 5 (Thread 0x7fa8cbfff700 (LWP 598))]
#0  __lll_lock_wait () at ../sysdeps/unix/sysv/linux/x86_64/lowlevellock.S:103
103     ../sysdeps/unix/sysv/linux/x86_64/lowlevellock.S: No such file or directory.

(gdb) bt
#0  __lll_lock_wait () at ../sysdeps/unix/sysv/linux/x86_64/lowlevellock.S:103
#1  0x0000000000415294 in __pthread_mutex_lock (mutex=0x4d34a0 <mutexA>) at
../nptl/pthread_mutex_lock.c:80
#2  0x0000000000401f27 in procB() () at pthread_create.c:688
#3  0x0000000000401fef in bar_four() () at pthread_create.c:688
#4  0x0000000000401ffb in foo_four() () at pthread_create.c:688
#5  0x000000000040200f in thread_four(void*) () at pthread_create.c:688
```

```
#6  0x00000000004137f3 in start_thread (arg=<optimized out>) at pthread_create.c:486
#7  0x000000000045512f in clone ()
```

```
(gdb) disassemble procB
Dump of assembler code for function _Z5procBv:
   0x0000000000401f0b <+0>:     push   %rbp
   0x0000000000401f0c <+1>:     mov    %rsp,%rbp
   0x0000000000401f0f <+4>:     lea    0xd15ca(%rip),%rdi        # 0x4d34e0 <mutexB>
   0x0000000000401f16 <+11>:    callq  0x415240 <__pthread_mutex_lock>
   0x0000000000401f1b <+16>:    lea    0xd157e(%rip),%rdi        # 0x4d34a0 <mutexA>
   0x0000000000401f22 <+23>:    callq  0x415240 <__pthread_mutex_lock>
   0x0000000000401f27 <+28>:    mov    $0x1e,%edi
   0x0000000000401f2c <+33>:    callq  0x4528c0 <sleep>
   0x0000000000401f31 <+38>:    lea    0xd1568(%rip),%rdi        # 0x4d34a0 <mutexA>
   0x0000000000401f38 <+45>:    callq  0x4160b0 <__pthread_mutex_unlock>
   0x0000000000401f3d <+50>:    lea    0xd159c(%rip),%rdi        # 0x4d34e0 <mutexB>
   0x0000000000401f44 <+57>:    callq  0x4160b0 <__pthread_mutex_unlock>
   0x0000000000401f49 <+62>:    nop
   0x0000000000401f4a <+63>:    pop    %rbp
   0x0000000000401f4b <+64>:    retq
End of assembler dump.
```

Note: We see thread #5 owns mutex 0x4d34e0 but is waiting for mutex 0x4d34a0.

5. Check **thread #3** and its waiting code:

```
(gdb) thread 3
[Switching to thread 3 (Thread 0x7fa8d106e700 (LWP 596))]
#0  __lll_lock_wait () at ../sysdeps/unix/sysv/linux/x86_64/lowlevellock.S:103
103     ../sysdeps/unix/sysv/linux/x86_64/lowlevellock.S: No such file or directory.
```

```
(gdb) bt
#0  __lll_lock_wait () at ../sysdeps/unix/sysv/linux/x86_64/lowlevellock.S:103
#1  0x0000000000415294 in __pthread_mutex_lock (mutex=0x4d34e0 <mutex>) at
../nptl/pthread_mutex_lock.c:80
#2  0x0000000000401eec in procA() ()
#3  0x0000000000401f8a in bar_two() ()
#4  0x0000000000401f96 in foo_two() ()
#5  0x0000000000401faa in thread_two(void*) ()
#6  0x00000000004137f3 in start_thread (arg=<optimized out>) at pthread_create.c:486
#7  0x000000000045512f in clone ()
```

```
(gdb) disassemble procA
Dump of assembler code for function _Z5procAv:
   0x0000000000401eb5 <+0>:     push   %rbp
   0x0000000000401eb6 <+1>:     mov    %rsp,%rbp
   0x0000000000401eb9 <+4>:     lea    0xd15e0(%rip),%rdi        # 0x4d34a0 <mutexA>
   0x0000000000401ec0 <+11>:    callq  0x415240 <__pthread_mutex_lock>
   0x0000000000401ec5 <+16>:    callq  0x401e8d <_Z5procCv>
   0x0000000000401eca <+21>:    lea    0xd15cf(%rip),%rdi        # 0x4d34a0 <mutexA>
   0x0000000000401ed1 <+28>:    callq  0x4160b0 <__pthread_mutex_unlock>
   0x0000000000401ed6 <+33>:    mov    $0x14,%edi
   0x0000000000401edb <+38>:    callq  0x4528c0 <sleep>
   0x0000000000401ee0 <+43>:    lea    0xd15f9(%rip),%rdi        # 0x4d34e0 <mutexB>
   0x0000000000401ee7 <+50>:    callq  0x415240 <__pthread_mutex_lock>
   0x0000000000401eec <+55>:    lea    0xd15ed(%rip),%rdi        # 0x4d34e0 <mutexB>
   0x0000000000401ef3 <+62>:    callq  0x4160b0 <__pthread_mutex_unlock>
   0x0000000000401ef8 <+67>:    jmp    0x401f09 <_Z5procAv+84>
   0x0000000000401efa <+69>:    mov    %rax,%rdi
   0x0000000000401efd <+72>:    callq  0x402ec0 <__cxa_begin_catch>
```

```
   0x0000000000401f02 <+77>:    callq  0x402f30 <__cxa_end_catch>
   0x0000000000401f07 <+82>:    jmp    0x401ed6 <_Z5procAv+33>
   0x0000000000401f09 <+84>:    pop    %rbp
   0x0000000000401f0a <+85>:    retq
End of assembler dump.
```

Note: We see that **thread #3** is waiting for **0x4d34e0** mutex but shouldn't own **0x4d34a0** mutex because it should have unlocked it unless something happened in **procC**. We also notice the *catch* exception processing which transfers execution for the block of code waiting for mutex **0x4d34e0.**

Note: We see C++ function names are mangled, so we can demangle them if necessary (however, it may affect some variable names like **mutexB**):

```
(gdb) set print asm-demangle on

(gdb) disassemble procA
Dump of assembler code for function _Z5procAv:
   0x0000000000401eb5 <+0>:     push   %rbp
   0x0000000000401eb6 <+1>:     mov    %rsp,%rbp
   0x0000000000401eb9 <+4>:     lea    0xd15e0(%rip),%rdi        # 0x4d34a0 <mutexA>
   0x0000000000401ec0 <+11>:    callq  0x415240 <__pthread_mutex_lock>
   0x0000000000401ec5 <+16>:    callq  0x401e8d <procC()>
   0x0000000000401eca <+21>:    lea    0xd15cf(%rip),%rdi        # 0x4d34a0 <mutexA>
   0x0000000000401ed1 <+28>:    callq  0x4160b0 <__pthread_mutex_unlock>
   0x0000000000401ed6 <+33>:    mov    $0x14,%edi
   0x0000000000401edb <+38>:    callq  0x4528c0 <sleep>
   0x0000000000401ee0 <+43>:    lea    0xd15f9(%rip),%rdi        # 0x4d34e0 <mutex>
   0x0000000000401ee7 <+50>:    callq  0x415240 <__pthread_mutex_lock>
   0x0000000000401eec <+55>:    lea    0xd15ed(%rip),%rdi        # 0x4d34e0 <mutex>
   0x0000000000401ef3 <+62>:    callq  0x4160b0 <__pthread_mutex_unlock>
   0x0000000000401ef8 <+67>:    jmp    0x401f09 <procA()+84>
   0x0000000000401efa <+69>:    mov    %rax,%rdi
   0x0000000000401efd <+72>:    callq  0x402ec0 <__cxa_begin_catch>
   0x0000000000401f02 <+77>:    callq  0x402f30 <__cxa_end_catch>
   0x0000000000401f07 <+82>:    jmp    0x401ed6 <procA()+33>
   0x0000000000401f09 <+84>:    pop    %rbp
   0x0000000000401f0a <+85>:    retq
End of assembler dump.
```

9. Disassemble *procC* code:

```
(gdb) disassemble procC
Dump of assembler code for function _Z5procCv:
   0x0000000000401e8d <+0>:     push   %rbp
   0x0000000000401e8e <+1>:     mov    %rsp,%rbp
   0x0000000000401e91 <+4>:     mov    $0x4,%edi
   0x0000000000401e96 <+9>:     callq  0x403420 <__cxa_allocate_exception>
   0x0000000000401e9b <+14>:    movl   $0x0,(%rax)
   0x0000000000401ea1 <+20>:    mov    $0x0,%edx
   0x0000000000401ea6 <+25>:    lea    0xcde33(%rip),%rsi        # 0x4cfce0 <typeinfo for int>
   0x0000000000401ead <+32>:    mov    %rax,%rdi
   0x0000000000401eb0 <+35>:    callq  0x402200 <__cxa_throw>
End of assembler dump.
```

Note: We see that code throws an exception, so perhaps it was caught in the caller *procA,* and the mutex *unlock* wasn't called, thus causing a deadlock.

10. Check if there was any exception processing:

```
(gdb) x/300a $rsp-2400
0x7fa8d106d368: 0x0     0x0
0x7fa8d106d378: 0x0     0x0
0x7fa8d106d388: 0x0     0x0
0x7fa8d106d398: 0x0     0x0
0x7fa8d106d3a8: 0x0     0x0
0x7fa8d106d3b8: 0x0     0x0
0x7fa8d106d3c8: 0x0     0x0
0x7fa8d106d3d8: 0x0     0x0
0x7fa8d106d3e8: 0x0     0x0
0x7fa8d106d3f8: 0x0     0x0
0x7fa8d106d408: 0x0     0x0
0x7fa8d106d418: 0x0     0x0
0x7fa8d106d428: 0x0     0x0
0x7fa8d106d438: 0x0     0x0
0x7fa8d106d448: 0x0     0x0
0x7fa8d106d458: 0x0     0x0
0x7fa8d106d468: 0x0     0x0
0x7fa8d106d478: 0x0     0x0
0x7fa8d106d488: 0x0     0x0
0x7fa8d106d498: 0x0     0x0
0x7fa8d106d4a8: 0x0     0x0
0x7fa8d106d4b8: 0x0     0x0
0x7fa8d106d4c8: 0x0     0x0
0x7fa8d106d4d8: 0x0     0x0
0x7fa8d106d4e8: 0x0     0x0
0x7fa8d106d4f8: 0x0     0x0
0x7fa8d106d508: 0x0     0x0
0x7fa8d106d518: 0x0     0x0
0x7fa8d106d528: 0x0     0x0
0x7fa8d106d538: 0x0     0x0
0x7fa8d106d548: 0x0     0x0
0x7fa8d106d558: 0x410d1d <fde_single_encoding_compare+93>       0x401850
<_GLOBAL__sub_I_eh_alloc.cc>
0x7fa8d106d568: 0x401840 <fini> 0x7fa8cc003370
0x7fa8d106d578: 0x1     0x7fa8cc003370
0x7fa8d106d588: 0x2     0x410cc0 <fde_single_encoding_compare>
0x7fa8d106d598: 0x410970 <frame_downheap+112>   0x7fa8cc001c98
0x7fa8d106d5a8: 0x4d3460 <object>       0x7fa8cc003380
0x7fa8d106d5b8: 0x9e    0xce0000027b
0x7fa8d106d5c8: 0x0     0x7fa8cc003370
0x7fa8d106d5d8: 0x4d3460 <object>       0x1dcb0
0x7fa8d106d5e8: 0x4cb   0x7fa8cc003360
0x7fa8d106d5f8: 0x410a51 <frame_heapsort+145>   0x27a8
0x7fa8d106d608: 0xc9abaa553021fb00      0x401834 <read_encoded_value_with_base.cold>
0x7fa8d106d618: 0x410cc0 <fde_single_encoding_compare>  0x4d3460 <object>
0x7fa8d106d628: 0x27    0x7fa8cc000bb0
0x7fa8d106d638: 0x41007d <_Unwind_RaiseException+61>    0x4c9768
0x7fa8d106d648: 0x411b56 <search_object+854>    0x0
0x7fa8d106d658: 0x7fa8d106d698  0x7fa8d106d6a0
0x7fa8d106d668: 0x7fa80000001b  0x0
0x7fa8d106d678: 0x7fa80000000b  0x7fa8d106dcf8
0x7fa8d106d688: 0x7fa8d106dd00  0x0
0x7fa8d106d698: 0x401eb5 <procA()>      0x56
0x7fa8d106d6a8: 0x0     0x7fa8d106dd48
0x7fa8d106d6b8: 0x4d3460 <object>       0x7fa8d106d7d0
0x7fa8d106d6c8: 0x7fa8d106db28  0x4160c0 <__pthread_key_create>
0x7fa8d106d6d8: 0x402838 <__gxx_personality_v0+184>     0x401ec9 <procA()+20>
```

```
0x7fa8d106d6e8: 0x7fa8cc000b80  0x601401eb5
--Type <RET> for more, q to quit, c to continue without paging--
0x7fa8d106d6f8: 0x0     0x4caa38
0x7fa8d106d708: 0x7fa8d106d701  0x7fa8d106dd60
0x7fa8d106d718: 0x401eb5 <procA()>      0x0
0x7fa8d106d728: 0x4bcdd1        0x4bcdd1
0x7fa8d106d738: 0xd106da80      0x0
0x7fa8d106d748: 0x1b    0x7fa8d106d7d0
0x7fa8d106d758: 0x40e940 <uw_frame_state_for+800>       0x0
0x7fa8d106d768: 0x9b00000000    0x4bcdb5
0x7fa8d106d778: 0x7fa8d106d788  0x7fa8d106d7d0
0x7fa8d106d788: 0x4caa38        0x7fa8d106d7d0
0x7fa8d106d798: 0x7fa8d106da80  0x4
0x7fa8d106d7a8: 0x7fa8cc000b80  0x7fa8d106d7d0
0x7fa8d106d7b8: 0x3     0x7fa8d106db70
0x7fa8d106d7c8: 0x40fa6b <_Unwind_RaiseException_Phase2+75>     0x0
0x7fa8d106d7d8: 0x0     0x0
0x7fa8d106d7e8: 0x0     0x0
0x7fa8d106d7f8: 0x0     0x0
0x7fa8d106d808: 0x0     0x0
0x7fa8d106d818: 0x0     0x0
0x7fa8d106d828: 0x0     0xfffffffffffffff0
0x7fa8d106d838: 0x1     0x0
0x7fa8d106d848: 0x0     0x0
0x7fa8d106d858: 0x0     0x0
0x7fa8d106d868: 0x0     0x0
0x7fa8d106d878: 0x0     0x0
0x7fa8d106d888: 0x0     0x0
0x7fa8d106d898: 0x0     0x0
0x7fa8d106d8a8: 0x0     0x0
0x7fa8d106d8b8: 0x0     0x0
0x7fa8d106d8c8: 0x0     0xfffffffffffffff8
0x7fa8d106d8d8: 0x1     0x0
0x7fa8d106d8e8: 0x0     0x0
0x7fa8d106d8f8: 0x10    0x6
0x7fa8d106d908: 0x0     0x1
0x7fa8d106d918: 0x401f0a <procA()+85>   0x402780 <__gxx_personality_v0>
0x7fa8d106d928: 0xfffffffffffffff8      0x1
0x7fa8d106d938: 0x10    0x11b1b
0x7fa8d106d948: 0x0     0x7fa8cc000b80
0x7fa8d106d958: 0x7fa8d106da80  0x7fa8d106dd30
0x7fa8d106d968: 0x7fa8d106db70  0x7fa8cc000b80
0x7fa8d106d978: 0x7fa8d106dd70  0x0
0x7fa8d106d988: 0x41031a <_Unwind_RaiseException+730>   0x7fa8d106dcf8
0x7fa8d106d998: 0x7fa8d106dd00  0x0
0x7fa8d106d9a8: 0x7fa8d106dd08  0x0
0x7fa8d106d9b8: 0x0     0x7fa8d106dd30
0x7fa8d106d9c8: 0x0     0x0
0x7fa8d106d9d8: 0x0     0x0
0x7fa8d106d9e8: 0x0     0x7fa8d106dd10
0x7fa8d106d9f8: 0x7fa8d106dd18  0x7fa8d106dd20
0x7fa8d106da08: 0x7fa8d106dd28  0x7fa8d106dd38
0x7fa8d106da18: 0x0     0x7fa8d106dd40
0x7fa8d106da28: 0x402237 <__cxa_throw+55>       0x0
0x7fa8d106da38: 0x0     0x0
0x7fa8d106da48: 0x410040 <_Unwind_RaiseException>       0x4000000000000000
0x7fa8d106da58: 0x0     0x0
0x7fa8d106da68: 0x0     0x0
0x7fa8d106da78: 0x0     0x7fa8d106dcf8
--Type <RET> for more, q to quit, c to continue without paging--
```

```
0x7fa8d106da88: 0x7fa8d106dd00  0x0
0x7fa8d106da98: 0x7fa8d106dd40  0x0
0x7fa8d106daa8: 0x0     0x7fa8d106dd60
0x7fa8d106dab8: 0x7fa8d106d978  0x0
0x7fa8d106dac8: 0x0     0x0
0x7fa8d106dad8: 0x0     0x7fa8d106dd50
0x7fa8d106dae8: 0x7fa8d106dd18  0x7fa8d106dd20
0x7fa8d106daf8: 0x7fa8d106dd28  0x7fa8d106dd68
0x7fa8d106db08: 0x0     0x7fa8d106dd70
0x7fa8d106db18: 0x401efa <procA()+69>   0x4caa38
0x7fa8d106db28: 0x0     0x0
0x7fa8d106db38: 0x401eb5 <procA()>      0x4000000000000000
0x7fa8d106db48: 0x0     0x0
0x7fa8d106db58: 0x0     0x0
0x7fa8d106db68: 0x0     0x3
0x7fa8d106db78: 0x0     0x0
0x7fa8d106db88: 0x0     0x0
0x7fa8d106db98: 0x0     0x0
0x7fa8d106dba8: 0x0     0x0
0x7fa8d106dbb8: 0x0     0x0
0x7fa8d106dbc8: 0x0     0xfffffffffffffff0
0x7fa8d106dbd8: 0x1     0x0
0x7fa8d106dbe8: 0x0     0x0
0x7fa8d106dbf8: 0x0     0x0
0x7fa8d106dc08: 0x0     0x0
0x7fa8d106dc18: 0x0     0x0
0x7fa8d106dc28: 0x0     0x0
0x7fa8d106dc38: 0x0     0x0
0x7fa8d106dc48: 0x0     0x0
0x7fa8d106dc58: 0x0     0x0
0x7fa8d106dc68: 0x0     0xfffffffffffffff8
0x7fa8d106dc78: 0x1     0x0
0x7fa8d106dc88: 0x0     0x0
0x7fa8d106dc98: 0x10    0x6
0x7fa8d106dca8: 0x0     0x1
0x7fa8d106dcb8: 0x401f0a <procA()+85>   0x402780 <__gxx_personality_v0>
```

Note: We see a reference 0x401efa <procA()+69> from the exception processing block in *procA* and also **0x402237 <__cxa_throw+55>**. We check whether the symbolic information we found is not coincidental:

```
(gdb) disassemble __cxa_throw
Dump of assembler code for function __cxa_throw:
   0x0000000000402200 <+0>:     push   %r12
   0x0000000000402202 <+2>:     mov    %rdx,%r12
   0x0000000000402205 <+5>:     push   %rbp
   0x0000000000402206 <+6>:     mov    %rsi,%rbp
   0x0000000000402209 <+9>:     push   %rbx
   0x000000000040220a <+10>:    mov    %rdi,%rbx
   0x000000000040220d <+13>:    nop
   0x000000000040220e <+14>:    callq  0x402d60 <__cxa_get_globals>
   0x0000000000402213 <+19>:    mov    %r12,%rdx
   0x0000000000402216 <+22>:    mov    %rbp,%rsi
   0x0000000000402219 <+25>:    mov    %rbx,%rdi
   0x000000000040221c <+28>:    addl   $0x1,0x8(%rax)
   0x0000000000402220 <+32>:    callq  0x4021b0 <__cxa_init_primary_exception>
   0x0000000000402225 <+37>:    movl   $0x1,(%rax)
   0x000000000040222b <+43>:    lea    0x60(%rax),%rbx
   0x000000000040222f <+47>:    mov    %rbx,%rdi
   0x0000000000402232 <+50>:    callq  0x410040 <_Unwind_RaiseException>
   0x0000000000402237 <+55>:    mov    %rbx,%rdi
```

```
   0x000000000040223a <+58>:    callq  0x402ec0 <__cxa_begin_catch>
   0x000000000040223f <+63>:    callq  0x4022f0 <std::terminate()>
End of assembler dump.
```

11. Since mutexes have owners, we can check their ownership instead of disassembly:

```
(gdb) print *(pthread_mutex_t *)&mutexA
$2 = {__data = {__lock = 2, __count = 0, __owner = 596, __nusers = 1, __kind = 0, __spins = 0,
__elision = 0, __list = {__prev = 0x0, __next = 0x0}},
  __size = "\002\000\000\000\000\000\000\000T\002\000\000\001", '\000' <repeats 26 times>,
__align = 2}

(gdb) print *(pthread_mutex_t *)&mutexB
$3 = {__data = {__lock = 2, __count = 0, __owner = 598, __nusers = 1, __kind = 0, __spins = 0,
__elision = 0, __list = {__prev = 0x0, __next = 0x0}},
  __size = "\002\000\000\000\000\000\000\000V\002\000\000\001", '\000' <repeats 26 times>,
__align = 2}
```

Note: We see their respective thread owners (LWP numbers).

```
(gdb) thread 5
[Switching to thread 5 (Thread 0x7fa8cbfff700 (LWP 598))]
#0  __lll_lock_wait () at ../sysdeps/unix/sysv/linux/x86_64/lowlevellock.S:103
103     in ../sysdeps/unix/sysv/linux/x86_64/lowlevellock.S

(gdb) bt
#0  __lll_lock_wait () at ../sysdeps/unix/sysv/linux/x86_64/lowlevellock.S:103
#1  0x0000000000415294 in __pthread_mutex_lock (mutex=0x4d34a0 <mutexA>) at
../nptl/pthread_mutex_lock.c:80
#2  0x0000000000401f27 in procB() () at pthread_create.c:688
#3  0x0000000000401fef in bar_four() () at pthread_create.c:688
#4  0x0000000000401ffb in foo_four() () at pthread_create.c:688
#5  0x000000000040200f in thread_four(void*) () at pthread_create.c:688
#6  0x00000000004137f3 in start_thread (arg=<optimized out>) at pthread_create.c:486
#7  0x000000000045512f in clone ()

(gdb) thread 3
[Switching to thread 3 (Thread 0x7fa8d106e700 (LWP 596))]
#0  __lll_lock_wait () at ../sysdeps/unix/sysv/linux/x86_64/lowlevellock.S:103
103     in ../sysdeps/unix/sysv/linux/x86_64/lowlevellock.S

(gdb) bt
#0  __lll_lock_wait () at ../sysdeps/unix/sysv/linux/x86_64/lowlevellock.S:103
#1  0x0000000000415294 in __pthread_mutex_lock (mutex=0x4d34e0 <mutex>) at
../nptl/pthread_mutex_lock.c:80
#2  0x0000000000401eec in procA() () at pthread_create.c:688
#3  0x0000000000401f8a in bar_two() () at pthread_create.c:688
#4  0x0000000000401f96 in foo_two() () at pthread_create.c:688
#5  0x0000000000401faa in thread_two(void*) () at pthread_create.c:688
#6  0x00000000004137f3 in start_thread (arg=<optimized out>) at pthread_create.c:486
#7  0x000000000045512f in clone ()
```

Note: We see the **mutex** name in the backtrace instead of **mutexB,** which can be discovered by disassembly after turning demangling off:

```
(gdb) set print asm-demangle off
```

```
(gdb) disass 0x0000000000401eec
Dump of assembler code for function _Z5procAv:
   0x0000000000401eb5 <+0>:     push   %rbp
   0x0000000000401eb6 <+1>:     mov    %rsp,%rbp
   0x0000000000401eb9 <+4>:     lea    0xd15e0(%rip),%rdi        # 0x4d34a0 <mutexA>
   0x0000000000401ec0 <+11>:    callq  0x415240 <__pthread_mutex_lock>
   0x0000000000401ec5 <+16>:    callq  0x401e8d <_Z5procCv>
   0x0000000000401eca <+21>:    lea    0xd15cf(%rip),%rdi        # 0x4d34a0 <mutexA>
   0x0000000000401ed1 <+28>:    callq  0x4160b0 <__pthread_mutex_unlock>
   0x0000000000401ed6 <+33>:    mov    $0x14,%edi
   0x0000000000401edb <+38>:    callq  0x4528c0 <sleep>
   0x0000000000401ee0 <+43>:    lea    0xd15f9(%rip),%rdi        # 0x4d34e0 <mutexB>
   0x0000000000401ee7 <+50>:    callq  0x415240 <__pthread_mutex_lock>
   0x0000000000401eec <+55>:    lea    0xd15ed(%rip),%rdi        # 0x4d34e0 <mutexB>
   0x0000000000401ef3 <+62>:    callq  0x4160b0 <__pthread_mutex_unlock>
   0x0000000000401ef8 <+67>:    jmp    0x401f09 <_Z5procAv+84>
   0x0000000000401efa <+69>:    mov    %rax,%rdi
   0x0000000000401efd <+72>:    callq  0x402ec0 <__cxa_begin_catch>
   0x0000000000401f02 <+77>:    callq  0x402f30 <__cxa_end_catch>
   0x0000000000401f07 <+82>:    jmp    0x401ed6 <_Z5procAv+33>
   0x0000000000401f09 <+84>:    pop    %rbp
   0x0000000000401f0a <+85>:    retq
End of assembler dump.
```

Deadlock (x64, GDB)

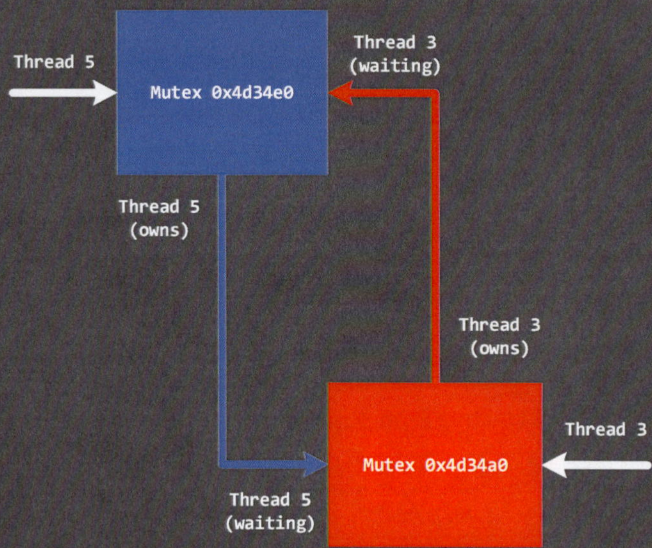

Exercise A11 (A64, GDB)

Goal: Learn how to identify synchronization wait chains, deadlocks, hidden and handled exceptions.

Patterns: Wait Chain (Mutex Objects); Deadlock (Mutex Objects).

1. Load the *App11.core.11410* dump file and *App11* executable from the A64/App11 directory:

```
~/ALCDA2/A64/App11$ gdb-multiarch -c App11.core.11410 -se App11
GNU gdb (Debian 8.2.1-2+b3) 8.2.1
Copyright (C) 2018 Free Software Foundation, Inc.
License GPLv3+: GNU GPL version 3 or later <http://gnu.org/licenses/gpl.html>
This is free software: you are free to change and redistribute it.
There is NO WARRANTY, to the extent permitted by law.
Type "show copying" and "show warranty" for details.
This GDB was configured as "x86_64-linux-gnu".
Type "show configuration" for configuration details.
For bug reporting instructions, please see:
<http://www.gnu.org/software/gdb/bugs/>.
Find the GDB manual and other documentation resources online at:
    <http://www.gnu.org/software/gdb/documentation/>.

For help, type "help".
Type "apropos word" to search for commands related to "word"...
Reading symbols from App11...(no debugging symbols found)...done.
[New LWP 11411]
[New LWP 11412]
[New LWP 11421]
[New LWP 11422]
[New LWP 11423]
[New LWP 11410]
Core was generated by `./App11'.
#0  0x000000000041ae24 in nanosleep ()
[Current thread is 1 (LWP 11411)]
```

2. Set logging to a file in case of lengthy output from some commands:

```
(gdb) set logging on App11.log
Copying output to App11.log.
```

3. List all thread stack traces and identify possible wait chains and deadlock:

```
(gdb) thread apply all bt

Thread 6 (LWP 11410):
#0  0x000000000041ae24 in nanosleep ()
#1  0x00000000004338b4 in sleep ()
#2  0x00000000004034e0 in main ()

Thread 5 (LWP 11423):
#0  0x000000000041ae24 in nanosleep ()
#1  0x00000000004338b4 in sleep ()
#2  0x00000000004033f0 in bar_five() ()
#3  0x0000000000403404 in foo_five() ()
#4  0x000000000040341c in thread_five(void*) ()
#5  0x00000000004130a4 in start_thread ()
#6  0x0000000000438760 in thread_start ()
```

```
Thread 4 (LWP 11422):
#0  0x000000000041a110 in __lll_lock_wait ()
#1  0x0000000000414ea4 in pthread_mutex_lock ()
#2  0x00000000004032a0 in procB() ()
#3  0x00000000004033a8 in bar_four() ()
#4  0x00000000004033bc in foo_four() ()
#5  0x00000000004033d4 in thread_four(void*) ()
#6  0x00000000004130a4 in start_thread ()
#7  0x0000000000438760 in thread_start ()

Thread 3 (LWP 11421):
#0  0x000000000041ae24 in nanosleep ()
#1  0x00000000004338b4 in sleep ()
#2  0x0000000000403364 in bar_three() ()
#3  0x0000000000403378 in foo_three() ()
#4  0x0000000000403390 in thread_three(void*) ()
#5  0x00000000004130a4 in start_thread ()
#6  0x0000000000438760 in thread_start ()

Thread 2 (LWP 11412):
#0  0x000000000041a110 in __lll_lock_wait ()
#1  0x0000000000414ea4 in pthread_mutex_lock ()
#2  0x000000000040325c in procA() ()
#3  0x000000000040331c in bar_two() ()
#4  0x0000000000403330 in foo_two() ()
#5  0x0000000000403348 in thread_two(void*) ()
#6  0x00000000004130a4 in start_thread ()
#7  0x0000000000438760 in thread_start ()

Thread 1 (LWP 11411):
#0  0x000000000041ae24 in nanosleep ()
#1  0x00000000004338b4 in sleep ()
#2  0x00000000004032d8 in bar_one() ()
#3  0x00000000004032ec in foo_one() ()
--Type <RET> for more, q to quit, c to continue without paging--
#4  0x0000000000403304 in thread_one(void*) ()
#5  0x00000000004130a4 in start_thread ()
#6  0x0000000000438760 in thread_start ()
```

4. Check **thread #4** and its waiting code:

```
(gdb) thread 4
[Switching to thread 4 (LWP 11422)]
#0  0x000000000041a110 in __lll_lock_wait ()

(gdb) bt
#0  0x000000000041a110 in __lll_lock_wait ()
#1  0x0000000000414ea4 in pthread_mutex_lock ()
#2  0x00000000004032a0 in procB() ()
#3  0x00000000004033a8 in bar_four() ()
#4  0x00000000004033bc in foo_four() ()
#5  0x00000000004033d4 in thread_four(void*) ()
#6  0x00000000004130a4 in start_thread ()
#7  0x0000000000438760 in thread_start ()
```

```
(gdb) disassemble procB
Dump of assembler code for function _Z5procBv:
   0x0000000000403280 <+0>:     stp     x29, x30, [sp, #-16]!
   0x0000000000403284 <+4>:     mov     x29, sp
   0x0000000000403288 <+8>:     adrp    x0, 0x4d1000 <main_arena+2128>
   0x000000000040328c <+12>:    add     x0, x0, #0x608
   0x0000000000403290 <+16>:    bl      0x414dbc <pthread_mutex_lock>
   0x0000000000403294 <+20>:    adrp    x0, 0x4d1000 <main_arena+2128>
   0x0000000000403298 <+24>:    add     x0, x0, #0x5d8
   0x000000000040329c <+28>:    bl      0x414dbc <pthread_mutex_lock>
   0x00000000004032a0 <+32>:    mov     w0, #0x1e                       // #30
   0x00000000004032a4 <+36>:    bl      0x4337a4 <sleep>
   0x00000000004032a8 <+40>:    adrp    x0, 0x4d1000 <main_arena+2128>
   0x00000000004032ac <+44>:    add     x0, x0, #0x5d8
   0x00000000004032b0 <+48>:    bl      0x416054 <pthread_mutex_unlock>
   0x00000000004032b4 <+52>:    adrp    x0, 0x4d1000 <main_arena+2128>
   0x00000000004032b8 <+56>:    add     x0, x0, #0x608
   0x00000000004032bc <+60>:    bl      0x416054 <pthread_mutex_unlock>
   0x00000000004032c0 <+64>:    ldp     x29, x30, [sp], #16
   0x00000000004032c4 <+68>:    ret
End of assembler dump.
```

Note: We see thread #4 owns the mutex 0x004d1000 + 0x608 but is waiting for the mutex 0x004d1000 + 0x5D8.

5. Check thread #2 and its waiting code:

```
(gdb) thread 2
[Switching to thread 2 (LWP 11412)]
#0  0x000000000041a110 in __lll_lock_wait ()

(gdb) bt
#0  0x000000000041a110 in __lll_lock_wait ()
#1  0x0000000000414ea4 in pthread_mutex_lock ()
#2  0x000000000040325c in procA() ()
#3  0x000000000040331c in bar_two() ()
#4  0x0000000000403330 in foo_two() ()
#5  0x0000000000403348 in thread_two(void*) ()
#6  0x00000000004130a4 in start_thread ()
#7  0x0000000000438760 in thread_start ()

(gdb) disassemble procA
Dump of assembler code for function _Z5procAv:
   0x0000000000403224 <+0>:     stp     x29, x30, [sp, #-16]!
   0x0000000000403228 <+4>:     mov     x29, sp
   0x000000000040322c <+8>:     adrp    x0, 0x4d1000 <main_arena+2128>
   0x0000000000403230 <+12>:    add     x0, x0, #0x5d8
   0x0000000000403234 <+16>:    bl      0x414dbc <pthread_mutex_lock>
   0x0000000000403238 <+20>:    bl      0x403200 <_Z5procCv>
   0x000000000040323c <+24>:    adrp    x0, 0x4d1000 <main_arena+2128>
   0x0000000000403240 <+28>:    add     x0, x0, #0x5d8
   0x0000000000403244 <+32>:    bl      0x416054 <pthread_mutex_unlock>
   0x0000000000403248 <+36>:    mov     w0, #0x14                       // #20
   0x000000000040324c <+40>:    bl      0x4337a4 <sleep>
   0x0000000000403250 <+44>:    adrp    x0, 0x4d1000 <main_arena+2128>
   0x0000000000403254 <+48>:    add     x0, x0, #0x608
   0x0000000000403258 <+52>:    bl      0x414dbc <pthread_mutex_lock>
   0x000000000040325c <+56>:    adrp    x0, 0x4d1000 <main_arena+2128>
   0x0000000000403260 <+60>:    add     x0, x0, #0x608
   0x0000000000403264 <+64>:    bl      0x416054 <pthread_mutex_unlock>
   0x0000000000403268 <+68>:    b       0x403278 <_Z5procAv+84>
```

```
   0x000000000040326c <+72>:    bl      0x4039b4 <__cxa_begin_catch>
   0x0000000000403270 <+76>:    bl      0x403a58 <__cxa_end_catch>
   0x0000000000403274 <+80>:    b       0x403248 <_Z5procAv+36>
   0x0000000000403278 <+84>:    ldp     x29, x30, [sp], #16
   0x000000000040327c <+88>:    ret
End of assembler dump.
```

Note: We see that **thread #2** is waiting for the `0x004d1000 + 0x608` mutex but shouldn't own the `0x004d1000 + 0x5D8` mutex because it should have unlocked it unless something happened in **procC**. We also notice the *catch* exception processing which transfers execution for the block of code waiting for the mutex `0x004d1000 + 0x608`.

Note: We see C++ function names are mangled, so we can demangle them if necessary:

```
(gdb) set print asm-demangle on
```

```
(gdb) disassemble procA
Dump of assembler code for function procA():
   0x0000000000403224 <+0>:     stp     x29, x30, [sp, #-16]!
   0x0000000000403228 <+4>:     mov     x29, sp
   0x000000000040322c <+8>:     adrp    x0, 0x4d1000 <main_arena+2128>
   0x0000000000403230 <+12>:    add     x0, x0, #0x5d8
   0x0000000000403234 <+16>:    bl      0x414dbc <pthread_mutex_lock>
   0x0000000000403238 <+20>:    bl      0x403200 <procC()>
   0x000000000040323c <+24>:    adrp    x0, 0x4d1000 <main_arena+2128>
   0x0000000000403240 <+28>:    add     x0, x0, #0x5d8
   0x0000000000403244 <+32>:    bl      0x416054 <pthread_mutex_unlock>
   0x0000000000403248 <+36>:    mov     w0, #0x14                       // #20
   0x000000000040324c <+40>:    bl      0x4337a4 <sleep>
   0x0000000000403250 <+44>:    adrp    x0, 0x4d1000 <main_arena+2128>
   0x0000000000403254 <+48>:    add     x0, x0, #0x608
   0x0000000000403258 <+52>:    bl      0x414dbc <pthread_mutex_lock>
   0x000000000040325c <+56>:    adrp    x0, 0x4d1000 <main_arena+2128>
   0x0000000000403260 <+60>:    add     x0, x0, #0x608
   0x0000000000403264 <+64>:    bl      0x416054 <pthread_mutex_unlock>
   0x0000000000403268 <+68>:    b       0x403278 <procA()+84>
   0x000000000040326c <+72>:    bl      0x4039b4 <__cxa_begin_catch>
   0x0000000000403270 <+76>:    bl      0x403a58 <__cxa_end_catch>
   0x0000000000403274 <+80>:    b       0x403248 <procA()+36>
   0x0000000000403278 <+84>:    ldp     x29, x30, [sp], #16
   0x000000000040327c <+88>:    ret
End of assembler dump.
```

6. Disassemble *procC* code:

```
(gdb) disassemble procC
Dump of assembler code for function procC():
   0x0000000000403200 <+0>:     stp     x29, x30, [sp, #-16]!
   0x0000000000403204 <+4>:     mov     x29, sp
   0x0000000000403208 <+8>:     mov     x0, #0x4                        // #4
   0x000000000040320c <+12>:    bl      0x403624 <__cxa_allocate_exception>
   0x0000000000403210 <+16>:    str     wzr, [x0]
   0x0000000000403214 <+20>:    adrp    x1, 0x4cf000 <vtable for std::exception+24>
   0x0000000000403218 <+24>:    add     x1, x1, #0x580
   0x000000000040321c <+28>:    mov     x2, #0x0                        // #0
   0x0000000000403220 <+32>:    bl      0x4047c0 <__cxa_throw>
End of assembler dump.
```

Note: We see that code throws an exception, so perhaps it was caught in the caller *procA,* and the mutex *unlock* wasn't called, thus causing a deadlock.

7. Check if there was any exception processing:

```
(gdb) x/512a $sp-0x1000
0xfffe0c03d7d0: 0x0     0x0
0xfffe0c03d7e0: 0x0     0x0
0xfffe0c03d7f0: 0x0     0x0
0xfffe0c03d800: 0x0     0x0
0xfffe0c03d810: 0x0     0x0
0xfffe0c03d820: 0x0     0x0
0xfffe0c03d830: 0x0     0x0
0xfffe0c03d840: 0x0     0x0
0xfffe0c03d850: 0x0     0x0
0xfffe0c03d860: 0x0     0x0
0xfffe0c03d870: 0x0     0x0
0xfffe0c03d880: 0x0     0x0
0xfffe0c03d890: 0x0     0x10
0xfffe0c03d8a0: 0xfffe0c03d8f0  0x40f8b0 <_Unwind_RaiseException+344>
0xfffe0c03d8b0: 0xfffe0c03dd80  0xfffe0c03e140
0xfffe0c03d8c0: 0xfffe04000b80  0xfffe0c03d9c0
0xfffe0c03d8d0: 0x0     0x1e
0xfffe0c03d8e0: 0x11b1b 0xfffe0c03e800
0xfffe0c03d8f0: 0xfffe0c03e800  0x40326c <procA()+72>
0xfffe0c03d900: 0xfffe04000b80  0x1
0xfffe0c03d910: 0x0     0x1
0xfffe0c03d920: 0xfffe0c03f070  0x0
0xfffe0c03d930: 0x4d0000        0x403338 <thread_two(void*)>
0xfffe0c03d940: 0x0     0xfffe0c03f760
0xfffe0c03d950: 0x2ba06f0       0x4e9558 <__default_pthread_attr>
0xfffe0c03d960: 0x10000 0x810000
0xfffe0c03d970: 0x0     0x0
0xfffe0c03d980: 0x0     0x0
0xfffe0c03d990: 0x0     0x0
0xfffe0c03d9a0: 0x0     0x0
0xfffe0c03d9b0: 0x0     0x40
0xfffe0c03d9c0: 0xfffe0c03d900  0xfffe0c03d908
0xfffe0c03d9d0: 0xfffe0c03d910  0xfffe0c03d918
0xfffe0c03d9e0: 0x0     0x0
0xfffe0c03d9f0: 0x0     0x0
0xfffe0c03da00: 0x0     0x0
0xfffe0c03da10: 0x0     0x0
0xfffe0c03da20: 0x0     0x0
0xfffe0c03da30: 0x0     0x0
0xfffe0c03da40: 0x0     0x0
0xfffe0c03da50: 0x0     0xfffe0c03d920
0xfffe0c03da60: 0xfffe0c03d928  0xfffe0c03d930
0xfffe0c03da70: 0xfffe0c03d938  0xfffe0c03d940
0xfffe0c03da80: 0xfffe0c03d948  0xfffe0c03d950
0xfffe0c03da90: 0xfffe0c03d958  0xfffe0c03d960
0xfffe0c03daa0: 0xfffe0c03d968  0xfffe0c03d8f0
0xfffe0c03dab0: 0xfffe0c03d8f8  0x0
0xfffe0c03dac0: 0x0     0x0
0xfffe0c03dad0: 0x0     0x0
--Type <RET> for more, q to quit, c to continue without paging--
0xfffe0c03dae0: 0x0     0x0
0xfffe0c03daf0: 0x0     0x0
0xfffe0c03db00: 0x0     0x0
0xfffe0c03db10: 0x0     0x0
```

```
0xfffe0c03db20: 0x0      0x0
0xfffe0c03db30: 0x0      0x0
0xfffe0c03db40: 0x0      0x0
0xfffe0c03db50: 0x0      0x0
0xfffe0c03db60: 0x0      0x0
0xfffe0c03db70: 0x0      0x0
0xfffe0c03db80: 0x0      0x0
0xfffe0c03db90: 0x0      0x0
0xfffe0c03dba0: 0x0      0x0
0xfffe0c03dbb0: 0x0      0x0
0xfffe0c03dbc0: 0x0      0x0
0xfffe0c03dbd0: 0x0      0x0
0xfffe0c03dbe0: 0x0      0x0
0xfffe0c03dbf0: 0x0      0x0
0xfffe0c03dc00: 0xfffe0c03d970  0xfffe0c03d978
0xfffe0c03dc10: 0xfffe0c03d980  0xfffe0c03d988
0xfffe0c03dc20: 0xfffe0c03d990  0xfffe0c03d998
0xfffe0c03dc30: 0xfffe0c03d9a0  0xfffe0c03d9a8
0xfffe0c03dc40: 0x0      0x0
0xfffe0c03dc50: 0x0      0x0
0xfffe0c03dc60: 0x0      0x0
0xfffe0c03dc70: 0x0      0x0
0xfffe0c03dc80: 0x0      0x0
0xfffe0c03dc90: 0x0      0x0
0xfffe0c03dca0: 0x0      0x0
0xfffe0c03dcb0: 0x0      0x0
0xfffe0c03dcc0: 0x0      0x0
0xfffe0c03dcd0: 0xfffe0c03e7c0  0x404850 <__cxa_throw+144>
0xfffe0c03dce0: 0x0      0x0
0xfffe0c03dcf0: 0x0      0x40f758 <_Unwind_RaiseException>
0xfffe0c03dd00: 0x4000000000000000      0x0
0xfffe0c03dd10: 0x0      0x0
0xfffe0c03dd20: 0x0      0x0
0xfffe0c03dd30: 0x0      0x0
0xfffe0c03dd40: 0x0      0x0
[...]
```

Note: We see a reference 0x40326c <procA()+72> from the exception processing block in *procA* and also **0x404850 <__cxa_throw+144>**. We check whether the symbolic information we found is not coincidental:

```
(gdb) disassemble __cxa_throw
Dump of assembler code for function __cxa_throw:
   0x00000000004047c0 <+0>:     stp     x29, x30, [sp, #-48]!
   0x00000000004047c4 <+4>:     mov     x29, sp
   0x00000000004047c8 <+8>:     stp     x19, x20, [sp, #16]
   0x00000000004047cc <+12>:    mov     x19, x0
   0x00000000004047d0 <+16>:    nop
   0x00000000004047d4 <+20>:    str     x1, [x29, #40]
   0x00000000004047d8 <+24>:    str     x2, [x29, #32]
   0x00000000004047dc <+28>:    bl      0x403c34 <__cxa_get_globals>
   0x00000000004047e0 <+32>:    ldr     w3, [x0, #8]
   0x00000000004047e4 <+36>:    ldr     x1, [x29, #40]
   0x00000000004047e8 <+40>:    ldr     x2, [x29, #32]
   0x00000000004047ec <+44>:    add     w3, w3, #0x1
   0x00000000004047f0 <+48>:    str     w3, [x0, #8]
   0x00000000004047f4 <+52>:    mov     w0, #0x1                        // #1
   0x00000000004047f8 <+56>:    stur    w0, [x19, #-128]
   0x00000000004047fc <+60>:    stur    x1, [x19, #-112]
   0x0000000000404800 <+64>:    stur    x2, [x19, #-104]
   0x0000000000404804 <+68>:    adrp    x0, 0x4cf000 <vtable for std::exception+24>
```

```
   0x0000000000404808 <+72>:    ldr     x0, [x0, #4016]
   0x000000000040480c <+76>:    mov     x1, #0x2b00                     // #11008
   0x0000000000404810 <+80>:    ldr     x0, [x0]
   0x0000000000404814 <+84>:    movk    x1, #0x432b, lsl #16
   0x0000000000404818 <+88>:    stur    x0, [x19, #-96]
   0x000000000040481c <+92>:    adrp    x0, 0x4cf000 <vtable for std::exception+24>
   0x0000000000404820 <+96>:    ldr     x0, [x0, #3960]
   0x0000000000404824 <+100>:   movk    x1, #0x5543, lsl #32
   0x0000000000404828 <+104>:   ldr     x0, [x0]
   0x000000000040482c <+108>:   movk    x1, #0x474e, lsl #48
   0x0000000000404830 <+112>:   stur    x0, [x19, #-88]
   0x0000000000404834 <+116>:   adrp    x0, 0x404000 <base_of_encoded_value(unsigned char,
_Unwind_Context*)+72>
   0x0000000000404838 <+120>:   sub     x20, x19, #0x20
   0x000000000040483c <+124>:   add     x0, x0, #0x75c
   0x0000000000404840 <+128>:   stur    x1, [x19, #-32]
   0x0000000000404844 <+132>:   stur    x0, [x19, #-24]
   0x0000000000404848 <+136>:   mov     x0, x20
   0x000000000040484c <+140>:   bl      0x40f758 <_Unwind_RaiseException>
   0x0000000000404850 <+144>:   mov     x0, x20
   0x0000000000404854 <+148>:   bl      0x4039b4 <__cxa_begin_catch>
   0x0000000000404858 <+152>:   bl      0x4046ec <std::terminate()>
End of assembler dump.
```

Note: Full debug symbols make it possible to find mutex ownership faster. We will do that in the next exercise, A12.

Deadlock (A64, GDB)

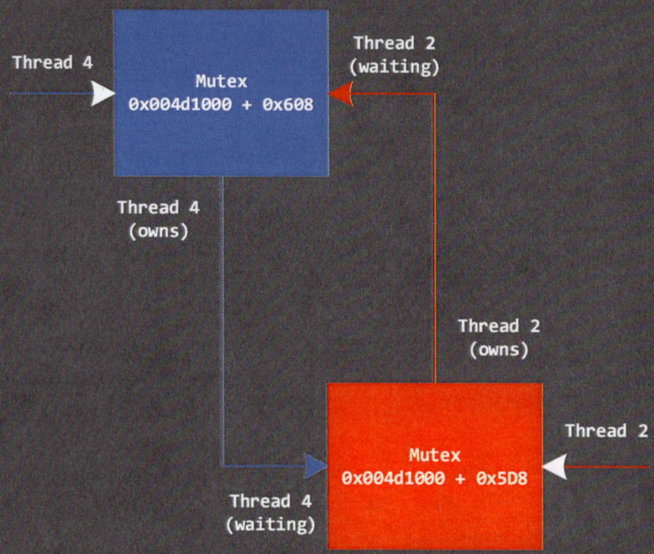

Exercise A11 (x64, WinDbg)

Goal: Learn how to identify synchronization wait chains, deadlocks, hidden and handled exceptions.

Patterns: Wait Chain (Mutex Objects); Deadlock (Mutex Objects); Disassembly Hole.

1. Launch WinDbg.

2. Load the *App11.core.594* dump file from the x64\App11 folder:

```
Microsoft (R) Windows Debugger Version 10.0.27725.1000 AMD64
Copyright (c) Microsoft Corporation. All rights reserved.


Loading Dump File [C:\ALCDA2\x64\App11\App11.core.594]
64-bit machine not using 64-bit API

************* Path validation summary **************
Response                         Time (ms)     Location
Deferred                                       srv*
OK                                             C:\ALCDA2\A64\App12\Symbols
Symbol search path is: srv*;C:\ALCDA2\A64\App12\Symbols
Executable search path is:
Generic Unix Version 0 UP Free x64
System Uptime: not available
Process Uptime: not available
..
*** WARNING: Unable to verify timestamp for App11
App11+0x52970:
00000000`00452970 cmp     rax,0FFFFFFFFFFFFF000h
```

3. Set logging to a file in case of lengthy output from some commands:

```
0:000> .logopen C:\ALCDA2\x64\App11\App11-WinDbg.log
Opened log file 'C:\ALCDA2\x64\App11\App11-WinDbg.log'
```

4. Specify the dump folder as the symbol path and reload symbols:

```
0:000> .symfix; .sympath+ C:\ALCDA2\x64\App11\
Symbol search path is: srv*;C:\ALCDA2\x64\App11\
Expanded Symbol search path is:
cache*;SRV*https://msdl.microsoft.com/download/symbols;c:\alcda2\x64\app11\

************* Path validation summary **************
Response                         Time (ms)     Location
Deferred                                       srv*
OK                                             C:\ALCDA2\x64\App11\
*** WARNING: Unable to verify timestamp for App11

0:000> .symopt+ 0x40
Symbol options are 0x30377:
  0x00000001 - SYMOPT_CASE_INSENSITIVE
  0x00000002 - SYMOPT_UNDNAME
  0x00000004 - SYMOPT_DEFERRED_LOADS
  0x00000010 - SYMOPT_LOAD_LINES
  0x00000020 - SYMOPT_OMAP_FIND_NEAREST
```

```
  0x00000040 - SYMOPT_LOAD_ANYTHING
  0x00000100 - SYMOPT_NO_UNQUALIFIED_LOADS
  0x00000200 - SYMOPT_FAIL_CRITICAL_ERRORS
  0x00010000 - SYMOPT_AUTO_PUBLICS
  0x00020000 - SYMOPT_NO_IMAGE_SEARCH
*** WARNING: Unable to verify timestamp for App11
0:000> .reload
..
*** WARNING: Unable to verify timestamp for App11

************* Symbol Loading Error Summary **************
Module name            Error
App11                  The system cannot find the file specified

You can troubleshoot most symbol related issues by turning on symbol loading diagnostics (!sym
noisy) and repeating the command that caused symbols to be loaded.
You should also verify that your symbol search path (.sympath) is correct.
```

Note: We ignore warnings and errors as they are not relevant for now.

5. List all thread stack traces and identify possible wait chains and deadlock:

```
0:000> ~*kL

Unable to get thread data for thread 0
.  0  Id: 252.252 Suspend: 0 Teb: 00000000`00000000 Unfrozen
 # Child-SP          RetAddr               Call Site
00 00007ffc`83b0c480 00000000`004528fa     App11!nanosleep+0x40
01 00007ffc`83b0c4b0 00000000`00402121     App11!sleep+0x3a
02 00007ffc`83b0c4f0 00000000`00417f11     App11!main+0xd6
03 00007ffc`83b0c540 00000000`00401d9a     App11!_libc_start_main+0x3d1
04 00007ffc`83b0c640 ffffffff`ffffffff     App11!start+0x2a
05 00007ffc`83b0c648 00000000`00000000     0xffffffff`ffffffff

Unable to get thread data for thread 1
   1  Id: 252.253 Suspend: 0 Teb: 00000000`00000000 Unfrozen
 # Child-SP          RetAddr               Call Site
00 00007fa8`d186ed10 00000000`004528fa     App11!nanosleep+0x40
01 00007fa8`d186ed40 00000000`00401f5a     App11!sleep+0x3a
02 00007fa8`d186ed80 00000000`00401f66     App11!bar_one+0xe
03 00007fa8`d186ed90 00000000`00401f7a     App11!foo_one+0x9
04 00007fa8`d186eda0 00000000`004137f3     App11!thread_one+0x11
05 00007fa8`d186edc0 00000000`0045512f     App11!start_thread+0xf3
06 00007fa8`d186ee80 ffffffff`ffffffff     App11!_clone+0x3f
07 00007fa8`d186ee88 00000000`00000000     0xffffffff`ffffffff

Unable to get thread data for thread 2
   2  Id: 252.254 Suspend: 0 Teb: 00000000`00000000 Unfrozen
 # Child-SP          RetAddr               Call Site
00 00007fa8`d106dcc8 00000000`00415294     App11!_lll_lock_wait+0x1c
01 00007fa8`d106dce0 00000000`00401eec     App11!__pthread_mutex_lock+0x54
02 00007fa8`d106dd70 00000000`00401f8a     App11!procA+0x37
03 00007fa8`d106dd80 00000000`00401f96     App11!bar_two+0x9
04 00007fa8`d106dd90 00000000`00401faa     App11!foo_two+0x9
05 00007fa8`d106dda0 00000000`004137f3     App11!thread_two+0x11
06 00007fa8`d106ddc0 00000000`0045512f     App11!start_thread+0xf3
07 00007fa8`d106de80 ffffffff`ffffffff     App11!_clone+0x3f
08 00007fa8`d106de88 00000000`00000000     0xffffffff`ffffffff
```

```
Unable to get thread data for thread 3
   3  Id: 252.255 Suspend: 0 Teb: 00000000`00000000 Unfrozen
 # Child-SP          RetAddr           Call Site
00 00007fa8`d086cd10 00000000`004528fa App11!nanosleep+0x40
01 00007fa8`d086cd40 00000000`00401fbf App11!sleep+0x3a
02 00007fa8`d086cd80 00000000`00401fcb App11!bar_three+0xe
03 00007fa8`d086cd90 00000000`00401fdf App11!foo_three+0x9
04 00007fa8`d086cda0 00000000`004137f3 App11!thread_three+0x11
05 00007fa8`d086cdc0 00000000`0045512f App11!start_thread+0xf3
06 00007fa8`d086ce80 ffffffff`ffffffff App11!_clone+0x3f
07 00007fa8`d086ce88 00000000`00000000 0xffffffff`ffffffff

Unable to get thread data for thread 4
   4  Id: 252.256 Suspend: 0 Teb: 00000000`00000000 Unfrozen
 # Child-SP          RetAddr           Call Site
00 00007fa8`cbffecc8 00000000`00415294 App11!_lll_lock_wait+0x1c
01 00007fa8`cbffece0 00000000`00401f27 App11!__pthread_mutex_lock+0x54
02 00007fa8`cbffed70 00000000`00401fef App11!procB+0x1c
03 00007fa8`cbffed80 00000000`00401ffb App11!bar_four+0x9
04 00007fa8`cbffed90 00000000`0040200f App11!foo_four+0x9
05 00007fa8`cbffeda0 00000000`004137f3 App11!thread_four+0x11
06 00007fa8`cbffedc0 00000000`0045512f App11!start_thread+0xf3
07 00007fa8`cbffee80 ffffffff`ffffffff App11!_clone+0x3f
08 00007fa8`cbffee88 00000000`00000000 0xffffffff`ffffffff

Unable to get thread data for thread 5
   5  Id: 252.257 Suspend: 0 Teb: 00000000`00000000 Unfrozen
 # Child-SP          RetAddr           Call Site
00 00007fa8`cb7fdd10 00000000`004528fa App11!nanosleep+0x40
01 00007fa8`cb7fdd40 00000000`00402024 App11!sleep+0x3a
02 00007fa8`cb7fdd80 00000000`00402030 App11!bar_five+0xe
03 00007fa8`cb7fdd90 00000000`00402044 App11!foo_five+0x9
04 00007fa8`cb7fdda0 00000000`004137f3 App11!thread_five+0x11
05 00007fa8`cb7fddc0 00000000`0045512f App11!start_thread+0xf3
06 00007fa8`cb7fde80 ffffffff`ffffffff App11!_clone+0x3f
07 00007fa8`cb7fde88 00000000`00000000 0xffffffff`ffffffff
```

6. Check **thread #4** and its waiting code:

```
0:000> ~4kL
 # Child-SP          RetAddr           Call Site
00 00007fa8`cbffecc8 00000000`00415294 App11!_lll_lock_wait+0x1c
01 00007fa8`cbffece0 00000000`00401f27 App11!__pthread_mutex_lock+0x54
02 00007fa8`cbffed70 00000000`00401fef App11!procB+0x1c
03 00007fa8`cbffed80 00000000`00401ffb App11!bar_four+0x9
04 00007fa8`cbffed90 00000000`0040200f App11!foo_four+0x9
05 00007fa8`cbffeda0 00000000`004137f3 App11!thread_four+0x11
06 00007fa8`cbffedc0 00000000`0045512f App11!start_thread+0xf3
07 00007fa8`cbffee80 ffffffff`ffffffff App11!_clone+0x3f
08 00007fa8`cbffee88 00000000`00000000 0xffffffff`ffffffff
```

```
0:000> ub 00000000`00401f27
App11!procA+0x54:
00000000`00401f09 pop     rbp
00000000`00401f0a ret
App11!procB:
00000000`00401f0b push    rbp
00000000`00401f0c mov     rbp,rsp
00000000`00401f0f lea     rdi,[App11!mutexB (00000000`004d34e0)]
00000000`00401f16 call    App11!__pthread_mutex_lock (00000000`00415240)
```

```
00000000`00401f1b lea      rdi,[App11!mutexA (00000000`004d34a0)]
00000000`00401f22 call     App11!__pthread_mutex_lock (00000000`00415240)
```

Note: We see thread #4 owns the mutex mutexB (00000000`004d34e0) but is waiting for the mutex mutexA (00000000`004d34a0).

7. Check thread #2 and its waiting code:

```
0:000> ~2kL
 # Child-SP          RetAddr               Call Site
00 00007fa8`d106dcc8 00000000`00415294     App11!_lll_lock_wait+0x1c
01 00007fa8`d106dce0 00000000`00401eec     App11!__pthread_mutex_lock+0x54
02 00007fa8`d106dd70 00000000`00401f8a     App11!procA+0x37
03 00007fa8`d106dd80 00000000`00401f96     App11!bar_two+0x9
04 00007fa8`d106dd90 00000000`00401faa     App11!foo_two+0x9
05 00007fa8`d106dda0 00000000`004137f3     App11!thread_two+0x11
06 00007fa8`d106ddc0 00000000`0045512f     App11!start_thread+0xf3
07 00007fa8`d106de80 ffffffff`ffffffff     App11!_clone+0x3f
08 00007fa8`d106de88 00000000`00000000     0xffffffff`ffffffff
```

```
0:000> uf App11!procA
App11!procA:
00000000`00401eb5 push    rbp
00000000`00401eb6 mov     rbp,rsp
00000000`00401eb9 lea     rdi,[App11!mutexA (00000000`004d34a0)]
00000000`00401ec0 call    App11!__pthread_mutex_lock (00000000`00415240)
00000000`00401ec5 call    App11!procC (00000000`00401e8d)
00000000`00401eca lea     rdi,[App11!mutexA (00000000`004d34a0)]
00000000`00401ed1 call    App11!__pthread_mutex_unlock (00000000`004160b0)
00000000`00401ed6 mov     edi,14h
00000000`00401edb call    App11!sleep (00000000`004528c0)
00000000`00401ee0 lea     rdi,[App11!mutexB (00000000`004d34e0)]
00000000`00401ee7 call    App11!__pthread_mutex_lock (00000000`00415240)
00000000`00401eec lea     rdi,[App11!mutexB (00000000`004d34e0)]
00000000`00401ef3 call    App11!__pthread_mutex_unlock (00000000`004160b0)
00000000`00401ef8 jmp     App11!procA+0x54 (00000000`00401f09)  Branch

App11!procA+0x54:
00000000`00401f09 pop     rbp
00000000`00401f0a ret
```

Note: There's a hole in function disassembly. We can disassemble the missing part manually:

```
0:000> u 00000000`00401ef8
App11!procA+0x43:
00000000`00401ef8 jmp     App11!procA+0x54 (00000000`00401f09)
00000000`00401efa mov     rdi,rax
00000000`00401efd call    App11!_cxa_begin_catch (00000000`00402ec0)
00000000`00401f02 call    App11!_cxa_end_catch (00000000`00402f30)
00000000`00401f07 jmp     App11!procA+0x21 (00000000`00401ed6)
00000000`00401f09 pop     rbp
00000000`00401f0a ret
App11!procB:
00000000`00401f0b push    rbp
```

Note: We put all reconstructed disassembly pieces together:

```
App11!procA:
00000000`00401eb5 push    rbp
00000000`00401eb6 mov     rbp,rsp
00000000`00401eb9 lea     rdi,[App11!mutexA (00000000`004d34a0)]
00000000`00401ec0 call    App11!__pthread_mutex_lock (00000000`00415240)
00000000`00401ec5 call    App11!procC (00000000`00401e8d)
00000000`00401eca lea     rdi,[App11!mutexA (00000000`004d34a0)]
00000000`00401ed1 call    App11!__pthread_mutex_unlock (00000000`004160b0)
00000000`00401ed6 mov     edi,14h
00000000`00401edb call    App11!sleep (00000000`004528c0)
00000000`00401ee0 lea     rdi,[App11!mutexB (00000000`004d34e0)]
00000000`00401ee7 call    App11!__pthread_mutex_lock (00000000`00415240)
00000000`00401eec lea     rdi,[App11!mutexB (00000000`004d34e0)]
00000000`00401ef3 call    App11!__pthread_mutex_unlock (00000000`004160b0)
00000000`00401ef8 jmp     App11!procA+0x54 (00000000`00401f09)  Branch
00000000`00401efa mov     rdi,rax
00000000`00401efd call    App11!_cxa_begin_catch (00000000`00402ec0)
00000000`00401f02 call    App11!_cxa_end_catch (00000000`00402f30)
00000000`00401f07 jmp     App11!procA+0x21 (00000000`00401ed6)
00000000`00401f09 pop     rbp
00000000`00401f0a ret
```

Note: We see that **thread #2** is waiting for the `mutexB (00000000`004d34e0)` mutex but shouldn't own the `mutexA (00000000`004d34a0)` mutex because it should have unlocked it unless something happened in **procC**. We also notice the *catch* exception processing which transfers execution for the block of code waiting for the mutex `mutexB (00000000`004d34e0)`.

8. Disassemble *procC* code:

```
0:000> uf App11!procC
App11!procC:
00000000`00401e8d push    rbp
00000000`00401e8e mov     rbp,rsp
00000000`00401e91 mov     edi,4
00000000`00401e96 call    App11!_cxa_allocate_exception (00000000`00403420)
00000000`00401e9b mov     dword ptr [rax],0
00000000`00401ea1 mov     edx,0
00000000`00401ea6 lea     rsi,[App11!typeinfo for int (00000000`004cfce0)]
00000000`00401ead mov     rdi,rax
00000000`00401eb0 call    App11!_cxa_throw (00000000`00402200)
00000000`00401eb5 push    rbp
00000000`00401eb6 mov     rbp,rsp
00000000`00401eb9 lea     rdi,[App11!mutexA (00000000`004d34a0)]
00000000`00401ec0 call    App11!__pthread_mutex_lock (00000000`00415240)
00000000`00401ec5 call    App11!procC (00000000`00401e8d)
00000000`00401eca lea     rdi,[App11!mutexA (00000000`004d34a0)]
00000000`00401ed1 call    App11!__pthread_mutex_unlock (00000000`004160b0)
00000000`00401ed6 mov     edi,14h
00000000`00401edb call    App11!sleep (00000000`004528c0)
00000000`00401ee0 lea     rdi,[App11!mutexB (00000000`004d34e0)]
00000000`00401ee7 call    App11!__pthread_mutex_lock (00000000`00415240)
00000000`00401eec lea     rdi,[App11!mutexB (00000000`004d34e0)]
00000000`00401ef3 call    App11!__pthread_mutex_unlock (00000000`004160b0)
00000000`00401ef8 jmp     App11!procA+0x54 (00000000`00401f09)  Branch

App11!procA+0x54:
00000000`00401f09 pop     rbp
```

```
00000000`00401f0a ret
```

Note: We see that code throws an exception, so perhaps it was caught in the caller *procA,* and the mutex *unlock* wasn't called, thus causing a deadlock.

9. Check if there was any exception processing (we use the **dpS** command to omit values without associated symbolic information):

```
0:000> ~2s
App11!_lll_lock_wait+0x1c:
00000000`0041665c mov      eax,edx

0:002> dpS rsp-2000 rsp
 00000000`00410d1d App11!fde_single_encoding_compare+0x5d
 00000000`00401850 App11!GLOBAL__sub_I_eh_alloc.cc
 00000000`00401840 App11!fini
 00000000`00410cc0 App11!fde_single_encoding_compare
 00000000`00410970 App11!frame_downheap+0x70
 00000000`004d3460 App11!object.6779
 00000000`004d3460 App11!object.6779
 00000000`00410a51 App11!frame_heapsort+0x91
 00000000`00401834 App11!read_encoded_value_with_base.cold.0
 00000000`00410cc0 App11!fde_single_encoding_compare
 00000000`004d3460 App11!object.6779
 00000000`0041007d App11!Unwind_RaiseException+0x3d
 00000000`004c9768 App11!_EH_FRAME_BEGIN__+0xc9e8
 00000000`00411b56 App11!search_object+0x356
 00000000`00401eb5 App11!procA
 00000000`004d3460 App11!object.6779
 00000000`004160c0 App11!__pthread_key_create [/build/glibc-vjB4T1/glibc-
2.28/nptl/pthread_key_create.c @ 28]
 00000000`00402838 App11!_gxx_personality_v0+0xb8
 00000000`00401ec9 App11!procA+0x14
 00000000`004caa38 App11!
 00000000`00401eb5 App11!procA
 00000000`004bcdd1 App11!_EH_FRAME_BEGIN__+0x51
 00000000`004bcdd1 App11!_EH_FRAME_BEGIN__+0x51
 00000000`0040e940 App11!uw_frame_state_for+0x320
 00000000`004bcdb5 App11!_EH_FRAME_BEGIN__+0x35
 00000000`004caa38 App11!
 00000000`0040fa6b App11!Unwind_RaiseException_Phase2+0x4b
 00000000`00401f0a App11!procA+0x55
 00000000`00402780 App11!_gxx_personality_v0
 00000000`0041031a App11!Unwind_RaiseException+0x2da
 00000000`00402237 App11!_cxa_throw+0x37
 00000000`00410040 App11!Unwind_RaiseException
 00000000`00401efa App11!procA+0x45
 00000000`004caa38 App11!
 00000000`00401eb5 App11!procA
 00000000`00401f0a App11!procA+0x55
 00000000`00402780 App11!_gxx_personality_v0
```

Note: We see a reference 00000000`00401efa App11!procA+0x45 from the exception processing block in *procA* and also **00000000`00402237 App11!_cxa_throw+0x37**. We check whether the symbolic information we found is not coincidental:

```
0:002> ub 00000000`00402237
App11!_cxa_throw+0x16:
00000000`00402216 mov     rsi,rbp
00000000`00402219 mov     rdi,rbx
00000000`0040221c add     dword ptr [rax+8],1
00000000`00402220 call    App11!_cxa_init_primary_exception (00000000`004021b0)
00000000`00402225 mov     dword ptr [rax],1
00000000`0040222b lea     rbx,[rax+60h]
00000000`0040222f mov     rdi,rbx
00000000`00402232 call    App11!Unwind_RaiseException (00000000`00410040)
```

```
0:002> ub 00000000`0041031a
App11!Unwind_RaiseException+0x2b4:
00000000`004102f4 test    dword ptr [rdi+48FFFFFEh],esi
00000000`004102fa mov     esi,ebx
00000000`004102fc mov     rdi,r14
00000000`004102ff call    App11!uw_install_context_1 (00000000`0040fc00)
00000000`00410304 mov     r8,qword ptr [rbp-218h]
00000000`0041030b mov     rdi,qword ptr [rbp-220h]
00000000`00410312 mov     rsi,r8
00000000`00410315 call    App11!Unwind_DebugHook (00000000`00410030)
```

```
0:002> ub 00000000`0040fa6b
App11!Unwind_RaiseException_Phase2+0x33:
00000000`0040fa53 je      App11!Unwind_RaiseException_Phase2+0x55 (00000000`0040fa75)
00000000`0040fa55 mov     esi,ebp
00000000`0040fa57 mov     r8,rbx
00000000`0040fa5a mov     rcx,r12
00000000`0040fa5d mov     rdx,qword ptr [r12]
00000000`0040fa61 or      esi,2
00000000`0040fa64 mov     edi,1
00000000`0040fa69 call    rax
```

13. Since mutexes have owners, we can check their ownership instead of disassembly:

```
0:002> dt -r pthread_mutex_t 00000000`004d34a0
App11!pthread_mutex_t
   +0x000 __data           : __pthread_mutex_s
      +0x000 __lock           : 0n2
      +0x004 __count          : 0
      +0x008 __owner          : 0n596
      +0x00c __nusers         : 1
      +0x010 __kind           : 0n0
      +0x014 __spins          : 0n0
      +0x016 __elision        : 0n0
      +0x018 __list           : __pthread_internal_list
         +0x000 __prev           : (null)
         +0x008 __next           : (null)
   +0x000 __size           : [40]  "???"
   +0x000 __align          : 0n2
```

```
0:002> dt -r pthread_mutex_t 00000000`004d34e0
App11!pthread_mutex_t
   +0x000 __data           : __pthread_mutex_s
      +0x000 __lock           : 0n2
      +0x004 __count          : 0
      +0x008 __owner          : 0n598
      +0x00c __nusers         : 1
      +0x010 __kind           : 0n0
      +0x014 __spins          : 0n0
```

```
    +0x016 __elision         : 0n0
    +0x018 __list            : __pthread_internal_list
       +0x000 __prev           : (null)
       +0x008 __next           : (null)
 +0x000 __size           : [40]  "???"
 +0x000 __align          : 0n2
```

Note: We see their respective thread owners (TID numbers).

```
0:002> ? 254
Evaluate expression: 596 = 00000000`00000254

0:002> ? 256
Evaluate expression: 598 = 00000000`00000256

(0:002> ~
Unable to get thread data for thread 0
#  0  Id: 252.252 Suspend: 0 Teb: 00000000`00000000 Unfrozen
Unable to get thread data for thread 1
   1  Id: 252.253 Suspend: 0 Teb: 00000000`00000000 Unfrozen
Unable to get thread data for thread 2
.  2  Id: 252.254 Suspend: 0 Teb: 00000000`00000000 Unfrozen
Unable to get thread data for thread 3
   3  Id: 252.255 Suspend: 0 Teb: 00000000`00000000 Unfrozen
Unable to get thread data for thread 4
   4  Id: 252.256 Suspend: 0 Teb: 00000000`00000000 Unfrozen
Unable to get thread data for thread 5
   5  Id: 252.257 Suspend: 0 Teb: 00000000`00000000 Unfrozen
```

14. We close logging before exiting WinDbg:

```
0:002> .logclose
Closing open log file 'C:\ALCDA2\x64\App11\App11-WinDbg.log
```

Deadlock (x64, WinDbg)

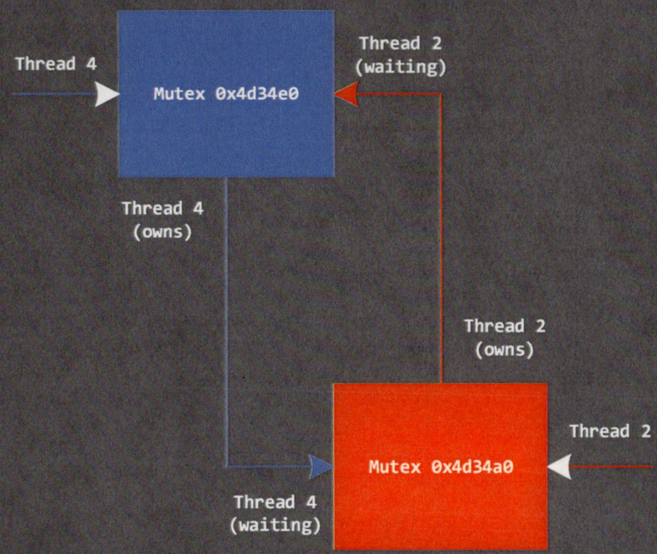

Exercise A11 (A64, WinDbg)

Goal: Learn how to identify synchronization wait chains, deadlocks, hidden and handled exceptions.

Patterns: Wait Chain (Mutex Objects); Deadlock (Mutex Objects); Disassembly Hole.

1. Launch WinDbg.

2. Load the *App11.core.11410* dump file from the A64\App11 folder:

```
Microsoft (R) Windows Debugger Version 10.0.27725.1000 AMD64
Copyright (c) Microsoft Corporation. All rights reserved.


Loading Dump File [C:\ALCDA2\A64\App11\App11.core.11410]
64-bit machine not using 64-bit API

************* Path validation summary **************
Response                         Time (ms)     Location
Deferred                                       srv*
Symbol search path is: srv*
Executable search path is:
Generic Unix Version 0 UP Free ARM 64-bit (AArch64)
System Uptime: not available
Process Uptime: not available
..
*** WARNING: Unable to verify timestamp for App11
App11+0x1ae24:
00000000`0041ae24 svc         #0
```

3. Set logging to a file in case of lengthy output from some commands:

```
0:000> .logopen C:\ALCDA2\A64\App11\App11-WinDbg.log
Opened log file 'C:\ALCDA2\A64\App11\App11-WinDbg.log'
```

4. Specify the dump folder as the symbol path and reload symbols:

```
0:000> .symfix; .sympath+ C:\ALCDA2\A64\App11\
Symbol search path is: srv*;C:\ALCDA2\A64\App11\
Expanded Symbol search path is:
cache*;SRV*https://msdl.microsoft.com/download/symbols;c:\alcda2\a64\app11\

************* Path validation summary **************
Response                         Time (ms)     Location
Deferred                                       srv*
OK                                             C:\ALCDA2\A64\App11\
*** WARNING: Unable to verify timestamp for App11
```

```
0:000> .reload
..
*** WARNING: Unable to verify timestamp for App11

************* Symbol Loading Error Summary **************
Module name            Error
App11                  The system cannot find the file specified

You can troubleshoot most symbol related issues by turning on symbol loading diagnostics (!sym
noisy) and repeating the command that caused symbols to be loaded.
You should also verify that your symbol search path (.sympath) is correct.
```

Note: We ignore warnings and errors as they are not relevant for now.

5. List all thread stack traces and identify possible wait chains and deadlock:

```
0:000> ~*k

Unable to get thread data for thread 0
.  0  Id: 2c92.2c93 Suspend: 0 Teb: 00000000`00000000 Unfrozen
 # Child-SP          RetAddr               Call Site
00 0000fffe`0c84e5e0 00000000`004338b4     App11!_libc_nanosleep+0x24
01 0000fffe`0c84e620 00000000`004032d8     App11!sleep+0x110
02 0000fffe`0c84e810 00000000`004032ec     App11!bar_one+0x10
03 0000fffe`0c84e820 00000000`00403304     App11!foo_one+0xc
04 0000fffe`0c84e830 00000000`004130a4     App11!thread_one+0x10
05 0000fffe`0c84e850 00000000`00438760     App11!start_thread+0xb4
06 0000fffe`0c84e980 ffffffff`ffffffff     App11!thread_start+0x30
07 0000fffe`0c84e980 00000000`00000000     0xffffffff`ffffffff

Unable to get thread data for thread 1
   1  Id: 2c92.2c94 Suspend: 0 Teb: 00000000`00000000 Unfrozen
 # Child-SP          RetAddr               Call Site
00 0000fffe`0c03e7d0 00000000`00414ea4     App11!_lll_lock_wait+0x3c
01 0000fffe`0c03e7d0 00000000`0040325c     App11!_pthread_mutex_lock+0xe8
02 0000fffe`0c03e800 00000000`0040331c     App11!procA+0x38
03 0000fffe`0c03e810 00000000`00403330     App11!bar_two+0xc
04 0000fffe`0c03e820 00000000`00403348     App11!foo_two+0xc
05 0000fffe`0c03e830 00000000`004130a4     App11!thread_two+0x10
06 0000fffe`0c03e850 00000000`00438760     App11!start_thread+0xb4
07 0000fffe`0c03e980 ffffffff`ffffffff     App11!thread_start+0x30
08 0000fffe`0c03e980 00000000`00000000     0xffffffff`ffffffff

Unable to get thread data for thread 2
   2  Id: 2c92.2c9d Suspend: 0 Teb: 00000000`00000000 Unfrozen
 # Child-SP          RetAddr               Call Site
00 0000fffe`0b82e5e0 00000000`004338b4     App11!_libc_nanosleep+0x24
01 0000fffe`0b82e620 00000000`00403364     App11!sleep+0x110
02 0000fffe`0b82e810 00000000`00403378     App11!bar_three+0x10
03 0000fffe`0b82e820 00000000`00403390     App11!foo_three+0xc
04 0000fffe`0b82e830 00000000`004130a4     App11!thread_three+0x10
05 0000fffe`0b82e850 00000000`00438760     App11!start_thread+0xb4
06 0000fffe`0b82e980 ffffffff`ffffffff     App11!thread_start+0x30
07 0000fffe`0b82e980 00000000`00000000     0xffffffff`ffffffff
```

```
Unable to get thread data for thread 3
   3  Id: 2c92.2c9e Suspend: 0 Teb: 00000000`00000000 Unfrozen
 # Child-SP          RetAddr               Call Site
00 0000fffe`0b01e7d0 00000000`00414ea4     App11!_lll_lock_wait+0x3c
01 0000fffe`0b01e7d0 00000000`004032a0     App11!_pthread_mutex_lock+0xe8
02 0000fffe`0b01e800 00000000`004033a8     App11!procB+0x20
03 0000fffe`0b01e810 00000000`004033bc     App11!bar_four+0xc
04 0000fffe`0b01e820 00000000`004033d4     App11!foo_four+0xc
05 0000fffe`0b01e830 00000000`004130a4     App11!thread_four+0x10
06 0000fffe`0b01e850 00000000`00438760     App11!start_thread+0xb4
07 0000fffe`0b01e980 ffffffff`ffffffff     App11!thread_start+0x30
08 0000fffe`0b01e980 00000000`00000000     0xffffffff`ffffffff

Unable to get thread data for thread 4
   4  Id: 2c92.2c9f Suspend: 0 Teb: 00000000`00000000 Unfrozen
 # Child-SP          RetAddr               Call Site
00 0000fffe`0a80e5e0 00000000`004338b4     App11!_libc_nanosleep+0x24
01 0000fffe`0a80e620 00000000`004033f0     App11!sleep+0x110
02 0000fffe`0a80e810 00000000`00403404     App11!bar_five+0x10
03 0000fffe`0a80e820 00000000`0040341c     App11!foo_five+0xc
04 0000fffe`0a80e830 00000000`004130a4     App11!thread_five+0x10
05 0000fffe`0a80e850 00000000`00438760     App11!start_thread+0xb4
06 0000fffe`0a80e980 ffffffff`ffffffff     App11!thread_start+0x30
07 0000fffe`0a80e980 00000000`00000000     0xffffffff`ffffffff

Unable to get thread data for thread 5
   5  Id: 2c92.2c92 Suspend: 0 Teb: 00000000`00000000 Unfrozen
 # Child-SP          RetAddr               Call Site
00 0000ffff`d8b393c0 00000000`004338b4     App11!_libc_nanosleep+0x24
01 0000ffff`d8b39400 00000000`004034e0     App11!sleep+0x110
02 0000ffff`d8b395f0 00000000`0041d0bc     App11!main+0xb8
03 0000ffff`d8b39640 00000000`004030a8     App11!_libc_start_main+0x304
04 0000ffff`d8b397a0 00000000`00000000     App11!start+0x4c
```

6. Check **thread #3** and its waiting code:

```
0:000> ~3k
 # Child-SP          RetAddr               Call Site
00 0000fffe`0b01e7d0 00000000`00414ea4     App11!_lll_lock_wait+0x3c
01 0000fffe`0b01e7d0 00000000`004032a0     App11!_pthread_mutex_lock+0xe8
02 0000fffe`0b01e800 00000000`004033a8     App11!procB+0x20
03 0000fffe`0b01e810 00000000`004033bc     App11!bar_four+0xc
04 0000fffe`0b01e820 00000000`004033d4     App11!foo_four+0xc
05 0000fffe`0b01e830 00000000`004130a4     App11!thread_four+0x10
06 0000fffe`0b01e850 00000000`00438760     App11!start_thread+0xb4
07 0000fffe`0b01e980 ffffffff`ffffffff     App11!thread_start+0x30
08 0000fffe`0b01e980 00000000`00000000     0xffffffff`ffffffff

0:000> uf 00000000`004032a0
App11!procB:
00000000`00403280 stp        fp,lr,[sp,#-0x10]!
00000000`00403284 mov        fp,sp
00000000`00403288 adrp       x0,App11!main_arena+0x850 (00000000`004d1000)
00000000`0040328c add        x0,x0,#0x608
00000000`00403290 bl         App11!_pthread_mutex_lock (00000000`00414dbc)
00000000`00403294 adrp       x0,App11!main_arena+0x850 (00000000`004d1000)
00000000`00403298 add        x0,x0,#0x5D8
00000000`0040329c bl         App11!_pthread_mutex_lock (00000000`00414dbc)
```

Note: We see thread #3 owns the mutex 00000000`004d1000 + 0x608 but is waiting for the mutex 00000000`004d1000 + 0x5D8.

7. Check thread #1 and its waiting code:

```
0:000> ~1k
 # Child-SP          RetAddr               Call Site
00 0000fffe`0c03e7d0 00000000`00414ea4     App11!_lll_lock_wait+0x3c
01 0000fffe`0c03e7d0 00000000`0040325c     App11!_pthread_mutex_lock+0xe8
02 0000fffe`0c03e800 00000000`0040331c     App11!procA+0x38
03 0000fffe`0c03e810 00000000`00403330     App11!bar_two+0xc
04 0000fffe`0c03e820 00000000`00403348     App11!foo_two+0xc
05 0000fffe`0c03e830 00000000`004130a4     App11!thread_two+0x10
06 0000fffe`0c03e850 00000000`00438760     App11!start_thread+0xb4
07 0000fffe`0c03e980 ffffffff`ffffffff     App11!thread_start+0x30
08 0000fffe`0c03e980 00000000`00000000     0xffffffff`ffffffff
```

```
0:000> uf App11!procA
App11!procA:
00000000`00403224 a9bf7bfd stp        fp,lr,[sp,#-0x10]!
00000000`00403228 910003fd mov        fp,sp
00000000`0040322c d0000660 adrp       x0,App11!main_arena+0x850 (00000000`004d1000)
00000000`00403230 91176000 add        x0,x0,#0x5D8
00000000`00403234 940046e2 bl         App11!_pthread_mutex_lock (00000000`00414dbc)
00000000`00403238 97fffff2 bl         App11!procC (00000000`00403200)
00000000`0040323c d0000660 adrp       x0,App11!main_arena+0x850 (00000000`004d1000)
00000000`00403240 91176000 add        x0,x0,#0x5D8
00000000`00403244 94004b84 bl         App11!_pthread_mutex_unlock (00000000`00416054)
00000000`00403248 52800280 mov        w0,#0x14
00000000`0040324c 9400c156 bl         App11!sleep (00000000`004337a4)
00000000`00403250 d0000660 adrp       x0,App11!main_arena+0x850 (00000000`004d1000)
00000000`00403254 91182000 add        x0,x0,#0x608
00000000`00403258 940046d9 bl         App11!_pthread_mutex_lock (00000000`00414dbc)
00000000`0040325c d0000660 adrp       x0,App11!main_arena+0x850 (00000000`004d1000)
00000000`00403260 91182000 add        x0,x0,#0x608
00000000`00403264 94004b7c bl         App11!_pthread_mutex_unlock (00000000`00416054)
00000000`00403268 14000004 b          App11!Z5procAv+0x54 (00000000`00403278)  Branch

App11!procA+0x54:
00000000`00403278 a8c17bfd ldp        fp,lr,[sp],#0x10
00000000`0040327c d65f03c0 ret
```

Note: There's a hole in function disassembly. We can disassemble the missing part manually:

```
0:000> u 00000000`00403268
App11!procA+0x44:
00000000`00403268 14000004 b          App11!procA+0x54 (00000000`00403278)
00000000`0040326c 940001d2 bl         App11!_cxa_begin_catch (00000000`004039b4)
00000000`00403270 940001fa bl         App11!_cxa_end_catch (00000000`00403a58)
00000000`00403274 17fffff5 b          App11!procA+0x24 (00000000`00403248)
00000000`00403278 a8c17bfd ldp        fp,lr,[sp],#0x10
00000000`0040327c d65f03c0 ret
App11!procB:
00000000`00403280 a9bf7bfd stp        fp,lr,[sp,#-0x10]!
00000000`00403284 910003fd mov        fp,sp
```

Note: We put all reconstructed disassembly pieces together:

```
App11!procA:
00000000`00403224 a9bf7bfd stp          fp,lr,[sp,#-0x10]!
00000000`00403228 910003fd mov          fp,sp
00000000`0040322c d0000660 adrp         x0,App11!main_arena+0x850 (00000000`004d1000)
00000000`00403230 91176000 add          x0,x0,#0x5D8
00000000`00403234 940046e2 bl           App11!_pthread_mutex_lock (00000000`00414dbc)
00000000`00403238 97fffff2 bl           App11!procC (00000000`00403200)
00000000`0040323c d0000660 adrp         x0,App11!main_arena+0x850 (00000000`004d1000)
00000000`00403240 91176000 add          x0,x0,#0x5D8
00000000`00403244 94004b84 bl           App11!_pthread_mutex_unlock (00000000`00416054)
00000000`00403248 52800280 mov          w0,#0x14
00000000`0040324c 9400c156 bl           App11!sleep (00000000`004337a4)
00000000`00403250 d0000660 adrp         x0,App11!main_arena+0x850 (00000000`004d1000)
00000000`00403254 91182000 add          x0,x0,#0x608
00000000`00403258 940046d9 bl           App11!_pthread_mutex_lock (00000000`00414dbc)
00000000`0040325c d0000660 adrp         x0,App11!main_arena+0x850 (00000000`004d1000)
00000000`00403260 91182000 add          x0,x0,#0x608
00000000`00403264 94004b7c bl           App11!_pthread_mutex_unlock (00000000`00416054)
00000000`00403268 14000004 b            App11!procA+0x54 (00000000`00403278)  Branch
00000000`0040326c 940001d2 bl           App11!_cxa_begin_catch (00000000`004039b4)
00000000`00403270 940001fa bl           App11!_cxa_end_catch (00000000`00403a58)
00000000`00403274 17fffff5 b            App11!procA+0x24 (00000000`00403248)
00000000`00403278 a8c17bfd ldp          fp,lr,[sp],#0x10
00000000`0040327c d65f03c0 ret
```

Note: We see that **thread #1** is waiting for the `00000000`004d1000 + 0x608` mutex but shouldn't own the **`00000000`004d1000 + 0x5D8`** mutex because it should have unlocked it unless something happened in **procC**. We also notice the *catch* exception processing which transfers execution for the block of code waiting for the mutex `00000000`004d1000 + 0x608`.

10. Disassemble *procC* code:

```
0:000> uf App11!procC
App11!procC:
00000000`00403200 a9bf7bfd stp          fp,lr,[sp,#-0x10]!
00000000`00403204 910003fd mov          fp,sp
00000000`00403208 d2800080 mov          x0,#4
00000000`0040320c 94000106 bl           App11!_cxa_allocate_exception (00000000`00403624)
00000000`00403210 b900001f str          wzr,[x0]
00000000`00403214 90000661 adrp         x1,App11!std::exception+0x18 (00000000`004cf000)
00000000`00403218 91160021 add          x1,x1,#0x580
00000000`0040321c d2800002 mov          x2,#0
00000000`00403220 94000568 bl           App11!_cxa_throw (00000000`004047c0)
00000000`00403224 a9bf7bfd stp          fp,lr,[sp,#-0x10]!
00000000`00403228 910003fd mov          fp,sp
00000000`0040322c d0000660 adrp         x0,App11!main_arena+0x850 (00000000`004d1000)
00000000`00403230 91176000 add          x0,x0,#0x5D8
00000000`00403234 940046e2 bl           App11!_pthread_mutex_lock (00000000`00414dbc)
00000000`00403238 97fffff2 bl           App11!procC (00000000`00403200)
00000000`0040323c d0000660 adrp         x0,App11!main_arena+0x850 (00000000`004d1000)
00000000`00403240 91176000 add          x0,x0,#0x5D8
00000000`00403244 94004b84 bl           App11!_pthread_mutex_unlock (00000000`00416054)
00000000`00403248 52800280 mov          w0,#0x14
00000000`0040324c 9400c156 bl           App11!sleep (00000000`004337a4)
00000000`00403250 d0000660 adrp         x0,App11!main_arena+0x850 (00000000`004d1000)
00000000`00403254 91182000 add          x0,x0,#0x608
00000000`00403258 940046d9 bl           App11!_pthread_mutex_lock (00000000`00414dbc)
```

```
00000000`0040325c d0000660 adrp         x0,App11!main_arena+0x850 (00000000`004d1000)
00000000`00403260 91182000 add          x0,x0,#0x608
00000000`00403264 94004b7c bl           App11!_pthread_mutex_unlock (00000000`00416054)
00000000`00403268 14000004 b            App11!procA+0x54 (00000000`00403278)  Branch

App11!procA+0x54:
00000000`00403278 a8c17bfd ldp          fp,lr,[sp],#0x10
00000000`0040327c d65f03c0 ret
```

Note: We see that code throws an exception, so perhaps it was caught in the caller *procA,* and the mutex *unlock* wasn't called, thus causing a deadlock.

11. Check if there was any exception processing (we use the **dpS** command to omit values without associated symbolic information):

```
0:000> ~1s
App11!_lll_lock_wait+0x3c:
00000000`0041a110 svc           #0

0:001> dpS sp-2000 sp
00000000`0040f150 App11!uw_update_context+0x18
 00000000`004e9558 App11!_default_pthread_attr
 00000000`004e3000 App11!ZL16emergency_buffer+0xfd90
 00000000`004e3000 App11!ZL16emergency_buffer+0xfd90
 00000000`00410ec0 App11!search_object+0x204
 00000000`004ad518 App11!$d+0x2c
 00000000`00410e48 App11!search_object+0x18c
 00000000`004117d0 App11!Unwind_Find_FDE+0x174
 00000000`004d15a8 App11!object.6205
 00000000`0040323b App11!procA+0x17
 00000000`004e3000 App11!ZL16emergency_buffer+0xfd90
 00000000`004cf000 App11!vtable for std::exception+0x18
 00000000`004e9558 App11!_default_pthread_attr
 00000000`0041178c App11!Unwind_Find_FDE+0x130
 00000000`004d15a8 App11!object.6205
 00000000`00403224 App11!procA
 00000000`00411778 App11!Unwind_Find_FDE+0x11c
 00000000`0040e374 App11!uw_frame_state_for+0x5cc
 00000000`00404228 App11!_gxx_personality_v0+0xf0
 00000000`0040f254 App11!Unwind_RaiseException_Phase2+0x70
 00000000`004e9558 App11!_default_pthread_attr
 00000000`0040f218 App11!Unwind_RaiseException_Phase2+0x34
 00000000`004bd09c App11!$d
 00000000`004e9558 App11!_default_pthread_attr
 00000000`0040f274 App11!Unwind_RaiseException_Phase2+0x90
 00000000`0040f89c App11!Unwind_RaiseException+0x144
 00000000`0040f8b0 App11!Unwind_RaiseException+0x158
 00000000`0040326c App11!procA+0x48
 00000000`004d0000 App11!+0x18
 00000000`00403338 App11!thread_two
 00000000`004e9558 App11!_default_pthread_attr
 00000000`00404850 App11!_cxa_throw+0x90
 00000000`0040f758 App11!Unwind_RaiseException
[...]
```

Note: We see a reference 00000000`0040326c App11!procA+0x48 from the exception processing block in *procA* and also **00000000`00404850 App11!_cxa_throw+0x90**. We check whether the symbolic information we found is not coincidental:

```
0:001> ub 00000000`00404850
App11!_cxa_throw+0x70:
00000000`00404830 f81a8260 stur       x0,[x19,#-0x58]
00000000`00404834 90000000 adrp
x0,App11!ZL21base_of_encoded_valuehP15_Unwind_Context+0x48 (00000000`00404000)
00000000`00404838 d1008274 sub        x20,x19,#0x20
00000000`0040483c 911d7000 add        x0,x0,#0x75C
00000000`00404840 f81e0261 stur       x1,[x19,#-0x20]
00000000`00404844 f81e8260 stur       x0,[x19,#-0x18]
00000000`00404848 aa1403e0 mov        x0,x20
00000000`0040484c 94002bc3 bl         App11!Unwind_RaiseException (00000000`0040f758)
```

```
0:001> ub 00000000`0040f8b0
App11!Unwind_RaiseException+0x138:
00000000`0040f890 mov          x0,x21
00000000`0040f894 mov          x1,x19
00000000`0040f898 bl           App11!Unwind_RaiseException_Phase2 (00000000`0040f1e4)
00000000`0040f89c cmp          w0,#7
00000000`0040f8a0 bne          App11!Unwind_RaiseException+0xc8 (00000000`0040f820)
00000000`0040f8a4 mov          x1,x19
00000000`0040f8a8 mov          x0,x22
00000000`0040f8ac bl           App11!uw_install_context_1 (00000000`0040f3a4)
```

```
0:001> ub 00000000`0040f89c
App11!Unwind_RaiseException+0x124:
00000000`0040f87c str          x0,[x21,#0x18]
00000000`0040f880 mov          x1,x22
00000000`0040f884 str          xzr,[x21,#0x10]
00000000`0040f888 mov          x0,x19
00000000`0040f88c bl           App11+0x280 (00000000`00400280)
00000000`0040f890 mov          x0,x21
00000000`0040f894 mov          x1,x19
00000000`0040f898 bl           App11!Unwind_RaiseException_Phase2 (00000000`0040f1e4)
```

```
0:001> ub 00000000`0040f274
App11!Unwind_RaiseException_Phase2+0x70:
00000000`0040f254 cmp          w0,#7
00000000`0040f258 beq          App11!Unwind_RaiseException_Phase2+0x98 (00000000`0040f27c)
00000000`0040f25c cmp          w0,#8
00000000`0040f260 bne          App11!Unwind_RaiseException_Phase2+0x94 (00000000`0040f278)
00000000`0040f264 cbnz         w21,App11!Unwind_RaiseException_Phase2+0xb0 (00000000`0040f294)
00000000`0040f268 mov          x0,x19
00000000`0040f26c mov          x1,x20
00000000`0040f270 bl           App11!uw_update_context (00000000`0040f138)
```

Note: Full debug symbols make it possible to find mutex ownership faster. We will do that in the next exercise, A12.

15. We close logging before exiting WinDbg:

```
0:001> .logclose
Closing open log file 'C:\ALCDA2\A64\App11\App11-WinDbg.log
```

Deadlock (A64, WinDbg)

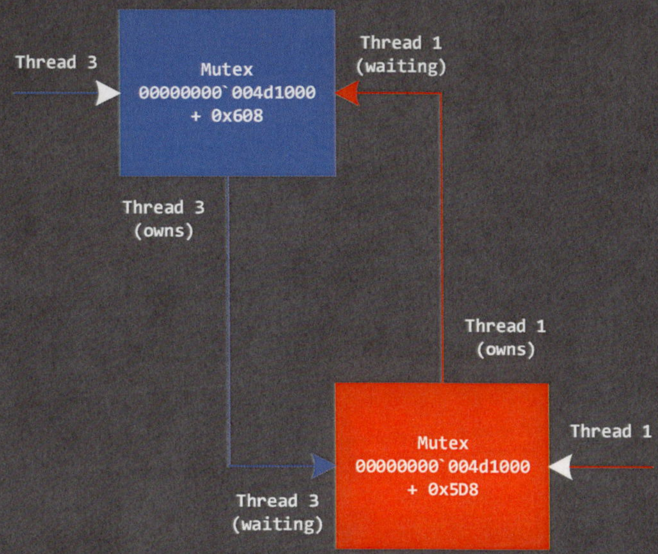

Mechanisms (Deadlock)

Exercise A12

- **Goal:** Learn how to dump memory for post-processing, get the list of functions and module variables, load symbols, disassemble with source code, inspect arguments, local variables, and types

- **Patterns:** Module Variable

- \ALCDA-Dumps\Exercise-A12-x64-GDB.pdf
- \ALCDA-Dumps\Exercise-A12-A64-GDB.pdf

- \ALCDA-Dumps\Exercise-A12-A64-WinDbg.pdf
- \ALCDA-Dumps\Exercise-A12-x64-WinDbg.pdf

Exercise A12 (x64, GDB)

Goal: Learn how to dump memory for post-processing, get the list of functions and module variables, load symbols, disassemble with source code, inspect arguments, local variables, and types.

Patterns: Module Variable.

1. Load the *App12.core.698* dump file and *App12* executable from the x64/App12 directory:

```
~/ALCDA2/x64/App12$ gdb -c App12.core.698 -se App12
GNU gdb (Debian 8.2.1-2+b3) 8.2.1
Copyright (C) 2018 Free Software Foundation, Inc.
License GPLv3+: GNU GPL version 3 or later <http://gnu.org/licenses/gpl.html>
This is free software: you are free to change and redistribute it.
There is NO WARRANTY, to the extent permitted by law.
Type "show copying" and "show warranty" for details.
This GDB was configured as "x86_64-linux-gnu".
Type "show configuration" for configuration details.
For bug reporting instructions, please see:
<http://www.gnu.org/software/gdb/bugs/>.
Find the GDB manual and other documentation resources online at:
    <http://www.gnu.org/software/gdb/documentation/>.

For help, type "help".
Type "apropos word" to search for commands related to "word"...
Reading symbols from App12...(no debugging symbols found)...done.
[New LWP 698]
[New LWP 699]
[New LWP 700]
[New LWP 701]
[New LWP 702]
[New LWP 703]
[Thread debugging using libthread_db enabled]
Using host libthread_db library "/lib/x86_64-linux-gnu/libthread_db.so.1".
Core was generated by `./App12'.
#0  0x0000000000452970 in nanosleep ()
[Current thread is 1 (Thread 0x1438880 (LWP 698))]
```

2. Set logging to a file in case of lengthy output from some commands:

```
(gdb) set logging on App12.log
Copying output to App12.log.
```

3. List all thread stack traces:

```
(gdb) thread apply all bt

Thread 6 (Thread 0x7fbcedc7f700 (LWP 703)):
#0  0x0000000000452970 in nanosleep ()
#1  0x00000000004528fa in sleep ()
#2  0x0000000000402024 in bar_five() ()
#3  0x0000000000402030 in foo_five() ()
#4  0x0000000000402044 in thread_five(void*) ()
#5  0x00000000004137f3 in start_thread ()
#6  0x000000000045512f in clone ()
```

```
Thread 5 (Thread 0x7fbcee480700 (LWP 702)):
#0  0x000000000041665c in __lll_lock_wait ()
#1  0x0000000000415294 in pthread_mutex_lock ()
#2  0x0000000000401f27 in procB() ()
#3  0x0000000000401fef in bar_four() ()
#4  0x0000000000401ffb in foo_four() ()
#5  0x000000000040200f in thread_four(void*) ()
#6  0x00000000004137f3 in start_thread ()
#7  0x000000000045512f in clone ()

Thread 4 (Thread 0x7fbceec81700 (LWP 701)):
#0  0x0000000000452970 in nanosleep ()
#1  0x00000000004528fa in sleep ()
#2  0x0000000000401fbf in bar_three() ()
#3  0x0000000000401fcb in foo_three() ()
#4  0x0000000000401fdf in thread_three(void*) ()
#5  0x00000000004137f3 in start_thread ()
#6  0x000000000045512f in clone ()

Thread 3 (Thread 0x7fbcef482700 (LWP 700)):
#0  0x000000000041665c in __lll_lock_wait ()
#1  0x0000000000415294 in pthread_mutex_lock ()
#2  0x0000000000401eec in procA() ()
#3  0x0000000000401f8a in bar_two() ()
#4  0x0000000000401f96 in foo_two() ()
#5  0x0000000000401faa in thread_two(void*) ()
#6  0x00000000004137f3 in start_thread ()
#7  0x000000000045512f in clone ()

Thread 2 (Thread 0x7fbcefc83700 (LWP 699)):
#0  0x0000000000452970 in nanosleep ()
#1  0x00000000004528fa in sleep ()
#2  0x0000000000401f5a in bar_one() ()
#3  0x0000000000401f66 in foo_one() ()
#4  0x0000000000401f7a in thread_one(void*) ()
#5  0x00000000004137f3 in start_thread ()
#6  0x000000000045512f in clone ()

Thread 1 (Thread 0x1438880 (LWP 698)):
#0  0x0000000000452970 in nanosleep ()
#1  0x00000000004528fa in sleep ()
#2  0x0000000000402121 in main ()
```

4. *App12* is an executable with stripped-off debug symbols. Change the symbol file to *App12.debug,* which is the same executable as *App12* but with debug symbols included:

```
(gdb) symbol-file App12.debug
Reading symbols from App12.debug...done.
```

5. List all thread stack traces again:

```
(gdb) thread apply all bt

Thread 6 (Thread 0x7fbcedc7f700 (LWP 703)):
#0  0x0000000000452970 in nanosleep ()
#1  0x00000000004528fa in sleep ()
#2  0x0000000000402024 in bar_five () at main.cpp:75
#3  0x0000000000402030 in foo_five () at main.cpp:75
#4  0x0000000000402044 in thread_five (arg=0x0) at main.cpp:75
#5  0x00000000004137f3 in start_thread (arg=<optimized out>) at pthread_create.c:486
```

```
#6  0x000000000045512f in clone ()

Thread 5 (Thread 0x7fbcee480700 (LWP 702)):
#0  __lll_lock_wait () at ../sysdeps/unix/sysv/linux/x86_64/lowlevellock.S:103
#1  0x0000000000415294 in __pthread_mutex_lock (mutex=0x4d34a0 <mutexA>) at
../nptl/pthread_mutex_lock.c:80
#2  0x0000000000401f27 in procB () at main.cpp:48
#3  0x0000000000401fef in bar_four () at main.cpp:74
#4  0x0000000000401ffb in foo_four () at main.cpp:74
#5  0x000000000040200f in thread_four (arg=0x0) at main.cpp:74
#6  0x00000000004137f3 in start_thread (arg=<optimized out>) at pthread_create.c:486
#7  0x000000000045512f in clone ()

Thread 4 (Thread 0x7fbceec81700 (LWP 701)):
#0  0x0000000000452970 in nanosleep ()
#1  0x00000000004528fa in sleep ()
#2  0x0000000000401fbf in bar_three () at main.cpp:73
#3  0x0000000000401fcb in foo_three () at main.cpp:73
#4  0x0000000000401fdf in thread_three (arg=0x0) at main.cpp:73
#5  0x00000000004137f3 in start_thread (arg=<optimized out>) at pthread_create.c:486
#6  0x000000000045512f in clone ()

Thread 3 (Thread 0x7fbcef482700 (LWP 700)):
#0  __lll_lock_wait () at ../sysdeps/unix/sysv/linux/x86_64/lowlevellock.S:103
#1  0x0000000000415294 in __pthread_mutex_lock (mutex=0x4d34e0 <mutex>) at
../nptl/pthread_mutex_lock.c:80
#2  0x0000000000401eec in procA () at main.cpp:41
#3  0x0000000000401f8a in bar_two () at main.cpp:72
#4  0x0000000000401f96 in foo_two () at main.cpp:72
#5  0x0000000000401faa in thread_two (arg=0x0) at main.cpp:72
#6  0x00000000004137f3 in start_thread (arg=<optimized out>) at pthread_create.c:486
#7  0x000000000045512f in clone ()

Thread 2 (Thread 0x7fbcefc83700 (LWP 699)):
#0  0x0000000000452970 in nanosleep ()
#1  0x00000000004528fa in sleep ()
#2  0x0000000000401f5a in bar_one () at main.cpp:71
#3  0x0000000000401f66 in foo_one () at main.cpp:71
#4  0x0000000000401f7a in thread_one (arg=0x0) at main.cpp:71
#5  0x00000000004137f3 in start_thread (arg=<optimized out>) at pthread_create.c:486
#6  0x000000000045512f in clone ()

Thread 1 (Thread 0x1438880 (LWP 698)):
#0  0x0000000000452970 in nanosleep ()
#1  0x00000000004528fa in sleep ()
#2  0x0000000000402121 in main (argc=1, argv=0x7ffee378a7d8) at main.cpp:91
```

6. Switch to thread #1 and its frame #2, and list arguments and locals:

```
(gdb) thread 1
[Switching to thread 1 (Thread 0x1438880 (LWP 698))]
#0  0x0000000000452970 in nanosleep ()

(gdb) bt
#0  0x0000000000452970 in nanosleep ()
#1  0x00000000004528fa in sleep ()
#2  0x0000000000402121 in main (argc=1, argv=0x7ffee378a7d8) at main.cpp:91

(gdb) frame 2
#2  0x0000000000402121 in main (argc=1, argv=0x7ffee378a7d8) at main.cpp:91
```

```
91          sleep(-1);
```

```
(gdb) info args
argc = 1
argv = 0x7ffee378a7d8
```

```
(gdb) info locals
No locals.
```

7. Examine the *argv* array:

```
(gdb) print argv[0]
$1 = 0x7ffee378b74e "./App12"
```

```
(gdb) print *argv@10
$2 = {0x7ffee378b74e "./App12", 0x0, 0x7ffee378b756 "SHELL=/bin/bash", 0x7ffee378b766
"HISTCONTROL=ignoreboth", 0x7ffee378b77d "WSL_DISTRO_NAME=Debian", 0x7ffee378b794
"NAME=DESKTOP-IS6V2L0",
  0x7ffee378b7a9 "PWD=/home/coredump/ALCDA2/x64/App12", 0x7ffee378b7cd "LOGNAME=coredump",
0x7ffee378b7de "MC_TMPDIR=/tmp/mc-coredump", 0x7ffee378b7f9 "MC_SID=14"}
```

8. Dump the region 0x4b0000 - 0x4bc000 to a binary file:

```
(gdb) dump memory mem.raw 0x4b0000 0x4bc000
```

9. List all functions:

```
(gdb) info functions
All defined functions:

File ../nptl/pthread_mutex_lock.c:
63:     int __pthread_mutex_lock(pthread_mutex_t *);
170:    static int __pthread_mutex_lock_full(pthread_mutex_t *);

File ../nptl/pthread_mutex_trylock.c:
34:     int __pthread_mutex_trylock(pthread_mutex_t *);

File ../nptl/sigaction.c:
22:     int __sigaction(int, const sigaction *, sigaction *);

File ../sysdeps/unix/sysv/linux/createthread.c:
49:     static int create_thread(pthread *, const pthread_attr *, _Bool *, void *, _Bool *);

File ../sysdeps/unix/sysv/linux/sigaction.c:
42:     int __libc_sigaction(int, const sigaction *, sigaction *);

File ../sysdeps/unix/sysv/linux/write.c:
24:     ssize_t __libc_write(int, const void *, size_t);

File ../sysdeps/unix/sysv/linux/x86/elision-conf.c:
75:     void _dl_tunable_set_elision_enable(tunable_val_t *);
97:     void _dl_tunable_set_elision_retry_try_xbegin(tunable_val_t *);
95:     void _dl_tunable_set_elision_skip_lock_busy(tunable_val_t *);
96:     void _dl_tunable_set_elision_skip_lock_internal_abort(tunable_val_t *);
98:     void _dl_tunable_set_elision_skip_trylock_internal_abort(tunable_val_t *);
104:    static void elision_init(int, char **, char **);

File ../sysdeps/unix/sysv/linux/x86/elision-lock.c:
45:     int __lll_lock_elision(int *, short *, int);
```

```
File ../sysdeps/unix/sysv/linux/x86/elision-trylock.c:
31:     int __lll_trylock_elision(int *, short *);

File ../sysdeps/unix/sysv/linux/x86/elision-unlock.c:
24:     int __lll_unlock_elision(int *, int);

File allocatestack.c:
787:    void __deallocate_stack(pthread *);
970:    pthread *__find_thread_by_id(pid_t);
810:    int __make_stacks_executable(void **);
1119:   int __nptl_setxid(xid_command *);
1098:   void __nptl_setxid_error(xid_command *, int);
293:    void __nptl_stacks_freeres(void);
1245:   void __pthread_init_static_tls(link_map *);
861:    void __reclaim_stacks(void);
1264:   void __wait_lookup_done(void);
316:    static int change_stack_perm(pthread *);
255:    static void free_stacks(size_t);
1015:   static void setxid_mark_thread(pthread *, xid_command *);
1072:   static int setxid_signal_thread(xid_command *, pthread *);
1052:   static void setxid_unmark_thread(pthread *, xid_command *);

File cleanup_compat.c:
39:     void _pthread_cleanup_pop(_pthread_cleanup_buffer *, int);
24:     void _pthread_cleanup_push(_pthread_cleanup_buffer *, void (*)(void *), void *);
--Type <RET> for more, q to quit, c to continue without paging--

File events.c:
24:     void __nptl_create_event(void);

File main.cpp:
75:     void bar_five();
74:     void bar_four();
71:     void bar_one();
73:     void bar_three();
72:     void bar_two();
75:     void foo_five();
74:     void foo_four();
71:     void foo_one();
73:     void foo_three();
72:     void foo_two();
79:     int main(int, char const**);
27:     void procA();
45:     void procB();
22:     void procC();
75:     void *thread_five(void*);
74:     void *thread_four(void*);
71:     void *thread_one(void*);
73:     void *thread_three(void*);
72:     void *thread_two(void*);

File nptl-init.c:
152:    void __nptl_set_robust(pthread *);
440:    size_t __pthread_get_minstack(const pthread_attr_t *);
269:    void __pthread_initialize_minimal_internal(void);
165:    static void sigcancel_handler(int, siginfo_t *, void *);
218:    static void sighandler_setxid(int, siginfo_t *, void *);

File pthread_cancel.c:
```

```
28:     int __pthread_cancel(pthread_t);

File pthread_create.c:
209:    pthread *__find_in_stack_list(pthread *);
344:    void __free_tcb(pthread *);
250:    void __nptl_deallocate_tsd(void);
632:    int __pthread_create_2_1(pthread_t *, const pthread_attr_t *, void *(*)(void *), void
*);
378:    static int start_thread(void *);

File pthread_getspecific.c:
24:     void *__pthread_getspecific(pthread_key_t);

File pthread_key_create.c:
25:     int __pthread_key_create(pthread_key_t *, void (*)(void *));

File pthread_key_delete.c:
25:     int __pthread_key_delete(pthread_key_t);

File pthread_mutex_init.c:
56:     int __pthread_mutex_init(pthread_mutex_t *, const pthread_mutexattr_t *);

File pthread_mutex_unlock.c:
354:    int __pthread_mutex_unlock(pthread_mutex_t *);
36:     int __pthread_mutex_unlock_usercnt(pthread_mutex_t *, int);
--Type <RET> for more, q to quit, c to continue without paging--
96:     static int __pthread_mutex_unlock_full(pthread_mutex_t *, int);

File pthread_once.c:
135:    int __pthread_once(pthread_once_t *, void (*)(void));
67:     static int __pthread_once_slow(pthread_once_t *, void (*)(void));
28:     static void clear_once_control(void *);

File pthread_setspecific.c:
25:     int __pthread_setspecific(pthread_key_t, const void *);

File tpp.c:
43:     void __init_sched_fifo_prio(void);
160:    int __pthread_current_priority(void);
52:     int __pthread_tpp_change_priority(int, int);

File unwind.c:
111:    void __pthread_unwind(__pthread_unwind_buf_t *);
132:    void __pthread_unwind_next(__pthread_unwind_buf_t *);
101:    static void unwind_cleanup(_Unwind_Reason_Code, _Unwind_Exception *);
39:     static _Unwind_Reason_Code unwind_stop(int, _Unwind_Action, _Unwind_Exception_Class,
_Unwind_Exception *, _Unwind_Context *, void *);

Non-debugging symbols:
0x00007ffee3797600  __vdso_gettimeofday
0x00007ffee3797600  gettimeofday
0x00007ffee3797730  __vdso_time
0x00007ffee3797730  time
0x00007ffee3797740  __vdso_clock_gettime
0x00007ffee3797740  clock_gettime
0x00007ffee37978a0  __vdso_clock_getres
0x00007ffee37978a0  clock_getres
0x00007ffee37978f0  __vdso_getcpu
0x00007ffee37978f0  getcpu
0x0000000000401000  _init
```

```
0x00000000004010f0  __cxxabiv1::__terminate(void (*)()) [clone .cold.0]
0x00000000004010fd  read_encoded_value_with_base(unsigned char, unsigned long, unsigned char
const*, unsigned long*) [clone .cold.4]
0x0000000000401102  __gxx_personality_v0.cold.5
0x000000000040110f  __cxa_call_unexpected.cold.6
0x00000000004011bc  (anonymous namespace)::pool::free(void*) [clone .constprop.2] [clone
.cold.5]
0x00000000004011cc  (anonymous namespace)::pool::allocate(unsigned long) [clone .constprop.3]
[clone .cold.6]
0x00000000004011dc  __gnu_cxx::__verbose_terminate_handler() [clone .cold.1]
0x000000000040125e  d_type.cold
0x0000000000401303  read_encoded_value_with_base.cold
0x0000000000401308  execute_cfa_program.cold
0x000000000040130d  execute_stack_op.cold
--Type <RET> for more, q to quit, c to continue without paging--q
Quit
```

10. We can also list all available types or specific types:

```
(gdb) info types pthread_mutex_t
All types matching regular expression "pthread_mutex_t":

File ../sysdeps/nptl/bits/pthreadtypes.h:
72:     typedef union {
    __pthread_mutex_s __data;
    char __size[40];
    long __align;
} pthread_mutex_t;

File /usr/include/x86_64-linux-gnu/bits/pthreadtypes.h:
68:     pthread_mutex_t;
72:     typedef pthread_mutex_t pthread_mutex_t;

(gdb) ptype pthread_mutex_t
type = union pthread_mutex_t {
    __pthread_mutex_s __data;
    char __size[40];
    long __align;
}

(gdb) ptype /o pthread_mutex_t
type = union pthread_mutex_t {
/*                    40 */    struct __pthread_mutex_s {
/*    0      |         4 */        int __lock;
/*    4      |         4 */        unsigned int __count;
/*    8      |         4 */        int __owner;
/*   12      |         4 */        unsigned int __nusers;
/*   16      |         4 */        int __kind;
/*   20      |         2 */        short __spins;
/*   22      |         2 */        short __elision;
/*   24      |        16 */        __pthread_list_t __list;

                                   /* total size (bytes):   40 */
                               } __data;
/*                    40 */    char __size[40];
/*                     8 */    long __align;

                               /* total size (bytes):   40 */
                             }
```

11. List all variables:

```
(gdb) info variables
All defined variables:

File ../nptl_db/db_info.c:
108:    const uint32_t _thread_db_const_thread_area;

File ../nptl_db/structs.def:
80:     const uint32_t _thread_db___nptl_initial_report_events[3];
78:     const uint32_t _thread_db___nptl_nthreads[3];
82:     const uint32_t _thread_db___pthread_keys[3];
96:     const uint32_t _thread_db_dtv_dtv[3];
113:    const uint32_t _thread_db_dtv_slotinfo_list_slotinfo[3];
93:     const uint32_t _thread_db_link_map_l_tls_modid[3];
94:     const uint32_t _thread_db_link_map_l_tls_offset[3];
62:     const uint32_t _thread_db_list_t_next[3];
63:     const uint32_t _thread_db_list_t_prev[3];
52:     const uint32_t _thread_db_pthread_cancelhandling[3];
56:     const uint32_t _thread_db_pthread_eventbuf[3];
57:     const uint32_t _thread_db_pthread_eventbuf_eventmask[3];
58:     const uint32_t _thread_db_pthread_eventbuf_eventmask_event_bits[3];
91:     const uint32_t _thread_db_pthread_key_data_level2_data[3];
48:     const uint32_t _thread_db_pthread_list[3];
59:     const uint32_t _thread_db_pthread_nextevent[3];
49:     const uint32_t _thread_db_pthread_report_events[3];
54:     const uint32_t _thread_db_pthread_schedparam_sched_priority[3];
53:     const uint32_t _thread_db_pthread_schedpolicy[3];
55:     const uint32_t _thread_db_pthread_specific[3];
51:     const uint32_t _thread_db_pthread_start_routine[3];
50:     const uint32_t _thread_db_pthread_tid[3];
61:     const uint32_t _thread_db_sizeof_list_t;
47:     const uint32_t _thread_db_sizeof_pthread;
90:     const uint32_t _thread_db_sizeof_pthread_key_data_level2;
68:     const uint32_t _thread_db_sizeof_td_eventbuf_t;
65:     const uint32_t _thread_db_sizeof_td_thr_events_t;
70:     const uint32_t _thread_db_td_eventbuf_t_eventdata[3];
69:     const uint32_t _thread_db_td_eventbuf_t_eventnum[3];
66:     const uint32_t _thread_db_td_thr_events_t_event_bits[3];

File ../sysdeps/unix/sysv/linux/x86/elision-conf.c:
33:     elision_config __elision_aconf;
56:     int __pthread_force_elision;
134:    void (* const__pthread_init_array[1])(int, char **, char **);

File allocatestack.c:
125:    list_t __stack_user;
121:    static uintptr_t in_flight_stack;
113:    static list_t stack_cache;
107:    static size_t stack_cache_actsize;
110:    static int stack_cache_lock;
106:    static size_t stack_cache_maxsize;
116:    static list_t stack_used;

File main.cpp:
20:     pthread_mutex_t mutexA;
20:     pthread_mutex_t mutexB;

File nptl-init.c:
44:     int *__libc_multiple_threads_ptr;
```

```
--Type <RET> for more, q to quit, c to continue without paging--
49:     size_t __static_tls_align_m1;
48:     size_t __static_tls_size;
212:    xid_command *__xidcmd;
266:    static _Bool __nptl_initial_report_events;
70:     static const char nptl_version[5];

File pthread_create.c:
53:     unsigned int __nptl_nthreads;
44:     int __pthread_debug;
50:     static pthread *__nptl_last_event;
47:     static td_thr_events_t __nptl_threads_events;

File pthread_mutex_init.c:
30:     static const pthread_mutexattr default_mutexattr;

File pthread_once.c:
24:     unsigned long __fork_generation;

File tpp.c:
30:     int __sched_fifo_max_prio;
29:     int __sched_fifo_min_prio;

File vars.c:
25:     pthread_attr __default_pthread_attr;
28:     int __default_pthread_attr_lock;
31:     int __is_smp;
41:     pthread_key_struct __pthread_keys[1024];
37:     int __pthread_multiple_threads;

Non-debugging symbols:
0x0000000000000000  __libc_resp
0x0000000000000008  _nl_current_LC_CTYPE
0x0000000000000010  __libc_tsd_LOCALE
0x0000000000000018  _nl_current_LC_MONETARY
0x0000000000000020  _nl_current_LC_NUMERIC
0x0000000000000028  (anonymous namespace)::get_global()::global
0x0000000000000038  __libc_errno
0x0000000000000040  __libc_tsd_CTYPE_TOLOWER
0x0000000000000048  __libc_tsd_CTYPE_TOUPPER
0x0000000000000050  __libc_tsd_CTYPE_B
0x0000000000000058  tcache
0x0000000000000060  tcache_shutting_down
0x0000000000000068  thread_arena
0x0000000000000070  current
0x0000000000000078  catch_hook
0x0000000000400000  __ehdr_start
0x0000000000400248  __rela_iplt_start
0x00000000004004d0  __rela_iplt_end
0x00000000004a1000  _IO_stdin_used
0x00000000004a1020  typeinfo name for __cxxabiv1::__fundamental_type_info
0x00000000004a1048  typeinfo name for void
0x00000000004a104a  typeinfo name for void*
0x00000000004a104d  typeinfo name for void const*
0x00000000004a1051  typeinfo name for bool
0x00000000004a1053  typeinfo name for bool*
0x00000000004a1056  typeinfo name for bool const*
0x00000000004a105a  typeinfo name for wchar_t
--Type <RET> for more, q to quit, c to continue without paging--q
Quit
```

12. List segment info (also **info files**):

```
(gdb) info target
Symbols from "/home/coredump/ALCDA2/x64/App12/App12.debug".
Local core dump file:
        `/home/coredump/ALCDA2/x64/App12/App12.core.698', file type elf64-x86-64.
        0x0000000000401000 - 0x00000000004a1000 is load1
        0x00000000004cc000 - 0x00000000004d4000 is load2
        0x00000000004d4000 - 0x00000000004da000 is load3
        0x0000000001438000 - 0x000000000145b000 is load4
        0x00007fbce8000000 - 0x00007fbce8021000 is load5
        0x00007fbce8021000 - 0x00007fbcec000000 is load6
        0x00007fbced47f000 - 0x00007fbced480000 is load7
        0x00007fbced480000 - 0x00007fbcedc80000 is load8
        0x00007fbcedc80000 - 0x00007fbcedc81000 is load9
        0x00007fbcedc81000 - 0x00007fbcee481000 is load10
        0x00007fbcee481000 - 0x00007fbcee482000 is load11
        0x00007fbcee482000 - 0x00007fbceec82000 is load12
        0x00007fbceec82000 - 0x00007fbceec83000 is load13
        0x00007fbceec83000 - 0x00007fbcef483000 is load14
        0x00007fbcef483000 - 0x00007fbcef484000 is load15
        0x00007fbcef484000 - 0x00007fbcefc84000 is load16
        0x00007ffee376b000 - 0x00007ffee378c000 is load17
        0x00007ffee3797000 - 0x00007ffee3798000 is load18
Local exec file:
        `/home/coredump/ALCDA2/x64/App12/App12', file type elf64-x86-64.
        Entry point: 0x401d70
        0x0000000000400200 - 0x0000000000400220 is .note.ABI-tag
        0x0000000000400220 - 0x0000000000400244 is .note.gnu.build-id
        0x0000000000400248 - 0x00000000004004d0 is .rela.plt
        0x0000000000401000 - 0x0000000000401017 is .init
        0x0000000000401018 - 0x00000000004010f0 is .plt
        0x00000000004010f0 - 0x000000000049f55b is .text
        0x000000000049f560 - 0x00000000004a0107 is __libc_freeres_fn
        0x00000000004a0108 - 0x00000000004a0111 is .fini
        0x00000000004a1000 - 0x00000000004bcd20 is .rodata
        0x00000000004bcd20 - 0x00000000004bcd21 is .stapsdt.base
        0x00000000004bcd28 - 0x00000000004caa38 is .eh_frame
        0x00000000004caa38 - 0x00000000004cac13 is .gcc_except_table
        0x00000000004cc848 - 0x00000000004cc870 is .tdata
        0x00000000004cc870 - 0x00000000004cc8c8 is .tbss
        0x00000000004cc870 - 0x00000000004cc878 is .preinit_array
        0x00000000004cc878 - 0x00000000004cc890 is .init_array
        0x00000000004cc890 - 0x00000000004cc8a0 is .fini_array
        0x00000000004cc8a0 - 0x00000000004d0ef4 is .data.rel.ro
        0x00000000004d0ef8 - 0x00000000004d1000 is .got
        0x00000000004d1000 - 0x00000000004d10f0 is .got.plt
        0x00000000004d1100 - 0x00000000004d2c48 is .data
        0x00000000004d2c48 - 0x00000000004d2ca8 is __libc_subfreeres
        0x00000000004d2cc0 - 0x00000000004d3428 is __libc_IO_vtables
        0x00000000004d3428 - 0x00000000004d3430 is __libc_atexit
        0x00000000004d3440 - 0x00000000004d9628 is .bss
        0x00000000004d9628 - 0x00000000004d9658 is __libc_freeres_ptrs
        0x00007ffee3797120 - 0x00007ffee3797164 is .hash in system-supplied DSO at 0x7ffee3797000
        0x00007ffee3797168 - 0x00007ffee37971b8 is .gnu.hash in system-supplied DSO at 0x7ffee3797000
        0x00007ffee37971b8 - 0x00007ffee37972d8 is .dynsym in system-supplied DSO at 0x7ffee3797000
        0x00007ffee37972d8 - 0x00007ffee379734a is .dynstr in system-supplied DSO at 0x7ffee3797000
        0x00007ffee379734a - 0x00007ffee3797362 is .gnu.version in system-supplied DSO at 0x7ffee3797000
        0x00007ffee3797368 - 0x00007ffee37973a0 is .gnu.version_d in system-supplied DSO at 0x7ffee3797000
        0x00007ffee37973a0 - 0x00007ffee37974b0 is .dynamic in system-supplied DSO at 0x7ffee3797000
        0x00007ffee37974b0 - 0x00007ffee3797504 is .note in system-supplied DSO at 0x7ffee3797000
        0x00007ffee3797504 - 0x00007ffee3797538 is .eh_frame_hdr in system-supplied DSO at 0x7ffee3797000
        0x00007ffee3797538 - 0x00007ffee37975fc is .eh_frame in system-supplied DSO at 0x7ffee3797000
--Type <RET> for more, q to quit, c to continue without paging--
        0x00007ffee3797600 - 0x00007ffee3797915 is .text in system-supplied DSO at 0x7ffee3797000
        0x00007ffee3797915 - 0x00007ffee379798a is .altinstructions in system-supplied DSO at 0x7ffee3797000
        0x00007ffee379798a - 0x00007ffee37979ae is .altinstr_replacement in system-supplied DSO at 0x7ffee3797000
```

13. With full debug symbols, we can also disassemble functions with source code annotations included:

```
(gdb) disassemble /s procA
Dump of assembler code for function procA():
main.cpp:
28      {
   0x0000000000401eb5 <+0>:     push   %rbp
   0x0000000000401eb6 <+1>:     mov    %rsp,%rbp

29          try
30          {
31              pthread_mutex_lock(&mutexA);
   0x0000000000401eb9 <+4>:     lea    0xd15e0(%rip),%rdi        # 0x4d34a0 <mutexA>
   0x0000000000401ec0 <+11>:    callq  0x415240 <__pthread_mutex_lock>

32              procC();
   0x0000000000401ec5 <+16>:    callq  0x401e8d <procC()>

33              pthread_mutex_unlock(&mutexA);
   0x0000000000401eca <+21>:    lea    0xd15cf(%rip),%rdi        # 0x4d34a0 <mutexA>
   0x0000000000401ed1 <+28>:    callq  0x4160b0 <__pthread_mutex_unlock>

36          {
37
38          }
39
40          sleep(20);
   0x0000000000401ed6 <+33>:    mov    $0x14,%edi
   0x0000000000401edb <+38>:    callq  0x4528c0 <sleep>

41          pthread_mutex_lock(&mutexB);
   0x0000000000401ee0 <+43>:    lea    0xd15f9(%rip),%rdi        # 0x4d34e0 <mutexB>
   0x0000000000401ee7 <+50>:    callq  0x415240 <__pthread_mutex_lock>

42          pthread_mutex_unlock(&mutexB);
   0x0000000000401eec <+55>:    lea    0xd15ed(%rip),%rdi        # 0x4d34e0 <mutexB>
   0x0000000000401ef3 <+62>:    callq  0x4160b0 <__pthread_mutex_unlock>

43      }
   0x0000000000401ef8 <+67>:    jmp    0x401f09 <procA()+84>

35          catch(...)
   0x0000000000401efa <+69>:    mov    %rax,%rdi
   0x0000000000401efd <+72>:    callq  0x402ec0 <__cxa_begin_catch>
   0x0000000000401f02 <+77>:    callq  0x402f30 <__cxa_end_catch>
   0x0000000000401f07 <+82>:    jmp    0x401ed6 <procA()+33>

43      }
   0x0000000000401f09 <+84>:    pop    %rbp
   0x0000000000401f0a <+85>:    retq
--Type <RET> for more, q to quit, c to continue without paging--c
End of assembler dump.
```

Exercise A12 (A64, GDB)

Goal: Learn how to dump memory for post-processing, get the list of functions and module variables, load symbols, disassemble with source code, inspect arguments, local variables, and types.

Patterns: Module Variable.

1. Load the *App12.core.17894* dump file and *App12* executable from the A64/App12 directory:

```
~/ALCDA2/A64/App12$ gdb-multiarch -c App12.core.17894 -se App12
GNU gdb (Debian 8.2.1-2+b3) 8.2.1
Copyright (C) 2018 Free Software Foundation, Inc.
License GPLv3+: GNU GPL version 3 or later <http://gnu.org/licenses/gpl.html>
This is free software: you are free to change and redistribute it.
There is NO WARRANTY, to the extent permitted by law.
Type "show copying" and "show warranty" for details.
This GDB was configured as "x86_64-linux-gnu".
Type "show configuration" for configuration details.
For bug reporting instructions, please see:
<http://www.gnu.org/software/gdb/bugs/>.
Find the GDB manual and other documentation resources online at:
    <http://www.gnu.org/software/gdb/documentation/>.

For help, type "help".
Type "apropos word" to search for commands related to "word".
[New LWP 17895]
[New LWP 17896]
[New LWP 17905]
[New LWP 17906]
[New LWP 17907]
[New LWP 17894]
Core was generated by `./App12'.
#0  0x000000000041ae24 in ?? ()
[Current thread is 1 (LWP 17895)]
```

2. Set logging to a file in case of lengthy output from some commands:

```
(gdb) set logging on App12.log
Copying output to App12.log.
```

3. List all thread stack traces:

```
(gdb) thread apply all bt

Thread 6 (LWP 17894):
#0  0x000000000041ae24 in ?? ()
#1  0x00000000004d0020 in ?? ()
Backtrace stopped: previous frame inner to this frame (corrupt stack?)

Thread 5 (LWP 17907):
#0  0x000000000041ae24 in ?? ()
Backtrace stopped: previous frame identical to this frame (corrupt stack?)

Thread 4 (LWP 17906):
#0  0x000000000041a110 in ?? ()
Backtrace stopped: previous frame identical to this frame (corrupt stack?)
```

```
Thread 3 (LWP 17905):
#0  0x000000000041ae24 in ?? ()
Backtrace stopped: previous frame identical to this frame (corrupt stack?)

Thread 2 (LWP 17896):
#0  0x000000000041a110 in ?? ()
Backtrace stopped: previous frame identical to this frame (corrupt stack?)

Thread 1 (LWP 17895):
#0  0x000000000041ae24 in ?? ()
Backtrace stopped: previous frame identical to this frame (corrupt stack?)
```

4. *App12* is an executable with stripped-off debug symbols. Change the symbol file to *Symbols/App12,* which is the same executable as *App12* but with debug symbols included:

```
(gdb) symbol-file Symbols/App12
Reading symbols from Symbols/App12...
```

5. List all thread stack traces again:

```
(gdb) thread apply all bt

Thread 6 (LWP 17894):
#0  0x000000000041ae24 in nanosleep ()
#1  0x00000000004338b4 in sleep ()
#2  0x00000000004034e0 in main (argc=1, argv=0xfffff841c0a8) at main.cpp:92

Thread 5 (LWP 17907):
#0  0x000000000041ae24 in nanosleep ()
#1  0x00000000004338b4 in sleep ()
#2  0x00000000004033f0 in bar_five () at main.cpp:76
#3  0x0000000000403404 in foo_five () at main.cpp:76
#4  0x000000000040341c in thread_five (arg=0x0) at main.cpp:76
#5  0x00000000004130a4 in start_thread ()
#6  0x0000000000438760 in thread_start ()

Thread 4 (LWP 17906):
#0  0x000000000041a110 in __lll_lock_wait ()
#1  0x0000000000414ea4 in pthread_mutex_lock ()
#2  0x00000000004032a0 in procB () at main.cpp:49
#3  0x00000000004033a8 in bar_four () at main.cpp:75
#4  0x00000000004033bc in foo_four () at main.cpp:75
#5  0x00000000004033d4 in thread_four (arg=0x0) at main.cpp:75
#6  0x00000000004130a4 in start_thread ()
#7  0x0000000000438760 in thread_start ()

Thread 3 (LWP 17905):
#0  0x000000000041ae24 in nanosleep ()
#1  0x00000000004338b4 in sleep ()
#2  0x0000000000403364 in bar_three () at main.cpp:74
#3  0x0000000000403378 in foo_three () at main.cpp:74
#4  0x0000000000403390 in thread_three (arg=0x0) at main.cpp:74
#5  0x00000000004130a4 in start_thread ()
#6  0x0000000000438760 in thread_start ()

Thread 2 (LWP 17896):
#0  0x000000000041a110 in __lll_lock_wait ()
#1  0x0000000000414ea4 in pthread_mutex_lock ()
#2  0x000000000040325c in procA () at main.cpp:42
#3  0x000000000040331c in bar_two () at main.cpp:73
```

```
#4  0x0000000000403330 in foo_two () at main.cpp:73
#5  0x0000000000403348 in thread_two (arg=0x0) at main.cpp:73
#6  0x00000000004130a4 in start_thread ()
#7  0x0000000000438760 in thread_start ()

Thread 1 (LWP 17895):
#0  0x000000000041ae24 in nanosleep ()
#1  0x00000000004338b4 in sleep ()
#2  0x00000000004032d8 in bar_one () at main.cpp:72
#3  0x00000000004032ec in foo_one () at main.cpp:72
--Type <RET> for more, q to quit, c to continue without paging--
#4  0x0000000000403304 in thread_one (arg=0x0) at main.cpp:72
#5  0x00000000004130a4 in start_thread ()
#6  0x0000000000438760 in thread_start ()
```

6. Having full symbols allows us to check the ownership of the mutex faster (this is a new process with the same source code as in the previous A11 exercise):

```
(gdb) disassemble procB
Dump of assembler code for function _Z5procBv:
   0x0000000000403280 <+0>:     stp     x29, x30, [sp, #-16]!
   0x0000000000403284 <+4>:     mov     x29, sp
   0x0000000000403288 <+8>:     adrp    x0, 0x4d1000 <main_arena+2128>
   0x000000000040328c <+12>:    add     x0, x0, #0x608
   0x0000000000403290 <+16>:    bl      0x414dbc <pthread_mutex_lock>
   0x0000000000403294 <+20>:    adrp    x0, 0x4d1000 <main_arena+2128>
   0x0000000000403298 <+24>:    add     x0, x0, #0x5d8
   0x000000000040329c <+28>:    bl      0x414dbc <pthread_mutex_lock>
   0x00000000004032a0 <+32>:    mov     w0, #0x1e                       // #30
   0x00000000004032a4 <+36>:    bl      0x4337a4 <sleep>
   0x00000000004032a8 <+40>:    adrp    x0, 0x4d1000 <main_arena+2128>
   0x00000000004032ac <+44>:    add     x0, x0, #0x5d8
   0x00000000004032b0 <+48>:    bl      0x414dbc <pthread_mutex_lock>
   0x00000000004032b4 <+52>:    adrp    x0, 0x4d1000 <main_arena+2128>
   0x00000000004032b8 <+56>:    add     x0, x0, #0x608
   0x00000000004032bc <+60>:    bl      0x414dbc <pthread_mutex_lock>
   0x00000000004032c0 <+64>:    ldp     x29, x30, [sp], #16
   0x00000000004032c4 <+68>:    ret
End of assembler dump.

(gdb) print (pthread_mutex_t *)0x4d15d8
$1 = (pthread_mutex_t *) 0x4d15d8 <mutexA>

(gdb) print *(pthread_mutex_t *)0x4d15d8
$2 = {__data = {__lock = 2, __count = 0, __owner = 17896, __nusers = 1, __kind = 0, __spins =
0, __list = {__prev = 0x0,
      __next = 0x0}}, __size = "\002\000\000\000\000\000\000\000\350E\000\000\001", '\000'
<repeats 34 times>, __align = 2}

(gdb) print mutexA
$2 = {__data = {__lock = 2, __count = 0, __owner = 17896, __nusers = 1, __kind = 0, __spins =
0, __list = {__prev = 0x0,
      __next = 0x0}}, __size = "\002\000\000\000\000\000\000\000\350E\000\000\001", '\000'
<repeats 34 times>, __align = 2}

(gdb) print mutexB
$3 = {__data = {__lock = 2, __count = 0, __owner = 17906, __nusers = 1, __kind = 0, __spins =
0, __list = {__prev = 0x0,
      __next = 0x0}}, __size = "\002\000\000\000\000\000\000\000\362E\000\000\001", '\000'
<repeats 34 times>, __align = 2}
```

7. Switch to thread #6 and its frame #2, and list arguments and locals:

```
(gdb) thread 6
[Switching to thread 6 (LWP 17894)]
#0  0x000000000041ae24 in nanosleep ()

(gdb) bt
#0  0x000000000041ae24 in nanosleep ()
#1  0x00000000004338b4 in sleep ()
#2  0x00000000004034e0 in main (argc=1, argv=0xfffff841c0a8) at main.cpp:92

(gdb) frame 2
#2  0x00000000004034e0 in main (argc=1, argv=0xfffff841c0a8) at main.cpp:92
92        main.cpp: No such file or directory.

(gdb) info args
argc = 1
argv = 0xfffff841c0a8

(gdb) info locals
No locals.
```

8. Examine the *argv* array:

```
(gdb) print argv[0]
$3 = 0xfffff841f6d7 "./App12"

(gdb) print *argv@10
$4 = {0xfffff841f6d7 "./App12", 0x0, 0xfffff841f6df "XDG_SESSION_ID=8954",
  0xfffff841f6f3 "HOSTNAME=instance-20211109-2004", 0xfffff841f713 "SELINUX_ROLE_REQUESTED=",
  0xfffff841f72b "TERM=xterm-256color", 0xfffff841f73f "SHELL=/bin/bash", 0xfffff841f74f
"HISTSIZE=1000",
  0xfffff841f75d "SSH_CLIENT=37.228.238.120 61014 22", 0xfffff841f780
"SELINUX_USE_CURRENT_RANGE="}
```

9. Dump the region 0x00400000 – 0x004e0000 to a binary file:

```
(gdb) dump memory mem.raw 0x00400000 0x004e0000
```

10. List all functions:

```
(gdb) info functions
All defined functions:

File main.cpp:
76:     void bar_five();
75:     void bar_four();
72:     void bar_one();
74:     void bar_three();
73:     void bar_two();
76:     void foo_five();
75:     void foo_four();
72:     void foo_one();
74:     void foo_three();
73:     void foo_two();
80:     int main(int, char const**);
28:     void procA();
46:     void procB();
23:     void procC();
```

```
76:     void *thread_five(void*);
75:     void *thread_four(void*);
72:     void *thread_one(void*);
74:     void *thread_three(void*);
73:     void *thread_two(void*);

Non-debugging symbols:
0x0000fffbfad70420  __kernel_clock_gettime
0x0000fffbfad704f8  __kernel_gettimeofday
0x0000fffbfad705a0  __kernel_clock_getres
0x0000fffbfad705b8  __kernel_rt_sigreturn
0x0000000000400250  _init
0x00000000004002c0  __pthread_mutex_lock_full
0x000000000040085c  __pthread_mutex_unlock_full
0x0000000000400cb8  __pthread_once_slow
0x0000000000400d9c  __pthread_mutex_cond_lock_full
0x0000000000401320  check_one_fd.part
0x00000000004013e0  new_heap
0x0000000000401568  arena_get2
0x0000000000401b28  arena_get_retry
0x0000000000401c14  sysmalloc
0x00000000004021d8  tcache_init.part
0x00000000004022d4  cancel_handler.part
0x00000000004022f8  put_locked_global.isra.3.part
0x000000000040231c  strip
0x00000000004023c0  read_int
0x000000000040242c  group_number
0x000000000040257c  _i18n_number_rewrite
0x00000000004027d0  _i18n_number_rewrite
0x0000000000402a24  search_list_add__
0x0000000000402a9c  nameserver_list_emplace__
0x0000000000402b48  is_trusted_path_normalize
--Type <RET> for more, q to quit, c to continue without paging-- q
Quit
```

11. We can also list all available types or specific types:

```
(gdb) info types pthread_mutex_t
All types matching regular expression "pthread_mutex_t":

File /usr/include/bits/pthreadtypes.h:
61:     pthread_mutex_t;
62:     pthread_mutex_t::__pthread_mutex_s;
75:     typedef pthread_mutex_t pthread_mutex_t;

(gdb) ptype pthread_mutex_t
type = union pthread_mutex_t {
    pthread_mutex_t::__pthread_mutex_s __data;
    char __size[48];
    long __align;
}

(gdb) ptype /o pthread_mutex_t
type = union pthread_mutex_t {
/*                40 */    struct pthread_mutex_t::__pthread_mutex_s {
/*    0      |     4 */        int __lock;
/*    4      |     4 */        unsigned int __count;
/*    8      |     4 */        int __owner;
/*   12      |     4 */        unsigned int __nusers;
/*   16      |     4 */        int __kind;
```

```
/*   20       |      4 */          int __spins;
/*   24       |     16 */          __pthread_list_t __list;

                                   /* total size (bytes):   40 */
                               } __data;
/*                  48 */      char __size[48];
/*                   8 */      long __align;

                               /* total size (bytes):   48 */
                             }
```

12. List all variables:

```
(gdb) info variables
All defined variables:

File main.cpp:
21:     pthread_mutex_t mutexA;
21:     pthread_mutex_t mutexB;

Non-debugging symbols:
0x0000000000000000  _TLS_MODULE_BASE_
0x0000000000000000  __libc_resp
0x0000000000000000  __resp
0x0000000000000008  _nl_current_LC_CTYPE
0x0000000000000010  __libc_tsd_LOCALE
0x0000000000000018  _nl_current_LC_MONETARY
0x0000000000000020  _nl_current_LC_NUMERIC
0x0000000000000028  (anonymous namespace)::get_global()::global
0x0000000000000038  __libc_errno
0x0000000000000038  errno
0x0000000000000040  __libc_tsd_CTYPE_B
0x0000000000000048  __libc_tsd_CTYPE_TOUPPER
0x0000000000000050  __libc_tsd_CTYPE_TOLOWER
0x0000000000000058  thread_arena
0x0000000000000060  tcache
0x0000000000000068  tcache_shutting_down
0x0000000000000070  current
0x0000000000000078  __h_errno
0x0000000000000078  __libc_h_errno
0x0000000000000080  data
0x00000000004001d8  __rela_iplt_start
0x0000000000400250  __rela_iplt_end
0x00000000004933e0  _IO_stdin_used
0x00000000004933e8  __dso_handle
0x00000000004933f0  typeinfo name for __gnu_cxx::__concurrence_lock_error
0x0000000000493418  typeinfo name for __gnu_cxx::__concurrence_unlock_error
0x0000000000493498  typeinfo name for std::exception
0x00000000004934a8  typeinfo name for std::bad_exception
0x00000000004934c0  typeinfo name for __cxxabiv1::__forced_unwind
0x00000000004934e0  typeinfo name for __cxxabiv1::__foreign_exception
0x0000000000493548  typeinfo name for __cxxabiv1::__fundamental_type_info
0x0000000000493570  typeinfo name for void
0x0000000000493578  typeinfo name for void*
0x0000000000493580  typeinfo name for void const*
0x0000000000493588  typeinfo name for bool
0x0000000000493590  typeinfo name for bool*
0x0000000000493598  typeinfo name for bool const*
0x00000000004935a0  typeinfo name for wchar_t
0x00000000004935a8  typeinfo name for wchar_t*
```

```
0x00000000004935b0  typeinfo name for wchar_t const*
0x00000000004935b8  typeinfo name for char16_t
0x00000000004935c0  typeinfo name for char16_t*
--Type <RET> for more, q to quit, c to continue without paging--q
Quit
```

13. List segment info (also **info files**):

```
(gdb) info target
Symbols from "/home/ubuntu/ALCDA2/A64/App12/Symbols/App12".
Local core dump file:
        `/home/ubuntu/ALCDA2/A64/App12/App12.core.17894', file type elf64-littleaarch64.
        0x0000000000400000 - 0x00000000004c0000 is load1
        0x00000000004c0000 - 0x00000000004e0000 is load2
        0x00000000004e0000 - 0x00000000004f0000 is load3
        0x000000003a6e0000 - 0x000000003a720000 is load4
        0x0000fffbf4000000 - 0x0000fffbf4030000 is load5
        0x0000fffbf4030000 - 0x0000fffbf8000000 is load6
        0x0000fffbf8510000 - 0x0000fffbf8520000 is load7
        0x0000fffbf8520000 - 0x0000fffbf8d20000 is load8
        0x0000fffbf8d20000 - 0x0000fffbf8d30000 is load9
        0x0000fffbf8d30000 - 0x0000fffbf9530000 is load10
        0x0000fffbf9530000 - 0x0000fffbf9540000 is load11
        0x0000fffbf9540000 - 0x0000fffbf9d40000 is load12
        0x0000fffbf9d40000 - 0x0000fffbf9d50000 is load13
        0x0000fffbf9d50000 - 0x0000fffbfa550000 is load14
        0x0000fffbfa550000 - 0x0000fffbfa560000 is load15
        0x0000fffbfa560000 - 0x0000fffbfad60000 is load16
        0x0000fffbfad70000 - 0x0000fffbfad80000 is load17
        0x0000ffffff83f0000 - 0x0000ffffff8420000 is load18
```

14. If we disassemble the *procA* function with the source code option, we don't get source code fragments because GDB can't find the location of *main.cpp*:

```
(gdb) disassemble /s procA
Dump of assembler code for function _Z5procAv:
main.cpp:
29      main.cpp: No such file or directory.
   0x0000000000403224 <+0>:     stp     x29, x30, [sp, #-16]!
   0x0000000000403228 <+4>:     mov     x29, sp

30      in main.cpp
31      in main.cpp
32      in main.cpp
   0x000000000040322c <+8>:     adrp    x0, 0x4d1000 <main_arena+2128>
   0x0000000000403230 <+12>:    add     x0, x0, #0x5d8
   0x0000000000403234 <+16>:    bl      0x414dbc <pthread_mutex_lock>

33      in main.cpp
   0x0000000000403238 <+20>:    bl      0x403200 <_Z5procCv>

34      in main.cpp
   0x000000000040323c <+24>:    adrp    x0, 0x4d1000 <main_arena+2128>
   0x0000000000403240 <+28>:    add     x0, x0, #0x5d8
   0x0000000000403244 <+32>:    bl      0x416054 <pthread_mutex_unlock>

37      in main.cpp
38      in main.cpp
39      in main.cpp
```

```
40      in main.cpp
41      in main.cpp
   0x0000000000403248 <+36>:    mov     w0, #0x14                       // #20
   0x000000000040324c <+40>:    bl      0x4337a4 <sleep>

42      in main.cpp
   0x0000000000403250 <+44>:    adrp    x0, 0x4d1000 <main_arena+2128>
   0x0000000000403254 <+48>:    add     x0, x0, #0x608
   0x0000000000403258 <+52>:    bl      0x414dbc <pthread_mutex_lock>

--Type <RET> for more, q to quit, c to continue without paging--
43      in main.cpp
   0x000000000040325c <+56>:    adrp    x0, 0x4d1000 <main_arena+2128>
   0x0000000000403260 <+60>:    add     x0, x0, #0x608
   0x0000000000403264 <+64>:    bl      0x416054 <pthread_mutex_unlock>
   0x0000000000403268 <+68>:    b       0x403278 <_Z5procAv+84>

36      in main.cpp
   0x000000000040326c <+72>:    bl      0x4039b4 <__cxa_begin_catch>
   0x0000000000403270 <+76>:    bl      0x403a58 <__cxa_end_catch>
   0x0000000000403274 <+80>:    b       0x403248 <_Z5procAv+36>

44      in main.cpp
   0x0000000000403278 <+84>:    ldp     x29, x30, [sp], #16
   0x000000000040327c <+88>:    ret
End of assembler dump.
```

Note: We can specify the source code directory:

```
(gdb) directory Source/
Source directories searched: /home/ubuntu/ALCDA2/A64/App12/Source: $cdir:$cwd
```

```
(gdb) disassemble /s procA
Dump of assembler code for function _Z5procAv:
main.cpp:
29      {
   0x0000000000403224 <+0>:     stp     x29, x30, [sp, #-16]!
   0x0000000000403228 <+4>:     mov     x29, sp

30          try
31          {
32              pthread_mutex_lock(&mutexA);
   0x000000000040322c <+8>:     adrp    x0, 0x4d1000 <main_arena+2128>
   0x0000000000403230 <+12>:    add     x0, x0, #0x5d8
   0x0000000000403234 <+16>:    bl      0x414dbc <pthread_mutex_lock>

33              procC();
   0x0000000000403238 <+20>:    bl      0x403200 <_Z5procCv>

34              pthread_mutex_unlock(&mutexA);
   0x000000000040323c <+24>:    adrp    x0, 0x4d1000 <main_arena+2128>
   0x0000000000403240 <+28>:    add     x0, x0, #0x5d8
   0x0000000000403244 <+32>:    bl      0x416054 <pthread_mutex_unlock>

37          {
38
39          }
40
41          sleep(20);
   0x0000000000403248 <+36>:    mov     w0, #0x14                       // #20
```

```
   0x000000000040324c <+40>:    bl      0x4337a4 <sleep>

42          pthread_mutex_lock(&mutexB);
   0x0000000000403250 <+44>:    adrp    x0, 0x4d1000 <main_arena+2128>
   0x0000000000403254 <+48>:    add     x0, x0, #0x608
   0x0000000000403258 <+52>:    bl      0x414dbc <pthread_mutex_lock>
--Type <RET> for more, q to quit, c to continue without paging--q
Quit
(gdb) disassemble /s procA
Dump of assembler code for function _Z5procAv:
main.cpp:
29      {
   0x0000000000403224 <+0>:     stp     x29, x30, [sp, #-16]!
   0x0000000000403228 <+4>:     mov     x29, sp

30          try
31          {
32              pthread_mutex_lock(&mutexA);
   0x000000000040322c <+8>:     adrp    x0, 0x4d1000 <main_arena+2128>
   0x0000000000403230 <+12>:    add     x0, x0, #0x5d8
   0x0000000000403234 <+16>:    bl      0x414dbc <pthread_mutex_lock>

33              procC();
   0x0000000000403238 <+20>:    bl      0x403200 <_Z5procCv>

34              pthread_mutex_unlock(&mutexA);
   0x000000000040323c <+24>:    adrp    x0, 0x4d1000 <main_arena+2128>
   0x0000000000403240 <+28>:    add     x0, x0, #0x5d8
   0x0000000000403244 <+32>:    bl      0x416054 <pthread_mutex_unlock>

37          {
38
39          }
40
41          sleep(20);
   0x0000000000403248 <+36>:    mov     w0, #0x14                       // #20
   0x000000000040324c <+40>:    bl      0x4337a4 <sleep>

42          pthread_mutex_lock(&mutexB);
   0x0000000000403250 <+44>:    adrp    x0, 0x4d1000 <main_arena+2128>
   0x0000000000403254 <+48>:    add     x0, x0, #0x608
   0x0000000000403258 <+52>:    bl      0x414dbc <pthread_mutex_lock>
--Type <RET> for more, q to quit, c to continue without paging--

43          pthread_mutex_unlock(&mutexB);
   0x000000000040325c <+56>:    adrp    x0, 0x4d1000 <main_arena+2128>
   0x0000000000403260 <+60>:    add     x0, x0, #0x608
   0x0000000000403264 <+64>:    bl      0x416054 <pthread_mutex_unlock>
   0x0000000000403268 <+68>:    b       0x403278 <_Z5procAv+84>

36          catch(...)
   0x000000000040326c <+72>:    bl      0x4039b4 <__cxa_begin_catch>
   0x0000000000403270 <+76>:    bl      0x403a58 <__cxa_end_catch>
   0x0000000000403274 <+80>:    b       0x403248 <_Z5procAv+36>

44      }
   0x0000000000403278 <+84>:    ldp     x29, x30, [sp], #16
   0x000000000040327c <+88>:    ret
End of assembler dump.
```

Exercise A12 (x64, WinDbg)

Goal: Learn how to dump memory for post-processing, get the list of functions and module variables, load symbols, disassemble with source code, inspect arguments, local variables, and types.

Patterns: Module Variable.

1. We have a core dump of the *App12* executable that was stripped of debugging information to run in production, and we also have an original executable in the App12\Symbols folder.

2. Launch WinDbg.

3. Load the *App12.core.698* dump file from the x64\App12 folder:

```
Microsoft (R) Windows Debugger Version 10.0.27725.1000 AMD64
Copyright (c) Microsoft Corporation. All rights reserved.


Loading Dump File [C:\ALCDA2\x64\App12\App12.core.698]
64-bit machine not using 64-bit API

************* Path validation summary **************
Response                         Time (ms)     Location
Deferred                                       srv*
Symbol search path is: srv*
Executable search path is:
Generic Unix Version 0 UP Free x64
System Uptime: not available
Process Uptime: not available
..
*** WARNING: Unable to verify timestamp for App12
App12+0x52970:
00000000`00452970 cmp     rax,0FFFFFFFFFFFFF000h
```

4. Set logging to a file in case of lengthy output from some commands:

```
0:000> .logopen C:\ALCDA2\x64\App12\App12-WinDbg.log
Opened log file 'C:\ALCDA2\x64\App12\App12-WinDbg.log'
```

5. Specify the folder for the symbol path and reload symbols:

```
0:000> .sympath+ C:\ALCDA2\x64\App12\Symbols\
Symbol search path is: srv*;C:\ALCDA2\x64\App12\Symbols\
Expanded Symbol search path is:
cache*;SRV*https://msdl.microsoft.com/download/symbols;c:\alcda2\x64\app12\symbols\

************* Path validation summary **************
Response                         Time (ms)     Location
Deferred                                       srv*
OK                                             C:\ALCDA2\x64\App12\Symbols\
*** WARNING: Unable to verify timestamp for App12
```

```
0:000> .symopt+ 0x40
Symbol options are 0x30377:
  0x00000001 - SYMOPT_CASE_INSENSITIVE
  0x00000002 - SYMOPT_UNDNAME
  0x00000004 - SYMOPT_DEFERRED_LOADS
  0x00000010 - SYMOPT_LOAD_LINES
  0x00000020 - SYMOPT_OMAP_FIND_NEAREST
  0x00000040 - SYMOPT_LOAD_ANYTHING
  0x00000100 - SYMOPT_NO_UNQUALIFIED_LOADS
  0x00000200 - SYMOPT_FAIL_CRITICAL_ERRORS
  0x00010000 - SYMOPT_AUTO_PUBLICS
  0x00020000 - SYMOPT_NO_IMAGE_SEARCH
*** WARNING: Unable to verify timestamp for App12

0:000> .reload
..
*** WARNING: Unable to verify timestamp for App12

************* Symbol Loading Error Summary **************
Module name            Error
App12                  The system cannot find the file specified

You can troubleshoot most symbol related issues by turning on symbol loading diagnostics (!sym
noisy) and repeating the command that caused symbols to be loaded.
You should also verify that your symbol search path (.sympath) is correct.
```

Note: We ignore warnings and errors as they are not relevant for now. Also, for x64, we need to specify the path ending with '\': C:\ALCDA2\x64\App12\Symbols\. Otherwise, the symbols from the separate folder are not loaded.

6. List all thread stack traces (we see that source code references are now included):

```
0:000> ~*k

Unable to get thread data for thread 0
.  0  Id: 2ba.2ba Suspend: 0 Teb: 00000000`00000000 Unfrozen
 # Child-SP          RetAddr           Call Site
00 00007ffe`e378a600 00000000`004528fa     App12!nanosleep+0x40
01 00007ffe`e378a630 00000000`00402121     App12!sleep+0x3a
02 00007ffe`e378a670 00000000`00417f11     App12!main+0xd6 [/home/coredump/ALCDA2/x64/App12/main.cpp @ 92]
03 00007ffe`e378a6c0 00000000`00401d9a     App12!_libc_start_main+0x3d1
04 00007ffe`e378a7c0 ffffffff`ffffffff     App12!start+0x2a
05 00007ffe`e378a7c8 00000000`00000000     0xffffffff`ffffffff

Unable to get thread data for thread 1
   1  Id: 2ba.2bb Suspend: 0 Teb: 00000000`00000000 Unfrozen
 # Child-SP          RetAddr           Call Site
00 00007fbc`efc82d10 00000000`004528fa     App12!nanosleep+0x40
01 00007fbc`efc82d40 00000000`00401f5a     App12!sleep+0x3a
02 00007fbc`efc82d80 00000000`00401f66     App12!bar_one+0xe [/home/coredump/ALCDA2/x64/App12/main.cpp @ 71]
03 00007fbc`efc82d90 00000000`00401f7a     App12!foo_one+0x9 [/home/coredump/ALCDA2/x64/App12/main.cpp @ 71]
04 00007fbc`efc82da0 00000000`004137f3     App12!thread_one+0x11 [/home/coredump/ALCDA2/x64/App12/main.cpp @ 71]
05 00007fbc`efc82dc0 00000000`0045512f     App12!start_thread+0xf3 [/build/glibc-vjB4T1/glibc-
2.28/nptl/pthread_create.c @ 487]
06 00007fbc`efc82e80 ffffffff`ffffffff     App12!_clone+0x3f
07 00007fbc`efc82e88 00000000`00000000     0xffffffff`ffffffff

Unable to get thread data for thread 2
   2  Id: 2ba.2bc Suspend: 0 Teb: 00000000`00000000 Unfrozen
 # Child-SP          RetAddr           Call Site
00 00007fbc`ef481cc8 00000000`00415294     App12!_lll_lock_wait+0x1c [/build/glibc-vjB4T1/glibc-
2.28/nptl/../sysdeps/unix/sysv/linux/x86_64/lowlevellock.S @ 103]
01 00007fbc`ef481ce0 00000000`00401eec     App12!__pthread_mutex_lock+0x54 [/build/glibc-vjB4T1/glibc-
2.28/nptl/../nptl/pthread_mutex_lock.c @ 80]
02 00007fbc`ef481d70 00000000`00401f8a     App12!procA+0x37 [/home/coredump/ALCDA2/x64/App12/main.cpp @ 42]
03 00007fbc`ef481d80 00000000`00401f96     App12!bar_two+0x9 [/home/coredump/ALCDA2/x64/App12/main.cpp @ 72]
04 00007fbc`ef481d90 00000000`00401faa     App12!foo_two+0x9 [/home/coredump/ALCDA2/x64/App12/main.cpp @ 72]
```

```
05 00007fbc`ef481da0 00000000`004137f3     App12!thread_two+0x11 [/home/coredump/ALCDA2/x64/App12/main.cpp @ 72]
06 00007fbc`ef481dc0 00000000`0045512f     App12!start_thread+0xf3 [/build/glibc-vjB4T1/glibc-
2.28/nptl/pthread_create.c @ 487]
07 00007fbc`ef481e80 ffffffff`ffffffff     App12!_clone+0x3f
08 00007fbc`ef481e88 00000000`00000000     0xffffffff`ffffffff

Unable to get thread data for thread 3
   3  Id: 2ba.2bd Suspend: 0 Teb: 00000000`00000000 Unfrozen
 # Child-SP          RetAddr               Call Site
00 00007fbc`eec80d10 00000000`004528fa     App12!nanosleep+0x40
01 00007fbc`eec80d40 00000000`00401fbf     App12!sleep+0x3a
02 00007fbc`eec80d80 00000000`00401fcb     App12!bar_three+0xe [/home/coredump/ALCDA2/x64/App12/main.cpp @ 73]
03 00007fbc`eec80d90 00000000`00401fdf     App12!foo_three+0x9 [/home/coredump/ALCDA2/x64/App12/main.cpp @ 73]
04 00007fbc`eec80da0 00000000`004137f3     App12!thread_three+0x11 [/home/coredump/ALCDA2/x64/App12/main.cpp @ 73]
05 00007fbc`eec80dc0 00000000`0045512f     App12!start_thread+0xf3 [/build/glibc-vjB4T1/glibc-
2.28/nptl/pthread_create.c @ 487]
06 00007fbc`eec80e80 ffffffff`ffffffff     App12!_clone+0x3f
07 00007fbc`eec80e88 00000000`00000000     0xffffffff`ffffffff

Unable to get thread data for thread 4
   4  Id: 2ba.2be Suspend: 0 Teb: 00000000`00000000 Unfrozen
 # Child-SP          RetAddr               Call Site
00 00007fbc`ee47fcc8 00000000`00415294     App12!_lll_lock_wait+0x1c [/build/glibc-vjB4T1/glibc-
2.28/nptl/../sysdeps/unix/sysv/linux/x86_64/lowlevellock.S @ 103]
01 00007fbc`ee47fce0 00000000`00401f27     App12!__pthread_mutex_lock+0x54 [/build/glibc-vjB4T1/glibc-
2.28/nptl/../nptl/pthread_mutex_lock.c @ 80]
02 00007fbc`ee47fd70 00000000`00401fef     App12!procB+0x1c [/home/coredump/ALCDA2/x64/App12/main.cpp @ 49]
03 00007fbc`ee47fd80 00000000`00401ffb     App12!bar_four+0x9 [/home/coredump/ALCDA2/x64/App12/main.cpp @ 74]
04 00007fbc`ee47fd90 00000000`0040200f     App12!foo_four+0x9 [/home/coredump/ALCDA2/x64/App12/main.cpp @ 74]
05 00007fbc`ee47fda0 00000000`004137f3     App12!thread_four+0x11 [/home/coredump/ALCDA2/x64/App12/main.cpp @ 74]
06 00007fbc`ee47fdc0 00000000`0045512f     App12!start_thread+0xf3 [/build/glibc-vjB4T1/glibc-
2.28/nptl/pthread_create.c @ 487]
07 00007fbc`ee47fe80 ffffffff`ffffffff     App12!_clone+0x3f
08 00007fbc`ee47fe88 00000000`00000000     0xffffffff`ffffffff

Unable to get thread data for thread 5
   5  Id: 2ba.2bf Suspend: 0 Teb: 00000000`00000000 Unfrozen
 # Child-SP          RetAddr               Call Site
00 00007fbc`edc7ed10 00000000`004528fa     App12!nanosleep+0x40
01 00007fbc`edc7ed40 00000000`00402024     App12!sleep+0x3a
02 00007fbc`edc7ed80 00000000`00402030     App12!bar_five+0xe [/home/coredump/ALCDA2/x64/App12/main.cpp @ 75]
03 00007fbc`edc7ed90 00000000`00402044     App12!foo_five+0x9 [/home/coredump/ALCDA2/x64/App12/main.cpp @ 75]
04 00007fbc`edc7eda0 00000000`004137f3     App12!thread_five+0x11 [/home/coredump/ALCDA2/x64/App12/main.cpp @ 75]
05 00007fbc`edc7edc0 00000000`0045512f     App12!start_thread+0xf3 [/build/glibc-vjB4T1/glibc-
2.28/nptl/pthread_create.c @ 487]
06 00007fbc`edc7ee80 ffffffff`ffffffff     App12!_clone+0x3f
07 00007fbc`edc7ee88 00000000`00000000     0xffffffff`ffffffff
```

7. If we want to omit them, we use this command variant:

```
0:000> kL
 # Child-SP          RetAddr               Call Site
00 00007ffe`e378a600 00000000`004528fa     App12!nanosleep+0x40
01 00007ffe`e378a630 00000000`00402121     App12!sleep+0x3a
02 00007ffe`e378a670 00000000`00417f11     App12!main+0xd6
03 00007ffe`e378a6c0 00000000`00401d9a     App12!_libc_start_main+0x3d1
04 00007ffe`e378a7c0 ffffffff`ffffffff     App12!start+0x2a
05 00007ffe`e378a7c8 00000000`00000000     0xffffffff`ffffffff
```

8. If we want to include parameters in the stack trace, we use another command variant:

```
0:000> kPL
 # Child-SP          RetAddr               Call Site
00 00007ffe`e378a600 00000000`004528fa     App12!nanosleep+0x40
01 00007ffe`e378a630 00000000`00402121     App12!sleep+0x3a
02 00007ffe`e378a670 00000000`00417f11     App12!main(
                    int argc = 0n1,
                    char ** argv = 0x00007ffe`e378a7d8)+0xd6
03 00007ffe`e378a6c0 00000000`00401d9a     App12!_libc_start_main+0x3d1
04 00007ffe`e378a7c0 ffffffff`ffffffff     App12!start+0x2a
05 00007ffe`e378a7c8 00000000`00000000     0xffffffff`ffffffff
```

9. Switch to frame #2, and list arguments and locals:

```
0:000> .frame /c /r 2
02 00007ffe`e378a670 00000000`00417f11     App12!main+0xd6
[/home/coredump/ALCDA2/x64/App12/main.cpp @ 92]
rax=fffffffffffffdfc rbx=00000000004004d0 rcx=0000000000452970
rdx=0000000000000000 rsi=00007ffee378a630 rdi=00007ffee378a630
rip=0000000000402121 rsp=00007ffee378a670 rbp=00007ffee378a6b0
 r8=0000000000000000  r9=00007fbcedc7f700 r10=00007fbcedc7f9d0
r11=0000000000000293 r12=00000000004185a0 r13=0000000000000000
r14=00000000004d1018 r15=0000000000000000
iopl=0         nv up ei ng nz ac pe cy
cs=0033  ss=002b  ds=0000  es=0000  fs=0000  gs=0000             efl=00000293
App12!main+0xd6:
00000000`00402121 mov     eax,0

0:000> dv /i /V
prv param  00007ffe`e378a67c @rbp-0x0034                  argc = 0n1
prv param  00007ffe`e378a670 @rbp-0x0040                  argv = 0x00007ffe`e378a7d8
```

10. Examine the *argv* array:

```
0:000> dpa 0x00007ffe`e378a7d8 L10
00007ffe`e378a7d8  00007ffe`e378b74e "./App12"
00007ffe`e378a7e0  00000000`00000000
00007ffe`e378a7e8  00007ffe`e378b756 "SHELL=/bin/bash"
00007ffe`e378a7f0  00007ffe`e378b766 "HISTCONTROL=ignoreboth"
00007ffe`e378a7f8  00007ffe`e378b77d "WSL_DISTRO_NAME=Debian"
00007ffe`e378a800  00007ffe`e378b794 "NAME=DESKTOP-IS6V2L0"
00007ffe`e378a808  00007ffe`e378b7a9 "PWD=/home/coredump/ALCDA2/x64/App12"
00007ffe`e378a810  00007ffe`e378b7cd "LOGNAME=coredump"
00007ffe`e378a818  00007ffe`e378b7de "MC_TMPDIR=/tmp/mc-coredump"
00007ffe`e378a820  00007ffe`e378b7f9 "MC_SID=14"
00007ffe`e378a828  00007ffe`e378b803 "HOME=/home/coredump"
00007ffe`e378a830  00007ffe`e378b817 "LANG=en_US.UTF-8"
00007ffe`e378a838  00007ffe`e378b828 "WSL_INTEROP=/run/WSL/8_interop"
00007ffe`e378a840  00007ffe`e378b847 "LS_COLORS=rs=0:di=01;34:ln=01;36:mh=00:pi=40;33:so=01;3"
00007ffe`e378a848  00007ffe`e378be29 "WAYLAND_DISPLAY=wayland-0"
00007ffe`e378a850  00007ffe`e378be43 "TERM=xterm-256color"
```

11. We can also specify the path to the source code (source code view should appear after resetting the context via the **.cxr** command and setting the frame without parameters):

```
0:000> .srcpath C:\ALCDA2\x64\App12
Source search path is: C:\ALCDA2\x64\App12

************* Path validation summary **************
Response                         Time (ms)     Location
OK                                             C:\ALCDA2\x64\App12

0:000> .cxr

0:000> .frame 2
```

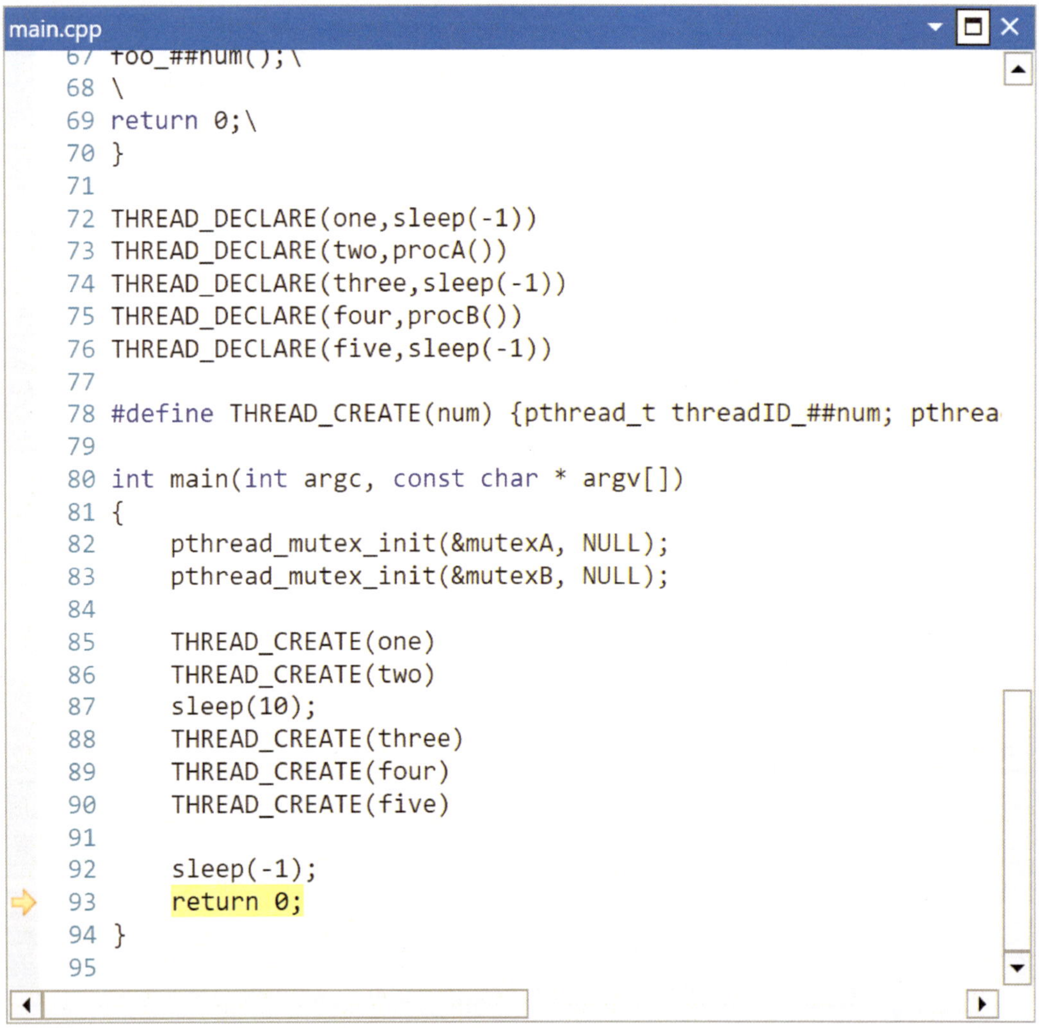

12. Dump the contents of the loaded *App12* module to a binary file:

```
0:000> lm
start             end                 module name
00000000`00400000 00000000`004d4000   App12      T (service symbols: DWARF Private Symbols)
c:\alcda2\x64\app12\symbols\App12
00007ffe`e3797000 00007ffe`e3798000   linux_vdso_so   (deferred)
```

```
0:000> .writemem C:\ALCDA2\x64\App12\mem.raw 00000000`00400000 00000000`004d4000
Writing d4001 bytes.
Unable to read memory at 00000000`00400800, file is incomplete
```

13. List all available symbols:

```
0:000> x App12!*
00000000`004d34a0 App12!mutexA = pthread_mutex_t
00000000`004d34e0 App12!mutexB = pthread_mutex_t
[...]
00000000`0040204b App12!main (int, char **)
00000000`00402033 App12!thread_five (int, char **)
00000000`00402027 App12!foo_five (int, char **)
00000000`00402016 App12!bar_five (int, char **)
00000000`00401ffe App12!thread_four (int, char **)
00000000`00401ff2 App12!foo_four (int, char **)
00000000`00401fe6 App12!bar_four (int, char **)
00000000`00401fce App12!thread_three (int, char **)
00000000`00401fc2 App12!foo_three (int, char **)
00000000`00401fb1 App12!bar_three (int, char **)
00000000`00401f99 App12!thread_two (int, char **)
00000000`00401f8d App12!foo_two (int, char **)
00000000`00401f81 App12!bar_two (int, char **)
00000000`00401f69 App12!thread_one (int, char **)
00000000`00401f5d App12!foo_one (int, char **)
00000000`00401f4c App12!bar_one (int, char **)
00000000`00401f0b App12!procB (int, char **)
00000000`00401eb5 App12!procA (int, char **)
00000000`00401e8d App12!procC (int, char **)
[...]
```

14. List all available types and functions/variables:

```
0:000> dt App12!*
[...]
          App12!pthread_mutex_t
[...]
000000000040204b  App12!main
0000000000402033  App12!thread_five
0000000000402027  App12!foo_five
0000000000402016  App12!bar_five
0000000000401ffe  App12!thread_four
0000000000401ff2  App12!foo_four
0000000000401fe6  App12!bar_four
0000000000401fce  App12!thread_three
0000000000401fc2  App12!foo_three
0000000000401fb1  App12!bar_three
0000000000401f99  App12!thread_two
0000000000401f8d  App12!foo_two
0000000000401f81  App12!bar_two
0000000000401f69  App12!thread_one
0000000000401f5d  App12!foo_one
0000000000401f4c  App12!bar_one
0000000000401f0b  App12!procB
0000000000401eb5  App12!procA
0000000000401e8d  App12!procC
[...]
```

15. We notice mutex waits on stack traces, and since mutexes have owners (thread IDs), we can check their ownership instead of disassembly to detect a deadlock as we did in the previous exercise A11 (we can use either **dx** or **dt** commands):

```
0:000> x App12!mutex*
00000000`004d34a0 App12!mutexA = pthread_mutex_t
00000000`004d34e0 App12!mutexB = pthread_mutex_t

0:000> dx mutexA
mutexA                 [Type: pthread_mutex_t]
    [+0x000] __data            [Type: __pthread_mutex_s]
    [+0x000] __size            : "???" [Type: char [40]]
    [+0x000] __align           : 2 [Type: long int]

0:000> dx mutexA.__data
mutexA.__data                  [Type: __pthread_mutex_s]
    [+0x000] __lock            : 2 [Type: int]
    [+0x004] __count           : 0x0 [Type: unsigned int]
    [+0x008] __owner           : 700 [Type: int]
    [+0x00c] __nusers          : 0x1 [Type: unsigned int]
    [+0x010] __kind            : 0 [Type: int]
    [+0x014] __spins           : 0 [Type: short int]
    [+0x016] __elision         : 0 [Type: short int]
    [+0x018] __list            [Type: __pthread_list_t]

0:000> ~~[0n700]kL
 # Child-SP          RetAddr               Call Site
00 00007fbc`ef481cc8 00000000`00415294     App12!_lll_lock_wait+0x1c
01 00007fbc`ef481ce0 00000000`00401eec     App12!__pthread_mutex_lock+0x54
02 00007fbc`ef481d70 00000000`00401f8a     App12!procA+0x37
03 00007fbc`ef481d80 00000000`00401f96     App12!bar_two+0x9
04 00007fbc`ef481d90 00000000`00401faa     App12!foo_two+0x9
05 00007fbc`ef481da0 00000000`004137f3     App12!thread_two+0x11
06 00007fbc`ef481dc0 00000000`0045512f     App12!start_thread+0xf3
07 00007fbc`ef481e80 ffffffff`ffffffff     App12!_clone+0x3f
08 00007fbc`ef481e88 00000000`00000000     0xffffffff`ffffffff

0:000> dt -r pthread_mutex_t 00000000`004d34a0
App12!pthread_mutex_t
   +0x000 __data           : __pthread_mutex_s
      +0x000 __lock           : 0n2
      +0x004 __count          : 0
      +0x008 __owner          : 0n700
      +0x00c __nusers         : 1
      +0x010 __kind           : 0n0
      +0x014 __spins          : 0n0
      +0x016 __elision        : 0n0
      +0x018 __list           : __pthread_internal_list
         +0x000 __prev           : (null)
         +0x008 __next           : (null)
   +0x000 __size           : [40]  "???"
   +0x000 __align          : 0n2
```

16. We close logging before exiting WinDbg:

```
0:000> .logclose
Closing open log file 'C:\ALCDA2\x64\App12\App12-WinDbg.log
```

Exercise A12 (A64, WinDbg)

Goal: Learn how to dump memory for post-processing, get the list of functions and module variables, load symbols, disassemble with source code, inspect arguments, local variables, and types.

Patterns: Module Variable.

1. We have a core dump of the *App12* executable that was stripped of debugging information to run in production, and we also have an original executable in the App12\Symbols folder.

2. Launch WinDbg.

3. Load *App12.core.17894* dump file from the A64\App12 folder:

```
Microsoft (R) Windows Debugger Version 10.0.27725.1000 AMD64
Copyright (c) Microsoft Corporation. All rights reserved.


Loading Dump File [C:\ALCDA2\A64\App12\App12.core.17894]
64-bit machine not using 64-bit API

************* Path validation summary **************
Response                         Time (ms)     Location
Deferred                                       srv*
Symbol search path is: srv*
Executable search path is:
Generic Unix Version 0 UP Free ARM 64-bit (AArch64)
System Uptime: not available
Process Uptime: not available
..
*** WARNING: Unable to verify timestamp for App12
App12+0x1ae24:
00000000`0041ae24 svc         #0
```

4. Set logging to a file in case of lengthy output from some commands:

```
0:000> .logopen C:\ALCDA2\A64\App12\App12-WinDbg.log
Opened log file 'C:\ALCDA2\A64\App12\App12-WinDbg.log'
```

5. Specify the folder for the symbol path and reload symbols:

```
0:000> .sympath+ C:\ALCDA2\A64\App12\Symbols
Symbol search path is: srv*;C:\ALCDA2\A64\App12\Symbols
Expanded Symbol search path is:
cache*;SRV*https://msdl.microsoft.com/download/symbols;c:\alcda2\a64\app12\symbols

************* Path validation summary **************
Response                         Time (ms)     Location
Deferred                                       srv*
OK                                             C:\ALCDA2\A64\App12\Symbols
*** WARNING: Unable to verify timestamp for App12
```

```
0:000> .reload
..
*** WARNING: Unable to verify timestamp for App12

************* Symbol Loading Error Summary **************
Module name            Error
App12                  The system cannot find the file specified

You can troubleshoot most symbol related issues by turning on symbol loading diagnostics (!sym
noisy) and repeating the command that caused symbols to be loaded.
You should also verify that your symbol search path (.sympath) is correct.
```

Note: We ignore warnings and errors as they are not relevant for now.

6. List all thread stack traces (we see that source code references are now included):

```
0:000> ~*k

Unable to get thread data for thread 0
.  0  Id: 45e6.45e7 Suspend: 0 Teb: 00000000`00000000 Unfrozen
 # Child-SP          RetAddr               Call Site
00 0000fffb`fad5e5e0 00000000`004338b4     App12!_libc_nanosleep+0x24
01 0000fffb`fad5e620 00000000`004032d8     App12!sleep+0x110
02 0000fffb`fad5e810 00000000`004032ec     App12!bar_one+0x10 [/home/opc/ALCDA2/App12\main.cpp @ 72]
03 0000fffb`fad5e820 00000000`00403304     App12!foo_one+0xc [/home/opc/ALCDA2/App12\main.cpp @ 72]
04 0000fffb`fad5e830 00000000`004130a4     App12!thread_one+0x10 [/home/opc/ALCDA2/App12\main.cpp @ 72]
05 0000fffb`fad5e850 00000000`00438760     App12!start_thread+0xb4
06 0000fffb`fad5e980 ffffffff`ffffffff     App12!thread_start+0x30
07 0000fffb`fad5e980 00000000`00000000     0xffffffff`ffffffff

Unable to get thread data for thread 1
   1  Id: 45e6.45e8 Suspend: 0 Teb: 00000000`00000000 Unfrozen
 # Child-SP          RetAddr               Call Site
00 0000fffb`fa54e7d0 00000000`00414ea4     App12!_lll_lock_wait+0x3c
01 0000fffb`fa54e7d0 00000000`0040325c     App12!_pthread_mutex_lock+0xe8
02 0000fffb`fa54e800 00000000`0040331c     App12!procA+0x38 [/home/opc/ALCDA2/App12\main.cpp @ 43]
03 0000fffb`fa54e810 00000000`00403330     App12!bar_two+0xc [/home/opc/ALCDA2/App12\main.cpp @ 73]
04 0000fffb`fa54e820 00000000`00403348     App12!foo_two+0xc [/home/opc/ALCDA2/App12\main.cpp @ 73]
05 0000fffb`fa54e830 00000000`004130a4     App12!thread_two+0x10 [/home/opc/ALCDA2/App12\main.cpp @ 73]
06 0000fffb`fa54e850 00000000`00438760     App12!start_thread+0xb4
07 0000fffb`fa54e980 ffffffff`ffffffff     App12!thread_start+0x30
08 0000fffb`fa54e980 00000000`00000000     0xffffffff`ffffffff

Unable to get thread data for thread 2
   2  Id: 45e6.45f1 Suspend: 0 Teb: 00000000`00000000 Unfrozen
 # Child-SP          RetAddr               Call Site
00 0000fffb`f9d3e5e0 00000000`004338b4     App12!_libc_nanosleep+0x24
01 0000fffb`f9d3e620 00000000`00403364     App12!sleep+0x110
02 0000fffb`f9d3e810 00000000`00403378     App12!bar_three+0x10 [/home/opc/ALCDA2/App12\main.cpp @ 74]
03 0000fffb`f9d3e820 00000000`00403390     App12!foo_three+0xc [/home/opc/ALCDA2/App12\main.cpp @ 74]
04 0000fffb`f9d3e830 00000000`004130a4     App12!thread_three+0x10 [/home/opc/ALCDA2/App12\main.cpp @ 74]
05 0000fffb`f9d3e850 00000000`00438760     App12!start_thread+0xb4
06 0000fffb`f9d3e980 ffffffff`ffffffff     App12!thread_start+0x30
07 0000fffb`f9d3e980 00000000`00000000     0xffffffff`ffffffff

Unable to get thread data for thread 3
   3  Id: 45e6.45f2 Suspend: 0 Teb: 00000000`00000000 Unfrozen
 # Child-SP          RetAddr               Call Site
00 0000fffb`f952e7d0 00000000`00414ea4     App12!_lll_lock_wait+0x3c
01 0000fffb`f952e7d0 00000000`004032a0     App12!_pthread_mutex_lock+0xe8
02 0000fffb`f952e800 00000000`004033a8     App12!procB+0x20 [/home/opc/ALCDA2/App12\main.cpp @ 50]
03 0000fffb`f952e810 00000000`004033bc     App12!bar_four+0xc [/home/opc/ALCDA2/App12\main.cpp @ 75]
04 0000fffb`f952e820 00000000`004033d4     App12!foo_four+0xc [/home/opc/ALCDA2/App12\main.cpp @ 75]
05 0000fffb`f952e830 00000000`004130a4     App12!thread_four+0x10 [/home/opc/ALCDA2/App12\main.cpp @ 75]
```

```
06 0000fffb`f952e850 00000000`00438760     App12!start_thread+0xb4
07 0000fffb`f952e980 ffffffff`ffffffff     App12!thread_start+0x30
08 0000fffb`f952e980 00000000`00000000     0xffffffff`ffffffff

Unable to get thread data for thread 4
   4  Id: 45e6.45f3 Suspend: 0 Teb: 00000000`00000000 Unfrozen
 # Child-SP          RetAddr               Call Site
00 0000fffb`f8d1e5e0 00000000`004338b4     App12!_libc_nanosleep+0x24
01 0000fffb`f8d1e620 00000000`004033f0     App12!sleep+0x110
02 0000fffb`f8d1e810 00000000`00403404     App12!bar_five+0x10 [/home/opc/ALCDA2/App12\main.cpp @ 76]
03 0000fffb`f8d1e820 00000000`0040341c     App12!foo_five+0xc [/home/opc/ALCDA2/App12\main.cpp @ 76]
04 0000fffb`f8d1e830 00000000`004130a4     App12!thread_five+0x10 [/home/opc/ALCDA2/App12\main.cpp @ 76]
05 0000fffb`f8d1e850 00000000`00438760     App12!start_thread+0xb4
06 0000fffb`f8d1e980 ffffffff`ffffffff     App12!thread_start+0x30
07 0000fffb`f8d1e980 00000000`00000000     0xffffffff`ffffffff

Unable to get thread data for thread 5
   5  Id: 45e6.45e6 Suspend: 0 Teb: 00000000`00000000 Unfrozen
 # Child-SP          RetAddr               Call Site
00 0000ffff`f841bcc0 00000000`004338b4     App12!_libc_nanosleep+0x24
01 0000ffff`f841bd00 00000000`004034e0     App12!sleep+0x110
02 0000ffff`f841bef0 00000000`0041d0bc     App12!main+0xb8 [/home/opc/ALCDA2/App12\main.cpp @ 93]
03 0000ffff`f841bf40 00000000`004030a8     App12!_libc_start_main+0x304
04 0000ffff`f841c0a0 00000000`00000000     App12!start+0x4c
```

7. If we want to omit them we use this command variant:

```
0:000> kL
 # Child-SP          RetAddr               Call Site
00 0000fffb`fad5e5e0 00000000`004338b4     App12!_libc_nanosleep+0x24
01 0000fffb`fad5e620 00000000`004032d8     App12!sleep+0x110
02 0000fffb`fad5e810 00000000`004032ec     App12!bar_one+0x10
03 0000fffb`fad5e820 00000000`00403304     App12!foo_one+0xc
04 0000fffb`fad5e830 00000000`004130a4     App12!thread_one+0x10
05 0000fffb`fad5e850 00000000`00438760     App12!start_thread+0xb4
06 0000fffb`fad5e980 ffffffff`ffffffff     App12!thread_start+0x30
07 0000fffb`fad5e980 00000000`00000000     0xffffffff`ffffffff
```

8. If we want to include parameters in the stack trace, we use another command variant:

```
0:000> ~5kPL
 # Child-SP          RetAddr               Call Site
00 0000ffff`f841bcc0 00000000`004338b4     App12!_libc_nanosleep+0x24
01 0000ffff`f841bd00 00000000`004034e0     App12!sleep+0x110
02 0000ffff`f841bef0 00000000`0041d0bc     App12!main(
                  int argc = 0n1,
                  char ** argv = 0x0000ffff`f841c0a8)+0xb8
03 0000ffff`f841bf40 00000000`004030a8     App12!_libc_start_main+0x304
04 0000ffff`f841c0a0 00000000`00000000     App12!start+0x4c
```

9. Switch to thread #5 and its frame #2, and list arguments and locals:

```
0:000> ~5s
App12!_libc_nanosleep+0x24:
00000000`0041ae24 d4000001 svc         #0
```

```
0:005> .frame /c /r 2
02 0000ffff`f841bef0 00000000`0041d0bc     App12!main+0xb8 [/home/opc/ALCDA2/App12\main.cpp @ 93]
 x0=0000ffff00000000   x1=0000ffff f841bd40   x2=000000003a6e0000   x3=000000003a6e0108
 x4=0000ffff f841bcb0   x5=000000003a6e06f0   x6=00000000ffffffbb   x7=0000000000000000
 x8=0000000000000065   x9=00000000004d07b0  x10=000000003a6e2670  x11=000000000003d990
x12=0000000000000002  x13=0000ffff f841bd70  x14=0000000000000008  x15=0000000000000000
x16=0000000000000000  x17=0000000000431dd0  x18=0000000000000110  x19=0000000000400250
x20=00000000004d0020  x21=0000000000400250  x22=0000000000000018  x23=00000000004e8000
x24=00000000004e8000  x25=0000000000000000  x26=000000000041d4f8  x27=000000000041d5b0
x28=0000000000000000   fp=0000ffff f841bef0   lr=00000000004034e0   sp=0000ffff f841bef0
 pc=00000000004034e0  psr=80001000 N--- EL0
App12!main+0xb8:
00000000`004034e0 52800000 mov       w0,#0
```

```
0:005> dv /i /V
prv param  0000ffff`f841bf0c @fp+0x001c              argc = 0n1
prv param  0000ffff`f841bf00 @fp+0x0010              argv = 0x0000ffff`f841c0a8
```

10. Examine the *argv* array:

```
0:005> dpa 0x0000ffff`f841c0a8 L10
0000ffff`f841c0a8  0000ffff`f841f6d7 "./App12"
0000ffff`f841c0b0  00000000`00000000
0000ffff`f841c0b8  0000ffff`f841f6df "XDG_SESSION_ID=8954"
0000ffff`f841c0c0  0000ffff`f841f6f3 "HOSTNAME=instance-20211109-2004"
0000ffff`f841c0c8  0000ffff`f841f713 "SELINUX_ROLE_REQUESTED="
0000ffff`f841c0d0  0000ffff`f841f72b "TERM=xterm-256color"
0000ffff`f841c0d8  0000ffff`f841f73f "SHELL=/bin/bash"
0000ffff`f841c0e0  0000ffff`f841f74f "HISTSIZE=1000"
0000ffff`f841c0e8  0000ffff`f841f75d "SSH_CLIENT=37.228.238.120 61014 22"
0000ffff`f841c0f0  0000ffff`f841f780 "SELINUX_USE_CURRENT_RANGE="
0000ffff`f841c0f8  0000ffff`f841f79b "SSH_TTY=/dev/pts/0"
0000ffff`f841c100  0000ffff`f841f7ae "USER=opc"
0000ffff`f841c108  0000ffff`f841f7b7 "LS_COLORS=rs=0:di=38;5;27:ln=38;5;51:mh=44;38;5;15:pi=4"
0000ffff`f841c110  0000ffff`f841fe6f "MAIL=/var/spool/mail/opc"
0000ffff`f841c118  0000ffff`f841fe88 "PATH=/usr/local/bin:/usr/bin:/usr/local/sbin:/usr/sbin:"
0000ffff`f841c120  0000ffff`f841fee2 "PWD=/home/opc/ALCDA2/App12"
```

11. We can also specify the path to the source code (the source code view should appear after resetting the context via the **.cxr** command and setting the frame without parameters):

```
0:005> .srcpath+ C:\ALCDA2\A64\App12\Source
Source search path is: C:\ALCDA2\A64\App12\Source

************* Path validation summary **************
Response                         Time (ms)     Location
OK                                             C:\ALCDA2\A64\App12\Source
```

```
0:005> .cxr
```

```
0:005> .frame 2
```

```
main.cpp
foo_##num();\
\
return 0;\
}

THREAD_DECLARE(one,sleep(-1))
THREAD_DECLARE(two,procA())
THREAD_DECLARE(three,sleep(-1))
THREAD_DECLARE(four,procB())
THREAD_DECLARE(five,sleep(-1))

#define THREAD_CREATE(num) {pthread_t threadID_##num; pthrea

int main(int argc, const char * argv[])
{
    pthread_mutex_init(&mutexA, NULL);
    pthread_mutex_init(&mutexB, NULL);

    THREAD_CREATE(one)
    THREAD_CREATE(two)
    sleep(10);
    THREAD_CREATE(three)
    THREAD_CREATE(four)
    THREAD_CREATE(five)

    sleep(-1);
    return 0;
}
```

12. Dump the contents of the loaded *App12* module to a binary file:

```
0:005> lm
start             end                 module name
00000000`00400000 00000000`004e0000   App12    T (service symbols: DWARF Private Symbols)
c:\alcda2\a64\app12\symbols\App12

0:005> .writemem C:\ALCDA2\A64\App12\mem.raw 00000000`00400000 00000000`004e0000
Writing e0001
bytes...............................................................................
................................................................................
................................................................................
................................................................................
.............................................................
```

13. List all available symbols:

```
0:005> x App12!*
00000000`004d15d8 App12!mutexA = pthread_mutex_t
00000000`004d1608 App12!mutexB = pthread_mutex_t
00000000`00000000 App12!__prev = <Memory access error>
00000000`00403200 App12!procC (int, char **)
00000000`00403224 App12!procA (int, char **)
00000000`00403280 App12!procB (int, char **)
00000000`004032c8 App12!bar_one (int, char **)
00000000`004032e0 App12!foo_one (int, char **)
```

```
00000000`004032f4 App12!thread_one (int, char **)
00000000`00403310 App12!bar_two (int, char **)
00000000`00403324 App12!foo_two (int, char **)
00000000`00403338 App12!thread_two (int, char **)
00000000`00403354 App12!bar_three (int, char **)
00000000`0040336c App12!foo_three (int, char **)
00000000`00403380 App12!thread_three (int, char **)
00000000`0040339c App12!bar_four (int, char **)
00000000`004033b0 App12!foo_four (int, char **)
00000000`004033c4 App12!thread_four (int, char **)
00000000`004033e0 App12!bar_five (int, char **)
00000000`004033f8 App12!foo_five (int, char **)
00000000`0040340c App12!thread_five (int, char **)
00000000`00403428 App12!main (int, char **)
[...]
```

14. List all available types and functions/variables:

```
0:005> dt App12!*
          App12!pthread_t
          App12!__pthread_internal_list
          App12!__pthread_list_t
          App12!pthread_mutex_t
          App12!__pthread_mutex_s
00000000004d15d8  App12!mutexA
00000000004d1608  App12!mutexB
          App12!__prev
0000000000403200  App12!procC
0000000000403224  App12!procA
0000000000403280  App12!procB
00000000004032c8  App12!bar_one
00000000004032e0  App12!foo_one
00000000004032f4  App12!thread_one
0000000000403310  App12!bar_two
0000000000403324  App12!foo_two
0000000000403338  App12!thread_two
0000000000403354  App12!bar_three
000000000040336c  App12!foo_three
0000000000403380  App12!thread_three
000000000040339c  App12!bar_four
00000000004033b0  App12!foo_four
00000000004033c4  App12!thread_four
00000000004033e0  App12!bar_five
00000000004033f8  App12!foo_five
000000000040340c  App12!thread_five
0000000000403428  App12!main
```

15. We notice mutex waits on stack traces, and since mutexes have owners (thread IDs), we can check their ownership instead of disassembly to detect a deadlock as we did in the previous exercise A11 (we can use either **dx** or **dt** commands):

```
0:005> x App12!mutex*
00000000`004d15d8 App12!mutexA = pthread_mutex_t
00000000`004d1608 App12!mutexB = pthread_mutex_t
```

```
0:005> dx mutexA
mutexA                      [Type: pthread_mutex_t]
    [+0x000] __data              [Type: __pthread_mutex_s]
    [+0x000] __size              : "???" [Type: char [48]]
    [+0x000] __align             : 2 [Type: long int]
```

```
0:005> dx mutexA.__data
mutexA.__data                 [Type: __pthread_mutex_s]
    [+0x000] __lock           : 2 [Type: int]
    [+0x004] __count          : 0x0 [Type: unsigned int]
    [+0x008] __owner          : 17896 [Type: int]
    [+0x00c] __nusers         : 0x1 [Type: unsigned int]
    [+0x010] __kind           : 0 [Type: int]
    [+0x014] __spins          : 0 [Type: int]
    [+0x018] __list           [Type: __pthread_list_t]

0:005> ~~[0n17896]k
 # Child-SP          RetAddr               Call Site
00 0000fffb`fa54e7d0 00000000`00414ea4     App12!_lll_lock_wait+0x3c
01 0000fffb`fa54e7d0 00000000`0040325c     App12!_pthread_mutex_lock+0xe8
02 0000fffb`fa54e800 00000000`0040331c     App12!procA+0x38
03 0000fffb`fa54e810 00000000`00403330     App12!bar_two+0xc
04 0000fffb`fa54e820 00000000`00403348     App12!foo_two+0xc
05 0000fffb`fa54e830 00000000`004130a4     App12!thread_two+0x10
06 0000fffb`fa54e850 00000000`00438760     App12!start_thread+0xb4
07 0000fffb`fa54e980 ffffffff`ffffffff     App12!thread_start+0x30
08 0000fffb`fa54e980 00000000`00000000     0xffffffff`ffffffff

0:005> dt -r pthread_mutex_t 00000000`004d15d8
App12!pthread_mutex_t
   +0x000 __data           : __pthread_mutex_s
      +0x000 __lock           : 0n2
      +0x004 __count          : 0
      +0x008 __owner          : 0n17896
      +0x00c __nusers         : 1
      +0x010 __kind           : 0n0
      +0x014 __spins          : 0n0
      +0x018 __list           : __pthread_internal_list
         +0x000 __prev           : (null)
         +0x008 __next           : (null)
   +0x000 __size           : [48]  "???"
   +0x000 __align          : 0n2
```

16. We close logging before exiting WinDbg:

```
0:005> .logclose
Closing open log file 'C:\ALCDA2\A64\App12\App12-WinDbg.log
```

Kernel Core Dumps

Exercises K1 – K5

Exercise K1

- **Goal:** Learn how to navigate a normal kernel dump
- **Patterns:** Manual Dump (Kernel); Stack Trace Collection
- \ALCDA-Dumps\Exercise-K1-x64-GDB.pdf
- \ALCDA-Dumps\Exercise-K1-A64-GDB.pdf
- \ALCDA-Dumps\Exercise-K1-A64-WinDbg.pdf
- \ALCDA-Dumps\Exercise-K1-x64-WinDbg.pdf

Exercise K1 (x64, GDB)

Goal: Learn how to navigate a normal kernel dump.

Patterns: Manual Dump (Kernel); Stack Trace Collection.

1. Install crash analysis tool:

```
~/ALCDA2/x64$ sudo apt install crash
```

2. Load the core dump *202412290014.kdump* from the x64/K1 directory and the matching *vmlinux-6.8.0-1018-azure* file from the x64/KSym directory:

```
~/ALCDA2/x64/K1$ crash 202412290014.kdump ../KSym/vmlinux-6.8.0-1018-azure

crash 8.0.6++
Copyright (C) 2002-2025  Red Hat, Inc.
Copyright (C) 2004, 2005, 2006, 2010  IBM Corporation
Copyright (C) 1999-2006  Hewlett-Packard Co
Copyright (C) 2005, 2006, 2011, 2012  Fujitsu Limited
Copyright (C) 2006, 2007  VA Linux Systems Japan K.K.
Copyright (C) 2005, 2011, 2020-2024  NEC Corporation
Copyright (C) 1999, 2002, 2007  Silicon Graphics, Inc.
Copyright (C) 1999, 2000, 2001, 2002  Mission Critical Linux, Inc.
Copyright (C) 2015, 2021  VMware, Inc.
This program is free software, covered by the GNU General Public License,
and you are welcome to change it and/or distribute copies of it under
certain conditions.  Enter "help copying" to see the conditions.
This program has absolutely no warranty.  Enter "help warranty" for details.

GNU gdb (GDB) 10.2
Copyright (C) 2021 Free Software Foundation, Inc.
License GPLv3+: GNU GPL version 3 or later <http://gnu.org/licenses/gpl.html>
This is free software: you are free to change and redistribute it.
There is NO WARRANTY, to the extent permitted by law.
Type "show copying" and "show warranty" for details.
This GDB was configured as "x86_64-pc-linux-gnu".
Type "show configuration" for configuration details.
Find the GDB manual and other documentation resources online at:
    <http://www.gnu.org/software/gdb/documentation/>.

For help, type "help".
Type "apropos word" to search for commands related to "word"...

      KERNEL: ../KSym/vmlinux-6.8.0-1018-azure
    DUMPFILE: 202412290014.kdump  [PARTIAL DUMP]
        CPUS: 4
        DATE: Sun Dec 29 00:12:36 GMT 2024
      UPTIME: 00:11:48
LOAD AVERAGE: 0.37, 0.19, 0.13
       TASKS: 634
    NODENAME: coredump-alcda
     RELEASE: 6.8.0-1018-azure
     VERSION: #21~22.04.1-Ubuntu SMP Fri Nov  8 00:21:25 UTC 2024
     MACHINE: x86_64  (2112 Mhz)
      MEMORY: 4 GB
```

```
    PANIC: "Kernel panic - not syncing: sysrq triggered crash"
      PID: 2278
  COMMAND: "bash"
     TASK: ffff991e03495100  [THREAD_INFO: ffff991e03495100]
      CPU: 0
    STATE: TASK_RUNNING (PANIC)

crash>
```

Note: If the *crash* tool fails to launch, it means that it is not up to date with the *vmlinux* kernel, and the latest version of the tool is required. You need to install it from the source as we did for WSL2 Debian (you may also need to install additional packages depending on your platform and previous installations):

```
$ git clone https://github.com/crash-utility/crash.git
$ sudo apt install build-essential wget libgmp-dev libmpfr-dev libmpc-dev flex bison texinfo zlib1g-dev libncurses-dev
$ cd crash
$ make
$ sudo make install
```

Note: For our x64 exercises, we built the *crash* tool on WSL2 Debian x64 using gcc 14.2.0 since the default *crash* tool installation didn't handle core dumps and symbols from the 6.8.x kernel well.

3. We can see the current thread from the process ID that led to the crash:

```
crash> bt
PID: 2278     TASK: ffff991e03495100  CPU: 0    COMMAND: "bash"
 #0 [ffffac1c46ca79b0] machine_kexec at ffffffff86a99db1
 #1 [ffffac1c46ca7a18] __crash_kexec at ffffffff86bf1e46
 #2 [ffffac1c46ca7ad8] panic at ffffffff86addf29
 #3 [ffffac1c46ca7b58] sysrq_handle_crash at ffffffff873fea05
 #4 [ffffac1c46ca7b68] __handle_sysrq at ffffffff873ff2d2
 #5 [ffffac1c46ca7bb0] write_sysrq_trigger at ffffffff873ffb2c
 #6 [ffffac1c46ca7be0] proc_reg_write at ffffffff86f31fce
 #7 [ffffac1c46ca7c00] vfs_write at ffffffff86e7e26f
 #8 [ffffac1c46ca7c98] ksys_write at ffffffff86e7e907
 #9 [ffffac1c46ca7cd8] __x64_sys_write at ffffffff86e7e9b9
#10 [ffffac1c46ca7ce8] x64_sys_call at ffffffff86a0651d
#11 [ffffac1c46ca7cf8] do_syscall_64 at ffffffff87abadac
#12 [ffffac1c46ca7f50] entry_SYSCALL_64_after_hwframe at ffffffff87c00130
    RIP: 00007d3b23914887  RSP: 00007fffee286ee8  RFLAGS: 00000246
    RAX: ffffffffffffffda  RBX: 0000000000000002  RCX: 00007d3b23914887
    RDX: 0000000000000002  RSI: 000057f2ab275ac0  RDI: 0000000000000001
    RBP: 000057f2ab275ac0   R8: 0000000000000000   R9: 000057f2ab275ac0
    R10: 00007d3b23a1ad00  R11: 0000000000000246  R12: 0000000000000002
    R13: 00007d3b23a1b780  R14: 00007d3b23a17600  R15: 00007d3b23a16a00
    ORIG_RAX: 0000000000000001  CS: 0033  SS: 002b
```

Note: User space addresses are not available in the kernel dump.

```
crash> sym 00007d3b23914887
sym: invalid address: 00007d3b23914887

crash> sym ffffffff86addf29
ffffffff86addf29 (T) panic+345 /build/linux-azure-6.8-2oiFiH/linux-azure-6.8-6.8.0/kernel/panic.c: 389
```

4. The tool has built-in help:

```
crash> help

*              files          mod            sbitmapq       union
alias          foreach        mount          search         vm
ascii          fuser          net            set            vtop
bpf            gdb            p              sig            waitq
bt             help           ps             struct         whatis
btop           ipcs           pte            swap           wr
dev            irq            ptob           sym            q
dis            kmem           ptov           sys
eval           list           rd             task
exit           log            repeat         timer
extend         mach           runq           tree

crash version: 8.0.6++   gdb version: 10.2
For help on any command above, enter "help <command>".
For help on input options, enter "help input".
For help on output options, enter "help output".
```

5. Print kernel message buffer before the crash (**dmesg** or **log**) with human-readable timestamps:

```
crash> dmesg -T
[Sun Dec 29 00:00:48 GMT 2024] Linux version 6.8.0-1018-azure (buildd@lcy02-amd64-013) (x86_64-linux-gnu-gcc-11
(Ubuntu 11.4.0-1ubuntu1~22.04) 11.4.0, GNU
 ld (GNU Binutils for Ubuntu) 2.38) #21~22.04.1-Ubuntu SMP Fri Nov  8 00:21:25 UTC 2024 (Ubuntu 6.8.0-1018.21~22.04.1-
azure 6.8.12)
[Sun Dec 29 00:00:48 GMT 2024] Command line: BOOT_IMAGE=/boot/vmlinuz-6.8.0-1018-azure root=UUID=89ee03ba-6808-4977-
a4fb-9b10174744f8 ro quiet splash crashkernel=512M-:192M vt.handoff=7
...
...
...
[Sun Dec 29 00:12:36 GMT 2024] sysrq: Trigger a crash
[Sun Dec 29 00:12:36 GMT 2024] Kernel panic - not syncing: sysrq triggered crash
[Sun Dec 29 00:12:36 GMT 2024] CPU: 0 PID: 2278 Comm: bash Kdump: loaded Not tainted 6.8.0-1018-azure #21~22.04.1-
Ubuntu
[Sun Dec 29 00:12:36 GMT 2024] Hardware name: Microsoft Corporation Virtual Machine/Virtual Machine, BIOS Hyper-V UEFI
Release v4.1 05/13/2024
[Sun Dec 29 00:12:36 GMT 2024] Call Trace:
[Sun Dec 29 00:12:36 GMT 2024]  <TASK>
[Sun Dec 29 00:12:36 GMT 2024]  dump_stack_lvl+0x27/0x70
[Sun Dec 29 00:12:36 GMT 2024]  dump_stack+0x10/0x20
[Sun Dec 29 00:12:36 GMT 2024]  panic+0x351/0x390
[Sun Dec 29 00:12:36 GMT 2024]  sysrq_handle_crash+0x15/0x20
[Sun Dec 29 00:12:36 GMT 2024]  __handle_sysrq+0xf2/0x290
[Sun Dec 29 00:12:36 GMT 2024]  write_sysrq_trigger+0x5c/0x80
[Sun Dec 29 00:12:36 GMT 2024]  proc_reg_write+0x5e/0xa0
[Sun Dec 29 00:12:36 GMT 2024]  ? __cond_resched+0x1a/0x50
[Sun Dec 29 00:12:36 GMT 2024]  vfs_write+0xef/0x410
[Sun Dec 29 00:12:36 GMT 2024]  ? __do_sys_newfstatat+0x3e/0x60
[Sun Dec 29 00:12:36 GMT 2024]  ksys_write+0x67/0xf0
[Sun Dec 29 00:12:36 GMT 2024]  __x64_sys_write+0x19/0x20
[Sun Dec 29 00:12:36 GMT 2024]  x64_sys_call+0x167d/0x20c0
[Sun Dec 29 00:12:36 GMT 2024]  do_syscall_64+0x7c/0x160
[Sun Dec 29 00:12:36 GMT 2024]  ? syscall_exit_to_user_mode+0x81/0x220
[Sun Dec 29 00:12:36 GMT 2024]  ? do_syscall_64+0x88/0x160
[Sun Dec 29 00:12:36 GMT 2024]  ? __check_object_size+0x1d/0x30
[Sun Dec 29 00:12:36 GMT 2024]  ? putname+0x57/0x70
[Sun Dec 29 00:12:36 GMT 2024]  ? do_sys_openat2+0x87/0xd0
[Sun Dec 29 00:12:36 GMT 2024]  ? syscall_exit_to_user_mode+0x81/0x220
[Sun Dec 29 00:12:36 GMT 2024]  ? do_syscall_64+0x88/0x160
[Sun Dec 29 00:12:36 GMT 2024]  ? syscall_exit_to_user_mode+0x81/0x220
[Sun Dec 29 00:12:36 GMT 2024]  ? do_syscall_64+0x88/0x160
[Sun Dec 29 00:12:36 GMT 2024]  ? do_syscall_64+0x88/0x160
[Sun Dec 29 00:12:36 GMT 2024]  ? clear_bhb_loop+0x45/0xa0
[Sun Dec 29 00:12:36 GMT 2024]  ? clear_bhb_loop+0x45/0xa0
[Sun Dec 29 00:12:36 GMT 2024]  ? clear_bhb_loop+0x45/0xa0
```

```
[Sun Dec 29 00:12:36 GMT 2024]  entry_SYSCALL_64_after_hwframe+0x78/0x80
[Sun Dec 29 00:12:36 GMT 2024] RIP: 0033:0x7d3b23914887
[Sun Dec 29 00:12:36 GMT 2024] Code: 10 00 f7 d8 64 89 02 48 c7 c0 ff ff ff ff eb b7 0f 1f 00 f3 0f 1e fa 64 8b 04 25
18 00 00 00 85 c0 75 10 b8 01 00 00 00 0f 05 <48> 3d 00 f0 ff ff 77 51 c3 48 83 ec 28 48 89 54 24 18 48 89 74 24
[Sun Dec 29 00:12:36 GMT 2024] RSP: 002b:00007fffee286ee8 EFLAGS: 00000246 ORIG_RAX: 0000000000000001
[Sun Dec 29 00:12:36 GMT 2024] RAX: ffffffffffffffda RBX: 0000000000000002 RCX: 00007d3b23914887
[Sun Dec 29 00:12:36 GMT 2024] RDX: 0000000000000002 RSI: 000057f2ab275ac0 RDI: 0000000000000001
[Sun Dec 29 00:12:36 GMT 2024] RBP: 000057f2ab275ac0 R08: 0000000000000000 R09: 000057f2ab275ac0
[Sun Dec 29 00:12:36 GMT 2024] R10: 00007d3b23a1ad00 R11: 0000000000000246 R12: 0000000000000002
[Sun Dec 29 00:12:36 GMT 2024] R13: 00007d3b23a1b780 R14: 00007d3b23a17600 R15: 00007d3b23a16a00
[Sun Dec 29 00:12:36 GMT 2024]  </TASK>
[Sun Dec 29 00:12:36 GMT 2024] Kernel Offset: 0x5a00000 from 0xffffffff81000000 (relocation range: 0xffffffff80000000-
0xffffffffbfffffff)
```

Note: Many commands have many options. Please check individual help entries.

```
crash> help dmesg
```

6. Check memory summary, computer, and network information:

```
crash> kmem -i
                 PAGES        TOTAL      PERCENTAGE
    TOTAL MEM   952170       3.6 GB         ----
         FREE   345855       1.3 GB   36% of TOTAL MEM
         USED   606315       2.3 GB   63% of TOTAL MEM
       SHARED   104781     409.3 MB   11% of TOTAL MEM
      BUFFERS    13305        52 MB    1% of TOTAL MEM
       CACHED   275999       1.1 GB   28% of TOTAL MEM
         SLAB    40934     159.9 MB    4% of TOTAL MEM

   TOTAL HUGE        0            0         ----
    HUGE FREE        0            0    0% of TOTAL HUGE

   TOTAL SWAP        0            0         ----
    SWAP USED        0            0    0% of TOTAL SWAP
    SWAP FREE        0            0    0% of TOTAL SWAP

 COMMIT LIMIT   476085       1.8 GB         ----
    COMMITTED  1332182       5.1 GB  279% of TOTAL LIMIT

crash> mach
          MACHINE TYPE: x86_64
           MEMORY SIZE: 4 GB
                  CPUS: 4
            HYPERVISOR: Hyper-V
       PROCESSOR SPEED: 2112 Mhz
                    HZ: 1000
             PAGE SIZE: 4096
   KERNEL VIRTUAL BASE: ffff991d00000000
   KERNEL VMALLOC BASE: ffffac1c40000000
   KERNEL VMEMMAP BASE: ffffe20180000000
      KERNEL START MAP: ffffffff80000000
   KERNEL MODULES BASE: ffffffffc0000000
     KERNEL STACK SIZE: 16384
        IRQ STACK SIZE: 16384
            IRQ STACKS:
                 CPU 0: ffffac1c40000000
                 CPU 1: ffffac1c4014d000
                 CPU 2: ffffac1c40019000
                 CPU 3: ffffac1c40181000
 DOUBLEFAULT STACK SIZE: 8192
```

```
    DOUBLEFAULT STACKS:
                 CPU 0: fffffe260c33c000
                 CPU 1: fffffe37c5b32000
                 CPU 2: fffffe4c43713000
                 CPU 3: fffffe2b8d19d000
        NMI STACK SIZE: 8192
            NMI STACKS:
                 CPU 0: fffffe260c33f000
                 CPU 1: fffffe37c5b35000
                 CPU 2: fffffe4c43716000
                 CPU 3: fffffe2b8d1a0000
      DEBUG STACK SIZE: 8192
          DEBUG STACKS:
                 CPU 0: fffffe260c342000
                 CPU 1: fffffe37c5b38000
                 CPU 2: fffffe4c43719000
                 CPU 3: fffffe2b8d1a3000
        MCE STACK SIZE: 8192
            MCE STACKS:
                 CPU 0: fffffe260c345000
                 CPU 1: fffffe37c5b3b000
                 CPU 2: fffffe4c4371c000
                 CPU 3: fffffe2b8d1a6000
         VC STACK SIZE: 8192
             VC STACKS:
                 CPU 0: fffffe260c348000 [unavailable]
                 CPU 1: fffffe37c5b3e000 [unavailable]
                 CPU 2: fffffe4c4371f000 [unavailable]
                 CPU 3: fffffe2b8d1a9000 [unavailable]
```

```
crash> net
   NET_DEVICE     NAME      IP ADDRESS(ES)
ffff991e00f89000  lo        127.0.0.1, ::1
ffff991d06a0a000  eth0      172.22.215.4, fe80::12c7:a888:fd35:18c2
```

7. List all processes:

```
crash> ps
      PID    PPID  CPU       TASK        ST  %MEM     VSZ    RSS  COMM
        0       0   0  ffffffff88c0fcc0  RU   0.0       0      0  [swapper/0]
>       0       0   1  ffff991e00825100  RU   0.0       0      0  [swapper/1]
>       0       0   2  ffff991e00820000  RU   0.0       0      0  [swapper/2]
>       0       0   3  ffff991e00822880  RU   0.0       0      0  [swapper/3]
        1       0   1  ffff991e00360000  IN   0.3  167064  12524  systemd
        2       0   1  ffff991e00362880  IN   0.0       0      0  [kthreadd]
...
...
...
     2046    1273   1  ffff991d58ce0000  IN   1.2  889248  53872  gmain
     2047    1273   1  ffff991d407d2880  IN   1.2  889248  53872  gdbus
     2048    1273   1  ffff991d50285100  IN   1.2  889248  53872  dconf worker
     2067    1273   0  ffff991d736b0000  IN   1.2  889248  53872  threaded-ml
     2068    2045   3  ffff991d33318000  IN   0.1   11252   5544  bash
     2079    1273   1  ffff991d2ed7a880  IN   9.7 5282320 421072  threaded-ml
     2094    1496   0  ffff991d33088000  IN   1.1  808880  46544  update-notifier
     2098    1496   0  ffff991d56b28000  IN   1.1  808880  46544  gmain
     2099    1496   1  ffff991d49ae2880  IN   1.1  808880  46544  gdbus
     2103    1496   1  ffff991d1084d100  IN   1.1  808880  46544  dconf worker
     2126    1496   3  ffff991d50262880  IN   1.1  808880  46544  threaded-ml
     2263       2   1  ffff991d49aa5100  ID   0.0       0      0  [kworker/u8:2]
```

```
   2266       2  0  ffff991d01b38000  ID   0.0        0        0  [kworker/0:0]
   2277    2068  3  ffff991d66fea880  IN   0.1    13492     5604  su
>  2278    2277  0  ffff991e03495100  RU   0.1    10236     4296  bash
   2285       2  2  ffff991d01b3a880  ID   0.0        0        0  [kworker/u8:0]
   2286    1273  0  ffff991d58d55100  IN   9.7  5282320   421072  pool-gnome-shel
```

8. List CPU queues:

```
crash> runq
CPU 0 RUNQUEUE: ffff991e03c33580
  CURRENT: PID: 2278   TASK: ffff991e03495100  COMMAND: "bash"
  RT PRIO_ARRAY: ffff991e03c33880
     [no tasks queued]
  CFS RB_ROOT: ffff991e03c336d0
     [no tasks queued]

CPU 1 RUNQUEUE: ffff991e03cb3580
  CURRENT: PID: 0      TASK: ffff991e00825100  COMMAND: "swapper/1"
  RT PRIO_ARRAY: ffff991e03cb3880
     [no tasks queued]
  CFS RB_ROOT: ffff991e03cb36d0
     [no tasks queued]

CPU 2 RUNQUEUE: ffff991e03d33580
  CURRENT: PID: 0      TASK: ffff991e00820000  COMMAND: "swapper/2"
  RT PRIO_ARRAY: ffff991e03d33880
     [no tasks queued]
  CFS RB_ROOT: ffff991e03d336d0
     [no tasks queued]

CPU 3 RUNQUEUE: ffff991e03db3580
  CURRENT: PID: 0      TASK: ffff991e00822880  COMMAND: "swapper/3"
  RT PRIO_ARRAY: ffff991e03db3880
     [no tasks queued]
  CFS RB_ROOT: ffff991e03db36d0
     [no tasks queued]
```

9. Set the current task to PID 2277 and, then to the task running to CPU 1, and then to the panicked task:

```
crash> set 2277
    PID: 2277
COMMAND: "su"
   TASK: ffff991d66fea880  [THREAD_INFO: ffff991d66fea880]
    CPU: 3
  STATE: TASK_INTERRUPTIBLE

crash> set -c 1
    PID: 0
COMMAND: "swapper/1"
   TASK: ffff991e00825100  (1 of 4)  [THREAD_INFO: ffff991e00825100]
    CPU: 1
  STATE: TASK_RUNNING (ACTIVE)
```

```
crash> set -p
    PID: 2278
COMMAND: "bash"
   TASK: ffff991e03495100  [THREAD_INFO: ffff991e03495100]
    CPU: 0
  STATE: TASK_RUNNING (PANIC)
```

10. Display the stack trace of the bash parent process without and with source code, and dump raw stack data:

```
crash> set 2068
    PID: 2068
COMMAND: "bash"
   TASK: ffff991d33318000  [THREAD_INFO: ffff991d33318000]
    CPU: 3
  STATE: TASK_INTERRUPTIBLE

crash> bt
PID: 2068     TASK: ffff991d33318000  CPU: 3    COMMAND: "bash"
 #0 [ffffac1c464d3bb0] __schedule at ffffffff87ace28a
 #1 [ffffac1c464d3c58] schedule at ffffffff87ace68e
 #2 [ffffac1c464d3c78] do_wait at ffffffff86ae5437
 #3 [ffffac1c464d3ca0] kernel_wait4 at ffffffff86ae5a2f
 #4 [ffffac1c464d3d38] __do_sys_wait4 at ffffffff86ae5b69
 #5 [ffffac1c464d3df8] __x64_sys_wait4 at ffffffff86ae5bac
 #6 [ffffac1c464d3e08] x64_sys_call at ffffffff86a05548
 #7 [ffffac1c464d3e18] do_syscall_64 at ffffffff87abadac
    RIP: 000078a64caea3ea  RSP: 00007ffdcd75b3f8  RFLAGS: 00000246
    RAX: ffffffffffffffda  RBX: 00000000000008e5  RCX: 000078a64caea3ea
    RDX: 000000000000000a  RSI: 00007ffdcd75b420  RDI: 00000000ffffffff
    RBP: 00005994c8d18d68   R8: 00005994ca06e800   R9: 0000000000000001
    R10: 0000000000000000  R11: 0000000000000246  R12: 000000000000000a
    R13: 00005994ca075470  R14: 00007ffdcd75b420  R15: 0000000000000001
    ORIG_RAX: 000000000000003d  CS: 0033  SS: 002b

crash> bt -l
PID: 2068     TASK: ffff991d33318000  CPU: 3    COMMAND: "bash"
 #0 [ffffac1c464d3bb0] __schedule at ffffffff87ace28a
    /build/linux-azure-6.8-2oiFiH/linux-azure-6.8-6.8.0/kernel/sched/core.c: 5399
 #1 [ffffac1c464d3c58] schedule at ffffffff87ace68e
    /build/linux-azure-6.8-2oiFiH/linux-azure-6.8-6.8.0/arch/x86/include/asm/bitops.h: 205
 #2 [ffffac1c464d3c78] do_wait at ffffffff86ae5437
    /build/linux-azure-6.8-2oiFiH/linux-azure-6.8-6.8.0/kernel/exit.c: 1624
 #3 [ffffac1c464d3ca0] kernel_wait4 at ffffffff86ae5a2f
    /build/linux-azure-6.8-2oiFiH/linux-azure-6.8-6.8.0/kernel/exit.c: 1786
 #4 [ffffac1c464d3d38] __do_sys_wait4 at ffffffff86ae5b69
    /build/linux-azure-6.8-2oiFiH/linux-azure-6.8-6.8.0/kernel/exit.c: 1813
 #5 [ffffac1c464d3df8] __x64_sys_wait4 at ffffffff86ae5bac
    /build/linux-azure-6.8-2oiFiH/linux-azure-6.8-6.8.0/kernel/exit.c: 1809
 #6 [ffffac1c464d3e08] x64_sys_call at ffffffff86a05548
    /build/linux-azure-6.8-2oiFiH/linux-azure-6.8-6.8.0/arch/x86/entry/syscall_64.c: 33
 #7 [ffffac1c464d3e18] do_syscall_64 at ffffffff87abadac
    /build/linux-azure-6.8-2oiFiH/linux-azure-6.8-6.8.0/arch/x86/entry/common.c: 52
    RIP: 000078a64caea3ea  RSP: 00007ffdcd75b3f8  RFLAGS: 00000246
    RAX: ffffffffffffffda  RBX: 00000000000008e5  RCX: 000078a64caea3ea
    RDX: 000000000000000a  RSI: 00007ffdcd75b420  RDI: 00000000ffffffff
    RBP: 00005994c8d18d68   R8: 00005994ca06e800   R9: 0000000000000001
    R10: 0000000000000000  R11: 0000000000000246  R12: 000000000000000a
    R13: 00005994ca075470  R14: 00007ffdcd75b420  R15: 0000000000000001
    ORIG_RAX: 000000000000003d  CS: 0033  SS: 002b
```

```
crash> bt -r
PID: 2068     TASK: ffff991d33318000  CPU: 3    COMMAND: "bash"
ffffac1c464d0000:  0000000057ac6e9d 0000000000000000
ffffac1c464d0010:  0000000000000000 0000000000000000
ffffac1c464d0020:  0000000000000000 0000000000000000
ffffac1c464d0030:  0000000000000000 0000000000000000
...
...
...
ffffac1c464d2ff0:  0000000000000000 0000000000000000
ffffac1c464d3000:  0000000000000000 0000000000000000
ffffac1c464d3010:  0000000000000000 0000000000000000
ffffac1c464d3020:  0000000000000000 0000000000000000
ffffac1c464d3030:  0000000000000000 0000000000000000
ffffac1c464d3040:  0000000000000000 0000000000000000
ffffac1c464d3050:  0000000000000000 ffffac1c464d3130
ffffac1c464d3060:  0000000000000003 ffff991e03db3580
ffffac1c464d3070:  0000000000000003 ffffac1c464d3310
ffffac1c464d3080:  ffffac1c464d3110 ffffac1c464d3160
ffffac1c464d3090:  0000000000000003 ffff991e03db3580
ffffac1c464d30a0:  ffffac1c464d3160 0000000000000003
ffffac1c464d30b0:  ffffac1c464d3140 update_sg_lb_stats+150
ffffac1c464d30c0:  ffff991e001cf428 ffff991e001cf400
ffffac1c464d30d0:  ffffac1c464d312c 0000000000000003
ffffac1c464d30e0:  00000000000000b7 ffff991e001cf840
ffffac1c464d30f0:  ffff991e001cf428 ffff991e001cf400
ffffac1c464d3100:  ffffac1c464d315c 0000000000000003
ffffac1c464d3110:  0000000000033580 ffffac1c464d31f8
ffffac1c464d3120:  ffff991e001cf400 ffffac1c464d3340
ffffac1c464d3130:  00000000000000fe ffffac1c464d3280
ffffac1c464d3140:  ffffac1c464d31e8 update_sd_lb_stats.constprop.0+239
ffffac1c464d3150:  0000000000000190 0000000000000002
ffffac1c464d3160:  ffffac1c464d31c0 696d304f0000020f
ffffac1c464d3170:  9fd13d8000000014 253a1ba00b0f6ae2
ffffac1c464d3180:  4f179c9d79de86ac 0000000000000000
ffffac1c464d3190:  ffffac1c464d32e0 ffffac1c464d3230
ffffac1c464d31a0:  ffff991e03c30720 ffffac1c464d32e0
ffffac1c464d31b0:  ffffac1c464d3220 chacha_block_generic+113
ffffac1c464d31c0:  79de86aca258d95d 5f9933da9fd13d80
ffffac1c464d31d0:  696d304ffff1ae8a 4f179c9d7a8b7939
ffffac1c464d31e0:  57660bb1a3e1dba0 0b0f6ae2253a1ba0
ffffac1c464d31f0:  3f9c44fea03c878d 6f2874d983c41e7e
ffffac1c464d3200:  0483c6faf5d47b00 ffff991e03c308a0
ffffac1c464d3210:  ffffac1c464d3270 6a675fd3464d3230
ffffac1c464d3220:  1889aa8600000014 21ff9c780266a162
ffffac1c464d3230:  20cb075dab48c3c2 0000000000000000
ffffac1c464d3240:  ffffac1c464d32e0 ffff991e03c30740
ffffac1c464d3250:  ffffac1c464d32e0 ffff991e00e6ba00
ffffac1c464d3260:  ffffac1c464d32d0 chacha_block_generic+113
ffffac1c464d3270:  ab48c3c23278428b f89312911889aa86
ffffac1c464d3280:  6a675fd394e56f79 20cb075d8e8b2c04
ffffac1c464d3290:  a65e19bd30db5300 0266a16221ff9c78
ffffac1c464d32a0:  07b64798e0cf024c 07933f9a909f38d3
ffffac1c464d32b0:  0483c6faf5d47b00 0000000000000040
ffffac1c464d32c0:  0000000000000020 ffff991e03c30740
ffffac1c464d32d0:  ffff991d3d2b9800 ffffac1c464d32e8
ffffac1c464d32e0:  ffff991e03db3680 ffff991d0ee9ae00
ffffac1c464d32f0:  000000979d959874 ffffac1c464d3360
ffffac1c464d3300:  newidle_balance+867 01ffac1c464d3348
ffffac1c464d3310:  ffff991e03db3680 ffffac1c464d3440
```

```
ffffac1c464d3320:  0000000000000000 0000000000000000
ffffac1c464d3330:  0483c6faf5d47b00 ffff991e03db3580
ffffac1c464d3340:  ffff991e03db3580 ffffac1c464d3440
ffffac1c464d3350:  ffffac1c464d33c0 psi_group_change+593
ffffac1c464d3360:  00000001464d33b0 000000979d959fe0
ffffac1c464d3370:  ffff991d0ec2f800 ffffac1c464d3388
ffffac1c464d3380:  _raw_spin_unlock_irqrestore+14 ffffac1c464d33d8
ffffac1c464d3390:  cgroup_rstat_updated+305 000000979d959fe0
ffffac1c464d33a0:  0000000000000003 ffff991e03da4014
ffffac1c464d33b0:  ffff991e03db3680 ffff991d0ee9ae00
ffffac1c464d33c0:  00000097a9336c10 ffffac1c464d3430
ffffac1c464d33d0:  newidle_balance+867 01ffac1c464d3418
ffffac1c464d33e0:  ffff991e03db3680 ffffac1c464d3510
ffffac1c464d33f0:  0000000000000000 0000000000000000
ffffac1c464d3400:  0483c6faf5d47b00 ffff991e03db3580
ffffac1c464d3410:  ffff991e03db3580 ffffac1c464d3510
ffffac1c464d3420:  ffffac1c464d3490 psi_group_change+593
ffffac1c464d3430:  00000001464d3480 00000097a93374a8
ffffac1c464d3440:  0000000300000000 00000000000208c0
ffffac1c464d3450:  0000000000000003 ffffffff00000000
ffffac1c464d3460:  psi_system       00000097a93374a8
ffffac1c464d3470:  0000000000000003 0000000000000014
ffffac1c464d3480:  0000000000000000 psi_system
ffffac1c464d3490:  ffffac1c464d34f0 psi_task_switch+217
ffffac1c464d34a0:  0000000000000000 ffffac1c464d34b8
ffffac1c464d34b0:  raw_spin_rq_unlock+16 ffffac1c464d34f0
ffffac1c464d34c0:  finish_task_switch+139 ffffcc1c3fda9900
ffffac1c464d34d0:  ffff991e03db3580 ffff991d33318000
ffffac1c464d34e0:  ffff991e00822880 0000000000000003
ffffac1c464d34f0:  ffffac1c464d3568 __schedule+642
ffffac1c464d3500:  ffff991d5dd20c00 ffffac1c464d3528
ffffac1c464d3510:  sysvec_hyperv_stimer0+78 0000000000000000
ffffac1c464d3520:  0000000000000000 ffffac1c464d3539
ffffac1c464d3530:  asm_sysvec_hyperv_stimer0+27 ffffac1c464d3700
ffffac1c464d3540:  0000000000000000 ffff991e0028f0c0
ffffac1c464d3550:  ffff991d66f56e00 ffffac1c464d3610
ffffac1c464d3560:  ffff991d5dd20c00 0000000000000000
ffffac1c464d3570:  tty_poll         ffffac1c464d3598
ffffac1c464d3580:  pty_write_room+57 0000000000000000
ffffac1c464d3590:  ffff991d5dd20c00 ffffac1c464d35a8
ffffac1c464d35a0:  ffff991d5dd20df8 ffffac1c464d35b8
ffffac1c464d35b0:  _raw_spin_unlock_irqrestore+14 ffffac1c464d35d8
ffffac1c464d35c0:  ffff991e03db3680 ffff991d0ee9ae00
ffffac1c464d35d0:  00000097cf455e2c ffffac1c464d3640
ffffac1c464d35e0:  newidle_balance+867 01ffac1c464d3628
ffffac1c464d35f0:  ffff991e03db3680 ffffac1c464d3720
ffffac1c464d3600:  0000000000000000 0000000000000000
ffffac1c464d3610:  ffffac1c464d3660 __raw_callee_save_hv_vcpu_is_preempted+21
ffffac1c464d3620:  0000000000000001 0000000000000008
ffffac1c464d3630:  0000000000000001 0000000000000000
ffffac1c464d3640:  0000000000000001 0000000000000001
ffffac1c464d3650:  0000000000000000 ffffac1c464d3680
ffffac1c464d3660:  _hv_do_fast_hypercall16.constprop.0+120 0000000000000001
ffffac1c464d3670:  00000000000000fb 0000000000000001
ffffac1c464d3680:  ffffac1c464d36a8 __send_ipi_one+99
ffffac1c464d3690:  0000000000000001 0000000000000001
ffffac1c464d36a0:  00000000000000fb ffffac1c464d36c8
ffffac1c464d36b0:  hv_send_ipi+24   ffff991e008f5138
ffffac1c464d36c0:  0000000000000001 ffffac1c464d36d8
ffffac1c464d36d0:  native_send_call_func_single_ipi+19 ffffac1c464d3708
```

```
ffffac1c464d36e0:  __smp_call_single_queue+200 ffff991e008f5100
ffffac1c464d36f0:  ffff991e008f5100 0000000000000001
ffffac1c464d3700:  ffff991e008f5d01 ffffac1c464d3750
ffffac1c464d3710:  ttwu_queue_wakelist+305 ffff991d33318aa0
ffffac1c464d3720:  0000000800000000 0000000000000000
ffffac1c464d3730:  0000000000000901 ffff991e07fd5600
ffffac1c464d3740:  ffffac1c464d3801 ffff991e07fd5600
ffffac1c464d3750:  0000000000000000 ffff991e03dbabc0
ffffac1c464d3760:  ffffe201819bf4c0 ffffac1c464d3848
ffffac1c464d3770:  rmqueue+1487     ffffac1c464d3798
ffffac1c464d3780:  schedule+46      0483c6faf5d47b00
ffffac1c464d3790:  ffff991e001dc000 0000000000000000
ffffac1c464d37a0:  ffff991e008f5100 ffff991e001dbc00
ffffac1c464d37b0:  ffff991df4571208 ffffac1c464d37c8
ffffac1c464d37c0:  wake_up_process+21 ffffac1c464d37f0
ffffac1c464d37d0:  kick_pool+101    ffff991e07fd5c00
ffffac1c464d37e0:  ffff991df4571210 0000000000000000
ffffac1c464d37f0:  ffffac1c464d3840 0000000000000283
ffffac1c464d3800:  0000000000000000 0000000000000032
ffffac1c464d3810:  0000000000000001 0000000000000032
ffffac1c464d3820:  ffff991d3338b000 000032fe3c06b740
ffffac1c464d3830:  ffffac1c464d3870 __mod_memcg_state+143
ffffac1c464d3840:  ffffe201819bf4c0 0000000000000001
ffffac1c464d3850:  ffff991d3338b000 0000000000000246
ffffac1c464d3860:  ffff991d3338b000 0000000000000001
ffffac1c464d3870:  ffffac1c464d3898 memcg_account_kmem+35
ffffac1c464d3880:  ffffe201819bf4c0 ffff991e01a0ff00
ffffac1c464d3890:  0000000000440dc0 ffffac1c464d38d8
ffffac1c464d38a0:  __memcg_kmem_charge_page+238 0000000007fd6e10
ffffac1c464d38b0:  0000000000000000 0000000000440dc0
ffffac1c464d38c0:  0000000000000000 ffffe201819bf4c0
ffffac1c464d38d0:  0000000000440dc0 ffffac1c464d3940
ffffac1c464d38e0:  __alloc_pages+437 ffff991e07fd6e00
ffffac1c464d38f0:  0000000000000000 ffff991e07fd6e00
ffffac1c464d3900:  0000000200000000 0000000000000000
ffffac1c464d3910:  0000000000000026 0000000000000001
ffffac1c464d3920:  0000000000000148 000032fe3c040a60
ffffac1c464d3930:  ffff991d3338b000 ffffac1c464d3988
ffffac1c464d3940:  __mod_memcg_lruvec_state+174 alloc_pages_mpol+145
ffffac1c464d3950:  memcg_account_kmem+35 0000000081f61dc0
ffffac1c464d3960:  0000000000000246 ffff991d02943000
ffffac1c464d3970:  0000000000000026 0000000000000001
ffffac1c464d3980:  ffff991d58ef0358 ffffac1c464d39b0
ffffac1c464d3990:  __mod_lruvec_state+55 ffffe201819bf4c0
ffffac1c464d39a0:  ffff991d7d877358 0000000000000001
ffffac1c464d39b0:  ffffac1c464d3a08 copy_present_pte+59
ffffac1c464d39c0:  ffff991d58c15c30 __pte_offset_map_lock+121
ffffac1c464d39d0:  ffff991d66fd3c30 ffff991d145fc0c0
ffffac1c464d39e0:  00007ffdcd786000 ffff991d58c15c30
ffffac1c464d39f0:  ffff991d66fd3c30 0000000000000009
ffffac1c464d3a00:  __cond_resched+26 00007ffdcd788000
ffffac1c464d3a10:  ffffac1c464d3ac8 copy_pte_range+592
ffffac1c464d3a20:  0000000000000000 ffff991d58ef0358
ffffac1c464d3a30:  ffff991d4065b700 ffffe20100000000
ffffac1c464d3a40:  0000000000000007 ffffac1c464d3a58
ffffac1c464d3a50:  _raw_spin_unlock_irqrestore+14 ffffac1c464d3a88
ffffac1c464d3a60:  tty_get_pgrp+82  ffff991d66f56e00
ffffac1c464d3a70:  0000000000000000 ffffac1c464d3a88
ffffac1c464d3a80:  put_pid+19       ffffac1c464d3ac0
ffffac1c464d3a90:  tty_jobctrl_ioctl+226 ffff991e03db3680
```

```
ffffac1c464d3aa0:  ffff991d0ee9ae00 000000980328c5bc
ffffac1c464d3ab0:  ffffac1c464d3b18 newidle_balance+867
ffffac1c464d3ac0:  01ffac1c464d3b00 ffff991e03db3680
ffffac1c464d3ad0:  ffffac1c464d3bf8 0000000000000000
ffffac1c464d3ae0:  0000000000000000 0483c6faf5d47b00
ffffac1c464d3af0:  ffff991e03db3580 ffff991e03db3580
ffffac1c464d3b00:  ffffac1c464d3bf8 ffffac1c464d3b78
ffffac1c464d3b10:  psi_group_change+593 00000001464d3b68
ffffac1c464d3b20:  000000980328cb34 0000000300000000
ffffac1c464d3b30:  00000000000208c0 0000000000000003
ffffac1c464d3b40:  ffffffff00000000 psi_system
ffffac1c464d3b50:  000000980328cb34 0000000000000003
ffffac1c464d3b60:  0000000000000014 0000000000000000
ffffac1c464d3b70:  psi_system       ffffac1c464d3bd8
ffffac1c464d3b80:  psi_task_switch+217 ffff991e00822880
ffffac1c464d3b90:  0100000000000009 ffff991d33318000
ffffac1c464d3ba0:  0000000000000000 ffffac1c00000001
ffffac1c464d3bb0:  0000000000000003 ffff991e00822880
ffffac1c464d3bc0:  ffff991d33318000 ffff991e03db3580
ffffac1c464d3bd0:  ffffcc1c3fda9900 ffffac1c464d3c50
ffffac1c464d3be0:  __schedule+634   ffffac1c464d3ca8
ffffac1c464d3bf0:  ffff991d33318aa0 ffffac1c464d3c38
ffffac1c464d3c00:  ffffffff00000004 cpu_bit_bitmap+4096
ffffac1c464d3c10:  0000000000000000 0000000000000002
ffffac1c464d3c20:  0483c6faf5d47b00 ffff991d33318000
ffffac1c464d3c30:  ffff991d33318000 ffffac1c464d3cd0
ffffac1c464d3c40:  0000000000000000 0000000000000000
ffffac1c464d3c50:  ffffac1c464d3c70 schedule+46
ffffac1c464d3c60:  ffff991d33318000 ffffac1c464d3ca8
ffffac1c464d3c70:  ffffac1c464d3c98 do_wait+183
ffffac1c464d3c80:  000000000000000e 00007ffdcd75b420
ffffac1c464d3c90:  0000000000000004 ffffac1c464d3d30
ffffac1c464d3ca0:  kernel_wait4+175 0000000e00000004
ffffac1c464d3cb0:  0000000000000000 0000000000000000
ffffac1c464d3cc0:  0483c6fa00000000 0000000000000000
ffffac1c464d3cd0:  0000000000000000 ffff991d33318000
ffffac1c464d3ce0:  child_wait_callback ffff991d503dda28
ffffac1c464d3cf0:  ffff991d503dda28 ffffac1c00000000
ffffac1c464d3d00:  0483c6faf5d47b00 ffffac1c464d3f58
ffffac1c464d3d10:  000000000000003d 000000000000003d
ffffac1c464d3d20:  0000000000000000 0000000000000000
ffffac1c464d3d30:  ffffac1c464d3df0 __do_sys_wait4+137
ffffac1c464d3d40:  ffff991d5dd20c00 0000000000005410
ffffac1c464d3d50:  ffff991d5dd20c00 00007ffdcd75b34c
ffffac1c464d3d60:  ffff991d66f56e00 ffffac1c464d3e08
ffffac1c464d3d70:  tty_ioctl+1602   do_wp_page+458
ffffac1c464d3d80:  ffff991d503dda00 ffffac1c464d3db8
ffffac1c464d3d90:  sigprocmask+184  0000000000390000
ffffac1c464d3da0:  0483c6faf5d47b00 0000000000000000
ffffac1c464d3db0:  _copy_to_user+37 ffffac1c464d3df0
ffffac1c464d3dc0:  __x64_sys_rt_sigprocmask+145 ffffac1c464d3f58
ffffac1c464d3dd0:  ffffac1c464d3f58 0483c6faf5d47b00
ffffac1c464d3de0:  000000000000003d 000000000000003d
ffffac1c464d3df0:  ffffac1c464d3e00 __x64_sys_wait4+28
ffffac1c464d3e00:  ffffac1c464d3e10 x64_sys_call+1704
ffffac1c464d3e10:  ffffac1c464d3f48 do_syscall_64+124
ffffac1c464d3e20:  ffffac1c464d3f58 ffffac1c464d3e50
ffffac1c464d3e30:  syscall_exit_to_user_mode+129 ffffac1c464d3f58
ffffac1c464d3e40:  0000000000000010 0000000000000010
ffffac1c464d3e50:  ffffac1c464d3f48 do_syscall_64+136
```

```
ffffac1c464d3e60:  mm_account_fault+94 0000000000000040
ffffac1c464d3e70:  0000000000001255 00005994ca06e800
ffffac1c464d3e80:  ffffac1c464d3f58 0000000000000000
ffffac1c464d3e90:  ffffac1c464d3ed0 handle_mm_fault+336
ffffac1c464d3ea0:  ffff991d4065b700 0000000000000255
ffffac1c464d3eb0:  0000000000000007 00005994ca06e800
ffffac1c464d3ec0:  ffff991d4065b700 ffffac1c464d3f58
ffffac1c464d3ed0:  ffffac1c464d3f18 do_user_addr_fault+829
ffffac1c464d3ee0:  ffffac1c464d3f08 irqentry_exit_to_user_mode+123
ffffac1c464d3ef0:  0000000000000000 ffffac1c464d3f58
ffffac1c464d3f00:  00005994ca06e800 ffffac1c464d3f18
ffffac1c464d3f10:  irqentry_exit+29 clear_bhb_loop+69
ffffac1c464d3f20:  clear_bhb_loop+69 clear_bhb_loop+69
ffffac1c464d3f30:  0000000000000000 0000000000000000
ffffac1c464d3f40:  0000000000000000 0000000000000000
ffffac1c464d3f50:  entry_SYSCALL_64_after_hwframe+120 0000000000000001
ffffac1c464d3f60:  00007ffdcd75b420 00005994ca075470
ffffac1c464d3f70:  000000000000000a 00005994c8d18d68
ffffac1c464d3f80:  00000000000008e5 0000000000000246
ffffac1c464d3f90:  0000000000000000 0000000000000001
ffffac1c464d3fa0:  00005994ca06e800 fffffffffffffda
ffffac1c464d3fb0:  000078a64caea3ea 000000000000000a
ffffac1c464d3fc0:  00007ffdcd75b420 00000000ffffffff
ffffac1c464d3fd0:  000000000000003d 000078a64caea3ea
ffffac1c464d3fe0:  0000000000000033 0000000000000246
ffffac1c464d3ff0:  00007ffdcd75b3f8 000000000000002b
```

```
crash> bt -f
PID: 2068     TASK: ffff991d33318000  CPU: 3    COMMAND: "bash"
 #0 [ffffac1c464d3bb0] __schedule at ffffffff87ace28a
    ffffac1c464d3bb8: ffff991e00822880 ffff991d33318000
    ffffac1c464d3bc8: ffff991e03db3580 ffffcc1c3fda9900
    ffffac1c464d3bd8: ffffac1c464d3c50 ffffffff87ace28a
    ffffac1c464d3be8: ffffac1c464d3ca8 ffff991d33318aa0
    ffffac1c464d3bf8: ffffac1c464d3c38 ffffffff00000004
    ffffac1c464d3c08: ffffffff87e15f40 0000000000000000
    ffffac1c464d3c18: 0000000000000002 0483c6faf5d47b00
    ffffac1c464d3c28: ffff991d33318000 ffff991d33318000
    ffffac1c464d3c38: ffffac1c464d3cd0 0000000000000000
    ffffac1c464d3c48: 0000000000000000 ffffac1c464d3c70
    ffffac1c464d3c58: ffffffff87ace68e
 #1 [ffffac1c464d3c58] schedule at ffffffff87ace68e
    ffffac1c464d3c60: ffff991d33318000 ffffac1c464d3ca8
    ffffac1c464d3c70: ffffac1c464d3c98 ffffffff86ae5437
 #2 [ffffac1c464d3c78] do_wait at ffffffff86ae5437
    ffffac1c464d3c80: 000000000000000e 00007ffdcd75b420
    ffffac1c464d3c90: 0000000000000004 ffffac1c464d3d30
    ffffac1c464d3ca0: ffffffff86ae5a2f
 #3 [ffffac1c464d3ca0] kernel_wait4 at ffffffff86ae5a2f
    ffffac1c464d3ca8: 0000000e00000004 0000000000000000
    ffffac1c464d3cb8: 0000000000000000 0483c6fa00000000
    ffffac1c464d3cc8: 0000000000000000 0000000000000000
    ffffac1c464d3cd8: ffff991d33318000 ffffffff86ae2c20
    ffffac1c464d3ce8: ffff991d503dda28 ffff991d503dda28
    ffffac1c464d3cf8: ffffac1c00000000 0483c6faf5d47b00
    ffffac1c464d3d08: ffffac1c464d3f58 000000000000003d
    ffffac1c464d3d18: 000000000000003d 0000000000000000
    ffffac1c464d3d28: 0000000000000000 ffffac1c464d3df0
    ffffac1c464d3d38: ffffffff86ae5b69
 #4 [ffffac1c464d3d38] __do_sys_wait4 at ffffffff86ae5b69
```

```
    ffffac1c464d3d40: ffff991d5dd20c00 0000000000005410
    ffffac1c464d3d50: ffff991d5dd20c00 00007ffdcd75b34c
    ffffac1c464d3d60: ffff991d66f56e00 ffffac1c464d3e08
    ffffac1c464d3d70: ffffffff873f0962 ffffffff86dc237a
    ffffac1c464d3d80: ffff991d503dda00 ffffac1c464d3db8
    ffffac1c464d3d90: ffffffff86af2818 0000000000390000
    ffffac1c464d3da0: 0483c6faf5d47b00 0000000000000000
    ffffac1c464d3db0: ffffffff871a82f5 ffffac1c464d3df0
    ffffac1c464d3dc0: ffffffff86af2aa1 ffffac1c464d3f58
    ffffac1c464d3dd0: ffffac1c464d3f58 0483c6faf5d47b00
    ffffac1c464d3de0: 000000000000003d 000000000000003d
    ffffac1c464d3df0: ffffac1c464d3e00 ffffffff86ae5bac
 #5 [ffffac1c464d3df8] __x64_sys_wait4 at ffffffff86ae5bac
    ffffac1c464d3e00: ffffac1c464d3e10 ffffffff86a05548
 #6 [ffffac1c464d3e08] x64_sys_call at ffffffff86a05548
    ffffac1c464d3e10: ffffac1c464d3f48 ffffffff87abadac
 #7 [ffffac1c464d3e18] do_syscall_64 at ffffffff87abadac
    RIP: 000078a64caea3ea  RSP: 00007ffdcd75b3f8  RFLAGS: 00000246
    RAX: ffffffffffffffda  RBX: 00000000000008e5  RCX: 000078a64caea3ea
    RDX: 000000000000000a  RSI: 00007ffdcd75b420  RDI: 00000000ffffffff
    RBP: 00005994c8d18d68   R8: 00005994ca06e800   R9: 0000000000000001
    R10: 0000000000000000  R11: 0000000000000246  R12: 000000000000000a
    R13: 00005994ca075470  R14: 00007ffdcd75b420  R15: 0000000000000001
    ORIG_RAX: 000000000000003d  CS: 0033  SS: 002b
```

11. Show virtual memory layout for the current process context:

```
crash> vm
PID: 2068     TASK: ffff991d33318000  CPU: 3    COMMAND: "bash"
       MM               PGD          RSS    TOTAL_VM
ffff991d4065b700  ffff991d56afc000  5544k    11252k
      VMA           START       END     FLAGS FILE
ffff991d735e7300 5994c8bc3000 5994c8bf2000 8000071 /usr/bin/bash
ffff991d735e7480 5994c8bf2000 5994c8cd1000 8000075 /usr/bin/bash
ffff991d735e7180 5994c8cd1000 5994c8d0b000 8000071 /usr/bin/bash
ffff991d735e73c0 5994c8d0c000 5994c8d10000 8100071 /usr/bin/bash
ffff991d735ea780 5994c8d10000 5994c8d19000 8100073 /usr/bin/bash
ffff991d735e7900 5994c8d19000 5994c8d24000 8100073
ffff991d66c5f6c0 5994c9f47000 5994ca0a8000 8100073
ffff991d735ea0c0 78a64c400000 78a64c973000 8000071 /usr/lib/locale/locale-archive
ffff991d735ea900 78a64ca00000 78a64ca28000 8000071 /usr/lib/x86_64-linux-gnu/libc.so.6
ffff991d735ead80 78a64ca28000 78a64cbbd000 8000075 /usr/lib/x86_64-linux-gnu/libc.so.6
ffff991d735ea240 78a64cbbd000 78a64cc15000 8000071 /usr/lib/x86_64-linux-gnu/libc.so.6
ffff991d735ea9c0 78a64cc15000 78a64cc16000 8000070 /usr/lib/x86_64-linux-gnu/libc.so.6
ffff991d735eae40 78a64cc16000 78a64cc1a000 8100071 /usr/lib/x86_64-linux-gnu/libc.so.6
ffff991d735ea000 78a64cc1a000 78a64cc1c000 8100073 /usr/lib/x86_64-linux-gnu/libc.so.6
ffff991d735eab40 78a64cc1c000 78a64cc29000 8100073
ffff991d735ea600 78a64ccdb000 78a64ccde000 8100073
ffff991d735e7a80 78a64ccde000 78a64ccec000 8000071 /usr/lib/x86_64-linux-gnu/libtinfo.so.6.3
ffff991d735e7cc0 78a64ccec000 78a64ccfd000 8000075 /usr/lib/x86_64-linux-gnu/libtinfo.so.6.3
ffff991d735e70c0 78a64ccfd000 78a64cd0b000 8000071 /usr/lib/x86_64-linux-gnu/libtinfo.so.6.3
ffff991d735e76c0 78a64cd0b000 78a64cd0f000 8100071 /usr/lib/x86_64-linux-gnu/libtinfo.so.6.3
ffff991d735eaa80 78a64cd0f000 78a64cd10000 8100073 /usr/lib/x86_64-linux-gnu/libtinfo.so.6.3
ffff991d735ea6c0 78a64cd19000 78a64cd20000 80000d1 /usr/lib/x86_64-linux-gnu/gconv/gconv-modules.cache
ffff991d735e7b40 78a64cd20000 78a64cd22000 8100073
ffff991d735e7f00 78a64cd22000 78a64cd24000 8000071 /usr/lib/x86_64-linux-gnu/ld-linux-x86-64.so.2
ffff991d735e7d80 78a64cd24000 78a64cd4e000 8000075 /usr/lib/x86_64-linux-gnu/ld-linux-x86-64.so.2
ffff991d735e79c0 78a64cd4e000 78a64cd59000 8000071 /usr/lib/x86_64-linux-gnu/ld-linux-x86-64.so.2
ffff991d735e7240 78a64cd5a000 78a64cd5c000 8100071 /usr/lib/x86_64-linux-gnu/ld-linux-x86-64.so.2
ffff991d735eacc0 78a64cd5c000 78a64cd5e000 8100073 /usr/lib/x86_64-linux-gnu/ld-linux-x86-64.so.2
ffff991d6f956480 7ffdcd73d000 7ffdcd75e000 100173
ffff991d735e7e40 7ffdcd784000 7ffdcd788000 c044411
ffff991d735e7c00 7ffdcd788000 7ffdcd78a000 8040075
```

12. List opened files for the current process context:

```
crash> files
PID: 2068     TASK: ffff991d33318000  CPU: 3    COMMAND: "bash"
ROOT: /    CWD: /home/coredump
 FD       FILE            DENTRY           INODE       TYPE PATH
  0 ffff991d66f56e00 ffff991d5286c900 ffff991d2ffa8500 CHR  /dev/pts/0
  1 ffff991d66f56e00 ffff991d5286c900 ffff991d2ffa8500 CHR  /dev/pts/0
  2 ffff991d66f56e00 ffff991d5286c900 ffff991d2ffa8500 CHR  /dev/pts/0
255 ffff991d66f56e00 ffff991d5286c900 ffff991d2ffa8500 CHR  /dev/pts/0
```

13. Dump memory contents as pointers without and with symbolic information:

```
crash> bt
PID: 2068     TASK: ffff991d33318000  CPU: 3    COMMAND: "bash"
 #0 [ffffac1c464d3bb0] __schedule at ffffffff87ace28a
 #1 [ffffac1c464d3c58] schedule at ffffffff87ace68e
 #2 [ffffac1c464d3c78] do_wait at ffffffff86ae5437
 #3 [ffffac1c464d3ca0] kernel_wait4 at ffffffff86ae5a2f
 #4 [ffffac1c464d3d38] __do_sys_wait4 at ffffffff86ae5b69
 #5 [ffffac1c464d3df8] __x64_sys_wait4 at ffffffff86ae5bac
 #6 [ffffac1c464d3e08] x64_sys_call at ffffffff86a05548
 #7 [ffffac1c464d3e18] do_syscall_64 at ffffffff87abadac
    RIP: 000078a64caea3ea  RSP: 00007ffdcd75b3f8  RFLAGS: 00000246
    RAX: ffffffffffffffda  RBX: 00000000000008e5  RCX: 000078a64caea3ea
    RDX: 000000000000000a  RSI: 00007ffdcd75b420  RDI: 00000000ffffffff
    RBP: 00005994c8d18d68   R8: 00005994ca06e800   R9: 0000000000000001
    R10: 0000000000000000  R11: 0000000000000246  R12: 000000000000000a
    R13: 00005994ca075470  R14: 00007ffdcd75b420  R15: 0000000000000001
    ORIG_RAX: 000000000000003d  CS: 0033  SS: 002b

crash> rd -64 ffffac1c464d3bb0 50
ffffac1c464d3bb0:  0000000000000003 ffff991e00822880   .........(......
ffffac1c464d3bc0:  ffff991d33318000 ffff991e03db3580   ..13.....5......
ffffac1c464d3bd0:  ffffcc1c3fda9900 ffffac1c464d3c50   ...?....P<MF....
ffffac1c464d3be0:  ffffffff87ace28a ffffac1c464d3ca8   .........<MF....
ffffac1c464d3bf0:  ffff991d33318aa0 ffffac1c464d3c38   ..13....8<MF....
ffffac1c464d3c00:  ffffffff00000004 ffffffff87e15f40   ........@_......
ffffac1c464d3c10:  0000000000000000 0000000000000002   ................
ffffac1c464d3c20:  0483c6faf5d47b00 ffff991d33318000   .{........13....
ffffac1c464d3c30:  ffff991d33318000 ffffac1c464d3cd0   ..13.....<MF....
ffffac1c464d3c40:  0000000000000000 0000000000000000   ................
ffffac1c464d3c50:  ffffac1c464d3c70 ffffffff87ace68e   p<MF............
ffffac1c464d3c60:  ffff991d33318000 ffffac1c464d3ca8   ..13.....<MF....
ffffac1c464d3c70:  ffffac1c464d3c98 ffffffff86ae5437   .<MF....7T......
ffffac1c464d3c80:  000000000000000e 00007ffdcd75b420   ........ .u.....
ffffac1c464d3c90:  0000000000000004 ffffac1c464d3d30   ........0=MF....
ffffac1c464d3ca0:  ffffffff86ae5a2f 0000000e00000004   /Z..............
ffffac1c464d3cb0:  0000000000000000 0000000000000000   ................
ffffac1c464d3cc0:  0483c6fa00000000 0000000000000000   ................
ffffac1c464d3cd0:  0000000000000000 ffff991d33318000   ..........13....
ffffac1c464d3ce0:  ffffffff86ae2c20 ffff991d503dda28    ,......(.=P....
ffffac1c464d3cf0:  ffff991d503dda28 ffffac1c00000000   (.=P............
ffffac1c464d3d00:  0483c6faf5d47b00 ffffac1c464d3f58   .{......X?MF....
ffffac1c464d3d10:  000000000000003d 000000000000003d   =.......=.......
ffffac1c464d3d20:  0000000000000000 0000000000000000   ................
ffffac1c464d3d30:  ffffac1c464d3df0 ffffffff86ae5b69   .=MF....i[......
```

```
crash> rd -SS -64 ffffac1c464d3bb0 50
ffffac1c464d3bb0:  0000000000000003 [ffff991e00822880:task_struct]
ffffac1c464d3bc0:  [ffff991d33318000:task_struct] ffff991e03db3580
ffffac1c464d3bd0:  ffffcc1c3fda9900 ffffac1c464d3c50
ffffac1c464d3be0:  __schedule+634   ffffac1c464d3ca8
ffffac1c464d3bf0:  [ffff991d33318aa0:task_struct] ffffac1c464d3c38
ffffac1c464d3c00:  ffffffff00000004 cpu_bit_bitmap+4096
ffffac1c464d3c10:  0000000000000000 0000000000000002
ffffac1c464d3c20:  0483c6faf5d47b00 [ffff991d33318000:task_struct]
ffffac1c464d3c30:  [ffff991d33318000:task_struct] ffffac1c464d3cd0
ffffac1c464d3c40:  0000000000000000 0000000000000000
ffffac1c464d3c50:  ffffac1c464d3c70 schedule+46
ffffac1c464d3c60:  [ffff991d33318000:task_struct] ffffac1c464d3ca8
ffffac1c464d3c70:  ffffac1c464d3c98 do_wait+183
ffffac1c464d3c80:  000000000000000e 00007ffdcd75b420
ffffac1c464d3c90:  0000000000000004 ffffac1c464d3d30
ffffac1c464d3ca0:  kernel_wait4+175 0000000e00000004
ffffac1c464d3cb0:  0000000000000000 0000000000000000
ffffac1c464d3cc0:  0483c6fa00000000 0000000000000000
ffffac1c464d3cd0:  0000000000000000 [ffff991d33318000:task_struct]
ffffac1c464d3ce0:  child_wait_callback [ffff991d503dda28:signal_cache]
ffffac1c464d3cf0:  [ffff991d503dda28:signal_cache] ffffac1c00000000
ffffac1c464d3d00:  0483c6faf5d47b00 ffffac1c464d3f58
ffffac1c464d3d10:  000000000000003d 000000000000003d
ffffac1c464d3d20:  0000000000000000 0000000000000000
ffffac1c464d3d30:  ffffac1c464d3df0 __do_sys_wait4+137
```

14. Verify the return address by disassembly:

```
crash> bt
PID: 2068     TASK: ffff991d33318000  CPU: 3    COMMAND: "bash"
 #0 [ffffac1c464d3bb0] __schedule at ffffffff87ace28a
 #1 [ffffac1c464d3c58] schedule at ffffffff87ace68e
 #2 [ffffac1c464d3c78] do_wait at ffffffff86ae5437
 #3 [ffffac1c464d3ca0] kernel_wait4 at ffffffff86ae5a2f
 #4 [ffffac1c464d3d38] __do_sys_wait4 at ffffffff86ae5b69
 #5 [ffffac1c464d3df8] __x64_sys_wait4 at ffffffff86ae5bac
 #6 [ffffac1c464d3e08] x64_sys_call at ffffffff86a05548
 #7 [ffffac1c464d3e18] do_syscall_64 at ffffffff87abadac
    RIP: 000078a64caea3ea  RSP: 00007ffdcd75b3f8  RFLAGS: 00000246
    RAX: ffffffffffffffda  RBX: 00000000000008e5  RCX: 000078a64caea3ea
    RDX: 000000000000000a  RSI: 00007ffdcd75b420  RDI: 00000000ffffffff
    RBP: 00005994c8d18d68   R8: 00005994ca06e800   R9: 0000000000000001
    R10: 0000000000000000  R11: 0000000000000246  R12: 000000000000000a
    R13: 00005994ca075470  R14: 00007ffdcd75b420  R15: 0000000000000001
    ORIG_RAX: 000000000000003d  CS: 0033  SS: 002b
```

```
crash> dis schedule
0xffffffff87ace660 <schedule>:  nopl   0x0(%rax,%rax,1) [FTRACE NOP]
0xffffffff87ace665 <schedule+5>:        push   %rbp
0xffffffff87ace666 <schedule+6>:        mov    %rsp,%rbp
0xffffffff87ace669 <schedule+9>:        push   %r12
0xffffffff87ace66b <schedule+11>:       push   %rbx
0xffffffff87ace66c <schedule+12>:       mov    %gs:0x32d40,%r12
0xffffffff87ace675 <schedule+21>:       mov    0x18(%r12),%eax
0xffffffff87ace67a <schedule+26>:       test   %eax,%eax
0xffffffff87ace67c <schedule+28>:       jne    0xffffffff87ace6c1 <schedule+97>
0xffffffff87ace67e <schedule+30>:       mov    %gs:0x32d40,%rbx
0xffffffff87ace687 <schedule+39>:       xor    %edi,%edi
0xffffffff87ace689 <schedule+41>:       call   0xffffffff87ace010 <__schedule>
0xffffffff87ace68e <schedule+46>:       mov    (%rbx),%rax
0xffffffff87ace691 <schedule+49>:       test   $0x8,%al
0xffffffff87ace693 <schedule+51>:       jne    0xffffffff87ace687 <schedule+39>
```

```
0xffffffff87ace695 <schedule+53>:     mov    0x2c(%r12),%eax
0xffffffff87ace69a <schedule+58>:     test   $0x30,%al
0xffffffff87ace69c <schedule+60>:     je     0xffffffff87ace6aa <schedule+74>
0xffffffff87ace69e <schedule+62>:     mov    %r12,%rdi
0xffffffff87ace6a1 <schedule+65>:     test   $0x20,%al
0xffffffff87ace6a3 <schedule+67>:     je     0xffffffff87ace6b3 <schedule+83>
0xffffffff87ace6a5 <schedule+69>:     call   0xffffffff86b07740 <wq_worker_running>
0xffffffff87ace6aa <schedule+74>:     pop    %rbx
0xffffffff87ace6ab <schedule+75>:     pop    %r12
0xffffffff87ace6ad <schedule+77>:     pop    %rbp
0xffffffff87ace6ae <schedule+78>:     ret
0xffffffff87ace6af <schedule+79>:     int3
0xffffffff87ace6b0 <schedule+80>:     int3
0xffffffff87ace6b1 <schedule+81>:     int3
0xffffffff87ace6b2 <schedule+82>:     int3
0xffffffff87ace6b3 <schedule+83>:     call   0xffffffff87197760 <io_wq_worker_running>
0xffffffff87ace6b8 <schedule+88>:     pop    %rbx
0xffffffff87ace6b9 <schedule+89>:     pop    %r12
0xffffffff87ace6bb <schedule+91>:     pop    %rbp
0xffffffff87ace6bc <schedule+92>:     ret
0xffffffff87ace6bd <schedule+93>:     int3
0xffffffff87ace6be <schedule+94>:     int3
0xffffffff87ace6bf <schedule+95>:     int3
0xffffffff87ace6c0 <schedule+96>:     int3
0xffffffff87ace6c1 <schedule+97>:     mov    0x2c(%r12),%eax
0xffffffff87ace6c6 <schedule+102>:    test   $0x20,%al
0xffffffff87ace6c8 <schedule+104>:    jne    0xffffffff87ace700 <schedule+160>
0xffffffff87ace6ca <schedule+106>:    test   $0x10,%al
0xffffffff87ace6cc <schedule+108>:    jne    0xffffffff87ace6f6 <schedule+150>
0xffffffff87ace6ce <schedule+110>:    mov    %gs:0x32d40,%rax
0xffffffff87ace6d7 <schedule+119>:    testb  $0x10,0x19(%rax)
0xffffffff87ace6db <schedule+123>:    jne    0xffffffff87ace70a <schedule+170>
0xffffffff87ace6dd <schedule+125>:    mov    0xcd0(%r12),%rdi
0xffffffff87ace6e5 <schedule+133>:    test   %rdi,%rdi
0xffffffff87ace6e8 <schedule+136>:    je     0xffffffff87ace67e <schedule+30>
0xffffffff87ace6ea <schedule+138>:    mov    $0x1,%esi
0xffffffff87ace6ef <schedule+143>:    call   0xffffffff87125ad0 <__blk_flush_plug>
0xffffffff87ace6f4 <schedule+148>:    jmp    0xffffffff87ace67e <schedule+30>
0xffffffff87ace6f6 <schedule+150>:    mov    %r12,%rdi
0xffffffff87ace6f9 <schedule+153>:    call   0xffffffff871977d0 <io_wq_worker_sleeping>
0xffffffff87ace6fe <schedule+158>:    jmp    0xffffffff87ace6ce <schedule+110>
0xffffffff87ace700 <schedule+160>:    mov    %r12,%rdi
0xffffffff87ace703 <schedule+163>:    call   0xffffffff86b077a0 <wq_worker_sleeping>
0xffffffff87ace708 <schedule+168>:    jmp    0xffffffff87ace6ce <schedule+110>
0xffffffff87ace70a <schedule+170>:    movzbl 0x151879f(%rip),%ebx        # 0xffffffff88fe6eb0 <__already_done.2>
0xffffffff87ace711 <schedule+177>:    cmp    $0x1,%bl
0xffffffff87ace714 <schedule+180>:    ja     0xffffffff87ace732 <schedule+210>
0xffffffff87ace716 <schedule+182>:    and    $0x1,%ebx
0xffffffff87ace719 <schedule+185>:    jne    0xffffffff87ace6dd <schedule+125>
0xffffffff87ace71b <schedule+187>:    mov    $0xffffffff8836ebf0,%rdi
0xffffffff87ace722 <schedule+194>:    movb   $0x1,0x1518787(%rip)        # 0xffffffff88fe6eb0 <__already_done.2>
0xffffffff87ace729 <schedule+201>:    call   0xffffffff86adda20 <__warn_printk>
0xffffffff87ace72e <schedule+206>:    ud2
0xffffffff87ace730 <schedule+208>:    jmp    0xffffffff87ace6dd <schedule+125>
0xffffffff87ace732 <schedule+210>:    movzbl %bl,%esi
0xffffffff87ace735 <schedule+213>:    mov    $0xffffffff88c8ea90,%rdi
0xffffffff87ace73c <schedule+220>:    call   0xffffffff87269920 <__ubsan_handle_load_invalid_value>
0xffffffff87ace741 <schedule+225>:    jmp    0xffffffff87ace716 <schedule+182>
```

Note: To emulate backward disassembly similar to the **ub** WinDbg command, use the **-r** flag:

```
crash> dis -r 0xffffffff87ace68e
0xffffffff87ace660 <schedule>:  nopl   0x0(%rax,%rax,1) [FTRACE NOP]
0xffffffff87ace665 <schedule+5>:        push   %rbp
0xffffffff87ace666 <schedule+6>:        mov    %rsp,%rbp
0xffffffff87ace669 <schedule+9>:        push   %r12
0xffffffff87ace66b <schedule+11>:       push   %rbx
0xffffffff87ace66c <schedule+12>:       mov    %gs:0x32d40,%r12
0xffffffff87ace675 <schedule+21>:       mov    0x18(%r12),%eax
0xffffffff87ace67a <schedule+26>:       test   %eax,%eax
0xffffffff87ace67c <schedule+28>:       jne    0xffffffff87ace6c1 <schedule+97>
```

```
0xffffffff87ace67e <schedule+30>:       mov    %gs:0x32d40,%rbx
0xffffffff87ace687 <schedule+39>:       xor    %edi,%edi
0xffffffff87ace689 <schedule+41>:       call   0xffffffff87ace010 <__schedule>
0xffffffff87ace68e <schedule+46>:       mov    (%rbx),%rax
```

15. Finally, we can see the backtrace of every PID/TID (task) in the system:

```
crash> foreach bt
PID: 0        TASK: ffffffff88c0fcc0  CPU: 0    COMMAND: "swapper/0"
 #0 [ffffffff88c03dc8] __schedule at ffffffff87ace28a
 #1 [ffffffff88c03e70] schedule_idle at ffffffff87aceb5a
 #2 [ffffffff88c03e88] do_idle at ffffffff86b51619
 #3 [ffffffff88c03ea8] cpu_startup_entry at ffffffff86b5184d
 #4 [ffffffff88c03ec0] rest_init at ffffffff87ac2aa7
 #5 [ffffffff88c03ee8] arch_call_rest_init at ffffffff890963ce
 #6 [ffffffff88c03ef8] start_kernel at ffffffff8909679a
 #7 [ffffffff88c03f18] x86_64_start_reservations at ffffffff890a2328
 #8 [ffffffff88c03f28] x86_64_start_kernel at ffffffff890a2470
 #9 [ffffffff88c03f50] secondary_startup_64_no_verify at ffffffff86a00279

PID: 0        TASK: ffff991e00825100  CPU: 1    COMMAND: "swapper/1"
 #0 [fffffe37c5b36e38] crash_nmi_callback at ffffffff86a875a7
 #1 [fffffe37c5b36e48] nmi_handle at ffffffff86a442cf
 #2 [fffffe37c5b36e98] default_do_nmi at ffffffff87abcb55
 #3 [fffffe37c5b36ec0] exc_nmi at ffffffff87abcdcb
 #4 [fffffe37c5b36ef0] end_repeat_nmi at ffffffff87c016a1
    [exception RIP: default_idle+11]
    RIP: ffffffff87ac1a1b  RSP: ffffac1c400d3e88  RFLAGS: 00000252
    RAX: ffff991e03caefa8  RBX: ffff991e00825100  RCX: 0000000000000001
    RDX: 0000000000000000  RSI: 0000000000000083  RDI: 000000000020139c
    RBP: ffffac1c400d3e90   R8: 0000000000000000   R9: 01364d9054fccc41
    R10: 0000000000000001  R11: 0000000000000000  R12: 0000000000000000
    R13: 0000000000000000  R14: 0000000000000000  R15: 0000000000000000
    ORIG_RAX: ffffffffffffffff  CS: 0010  SS: 0018
--- <NMI exception stack> ---
 #5 [ffffac1c400d3e88] default_idle at ffffffff87ac1a1b
 #6 [ffffac1c400d3e88] arch_cpu_idle at ffffffff87ac1ac9
 #7 [ffffac1c400d3e98] default_idle_call at ffffffff87ac1d3c
 #8 [ffffac1c400d3ea8] cpuidle_idle_call at ffffffff86b51512
 #9 [ffffac1c400d3ee8] do_idle at ffffffff86b515e2
#10 [ffffac1c400d3f08] cpu_startup_entry at ffffffff86b5184d
#11 [ffffac1c400d3f20] start_secondary at ffffffff86a8a950
#12 [ffffac1c400d3f50] secondary_startup_64_no_verify at ffffffff86a00279

PID: 0        TASK: ffff991e00820000  CPU: 2    COMMAND: "swapper/2"
 #0 [fffffe4c43717e38] crash_nmi_callback at ffffffff86a875a7
 #1 [fffffe4c43717e48] nmi_handle at ffffffff86a442cf
 #2 [fffffe4c43717e98] default_do_nmi at ffffffff87abcb55
 #3 [fffffe4c43717ec0] exc_nmi at ffffffff87abcdcb
 #4 [fffffe4c43717ef0] end_repeat_nmi at ffffffff87c016a1
    [exception RIP: default_idle+11]
    RIP: ffffffff87ac1a1b  RSP: ffffac1c400dbe88  RFLAGS: 00000246
    RAX: ffff991e03d2efa8  RBX: ffff991e00820000  RCX: 0000000000000001
    RDX: 0000000000000000  RSI: 0000000000000083  RDI: 00000000001d8a94
    RBP: ffffac1c400dbe90   R8: 0000000000000000   R9: 01364d9054fccc41
    R10: 0000000000000001  R11: 0000000000000000  R12: 0000000000000000
    R13: 0000000000000000  R14: 0000000000000000  R15: 0000000000000000
    ORIG_RAX: ffffffffffffffff  CS: 0010  SS: 0018
--- <NMI exception stack> ---
 #5 [ffffac1c400dbe88] default_idle at ffffffff87ac1a1b
```

```
 #6 [ffffac1c400dbe88] arch_cpu_idle at ffffffff87ac1ac9
 #7 [ffffac1c400dbe98] default_idle_call at ffffffff87ac1d3c
 #8 [ffffac1c400dbea8] cpuidle_idle_call at ffffffff86b51512
 #9 [ffffac1c400dbee8] do_idle at ffffffff86b515e2
#10 [ffffac1c400dbf08] cpu_startup_entry at ffffffff86b5184d
#11 [ffffac1c400dbf20] start_secondary at ffffffff86a8a950
#12 [ffffac1c400dbf50] secondary_startup_64_no_verify at ffffffff86a00279

PID: 0        TASK: ffff991e00822880  CPU: 3    COMMAND: "swapper/3"
 #0 [fffffe2b8d1a1e38] crash_nmi_callback at ffffffff86a875a7
 #1 [fffffe2b8d1a1e48] nmi_handle at ffffffff86a442cf
 #2 [fffffe2b8d1a1e98] default_do_nmi at ffffffff87abcb55
 #3 [fffffe2b8d1a1ec0] exc_nmi at ffffffff87abcdcb
 #4 [fffffe2b8d1a1ef0] end_repeat_nmi at ffffffff87c016a1
    [exception RIP: default_idle+11]
    RIP: ffffffff87ac1a1b  RSP: ffffac1c400e3e88  RFLAGS: 00000242
    RAX: ffff991e03daefa8  RBX: ffff991e00822880  RCX: 0000000000000001
    RDX: 0000000000000000  RSI: 0000000000000083  RDI: 00000000001943b4
    RBP: ffffac1c400e3e90   R8: 0000000000000000   R9: 01364d9054fccc41
    R10: 0000000000000001  R11: 0000000000000000  R12: 0000000000000000
    R13: 0000000000000000  R14: 0000000000000000  R15: 0000000000000000
    ORIG_RAX: ffffffffffffffff  CS: 0010  SS: 0018
--- <NMI exception stack> ---
 #5 [ffffac1c400e3e88] default_idle at ffffffff87ac1a1b
 #6 [ffffac1c400e3e88] arch_cpu_idle at ffffffff87ac1ac9
 #7 [ffffac1c400e3e98] default_idle_call at ffffffff87ac1d3c
 #8 [ffffac1c400e3ea8] cpuidle_idle_call at ffffffff86b51512
 #9 [ffffac1c400e3ee8] do_idle at ffffffff86b515e2
#10 [ffffac1c400e3f08] cpu_startup_entry at ffffffff86b5184d
#11 [ffffac1c400e3f20] start_secondary at ffffffff86a8a950
#12 [ffffac1c400e3f50] secondary_startup_64_no_verify at ffffffff86a00279

PID: 1        TASK: ffff991e00360000  CPU: 1    COMMAND: "systemd"
 #0 [ffffac1c400439b0] __schedule at ffffffff87ace28a
 #1 [ffffac1c40043a58] schedule at ffffffff87ace68e
 #2 [ffffac1c40043a78] schedule_hrtimeout_range_clock at ffffffff87ad4679
 #3 [ffffac1c40043af0] schedule_hrtimeout_range at ffffffff87ad46b3
 #4 [ffffac1c40043b00] ep_poll at ffffffff86ee7cac
 #5 [ffffac1c40043ba0] do_epoll_wait at ffffffff86ee7dcb
 #6 [ffffac1c40043be0] __x64_sys_epoll_wait at ffffffff86ee8580
 #7 [ffffac1c40043c30] x64_sys_call at ffffffff86a068a4
 #8 [ffffac1c40043c40] do_syscall_64 at ffffffff87abadac
 #9 [ffffac1c40043ea8] do_syscall_64 at ffffffff87abadb8
#10 [ffffac1c40043f50] entry_SYSCALL_64_after_hwframe at ffffffff87c00130
    RIP: 00007b61df525e2e  RSP: 00007fff26670f60  RFLAGS: 00000293
    RAX: ffffffffffffffda  RBX: 00005760a2e5a890  RCX: 00007b61df525e2e
    RDX: 000000000000016a  RSI: 00005760a30c9700  RDI: 0000000000000004
    RBP: 0000000000000001   R8: 0000000000000000   R9: 0000000000000000
    R10: 00000000ffffffff  R11: 0000000000000293  R12: 00000000000008f2
    R13: 000000000000016a  R14: 00000000000000e5  R15: 00005760a2e5aa20
    ORIG_RAX: 00000000000000e8  CS: 0033  SS: 002b

PID: 2        TASK: ffff991e00362880  CPU: 1    COMMAND: "kthreadd"
 #0 [ffffac1c4004bdc8] __schedule at ffffffff87ace28a
 #1 [ffffac1c4004be70] schedule at ffffffff87ace68e
 #2 [ffffac1c4004be90] kthreadd at ffffffff86b103e2
 #3 [ffffac1c4004bf28] ret_from_fork at ffffffff86a4f459
 #4 [ffffac1c4004bf50] ret_from_fork_asm at ffffffff86a04e5b

PID: 3        TASK: ffff991e00365100  CPU: 0    COMMAND: "pool_workqueue_"
```

```
 #0 [ffffac1c40053de8] __schedule at ffffffff87ace28a
 #1 [ffffac1c40053e90] schedule at ffffffff87ace68e
 #2 [ffffac1c40053eb0] kthread_worker_fn at ffffffff86b0fa96
 #3 [ffffac1c40053ee8] kthread at ffffffff86b0ff93
 #4 [ffffac1c40053f28] ret_from_fork at ffffffff86a4f459
 #5 [ffffac1c40053f50] ret_from_fork_asm at ffffffff86a04e5b

PID: 4        TASK: ffff991e00380000  CPU: 0    COMMAND: "kworker/R-rcu_g"
 #0 [ffffac1c4005bdb8] __schedule at ffffffff87ace28a
 #1 [ffffac1c4005be60] schedule at ffffffff87ace68e
 #2 [ffffac1c4005be80] rescuer_thread at ffffffff86b058b2
 #3 [ffffac1c4005bee8] kthread at ffffffff86b0ff93
 #4 [ffffac1c4005bf28] ret_from_fork at ffffffff86a4f459
 #5 [ffffac1c4005bf50] ret_from_fork_asm at ffffffff86a04e5b

PID: 5        TASK: ffff991e00382880  CPU: 0    COMMAND: "kworker/R-rcu_p"
 #0 [ffffac1c40063db8] __schedule at ffffffff87ace28a
 #1 [ffffac1c40063e60] schedule at ffffffff87ace68e
 #2 [ffffac1c40063e80] rescuer_thread at ffffffff86b058b2
 #3 [ffffac1c40063ee8] kthread at ffffffff86b0ff93
 #4 [ffffac1c40063f28] ret_from_fork at ffffffff86a4f459
 #5 [ffffac1c40063f50] ret_from_fork_asm at ffffffff86a04e5b

PID: 6        TASK: ffff991e00385100  CPU: 0    COMMAND: "kworker/R-slub_"
 #0 [ffffac1c4006bdb8] __schedule at ffffffff87ace28a
 #1 [ffffac1c4006be60] schedule at ffffffff87ace68e
 #2 [ffffac1c4006be80] rescuer_thread at ffffffff86b058b2
 #3 [ffffac1c4006bee8] kthread at ffffffff86b0ff93
 #4 [ffffac1c4006bf28] ret_from_fork at ffffffff86a4f459
 #5 [ffffac1c4006bf50] ret_from_fork_asm at ffffffff86a04e5b

PID: 7        TASK: ffff991e003ed100  CPU: 0    COMMAND: "kworker/R-netns"
 #0 [ffffac1c40073db8] __schedule at ffffffff87ace28a
 #1 [ffffac1c40073e60] schedule at ffffffff87ace68e
 #2 [ffffac1c40073e80] rescuer_thread at ffffffff86b058b2
 #3 [ffffac1c40073ee8] kthread at ffffffff86b0ff93
 #4 [ffffac1c40073f28] ret_from_fork at ffffffff86a4f459
 #5 [ffffac1c40073f50] ret_from_fork_asm at ffffffff86a04e5b

PID: 9        TASK: ffff991e003ea880  CPU: 0    COMMAND: "kworker/0:0H"
 #0 [ffffac1c40083dd0] __schedule at ffffffff87ace28a
 #1 [ffffac1c40083e78] schedule at ffffffff87ace68e
 #2 [ffffac1c40083e98] worker_thread at ffffffff86b05baf
 #3 [ffffac1c40083ee8] kthread at ffffffff86b0ff93
 #4 [ffffac1c40083f28] ret_from_fork at ffffffff86a4f459
 #5 [ffffac1c40083f50] ret_from_fork_asm at ffffffff86a04e5b

PID: 10       TASK: ffff991e003f0000  CPU: 0    COMMAND: "kworker/0:1"
 #0 [ffffac1c4008bdd0] __schedule at ffffffff87ace28a
 #1 [ffffac1c4008be78] schedule at ffffffff87ace68e
 #2 [ffffac1c4008be98] worker_thread at ffffffff86b05baf
 #3 [ffffac1c4008bee8] kthread at ffffffff86b0ff93
 #4 [ffffac1c4008bf28] ret_from_fork at ffffffff86a4f459
 #5 [ffffac1c4008bf50] ret_from_fork_asm at ffffffff86a04e5b

PID: 12       TASK: ffff991e003f5100  CPU: 0    COMMAND: "kworker/R-mm_pe"
 #0 [ffffac1c4009bdb8] __schedule at ffffffff87ace28a
 #1 [ffffac1c4009be60] schedule at ffffffff87ace68e
 #2 [ffffac1c4009be80] rescuer_thread at ffffffff86b058b2
 #3 [ffffac1c4009bee8] kthread at ffffffff86b0ff93
```

```
 #4 [ffffac1c4009bf28] ret_from_fork at ffffffff86a4f459
 #5 [ffffac1c4009bf50] ret_from_fork_asm at ffffffff86a04e5b

PID: 13       TASK: ffff991e00805100  CPU: 0    COMMAND: "rcu_tasks_rude_"
 #0 [ffffac1c400a3db8] __schedule at ffffffff87ace28a
 #1 [ffffac1c400a3e60] schedule at ffffffff87ace68e
 #2 [ffffac1c400a3e80] rcu_tasks_one_gp at ffffffff86b9b2dc
 #3 [ffffac1c400a3eb8] rcu_tasks_kthread at ffffffff86b9ba44
 #4 [ffffac1c400a3ee8] kthread at ffffffff86b0ff93
 #5 [ffffac1c400a3f28] ret_from_fork at ffffffff86a4f459
 #6 [ffffac1c400a3f50] ret_from_fork_asm at ffffffff86a04e5b

PID: 14       TASK: ffff991e00800000  CPU: 0    COMMAND: "rcu_tasks_trace"
 #0 [ffffac1c400abdb8] __schedule at ffffffff87ace28a
 #1 [ffffac1c400abe60] schedule at ffffffff87ace68e
 #2 [ffffac1c400abe80] rcu_tasks_one_gp at ffffffff86b9b2dc
 #3 [ffffac1c400abeb8] rcu_tasks_kthread at ffffffff86b9ba44
 #4 [ffffac1c400abee8] kthread at ffffffff86b0ff93
 #5 [ffffac1c400abf28] ret_from_fork at ffffffff86a4f459
 #6 [ffffac1c400abf50] ret_from_fork_asm at ffffffff86a04e5b

PID: 15       TASK: ffff991e00802880  CPU: 0    COMMAND: "ksoftirqd/0"
 #0 [ffffac1c400b3df8] __schedule at ffffffff87ace28a
 #1 [ffffac1c400b3ea0] schedule at ffffffff87ace68e
 #2 [ffffac1c400b3ec0] smpboot_thread_fn at ffffffff86b1bbdf
 #3 [ffffac1c400b3ee8] kthread at ffffffff86b0ff93
 #4 [ffffac1c400b3f28] ret_from_fork at ffffffff86a4f459
 #5 [ffffac1c400b3f50] ret_from_fork_asm at ffffffff86a04e5b

PID: 16       TASK: ffff991e0080d100  CPU: 1    COMMAND: "rcu_sched"
 #0 [ffffac1c400bbde0] __schedule at ffffffff87ace28a
 #1 [ffffac1c400bbe88] schedule at ffffffff87ace68e
 #2 [ffffac1c400bbea8] rcu_gp_kthread at ffffffff86baccf8
 #3 [ffffac1c400bbee8] kthread at ffffffff86b0ff93
 #4 [ffffac1c400bbf28] ret_from_fork at ffffffff86a4f459
 #5 [ffffac1c400bbf50] ret_from_fork_asm at ffffffff86a04e5b

PID: 17       TASK: ffff991e00808000  CPU: 0    COMMAND: "migration/0"
 #0 [ffffac1c400c3df8] __schedule at ffffffff87ace28a
 #1 [ffffac1c400c3ea0] schedule at ffffffff87ace68e
 #2 [ffffac1c400c3ec0] smpboot_thread_fn at ffffffff86b1bbdf
 #3 [ffffac1c400c3ee8] kthread at ffffffff86b0ff93
 #4 [ffffac1c400c3f28] ret_from_fork at ffffffff86a4f459
 #5 [ffffac1c400c3f50] ret_from_fork_asm at ffffffff86a04e5b

PID: 18       TASK: ffff991e0080a880  CPU: 0    COMMAND: "idle_inject/0"
 #0 [ffffac1c400cbdf8] __schedule at ffffffff87ace28a
 #1 [ffffac1c400cbea0] schedule at ffffffff87ace68e
 #2 [ffffac1c400cbec0] smpboot_thread_fn at ffffffff86b1bbdf
 #3 [ffffac1c400cbee8] kthread at ffffffff86b0ff93
 #4 [ffffac1c400cbf28] ret_from_fork at ffffffff86a4f459
 #5 [ffffac1c400cbf50] ret_from_fork_asm at ffffffff86a04e5b

PID: 19       TASK: ffff991e0082a880  CPU: 0    COMMAND: "cpuhp/0"
 #0 [ffffac1c400ebdf8] __schedule at ffffffff87ace28a
 #1 [ffffac1c400ebea0] schedule at ffffffff87ace68e
 #2 [ffffac1c400ebec0] smpboot_thread_fn at ffffffff86b1bbdf
 #3 [ffffac1c400ebee8] kthread at ffffffff86b0ff93
 #4 [ffffac1c400ebf28] ret_from_fork at ffffffff86a4f459
 #5 [ffffac1c400ebf50] ret_from_fork_asm at ffffffff86a04e5b
```

```
PID: 20        TASK: ffff991e0082d100  CPU: 2    COMMAND: "cpuhp/2"
 #0 [ffffac1c400f3df8] __schedule at ffffffff87ace28a
 #1 [ffffac1c400f3ea0] schedule at ffffffff87ace68e
 #2 [ffffac1c400f3ec0] smpboot_thread_fn at ffffffff86b1bbdf
 #3 [ffffac1c400f3ee8] kthread at ffffffff86b0ff93
 #4 [ffffac1c400f3f28] ret_from_fork at ffffffff86a4f459
 #5 [ffffac1c400f3f50] ret_from_fork_asm at ffffffff86a04e5b

PID: 21        TASK: ffff991e00828000  CPU: 2    COMMAND: "idle_inject/2"
 #0 [ffffac1c400fbdf8] __schedule at ffffffff87ace28a
 #1 [ffffac1c400fbea0] schedule at ffffffff87ace68e
 #2 [ffffac1c400fbec0] smpboot_thread_fn at ffffffff86b1bbdf
 #3 [ffffac1c400fbee8] kthread at ffffffff86b0ff93
 #4 [ffffac1c400fbf28] ret_from_fork at ffffffff86a4f459
 #5 [ffffac1c400fbf50] ret_from_fork_asm at ffffffff86a04e5b

PID: 22        TASK: ffff991e00832880  CPU: 2    COMMAND: "migration/2"
 #0 [ffffac1c40103df8] __schedule at ffffffff87ace28a
 #1 [ffffac1c40103ea0] schedule at ffffffff87ace68e
 #2 [ffffac1c40103ec0] smpboot_thread_fn at ffffffff86b1bbdf
 #3 [ffffac1c40103ee8] kthread at ffffffff86b0ff93
 #4 [ffffac1c40103f28] ret_from_fork at ffffffff86a4f459
 #5 [ffffac1c40103f50] ret_from_fork_asm at ffffffff86a04e5b

PID: 23        TASK: ffff991e00835100  CPU: 2    COMMAND: "ksoftirqd/2"
 #0 [ffffac1c4010bdf8] __schedule at ffffffff87ace28a
 #1 [ffffac1c4010bea0] schedule at ffffffff87ace68e
 #2 [ffffac1c4010bec0] smpboot_thread_fn at ffffffff86b1bbdf
 #3 [ffffac1c4010bee8] kthread at ffffffff86b0ff93
 #4 [ffffac1c4010bf28] ret_from_fork at ffffffff86a4f459
 #5 [ffffac1c4010bf50] ret_from_fork_asm at ffffffff86a04e5b

PID: 25        TASK: ffff991e0083a880  CPU: 2    COMMAND: "kworker/2:0H"
 #0 [ffffac1c4011bdd0] __schedule at ffffffff87ace28a
 #1 [ffffac1c4011be78] schedule at ffffffff87ace68e
 #2 [ffffac1c4011be98] worker_thread at ffffffff86b05baf
 #3 [ffffac1c4011bee8] kthread at ffffffff86b0ff93
 #4 [ffffac1c4011bf28] ret_from_fork at ffffffff86a4f459
 #5 [ffffac1c4011bf50] ret_from_fork_asm at ffffffff86a04e5b

PID: 26        TASK: ffff991e0083d100  CPU: 1    COMMAND: "cpuhp/1"
 #0 [ffffac1c40123df8] __schedule at ffffffff87ace28a
 #1 [ffffac1c40123ea0] schedule at ffffffff87ace68e
 #2 [ffffac1c40123ec0] smpboot_thread_fn at ffffffff86b1bbdf
 #3 [ffffac1c40123ee8] kthread at ffffffff86b0ff93
 #4 [ffffac1c40123f28] ret_from_fork at ffffffff86a4f459
 #5 [ffffac1c40123f50] ret_from_fork_asm at ffffffff86a04e5b

PID: 27        TASK: ffff991e00838000  CPU: 1    COMMAND: "idle_inject/1"
 -- MORE --  forward: <SPACE>, <ENTER> or j  backward: b or k  quit: qq
```

16. Individual process/thread (task) structures of interest can also be explored:

```
crash> task ffff991e0083d100
PID: 26       TASK: ffff991e0083d100  CPU: 1    COMMAND: "cpuhp/1"
struct task_struct {
  thread_info = {
    flags = 16384,
    syscall_work = 0,
    status = 0,
    cpu = 1
  },
  __state = 1,
  saved_state = 0,
  stack = 0xffffac1c40120000,
  usage = {
    refs = {
      counter = 2
    }
  },
  flags = 69238848,
  ptrace = 0,
  on_cpu = 0,
  wake_entry = {
    llist = {
      next = 0x0
    },
    {
      u_flags = 48,
      a_flags = {
        counter = 48
      }
    },
    src = 0,
    dst = 0
  },
  wakee_flips = 2,
  wakee_flip_decay_ts = 4294669276,
  last_wakee = 0xffff991d06998000,
  recent_used_cpu = 0,
  wake_cpu = 1,
  on_rq = 0,
  prio = 120,
  static_prio = 120,
  normal_prio = 120,
  rt_priority = 0,
  se = {
    load = {
      weight = 1048576,
      inv_weight = 4194304
    },
    run_node = {
      __rb_parent_color = 1,
      rb_right = 0x0,
      rb_left = 0x0
    },
 -- MORE --  forward: <SPACE>, <ENTER> or j  backward: b or k  quit: qq
```

Exercise K1 (A64, GDB)

Goal: Learn how to navigate a normal kernel dump.

Patterns: Manual Dump (Kernel); Stack Trace Collection.

1. Install crash analysis tool:

```
~/ALCDA2/A64$ sudo apt install crash
```

2. Load the core dump *202412291058.kdump* from the A64/K1 directory and the matching *vmlinux-6.8.0-1018-oracle* file from the A64/KSym directory:

```
~/ALCDA2/A64/K1$ crash 202412291058.kdump ../KSym/vmlinux-6.8.0-1018-oracle
```

```
crash 8.0.6++
Copyright (C) 2002-2025  Red Hat, Inc.
Copyright (C) 2004, 2005, 2006, 2010  IBM Corporation
Copyright (C) 1999-2006  Hewlett-Packard Co
Copyright (C) 2005, 2006, 2011, 2012  Fujitsu Limited
Copyright (C) 2006, 2007  VA Linux Systems Japan K.K.
Copyright (C) 2005, 2011, 2020-2024  NEC Corporation
Copyright (C) 1999, 2002, 2007  Silicon Graphics, Inc.
Copyright (C) 1999, 2000, 2001, 2002  Mission Critical Linux, Inc.
Copyright (C) 2015, 2021  VMware, Inc.
This program is free software, covered by the GNU General Public License,
and you are welcome to change it and/or distribute copies of it under
certain conditions.  Enter "help copying" to see the conditions.
This program has absolutely no warranty.  Enter "help warranty" for details.

GNU gdb (GDB) 10.2
Copyright (C) 2021 Free Software Foundation, Inc.
License GPLv3+: GNU GPL version 3 or later <http://gnu.org/licenses/gpl.html>
This is free software: you are free to change and redistribute it.
There is NO WARRANTY, to the extent permitted by law.
Type "show copying" and "show warranty" for details.
This GDB was configured as "aarch64-unknown-linux-gnu".
Type "show configuration" for configuration details.
Find the GDB manual and other documentation resources online at:
    <http://www.gnu.org/software/gdb/documentation/>.

For help, type "help".
Type "apropos word" to search for commands related to "word"...

      KERNEL: ../KSym/vmlinux-6.8.0-1018-oracle
    DUMPFILE: 202412291058.kdump  [PARTIAL DUMP]
        CPUS: 2
        DATE: Sun Dec 29 10:51:17 UTC 2024
      UPTIME: 00:01:13
LOAD AVERAGE: 0.79, 0.39, 0.14
       TASKS: 214
    NODENAME: instance-20230624-1144
     RELEASE: 6.8.0-1018-oracle
     VERSION: #19~22.04.1-Ubuntu SMP Mon Dec  9 23:49:53 UTC 2024
     MACHINE: aarch64  (unknown Mhz)
      MEMORY: 12 GB
```

```
      PANIC: "Kernel panic - not syncing: sysrq triggered crash"
        PID: 1206
    COMMAND: "tee"
       TASK: ffff0000c413c400  [THREAD_INFO: ffff0000c413c400]
        CPU: 0
      STATE: TASK_RUNNING (PANIC)

crash>
```

Note: If the *crash* tool fails to launch, it means that it is not up to date with the *vmlinux* kernel, and the latest version of the tool is required. You need to install it from the source as we did for WSL2 Debian (you may also need to install additional packages depending on your platform and previous installations):

```
$ git clone https://github.com/crash-utility/crash.git
$ sudo apt install build-essential wget libgmp-dev libmpfr-dev libmpc-dev flex bison
$ sudo apt install texinfo
$ sudo apt install zlib1g-dev
$ cd crash
$ make
$ sudo make install
```

Note: For our A64 exercises, we built the *crash* tool on Ubuntu 22.04 arm64, using gcc 11.4.0, since the default *crash* tool installation didn't handle core dumps and symbols from the 6.8.x kernel well.

3. We can see the current thread from the process ID that led to the crash:

```
crash> bt
PID: 1206     TASK: ffff0000c413c400  CPU: 0    COMMAND: "tee"
 #0 [ffff800085a538f0] machine_kexec at ffff80008003fdcc
 #1 [ffff800085a53920] __crash_kexec at ffff80008020b600
 #2 [ffff800085a53aa0] panic at ffff8000800c83dc
 #3 [ffff800085a53b80] sysrq_handle_crash at ffff800080d326e4
 #4 [ffff800085a53b90] __handle_sysrq at ffff800080d33494
 #5 [ffff800085a53c20] write_sysrq_trigger at ffff800080d34070
 #6 [ffff800085a53c60] proc_reg_write at ffff8000805f22c8
 #7 [ffff800085a53c80] vfs_write at ffff80008051026c
 #8 [ffff800085a53d20] ksys_write at ffff800080510724
 #9 [ffff800085a53d60] __arm64_sys_write at ffff8000805107f8
#10 [ffff800085a53e10] invoke_syscall at ffff8000800313bc
#11 [ffff800085a53e40] el0_svc_common.constprop.0 at ffff8000800314b4
#12 [ffff800085a53e70] do_el0_svc at ffff8000800315cc
#13 [ffff800085a53e80] el0_svc at ffff8000815dd9e4
#14 [ffff800085a53ea0] el0t_64_sync_handler at ffff8000815ddff8
#15 [ffff800085a53fe0] el0t_64_sync at ffff80008001163c
     PC: 0000e7f34d0a7e10   LR: 0000e7f34d04507c   SP: 0000ffffeeaaf690
    X29: 0000ffffeeaaf690  X28: 0000000000000001  X27: 0000ad6112dc5ad8
    X26: 0000ad61176932c0  X25: 0000ad61176932c0  X24: 0000000000000002
    X23: 0000ffffeeaaf838  X22: 0000e7f34d1b3640  X21: 0000ad61176932c0
    X20: 0000ffffeeaaf838  X19: 0000000000000003  X18: 0000000000000000
    X17: 0000e7f34d043f90  X16: 0000ad6112dc5df0  X15: 0000000000000000
    X14: ffffffffffffffff  X13: 006f6d2e736c6974  X12: 7565726f632f5345
    X11: 0101010101010101  X10: 00000000000001b0   X9: 000000000000000b
     X8: 0000000000000040   X7: 0000000000000001   X6: 0000000000000000
     X5: 00000000fbad2c87   X4: 00000000ffffffff   X3: 0000e7f34d1b2e80
     X2: 0000000000000002   X1: 0000ffffeeaaf838   X0: 0000000000000003
    ORIG_X0: 0000000000000003  SYSCALLNO: 40  PSTATE: 20001000
```

Note: User space addresses are not available in the kernel dump.

```
crash> sym 0000e7f34d0a7e10
sym: invalid address: 0000e7f34d0a7e10

crash> sym ffff8000800c83dc
ffff8000800c83dc (T) panic+844 /build/linux-oracle-6.8-EzVzJ2/linux-oracle-6.8-
6.8.0/kernel/panic.c: 387
```

4. The tool has built-in help:

```
crash> help

*              files          mod            sbitmapq       union
alias          foreach        mount          search         vm
ascii          fuser          net            set            vtop
bpf            gdb            p              sig            waitq
bt             help           ps             struct         whatis
btop           ipcs           pte            swap           wr
dev            irq            ptob           sym            q
dis            kmem           ptov           sys
eval           list           rd             task
exit           log            repeat         timer
extend         mach           runq           tree

crash version: 8.0.6++   gdb version: 10.2
For help on any command above, enter "help <command>".
For help on input options, enter "help input".
For help on output options, enter "help output".
```

5. Print kernel message buffer before the crash (**dmesg** or **log**) with human-readable timestamps:

```
crash> dmesg -T
[Sun Dec 29 10:50:04 UTC 2024] Booting Linux on physical CPU 0x0000000000 [0x413fd0c1]
[Sun Dec 29 10:50:04 UTC 2024] Linux version 6.8.0-1018-oracle (buildd@bos03-arm64-112) (aarch64-linux-gnu-gcc-11
(Ubuntu 11.4.0-1ubuntu1~22.04) 11.4.0, GNU ld (GNU Binutils for Ubuntu) 2.38) #19~22.04.1-Ubuntu SMP Mon Dec  9
23:49:53 UTC 2024 (Ubuntu 6.8.0-1018.19~22.04.1-oracle 6.8.12)
...
...
...
[Sun Dec 29 10:51:17 UTC 2024] sysrq: Trigger a crash
[Sun Dec 29 10:51:17 UTC 2024] Kernel panic - not syncing: sysrq triggered crash
[Sun Dec 29 10:51:17 UTC 2024] CPU: 0 PID: 1206 Comm: tee Kdump: loaded Not tainted 6.8.0-1018-oracle #19~22.04.1-
Ubuntu
[Sun Dec 29 10:51:17 UTC 2024] Hardware name: QEMU KVM Virtual Machine, BIOS 1.6.6 08/22/2023
[Sun Dec 29 10:51:17 UTC 2024] Call trace:
[Sun Dec 29 10:51:17 UTC 2024]  dump_backtrace+0xa0/0x148
[Sun Dec 29 10:51:17 UTC 2024]  show_stack+0x20/0x48
[Sun Dec 29 10:51:17 UTC 2024]  dump_stack_lvl+0x38/0x130
[Sun Dec 29 10:51:17 UTC 2024]  dump_stack+0x18/0x30
[Sun Dec 29 10:51:17 UTC 2024]  panic+0x3a4/0x428
[Sun Dec 29 10:51:17 UTC 2024]  sysrq_handle_crash+0x20/0x28
[Sun Dec 29 10:51:17 UTC 2024]  __handle_sysrq+0xb8/0x308
[Sun Dec 29 10:51:17 UTC 2024]  write_sysrq_trigger+0x154/0x200
[Sun Dec 29 10:51:17 UTC 2024]  proc_reg_write+0xcc/0x150
[Sun Dec 29 10:51:17 UTC 2024]  vfs_write+0xd8/0x3b8
[Sun Dec 29 10:51:17 UTC 2024]  ksys_write+0x70/0x120
[Sun Dec 29 10:51:17 UTC 2024]  __arm64_sys_write+0x24/0x48
[Sun Dec 29 10:51:17 UTC 2024]  invoke_syscall+0x78/0x128
[Sun Dec 29 10:51:17 UTC 2024]  el0_svc_common.constprop.0+0x48/0x138
[Sun Dec 29 10:51:17 UTC 2024]  do_el0_svc+0x28/0x58
[Sun Dec 29 10:51:17 UTC 2024]  el0_svc+0x40/0x168
[Sun Dec 29 10:51:17 UTC 2024]  el0t_64_sync_handler+0x15c/0x178
[Sun Dec 29 10:51:17 UTC 2024]  el0t_64_sync+0x1a8/0x1b0
[Sun Dec 29 10:51:17 UTC 2024] SMP: stopping secondary CPUs
```

```
[Sun Dec 29 10:51:17 UTC 2024] Kernel Offset: disabled
[Sun Dec 29 10:51:17 UTC 2024] CPU features: 0x1,00000020,7002014a,2101720b
[Sun Dec 29 10:51:17 UTC 2024] Memory Limit: none
[Sun Dec 29 10:51:28 UTC 2024] Starting crashdump kernel...
[Sun Dec 29 10:51:28 UTC 2024] Bye!
```

Note: Many commands have many options. Please check individual help entries.

```
crash> help dmesg
```

6. Check memory summary, computer, and network information:

```
crash> kmem -i
                PAGES        TOTAL      PERCENTAGE
    TOTAL MEM  2923527      11.2 GB         ----
         FREE  2666051      10.2 GB   91% of TOTAL MEM
         USED   257476    1005.8 MB    8% of TOTAL MEM
       SHARED    34920     136.4 MB    1% of TOTAL MEM
      BUFFERS     6912        27 MB    0% of TOTAL MEM
       CACHED   192581     752.3 MB    6% of TOTAL MEM
         SLAB    21093      82.4 MB    0% of TOTAL MEM

   TOTAL HUGE        0            0         ----
    HUGE FREE        0            0    0% of TOTAL HUGE

   TOTAL SWAP        0            0         ----
    SWAP USED        0            0    0% of TOTAL SWAP
    SWAP FREE        0            0    0% of TOTAL SWAP

 COMMIT LIMIT  1461763       5.6 GB         ----
    COMMITTED        0            0    0% of TOTAL LIMIT

crash> mach
       MACHINE TYPE: aarch64
        MEMORY SIZE: 12 GB
               CPUS: 2
                 HZ: 1000
          PAGE SIZE: 4096
KERNEL VIRTUAL BASE: ffff000000000000
KERNEL MODULES BASE: ffff800000000000
KERNEL VMALLOC BASE: ffff800080000000
KERNEL VMEMMAP BASE: fffffc0000000000
  KERNEL STACK SIZE: 16384
     IRQ STACK SIZE: 16384
         IRQ STACKS:
              CPU 0: ffff800080000000
              CPU 1: ffff800080008000
OVERFLOW STACK SIZE: 4096
    OVERFLOW STACKS:
              CPU 0: ffff0002fe76f310
              CPU 1: ffff0002fe7a5310

crash> net
   NET_DEVICE     NAME     IP ADDRESS(ES)
ffff0000c0af4000  lo       127.0.0.1, ::1
ffff0000c0b55000  enp0s6   10.0.0.248, fe80::17ff:fe03:cbc6
```

7. List all processes:

```
crash> ps
      PID    PPID  CPU       TASK        ST  %MEM     VSZ    RSS  COMM
        0       0   0  ffff800083239ac0  RU   0.0       0      0  [swapper/0]
>       0       0   1  ffff0000c0582200  RU   0.0       0      0  [swapper/1]
        1       0   1  ffff0000c03bc400  IN   0.1  101336  11264  systemd
        2       0   0  ffff0000c03ba200  IN   0.0       0      0  [kthreadd]
...
...
...
     1106     959   1  ffff0000c4838000  IN   0.0   18404   6644  sshd
     1113    1105   0  ffff0000c483a200  IN   0.1 1237944  17912  gomon
     1115    1106   1  ffff0000c483c400  IN   0.0    8720   4860  bash
     1123    1105   1  ffff0000c45d4400  IN   0.1 1237944  17912  gomon
     1125    1105   1  ffff0000c45d2200  IN   0.1 1237944  17912  gomon
     1126    1105   1  ffff0000c4860000  IN   0.1 1237944  17912  gomon
     1146       1   1  ffff0000c45c2200  IN   0.2 1319816  32180  snapd
     1147    1105   1  ffff0000c4134400  IN   0.1 1237944  17912  gomon
     1148    1105   0  ffff0000c6be4400  IN   0.1 1237944  17912  gomon
     1149    1105   1  ffff0000c4870000  IN   0.1 1237944  17912  gomon
     1200    1105   0  ffff0000c4138000  IN   0.1 1237944  17912  gomon
     1201     888   1  ffff0000c485c400  IN   0.1   15136   8336  sshd
     1202    1201   0  ffff0000c413a200  IN   0.0   15136   6808  sshd
     1204    1115   1  ffff0000c485a200  IN   0.0   13368   4780  sudo
     1205    1204   1  ffff0000c4858000  IN   0.0   13368   1768  sudo
>    1206    1205   0  ffff0000c413c400  RU   0.0    5604   1596  tee
```

8. List CPU queues:

```
crash> runq
CPU 0 RUNQUEUE: ffff0002fe784b80
  CURRENT: PID: 1206   TASK: ffff0000c413c400  COMMAND: "tee"
  RT PRIO_ARRAY: ffff0002fe784e80
     [no tasks queued]
  CFS RB_ROOT: ffff0002fe784cd0
     [120] PID: 117    TASK: ffff0000c91d8000  COMMAND: "kworker/0:2"

CPU 1 RUNQUEUE: ffff0002fe7bab80
  CURRENT: PID: 0      TASK: ffff0000c0582200  COMMAND: "swapper/1"
  RT PRIO_ARRAY: ffff0002fe7bae80
     [no tasks queued]
  CFS RB_ROOT: ffff0002fe7bacd0
     [no tasks queued]
```

9. Set the current task to PID 1205 and, then to the task running to CPU 1, and then to the panicked task:

```
crash> set 1205
    PID: 1205
COMMAND: "sudo"
   TASK: ffff0000c4858000  [THREAD_INFO: ffff0000c4858000]
    CPU: 1
  STATE: TASK_INTERRUPTIBLE
```

```
crash> set -c 1
    PID: 0
COMMAND: "swapper/1"
   TASK: ffff0000c0582200  (1 of 2)  [THREAD_INFO: ffff0000c0582200]
    CPU: 1
```

```
  STATE: TASK_RUNNING (ACTIVE)

rash> set -p
    PID: 1206
COMMAND: "tee"
   TASK: ffff0000c413c400  [THREAD_INFO: ffff0000c413c400]
    CPU: 0
  STATE: TASK_RUNNING (PANIC)
```

10. Display the stack trace of the bash parent process without and with source code, and dump raw stack data:

```
crash> set 1115
    PID: 1115
COMMAND: "bash"
   TASK: ffff0000c483c400  [THREAD_INFO: ffff0000c483c400]
    CPU: 1
  STATE: TASK_INTERRUPTIBLE

crash> bt
PID: 1115     TASK: ffff0000c483c400  CPU: 1    COMMAND: "bash"
 #0 [ffff800085b139a0] __switch_to at ffff8000815e7e1c
 #1 [ffff800085b139c0] __schedule at ffff8000815e8168
 #2 [ffff800085b13a60] schedule at ffff8000815e862c
 #3 [ffff800085b13a90] do_wait at ffff8000800d1958
 #4 [ffff800085b13ac0] kernel_wait4 at ffff8000800d2434
 #5 [ffff800085b13b60] __do_sys_wait4 at ffff8000800d2618
 #6 [ffff800085b13c20] __arm64_sys_wait4 at ffff8000800d2668
 #7 [ffff800085b13e10] invoke_syscall at ffff8000800313bc
 #8 [ffff800085b13e40] el0_svc_common.constprop.0 at ffff8000800314b4
 #9 [ffff800085b13e70] do_el0_svc at ffff8000800315cc
#10 [ffff800085b13e80] el0_svc at ffff8000815dd9e4
#11 [ffff800085b13ea0] el0t_64_sync_handler at ffff8000815ddff8
#12 [ffff800085b13fe0] el0t_64_sync at ffff80008001163c
     PC: 0000f4897a3767b8   LR: 0000c4592f6b548c   SP: 0000ffff1ca8380
    X29: 0000ffff1ca8380  X28: 0000000000000000  X27: 000000000000000a
    X26: 0000c4592f70d464  X25: 0000c4592f715e5c  X24: 0000c4592f70c000
    X23: 0000f4897a4e47e0  X22: 0000c4592f715140  X21: 0000c4592f717000
    X20: ffffffffffffffff  X19: 000000000000000a  X18: 0000000000000000
    X17: 0000f4897a376750  X16: 0000c4592f70ba48  X15: 0000000000000005
    X14: 0000000000000001  X13: 0000000000000000  X12: 0000000000000001
    X11: 0000000000000000  X10: 0000c4592f70c000   X9: 0000000000000000
     X8: 0000000000000104   X7: 0000000000000000   X6: 0000000000000001
     X5: 0000c4592f717e54   X4: 0000f4897a4e4020   X3: 0000000000000000
     X2: 000000000000000a   X1: 0000ffff1ca8450   X0: ffffffffffffffff
    ORIG_X0: ffffffffffffffff  SYSCALLNO: 104  PSTATE: 60001000

crash> bt -l
PID: 1115     TASK: ffff0000c483c400  CPU: 1    COMMAND: "bash"
 #0 [ffff800085b139a0] __switch_to at ffff8000815e7e1c
    /build/linux-oracle-6.8-EzVzJ2/linux-oracle-6.8-6.8.0/arch/arm64/kernel/process.c: 556
 #1 [ffff800085b139c0] __schedule at ffff8000815e8168
    /build/linux-oracle-6.8-EzVzJ2/linux-oracle-6.8-6.8.0/kernel/sched/core.c: 5396
 #2 [ffff800085b13a60] schedule at ffff8000815e862c
    /build/linux-oracle-6.8-EzVzJ2/linux-oracle-6.8-6.8.0/kernel/sched/core.c: 6803
 #3 [ffff800085b13a90] do_wait at ffff8000800d1958
    /build/linux-oracle-6.8-EzVzJ2/linux-oracle-6.8-6.8.0/kernel/exit.c: 1632
 #4 [ffff800085b13ac0] kernel_wait4 at ffff8000800d2434
    /build/linux-oracle-6.8-EzVzJ2/linux-oracle-6.8-6.8.0/kernel/exit.c: 1786
 #5 [ffff800085b13b60] __do_sys_wait4 at ffff8000800d2618
    /build/linux-oracle-6.8-EzVzJ2/linux-oracle-6.8-6.8.0/kernel/exit.c: 1814
```

```
 #6 [ffff800085b13c20] __arm64_sys_wait4 at ffff8000800d2668
    /build/linux-oracle-6.8-EzVzJ2/linux-oracle-6.8-6.8.0/kernel/exit.c: 1810
 #7 [ffff800085b13e10] invoke_syscall at ffff8000800313bc
    /build/linux-oracle-6.8-EzVzJ2/linux-oracle-6.8-6.8.0/arch/arm64/kernel/syscall.c: 37
 #8 [ffff800085b13e40] el0_svc_common.constprop.0 at ffff8000800314b4
    /build/linux-oracle-6.8-EzVzJ2/linux-oracle-6.8-6.8.0/arch/arm64/kernel/syscall.c: 134
 #9 [ffff800085b13e70] do_el0_svc at ffff8000800315cc
    /build/linux-oracle-6.8-EzVzJ2/linux-oracle-6.8-6.8.0/arch/arm64/kernel/syscall.c: 153
#10 [ffff800085b13e80] el0_svc at ffff8000815dd9e4
    /build/linux-oracle-6.8-EzVzJ2/linux-oracle-6.8-6.8.0/arch/arm64/kernel/entry-common.c: 678
#11 [ffff800085b13ea0] el0t_64_sync_handler at ffff8000815ddff8
    /build/linux-oracle-6.8-EzVzJ2/linux-oracle-6.8-6.8.0/arch/arm64/kernel/entry-common.c: 696
#12 [ffff800085b13fe0] el0t_64_sync at ffff80008001163c
    /build/linux-oracle-6.8-EzVzJ2/linux-oracle-6.8-6.8.0/arch/arm64/kernel/entry.S: 598
     PC: 0000f4897a3767b8   LR: 0000c4592f6b548c   SP: 0000fffff1ca8380
    X29: 0000fffff1ca8380  X28: 0000000000000000  X27: 000000000000000a
    X26: 0000c4592f70d464  X25: 0000c4592f715e5c  X24: 0000c4592f70c000
    X23: 0000f4897a4e47e0  X22: 0000c4592f715140  X21: 0000c4592f717000
    X20: ffffffffffffffff  X19: 000000000000000a  X18: 0000000000000000
    X17: 0000f4897a376750  X16: 0000c4592f70ba48  X15: 0000000000000005
    X14: 0000000000000001  X13: 0000000000000000  X12: 0000000000000001
    X11: 0000000000000000  X10: 0000c4592f70c000   X9: 0000000000000000
     X8: 0000000000000104   X7: 0000000000000000   X6: 0000000000000001
     X5: 0000c4592f717e54   X4: 0000f4897a4e4020   X3: 0000000000000000
     X2: 000000000000000a   X1: 0000fffff1ca8450   X0: ffffffffffffffff
    ORIG_X0: ffffffffffffffff  SYSCALLNO: 104  PSTATE: 60001000
```

```
crash> bt -r
PID: 1115     TASK: ffff0000c483c400  CPU: 1    COMMAND: "bash"
ffff800085b10000:  0000000057ac6e9d 0000000000000000
ffff800085b10010:  0000000000000000 0000000000000000
ffff800085b10020:  0000000000000000 0000000000000000
ffff800085b10030:  0000000000000000 0000000000000000...
...
...
ffff800085b12a50:  0000000000000000 0000000000000000
ffff800085b12a60:  0000000000000000 0000000000000000
ffff800085b12a70:  0000000000000000 0000000000000000
ffff800085b12a80:  0000000000000000 0000000000000000
ffff800085b12a90:  0000000000000000 0000000000000000
ffff800085b12aa0:  ffff800085b12ac0 __update_load_avg_se+604
ffff800085b12ab0:  ffff0000c907a2c0 ffff0000c907a380
ffff800085b12ac0:  ffff800085b12b30 update_load_avg+1380
ffff800085b12ad0:  ffff800085b12b30 update_load_avg+112
ffff800085b12ae0:  ffff0002fe784c80 ffff0000c907a2c0
ffff800085b12af0:  0000000221a22380 0000000000000005
ffff800085b12b00:  0000000000000000 0000000000000001
ffff800085b12b10:  0000000000000000 cpu_number
ffff800085b12b20:  ffff0000c01a4c00 ffff0000c030b400
ffff800085b12b30:  ffff800085b12b80 enqueue_entity+76
ffff800085b12b40:  ffff800085b12b70 __enqueue_entity+384
ffff800085b12b50:  ffff0002fe784c80 ffff0000c907a2c0
ffff800085b12b60:  0000000000000009 ffff0000c0336800
ffff800085b12b70:  ffff800085b12b80 enqueue_entity+232
ffff800085b12b80:  ffff800085b12be0 enqueue_task_fair+136
ffff800085b12b90:  ffff800085b12bf0 check_preempt_wakeup_fair+320
ffff800085b12ba0:  ffff0000c907a2c0 ffff0002fe784c80
ffff800085b12bb0:  0000000000000000 ffff0000c907a2c0
ffff800085b12bc0:  ffff0002fe784b80 ffff0000c483c400
ffff800085b12bd0:  ffff0000c483c4c0 cpu_number
```

```
ffff800085b12be0:  ffff0000c01a4c00 ffff0000c907a2c0
ffff800085b12bf0:  ffff800085b12c40 wakeup_preempt+168
ffff800085b12c00:  ffff0002fe784b80 ffff0002fe784b80
ffff800085b12c10:  0000000000000000 ffff800085b12cf8
ffff800085b12c20:  ffff80027bedf000 0000000000000000
ffff800085b12c30:  0000000000000000 ttwu_do_activate+104
ffff800085b12c40:  ffff800085b12c60 ttwu_do_activate+128
ffff800085b12c50:  ffff0000c907a200 ffff800085b12cf8
ffff800085b12c60:  ffff800085b12ca0 try_to_wake_up+524
ffff800085b12c70:  ffff0000c907a200 ffff0002fe784b80
ffff800085b12c80:  0000000000000000 00000000000000c0
ffff800085b12c90:  ffff800085b12d00 update_load_avg+1380
ffff800085b12ca0:  ffff800085b12d00 update_load_avg+112
ffff800085b12cb0:  ffff0002fe784c80 ffff0000c907a2c0
ffff800085b12cc0:  ffff0002fe784b80 ffff0000c907a200
ffff800085b12cd0:  fair_sched_class ffff0002fe784c80
ffff800085b12ce0:  ffff0000c483cb20 0000000000000000
ffff800085b12cf0:  cpu_number       __per_cpu_offset
ffff800085b12d00:  ffff800085b12d50 set_next_entity+232
ffff800085b12d10:  ffff0000c907a2c0 ffff0002fe784c80
ffff800085b12d20:  ffff0002fe784c80 ffff0002fe784b80
ffff800085b12d30:  0000000000000000 ffff0000c907a200
ffff800085b12d40:  ffff0002fe784c80 ffff0000c0336800
ffff800085b12d50:  ffff800085b12dc0 update_load_avg+1380
ffff800085b12d60:  ffff800085b12dc0 update_load_avg+112
ffff800085b12d70:  ffff0002fe784c80 ffff0000c907a2c0
ffff800085b12d80:  0000000221a96050 0000000000000005
ffff800085b12d90:  0000000000000000 0000000000000001
ffff800085b12da0:  ffff800085b12df0 update_sg_lb_stats+236
ffff800085b12db0:  ffff800085b12f0c ffff800085b13110
ffff800085b12dc0:  nr_cpu_ids       0000000000000009
ffff800085b12dd0:  __per_cpu_offset ffff0002fe784b80
ffff800085b12de0:  ffff800085b12f0c ffff800085b13110
ffff800085b12df0:  ffff800085b12ec0 update_sd_lb_stats.constprop.0+256
ffff800085b12e00:  ffff800085b12f98 ffff0000c0231e40
ffff800085b12e10:  ffff800085b13110 0000000000000002
ffff800085b12e20:  ffff800085b13020 bit_wait_table+3712
ffff800085b12e30:  0000000000000001 ffff0000c01c5a00
ffff800085b12e40:  0000000000000002 0000000000000000
ffff800085b12e50:  ffff800085b12ec0 runqueues
ffff800085b12e60:  ffff800085b12ec0 update_sd_lb_stats.constprop.0+276
ffff800085b12e70:  ffff800085b12f98 ffff0000c0231e40
ffff800085b12e80:  ffff800085b13110 0000000000000002
ffff800085b12e90:  ffff800085b13020 bit_wait_table+3712
ffff800085b12ea0:  0000000000000001 ffff0000c01c5a00
ffff800085b12eb0:  ffff800085b12ee0 virtqueue_add_split+1072
ffff800085b12ec0:  ffff800085b12f70 find_busiest_group+80
ffff800085b12ed0:  ffff800085b13110 ffff0002fe7a7c40
ffff800085b12ee0:  ffff800085b13168 0000000000000001
ffff800085b12ef0:  bit_wait_table+3712 load_balance_mask
ffff800085b12f00:  0000000000000003 0000000000000001
ffff800085b12f10:  0000000000000000 0000000000000009
ffff800085b12f20:  0000000000000400 0000000000000009
ffff800085b12f30:  0000000000000000 0000000100000001
ffff800085b12f40:  0000000100000000 0000000000000000
ffff800085b12f50:  0000000000000000 0000000000000000
ffff800085b12f60:  0000000000000000 3fbe42f52288d100
ffff800085b12f70:  ffff800085b12fc0 update_sg_lb_stats+236
ffff800085b12f80:  ffff800085b130dc ffff800085b132e0
ffff800085b12f90:  nr_cpu_ids       0000000000000203
```

```
ffff800085b12fa0:  ffff800085b12fc0 update_sg_lb_stats+720
ffff800085b12fb0:  ffff800085b130dc ffff800085b132e0
ffff800085b12fc0:  ffff800085b13090 update_sd_lb_stats.constprop.0+256
ffff800085b12fd0:  ffff800085b13168 ffff0000c0231ec0
ffff800085b12fe0:  ffff800085b132e0 0000000000000022
ffff800085b12ff0:  ffff800085b131f0 bit_wait_table+3712
ffff800085b13000:  0000000000000001 ffff0000c01c4000
ffff800085b13010:  0000000000000002 0000000000000000
ffff800085b13020:  0000000000000000 runqueues
ffff800085b13030:  ffff800085b13090 update_sd_lb_stats.constprop.0+276
ffff800085b13040:  ffff0000c0231e40 runqueues
ffff800085b13050:  ffff800085b132e0 0000000000000022
ffff800085b13060:  0000000000000000 sysctl_numa_balancing_scan_delay+584
ffff800085b13070:  0000000000000000 3fbe42f52288d100
ffff800085b13080:  ffff800085b13180 newidle_balance+492
ffff800085b13090:  ffff800085b13140 find_busiest_group+80
ffff800085b130a0:  ffff800085b132e0 ffff0002fe771c40
ffff800085b130b0:  ffff800085b13338 0000000000000000
ffff800085b130c0:  bit_wait_table+3712 load_balance_mask
ffff800085b130d0:  00000000fffbea54 0000000000000000
ffff800085b130e0:  0000000000000000 0000000000000203
ffff800085b130f0:  0000000000000400 0000000000000176
ffff800085b13100:  0000000000000187 0000000000000000
ffff800085b13110:  0000000100000000 0000000000000000
ffff800085b13120:  0000000000000000 0000000000000000
ffff800085b13130:  0000000000000000 3fbe42f52288d100
ffff800085b13140:  ffff800085b13250 load_balance+260
ffff800085b13150:  ffff0002fe784b80 ffff0002fe771c40
ffff800085b13160:  ffff800085b13180 0000000000000000
ffff800085b13170:  ffff0000c0231e40 0000000000000221
ffff800085b13180:  0000000000000800 0000000000000000
ffff800085b13190:  0000000000000000 0000000000000000
ffff800085b131a0:  0000000000000000 0000000000000000
ffff800085b131b0:  0000000000000000 0000000000000000
ffff800085b131c0:  0000000000000000 00000000ffffffff
ffff800085b131d0:  0000000000000000 0000000000000000
ffff800085b131e0:  0000000000000000 0000000000000000
ffff800085b131f0:  0000000000000000 000000000000001e
ffff800085b13200:  0000000000000400 0000000000000022
ffff800085b13210:  0000000000000030 0000000000000000
ffff800085b13220:  ffff800085b13290 __cgroup_account_cputime+68
ffff800085b13230:  ffff800085b132b0 pick_next_task_fair+88
ffff800085b13240:  fair_sched_class ffff0002fe784b80
ffff800085b13250:  ffff0000c483c400 ffff0002fe784b80
ffff800085b13260:  ffff800085b13460 ffff0002fe784c80
ffff800085b13270:  fair_sched_class ffff0002fe784c80
ffff800085b13280:  ffff0000c483cb20 0000000000000000
ffff800085b13290:  ffff800085b13460 0000000100000009
ffff800085b132a0:  ffff800085b132f0 3fbe42f52288d100
ffff800085b132b0:  ffff800085b132f0 put_prev_task_fair+44
ffff800085b132c0:  ffff0000c0336800 ffff0002fe784b80
ffff800085b132d0:  ffff0000c483c400 ffff800085b13460
ffff800085b132e0:  ffff800085b13390 psi_task_switch+156
ffff800085b132f0:  ffff800085b13370 rmqueue+812
ffff800085b13300:  ffff0002fe7f3540 ffff0002fe78af00
ffff800085b13310:  00000000001ef443 0000000000000001
ffff800085b13320:  0000000000000100 0000000000540dc0
ffff800085b13330:  ffff800085b13560 ffff0002fe7f3540
ffff800085b13340:  0000000000000901 0000000000000001
ffff800085b13350:  types__process_vm_readv+48 pcpu_drain_mutex+1768
```

```
ffff800085b13360:   ffff800085b13370 rmqueue+908
ffff800085b13370:   ffff800085b13470 get_page_from_freelist+416
ffff800085b13380:   ffff0002fe7f4c80 0000000000000000
ffff800085b13390:   00000000001ef443 0000000000000000
ffff800085b133a0:   0000000000000100 0000000000540dc0
ffff800085b133b0:   ffff800085b13560 ffff0002fe7f3540
ffff800085b133c0:   0000000000000901 0000000000000001
ffff800085b133d0:   ffff800085b13440 __mod_memcg_state+172
ffff800085b133e0:   cpu_number       0000000000000001
ffff800085b133f0:   00007bfd740e2ee8 ffff0000c8203000
ffff800085b13400:   00007bfd740e2d40 0000000000440dc0
ffff800085b13410:   0000000000540dc0 page_group_by_mobility_disabled
ffff800085b13420:   ffff800085b13470 update_sg_lb_stats+236
ffff800085b13430:   ffff800085b1358c ffff800085b13790
ffff800085b13440:   nr_cpu_ids       0000000000000200
ffff800085b13450:   __per_cpu_offset ffff0002fe784b80
ffff800085b13460:   ffff800085b1358c ffff800085b13790
ffff800085b13470:   ffff800085b13540 update_sd_lb_stats.constprop.0+256
ffff800085b13480:   ffff800085b13618 ffff0000c0231e40
ffff800085b13490:   ffff800085b13790 0000000000000014
ffff800085b134a0:   ffff800085b136a0 bit_wait_table+3712
ffff800085b134b0:   0000000000000001 ffff0000c01c5a00
ffff800085b134c0:   0000000000000002 ffff0000c483c400
ffff800085b134d0:   0000000000000002 runqueues
ffff800085b134e0:   ffff800085b13540 update_sd_lb_stats.constprop.0+276
ffff800085b134f0:   ffff800085b13618 ffff0000c0231e40
ffff800085b13500:   ffff800085b13790 0000000000000014
ffff800085b13510:   ffff800085b136a0 bit_wait_table+3712
ffff800085b13520:   0000000000000001 ffff0000c01c5a00
ffff800085b13530:   __per_cpu_offset ffff0002fe7bab80
ffff800085b13540:   ffff800085b135f0 find_busiest_group+80
ffff800085b13550:   ffff800085b13790 ffff0002fe7a7c40
ffff800085b13560:   ffff800085b137e8 0000000000000001
ffff800085b13570:   bit_wait_table+3712 load_balance_mask
ffff800085b13580:   ffff800085b13780 0000000083226000
ffff800085b13590:   0000000000000000 0000000000000200
ffff800085b135a0:   0000000000000400 0000000000000101
ffff800085b135b0:   0000000000000101 0000000100000001
ffff800085b135c0:   0000000100000000 0000000000000000
ffff800085b135d0:   0000000000000000 0000000000000000
ffff800085b135e0:   0000000000000000 3fbe42f52288d100
ffff800085b135f0:   ffff800085b13700 load_balance+260
ffff800085b13600:   ffff0002fe7bab80 ffff0002fe7a7c40
ffff800085b13610:   00000000001ef443 ffff0000c0231e40
ffff800085b13620:   ffff0000c0231ec0 0000000000000209
ffff800085b13630:   0000000000000800 0000000000000000
ffff800085b13640:   0000000000000000 0000000000000000
ffff800085b13650:   0000000000000200 0000000000000400
ffff800085b13660:   0000000000000101 0000000000000101
ffff800085b13670:   0000000100000001 0000000100000000
ffff800085b13680:   0000000000000000 0000000000000000
ffff800085b13690:   0000000000000000 0000000000000000
ffff800085b136a0:   0000000000000000 0000000000000009
ffff800085b136b0:   0000000000000400 0000000000000014
ffff800085b136c0:   0000000000000014 0000000000000000
ffff800085b136d0:   0000000100000000 0000000000000000
ffff800085b136e0:   0000000000000000 0000000000000000
ffff800085b136f0:   0000000000000000 3fbe42f52288d100
ffff800085b13700:   ffff800085b13800 newidle_balance+492
ffff800085b13710:   ffff0000c01c5a00 0000000000000001
```

```
ffff800085b13720:  000000111e6b3968 0000000000000000
ffff800085b13730:  bit_wait_table+3712 sysctl_sched_migration_cost
ffff800085b13740:  0000000000000001 ffff0002fe7bab80
ffff800085b13750:  00000000fffc8a39 ffff0000c483c400
ffff800085b13760:  0000000000000000 0000000000000002
ffff800085b13770:  ffff0002fe7a7c40 normalized_sysctl_sched_base_slice+740
ffff800085b13780:  ffff800085b137e0 sched_clock+16
ffff800085b13790:  ffff0000c01c5a00 0000000000000001
ffff800085b137a0:  000000111e6b3968 0000000000000000
ffff800085b137b0:  bit_wait_table+3712 sysctl_sched_migration_cost
ffff800085b137c0:  0000000000000001 ffff0002fe7a7c40
ffff800085b137d0:  0000000000000000 0000000000000020
ffff800085b137e0:  ffff800085b13800 newidle_balance+804
ffff800085b137f0:  0000000000000000 0000000000000001
ffff800085b13800:  ffff800085b13880 pick_next_task_fair+88
ffff800085b13810:  fair_sched_class ffff0002fe7bab80
ffff800085b13820:  ffff0000c483c400 ffff0002fe7bab80
ffff800085b13830:  ffff800085b13a30 ffff0002fe7bac80
ffff800085b13840:  fair_sched_class ffff0002fe7bac80
ffff800085b13850:  ffff0000c483cb20 ffff0000c483c400
ffff800085b13860:  ffff800085b13a30 000000018013eb64
ffff800085b13870:  00000001c0337c00 3fbe42f52288d100
ffff800085b13880:  ffff800085b138c0 put_prev_task_fair+44
ffff800085b13890:  ffff0000c0337c00 ffff0002fe7bab80
ffff800085b138a0:  ffff0000c483c400 ffff800085b13a30
ffff800085b138b0:  ffff800085b13960 psi_task_switch+156
ffff800085b138c0:  0000000000000000 psi_system
ffff800085b138d0:  000000111e6b3eb8 0000000000000001
ffff800085b138e0:  0000000000000014 0000000000000001
ffff800085b138f0:  0000000000000000 ffff0000c483c400
ffff800085b13900:  ffff800085b13940 fpsimd_thread_switch+348
ffff800085b13910:  ffff0000c0582200 ffff0000c483c400
ffff800085b13920:  ffff0000c0582200 0000000000000000
ffff800085b13930:  00007bfd740e41c8 ffff0000c42f1900
ffff800085b13940:  ffff800085b139a0 __switch_to+32
ffff800085b13950:  ffff0000c0582200 ffff0000c483c400
ffff800085b13960:  ffff800085b13980 erratum_1418040_thread_switch+36
ffff800085b13970:  ffff0000c0582200 ffff0000c483c400
ffff800085b13980:  ffff800085b139a0 __switch_to+92
ffff800085b13990:  ffff0000c0582200 ffff0000c483c400
ffff800085b139a0:  ffff800085b139c0 __schedule+660
ffff800085b139b0:  ffff0002fe7bab80 ffff0000c483c400
ffff800085b139c0:  ffff800085b13a60 schedule+48
ffff800085b139d0:  ffff0000c483c400 ffff0000c483c400
ffff800085b139e0:  0000000000000001 ffff800085b13b28
ffff800085b139f0:  0000000000000000 0000000000000000
ffff800085b13a00:  0000000000000000 0000000000000000
ffff800085b13a10:  0000000000000000 ffff800085b13b00
ffff800085b13a20:  ffff0000c483c400 ffff0000c483c400
ffff800085b13a30:  ffff800085b13a98 ffff800000000004
ffff800085b13a40:  cpu_bit_bitmap+128 0000000000000000
ffff800085b13a50:  0000000000000002 3fbe42f52288d100
ffff800085b13a60:  ffff800085b13a90 do_wait+204
ffff800085b13a70:  ffff0000c483c400 ffff800085b13b00
ffff800085b13a80:  0000000000000000 0000000000000000
ffff800085b13a90:  ffff800085b13ac0 kernel_wait4+152
ffff800085b13aa0:  000000000000000e 0000ffffff1ca8450
ffff800085b13ab0:  0000000000000004 0000000000000000
ffff800085b13ac0:  ffff800085b13b60 __do_sys_wait4+220
ffff800085b13ad0:  ffff800085b13eb0 ffff80027bf15000
```

```
ffff800085b13ae0:  ffff0000c483c400 0000f4897a3767b8
ffff800085b13af0:  0000000060001000 0000000000000215
ffff800085b13b00:  0000000e00000004 0000000000000000
ffff800085b13b10:  0000000000000000 ffff800000000000
ffff800085b13b20:  0000000000000000 0000f48900000000
ffff800085b13b30:  ffff0000c483c400 child_wait_callback
ffff800085b13b40:  ffff0000c6549b28 ffff0000c6549b28
ffff800085b13b50:  0000000000000000 3fbe42f52288d100
ffff800085b13b60:  ffff800085b13c20 __arm64_sys_wait4+44
ffff800085b13b70:  ffff800085b13eb0 ffff80027bf15000
ffff800085b13b80:  000000009600004f ffff800085b13c40
ffff800085b13b90:  0000f4897a4e47c8 vdso_end+360
ffff800085b13ba0:  0000000080400005 ffff800085b13eb0
ffff800085b13bb0:  ffff0000c483c400 0000000000000000
ffff800085b13bc0:  0000000000000000 0000f4897a3767b8
ffff800085b13bd0:  ffff800085b13c00 el1_abort+76
ffff800085b13be0:  ffff800085b13c40 000000009600004f
ffff800085b13bf0:  ffff800085b13c00 el1_abort+92
ffff800085b13c00:  ffff800085b13c30 el1h_64_sync_handler+376
ffff800085b13c10:  0000f4897a4e47c8 3fbe42f52288d100
ffff800085b13c20:  ffff800085b13e10 invoke_syscall+120
ffff800085b13c30:  ffff800085b13d70 el1h_64_sync+124
ffff800085b13c40:  0000000000000000 0000000000000000
ffff800085b13c50:  0000000000000000 0000000000000000
ffff800085b13c60:  0000000000000000 0000000000000000
ffff800085b13c70:  0000000000000000 0000000000000000
ffff800085b13c80:  0000000000000000 __rseq_handle_notify_resume+396
ffff800085b13c90:  0000000000000000 0000000000000000
ffff800085b13ca0:  0000000000000000 0000000000000000
ffff800085b13cb0:  0000000000000000 0000000000000000
ffff800085b13cc0:  0000000000000000 0000000000000000
ffff800085b13cd0:  0000000000000000 0000f4897a4e47c8
ffff800085b13ce0:  0000000000000000 0000000000000000
ffff800085b13cf0:  0000f4897a3767b8 0000000060001000
ffff800085b13d00:  ffff800085b13eb0 ffff0000c483c400
ffff800085b13d10:  0000000000000000 0000000000000000
ffff800085b13d20:  ffff0000c483c400 ffff800085b13d90
ffff800085b13d30:  clear_rseq_cs+76 ffff800085b13d90
ffff800085b13d40:  clear_rseq_cs+76 0000000080400005
ffff800085b13d50:  ffff800085b13d80 handle_mm_fault+428
ffff800085b13d60:  ffff800085b13db0 __rseq_handle_notify_resume+304
ffff800085b13d70:  000000000000000c ffff0000c483c400
ffff800085b13d80:  0000000000000000 0000f4897a3767b8
ffff800085b13d90:  0000000060001000 ffff800085b13eb0
ffff800085b13da0:  ffff0000c483c400 0000000000000000
ffff800085b13db0:  ffff800085b13e50 do_notify_resume+256
ffff800085b13dc0:  000000000000000c ffff0000c483c400
ffff800085b13dd0:  ffff800085b13eb0 0000000000000041
ffff800085b13de0:  0000000060001000 0000000000000000
ffff800085b13df0:  0000000000000000 0000000000000000
ffff800085b13e00:  ffff800085b13eb0 0000000000000041
ffff800085b13e10:  ffff800085b13e40 el0_svc_common.constprop.0+72
ffff800085b13e20:  ffff800085b13eb0 ffff80027bf15000
ffff800085b13e30:  ffff0000c483c400 fpsimd_restore_current_state+280
ffff800085b13e40:  ffff800085b13e70 do_el0_svc+40
ffff800085b13e50:  ffff800085b13eb0 ffff80027bf15000
ffff800085b13e60:  00000000ffffffff ffff80027bedf000
ffff800085b13e70:  ffff800085b13e80 el0_svc+64
ffff800085b13e80:  ffff800085b13ea0 el0t_64_sync_handler+348
ffff800085b13e90:  0000000000000000 el0t_64_irq_handler+16
```

```
ffff800085b13ea0:  ffff800085b13fe0 el0t_64_sync+424
ffff800085b13eb0:  ffffffffffffffff 0000fffff1ca8450
ffff800085b13ec0:  000000000000000a 0000000000000000
ffff800085b13ed0:  0000f4897a4e4020 0000c4592f717e54
ffff800085b13ee0:  0000000000000001 0000000000000000
ffff800085b13ef0:  0000000000000104 0000000000000000
ffff800085b13f00:  0000c4592f70c000 0000000000000000
ffff800085b13f10:  0000000000000001 0000000000000000
ffff800085b13f20:  0000000000000001 0000000000000005
ffff800085b13f30:  0000c4592f70ba48 0000f4897a376750
ffff800085b13f40:  0000000000000000 000000000000000a
ffff800085b13f50:  ffffffffffffffff 0000c4592f717000
ffff800085b13f60:  0000c4592f715140 0000f4897a4e47e0
ffff800085b13f70:  0000c4592f70c000 0000c4592f715e5c
ffff800085b13f80:  0000c4592f70d464 000000000000000a
ffff800085b13f90:  0000000000000000 0000fffff1ca8380
ffff800085b13fa0:  0000c4592f6b548c 0000fffff1ca8380
ffff800085b13fb0:  0000f4897a3767b8 0000000060001000
ffff800085b13fc0:  ffffffffffffffff 0000000000000104
ffff800085b13fd0:  0000000000000000 0000000000000000
ffff800085b13fe0:  0000000000000000 0000000000000000
ffff800085b13ff0:  0000000000000000 0000000000000000

crash> bt -f
PID: 1115     TASK: ffff0000c483c400  CPU: 1    COMMAND: "bash"
 #0 [ffff800085b139a0] __switch_to at ffff8000815e7e1c
    ffff800085b139a0: ffff800085b139c0 ffff8000815e816c
    ffff800085b139b0: ffff0002fe7bab80 ffff0000c483c400
 #1 [ffff800085b139c0] __schedule at ffff8000815e8168
    ffff800085b139c0: ffff800085b13a60 ffff8000815e8630
    ffff800085b139d0: ffff0000c483c400 ffff0000c483c400
    ffff800085b139e0: 0000000000000001 ffff800085b13b28
    ffff800085b139f0: 0000000000000000 0000000000000000
    ffff800085b13a00: 0000000000000000 0000000000000000
    ffff800085b13a10: 0000000000000000 ffff800085b13b00
    ffff800085b13a20: ffff0000c483c400 ffff0000c483c400
    ffff800085b13a30: ffff800085b13a98 ffff800000000004
    ffff800085b13a40: ffff80008162c9d8 0000000000000000
    ffff800085b13a50: 0000000000000002 3fbe42f52288d100
 #2 [ffff800085b13a60] schedule at ffff8000815e862c
    ffff800085b13a60: ffff800085b13a90 ffff8000800d195c
    ffff800085b13a70: ffff0000c483c400 ffff800085b13b00
    ffff800085b13a80: 0000000000000000 0000000000000000
 #3 [ffff800085b13a90] do_wait at ffff8000800d1958
    ffff800085b13a90: ffff800085b13ac0 ffff8000800d2438
    ffff800085b13aa0: 000000000000000e 0000fffff1ca8450
    ffff800085b13ab0: 0000000000000004 0000000000000000
 #4 [ffff800085b13ac0] kernel_wait4 at ffff8000800d2434
    ffff800085b13ac0: ffff800085b13b60 ffff8000800d261c
    ffff800085b13ad0: ffff800085b13eb0 ffff80027bf15000
    ffff800085b13ae0: ffff0000c483c400 0000f4897a3767b8
    ffff800085b13af0: 0000000060001000 0000000000000215
    ffff800085b13b00: 0000000e00000004 0000000000000000
    ffff800085b13b10: 0000000000000000 ffff800000000000
    ffff800085b13b20: 0000000000000000 0000f48900000000
    ffff800085b13b30: ffff0000c483c400 ffff8000800ce820
    ffff800085b13b40: ffff0000c6549b28 ffff0000c6549b28
    ffff800085b13b50: 0000000000000000 3fbe42f52288d100
 #5 [ffff800085b13b60] __do_sys_wait4 at ffff8000800d2618
    ffff800085b13b60: ffff800085b13c20 ffff8000800d266c
```

```
    ffff800085b13b70: ffff800085b13eb0 ffff80027bf15000
    ffff800085b13b80: 000000009600004f ffff800085b13c40
    ffff800085b13b90: 0000f4897a4e47c8 ffff80008161b168
    ffff800085b13ba0: 0000000080400005 ffff800085b13eb0
    ffff800085b13bb0: ffff0000c483c400 0000000000000000
    ffff800085b13bc0: 0000000000000000 0000f4897a3767b8
    ffff800085b13bd0: ffff800085b13c00 ffff8000815dbdc4
    ffff800085b13be0: ffff800085b13c40 000000009600004f
    ffff800085b13bf0: ffff800085b13c00 ffff8000815dbdd4
    ffff800085b13c00: ffff800085b13c30 ffff8000815ddd90
    ffff800085b13c10: 0000f4897a4e47c8 3fbe42f52288d100
 #6 [ffff800085b13c20] __arm64_sys_wait4 at ffff8000800d2668
    ffff800085b13c20: ffff800085b13e10 ffff8000800313c0
    ffff800085b13c30: ffff800085b13d70 ffff800080011314
    ffff800085b13c40: 0000000000000000 0000000000000000
    ffff800085b13c50: 0000000000000000 0000000000000000
    ffff800085b13c60: 0000000000000000 0000000000000000
    ffff800085b13c70: 0000000000000000 0000000000000000
    ffff800085b13c80: 0000000000000000 ffff8000803bbc9c
    ffff800085b13c90: 0000000000000000 0000000000000000
    ffff800085b13ca0: 0000000000000000 0000000000000000
    ffff800085b13cb0: 0000000000000000 0000000000000000
    ffff800085b13cc0: 0000000000000000 0000000000000000
    ffff800085b13cd0: 0000000000000000 0000f4897a4e47c8
    ffff800085b13ce0: 0000000000000000 0000000000000000
    ffff800085b13cf0: 0000f4897a3767b8 0000000060001000
    ffff800085b13d00: ffff800085b13eb0 ffff0000c483c400
    ffff800085b13d10: 0000000000000000 0000000000000000
    ffff800085b13d20: ffff0000c483c400 ffff800085b13d90
    ffff800085b13d30: ffff8000803baf1c ffff800085b13d90
    ffff800085b13d40: ffff8000803baf1c 0000000080400005
    ffff800085b13d50: ffff800085b13d80 ffff80008043b45c
    ffff800085b13d60: ffff800085b13db0 ffff8000803bbc40
    ffff800085b13d70: 000000000000000c ffff0000c483c400
    ffff800085b13d80: 0000000000000000 0000f4897a3767b8
    ffff800085b13d90: 0000000060001000 ffff800085b13eb0
    ffff800085b13da0: ffff0000c483c400 0000000000000000
    ffff800085b13db0: ffff800085b13e50 ffff8000800251a0
    ffff800085b13dc0: 000000000000000c ffff0000c483c400
    ffff800085b13dd0: ffff800085b13eb0 0000000000000041
    ffff800085b13de0: 0000000060001000 0000000000000000
    ffff800085b13df0: 0000000000000000 0000000000000000
    ffff800085b13e00: ffff800085b13eb0 0000000000000041
 #7 [ffff800085b13e10] invoke_syscall at ffff8000800313bc
    ffff800085b13e10: ffff800085b13e40 ffff8000800314b8
    ffff800085b13e20: ffff800085b13eb0 ffff80027bf15000
    ffff800085b13e30: ffff0000c483c400 ffff800080019f88
 #8 [ffff800085b13e40] el0_svc_common.constprop.0 at ffff8000800314b4
    ffff800085b13e40: ffff800085b13e70 ffff8000800315d0
    ffff800085b13e50: ffff800085b13eb0 ffff80027bf15000
    ffff800085b13e60: 00000000ffffffff ffff80027bedf000
 #9 [ffff800085b13e70] do_el0_svc at ffff8000800315cc
    ffff800085b13e70: ffff800085b13e80 ffff8000815dd9e8
#10 [ffff800085b13e80] el0_svc at ffff8000815dd9e4
    ffff800085b13e80: ffff800085b13ea0 ffff8000815ddffc
    ffff800085b13e90: 0000000000000000 ffff8000815de028
#11 [ffff800085b13ea0] el0t_64_sync_handler at ffff8000815ddff8
    ffff800085b13ea0: ffff800085b13fe0 ffff800080011640
    ffff800085b13eb0: ffffffffffffffff 0000fffff1ca8450
    ffff800085b13ec0: 000000000000000a 0000000000000000
```

```
    ffff800085b13ed0: 0000f4897a4e4020 0000c4592f717e54
    ffff800085b13ee0: 0000000000000001 0000000000000000
    ffff800085b13ef0: 0000000000000104 0000000000000000
    ffff800085b13f00: 0000c4592f70c000 0000000000000000
    ffff800085b13f10: 0000000000000001 0000000000000000
    ffff800085b13f20: 0000000000000001 0000000000000005
    ffff800085b13f30: 0000c4592f70ba48 0000f4897a376750
    ffff800085b13f40: 0000000000000000 000000000000000a
    ffff800085b13f50: ffffffffffffffff 0000c4592f717000
    ffff800085b13f60: 0000c4592f715140 0000f4897a4e47e0
    ffff800085b13f70: 0000c4592f70c000 0000c4592f715e5c
    ffff800085b13f80: 0000c4592f70d464 000000000000000a
    ffff800085b13f90: 0000000000000000 0000fffff1ca8380
    ffff800085b13fa0: 0000c4592f6b548c 0000fffff1ca8380
    ffff800085b13fb0: 0000f4897a3767b8 0000000060001000
    ffff800085b13fc0: ffffffffffffffff 0000000000000104
    ffff800085b13fd0: 0000000000000000 0000000000000000
#12 [ffff800085b13fe0] el0t_64_sync at ffff80008001163c
     PC: 0000f4897a3767b8   LR: 0000c4592f6b548c   SP: 0000fffff1ca8380
    X29: 0000fffff1ca8380  X28: 0000000000000000  X27: 000000000000000a
    X26: 0000c4592f70d464  X25: 0000c4592f715e5c  X24: 0000c4592f70c000
    X23: 0000f4897a4e47e0  X22: 0000c4592f715140  X21: 0000c4592f717000
    X20: ffffffffffffffff  X19: 000000000000000a  X18: 0000000000000000
    X17: 0000f4897a376750  X16: 0000c4592f70ba48  X15: 0000000000000005
    X14: 0000000000000001  X13: 0000000000000000  X12: 0000000000000001
    X11: 0000000000000000  X10: 0000c4592f70c000   X9: 0000000000000000
     X8: 0000000000000104   X7: 0000000000000000   X6: 0000000000000001
     X5: 0000c4592f717e54   X4: 0000f4897a4e4020   X3: 0000000000000000
     X2: 000000000000000a   X1: 0000fffff1ca8450   X0: ffffffffffffffff
    ORIG_X0: ffffffffffffffff  SYSCALLNO: 104  PSTATE: 60001000
```

11. Show virtual memory layout for the current process context:

```
crash> vm
PID: 1115     TASK: ffff0000c483c400  CPU: 1    COMMAND: "bash"
       MM               PGD          RSS    TOTAL_VM
ffff0000c42f1900  ffff0000c5a44000  4860k    8720k
      VMA           START         END     FLAGS FILE
ffff0000c83f3c00 c4592f5b0000 c4592f6f9000     75 /usr/bin/bash
ffff0000c83f3f00 c4592f708000 c4592f70d000 100071 /usr/bin/bash
ffff0000c48df540 c4592f70d000 c4592f716000 100073 /usr/bin/bash
ffff0000c83f3180 c4592f716000 c4592f721000 200100073
ffff0000c83b46c0 c45952d7f000 c45952f0f000 200100073
ffff0000c48dfe40 f48979e00000 f4897a0e9000     71 /usr/lib/locale/locale-archive
ffff0000c839ac00 f4897a269000 f4897a2c0000     71 /usr/lib/locale/C.utf8/LC_CTYPE
ffff0000c48df900 f4897a2c0000 f4897a448000     75 /usr/lib/aarch64-linux-gnu/libc.so.6
ffff0000c48df180 f4897a448000 f4897a457000     70 /usr/lib/aarch64-linux-gnu/libc.so.6
ffff0000c48df300 f4897a457000 f4897a45b000 100071 /usr/lib/aarch64-linux-gnu/libc.so.6
ffff0000c48df000 f4897a45b000 f4897a45d000 100073 /usr/lib/aarch64-linux-gnu/libc.so.6
ffff0000c48df3c0 f4897a45d000 f4897a469000 100073
ffff0000c839a600 f4897a46e000 f4897a46f000     71 /usr/lib/locale/C.utf8/LC_NUMERIC
ffff0000c839a240 f4897a46f000 f4897a470000     71 /usr/lib/locale/C.utf8/LC_TIME
ffff0000c83f36c0 f4897a470000 f4897a49c000     75 /usr/lib/aarch64-linux-gnu/libtinfo.so.6.3
ffff0000c83f3cc0 f4897a49c000 f4897a4ab000     70 /usr/lib/aarch64-linux-gnu/libtinfo.so.6.3
ffff0000c83f3e40 f4897a4ab000 f4897a4af000 100071 /usr/lib/aarch64-linux-gnu/libtinfo.so.6.3
ffff0000c48df0c0 f4897a4af000 f4897a4b0000 100073 /usr/lib/aarch64-linux-gnu/libtinfo.so.6.3
ffff0000c839a840 f4897a4b0000 f4897a4b1000     71 /usr/lib/locale/C.utf8/LC_COLLATE
ffff0000c48df6c0 f4897a4b1000 f4897a4b8000     d1 /usr/lib/aarch64-linux-gnu/gconv/gconv-modules.cache
ffff0000c83f3780 f4897a4b8000 f4897a4e3000     75 /usr/lib/aarch64-linux-gnu/ld-linux-aarch64.so.1
ffff0000c839acc0 f4897a4e3000 f4897a4e4000     71 /usr/lib/locale/C.utf8/LC_MONETARY
ffff0000c48dfd80 f4897a4e4000 f4897a4e6000 100073
ffff0000c48dff00 f4897a4e6000 f4897a4e7000     71 /usr/lib/locale/C.utf8/LC_MESSAGES/SYS_LC_MESSAGES
ffff0000c48dfc00 f4897a4e7000 f4897a4e8000     71 /usr/lib/locale/C.utf8/LC_PAPER
```

```
ffff0000c48df600 f4897a4e8000 f4897a4e9000      71 /usr/lib/locale/C.utf8/LC_NAME
ffff0000c48df240 f4897a4e9000 f4897a4ea000      71 /usr/lib/locale/C.utf8/LC_ADDRESS
ffff0000c48df840 f4897a4ea000 f4897a4eb000      71 /usr/lib/locale/C.utf8/LC_TELEPHONE
ffff0000c48dfcc0 f4897a4eb000 f4897a4ec000      71 /usr/lib/locale/C.utf8/LC_MEASUREMENT
ffff0000c48df9c0 f4897a4ec000 f4897a4ed000      71 /usr/lib/locale/C.utf8/LC_IDENTIFICATION
ffff0000c83f3d80 f4897a4ed000 f4897a4ef000 100073
ffff0000c83f3300 f4897a4ef000 f4897a4f1000  40411
ffff0000c83f33c0 f4897a4f1000 f4897a4f2000  40075
ffff0000c83f3480 f4897a4f2000 f4897a4f4000 100071 /usr/lib/aarch64-linux-gnu/ld-linux-aarch64.so.1
ffff0000c48dfa80 f4897a4f4000 f4897a4f6000 100073 /usr/lib/aarch64-linux-gnu/ld-linux-aarch64.so.1
ffff0000c5956300 fffff1c89000 fffff1caa000 200100173
```

12. List opened files for the current process context:

```
crash> files
PID: 1115     TASK: ffff0000c483c400  CPU: 1    COMMAND: "bash"
ROOT: /    CWD: /home/ubuntu
 FD       FILE            DENTRY           INODE       TYPE PATH
  0 ffff0000c82db600 ffff0000c3072b40 ffff0000c32d3180 CHR  /dev/pts/0
  1 ffff0000c82db600 ffff0000c3072b40 ffff0000c32d3180 CHR  /dev/pts/0
  2 ffff0000c82db600 ffff0000c3072b40 ffff0000c32d3180 CHR  /dev/pts/0
255 ffff0000c82db600 ffff0000c3072b40 ffff0000c32d3180 CHR  /dev/pts/0
```

13. Dump memory contents as pointers without and with symbolic information:

```
crash> bt
PID: 1115     TASK: ffff0000c483c400  CPU: 1    COMMAND: "bash"
 #0 [ffff800085b139a0] __switch_to at ffff8000815e7e1c
 #1 [ffff800085b139c0] __schedule at ffff8000815e8168
 #2 [ffff800085b13a60] schedule at ffff8000815e862c
 #3 [ffff800085b13a90] do_wait at ffff8000800d1958
 #4 [ffff800085b13ac0] kernel_wait4 at ffff8000800d2434
 #5 [ffff800085b13b60] __do_sys_wait4 at ffff8000800d2618
 #6 [ffff800085b13c20] __arm64_sys_wait4 at ffff8000800d2668
 #7 [ffff800085b13e10] invoke_syscall at ffff8000800313bc
 #8 [ffff800085b13e40] el0_svc_common.constprop.0 at ffff8000800314b4
 #9 [ffff800085b13e70] do_el0_svc at ffff8000800315cc
#10 [ffff800085b13e80] el0_svc at ffff8000815dd9e4
#11 [ffff800085b13ea0] el0t_64_sync_handler at ffff8000815ddff8
#12 [ffff800085b13fe0] el0t_64_sync at ffff80008001163c
     PC: 0000f4897a3767b8   LR: 0000c4592f6b548c   SP: 0000fffff1ca8380
    X29: 0000fffff1ca8380  X28: 0000000000000000  X27: 000000000000000a
    X26: 0000c4592f70d464  X25: 0000c4592f715e5c  X24: 0000c4592f70c000
    X23: 0000f4897a4e47e0  X22: 0000c4592f715140  X21: 0000c4592f717000
    X20: ffffffffffffffff  X19: 000000000000000a  X18: 0000000000000000
    X17: 0000f4897a376750  X16: 0000c4592f70ba48  X15: 0000000000000005
    X14: 0000000000000001  X13: 0000000000000000  X12: 0000000000000001
    X11: 0000000000000000  X10: 0000c4592f70c000   X9: 0000000000000000
     X8: 0000000000000104   X7: 0000000000000000   X6: 0000000000000001
     X5: 0000c4592f717e54   X4: 0000f4897a4e4020   X3: 0000000000000000
     X2: 000000000000000a   X1: 0000fffff1ca8450   X0: ffffffffffffffff
    ORIG_X0: ffffffffffffffff  SYSCALLNO: 104  PSTATE: 60001000

crash> rd -64 ffff800085b139c0 50
ffff800085b139c0:  ffff800085b13a60 ffff8000815e8630   `:......0.^.....
ffff800085b139d0:  ffff0000c483c400 ffff0000c483c400   ................
ffff800085b139e0:  0000000000000001 ffff800085b13b28   ........(;......
ffff800085b139f0:  0000000000000000 0000000000000000   ................
ffff800085b13a00:  0000000000000000 0000000000000000   ................
ffff800085b13a10:  0000000000000000 ffff800085b13b00   .........;......
```

```
ffff800085b13a20:  ffff0000c483c400 ffff0000c483c400   ................
ffff800085b13a30:  ffff800085b13a98 ffff800000000004   .:..............
ffff800085b13a40:  ffff80008162c9d8 0000000000000000   ..b.............
ffff800085b13a50:  0000000000000002 3fbe42f52288d100   ..........".B.?
ffff800085b13a60:  ffff800085b13a90 ffff8000800d195c   .:......\.......
ffff800085b13a70:  ffff0000c483c400 ffff800085b13b00   .........;......
ffff800085b13a80:  0000000000000000 0000000000000000   ................
ffff800085b13a90:  ffff800085b13ac0 ffff8000800d2438   .:......8$......
ffff800085b13aa0:  000000000000000e 0000ffffff1ca8450   ........P.......
ffff800085b13ab0:  0000000000000004 0000000000000000   ................
ffff800085b13ac0:  ffff800085b13b60 ffff8000800d261c   `;......&.......
ffff800085b13ad0:  ffff800085b13eb0 ffff80027bf15000   .>......P.{....
ffff800085b13ae0:  ffff0000c483c400 0000f4897a3767b8   .........g7z....
ffff800085b13af0:  0000000060001000 0000000000000215   ...`............
ffff800085b13b00:  0000000e00000004 0000000000000000   ................
ffff800085b13b10:  0000000000000000 ffff800000000000   ................
ffff800085b13b20:  0000000000000000 0000f48900000000   ................
ffff800085b13b30:  ffff0000c483c400 ffff8000800ce820   ........ .......
ffff800085b13b40:  ffff0000c6549b28 ffff0000c6549b28   (.T.....(.T.....
```

```
crash> rd -SS -64 ffff800085b139c0 50
ffff800085b139c0:  ffff800085b13a60 schedule+48
ffff800085b139d0:  [ffff0000c483c400:task_struct] [ffff0000c483c400:task_struct]
ffff800085b139e0:  0000000000000001 ffff800085b13b28
ffff800085b139f0:  0000000000000000 0000000000000000
ffff800085b13a00:  0000000000000000 0000000000000000
ffff800085b13a10:  0000000000000000 ffff800085b13b00
ffff800085b13a20:  [ffff0000c483c400:task_struct] [ffff0000c483c400:task_struct]
ffff800085b13a30:  ffff800085b13a98 ffff800000000004
ffff800085b13a40:  cpu_bit_bitmap+128 0000000000000000
ffff800085b13a50:  0000000000000002 3fbe42f52288d100
ffff800085b13a60:  ffff800085b13a90 do_wait+204
ffff800085b13a70:  [ffff0000c483c400:task_struct] ffff800085b13b00
ffff800085b13a80:  0000000000000000 0000000000000000
ffff800085b13a90:  ffff800085b13ac0 kernel_wait4+152
ffff800085b13aa0:  000000000000000e 0000ffffff1ca8450
ffff800085b13ab0:  0000000000000004 0000000000000000
ffff800085b13ac0:  ffff800085b13b60 __do_sys_wait4+220
ffff800085b13ad0:  ffff800085b13eb0 ffff80027bf15000
ffff800085b13ae0:  [ffff0000c483c400:task_struct] 0000f4897a3767b8
ffff800085b13af0:  0000000060001000 0000000000000215
ffff800085b13b00:  0000000e00000004 0000000000000000
ffff800085b13b10:  0000000000000000 ffff800000000000
ffff800085b13b20:  0000000000000000 0000f48900000000
ffff800085b13b30:  [ffff0000c483c400:task_struct] child_wait_callback
ffff800085b13b40:  [ffff0000c6549b28:signal_cache] [ffff0000c6549b28:signal_cache]
```

14. Verify the return address by disassembly:

```
crash> bt
PID: 1115     TASK: ffff0000c483c400  CPU: 1    COMMAND: "bash"
 #0 [ffff800085b139a0] __switch_to at ffff8000815e7e1c
 #1 [ffff800085b139c0] __schedule at ffff8000815e8168
 #2 [ffff800085b13a60] schedule at ffff8000815e862c
 #3 [ffff800085b13a90] do_wait at ffff8000800d1958
 #4 [ffff800085b13ac0] kernel_wait4 at ffff8000800d2434
 #5 [ffff800085b13b60] __do_sys_wait4 at ffff8000800d2618
 #6 [ffff800085b13c20] __arm64_sys_wait4 at ffff8000800d2668
 #7 [ffff800085b13e10] invoke_syscall at ffff8000800313bc
 #8 [ffff800085b13e40] el0_svc_common.constprop.0 at ffff8000800314b4
```

```
 #9 [ffff800085b13e70] do_el0_svc at ffff8000800315cc
#10 [ffff800085b13e80] el0_svc at ffff8000815dd9e4
#11 [ffff800085b13ea0] el0t_64_sync_handler at ffff8000815ddff8
#12 [ffff800085b13fe0] el0t_64_sync at ffff80008001163c
     PC: 0000f4897a3767b8   LR: 0000c4592f6b548c   SP: 0000fffff1ca8380
    X29: 0000fffff1ca8380  X28: 0000000000000000  X27: 000000000000000a
    X26: 0000c4592f70d464  X25: 0000c4592f715e5c  X24: 0000c4592f70c000
    X23: 0000f4897a4e47e0  X22: 0000c4592f715140  X21: 0000c4592f717000
    X20: ffffffffffffffff  X19: 000000000000000a  X18: 0000000000000000
    X17: 0000f4897a376750  X16: 0000c4592f70ba48  X15: 0000000000000005
    X14: 0000000000000001  X13: 0000000000000000  X12: 0000000000000001
    X11: 0000000000000000  X10: 0000c4592f70c000   X9: 0000000000000000
     X8: 0000000000000104   X7: 0000000000000000   X6: 0000000000000001
     X5: 0000c4592f717e54   X4: 0000f4897a4e4020   X3: 0000000000000000
     X2: 000000000000000a   X1: 0000fffff1ca8450   X0: ffffffffffffffff
    ORIG_X0: ffffffffffffffff  SYSCALLNO: 104  PSTATE: 60001000
```

```
crash> dis schedule
0xffff8000815e8600 <schedule>:  mov     x9, x30
0xffff8000815e8604 <schedule+4>:        nop
0xffff8000815e8608 <schedule+8>:        paciasp
0xffff8000815e860c <schedule+12>:       stp     x29, x30, [sp, #-48]!
0xffff8000815e8610 <schedule+16>:       mov     x29, sp
0xffff8000815e8614 <schedule+20>:       stp     x19, x20, [sp, #16]
0xffff8000815e8618 <schedule+24>:       mrs     x19, sp_el0
0xffff8000815e861c <schedule+28>:       ldr     w0, [x19, #32]
0xffff8000815e8620 <schedule+32>:       cbnz    w0, 0xffff8000815e8670 <schedule+112>
0xffff8000815e8624 <schedule+36>:       mrs     x20, sp_el0
0xffff8000815e8628 <schedule+40>:       mov     w0, #0x0                        // #0
0xffff8000815e862c <schedule+44>:       bl      0xffff8000815e7ed8 <__schedule>
0xffff8000815e8630 <schedule+48>:       ldr     x0, [x20]
0xffff8000815e8634 <schedule+52>:       tbnz    w0, #1, 0xffff8000815e8628 <schedule+40>
0xffff8000815e8638 <schedule+56>:       ldr     w0, [x19, #52]
0xffff8000815e863c <schedule+60>:       tst     w0, #0x30
0xffff8000815e8640 <schedule+64>:       b.eq    0xffff8000815e8650 <schedule+80>  // b.none
0xffff8000815e8644 <schedule+68>:       tbz     w0, #5, 0xffff8000815e869c <schedule+156>
0xffff8000815e8648 <schedule+72>:       mov     x0, x19
0xffff8000815e864c <schedule+76>:       bl      0xffff8000800fc080 <wq_worker_running>
0xffff8000815e8650 <schedule+80>:       ldp     x19, x20, [sp, #16]
0xffff8000815e8654 <schedule+84>:       ldp     x29, x30, [sp], #48
0xffff8000815e8658 <schedule+88>:       autiasp
0xffff8000815e865c <schedule+92>:       mov     x0, #0x0                        // #0
0xffff8000815e8660 <schedule+96>:       mov     x1, #0x0                        // #0
0xffff8000815e8664 <schedule+100>:      mov     x16, #0x0                       // #0
0xffff8000815e8668 <schedule+104>:      mov     x17, #0x0                       // #0
0xffff8000815e866c <schedule+108>:      ret
0xffff8000815e8670 <schedule+112>:      ldr     w0, [x19, #52]
0xffff8000815e8674 <schedule+116>:      tbnz    w0, #5, 0xffff8000815e86d0 <schedule+208>
0xffff8000815e8678 <schedule+120>:      tbnz    w0, #4, 0xffff8000815e86c4 <schedule+196>
0xffff8000815e867c <schedule+124>:      mrs     x0, sp_el0
0xffff8000815e8680 <schedule+128>:      ldr     w0, [x0, #32]
0xffff8000815e8684 <schedule+132>:      tbnz    w0, #12, 0xffff8000815e86dc <schedule+220>
0xffff8000815e8688 <schedule+136>:      ldr     x0, [x19, #2352]
0xffff8000815e868c <schedule+140>:      cbz     x0, 0xffff8000815e8624 <schedule+36>
0xffff8000815e8690 <schedule+144>:      mov     w1, #0x1                        // #1
0xffff8000815e8694 <schedule+148>:      bl      0xffff80008084b378 <__blk_flush_plug>
0xffff8000815e8698 <schedule+152>:      b       0xffff8000815e8624 <schedule+36>
0xffff8000815e869c <schedule+156>:      mov     x0, x19
0xffff8000815e86a0 <schedule+160>:      bl      0xffff8000808d95b8 <io_wq_worker_running>
0xffff8000815e86a4 <schedule+164>:      ldp     x19, x20, [sp, #16]
0xffff8000815e86a8 <schedule+168>:      ldp     x29, x30, [sp], #48
0xffff8000815e86ac <schedule+172>:      autiasp
0xffff8000815e86b0 <schedule+176>:      mov     x0, #0x0                        // #0
0xffff8000815e86b4 <schedule+180>:      mov     x1, #0x0                        // #0
0xffff8000815e86b8 <schedule+184>:      mov     x16, #0x0                       // #0
0xffff8000815e86bc <schedule+188>:      mov     x17, #0x0                       // #0
0xffff8000815e86c0 <schedule+192>:      ret
0xffff8000815e86c4 <schedule+196>:      mov     x0, x19
0xffff8000815e86c8 <schedule+200>:      bl      0xffff8000808d96d0 <io_wq_worker_sleeping>
0xffff8000815e86cc <schedule+204>:      b       0xffff8000815e867c <schedule+124>
0xffff8000815e86d0 <schedule+208>:      mov     x0, x19
```

```
0xffff8000815e86d4 <schedule+212>:      bl      0xffff8000800fc100 <wq_worker_sleeping>
0xffff8000815e86d8 <schedule+216>:      b       0xffff8000815e867c <schedule+124>
0xffff8000815e86dc <schedule+220>:      adrp    x20, 0xffff8000836c6000 <event_class_netlink_extack+8>
0xffff8000815e86e0 <schedule+224>:      add     x20, x20, #0x7f2
0xffff8000815e86e4 <schedule+228>:      str     x21, [sp, #32]
0xffff8000815e86e8 <schedule+232>:      ldrb    w21, [x20, #9]
0xffff8000815e86ec <schedule+236>:      cmp     w21, #0x1
0xffff8000815e86f0 <schedule+240>:      b.hi    0xffff8000815e8720 <schedule+288>  // b.pmore
0xffff8000815e86f4 <schedule+244>:      tbz     w21, #0, 0xffff8000815e8700 <schedule+256>
0xffff8000815e86f8 <schedule+248>:      ldr     x21, [sp, #32]
0xffff8000815e86fc <schedule+252>:      b       0xffff8000815e8688 <schedule+136>
0xffff8000815e8700 <schedule+256>:      mov     w1, #0x1                        // #1
0xffff8000815e8704 <schedule+260>:      adrp    x0, 0xffff800081c8e000
0xffff8000815e8708 <schedule+264>:      add     x0, x0, #0xf38
0xffff8000815e870c <schedule+268>:      strb    w1, [x20, #9]
0xffff8000815e8710 <schedule+272>:      bl      0xffff8000800c7e60 <__warn_printk>
0xffff8000815e8714 <schedule+276>:      brk     #0x800
0xffff8000815e8718 <schedule+280>:      ldr     x21, [sp, #32]
0xffff8000815e871c <schedule+284>:      b       0xffff8000815e8688 <schedule+136>
0xffff8000815e8720 <schedule+288>:      adrp    x0, 0xffff800083261000 <event_enter__setgroups+40>
0xffff8000815e8724 <schedule+292>:      add     x0, x0, #0x270
0xffff8000815e8728 <schedule+296>:      add     x0, x0, #0xda8
0xffff8000815e872c <schedule+300>:      and     x1, x21, #0xff
0xffff8000815e8730 <schedule+304>:      bl      0xffff8000809b9920 <__ubsan_handle_load_invalid_value>
0xffff8000815e8734 <schedule+308>:      b       0xffff8000815e86f4 <schedule+244>
```

Note: To emulate backward disassembly similar to the **ub** WinDbg command, use the **-r** flag:

```
crash> dis -r 0xffff8000815e862c
0xffff8000815e8600 <schedule>:  mov     x9, x30
0xffff8000815e8604 <schedule+4>:        nop
0xffff8000815e8608 <schedule+8>:        paciasp
0xffff8000815e860c <schedule+12>:       stp     x29, x30, [sp, #-48]!
0xffff8000815e8610 <schedule+16>:       mov     x29, sp
0xffff8000815e8614 <schedule+20>:       stp     x19, x20, [sp, #16]
0xffff8000815e8618 <schedule+24>:       mrs     x19, sp_el0
0xffff8000815e861c <schedule+28>:       ldr     w0, [x19, #32]
0xffff8000815e8620 <schedule+32>:       cbnz    w0, 0xffff8000815e8670 <schedule+112>
0xffff8000815e8624 <schedule+36>:       mrs     x20, sp_el0
0xffff8000815e8628 <schedule+40>:       mov     w0, #0x0                        // #0
0xffff8000815e862c <schedule+44>:       bl      0xffff8000815e7ed8 <__schedule>
```

15. Finally, we can see the backtrace of every PID/TID (task) in the system:

```
crash> foreach bt
PID: 0        TASK: ffff800083239ac0  CPU: 0    COMMAND: "swapper/0"
 #0 [ffff800083223cf0] __switch_to at ffff8000815e7e1c
 #1 [ffff800083223d10] __schedule at ffff8000815e8168
 #2 [ffff800083223db0] schedule_idle at ffff8000815e8b8c
 #3 [ffff800083223dd0] do_idle at ffff80008014fa8c
 #4 [ffff800083223e00] cpu_startup_entry at ffff80008014fd08
 #5 [ffff800083223e20] rest_init at ffff8000815e0f94
 #6 [ffff800083223e50] arch_call_rest_init at ffff8000825f17e4
 #7 [ffff800083223e60] start_kernel at ffff8000825f1bb8

PID: 0        TASK: ffff0000c0582200  CPU: 1    COMMAND: "swapper/1"
 #0 [ffff80008000bd10] crash_save_cpu at ffff80008020ba9c
 #1 [ffff80008000bed0] ipi_cpu_crash_stop at ffff80008002ee0c
 #2 [ffff80008000bef0] do_handle_IPI at ffff80008002f2ec
 #3 [ffff80008000bf40] ipi_handler at ffff80008002f498
 #4 [ffff80008000bf50] handle_percpu_devid_irq at ffff800080190c94
 #5 [ffff80008000bfa0] generic_handle_domain_irq at ffff800080185408
 #6 [ffff80008000bfb0] __gic_handle_irq_from_irqson at ffff8000809c834c
 #7 [ffff80008000bfe0] gic_handle_irq at ffff8000800102b0
```

```
--- <IRQ stack> ---
 #8 [ffff800083953c30] call_on_irq_stack at ffff800080017460
 #9 [ffff800083953c40] do_interrupt_handler at ffff80008001ae6c
#10 [ffff800083953c60] el1_interrupt at ffff8000815dc178
#11 [ffff800083953c80] el1h_64_irq_handler at ffff8000815dddd4
#12 [ffff800083953dc0] el1h_64_irq at ffff800080011390
#13 [ffff800083953de0] default_idle_call at ffff8000815e0b18
#14 [ffff800083953e00] cpuidle_idle_call at ffff80008014f950
#15 [ffff800083953e40] do_idle at ffff80008014fa68
#16 [ffff800083953e70] cpu_startup_entry at ffff80008014fd0c
#17 [ffff800083953e90] secondary_start_kernel at ffff80008002f7bc

PID: 1      TASK: ffff0000c03bc400  CPU: 1    COMMAND: "systemd"
 #0 [ffff80008387b8d0] __switch_to at ffff8000815e7e1c
 #1 [ffff80008387b8f0] __schedule at ffff8000815e8168
 #2 [ffff80008387b990] schedule at ffff8000815e862c
 #3 [ffff80008387b9c0] schedule_hrtimeout_range_clock at ffff8000815f16f0
 #4 [ffff80008387ba40] schedule_hrtimeout_range at ffff8000815f1728
 #5 [ffff80008387ba50] ep_poll at ffff800080597910
 #6 [ffff80008387bb00] do_epoll_wait at ffff800080597b94
 #7 [ffff80008387bb40] do_epoll_pwait at ffff800080597d00
 #8 [ffff80008387bb60] __arm64_sys_epoll_pwait at ffff800080598174
 #9 [ffff80008387be10] invoke_syscall at ffff8000800313bc
#10 [ffff80008387be40] el0_svc_common.constprop.0 at ffff8000800314b4
#11 [ffff80008387be70] do_el0_svc at ffff8000800315cc
#12 [ffff80008387be80] el0_svc at ffff8000815dd9e4
crash> foreach bt
PID: 0      TASK: ffff800083239ac0  CPU: 0    COMMAND: "swapper/0"
 #0 [ffff800083223cf0] __switch_to at ffff8000815e7e1c
 #1 [ffff800083223d10] __schedule at ffff8000815e8168
 #2 [ffff800083223db0] schedule_idle at ffff8000815e8b8c
 #3 [ffff800083223dd0] do_idle at ffff80008014fa8c
 #4 [ffff800083223e00] cpu_startup_entry at ffff80008014fd08
 #5 [ffff800083223e20] rest_init at ffff8000815e0f94
 #6 [ffff800083223e50] arch_call_rest_init at ffff8000825f17e4
 #7 [ffff800083223e60] start_kernel at ffff8000825f1bb8

PID: 0      TASK: ffff0000c0582200  CPU: 1    COMMAND: "swapper/1"
 #0 [ffff80008000bd10] crash_save_cpu at ffff80008020ba9c
 #1 [ffff80008000bed0] ipi_cpu_crash_stop at ffff80008002ee0c
 #2 [ffff80008000bef0] do_handle_IPI at ffff80008002f2ec
 #3 [ffff80008000bf40] ipi_handler at ffff80008002f498
 #4 [ffff80008000bf50] handle_percpu_devid_irq at ffff800080190c94
 #5 [ffff80008000bfa0] generic_handle_domain_irq at ffff800080185408
 #6 [ffff80008000bfb0] __gic_handle_irq_from_irqson at ffff8000809c834c
 #7 [ffff80008000bfe0] gic_handle_irq at ffff8000800102b0
--- <IRQ stack> ---
 #8 [ffff800083953c30] call_on_irq_stack at ffff800080017460
 #9 [ffff800083953c40] do_interrupt_handler at ffff80008001ae6c
#10 [ffff800083953c60] el1_interrupt at ffff8000815dc178
#11 [ffff800083953c80] el1h_64_irq_handler at ffff8000815dddd4
#12 [ffff800083953dc0] el1h_64_irq at ffff800080011390
#13 [ffff800083953de0] default_idle_call at ffff8000815e0b18
#14 [ffff800083953e00] cpuidle_idle_call at ffff80008014f950
#15 [ffff800083953e40] do_idle at ffff80008014fa68
#16 [ffff800083953e70] cpu_startup_entry at ffff80008014fd0c
#17 [ffff800083953e90] secondary_start_kernel at ffff80008002f7bc

PID: 1      TASK: ffff0000c03bc400  CPU: 1    COMMAND: "systemd"
 #0 [ffff80008387b8d0] __switch_to at ffff8000815e7e1c
```

```
 #1 [ffff80008387b8f0] __schedule at ffff8000815e8168
 #2 [ffff80008387b990] schedule at ffff8000815e862c
 #3 [ffff80008387b9c0] schedule_hrtimeout_range_clock at ffff8000815f16f0
 #4 [ffff80008387ba40] schedule_hrtimeout_range at ffff8000815f1728
 #5 [ffff80008387ba50] ep_poll at ffff800080597910
 #6 [ffff80008387bb00] do_epoll_wait at ffff800080597b94
 #7 [ffff80008387bb40] do_epoll_pwait at ffff800080597d00
 #8 [ffff80008387bb60] __arm64_sys_epoll_pwait at ffff800080598174
 #9 [ffff80008387be10] invoke_syscall at ffff8000800313bc
#10 [ffff80008387be40] el0_svc_common.constprop.0 at ffff8000800314b4
#11 [ffff80008387be70] do_el0_svc at ffff8000800315cc
#12 [ffff80008387be80] el0_svc at ffff8000815dd9e4
#13 [ffff80008387bea0] el0t_64_sync_handler at ffff8000815ddff8
#14 [ffff80008387bfe0] el0t_64_sync at ffff80008001163c
     PC: 0000fdc20d5a607c   LR: 0000fdc20d5a6058   SP: 0000ffffe75719a0
    X29: 0000ffffe75719a0  X28: ffffffffffffffff  X27: 000000000000041a
    X26: 0000000000000069  X25: 00000000000000c0  X24: 0000fdc20dadafe0
    X23: 0000bc53159a8580  X22: 0000000000000000  X21: 0000000000000004
    X20: 00000000000000c0  X19: ffffffffffffffff  X18: 0000000000000001
    X17: 0000fdc20d5a6320  X16: 0000fdc20dac6618  X15: 0000bc53157c9808
    X14: 0000000000000000  X13: 0000000000000000  X12: 0000000000000000
    X11: 0000000000000000  X10: fffffffe1821f10   X9: 0000000000000000
     X8: 0000000000000016   X7: 7f7f7f7f7f7f7f7f   X6: 0000000000000000
     X5: 0000000000000008   X4: 0000000000000000   X3: ffffffffffffffff
     X2: 00000000000000c0   X1: 0000bc53159a8580   X0: 0000000000000004
    ORIG_X0: 0000000000000004  SYSCALLNO: 16  PSTATE: 80001000

PID: 2        TASK: ffff0000c03ba200  CPU: 0    COMMAND: "kthreadd"
 #0 [ffff80008389bd50] __switch_to at ffff8000815e7e1c
 #1 [ffff80008389bd70] __schedule at ffff8000815e8168
 #2 [ffff80008389be10] schedule at ffff8000815e862c
 #3 [ffff80008389be40] kthreadd at ffff80008010828c

PID: 3        TASK: ffff0000c03b8000  CPU: 1    COMMAND: "pool_workqueue_"
 #0 [ffff8000838bbd30] __switch_to at ffff8000815e7e1c
 #1 [ffff8000838bbd50] __schedule at ffff8000815e8168
 #2 [ffff8000838bbdf0] schedule at ffff8000815e862c
 #3 [ffff8000838bbe20] kthread_worker_fn at ffff800080106460
 #4 [ffff8000838bbe70] kthread at ffff800080107f2c

PID: 4        TASK: ffff0000c0448000  CPU: 0    COMMAND: "kworker/R-rcu_g"
 #0 [ffff8000838dbd00] __switch_to at ffff8000815e7e1c
 #1 [ffff8000838dbd20] __schedule at ffff8000815e8168
 #2 [ffff8000838dbdc0] schedule at ffff8000815e862c
 #3 [ffff8000838dbdf0] rescuer_thread at ffff8000800fa280
 #4 [ffff8000838dbe70] kthread at ffff800080107f2c

PID: 5        TASK: ffff0000c044c400  CPU: 0    COMMAND: "kworker/R-rcu_p"
 #0 [ffff8000838e3d00] __switch_to at ffff8000815e7e1c
 #1 [ffff8000838e3d20] __schedule at ffff8000815e8168
 #2 [ffff8000838e3dc0] schedule at ffff8000815e862c
 #3 [ffff8000838e3df0] rescuer_thread at ffff8000800fa280
 #4 [ffff8000838e3e70] kthread at ffff800080107f2c

PID: 6        TASK: ffff0000c044a200  CPU: 0    COMMAND: "kworker/R-slub_"
 #0 [ffff8000838ebd00] __switch_to at ffff8000815e7e1c
 #1 [ffff8000838ebd20] __schedule at ffff8000815e8168
 #2 [ffff8000838ebdc0] schedule at ffff8000815e862c
 #3 [ffff8000838ebdf0] rescuer_thread at ffff8000800fa280
 #4 [ffff8000838ebe70] kthread at ffff800080107f2c
```

```
PID: 7        TASK: ffff0000c0454400  CPU: 0    COMMAND: "kworker/R-netns"
 #0 [ffff8000838f3d00] __switch_to at ffff8000815e7e1c
 #1 [ffff8000838f3d20] __schedule at ffff8000815e8168
 #2 [ffff8000838f3dc0] schedule at ffff8000815e862c
 #3 [ffff8000838f3df0] rescuer_thread at ffff8000800fa280
 #4 [ffff8000838f3e70] kthread at ffff800080107f2c

PID: 8        TASK: ffff0000c0452200  CPU: 0    COMMAND: "kworker/0:0"
 #0 [ffff8000838fbd10] __switch_to at ffff8000815e7e1c
 #1 [ffff8000838fbd30] __schedule at ffff8000815e8168
 #2 [ffff8000838fbdd0] schedule at ffff8000815e862c
 #3 [ffff8000838fbe00] worker_thread at ffff8000800fb424
 #4 [ffff8000838fbe70] kthread at ffff800080107f2c

PID: 9        TASK: ffff0000c0450000  CPU: 0    COMMAND: "kworker/0:0H"
 #0 [ffff800083903d10] __switch_to at ffff8000815e7e1c
 #1 [ffff800083903d30] __schedule at ffff8000815e8168
 #2 [ffff800083903dd0] schedule at ffff8000815e862c
 #3 [ffff800083903e00] worker_thread at ffff8000800fb424
 #4 [ffff800083903e70] kthread at ffff800080107f2c

PID: 10       TASK: ffff0000c0458000  CPU: 0    COMMAND: "kworker/0:1"
 #0 [ffff80008390bd10] __switch_to at ffff8000815e7e1c
 #1 [ffff80008390bd30] __schedule at ffff8000815e8168
 #2 [ffff80008390bdd0] schedule at ffff8000815e862c
 #3 [ffff80008390be00] worker_thread at ffff8000800fb424
 #4 [ffff80008390be70] kthread at ffff800080107f2c

PID: 11       TASK: ffff0000c045c400  CPU: 1    COMMAND: "kworker/u4:0"
 #0 [ffff800083913d10] __switch_to at ffff8000815e7e1c
 #1 [ffff800083913d30] __schedule at ffff8000815e8168
 #2 [ffff800083913dd0] schedule at ffff8000815e862c
 #3 [ffff800083913e00] worker_thread at ffff8000800fb424
 #4 [ffff800083913e70] kthread at ffff800080107f2c

PID: 12       TASK: ffff0000c045a200  CPU: 0    COMMAND: "kworker/R-mm_pe"
 #0 [ffff80008391bd00] __switch_to at ffff8000815e7e1c
 #1 [ffff80008391bd20] __schedule at ffff8000815e8168
 #2 [ffff80008391bdc0] schedule at ffff8000815e862c
 #3 [ffff80008391bdf0] rescuer_thread at ffff8000800fa280
 #4 [ffff80008391be70] kthread at ffff800080107f2c

PID: 13       TASK: ffff0000c0460000  CPU: 0    COMMAND: "rcu_tasks_rude_"
 #0 [ffff800083923ce0] __switch_to at ffff8000815e7e1c
 #1 [ffff800083923d00] __schedule at ffff8000815e8168
 #2 [ffff800083923da0] schedule at ffff8000815e862c
 #3 [ffff800083923dd0] rcu_tasks_one_gp at ffff8000801a2fcc
 #4 [ffff800083923e10] rcu_tasks_kthread at ffff8000801a31c0
 #5 [ffff800083923e70] kthread at ffff800080107f2c

PID: 14       TASK: ffff0000c0464400  CPU: 0    COMMAND: "rcu_tasks_trace"
 #0 [ffff80008392bce0] __switch_to at ffff8000815e7e1c
 #1 [ffff80008392bd00] __schedule at ffff8000815e8168
 #2 [ffff80008392bda0] schedule at ffff8000815e862c
 #3 [ffff80008392bdd0] rcu_tasks_one_gp at ffff8000801a2fcc
 #4 [ffff80008392be10] rcu_tasks_kthread at ffff8000801a31c0
 #5 [ffff80008392be70] kthread at ffff800080107f2c

PID: 15       TASK: ffff0000c0462200  CPU: 0    COMMAND: "ksoftirqd/0"
```

```
 #0 [ffff800083933d40] __switch_to at ffff8000815e7e1c
 #1 [ffff800083933d60] __schedule at ffff8000815e8168
 #2 [ffff800083933e00] schedule at ffff8000815e862c
 #3 [ffff800083933e30] smpboot_thread_fn at ffff800080111bd0
 #4 [ffff800083933e70] kthread at ffff800080107f2c

PID: 16       TASK: ffff0000c0570000  CPU: 1    COMMAND: "rcu_sched"
 #0 [ffff80008393bc10] __switch_to at ffff8000815e7e1c
 #1 [ffff80008393bc30] __schedule at ffff8000815e8168
 #2 [ffff80008393bcd0] schedule at ffff8000815e862c
 #3 [ffff80008393bd00] schedule_timeout at ffff8000815f1364
 #4 [ffff80008393bd80] rcu_gp_fqs_loop at ffff8000801af078
 #5 [ffff80008393be00] rcu_gp_kthread at ffff8000801b6d7c
 #6 [ffff80008393be70] kthread at ffff800080107f2c

PID: 17       TASK: ffff0000c0574400  CPU: 0    COMMAND: "migration/0"
 #0 [ffff800083943d40] __switch_to at ffff8000815e7e1c
 #1 [ffff800083943d60] __schedule at ffff8000815e8168
 #2 [ffff800083943e00] schedule at ffff8000815e862c
 #3 [ffff800083943e30] smpboot_thread_fn at ffff800080111bd0
 #4 [ffff800083943e70] kthread at ffff800080107f2c

PID: 18       TASK: ffff0000c0572200  CPU: 0    COMMAND: "idle_inject/0"
 #0 [ffff80008394bd40] __switch_to at ffff8000815e7e1c
 #1 [ffff80008394bd60] __schedule at ffff8000815e8168
 #2 [ffff80008394be00] schedule at ffff8000815e862c
 #3 [ffff80008394be30] smpboot_thread_fn at ffff800080111bd0
 #4 [ffff80008394be70] kthread at ffff800080107f2c

PID: 19       TASK: ffff0000c0580000  CPU: 0    COMMAND: "cpuhp/0"
 #0 [ffff80008395bd40] __switch_to at ffff8000815e7e1c
 #1 [ffff80008395bd60] __schedule at ffff8000815e8168
 #2 [ffff80008395be00] schedule at ffff8000815e862c
 #3 [ffff80008395be30] smpboot_thread_fn at ffff800080111bd0
 #4 [ffff80008395be70] kthread at ffff800080107f2c

PID: 20       TASK: ffff0000c0584400  CPU: 1    COMMAND: "cpuhp/1"
 #0 [ffff800083963d40] __switch_to at ffff8000815e7e1c
 #1 [ffff800083963d60] __schedule at ffff8000815e8168
 #2 [ffff800083963e00] schedule at ffff8000815e862c
 #3 [ffff800083963e30] smpboot_thread_fn at ffff800080111bd0
 #4 [ffff800083963e70] kthread at ffff800080107f2c

PID: 21       TASK: ffff0000c058a200  CPU: 1    COMMAND: "idle_inject/1"
 #0 [ffff80008396bd40] __switch_to at ffff8000815e7e1c
 #1 [ffff80008396bd60] __schedule at ffff8000815e8168
 #2 [ffff80008396be00] schedule at ffff8000815e862c
 #3 [ffff80008396be30] smpboot_thread_fn at ffff800080111bd0
 #4 [ffff80008396be70] kthread at ffff800080107f2c

PID: 22       TASK: ffff0000c0588000  CPU: 1    COMMAND: "migration/1"
 #0 [ffff800083973d40] __switch_to at ffff8000815e7e1c
 #1 [ffff800083973d60] __schedule at ffff8000815e8168
 #2 [ffff800083973e00] schedule at ffff8000815e862c
 #3 [ffff800083973e30] smpboot_thread_fn at ffff800080111bd0
 #4 [ffff800083973e70] kthread at ffff800080107f2c

PID: 23       TASK: ffff0000c058c400  CPU: 1    COMMAND: "ksoftirqd/1"
 -- MORE --  forward: <SPACE>, <ENTER> or j  backward: b or k  quit: qq
```

16. Individual process/thread (task) structures of interest can also be explored:

```
crash> task ffff0000c0584400
struct task_struct {
  thread_info = {
    flags = 8,
    ttbr0 = 13620928512,
    {
      preempt_count = 4294967296,
      preempt = {
        count = 0,
        need_resched = 1
      }
    },
    cpu = 1
  },
  __state = 1,
  saved_state = 0,
  stack = 0xffff800083960000,
  usage = {
    refs = {
      counter = 2
    }
  },
  flags = 69238848,
  ptrace = 0,
  on_cpu = 0,
  wake_entry = {
    llist = {
      next = 0x0
    },
    {
      u_flags = 48,
      a_flags = {
        counter = 48
      }
    },
    src = 0,
    dst = 0
  },
  wakee_flips = 0,
  wakee_flip_decay_ts = 4294668347,
  last_wakee = 0xffff0000c03bc400,
  recent_used_cpu = 0,
  wake_cpu = 1,
  on_rq = 0,
  prio = 120,
 -- MORE --  forward: <SPACE>, <ENTER> or j  backward: b or k  quit: qq
```

Exercise K1 (x64, WinDbg)

Goal: Learn how to navigate a normal kernel dump.

Patterns: Manual Dump (Kernel); Stack Trace Collection.

1. Copy the *vmlinux-6.8.0-1018-azure* file in the x64/KSym directory to the *vmlinux* file.

2. Launch WinDbg. Load the core dump *202412290014.kdump* from the x64/K1 directory and set the symbol path to the x64/KSym directory (there may be some delay/unresponsiveness when you type the **.reload** command):

```
Microsoft (R) Windows Debugger Version 10.0.27725.1000 AMD64
Copyright (c) Microsoft Corporation. All rights reserved.


Loading Dump File [C:\ALCDA2\x64\K1\202412290014.kdump]
64-bit machine not using 64-bit API

************* Path validation summary **************
Response                         Time (ms)     Location
Deferred                                       srv*
Symbol search path is: srv*
Executable search path is:
Generic Unix Kernel Version 0 MP (4 procs) Free x64
Primary image base = 0xffffffff`86a00000 Loaded module list = 0x00000000`00000000
System Uptime: not available
Loading Kernel Symbols

Loading User Symbols

ReadVirtual() failed in GetXStateConfiguration() first read attempt (error == 0.)
For analysis of this file, run !analyze -v
ffffffff`86bf1dc4 mov     qword ptr [rdi+80h],rax ds:ffffac1c`46ca7aa0=ffffffff86bf1dc4

0: kd> .sympath C:\ALCDA2\x64\KSym\
Symbol search path is: C:\ALCDA2\x64\KSym\
Expanded Symbol search path is: c:\alcda2\x64\ksym\

************* Path validation summary **************
Response                         Time (ms)     Location
OK                                             C:\ALCDA2\x64\KSym\

0: kd> .reload
Loading Kernel Symbols
.*** WARNING: Unable to verify timestamp for vmlinux
..............................................................
....
Loading User Symbols


************* Symbol Loading Error Summary **************
Module name            Error
vmlinux                The system cannot find the file specified

You can troubleshoot most symbol related issues by turning on symbol loading diagnostics (!sym
noisy) and repeating the command that caused symbols to be loaded.
You should also verify that your symbol search path (.sympath) is correct.
```

3. We can see the current process stack trace that led to the crash (we omit source code references) and verify the correctness of the stack trace:

```
0: kd> kL
 # Child-SP          RetAddr               Call Site
00 ffffac1c`46ca7a18 ffffffff`86bf1e46     vmlinux!crash_setup_regs+0x74
01 ffffac1c`46ca7a20 ffffffff`86addf29     vmlinux!__crash_kexec+0x66
02 ffffac1c`46ca7ae0 ffffffff`873fea05 (T) vmlinux!panic+0x159
03 ffffac1c`46ca7b60 ffffffff`873ff2d2     vmlinux!sysrq_handle_crash+0x10
04 ffffac1c`46ca7b70 ffffffff`873ffb2c     vmlinux!__handle_sysrq+0xf2
05 ffffac1c`46ca7bb8 ffffffff`86f31fce     vmlinux!write_sysrq_trigger+0x5c
06 ffffac1c`46ca7be8 ffffffff`86e7e26f     vmlinux!proc_reg_write+0x5e
07 ffffac1c`46ca7c08 ffffffff`86e7e907     vmlinux!vfs_write+0xef
08 ffffac1c`46ca7ca0 ffffffff`86e7e9b9     vmlinux!ksys_write+0x67
09 ffffac1c`46ca7ce0 ffffffff`86a0651d     vmlinux!__x64_sys_write+0x19
0a ffffac1c`46ca7cf0 ffffffff`87abadac     vmlinux!x64_sys_call+0x167d
0b ffffac1c`46ca7d00 ffffffff`87c00130     vmlinux!do_syscall_64+0x7c
0c ffffac1c`46ca7f58 00007d3b`23914887     vmlinux!entry_SYSCALL_64_after_hwframe+0x78
0d 00007fff`ee286ee8 00000000`00000000     0x00007d3b`23914887

0: kd> ub ffffffff`86addf29
vmlinux!panic+0x135:
ffffffff`86addf05 xor     esi,esi
ffffffff`86addf07 mov     rdi,0FFFFFFFF8966F450h
ffffffff`86addf0e call    vmlinux!atomic_notifier_call_chain (ffffffff`86b17b60)
ffffffff`86addf13 call    vmlinux!panic_print_sys_info (ffffffff`86addbc0)
ffffffff`86addf18 mov     edi,1
ffffffff`86addf1d call    vmlinux!kmsg_dump (ffffffff`86b847d0)
ffffffff`86addf22 xor     edi,edi
ffffffff`86addf24 call    vmlinux!__crash_kexec (ffffffff`86bf1de0)
```

Note: User space addresses are not available in the kernel dump.

```
0: kd> dp 00007d3b`23914887
00007d3b`23914887  ????????`???????? ????????`????????
00007d3b`23914897  ????????`???????? ????????`????????
00007d3b`239148a7  ????????`???????? ????????`????????
00007d3b`239148b7  ????????`???????? ????????`????????
00007d3b`239148c7  ????????`???????? ????????`????????
00007d3b`239148d7  ????????`???????? ????????`????????
00007d3b`239148e7  ????????`???????? ????????`????????
00007d3b`239148f7  ????????`???????? ????????`????????

0: kd> dp ffffffff`86addf29
ffffffff`86addf29  c62de800`0a6342e8 0a64d6e8`ff31006b
ffffffff`86addf39  2002b915`1f05f600 83480000`013a850f
ffffffff`86addf49  840f0002`b914f13d 150d358b`0000011c
ffffffff`86addf59  f63145ed`314502b9 0000008b`8f0ff685
ffffffff`86addf69  c08502b9`14f9058b 021ae5df`058b1674
ffffffff`86addf79  0c058906`74fff883 0003b9a7`e802b93f
ffffffff`86addf89  488966f4`c0c6c748 74e88836`a4e0c7c7
ffffffff`86addf99  bc05c7ff`31000a18 e8000000`0102554f
```

4. We can list modules, for example, to determine the kernel range and get the core file information:

```
0: kd> lm
start             end                 module name
ffffffff`86a00000 ffffffff`8a400000   vmlinux  T (service symbols: DWARF Private Symbols)        c:\alcda2\x64\ksym\vmlinux
ffffffff`c0980000 ffffffff`c098b000   crct10dif_pclmul   (deferred)
ffffffff`c098c000 ffffffff`c0997000   nls_iso8859_1   (deferred)
ffffffff`c0998000 ffffffff`c099f000   binfmt_misc   (deferred)

0: kd> !vmcoreinfo
VMCOREINFO:
    OSRELEASE=6.8.0-1018-azure
    BUILD-ID=ab457c81cb2411972a9ce2c82a4a04849f1f92e6
    PAGESIZE=4096
    SYMBOL(init_uts_ns)=ffffffff88fd6980
    OFFSET(uts_namespace.name)=0
    SYMBOL(node_online_map)=ffffffff890349e0
    SYMBOL(swapper_pg_dir)=ffffffff88c38000
    SYMBOL(_stext)=ffffffff86a00000
    SYMBOL(vmap_area_list)=ffffffff88e37490
    SYMBOL(mem_section)=ffff991e07fd1000
    LENGTH(mem_section)=2048
    SIZE(mem_section)=16
    OFFSET(mem_section.section_mem_map)=0
    NUMBER(SECTION_SIZE_BITS)=27
    NUMBER(MAX_PHYSMEM_BITS)=46
    SIZE(page)=64
    SIZE(pglist_data)=174464
    SIZE(zone)=1536
    SIZE(free_area)=88
    SIZE(list_head)=16
    SIZE(nodemask_t)=128
    OFFSET(page.flags)=0
    OFFSET(page._refcount)=52
    OFFSET(page.mapping)=24
    OFFSET(page.lru)=8
    OFFSET(page._mapcount)=48
    OFFSET(page.private)=40
    OFFSET(page.compound_head)=8
    OFFSET(pglist_data.node_zones)=0
    OFFSET(pglist_data.nr_zones)=171552
    OFFSET(pglist_data.node_start_pfn)=171560
    OFFSET(pglist_data.node_spanned_pages)=171576
    OFFSET(pglist_data.node_id)=171584
    OFFSET(zone.free_area)=256
    OFFSET(zone.vm_stat)=1344
    OFFSET(zone.spanned_pages)=152
    OFFSET(free_area.free_list)=0
    OFFSET(list_head.next)=0
    OFFSET(list_head.prev)=8
    OFFSET(vmap_area.va_start)=0
    OFFSET(vmap_area.list)=40
    LENGTH(zone.free_area)=11
    SYMBOL(prb)=ffffffff88c9d780
    SYMBOL(printk_rb_static)=ffffffff88c9d7a0
    SYMBOL(clear_seq)=ffffffff896b7220
    SIZE(printk_ringbuffer)=88
    OFFSET(printk_ringbuffer.desc_ring)=0
    OFFSET(printk_ringbuffer.text_data_ring)=48
    OFFSET(printk_ringbuffer.fail)=80
    SIZE(prb_desc_ring)=48
```

```
OFFSET(prb_desc_ring.count_bits)=0
OFFSET(prb_desc_ring.descs)=8
OFFSET(prb_desc_ring.infos)=16
OFFSET(prb_desc_ring.head_id)=24
OFFSET(prb_desc_ring.tail_id)=32
SIZE(prb_desc)=24
OFFSET(prb_desc.state_var)=0
OFFSET(prb_desc.text_blk_lpos)=8
SIZE(prb_data_blk_lpos)=16
OFFSET(prb_data_blk_lpos.begin)=0
OFFSET(prb_data_blk_lpos.next)=8
SIZE(printk_info)=88
OFFSET(printk_info.seq)=0
OFFSET(printk_info.ts_nsec)=8
OFFSET(printk_info.text_len)=16
OFFSET(printk_info.caller_id)=20
OFFSET(printk_info.dev_info)=24
SIZE(dev_printk_info)=64
OFFSET(dev_printk_info.subsystem)=0
LENGTH(printk_info_subsystem)=16
OFFSET(dev_printk_info.device)=16
LENGTH(printk_info_device)=48
SIZE(prb_data_ring)=32
OFFSET(prb_data_ring.size_bits)=0
OFFSET(prb_data_ring.data)=8
OFFSET(prb_data_ring.head_lpos)=16
OFFSET(prb_data_ring.tail_lpos)=24
SIZE(atomic_long_t)=8
OFFSET(atomic_long_t.counter)=0
SIZE(latched_seq)=24
OFFSET(latched_seq.val)=8
LENGTH(free_area.free_list)=5
NUMBER(NR_FREE_PAGES)=0
NUMBER(PG_lru)=5
NUMBER(PG_private)=15
NUMBER(PG_swapcache)=12
NUMBER(PG_swapbacked)=19
NUMBER(PG_slab)=11
NUMBER(PG_hwpoison)=23
NUMBER(PG_head_mask)=64
NUMBER(PAGE_BUDDY_MAPCOUNT_VALUE)=-129
NUMBER(PAGE_HUGETLB_MAPCOUNT_VALUE)=-2049
NUMBER(PAGE_OFFLINE_MAPCOUNT_VALUE)=-257
SYMBOL(kallsyms_names)=ffffffff87f7af48
SYMBOL(kallsyms_num_syms)=ffffffff87f7af40
SYMBOL(kallsyms_token_table)=ffffffff881fb2a8
SYMBOL(kallsyms_token_index)=ffffffff881fb620
SYMBOL(kallsyms_offsets)=ffffffff881fb820
SYMBOL(kallsyms_relative_base)=ffffffff882b9598
NUMBER(phys_base)=538968064
SYMBOL(init_top_pgt)=ffffffff88c38000
NUMBER(pgtable_l5_enabled)=0
SYMBOL(node_data)=ffffffff8902faa0
LENGTH(node_data)=1024
KERNELOFFSET=5a00000
NUMBER(KERNEL_IMAGE_SIZE)=1073741824
NUMBER(sme_mask)=0
CRASHTIME=1735431156
```

5. We can also check backtraces from other CPUs:

```
0: kd> ~1s
WARNING: Unable to reset page directories

1: kd> kL
 # Child-SP          RetAddr               Call Site
00 (Inline Function) --------`--------     vmlinux!native_irq_disable
01 (Inline Function) --------`--------     vmlinux!arch_local_irq_disable
02 ffffac1c`400d3e88 ffffffff`87ac1ac9     vmlinux!default_idle+0xb
03 ffffac1c`400d3e90 ffffffff`87ac1d3c     vmlinux!arch_cpu_idle+0x9
04 ffffac1c`400d3ea0 ffffffff`86b51512     vmlinux!default_idle_call+0x2c
05 ffffac1c`400d3eb0 ffffffff`86b515e2     vmlinux!cpuidle_idle_call+0x132
06 ffffac1c`400d3ef0 ffffffff`86b5184d     vmlinux!do_idle+0x82
07 ffffac1c`400d3f10 ffffffff`86a8a950     vmlinux!cpu_startup_entry+0x2d
08 ffffac1c`400d3f28 ffffffff`86a00279     vmlinux!start_secondary+0x120
09 ffffac1c`400d3f58 00000000`00000000     vmlinux!secondary_startup_64_no_verify+0x184

1: kd> ~2s
WARNING: Unable to reset page directories

2: kd> kL
 # Child-SP          RetAddr               Call Site
00 (Inline Function) --------`--------     vmlinux!native_irq_disable
01 (Inline Function) --------`--------     vmlinux!arch_local_irq_disable
02 ffffac1c`400dbe88 ffffffff`87ac1ac9     vmlinux!default_idle+0xb
03 ffffac1c`400dbe90 ffffffff`87ac1d3c     vmlinux!arch_cpu_idle+0x9
04 ffffac1c`400dbea0 ffffffff`86b51512     vmlinux!default_idle_call+0x2c
05 ffffac1c`400dbeb0 ffffffff`86b515e2     vmlinux!cpuidle_idle_call+0x132
06 ffffac1c`400dbef0 ffffffff`86b5184d     vmlinux!do_idle+0x82
07 ffffac1c`400dbf10 ffffffff`86a8a950     vmlinux!cpu_startup_entry+0x2d
08 ffffac1c`400dbf28 ffffffff`86a00279     vmlinux!start_secondary+0x120
09 ffffac1c`400dbf58 00000000`00000000     vmlinux!secondary_startup_64_no_verify+0x184

2: kd> ~3s
WARNING: Unable to reset page directories

3: kd> kL
 # Child-SP          RetAddr               Call Site
00 (Inline Function) --------`--------     vmlinux!native_irq_disable
01 (Inline Function) --------`--------     vmlinux!arch_local_irq_disable
02 ffffac1c`400e3e88 ffffffff`87ac1ac9     vmlinux!default_idle+0xb
03 ffffac1c`400e3e90 ffffffff`87ac1d3c     vmlinux!arch_cpu_idle+0x9
04 ffffac1c`400e3ea0 ffffffff`86b51512     vmlinux!default_idle_call+0x2c
05 ffffac1c`400e3eb0 ffffffff`86b515e2     vmlinux!cpuidle_idle_call+0x132
06 ffffac1c`400e3ef0 ffffffff`86b5184d     vmlinux!do_idle+0x82
07 ffffac1c`400e3f10 ffffffff`86a8a950     vmlinux!cpu_startup_entry+0x2d
08 ffffac1c`400e3f28 ffffffff`86a00279     vmlinux!start_secondary+0x120
09 ffffac1c`400e3f58 00000000`00000000     vmlinux!secondary_startup_64_no_verify+0x184

3: kd> ~4s
4 is not a valid processor number

3: kd> ~0s
WARNING: Unable to reset page directories
```

6. To see the kernel log messages you can use the **!log** command (please refer to GDB exercises for log analysis examples). Another useful command is **!runq**:

```
0: kd> !runq
@$runq()
    [0x0]              : CPU 0 run queue [current = 'bash' (8e6)]
        Cpu                : 0x0
        RunQueue           [Type: rq]
        CurrentTask        : bash [Type: task_struct]
        RTTasks
        CfsTasks
    [0x1]              : CPU 1 run queue [current = 'swapper/1' (0)]
        Cpu                : 0x1
        RunQueue           [Type: rq]
        CurrentTask        : swapper/1 [Type: task_struct]
        RTTasks
        CfsTasks
    [0x2]              : CPU 2 run queue [current = 'swapper/2' (0)]
        Cpu                : 0x2
        RunQueue           [Type: rq]
        CurrentTask        : swapper/2 [Type: task_struct]
        RTTasks
        CfsTasks
    [0x3]              : CPU 3 run queue [current = 'swapper/3' (0)]
        Cpu                : 0x3
        RunQueue           [Type: rq]
        CurrentTask        : swapper/3 [Type: task_struct]
        RTTasks
        CfsTasks
```

Note: Please use this Microsoft page[3] for additional commands available from the *LinuxKernel.js* script (but most commands fail with an internal error at the time of this writing and this core dump).

7. If you want to dump raw stack data (or any memory), you can use the **dps** and **dpp** commands:

```
0: kd> r
rax=0000000000000000 rbx=0000000000000016 rcx=0000000000000000
rdx=0000000000000001 rsi=0000000000000000 rdi=ffffac1c46ca7a20
rip=ffffffff86bf1dc4 rsp=ffffac1c46ca7a18 rbp=ffffac1c46ca7ad0
 r8=0000000000000000  r9=ffff991e02cbf30c r10=ffffac1c46ca79e8
r11=00000000000010c0 r12=0000000000000001 r13=0000000000000015
r14=ffffffff8966f4c0 r15=0000000000000000
iopl=0         nv up di pl zr na po nc
cs=0010  ss=0018  ds=0000  es=0000  fs=0000  gs=0000             efl=00000046
vmlinux!crash_setup_regs+0x74:
ffffffff`86bf1dc4 mov     qword ptr [rdi+80h],rax ds:ffffac1c`46ca7aa0=ffffffff86bf1dc4

0: kd> dps ffffac1c46ca7a18 L20
ffffac1c`46ca7a18  ffffffff`86bf1e46 vmlinux!__crash_kexec+0x66 [/build/linux-azure-6.8-
2oiFiH/linux-azure-6.8-6.8.0/include/linux/atomic/atomic-arch-fallback.h @ 524]
ffffac1c`46ca7a20  00000000`00000000
ffffac1c`46ca7a28  ffffffff`8966f4c0 vmlinux!buf.2
ffffac1c`46ca7a30  00000000`00000015
ffffac1c`46ca7a38  00000000`00000001
ffffac1c`46ca7a40  ffffac1c`46ca7ad0
ffffac1c`46ca7a48  00000000`00000016
```

[3] https://learn.microsoft.com/en-us/windows-hardware/drivers/debugger/linux-crash-dumps

```
ffffac1c`46ca7a50  00000000`000010c0
ffffac1c`46ca7a58  ffffac1c`46ca79e8
ffffac1c`46ca7a60  ffff991e`02cbf30c
ffffac1c`46ca7a68  00000000`00000000
ffffac1c`46ca7a70  00000000`00000000
ffffac1c`46ca7a78  00000000`00000000
ffffac1c`46ca7a80  00000000`00000001
ffffac1c`46ca7a88  00000000`00000000
ffffac1c`46ca7a90  ffffac1c`46ca7a20
ffffac1c`46ca7a98  ffffffff`8966f4c0 vmlinux!buf.2
ffffac1c`46ca7aa0  ffffffff`86bf1dc4 vmlinux!crash_setup_regs+0x74 [/build/linux-azure-6.8-
2oiFiH/linux-azure-6.8-6.8.0/arch/x86/include/asm/kexec.h @ 115]
ffffac1c`46ca7aa8  00000000`00000010
ffffac1c`46ca7ab0  00000000`00000046
ffffac1c`46ca7ab8  ffffac1c`46ca7a18
ffffac1c`46ca7ac0  00000000`00000018
ffffac1c`46ca7ac8  adb02142`bd5d6d00
ffffac1c`46ca7ad0  ffffac1c`46ca7b50
ffffac1c`46ca7ad8  ffffffff`86addf29 vmlinux!panic+0x159
ffffac1c`46ca7ae0  ffffac1c`00000008
ffffac1c`46ca7ae8  ffffac1c`46ca7b60
ffffac1c`46ca7af0  ffffac1c`46ca7b00
ffffac1c`46ca7af8  adb02142`bd5d6d00
ffffac1c`46ca7b00  ffffac1c`46ca7b60
ffffac1c`46ca7b08  ffff991e`03c20a00
ffffac1c`46ca7b10  00000000`00000000

0: kd> dpp ffffac1c46ca7a18 L20
ffffac1c`46ca7a18  ffffffff`86bf1e46 000002ad`0e5c05c7
ffffac1c`46ca7a20  00000000`00000000
ffffac1c`46ca7a28  ffffffff`8966f4c0 72742071`72737973
ffffac1c`46ca7a30  00000000`00000015
ffffac1c`46ca7a38  00000000`00000001
ffffac1c`46ca7a40  ffffac1c`46ca7ad0 ffffac1c`46ca7b50
ffffac1c`46ca7a48  00000000`00000016
ffffac1c`46ca7a50  00000000`000010c0
ffffac1c`46ca7a58  ffffac1c`46ca79e8 adb02142`bd5d6d00
ffffac1c`46ca7a60  ffff991e`02cbf30c 1d6b6daa`a7309d9f
ffffac1c`46ca7a68  00000000`00000000
ffffac1c`46ca7a70  00000000`00000000
ffffac1c`46ca7a78  00000000`00000000
ffffac1c`46ca7a80  00000000`00000001
ffffac1c`46ca7a88  00000000`00000000
ffffac1c`46ca7a90  ffffac1c`46ca7a20 00000000`00000000
ffffac1c`46ca7a98  ffffffff`8966f4c0 72742071`72737973
ffffac1c`46ca7aa0  ffffffff`86bf1dc4 c3000000`80878948
ffffac1c`46ca7aa8  00000000`00000010
ffffac1c`46ca7ab0  00000000`00000046
ffffac1c`46ca7ab8  ffffac1c`46ca7a18 ffffffff`86bf1e46 vmlinux!__crash_kexec+0x66
[/build/linux-azure-6.8-2oiFiH/linux-azure-6.8-6.8.0/include/linux/atomic/atomic-arch-
fallback.h @ 524]
ffffac1c`46ca7ac0  00000000`00000018
ffffac1c`46ca7ac8  adb02142`bd5d6d00
ffffac1c`46ca7ad0  ffffac1c`46ca7b50 ffffac1c`46ca7b60
ffffac1c`46ca7ad8  ffffffff`86addf29 c62de800`0a6342e8
ffffac1c`46ca7ae0  ffffac1c`00000008
ffffac1c`46ca7ae8  ffffac1c`46ca7b60 ffffac1c`46ca7ba8
ffffac1c`46ca7af0  ffffac1c`46ca7b00 ffffac1c`46ca7b60
ffffac1c`46ca7af8  adb02142`bd5d6d00
ffffac1c`46ca7b00  ffffac1c`46ca7b60 ffffac1c`46ca7ba8
```

```
ffffac1c`46ca7b08  ffff991e`03c20a00 00000000`00000000
ffffac1c`46ca7b10  00000000`00000000

0: kd> dc ffffac1c46ca7a18
ffffac1c`46ca7a18  86bf1e46 ffffffff 00000000 00000000  F...............
ffffac1c`46ca7a28  8966f4c0 ffffffff 00000015 00000000  ..f.............
ffffac1c`46ca7a38  00000001 00000000 46ca7ad0 ffffac1c  .........z.F....
ffffac1c`46ca7a48  00000016 00000000 000010c0 00000000  ................
ffffac1c`46ca7a58  46ca79e8 ffffac1c 02cbf30c ffff991e  .y.F............
ffffac1c`46ca7a68  00000000 00000000 00000000 00000000  ................
ffffac1c`46ca7a78  00000000 00000000 00000001 00000000  ................
ffffac1c`46ca7a88  00000000 00000000 46ca7a20 ffffac1c  ........ z.F....

0: kd> db ffffac1c46ca7a18
ffffac1c`46ca7a18  46 1e bf 86 ff ff ff ff-00 00 00 00 00 00 00 00  F...............
ffffac1c`46ca7a28  c0 f4 66 89 ff ff ff ff-15 00 00 00 00 00 00 00  ..f.............
ffffac1c`46ca7a38  01 00 00 00 00 00 00 00-d0 7a ca 46 1c ac ff ff  .........z.F....
ffffac1c`46ca7a48  16 00 00 00 00 00 00 00-c0 10 00 00 00 00 00 00  ................
ffffac1c`46ca7a58  e8 79 ca 46 1c ac ff ff-0c f3 cb 02 1e 99 ff ff  .y.F............
ffffac1c`46ca7a68  00 00 00 00 00 00 00 00-00 00 00 00 00 00 00 00  ................
ffffac1c`46ca7a78  00 00 00 00 00 00 00 00-01 00 00 00 00 00 00 00  ................
ffffac1c`46ca7a88  00 00 00 00 00 00 00 00-20 7a ca 46 1c ac ff ff  ........ z.F....

0: kd> da ffffac1c46ca7a18
ffffac1c`46ca7a18  "F......."

0: kd> dpa ffffac1c46ca7a18
ffffac1c`46ca7a18  ffffffff`86bf1e46 "..\..."
ffffac1c`46ca7a20  00000000`00000000
ffffac1c`46ca7a28  ffffffff`8966f4c0 "sysrq triggered crash"
ffffac1c`46ca7a30  00000000`00000015
ffffac1c`46ca7a38  00000000`00000001
ffffac1c`46ca7a40  ffffac1c`46ca7ad0 "P{.F....)........"
ffffac1c`46ca7a48  00000000`00000016
ffffac1c`46ca7a50  00000000`000010c0
ffffac1c`46ca7a58  ffffac1c`46ca79e8 ""
ffffac1c`46ca7a60  ffff991e`02cbf30c "..0..mk..EA.G?...S..~..GD...#..........V.-.. <}.K....."
ffffac1c`46ca7a68  00000000`00000000
ffffac1c`46ca7a70  00000000`00000000
ffffac1c`46ca7a78  00000000`00000000
ffffac1c`46ca7a80  00000000`00000001
ffffac1c`46ca7a88  00000000`00000000
ffffac1c`46ca7a90  ffffac1c`46ca7a20 ""
```

Exercise K1 (A64, WinDbg)

Goal: Learn how to navigate a normal kernel dump.

Patterns: Manual Dump (Kernel); Stack Trace Collection.

1. Copy the *vmlinux-6.8.0-1018-oracle* file in the A64/KSym directory to the *vmlinux* file.

2. Launch WinDbg. Load the core dump *202412291058.kdump* from the A64/K1 directory and set the symbol path to the A64/KSym directory (there may be some delay/unresponsiveness when you type the **.reload** command):

```
Microsoft (R) Windows Debugger Version 10.0.27725.1000 AMD64
Copyright (c) Microsoft Corporation. All rights reserved.


Loading Dump File [C:\ALCDA2\A64\K1\202412291058.kdump]
64-bit machine not using 64-bit API

************* Path validation summary **************
Response                         Time (ms)     Location
OK                                             C:\ALCDA2\x64\KSym\
Symbol search path is: C:\ALCDA2\x64\KSym\
Executable search path is:
Generic Unix Kernel Version 0 MP (2 procs) Free ARM 64-bit (AArch64)
Primary image base = 0xffff8000`80010000 Loaded module list = 0x00000000`00000000
System Uptime: not available
Loading Kernel Symbols

Loading User Symbols

For analysis of this file, run !analyze -v
ffff8000`802097d0 stp         x1,x0,[x2,#0x100]

0: kd> .sympath C:\ALCDA2\A64\KSym\
Symbol search path is: C:\ALCDA2\A64\KSym\
Expanded Symbol search path is: c:\alcda2\a64\ksym\

************* Path validation summary **************
Response                         Time (ms)     Location
OK                                             C:\ALCDA2\A64\KSym\
```

3. We can see the current process stack trace that led to the crash (we omit source code references) and verify the correctness of the stack trace:

```
0: kd> kL
 # Child-SP          RetAddr               Call Site
00 ffff8000`85a53920 ffff8000`8020b5f0     vmlinux!crash_setup_regs+0xa0
01 ffff8000`85a53920 ffff8000`800c83e0     vmlinux!__crash_kexec+0x60
02 ffff8000`85a53aa0 ffff8000`80d326e8 (T) vmlinux!panic+0x350
03 ffff8000`85a53b80 ffff8000`80d33498     vmlinux!sysrq_handle_crash+0x1c
04 ffff8000`85a53b90 ffff8000`80d34074     vmlinux!__handle_sysrq+0xb8
05 ffff8000`85a53c20 ffff8000`805f22cc     vmlinux!write_sysrq_trigger+0x154
06 ffff8000`85a53c60 ffff8000`80510270     vmlinux!proc_reg_write+0xcc
07 ffff8000`85a53c80 ffff8000`80510728     vmlinux!vfs_write+0xd8
08 ffff8000`85a53d20 ffff8000`805107fc     vmlinux!ksys_write+0x70
09 ffff8000`85a53d60 ffff8000`800313c0     vmlinux!__arm64_sys_write+0x24
```

```
0a ffff8000`85a53d70 ffff8000`800314b8     vmlinux!invoke_syscall+0x78
0b ffff8000`85a53e40 ffff8000`800315d0     vmlinux!el0_svc_common+0x48
0c ffff8000`85a53e70 ffff8000`815dd9e8     vmlinux!do_el0_svc+0x28
0d ffff8000`85a53e80 ffff8000`815ddffc     vmlinux!el0_svc+0x40
0e ffff8000`85a53ea0 ffff8000`80011640     vmlinux!el0t_64_sync_handler+0x15c
0f ffff8000`85a53eb0 00000000`00000000     vmlinux!el0t_64_sync+0x1a8
```

```
0: kd> ub ffff8000`800c83e0
vmlinux!panic+0x330 [/build/linux-oracle-6.8-EzVzJ2/linux-oracle-6.8-6.8.0/kernel/panic.c @
405]:
ffff8000`800c83c0 add          x0,x0,#0xA08
ffff8000`800c83c4 str          x0,[x22,#0x458]
ffff8000`800c83c8 b            vmlinux!panic+0x188 (ffff8000`800c8218)
ffff8000`800c83cc mov          w0,#1
ffff8000`800c83d0 bl           vmlinux!console_flush_on_panic (ffff8000`80181630)
ffff8000`800c83d4 b            vmlinux!panic+0x180 (ffff8000`800c8210)
ffff8000`800c83d8 mov          x0,#0
ffff8000`800c83dc bl           vmlinux!__crash_kexec (ffff8000`8020b590)
```

4. We can list modules, for example, to determine the kernel range and get the core file information:

```
0: kd> lm
start             end                 module name
ffff8000`7b870000 ffff8000`7b875000   aes_ce_cipher   (deferred)
ffff8000`7b876000 ffff8000`7b889000   aes_neon_blk   (no symbols)
ffff8000`7b87a000 ffff8000`7b884000   aes_ce_blk   (deferred)
ffff8000`7b88a000 ffff8000`7b892000   aes_neon_bs   (deferred)
ffff8000`7b893000 ffff8000`7b89a000   xhci_pci_renesas   (deferred)
ffff8000`7b89d000 ffff8000`7b8a8000   sha1_ce   (no symbols)
ffff8000`7b8a1000 ffff8000`7b8a6000   virtio_dma_buf   (deferred)
ffff8000`7b8a9000 ffff8000`7b8e2000   sm4   (no symbols)
ffff8000`7b8ab000 ffff8000`7b8b2000   xhci_pci   (deferred)
ffff8000`7b8b5000 ffff8000`7b8e4000   ghash_ce   (no symbols)
ffff8000`7b8bc000 ffff8000`7b8d3000   virtio_gpu   (deferred)
ffff8000`7b8d8000 ffff8000`7b8e0000   sha256_arm64   (deferred)
ffff8000`7b8e5000 ffff8000`7b8eb000   sha2_ce   (deferred)
ffff8000`7b8ec000 ffff8000`7b8f1000   polyval_generic   (deferred)
ffff8000`7b8f2000 ffff8000`7b907000   raid0   (no symbols)
ffff8000`7b8f6000 ffff8000`7b8fb000   polyval_ce   (deferred)
ffff8000`7b900000 ffff8000`7b905000   crct10dif_ce   (deferred)
ffff8000`7b90a000 ffff8000`7b92a000   libcrc32c   (no symbols)
ffff8000`7b90f000 ffff8000`7b920000   raid1   (deferred)
ffff8000`7b923000 ffff8000`7b928000   async_xor   (deferred)
ffff8000`7b92f000 ffff8000`7b94c000   raid6_pq   (deferred)
ffff8000`7b952000 ffff8000`7b957000   xor_neon   (deferred)
ffff8000`7b95a000 ffff8000`7b967000   iscsi_boot_sysfs   (no symbols)
ffff8000`7b95e000 ffff8000`7b963000   xor   (deferred)
ffff8000`7b968000 ffff8000`7b96d000   async_tx   (deferred)
ffff8000`7b972000 ffff8000`7b985000   iscsi_ibft   (no symbols)
ffff8000`7b97a000 ffff8000`7b97f000   async_pq   (deferred)
ffff8000`7b986000 ffff8000`7b98b000   async_memcpy   (deferred)
ffff8000`7b992000 ffff8000`7b998000   async_raid6_recov   (deferred)
ffff8000`7b99f000 ffff8000`7b9d6000   raid456   (deferred)
ffff8000`7b9d9000 ffff8000`7b9e7000   raid10   (deferred)
ffff8000`7b9e8000 ffff8000`7ba10000   scsi_transport_iscsi   (deferred)
ffff8000`7ba11000 ffff8000`7ba17000   iscsi_tcp   (deferred)
ffff8000`7ba1a000 ffff8000`7ba76000   hid_generic   (no symbols)
ffff8000`7ba21000 ffff8000`7ba33000   libiscsi   (deferred)
ffff8000`7ba3b000 ffff8000`7ba42000   libiscsi_tcp   (deferred)
ffff8000`7ba45000 ffff8000`7ba72000   hid   (deferred)
ffff8000`7ba77000 ffff8000`7ba8d000   blake2b_generic   (no symbols)
ffff8000`7ba7c000 ffff8000`7ba88000   usbhid   (deferred)
ffff8000`7ba92000 ffff8000`7bc5d000   btrfs   (deferred)
ffff8000`7bc61000 ffff8000`7bc6d000   autofs4   (deferred)
ffff8000`7bc70000 ffff8000`7bc98000   ip_tables   (no symbols)
ffff8000`7bc77000 ffff8000`7bc88000   x_tables   (deferred)
ffff8000`7bc8b000 ffff8000`7bc90000   efi_pstore   (deferred)
ffff8000`7bc9b000 ffff8000`7bca1000   scsi_dh_alua   (deferred)
ffff8000`7bca4000 ffff8000`7bca9000   scsi_dh_emc   (deferred)
ffff8000`7bcae000 ffff8000`7bcb4000   scsi_dh_rdac   (deferred)
ffff8000`7bcb5000 ffff8000`7bcd0000   sch_fq_codel   (no symbols)
ffff8000`7bcb9000 ffff8000`7bcc3000   dm_multipath   (deferred)
```

```
ffff8000`7bcc6000 ffff8000`7bccb000   input_leds   (deferred)
ffff8000`7bcd1000 ffff8000`7bce3000   nls_iso8859_1   (no symbols)
ffff8000`7bcd5000 ffff8000`7bcdf000   joydev     (deferred)
ffff8000`7bce4000 ffff8000`7bcec000   binfmt_misc   (deferred)
ffff8000`7bcef000 ffff8000`7bcf6000   nfnetlink    (deferred)
ffff8000`7bcf7000 ffff8000`7bd47000   nf_tables    (deferred)
ffff8000`7bd5c000 ffff8000`7bd64000   nft_compat    (deferred)
ffff8000`7bd67000 ffff8000`7be9e000   xt_state   (no symbols)
ffff8000`7bd6a000 ffff8000`7be10000   sunrpc     (deferred)
ffff8000`7be11000 ffff8000`7be16000   xt_tcpudp    (deferred)
ffff8000`7be19000 ffff8000`7be20000   nf_reject_ipv4    (deferred)
ffff8000`7be21000 ffff8000`7be30000   xt_owner   (no symbols)
ffff8000`7be25000 ffff8000`7be2a000   ipt_REJECT   (deferred)
ffff8000`7be2b000 ffff8000`7be32000   xt_comment   (deferred)
ffff8000`7be4e000 ffff8000`7be53000   nf_defrag_ipv4    (deferred)
ffff8000`7be54000 ffff8000`7be63000   xt_conntrack   (no symbols)
ffff8000`7be58000 ffff8000`7be5f000   nf_defrag_ipv6    (deferred)
ffff8000`7be67000 ffff8000`7be9a000   nf_conntrack   (deferred)
ffff8000`80000000 ffff8000`8386a010   vmlinux  T (service symbols: DWARF Private Symbols)        c:\alcda2\a64\ksym\vmlinux
```

```
0: kd> !vmcoreinfo
VMCOREINFO:
     OSRELEASE=6.8.0-1018-oracle
     BUILD-ID=6d7cb96ecca23ed59445043a74fa8eeea1a7426f
     PAGESIZE=4096
     SYMBOL(init_uts_ns)=ffff8000836bb1e0
     OFFSET(uts_namespace.name)=0
     SYMBOL(node_online_map)=ffff80008322ec20
     SYMBOL(swapper_pg_dir)=ffff8000825ef000
     SYMBOL(_stext)=ffff800080010000
     SYMBOL(vmap_area_list)=ffff8000833b4c50
     SYMBOL(mem_section)=ffff0002fe7e25c0
     LENGTH(mem_section)=8192
     SIZE(mem_section)=16
     OFFSET(mem_section.section_mem_map)=0
     NUMBER(SECTION_SIZE_BITS)=27
     NUMBER(MAX_PHYSMEM_BITS)=48
     SIZE(page)=64
     SIZE(pglist_data)=23104
     SIZE(zone)=1984
     SIZE(free_area)=104
     SIZE(list_head)=16
     SIZE(nodemask_t)=8
     OFFSET(page.flags)=0
     OFFSET(page._refcount)=52
     OFFSET(page.mapping)=24
     OFFSET(page.lru)=8
     OFFSET(page._mapcount)=48
     OFFSET(page.private)=40
     OFFSET(page.compound_head)=8
     OFFSET(pglist_data.node_zones)=0
     OFFSET(pglist_data.nr_zones)=20192
     OFFSET(pglist_data.node_start_pfn)=20200
     OFFSET(pglist_data.node_spanned_pages)=20216
     OFFSET(pglist_data.node_id)=20224
     OFFSET(zone.free_area)=256
     OFFSET(zone.vm_stat)=1792
     OFFSET(zone.spanned_pages)=152
     OFFSET(free_area.free_list)=0
     OFFSET(list_head.next)=0
     OFFSET(list_head.prev)=8
     OFFSET(vmap_area.va_start)=0
     OFFSET(vmap_area.list)=40
     LENGTH(zone.free_area)=14
     SYMBOL(prb)=ffff80008326fbf0
```

```
SYMBOL(printk_rb_static)=ffff80008326ff00
SYMBOL(clear_seq)=ffff800083754128
SIZE(printk_ringbuffer)=88
OFFSET(printk_ringbuffer.desc_ring)=0
OFFSET(printk_ringbuffer.text_data_ring)=48
OFFSET(printk_ringbuffer.fail)=80
SIZE(prb_desc_ring)=48
OFFSET(prb_desc_ring.count_bits)=0
OFFSET(prb_desc_ring.descs)=8
OFFSET(prb_desc_ring.infos)=16
OFFSET(prb_desc_ring.head_id)=24
OFFSET(prb_desc_ring.tail_id)=32
SIZE(prb_desc)=24
OFFSET(prb_desc.state_var)=0
OFFSET(prb_desc.text_blk_lpos)=8
SIZE(prb_data_blk_lpos)=16
OFFSET(prb_data_blk_lpos.begin)=0
OFFSET(prb_data_blk_lpos.next)=8
SIZE(printk_info)=88
OFFSET(printk_info.seq)=0
OFFSET(printk_info.ts_nsec)=8
OFFSET(printk_info.text_len)=16
OFFSET(printk_info.caller_id)=20
OFFSET(printk_info.dev_info)=24
SIZE(dev_printk_info)=64
OFFSET(dev_printk_info.subsystem)=0
LENGTH(printk_info_subsystem)=16
OFFSET(dev_printk_info.device)=16
LENGTH(printk_info_device)=48
SIZE(prb_data_ring)=32
OFFSET(prb_data_ring.size_bits)=0
OFFSET(prb_data_ring.data)=8
OFFSET(prb_data_ring.head_lpos)=16
OFFSET(prb_data_ring.tail_lpos)=24
SIZE(atomic_long_t)=8
OFFSET(atomic_long_t.counter)=0
SIZE(latched_seq)=24
OFFSET(latched_seq.val)=8
LENGTH(free_area.free_list)=6
NUMBER(NR_FREE_PAGES)=0
NUMBER(PG_lru)=5
NUMBER(PG_private)=15
NUMBER(PG_swapcache)=12
NUMBER(PG_swapbacked)=19
NUMBER(PG_slab)=11
NUMBER(PG_hwpoison)=22
NUMBER(PG_head_mask)=64
NUMBER(PAGE_BUDDY_MAPCOUNT_VALUE)=-129
NUMBER(PAGE_HUGETLB_MAPCOUNT_VALUE)=-2049
NUMBER(PAGE_OFFLINE_MAPCOUNT_VALUE)=-257
SYMBOL(kallsyms_names)=ffff800081972758
SYMBOL(kallsyms_num_syms)=ffff800081972750
SYMBOL(kallsyms_token_table)=ffff800081b63890
SYMBOL(kallsyms_token_index)=ffff800081b63c58
SYMBOL(kallsyms_offsets)=ffff800081b63e58
SYMBOL(kallsyms_relative_base)=ffff800081c02258
NUMBER(VA_BITS)=48
NUMBER(MODULES_VADDR)=0xffff800000000000
NUMBER(MODULES_END)=0xffff800080000000
NUMBER(VMALLOC_START)=0xffff800080000000
```

```
NUMBER(VMALLOC_END)=0xfffffbfff0000000
NUMBER(VMEMMAP_START)=0xfffffc0000000000
NUMBER(VMEMMAP_END)=0xfffffe0000000000
NUMBER(kimage_voffset)=0xffff7ffd56800000
NUMBER(PHYS_OFFSET)=0x40000000
NUMBER(TCR_EL1_T1SZ)=0x10
KERNELOFFSET=0
NUMBER(KERNELPACMASK)=0x0
CRASHTIME=1735469477
```

5. We can also check backtraces from other CPUs:

```
0: kd> ~1s
WARNING: Unable to reset page directories

1: kd> kL
 # Child-SP          RetAddr               Call Site
00 ffff8000`83953de0 ffff8000`8014f954     vmlinux!default_idle_call+0x54
01 ffff8000`83953e00 ffff8000`8014fa6c     vmlinux!cpuidle_idle_call+0x194
02 ffff8000`83953e40 ffff8000`8014fd10     vmlinux!do_idle+0xac
03 ffff8000`83953e70 ffff8000`8002f7c0     vmlinux!cpu_startup_entry+0x40
04 ffff8000`83953e90 ffff8000`800431c0     vmlinux!secondary_start_kernel+0xe8
05 ffff8000`83953eb0 00000000`00000000     vmlinux!_secondary_switched+0xb8

1: kd> ~2s
2 is not a valid processor number

1: kd> ~0s
WARNING: Unable to reset page directories
```

6. To see the kernel log messages you can use the **!log** command (please refer to GDB exercises for log analysis examples). Another useful command is **!run**:

```
0: kd> !runq
@$runq()
    [0x0]            : CPU 0 run queue [current = 'tee' (4b6)]
        Cpu              : 0x0
        RunQueue         [Type: rq]
        CurrentTask      : tee [Type: task_struct]
        RTTasks
        CfsTasks
            [0x75]           : kworker/0:2 [Type: task_struct]
    [0x1]            : CPU 1 run queue [current = 'swapper/1' (0)]
        Cpu              : 0x1
        RunQueue         [Type: rq]
        CurrentTask      : swapper/1 [Type: task_struct]
        RTTasks
        CfsTasks
```

Note: Please use this Microsoft page[4] for additional commands available from the *LinuxKernel.js* script (but most commands fail with an internal error at the time of this writing and this core dump).

[4] https://learn.microsoft.com/en-us/windows-hardware/drivers/debugger/linux-crash-dumps

7. If you want to dump raw stack data (or any memory), you can use the **dps** and **dpp** commands:

```
0: kd> r
 x0=ffff800085a53948   x1=0000000000000000   x2=ffff800085a53948   x3=ffff8000837979a0
 x4=0000000000000000   x5=0000000000000000   x6=0000000000000000   x7=0000000000000000
 x8=0000000000000000   x9=ffff8000800c83e0  x10=c3f4450c59576232  x11=03fb355d88181a17
x12=16cdbdf007125184  x13=3165bee26289375b  x14=4e5556c504136451  x15=51840dfc495348ae
x16=0000000000000000  x17=0000000000000000  x18=0000000000000000  x19=ffff800083797990
x20=ffff800083797000  x21=0000000000000001  x22=ffff80008374c4c0  x23=0000000000000004
x24=0000000000000000  x25=0000000000000000  x26=ffff8000835da8c0  x27=0000000000000000
x28=ffff0000c413c400   fp=ffff800085a53920   lr=ffff80008020b5f0   sp=ffff800085a53920
 pc=ffff8000802097d0  psr=600000c5 -ZC- EL1
vmlinux!crash_setup_regs+0xa0:
ffff8000`802097d0 stp          x1,x0,[x2,#0x100]

0: kd> dps ffff800085a53920 L20
ffff8000`85a53920  ffff8000`85a53aa0
ffff8000`85a53928  ffff8000`800c83e0 vmlinux!panic+0x350 [/build/linux-oracle-6.8-EzVzJ2/linux-oracle-6.8-6.8.0/kernel/panic.c @ 387]
ffff8000`85a53930  ffff8000`83251c30 vmlinux!kern_panic_table
ffff8000`85a53938  00000000`00000015
ffff8000`85a53940  00000000`00000000
ffff8000`85a53948  ffff8000`85a53948
ffff8000`85a53950  00000000`00000000
ffff8000`85a53958  ffff8000`85a53948
ffff8000`85a53960  ffff8000`837979a0 vmlinux!_kexec_lock
ffff8000`85a53968  00000000`00000000
ffff8000`85a53970  00000000`00000000
ffff8000`85a53978  00000000`00000000
ffff8000`85a53980  00000000`00000000
ffff8000`85a53988  00000000`00000000
ffff8000`85a53990  ffff8000`800c83e0 vmlinux!panic+0x350 [/build/linux-oracle-6.8-EzVzJ2/linux-oracle-6.8-6.8.0/kernel/panic.c @ 387]
ffff8000`85a53998  c3f4450c`59576232
ffff8000`85a539a0  03fb355d`88181a17
ffff8000`85a539a8  16cdbdf0`07125184
ffff8000`85a539b0  3165bee2`6289375b
ffff8000`85a539b8  4e5556c5`04136451
ffff8000`85a539c0  51840dfc`495348ae
ffff8000`85a539c8  00000000`00000000
ffff8000`85a539d0  00000000`00000000
ffff8000`85a539d8  00000000`00000000
ffff8000`85a539e0  ffff8000`83797990 vmlinux!kexec_crash_image
ffff8000`85a539e8  ffff8000`83797000 vmlinux!posix_timers_hashtable+0xc50
ffff8000`85a539f0  00000000`00000001
ffff8000`85a539f8  ffff8000`8374c4c0 vmlinux!warn_count
ffff8000`85a53a00  00000000`00000004
ffff8000`85a53a08  00000000`00000000
ffff8000`85a53a10  00000000`00000000
ffff8000`85a53a18  ffff8000`835da8c0 vmlinux!sysrq_reset_seq_version

0: kd> dpp ffff800085a53920 L20
ffff8000`85a53920  ffff8000`85a53aa0 ffff8000`85a53b80
ffff8000`85a53928  ffff8000`800c83e0 52800020`17ffff86
ffff8000`85a53930  ffff8000`83251c30 ffff8000`81c8a018 vmlinux!$d+0x268
ffff8000`85a53938  00000000`00000015
ffff8000`85a53940  00000000`00000000
ffff8000`85a53948  ffff8000`85a53948 ffff8000`85a53948
ffff8000`85a53950  00000000`00000000
ffff8000`85a53958  ffff8000`85a53948 ffff8000`85a53948
```

```
ffff8000`85a53960  ffff8000`837979a0 00000000`00000001
ffff8000`85a53968  00000000`00000000
ffff8000`85a53970  00000000`00000000
ffff8000`85a53978  00000000`00000000
ffff8000`85a53980  00000000`00000000
ffff8000`85a53988  00000000`00000000
ffff8000`85a53990  ffff8000`800c83e0 52800020`17ffff86
ffff8000`85a53998  c3f4450c`59576232
ffff8000`85a539a0  03fb355d`88181a17
ffff8000`85a539a8  16cdbdf0`07125184
ffff8000`85a539b0  3165bee2`6289375b
ffff8000`85a539b8  4e5556c5`04136451
ffff8000`85a539c0  51840dfc`495348ae
ffff8000`85a539c8  00000000`00000000
ffff8000`85a539d0  00000000`00000000
ffff8000`85a539d8  00000000`00000000
ffff8000`85a539e0  ffff8000`83797990 ffff0000`c180a400
ffff8000`85a539e8  ffff8000`83797000 00000000`00000000
ffff8000`85a539f0  00000000`00000001
ffff8000`85a539f8  ffff8000`8374c4c0 00000000`00000000
ffff8000`85a53a00  00000000`00000004
ffff8000`85a53a08  00000000`00000000
ffff8000`85a53a10  00000000`00000000
ffff8000`85a53a18  ffff8000`835da8c0 00000000`00000001

0: kd> dc ffff800085a53920
ffff8000`85a53920  85a53aa0 ffff8000 800c83e0 ffff8000  .:..............
ffff8000`85a53930  83251c30 ffff8000 00000015 00000000  0.%.............
ffff8000`85a53940  00000000 00000000 85a53948 ffff8000  ........H9......
ffff8000`85a53950  00000000 00000000 85a53948 ffff8000  ........H9......
ffff8000`85a53960  837979a0 ffff8000 00000000 00000000  .yy.............
ffff8000`85a53970  00000000 00000000 00000000 00000000  ................
ffff8000`85a53980  00000000 00000000 00000000 00000000  ................
ffff8000`85a53990  800c83e0 ffff8000 59576232 c3f4450c  ........2bWY.E..

0: kd> db ffff800085a53920
ffff8000`85a53920  a0 3a a5 85 00 80 ff ff-e0 83 0c 80 00 80 ff ff  .:..............
ffff8000`85a53930  30 1c 25 83 00 80 ff ff-15 00 00 00 00 00 00 00  0.%.............
ffff8000`85a53940  00 00 00 00 00 00 00 00-48 39 a5 85 00 80 ff ff  ........H9......
ffff8000`85a53950  00 00 00 00 00 00 00 00-48 39 a5 85 00 80 ff ff  ........H9......
ffff8000`85a53960  a0 79 79 83 00 80 ff ff-00 00 00 00 00 00 00 00  .yy.............
ffff8000`85a53970  00 00 00 00 00 00 00 00-00 00 00 00 00 00 00 00  ................
ffff8000`85a53980  00 00 00 00 00 00 00 00-00 00 00 00 00 00 00 00  ................
ffff8000`85a53990  e0 83 0c 80 00 80 ff ff-32 62 57 59 0c 45 f4 c3  ........2bWY.E..

0: kd> dw ffff800085a53920
ffff8000`85a53920  3aa0 85a5 8000 ffff 83e0 800c 8000 ffff
ffff8000`85a53930  1c30 8325 8000 ffff 0015 0000 0000 0000
ffff8000`85a53940  0000 0000 0000 0000 3948 85a5 8000 ffff
ffff8000`85a53950  0000 0000 0000 0000 3948 85a5 8000 ffff
ffff8000`85a53960  79a0 8379 8000 ffff 0000 0000 0000 0000
ffff8000`85a53970  0000 0000 0000 0000 0000 0000 0000 0000
ffff8000`85a53980  0000 0000 0000 0000 0000 0000 0000 0000
ffff8000`85a53990  83e0 800c 8000 ffff 6232 5957 450c c3f4
```

```
0: kd> dd ffff800085a53920
ffff8000`85a53920  85a53aa0 ffff8000 800c83e0 ffff8000
ffff8000`85a53930  83251c30 ffff8000 00000015 00000000
ffff8000`85a53940  00000000 00000000 85a53948 ffff8000
ffff8000`85a53950  00000000 00000000 85a53948 ffff8000
ffff8000`85a53960  837979a0 ffff8000 00000000 00000000
ffff8000`85a53970  00000000 00000000 00000000 00000000
ffff8000`85a53980  00000000 00000000 00000000 00000000
ffff8000`85a53990  800c83e0 ffff8000 59576232 c3f4450c

0: kd> da ffff800085a53920
ffff8000`85a53920  ".:.."

0: kd> dpa ffff800085a53920
ffff8000`85a53920  ffff8000`85a53aa0 ".;.."
ffff8000`85a53928  ffff8000`800c83e0 ".... "
ffff8000`85a53930  ffff8000`83251c30 "...."
ffff8000`85a53938  00000000`00000015
ffff8000`85a53940  00000000`00000000
ffff8000`85a53948  ffff8000`85a53948 "H9.."
ffff8000`85a53950  00000000`00000000
ffff8000`85a53958  ffff8000`85a53948 "H9.."
ffff8000`85a53960  ffff8000`837979a0 "."
ffff8000`85a53968  00000000`00000000
ffff8000`85a53970  00000000`00000000
ffff8000`85a53978  00000000`00000000
ffff8000`85a53980  00000000`00000000
ffff8000`85a53988  00000000`00000000
ffff8000`85a53990  ffff8000`800c83e0 ".... "
ffff8000`85a53998  c3f4450c`59576232
```

Exercise K2

- **Goal:** Learn how to navigate a problem kernel dump
- **Patterns:** Exception Stack Trace; Exception Module; NULL Pointer (Data); Execution Residue (Kernel Space); Value References
- \ALCDA-Dumps\Exercise-K2-x64-GDB.pdf
- \ALCDA-Dumps\Exercise-K2-A64-GDB.pdf
- \ALCDA-Dumps\Exercise-K2-A64-WinDbg.pdf
- \ALCDA-Dumps\Exercise-K2-x64-WinDbg.pdf

Exercise K2 (x64, GDB)

Goal: Learn how to navigate a problem kernel dump.

Patterns: Exception Stack Trace; Exception Module; NULL Pointer (Data); Execution Residue (Kernel Space); Value References.

1. Load the core dump *202501041608.kdump* from the x64/K2 directory and the matching *vmlinux-6.8.0-1018-azure* file from the x64/KSym directory:

```
~/ALCDA2/x64/K2$ crash 202501041608.kdump ../KSym/vmlinux-6.8.0-1018-azure
```

```
crash 8.0.6++
Copyright (C) 2002-2025  Red Hat, Inc.
Copyright (C) 2004, 2005, 2006, 2010  IBM Corporation
Copyright (C) 1999-2006  Hewlett-Packard Co
Copyright (C) 2005, 2006, 2011, 2012  Fujitsu Limited
Copyright (C) 2006, 2007  VA Linux Systems Japan K.K.
Copyright (C) 2005, 2011, 2020-2024  NEC Corporation
Copyright (C) 1999, 2002, 2007  Silicon Graphics, Inc.
Copyright (C) 1999, 2000, 2001, 2002  Mission Critical Linux, Inc.
Copyright (C) 2015, 2021  VMware, Inc.
This program is free software, covered by the GNU General Public License,
and you are welcome to change it and/or distribute copies of it under
certain conditions.  Enter "help copying" to see the conditions.
This program has absolutely no warranty.  Enter "help warranty" for details.

GNU gdb (GDB) 10.2
Copyright (C) 2021 Free Software Foundation, Inc.
License GPLv3+: GNU GPL version 3 or later <http://gnu.org/licenses/gpl.html>
This is free software: you are free to change and redistribute it.
There is NO WARRANTY, to the extent permitted by law.
Type "show copying" and "show warranty" for details.
This GDB was configured as "x86_64-pc-linux-gnu".
Type "show configuration" for configuration details.
Find the GDB manual and other documentation resources online at:
    <http://www.gnu.org/software/gdb/documentation/>.

For help, type "help".
Type "apropos word" to search for commands related to "word"...

      KERNEL: ../KSym/vmlinux-6.8.0-1018-azure  [TAINTED]
    DUMPFILE: 202501041608.kdump  [PARTIAL DUMP]
        CPUS: 4
        DATE: Sat Jan  4 16:06:42 GMT 2025
      UPTIME: 00:18:42
LOAD AVERAGE: 0.08, 0.11, 0.11
       TASKS: 631
    NODENAME: coredump-alcda
     RELEASE: 6.8.0-1018-azure
     VERSION: #21~22.04.1-Ubuntu SMP Fri Nov  8 00:21:25 UTC 2024
     MACHINE: x86_64  (2112 Mhz)
      MEMORY: 4 GB
       PANIC: "Kernel panic - not syncing: Fatal exception"
         PID: 3856
     COMMAND: "insmod"
        TASK: ffff8fb95ad50000  [THREAD_INFO: ffff8fb95ad50000]
```

```
          CPU: 3
        STATE: TASK_RUNNING (PANIC)

crash>
```

2. We check the log for details, and at the end, we find the bug description, crash RIP that points to the problem source code, the stack pointer, and the stack trace:

```
crash> log -T
[Sat Jan  4 15:48:00 GMT 2025] Linux version 6.8.0-1018-azure (buildd@lcy02-amd64-013) (x86_64-linux-gnu-gcc-11 (Ubuntu 11.4.0-1ubuntu1~22.04) 11.4.0, GNU ld (GNU Binutils for Ubuntu) 2.38) #21~22.04.1-Ubuntu SMP Fri Nov  8 00:21:25 UTC 2024 (Ubuntu 6.8.0-1018.21~22.04.1-azure 6.8.12)
[Sat Jan  4 15:48:00 GMT 2025] Command line: BOOT_IMAGE=/boot/vmlinuz-6.8.0-1018-azure root=UUID=89ee03ba-6808-4977-a4fb-9b10174744f8 ro quiet splash crashkernel=512M-:192M vt.handoff=7
...
...
...
[Sat Jan  4 16:06:42 GMT 2025] BUG: kernel NULL pointer dereference, address: 0000000000000000
[Sat Jan  4 16:06:42 GMT 2025] #PF: supervisor write access in kernel mode
[Sat Jan  4 16:06:42 GMT 2025] #PF: error_code(0x0002) - not-present page
[Sat Jan  4 16:06:42 GMT 2025] PGD 0 P4D 0
[Sat Jan  4 16:06:42 GMT 2025] Oops: 0002 [#1] SMP PTI
[Sat Jan  4 16:06:42 GMT 2025] CPU: 3 PID: 3856 Comm: insmod Kdump: loaded Tainted: G           OE      6.8.0-1018-azure #21~22.04.1-Ubuntu
[Sat Jan  4 16:06:42 GMT 2025] Hardware name: Microsoft Corporation Virtual Machine/Virtual Machine, BIOS Hyper-V UEFI Release v4.1 05/13/2024
[Sat Jan  4 16:06:42 GMT 2025] RIP: 0010:init_module+0x8/0x20 [mod_a]
[Sat Jan  4 16:06:42 GMT 2025] Code: Unable to access opcode bytes at 0xffffffffc0809fee.
[Sat Jan  4 16:06:42 GMT 2025] RSP: 0018:ffffa73508bebbc8 EFLAGS: 00010246
[Sat Jan  4 16:06:42 GMT 2025] RAX: 0000000000000000 RBX: 0000000000000000 RCX: 0000000000000000
[Sat Jan  4 16:06:42 GMT 2025] RDX: 0000000000000000 RSI: ffffffff9b7be8e7 RDI: ffffffffc080a010
[Sat Jan  4 16:06:42 GMT 2025] RBP: ffffa73508bebc38 R08: 0000000000000020 R09: 0000000000000000
[Sat Jan  4 16:06:42 GMT 2025] R10: ffffa73508bebc48 R11: 0000000000000000 R12: ffffffffc080a010
[Sat Jan  4 16:06:42 GMT 2025] R13: ffff8fb906f2e160 R14: 0000000000000000 R15: 0000000000000000
[Sat Jan  4 16:06:42 GMT 2025] FS:  00007e01bbc08c40(0000) GS:ffff8fba03d80000(0000) knlGS:0000000000000000
[Sat Jan  4 16:06:42 GMT 2025] CS:  0010 DS: 0000 ES: 0000 CR0: 0000000080050033
[Sat Jan  4 16:06:42 GMT 2025] CR2: ffffffffc0809fee CR3: 00000000e5fe006 CR4: 00000000003706f0
[Sat Jan  4 16:06:42 GMT 2025] DR0: 0000000000000000 DR1: 0000000000000000 DR2: 0000000000000000
[Sat Jan  4 16:06:42 GMT 2025] DR3: 0000000000000000 DR6: 00000000fffe0ff0 DR7: 0000000000000400
[Sat Jan  4 16:06:42 GMT 2025] Call Trace:
[Sat Jan  4 16:06:42 GMT 2025]  <TASK>
[Sat Jan  4 16:06:42 GMT 2025]  ? show_regs+0x6a/0x80
[Sat Jan  4 16:06:42 GMT 2025]  ? __die+0x25/0x70
[Sat Jan  4 16:06:42 GMT 2025]  ? page_fault_oops+0x79/0x180
[Sat Jan  4 16:06:42 GMT 2025]  ? __kernfs_new_node+0x15f/0x1d0
[Sat Jan  4 16:06:42 GMT 2025]  ? do_user_addr_fault+0x2fe/0x640
[Sat Jan  4 16:06:42 GMT 2025]  ? down_write+0x13/0x60
[Sat Jan  4 16:06:42 GMT 2025]  ? exc_page_fault+0x74/0x160
[Sat Jan  4 16:06:42 GMT 2025]  ? asm_exc_page_fault+0x27/0x30
[Sat Jan  4 16:06:42 GMT 2025]  ? __pfx_init_module+0x10/0x10 [mod_a]
[Sat Jan  4 16:06:42 GMT 2025]  ? do_init_module+0x57/0x2a0
[Sat Jan  4 16:06:42 GMT 2025]  ? __pfx_init_module+0x10/0x10 [mod_a]
[Sat Jan  4 16:06:42 GMT 2025]  ? init_module+0x8/0x20 [mod_a]
[Sat Jan  4 16:06:42 GMT 2025]  ? do_one_initcall+0x46/0x2d0
[Sat Jan  4 16:06:42 GMT 2025]  ? kmalloc_trace+0x131/0x310
[Sat Jan  4 16:06:42 GMT 2025]  ? do_init_module+0x57/0x2a0
[Sat Jan  4 16:06:42 GMT 2025]  do_init_module+0x99/0x2a0
[Sat Jan  4 16:06:42 GMT 2025]  load_module+0xccc/0xe50
[Sat Jan  4 16:06:42 GMT 2025]  ? security_kernel_post_read_file+0x5c/0x70
[Sat Jan  4 16:06:42 GMT 2025]  init_module_from_file+0x9a/0xf0
[Sat Jan  4 16:06:42 GMT 2025]  ? init_module_from_file+0x9a/0xf0
[Sat Jan  4 16:06:42 GMT 2025]  idempotent_init_module+0x10b/0x200
[Sat Jan  4 16:06:42 GMT 2025]  __x64_sys_finit_module+0x60/0xc0
[Sat Jan  4 16:06:42 GMT 2025]  x64_sys_call+0x1954/0x20c0
[Sat Jan  4 16:06:42 GMT 2025]  do_syscall_64+0x7c/0x160
[Sat Jan  4 16:06:42 GMT 2025]  ? irqentry_exit+0x1d/0x30
[Sat Jan  4 16:06:42 GMT 2025]  ? clear_bhb_loop+0x45/0xa0
[Sat Jan  4 16:06:42 GMT 2025]  ? clear_bhb_loop+0x45/0xa0
[Sat Jan  4 16:06:42 GMT 2025]  ? clear_bhb_loop+0x45/0xa0
[Sat Jan  4 16:06:42 GMT 2025]  entry_SYSCALL_64_after_hwframe+0x78/0x80
[Sat Jan  4 16:06:42 GMT 2025] RIP: 0033:0x7e01bb31e88d
```

```
[Sat Jan  4 16:06:42 GMT 2025] Code: 5b 41 5c c3 66 0f 1f 84 00 00 00 00 00 f3 0f 1e fa 48 89 f8 48 89 f7 48 89 d6 48
89 ca 4d 89 c2 4d 89 c8 4c 8b 4c 24 08 0f 05 <48> 3d 01 f0 ff ff 73 01 c3 48 8b 0d 73 b5 0f 00 f7 d8 64 89 01 48
[Sat Jan  4 16:06:42 GMT 2025] RSP: 002b:00007fff12fdbac8 EFLAGS: 00000246 ORIG_RAX: 0000000000000139
[Sat Jan  4 16:06:42 GMT 2025] RAX: ffffffffffffffda RBX: 0000633b1701e780 RCX: 00007e01bb31e88d
[Sat Jan  4 16:06:42 GMT 2025] RDX: 0000000000000000 RSI: 0000633b160a1cd2 RDI: 0000000000000003
[Sat Jan  4 16:06:42 GMT 2025] RBP: 0000000000000000 R08: 0000000000000000 R09: 0000000000000000
[Sat Jan  4 16:06:42 GMT 2025] R10: 0000000000000003 R11: 0000000000000246 R12: 0000633b160a1cd2
[Sat Jan  4 16:06:42 GMT 2025] R13: 0000633b17021430 R14: 0000633b160a0888 R15: 0000633b1701e890
[Sat Jan  4 16:06:42 GMT 2025]  </TASK>
[Sat Jan  4 16:06:42 GMT 2025] Modules linked in: mod_a(OE+) binfmt_misc nls_iso8859_1 crct10dif_pclmul crc32_pclmul
polyval_clmulni polyval_generic ghash_clmulni_intel sha256_ssse3 sha1_ssse3 aesni_intel crypto_simd cryptd serio_raw
hyperv_drm joydev sch_fq_codel hv_sock vsock msr parport_pc ppdev lp parport efi_pstore ip_tables x_tables autofs4
btrfs blake2b_generic xor raid6_pq libcrc32c hid_generic hid_hyperv hv_netvsc hid hyperv_keyboard
[Sat Jan  4 16:06:42 GMT 2025] CR2: 0000000000000000
[Sat Jan  4 16:06:42 GMT 2025] ---[ end trace 0000000000000000 ]---
[Sat Jan  4 16:06:42 GMT 2025] RIP: 0010:init_module+0x8/0x20 [mod_a]
[Sat Jan  4 16:06:42 GMT 2025] Code: Unable to access opcode bytes at 0xffffffffc0809fee.
[Sat Jan  4 16:06:42 GMT 2025] RSP: 0018:ffffa73508bebbc8 EFLAGS: 00010246
[Sat Jan  4 16:06:42 GMT 2025] RAX: 0000000000000000 RBX: 0000000000000000 RCX: 0000000000000000
[Sat Jan  4 16:06:42 GMT 2025] RDX: 0000000000000000 RSI: ffffffff9b7be8e7 RDI: ffffffffc080a010
[Sat Jan  4 16:06:42 GMT 2025] RBP: ffffa73508bebc38 R08: 0000000000000020 R09: 0000000000000000
[Sat Jan  4 16:06:42 GMT 2025] R10: ffffa73508bebc48 R11: 0000000000000000 R12: ffffffffc080a010
[Sat Jan  4 16:06:42 GMT 2025] R13: ffff8fb906f2e160 R14: 0000000000000000 R15: 0000000000000000
[Sat Jan  4 16:06:42 GMT 2025] FS:  00007e01bbc08c40(0000) GS:ffff8fba03d80000(0000) knlGS:0000000000000000
[Sat Jan  4 16:06:42 GMT 2025] CS:  0010 DS: 0000 ES: 0000 CR0: 0000000080050033
[Sat Jan  4 16:06:42 GMT 2025] CR2: ffffffffc0809fee CR3: 00000000e5fe006 CR4: 00000000003706f0
[Sat Jan  4 16:06:42 GMT 2025] DR0: 0000000000000000 DR1: 0000000000000000 DR2: 0000000000000000
[Sat Jan  4 16:06:42 GMT 2025] DR3: 0000000000000000 DR6: 00000000fffe0ff0 DR7: 0000000000000400
[Sat Jan  4 16:06:42 GMT 2025] Kernel panic - not syncing: Fatal exception
[Sat Jan  4 16:06:42 GMT 2025] Kernel Offset: 0x1a600000 from 0xffffffff81000000 (relocation range:
0xffffffff80000000-0xffffffffbfffffff)
```

3. We also get an exception stack trace from the tool where we have more information without and with source code references:

```
crash> bt
PID: 3856      TASK: ffff8fb95ad50000  CPU: 3    COMMAND: "insmod"
 #0 [ffffa73508beb868] machine_kexec at ffffffff9b699db1
 #1 [ffffa73508beb8d0] __crash_kexec at ffffffff9b7f1e46
 #2 [ffffa73508beb990] panic at ffffffff9b6ddf29
 #3 [ffffa73508beba10] oops_end at ffffffff9b643287
 #4 [ffffa73508beba38] page_fault_oops at ffffffff9b6b1000
 #5 [ffffa73508beba98] do_user_addr_fault at ffffffff9b6b1a0e
 #6 [ffffa73508bebae0] exc_page_fault at ffffffff9c6bfd44
 #7 [ffffa73508bebb10] asm_exc_page_fault at ffffffff9c800bc7
    [exception RIP: init_module+8]
    RIP: ffffffffc080a018  RSP: ffffa73508bebbc8  RFLAGS: 00010246
    RAX: 0000000000000000  RBX: 0000000000000000  RCX: 0000000000000000
    RDX: 0000000000000000  RSI: ffffffff9b7be8e7  RDI: ffffffffc080a010
    RBP: ffffa73508bebc38   R8: 0000000000000020   R9: 0000000000000000
    R10: ffffa73508bebc48  R11: 0000000000000000  R12: ffffffffc080a010
    R13: ffff8fb906f2e160  R14: 0000000000000000  R15: 0000000000000000
    ORIG_RAX: ffffffffffffffff  CS: 0010  SS: 0018
 #8 [ffffa73508bebbd0] do_one_initcall at ffffffff9b6029f6
 #9 [ffffa73508bebc40] do_init_module at ffffffff9b7be929
#10 [ffffa73508bebc68] load_module at ffffffff9b7c09ac
#11 [ffffa73508bebd38] init_module_from_file at ffffffff9b7c0e3a
#12 [ffffa73508bebe18] idempotent_init_module at ffffffff9b7c0fab
#13 [ffffa73508bebea0] __x64_sys_finit_module at ffffffff9b7c11e0
#14 [ffffa73508bebed8] x64_sys_call at ffffffff9b6067f4
#15 [ffffa73508bebee8] do_syscall_64 at ffffffff9c6badac
#16 [ffffa73508bebf50] entry_SYSCALL_64_after_hwframe at ffffffff9c800130
    RIP: 00007e01bb31e88d  RSP: 00007fff12fdbac8  RFLAGS: 00000246
    RAX: ffffffffffffffda  RBX: 0000633b1701e780  RCX: 00007e01bb31e88d
    RDX: 0000000000000000  RSI: 0000633b160a1cd2  RDI: 0000000000000003
```

```
    RBP: 0000000000000000   R8: 0000000000000000   R9: 0000000000000000
    R10: 0000000000000003  R11: 0000000000000246  R12: 0000633b160a1cd2
    R13: 0000633b17021430  R14: 0000633b160a0888  R15: 0000633b1701e890
    ORIG_RAX: 0000000000000139  CS: 0033  SS: 002b
```

```
crash> bt -l
PID: 3856     TASK: ffff8fb95ad50000  CPU: 3    COMMAND: "insmod"
 #0 [ffffa73508beb868] machine_kexec at ffffffff9b699db1
    /build/linux-azure-6.8-2oiFiH/linux-azure-6.8-6.8.0/arch/x86/kernel/machine_kexec_64.c: 364
 #1 [ffffa73508beb8d0] __crash_kexec at ffffffff9b7f1e46
    /build/linux-azure-6.8-2oiFiH/linux-azure-6.8-6.8.0/include/linux/atomic/atomic-arch-
fallback.h: 524
 #2 [ffffa73508beb990] panic at ffffffff9b6ddf29
    /build/linux-azure-6.8-2oiFiH/linux-azure-6.8-6.8.0/kernel/panic.c: 389
 #3 [ffffa73508beba10] oops_end at ffffffff9b643287
    /build/linux-azure-6.8-2oiFiH/linux-azure-6.8-6.8.0/arch/x86/kernel/dumpstack.c: 392
 #4 [ffffa73508beba38] page_fault_oops at ffffffff9b6b1000
    /build/linux-azure-6.8-2oiFiH/linux-azure-6.8-6.8.0/arch/x86/mm/fault.c: 710
 #5 [ffffa73508beba98] do_user_addr_fault at ffffffff9b6b1a0e
    /build/linux-azure-6.8-2oiFiH/linux-azure-6.8-6.8.0/arch/x86/mm/fault.c: 1224
 #6 [ffffa73508bebae0] exc_page_fault at ffffffff9c6bfd44
    /build/linux-azure-6.8-2oiFiH/linux-azure-6.8-6.8.0/arch/x86/include/asm/irqflags.h: 37
 #7 [ffffa73508bebb10] asm_exc_page_fault at ffffffff9c800bc7
    /build/linux-azure-6.8-2oiFiH/linux-azure-6.8-6.8.0/arch/x86/include/asm/idtentry.h: 570
    [exception RIP: init_module+8]
    RIP: ffffffffc080a018  RSP: ffffa73508bebbc8  RFLAGS: 00010246
    RAX: 0000000000000000  RBX: 0000000000000000  RCX: 0000000000000000
    RDX: 0000000000000000  RSI: ffffffff9b7be8e7  RDI: ffffffffc080a010
    RBP: ffffa73508bebc38   R8: 0000000000000020   R9: 0000000000000000
    R10: ffffa73508bebc48  R11: 0000000000000000  R12: ffffffffc080a010
    R13: ffff8fb906f2e160  R14: 0000000000000000  R15: 0000000000000000
    ORIG_RAX: ffffffffffffffff  CS: 0010  SS: 0018
 #8 [ffffa73508bebbd0] do_one_initcall at ffffffff9b6029f6
    /build/linux-azure-6.8-2oiFiH/linux-azure-6.8-6.8.0/init/main.c: 1243
 #9 [ffffa73508bebc40] do_init_module at ffffffff9b7be929
    /build/linux-azure-6.8-2oiFiH/linux-azure-6.8-6.8.0/kernel/module/main.c: 2538
#10 [ffffa73508bebc68] load_module at ffffffff9b7c09ac
    /build/linux-azure-6.8-2oiFiH/linux-azure-6.8-6.8.0/kernel/module/main.c: 2989
#11 [ffffa73508bebd38] init_module_from_file at ffffffff9b7c0e3a
    /build/linux-azure-6.8-2oiFiH/linux-azure-6.8-6.8.0/kernel/module/main.c: 3157
#12 [ffffa73508bebe18] idempotent_init_module at ffffffff9b7c0fab
    /build/linux-azure-6.8-2oiFiH/linux-azure-6.8-6.8.0/kernel/module/main.c: 3173
#13 [ffffa73508bebea0] __x64_sys_finit_module at ffffffff9b7c11e0
    /build/linux-azure-6.8-2oiFiH/linux-azure-6.8-6.8.0/include/linux/file.h: 45
#14 [ffffa73508bebed8] x64_sys_call at ffffffff9b6067f4
    /build/linux-azure-6.8-2oiFiH/linux-azure-6.8-6.8.0/arch/x86/entry/syscall_64.c: 33
#15 [ffffa73508bebee8] do_syscall_64 at ffffffff9c6badac
    /build/linux-azure-6.8-2oiFiH/linux-azure-6.8-6.8.0/arch/x86/entry/common.c: 52
#16 [ffffa73508bebf50] entry_SYSCALL_64_after_hwframe at ffffffff9c800130
    /build/linux-azure-6.8-2oiFiH/linux-azure-6.8-6.8.0/arch/x86/entry/entry_64.S: 130
    RIP: 00007e01bb31e88d  RSP: 00007fff12fdbac8  RFLAGS: 00000246
    RAX: ffffffffffffffda  RBX: 0000633b1701e780  RCX: 00007e01bb31e88d
    RDX: 0000000000000000  RSI: 0000633b160a1cd2  RDI: 0000000000000003
    RBP: 0000000000000000   R8: 0000000000000000   R9: 0000000000000000
    R10: 0000000000000003  R11: 0000000000000246  R12: 0000633b160a1cd2
    R13: 0000633b17021430  R14: 0000633b160a0888  R15: 0000633b1701e890
    ORIG_RAX: 0000000000000139  CS: 0033  SS: 002b
```

4. If we disassemble the problem RIP address or function, we confirm NULL pointer dereference (we also see that the code was optimized as we don't see our module function calls from *init_module* that led to the exception):

```
crash> dis ffffffffc080a018
0xffffffffc080a018 <init_module+8>:     movl   $0x1,0x0

crash> dis init_module+8
0xffffffffc080a018 <init_module+8>:     movl   $0x1,0x0

crash> dis init_module
0xffffffffc080a010 <init_module>:       nopl   0x0(%rax,%rax,1) [FTRACE NOP]
0xffffffffc080a015 <init_module+5>:     push   %rbp
0xffffffffc080a016 <init_module+6>:     xor    %eax,%eax
0xffffffffc080a018 <init_module+8>:     movl   $0x1,0x0
0xffffffffc080a023 <init_module+19>:    mov    %rsp,%rbp
0xffffffffc080a026 <init_module+22>:    pop    %rbp
0xffffffffc080a027 <init_module+23>:    ret
0xffffffffc080a028 <init_module+24>:    int3
0xffffffffc080a029 <init_module+25>:    int3
0xffffffffc080a02a <init_module+26>:    int3
0xffffffffc080a02b <init_module+27>:    int3
0xffffffffc080a02c <init_module+28>:    nopl   0x0(%rax)
```

5. Now, we dump the raw stack region around the stack pointer to see exception processing execution residue:

```
crash> rd -SS -64 ffffa73508bebb08 50
ffffa73508bebb08:  ffffa73508bebb19 asm_exc_page_fault+39
ffffa73508bebb18:  0000000000000000 0000000000000000
ffffa73508bebb28:  [ffff8fb906f2e160:kmalloc-rnd-03-32] init_module
ffffa73508bebb38:  ffffa73508bebc38 0000000000000000
ffffa73508bebb48:  0000000000000000 ffffa73508bebc48
ffffa73508bebb58:  0000000000000000 0000000000000020
ffffa73508bebb68:  0000000000000000 0000000000000000
ffffa73508bebb78:  0000000000000000 do_init_module+87
ffffa73508bebb88:  init_module      ffffffffffffffff
ffffa73508bebb98:  init_module+8    0000000000000010
ffffa73508bebba8:  0000000000010246 ffffa73508bebbc8
ffffa73508bebbb8:  0000000000000018 0000000000000000
ffffa73508bebbc8:  ffffa73508bebc38 do_one_initcall+70
ffffa73508bebbd8:  kmalloc_trace+305 0000000000000000
ffffa73508bebbe8:  do_init_module+87 [ffff8fb906f2e160:kmalloc-rnd-03-32]
ffffa73508bebbf8:  ffab5278ba580500 0000000000000000
ffffa73508bebc08:  ffffa73508bebc48 __this_module
ffffa73508bebc18:  ffab5278ba580500 0000000000000000
ffffa73508bebc28:  __this_module    [ffff8fb906f2e160:kmalloc-rnd-03-32]
ffffa73508bebc38:  ffffa73508bebc60 do_init_module+153
ffffa73508bebc48:  0000000000000000 ffffa73508bebd60
ffffa73508bebc58:  0000000000000000 ffffa73508bebd30
ffffa73508bebc68:  load_module+3276 000000000029f328
ffffa73508bebc78:  0000000000000000 __this_module
ffffa73508bebc88:  ffffffff00000000 ffffffff00000000
```

6. Search for the address ffffffffc080a018 in kernel space:

```
crash> search ffffffffc080a018
ffff8fb935e08200: ffffffffc080a018
ffff8fb96cb66b98: ffffffffc080a018
ffffa73508bebb98: ffffffffc080a018
ffffffff9e208200: ffffffffc080a018
```

Note: We see that the address was also found in the raw stack region we inspected in step #5.

7. We can also search for strings; for example, search for "bad" as a value and string:

```
crash> search "bad"
ffff8fb90733dbc0: bad
ffff8fb907585d60: bad
ffff8fb908885d60: bad
ffff8fb908b05d60: bad
ffff8fb908b85d60: bad
ffff8fb91ca09408: bad
ffff8fb91dc9f1b8: bad
ffff8fb93ecc5550: bad
ffff8fb93ecc5590: bad
ffff8fb93ecc55a8: bad
...
...
...

crash> rd ffff8fb908b05d60
ffff8fb908b05d60:  0000000000000bad                    ........

crash> search -c "bad"
ffff8fb90163e589: badge.badge.name...........0...Japanese symbol for begin
ffff8fb90163e58f: badge.name...........0...Japanese symbol for beginner.be
ffff8fb9019819d8: bad_optional_access.so.20210324.0.0....................
ffff8fb901d4ef68: badger.honey badger.pester..........!...>...paw prints.f
ffff8fb901d4ef75: badger.pester..........!...>...paw prints.feet.paw.print
ffff8fb901da8fd0: bad device descriptor (%d)..%04X:%04X:%04X.%04X.
ffff8fb901eb638d: bados.BB.flag..........!..........flag: Bangladesh.BD.f
ffff8fb902647aba: badwaita-1.so.0.......................................
ffff8fb9057e140c: badminton.birdie.game.racquet.shuttlecock.... ......2...
ffff8fb906a7bb4b: badf40d6b8de3311e632045370588e0b23b7a480eb5dc10db65d1b4b
ffff8fb906a87030: badf8fd66b77495f8d94...........................bin:cf13
ffff8fb906a87220: bada..........................bin:cb340011afeb0d74c4a5
ffff8fb906a8738a: bada7768e649d047ff9b1f660c...........................bi
ffff8fb906a87c34: bad0a89bf4c7bfbf.........................bin:e6856f13
ffff8fb906a9c7f3: badafce4356206c85f73e22456eae4ed6ee77f6a9e11a078c.......
ffff8fb9092779b6: bad roots..6ignoring data csums..6setting datacow..6not
ffff8fb909277b14: badroots.ignoredatacsums..6using free-space-tree..6resiz
ffff8fb9092784d4: badroots.idatacsums.all.v1.v2.sync.async.panic.bug.btrfs
ffff8fb909279fea: badroots.ignoredatacsu
ffff8fb90927a200: bad tree block start %llu.&eb->lock.btrfs.fs/btrfs/volum
...
...
...
```

Exercise K2 (A64, GDB)

Goal: Learn how to navigate a problem kernel dump.

Patterns: Exception Stack Trace; Exception Module; NULL Pointer (Data); Execution Residue (Kernel Space); Value References.

1. Load the core dump *202501041634.kdump* from the A64/K2 directory and the matching *vmlinux-6.8.0-1018-oracle* file from the A64/KSym directory:

```
~/ALCDA2/A64/K2$ crash 202501041634.kdump ../KSym/vmlinux-6.8.0-1018-oracle
```

```
crash 8.0.6++
Copyright (C) 2002-2025  Red Hat, Inc.
Copyright (C) 2004, 2005, 2006, 2010  IBM Corporation
Copyright (C) 1999-2006  Hewlett-Packard Co
Copyright (C) 2005, 2006, 2011, 2012  Fujitsu Limited
Copyright (C) 2006, 2007  VA Linux Systems Japan K.K.
Copyright (C) 2005, 2011, 2020-2024  NEC Corporation
Copyright (C) 1999, 2002, 2007  Silicon Graphics, Inc.
Copyright (C) 1999, 2000, 2001, 2002  Mission Critical Linux, Inc.
Copyright (C) 2015, 2021  VMware, Inc.
This program is free software, covered by the GNU General Public License,
and you are welcome to change it and/or distribute copies of it under
certain conditions.  Enter "help copying" to see the conditions.
This program has absolutely no warranty.  Enter "help warranty" for details.

GNU gdb (GDB) 10.2
Copyright (C) 2021 Free Software Foundation, Inc.
License GPLv3+: GNU GPL version 3 or later <http://gnu.org/licenses/gpl.html>
This is free software: you are free to change and redistribute it.
There is NO WARRANTY, to the extent permitted by law.
Type "show copying" and "show warranty" for details.
This GDB was configured as "aarch64-unknown-linux-gnu".
Type "show configuration" for configuration details.
Find the GDB manual and other documentation resources online at:
    <http://www.gnu.org/software/gdb/documentation/>.

For help, type "help".
Type "apropos word" to search for commands related to "word"...

      KERNEL: ../KSym/vmlinux-6.8.0-1018-oracle  [TAINTED]
    DUMPFILE: 202501041634.kdump  [PARTIAL DUMP]
        CPUS: 2
        DATE: Sat Jan  4 16:27:25 UTC 2025
      UPTIME: 6 days, 05:28:12
LOAD AVERAGE: 0.38, 0.08, 0.03
       TASKS: 214
    NODENAME: instance-20230624-1144
     RELEASE: 6.8.0-1018-oracle
     VERSION: #19~22.04.1-Ubuntu SMP Mon Dec  9 23:49:53 UTC 2024
     MACHINE: aarch64  (unknown Mhz)
      MEMORY: 12 GB
       PANIC: "Kernel panic - not syncing: Oops: Fatal exception" (check log for details)
         PID: 177806
     COMMAND: "insmod"
        TASK: ffff0000c72e2200  [THREAD_INFO: ffff0000c72e2200]
```

```
    CPU: 0
   STATE: TASK_RUNNING (PANIC)

crash>
```

2. We check the log for details as suggested, and at the end, we find the bug description, crash PC that points to the problem source code, the stack pointer, and the stack trace:

```
crash> log -T
[Sun Dec 29 10:59:13 UTC 2024] Booting Linux on physical CPU 0x0000000000 [0x413fd0c1]
[Sun Dec 29 10:59:13 UTC 2024] Linux version 6.8.0-1018-oracle (buildd@bos03-arm64-112) (aarch64-linux-gnu-gcc-11
(Ubuntu 11.4.0-1ubuntu1~22.04) 11.4.0, GNU ld (GNU Binutils for Ubuntu) 2.38) #19~22.04.1-Ubuntu SMP Mon Dec  9
23:49:53 UTC 2024 (Ubuntu 6.8.0-1018.19~22.04.1-oracle 6.8.12)
...
...
...
[Sat Jan  4 16:27:13 UTC 2025] Unable to handle kernel NULL pointer dereference at virtual address 0000000000000000
[Sat Jan  4 16:27:13 UTC 2025] Mem abort info:
[Sat Jan  4 16:27:13 UTC 2025]   ESR = 0x0000000096000044
[Sat Jan  4 16:27:13 UTC 2025]   EC = 0x25: DABT (current EL), IL = 32 bits
[Sat Jan  4 16:27:13 UTC 2025]   SET = 0, FnV = 0
[Sat Jan  4 16:27:13 UTC 2025]   EA = 0, S1PTW = 0
[Sat Jan  4 16:27:13 UTC 2025]   FSC = 0x04: level 0 translation fault
[Sat Jan  4 16:27:13 UTC 2025] Data abort info:
[Sat Jan  4 16:27:13 UTC 2025]   ISV = 0, ISS = 0x00000044, ISS2 = 0x00000000
[Sat Jan  4 16:27:13 UTC 2025]   CM = 0, WnR = 1, TnD = 0, TagAccess = 0
[Sat Jan  4 16:27:13 UTC 2025]   GCS = 0, Overlay = 0, DirtyBit = 0, Xs = 0
[Sat Jan  4 16:27:13 UTC 2025] user pgtable: 4k pages, 48-bit VAs, pgdp=000000010ba73000
[Sat Jan  4 16:27:13 UTC 2025] [0000000000000000] pgd=0000000000000000, p4d=0000000000000000
[Sat Jan  4 16:27:13 UTC 2025] Internal error: Oops: 0000000096000044 [#1] SMP
[Sat Jan  4 16:27:13 UTC 2025] Modules linked in: mod_a(OE+) tls xt_comment xt_owner ipt_REJECT nf_reject_ipv4
xt_tcpudp xt_state xt_conntrack nf_conntrack nf_defrag_ipv6 sunrpc nf_defrag_ipv4 nft_compat nf_tables nfnetlink
binfmt_misc nls_iso8859_1 joydev input_leds sch_fq_codel dm_multipath scsi_dh_rdac scsi_dh_emc scsi_dh_alua efi_pstore
ip_tables x_tables autofs4 btrfs blake2b_generic iscsi_tcp libiscsi_tcp libiscsi scsi_transport_iscsi iscsi_ibft
iscsi_boot_sysfs hid_generic usbhid hid raid10 raid456 async_raid6_recov async_memcpy async_pq async_xor async_tx xor
xor_neon raid6_pq libcrc32c raid1 raid0 crct10dif_ce polyval_ce polyval_generic ghash_ce sm4 sha2_ce sha256_arm64
sha1_ce xhci_pci virtio_gpu virtio_dma_buf xhci_pci_renesas aes_neon_bs aes_neon_blk aes_ce_blk aes_ce_cipher
[Sat Jan  4 16:27:13 UTC 2025] CPU: 0 PID: 177806 Comm: insmod Kdump: loaded Tainted: G           OE      6.8.0-1018-
oracle #19~22.04.1-Ubuntu
[Sat Jan  4 16:27:13 UTC 2025] Hardware name: QEMU KVM Virtual Machine, BIOS 1.6.6 08/22/2023
[Sat Jan  4 16:27:13 UTC 2025] pstate: 40400005 (nZcv daif +PAN -UAO -TCO -DIT -SSBS BTYPE=--)
[Sat Jan  4 16:27:13 UTC 2025] pc : init_module+0x14/0x30 [mod_a]
[Sat Jan  4 16:27:13 UTC 2025] lr : do_one_initcall+0x4c/0x328
[Sat Jan  4 16:27:13 UTC 2025] sp : ffff800085aa39c0
[Sat Jan  4 16:27:13 UTC 2025] x29: ffff800085aa39c0 x28: 0000000000000000 x27: 0000000000000000
[Sat Jan  4 16:27:13 UTC 2025] x26: 0000000000000000 x25: ffff80007beaf058 x24: ffff80008335b8c8
[Sat Jan  4 16:27:13 UTC 2025] x23: ffff80007beaf040 x22: 0000000000000000 x21: ffff80008335b8c8
[Sat Jan  4 16:27:13 UTC 2025] x20: ffff0000ca4c1ea0 x19: ffff80007bead008 x18: 0000000000000000
[Sat Jan  4 16:27:13 UTC 2025] x17: 0000000000000000 x16: 0000000000000000 x15: 0000000000000000
[Sat Jan  4 16:27:13 UTC 2025] x14: 0000000000000000 x13: 0064692d646c6975 x12: 622e756e672e6574
[Sat Jan  4 16:27:13 UTC 2025] x11: 0000000000000000 x10: 0000000000000000 x9 : ffff800080015374
[Sat Jan  4 16:27:13 UTC 2025] x8 : 0000000000000000 x7 : 0000000000000000 x6 : 0000000000000000
[Sat Jan  4 16:27:13 UTC 2025] x5 : 0000000000000000 x4 : 0000000000000000 x3 : 0000000000000000
[Sat Jan  4 16:27:13 UTC 2025] x2 : 0000000000000001 x1 : 0000000000000000 x0 : 0000000000000000
[Sat Jan  4 16:27:13 UTC 2025] Call trace:
[Sat Jan  4 16:27:13 UTC 2025]  init_module+0x14/0x30 [mod_a]
[Sat Jan  4 16:27:13 UTC 2025]  do_init_module+0xa0/0x280
[Sat Jan  4 16:27:13 UTC 2025]  load_module+0x7c4/0x8c8
[Sat Jan  4 16:27:13 UTC 2025]  init_module_from_file+0x90/0x108
[Sat Jan  4 16:27:13 UTC 2025]  idempotent_init_module+0x1d0/0x390
[Sat Jan  4 16:27:13 UTC 2025]  __arm64_sys_finit_module+0x70/0xf8
[Sat Jan  4 16:27:13 UTC 2025]  invoke_syscall+0x78/0x128
[Sat Jan  4 16:27:13 UTC 2025]  el0_svc_common.constprop.0+0x48/0x138
[Sat Jan  4 16:27:13 UTC 2025]  do_el0_svc+0x28/0x58
[Sat Jan  4 16:27:13 UTC 2025]  el0_svc+0x40/0x168
[Sat Jan  4 16:27:13 UTC 2025]  el0t_64_sync_handler+0x15c/0x178
[Sat Jan  4 16:27:13 UTC 2025]  el0t_64_sync+0x1a8/0x1b0
[Sat Jan  4 16:27:13 UTC 2025] Code: d503201f d2800001 52800022 52800000 (b9000022)
[Sat Jan  4 16:27:13 UTC 2025] ---[ end trace 0000000000000000 ]---
[Sat Jan  4 16:27:24 UTC 2025] Kernel panic - not syncing: Oops: Fatal exception
[Sat Jan  4 16:27:24 UTC 2025] SMP: stopping secondary CPUs
[Sat Jan  4 16:27:24 UTC 2025] Kernel Offset: disabled
```

```
[Sat Jan  4 16:27:24 UTC 2025] CPU features: 0x1,00000020,7002014a,2101720b
[Sat Jan  4 16:27:25 UTC 2025] Memory Limit: none
[Sat Jan  4 16:27:38 UTC 2025] Starting crashdump kernel...
[Sat Jan  4 16:27:38 UTC 2025] Bye!
```

3. We also get an exception stack trace from the tool where we have more information without and with source code references:

```
crash> bt
PID: 177806   TASK: ffff0000c72e2200  CPU: 0    COMMAND: "insmod"
 #0 [ffff800085aa33f0] machine_kexec at ffff80008003fdcc
 #1 [ffff800085aa3420] __crash_kexec at ffff80008020b600
 #2 [ffff800085aa35a0] panic at ffff8000800c83dc
 #3 [ffff800085aa3680] die at ffff800080025f94
 #4 [ffff800085aa3730] die_kernel_fault at ffff800080043c30
 #5 [ffff800085aa3760] __do_kernel_fault at ffff8000800441e8
 #6 [ffff800085aa3790] do_page_fault at ffff8000815f5944
 #7 [ffff800085aa37f0] do_translation_fault at ffff8000815f5cc0
 #8 [ffff800085aa3800] do_mem_abort at ffff800080043d40
 #9 [ffff800085aa3830] el1_abort at ffff8000815dbdc0
#10 [ffff800085aa3860] el1h_64_sync_handler at ffff8000815ddd8c
#11 [ffff800085aa39a0] el1h_64_sync at ffff800080011310
#12 [ffff800085aa39c0] init_module at ffff80007bead018 [mod_a]
#13 [ffff800085aa3a40] do_init_module at ffff8000801c915c
#14 [ffff800085aa3a70] load_module at ffff8000801cadb8
#15 [ffff800085aa3b40] init_module_from_file at ffff8000801cb11c
#16 [ffff800085aa3c10] idempotent_init_module at ffff8000801cb364
#17 [ffff800085aa3cc0] __arm64_sys_finit_module at ffff8000801cb594
#18 [ffff800085aa3e10] invoke_syscall at ffff8000800313bc
#19 [ffff800085aa3e40] el0_svc_common.constprop.0 at ffff8000800314b4
#20 [ffff800085aa3e70] do_el0_svc at ffff8000800315cc
#21 [ffff800085aa3e80] el0_svc at ffff8000815dd9e4
#22 [ffff800085aa3ea0] el0t_64_sync_handler at ffff8000815ddff8
#23 [ffff800085aa3fe0] el0t_64_sync at ffff80008001163c
     PC: 0000fb1d2d531c28   LR: 0000bab4b81b7364   SP: 0000ffff994dab0
    X29: 0000ffff994dab0  X28: 0000000000000000  X27: 0000bab4b81d4c48
    X26: 0000ffff994dda0  X25: 0000000000000000  X24: 0000000000000000
    X23: 0000bab4df2b1430  X22: 0000000000000000  X21: 0000bab4df2ae7b0
    X20: 0000bab4df2ae8c0  X19: 0000bab4b81bcfc8  X18: 0000000000000000
    X17: 0000fb1d2d531c00  X16: 0000bab4b81d5d48  X15: 0000bab4df2ae020
    X14: 0000000000000040  X13: 8deb6cdb0115a384  X12: 0000000000000001
    X11: 0000000000000000  X10: 0000000000000000   X9: 0000000000000000
     X8: 0000000000000111   X7: 0000ffff994da56   X6: 0000ffff994da56
     X5: 00000000005a587a   X4: 0000000000000000   X3: 0000000000000001
     X2: 0000000000000000   X1: 0000bab4b81bcfc8   X0: 0000000000000003
    ORIG_X0: 0000000000000003  SYSCALLNO: 111  PSTATE: 40001000

crash> bt -l
PID: 177806   TASK: ffff0000c72e2200  CPU: 0    COMMAND: "insmod"
 #0 [ffff800085aa33f0] machine_kexec at ffff80008003fdcc
    /build/linux-oracle-6.8-EzVzJ2/linux-oracle-6.8-6.8.0/arch/arm64/kernel/machine_kexec.c:
177
 #1 [ffff800085aa3420] __crash_kexec at ffff80008020b600
    /build/linux-oracle-6.8-EzVzJ2/linux-oracle-6.8-6.8.0/kernel/kexec_core.c: 1052
 #2 [ffff800085aa35a0] panic at ffff8000800c83dc
    /build/linux-oracle-6.8-EzVzJ2/linux-oracle-6.8-6.8.0/kernel/panic.c: 387
 #3 [ffff800085aa3680] die at ffff800080025f94
    /build/linux-oracle-6.8-EzVzJ2/linux-oracle-6.8-6.8.0/arch/arm64/kernel/traps.c: 234
 #4 [ffff800085aa3730] die_kernel_fault at ffff800080043c30
    /build/linux-oracle-6.8-EzVzJ2/linux-oracle-6.8-6.8.0/arch/arm64/mm/fault.c: 320
```

```
 #5 [ffff800085aa3760] __do_kernel_fault at ffff8000800441e8
    /build/linux-oracle-6.8-EzVzJ2/linux-oracle-6.8-6.8.0/arch/arm64/mm/fault.c: 418
 #6 [ffff800085aa3790] do_page_fault at ffff8000815f5944
    /build/linux-oracle-6.8-EzVzJ2/linux-oracle-6.8-6.8.0/arch/arm64/mm/fault.c: 701
 #7 [ffff800085aa37f0] do_translation_fault at ffff8000815f5cc0
    /build/linux-oracle-6.8-EzVzJ2/linux-oracle-6.8-6.8.0/arch/arm64/mm/fault.c: 712
 #8 [ffff800085aa3800] do_mem_abort at ffff800080043d40
    /build/linux-oracle-6.8-EzVzJ2/linux-oracle-6.8-6.8.0/arch/arm64/mm/fault.c: 848
 #9 [ffff800085aa3830] el1_abort at ffff8000815dbdc0
    /build/linux-oracle-6.8-EzVzJ2/linux-oracle-6.8-6.8.0/arch/arm64/kernel/entry-common.c: 398
#10 [ffff800085aa3860] el1h_64_sync_handler at ffff8000815ddd8c
    /build/linux-oracle-6.8-EzVzJ2/linux-oracle-6.8-6.8.0/arch/arm64/kernel/entry-common.c: 458
#11 [ffff800085aa39a0] el1h_64_sync at ffff800080011310
    /build/linux-oracle-6.8-EzVzJ2/linux-oracle-6.8-6.8.0/arch/arm64/kernel/entry.S: 593
#12 [ffff800085aa39c0] init_module at ffff80007bead018 [mod_a]
#13 [ffff800085aa3a40] do_init_module at ffff8000801c915c
    /build/linux-oracle-6.8-EzVzJ2/linux-oracle-6.8-6.8.0/kernel/module/main.c: 2538
#14 [ffff800085aa3a70] load_module at ffff8000801cadb8
    /build/linux-oracle-6.8-EzVzJ2/linux-oracle-6.8-6.8.0/kernel/module/main.c: 2989
#15 [ffff800085aa3b40] init_module_from_file at ffff8000801cb11c
    /build/linux-oracle-6.8-EzVzJ2/linux-oracle-6.8-6.8.0/kernel/module/main.c: 3178
#16 [ffff800085aa3c10] idempotent_init_module at ffff8000801cb364
    /build/linux-oracle-6.8-EzVzJ2/linux-oracle-6.8-6.8.0/kernel/module/main.c: 3190
#17 [ffff800085aa3cc0] __arm64_sys_finit_module at ffff8000801cb594
    /build/linux-oracle-6.8-EzVzJ2/linux-oracle-6.8-6.8.0/kernel/module/main.c: 3217
#18 [ffff800085aa3e10] invoke_syscall at ffff8000800313bc
    /build/linux-oracle-6.8-EzVzJ2/linux-oracle-6.8-6.8.0/arch/arm64/kernel/syscall.c: 37
#19 [ffff800085aa3e40] el0_svc_common.constprop.0 at ffff8000800314b4
    /build/linux-oracle-6.8-EzVzJ2/linux-oracle-6.8-6.8.0/arch/arm64/kernel/syscall.c: 134
#20 [ffff800085aa3e70] do_el0_svc at ffff8000800315cc
    /build/linux-oracle-6.8-EzVzJ2/linux-oracle-6.8-6.8.0/arch/arm64/kernel/syscall.c: 153
#21 [ffff800085aa3e80] el0_svc at ffff8000815dd9e4
    /build/linux-oracle-6.8-EzVzJ2/linux-oracle-6.8-6.8.0/arch/arm64/kernel/entry-common.c: 678
#22 [ffff800085aa3ea0] el0t_64_sync_handler at ffff8000815ddff8
    /build/linux-oracle-6.8-EzVzJ2/linux-oracle-6.8-6.8.0/arch/arm64/kernel/entry-common.c: 696
#23 [ffff800085aa3fe0] el0t_64_sync at ffff80008001163c
    /build/linux-oracle-6.8-EzVzJ2/linux-oracle-6.8-6.8.0/arch/arm64/kernel/entry.S: 598
     PC: 0000fb1d2d531c28   LR: 0000bab4b81b7364   SP: 0000ffffff994dab0
    X29: 0000ffffff994dab0  X28: 0000000000000000  X27: 0000bab4b81d4c48
    X26: 0000ffffff994dda0  X25: 0000000000000000  X24: 0000000000000000
    X23: 0000bab4df2b1430  X22: 0000000000000000  X21: 0000bab4df2ae7b0
    X20: 0000bab4df2ae8c0  X19: 0000bab4b81bcfc8  X18: 0000000000000000
    X17: 0000fb1d2d531c00  X16: 0000bab4b81d5d48  X15: 0000bab4df2ae020
    X14: 0000000000000040  X13: 8deb6cdb0115a384  X12: 0000000000000001
    X11: 0000000000000000  X10: 0000000000000000   X9: 0000000000000000
     X8: 0000000000000111   X7: 0000ffffff994da56   X6: 0000ffffff994da56
     X5: 00000000005a587a   X4: 0000000000000000   X3: 0000000000000001
     X2: 0000000000000000   X1: 0000bab4b81bcfc8   X0: 0000000000000003
    ORIG_X0: 0000000000000003  SYSCALLNO: 111  PSTATE: 40001000
```

4. If we disassemble the problem PC address or function, we confirm NULL pointer dereference (we also see that the code was optimized as we don't see our module function calls from *init_module* that led to the exception):

```
crash> dis ffff80007bead018
0xffff80007bead018 <init_module+16>:    mov     w0, #0x0                        // #0
```

```
crash> dis init_module
0xffff80007bead008 <init_module>:       mov     x9, x30
0xffff80007bead00c <init_module+4>:     nop
0xffff80007bead010 <init_module+8>:     mov     x1, #0x0                        // #0
0xffff80007bead014 <init_module+12>:    mov     w2, #0x1                        // #1
0xffff80007bead018 <init_module+16>:    mov     w0, #0x0                        // #0
0xffff80007bead01c <init_module+20>:    str     w2, [x1]
0xffff80007bead020 <init_module+24>:    mov     x1, #0x0                        // #0
0xffff80007bead024 <init_module+28>:    mov     x2, #0x0                        // #0
0xffff80007bead028 <init_module+32>:    ret
0xffff80007bead02c <init_module+36>:    nop
0xffff80007bead030 <init_module+40>:    .inst   0x81634280 ; undefined
0xffff80007bead034 <init_module+44>:    .inst   0xffff8000 ; undefined
```

Note: We see that the real PC for the fault is `init_module+20`.

5. Now, we dump the raw stack region around the stack pointer to see exception processing execution residue:

```
crash> rd -SS -64 ffff800085aa3800 80
ffff800085aa3800:  ffff800085aa3830 el1_abort+76
ffff800085aa3810:  ffff800085aa3870 0000000096000044
ffff800085aa3820:  0000000000000000 init_module+20
ffff800085aa3830:  ffff800085aa3860 el1h_64_sync_handler+376
ffff800085aa3840:  init_module      [ffff0000ca4c1ea0:kmalloc-rnd-09-32]
ffff800085aa3850:  ffff800085aa39c0 __this_module+1160
ffff800085aa3860:  ffff800085aa39a0 el1h_64_sync+124
ffff800085aa3870:  0000000000000000 0000000000000000
ffff800085aa3880:  0000000000000001 0000000000000000
ffff800085aa3890:  0000000000000000 0000000000000000
ffff800085aa38a0:  0000000000000000 0000000000000000
ffff800085aa38b0:  0000000000000000 do_one_initcall+76
ffff800085aa38c0:  0000000000000000 0000000000000000
ffff800085aa38d0:  622e756e672e6574 0064692d646c6975
ffff800085aa38e0:  0000000000000000 0000000000000000
ffff800085aa38f0:  0000000000000000 0000000000000000
ffff800085aa3900:  0000000000000000 init_module
ffff800085aa3910:  [ffff0000ca4c1ea0:kmalloc-rnd-09-32] module_notify_list
ffff800085aa3920:  0000000000000000 __this_module
ffff800085aa3930:  module_notify_list __this_module+24
ffff800085aa3940:  0000000000000000 0000000000000000
ffff800085aa3950:  0000000000000000 ffff800085aa39c0
ffff800085aa3960:  do_one_initcall+76 ffff800085aa39c0
ffff800085aa3970:  init_module+20   0000000040400005
ffff800085aa3980:  ffff800085aa39d0 kvfree+80
ffff800085aa3990:  [ffff0000c0310600:kmalloc-rnd-04-512] fffffc00032ff040
ffff800085aa39a0:  ffff800085aa39c0 init_module+20
ffff800085aa39b0:  0000000000000027 0000000000000000
ffff800085aa39c0:  ffff800085aa3a40 do_init_module+160
ffff800085aa39d0:  __this_module    [ffff0000ca4c1ea0:kmalloc-rnd-09-32]
ffff800085aa39e0:  module_notify_list ffff800085aa3b78
ffff800085aa39f0:  __this_module    0000000000000000
ffff800085aa3a00:  module_notify_list ffff800085aa3b78
ffff800085aa3a10:  __this_module    module_notify_list
ffff800085aa3a20:  __this_module+24 0000000000000000
ffff800085aa3a30:  [ffff0000ca4c1ea0:kmalloc-rnd-09-32] 60066b6b1c517d00
ffff800085aa3a40:  ffff800085aa3a70 load_module+1988
ffff800085aa3a50:  0000000000000000 0000000000000000
ffff800085aa3a60:  0000000000000000 ffff800085aa3b78
```

6. Search for the address search **init_module+20** in kernel space:

```
crash> search init_module+20
ffff00013a197828: ffff80007bead01c (init_module+20)
ffff00013a197970: ffff80007bead01c (init_module+20)
ffff00013a1979a8: ffff80007bead01c (init_module+20)
ffff800085aa3828: ffff80007bead01c (init_module+20)
ffff800085aa3970: ffff80007bead01c (init_module+20)
ffff800085aa39a8: ffff80007bead01c (init_module+20)
```

Note: We see that the address was also found in the raw stack region we inspected in step #5.

7. We can also search for strings; for example, search for "bad" as a value and string:

```
crash> search "bad"
ffff0000c06bede8: bad
ffff0000c1088c18: bad
ffff0000c1088c20: bad
ffff0000c1102eb0: bad
ffff0000c3d20270: bad
ffff0000c4402eb0: bad
ffff0000c58205d8: bad
ffff0000c5820858: bad
ffff0000c5ea3f58: bad
ffff0000c5ea3fc8: bad
ffff0000c5ea4a00: bad
...
...
...

crash> rd ffff0000c1102eb0
ffff0000c1102eb0:  0000000000000bad                    ........

crash> search -c "bad"
ffff0000c05a7786: badc5b4a018cb39e7e5816a825...........................
ffff0000c063a4b8: bados|.......Belem.......Belize.......Blanc-Sablon....
ffff0000c063aebf: bad.......Atyrau<.......Baghdadf.......Bahrain.......B
ffff0000c063b5ae: bad.......Atyrau.......Baghdad.......Bahrain.......B
ffff0000c063ebb3: badosa.......Belem.......Belize.......Blanc-Sablon....
ffff0000c1a4535c: baddddrrrrrrrrrrrrrrrrrrrrrrrrrrrrrrrrrrrrrrrrrrrrrrr
ffff0000c1a4c79d: bad type %d!.......%p......&wq->queue......autofs4:pid:%
ffff0000c1dcb5fd: bad.......Atyrau.......Baghdad;.......Bahrain_.......B
ffff0000c2d2f638: bad-regnum.exp...................................
ffff0000c3eee63d: bad0000-f02bcbba2000.......................Ke......hd..
ffff0000c52dfce4: bad_verifier................svc_replace_page_err........
ffff0000c56d1424: bad_callhdr.rpc_buffers.....memory.events....note.Linux.
ffff0000c56d1ea5: bad_creds..memory.reclaim..__jump_table....cpu.weight...
ffff0000c6576970: bad device descriptor (%d)......%04X:%04X:%04X.%04X.....
ffff0000c65be2ff: bad disk number %d - aborting!....4md/raid0:%s: multiple
ffff0000c710a137: bad.......Atyrau.......Baghdad.......Bahrain.......B
ffff0000c71142d9: bados.......Belem.......Belize.......Blanc-Sablon7...
ffff0000c7114cd4: bad.......Atyrau.......Baghdad.......Bahrain.......B
ffff0000c81b2879: bad|.......Atyrau.......Baghdad.......Bahrain.......B
ffff0000c81b3777: badosh.......Belem.......Belize.......Blanc-Sablon....
ffff0000c81b4e7e: badosM.......Belemq.......Belize.......Blanc-Sablon....
ffff0000c81b7b63: bados..........*d.%............/../America/Belem........
...
...
...
```

Exercise K2 (x64, WinDbg)

Goal: Learn how to navigate a problem kernel dump.

Patterns: Exception Stack Trace; Exception Module; NULL Pointer (Data); Execution Residue (Kernel Space); Value References.

1. Copy the *vmlinux-6.8.0-1018-azure* file in the x64/KSym directory to the *vmlinux* file.

2. Launch WinDbg. Load the core dump *202501041608.kdump* from the x64/K2 directory and set the symbol path to the x64/KSym directory (there may be some delay/unresponsiveness when you type the **.reload** command):

```
Microsoft (R) Windows Debugger Version 10.0.27725.1000 AMD64
Copyright (c) Microsoft Corporation. All rights reserved.


Loading Dump File [C:\ALCDA2\x64\K2\202501041608.kdump]
64-bit machine not using 64-bit API

************* Path validation summary **************
Response                         Time (ms)     Location
OK                                             C:\ALCDA2\A64\KSym\
Symbol search path is: C:\ALCDA2\A64\KSym\
Executable search path is:
Generic Unix Kernel Version 0 MP (4 procs) Free x64
Primary image base = 0xffffffff`9b600000 Loaded module list = 0x00000000`00000000
System Uptime: not available
Loading Kernel Symbols

Loading User Symbols

ReadVirtual() failed in GetXStateConfiguration() first read attempt (error == 0.)
For analysis of this file, run !analyze -v
ffffffff`9c6c1a1b cli

0: kd> .sympath C:\ALCDA2\x64\KSym\
Symbol search path is: C:\ALCDA2\x64\KSym\
Expanded Symbol search path is: c:\alcda2\x64\ksym\

************* Path validation summary **************
Response                         Time (ms)     Location
OK                                             C:\ALCDA2\x64\KSym\

0: kd> .reload
Loading Kernel Symbols
.*** WARNING: Unable to verify timestamp for vmlinux

Loading User Symbols


************* Symbol Loading Error Summary **************
Module name            Error
vmlinux                The system cannot find the file specified

You can troubleshoot most symbol related issues by turning on symbol loading diagnostics (!sym
noisy) and repeating the command that caused symbols to be loaded.
```

You should also verify that your symbol search path (.sympath) is correct.

3. We see the kernel log messages using the **!log** command and find the bug description, crash RIP that points to the problem source code, the stack pointer, and the stack trace:

```
0: kd> !log
@$log()
    [0x0]            : [     0.000000] Linux version 6.8.0-1018-azure (buildd@lcy02-amd64-013) (x86_64-linux-gnu-gcc-11 (Ubuntu 11.4.0-1ubuntu1~22.04) 11.4.0, GNU ld (GNU Binutils for Ubuntu) 2.38) #21~22.04.1-Ubuntu SMP Fri Nov  8 00:21:25 UTC 2024 (Ubuntu 6.8.0-1018.21~22.04.1-azure 6.8.12)
    [0x1]            : [     0.000000] Command line: BOOT_IMAGE=/boot/vmlinuz-6.8.0-1018-azure root=UUID=89ee03ba-6808-4977-a4fb-9b10174744f8 ro quiet splash crashkernel=512M-:192M vt.handoff=7
    [0x2]            : [     0.000000] KERNEL supported cpus:
...
...
...
    [0x232]          : [  1122.792418] BUG: kernel NULL pointer dereference, address: 0000000000000000
    [0x233]          : [  1122.792423] #PF: supervisor write access in kernel mode
    [0x234]          : [  1122.792425] #PF: error_code(0x0002) - not-present page
    [0x235]          : [  1122.792427] PGD 0 P4D 0
    [0x236]          : [  1122.792430] Oops: 0002 [#1] SMP PTI
    [0x237]          : [  1122.792434] CPU: 3 PID: 3856 Comm: insmod Kdump: loaded Tainted: G           OE      6.8.0-1018-azure #21~22.04.1-Ubuntu
    [0x238]          : [  1122.792437] Hardware name: Microsoft Corporation Virtual Machine/Virtual Machine, BIOS Hyper-V UEFI Release v4.1 05/13/2024
    [0x239]          : [  1122.792439] RIP: 0010:init_module+0x8/0x20 [mod_a]
    [0x23a]          : [  1122.792446] Code: Unable to access opcode bytes at 0xffffffffc0809fee.
    [0x23b]          : [  1122.792447] RSP: 0018:ffffa73508bebbc8 EFLAGS: 00010246
    [0x23c]          : [  1122.792450] RAX: 0000000000000000 RBX: 0000000000000000 RCX: 0000000000000000
    [0x23d]          : [  1122.792452] RDX: 0000000000000000 RSI: ffffffff9b7be8e7 RDI: ffffffffc080a010
    [0x23e]          : [  1122.792453] RBP: ffffa73508bebc38 R08: 0000000000000020 R09: 0000000000000000
    [0x23f]          : [  1122.792455] R10: ffffa73508bebc48 R11: 0000000000000000 R12: ffffffffc080a010
    [0x240]          : [  1122.792457] R13: ffff8fb906f2e160 R14: 0000000000000000 R15: 0000000000000000
    [0x241]          : [  1122.792460] FS:  00007e01bbc08c40(0000) GS:ffff8fba03d80000(0000) knlGS:0000000000000000
    [0x242]          : [  1122.792462] CS:  0010 DS: 0000 ES: 0000 CR0: 0000000080050033
    [0x243]          : [  1122.792464] CR2: ffffffffc0809fee CR3: 000000000e5fe006 CR4: 00000000003706f0
    [0x244]          : [  1122.792466] DR0: 0000000000000000 DR1: 0000000000000000 DR2: 0000000000000000
    [0x245]          : [  1122.792467] DR3: 0000000000000000 DR6: 00000000fffe0ff0 DR7: 0000000000000400
    [0x246]          : [  1122.792469] Call Trace:
    [0x247]          : [  1122.792470]  <TASK>
    [0x248]          : [  1122.792473]  ? show_regs+0x6a/0x80
    [0x249]          : [  1122.792479]  ? __die+0x25/0x70
    [0x24a]          : [  1122.792482]  ? page_fault_oops+0x79/0x180
    [0x24b]          : [  1122.792485]  ? __kernfs_new_node+0x15f/0x1d0
    [0x24c]          : [  1122.792489]  ? do_user_addr_fault+0x2fe/0x640
    [0x24d]          : [  1122.792491]  ? down_write+0x13/0x60
    [0x24e]          : [  1122.792495]  ? exc_page_fault+0x74/0x160
    [0x24f]          : [  1122.792499]  ? asm_exc_page_fault+0x27/0x30
    [0x250]          : [  1122.792504]  ? __pfx_init_module+0x10/0x10 [mod_a]
    [0x251]          : [  1122.792509]  ? do_init_module+0x57/0x2a0
    [0x252]          : [  1122.792513]  ? __pfx_init_module+0x10/0x10 [mod_a]
    [0x253]          : [  1122.792518]  ? init_module+0x8/0x20 [mod_a]
    [0x254]          : [  1122.792522]  ? do_one_initcall+0x46/0x2d0
    [0x255]          : [  1122.792526]  ? kmalloc_trace+0x131/0x310
    [0x256]          : [  1122.792530]  ? do_init_module+0x57/0x2a0
    [0x257]          : [  1122.792533]  do_init_module+0x99/0x2a0
    [...]

    [0x258]          : [  1122.792536]  load_module+0xccc/0xe50
    [0x259]          : [  1122.792539]  ? security_kernel_post_read_file+0x5c/0x70
    [0x25a]          : [  1122.792544]  init_module_from_file+0x9a/0xf0
    [0x25b]          : [  1122.792547]  ? init_module_from_file+0x9a/0xf0
    [0x25c]          : [  1122.792551]  idempotent_init_module+0x10b/0x200
    [0x25d]          : [  1122.792555]  __x64_sys_finit_module+0x60/0xc0
    [0x25e]          : [  1122.792558]  x64_sys_call+0x1954/0x20c0
    [0x25f]          : [  1122.792560]  do_syscall_64+0x7c/0x160
    [0x260]          : [  1122.792563]  ? irqentry_exit+0x1d/0x30
    [0x261]          : [  1122.792566]  ? clear_bhb_loop+0x45/0xa0
    [0x262]          : [  1122.792568]  ? clear_bhb_loop+0x45/0xa0
    [0x263]          : [  1122.792570]  ? clear_bhb_loop+0x45/0xa0
    [0x264]          : [  1122.792572]  entry_SYSCALL_64_after_hwframe+0x78/0x80
    [0x265]          : [  1122.792575] RIP: 0033:0x7e01bb31e88d
```

```
    [0x266]         : [  1122.792582] Code: 5b 41 5c c3 66 0f 1f 84 00 00 00 00 00 f3 0f 1e fa 48 89 f8 48 89 f7 48
89 d6 48 89 ca 4d 89 c2 4d 89 c8 4c 8b 4c 24 08 0f 05 <48> 3d 01 f0 ff ff 73 01 c3 48 8b 0d 73 b5 0f 00 f7 d8 64 89 01
48
    [0x267]         : [  1122.792584] RSP: 002b:00007fff12fdbac8 EFLAGS: 00000246 ORIG_RAX: 0000000000000139
    [0x268]         : [  1122.792587] RAX: ffffffffffffffda RBX: 0000633b1701e780 RCX: 00007e01bb31e88d
    [0x269]         : [  1122.792589] RDX: 0000000000000000 RSI: 0000633b160a1cd2 RDI: 0000000000000003
    [0x26a]         : [  1122.792590] RBP: 0000000000000000 R08: 0000000000000000 R09: 0000000000000000
    [0x26b]         : [  1122.792592] R10: 0000000000000003 R11: 0000000000000246 R12: 0000633b160a1cd2
    [0x26c]         : [  1122.792593] R13: 0000633b17021430 R14: 0000633b160a0888 R15: 0000633b1701e890
    [0x26d]         : [  1122.792596]  </TASK>
    [0x26e]         : [  1122.792597] Modules linked in: mod_a(OE+) binfmt_misc nls_iso8859_1 crct10dif_pclmul
crc32_pclmul polyval_clmulni polyval_generic ghash_clmulni_intel sha256_ssse3 sha1_ssse3 aesni_intel crypto_simd
cryptd serio_raw hyperv_drm joydev sch_fq_codel hv_sock vsock msr parport_pc ppdev lp parport efi_pstore ip_tables
x_tables autofs4 btrfs blake2b_generic xor raid6_pq libcrc32c hid_generic hid_hyperv hv_netvsc hid hyperv_keyboard
    [0x26f]         : [  1122.792628] CR2: 0000000000000000
    [0x270]         : [  1122.792630] ---[ end trace 0000000000000000 ]---
    [0x271]         : [  1122.949237] RIP: 0010:init_module+0x8/0x20 [mod_a]
    [0x272]         : [  1122.949261] Code: Unable to access opcode bytes at 0xffffffffc0809fee.
    [0x273]         : [  1122.949264] RSP: 0018:ffffa73508bebbc8 EFLAGS: 00010246
    [0x274]         : [  1122.949268] RAX: 0000000000000000 RBX: 0000000000000000 RCX: 0000000000000000
    [0x275]         : [  1122.949270] RDX: 0000000000000000 RSI: ffffffff9b7be8e7 RDI: ffffffffc080a010
    [0x276]         : [  1122.949271] RBP: ffffa73508bebc38 R08: 0000000000000020 R09: 0000000000000000
    [0x277]         : [  1122.949273] R10: ffffa73508bebc48 R11: 0000000000000000 R12: ffffffffc080a010
    [0x278]         : [  1122.949275] R13: ffff8fb906f2e160 R14: 0000000000000000 R15: 0000000000000000
    [0x279]         : [  1122.949278] FS:  00007e01bbc08c40(0000) GS:ffff8fba03d80000(0000) knlGS:0000000000000000
    [0x27a]         : [  1122.949281] CS:  0010 DS: 0000 ES: 0000 CR0: 0000000080050033
    [0x27b]         : [  1122.949283] CR2: ffffffffc0809fee CR3: 000000000e5fe006 CR4: 00000000003706f0
    [0x27c]         : [  1122.949285] DR0: 0000000000000000 DR1: 0000000000000000 DR2: 0000000000000000
    [0x27d]         : [  1122.949286] DR3: 0000000000000000 DR6: 00000000fffe0ff0 DR7: 0000000000000400
    [0x27e]         : [  1122.949289] Kernel panic - not syncing: Fatal exception
```

4. Unfortunately, in this dump, we can only inspect the raw stack region around the stack pointer to see exception processing execution residue:

```
0: kd> dps ffffa73508bebbc8-100 L50
ffffa735`08bebac8  00000000`00000002
ffffa735`08bebad0  00000000`00000000
ffffa735`08bebad8  ffffa735`08bebb08
ffffa735`08bebae0  ffffffff`9c6bfd44 vmlinux!exc_page_fault+0x74 [/build/linux-azure-6.8-
2oiFiH/linux-azure-6.8-6.8.0/arch/x86/include/asm/irqflags.h @ 37]
ffffa735`08bebae8  00000000`00000000
ffffa735`08bebaf0  00000000`00000000
ffffa735`08bebaf8  00000000`00000000
ffffa735`08bebb00  00000000`00000000
ffffa735`08bebb08  ffffa735`08bebb19
ffffa735`08bebb10  ffffffff`9c800bc7 vmlinux!asm_exc_page_fault+0x27 [/build/linux-azure-6.8-
2oiFiH/linux-azure-6.8-6.8.0/arch/x86/include/asm/idtentry.h @ 570]
ffffa735`08bebb18  00000000`00000000
ffffa735`08bebb20  00000000`00000000
ffffa735`08bebb28  ffff8fb9`06f2e160
ffffa735`08bebb30  ffffffff`c080a010
ffffa735`08bebb38  ffffa735`08bebc38
ffffa735`08bebb40  00000000`00000000
ffffa735`08bebb48  00000000`00000000
ffffa735`08bebb50  ffffa735`08bebc48
ffffa735`08bebb58  00000000`00000000
ffffa735`08bebb60  00000000`00000020
ffffa735`08bebb68  00000000`00000000
ffffa735`08bebb70  00000000`00000000
ffffa735`08bebb78  00000000`00000000
ffffa735`08bebb80  ffffffff`9b7be8e7 vmlinux!do_init_module+0x57
ffffa735`08bebb88  ffffffff`c080a010
ffffa735`08bebb90  ffffffff`ffffffff
ffffa735`08bebb98  ffffffff`c080a018
ffffa735`08bebba0  00000000`00000010
ffffa735`08bebba8  00000000`00010246
```

```
ffffa735`08bebbb0  ffffa735`08bebbc8
ffffa735`08bebbb8  00000000`00000018
ffffa735`08bebbc0  00000000`00000000
ffffa735`08bebbc8  ffffa735`08bebc38
ffffa735`08bebbd0  ffffffff`9b6029f6 vmlinux!do_one_initcall+0x46 [/build/linux-azure-6.8-2oiFiH/linux-azure-6.8-6.8.0/init/main.c @ 1243]
ffffa735`08bebbd8  ffffffff`9ba01ec1 vmlinux!kmalloc_trace+0x131 [/build/linux-azure-6.8-2oiFiH/linux-azure-6.8-6.8.0/arch/x86/include/asm/jump_label.h @ 55]
ffffa735`08bebbe0  00000000`00000000
ffffa735`08bebbe8  ffffffff`9b7be8e7 vmlinux!do_init_module+0x57
ffffa735`08bebbf0  ffff8fb9`06f2e160
ffffa735`08bebbf8  ffab5278`ba580500
ffffa735`08bebc00  00000000`00000000
ffffa735`08bebc08  ffffa735`08bebc48
ffffa735`08bebc10  ffffffff`c080c040
ffffa735`08bebc18  ffab5278`ba580500
ffffa735`08bebc20  00000000`00000000
ffffa735`08bebc28  ffffffff`c080c040
ffffa735`08bebc30  ffff8fb9`06f2e160
ffffa735`08bebc38  ffffa735`08bebc60
ffffa735`08bebc40  ffffffff`9b7be929 vmlinux!do_init_module+0x99
ffffa735`08bebc48  00000000`00000000
ffffa735`08bebc50  ffffa735`08bebd60
ffffa735`08bebc58  00000000`00000000
ffffa735`08bebc60  ffffa735`08bebd30
ffffa735`08bebc68  ffffffff`9b7c09ac vmlinux!load_module+0xccc
ffffa735`08bebc70  00000000`0029f328
ffffa735`08bebc78  00000000`00000000
ffffa735`08bebc80  ffffffff`c080c040
ffffa735`08bebc88  ffffffff`00000000
ffffa735`08bebc90  ffffffff`00000000
ffffa735`08bebc98  ffffffff`c080c040
ffffa735`08bebca0  00000000`00029100
ffffa735`08bebca8  ffffa735`08bebce0
ffffa735`08bebcb0  ffffffff`9bc5818c vmlinux!security_kernel_post_read_file+0x5c [/build/linux-azure-6.8-2oiFiH/linux-azure-6.8-6.8.0/security/security.c @ 3309]
ffffa735`08bebcb8  00000000`00029100
ffffa735`08bebcc0  00000000`00029100
ffffa735`08bebcc8  00000000`7fffffff
ffffa735`08bebcd0  00000000`00000000
ffffa735`08bebcd8  ffff8fb9`00000000
ffffa735`08bebce0  00000000`00000000
ffffa735`08bebce8  ffffffff`00000000
ffffa735`08bebcf0  ffffa735`08c45000
ffffa735`08bebcf8  ffab5278`ba580500
ffffa735`08bebd00  00000000`000000f2
ffffa735`08bebd08  ffffa735`08bebd50
ffffa735`08bebd10  0000633b`160a1cd2
ffffa735`08bebd18  00000000`00000000
ffffa735`08bebd20  ffffa735`08bebd60
ffffa735`08bebd28  ffff8fb9`a85d7028
ffffa735`08bebd30  ffffa735`08bebe10
ffffa735`08bebd38  ffffffff`9b7c0e3a vmlinux!init_module_from_file+0x9a [/build/linux-azure-6.8-2oiFiH/linux-azure-6.8-6.8.0/kernel/module/main.c @ 3157]
ffffa735`08bebd40  ffffa735`08bebe10
```

5. Search for the address ffffa735`08bebbc8 in kernel space:

```
0: kd> lm
start             end                 module name
ffffffff`9b600000 ffffffff`9f000000   vmlinux   T (service symbols: DWARF Private Symbols)
c:\alcda2\x64\ksym\vmlinux

0: kd> s-q ffffffff`9b600000 ffffffff`9f000000 ffffa735`08bebbc8
ffffffff`9e208218  ffffa735`08bebbc8 00000000`00000018
```

6. We can also search for particular strings and for any ASCII string fragment of three or more characters that doesn't contain non-ASCII characters (please don't forget about the little-endian system where the least significant digit comes first in a byte stream):

```
0: kd> s-a ffffffff`9b600000 ffffffff`9f000000 "bad"
ffffffff`9ba037d1  62 61 64 48 8b 50 08 4c-3b 70 10 75 48 8b 4f 28  badH.P.L;p.uH.O(
ffffffff`9ba192e0  62 61 64 49 8b 41 08 a8-01 0f 85 98 00 00 00 66  badI.A.........f
ffffffff`9ba19343  62 61 64 eb a9 41 f7 c1-ff 0f 00 00 75 a0 49 8b  bad..A......u.I.
ffffffff`9ca01325  62 61 64 5f 76 73 79 73-63 61 6c 6c 00 00 00 00  bad_vsyscall....
ffffffff`9ca0598c  62 61 64 5f 69 72 71 00-00 00 00 00 69 72 71 5f  bad_irq.....irq_
ffffffff`9caf4774  62 61 64 62 6c 6f 63 6b-00 00 00 00 6e 76 64 69  badblock....nvdi
ffffffff`9caf4787  62 61 64 62 6c 6f 63 6b-73 5f 70 6f 70 75 6c 61  badblocks_popula
ffffffff`9caf47aa  62 61 64 62 6c 6f 63 6b-73 00 00 00 00 00 00 00  badblocks.......m
...
...
...

0: kd> s-sa ffffffff`9b600000 ffffffff`9f000000
ffffffff`9b600198  "2H1"
ffffffff`9b60019f  "]o%"
ffffffff`9b6001ac  " /c"
ffffffff`9b6002a9  "Authu"
ffffffff`9b6002b1  "entiu"
ffffffff`9b6002b9  "cAMDu"
ffffffff`9b6002c7  "GenuuE"
ffffffff`9b6002cf  "ineIu="
ffffffff`9b6002d7  "ntelu5"
...
...
...

0: kd> dc ffffffff`9b6002a9
ffffffff`9b6002a9  68747541 fa811675 69746e65 f9810e75  Authu...entiu...
ffffffff`9b6002b9  444d4163 bf660675 4deb0001 6547fb81  cAMDu.f....M..Ge
ffffffff`9b6002c9  4575756e 6e69fa81 3d754965 746ef981  nuuE..ineIu=..nt
ffffffff`9b6002d9  35756c65 000001b8 89a20f00 0f0025c1  elu5.........%..
ffffffff`9b6002e9  e8c10ff0 06f88308 1d721077 00f0e181  ........w.r.....
ffffffff`9b6002f9  e9c1000f 0df98304 a0b90f72 0f000001  ........r.......
ffffffff`9b600309  f2ba0f32 0f027302 0001b830 a20f0000  2....s..0.......
ffffffff`9b600319  8169e281 f2810700 07008169 00b84f75  ..i.....i...uO..
```

Exercise K2 (A64, WinDbg)

Goal: Learn how to navigate a problem kernel dump.

Patterns: Exception Stack Trace; Exception Module; NULL Pointer (Data); Execution Residue (Kernel Space); Value References.

1. Copy the *vmlinux-6.8.0-1018-oracle* file in the A64/KSym directory to the *vmlinux* file.

2. Launch WinDbg. Load the core dump *202501041634.kdump* from the A64/K2 directory and set the symbol path to the A64/KSym directory (there may be some delay/unresponsiveness when you type the **.reload** command):

```
Microsoft (R) Windows Debugger Version 10.0.27725.1000 AMD64
Copyright (c) Microsoft Corporation. All rights reserved.


Loading Dump File [C:\ALCDA2\A64\K2\202501041634.kdump]
64-bit machine not using 64-bit API

************* Path validation summary **************
Response                         Time (ms)     Location
OK                                             C:\ALCDA2\x64\KSym\
Symbol search path is: C:\ALCDA2\x64\KSym\
Executable search path is:
Generic Unix Kernel Version 0 MP (2 procs) Free ARM 64-bit (AArch64)
Primary image base = 0xffff8000`80010000 Loaded module list = 0x00000000`00000000
System Uptime: not available
Loading Kernel Symbols

Loading User Symbols

For analysis of this file, run !analyze -v
ffff8000`802097d0 stp         x1,x0,[x2,#0x100]

0: kd> .sympath C:\ALCDA2\A64\KSym\
Symbol search path is: C:\ALCDA2\A64\KSym\
Expanded Symbol search path is: c:\alcda2\a64\ksym\

************* Path validation summary **************
Response                         Time (ms)     Location
OK                                             C:\ALCDA2\A64\KSym\

0: kd> .reload
Loading Kernel Symbols
.*** WARNING: Unable to verify timestamp for vmlinux

Loading User Symbols


************* Symbol Loading Error Summary **************
Module name            Error
vmlinux                The system cannot find the file specified

You can troubleshoot most symbol related issues by turning on symbol loading diagnostics (!sym
noisy) and repeating the command that caused symbols to be loaded.
You should also verify that your symbol search path (.sympath) is correct.
```

3. We see the kernel log messages using the **!log** command and find the bug description, crash PC that points to the problem source code, the stack pointer, and the stack trace. Please refer to GDB exercises for log analysis examples.

4. We can get an exception stack trace from this dump:

```
0: kd> kL
 # Child-SP          RetAddr           Call Site
00 ffff8000`85aa3420 ffff8000`8020b5f0 vmlinux!crash_setup_regs+0xa0
01 ffff8000`85aa3420 ffff8000`800c83e0 vmlinux!__crash_kexec+0x60
02 ffff8000`85aa35a0 ffff8000`80025f98 vmlinux!panic+0x350
03 ffff8000`85aa3680 ffff8000`80043c34 vmlinux!die+0x2d8
04 ffff8000`85aa3730 ffff8000`800441ec vmlinux!die_kernel_fault+0x10c
05 ffff8000`85aa3760 ffff8000`815f5948 vmlinux!__do_kernel_fault+0x1bc
06 ffff8000`85aa3790 ffff8000`815f5cc4 vmlinux!do_page_fault+0x220
07 ffff8000`85aa37f0 ffff8000`80043d44 vmlinux!do_translation_fault+0x74
08 ffff8000`85aa3800 ffff8000`815dbdc4 vmlinux!do_mem_abort+0x4c
09 ffff8000`85aa3830 ffff8000`815ddd90 vmlinux!el1_abort+0x4c
0a ffff8000`85aa3860 ffff8000`80011314 vmlinux!el1h_64_sync_handler+0x178
0b ffff8000`85aa3870 ffff8000`7bead01c vmlinux!el1h_64_sync+0x7c
0c ffff8000`85aa39c0 ffff8000`801c9160 mod_a+0x1c
0d ffff8000`85aa3a40 ffff8000`801cadbc vmlinux!do_init_module+0xa0
0e ffff8000`85aa3a70 ffff8000`801cb120 vmlinux!load_module+0x7c4
0f ffff8000`85aa3b40 ffff8000`801cb368 vmlinux!init_module_from_file+0x90
10 ffff8000`85aa3c10 ffff8000`801cb598 vmlinux!idempotent_init_module+0x1d0
11 ffff8000`85aa3cc0 ffff8000`800313c0 vmlinux!__arm64_sys_finit_module+0x70
12 ffff8000`85aa3cf0 ffff8000`800314b8 vmlinux!invoke_syscall+0x78
13 ffff8000`85aa3e40 ffff8000`800315d0 vmlinux!el0_svc_common+0x48
14 ffff8000`85aa3e70 ffff8000`815dd9e8 vmlinux!do_el0_svc+0x28
15 ffff8000`85aa3e80 ffff8000`815ddffc vmlinux!el0_svc+0x40
16 ffff8000`85aa3ea0 ffff8000`80011640 vmlinux!el0t_64_sync_handler+0x15c
17 ffff8000`85aa3eb0 00000000`00000000 vmlinux!el0t_64_sync+0x1a8
```

5. We can also see the problem module in the module list:

```
0: kd> lm
start             end                 module name
ffff8000`7b870000 ffff8000`7b875000   aes_ce_cipher   (deferred)
ffff8000`7b876000 ffff8000`7b880000   aes_ce_blk   (deferred)
ffff8000`7b881000 ffff8000`7b889000   aes_neon_blk   (deferred)
ffff8000`7b88a000 ffff8000`7b892000   aes_neon_bs   (deferred)
ffff8000`7b893000 ffff8000`7b89a000   xhci_pci_renesas   (deferred)
ffff8000`7b89d000 ffff8000`7b8a2000   virtio_dma_buf   (deferred)
ffff8000`7b8a3000 ffff8000`7b8ba000   virtio_gpu   (deferred)
ffff8000`7b8bd000 ffff8000`7b8c2000   polyval_generic   (deferred)
ffff8000`7b8c3000 ffff8000`7b8d2000   polyval_ce   (no symbols)
ffff8000`7b8c7000 ffff8000`7b8ce000   xhci_pci   (deferred)
ffff8000`7b8d3000 ffff8000`7b905000   raid0      (no symbols)
ffff8000`7b8d8000 ffff8000`7b8dd000   sha1_ce    (deferred)
ffff8000`7b8de000 ffff8000`7b8ec000   sm4        (no symbols)
ffff8000`7b8e2000 ffff8000`7b8ea000   sha256_arm64   (deferred)
ffff8000`7b8ef000 ffff8000`7b8f5000   sha2_ce    (deferred)
ffff8000`7b8f6000 ffff8000`7b8fc000   ghash_ce   (deferred)
ffff8000`7b8fd000 ffff8000`7b902000   crct10dif_ce   (deferred)
ffff8000`7b908000 ffff8000`7b928000   libcrc32c   (no symbols)
ffff8000`7b90d000 ffff8000`7b91e000   raid1      (deferred)
ffff8000`7b921000 ffff8000`7b926000   xor        (deferred)
ffff8000`7b929000 ffff8000`7b94c000   async_pq   (no symbols)
```

```
ffff8000`7b92d000 ffff8000`7b94a000   raid6_pq   (deferred)
ffff8000`7b950000 ffff8000`7b955000   xor_neon   (deferred)
ffff8000`7b960000 ffff8000`7b965000   async_tx   (deferred)
ffff8000`7b96c000 ffff8000`7b971000   async_xor   (deferred)
ffff8000`7b974000 ffff8000`7ba09000   hid_generic   (no symbols)
ffff8000`7b978000 ffff8000`7b97d000   async_memcpy   (deferred)
ffff8000`7b984000 ffff8000`7b98a000   async_raid6_recov   (deferred)
ffff8000`7b98d000 ffff8000`7ba0f000   iscsi_boot_sysfs   (no symbols)
ffff8000`7b991000 ffff8000`7b9c8000   raid456    (deferred)
ffff8000`7b9cb000 ffff8000`7b9d9000   raid10     (deferred)
ffff8000`7b9da000 ffff8000`7ba07000   hid        (deferred)
ffff8000`7ba11000 ffff8000`7ba23000   usbhid     (deferred)
ffff8000`7ba29000 ffff8000`7ba2e000   iscsi_ibft   (deferred)
ffff8000`7ba2f000 ffff8000`7ba52000   scsi_transport_iscsi   (deferred)
ffff8000`7ba55000 ffff8000`7ba5c000   blake2b_generic   (deferred)
ffff8000`7ba67000 ffff8000`7ba7d000   libiscsi   (deferred)
ffff8000`7ba80000 ffff8000`7ba99000   autofs4    (no symbols)
ffff8000`7ba89000 ffff8000`7ba92000   libiscsi_tcp   (deferred)
ffff8000`7ba9b000 ffff8000`7baa3000   iscsi_tcp   (deferred)
ffff8000`7baa6000 ffff8000`7bc71000   btrfs      (deferred)
ffff8000`7bc72000 ffff8000`7bc9a000   ip_tables   (no symbols)
ffff8000`7bc79000 ffff8000`7bc8a000   x_tables   (deferred)
ffff8000`7bc8d000 ffff8000`7bc92000   efi_pstore   (deferred)
ffff8000`7bc9d000 ffff8000`7bca3000   scsi_dh_alua   (deferred)
ffff8000`7bca6000 ffff8000`7bcab000   scsi_dh_emc   (deferred)
ffff8000`7bcb0000 ffff8000`7bcb6000   scsi_dh_rdac   (deferred)
ffff8000`7bcbb000 ffff8000`7bcc2000   dm_multipath   (deferred)
ffff8000`7bcc5000 ffff8000`7bccd000   sch_fq_codel   (deferred)
ffff8000`7bcce000 ffff8000`7bcd3000   input_leds   (deferred)
ffff8000`7bcd4000 ffff8000`7bce6000   nls_iso8859_1   (no symbols)
ffff8000`7bcd8000 ffff8000`7bce2000   joydev     (deferred)
ffff8000`7bce7000 ffff8000`7bcef000   binfmt_misc   (deferred)
ffff8000`7bcf2000 ffff8000`7bcf9000   nfnetlink   (deferred)
ffff8000`7bcfa000 ffff8000`7bd4a000   nf_tables   (deferred)
ffff8000`7bd4d000 ffff8000`7bd52000   nf_defrag_ipv4   (deferred)
ffff8000`7bd55000 ffff8000`7be98000   xt_conntrack   (no symbols)
ffff8000`7bd59000 ffff8000`7be22000   xt_state   (no symbols)
ffff8000`7bd5b000 ffff8000`7be5e000   nf_defrag_ipv6   (no symbols)
ffff8000`7bd5f000 ffff8000`7bd67000   nft_compat   (deferred)
ffff8000`7bd68000 ffff8000`7be1e000   sunrpc     (deferred)
ffff8000`7be23000 ffff8000`7be28000   xt_tcpudp   (deferred)
ffff8000`7be2b000 ffff8000`7be32000   nf_reject_ipv4   (deferred)
ffff8000`7be33000 ffff8000`7be42000   xt_owner   (no symbols)
ffff8000`7be37000 ffff8000`7be3c000   ipt_REJECT   (deferred)
ffff8000`7be3d000 ffff8000`7be44000   xt_comment   (deferred)
ffff8000`7be45000 ffff8000`7beaa000   tls        (no symbols)
ffff8000`7be61000 ffff8000`7be94000   nf_conntrack   (deferred)
ffff8000`7bead000 ffff8000`7beb2000   mod_a     T (no symbols)
ffff8000`80000000 ffff8000`8386a010   vmlinux  T (service symbols: DWARF Private Symbols)
c:\alcda2\a64\ksym\vmlinux
```

6. Either by setting the frame or disassembling the return address, we see the problem instruction (we should not trust the values of volatile registers like X1 in the registry value output):

```
0: kd> u ffff8000`7bead01c
mod_a+0x1c:
ffff8000`7bead01c str           w2,[x1]
ffff8000`7bead020 mov           x1,#0
ffff8000`7bead024 mov           x2,#0
ffff8000`7bead028 ret
```

```
ffff8000`7bead02c nop
ffff8000`7bead030 ???
ffff8000`7bead034 ???
ffff8000`7bead038 mov         x9,lr
```

```
0: kd> .frame /c c
0c ffff8000`85aa39c0 ffff8000`801c9160     mod_a+0x1c
 x0=ffff800085aa3448   x1=0000000000000000   x2=ffff800085aa3448   x3=ffff8000837979a0
 x4=0000000000000000   x5=0000000000000000   x6=0000000000000000   x7=0000000000000000
 x8=0000000000000000   x9=ffff8000800c83e0  x10=6457e8635d44296b  x11=17fabb5c6be64724
x12=3485b381f9ea51ab  x13=eb38b5d41acf614d  x14=51ab4bf530ceb440  x15=614d3485b381f9ea
x16=0000000000000000  x17=0000000000000000  x18=0000000000000000  x19=ffff80007bead008
x20=ffff0000ca4c1ea0  x21=ffff800085aa39c0  x22=ffff80007bead01c  x23=0000000040400005
x24=ffff80008335b8c8  x25=ffff80007beaf058  x26=0000000000000000  x27=0000000000000000
x28=ffff0000c72e2200   fp=ffff800085aa39c0   lr=ffff800080011314   sp=ffff800085aa39c0
 pc=ffff80007bead01c  psr=600000c5 -ZC- EL1
mod_a+0x1c:
ffff8000`7bead01c str         w2,[x1]
```

7. Now, we dump the raw stack region around the stack pointer to see exception processing execution residue:

```
0: kd> dps ffff800085aa39c0-300 L120
0
ffff8000`85aa36c0  ffff8000`7beaf058 mod_a+0x2058
ffff8000`85aa36c8  00000000`00000000
ffff8000`85aa36d0  00000000`00000000
ffff8000`85aa36d8  ffff0000`c72e2200
ffff8000`85aa36e0  00000000`00000000
ffff8000`85aa36e8  b9000022`00000000
ffff8000`85aa36f0  32333035`64aa3730
ffff8000`85aa36f8  30383264`20663130
ffff8000`85aa3700  38323520`31303030
ffff8000`85aa3708  32352032`32303030
ffff8000`85aa3710  28203030`30303038
ffff8000`85aa3718  32323030`30303962
ffff8000`85aa3720  00000000`00002029
ffff8000`85aa3728  60066b6b`1c517d00
ffff8000`85aa3730  ffff8000`85aa3760
ffff8000`85aa3738  ffff8000`800441ec vmlinux!__do_kernel_fault+0x1bc [/build/linux-oracle-6.8-
EzVzJ2/linux-oracle-6.8-6.8.0/arch/arm64/mm/fault.c @ 270]
ffff8000`85aa3740  00000000`96000044
ffff8000`85aa3748  ffff8000`85aa3870
ffff8000`85aa3750  ffff8000`81c811c0 vmlinux!$d+0x388
ffff8000`85aa3758  00000000`00000000
ffff8000`85aa3760  ffff8000`85aa3790
ffff8000`85aa3768  ffff8000`815f5948 vmlinux!do_page_fault+0x220 [/build/linux-oracle-6.8-
EzVzJ2/linux-oracle-6.8-6.8.0/arch/arm64/mm/fault.c @ 703]
ffff8000`85aa3770  ffff8000`85aa3870
ffff8000`85aa3778  00000000`00000000
ffff8000`85aa3780  00000000`00000000
ffff8000`85aa3788  00000000`96000044
ffff8000`85aa3790  ffff8000`85aa37f0
ffff8000`85aa3798  ffff8000`815f5cc4 vmlinux!do_translation_fault+0x74 [/build/linux-oracle-
6.8-EzVzJ2/linux-oracle-6.8-6.8.0/arch/arm64/mm/fault.c @ 716]
ffff8000`85aa37a0  00000000`96000044
ffff8000`85aa37a8  ffff8000`85aa3870
ffff8000`85aa37b0  00000000`00000000
ffff8000`85aa37b8  ffff8000`8161b060 vmlinux!fault_info+0x60
ffff8000`85aa37c0  00000000`40400005
ffff8000`85aa37c8  ffff8000`8335b8c8 vmlinux!module_notify_list
```

```
ffff8000`85aa37d0  ffff8000`7beaf058 mod_a+0x2058
ffff8000`85aa37d8  00000000`00000000
ffff8000`85aa37e0  00000000`00000000
ffff8000`85aa37e8  ffff8000`80610e44 vmlinux!__kernfs_new_node+0x15c [/build/linux-oracle-6.8-EzVzJ2/linux-oracle-6.8-6.8.0/fs/kernfs/dir.c @ 664]
ffff8000`85aa37f0  ffff8000`85aa3800
ffff8000`85aa37f8  ffff8000`80043d44 vmlinux!do_mem_abort+0x4c [/build/linux-oracle-6.8-EzVzJ2/linux-oracle-6.8-6.8.0/arch/arm64/mm/fault.c @ 848]
ffff8000`85aa3800  ffff8000`85aa3830
ffff8000`85aa3808  ffff8000`815dbdc4 vmlinux!el1_abort+0x4c [/build/linux-oracle-6.8-EzVzJ2/linux-oracle-6.8-6.8.0/arch/arm64/include/asm/daifflags.h @ 28]
ffff8000`85aa3810  ffff8000`85aa3870
ffff8000`85aa3818  00000000`96000044
ffff8000`85aa3820  00000000`00000000
ffff8000`85aa3828  ffff8000`7bead01c mod_a+0x1c
ffff8000`85aa3830  ffff8000`85aa3860
ffff8000`85aa3838  ffff8000`815ddd90 vmlinux!el1h_64_sync_handler+0x178 [/build/linux-oracle-6.8-EzVzJ2/linux-oracle-6.8-6.8.0/arch/arm64/kernel/entry-common.c @ 486]
ffff8000`85aa3840  ffff8000`7bead008 mod_a+0x8
ffff8000`85aa3848  ffff0000`ca4c1ea0
ffff8000`85aa3850  ffff8000`85aa39c0
ffff8000`85aa3858  ffff8000`7beaf4c8 mod_a+0x24c8
ffff8000`85aa3860  ffff8000`85aa39a0
ffff8000`85aa3868  ffff8000`80011314 vmlinux!el1h_64_sync+0x7c [/build/linux-oracle-6.8-EzVzJ2/linux-oracle-6.8-6.8.0/arch/arm64/kernel/entry.S @ 593]
ffff8000`85aa3870  00000000`00000000
ffff8000`85aa3878  00000000`00000000
ffff8000`85aa3880  00000000`00000001
ffff8000`85aa3888  00000000`00000000
ffff8000`85aa3890  00000000`00000000
ffff8000`85aa3898  00000000`00000000
ffff8000`85aa38a0  00000000`00000000
ffff8000`85aa38a8  00000000`00000000
ffff8000`85aa38b0  00000000`00000000
ffff8000`85aa38b8  ffff8000`80015374 vmlinux!do_one_initcall+0x4c [/build/linux-oracle-6.8-EzVzJ2/linux-oracle-6.8-6.8.0/init/main.c @ 1243]
ffff8000`85aa38c0  00000000`00000000
ffff8000`85aa38c8  00000000`00000000
ffff8000`85aa38d0  622e756e`672e6574
ffff8000`85aa38d8  0064692d`646c6975
ffff8000`85aa38e0  00000000`00000000
ffff8000`85aa38e8  00000000`00000000
ffff8000`85aa38f0  00000000`00000000
ffff8000`85aa38f8  00000000`00000000
ffff8000`85aa3900  00000000`00000000
ffff8000`85aa3908  ffff8000`7bead008 mod_a+0x8
ffff8000`85aa3910  ffff0000`ca4c1ea0
ffff8000`85aa3918  ffff8000`8335b8c8 vmlinux!module_notify_list
ffff8000`85aa3920  00000000`00000000
ffff8000`85aa3928  ffff8000`7beaf040 mod_a+0x2040
ffff8000`85aa3930  ffff8000`8335b8c8 vmlinux!module_notify_list
ffff8000`85aa3938  ffff8000`7beaf058 mod_a+0x2058
ffff8000`85aa3940  00000000`00000000
ffff8000`85aa3948  00000000`00000000
ffff8000`85aa3950  00000000`00000000
ffff8000`85aa3958  ffff8000`85aa39c0
ffff8000`85aa3960  ffff8000`80015374 vmlinux!do_one_initcall+0x4c [/build/linux-oracle-6.8-EzVzJ2/linux-oracle-6.8-6.8.0/init/main.c @ 1243]
ffff8000`85aa3968  ffff8000`85aa39c0
ffff8000`85aa3970  ffff8000`7bead01c mod_a+0x1c
```

```
ffff8000`85aa3978  00000000`40400005
ffff8000`85aa3980  ffff8000`85aa39d0
ffff8000`85aa3988  ffff8000`80401920 vmlinux!kvfree+0x50 [/build/linux-oracle-6.8-EzVzJ2/linux-
oracle-6.8-6.8.0/mm/util.c @ 664]
ffff8000`85aa3990  ffff0000`c0310600
ffff8000`85aa3998  fffffc00`032ff040
ffff8000`85aa39a0  ffff8000`85aa39c0
ffff8000`85aa39a8  ffff8000`7bead01c mod_a+0x1c
ffff8000`85aa39b0  00000000`00000027
ffff8000`85aa39b8  00000000`00000000
ffff8000`85aa39c0  ffff8000`85aa3a40
ffff8000`85aa39c8  ffff8000`801c9160 vmlinux!do_init_module+0xa0 [/build/linux-oracle-6.8-
EzVzJ2/linux-oracle-6.8-6.8.0/kernel/module/main.c @ 2538]
ffff8000`85aa39d0  ffff8000`7beaf040 mod_a+0x2040
ffff8000`85aa39d8  ffff0000`ca4c1ea0
ffff8000`85aa39e0  ffff8000`8335b8c8 vmlinux!module_notify_list
ffff8000`85aa39e8  ffff8000`85aa3b78
ffff8000`85aa39f0  ffff8000`7beaf040 mod_a+0x2040
ffff8000`85aa39f8  00000000`00000000
ffff8000`85aa3a00  ffff8000`8335b8c8 vmlinux!module_notify_list
ffff8000`85aa3a08  ffff8000`85aa3b78
ffff8000`85aa3a10  ffff8000`7beaf040 mod_a+0x2040
ffff8000`85aa3a18  ffff8000`8335b8c8 vmlinux!module_notify_list
ffff8000`85aa3a20  ffff8000`7beaf058 mod_a+0x2058
ffff8000`85aa3a28  00000000`00000000
ffff8000`85aa3a30  ffff0000`ca4c1ea0
ffff8000`85aa3a38  60066b6b`1c517d00
ffff8000`85aa3a40  ffff8000`85aa3a70
ffff8000`85aa3a48  ffff8000`801cadbc vmlinux!load_module+0x7c4 [/build/linux-oracle-6.8-
EzVzJ2/linux-oracle-6.8-6.8.0/kernel/module/main.c @ 2989]
ffff8000`85aa3a50  00000000`00000000
ffff8000`85aa3a58  00000000`00000000
ffff8000`85aa3a60  00000000`00000000
ffff8000`85aa3a68  ffff8000`85aa3b78
ffff8000`85aa3a70  ffff8000`85aa3b40
ffff8000`85aa3a78  ffff8000`801cb120 vmlinux!init_module_from_file+0x90 [/build/linux-oracle-
6.8-EzVzJ2/linux-oracle-6.8-6.8.0/kernel/module/main.c @ 3178]
ffff8000`85aa3a80  00000000`00026ae0
ffff8000`85aa3a88  00000000`00000000
ffff8000`85aa3a90  0000bab4`b81bcfc8
ffff8000`85aa3a98  00000000`00000000
ffff8000`85aa3aa0  ffff0000`c952b700
ffff8000`85aa3aa8  ffff0001`ce342628
ffff8000`85aa3ab0  ffff8000`83795590 vmlinux!idem_hash
ffff8000`85aa3ab8  ffff8000`837955d8 vmlinux!idem_hash+0x48
ffff8000`85aa3ac0  00000000`00000048
ffff8000`85aa3ac8  ffff0000`c72e2200
ffff8000`85aa3ad0  ffff8000`85aa3b38
ffff8000`85aa3ad8  ffff8000`00000001
ffff8000`85aa3ae0  ffff0000`c952b700
ffff8000`85aa3ae8  00000000`00000000
ffff8000`85aa3af0  0000bab4`b81bcfc8
ffff8000`85aa3af8  00000000`00000000
ffff8000`85aa3b00  ffff0000`c952b700
ffff8000`85aa3b08  ffff0001`ce342628
ffff8000`85aa3b10  ffff8000`83795590 vmlinux!idem_hash
ffff8000`85aa3b18  00000000`00000000
ffff8000`85aa3b20  00000000`00000000
ffff8000`85aa3b28  00000000`00000000
ffff8000`85aa3b30  00000000`00000000
```

```
ffff8000`85aa3b38  60066b6b`1c517d00
ffff8000`85aa3b40  ffff8000`85aa3c10
ffff8000`85aa3b48  ffff8000`801cb368 vmlinux!idempotent_init_module+0x1d0 [/build/linux-oracle-
6.8-EzVzJ2/linux-oracle-6.8-6.8.0/kernel/module/main.c @ 3190]
ffff8000`85aa3b50  00000000`80b583eb
ffff8000`85aa3b58  ffff8000`83795578 vmlinux!module_blacklist
ffff8000`85aa3b60  0000bab4`b81bcfc8
ffff8000`85aa3b68  ffffffff`fffffffc
ffff8000`85aa3b70  ffff8000`85d65000
ffff8000`85aa3b78  ffff8000`85d65640
ffff8000`85aa3b80  ffff8000`85d65100
ffff8000`85aa3b88  ffff8000`85d65000
ffff8000`85aa3b90  00000000`00026ae0
ffff8000`85aa3b98  ffff8000`85d8b2a0
ffff8000`85aa3ba0  ffff8000`85d8b130
ffff8000`85aa3ba8  ffff8000`85d79a80
ffff8000`85aa3bb0  00000000`00000540
ffff8000`85aa3bb8  00000000`00000660
ffff8000`85aa3bc0  00000000`00000510
ffff8000`85aa3bc8  00000000`000006a4
ffff8000`85aa3bd0  00000000`00000000
ffff8000`85aa3bd8  00000000`000004f0
ffff8000`85aa3be0  00000000`00000000
ffff8000`85aa3be8  00000000`00000000
ffff8000`85aa3bf0  0000001f`0000001e
ffff8000`85aa3bf8  0000000e`00000005
ffff8000`85aa3c00  00000000`0000000a
ffff8000`85aa3c08  60066b6b`1c517d00
ffff8000`85aa3c10  ffff8000`85aa3cc0
ffff8000`85aa3c18  ffff8000`801cb598 vmlinux!__arm64_sys_finit_module+0x70 [/build/linux-
oracle-6.8-EzVzJ2/linux-oracle-6.8-6.8.0/kernel/module/main.c @ 3217]
ffff8000`85aa3c20  00000000`00000000
ffff8000`85aa3c28  ffff0000`c952b700
ffff8000`85aa3c30  ffff0000`c952b700
ffff8000`85aa3c38  0000fb1d`2d531c28
ffff8000`85aa3c40  00000000`40001000
ffff8000`85aa3c48  00000000`00000000
ffff8000`85aa3c50  00000000`00000000
ffff8000`85aa3c58  00000000`00000000
ffff8000`85aa3c60  00000000`00000000
ffff8000`85aa3c68  ffff8000`800dc86c vmlinux!capable+0x3c [/build/linux-oracle-6.8-
EzVzJ2/linux-oracle-6.8-6.8.0/kernel/capability.c @ 367]
ffff8000`85aa3c70  ffff0000`c72e2200
ffff8000`85aa3c78  ffff0001`ce342628
ffff8000`85aa3c80  00000000`00000000
ffff8000`85aa3c88  ffff8000`837955d8 vmlinux!idem_hash+0x48
ffff8000`85aa3c90  00000000`00000000
ffff8000`85aa3c98  00000000`00000000
ffff8000`85aa3ca0  ffff8000`85aa3ca0
ffff8000`85aa3ca8  ffff8000`85aa3ca0
ffff8000`85aa3cb0  ffff8000`fffffffc
ffff8000`85aa3cb8  60066b6b`1c517d00
ffff8000`85aa3cc0  ffff8000`85aa3e10
ffff8000`85aa3cc8  ffff8000`800313c0 vmlinux!invoke_syscall+0x78 [/build/linux-oracle-6.8-
EzVzJ2/linux-oracle-6.8-6.8.0/arch/arm64/include/asm/current.h @ 19]
ffff8000`85aa3cd0  ffff8000`85aa3eb0
ffff8000`85aa3cd8  ffff8002`7bedf000
ffff8000`85aa3ce0  ffff0000`c72e2200
ffff8000`85aa3ce8  00000000`00000001
ffff8000`85aa3cf0  ffff8000`82890008 vmlinux!cpu_number
```

```
ffff8000`85aa3cf8  ffff0001`2ea4a000
ffff8000`85aa3d00  00000000`00000000
ffff8000`85aa3d08  ffff0000`c72e2200
ffff8000`85aa3d10  00000000`00000007
ffff8000`85aa3d18  ffff0000`c6bd2cc0
ffff8000`85aa3d20  00000000`00001a54
ffff8000`85aa3d28  ffff0001`2ec2ce00
ffff8000`85aa3d30  ffff0001`31f4f690
ffff8000`85aa3d38  00000000`00000000
ffff8000`85aa3d40  ffff8000`85aa3d70
ffff8000`85aa3d48  ffff8000`8043b45c vmlinux!handle_mm_fault+0x1ac [/build/linux-oracle-6.8-
EzVzJ2/linux-oracle-6.8-6.8.0/arch/arm64/include/asm/alternative-macros.h @ 250]
ffff8000`85aa3d50  00000000`00000100
ffff8000`85aa3d58  00000000`00001254
ffff8000`85aa3d60  0000bab4`b81c0b90
ffff8000`85aa3d68  ffff8000`85aa3eb0
ffff8000`85aa3d70  ffff8000`85aa3dd0
ffff8000`85aa3d78  ffff8000`815f584c vmlinux!do_page_fault+0x124 [/build/linux-oracle-6.8-
EzVzJ2/linux-oracle-6.8-6.8.0/arch/arm64/mm/fault.c @ 602]
ffff8000`85aa3d80  ffff8000`85aa3eb0
ffff8000`85aa3d88  0000bab4`b81c0b90
ffff8000`85aa3d90  0000bab4`b81c0b90
ffff8000`85aa3d98  00000000`92000007
ffff8000`85aa3da0  ffff0000`ca1b8f00
ffff8000`85aa3da8  00000000`00000254
ffff8000`85aa3db0  00000000`00000007
ffff8000`85aa3db8  00000000`00000000
ffff8000`85aa3dc0  0e000101`00000000
ffff8000`85aa3dc8  00001254`1c517d00
ffff8000`85aa3dd0  ffff8000`85aa3e30
ffff8000`85aa3dd8  ffff8000`815f5cc4 vmlinux!do_translation_fault+0x74 [/build/linux-oracle-
6.8-EzVzJ2/linux-oracle-6.8-6.8.0/arch/arm64/mm/fault.c @ 716]
ffff8000`85aa3de0  00000000`92000007
ffff8000`85aa3de8  ffff8000`85aa3eb0
ffff8000`85aa3df0  0000bab4`b81c0b90
ffff8000`85aa3df8  ffff8000`8161b0a8 vmlinux!fault_info+0xa8
ffff8000`85aa3e00  00000000`80001000
ffff8000`85aa3e08  00000000`00000000
ffff8000`85aa3e10  ffff8000`85aa3e40
ffff8000`85aa3e18  ffff8000`800314b8 vmlinux!el0_svc_common+0x48 [/build/linux-oracle-6.8-
EzVzJ2/linux-oracle-6.8-6.8.0/include/linux/thread_info.h @ 127]
ffff8000`85aa3e20  ffff8000`85aa3eb0
ffff8000`85aa3e28  ffff8002`7bedf000
ffff8000`85aa3e30  ffff0000`c72e2200
ffff8000`85aa3e38  ffff8000`80043d44 vmlinux!do_mem_abort+0x4c [/build/linux-oracle-6.8-
EzVzJ2/linux-oracle-6.8-6.8.0/arch/arm64/mm/fault.c @ 848]
ffff8000`85aa3e40  ffff8000`85aa3e70
ffff8000`85aa3e48  ffff8000`800315d0 vmlinux!do_el0_svc+0x28 [/build/linux-oracle-6.8-
EzVzJ2/linux-oracle-6.8-6.8.0/arch/arm64/kernel/syscall.c @ 154]
ffff8000`85aa3e50  ffff8000`85aa3eb0
ffff8000`85aa3e58  ffff8002`7bedf000
ffff8000`85aa3e60  00000000`ffffffff
ffff8000`85aa3e68  0000fb1d`2d4e1758
ffff8000`85aa3e70  ffff8000`85aa3e80
ffff8000`85aa3e78  ffff8000`815dd9e8 vmlinux!el0_svc+0x40 [/build/linux-oracle-6.8-
EzVzJ2/linux-oracle-6.8-6.8.0/arch/arm64/include/asm/daifflags.h @ 28]
ffff8000`85aa3e80  ffff8000`85aa3ea0
ffff8000`85aa3e88  ffff8000`815ddffc vmlinux!el0t_64_sync_handler+0x15c [/build/linux-oracle-
6.8-EzVzJ2/linux-oracle-6.8-6.8.0/arch/arm64/kernel/entry-common.c @ 697]
ffff8000`85aa3e90  00000000`00000000
```

```
ffff8000`85aa3e98  ffff8000`815de028 vmlinux!el0t_64_irq_handler+0x10 [/build/linux-oracle-6.8-EzVzJ2/linux-oracle-6.8-6.8.0/arch/arm64/kernel/entry-common.c @ 774]
ffff8000`85aa3ea0  ffff8000`85aa3fe0
ffff8000`85aa3ea8  ffff8000`80011640 vmlinux!el0t_64_sync+0x1a8 [/build/linux-oracle-6.8-EzVzJ2/linux-oracle-6.8-6.8.0/arch/arm64/kernel/entry.S @ 598]
ffff8000`85aa3eb0  00000000`00000003
ffff8000`85aa3eb8  0000bab4`b81bcfc8
ffff8000`85aa3ec0  00000000`00000000
ffff8000`85aa3ec8  00000000`00000001
ffff8000`85aa3ed0  00000000`00000000
ffff8000`85aa3ed8  00000000`005a587a
ffff8000`85aa3ee0  0000ffff`f994da56
ffff8000`85aa3ee8  0000ffff`f994da56
ffff8000`85aa3ef0  00000000`00000111
ffff8000`85aa3ef8  00000000`00000000
ffff8000`85aa3f00  00000000`00000000
ffff8000`85aa3f08  00000000`00000000
ffff8000`85aa3f10  00000000`00000001
ffff8000`85aa3f18  8deb6cdb`0115a384
ffff8000`85aa3f20  00000000`00000040
ffff8000`85aa3f28  0000bab4`df2ae020
ffff8000`85aa3f30  0000bab4`b81d5d48
ffff8000`85aa3f38  0000fb1d`2d531c00
ffff8000`85aa3f40  00000000`00000000
ffff8000`85aa3f48  0000bab4`b81bcfc8
ffff8000`85aa3f50  0000bab4`df2ae8c0
ffff8000`85aa3f58  0000bab4`df2ae7b0
ffff8000`85aa3f60  00000000`00000000
ffff8000`85aa3f68  0000bab4`df2b1430
ffff8000`85aa3f70  00000000`00000000
ffff8000`85aa3f78  00000000`00000000
ffff8000`85aa3f80  0000ffff`f994dda0
ffff8000`85aa3f88  0000bab4`b81d4c48
ffff8000`85aa3f90  00000000`00000000
ffff8000`85aa3f98  0000ffff`f994dab0
ffff8000`85aa3fa0  0000bab4`b81b7364
ffff8000`85aa3fa8  0000ffff`f994dab0
ffff8000`85aa3fb0  0000fb1d`2d531c28
ffff8000`85aa3fb8  00000000`40001000
```

8. Search for the address **ffff8000`7bead01c** in kernel space:

```
0: kd> s-q ffff8000`80000000 ffff8000`90000000-1 ffff8000`7bead01c
ffff8000`85aa3828  ffff8000`7bead01c ffff8000`85aa3860
ffff8000`85aa3970  ffff8000`7bead01c 00000000`40400005
ffff8000`85aa39a8  ffff8000`7bead01c 00000000`00000027
```

Note: We see that the address was also found in the raw stack region we inspected in step #7.

9. We can also search for particular strings and for any ASCII string fragment of three or more characters that doesn't contain non-ASCII characters (please don't forget about the little-endian system where the least significant digit comes first in a byte stream):

```
0: kd> s-a ffff8000`80000000 ffff8000`8386a010 "bad"
ffff8000`818d765c  62 61 64 62 6c 6f 63 6b-00 00 00 00 6e 76 64 69  badblock....nvdi
ffff8000`818d766f  62 61 64 62 6c 6f 63 6b-73 5f 70 6f 70 75 6c 61  badblocks_popula
ffff8000`818d76c2  62 61 64 62 6c 6f 63 6b-73 00 00 00 00 00 6e 64  badblocks.....nd
ffff8000`818dc5fc  62 61 64 20 62 79 20 61-70 70 6c 69 63 61 74 69  bad by applicati
ffff8000`8196f83c  62 61 64 5f 6d 61 70 00-00 00 00 00 67 65 74 5f  bad_map.....get_
ffff8000`81971158  62 61 64 20 69 66 69 6e-64 65 78 00 00 00 00 00  bad ifindex.....
ffff8000`81c79cd8  62 61 64 20 64 61 74 61-20 63 68 65 63 6b 73 75  bad data checksu
ffff8000`81c7f037  62 61 64 20 63 6f 6d 70-61 74 20 73 79 73 63 61  bad compat sysca
ffff8000`81c901a2  62 61 64 3a 20 73 63 68-65 64 75 6c 69 6e 67 20  bad: scheduling 
ffff8000`81c93c6a  62 61 64 20 6f 70 74 69-6f 6e 20 73 74 72 69 6e  bad option strin
ffff8000`81c971ba  62 61 64 20 43 50 55 20-72 61 6e 67 65 2c 20 61  bad CPU range, a
ffff8000`81ca43f4  62 61 64 20 77 69 64 74-68 20 25 7a 75 0a 00 00  bad width %zu...
...
...
...

0: kd> s-sa ffff8000`80000000 ffff8000`8386a010
ffff8000`80002c10  "83D"
ffff8000`80002cf0  "83D"
ffff8000`80002d20  "83D"
ffff8000`80002d50  "83D"
ffff8000`80002fa8  "t(-"
ffff8000`80003018  "t(-"
ffff8000`80003078  "t(-"
ffff8000`800032ff  "1@3"
ffff8000`80003448  "HY-"
ffff8000`80003512  "+RS"
ffff8000`800035b2  "+RS"
ffff8000`80003630  "@%w""
...
...
...

0: kd> dc ffff8000`80002c10
ffff8000`80002c10  83443338 ffff8000 00000008 00000000  83D.............
ffff8000`80002c20  00000001 00000000 00000008 00000000  ................
ffff8000`80002c30  80002c50 ffff8000 809c6138 ffff8000  P,......8a......
ffff8000`80002c40  00000000 00000000 c02424a0 ffff0000  .........$$.....
ffff8000`80002c50  80002cc0 ffff8000 8019ddec ffff8000  .,..............
ffff8000`80002c60  8162c9d8 ffff8000 c02424a0 ffff0000  ..b......$$.....
ffff8000`80002c70  802046d4 ffff8000 00000001 00000000  .F .............
ffff8000`80002c80  80002ca0 ffff8000 801539b0 ffff8000  .,.......9......
```

Exercise K3

- **Goal:** Learn how to recognize problems with kernel threads, identify their owner module, follow call chains, and reconstruct a stack trace if necessary
- **Patterns:** Origin Module; NULL Pointer (Code); Hidden Call
- \ALCDA-Dumps\Exercise-K3-x64-GDB.pdf
- \ALCDA-Dumps\Exercise-K3-A64-GDB.pdf
- \ALCDA-Dumps\Exercise-K3-A64-WinDbg.pdf
- \ALCDA-Dumps\Exercise-K3-x64-WinDbg.pdf

Exercise K3 (x64, GDB)

Goal: Learn how to recognize problems with kernel threads, identify their owner module, and follow call chains.

Patterns: Origin Module; NULL Pointer (Code); Hidden Call.

1. Load the core dump *202501051138.kdump* from the x64/K3 directory and the matching *vmlinux-6.8.0-1018-azure* file from the x64/KSym directory:

```
~/ALCDA2/x64/K3$ crash 202501051138.kdump ../KSym/vmlinux-6.8.0-1018-azure

crash 8.0.6++
Copyright (C) 2002-2025  Red Hat, Inc.
Copyright (C) 2004, 2005, 2006, 2010  IBM Corporation
Copyright (C) 1999-2006  Hewlett-Packard Co
Copyright (C) 2005, 2006, 2011, 2012  Fujitsu Limited
Copyright (C) 2006, 2007  VA Linux Systems Japan K.K.
Copyright (C) 2005, 2011, 2020-2024  NEC Corporation
Copyright (C) 1999, 2002, 2007  Silicon Graphics, Inc.
Copyright (C) 1999, 2000, 2001, 2002  Mission Critical Linux, Inc.
Copyright (C) 2015, 2021  VMware, Inc.
This program is free software, covered by the GNU General Public License,
and you are welcome to change it and/or distribute copies of it under
certain conditions.  Enter "help copying" to see the conditions.
This program has absolutely no warranty.  Enter "help warranty" for details.

GNU gdb (GDB) 10.2
Copyright (C) 2021 Free Software Foundation, Inc.
License GPLv3+: GNU GPL version 3 or later <http://gnu.org/licenses/gpl.html>
This is free software: you are free to change and redistribute it.
There is NO WARRANTY, to the extent permitted by law.
Type "show copying" and "show warranty" for details.
This GDB was configured as "x86_64-pc-linux-gnu".
Type "show configuration" for configuration details.
Find the GDB manual and other documentation resources online at:
    <http://www.gnu.org/software/gdb/documentation/>.

For help, type "help".
Type "apropos word" to search for commands related to "word"...

      KERNEL: ../KSym/vmlinux-6.8.0-1018-azure  [TAINTED]
    DUMPFILE: 202501051138.kdump  [PARTIAL DUMP]
        CPUS: 4
        DATE: Sun Jan  5 11:36:54 GMT 2025
      UPTIME: 06:30:00
LOAD AVERAGE: 0.37, 0.11, 0.03
       TASKS: 628
    NODENAME: coredump-alcda
     RELEASE: 6.8.0-1018-azure
     VERSION: #21~22.04.1-Ubuntu SMP Fri Nov  8 00:21:25 UTC 2024
     MACHINE: x86_64  (2112 Mhz)
      MEMORY: 4 GB
       PANIC: "Kernel panic - not syncing: Fatal exception"
         PID: 6611
     COMMAND: "mod_b thread"
        TASK: ffff9ef251598000  [THREAD_INFO: ffff9ef251598000]
         CPU: 2
```

```
STATE: TASK_RUNNING (PANIC)

crash>
```

2. We check the log for details, and at the end, we find the bug description, crash RIP, the stack pointer, and the stack trace:

```
crash> log -T
[Sun Jan  5 05:06:54 GMT 2025] Linux version 6.8.0-1018-azure (buildd@lcy02-amd64-013) (x86_64-linux-gnu-gcc-11 (Ubuntu 11.4.0-1ubuntu1~22.04) 11.4.0, GNU ld (GNU Binutils for Ubuntu) 2.38) #21~22.04.1-Ubuntu SMP Fri Nov  8 00:21:25 UTC 2024 (Ubuntu 6.8.0-1018.21~22.04.1-azure 6.8.12)
[Sun Jan  5 05:06:54 GMT 2025] Command line: BOOT_IMAGE=/boot/vmlinuz-6.8.0-1018-azure root=UUID=89ee03ba-6808-4977-a4fb-9b10174744f8 ro quiet splash crashkernel=512M-:192M vt.handoff=7
...
...
...
[Sun Jan  5 11:36:53 GMT 2025] BUG: kernel NULL pointer dereference, address: 0000000000000000
[Sun Jan  5 11:36:53 GMT 2025] #PF: supervisor instruction fetch in kernel mode
[Sun Jan  5 11:36:53 GMT 2025] #PF: error_code(0x0010) - not-present page
[Sun Jan  5 11:36:53 GMT 2025] PGD 0 P4D 0
[Sun Jan  5 11:36:53 GMT 2025] Oops: 0010 [#1] SMP PTI
[Sun Jan  5 11:36:53 GMT 2025] CPU: 2 PID: 6611 Comm: mod_b thread Kdump: loaded Tainted: G           OE      6.8.0-1018-azure #21~22.04.1-Ubuntu
[Sun Jan  5 11:36:53 GMT 2025] Hardware name: Microsoft Corporation Virtual Machine/Virtual Machine, BIOS Hyper-V UEFI Release v4.1 05/13/2024
[Sun Jan  5 11:36:53 GMT 2025] RIP: 0010:0x0
[Sun Jan  5 11:36:53 GMT 2025] Code: Unable to access opcode bytes at 0xffffffffffffffd6.
[Sun Jan  5 11:36:53 GMT 2025] RSP: 0018:ffffbaeb8567beb8 EFLAGS: 00010246
[Sun Jan  5 11:36:53 GMT 2025] RAX: 0000000000000000 RBX: ffff9ef251598000 RCX: 0000000000000000
[Sun Jan  5 11:36:53 GMT 2025] RDX: 0000000000000000 RSI: 0000000000000286 RDI: 0000000000000000
[Sun Jan  5 11:36:53 GMT 2025] RBP: ffffbaeb8567bec0 R08: 0000000000000000 R09: 0000000000000000
[Sun Jan  5 11:36:53 GMT 2025] R10: 0000000000000002 R11: 0000000000000000 R12: ffff9ef28083ad80
[Sun Jan  5 11:36:53 GMT 2025] R13: ffffbaeb856db8b8 R14: ffff9ef2347a6600 R15: ffffffffc07a5010
[Sun Jan  5 11:36:53 GMT 2025] FS:  0000000000000000(0000) GS:ffff9ef303d00000(0000) knlGS:0000000000000000
[Sun Jan  5 11:36:53 GMT 2025] CS:  0010 DS: 0000 ES: 0000 CR0: 0000000080050033
[Sun Jan  5 11:36:53 GMT 2025] CR2: ffffffffffffffd6 CR3: 000000003e5d0006 CR4: 00000000003706f0
[Sun Jan  5 11:36:53 GMT 2025] DR0: 0000000000000000 DR1: 0000000000000000 DR2: 0000000000000000
[Sun Jan  5 11:36:53 GMT 2025] DR3: 0000000000000000 DR6: 00000000fffe0ff0 DR7: 0000000000000400
[Sun Jan  5 11:36:53 GMT 2025] Call Trace:
[Sun Jan  5 11:36:53 GMT 2025]  <TASK>
[Sun Jan  5 11:36:53 GMT 2025]  ? show_regs+0x6a/0x80
[Sun Jan  5 11:36:53 GMT 2025]  ? __die+0x25/0x70
[Sun Jan  5 11:36:53 GMT 2025]  ? page_fault_oops+0x79/0x180
[Sun Jan  5 11:36:53 GMT 2025]  ? do_user_addr_fault+0x2fe/0x640
[Sun Jan  5 11:36:53 GMT 2025]  ? raw_spin_rq_unlock+0x10/0x30
[Sun Jan  5 11:36:53 GMT 2025]  ? exc_page_fault+0x74/0x160
[Sun Jan  5 11:36:53 GMT 2025]  ? asm_exc_page_fault+0x27/0x30
[Sun Jan  5 11:36:53 GMT 2025]  ? __pfx_kthread_f+0x10/0x10 [mod_b]
[Sun Jan  5 11:36:53 GMT 2025]  bar+0xd/0xf40 [mod_b]
[Sun Jan  5 11:36:53 GMT 2025]  foo+0xe/0x20 [mod_b]
[Sun Jan  5 11:36:53 GMT 2025]  kthread_f+0x18/0x20 [mod_b]
[Sun Jan  5 11:36:53 GMT 2025]  kthread+0xd3/0x100
[Sun Jan  5 11:36:53 GMT 2025]  ? __pfx_kthread+0x10/0x10
[Sun Jan  5 11:36:53 GMT 2025]  ret_from_fork+0x39/0x60
[Sun Jan  5 11:36:53 GMT 2025]  ? __pfx_kthread+0x10/0x10
[Sun Jan  5 11:36:53 GMT 2025]  ret_from_fork_asm+0x1b/0x30
[Sun Jan  5 11:36:53 GMT 2025]  </TASK>
[Sun Jan  5 11:36:53 GMT 2025] Modules linked in: mod_b(OE) binfmt_misc crct10dif_pclmul crc32_pclmul polyval_clmulni nls_iso8859_1 polyval_generic ghash_clmulni_intel sha256_ssse3 sha1_ssse3 aesni_intel crypto_simd cryptd serio_raw hyperv_drm joydev sch_fq_codel hv_sock vsock msr parport_pc ppdev lp parport efi_pstore ip_tables x_tables autofs4 btrfs blake2b_generic xor raid6_pq libcrc32c hid_generic hid_hyperv hyperv_keyboard hv_netvsc hid
[Sun Jan  5 11:36:53 GMT 2025] CR2: 0000000000000000
[Sun Jan  5 11:36:53 GMT 2025] ---[ end trace 0000000000000000 ]---
[Sun Jan  5 11:36:54 GMT 2025] RIP: 0010:0x0
[Sun Jan  5 11:36:54 GMT 2025] Code: Unable to access opcode bytes at 0xffffffffffffffd6.
[Sun Jan  5 11:36:54 GMT 2025] RSP: 0018:ffffbaeb8567beb8 EFLAGS: 00010246
[Sun Jan  5 11:36:54 GMT 2025] RAX: 0000000000000000 RBX: ffff9ef251598000 RCX: 0000000000000000
[Sun Jan  5 11:36:54 GMT 2025] RDX: 0000000000000000 RSI: 0000000000000286 RDI: 0000000000000000
[Sun Jan  5 11:36:54 GMT 2025] RBP: ffffbaeb8567bec0 R08: 0000000000000000 R09: 0000000000000000
[Sun Jan  5 11:36:54 GMT 2025] R10: 0000000000000002 R11: 0000000000000000 R12: ffff9ef28083ad80
[Sun Jan  5 11:36:54 GMT 2025] R13: ffffbaeb856db8b8 R14: ffff9ef2347a6600 R15: ffffffffc07a5010
[Sun Jan  5 11:36:54 GMT 2025] FS:  0000000000000000(0000) GS:ffff9ef303d00000(0000) knlGS:0000000000000000
```

```
[Sun Jan  5 11:36:54 GMT 2025] CS:  0010 DS: 0000 ES: 0000 CR0: 0000000080050033
[Sun Jan  5 11:36:54 GMT 2025] CR2: ffffffffffffffd6 CR3: 000000003e5d0006 CR4: 00000000003706f0
[Sun Jan  5 11:36:54 GMT 2025] DR0: 0000000000000000 DR1: 0000000000000000 DR2: 0000000000000000
[Sun Jan  5 11:36:54 GMT 2025] DR3: 0000000000000000 DR6: 00000000fffe0ff0 DR7: 0000000000000400
[Sun Jan  5 11:36:54 GMT 2025] Kernel panic - not syncing: Fatal exception
[Sun Jan  5 11:36:54 GMT 2025] Kernel Offset: 0x1f600000 from 0xffffffff81000000 (relocation range:
0xffffffff80000000-0xffffffffbfffffff)
```

3. We also get an exception stack trace from the tool where we have more information without and with source code references (we use **-sx** to include offsets):

```
crash> bt -sx
PID: 6611     TASK: ffff9ef251598000  CPU: 2    COMMAND: "mod_b thread"
 #0 [ffffbaeb8567bb58] machine_kexec+0x171 at ffffffffa0699db1
 #1 [ffffbaeb8567bbc0] __crash_kexec+0x66 at ffffffffa07f1e46
 #2 [ffffbaeb8567bc80] panic+0x159 at ffffffffa06ddf29
 #3 [ffffbaeb8567bd00] oops_end+0xa7 at ffffffffa0643287
 #4 [ffffbaeb8567bd28] page_fault_oops+0xa0 at ffffffffa06b1000
 #5 [ffffbaeb8567bd88] do_user_addr_fault+0x2fe at ffffffffa06b1a0e
 #6 [ffffbaeb8567bdd0] exc_page_fault+0x74 at ffffffffa16bfd44
 #7 [ffffbaeb8567be00] asm_exc_page_fault+0x27 at ffffffffa1800bc7
 #8 [ffffbaeb8567beb8] bar+0xd at ffffffffc07a50cd [mod_b]
 #9 [ffffbaeb8567bec8] foo+0xe at ffffffffc07a509e [mod_b]
#10 [ffffbaeb8567bed8] kthread_f+0x18 at ffffffffc07a5028 [mod_b]
#11 [ffffbaeb8567bee8] kthread+0xd3 at ffffffffa070ff93
#12 [ffffbaeb8567bf28] ret_from_fork+0x39 at ffffffffa064f459
#13 [ffffbaeb8567bf50] ret_from_fork_asm+0x1b at ffffffffa0604e5b
```

4. However, the problem RIP address is 0, so we need to look at the call stack below **asm_exc_page_fault**:

```
crash> dis bar
dis: invalid kernel virtual address: ffffffffc07a6000  type: "gdb_readmem_callback"
dis: invalid kernel virtual address: ffffffffc07a6000  type: "gdb_readmem_callback"
0xffffffffc07a50c0 <bar>:       nopl   0x0(%rax,%rax,1) [FTRACE NOP]
0xffffffffc07a50c5 <bar+5>:     push   %rbp
0xffffffffc07a50c6 <bar+6>:     xor    %eax,%eax
0xffffffffc07a50c8 <bar+8>:     mov    %rsp,%rbp
0xffffffffc07a50cb <bar+11>:    call   *%rax
0xffffffffc07a50cd <bar+13>:    nopl   (%rax)
0xffffffffc07a50d0 <bar+16>:    pop    %rbp
0xffffffffc07a50d1 <bar+17>:    ret
0xffffffffc07a50d2 <bar+18>:    int3
0xffffffffc07a50d3 <bar+19>:    int3
0xffffffffc07a50d4 <bar+20>:    int3
0xffffffffc07a50d5 <bar+21>:    int3
0xffffffffc07a50d6 <bar+22>:    add    %al,(%rax)
0xffffffffc07a50d8 <bar+24>:    add    %al,(%rax)
...
...
...
 -- MORE --  forward: <SPACE>, <ENTER> or j  backward: b or k  quit: qq
```

Note: Depending on the kernel and compiler versions, it may be somewhat complicated, for example, from the previous edition:

```
crash> bt -sx
PID: 2189   TASK: ffff8facda610000  CPU: 1   COMMAND: "mod_b thread"
 #0 [ffffbb1d00b1fcd8] machine_kexec+0x1bb at ffffffffb726436b
 #1 [ffffbb1d00b1fd30] __crash_kexec+0x6d at ffffffffb733aaad
 #2 [ffffbb1d00b1fdf8] crash_kexec+0x35 at ffffffffb733bbe5
 #3 [ffffbb1d00b1fe08] oops_end+0x9b at ffffffffb722da9b
 #4 [ffffbb1d00b1fe28] exc_page_fault+0x78 at ffffffffb7ab6c98
 #5 [ffffbb1d00b1fe50] asm_exc_page_fault+0x1e at ffffffffb7c00ade
 #6 [ffffbb1d00b1ff08] kthread_f+0x14 at ffffffffc0a0e014 [mod_b]
 #7 [ffffbb1d00b1ff10] kthread+0x11b at ffffffffb72ac91b
 #8 [ffffbb1d00b1ff50] ret_from_fork+0x22 at ffffffffb7204442

crash> dis kthread_f
0xffffffffc0a0e000 <kthread_f>: nopl   0x0(%rax,%rax,1) [FTRACE NOP]
0xffffffffc0a0e005 <kthread_f+5>:       mov    $0x2710,%edi
0xffffffffc0a0e00a <kthread_f+10>:      call   0xffffffffb7317cf0 <msleep>
0xffffffffc0a0e00f <kthread_f+15>:      call   0xffffffffc0a0e060
0xffffffffc0a0e014 <kthread_f+20>:      xor    %eax,%eax
0xffffffffc0a0e016 <kthread_f+22>:      ret
0xffffffffc0a0e017 <kthread_f+23>:      nopw   0x0(%rax,%rax,1)

crash> dis 0xffffffffc0a0e060
0xffffffffc0a0e060 <foo>:       nopl   0x0(%rax,%rax,1) [FTRACE NOP]
0xffffffffc0a0e065 <foo+5>:     jmp    0xffffffffc0a0e070 <bar>
0xffffffffc0a0e06a <foo+10>:    nopw   0x0(%rax,%rax,1)

crash> dis 0xffffffffc0a0e070
0xffffffffc0a0e070 <bar>:       nopl   0x0(%rax,%rax,1) [FTRACE NOP]
0xffffffffc0a0e075 <bar+5>:     xor    %eax,%eax
0xffffffffc0a0e077 <bar+7>:     jmp    0xffffffffb7e01ca0 <__x86_indirect_thunk_rax>
0xffffffffc0a0e07c <bar+12>:    add    %al,(%rax)
0xffffffffc0a0e07e <bar+14>:    add    %al,(%rax)
...
...
...
crash> dis 0xffffffffb7e01ca0
0xffffffffb7e01ca0 <__x86_indirect_thunk_rax>: jmp    0xffffffffb7e01ca5 <__x86_retpoline_rax>
0xffffffffb7e01ca2 <__x86_indirect_thunk_rax+2>:       nopl   (%rax)

crash> dis 0xffffffffb7e01ca5
0xffffffffb7e01ca5 <__x86_retpoline_rax>:      call   0xffffffffb7e01cb1 <__x86_retpoline_rax+12>
0xffffffffb7e01caa <__x86_retpoline_rax+5>:    pause
0xffffffffb7e01cac <__x86_retpoline_rax+7>:    lfence
0xffffffffb7e01caf <__x86_retpoline_rax+10>:   jmp    0xffffffffb7e01caa <__x86_retpoline_rax+5>
0xffffffffb7e01cb1 <__x86_retpoline_rax+12>:   mov    %rax,(%rsp)
0xffffffffb7e01cb5 <__x86_retpoline_rax+16>:   ret
```

Note: Since the **ret** instruction takes its return address from **(%rsp)** value, the %RSP-8 from message output should point to memory value 0 (we need to subtract 8 bytes from %RSP address because %RSP is incremented before transferring execution to the stored return address):

```
[Sat Jun 25 19:22:31 BST 2022] RSP: 0018:ffffbb1d00b1ff08 EFLAGS: 00010246

crash> rd ffffbb1d00b1ff00
ffffbb1d00b1ff00:  0000000000000000                    ........
```

Exercise K3 (A64, GDB)

Goal: Learn how to recognize problems with kernel threads, identify their owner module, and follow call chains.

Patterns: Origin Module; NULL Pointer (Code); Hidden Call.

1. Load the core dump *202501051206.kdump* from the A64/K3 directory and the matching *vmlinux-6.8.0-1018-oracle* file from the A64/KSym directory:

```
~/ALCDA2/A64/K3$ crash 202501051206.kdump ../KSym/vmlinux-6.8.0-1018-oracle

crash 8.0.6++
Copyright (C) 2002-2025  Red Hat, Inc.
Copyright (C) 2004, 2005, 2006, 2010  IBM Corporation
Copyright (C) 1999-2006  Hewlett-Packard Co
Copyright (C) 2005, 2006, 2011, 2012  Fujitsu Limited
Copyright (C) 2006, 2007  VA Linux Systems Japan K.K.
Copyright (C) 2005, 2011, 2020-2024  NEC Corporation
Copyright (C) 1999, 2002, 2007  Silicon Graphics, Inc.
Copyright (C) 1999, 2000, 2001, 2002  Mission Critical Linux, Inc.
Copyright (C) 2015, 2021  VMware, Inc.
This program is free software, covered by the GNU General Public License,
and you are welcome to change it and/or distribute copies of it under
certain conditions.  Enter "help copying" to see the conditions.
This program has absolutely no warranty.  Enter "help warranty" for details.

GNU gdb (GDB) 10.2
Copyright (C) 2021 Free Software Foundation, Inc.
License GPLv3+: GNU GPL version 3 or later <http://gnu.org/licenses/gpl.html>
This is free software: you are free to change and redistribute it.
There is NO WARRANTY, to the extent permitted by law.
Type "show copying" and "show warranty" for details.
This GDB was configured as "aarch64-unknown-linux-gnu".
Type "show configuration" for configuration details.
Find the GDB manual and other documentation resources online at:
    <http://www.gnu.org/software/gdb/documentation/>.

For help, type "help".
Type "apropos word" to search for commands related to "word"...

      KERNEL: ../KSym/vmlinux-6.8.0-1018-oracle  [TAINTED]
    DUMPFILE: 202501051206.kdump  [PARTIAL DUMP]
        CPUS: 2
        DATE: Sun Jan  5 12:05:59 UTC 2025
      UPTIME: 19:30:55
LOAD AVERAGE: 0.44, 0.14, 0.04
       TASKS: 215
    NODENAME: instance-20230624-1144
     RELEASE: 6.8.0-1018-oracle
     VERSION: #19~22.04.1-Ubuntu SMP Mon Dec  9 23:49:53 UTC 2024
     MACHINE: aarch64  (unknown Mhz)
      MEMORY: 12 GB
       PANIC: "Kernel panic - not syncing: Oops: Fatal exception" (check log for details)
         PID: 11894
     COMMAND: "mod_b thread"
        TASK: ffff0000c0448000  [THREAD_INFO: ffff0000c0448000]
         CPU: 1
```

```
        STATE: TASK_RUNNING (PANIC)

crash>
```

2. We check the log for details, and at the end, we find the bug description, crash PC, the stack pointer, and the stack trace:

```
crash> log -T
[Sat Jan  4 16:35:04 UTC 2025] Booting Linux on physical CPU 0x0000000000 [0x413fd0c1]
[Sat Jan  4 16:35:04 UTC 2025] Linux version 6.8.0-1018-oracle (buildd@bos03-arm64-112) (aarch64-linux-gnu-gcc-11
(Ubuntu 11.4.0-1ubuntu1~22.04) 11.4.0, GNU ld (GNU Binutils for Ubuntu) 2.38) #19~22.04.1-Ubuntu SMP Mon Dec  9
23:49:53 UTC 2024 (Ubuntu 6.8.0-1018.19~22.04.1-oracle 6.8.12)
[Sat Jan  4 16:35:04 UTC 2025] KASLR disabled due to lack of seed
...
...
...
[Sun Jan  5 12:05:42 UTC 2025] Unable to handle kernel NULL pointer dereference at virtual address 0000000000000000
[Sun Jan  5 12:05:42 UTC 2025] Mem abort info:
[Sun Jan  5 12:05:42 UTC 2025]   ESR = 0x0000000086000004
[Sun Jan  5 12:05:42 UTC 2025]   EC = 0x21: IABT (current EL), IL = 32 bits
[Sun Jan  5 12:05:42 UTC 2025]   SET = 0, FnV = 0
[Sun Jan  5 12:05:42 UTC 2025]   EA = 0, S1PTW = 0
[Sun Jan  5 12:05:42 UTC 2025]   FSC = 0x04: level 0 translation fault
[Sun Jan  5 12:05:42 UTC 2025] user pgtable: 4k pages, 48-bit VAs, pgdp=0000000105a7b000
[Sun Jan  5 12:05:42 UTC 2025] [0000000000000000] pgd=0000000000000000, p4d=0000000000000000
[Sun Jan  5 12:05:42 UTC 2025] Internal error: Oops: 0000000086000004 [#1] SMP
[Sun Jan  5 12:05:42 UTC 2025] Modules linked in: mod_b(OE) tls xt_comment xt_owner ipt_REJECT nf_reject_ipv4
xt_tcpudp xt_state xt_conntrack nf_conntrack sunrpc nf_defrag_ipv6 nf_defrag_ipv4 binfmt_misc nft_compat nf_tables
nfnetlink nls_iso8859_1 joydev input_leds sch_fq_codel dm_multipath scsi_dh_rdac scsi_dh_emc scsi_dh_alua efi_pstore
ip_tables x_tables autofs4 btrfs blake2b_generic iscsi_tcp libiscsi_tcp libiscsi scsi_transport_iscsi iscsi_ibft
iscsi_boot_sysfs raid10 raid456 async_raid6_recov async_memcpy async_pq async_xor async_tx xor xor_neon raid6_pq
libcrc32c raid1 raid0 hid_generic usbhid hid crct10dif_ce polyval_ce polyval_generic ghash_ce sm4 sha2_ce sha256_arm64
sha1_ce xhci_pci virtio_gpu xhci_pci_renesas virtio_dma_buf aes_neon_bs aes_neon_blk aes_ce_blk aes_ce_cipher
[Sun Jan  5 12:05:42 UTC 2025] CPU: 1 PID: 11894 Comm: mod_b thread Kdump: loaded Tainted: G           OE      6.8.0-
1018-oracle #19~22.04.1-Ubuntu
[Sun Jan  5 12:05:42 UTC 2025] Hardware name: QEMU KVM Virtual Machine, BIOS 1.6.6 08/22/2023
[Sun Jan  5 12:05:42 UTC 2025] pstate: 60400005 (nZCv daif +PAN -UAO -TCO -DIT -SSBS BTYPE=--)
[Sun Jan  5 12:05:42 UTC 2025] pc : 0x0
[Sun Jan  5 12:05:42 UTC 2025] lr : bar+0x1c/0xf18 [mod_b]
[Sun Jan  5 12:05:42 UTC 2025] sp : ffff800085a23e40
[Sun Jan  5 12:05:42 UTC 2025] x29: ffff800085a23e40 x28: 0000000000000000 x27: 0000000000000000
[Sun Jan  5 12:05:42 UTC 2025] x26: 0000000000000000 x25: 0000000000000000 x24: 0000000000000000
[Sun Jan  5 12:05:42 UTC 2025] x23: ffff80007bead008 x22: ffff0000c0448000 x21: ffff800085a139d8
[Sun Jan  5 12:05:42 UTC 2025] x20: ffff0000c9454480 x19: ffff0000cb8903c0 x18: 0000000000000000
[Sun Jan  5 12:05:42 UTC 2025] x17: 0000000000000000 x16: 0000000000000000 x15: 0000000000000000
[Sun Jan  5 12:05:42 UTC 2025] x14: 0000000000000000 x13: 0000000000000000 x12: 0000000000000000
[Sun Jan  5 12:05:42 UTC 2025] x11: 0000000000000000 x10: 0000000000001b70 x9 : ffff80007bead0c8
[Sun Jan  5 12:05:42 UTC 2025] x8 : ffff0000c0449bd0 x7 : 0000000000000000 x6 : 0000000000000000
[Sun Jan  5 12:05:42 UTC 2025] x5 : 0000000000000000 x4 : 0000000000000000 x3 : 0000000000000000
[Sun Jan  5 12:05:42 UTC 2025] x2 : 0000000000000000 x1 : 0000000000000000 x0 : 0000000000000000
[Sun Jan  5 12:05:42 UTC 2025] Call trace:
[Sun Jan  5 12:05:42 UTC 2025]  0x0
[Sun Jan  5 12:05:42 UTC 2025]  foo+0x18/0x38 [mod_b]
[Sun Jan  5 12:05:42 UTC 2025]  kthread_f+0x20/0x40 [mod_b]
[Sun Jan  5 12:05:42 UTC 2025]  kthread+0xe0/0xf0
[Sun Jan  5 12:05:42 UTC 2025]  ret_from_fork+0x10/0x20
[Sun Jan  5 12:05:42 UTC 2025] Code: ???????? ???????? ???????? ???????? (????????)
[Sun Jan  5 12:05:42 UTC 2025] ---[ end trace 0000000000000000 ]---
[Sun Jan  5 12:05:59 UTC 2025] Kernel panic - not syncing: Oops: Fatal exception
[Sun Jan  5 12:05:59 UTC 2025] SMP: stopping secondary CPUs
[Sun Jan  5 12:05:59 UTC 2025] Kernel Offset: disabled
[Sun Jan  5 12:05:59 UTC 2025] CPU features: 0x1,00000020,7002014a,2101720b
[Sun Jan  5 12:05:59 UTC 2025] Memory Limit: none
[Sun Jan  5 12:06:18 UTC 2025] Starting crashdump kernel...
[Sun Jan  5 12:06:18 UTC 2025] Bye!
```

3. We also get an exception stack trace from the tool where we have more information (we use **-sx** to include offsets):

```
crash> bt -sx
PID: 11894    TASK: ffff0000c0448000  CPU: 1    COMMAND: "mod_b thread"
 #0 [ffff800085a23870] machine_kexec+0x54 at ffff80008003fdcc
 #1 [ffff800085a238a0] __crash_kexec+0x70 at ffff80008020b600
 #2 [ffff800085a23a20] panic+0x34c at ffff8000800c83dc
 #3 [ffff800085a23b00] die+0x2d4 at ffff800080025f94
 #4 [ffff800085a23bb0] die_kernel_fault+0x108 at ffff800080043c30
 #5 [ffff800085a23be0] __do_kernel_fault+0x1b8 at ffff8000800441e8
 #6 [ffff800085a23c10] do_page_fault+0x21c at ffff8000815f5944
 #7 [ffff800085a23c70] do_translation_fault+0x70 at ffff8000815f5cc0
 #8 [ffff800085a23c80] do_mem_abort+0x48 at ffff800080043d40
 #9 [ffff800085a23cb0] el1_abort+0x48 at ffff8000815dbdc0
#10 [ffff800085a23ce0] el1h_64_sync_handler+0x174 at ffff8000815ddd8c
#11 [ffff800085a23e20] el1h_64_sync+0x78 at ffff800080011310
#12 [ffff800085a23e40] (null) at fffffffffffffffc
#13 [ffff800085a23e50] foo+0x14 at ffff80007bead0c4 [mod_b]
#14 [ffff800085a23e60] kthread_f+0x1c at ffff80007bead024 [mod_b]
#15 [ffff800085a23e70] kthread+0xdc at ffff800080107f2c
```

4. However, the problem PC address is 0, so we need to look at the call stack below **el1h_64_sync** and follow the function calls (we see the **bar+0x1c** return address in LR):

```
crash> dis foo
0xffff80007bead0b0 <foo>:       mov     x9, x30
0xffff80007bead0b4 <foo+4>:     nop
0xffff80007bead0b8 <foo+8>:     paciasp
0xffff80007bead0bc <foo+12>:    stp     x29, x30, [sp, #-16]!
0xffff80007bead0c0 <foo+16>:    mov     x29, sp
0xffff80007bead0c4 <foo+20>:    bl      0xffff80007bead0e8 <bar>
0xffff80007bead0c8 <foo+24>:    ldp     x29, x30, [sp], #16
0xffff80007bead0cc <foo+28>:    autiasp
0xffff80007bead0d0 <foo+32>:    mov     x16, #0x0                       // #0
0xffff80007bead0d4 <foo+36>:    mov     x17, #0x0                       // #0
0xffff80007bead0d8 <foo+40>:    ret
0xffff80007bead0dc <foo+44>:    nop
0xffff80007bead0e0 <foo+48>:    .inst   0x81634280 ; undefined
0xffff80007bead0e4 <foo+52>:    .inst   0xffff8000 ; undefined

crash> dis bar
dis: invalid kernel virtual address: ffff80007beae000  type: "gdb_readmem_callback"
dis: invalid kernel virtual address: ffff80007beae000  type: "gdb_readmem callback"
0xffff80007bead0e8 <bar>:       mov     x9, x30
0xffff80007bead0ec <bar+4>:     nop
0xffff80007bead0f0 <bar+8>:     paciasp
0xffff80007bead0f4 <bar+12>:    stp     x29, x30, [sp, #-16]!
0xffff80007bead0f8 <bar+16>:    mov     x0, #0x0                        // #0
0xffff80007bead0fc <bar+20>:    mov     x29, sp
0xffff80007bead100 <bar+24>:    blr     x0
0xffff80007bead104 <bar+28>:    ldp     x29, x30, [sp], #16
0xffff80007bead108 <bar+32>:    autiasp
...
...
...
 -- MORE --  forward: <SPACE>, <ENTER> or j  backward: b or k  quit: qq
```

Exercise K3 (x64, WinDbg)

Goal: Learn how to recognize problems with kernel threads and identify their owner module.

Patterns: Origin Module; NULL Pointer (Code); Hidden Call.

1. Copy the *vmlinux-6.8.0-1018-azure* file in the x64/KSym directory to the *vmlinux* file.

2. Launch WinDbg. Load the core dump *202501051138.kdump* from the x64/K3 directory and set the symbol path to the x64/KSym directory (there may be some delay/unresponsiveness when you type the **.reload** command):

```
Microsoft (R) Windows Debugger Version 10.0.27725.1000 AMD64
Copyright (c) Microsoft Corporation. All rights reserved.


Loading Dump File [C:\ALCDA2\x64\K3\202501051138.kdump]
64-bit machine not using 64-bit API

************* Path validation summary **************
Response                         Time (ms)     Location
OK                                             C:\ALCDA2\A64\KSym\
Symbol search path is: C:\ALCDA2\A64\KSym\
Executable search path is:
Generic Unix Kernel Version 0 MP (4 procs) Free x64
Primary image base = 0xffffffff`a0600000 Loaded module list = 0x00000000`00000000
System Uptime: not available
Loading Kernel Symbols

Loading User Symbols

ReadVirtual() failed in GetXStateConfiguration() first read attempt (error == 0.)
For analysis of this file, run !analyze -v
ffffffff`a16c1a1b cli

0: kd> .sympath C:\ALCDA2\x64\KSym\
Symbol search path is: C:\ALCDA2\x64\KSym\
Expanded Symbol search path is: c:\alcda2\x64\ksym\

************* Path validation summary **************
Response                         Time (ms)     Location
OK                                             C:\ALCDA2\x64\KSym\

0: kd> .reload
Loading Kernel Symbols
.*** WARNING: Unable to verify timestamp for vmlinux

Loading User Symbols


************* Symbol Loading Error Summary **************
Module name            Error
vmlinux                The system cannot find the file specified

You can troubleshoot most symbol related issues by turning on symbol loading diagnostics (!sym
noisy) and repeating the command that caused symbols to be loaded.
You should also verify that your symbol search path (.sympath) is correct.
```

3. We check the log for details, and at the end, we find the bug description, crash RIP, the stack pointer, and the stack trace:

```
0: kd> !log
@$log()
    [0x0]            : [     0.000000] Linux version 6.8.0-1018-azure (buildd@lcy02-amd64-013) (x86_64-linux-gnu-gcc-11 (Ubuntu 11.4.0-1ubuntu1~22.04) 11.4.0, GNU ld (GNU Binutils for Ubuntu) 2.38) #21~22.04.1-Ubuntu SMP Fri Nov  8 00:21:25 UTC 2024 (Ubuntu 6.8.0-1018.21~22.04.1-azure 6.8.12)
    [0x1]            : [     0.000000] Command line: BOOT_IMAGE=/boot/vmlinuz-6.8.0-1018-azure root=UUID=89ee03ba-6808-4977-a4fb-9b10174744f8 ro quiet splash crashkernel=512M-:192M vt.handoff=7
...
...
...
    [0x230]          : [ 23399.998839] BUG: kernel NULL pointer dereference, address: 0000000000000000
    [0x231]          : [ 23399.998850] #PF: supervisor instruction fetch in kernel mode
    [0x232]          : [ 23399.998854] #PF: error_code(0x0010) - not-present page
    [0x233]          : [ 23399.998861] PGD 0 P4D 0
    [0x234]          : [ 23399.998865] Oops: 0010 [#1] SMP PTI
    [0x235]          : [ 23399.998870] CPU: 2 PID: 6611 Comm: mod_b thread Kdump: loaded Tainted: G           OE
6.8.0-1018-azure #21~22.04.1-Ubuntu
    [0x236]          : [ 23399.998874] Hardware name: Microsoft Corporation Virtual Machine/Virtual Machine, BIOS
Hyper-V UEFI Release v4.1 05/13/2024
    [0x237]          : [ 23399.998876] RIP: 0010:0x0
    [0x238]          : [ 23399.998891] Code: Unable to access opcode bytes at 0xffffffffffffffd6.
    [0x239]          : [ 23399.998893] RSP: 0018:ffffbaeb8567beb8 EFLAGS: 00010246
    [0x23a]          : [ 23399.998896] RAX: 0000000000000000 RBX: ffff9ef251598000 RCX: 0000000000000000
    [0x23b]          : [ 23399.998898] RDX: 0000000000000000 RSI: 0000000000000286 RDI: 0000000000000000
    [0x23c]          : [ 23399.998900] RBP: ffffbaeb8567bec0 R08: 0000000000000000 R09: 0000000000000000
    [0x23d]          : [ 23399.998902] R10: 0000000000000002 R11: 0000000000000000 R12: ffff9ef28083ad80
    [0x23e]          : [ 23399.998905] R13: ffffbaeb856db8b8 R14: ffff9ef2347a6600 R15: ffffffffc07a5010
    [0x23f]          : [ 23399.998909] FS:  0000000000000000(0000) GS:ffff9ef303d00000(0000) knlGS:0000000000000000
    [0x240]          : [ 23399.998912] CS:  0010 DS: 0000 ES: 0000 CR0: 0000000080050033
    [0x241]          : [ 23399.998915] CR2: ffffffffffffffd6 CR3: 000000003e5d0006 CR4: 00000000003706f0
    [0x242]          : [ 23399.998917] DR0: 0000000000000000 DR1: 0000000000000000 DR2: 0000000000000000
    [0x243]          : [ 23399.998919] DR3: 0000000000000000 DR6: 00000000fffe0ff0 DR7: 0000000000000400
    [0x244]          : [ 23399.998920] Call Trace:
    [0x245]          : [ 23399.998923]  <TASK>
    [0x246]          : [ 23399.998926]  ? show_regs+0x6a/0x80
    [0x247]          : [ 23399.998933]  ? __die+0x25/0x70
    [0x248]          : [ 23399.998937]  ? page_fault_oops+0x79/0x180
    [0x249]          : [ 23399.998941]  ? do_user_addr_fault+0x2fe/0x640
    [0x24a]          : [ 23399.998944]  ? raw_spin_rq_unlock+0x10/0x30
    [0x24b]          : [ 23399.998949]  ? exc_page_fault+0x74/0x160
    [0x24c]          : [ 23399.998954]  ? asm_exc_page_fault+0x27/0x30
    [0x24d]          : [ 23399.998962]  ? __pfx_kthread_f+0x10/0x10 [mod_b]
    [0x24e]          : [ 23399.998970]  bar+0xd/0xf40 [mod_b]
    [0x24f]          : [ 23399.998976]  foo+0xe/0x20 [mod_b]
    [0x250]          : [ 23399.998981]  kthread_f+0x18/0x20 [mod_b]
    [0x251]          : [ 23399.998986]  kthread+0xd3/0x100
    [0x252]          : [ 23399.998990]  ? __pfx_kthread+0x10/0x10
    [0x253]          : [ 23399.998993]  ret_from_fork+0x39/0x60
    [0x254]          : [ 23399.998997]  ? __pfx_kthread+0x10/0x10
    [0x255]          : [ 23399.998999]  ret_from_fork_asm+0x1b/0x30
    [0x256]          : [ 23399.999004]  </TASK>
    [0x257]          : [ 23399.999006] Modules linked in: mod_b(OE) binfmt_misc crct10dif_pclmul crc32_pclmul
polyval_clmulni nls_iso8859_1 polyval_generic ghash_clmulni_intel sha256_ssse3 sha1_ssse3 aesni_intel crypto_simd
cryptd serio_raw hyperv_drm joydev sch_fq_codel hv_sock vsock msr parport_pc ppdev lp parport efi_pstore ip_tables
x_tables autofs4 btrfs blake2b_generic xor raid6_pq libcrc32c hid_generic hid_hyperv hyperv_keyboard hv_netvsc hid
    [...]
0: kd> dx -r1  -c 600 @$log()
@$log()
    [0x258]          : [ 23399.999045] CR2: 0000000000000000
    [0x259]          : [ 23399.999048] ---[ end trace 0000000000000000 ]---
    [0x25a]          : [ 23400.169199] RIP: 0010:0x0
    [0x25b]          : [ 23400.169235] Code: Unable to access opcode bytes at 0xffffffffffffffd6.
    [0x25c]          : [ 23400.169238] RSP: 0018:ffffbaeb8567beb8 EFLAGS: 00010246
    [0x25d]          : [ 23400.169245] RAX: 0000000000000000 RBX: ffff9ef251598000 RCX: 0000000000000000
    [0x25e]          : [ 23400.169249] RDX: 0000000000000000 RSI: 0000000000000286 RDI: 0000000000000000
    [0x25f]          : [ 23400.169252] RBP: ffffbaeb8567bec0 R08: 0000000000000000 R09: 0000000000000000
    [0x260]          : [ 23400.169255] R10: 0000000000000002 R11: 0000000000000000 R12: ffff9ef28083ad80
    [0x261]          : [ 23400.169258] R13: ffffbaeb856db8b8 R14: ffff9ef2347a6600 R15: ffffffffc07a5010
    [0x262]          : [ 23400.169265] FS:  0000000000000000(0000) GS:ffff9ef303d00000(0000) knlGS:0000000000000000
    [0x263]          : [ 23400.169269] CS:  0010 DS: 0000 ES: 0000 CR0: 0000000080050033
```

```
    [0x264]          : [ 23400.169273] CR2: ffffffffffffffd6 CR3: 000000003e5d0006 CR4: 00000000003706f0
    [0x265]          : [ 23400.169277] DR0: 0000000000000000 DR1: 0000000000000000 DR2: 0000000000000000
    [0x266]          : [ 23400.169280] DR3: 0000000000000000 DR6: 00000000fffe0ff0 DR7: 0000000000000400
    [0x267]          : [ 23400.169284] Kernel panic - not syncing: Fatal exception
```

4. Unfortunately, we are not able to get either the stack trace on CPU 2 or raw stack data around RSP in this dump, so we explore more WinDbg commands in this exercise.

5. We can get the problem task info:

```
0: kd> !runq
@$runq()
    [0x0]               : CPU 0 run queue [current = 'swapper/0' (0)]
        Cpu                 : 0x0
        RunQueue            [Type: rq]
        CurrentTask         : swapper/0 [Type: task_struct]
        RTTasks
        CfsTasks
    [0x1]               : CPU 1 run queue [current = 'swapper/1' (0)]
        Cpu                 : 0x1
        RunQueue            [Type: rq]
        CurrentTask         : swapper/1 [Type: task_struct]
        RTTasks
        CfsTasks
    [0x2]               : CPU 2 run queue [current = 'mod_b thread' (19d3)]
        Cpu                 : 0x2
        RunQueue            [Type: rq]
        CurrentTask         : mod_b thread [Type: task_struct]
        RTTasks
        CfsTasks
            [0x1740]            : kworker/2:1 [Type: task_struct]
    [0x3]               : CPU 3 run queue [current = 'swapper/3' (0)]
        Cpu                 : 0x3
        RunQueue            [Type: rq]
        CurrentTask         : swapper/3 [Type: task_struct]
        RTTasks
        CfsTasks

0: kd> dx -r1 @$runq()[2].CurrentTask
@$runq()[2].CurrentTask                        : mod_b thread [Type: task_struct]
    [+0x000] thread_info      [Type: thread_info]
    [+0x018] __state          : 0x0 [Type: unsigned int]
    [+0x01c] saved_state      : 0x0 [Type: unsigned int]
    [+0x020] stack            : 0xffffbaeb85678000 [Type: void *]
    [+0x028] usage            [Type: refcount_t]
    [+0x02c] flags            : 0x208040 [Type: unsigned int]
    [+0x030] ptrace           : 0x0 [Type: unsigned int]
    [+0x034] on_cpu           : 1 [Type: int]
...
...
...
```

6. We can get the list of available symbols, such as variables and functions, using the **x** command. However, it is better to restrict the output to some pattern, and it still takes some time to see the output:

```
0: kd> x vmlinux!*task*
ffffffff`a280fcc0 vmlinux!init_task = swapper/0
ffffffff`a2815210 vmlinux!__SCK__x86_pmu_sched_task = static_call_key
ffffffff`a2815200 vmlinux!__SCK__x86_pmu_swap_task_ctx = static_call_key
ffffffff`a20f2fe0 vmlinux!__tpstrtab_task_newtask = char [13] "task_newtask"
ffffffff`a2be8940 vmlinux!__tracepoint_task_newtask = tracepoint
ffffffff`a287c750 vmlinux!__SCK__tp_func_task_newtask = static_call_key
...
...
...
ffffffff`a06f6580 vmlinux!force_sig_info_to_task (void)
ffffffff`a06f3d50 vmlinux!task_join_group_stop (void)
ffffffff`a06f14b0 vmlinux!task_participate_group_stop (void)
ffffffff`a06f3be0 vmlinux!task_set_jobctl_pending (void)
ffffffff`a06f3c60 vmlinux!task_clear_jobctl_trapping (void)
ffffffff`a06f3cc0 vmlinux!task_clear_jobctl_pending (void)
...
...
...
ffffffff`a0b3c130 vmlinux!_pfx_proc_task_name = <no type information>
ffffffff`a1165220 vmlinux!_pfx___traceiter_ata_sff_flush_pio_task = <no type information>
ffffffff`a096ce20 vmlinux!_probestub_finish_task_reaping = <no type information>
ffffffff`a070c340 vmlinux!_pfx_task_work_cancel = <no type information>
ffffffff`a0838f00 vmlinux!_pfx_kdb_task_state = <no type information>
```

7. Unfortunately, the **dt** command to list data types (even patterns) loops infinitely, repeating the same data, so you may need to break it and wait for the current cycle to finish:

```
0: kd> dt vmlinux!*task*
          vmlinux!task_struct
          vmlinux!arch_uprobe_task
          vmlinux!uprobe_task_state
          vmlinux!uprobe_task
          vmlinux!task_cputime
          vmlinux!task_io_accounting
          vmlinux!rv_task_monitor
          vmlinux!dl_server_has_tasks_f
          vmlinux!task_delay_info
          vmlinux!task_cputime_atomic
          vmlinux!taskstats
          vmlinux!task_struct
...
...
...

0: kd> dt -r task_struct
vmlinux!task_struct
   +0x000 thread_info      : thread_info
      +0x000 flags            : Uint8B
      +0x008 syscall_work     : Uint8B
      +0x010 status           : Uint4B
      +0x014 cpu              : Uint4B
   +0x018 __state          : Uint4B
...
...
...
```

Exercise K3 (A64, WinDbg)

Goal: Learn how to recognize problems with kernel threads, identify their owner module, follow call chains, and reconstruct a stack trace if necessary.

Patterns: Origin Module; NULL Pointer (Code); Hidden Call.

1. Copy the *vmlinux-6.8.0-1018-oracle* file in the A64/KSym directory to the *vmlinux* file.

2. Launch WinDbg. Load the core dump *202501051206.kdump* from the A64/K3 directory and set the symbol path to the A64/KSym directory (there may be some delay/unresponsiveness when you type the **.reload** command):

```
Microsoft (R) Windows Debugger Version 10.0.27725.1000 AMD64
Copyright (c) Microsoft Corporation. All rights reserved.


Loading Dump File [C:\ALCDA2\A64\K3\202501051206.kdump]
64-bit machine not using 64-bit API

************* Path validation summary **************
Response                         Time (ms)     Location
OK                                             C:\ALCDA2\x64\KSym\
Symbol search path is: C:\ALCDA2\x64\KSym\
Executable search path is:
Generic Unix Kernel Version 0 MP (2 procs) Free ARM 64-bit (AArch64)
Primary image base = 0xffff8000`80010000 Loaded module list = 0x00000000`00000000
System Uptime: not available
Loading Kernel Symbols

Loading User Symbols

For analysis of this file, run !analyze -v
ffff8000`815e0b1c ldp         fp,lr,[sp],#0x20

0: kd> .sympath C:\ALCDA2\A64\KSym\
Symbol search path is: C:\ALCDA2\A64\KSym\
Expanded Symbol search path is: c:\alcda2\a64\ksym\

************* Path validation summary **************
Response                         Time (ms)     Location
OK                                             C:\ALCDA2\A64\KSym\

0: kd> .reload
Loading Kernel Symbols
.*** WARNING: Unable to verify timestamp for vmlinux

Loading User Symbols


************* Symbol Loading Error Summary **************
Module name            Error
vmlinux                The system cannot find the file specified

You can troubleshoot most symbol related issues by turning on symbol loading diagnostics (!sym
noisy) and repeating the command that caused symbols to be loaded.
You should also verify that your symbol search path (.sympath) is correct.
```

3. We check the log for details, and at the end, we find the bug description, crash PC, the stack pointer, and the stack trace:

```
0: kd> !log
@$log()
    [0x0]            : [     0.000000] Booting Linux on physical CPU 0x0000000000 [0x413fd0c1]
    [0x1]            : [     0.000000] Linux version 6.8.0-1018-oracle (buildd@bos03-arm64-112) (aarch64-linux-gnu-gcc-11 (Ubuntu 11.4.0-1ubuntu1~22.04) 11.4.0, GNU ld (GNU Binutils for Ubuntu) 2.38) #19~22.04.1-Ubuntu SMP Mon Dec  9 23:49:53 UTC 2024 (Ubuntu 6.8.0-1018.19~22.04.1-oracle 6.8.12)
...
...
...
    [0x3e3]          : [ 70238.552856] Unable to handle kernel NULL pointer dereference at virtual address 0000000000000000
    [0x3e4]          : [ 70238.556413] Mem abort info:
    [0x3e5]          : [ 70238.556663]   ESR = 0x0000000086000004
    [0x3e6]          : [ 70238.557036]   EC = 0x21: IABT (current EL), IL = 32 bits
    [0x3e7]          : [ 70238.557518]   SET = 0, FnV = 0
    [...]
0: kd> dx -r1  -c 1000 @$log()
@$log()
    [0x3e8]          : [ 70238.557806]   EA = 0, S1PTW = 0
    [0x3e9]          : [ 70238.558093]   FSC = 0x04: level 0 translation fault
    [0x3ea]          : [ 70238.558517] user pgtable: 4k pages, 48-bit VAs, pgdp=0000000105a7b000
    [0x3eb]          : [ 70238.559103] [0000000000000000] pgd=0000000000000000, p4d=0000000000000000
    [0x3ec]          : [ 70238.559713] Internal error: Oops: 0000000086000004 [#1] SMP
    [0x3ed]          : [ 70238.560232] Modules linked in: mod_b(OE) tls xt_comment xt_owner ipt_REJECT nf_reject_ipv4 xt_tcpudp xt_state xt_conntrack nf_conntrack sunrpc nf_defrag_ipv6 nf_defrag_ipv4 binfmt_misc nft_compat nf_tables nfnetlink nls_iso8859_1 joydev input_leds sch_fq_codel dm_multipath scsi_dh_rdac scsi_dh_emc scsi_dh_alua efi_pstore ip_tables x_tables autofs4 btrfs blake2b_generic iscsi_tcp libiscsi_tcp libiscsi scsi_transport_iscsi iscsi_ibft iscsi_boot_sysfs raid10 raid456 async_raid6_recov async_memcpy async_...
    [0x3ee]          : [ 70238.579988] CPU: 1 PID: 11894 Comm: mod_b thread Kdump: loaded Tainted: G           OE 6.8.0-1018-oracle #19~22.04.1-Ubuntu
    [0x3ef]          : [ 70238.582552] Hardware name: QEMU KVM Virtual Machine, BIOS 1.6.6 08/22/2023
    [0x3f0]          : [ 70238.583247] pstate: 60400005 (nZCv daif +PAN -UAO -TCO -DIT -SSBS BTYPE=--)
    [0x3f1]          : [ 70238.583949] pc : 0x0
    [0x3f2]          : [ 70238.584201] lr : bar+0x1c/0xf18 [mod_b]
    [0x3f3]          : [ 70238.584955] sp : ffff800085a23e40
    [0x3f4]          : [ 70238.585729] x29: ffff800085a23e40 x28: 0000000000000000 x27: 0000000000000000
    [0x3f5]          : [ 70238.587411] x26: 0000000000000000 x25: 0000000000000000 x24: 0000000000000000
    [0x3f6]          : [ 70238.589040] x23: ffff80007bead008 x22: ffff0000c0448000 x21: ffff800085a139d8
    [0x3f7]          : [ 70238.590821] x20: ffff0000c9454480 x19: ffff0000cb8903c0 x18: 0000000000000000
    [0x3f8]          : [ 70238.591564] x17: 0000000000000000 x16: 0000000000000000 x15: 0000000000000000
    [0x3f9]          : [ 70238.592281] x14: 0000000000000000 x13: 0000000000000000 x12: 0000000000000000
    [0x3fa]          : [ 70238.593707] x11: 0000000000000000 x10: 0000000000001b70 x9 : ffff80007bead0c8
    [0x3fb]          : [ 70238.595355] x8 : ffff0000c0449bd0 x7 : 0000000000000000 x6 : 0000000000000000
    [0x3fc]          : [ 70238.596962] x5 : 0000000000000000 x4 : 0000000000000000 x3 : 0000000000000000
    [0x3fd]          : [ 70238.598450] x2 : 0000000000000000 x1 : 0000000000000000 x0 : 0000000000000000
    [0x3fe]          : [ 70238.612592] Call trace:
    [0x3ff]          : [ 70238.613248]  0x0
    [0x400]          : [ 70238.613658]  foo+0x18/0x38 [mod_b]
    [0x401]          : [ 70238.614676]  kthread_f+0x20/0x40 [mod_b]
    [0x402]          : [ 70238.615348]  kthread+0xe0/0xf0
    [0x403]          : [ 70238.616298]  ret_from_fork+0x10/0x20
    [0x404]          : [ 70238.617060] Code: ???????? ???????? ???????? ???????? (????????)
    [0x405]          : [ 70238.618570] ---[ end trace 0000000000000000 ]---
    [0x406]          : [ 70255.524771] Kernel panic - not syncing: Oops: Fatal exception
    [0x407]          : [ 70255.528478] SMP: stopping secondary CPUs
    [0x408]          : [ 70255.530542] Kernel Offset: disabled
    [0x409]          : [ 70255.532863] CPU features: 0x1,00000020,7002014a,2101720b
    [0x40a]          : [ 70255.534935] Memory Limit: none
    [0x40b]          : [ 70274.138950] Starting crashdump kernel...
```

4. Unfortunately, we are not able to get the stack trace on CPU 1 beyond exception processing:

```
0: kd> ~1s
WARNING: Unable to reset page directories
```

```
1: kd> kL
 # Child-SP          RetAddr               Call Site
00 ffff8000`85a238a0 ffff8000`8020b5f0     vmlinux!crash_setup_regs+0xa0
01 ffff8000`85a238a0 ffff8000`800c83e0     vmlinux!__crash_kexec+0x60
02 ffff8000`85a23a20 ffff8000`80025f98     vmlinux!panic+0x350
03 ffff8000`85a23b00 ffff8000`80043c34     vmlinux!die+0x2d8
04 ffff8000`85a23bb0 ffff8000`800441ec     vmlinux!die_kernel_fault+0x10c
05 ffff8000`85a23be0 ffff8000`815f5948     vmlinux!__do_kernel_fault+0x1bc
06 ffff8000`85a23c10 ffff8000`815f5cc4     vmlinux!do_page_fault+0x220
07 ffff8000`85a23c70 ffff8000`80043d44     vmlinux!do_translation_fault+0x74
08 ffff8000`85a23c80 ffff8000`815dbdc4     vmlinux!do_mem_abort+0x4c
09 ffff8000`85a23cb0 ffff8000`815ddd90     vmlinux!el1_abort+0x4c
0a ffff8000`85a23ce0 ffff8000`80011314     vmlinux!el1h_64_sync_handler+0x178
0b ffff8000`85a23cf0 00000000`00000000     vmlinux!el1h_64_sync+0x7c
```

5. But we can dump raw stack data around the SP value in the log and reconstruct the partial stack trace from the sequence of the saved FP values:

```
1: kd> dps ffff800085a23e40-200 L50
ffff8000`85a23c40  00000000`60400005
ffff8000`85a23c48  00000000`00000000
ffff8000`85a23c50  ffff8000`83239ac0 vmlinux!init_task
ffff8000`85a23c58  ffff8000`82890008 vmlinux!cpu_number
ffff8000`85a23c60  ffff8000`85a23c90
ffff8000`85a23c68  00000001`8017021c
ffff8000`85a23c70  ffff8000`85a23c80
ffff8000`85a23c78  ffff8000`80043d44 vmlinux!do_mem_abort+0x4c [/build/linux-oracle-6.8-
EzVzJ2/linux-oracle-6.8-6.8.0/arch/arm64/mm/fault.c @ 848]
ffff8000`85a23c80  ffff8000`85a23cb0
ffff8000`85a23c88  ffff8000`815dbdc4 vmlinux!el1_abort+0x4c [/build/linux-oracle-6.8-
EzVzJ2/linux-oracle-6.8-6.8.0/arch/arm64/include/asm/daifflags.h @ 28]
ffff8000`85a23c90  ffff8000`85a23cf0
ffff8000`85a23c98  00000000`86000004
ffff8000`85a23ca0  00000000`00000000
ffff8000`85a23ca8  00000000`00000000
ffff8000`85a23cb0  ffff8000`85a23ce0
ffff8000`85a23cb8  ffff8000`815ddd90 vmlinux!el1h_64_sync_handler+0x178 [/build/linux-oracle-
6.8-EzVzJ2/linux-oracle-6.8-6.8.0/arch/arm64/kernel/entry-common.c @ 486]
ffff8000`85a23cc0  ffff0000`cb8903c0
ffff8000`85a23cc8  ffff0000`c9454480
ffff8000`85a23cd0  ffff8000`85a23e40
ffff8000`85a23cd8  ffff8000`83261270 vmlinux!$d
ffff8000`85a23ce0  ffff8000`85a23e20
ffff8000`85a23ce8  ffff8000`80011314 vmlinux!el1h_64_sync+0x7c [/build/linux-oracle-6.8-
EzVzJ2/linux-oracle-6.8-6.8.0/arch/arm64/kernel/entry.S @ 593]
ffff8000`85a23cf0  00000000`00000000
ffff8000`85a23cf8  00000000`00000000
ffff8000`85a23d00  00000000`00000000
ffff8000`85a23d08  00000000`00000000
ffff8000`85a23d10  00000000`00000000
ffff8000`85a23d18  00000000`00000000
ffff8000`85a23d20  00000000`00000000
ffff8000`85a23d28  00000000`00000000
ffff8000`85a23d30  ffff0000`c0449bd0
ffff8000`85a23d38  ffff8000`7bead0c8 mod_b+0xc8
ffff8000`85a23d40  00000000`00001b70
ffff8000`85a23d48  00000000`00000000
ffff8000`85a23d50  00000000`00000000
ffff8000`85a23d58  00000000`00000000
```

```
ffff8000`85a23d60  00000000`00000000
ffff8000`85a23d68  00000000`00000000
ffff8000`85a23d70  00000000`00000000
ffff8000`85a23d78  00000000`00000000
ffff8000`85a23d80  00000000`00000000
ffff8000`85a23d88  ffff0000`cb8903c0
ffff8000`85a23d90  ffff0000`c9454480
ffff8000`85a23d98  ffff8000`85a139d8
ffff8000`85a23da0  ffff0000`c0448000
ffff8000`85a23da8  ffff8000`7bead008 mod_b+0x8
ffff8000`85a23db0  00000000`00000000
ffff8000`85a23db8  00000000`00000000
ffff8000`85a23dc0  00000000`00000000
ffff8000`85a23dc8  00000000`00000000
ffff8000`85a23dd0  00000000`00000000
ffff8000`85a23dd8  ffff8000`85a23e40
ffff8000`85a23de0  ffff8000`7bead104 mod_b+0x104
ffff8000`85a23de8  ffff8000`85a23e40
ffff8000`85a23df0  00000000`00000000
ffff8000`85a23df8  00000000`60400005
ffff8000`85a23e00  00000000`00000000
ffff8000`85a23e08  dead0000`00000122
ffff8000`85a23e10  00000000`00000000
ffff8000`85a23e18  00000001`042b2d06
ffff8000`85a23e20  ffff8000`85a23e40
ffff8000`85a23e28  00000000`00000000
ffff8000`85a23e30  ffff0000`c0448000
ffff8000`85a23e38  00000000`00000000
ffff8000`85a23e40  ffff8000`85a23e50
ffff8000`85a23e48  ffff8000`7bead0c8 mod_b+0xc8
ffff8000`85a23e50  ffff8000`85a23e60
ffff8000`85a23e58  ffff8000`7bead028 mod_b+0x28
ffff8000`85a23e60  ffff8000`85a23e70
ffff8000`85a23e68  ffff8000`80107f30 vmlinux!kthread+0xe0 [/build/linux-oracle-6.8-
EzVzJ2/linux-oracle-6.8-6.8.0/kernel/kthread.c @ 388]
ffff8000`85a23e70  ffff8000`85a23fe0
ffff8000`85a23e78  ffff8000`80017430 vmlinux!ret_from_fork+0x10 [/build/linux-oracle-6.8-
EzVzJ2/linux-oracle-6.8-6.8.0/arch/arm64/kernel/entry.S @ 861]
ffff8000`85a23e80  ffff8000`80107e50 vmlinux!kthread [/build/linux-oracle-6.8-EzVzJ2/linux-
oracle-6.8-6.8.0/kernel/kthread.c @ 341]
ffff8000`85a23e88  ffff0000`cb8903c0
ffff8000`85a23e90  00000000`00000000
ffff8000`85a23e98  00000000`00000000
...
```

6. If we disassemble backward the top found return address, we see the NULL pointer function call:

```
1: kd> ub ffff8000`7bead104
mod_b+0xe4:
ffff8000`7bead0e4 ???
ffff8000`7bead0e8 mov          x9,lr
ffff8000`7bead0ec nop
ffff8000`7bead0f0 paciasp
ffff8000`7bead0f4 stp          fp,lr,[sp,#-0x10]!
ffff8000`7bead0f8 mov          x0,#0
ffff8000`7bead0fc mov          fp,sp
ffff8000`7bead100 blr          x0
```

Exercise K4

- **Goal:** Learn how to identify spiking kernel threads
- **Patterns:** Stack Trace Collection (CPUs); Interrupt Stack; Active Thread; Spiking Thread
- \ALCDA-Dumps\Exercise-K4-x64-GDB.pdf
- \ALCDA-Dumps\Exercise-K4-A64-GDB.pdf
- \ALCDA-Dumps\Exercise-K4-A64-WinDbg.pdf

Exercise K4 (x64, GDB)

Goal: Learn how to identify spiking kernel threads.

Patterns: Stack Trace Collection (CPUs); Interrupt Stack; Active Thread; Spiking Thread.

1. Load the core dump *202501051800.kdump* from the x64/K4 directory and the matching *vmlinux-6.8.0-1018-azure* file from the x64/KSym directory:

```
~/ALCDA2/x64/K4$ crash 202501051800.kdump ../KSym/vmlinux-6.8.0-1018-azure

crash 8.0.6++
Copyright (C) 2002-2025  Red Hat, Inc.
Copyright (C) 2004, 2005, 2006, 2010  IBM Corporation
Copyright (C) 1999-2006  Hewlett-Packard Co
Copyright (C) 2005, 2006, 2011, 2012  Fujitsu Limited
Copyright (C) 2006, 2007  VA Linux Systems Japan K.K.
Copyright (C) 2005, 2011, 2020-2024  NEC Corporation
Copyright (C) 1999, 2002, 2007  Silicon Graphics, Inc.
Copyright (C) 1999, 2000, 2001, 2002  Mission Critical Linux, Inc.
Copyright (C) 2015, 2021  VMware, Inc.
This program is free software, covered by the GNU General Public License,
and you are welcome to change it and/or distribute copies of it under
certain conditions.  Enter "help copying" to see the conditions.
This program has absolutely no warranty.  Enter "help warranty" for details.

GNU gdb (GDB) 10.2
Copyright (C) 2021 Free Software Foundation, Inc.
License GPLv3+: GNU GPL version 3 or later <http://gnu.org/licenses/gpl.html>
This is free software: you are free to change and redistribute it.
There is NO WARRANTY, to the extent permitted by law.
Type "show copying" and "show warranty" for details.
This GDB was configured as "x86_64-pc-linux-gnu".
Type "show configuration" for configuration details.
Find the GDB manual and other documentation resources online at:
    <http://www.gnu.org/software/gdb/documentation/>.

For help, type "help".
Type "apropos word" to search for commands related to "word"...

      KERNEL: ../KSym/vmlinux-6.8.0-1018-azure  [TAINTED]
    DUMPFILE: 202501051800.kdump  [PARTIAL DUMP]
        CPUS: 4
        DATE: Sun Jan  5 17:58:25 GMT 2025
      UPTIME: 00:10:19
LOAD AVERAGE: 14.95, 11.01, 5.31
       TASKS: 640
    NODENAME: coredump-alcda
     RELEASE: 6.8.0-1018-azure
     VERSION: #21~22.04.1-Ubuntu SMP Fri Nov  8 00:21:25 UTC 2024
     MACHINE: x86_64  (2112 Mhz)
      MEMORY: 4 GB
       PANIC: "Kernel panic - not syncing: sysrq triggered crash"
         PID: 2443
     COMMAND: "bash"
        TASK: ffff8c475f2b2880  [THREAD_INFO: ffff8c475f2b2880]
         CPU: 2
```

```
    STATE: TASK_RUNNING (PANIC)

crash>
```

2. Since this is a manual dump, we check stack traces on all CPUs:

```
crash> bt -a
PID: 2411     TASK: ffff8c47735ed100  CPU: 0    COMMAND: "mod_c thread"
 #0 [fffffe3101831e38] crash_nmi_callback at ffffffffaa8875a7
 #1 [fffffe3101831e48] nmi_handle at ffffffffaa8442cf
 #2 [fffffe3101831e98] default_do_nmi at ffffffffab8bcb55
 #3 [fffffe3101831ec0] exc_nmi at ffffffffab8bcdcb
 #4 [fffffe3101831ef0] end_repeat_nmi at ffffffffaba016a1
    [exception RIP: foo+9]
    RIP: ffffffffc0606099  RSP: ffffa415402a3ed0  RFLAGS: 00000246
    RAX: 0000000000000000  RBX: ffff8c47735ed100  RCX: 0000000000000001
    RDX: 0000000000000000  RSI: 0000000000000286  RDI: 0000000000000000
    RBP: ffffa415402a3ed0   R8: 0000000000000000   R9: 0000000000000000
    R10: 0000000000000001  R11: 0000000000000000  R12: ffff8c48001d0600
    R13: ffffa41546c2b9b8  R14: ffff8c4800882200  R15: ffffffffc0606010
    ORIG_RAX: ffffffffffffffff  CS: 0010  SS: 0018
--- <NMI exception stack> ---
 #5 [ffffa415402a3ed0] foo at ffffffffc0606099 [mod_c]
 #6 [ffffa415402a3ed8] kthread_f at ffffffffc0606028 [mod_c]
 #7 [ffffa415402a3ee8] kthread at ffffffffaa90ff93
 #8 [ffffa415402a3f28] ret_from_fork at ffffffffaa84f459
 #9 [ffffa415402a3f50] ret_from_fork_asm at ffffffffaa804e5b

PID: 0        TASK: ffff8c480083d100  CPU: 1    COMMAND: "swapper/1"
 #0 [fffffe17fde15e38] crash_nmi_callback at ffffffffaa8875a7
 #1 [fffffe17fde15e48] nmi_handle at ffffffffaa8442cf
 #2 [fffffe17fde15e98] default_do_nmi at ffffffffab8bcb55
 #3 [fffffe17fde15ec0] exc_nmi at ffffffffab8bcdcb
 #4 [fffffe17fde15ef0] end_repeat_nmi at ffffffffaba016a1
    [exception RIP: default_idle+11]
    RIP: ffffffffab8c1a1b  RSP: ffffa415400d3e88  RFLAGS: 00000256
    RAX: ffff8c4803caefa8  RBX: ffff8c480083d100  RCX: ffff8c4703fae2f0
    RDX: 0000000000000000  RSI: 0000000000000001  RDI: 000000000075f27c
    RBP: ffffa415400d3e90   R8: 000000902f84230c   R9: 01364d9054fccc41
    R10: 0000000000000000  R11: 0000000000000000  R12: 0000000000000000
    R13: 0000000000000000  R14: 0000000000000000  R15: 0000000000000000
    ORIG_RAX: ffffffffffffffff  CS: 0010  SS: 0018
--- <NMI exception stack> ---
 #5 [ffffa415400d3e88] default_idle at ffffffffab8c1a1b
 #6 [ffffa415400d3e88] arch_cpu_idle at ffffffffab8c1ac9
 #7 [ffffa415400d3e98] default_idle_call at ffffffffab8c1d3c
 #8 [ffffa415400d3ea8] cpuidle_idle_call at ffffffffaa951512
 #9 [ffffa415400d3ee8] do_idle at ffffffffaa9515e2
#10 [ffffa415400d3f08] cpu_startup_entry at ffffffffaa95184d
#11 [ffffa415400d3f20] start_secondary at ffffffffaa88a950
#12 [ffffa415400d3f50] secondary_startup_64_no_verify at ffffffffaa800279

PID: 2443     TASK: ffff8c475f2b2880  CPU: 2    COMMAND: "bash"
 #0 [ffffa41540ca7928] machine_kexec at ffffffffaa899db1
 #1 [ffffa41540ca7990] __crash_kexec at ffffffffaa9f1e46
 #2 [ffffa41540ca7a50] panic at ffffffffaa8ddf29
 #3 [ffffa41540ca7ad0] sysrq_handle_crash at ffffffffab1fea05
 #4 [ffffa41540ca7ae0] __handle_sysrq at ffffffffab1ff2d2
 #5 [ffffa41540ca7b28] write_sysrq_trigger at ffffffffab1ffb2c
 #6 [ffffa41540ca7b58] proc_reg_write at ffffffffaad31fce
```

```
 #7 [ffffa41540ca7b78] vfs_write at ffffffffaac7e26f
 #8 [ffffa41540ca7c10] ksys_write at ffffffffaac7e907
 #9 [ffffa41540ca7c50] __x64_sys_write at ffffffffaac7e9b9
#10 [ffffa41540ca7c60] x64_sys_call at ffffffffaa80651d
#11 [ffffa41540ca7c70] do_syscall_64 at ffffffffab8badac
#12 [ffffa41540ca7f50] entry_SYSCALL_64_after_hwframe at ffffffffaba00130
    RIP: 000078a595114887  RSP: 00007ffe3703f6e8  RFLAGS: 00000246
    RAX: ffffffffffffffda  RBX: 0000000000000002  RCX: 000078a595114887
    RDX: 0000000000000002  RSI: 00005e5b490f1f00  RDI: 0000000000000001
    RBP: 00005e5b490f1f00   R8: 0000000000000000   R9: 00005e5b490f1f00
    R10: 000078a59521afb0  R11: 0000000000000246  R12: 0000000000000002
    R13: 000078a59521b780  R14: 000078a595217600  R15: 000078a595216a00
    ORIG_RAX: 0000000000000001  CS: 0033  SS: 002b

PID: 0        TASK: ffff8c4800838000  CPU: 3    COMMAND: "swapper/3"
 #0 [fffffe7284bcce38] crash_nmi_callback at ffffffffaa8875a7
 #1 [fffffe7284bcce48] nmi_handle at ffffffffaa8442cf
 #2 [fffffe7284bcce98] default_do_nmi at ffffffffab8bcb55
 #3 [fffffe7284bccec0] exc_nmi at ffffffffab8bcdcb
 #4 [fffffe7284bccef0] end_repeat_nmi at ffffffffaba016a1
    [exception RIP: default_idle+11]
    RIP: ffffffffab8c1a1b  RSP: ffffa415400e3e88  RFLAGS: 00000246
    RAX: ffff8c4803daefa8  RBX: ffff8c4800838000  RCX: ffff8c47019f9a70
    RDX: 0000000000000000  RSI: 0000000000000003  RDI: 000000000075bcc4
    RBP: ffffa415400e3e90   R8: 000000902f830328   R9: 01364d9054fccc41
    R10: 0000000000000000  R11: 0000000000000000  R12: 0000000000000000
    R13: 0000000000000000  R14: 0000000000000000  R15: 0000000000000000
    ORIG_RAX: ffffffffffffffff  CS: 0010  SS: 0018
--- <NMI exception stack> ---
 #5 [ffffa415400e3e88] default_idle at ffffffffab8c1a1b
 #6 [ffffa415400e3e88] arch_cpu_idle at ffffffffab8c1ac9
 #7 [ffffa415400e3e98] default_idle_call at ffffffffab8c1d3c
 #8 [ffffa415400e3ea8] cpuidle_idle_call at ffffffffaa951512
 #9 [ffffa415400e3ee8] do_idle at ffffffffaa9515e2
#10 [ffffa415400e3f08] cpu_startup_entry at ffffffffaa95184d
#11 [ffffa415400e3f20] start_secondary at ffffffffaa88a950
#12 [ffffa415400e3f50] secondary_startup_64_no_verify at ffffffffaa800279
```

Note: We see PID 2411 was interrupted on CPU 0. PID: 2443 stack trace is a manual dump generation command. The rest of the PIDs are idle threads.

3. We can check the process tree and CPU consumption:

```
crash> ps -p 2411
PID: 0        TASK: ffffffffaca0fcc0  CPU: 0    COMMAND: "swapper/0"
 PID: 2        TASK: ffff8c4800378000  CPU: 0    COMMAND: "kthreadd"
  PID: 2411     TASK: ffff8c47735ed100  CPU: 0    COMMAND: "mod_c thread"

crash> ps -t 2411
PID: 2411     TASK: ffff8c47735ed100  CPU: 0    COMMAND: "mod_c thread"
    RUN TIME: 00:07:48
  START TIME: 151212130984
       UTIME: 0
       STIME: 456023000000
```

4. Just **ps** command also shows running PIDs:

```
crash> ps
      PID    PPID  CPU       TASK        ST  %MEM     VSZ    RSS  COMM
        0       0   0  ffffffffaca0fcc0  RU   0.0       0      0  [swapper/0]
>       0       0   1  ffff8c480083d100  RU   0.0       0      0  [swapper/1]
        0       0   2  ffff8c480083a880  RU   0.0       0      0  [swapper/2]
>       0       0   3  ffff8c4800838000  RU   0.0       0      0  [swapper/3]
        1       0   3  ffff8c480037a880  UN   0.3  167084  12508  systemd
        2       0   0  ffff8c4800378000  IN   0.0       0      0  [kthreadd]
...
...
...
     2396    1502   1  ffff8c4704ae8000  IN   1.1  808872  46756  threaded-ml
>    2411       2   0  ffff8c47735ed100  RU   0.0       0      0  [mod_c thread]
     2413    2063   3  ffff8c477a8a8000  IN   0.1   13208   4256  top
     2423    1277   2  ffff8c477a89d100  ZO   0.0       0      0  gnome-terminal
     2430    2041   3  ffff8c470eec0000  IN   0.1   11008   5260  bash
     2437       1   2  ffff8c470eed5100  UN   0.4   48412  17820  journal-offline
     2438       1   2  ffff8c470eeb0000  UN   0.4   48412  17820  journal-offline
     2442    2430   2  ffff8c47037ed100  IN   0.1   13488   5584  su
>    2443    2442   2  ffff8c475f2b2880  RU   0.1   10236   4400  bash
     2455    1277   2  ffff8c470cff8000  UN  10.3 5311176 445000  pool-gnome-shel
     2457       1   2  ffff8c47598e2880  IN   0.3  393084  13384  pool-udisksd
```

5. We can also see our problem thread in the log because the watchdog reported it:

```
crash> log -T
[Sun Jan  5 17:48:06 GMT 2025] Linux version 6.8.0-1018-azure (buildd@lcy02-amd64-013) (x86_64-linux-gnu-gcc-11
(Ubuntu 11.4.0-1ubuntu1~22.04) 11.4.0, GNU ld (GNU Binutils for Ubuntu) 2.38) #21~22.04.1-Ubuntu SMP Fri Nov  8
00:21:25 UTC 2024 (Ubuntu 6.8.0-1018.21~22.04.1-azure 6.8.12)
[Sun Jan  5 17:48:06 GMT 2025] Command line: BOOT_IMAGE=/boot/vmlinuz-6.8.0-1018-azure root=UUID=89ee03ba-6808-4977-
a4fb-9b10174744f8 ro quiet splash crashkernel=512M-:192M vt.handoff=7
...
...
...
[Sun Jan  5 17:57:34 GMT 2025] RIP: 0010:foo+0x9/0xf70 [mod_c]
[Sun Jan  5 17:57:34 GMT 2025] Code: fd e5 32 ea 31 c0 5d c3 cc cc cc cc 0f 1f 44 00 00 90 90 90 90 90 90 90 90 90 90
90 90 90 90 90 90 0f 1f 44 00 00 55 48 89 e5 <eb> fe 00 00 00 00 00 00 00 00 00 00 00 00 00 00 00 00 00 00 00
[Sun Jan  5 17:57:34 GMT 2025] RSP: 0018:ffffa415402a3ed0 EFLAGS: 00000246
[Sun Jan  5 17:57:34 GMT 2025] RAX: 0000000000000000 RBX: ffff8c47735ed100 RCX: 0000000000000001
[Sun Jan  5 17:57:34 GMT 2025] RDX: 0000000000000000 RSI: 0000000000000286 RDI: 0000000000000000
[Sun Jan  5 17:57:34 GMT 2025] RBP: ffffa415402a3ed0 R08: 0000000000000000 R09: 0000000000000000
[Sun Jan  5 17:57:34 GMT 2025] R10: 0000000000000001 R11: 0000000000000000 R12: ffff8c48001d0600
[Sun Jan  5 17:57:34 GMT 2025] R13: ffffa41546c2b9b8 R14: ffff8c4800882200 R15: ffffffffc0606010
[Sun Jan  5 17:57:34 GMT 2025] FS:  0000000000000000(0000) GS:ffff8c4803c00000(0000) knlGS:0000000000000000
[Sun Jan  5 17:57:34 GMT 2025] CS:  0010 DS: 0000 ES: 0000 CR0: 0000000080050033
[Sun Jan  5 17:57:34 GMT 2025] CR2: 00005bf7b867fca8 CR3: 0000000006b58005 CR4: 00000000003706f0
[Sun Jan  5 17:57:34 GMT 2025] DR0: 0000000000000000 DR1: 0000000000000000 DR2: 0000000000000000
[Sun Jan  5 17:57:34 GMT 2025] DR3: 0000000000000000 DR6: 00000000fffe0ff0 DR7: 0000000000000400
[Sun Jan  5 17:57:34 GMT 2025] Call Trace:
[Sun Jan  5 17:57:34 GMT 2025]  <IRQ>
[Sun Jan  5 17:57:34 GMT 2025]  ? show_regs+0x6a/0x80
[Sun Jan  5 17:57:34 GMT 2025]  ? watchdog_timer_fn+0x1ec/0x270
[Sun Jan  5 17:57:34 GMT 2025]  ? __pfx_watchdog_timer_fn+0x10/0x10
[Sun Jan  5 17:57:34 GMT 2025]  ? __hrtimer_run_queues+0x10e/0x240
[Sun Jan  5 17:57:34 GMT 2025]  ? clockevents_program_event+0xaa/0x130
[Sun Jan  5 17:57:34 GMT 2025]  ? hrtimer_interrupt+0x101/0x240
[Sun Jan  5 17:57:34 GMT 2025]  ? hv_stimer0_isr+0x1d/0x30
[Sun Jan  5 17:57:34 GMT 2025]  ? __sysvec_hyperv_stimer0+0x2f/0x60
[Sun Jan  5 17:57:34 GMT 2025]  ? sysvec_hyperv_stimer0+0x7b/0x90
[Sun Jan  5 17:57:34 GMT 2025]  </IRQ>
[Sun Jan  5 17:57:34 GMT 2025]  <TASK>
[Sun Jan  5 17:57:34 GMT 2025]  ? asm_sysvec_hyperv_stimer0+0x1b/0x20
[Sun Jan  5 17:57:34 GMT 2025]  ? __pfx_kthread_f+0x10/0x10 [mod_c]
[Sun Jan  5 17:57:34 GMT 2025]  ? foo+0x9/0xf70 [mod_c]
[Sun Jan  5 17:57:34 GMT 2025]  kthread_f+0x18/0x20 [mod_c]
```

```
[Sun Jan  5 17:57:34 GMT 2025]  kthread+0xd3/0x100
[Sun Jan  5 17:57:34 GMT 2025]  ? __pfx_kthread+0x10/0x10
[Sun Jan  5 17:57:34 GMT 2025]  ret_from_fork+0x39/0x60
[Sun Jan  5 17:57:34 GMT 2025]  ? __pfx_kthread+0x10/0x10
[Sun Jan  5 17:57:34 GMT 2025]  ret_from_fork_asm+0x1b/0x30
[Sun Jan  5 17:57:34 GMT 2025]  </TASK>
[Sun Jan  5 17:57:48 GMT 2025] rcu: INFO: rcu_sched self-detected stall on CPU
[Sun Jan  5 17:57:48 GMT 2025] rcu:     0-....: (418439 ticks this GP) idle=c04c/1/0x4000000000000000
softirq=16085/16085 fqs=104069
[Sun Jan  5 17:57:48 GMT 2025] rcu:              hardirqs   softirqs   csw/system
[Sun Jan  5 17:57:48 GMT 2025] rcu:      number:        0      10455          0
[Sun Jan  5 17:57:48 GMT 2025] rcu:     cputime:        0         97     388453   ==> 390002(ms)
[Sun Jan  5 17:57:48 GMT 2025] rcu:     (t=420006 jiffies g=22273 q=9893 ncpus=4)
[Sun Jan  5 17:57:48 GMT 2025] CPU: 0 PID: 2411 Comm: mod_c thread Kdump: loaded Tainted: G           OEL     6.8.0-
1018-azure #21~22.04.1-Ubuntu
[Sun Jan  5 17:57:48 GMT 2025] Hardware name: Microsoft Corporation Virtual Machine/Virtual Machine, BIOS Hyper-V UEFI
Release v4.1 05/13/2024
[Sun Jan  5 17:57:48 GMT 2025] RIP: 0010:foo+0x9/0xf70 [mod_c]
[Sun Jan  5 17:57:48 GMT 2025] Code: fd e5 32 ea 31 c0 5d c3 cc cc cc cc 0f 1f 44 00 00 90 90 90 90 90 90 90 90 90 90
90 90 90 90 90 90 0f 1f 44 00 00 55 48 89 e5 <eb> fe 00 00 00 00 00 00 00 00 00 00 00 00 00 00 00 00 00 00 00
[Sun Jan  5 17:57:48 GMT 2025] RSP: 0018:ffffa415402a3ed0 EFLAGS: 00000246
[Sun Jan  5 17:57:48 GMT 2025] RAX: 0000000000000000 RBX: ffff8c47735ed100 RCX: 0000000000000001
[Sun Jan  5 17:57:48 GMT 2025] RDX: 0000000000000000 RSI: 0000000000000286 RDI: 0000000000000000
[Sun Jan  5 17:57:48 GMT 2025] RBP: ffffa415402a3ed0 R08: 0000000000000000 R09: 0000000000000000
[Sun Jan  5 17:57:48 GMT 2025] R10: 0000000000000001 R11: 0000000000000000 R12: ffff8c48001d0600
[Sun Jan  5 17:57:48 GMT 2025] R13: ffffa41546c2b9b8 R14: ffff8c4800882200 R15: ffffffffc0606010
[Sun Jan  5 17:57:48 GMT 2025] FS:  0000000000000000(0000) GS:ffff8c4803c00000(0000) knlGS:0000000000000000
[Sun Jan  5 17:57:48 GMT 2025] CS:  0010 DS: 0000 ES: 0000 CR0: 0000000080050033
[Sun Jan  5 17:57:48 GMT 2025] CR2: 00005bf7b867fca8 CR3: 0000000006b58005 CR4: 00000000003706f0
[Sun Jan  5 17:57:48 GMT 2025] DR0: 0000000000000000 DR1: 0000000000000000 DR2: 0000000000000000
[Sun Jan  5 17:57:48 GMT 2025] DR3: 0000000000000000 DR6: 00000000fffe0ff0 DR7: 0000000000000400
[Sun Jan  5 17:57:48 GMT 2025] Call Trace:
[Sun Jan  5 17:57:48 GMT 2025]  <IRQ>
[Sun Jan  5 17:57:48 GMT 2025]  ? show_regs+0x6a/0x80
[Sun Jan  5 17:57:48 GMT 2025]  ? dump_cpu_task+0x71/0x90
[Sun Jan  5 17:57:48 GMT 2025]  ? rcu_dump_cpu_stacks+0xe8/0x180
[Sun Jan  5 17:57:48 GMT 2025]  ? print_cpu_stall+0x131/0x290
[Sun Jan  5 17:57:48 GMT 2025]  ? check_cpu_stall+0x133/0x230
[Sun Jan  5 17:57:48 GMT 2025]  ? rcu_pending+0x32/0x1e0
[Sun Jan  5 17:57:48 GMT 2025]  ? rcu_sched_clock_irq+0x150/0x280
[Sun Jan  5 17:57:48 GMT 2025]  ? update_process_times+0x63/0xa0
[Sun Jan  5 17:57:48 GMT 2025]  ? tick_sched_handle+0x28/0x70
[Sun Jan  5 17:57:48 GMT 2025]  ? tick_nohz_highres_handler+0x77/0x90
[Sun Jan  5 17:57:48 GMT 2025]  ? __pfx_tick_nohz_highres_handler+0x10/0x10
[Sun Jan  5 17:57:48 GMT 2025]  ? __hrtimer_run_queues+0x10e/0x240
[Sun Jan  5 17:57:48 GMT 2025]  ? clockevents_program_event+0xaa/0x130
[Sun Jan  5 17:57:48 GMT 2025]  ? hrtimer_interrupt+0x101/0x240
[Sun Jan  5 17:57:48 GMT 2025]  ? hv_stimer0_isr+0x1d/0x30
[Sun Jan  5 17:57:48 GMT 2025]  ? __sysvec_hyperv_stimer0+0x2f/0x60
[Sun Jan  5 17:57:48 GMT 2025]  ? sysvec_hyperv_stimer0+0x7b/0x90
[Sun Jan  5 17:57:48 GMT 2025]  </IRQ>
[Sun Jan  5 17:57:48 GMT 2025]  <TASK>
[Sun Jan  5 17:57:48 GMT 2025]  ? asm_sysvec_hyperv_stimer0+0x1b/0x20
[Sun Jan  5 17:57:48 GMT 2025]  ? __pfx_kthread_f+0x10/0x10 [mod_c]
[Sun Jan  5 17:57:48 GMT 2025]  ? foo+0x9/0xf70 [mod_c]
[Sun Jan  5 17:57:48 GMT 2025]  kthread_f+0x18/0x20 [mod_c]
[Sun Jan  5 17:57:48 GMT 2025]  kthread+0xd3/0x100
[Sun Jan  5 17:57:48 GMT 2025]  ? __pfx_kthread+0x10/0x10
[Sun Jan  5 17:57:48 GMT 2025]  ret_from_fork+0x39/0x60
[Sun Jan  5 17:57:48 GMT 2025]  ? __pfx_kthread+0x10/0x10
[Sun Jan  5 17:57:48 GMT 2025]  ret_from_fork_asm+0x1b/0x30
[Sun Jan  5 17:57:48 GMT 2025]  </TASK>
[Sun Jan  5 17:58:14 GMT 2025] watchdog: BUG: soft lockup - CPU#0 stuck for 417s! [mod_c thread:2411]
[Sun Jan  5 17:58:14 GMT 2025] Modules linked in: mod_c(OE) binfmt_misc nls_iso8859_1 crct10dif_pclmul crc32_pclmul
polyval_clmulni polyval_generic ghash_clmulni_intel sha256_ssse3 sha1_ssse3 aesni_intel crypto_simd cryptd serio_raw
hyperv_drm joydev sch_fq_codel hv_sock vsock msr parport_pc ppdev lp parport efi_pstore ip_tables x_tables autofs4
btrfs blake2b_generic xor raid6_pq libcrc32c hid_generic hid_hyperv hid hv_netvsc hyperv_keyboard
[Sun Jan  5 17:58:14 GMT 2025] CPU: 0 PID: 2411 Comm: mod_c thread Kdump: loaded Tainted: G           OEL     6.8.0-
1018-azure #21~22.04.1-Ubuntu
[Sun Jan  5 17:58:14 GMT 2025] Hardware name: Microsoft Corporation Virtual Machine/Virtual Machine, BIOS Hyper-V UEFI
Release v4.1 05/13/2024
[Sun Jan  5 17:58:14 GMT 2025] RIP: 0010:foo+0x9/0xf70 [mod_c]
[Sun Jan  5 17:58:14 GMT 2025] Code: fd e5 32 ea 31 c0 5d c3 cc cc cc cc 0f 1f 44 00 00 90 90 90 90 90 90 90 90 90 90
90 90 90 90 90 90 0f 1f 44 00 00 55 48 89 e5 <eb> fe 00 00 00 00 00 00 00 00 00 00 00 00 00 00 00 00 00 00 00
[Sun Jan  5 17:58:14 GMT 2025] RSP: 0018:ffffa415402a3ed0 EFLAGS: 00000246
[Sun Jan  5 17:58:14 GMT 2025] RAX: 0000000000000000 RBX: ffff8c47735ed100 RCX: 0000000000000001
```

```
[Sun Jan  5 17:58:14 GMT 2025] RDX: 0000000000000000 RSI: 0000000000000286 RDI: 0000000000000000
[Sun Jan  5 17:58:14 GMT 2025] RBP: ffffa415402a3ed0 R08: 0000000000000000 R09: 0000000000000000
[Sun Jan  5 17:58:14 GMT 2025] R10: 0000000000000001 R11: 0000000000000000 R12: ffff8c48001d0600
[Sun Jan  5 17:58:14 GMT 2025] R13: ffffa41546c2b9b8 R14: ffff8c4800882200 R15: ffffffffc0606010
[Sun Jan  5 17:58:14 GMT 2025] FS:  0000000000000000(0000) GS:ffff8c4803c00000(0000) knlGS:0000000000000000
[Sun Jan  5 17:58:14 GMT 2025] CS:  0010 DS: 0000 ES: 0000 CR0: 0000000080050033
[Sun Jan  5 17:58:14 GMT 2025] CR2: 00005bf7b867fca8 CR3: 0000000006b58005 CR4: 00000000003706f0
[Sun Jan  5 17:58:14 GMT 2025] DR0: 0000000000000000 DR1: 0000000000000000 DR2: 0000000000000000
[Sun Jan  5 17:58:14 GMT 2025] DR3: 0000000000000000 DR6: 00000000fffe0ff0 DR7: 0000000000000400
[Sun Jan  5 17:58:14 GMT 2025] Call Trace:
[Sun Jan  5 17:58:14 GMT 2025]  <IRQ>
[Sun Jan  5 17:58:14 GMT 2025]  ? show_regs+0x6a/0x80
[Sun Jan  5 17:58:14 GMT 2025]  ? watchdog_timer_fn+0x1ec/0x270
[Sun Jan  5 17:58:14 GMT 2025]  ? __pfx_watchdog_timer_fn+0x10/0x10
[Sun Jan  5 17:58:14 GMT 2025]  ? __hrtimer_run_queues+0x10e/0x240
[Sun Jan  5 17:58:14 GMT 2025]  ? clockevents_program_event+0xaa/0x130
[Sun Jan  5 17:58:14 GMT 2025]  ? hrtimer_interrupt+0x101/0x240
[Sun Jan  5 17:58:14 GMT 2025]  ? hv_stimer0_isr+0x1d/0x30
[Sun Jan  5 17:58:14 GMT 2025]  ? __sysvec_hyperv_stimer0+0x2f/0x60
[Sun Jan  5 17:58:14 GMT 2025]  ? sysvec_hyperv_stimer0+0x7b/0x90
[Sun Jan  5 17:58:14 GMT 2025]  </IRQ>
[Sun Jan  5 17:58:14 GMT 2025]  <TASK>
[Sun Jan  5 17:58:14 GMT 2025]  ? asm_sysvec_hyperv_stimer0+0x1b/0x20
[Sun Jan  5 17:58:14 GMT 2025]  ? __pfx_kthread_f+0x10/0x10 [mod_c]
[Sun Jan  5 17:58:14 GMT 2025]  ? foo+0x9/0xf70 [mod_c]
[Sun Jan  5 17:58:14 GMT 2025]  kthread_f+0x18/0x20 [mod_c]
[Sun Jan  5 17:58:14 GMT 2025]  kthread+0xd3/0x100
[Sun Jan  5 17:58:14 GMT 2025]  ? __pfx_kthread+0x10/0x10
[Sun Jan  5 17:58:14 GMT 2025]  ret_from_fork+0x39/0x60
[Sun Jan  5 17:58:14 GMT 2025]  ? __pfx_kthread+0x10/0x10
[Sun Jan  5 17:58:14 GMT 2025]  ret_from_fork_asm+0x1b/0x30
[Sun Jan  5 17:58:14 GMT 2025]  </TASK>
[Sun Jan  5 17:58:25 GMT 2025] sysrq: Trigger a crash
[Sun Jan  5 17:58:25 GMT 2025] Kernel panic - not syncing: sysrq triggered crash
[Sun Jan  5 17:58:25 GMT 2025] CPU: 2 PID: 2443 Comm: bash Kdump: loaded Tainted: G           OEL     6.8.0-1018-azure #21~22.04.1-Ubuntu
[Sun Jan  5 17:58:25 GMT 2025] Hardware name: Microsoft Corporation Virtual Machine/Virtual Machine, BIOS Hyper-V UEFI Release v4.1 05/13/2024
[Sun Jan  5 17:58:25 GMT 2025] Call Trace:
[Sun Jan  5 17:58:25 GMT 2025]  <TASK>
[Sun Jan  5 17:58:25 GMT 2025]  dump_stack_lvl+0x27/0x70
[Sun Jan  5 17:58:25 GMT 2025]  dump_stack+0x10/0x20
[Sun Jan  5 17:58:25 GMT 2025]  panic+0x351/0x390
[Sun Jan  5 17:58:25 GMT 2025]  sysrq_handle_crash+0x15/0x20
[Sun Jan  5 17:58:25 GMT 2025]  __handle_sysrq+0xf2/0x290
[Sun Jan  5 17:58:25 GMT 2025]  write_sysrq_trigger+0x5c/0x80
[Sun Jan  5 17:58:25 GMT 2025]  proc_reg_write+0x5e/0xa0
[Sun Jan  5 17:58:25 GMT 2025]  ? __cond_resched+0x1a/0x50
[Sun Jan  5 17:58:25 GMT 2025]  vfs_write+0xef/0x410
[Sun Jan  5 17:58:25 GMT 2025]  ? do_syscall_64+0x88/0x160
[Sun Jan  5 17:58:25 GMT 2025]  ? syscall_exit_to_user_mode+0x81/0x220
[Sun Jan  5 17:58:25 GMT 2025]  ksys_write+0x67/0xf0
[Sun Jan  5 17:58:25 GMT 2025]  __x64_sys_write+0x19/0x20
[Sun Jan  5 17:58:25 GMT 2025]  x64_sys_call+0x167d/0x20c0
[Sun Jan  5 17:58:25 GMT 2025]  do_syscall_64+0x7c/0x160
[Sun Jan  5 17:58:25 GMT 2025]  ? cp_new_stat+0x152/0x180
[Sun Jan  5 17:58:25 GMT 2025]  ? __do_sys_newfstatat+0x3e/0x60
[Sun Jan  5 17:58:25 GMT 2025]  ? syscall_exit_to_user_mode+0x81/0x220
[Sun Jan  5 17:58:25 GMT 2025]  ? do_syscall_64+0x88/0x160
[Sun Jan  5 17:58:25 GMT 2025]  ? filp_flush+0x5d/0x90
[Sun Jan  5 17:58:25 GMT 2025]  ? syscall_exit_to_user_mode+0x81/0x220
[Sun Jan  5 17:58:25 GMT 2025]  ? do_syscall_64+0x88/0x160
[Sun Jan  5 17:58:25 GMT 2025]  ? syscall_exit_to_user_mode+0x81/0x220
[Sun Jan  5 17:58:25 GMT 2025]  ? do_syscall_64+0x88/0x160
[Sun Jan  5 17:58:25 GMT 2025]  ? syscall_exit_to_user_mode+0x81/0x220
[Sun Jan  5 17:58:25 GMT 2025]  ? do_syscall_64+0x88/0x160
[Sun Jan  5 17:58:25 GMT 2025]  ? clear_bhb_loop+0x45/0xa0
[Sun Jan  5 17:58:25 GMT 2025]  ? clear_bhb_loop+0x45/0xa0
[Sun Jan  5 17:58:25 GMT 2025]  ? clear_bhb_loop+0x45/0xa0
[Sun Jan  5 17:58:25 GMT 2025]  entry_SYSCALL_64_after_hwframe+0x78/0x80
[Sun Jan  5 17:58:25 GMT 2025] RIP: 0033:0x78a595114887
[Sun Jan  5 17:58:25 GMT 2025] Code: 10 00 f7 d8 64 89 02 48 c7 c0 ff ff ff ff eb b7 0f 1f 00 f3 0f 1e fa 64 8b 04 25 18 00 00 00 85 c0 75 10 b8 01 00 00 00 0f 05 <48> 3d 00 f0 ff ff 77 51 c3 48 83 ec 28 48 89 54 24 18 48 89 74 24
[Sun Jan  5 17:58:25 GMT 2025] RSP: 002b:00007ffe3703f6e8 EFLAGS: 00000246 ORIG_RAX: 0000000000000001
[Sun Jan  5 17:58:25 GMT 2025] RAX: ffffffffffffffda RBX: 0000000000000002 RCX: 000078a595114887
[Sun Jan  5 17:58:25 GMT 2025] RDX: 0000000000000002 RSI: 00005e5b490f1f00 RDI: 0000000000000001
```

```
[Sun Jan  5 17:58:25 GMT 2025] RBP: 00005e5b490f1f00 R08: 0000000000000000 R09: 00005e5b490f1f00
[Sun Jan  5 17:58:25 GMT 2025] R10: 000078a59521afb0 R11: 0000000000000246 R12: 0000000000000002
[Sun Jan  5 17:58:25 GMT 2025] R13: 000078a59521b780 R14: 000078a595217600 R15: 000078a595216a00
[Sun Jan  5 17:58:25 GMT 2025]  </TASK>
[Sun Jan  5 17:58:25 GMT 2025] Kernel Offset: 0x29800000 from 0xffffffff81000000 (relocation range:
0xffffffff80000000-0xffffffffbfffffff)
```

6. If we look at the interrupted **foo+0x9** location (also shown as called from **kthread_f** with **kthread_f+0x18** return address), we see it cycles indefinitely:

```
crash> dis foo+0x9
0xffffffffc0606099 <foo+9>:      jmp    0xffffffffc0606099 <foo+9>

crash> dis kthread_f
0xffffffffc0606010 <kthread_f>: nopl   0x0(%rax,%rax,1) [FTRACE NOP]
0xffffffffc0606015 <kthread_f+5>:       push   %rbp
0xffffffffc0606016 <kthread_f+6>:       mov    $0x2710,%edi
0xffffffffc060601b <kthread_f+11>:      mov    %rsp,%rbp
0xffffffffc060601e <kthread_f+14>:      call   0xffffffffaa9cbd40 <msleep>
0xffffffffc0606023 <kthread_f+19>:      call   0xffffffffc0606090 <foo>
0xffffffffc0606028 <kthread_f+24>:      xor    %eax,%eax
0xffffffffc060602a <kthread_f+26>:      pop    %rbp
0xffffffffc060602b <kthread_f+27>:      ret
0xffffffffc060602c <kthread_f+28>:      int3
0xffffffffc060602d <kthread_f+29>:      int3
0xffffffffc060602e <kthread_f+30>:      int3
0xffffffffc060602f <kthread_f+31>:      int3

crash> dis 0xffffffffc0606090 8
0xffffffffc0606090 <foo>:       nopl   0x0(%rax,%rax,1) [FTRACE NOP]
0xffffffffc0606095 <foo+5>:     push   %rbp
0xffffffffc0606096 <foo+6>:     mov    %rsp,%rbp
0xffffffffc0606099 <foo+9>:     jmp    0xffffffffc0606099 <foo+9>
0xffffffffc060609b <foo+11>:    add    %al,(%rax)
0xffffffffc060609d <foo+13>:    add    %al,(%rax)
0xffffffffc060609f <foo+15>:    add    %al,(%rax)
0xffffffffc06060a1 <foo+17>:    add    %al,(%rax)
```

Exercise K4 (A64, GDB)

Goal: Learn how to identify spiking kernel threads.

Patterns: Stack Trace Collection (CPUs); Interrupt Stack; Active Thread; Spiking Thread.

1. Load the core dump *202501051833.kdump* from the A64/K4 directory and the matching *vmlinux-6.8.0-1018-oracle* file from the A64/KSym directory:

```
~/ALCDA2/A64/K4$ crash 202501051833.kdump ../KSym/vmlinux-6.8.0-1018-oracle

crash 8.0.6++
Copyright (C) 2002-2025  Red Hat, Inc.
Copyright (C) 2004, 2005, 2006, 2010  IBM Corporation
Copyright (C) 1999-2006  Hewlett-Packard Co
Copyright (C) 2005, 2006, 2011, 2012  Fujitsu Limited
Copyright (C) 2006, 2007  VA Linux Systems Japan K.K.
Copyright (C) 2005, 2011, 2020-2024  NEC Corporation
Copyright (C) 1999, 2002, 2007  Silicon Graphics, Inc.
Copyright (C) 1999, 2000, 2001, 2002  Mission Critical Linux, Inc.
Copyright (C) 2015, 2021  VMware, Inc.
This program is free software, covered by the GNU General Public License,
and you are welcome to change it and/or distribute copies of it under
certain conditions.  Enter "help copying" to see the conditions.
This program has absolutely no warranty.  Enter "help warranty" for details.

GNU gdb (GDB) 10.2
Copyright (C) 2021 Free Software Foundation, Inc.
License GPLv3+: GNU GPL version 3 or later <http://gnu.org/licenses/gpl.html>
This is free software: you are free to change and redistribute it.
There is NO WARRANTY, to the extent permitted by law.
Type "show copying" and "show warranty" for details.
This GDB was configured as "aarch64-unknown-linux-gnu".
Type "show configuration" for configuration details.
Find the GDB manual and other documentation resources online at:
    <http://www.gnu.org/software/gdb/documentation/>.

For help, type "help".
Type "apropos word" to search for commands related to "word"...

      KERNEL: ../KSym/vmlinux-6.8.0-1018-oracle  [TAINTED]
    DUMPFILE: 202501051833.kdump  [PARTIAL DUMP]
        CPUS: 2
        DATE: Sun Jan  5 18:25:48 UTC 2025
      UPTIME: 06:18:41
LOAD AVERAGE: 5.94, 3.43, 1.43
       TASKS: 207
    NODENAME: instance-20230624-1144
     RELEASE: 6.8.0-1018-oracle
     VERSION: #19~22.04.1-Ubuntu SMP Mon Dec  9 23:49:53 UTC 2024
     MACHINE: aarch64  (unknown Mhz)
      MEMORY: 12 GB
       PANIC: "Kernel panic - not syncing: sysrq triggered crash"
         PID: 6089
     COMMAND: "bash"
        TASK: ffff0000c9e54400  [THREAD_INFO: ffff0000c9e54400]
         CPU: 0
```

```
        STATE: TASK_RUNNING (PANIC)

crash>
```

2. Since this is a manual dump, we check stack traces on all CPUs:

```
crash> bt -a
PID: 6089     TASK: ffff0000c9e54400  CPU: 0    COMMAND: "bash"
 #0 [ffff8000859938b0] machine_kexec at ffff80008003fdcc
 #1 [ffff8000859938e0] __crash_kexec at ffff80008020b600
 #2 [ffff800085993a60] panic at ffff8000800c83dc
 #3 [ffff800085993b40] sysrq_handle_crash at ffff800080d326e4
 #4 [ffff800085993b50] __handle_sysrq at ffff800080d33494
 #5 [ffff800085993be0] write_sysrq_trigger at ffff800080d34070
 #6 [ffff800085993c20] proc_reg_write at ffff8000805f22c8
 #7 [ffff800085993c40] vfs_write at ffff80008051026c
 #8 [ffff800085993ce0] ksys_write at ffff800080510724
 #9 [ffff800085993d20] __arm64_sys_write at ffff8000805107f8
#10 [ffff800085993e10] invoke_syscall at ffff8000800313bc
#11 [ffff800085993e40] el0_svc_common.constprop.0 at ffff8000800314b4
#12 [ffff800085993e70] do_el0_svc at ffff8000800315cc
#13 [ffff800085993e80] el0_svc at ffff8000815dd9e4
#14 [ffff800085993ea0] el0t_64_sync_handler at ffff8000815ddff8
#15 [ffff800085993fe0] el0t_64_sync at ffff80008001163c
     PC: 0000e6c14cda7e10   LR: 0000e6c14cd4507c   SP: 0000ffffec63f860
    X29: 0000ffffec63f860  X28: 0000000000000000  X27: 0000c3438bb3b000
    X26: 0000c3438bb01468  X25: 0000c3438bb45810  X24: 0000000000000002
    X23: 0000c343bf885410  X22: 0000e6c14cef77e0  X21: 0000e6c14ce6c5d8
    X20: 0000c343bf885410  X19: 0000000000000001  X18: 0000000000000001
    X17: 0000e6c14cd41d40  X16: 0000e6c14cd46460  X15: 0000c343bf834208
    X14: 0000000000000410  X13: c310400c6fd54f5b  X12: 0000000000000001
    X11: 0000000000000000  X10: 0000000000000000   X9: 0000000000000001
     X8: 0000000000000040   X7: 0000000000000000   X6: 000000000000021a
     X5: 00000000fbad2a84   X4: 00000000ffffffff   X3: 0000e6c14cef7020
     X2: 0000000000000002   X1: 0000c343bf885410   X0: 0000000000000001
    ORIG_X0: 0000000000000001  SYSCALLNO: 40  PSTATE: 20001000

PID: 6060     TASK: ffff0000c83dc400  CPU: 1    COMMAND: "mod_c thread"
 #0 [ffff80008000bd10] crash_save_cpu at ffff80008020ba9c
 #1 [ffff80008000bed0] ipi_cpu_crash_stop at ffff80008002ee0c
 #2 [ffff80008000bef0] do_handle_IPI at ffff80008002f2ec
 #3 [ffff80008000bf40] ipi_handler at ffff80008002f498
 #4 [ffff80008000bf50] handle_percpu_devid_irq at ffff800080190c94
 #5 [ffff80008000bfa0] generic_handle_domain_irq at ffff800080185408
 #6 [ffff80008000bfb0] __gic_handle_irq_from_irqson at ffff8000809c834c
 #7 [ffff80008000bfe0] gic_handle_irq at ffff8000800102b0
--- <IRQ stack> ---
 #8 [ffff800085953cb0] call_on_irq_stack at ffff800080017460
 #9 [ffff800085953cc0] do_interrupt_handler at ffff80008001ae6c
#10 [ffff800085953ce0] el1_interrupt at ffff8000815dc178
#11 [ffff800085953d00] el1h_64_irq_handler at ffff8000815dddd4
#12 [ffff800085953e40] el1h_64_irq at ffff800080011390
#13 [ffff800085953e60] foo at ffff80007beaa0b4 [mod_c]
#14 [ffff800085953e70] kthread at ffff800080107f2c
```

Note: We see PID 6060 was interrupted on CPU 1. PID: 6089 stack trace is a manual dump generation command.

3. We can check the process tree and CPU consumption:

```
crash> ps -p 6060
PID: 0        TASK: ffff800083239ac0  CPU: 0    COMMAND: "swapper/0"
 PID: 2        TASK: ffff0000c044a200  CPU: 0    COMMAND: "kthreadd"
  PID: 6060     TASK: ffff0000c83dc400  CPU: 1    COMMAND: "mod_c thread"
```

```
crash> ps -t 6060
PID: 6060     TASK: ffff0000c83dc400  CPU: 1    COMMAND: "mod_c thread"
    RUN TIME: 00:04:20
  START TIME: 22461712515069
       UTIME: 0
       STIME: 248767000000
```

4. Just **ps** command also shows running PIDs:

```
crash> ps
      PID    PPID  CPU       TASK        ST  %MEM     VSZ    RSS  COMM
        0       0   0  ffff800083239ac0  RU   0.0       0      0  [swapper/0]
        0       0   1  ffff0000c058a200  RU   0.0       0      0  [swapper/1]
        1       0   0  ffff0000c0448000  IN   0.1  166876  11272  systemd
        2       0   0  ffff0000c044a200  IN   0.0       0      0  [kthreadd]
...
...
...
     5716     854   0  ffff0000c8e74400  IN   0.1   18108   9636  sshd
     5719       1   0  ffff0000c0598000  IN   0.1   17220   9048  systemd
     5720    5719   1  ffff0000c059a200  IN   0.0  170908   5568  (sd-pam)
     5781    5716   0  ffff0000c5800000  IN   0.0   18404   6644  sshd
     5782    5781   0  ffff0000c5ba0000  IN   0.0    9368   5700  bash
     5791       2   0  ffff0000c505a200  ID   0.0       0      0  [kworker/u4:2]
>    6060       2   1  ffff0000c83dc400  RU   0.0       0      0  [mod_c thread]
     6062       2   0  ffff0000c5af4400  ID   0.0       0      0  [kworker/0:2]
     6079       2   0  ffff0000c6398000  ID   0.0       0      0  [kworker/u4:1]
     6088    5782   0  ffff0000c63a4400  IN   0.0   12416   4432  su
>    6089    6088   0  ffff0000c9e54400  RU   0.0    7516   3712  bash
```

5. We can also see our problem thread in the log because the watchdog reported it:

```
crash> log -T
[Sun Jan  5 12:07:07 UTC 2025] Booting Linux on physical CPU 0x0000000000 [0x413fd0c1]
[Sun Jan  5 12:07:07 UTC 2025] Linux version 6.8.0-1018-oracle (buildd@bos03-arm64-112) (aarch64-linux-gnu-gcc-11
(Ubuntu 11.4.0-1ubuntu1~22.04) 11.4.0, GNU ld (GNU Binutils for Ubuntu) 2.38) #19~22.04.1-Ubuntu SMP Mon Dec  9
23:49:53 UTC 2024 (Ubuntu 6.8.0-1018.19~22.04.1-oracle 6.8.12)
...
...
...
[Sun Jan  5 18:25:07 UTC 2025] CPU: 1 PID: 6060 Comm: mod_c thread Kdump: loaded Tainted: G           OEL     6.8.0-
1018-oracle #19~22.04.1-Ubuntu
[Sun Jan  5 18:25:07 UTC 2025] Hardware name: QEMU KVM Virtual Machine, BIOS 1.6.6 08/22/2023
[Sun Jan  5 18:25:07 UTC 2025] pstate: 60400005 (nZCv daif +PAN -UAO -TCO -DIT -SSBS BTYPE=--)
[Sun Jan  5 18:25:07 UTC 2025] pc : foo+0x8/0xf50 [mod_c]
[Sun Jan  5 18:25:07 UTC 2025] lr : kthread_f+0x20/0x40 [mod_c]
[Sun Jan  5 18:25:07 UTC 2025] sp : ffff800085953e60
[Sun Jan  5 18:25:07 UTC 2025] x29: ffff800085953e60 x28: 0000000000000000 x27: 0000000000000000
[Sun Jan  5 18:25:07 UTC 2025] x26: 0000000000000000 x25: 0000000000000000 x24: 0000000000000000
[Sun Jan  5 18:25:07 UTC 2025] x23: ffff80007beaa008 x22: ffff0000c83dc400 x21: ffff800085b53968
[Sun Jan  5 18:25:07 UTC 2025] x20: ffff0000caa96b00 x19: ffff0000c0567b40 x18: 0000000000000000
[Sun Jan  5 18:25:07 UTC 2025] x17: 0000000000000000 x16: 0000000000000000 x15: 0000000000000000
[Sun Jan  5 18:25:07 UTC 2025] x14: 0000000000000000 x13: 0000000000000030 x12: 0000000000000000
[Sun Jan  5 18:25:07 UTC 2025] x11: 0000000000000000 x10: 0000000000001b70 x9 : ffff80007beaa028
[Sun Jan  5 18:25:07 UTC 2025] x8 : ffff0000c83ddfd0 x7 : 0000000000000000 x6 : 0000000000000000
```

```
[Sun Jan  5 18:25:07 UTC 2025] x5 : 0000000000000000 x4 : 0000000000000000 x3 : 0000000000000000
[Sun Jan  5 18:25:07 UTC 2025] x2 : 0000000000000000 x1 : 0000000000000000 x0 : 0000000000000000
[Sun Jan  5 18:25:07 UTC 2025] Call trace:
[Sun Jan  5 18:25:07 UTC 2025]  foo+0x8/0xf50 [mod_c]
[Sun Jan  5 18:25:07 UTC 2025]  kthread+0xe0/0xf0
[Sun Jan  5 18:25:07 UTC 2025]  ret_from_fork+0x10/0x20
[Sun Jan  5 18:25:31 UTC 2025] watchdog: BUG: soft lockup - CPU#1 stuck for 216s! [mod_c thread:6060]
[Sun Jan  5 18:25:31 UTC 2025] Modules linked in: mod_c(OE) tls xt_comment xt_owner ipt_REJECT nf_reject_ipv4
xt_tcpudp xt_state xt_conntrack nf_conntrack nf_defrag_ipv6 nf_defrag_ipv4 nft_compat sunrpc nf_tables nfnetlink
binfmt_misc nls_iso8859_1 input_leds joydev dm_multipath scsi_dh_rdac scsi_dh_emc scsi_dh_alua sch_fq_codel efi_pstore
ip_tables x_tables autofs4 btrfs blake2b_generic iscsi_tcp libiscsi_tcp libiscsi scsi_transport_iscsi iscsi_ibft
iscsi_boot_sysfs hid_generic usbhid hid raid10 raid456 async_raid6_recov async_memcpy async_pq async_xor async_tx xor
xor_neon raid6_pq libcrc32c raid1 raid0 crct10dif_ce polyval_ce polyval_generic ghash_ce sm4 sha2_ce sha256_arm64
sha1_ce virtio_gpu xhci_pci virtio_dma_buf xhci_pci_renesas aes_neon_bs aes_neon_blk aes_ce_blk aes_ce_cipher
[Sun Jan  5 18:25:31 UTC 2025] CPU: 1 PID: 6060 Comm: mod_c thread Kdump: loaded Tainted: G           OEL     6.8.0-
1018-oracle #19~22.04.1-Ubuntu
[Sun Jan  5 18:25:31 UTC 2025] Hardware name: QEMU KVM Virtual Machine, BIOS 1.6.6 08/22/2023
[Sun Jan  5 18:25:31 UTC 2025] pstate: 60400005 (nZCv daif +PAN -UAO -TCO -DIT -SSBS BTYPE=--)
[Sun Jan  5 18:25:31 UTC 2025] pc : foo+0x8/0xf50 [mod_c]
[Sun Jan  5 18:25:31 UTC 2025] lr : kthread_f+0x20/0x40 [mod_c]
[Sun Jan  5 18:25:31 UTC 2025] sp : ffff800085953e60
[Sun Jan  5 18:25:31 UTC 2025] x29: ffff800085953e60 x28: 0000000000000000 x27: 0000000000000000
[Sun Jan  5 18:25:31 UTC 2025] x26: 0000000000000000 x25: 0000000000000000 x24: 0000000000000000
[Sun Jan  5 18:25:31 UTC 2025] x23: ffff80007beaa008 x22: ffff0000c83dc400 x21: ffff800085b53968
[Sun Jan  5 18:25:31 UTC 2025] x20: ffff0000caa96b00 x19: ffff0000c0567b40 x18: 0000000000000000
[Sun Jan  5 18:25:31 UTC 2025] x17: 0000000000000000 x16: 0000000000000000 x15: 0000000000000000
[Sun Jan  5 18:25:31 UTC 2025] x14: 0000000000000000 x13: 0000000000000030 x12: 0000000000000000
[Sun Jan  5 18:25:31 UTC 2025] x11: 0000000000000000 x10: 0000000000001b70 x9 : ffff80007beaa028
[Sun Jan  5 18:25:31 UTC 2025] x8 : ffff0000c83ddfd0 x7 : 0000000000000000 x6 : 0000000000000000
[Sun Jan  5 18:25:31 UTC 2025] x5 : 0000000000000000 x4 : 0000000000000000 x3 : 0000000000000000
[Sun Jan  5 18:25:31 UTC 2025] x2 : 0000000000000000 x1 : 0000000000000000 x0 : 0000000000000000
[Sun Jan  5 18:25:31 UTC 2025] Call trace:
[Sun Jan  5 18:25:31 UTC 2025]  foo+0x8/0xf50 [mod_c]
[Sun Jan  5 18:25:31 UTC 2025]  kthread+0xe0/0xf0
[Sun Jan  5 18:25:31 UTC 2025]  ret_from_fork+0x10/0x20
[Sun Jan  5 18:25:42 UTC 2025] rcu: INFO: rcu_sched self-detected stall on CPU
[Sun Jan  5 18:25:42 UTC 2025] rcu:     1-....: (239926 ticks this GP) idle=9f34/1/0x4000000000000000
softirq=101207/101207 fqs=59970
[Sun Jan  5 18:25:42 UTC 2025] rcu:              hardirqs   softirqs   csw/system
[Sun Jan  5 18:25:42 UTC 2025] rcu:      number:   210788       6139            0
[Sun Jan  5 18:25:42 UTC 2025] rcu:     cputime:        0         15       209923   ==> 210010(ms)
[Sun Jan  5 18:25:42 UTC 2025] rcu:     (t=240013 jiffies g=124949 q=7750 ncpus=2)
[Sun Jan  5 18:25:42 UTC 2025] CPU: 1 PID: 6060 Comm: mod_c thread Kdump: loaded Tainted: G           OEL     6.8.0-
1018-oracle #19~22.04.1-Ubuntu
[Sun Jan  5 18:25:42 UTC 2025] Hardware name: QEMU KVM Virtual Machine, BIOS 1.6.6 08/22/2023
[Sun Jan  5 18:25:42 UTC 2025] pstate: 60400005 (nZCv daif +PAN -UAO -TCO -DIT -SSBS BTYPE=--)
[Sun Jan  5 18:25:42 UTC 2025] pc : foo+0x8/0xf50 [mod_c]
[Sun Jan  5 18:25:42 UTC 2025] lr : kthread_f+0x20/0x40 [mod_c]
[Sun Jan  5 18:25:42 UTC 2025] sp : ffff800085953e60
[Sun Jan  5 18:25:42 UTC 2025] x29: ffff800085953e60 x28: 0000000000000000 x27: 0000000000000000
[Sun Jan  5 18:25:42 UTC 2025] x26: 0000000000000000 x25: 0000000000000000 x24: 0000000000000000
[Sun Jan  5 18:25:42 UTC 2025] x23: ffff80007beaa008 x22: ffff0000c83dc400 x21: ffff800085b53968
[Sun Jan  5 18:25:42 UTC 2025] x20: ffff0000caa96b00 x19: ffff0000c0567b40 x18: 0000000000000000
[Sun Jan  5 18:25:42 UTC 2025] x17: 0000000000000000 x16: 0000000000000000 x15: 0000000000000000
[Sun Jan  5 18:25:42 UTC 2025] x14: 0000000000000000 x13: 0000000000000030 x12: 0000000000000000
[Sun Jan  5 18:25:42 UTC 2025] x11: 0000000000000000 x10: 0000000000001b70 x9 : ffff80007beaa028
[Sun Jan  5 18:25:42 UTC 2025] x8 : ffff0000c83ddfd0 x7 : 0000000000000000 x6 : 0000000000000000
[Sun Jan  5 18:25:42 UTC 2025] x5 : 0000000000000000 x4 : 0000000000000000 x3 : 0000000000000000
[Sun Jan  5 18:25:42 UTC 2025] x2 : 0000000000000000 x1 : 0000000000000000 x0 : 0000000000000000
[Sun Jan  5 18:25:42 UTC 2025] Call trace:
[Sun Jan  5 18:25:42 UTC 2025]  foo+0x8/0xf50 [mod_c]
[Sun Jan  5 18:25:42 UTC 2025]  kthread+0xe0/0xf0
[Sun Jan  5 18:25:42 UTC 2025]  ret_from_fork+0x10/0x20
[Sun Jan  5 18:25:48 UTC 2025] sysrq: Trigger a crash
[Sun Jan  5 18:25:48 UTC 2025] Kernel panic - not syncing: sysrq triggered crash
[Sun Jan  5 18:25:48 UTC 2025] CPU: 0 PID: 6089 Comm: bash Kdump: loaded Tainted: G           OEL     6.8.0-1018-
oracle #19~22.04.1-Ubuntu
[Sun Jan  5 18:25:48 UTC 2025] Hardware name: QEMU KVM Virtual Machine, BIOS 1.6.6 08/22/2023
[Sun Jan  5 18:25:48 UTC 2025] Call trace:
[Sun Jan  5 18:25:48 UTC 2025]  dump_backtrace+0xa0/0x148
[Sun Jan  5 18:25:48 UTC 2025]  show_stack+0x20/0x48
[Sun Jan  5 18:25:48 UTC 2025]  dump_stack_lvl+0x38/0x130
[Sun Jan  5 18:25:48 UTC 2025]  dump_stack+0x18/0x30
[Sun Jan  5 18:25:48 UTC 2025]  panic+0x3a4/0x428
[Sun Jan  5 18:25:48 UTC 2025]  sysrq_handle_crash+0x20/0x28
[Sun Jan  5 18:25:48 UTC 2025]  __handle_sysrq+0xb8/0x308
```

```
[Sun Jan  5 18:25:48 UTC 2025]  write_sysrq_trigger+0x154/0x200
[Sun Jan  5 18:25:48 UTC 2025]  proc_reg_write+0xcc/0x150
[Sun Jan  5 18:25:48 UTC 2025]  vfs_write+0xd8/0x3b8
[Sun Jan  5 18:25:48 UTC 2025]  ksys_write+0x70/0x120
[Sun Jan  5 18:25:48 UTC 2025]  __arm64_sys_write+0x24/0x48
[Sun Jan  5 18:25:48 UTC 2025]  invoke_syscall+0x78/0x128
[Sun Jan  5 18:25:48 UTC 2025]  el0_svc_common.constprop.0+0x48/0x138
[Sun Jan  5 18:25:48 UTC 2025]  do_el0_svc+0x28/0x58
[Sun Jan  5 18:25:48 UTC 2025]  el0_svc+0x40/0x168
[Sun Jan  5 18:25:48 UTC 2025]  el0t_64_sync_handler+0x15c/0x178
[Sun Jan  5 18:25:48 UTC 2025]  el0t_64_sync+0x1a8/0x1b0
[Sun Jan  5 18:25:48 UTC 2025] SMP: stopping secondary CPUs
[Sun Jan  5 18:25:48 UTC 2025] Kernel Offset: disabled
[Sun Jan  5 18:25:48 UTC 2025] CPU features: 0x1,00000020,7002014a,2101720b
[Sun Jan  5 18:25:48 UTC 2025] Memory Limit: none
[Sun Jan  5 18:26:09 UTC 2025] Starting crashdump kernel...
[Sun Jan  5 18:26:09 UTC 2025] Bye!
```

6. If we look at the interrupted **foo+0x8** location (also shown as called from **kthread_f** with the **kthread_f+0x20** return address in LR), we see it cycles indefinitely:

```
crash> dis foo+0x8
0xffff80007beaa0b8 <foo+8>:      b       0xffff80007beaa0b8 <foo+8>

crash> dis kthread_f
0xffff80007beaa008 <kthread_f>: mov      x9, x30
0xffff80007beaa00c <kthread_f+4>:        nop
0xffff80007beaa010 <kthread_f+8>:        paciasp
0xffff80007beaa014 <kthread_f+12>:       mov      w0, #0x2710                     // #10000
0xffff80007beaa018 <kthread_f+16>:       stp      x29, x30, [sp, #-16]!
0xffff80007beaa01c <kthread_f+20>:       mov      x29, sp
0xffff80007beaa020 <kthread_f+24>:       bl       0xffff8000801d9380 <msleep>
0xffff80007beaa024 <kthread_f+28>:       bl       0xffff80007beaa0b0 <foo>
0xffff80007beaa028 <kthread_f+32>:       mov      w0, #0x0                        // #0
0xffff80007beaa02c <kthread_f+36>:       ldp      x29, x30, [sp], #16
0xffff80007beaa030 <kthread_f+40>:       autiasp
0xffff80007beaa034 <kthread_f+44>:       mov      x16, #0x0                       // #0
0xffff80007beaa038 <kthread_f+48>:       mov      x17, #0x0                       // #0
0xffff80007beaa03c <kthread_f+52>:       ret
0xffff80007beaa040 <kthread_f+56>:       .inst    0x81634280 ; undefined
0xffff80007beaa044 <kthread_f+60>:       .inst    0xffff8000 ; undefined

crash> dis 0xffff80007beaa0b0 4
0xffff80007beaa0b0 <foo>:        mov     x9, x30
0xffff80007beaa0b4 <foo+4>:      nop
0xffff80007beaa0b8 <foo+8>:      b       0xffff80007beaa0b8 <foo+8>
0xffff80007beaa0bc <foo+12>:     udf     #0
```

Exercise K4 (A64, WinDbg)

Goal: Learn how to identify spiking kernel threads.

Patterns: Stack Trace Collection (CPUs); Interrupt Stack; Active Thread; Spiking Thread.

1. Copy the *vmlinux-6.8.0-1018-oracle* file in the A64/KSym directory to the *vmlinux* file.

2. Launch WinDbg. Load the core dump *202501051833.kdump* from the A64/K4 directory and set the symbol path to the A64/KSym directory (there may be some delay/unresponsiveness when you type the **.reload** command):

```
Microsoft (R) Windows Debugger Version 10.0.27725.1000 AMD64
Copyright (c) Microsoft Corporation. All rights reserved.


Loading Dump File [C:\ALCDA2\A64\K4\202501051833.kdump]
64-bit machine not using 64-bit API

************* Path validation summary **************
Response                         Time (ms)     Location
Deferred                                       srv*
Symbol search path is: srv*
Executable search path is:
Generic Unix Kernel Version 0 MP (2 procs) Free ARM 64-bit (AArch64)
Primary image base = 0xffff8000`80010000 Loaded module list = 0x00000000`00000000
System Uptime: not available
Loading Kernel Symbols

Loading User Symbols

For analysis of this file, run !analyze -v
ffff8000`802097d0 stp         x1,x0,[x2,#0x100]

0: kd> .sympath C:\ALCDA2\A64\KSym\
Symbol search path is: C:\ALCDA2\A64\KSym\
Expanded Symbol search path is: c:\alcda2\a64\ksym\

************* Path validation summary **************
Response                         Time (ms)     Location
OK                                             C:\ALCDA2\A64\KSym\

0: kd> .reload
Loading Kernel Symbols
.*** WARNING: Unable to verify timestamp for vmlinux

Loading User Symbols


************* Symbol Loading Error Summary **************
Module name            Error
vmlinux                The system cannot find the file specified

You can troubleshoot most symbol related issues by turning on symbol loading diagnostics (!sym
noisy) and repeating the command that caused symbols to be loaded.
You should also verify that your symbol search path (.sympath) is correct.
```

3. The CPU 0 thread stack trace is expected for manual dump generation:

```
0: kd> kL
 # Child-SP          RetAddr               Call Site
00 ffff8000`859938e0 ffff8000`8020b5f0     vmlinux!crash_setup_regs+0xa0
01 ffff8000`859938e0 ffff8000`800c83e0     vmlinux!__crash_kexec+0x60
02 ffff8000`85993a60 ffff8000`80d326e8 (T) vmlinux!panic+0x350
03 ffff8000`85993b40 ffff8000`80d33498     vmlinux!sysrq_handle_crash+0x1c
04 ffff8000`85993b50 ffff8000`80d34074     vmlinux!__handle_sysrq+0xb8
05 ffff8000`85993be0 ffff8000`805f22cc     vmlinux!write_sysrq_trigger+0x154
06 ffff8000`85993c20 ffff8000`80510270     vmlinux!proc_reg_write+0xcc
07 ffff8000`85993c40 ffff8000`80510728     vmlinux!vfs_write+0xd8
08 ffff8000`85993ce0 ffff8000`805107fc     vmlinux!ksys_write+0x70
09 ffff8000`85993d20 ffff8000`800313c0     vmlinux!__arm64_sys_write+0x24
0a ffff8000`85993d30 ffff8000`800314b8     vmlinux!invoke_syscall+0x78
0b ffff8000`85993e40 ffff8000`800315d0     vmlinux!el0_svc_common+0x48
0c ffff8000`85993e70 ffff8000`815dd9e8     vmlinux!do_el0_svc+0x28
0d ffff8000`85993e80 ffff8000`815ddffc     vmlinux!el0_svc+0x40
0e ffff8000`85993ea0 ffff8000`80011640     vmlinux!el0t_64_sync_handler+0x15c
0f ffff8000`85993eb0 00000000`00000000     vmlinux!el0t_64_sync+0x1a8
```

4. The CPU 1 thread stack trace shows an active thread with an infinite loop:

```
0: kd> ~1s
WARNING: Unable to reset page directories

1: kd> kL
 # Child-SP          RetAddr               Call Site
00 ffff8000`85953e60 ffff8000`80107f30     mod_c+0xb8
01 ffff8000`85953e70 ffff8000`80017430     vmlinux!kthread+0xe0
02 ffff8000`85953eb0 00000000`00000000     vmlinux!ret_from_fork+0x10

1: kd> r
 x0=0000000000000000  x1=0000000000000000  x2=0000000000000000  x3=0000000000000000
 x4=0000000000000000  x5=0000000000000000  x6=0000000000000000  x7=0000000000000000
 x8=ffff0000c83ddfd0  x9=ffff80007beaa028 x10=0000000000001b70 x11=0000000000000000
x12=0000000000000000 x13=0000000000000030 x14=0000000000000000 x15=0000000000000000
x16=0000000000000000 x17=0000000000000000 x18=0000000000000000 x19=ffff0000c0567b40
x20=ffff0000caa96b00 x21=ffff800085b53968 x22=ffff0000c83dc400 x23=ffff80007beaa008
x24=0000000000000000 x25=0000000000000000 x26=0000000000000000 x27=0000000000000000
x28=0000000000000000  fp=ffff800085953e60  lr=ffff80007beaa028  sp=ffff800085953e60
 pc=ffff80007beaa0b8 psr=60400005 -ZC- EL1
mod_c+0xb8:
ffff8000`7beaa0b8 b            mod_c+0xb8 (ffff8000`7beaa0b8)
```

Exercise K5

- **Goal:** Learn how to identify kernel stack overflow and kernel stack boundaries
- **Patterns:** Stack Overflow (Kernel Mode)
- \ALCDA-Dumps\Exercise-K5-x64-GDB.pdf
- \ALCDA-Dumps\Exercise-K5-A64-GDB.pdf
- \ALCDA-Dumps\Exercise-K5-A64-WinDbg.pdf
- \ALCDA-Dumps\Exercise-K5-x64-WinDbg.pdf

Exercise K5 (x64, GDB)

Goal: Learn how to identify kernel stack overflow and kernel stack boundaries.

Patterns: Stack Overflow (Kernel Mode); Debugger Bug.

1. Load the core dump *202501051854.kdump* from the x64/K5 directory and the matching *vmlinux-6.8.0-1018-azure* file from the x64/KSym directory:

```
~/ALCDA2/x64/K5$ crash 202501051854.kdump ../KSym/vmlinux-6.8.0-1018-azure

crash 8.0.6++
Copyright (C) 2002-2025  Red Hat, Inc.
Copyright (C) 2004, 2005, 2006, 2010  IBM Corporation
Copyright (C) 1999-2006  Hewlett-Packard Co
Copyright (C) 2005, 2006, 2011, 2012  Fujitsu Limited
Copyright (C) 2006, 2007  VA Linux Systems Japan K.K.
Copyright (C) 2005, 2011, 2020-2024  NEC Corporation
Copyright (C) 1999, 2002, 2007  Silicon Graphics, Inc.
Copyright (C) 1999, 2000, 2001, 2002  Mission Critical Linux, Inc.
Copyright (C) 2015, 2021  VMware, Inc.
This program is free software, covered by the GNU General Public License,
and you are welcome to change it and/or distribute copies of it under
certain conditions.  Enter "help copying" to see the conditions.
This program has absolutely no warranty.  Enter "help warranty" for details.

GNU gdb (GDB) 10.2
Copyright (C) 2021 Free Software Foundation, Inc.
License GPLv3+: GNU GPL version 3 or later <http://gnu.org/licenses/gpl.html>
This is free software: you are free to change and redistribute it.
There is NO WARRANTY, to the extent permitted by law.
Type "show copying" and "show warranty" for details.
This GDB was configured as "x86_64-pc-linux-gnu".
Type "show configuration" for configuration details.
Find the GDB manual and other documentation resources online at:
    <http://www.gnu.org/software/gdb/documentation/>.

For help, type "help".
Type "apropos word" to search for commands related to "word"...

      KERNEL: ../KSym/vmlinux-6.8.0-1018-azure  [TAINTED]
    DUMPFILE: 202501051854.kdump  [PARTIAL DUMP]
        CPUS: 4
        DATE: Sun Jan  5 18:50:04 GMT 2025
      UPTIME: 00:47:49
LOAD AVERAGE: 0.25, 0.08, 0.02
       TASKS: 632
    NODENAME: coredump-alcda
     RELEASE: 6.8.0-1018-azure
     VERSION: #21~22.04.1-Ubuntu SMP Fri Nov  8 00:21:25 UTC 2024
     MACHINE: x86_64  (2112 Mhz)
      MEMORY: 4 GB
       PANIC: "Kernel panic - not syncing: Fatal exception in interrupt"
         PID: 2662
     COMMAND: "mod_d thread"
        TASK: ffff97e515058000  [THREAD_INFO: ffff97e515058000]
         CPU: 0
```

```
   STATE: TASK_RUNNING (PANIC)

crash>
```

2. The backtrace shows recursive calls and double fault pointing to stack overflow:

```
crash> bt
PID: 2662     TASK: ffff97e515058000  CPU: 0    COMMAND: "mod_d thread"
 #0 [fffffe71f147acc0] machine_kexec at ffffffffa8c99db1
 #1 [fffffe71f147ad28] __crash_kexec at ffffffffa8df1e46
 #2 [fffffe71f147ade8] panic at ffffffffa8cddf29
 #3 [fffffe71f147ae68] oops_end at ffffffffa8c432c2
 #4 [fffffe71f147ae90] die at ffffffffa8c43cd3
 #5 [fffffe71f147aec0] handle_stack_overflow at ffffffffa8c3e9ee
 #6 [fffffe71f147aef0] exc_double_fault at ffffffffa9cbb861
 #7 [fffffe71f147af50] asm_exc_double_fault at ffffffffa9e00caf
    [exception RIP: foo+15]
    RIP: ffffffffc090a0af  RSP: ffffac1e40174000  RFLAGS: 00010246
    RAX: 0000000000000000  RBX: 0000000000000000  RCX: 0000000000000000
    RDX: 0000000000000000  RSI: 0000000000000286  RDI: 0000000000000000
    RBP: ffffac1e40174010   R8: 0000029c0eec1164   R9: 0000000000000000
    R10: 0000000000000001  R11: 0000000000000000  R12: ffff97e5c08c2a80
    R13: ffffac1e47b7b868  R14: ffff97e5c092ee80  R15: ffffffffc090a010
    ORIG_RAX: ffffffffffffffff  CS: 0010  SS: 0018
--- <DOUBLEFAULT exception stack> ---
 #8 [ffffac1e40174000] foo at ffffffffc090a0af [mod_d]
 #9 [ffffac1e40174018] bar at ffffffffc090a0f4 [mod_d]
#10 [ffffac1e40174038] foo at ffffffffc090a0b4 [mod_d]
#11 [ffffac1e40174058] bar at ffffffffc090a0f4 [mod_d]
#12 [ffffac1e40174078] foo at ffffffffc090a0b4 [mod_d]
#13 [ffffac1e40174098] bar at ffffffffc090a0f4 [mod_d]
#14 [ffffac1e401740b8] foo at ffffffffc090a0b4 [mod_d]
#15 [ffffac1e401740d8] bar at ffffffffc090a0f4 [mod_d]
#16 [ffffac1e401740f8] foo at ffffffffc090a0b4 [mod_d]
#17 [ffffac1e40174118] bar at ffffffffc090a0f4 [mod_d]
#18 [ffffac1e40174138] foo at ffffffffc090a0b4 [mod_d]
#19 [ffffac1e40174158] bar at ffffffffc090a0f4 [mod_d]
#20 [ffffac1e40174178] foo at ffffffffc090a0b4 [mod_d]
#21 [ffffac1e40174198] bar at ffffffffc090a0f4 [mod_d]
#22 [ffffac1e401741b8] foo at ffffffffc090a0b4 [mod_d]
#23 [ffffac1e401741d8] bar at ffffffffc090a0f4 [mod_d]
#24 [ffffac1e401741f8] foo at ffffffffc090a0b4 [mod_d]
#25 [ffffac1e40174218] bar at ffffffffc090a0f4 [mod_d]
#26 [ffffac1e40174238] foo at ffffffffc090a0b4 [mod_d]
#27 [ffffac1e40174258] bar at ffffffffc090a0f4 [mod_d]
#28 [ffffac1e40174278] foo at ffffffffc090a0b4 [mod_d]
#29 [ffffac1e40174298] bar at ffffffffc090a0f4 [mod_d]
#30 [ffffac1e401742b8] foo at ffffffffc090a0b4 [mod_d]
#31 [ffffac1e401742d8] bar at ffffffffc090a0f4 [mod_d]
#32 [ffffac1e401742f8] foo at ffffffffc090a0b4 [mod_d]
#33 [ffffac1e40174318] bar at ffffffffc090a0f4 [mod_d]
#34 [ffffac1e40174338] foo at ffffffffc090a0b4 [mod_d]
#35 [ffffac1e40174358] bar at ffffffffc090a0f4 [mod_d]
#36 [ffffac1e40174378] foo at ffffffffc090a0b4 [mod_d]
-- MORE --  forward: <SPACE>, <ENTER> or j  backward: b or k  quit: qq
```

Note: A different stack region is used for the overflow stack processing since there is no space in the original stack region.

3. We can get the stack limit from the task structure (on x64 systems, the stack is 4 4K pages, 0x4000 bytes):

```
crash> mach
          MACHINE TYPE: x86_64
           MEMORY SIZE: 4 GB
                  CPUS: 4
            HYPERVISOR: Hyper-V
       PROCESSOR SPEED: 2112 Mhz
                    HZ: 1000
             PAGE SIZE: 4096
   KERNEL VIRTUAL BASE: ffff97e4c0000000
   KERNEL VMALLOC BASE: ffffac1e40000000
   KERNEL VMEMMAP BASE: ffffebb4c0000000
      KERNEL START MAP: ffffffff80000000
   KERNEL MODULES BASE: ffffffffc0000000
     KERNEL STACK SIZE: 16384
...
...
...

crash> task
PID: 2662     TASK: ffff97e515058000  CPU: 0    COMMAND: "mod_d thread"
struct task_struct {
  thread_info = {
    flags = 16384,
    syscall_work = 0,
    status = 0,
    cpu = 0
  },
  __state = 0,
  saved_state = 0,
  stack = 0xffffac1e40174000,
  usage = {
    refs = {
      counter = 1
    }
  },
  flags = 2129984,
  ptrace = 0,
  on_cpu = 1,
  wake_entry = {
    llist = {
      next = 0x0
    },
    {
      u_flags = 48,
      a_flags = {
        counter = 48
      }
    },
    src = 0,
    dst = 0
  },
  wakee_flips = 1,
  wakee_flip_decay_ts = 4297526484,
  last_wakee = 0xffff97e51505d100,
  recent_used_cpu = 1,
  wake_cpu = 0,
  on_rq = 1,
  prio = 120,
```

```
  static_prio = 120,
  normal_prio = 120,
  rt_priority = 0,
  se = {
    load = {
      weight = 1048576,
      inv_weight = 4194304
    },
 -- MORE --  forward: <SPACE>, <ENTER> or j  backward: b or k  quit: qq
```

Note: We see from the backtrace that RSP reached stack region limit **0xffffac1e40174000**.

4. The stack region base is **0xffffac1e40174000** + 0x4000 = **0xffffac1e40178000**. We can specify the RSP hint to the **bt** command to get to the bottom of the stack trace (we choose a close address to the bottom, **0xffffac1e40178000** – 0x200 = **0xffffac1e40177e00**):

```
crash> bt -S 0xffffac1e40177e00
Segmentation fault (core dumped)
```

Note: Oops, we see the debugger bug. This crash also happened on the original Ubuntu, where the core dump was collected. On your system, this may work though. On our WSL Debian or the original Ubuntu system, we then dump the raw stack data as a workaround to see the bottom of the stack trace:

```
crash> rd -SS -64 0xffffac1e40177e00 64
ffffac1e40177e00:  0000000000000000 [ffff97e5c08c2a80:kmalloc-rnd-11-64]
ffffac1e40177e10:  ffffac1e40177e30 bar+20
ffffac1e40177e20:  0000000000000000 [ffff97e5c08c2a80:kmalloc-rnd-11-64]
ffffac1e40177e30:  ffffac1e40177e50 foo+20
ffffac1e40177e40:  0000000000000000 [ffff97e5c08c2a80:kmalloc-rnd-11-64]
ffffac1e40177e50:  ffffac1e40177e70 bar+20
ffffac1e40177e60:  0000000000000000 [ffff97e5c08c2a80:kmalloc-rnd-11-64]
ffffac1e40177e70:  ffffac1e40177e90 foo+20
ffffac1e40177e80:  0000000000000000 [ffff97e5c08c2a80:kmalloc-rnd-11-64]
ffffac1e40177e90:  ffffac1e40177eb0 bar+20
ffffac1e40177ea0:  0000000000000000 [ffff97e5c08c2a80:kmalloc-rnd-11-64]
ffffac1e40177eb0:  ffffac1e40177ed0 foo+20
ffffac1e40177ec0:  [ffff97e515058000:task_struct] [ffff97e5c08c2a80:kmalloc-rnd-11-64]
ffffac1e40177ed0:  ffffac1e40177ee0 kthread_f+26
ffffac1e40177ee0:  ffffac1e40177f20 kthread+211
ffffac1e40177ef0:  0000000000000000 kthread
ffffac1e40177f00:  ffffac1e40177f58 [ffff97e5c08c2a80:kmalloc-rnd-11-64]
ffffac1e40177f10:  0000000000000000 0000000000000000
ffffac1e40177f20:  ffffac1e40177f48 ret_from_fork+57
ffffac1e40177f30:  kthread          [ffff97e5c08c2a80:kmalloc-rnd-11-64]
ffffac1e40177f40:  0000000000000000 ffffac1e40177f59
ffffac1e40177f50:  ret_from_fork_asm+27 0000000000000000
ffffac1e40177f60:  0000000000000000 0000000000000000
ffffac1e40177f70:  0000000000000000 0000000000000000
ffffac1e40177f80:  0000000000000000 0000000000000000
ffffac1e40177f90:  0000000000000000 0000000000000000
ffffac1e40177fa0:  0000000000000000 0000000000000000
ffffac1e40177fb0:  0000000000000000 0000000000000000
ffffac1e40177fc0:  0000000000000000 0000000000000000
ffffac1e40177fd0:  0000000000000000 0000000000000000
ffffac1e40177fe0:  0000000000000000 0000000000000000
ffffac1e40177ff0:  0000000000000000 0000000000000000
```

5. If we disassemble *foo* and *bar,* we see they call each other:

```
crash> dis foo 20
0xffffffffc090a0a0 <foo>:       nopl   0x0(%rax,%rax,1) [FTRACE NOP]
0xffffffffc090a0a5 <foo+5>:     push   %rbp
0xffffffffc090a0a6 <foo+6>:     mov    %rsp,%rbp
0xffffffffc090a0a9 <foo+9>:     push   %r12
0xffffffffc090a0ab <foo+11>:    push   %rbx
0xffffffffc090a0ac <foo+12>:    mov    %rdi,%rbx
0xffffffffc090a0af <foo+15>:    call   0xffffffffc090a0e0 <bar>
0xffffffffc090a0b4 <foo+20>:    lea    0x1(%rbx),%rdi
0xffffffffc090a0b8 <foo+24>:    mov    %rax,%r12
0xffffffffc090a0bb <foo+27>:    call   0xffffffffc090a0e0 <bar>
0xffffffffc090a0c0 <foo+32>:    pop    %rbx
0xffffffffc090a0c1 <foo+33>:    add    %r12,%rax
0xffffffffc090a0c4 <foo+36>:    pop    %r12
0xffffffffc090a0c6 <foo+38>:    pop    %rbp
0xffffffffc090a0c7 <foo+39>:    ret
0xffffffffc090a0c8 <foo+40>:    int3
0xffffffffc090a0c9 <foo+41>:    int3
0xffffffffc090a0ca <foo+42>:    int3
0xffffffffc090a0cb <foo+43>:    int3
0xffffffffc090a0cc <foo+44>:    nopl   0x0(%rax)

crash> dis bar 20
0xffffffffc090a0e0 <bar>:       nopl   0x0(%rax,%rax,1) [FTRACE NOP]
0xffffffffc090a0e5 <bar+5>:     push   %rbp
0xffffffffc090a0e6 <bar+6>:     mov    %rsp,%rbp
0xffffffffc090a0e9 <bar+9>:     push   %r12
0xffffffffc090a0eb <bar+11>:    push   %rbx
0xffffffffc090a0ec <bar+12>:    mov    %rdi,%rbx
0xffffffffc090a0ef <bar+15>:    call   0xffffffffc090a0a0 <foo>
0xffffffffc090a0f4 <bar+20>:    lea    0x1(%rbx),%rdi
0xffffffffc090a0f8 <bar+24>:    mov    %rax,%r12
0xffffffffc090a0fb <bar+27>:    call   0xffffffffc090a0a0 <foo>
0xffffffffc090a100 <bar+32>:    pop    %rbx
0xffffffffc090a101 <bar+33>:    add    %r12,%rax
0xffffffffc090a104 <bar+36>:    pop    %r12
0xffffffffc090a106 <bar+38>:    pop    %rbp
0xffffffffc090a107 <bar+39>:    ret
0xffffffffc090a108 <bar+40>:    int3
0xffffffffc090a109 <bar+41>:    int3
0xffffffffc090a10a <bar+42>:    int3
0xffffffffc090a10b <bar+43>:    int3
0xffffffffc090a10c <bar+44>:    add    %al,(%rax)
```

Exercise K5 (A64, GDB)

Goal: Learn how to identify kernel stack overflow and kernel stack boundaries.

Patterns: Stack Overflow (Kernel Mode).

1. Load the core dump *202501051903.kdump* from the A64/K5 directory and the matching *vmlinux-6.8.0-1018-oracle* file from the A64/KSym directory:

```
~/ALCDA2/A64/K5$ crash 202501051903.kdump ../KSym/vmlinux-6.8.0-1018-oracle

crash 8.0.6++
Copyright (C) 2002-2025  Red Hat, Inc.
Copyright (C) 2004, 2005, 2006, 2010  IBM Corporation
Copyright (C) 1999-2006  Hewlett-Packard Co
Copyright (C) 2005, 2006, 2011, 2012  Fujitsu Limited
Copyright (C) 2006, 2007  VA Linux Systems Japan K.K.
Copyright (C) 2005, 2011, 2020-2024  NEC Corporation
Copyright (C) 1999, 2002, 2007  Silicon Graphics, Inc.
Copyright (C) 1999, 2000, 2001, 2002  Mission Critical Linux, Inc.
Copyright (C) 2015, 2021  VMware, Inc.
This program is free software, covered by the GNU General Public License,
and you are welcome to change it and/or distribute copies of it under
certain conditions.  Enter "help copying" to see the conditions.
This program has absolutely no warranty.  Enter "help warranty" for details.

GNU gdb (GDB) 10.2
Copyright (C) 2021 Free Software Foundation, Inc.
License GPLv3+: GNU GPL version 3 or later <http://gnu.org/licenses/gpl.html>
This is free software: you are free to change and redistribute it.
There is NO WARRANTY, to the extent permitted by law.
Type "show copying" and "show warranty" for details.
This GDB was configured as "aarch64-unknown-linux-gnu".
Type "show configuration" for configuration details.
Find the GDB manual and other documentation resources online at:
    <http://www.gnu.org/software/gdb/documentation/>.

For help, type "help".
Type "apropos word" to search for commands related to "word"...

      KERNEL: ../KSym/vmlinux-6.8.0-1018-oracle  [TAINTED]
    DUMPFILE: 202501051903.kdump  [PARTIAL DUMP]
        CPUS: 2
        DATE: Sun Jan  5 19:02:43 UTC 2025
      UPTIME: 00:29:09
LOAD AVERAGE: 0.15, 0.03, 0.01
       TASKS: 211
    NODENAME: instance-20230624-1144
     RELEASE: 6.8.0-1018-oracle
     VERSION: #19~22.04.1-Ubuntu SMP Mon Dec  9 23:49:53 UTC 2024
     MACHINE: aarch64  (unknown Mhz)
      MEMORY: 12 GB
       PANIC: "Kernel panic - not syncing: kernel stack overflow"
         PID: 1955
     COMMAND: "mod_d thread"
        TASK: ffff0000c71da200  [THREAD_INFO: ffff0000c71da200]
         CPU: 1
```

```
    STATE: TASK_RUNNING (PANIC)

crash>
```

Note: Here the panic description tells us about stack overflow explicitly.

2. The backtrace shows recursive calls and double fault pointing to stack overflow:

```
crash> bt
PID: 1955    TASK: ffff0000c71da200  CPU: 1    COMMAND: "mod_d thread"
 #0 [ffff0002fe7a5ee0] crash_setup_regs at ffff8000802097cc
 #1 [ffff0002fe7a6060] panic at ffff8000800c83dc
 #2 [ffff0002fe7a6140] nmi_panic at ffff8000800c8504
 #3 [ffff0002fe7a6150] panic_bad_stack at ffff8000800276c8
 #4 [ffff0002fe7a6190] handle_bad_stack at ffff8000815de3c0
 #5 [ffff0002fe7a62f0] __bad_stack at ffff80008001108c
     PC: ffff80007be440d8  [foo+32]
     LR: 0000000000000000  [unknown or invalid address]
     SP: ffff800085c10000  PSTATE: ffff800085c10000
    X29: 0000000000000000  X28: 0000000000000000  X27: 0000000000000000
    X26: 0000000000000000  X25: ffff80007be44008  X24: ffff0000c71da200
    X23: ffff800085a8b718  X22: 0000000000000000  X21: ffff0000c01b97c0
    X20: 0000000000000000  X19: 0000000000000000  X18: 0000000000000000
    X17: 0000000000000000  X16: 0000000000000000  X15: 0000000000000000
    X14: 0000000000000000  X13: 0000000000000000  X12: 0000000000001b70
    X11: ffff80007be440d8  X10: ffff0000c71dbdd0   X9: 0000000000000000
     X8: 0000000000000000   X7: 0000000000000000   X6: 0000000000000000
     X5: 0000000000000000   X4: 0000000000000000   X3: 0000000000000000
     X2: 0000000000000000   X1: 0000000000000000   X0: ffff0002fe7a6310
--- <Overflow stack> ---
 #6 [ffff800085c10000] bar at ffff80007be44110 [mod_d]
 #7 [ffff800085c10020] bar at ffff80007be44124 [mod_d]
 #8 [ffff800085c10040] foo at ffff80007be440d4 [mod_d]
 #9 [ffff800085c10060] bar at ffff80007be44124 [mod_d]
#10 [ffff800085c10080] foo at ffff80007be440d4 [mod_d]
#11 [ffff800085c100a0] bar at ffff80007be44124 [mod_d]
#12 [ffff800085c100c0] foo at ffff80007be440d4 [mod_d]
#13 [ffff800085c100e0] bar at ffff80007be44124 [mod_d]
#14 [ffff800085c10100] foo at ffff80007be440d4 [mod_d]
#15 [ffff800085c10120] bar at ffff80007be44124 [mod_d]
#16 [ffff800085c10140] foo at ffff80007be440d4 [mod_d]
#17 [ffff800085c10160] bar at ffff80007be44124 [mod_d]
#18 [ffff800085c10180] foo at ffff80007be440d4 [mod_d]
#19 [ffff800085c101a0] bar at ffff80007be44124 [mod_d]
#20 [ffff800085c101c0] foo at ffff80007be440d4 [mod_d]
#21 [ffff800085c101e0] bar at ffff80007be44124 [mod_d]
#22 [ffff800085c10200] foo at ffff80007be440d4 [mod_d]
#23 [ffff800085c10220] bar at ffff80007be44124 [mod_d]
#24 [ffff800085c10240] foo at ffff80007be440d4 [mod_d]
#25 [ffff800085c10260] bar at ffff80007be44124 [mod_d]
#26 [ffff800085c10280] foo at ffff80007be440d4 [mod_d]
#27 [ffff800085c102a0] bar at ffff80007be44124 [mod_d]
#28 [ffff800085c102c0] foo at ffff80007be440d4 [mod_d]
#29 [ffff800085c102e0] bar at ffff80007be44124 [mod_d]
-- MORE --  forward: <SPACE>, <ENTER> or j  backward: b or k  quit: qq
```

Note: A different stack region is used for the overflow stack processing since there is no space in the original stack region.

3. We can get the stack limit from the task structure (on A64 systems, the stack is 4 4K pages, 0x4000 bytes):

```
crash> mach
       MACHINE TYPE: aarch64
        MEMORY SIZE: 12 GB
               CPUS: 2
                 HZ: 1000
          PAGE SIZE: 4096
KERNEL VIRTUAL BASE: ffff000000000000
KERNEL MODULES BASE: ffff800000000000
KERNEL VMALLOC BASE: ffff800080000000
KERNEL VMEMMAP BASE: fffffc0000000000
  KERNEL STACK SIZE: 16384
...
...
...

crash> task
PID: 1955     TASK: ffff0000c71da200  CPU: 1    COMMAND: "mod_d thread"
struct task_struct {
  thread_info = {
    flags = 8,
    ttbr0 = 13620928512,
    {
      preempt_count = 4296081408,
      preempt = {
        count = 1114112,
        need_resched = 1
      }
    },
    cpu = 1
  },
  __state = 0,
  saved_state = 0,
  stack = 0xffff800085c10000,
  usage = {
    refs = {
      counter = 1
    }
  },
  flags = 2129984,
  ptrace = 0,
  on_cpu = 1,
  wake_entry = {
    llist = {
      next = 0x0
    },
    {
      u_flags = 48,
      a_flags = {
        counter = 48
      }
    },
    src = 0,
    dst = 0
  },
  wakee_flips = 1,
  wakee_flip_decay_ts = 4296406599,
  last_wakee = 0xffff0000c752a200,
  recent_used_cpu = 0,
```

```
  wake_cpu = 1,
  on_rq = 1,
  prio = 120,
 -- MORE --  forward: <SPACE>, <ENTER> or j  backward: b or k  quit: qq
```

Note: We see from the backtrace that RSP reached stack region limit **0xffff800085c10000**.

4. The stack region base is **0xffff800085c10000** + 0x4000 = **0xffff800085c14000**. We can specify the RSP hint to the **bt** command to get to the bottom of the stack trace (we choose a close address to the bottom, **0xffff800085c14000** – 0x300 = **0xffff800085c13d00**):

```
crash> bt -S 0xffff800085c13d00
#0 [ffff800085c13eb0] (null) at ffff800085c13d1c

crash> bt -S 0xffff800085c13d08
PID: 1955     TASK: ffff0000c71da200  CPU: 1    COMMAND: "mod_d thread"
 #0 [ffff800085c13d20] bar at ffff80007be44124 [mod_d]
 #1 [ffff800085c13d40] foo at ffff80007be440d4 [mod_d]
 #2 [ffff800085c13d60] bar at ffff80007be44124 [mod_d]
 #3 [ffff800085c13d80] foo at ffff80007be440d4 [mod_d]
 #4 [ffff800085c13da0] bar at ffff80007be44124 [mod_d]
 #5 [ffff800085c13dc0] foo at ffff80007be440d4 [mod_d]
 #6 [ffff800085c13de0] bar at ffff80007be44124 [mod_d]
 #7 [ffff800085c13e00] foo at ffff80007be440d4 [mod_d]
 #8 [ffff800085c13e20] bar at ffff80007be44124 [mod_d]
 #9 [ffff800085c13e40] foo at ffff80007be440d4 [mod_d]
#10 [ffff800085c13e60] kthread_f at ffff80007be44028 [mod_d]
#11 [ffff800085c13e70] kthread at ffff800080107f2c
```

Note: On some systems, we may see the debugger bug like a segmentation fault. We then dump the raw stack data as a workaround to see the bottom of the stack trace:

```
crash> rd -SS -64 0xffff800085c13d00 64
ffff800085c13d00:  ffff800085c13d20 bar+32
ffff800085c13d10:  [ffff0000c01b97c0:kmalloc-rnd-04-64] 0000000000000000
ffff800085c13d20:  ffff800085c13d40 foo+32
ffff800085c13d30:  [ffff0000c01b97c0:kmalloc-rnd-04-64] 0000000000000000
ffff800085c13d40:  ffff800085c13d60 bar+32
ffff800085c13d50:  [ffff0000c01b97c0:kmalloc-rnd-04-64] 0000000000000000
ffff800085c13d60:  ffff800085c13d80 foo+32
ffff800085c13d70:  [ffff0000c01b97c0:kmalloc-rnd-04-64] 0000000000000000
ffff800085c13d80:  ffff800085c13da0 bar+32
ffff800085c13d90:  [ffff0000c01b97c0:kmalloc-rnd-04-64] 0000000000000000
ffff800085c13da0:  ffff800085c13dc0 foo+32
ffff800085c13db0:  [ffff0000c01b97c0:kmalloc-rnd-04-64] 0000000000000000
ffff800085c13dc0:  ffff800085c13de0 bar+32
ffff800085c13dd0:  [ffff0000c01b97c0:kmalloc-rnd-04-64] 0000000000000000
ffff800085c13de0:  ffff800085c13e00 foo+32
ffff800085c13df0:  [ffff0000c01b97c0:kmalloc-rnd-04-64] 0000000000000000
ffff800085c13e00:  ffff800085c13e20 bar+32
ffff800085c13e10:  [ffff0000c01b97c0:kmalloc-rnd-04-64] 0000000000000000
ffff800085c13e20:  ffff800085c13e40 foo+32
ffff800085c13e30:  [ffff0000c01b97c0:kmalloc-rnd-04-64] 0000000000000000
ffff800085c13e40:  ffff800085c13e60 kthread_f+36
ffff800085c13e50:  [ffff0000c01b97c0:kmalloc-rnd-04-64] [ffff0000c5779d00:kmalloc-rnd-01-128]
ffff800085c13e60:  ffff800085c13e70 kthread+224
ffff800085c13e70:  ffff800085c13fe0 ret_from_fork+16
```

```
ffff800085c13e80:  kthread          [ffff0000c01b97c0:kmalloc-rnd-04-64]
ffff800085c13e90:  0000000000000000 0000000000000000
ffff800085c13ea0:  0000000000000000 0000000000000000
ffff800085c13eb0:  0000000000000000 0000000000000000
ffff800085c13ec0:  0000000000000000 0000000000000000
ffff800085c13ed0:  0000000000000000 0000000000000000
ffff800085c13ee0:  0000000000000000 0000000000000000
ffff800085c13ef0:  0000000000000000 0000000000000000
```

5. If we disassemble *foo* and *bar,* we see they call each other:

```
crash> dis foo 20
0xffff80007be440b8 <foo>:       mov     x9, x30
0xffff80007be440bc <foo+4>:     nop
0xffff80007be440c0 <foo+8>:     paciasp
0xffff80007be440c4 <foo+12>:    stp     x29, x30, [sp, #-32]!
0xffff80007be440c8 <foo+16>:    mov     x29, sp
0xffff80007be440cc <foo+20>:    stp     x19, x20, [sp, #16]
0xffff80007be440d0 <foo+24>:    mov     x20, x0
0xffff80007be440d4 <foo+28>:    bl      0xffff80007be44108 <bar>
0xffff80007be440d8 <foo+32>:    mov     x19, x0
0xffff80007be440dc <foo+36>:    add     x0, x20, #0x1
0xffff80007be440e0 <foo+40>:    bl      0xffff80007be44108 <bar>
0xffff80007be440e4 <foo+44>:    add     x0, x19, x0
0xffff80007be440e8 <foo+48>:    ldp     x19, x20, [sp, #16]
0xffff80007be440ec <foo+52>:    ldp     x29, x30, [sp], #32
0xffff80007be440f0 <foo+56>:    autiasp
0xffff80007be440f4 <foo+60>:    mov     x16, #0x0                       // #0
0xffff80007be440f8 <foo+64>:    mov     x17, #0x0                       // #0
0xffff80007be440fc <foo+68>:    ret
0xffff80007be44100 <foo+72>:    .inst   0x81634280 ; undefined
0xffff80007be44104 <foo+76>:    .inst   0xffff8000 ; undefined

crash> dis bar 20
0xffff80007be44108 <bar>:       mov     x9, x30
0xffff80007be4410c <bar+4>:     nop
0xffff80007be44110 <bar+8>:     paciasp
0xffff80007be44114 <bar+12>:    stp     x29, x30, [sp, #-32]!
0xffff80007be44118 <bar+16>:    mov     x29, sp
0xffff80007be4411c <bar+20>:    stp     x19, x20, [sp, #16]
0xffff80007be44120 <bar+24>:    mov     x20, x0
0xffff80007be44124 <bar+28>:    bl      0xffff80007be440b8 <foo>
0xffff80007be44128 <bar+32>:    mov     x19, x0
0xffff80007be4412c <bar+36>:    add     x0, x20, #0x1
0xffff80007be44130 <bar+40>:    bl      0xffff80007be440b8 <foo>
0xffff80007be44134 <bar+44>:    add     x0, x19, x0
0xffff80007be44138 <bar+48>:    ldp     x19, x20, [sp, #16]
0xffff80007be4413c <bar+52>:    ldp     x29, x30, [sp], #32
0xffff80007be44140 <bar+56>:    autiasp
0xffff80007be44144 <bar+60>:    mov     x16, #0x0                       // #0
0xffff80007be44148 <bar+64>:    mov     x17, #0x0                       // #0
0xffff80007be4414c <bar+68>:    ret
0xffff80007be44150 <bar+72>:    udf     #0
0xffff80007be44154 <bar+76>:    udf     #0
```

Exercise K5 (x64, WinDbg)

Goal: Learn how to identify kernel stack overflow and kernel stack boundaries.

Patterns: Stack Overflow (Kernel Mode); Debugger Bug.

1. Copy the *vmlinux-6.8.0-1018-azure* file in the x64/KSym directory to the *vmlinux* file.

2. Launch WinDbg. Load the core dump *202501051854.kdump* from the x64/K5 directory and set the symbol path to the x64/KSym directory (there may be some delay/unresponsiveness when you type the **.reload** command):

```
Microsoft (R) Windows Debugger Version 10.0.27725.1000 AMD64
Copyright (c) Microsoft Corporation. All rights reserved.


Loading Dump File [C:\ALCDA2\x64\K5\202501051854.kdump]
64-bit machine not using 64-bit API

************* Path validation summary **************
Response                         Time (ms)     Location
Deferred                                       srv*
Symbol search path is: srv*
Executable search path is:
Generic Unix Kernel Version 0 MP (4 procs) Free x64
Primary image base = 0xffffffff`a8c00000 Loaded module list = 0x00000000`00000000
System Uptime: not available
Loading Kernel Symbols

Loading User Symbols

ReadVirtual() failed in GetXStateConfiguration() first read attempt (error == 0.)
For analysis of this file, run !analyze -v
ffffffff`a8df1dc4 mov     qword ptr [rdi+80h],rax ds:fffffe71`f147adb0=ffffffffa8df1dc4

0: kd> .sympath C:\ALCDA2\x64\KSym\
Symbol search path is: C:\ALCDA2\x64\KSym\
Expanded Symbol search path is: c:\alcda2\x64\ksym\

************* Path validation summary **************
Response                         Time (ms)     Location
OK                                             C:\ALCDA2\x64\KSym\

0: kd> .reload
Loading Kernel Symbols
.*** WARNING: Unable to verify timestamp for vmlinux

Loading User Symbols


************* Symbol Loading Error Summary **************
Module name            Error
vmlinux                The system cannot find the file specified

You can troubleshoot most symbol related issues by turning on symbol loading diagnostics (!sym
noisy) and repeating the command that caused symbols to be loaded.
You should also verify that your symbol search path (.sympath) is correct.
```

3. We see the presence of the double fault and stack overflow processing in the stack trace:

```
0: kd> kL
 # Child-SP          RetAddr               Call Site
00 ffffe71`f147ad28 ffffffff`a8df1e46     vmlinux!crash_setup_regs+0x74
01 ffffe71`f147ad30 ffffffff`a8cddf29     vmlinux!__crash_kexec+0x66
02 ffffe71`f147adf0 ffffffff`a8c432c2 (T) vmlinux!panic+0x159
03 ffffe71`f147ae70 ffffffff`a8c43cd3     vmlinux!oops_end+0xdd
04 ffffe71`f147ae98 ffffffff`a8c3e9ee     vmlinux!die+0x83
05 ffffe71`f147aec8 ffffffff`a9cbb861     vmlinux!handle_stack_overflow+0x4e
06 ffffe71`f147aef8 ffffffff`a9e00caf     vmlinux!exc_double_fault+0x101
07 ffffe71`f147af58 00000000`00000000     vmlinux!asm_exc_double_fault+0x1f
```

Note: A different stack region is used for the overflow stack processing since there is no space in the original stack region.

4. We check the system log for the thread stack that experienced the stack overflow:

```
0: kd> !log
@$log()
    [0x0]           : [     0.000000] Linux version 6.8.0-1018-azure (buildd@lcy02-amd64-013) (x86_64-linux-gnu-gcc-11 (Ubuntu 11.4.0-1ubuntu1~22.04) 11.4.0, GNU ld (GNU Binutils for Ubuntu) 2.38) #21~22.04.1-Ubuntu SMP Fri Nov  8 00:21:25 UTC 2024 (Ubuntu 6.8.0-1018.21~22.04.1-azure 6.8.12)
    [0x1]           : [     0.000000] Command line: BOOT_IMAGE=/boot/vmlinuz-6.8.0-1018-azure root=UUID=89ee03ba-6808-4977-a4fb-9b10174744f8 ro quiet splash crashkernel=512M-:192M vt.handoff=7
...
...
...
   [0x232]          : [  2869.288516] BUG: TASK stack guard page was hit at 000000005f654585 (stack is 0000000074e03375..000000007988dffc)
    [0x233]         : [  2869.288527] stack guard page: 0000 [#1] SMP PTI
    [0x234]         : [  2869.288534] CPU: 0 PID: 2662 Comm: mod_d thread Kdump: loaded Tainted: G           OE      6.8.0-1018-azure #21~22.04.1-Ubuntu
    [0x235]         : [  2869.288537] Hardware name: Microsoft Corporation Virtual Machine/Virtual Machine, BIOS Hyper-V UEFI Release v4.1 05/13/2024
    [0x236]         : [  2869.288539] RIP: 0010:foo+0xf/0x30 [mod_d]
    [0x237]         : [  2869.288550] Code: 5d c3 cc cc cc cc 0f 1f 44 00 00 90 90 90 90 90 90 90 90 90 90 90 90 90 90 90 90 0f 1f 44 00 00 55 48 89 e5 41 54 53 48 89 fb <e8> 2c 00 00 00 48 8d 7b 01 49 89 c4 e8 20 00 00 00 5b 4c 01 e0 41
    [0x238]         : [  2869.288552] RSP: 0018:ffffac1e40174000 EFLAGS: 00010246
    [0x239]         : [  2869.288554] RAX: 0000000000000000 RBX: 0000000000000000 RCX: 0000000000000000
    [0x23a]         : [  2869.288556] RDX: 0000000000000000 RSI: 0000000000000286 RDI: 0000000000000000
    [0x23b]         : [  2869.288557] RBP: ffffac1e40174010 R08: 0000029c0eec1164 R09: 0000000000000000
    [0x23c]         : [  2869.288558] R10: 0000000000000001 R11: 0000000000000000 R12: ffff97e5c08c2a80
    [0x23d]         : [  2869.288559] R13: ffffac1e47b7b868 R14: ffff97e5c092ee80 R15: ffffffffc090a010
    [0x23e]         : [  2869.288562] FS:  0000000000000000(0000) GS:ffff97e5c3c00000(0000) knlGS:0000000000000000
    [0x23f]         : [  2869.288564] CS:  0010 DS: 0000 ES: 0000 CR0: 0000000080050033
    [0x240]         : [  2869.288565] CR2: ffffac1e40173ff8 CR3: 000000003d222006 CR4: 00000000003706f0
    [0x241]         : [  2869.288567] DR0: 0000000000000000 DR1: 0000000000000000 DR2: 0000000000000000
    [0x242]         : [  2869.288568] DR3: 0000000000000000 DR6: 00000000fffe0ff0 DR7: 0000000000000400
    [0x243]         : [  2869.288569] Call Trace:
    [0x244]         : [  2869.288570]  <#DF>
    [0x245]         : [  2869.288573]  ? show_regs+0x6a/0x80
    [0x246]         : [  2869.288579]  ? die+0x38/0xa0
    [0x247]         : [  2869.288582]  ? handle_stack_overflow+0x4e/0x60
    [0x248]         : [  2869.288585]  ? exc_double_fault+0x101/0x190
    [0x249]         : [  2869.288589]  ? asm_exc_double_fault+0x1f/0x30
    [0x24a]         : [  2869.288594]  ? __pfx_kthread_f+0x10/0x10 [mod_d]
    [0x24b]         : [  2869.288600]  ? foo+0xf/0x30 [mod_d]
    [0x24c]         : [  2869.288604]  </#DF>
    [0x24d]         : [  2869.288605]  <TASK>
    [0x24e]         : [  2869.288606]  bar+0x14/0xf20 [mod_d]
    [0x24f]         : [  2869.288610]  foo+0x14/0x30 [mod_d]
    [0x250]         : [  2869.288614]  bar+0x14/0xf20 [mod_d]
    [0x251]         : [  2869.288618]  foo+0x14/0x30 [mod_d]
    [0x252]         : [  2869.288623]  bar+0x14/0xf20 [mod_d]
    [0x253]         : [  2869.288627]  foo+0x14/0x30 [mod_d]
    [0x254]         : [  2869.288631]  bar+0x14/0xf20 [mod_d]
```

```
[0x255]         : [  2869.288635]  foo+0x14/0x30 [mod_d]
[0x256]         : [  2869.288639]  bar+0x14/0xf20 [mod_d]
[0x257]         : [  2869.288643]  foo+0x14/0x30 [mod_d]
[...]
```

Note: We see that RSP reached stack region limit **0xffffac1e40174000**.

5. We can continue expanding the log and see the bottom of the stack trace:

```
...
...
...
    [0x439]         : [  2869.290715]  foo+0x14/0x30 [mod_d]
    [0x43a]         : [  2869.290719]  bar+0x14/0xf20 [mod_d]
    [0x43b]         : [  2869.290723]  foo+0x14/0x30 [mod_d]
    [0x43c]         : [  2869.290727]  bar+0x14/0xf20 [mod_d]
    [0x43d]         : [  2869.290731]  foo+0x14/0x30 [mod_d]
    [0x43e]         : [  2869.290736]  bar+0x14/0xf20 [mod_d]
    [0x43f]         : [  2869.290740]  foo+0x14/0x30 [mod_d]
    [0x440]         : [  2869.290744]  bar+0x14/0xf20 [mod_d]
    [0x441]         : [  2869.290748]  foo+0x14/0x30 [mod_d]
    [0x442]         : [  2869.290752]  bar+0x14/0xf20 [mod_d]
    [0x443]         : [  2869.290756]  foo+0x14/0x30 [mod_d]
    [0x444]         : [  2869.290761]  kthread_f+0x1a/0x30 [mod_d]
    [0x445]         : [  2869.290765]  kthread+0xd3/0x100
    [0x446]         : [  2869.290769]  ? __pfx_kthread+0x10/0x10
    [0x447]         : [  2869.290771]  ret_from_fork+0x39/0x60
    [0x448]         : [  2869.290775]  ? __pfx_kthread+0x10/0x10
    [0x449]         : [  2869.290776]  ret_from_fork_asm+0x1b/0x30
    [0x44a]         : [  2869.290780]  </TASK>
...
...
...
```

Exercise K5 (A64, WinDbg)

Goal: Learn how to identify kernel stack overflow and kernel stack boundaries.

Patterns: Stack Overflow (Kernel Mode); Debugger Bug.

1. Copy the *vmlinux-6.8.0-1018-oracle* file in the A64/KSym directory to the *vmlinux* file.

2. Launch WinDbg. Load the core dump *202501051903.kdump* from the A64/K5 directory and set the symbol path to the A64/KSym directory (there may be some delay/unresponsiveness when you type the **.reload** command):

```
Microsoft (R) Windows Debugger Version 10.0.27725.1000 AMD64
Copyright (c) Microsoft Corporation. All rights reserved.


Loading Dump File [C:\ALCDA2\A64\K5\202501051903.kdump]
64-bit machine not using 64-bit API

************* Path validation summary **************
Response                         Time (ms)     Location
OK                                             C:\ALCDA2\x64\KSym\
Symbol search path is: C:\ALCDA2\x64\KSym\
Executable search path is:
Generic Unix Kernel Version 0 MP (2 procs) Free ARM 64-bit (AArch64)
Primary image base = 0xffff8000`80010000 Loaded module list = 0x00000000`00000000
System Uptime: not available
Loading Kernel Symbols

Loading User Symbols

For analysis of this file, run !analyze -v
ffff8000`815e0b1c ldp         fp,lr,[sp],#0x20

0: kd> .sympath C:\ALCDA2\A64\KSym\
Symbol search path is: C:\ALCDA2\A64\KSym\
Expanded Symbol search path is: c:\alcda2\a64\ksym\

************* Path validation summary **************
Response                         Time (ms)     Location
OK                                             C:\ALCDA2\A64\KSym\

0: kd> .reload
Loading Kernel Symbols
.*** WARNING: Unable to verify timestamp for vmlinux

Loading User Symbols


************* Symbol Loading Error Summary **************
Module name            Error
vmlinux                The system cannot find the file specified

You can troubleshoot most symbol related issues by turning on symbol loading diagnostics (!sym
noisy) and repeating the command that caused symbols to be loaded.
You should also verify that your symbol search path (.sympath) is correct.
```

3. We see the presence of bad stack processing in the stack trace on CPU 1:

```
0: kd> !runq
@$runq()
    [0x0]              : CPU 0 run queue [current = 'swapper/0' (0)]
        Cpu              : 0x0
        RunQueue         [Type: rq]
        CurrentTask      : swapper/0 [Type: task_struct]
        RTTasks
        CfsTasks
    [0x1]              : CPU 1 run queue [current = 'mod_d thread' (7a3)]
        Cpu              : 0x1
        RunQueue         [Type: rq]
        CurrentTask      : mod_d thread [Type: task_struct]
        RTTasks
        CfsTasks

0: kd> ~1s
WARNING: Unable to reset page directories

1: kd> kL
 # Child-SP          RetAddr               Call Site
00 ffff0002`fe7a5ee0 ffff8000`8020b5f0     vmlinux!crash_setup_regs+0xa0
01 ffff0002`fe7a5ee0 ffff8000`800c83e0     vmlinux!__crash_kexec+0x60
02 ffff0002`fe7a6060 ffff8000`800c8508     vmlinux!panic+0x350
03 ffff0002`fe7a6140 ffff8000`800276cc     vmlinux!nmi_panic+0x50
04 ffff0002`fe7a6150 ffff8000`815de3c4 (T) vmlinux!panic_bad_stack+0xec
05 ffff0002`fe7a6190 ffff8000`80011090     vmlinux!handle_bad_stack+0x30
06 ffff0002`fe7a61c0 00000000`00000000     vmlinux!_bad_stack+0x90
```

Note: A different stack region is used for the bad stack processing since there is no space in the original stack region.

4. We check the system log for the thread stack that experienced the stack overflow:

```
0: kd> !log
@$log()
    [0x0]            : [    0.000000] Booting Linux on physical CPU 0x0000000000 [0x413fd0c1]
    [0x1]            : [    0.000000] Linux version 6.8.0-1018-oracle (buildd@bos03-arm64-112) (aarch64-linux-gnu-
gcc-11 (Ubuntu 11.4.0-1ubuntu1~22.04) 11.4.0, GNU ld (GNU Binutils for Ubuntu) 2.38) #19~22.04.1-Ubuntu SMP Mon Dec  9
23:49:53 UTC 2024 (Ubuntu 6.8.0-1018.19~22.04.1-oracle 6.8.12)
...
...
...
    [0x3e3]          : [ 1749.735686] Insufficient stack space to handle exception!
    [0x3e4]          : [ 1749.735690] ESR: 0x0000000096000047 -- DABT (current EL)
    [0x3e5]          : [ 1749.735693] FAR: 0xffff800085c0ffe0
    [0x3e6]          : [ 1749.735695] Task stack:     [0xffff800085c10000..0xffff800085c14000]
    [0x3e7]          : [ 1749.735696] IRQ stack:      [0xffff800080008000..0xffff80008000c000]
    [...]
1: kd> dx -r1  -c 1000 @$log()
@$log()
    [0x3e8]          : [ 1749.735698] Overflow stack: [0xffff0002fe7a5310..0xffff0002fe7a6310]
    [0x3e9]          : [ 1749.735701] CPU: 1 PID: 1955 Comm: mod_d thread Kdump: loaded Tainted: G           OE
6.8.0-1018-oracle #19~22.04.1-Ubuntu
    [0x3ea]          : [ 1749.735706] Hardware name: QEMU KVM Virtual Machine, BIOS 1.6.6 08/22/2023
    [0x3eb]          : [ 1749.735707] pstate: 60400005 (nZCv daif +PAN -UAO -TCO -DIT -SSBS BTYPE=--)
    [0x3ec]          : [ 1749.735711] pc : bar+0xc/0xef8 [mod_d]
    [0x3ed]          : [ 1749.735720] lr : foo+0x20/0x50 [mod_d]
    [0x3ee]          : [ 1749.735723] sp : ffff800085c10000
    [0x3ef]          : [ 1749.735724] x29: ffff800085c10000 x28: 0000000000000000 x27: 0000000000000000
    [0x3f0]          : [ 1749.735729] x26: 0000000000000000 x25: 0000000000000000 x24: 0000000000000000
    [0x3f1]          : [ 1749.735733] x23: ffff80007be44008 x22: ffff0000c71da200 x21: ffff800085a8b718
    [0x3f2]          : [ 1749.735736] x20: 0000000000000000 x19: ffff0000c01b97c0 x18: 0000000000000000
    [0x3f3]          : [ 1749.735740] x17: 0000000000000000 x16: 0000000000000000 x15: 0000000000000000
```

```
[0x3f4]        : [  1749.735743] x14: 0000000000000000 x13: 0000000000000000 x12: 0000000000000000
[0x3f5]        : [  1749.735746] x11: 0000000000000000 x10: 0000000000001b70 x9 : ffff80007be440d8
[0x3f6]        : [  1749.735750] x8 : ffff0000c71dbdd0 x7 : 0000000000000000 x6 : 0000000000000000
[0x3f7]        : [  1749.735753] x5 : 0000000000000000 x4 : 0000000000000000 x3 : 0000000000000000
[0x3f8]        : [  1749.735756] x2 : 0000000000000000 x1 : 0000000000000000 x0 : 0000000000000000
[0x3f9]        : [  1749.735761] Kernel panic - not syncing: kernel stack overflow
[0x3fa]        : [  1749.735763] CPU: 1 PID: 1955 Comm: mod_d thread Kdump: loaded Tainted: G           OE
6.8.0-1018-oracle #19~22.04.1-Ubuntu
[0x3fb]        : [  1749.735766] Hardware name: QEMU KVM Virtual Machine, BIOS 1.6.6 08/22/2023
[0x3fc]        : [  1749.735768] Call trace:
[0x3fd]        : [  1749.735770]  dump_backtrace+0xa0/0x148
[0x3fe]        : [  1749.735775]  show_stack+0x20/0x48
[0x3ff]        : [  1749.735778]  dump_stack_lvl+0x38/0x130
[0x400]        : [  1749.735783]  dump_stack+0x18/0x30
[0x401]        : [  1749.735785]  panic+0x3a4/0x428
[0x402]        : [  1749.735790]  nmi_panic+0x50/0xc8
[0x403]        : [  1749.735794]  panic_bad_stack+0xec/0x108
[0x404]        : [  1749.735797]  handle_bad_stack+0x34/0x38
[0x405]        : [  1749.735802]  __bad_stack+0x90/0x98
[0x406]        : [  1749.735805]  bar+0xc/0xef8 [mod_d]
[0x407]        : [  1749.735807]  bar+0x20/0xef8 [mod_d]
[0x408]        : [  1749.735809]  foo+0x20/0x50 [mod_d]
[0x409]        : [  1749.735812]  bar+0x20/0xef8 [mod_d]
[0x40a]        : [  1749.735814]  foo+0x20/0x50 [mod_d]
[0x40b]        : [  1749.735816]  bar+0x20/0xef8 [mod_d]
[0x40c]        : [  1749.735818]  foo+0x20/0x50 [mod_d]
[0x40d]        : [  1749.735821]  bar+0x20/0xef8 [mod_d]
[0x40e]        : [  1749.735823]  foo+0x20/0x50 [mod_d]
[0x40f]        : [  1749.735825]  bar+0x20/0xef8 [mod_d]
[0x410]        : [  1749.735827]  foo+0x20/0x50 [mod_d]
[0x411]        : [  1749.735829]  bar+0x20/0xef8 [mod_d]
[0x412]        : [  1749.735831]  foo+0x20/0x50 [mod_d]
[0x413]        : [  1749.735833]  bar+0x20/0xef8 [mod_d]
[0x414]        : [  1749.735836]  foo+0x20/0x50 [mod_d]
[0x415]        : [  1749.735838]  bar+0x20/0xef8 [mod_d]
[0x416]        : [  1749.735840]  foo+0x20/0x50 [mod_d]
[0x417]        : [  1749.735842]  bar+0x20/0xef8 [mod_d]
[0x418]        : [  1749.735844]  foo+0x20/0x50 [mod_d]
[0x419]        : [  1749.735846]  bar+0x20/0xef8 [mod_d]
[0x41a]        : [  1749.735848]  foo+0x20/0x50 [mod_d]
[0x41b]        : [  1749.735851]  bar+0x20/0xef8 [mod_d]
[0x41c]        : [  1749.735853]  foo+0x20/0x50 [mod_d]
[0x41d]        : [  1749.735855]  bar+0x20/0xef8 [mod_d]
[0x41e]        : [  1749.735857]  foo+0x20/0x50 [mod_d]
[0x41f]        : [  1749.735859]  bar+0x20/0xef8 [mod_d]
[0x420]        : [  1749.735861]  foo+0x20/0x50 [mod_d]
[0x421]        : [  1749.735863]  bar+0x20/0xef8 [mod_d]
[0x422]        : [  1749.735866]  foo+0x20/0x50 [mod_d]
[0x423]        : [  1749.735868]  bar+0x20/0xef8 [mod_d]
[0x424]        : [  1749.735870]  foo+0x20/0x50 [mod_d]
[0x425]        : [  1749.735872]  bar+0x20/0xef8 [mod_d]
[0x426]        : [  1749.735874]  foo+0x20/0x50 [mod_d]
[0x427]        : [  1749.735876]  bar+0x20/0xef8 [mod_d]
[0x428]        : [  1749.735878]  foo+0x20/0x50 [mod_d]
[0x429]        : [  1749.735881]  bar+0x20/0xef8 [mod_d]
[0x42a]        : [  1749.735883]  foo+0x20/0x50 [mod_d]
[0x42b]        : [  1749.735885]  bar+0x20/0xef8 [mod_d]
[0x42c]        : [  1749.735887]  foo+0x20/0x50 [mod_d]
[0x42d]        : [  1749.735889]  bar+0x20/0xef8 [mod_d]
[0x42e]        : [  1749.735891]  foo+0x20/0x50 [mod_d]
[0x42f]        : [  1749.735893]  bar+0x20/0xef8 [mod_d]
[0x430]        : [  1749.735896]  foo+0x20/0x50 [mod_d]
[0x431]        : [  1749.735898]  bar+0x20/0xef8 [mod_d]
[0x432]        : [  1749.735900]  foo+0x20/0x50 [mod_d]
[0x433]        : [  1749.735902]  bar+0x20/0xef8 [mod_d]
[0x434]        : [  1749.735904]  foo+0x20/0x50 [mod_d]
[0x435]        : [  1749.735907]  bar+0x20/0xef8 [mod_d]
[0x436]        : [  1749.735909]  foo+0x20/0x50 [mod_d]
[0x437]        : [  1749.735911]  bar+0x20/0xef8 [mod_d]
[0x438]        : [  1749.735913]  foo+0x20/0x50 [mod_d]
[0x439]        : [  1749.735915]  bar+0x20/0xef8 [mod_d]
[0x43a]        : [  1749.735917]  foo+0x20/0x50 [mod_d]
[0x43b]        : [  1749.735919]  bar+0x20/0xef8 [mod_d]
[0x43c]        : [  1749.735921]  foo+0x20/0x50 [mod_d]
[0x43d]        : [  1749.735924]  bar+0x20/0xef8 [mod_d]
[0x43e]        : [  1749.735926]  foo+0x20/0x50 [mod_d]
```

```
    [0x43f]          : [  1749.735928] bar+0x20/0xef8 [mod_d]
    [0x440]          : [  1749.735930] foo+0x20/0x50 [mod_d]
    [0x441]          : [  1749.735932] bar+0x20/0xef8 [mod_d]
    [0x442]          : [  1749.735934] foo+0x20/0x50 [mod_d]
    [0x443]          : [  1749.735936] bar+0x20/0xef8 [mod_d]
    [0x444]          : [  1749.735939] foo+0x20/0x50 [mod_d]
    [0x445]          : [  1749.735941] bar+0x20/0xef8 [mod_d]
    [0x446]          : [  1749.735943] foo+0x20/0x50 [mod_d]
    [0x447]          : [  1749.735945] bar+0x20/0xef8 [mod_d]
    [0x448]          : [  1749.735947] foo+0x20/0x50 [mod_d]
    [0x449]          : [  1749.735949] bar+0x20/0xef8 [mod_d]
    [0x44a]          : [  1749.735952] foo+0x20/0x50 [mod_d]
    [0x44b]          : [  1749.735954] bar+0x20/0xef8 [mod_d]
    [...]
...
...
...
    [0x5f1]          : [  1749.736473] bar+0x20/0xef8 [mod_d]
    [0x5f2]          : [  1749.736474] foo+0x20/0x50 [mod_d]
    [0x5f3]          : [  1749.736475] bar+0x20/0xef8 [mod_d]
    [0x5f4]          : [  1749.736476] foo+0x20/0x50 [mod_d]
    [0x5f5]          : [  1749.736477] bar+0x20/0xef8 [mod_d]
    [0x5f6]          : [  1749.736478] foo+0x20/0x50 [mod_d]
    [0x5f7]          : [  1749.736479] bar+0x20/0xef8 [mod_d]
    [0x5f8]          : [  1749.736481] foo+0x20/0x50 [mod_d]
    [0x5f9]          : [  1749.736482] kthread_f+0x24/0x48 [mod_d]
    [0x5fa]          : [  1749.736483] kthread+0xe0/0xf0
    [0x5fb]          : [  1749.736485] ret_from_fork+0x10/0x20
    [0x5fc]          : [  1749.736488] SMP: stopping secondary CPUs
    [0x5fd]          : [  1749.736516] Kernel Offset: disabled
    [0x5fe]          : [  1749.736517] CPU features: 0x1,00000020,7002014a,2101720b
    [0x5ff]          : [  1749.736519] Memory Limit: none
    [0x600]          : [  1787.499252] Starting crashdump kernel...
```

Note: We see that RSP reached stack region limit **0xffff800085c10000**. We also see the base of the stack region: 0xffff800085c14000.

5. To get recursive function call addresses, we dump the execution residue from the limit address and below the base address:

```
1: kd> dps 0xffff800085c10000 L20
ffff8000`85c10000  ffff8000`85c10020
ffff8000`85c10008  ffff8000`7be44128 mod_d+0x128
ffff8000`85c10010  ffff0000`c01b97c0
ffff8000`85c10018  00000000`00000000
ffff8000`85c10020  ffff8000`85c10040
ffff8000`85c10028  ffff8000`7be440d8 mod_d+0xd8
ffff8000`85c10030  ffff0000`c01b97c0
ffff8000`85c10038  00000000`00000000
ffff8000`85c10040  ffff8000`85c10060
ffff8000`85c10048  ffff8000`7be44128 mod_d+0x128
ffff8000`85c10050  ffff0000`c01b97c0
ffff8000`85c10058  00000000`00000000
ffff8000`85c10060  ffff8000`85c10080
ffff8000`85c10068  ffff8000`7be440d8 mod_d+0xd8
ffff8000`85c10070  ffff0000`c01b97c0
ffff8000`85c10078  00000000`00000000
ffff8000`85c10080  ffff8000`85c100a0
ffff8000`85c10088  ffff8000`7be44128 mod_d+0x128
ffff8000`85c10090  ffff0000`c01b97c0
ffff8000`85c10098  00000000`00000000
ffff8000`85c100a0  ffff8000`85c100c0
ffff8000`85c100a8  ffff8000`7be440d8 mod_d+0xd8
ffff8000`85c100b0  ffff0000`c01b97c0
ffff8000`85c100b8  00000000`00000000
```

```
ffff8000`85c100c0  ffff8000`85c100e0
ffff8000`85c100c8  ffff8000`7be44128 mod_d+0x128
ffff8000`85c100d0  ffff0000`c01b97c0
ffff8000`85c100d8  00000000`00000000
ffff8000`85c100e0  ffff8000`85c10100
ffff8000`85c100e8  ffff8000`7be440d8 mod_d+0xd8
ffff8000`85c100f0  ffff0000`c01b97c0
ffff8000`85c100f8  00000000`00000000

1: kd> dps 0xffff800085c14000-300 L40
ffff8000`85c13d00  ffff8000`85c13d20
ffff8000`85c13d08  ffff8000`7be44128 mod_d+0x128
ffff8000`85c13d10  ffff0000`c01b97c0
ffff8000`85c13d18  00000000`00000000
ffff8000`85c13d20  ffff8000`85c13d40
ffff8000`85c13d28  ffff8000`7be440d8 mod_d+0xd8
ffff8000`85c13d30  ffff0000`c01b97c0
ffff8000`85c13d38  00000000`00000000
ffff8000`85c13d40  ffff8000`85c13d60
ffff8000`85c13d48  ffff8000`7be44128 mod_d+0x128
ffff8000`85c13d50  ffff0000`c01b97c0
ffff8000`85c13d58  00000000`00000000
ffff8000`85c13d60  ffff8000`85c13d80
ffff8000`85c13d68  ffff8000`7be440d8 mod_d+0xd8
ffff8000`85c13d70  ffff0000`c01b97c0
ffff8000`85c13d78  00000000`00000000
ffff8000`85c13d80  ffff8000`85c13da0
ffff8000`85c13d88  ffff8000`7be44128 mod_d+0x128
ffff8000`85c13d90  ffff0000`c01b97c0
ffff8000`85c13d98  00000000`00000000
ffff8000`85c13da0  ffff8000`85c13dc0
ffff8000`85c13da8  ffff8000`7be440d8 mod_d+0xd8
ffff8000`85c13db0  ffff0000`c01b97c0
ffff8000`85c13db8  00000000`00000000
ffff8000`85c13dc0  ffff8000`85c13de0
ffff8000`85c13dc8  ffff8000`7be44128 mod_d+0x128
ffff8000`85c13dd0  ffff0000`c01b97c0
ffff8000`85c13dd8  00000000`00000000
ffff8000`85c13de0  ffff8000`85c13e00
ffff8000`85c13de8  ffff8000`7be440d8 mod_d+0xd8
ffff8000`85c13df0  ffff0000`c01b97c0
ffff8000`85c13df8  00000000`00000000
ffff8000`85c13e00  ffff8000`85c13e20
ffff8000`85c13e08  ffff8000`7be44128 mod_d+0x128
ffff8000`85c13e10  ffff0000`c01b97c0
ffff8000`85c13e18  00000000`00000000
ffff8000`85c13e20  ffff8000`85c13e40
ffff8000`85c13e28  ffff8000`7be440d8 mod_d+0xd8
ffff8000`85c13e30  ffff0000`c01b97c0
ffff8000`85c13e38  00000000`00000000
ffff8000`85c13e40  ffff8000`85c13e60
ffff8000`85c13e48  ffff8000`7be4402c mod_d+0x2c
ffff8000`85c13e50  ffff0000`c01b97c0
ffff8000`85c13e58  ffff0000`c5779d00
ffff8000`85c13e60  ffff8000`85c13e70
ffff8000`85c13e68  ffff8000`80107f30 vmlinux!kthread+0xe0 [/build/linux-oracle-6.8-EzVzJ2/linux-oracle-6.8-6.8.0/kernel/kthread.c @ 388]
ffff8000`85c13e70  ffff8000`85c13fe0
ffff8000`85c13e78  ffff8000`80017430 vmlinux!ret_from_fork+0x10 [/build/linux-oracle-6.8-EzVzJ2/linux-oracle-6.8-6.8.0/arch/arm64/kernel/entry.S @ 861]
```

```
ffff8000`85c13e80  ffff8000`80107e50 vmlinux!kthread [/build/linux-oracle-6.8-EzVzJ2/linux-oracle-6.8-6.8.0/kernel/kthread.c @ 341]
ffff8000`85c13e88  ffff0000`c01b97c0
ffff8000`85c13e90  00000000`00000000
ffff8000`85c13e98  00000000`00000000
ffff8000`85c13ea0  00000000`00000000
ffff8000`85c13ea8  00000000`00000000
ffff8000`85c13eb0  00000000`00000000
ffff8000`85c13eb8  00000000`00000000
ffff8000`85c13ec0  00000000`00000000
ffff8000`85c13ec8  00000000`00000000
ffff8000`85c13ed0  00000000`00000000
ffff8000`85c13ed8  00000000`00000000
ffff8000`85c13ee0  00000000`00000000
ffff8000`85c13ee8  00000000`00000000
ffff8000`85c13ef0  00000000`00000000
ffff8000`85c13ef8  00000000`00000000
```

6. If we disassemble mod_d+0xd8 and mod_d+0x128, we see two code fragments call each other:

```
1: kd> ub mod_d+0xd8
mod_d+0xb8:
ffff8000`7be440b8 mov         x9,lr
ffff8000`7be440bc nop
ffff8000`7be440c0 paciasp
ffff8000`7be440c4 stp         fp,lr,[sp,#-0x20]!
ffff8000`7be440c8 mov         fp,sp
ffff8000`7be440cc stp         x19,x20,[sp,#0x10]
ffff8000`7be440d0 mov         x20,x0
ffff8000`7be440d4 bl          mod_d+0x108 (ffff8000`7be44108)
```

```
1: kd> ub mod_d+0x128
mod_d+0x108:
ffff8000`7be44108 mov         x9,lr
ffff8000`7be4410c nop
ffff8000`7be44110 paciasp
ffff8000`7be44114 stp         fp,lr,[sp,#-0x20]!
ffff8000`7be44118 mov         fp,sp
ffff8000`7be4411c stp         x19,x20,[sp,#0x10]
ffff8000`7be44120 mov         x20,x0
ffff8000`7be44124 bl          mod_d+0xb8 (ffff8000`7be440b8)
```

Follow-up Courses

Advanced Linux Core Dump Analysis with Data Structures

Accelerated Linux Disassembly, Reconstruction, and Reversing

Accelerated Linux Debugging^4

Accelerated Linux API for Software Diagnostics

Accelerated C & C++ for Linux Diagnostics

Advanced Linux Core Dump Analysis with Data Structures
https://www.patterndiagnostics.com/advanced-linux-core-dump-analysis

Accelerated Linux Disassembly, Reconstruction, and Reversing
https://www.patterndiagnostics.com/accelerated-linux-disassembly-reconstruction-reversing-book

Accelerated Linux Debugging^4
https://www.patterndiagnostics.com/accelerated-linux-debugging-4d

Accelerated Linux API for Software Diagnostics
https://www.patterndiagnostics.com/accelerated-linux-api-book

Accelerated C & C++ for Linux Diagnostics
https://www.patterndiagnostics.com/accelerated-c-cpp-linux-diagnostics

Rust Core Dump Analysis

Memory Thinking for Rust

Accelerated Rust Linux Core Dump Analysis

Memory Thinking for Rust
https://www.patterndiagnostics.com/memory-thinking-rust

Accelerated Rust Linux Core Dump Analysis
https://www.patterndiagnostics.com/accelerated-rust-linux-core-dump-analysis

Python Core Dump Analysis

Python Debugging for AI, Machine Learning, and Cloud Computing
https://link.springer.com/book/10.1007/978-1-4842-9745-2

Educative Courses

Debugging, Disassembly & Reversing in Linux for x64 Architecture

Foundations of Linux ARM64: Debug, Disassemble, and Reverse

Accelerated Linux Core Dump Analysis

Debugging, Disassembly & Reversing in Linux for x64 Architecture
https://www.educative.io/courses/guide-learning-software-trace-log-analysis-patterns

Foundations of Linux ARM64: Debug, Disassemble, and Reverse
https://www.educative.io/courses/foundations-of-linux-arm64-debug-disassemble-and-reverse

Accelerated Linux Core Dump Analysis
https://www.educative.io/courses/accelerated-linux-core-dump-analysis

Pattern Links (Linux and GDB)

Active Thread
C++ Exception
Critical Region
Divide by Zero
Execution Residue
High Contention
Memory Leak
Local Buffer Overflow
Module Hint
Not My Version
NULL Pointer (Data)
Self-Diagnosis
Stack Overflow (User Mode)
Stack Trace Collection
Regular Data
Near Exception
Invalid Pointer
Past Stack Trace
Exception Stack Trace
Value References
Hidden Call
Interrupt Stack
Truncated Stack Trace
Disassembly Ambiguity
Wild Pointer
Debugger Bug

Annotated Disassembly
Coincidental Symbolic Information
Deadlock (Mutex Objects, User Space)
Environment Hint
Handled Exception
Dynamic Memory Corruption
Lateral Damage
Manual Dump (Process) / (Kernel)
Module Variable
NULL Pointer (Code)
Paratext
Spiking Thread
Stack Trace
Wait Chain (General)
Multiple Exceptions
Wait Chain (Mutex Objects)
Disassembly Hole
Deadlock (Mutex Objects, Kernel Space)
Origin Module
Stack Trace Collection (CPUs)
Stack Overflow (Kernel Mode)
Unrecognizable Symbolic Information
Crash Signature
Well-Tested Function
Historical Information
Exception Module

Here is the link to pattern descriptions and additional GDB examples:

http://www.dumpanalysis.org/blog/index.php/category/core-dump-analysis/

Selected pattern descriptions are provided at the end of this book.

Resources

- DumpAnalysis.org / SoftwareDiagnostics.Institute / PatternDiagnostics.com
- Debugging.TV / YouTube.com/DebuggingTV / YouTube.com/PatternDiagnostics
- Rosetta Stone for Debuggers
- Accelerated macOS Core Dump Analysis (also covers LLDB)
- GDB Pocket Reference
- GDB
- Intel® 64 and IA-32 Architectures Software Developer Manuals
- A64 Instruction Set Architecture
- A64 Base Instructions
- Encyclopedia of Crash Dump Analysis Patterns, Third Edition
- Memory Dump Analysis Anthology (Diagnomicon) (some articles in volumes 1, 7, 9A cover GDB)

WinDbg quick links
http://WinDbg.org

Software Diagnostics Institute
https://www.dumpanalysis.org

Debugging.TV
http://debugging.tv

Pattern Diagnostics Seminars
https://www.youtube.com/PatternDiagnostics

Software Diagnostics Services
https://www.patterndiagnostics.com

Encyclopedia of Crash Dump Analysis Patterns, 3rd edition
https://www.patterndiagnostics.com/encyclopedia-crash-dump-analysis-patterns

Memory Dump Analysis Anthology
https://www.patterndiagnostics.com/ultimate-memory-analysis-reference

Rosetta Stone for Debuggers
https://www.dumpanalysis.org/rosetta-stone-debuggers

Accelerated macOS Core Dump Analysis
https://www.patterndiagnostics.com/accelerated-macosx-core-dump-analysis-book

GDB
https://www.sourceware.org/gdb/

Intel® 64 and IA-32 Architectures Software Developer Manuals
https://www.intel.com/content/www/us/en/developer/articles/technical/intel-sdm.html

A64 Instruction Set Architecture
https://developer.arm.com/documentation/102374/latest/

A64 Base Instructions
https://developer.arm.com/documentation/ddi0596/2021-12/Base-Instructions?lang=en

Selected Q&A

Q. What is **anon** in the *pmap* output?

A. This is anonymous memory that doesn't have filesystem backing. For example, memory allocated by *malloc* and thread stacks is **anon**.

Q. What does 'at' mean in the **maintenance info sections** command output?

A. This might be related to section descriptions in object files. These numbers can be safely ignored in our analysis exercises. For further information, please see Binary File Descriptor library: https://en.wikipedia.org/wiki/Binary_File_Descriptor_library

Q. If we don't have the *pmap* output as an input for debugging, is there any method or sequence to know the *.data* region from the **maintenance info sections** command?

A. The output of the command contains the range of the *.data* section in the **Exec file** portion.

Q. Can we dump C/C++ code together with disassembly?

A. Yes, we can specify the **/s** option if symbols are available:

```
(gdb) disassemble /s main
Dump of assembler code for function main:
main.c:
64      {
   0x0000000000400888 <+0>:     stp     x29, x30, [sp, #-48]!
   0x000000000040088c <+4>:     mov     x29, sp
   0x0000000000400890 <+8>:     str     w0, [sp, #28]
   0x0000000000400894 <+12>:    str     x1, [sp, #16]
   0x0000000000400898 <+16>:    adrp    x0, 0x49c000 <tunable_list+1312>
   0x000000000040089c <+20>:    ldr     x0, [x0, #3024]
   0x00000000004008a0 <+24>:    ldr     x1, [x0]
   0x00000000004008a4 <+28>:    str     x1, [sp, #40]
   0x00000000004008a8 <+32>:    mov     x1, #0x0                        // #0

65              THREAD_CREATE(one)
   0x00000000004008ac <+36>:    add     x4, sp, #0x20
   0x00000000004008b0 <+40>:    mov     x3, #0x0                        // #0
   0x00000000004008b4 <+44>:    adrp    x0, 0x400000
   0x00000000004008b8 <+48>:    add     x2, x0, #0x754
   0x00000000004008bc <+52>:    mov     x1, #0x0                        // #0
   0x00000000004008c0 <+56>:    mov     x0, x4
   0x00000000004008c4 <+60>:    bl      0x40ee00 <pthread_create>

66              THREAD_CREATE(two)
   0x00000000004008c8 <+64>:    add     x4, sp, #0x20
   0x00000000004008cc <+68>:    mov     x3, #0x0                        // #0
   0x00000000004008d0 <+72>:    adrp    x0, 0x400000
   0x00000000004008d4 <+76>:    add     x2, x0, #0x798
   0x00000000004008d8 <+80>:    mov     x1, #0x0                        // #0
   0x00000000004008dc <+84>:    mov     x0, x4
   0x00000000004008e0 <+88>:    bl      0x40ee00 <pthread_create>

67              THREAD_CREATE(three)
   0x00000000004008e4 <+92>:    add     x4, sp, #0x20
   0x00000000004008e8 <+96>:    mov     x3, #0x0                        // #0
   0x00000000004008ec <+100>:   adrp    x0, 0x400000
   0x00000000004008f0 <+104>:   add     x2, x0, #0x7e0
```

```
   0x00000000004008f4 <+108>:   mov     x1, #0x0                        // #0
   0x00000000004008f8 <+112>:   mov     x0, x4
   0x00000000004008fc <+116>:   bl      0x40ee00 <pthread_create>

68          THREAD_CREATE(four)
   0x0000000000400900 <+120>:   add     x4, sp, #0x20
--Type <RET> for more, q to quit, c to continue without paging--
   0x0000000000400904 <+124>:   mov     x3, #0x0                        // #0
   0x0000000000400908 <+128>:   adrp    x0, 0x400000
   0x000000000040090c <+132>:   add     x2, x0, #0x824
   0x0000000000400910 <+136>:   mov     x1, #0x0                        // #0
   0x0000000000400914 <+140>:   mov     x0, x4
   0x0000000000400918 <+144>:   bl      0x40ee00 <pthread_create>

69          THREAD_CREATE(five)
   0x000000000040091c <+148>:   add     x4, sp, #0x20
   0x0000000000400920 <+152>:   mov     x3, #0x0                        // #0
   0x0000000000400924 <+156>:   adrp    x0, 0x400000
   0x0000000000400928 <+160>:   add     x2, x0, #0x86c
   0x000000000040092c <+164>:   mov     x1, #0x0                        // #0
   0x0000000000400930 <+168>:   mov     x0, x4
   0x0000000000400934 <+172>:   bl      0x40ee00 <pthread_create>

70
71          sleep(3);
   0x0000000000400938 <+176>:   mov     w0, #0x3                        // #3
   0x000000000040093c <+180>:   bl      0x41c490 <sleep>

72          return 0;
   0x0000000000400940 <+184>:   mov     w0, #0x0                        // #0

73      }
   0x0000000000400944 <+188>:   mov     w1, w0
   0x0000000000400948 <+192>:   adrp    x0, 0x49c000 <tunable_list+1312>
   0x000000000040094c <+196>:   ldr     x0, [x0, #3024]
   0x0000000000400950 <+200>:   ldr     x3, [sp, #40]
   0x0000000000400954 <+204>:   ldr     x2, [x0]
   0x0000000000400958 <+208>:   subs    x3, x3, x2
   0x000000000040095c <+212>:   mov     x2, #0x0                        // #0
   0x0000000000400960 <+216>:   b.eq    0x400968 <main+224>  // b.none
   0x0000000000400964 <+220>:   bl      0x41f930 <__stack_chk_fail_local>
   0x0000000000400968 <+224>:   mov     w0, w1
   0x000000000040096c <+228>:   ldp     x29, x30, [sp], #48
   0x0000000000400970 <+232>:   ret
End of assembler dump.
```

Q. Is this crash tool procedure to analyze Linux kernel core dumps also working for ESXi?

A. It should work if core dumps are generated with this tool: https://flings.vmware.com/vmss2core.

Q. Is there an **!analyze** equivalent command in GDB?

A. You can use GDB scripting to emulate some functionality. Crash tool shows some analysis information summary when you open a kernel core dump.

Q. Is it possible to use scripts in GDB?

A. Yes, for example, in the past, I wrote the following script to emulate the WinDbg **dpp** command (*UserCommands.txt*):

```
define dpp
    set $i = 0
    set $p = $arg0
    while $i < $arg1
        printf "%p: ", $p
        x/ga *(long *)$p
        set $i = $i + 1
        set $p = $p + 8
    end
end
```

We load the file in GDB and execute the **dpp** command supplying the initial address and the number of addresses to iterate (we also double-check its correctness):

```
(gdb) source UserCommands.txt

(gdb) dpp 0x7ffdf45637f8 10
0x7ffdf45637f8: 0x7ffdf4565756: 0x622f3d4c4c454853
0x7ffdf4563800: 0x7ffdf4565766: 0x544e4f4354534948
0x7ffdf4563808: 0x7ffdf456577d: 0x545349445f4c5357
0x7ffdf4563810: 0x7ffdf4565794: 0x5345443d454d414e
0x7ffdf4563818: 0x7ffdf45657a9: 0x6d6f682f3d445750
0x7ffdf4563820: 0x7ffdf45657c7: 0x3d454d414e474f4c
0x7ffdf4563828: 0x7ffdf45657d8: 0x4944504d545f434d
0x7ffdf4563830: 0x7ffdf45657f3: 0x313d4449535f434d
0x7ffdf4563838: 0x7ffdf45657fe: 0x6f682f3d454d4f48
0x7ffdf4563840: 0x7ffdf4565812: 0x5f6e653d474e414c

(gdb) x/a 0x7ffdf4563840
0x7ffdf4563840: 0x7ffdf4565812

(gdb) x/a  0x7ffdf4565812
0x7ffdf4565812: 0x5f6e653d474e414c
```

Q. Is I/O or PCI-mapped memory included in process core dumps?

A. Certain memory-mapped I/O pages like frame buffer are excluded from dumping according to a man page: https://man7.org/linux/man-pages/man5/core.5.html

Q. Is there a way to know how much each function takes space on a stack?

A. In WinDbg, it is possible by using the **kf** command variant:

```
0:000> kf
 #   Memory  Child-SP          RetAddr               Call Site
00           0000fffc`cd38e5f0 00000000`00424cb4     App1!_libc_nanosleep+0x24
01        40 0000fffc`cd38e630 00000000`004031f8     App1!sleep+0x110
02       1f0 0000fffc`cd38e820 00000000`0040320c     App1!bar_one+0x10
03        10 0000fffc`cd38e830 00000000`00403224     App1!foo_one+0xc
04        10 0000fffc`cd38e840 00000000`00404c34     App1!thread_one+0x10
05        20 0000fffc`cd38e860 00000000`00429b60     App1!start_thread+0xb4
06       130 0000fffc`cd38e990 ffffffff`ffffffff     App1!thread_start+0x30
07         0 0000fffc`cd38e990 00000000`00000000     0xffffffff`ffffffff
```

In GDB, it is possible by examining the stack pointer for each frame and calculating the difference.

Q. In case of multiple threads, will GDB show the thread that got a signal or another thread?

A. The thread that got a signal is thread #1 in the output of the **info threads** command.

Q. Sometimes, we get truncated core dumps. When does this happen?

A. This could be insufficient disk space or configured limit. Also, it could be that certain regions are excluded from dumping or by a dump filter (see the core man page referenced earlier).

Q. What happens if process memory is relocated?

A. You can add symbol offsets (-o option) for symbol-file and add-symbol-file GDB commands.

Q. Can I search for a pattern in the dump?

A. Yes, the **find** command for GDB and the **s** command for WinDbg. The two exercises, A1, contain corresponding examples.

Q. Can I dump entire memory contents from a core dump? For example, I want to examine the entire contents of the memory in one command.

A. The **find** command for GDB stops at invalid memory. The **s** command for WinDbg continues, although it may have memory size limitations. The **search** command in the *crash* wrapper may be used for the entire available kernel memory search.

Q. If a thread is in kernel context, do we get to know any info on what kernel function it was executing?

A. We can see from the top frame and get an idea, for example:

```
(gdb) info threads
  Id   Target Id         Frame
* 1    LWP 9             0x00007facb3d2a437 in __GI___waitpid (pid=-1, stat_loc=0x7ffc6b178670,
options=10)
    at ../sysdeps/unix/sysv/linux/waitpid.c:30

(gdb) bt
#0  0x00007facb3d2a437 in __GI___waitpid (pid=-1, stat_loc=0x7ffc6b178670, options=10)
    at ../sysdeps/unix/sysv/linux/waitpid.c:30
#1  0x00005637dc4e8869 in ?? ()
#2  0x00005637dc4e9cc3 in wait_for ()
#3  0x00005637dc4d7b85 in execute_command_internal ()
#4  0x00005637dc4d7df2 in execute_command ()
#5  0x00005637dc4bf833 in reader_loop ()
#6  0x00005637dc4be104 in main ()
```

Q. Sometimes, GDB says that it optimized away some local variables. Does it mean it doesn't use a stack for those variables (and uses registers)?

A. Yes, the values are in registers. Another optimization type I encountered in the past is reusing stack locations for different variables.

Q. Can I search for an address?

A. Yes, addresses are just 64-bit values, so you need to specify the **/g** option for the GDB **find** command, the option **-64** for the **search** command in the *crash* tool, and the **q** type in the WinDbg **s** command. For example, see exercises App1 and K2.

Q. I got this output when I tried to load Exercise K1 core dump:

```
WARNING: kernel relocated [500MB]: patching 105514 gdb minimal_symbol values

      KERNEL: ../KSym/vmlinux-5.10.0-10-amd64
    DUMPFILE: dump.202201020022  [PARTIAL DUMP]
        CPUS: 4
        DATE: Sun Jan  2 00:19:33 2022
      UPTIME: 00:12:07
LOAD AVERAGE: 0.09, 0.07, 0.08
       TASKS: 454
    NODENAME: coredump
     RELEASE: 5.10.0-10-amd64
     VERSION: #1 SMP Debian 5.10.84-1 (2021-12-08)
     MACHINE: x86_64  (1991 Mhz)
      MEMORY: 4 GB
       PANIC:
crash: cannot determine length of symbol: log_end
```

A. Your distribution *crash* tool is older than the kernel. Therefore, you need to build the *crash* tool from the source. Please check the steps in exercise K1.

Q. When I load *x64\App1.core.253* in WinDbg, set the symbol path, and reload, I get only this stack trace:

```
0:000> k
 # Child-SP          RetAddr               Call Site
00 00007ffd`f4563610 00000000`00000000     App1+0x41a10
```

A. There's a problem at the time of this writing with the gcore-generated dumps on the latest Debian WSL2 distribution used for x64 exercises. It can be resolved by using the SYMOPT_LOAD_ANYTHING option and making sure that *App1* is in the search path:

```
0:000> .symopt+ 0x40
Symbol options are 0x30377:
  0x00000001 - SYMOPT_CASE_INSENSITIVE
  0x00000002 - SYMOPT_UNDNAME
  0x00000004 - SYMOPT_DEFERRED_LOADS
  0x00000010 - SYMOPT_LOAD_LINES
  0x00000020 - SYMOPT_OMAP_FIND_NEAREST
  0x00000040 - SYMOPT_LOAD_ANYTHING
  0x00000100 - SYMOPT_NO_UNQUALIFIED_LOADS
  0x00000200 - SYMOPT_FAIL_CRITICAL_ERRORS
  0x00010000 - SYMOPT_AUTO_PUBLICS
  0x00020000 - SYMOPT_NO_IMAGE_SEARCH

0:000> .reload
.
Unable to load image /home/coredump/ALCDA/App1/App1, Win32 error 0n2
*** WARNING: Unable to verify timestamp for App1

************* Symbol Loading Error Summary **************
```

```
Module name              Error
App1                     The system cannot find the file specified

You can troubleshoot most symbol related issues by turning on symbol loading diagnostics (!sym
noisy) and repeating the command that caused symbols to be loaded.
You should also verify that your symbol search path (.sympath) is correct.

0:000> k
 # Child-SP          RetAddr               Call Site
00 00007ffd`f4563610 00000000`0044199a     App1!nanosleep+0x40
01 00007ffd`f4563640 00000000`00401d92     App1!sleep+0x3a
02 00007ffd`f4563680 00000000`00407581     App1!main+0xaa
03 00007ffd`f45636d0 00000000`00401aba     App1!_libc_start_main+0x3d1
04 00007ffd`f45637d0 ffffffff`ffffffff     App1!start+0x2a
05 00007ffd`f45637d8 00000000`00000000     0xffffffff`ffffffff
```

App Source Code

App0

```
//
//  main.c
//  App0 - Exercise 0 - Testing Linux GDB
//
//  Copyright (c) 2015 - 2022 Software Diagnostics Services. All rights reserved.
//
//  Build:
//
//      gcc main.c -pthread -static -o App0
//

#include <stdlib.h>

void bar()
{
    abort();
}

void foo()
{
    bar();
}

int main(int argc, const char * argv[])
{
    foo();
    return 0;
}
```

App1

```
//
//  main.c
//  App1 - Normal application with multiple threads
//
//  Copyright (c) 2015 - 2022 Software Diagnostics Services. All rights reserved.
//
//  Build:
//
//      gcc main.c -pthread -static -o App1
//      gcc main.c -pthread -o App1.shared
//

#include <stdio.h>
#include <pthread.h>
#include <unistd.h>
#include <string.h>
#include <stdlib.h>

#define THREAD_DECLARE(num) void bar_##num()\
{\
    sleep(-1);\
}\
\
void foo_##num()\
{\
    bar_##num();\
}\
\
void * thread_##num (void *arg)\
{\
    foo_##num();\
\
    return 0;\
}

THREAD_DECLARE(one)
THREAD_DECLARE(two)
THREAD_DECLARE(three)
THREAD_DECLARE(four)
THREAD_DECLARE(five)

#define THREAD_CREATE(num) {pthread_t threadID_##num; pthread_create (&threadID_##num, NULL,
thread_##num, NULL);}

int main(int argc, const char * argv[])
{
    THREAD_CREATE(one)
    THREAD_CREATE(two)
    THREAD_CREATE(three)
    THREAD_CREATE(four)
    THREAD_CREATE(five)

    sleep(-1);
    return 0;
}
```

App2D

```
//
//  main.c
//  App2D - Shows NULL data pointer exception
//
//  Copyright (c) 2015 - 2022 Software Diagnostics Services. All rights reserved.
//
//  Build:
//
//      gcc main.c -pthread -static -o App2D
//

#include <stdio.h>
#include <pthread.h>
#include <unistd.h>
#include <string.h>
#include <stdlib.h>

void procA()
{
    int *p = NULL;

    *p = 1;
}

void procB()
{
    sleep(1);

    void (*pf)() = NULL;

    pf();
}

#define THREAD_DECLARE(num,func) void bar_##num()\
{\
func;\
}\
\
void foo_##num()\
{\
bar_##num();\
}\
\
void * thread_##num (void *arg)\
{\
foo_##num();\
\
return 0;\
}

THREAD_DECLARE(one,sleep(-1))
THREAD_DECLARE(two,procA())
THREAD_DECLARE(three,sleep(-1))
THREAD_DECLARE(four,procB())
THREAD_DECLARE(five,sleep(-1))
```

```
#define THREAD_CREATE(num) {pthread_t threadID_##num; pthread_create (&threadID_##num, NULL,
thread_##num, NULL);}

int main(int argc, const char * argv[])
{
    THREAD_CREATE(one)
    THREAD_CREATE(two)
    THREAD_CREATE(three)
    THREAD_CREATE(four)
    THREAD_CREATE(five)

    sleep(3);
    return 0;
}
```

App2C

```
//
// main.c
// App2C - Shows NULL code pointer exception
//
// Copyright (c) 2015 - 2022 Software Diagnostics Services. All rights reserved.
//
// Build:
//
//     gcc main.c -pthread -static -o App2C
//

#include <stdio.h>
#include <pthread.h>
#include <unistd.h>
#include <string.h>
#include <stdlib.h>

void procA()
{
    sleep(2);

    int *p = NULL;

    *p = 1;
}

void procB()
{
    sleep(1);

    void (*pf)() = NULL;

    pf();
}

#define THREAD_DECLARE(num,func) void bar_##num()\
{\
func;\
}\
\
void foo_##num()\
{\
bar_##num();\
}\
\
void * thread_##num (void *arg)\
{\
foo_##num();\
\
return 0;\
}

THREAD_DECLARE(one,sleep(-1))
THREAD_DECLARE(two,procA())
THREAD_DECLARE(three,sleep(-1))
THREAD_DECLARE(four,procB())
THREAD_DECLARE(five,sleep(-1))
```

```
#define THREAD_CREATE(num) {pthread_t threadID_##num; pthread_create (&threadID_##num, NULL,
thread_##num, NULL);}

int main(int argc, const char * argv[])
{
    THREAD_CREATE(one)
    THREAD_CREATE(two)
    THREAD_CREATE(three)
    THREAD_CREATE(four)
    THREAD_CREATE(five)

    sleep(3);
    return 0;
}
```

App2S

```
//
//   main.c
//   App2S - Shows how to use external debugging information
//
//   Copyright (c) 2015 - 2022 Software Diagnostics Services. All rights reserved.
//
//   Build:
//
//       gcc main.c -g -pthread -static -o App2S
//       cp App2S App2S.debug
//       objcopy --strip-debug App2S
//

#include <stdio.h>
#include <pthread.h>
#include <unistd.h>
#include <string.h>
#include <stdlib.h>

void procA()
{
    sleep(1);

    int *p = NULL;

    *p = 1;
}

void procB()
{
    sleep(2);

    void (*pf)() = NULL;

    pf();
}

#define THREAD_DECLARE(num,func) void bar_##num()\
{\
func;\
}\
\
void foo_##num()\
{\
bar_##num();\
}\
\
void * thread_##num (void *arg)\
{\
foo_##num();\
\
return 0;\
}

THREAD_DECLARE(one,sleep(-1))
THREAD_DECLARE(two,procA())
THREAD_DECLARE(three,sleep(-1))
THREAD_DECLARE(four,procB())
```

```
THREAD_DECLARE(five,sleep(-1))

#define THREAD_CREATE(num) {pthread_t threadID_##num; pthread_create (&threadID_##num, NULL,
thread_##num, NULL);}

int main(int argc, const char * argv[])
{
    THREAD_CREATE(one)
    THREAD_CREATE(two)
    THREAD_CREATE(three)
    THREAD_CREATE(four)
    THREAD_CREATE(five)

    sleep(3);
    return 0;
}
```

App3

```
//
//  main.c
//  App3 - Spiking Thread pattern
//
//  Copyright (c) 2015 - 2022 Software Diagnostics Services. All rights reserved.
//
//  Build:
//
//      gcc main.c -pthread -lm -static -o App3
//

#include <stdio.h>
#include <pthread.h>
#include <unistd.h>
#include <string.h>
#include <stdlib.h>
#include <math.h>

void procA()
{
    while (1)
    {
        sleep(1);
    }
}

void procB()
{
    double d = 1.0/3.0;
    while (1)
    {
        d = sqrt(d);
    }
}

#define THREAD_DECLARE(num,func) void bar_##num()\
{\
func;\
}\
\
void foo_##num()\
{\
bar_##num();\
}\
\
void * thread_##num (void *arg)\
{\
foo_##num();\
\
return 0;\
}

THREAD_DECLARE(one,sleep(-1))
THREAD_DECLARE(two,sleep(-1))
THREAD_DECLARE(three,procA())
THREAD_DECLARE(four,sleep(-1))
THREAD_DECLARE(five,procB())
```

```
#define THREAD_CREATE(num) {pthread_t threadID_##num; pthread_create (&threadID_##num, NULL,
thread_##num, NULL);}

int main(int argc, const char * argv[])
{
    THREAD_CREATE(one)
    THREAD_CREATE(two)
    THREAD_CREATE(three)
    THREAD_CREATE(four)
    THREAD_CREATE(five)

    sleep(-1);
    return 0;
}
```

App4

```
//
//  main.c
//  App4 - Heap Corruption pattern
//
//  Copyright (c) 2015 - 2022 Software Diagnostics Services. All rights reserved.
//
//  Build:
//
//      gcc main.c -pthread -static -o App4
//

#include <stdio.h>
#include <pthread.h>
#include <unistd.h>
#include <string.h>
#include <stdlib.h>

void proc()
{
    sleep(1);

    char *p1 = (char *) malloc (256);
    char *p2 = (char *) malloc (256);
    char *p3 = (char *) malloc (256);
    char *p4 = (char *) malloc (256);
    char *p5 = (char *) malloc (256);
    char *p6 = (char *) malloc (256);
    char *p7 = (char *) malloc (256);

    free(p6);
    free(p4);
    free(p2);

    strcpy(p2, "Hello Crash2! Hello Crash2! Hello Crash2! Hello Crash2! Hello Crash2!");
    strcpy(p4, "Hello Crash4! Hello Crash4! Hello Crash4! Hello Crash4! Hello Crash4! Hello
Crash4!");
    strcpy(p6, "Hello Crash6! Hello Crash6! Hello Crash6! Hello Crash6! Hello Crash6! Hello
Crash6! Hello Crash6!");

    p2 = (char *) malloc (256);
    p4 = (char *) malloc (256);
    p6 = (char *) malloc (256);

    sleep(300);

    free (p7);
    free (p6);
    free (p5);
    free (p4);
    free (p3);
    free (p2);
    free (p1);

    sleep(-1);
}
```

```
#define THREAD_DECLARE(num,func) void bar_##num()\
{\
func;\
}\
\
void foo_##num()\
{\
bar_##num();\
}\
\
void * thread_##num (void *arg)\
{\
foo_##num();\
\
return 0;\
}

THREAD_DECLARE(one,sleep(-1))
THREAD_DECLARE(two,sleep(-1))
THREAD_DECLARE(three,proc())
THREAD_DECLARE(four,sleep(-1))
THREAD_DECLARE(five,sleep(-1))

#define THREAD_CREATE(num) {pthread_t threadID_##num; pthread_create (&threadID_##num, NULL,
thread_##num, NULL);}

int main(int argc, const char * argv[])
{
    THREAD_CREATE(one)
    THREAD_CREATE(two)
    THREAD_CREATE(three)
    THREAD_CREATE(four)
    THREAD_CREATE(five)

    sleep(-1);
    return 0;
}
```

App5

```
//
//  main.c
//  App5 - Local Buffer Overflow
//
//  Copyright (c) 2015 - 2022 Software Diagnostics Services. All rights reserved.
//
//  Build:
//
//      gcc main.c -pthread -static -o App5
//

#include <stdio.h>
#include <pthread.h>
#include <unistd.h>
#include <string.h>
#include <stdlib.h>

void procB(char *buffer)
{
    sleep(1);
    char data[100] = "My New Bigger Buffer";
    memcpy (buffer, data, sizeof(data));
}

void procA()
{
    char data[10] = "My Buffer";
    procB(data);
}

#define THREAD_DECLARE(num,func) void bar_##num()\
{\
func;\
}\
\
void foo_##num()\
{\
bar_##num();\
}\
\
void * thread_##num (void *arg)\
{\
foo_##num();\
\
return 0;\
}

THREAD_DECLARE(one,procA())
THREAD_DECLARE(two,sleep(-1))
THREAD_DECLARE(three,sleep(-1))
THREAD_DECLARE(four,sleep(-1))
THREAD_DECLARE(five,sleep(-1))

#define THREAD_CREATE(num) {pthread_t threadID_##num; pthread_create (&threadID_##num, NULL,
thread_##num, NULL);}
```

```
int main(int argc, const char * argv[])
{
    THREAD_CREATE(one)
    THREAD_CREATE(two)
    THREAD_CREATE(three)
    THREAD_CREATE(four)
    THREAD_CREATE(five)

    sleep(-1);
    return 0;
}
```

App6

```
//
//  main.c
//  App6 - Stack Overflow
//
//  Copyright (c) 2015 - 2022 Software Diagnostics Services. All rights reserved.
//
//  Build:
//
//      gcc main.c -pthread -static -o App6
//

#include <stdio.h>
#include <pthread.h>
#include <unistd.h>
#include <string.h>
#include <stdlib.h>

void procF(int i)
{
    int buffer[128] = {-1, 0, i+1, 0, -1};

    procF(buffer[2]);
}

void procE()
{
    procF(1);
}

#define THREAD_DECLARE(num,func) void bar_##num()\
{\
sleep(300);\
func;\
}\
\
void foo_##num()\
{\
bar_##num();\
}\
\
void * thread_##num (void *arg)\
{\
foo_##num();\
\
return 0;\
}

THREAD_DECLARE(one,procE())
THREAD_DECLARE(two,sleep(-1))
THREAD_DECLARE(three,sleep(-1))
THREAD_DECLARE(four,sleep(-1))
THREAD_DECLARE(five,sleep(-1))

#define THREAD_CREATE(num) {pthread_t threadID_##num; pthread_create (&threadID_##num, NULL,
thread_##num, NULL);}
```

```
int main(int argc, const char * argv[])
{
    THREAD_CREATE(one)
    THREAD_CREATE(two)
    THREAD_CREATE(three)
    THREAD_CREATE(four)
    THREAD_CREATE(five)

    sleep(-1);
    return 0;
}
```

App7

```
//
//  main.c
//  App7 - Divide by Zero and Active Threads
//
//  Copyright (c) 2015 - 2022 Software Diagnostics Services. All rights reserved.
//
//  Build:
//      gcc main.c -pthread -static -o App7

#include <stdio.h>
#include <pthread.h>
#include <unistd.h>
#include <string.h>
#include <stdlib.h>

void procF(int i)
{
    int buffer[1024] = {-1, 0, i+1, 0, -1};

    procF(buffer[2]);
}

void procE()
{
    procF(1);
}

int procD(int a, int b)
{
    return a/b;
}

int procC()
{
    return procD(1,0);
}

void procB(char *buffer)
{
    char data[100] = "My New Bigger Buffer";
    memcpy (buffer, data, sizeof(data));
}

void procA()
{
    char data[10] = "My Buffer";
    procB(data);
}
```

```
#define THREAD_DECLARE(num,func) void bar_##num()\
{\
sleep(10);\
func;\
}\
\
void foo_##num()\
{\
bar_##num();\
}\
\
void * thread_##num (void *arg)\
{\
foo_##num();\
\
return 0;\
}

THREAD_DECLARE(one,procA())
THREAD_DECLARE(two,sleep(-1))
THREAD_DECLARE(three,procC())
THREAD_DECLARE(four,sleep(-1))
THREAD_DECLARE(five,procE())

#define THREAD_CREATE(num) {pthread_t threadID_##num; pthread_create (&threadID_##num, NULL,
thread_##num, NULL);}

int main(int argc, const char * argv[])
{
    THREAD_CREATE(one)
    THREAD_CREATE(two)
    THREAD_CREATE(three)
    THREAD_CREATE(four)
    THREAD_CREATE(five)

    sleep(-1);
    return 0;
}
```

App8

```
//
//  main.cpp
//  App8 - C++ Exception, Execution Residue, Handled Exception
//
//  Copyright (c) 2015 - 2022 Software Diagnostics Services. All rights reserved.
//
//  Build:
//
//      g++ main.cpp -pthread -static -o App8
//

#include <string>
#include <unistd.h>

#define def_call(name,x,y) void name##_##x() { name##_##y(); }
#define def_final(name,x) void name##_##x() { }
#define def_init(name,y,size) void name() { int arr[size]; name##_##y(); *arr=0; }

def_final(work,9)
def_call(work,8,9)
def_call(work,7,8)
def_call(work,6,7)
def_call(work,5,6)
def_call(work,4,5)
def_call(work,3,4)
def_call(work,2,3)
def_call(work,1,2)
def_init(work,1,256)

class Exception
{
    int code;
    std::string description;

public:
    Exception(int _code, std::string _desc) : code(_code), description(_desc) {}
};

void procB()
{
    throw new Exception(5, "Access Denied");
}

void procNB()
{
    work();
}

void procA()
{
    procB();
}

void procNA()
{
    procNB();
}
```

```
void procH()
{
    try {
        procA();
    } catch (...) {
        sleep(-1);
    }
}

void procNH()
{
    sleep(10);
    procA();
}

void procNE()
{
    try {
        procNA();
    }
    catch (...)
    {
    }
    sleep(-1);
}

#define THREAD_DECLARE(num,func) void bar_##num()\
{\
func;\
}\
\
void foo_##num()\
{\
bar_##num();\
}\
\
void * thread_##num (void *arg)\
{\
foo_##num();\
\
return 0;\
}

THREAD_DECLARE(one,procNH())
THREAD_DECLARE(two,procNE())
THREAD_DECLARE(three,procH())
THREAD_DECLARE(four,procNE())
THREAD_DECLARE(five,procNE())

#define THREAD_CREATE(num) {pthread_t threadID_##num; pthread_create (&threadID_##num, NULL,
thread_##num, NULL);}
```

```
int main(int argc, const char * argv[])
{
    THREAD_CREATE(one)
    THREAD_CREATE(two)
    THREAD_CREATE(three)
    THREAD_CREATE(four)
    THREAD_CREATE(five)

    sleep(-1);
    return 0;
}
```

App9

```
//
//  main.c
//  App9 - Heap Leak pattern
//
//  Copyright (c) 2015 - 2022 Software Diagnostics Services. All rights reserved.
//
//  Build:
//
//      gcc main.c -pthread -static -o App9
//

#include <stdio.h>
#include <pthread.h>
#include <unistd.h>
#include <string.h>
#include <stdlib.h>

void procD()
{
}

typedef void (**PFUNC)();

void procC(int iter)
{
    for (int i = 0; i < iter; ++i)
    {
        char *p = malloc(256);
        strcpy(p, "allocated memory");

        *(PFUNC)(p + 32) = &procD;
    }
}

void procB()
{
    procC(250000);
    sleep(300);
    procC(250000);
    sleep(-1);
}

void procA()
{
    procC(5000);
    sleep(300);
    procB();
}
```

```
#define THREAD_DECLARE(num,func) void bar_##num()\
{\
func;\
}\
\
void foo_##num()\
{\
bar_##num();\
}\
\
void * thread_##num (void *arg)\
{\
foo_##num();\
\
return 0;\
}

THREAD_DECLARE(one,sleep(-1))
THREAD_DECLARE(two,procA())
THREAD_DECLARE(three,sleep(-1))
THREAD_DECLARE(four,sleep(-1))
THREAD_DECLARE(five,sleep(-1))

#define THREAD_CREATE(num) {pthread_t threadID_##num; pthread_create (&threadID_##num, NULL,
thread_##num, NULL);}

int main(int argc, const char * argv[])
{
    THREAD_CREATE(one)
    THREAD_CREATE(two)
    THREAD_CREATE(three)
    THREAD_CREATE(four)
    THREAD_CREATE(five)

    sleep(-1);
    return 0;
}
```

App10

```
//
//  main.c
//  App10 - Heap Corruption, Heap Contention, Critical Region, Wait Chains, Self-Diagnostics
patterns
//
//  Copyright (c) 2015 - 2022 Software Diagnostics Services. All rights reserved.
//
//  Build:
//
//      gcc main.c -pthread -static -o App10
//

#include <stdio.h>
#include <pthread.h>
#include <unistd.h>
#include <string.h>
#include <stdlib.h>

#define ARR_SIZE 10000

char *pAllocBuf [ARR_SIZE] = {0};

void proc()
{
    while (1)
    {
        int idx = rand()%ARR_SIZE;
        int malloc_size = rand()%ARR_SIZE;

        if (pAllocBuf[idx])
        {
            free(pAllocBuf[idx]);
            pAllocBuf[idx] = 0;
        }

        pAllocBuf[idx] = malloc(malloc_size);
    }
}

#define THREAD_DECLARE(num,func) void bar_##num()\
{\
func;\
}\
\
void foo_##num()\
{\
bar_##num();\
}\
\
void * thread_##num (void *arg)\
{\
foo_##num();\
\
return 0;\
}
```

```
THREAD_DECLARE(one,proc())
THREAD_DECLARE(two,proc())
THREAD_DECLARE(three,proc())
THREAD_DECLARE(four,proc())
THREAD_DECLARE(five,proc())

#define THREAD_CREATE(num) {pthread_t threadID_##num; pthread_create (&threadID_##num, NULL,
thread_##num, NULL);}

int main(int argc, const char * argv[])
{
    THREAD_CREATE(one)
    THREAD_CREATE(two)
    THREAD_CREATE(three)
    THREAD_CREATE(four)
    THREAD_CREATE(five)

    sleep(-1);
    return 0;
}
```

App11 / App12

```
//
//  main.c
//  App11 - Wait Chains, Deadlock, Handled Exception patterns
//
//  Copyright (c) 2015 - 2022 Software Diagnostics Services. All rights reserved.
//
//  Build (App11):
//
//      g++ main.cpp -pthread -static -o App11
//
//  Build (App12):
//
//      g++ main.cpp -g -pthread -static -o App12
//      cp App12 App12.debug
//      objcopy --strip-debug App12
//

#include <stdio.h>
#include <pthread.h>
#include <unistd.h>
#include <string.h>
#include <stdlib.h>

pthread_mutex_t mutexA, mutexB;

void procC()
{
    throw 0;
}

void procA()
{
    try
    {
        pthread_mutex_lock(&mutexA);
        procC();
        pthread_mutex_unlock(&mutexA);
    }
    catch(...)
    {

    }

    sleep(20);
    pthread_mutex_lock(&mutexB);
    pthread_mutex_unlock(&mutexB);
}

void procB()
{
    pthread_mutex_lock(&mutexB);
    pthread_mutex_lock(&mutexA);
    sleep(30);
    pthread_mutex_unlock(&mutexA);
    pthread_mutex_unlock(&mutexB);
}
```

```
#define THREAD_DECLARE(num,func) void bar_##num()\
{\
func;\
}\
\
void foo_##num()\
{\
bar_##num();\
}\
\
void * thread_##num (void *arg)\
{\
foo_##num();\
\
return 0;\
}

THREAD_DECLARE(one,sleep(-1))
THREAD_DECLARE(two,procA())
THREAD_DECLARE(three,sleep(-1))
THREAD_DECLARE(four,procB())
THREAD_DECLARE(five,sleep(-1))

#define THREAD_CREATE(num) {pthread_t threadID_##num; pthread_create (&threadID_##num, NULL,
thread_##num, NULL);}

int main(int argc, const char * argv[])
{
    pthread_mutex_init(&mutexA, NULL);
    pthread_mutex_init(&mutexB, NULL);

    THREAD_CREATE(one)
    THREAD_CREATE(two)
    sleep(10);
    THREAD_CREATE(three)
    THREAD_CREATE(four)
    THREAD_CREATE(five)

    sleep(-1);
    return 0;
}
```

```
//
// mod_a.c
// Models NULL Pointer (Data) memory analysis pattern in kernel space
//
// Copyright (c) 2022 Software Diagnostics Services. All rights reserved.
//

#include <linux/module.h>

void foo(void);
void bar(void);

int init_module(void)
{
    foo();

    return 0;
}

void bar(void)
{
    int *pi = NULL;
    *pi = 1;
}

void foo(void)
{
    bar();
}

MODULE_LICENSE("GPL");
```

```
//
// mod_b.c
// Models Null Pointer (Code) memory analysis pattern in kernel space
//
// Copyright (c) 2022 Software Diagnostics Services. All rights reserved.
//

#include <linux/module.h>
#include <linux/kernel.h>
#include <linux/init.h>
#include <linux/kthread.h>
#include <linux/sched.h>
#include <linux/delay.h>

void foo(void);

int kthread_f(void *arg)
{
    msleep(10000);

    foo();

    return 0;
}

int init_module(void)
{
    struct task_struct *ts;

    ts = kthread_run(kthread_f, NULL, "mod_b thread");

    if (IS_ERR(ts))
    {
    return PTR_ERR(ts);
    }

    return 0;
}
```

```c
//
// foo.c
//

MODULE_LICENSE("GPL");

#include <linux/module.h>

void bar(void);

void foo(void)
{
    bar();
}

//
// bar.c
//

MODULE_LICENSE("GPL");

#include <linux/module.h>
#include <linux/kernel.h>

void bar(void)
{
    int (*pf)(void) = NULL;
    pf();
}

MODULE_LICENSE("GPL");
```

```
//
// mod_c.c
// Models Spiking Thread memory analysis pattern in kernel space
//
// Copyright (c) 2022 Software Diagnostics Services. All rights reserved.
//

#include <linux/module.h>
#include <linux/kernel.h>
#include <linux/init.h>
#include <linux/kthread.h>
#include <linux/sched.h>
#include <linux/delay.h>

void foo(void);

int kthread_f(void *arg)
{
    msleep(10000);

    foo();

    return 0;
}

int init_module(void)
{
    struct task_struct *ts;

    ts = kthread_run(kthread_f, NULL, "mod_c thread");

    if (IS_ERR(ts))
    {
    return PTR_ERR(ts);
    }

    return 0;
}
```

```c
//
// foo.c
//

MODULE_LICENSE("GPL");

#include <linux/module.h>

void foo(void)
{
    while (1);
}

MODULE_LICENSE("GPL");
```

K5

```
//
// mod_d.c
// Models Stack Overflow (Kernel Mode) memory analysis pattern
//
// Copyright (c) 2022 Software Diagnostics Services. All rights reserved.
//

#include <linux/module.h>
#include <linux/kernel.h>
#include <linux/init.h>
#include <linux/kthread.h>
#include <linux/sched.h>
#include <linux/delay.h>

long foo(long n);

int kthread_f(void *arg)
{
    msleep(10000);

    foo(0);

    return 0;
}

int init_module(void)
{
    struct task_struct *ts;

    ts = kthread_run(kthread_f, NULL, "mod_d thread");

    if (IS_ERR(ts))
    {
        return PTR_ERR(ts);
    }

    return 0;
}

MODULE_LICENSE("GPL");
```

```c
//
// foo.c
//

#include <linux/module.h>

long bar(long n);

long foo(long n)
{
    return bar(n) + bar(n + 1);
}

//
// bar.c
//

MODULE_LICENSE("GPL");

#include <linux/module.h>
#include <linux/kernel.h>

long foo(long n);

long bar(long n)
{
    return foo(n) + foo(n + 1);
}

MODULE_LICENSE("GPL");
```

Selected Analysis Patterns

(edited articles from Software Diagnostics Institute, www.DumpAnalysis.org)

NULL Pointer (Data)

This pattern is a Linux variant of **NULL Pointer** (data) pattern previously described for Mac OS X[5] and Windows[6] platforms:

```
(gdb) bt
#0  0x0000000000400500 in procA ()
#1  0x000000000040057a in bar_two ()
#2  0x000000000040058a in foo_two ()
#3  0x00000000004005a2 in thread_two ()
#4  0x0000000000401630 in start_thread (arg=<optimized out>)
at pthread_create.c:304
#5  0x00000000004324e9 in clone ()
#6  0x0000000000000000 in ?? ()

(gdb) x/i 0x400500
=> 0x400500 <procA+16>: movl   $0x1,(%rax)

(gdb) info r $rax
rax            0x0 0

(gdb) x $rax
0x0: Cannot access memory at address 0x0
```

[5] https://www.dumpanalysis.org/blog/index.php/2012/03/25/crash-dump-analysis-patterns-part-6b-mac-os-x/

[6] https://www.dumpanalysis.org/blog/index.php/2009/04/14/crash-dump-analysis-patterns-part-6b/

Incomplete Stack Trace

Users of WinDbg debugger accustomed to full thread stack traces will wonder whether a thread starts from *main*:

```
(gdb) bt
#0  0x000000000042fed1 in nanosleep ()
#1  0x000000000042fda0 in sleep ()
#2  0x000000000040078a in main ()
```

Of course, not, and by default, a stack trace is shown starting from the *main* function. You can change this behavior by using the following command:

```
(gdb) set backtrace past-main
```

Now we see an additional frame:

```
(gdb) bt
#0  0x000000000042fed1 in nanosleep ()
#1  0x000000000042fda0 in sleep ()
#2  0x000000000040078a in main ()
#3  0x0000000000405283 in __libc_start_main ()
#4  0x00000000004003e9 in _start ()
```

Stack Trace

This pattern is a Linux variant of **Stack Trace** pattern previously described for Mac OS X[7] and Windows[8] platforms. Here we show a stack trace when debug symbols are not available (stripped executable) and also how to apply debug symbols from the executable where they were preserved:

```
(gdb) bt
#0 0x000000000043e4f1 in nanosleep ()
#1 0x000000000043e3c0 in sleep ()
#2 0x0000000000400789 in main ()

(gdb) symbol-file ./App/App.debug
Reading symbols from /home/Apps/App/App.debug...done.

(gdb) bt
#0 0x000000000043e4f1 in nanosleep ()
#1 0x000000000043e3c0 in sleep ()
#2 0x0000000000400789 in main (argc=1, argv=0x7fff5d1572d8) at main.cpp:85
```

---

[7] https://www.dumpanalysis.org/blog/index.php/2012/03/25/crash-dump-analysis-patterns-part-25-mac-os-x/

[8] https://www.dumpanalysis.org/blog/index.php/2007/09/10/crash-dump-analysis-patterns-part-25/

NULL Pointer (Code)

This pattern is a Linux variant of **NULL Pointer** (code) pattern previously described for Mac OS X[9] and Windows[10] platforms:

```
(gdb) bt
#0  0x0000000000000000 in ?? ()
#1  0x0000000000400531 in procB ()
#2  0x00000000004005f8 in bar_four ()
#3  0x0000000000400608 in foo_four ()
#4  0x0000000000400620 in thread_four ()
#5  0x0000000000401630 in start_thread (arg=<optimized out>)
at pthread_create.c:304
#6  0x00000000004324e9 in clone ()
#7  0x0000000000000000 in ?? ()

(gdb) disassemble procB
Dump of assembler code for function procB:
0x0000000000400516 <+0>: push   %rbp
0x0000000000400517 <+1>: mov    %rsp,%rbp
0x000000000040051a <+4>: sub    $0x10,%rsp
0x000000000040051e <+8>: movq   $0x0,-0x8(%rbp)
0x0000000000400526 <+16>: mov    -0x8(%rbp),%rdx
0x000000000040052a <+20>: mov    $0x0,%eax
0x000000000040052f <+25>: callq  *%rdx
0x0000000000400531 <+27>: leaveq
0x0000000000400532 <+28>: retq
End of assembler dump.

(gdb) info r rdx
rdx            0x0 0
```

---

[9] https://www.dumpanalysis.org/blog/index.php/2012/05/03/crash-dump-analysis-patterns-part-6a-mac-os-x/

[10] https://www.dumpanalysis.org/blog/index.php/2008/04/28/crash-dump-analysis-patterns-part-6a/

Spiking Thread

This pattern is a variant of **Spiking Thread** pattern previously described for Mac OS X[11] and Windows[12] platforms:

```
(gdb) info threads
Id Target Id Frame
6 LWP 3712 0x00000000004329d1 in nanosleep ()
5 LWP 3717 0x00000000004007a3 in isnan ()
4 LWP 3716 0x00000000004329d1 in nanosleep ()
3 LWP 3715 0x00000000004329d1 in nanosleep ()
2 LWP 3714 0x00000000004329d1 in nanosleep ()
* 1 LWP 3713 0x00000000004329d1 in nanosleep ()
```

We notice a non-waiting thread and switch to it:

```
(gdb) thread 5
[Switching to thread 5 (LWP 3717)]
#0 0x00000000004007a3 in isnan ()

(gdb) bt
#0 0x00000000004007a3 in isnan ()
#1 0x0000000000400743 in sqrt ()
#2 0x0000000000400528 in procB ()
#3 0x0000000000400639 in bar_five ()
#4 0x0000000000400649 in foo_five ()
#5 0x0000000000400661 in thread_five ()
#6 0x0000000000403e30 in start_thread ()
#7 0x0000000000435089 in clone ()
#8 0x0000000000000000 in ?? ()
```

If we disassemble the return address for *procB* function to come back from *sqrt* call, we see an infinite loop:

```
(gdb) disassemble 0x400528
Dump of assembler code for function procB:
0x0000000000400500 <+0>: push   %rbp
0x0000000000400501 <+1>: mov    %rsp,%rbp
0x0000000000400504 <+4>: sub    $0x20,%rsp
0x0000000000400508 <+8>: movabs $0x3fd5555555555555,%rax
0x0000000000400512 <+18>: mov    %rax,-0x8(%rbp)
0x0000000000400516 <+22>: mov    -0x8(%rbp),%rax
0x000000000040051a <+26>: mov    %rax,-0x18(%rbp)
0x000000000040051e <+30>: movsd  -0x18(%rbp),%xmm0
0x0000000000400523 <+35>: callq  0x400710 <sqrt>
0x0000000000400528 <+40>: movsd  %xmm0,-0x18(%rbp)
0x000000000040052d <+45>: mov    -0x18(%rbp),%rax
0x0000000000400531 <+49>: mov    %rax,-0x8(%rbp)
0x0000000000400535 <+53>: jmp    0x400516 <procB+22>
End of assembler dump.
```

[11] https://www.dumpanalysis.org/blog/index.php/2012/05/09/crash-dump-analysis-patterns-part-14-mac-os-x/

[12] https://www.dumpanalysis.org/blog/index.php/2007/05/11/crash-dump-analysis-patterns-part-14/

Dynamic Memory Corruption (Process Heap)

This pattern is a Linux variant of **Dynamic Memory Corruption** (process heap) pattern previously described for Mac OS X[13] and Windows[14] platforms.

The corruption may be internal to heap structures with a subsequent memory access violation:

```
(gdb) bt
#0  0x000000000041482e in _int_malloc ()
#1  0x0000000000416d88 in malloc ()
#2  0x00000000004005dc in proc ()
#3  0x00000000004006ee in bar_three ()
#4  0x00000000004006fe in foo_three ()
#5  0x0000000000400716 in thread_three ()
#6  0x0000000000401760 in start_thread (arg=<optimized out>)
at pthread_create.c:304
#7  0x0000000000432609 in clone ()
#8  0x0000000000000000 in ?? ()

(gdb) x/i $rip
=> 0x41482e <_int_malloc+622>: mov    %rbx,0x10(%r12)

(gdb) x $r12+0x10
0x21687371: Cannot access memory at address 0x21687371

(gdb) p (char[4])0x21687371
$1 = "qsh!"
```

Or it may be detected with a diagnostic message (similar to double free):

```
(gdb) bt
#0  0x000000000043ef65 in raise ()
#1  0x0000000000409fc0 in abort ()
#2  0x000000000040bf5b in __libc_message ()
#3  0x0000000000412042 in malloc_printerr ()
#4  0x0000000000416c27 in free ()
#5  0x0000000000400586 in proc ()
#6  0x000000000040067e in bar_four ()
#7  0x000000000040068e in foo_four ()
#8  0x00000000004006a6 in thread_four ()
#9  0x00000000004016c0 in start_thread (arg=<optimized out>)
at pthread_create.c:304
#10 0x0000000000432589 in clone ()
#11 0x0000000000000000 in ?? ()
```

---

[13] https://www.dumpanalysis.org/blog/index.php/2012/05/27/crash-dump-analysis-patterns-part-2-mac-os-x/

[14] https://www.dumpanalysis.org/blog/index.php/2006/10/31/crash-dump-analysis-patterns-part-2/

Execution Residue (User Space)

This pattern is a Linux variant of **Execution Residue** pattern previously described for Mac OS X[15] and Windows[16] platforms. This residue is symbolic information left in a stack region, including ASCII and UNICODE fragments or pointers to them, for example, return addresses from past function calls:

```
(gdb) bt
#0  0x00000000004431f1 in nanosleep ()
#1  0x00000000004430c0 in sleep ()
#2  0x0000000000400771 in procNE() ()
#3  0x00000000004007aa in bar_two() ()
#4  0x00000000004007b5 in foo_two() ()
#5  0x00000000004007c8 in thread_two(void*) ()
#6  0x00000000004140f0 in start_thread (arg=<optimized out>)
at pthread_create.c:304
#7  0x0000000000445879 in clone ()
#8  0x0000000000000000 in ?? ()

(gdb) x/512a $rsp-2000
0x7f4cacc42360: 0x0 0x0
0x7f4cacc42370: 0x0 0x0
0x7f4cacc42380: 0x0 0x0
0x7f4cacc42390: 0x0 0x0
[...]
0x7f4cacc42830: 0x0 0x0
0x7f4cacc42840: 0x0 0x0
0x7f4cacc42850: 0x0 0x0
0x7f4cacc42860: 0x7f4cacc42870 0x4005af <_Z6work_8v+9>
0x7f4cacc42870: 0x7f4cacc42880 0x4005ba <_Z6work_7v+9>
0x7f4cacc42880: 0x7f4cacc42890 0x4005c5 <_Z6work_6v+9>
0x7f4cacc42890: 0x7f4cacc428a0 0x4005d0 <_Z6work_5v+9>
0x7f4cacc428a0: 0x7f4cacc428b0 0x4005db <_Z6work_4v+9>
0x7f4cacc428b0: 0x7f4cacc428c0 0x4005e6 <_Z6work_3v+9>
0x7f4cacc428c0: 0x7f4cacc428d0 0x4005f1 <_Z6work_2v+9>
0x7f4cacc428d0: 0x7f4cacc428e0 0x4005fc <_Z6work_1v+9>
0x7f4cacc428e0: 0x7f4cacc42cf0 0x40060e <_Z4workv+16>
0x7f4cacc428f0: 0x0 0x0
0x7f4cacc42900: 0x0 0x0
0x7f4cacc42910: 0x0 0x0
[...]
0x7f4cacc42af0: 0x0 0x0
0x7f4cacc42b00: 0x0 0x0
0x7f4cacc42b10: 0x0 0x0
0x7f4cacc42b20: 0x0 0x4431e6 <nanosleep+38>
0x7f4cacc42b30: 0x0 0x4430c0 <sleep+224>
0x7f4cacc42b40: 0x0 0x0
0x7f4cacc42b50: 0x0 0x0
0x7f4cacc42b60: 0x0 0x0
0x7f4cacc42b70: 0x0 0x0
[...]
0x7f4cacc42cb0: 0x0 0x0
0x7f4cacc42cc0: 0x0 0x0
0x7f4cacc42cd0: 0x0 0x0
0x7f4cacc42ce0: 0xfffffed2 0x3ad3affa
0x7f4cacc42cf0: 0x7f4cacc42d00 0x0
```

---

[15] https://www.dumpanalysis.org/blog/index.php/2012/06/05/crash-dump-analysis-patterns-part-60-mac-os-x/

[16] https://www.dumpanalysis.org/blog/index.php/2008/04/29/crash-dump-analysis-patterns-part-60/

```
0x7f4cacc42d00: 0x7f4cacc42d20 0x49c740 <default_attr>
0x7f4cacc42d10: 0x7f4cacc439c0 0x400771 <_Z6procNEv+19>
0x7f4cacc42d20: 0x7f4cacc42d30 0x4007aa <_Z7bar_twov+9>
0x7f4cacc42d30: 0x7f4cacc42d40 0x4007b5 <_Z7foo_twov+9>
0x7f4cacc42d40: 0x7f4cacc42d60 0x4007c8 <_Z10thread_twoPv+17>
0x7f4cacc42d50: 0x0 0x0
0x7f4cacc42d60: 0x0 0x4140f0 <start_thread+208>
0x7f4cacc42d70: 0x0 0x7f4cacc43700
0x7f4cacc42d80: 0x0 0x0
0x7f4cacc42d90: 0x0 0x0
[...]
```

However, supposed return addresses need to be checked for **Coincidental Symbolic Information** pattern.

Coincidental Symbolic Information

This pattern is a Linux variant of **Coincidental Symbolic Information** pattern previously described for Mac OS X[17] and Windows[18] platforms. The idea is the same: to disassemble the address to see if the preceding instruction is a call. If it is indeed, then most likely the symbolic address is a return address from past **Execution Residue**:

```
(gdb) x/i 0x4005e6
0x4005e6 <_Z6work_3v+9>: pop    %rbp

(gdb) disassemble 0x4005e6
Dump of assembler code for function _Z6work_3v:
0x00000000004005dd <+0>: push   %rbp
0x00000000004005de <+1>: mov    %rsp,%rbp
0x00000000004005e1 <+4>: callq  0x4005d2 <_Z6work_4v>
0x00000000004005e6 <+9>: pop    %rbp
0x00000000004005e7 <+10>: retq
End of assembler dump.

(gdb) x/4i 0x49c740-4
0x49c73c: add    %al,(%rax)
0x49c73e: add    %al,(%rax)
0x49c740 <default_attr>: add    %al,(%rax)
0x49c742 <default_attr+2>: add    %al,(%rax)
```

[17] https://www.dumpanalysis.org/blog/index.php/2012/06/09/crash-dump-analysis-patterns-part-24-mac-os-x/

[18] https://www.dumpanalysis.org/blog/index.php/2007/08/30/crash-dump-analysis-patterns-part-24/

Stack Overflow (User Mode)

This pattern is a Linux variant of **Stack Overflow** (user mode) pattern previously described for Mac OS X[19] and Windows[20] platforms:

```
(gdb) bt
#0  0x00000000004004fb in procF ()
#1  0x000000000040054b in procF ()
#2  0x000000000040054b in procF ()
#3  0x000000000040054b in procF ()
#4  0x000000000040054b in procF ()
#5  0x000000000040054b in procF ()
#6  0x000000000040054b in procF ()
#7  0x000000000040054b in procF ()
#8  0x000000000040054b in procF ()
#9  0x000000000040054b in procF ()
#10 0x000000000040054b in procF ()
#11 0x000000000040054b in procF ()
#12 0x000000000040054b in procF ()
[...]

(gdb) bt -10
#15409 0x000000000040054b in procF ()
#15410 0x000000000040054b in procF ()
#15411 0x000000000040054b in procF ()
#15412 0x000000000040055b in procE ()
#15413 0x0000000000400575 in bar_one ()
#15414 0x0000000000400585 in foo_one ()
#15415 0x000000000040059d in thread_one ()
#15416 0x0000000000401690 in start_thread (arg=<optimized out>)
at pthread_create.c:304
#15417 0x0000000000432549 in clone ()
#15418 0x0000000000000000 in ?? ()
```

In case of a stack overflow, the stack pointer is decremented beyond the stack region boundary into a non-accessible region, so any stack memory access triggers an access violation:

```
(gdb) x $rsp
0x7eff46109ec0: 0x0

(gdb) frame 1
#1  0x000000000040054b in procF ()

(gdb) x $rsp
0x7eff4610a0e0: 0x0

(gdb) maintenance info sections
[...]
Core file:
[...]
0x7eff46109000->0x7eff4610a000 at 0x02034000: load13 ALLOC LOAD READONLY HAS_CONTENTS
0x7eff4610a000->0x7eff4690a000 at 0x02035000: load14 ALLOC LOAD HAS_CONTENTS
[...]
```

---

[19] https://www.dumpanalysis.org/blog/index.php/2012/07/17/crash-dump-analysis-patterns-part-16b-mac-os-x/

[20] https://www.dumpanalysis.org/blog/index.php/2008/06/10/crash-dump-analysis-patterns-part-16b/

Divide by Zero (User Mode)

This pattern is a Linux variant of **Divide by Zero** (user mode) pattern previously described for Mac OS X[21] and Windows[22] platforms:

```
GNU gdb (GDB)
[...]
Program terminated with signal 8, Arithmetic exception.
#0 0x000000000040056f in procD ()

(gdb) x/i $rip
=> 0x40056f <procD+18>: idivl -0x8(%rbp)

(gdb) info r $rax
rax 0x1 1

(gdb) x/w $rbp-0x8
0x7f0f6806bd28: 0x00000000
```

[21] https://www.dumpanalysis.org/blog/index.php/2012/07/18/crash-dump-analysis-patterns-part-78a-mac-os-x/

[22] https://www.dumpanalysis.org/blog/index.php/2008/12/01/crash-dump-analysis-patterns-part-78a/

Local Buffer Overflow (User Space)

This pattern is a Linux variant of **Local Buffer Overflow** pattern previously described for Mac OS X[23] and Windows[24] platforms. Most of the time, simple mistakes in using memory and string manipulation functions are easily detected by the runtime. The more sophisticated example which overwrites stack trace without being detected involves overwriting indirectly via a pointer to a local buffer passed to the called function. In such cases, we might see incorrect and truncated stack traces:

```
(gdb) bt
#0  0x0000000000000000 in ?? ()
#1  0x0000000000000000 in ?? ()

(gdb) x/100a $rsp
[...]
0x7fc3dd9dece8: 0x0 0x0
0x7fc3dd9decf8: 0x0 0x0
0x7fc3dd9ded08: 0x0 0x0
0x7fc3dd9ded18: 0x0 0x0
0x7fc3dd9ded28: 0x7fc3dd9ded48 0x4005cc <procA+40>
0x7fc3dd9ded38: 0x422077654e20794d 0x7542207265676769
0x7fc3dd9ded48: 0x72656666 0x0
0x7fc3dd9ded58: 0x0 0x0
0x7fc3dd9ded68: 0x0 0x0
0x7fc3dd9ded78: 0x0 0x0
[...]
```

[23] https://www.dumpanalysis.org/blog/index.php/2012/07/19/crash-dump-analysis-patterns-part-36-mac-os-x/

[24] https://www.dumpanalysis.org/blog/index.php/2007/11/14/crash-dump-analysis-patterns-part-36/

C++ Exception

This pattern is a Linux variant of **C++ Exception** pattern previously described for Mac OS X[25] and Windows[26] platforms:

```
(gdb) bt
#0 0x00007f0a1d0e5165 in *__GI_raise ()
at ../nptl/sysdeps/unix/sysv/linux/raise.c:64
#1 0x00007f0a1d0e83e0 in *__GI_abort () at abort.c:92
#2 0x00007f0a1db5789d in __gnu_cxx::__verbose_terminate_handler() ()
from /usr/lib/x86_64-linux-gnu/libstdc++.so.6
#3 0x00007f0a1db55996 in ?? () from /usr/lib/x86_64-linux-gnu/libstdc++.so.6
#4 0x00007f0a1db559c3 in std::terminate() ()
from /usr/lib/x86_64-linux-gnu/libstdc++.so.6
#5 0x00007f0a1db55bee in __cxa_throw ()
from /usr/lib/x86_64-linux-gnu/libstdc++.so.6
#6 0x0000000000400dcf in procB() ()
#7 0x0000000000400e26 in procA() ()
#8 0x0000000000400e88 in procNH() ()
#9 0x0000000000400ea8 in bar_one() ()
#10 0x0000000000400eb3 in foo_one() ()
#11 0x0000000000400ec6 in thread_one(void*) ()
#12 0x00007f0a1d444b50 in start_thread ()
#13 0x00007f0a1d18e95d in clone ()
at ../sysdeps/unix/sysv/linux/x86_64/clone.S:112
#14 0x0000000000000000 in ?? ()
```

[25] https://www.dumpanalysis.org/blog/index.php/2012/07/20/crash-dump-analysis-patterns-part-77-mac-os-x/

[26] https://www.dumpanalysis.org/blog/index.php/2008/10/21/crash-dump-analysis-patterns-part-77/

Paratext

This pattern is Linux variant of **Paratext** pattern for Mac OS X[27]. Because of debugger tool limitations, additional software logs and the output of other tools may help in memory dump analysis. Typical examples of such pattern usage can be the list of modules with version and path info, application crash-specific information from instrumentation tools such as *Valgrind*, memory region names with attribution and boundaries, and CPU usage information. For example, *top* and *pmap* commands output:

```
top - 22:32:00 up 23 min,  1 user,  load average: 0.95, 0.38, 0.17
Tasks:  64 total,   1 running,  63 sleeping,   0 stopped,   0 zombie
%Cpu(s):100.0 us,  0.0 sy,  0.0 ni,  0.0 id,  0.0 wa,  0.0 hi,  0.0 si,  0.0 st
KiB Mem:    505464 total,   174140 used,   331324 free,    11872 buffers
KiB Swap:   223228 total,        0 used,   223228 free,   122696 cached

  PID USER      PR  NI  VIRT  RES  SHR S  %CPU %MEM    TIME+  COMMAND
 3712 training  20   0 42040    4    0 S  99.9  0.0   2:06.33 App3
    1 root      20   0 10648  836  704 S   0.0  0.2   0:01.34 init
    2 root      20   0     0    0    0 S   0.0  0.0   0:00.00 kthreadd
    3 root      20   0     0    0    0 S   0.0  0.0   0:00.03 ksoftirqd/0
    5 root      20   0     0    0    0 S   0.0  0.0   0:00.00 kworker/u:0
    6 root      rt   0     0    0    0 S   0.0  0.0   0:00.00 migration/0
    7 root      rt   0     0    0    0 S   0.0  0.0   0:00.01 watchdog/0
    8 root       0 -20     0    0    0 S   0.0  0.0   0:00.00 cpuset
    9 root       0 -20     0    0    0 S   0.0  0.0   0:00.00 khelper
   10 root      20   0     0    0    0 S   0.0  0.0   0:00.00 kdevtmpfs
   11 root       0 -20     0    0    0 S   0.0  0.0   0:00.00 netns
   12 root      20   0     0    0    0 S   0.0  0.0   0:00.01 sync_supers
   13 root      20   0     0    0    0 S   0.0  0.0   0:00.00 bdi-default
   14 root       0 -20     0    0    0 S   0.0  0.0   0:00.00 kintegrityd
   15 root       0 -20     0    0    0 S   0.0  0.0   0:00.00 kblockd
   16 root      20   0     0    0    0 S   0.0  0.0   0:00.00 khungtaskd
   17 root      20   0     0    0    0 S   0.0  0.0   0:00.00 kswapd0
   18 root      25   5     0    0    0 S   0.0  0.0   0:00.00 ksmd
```

```
14039: ./App1.shared
0000000000400000 4K r-x-- /home/training/ALCDA/App1/App1.shared
0000000000600000 4K rw--- /home/training/ALCDA/App1/App1.shared
0000000000611000 132K rw--- [ anon ]
00007fe8999a6000 4K ----- [ anon ]
00007fe8999a7000 8192K rw--- [ anon ]
00007fe89a1a7000 4K ----- [ anon ]
00007fe89a1a8000 8192K rw--- [ anon ]
00007fe89a9a8000 4K ----- [ anon ]
00007fe89a9a9000 8192K rw--- [ anon ]
00007fe89b1a9000 4K ----- [ anon ]
00007fe89b1aa000 8192K rw--- [ anon ]
00007fe89b9aa000 4K ----- [ anon ]
00007fe89b9ab000 8192K rw--- [ anon ]
00007fe89c1ab000 1540K r-x-- /lib/x86_64-linux-gnu/libc-2.13.so
00007fe89c32c000 2048K ----- /lib/x86_64-linux-gnu/libc-2.13.so
00007fe89c52c000 16K r---- /lib/x86_64-linux-gnu/libc-2.13.so
00007fe89c530000 4K rw--- /lib/x86_64-linux-gnu/libc-2.13.so
00007fe89c531000 20K rw--- [ anon ]
00007fe89c536000 92K r-x-- /lib/x86_64-linux-gnu/libpthread-2.13.so
00007fe89c54d000 2044K ----- /lib/x86_64-linux-gnu/libpthread-2.13.so
00007fe89c74c000 4K r---- /lib/x86_64-linux-gnu/libpthread-2.13.so
00007fe89c74d000 4K rw--- /lib/x86_64-linux-gnu/libpthread-2.13.so
00007fe89c74e000 16K rw--- [ anon ]
00007fe89c752000 128K r-x-- /lib/x86_64-linux-gnu/ld-2.13.so
00007fe89c966000 12K rw--- [ anon ]
00007fe89c96f000 8K rw--- [ anon ]
00007fe89c971000 4K r---- /lib/x86_64-linux-gnu/ld-2.13.so
00007fe89c972000 4K rw--- /lib/x86_64-linux-gnu/ld-2.13.so
00007fe89c973000 4K rw--- [ anon ]
00007ffd458c1000 132K rw--- [ stack ]
00007ffd459e9000 4K r-x-- [ anon ]
```

---

[27] https://www.dumpanalysis.org/blog/index.php/2012/07/28/crash-dump-analysis-patterns-part-180-mac-os-x/

```
ffffffffff600000 4K r-x-- [ anon ]
total 47208K
```

Active Thread

Here we publish a Linux variant of **Active Thread** pattern that was previously introduced for Mac OS X[28] and Windows[29]. Basically, it is a thread that is not waiting, sleeping, or suspended (most threads are). However, from a memory dump, it is not possible to find out whether it was **Spiking Thread** at the dump generation time (unless we have a set of memory snapshots and in each one, we have the same or similar backtrace), and we don't have any **Paratext** with CPU consumption stats for threads. For example, in one core dump, we have this thread:

```
(gdb) info threads
Id Target Id Frame
6 Thread 0x7f560d467700 (LWP 3483) 0x00000000004324a9 in clone ()
5 Thread 0x7f560c465700 (LWP 3485) 0x000000000042fe31 in nanosleep ()
4 Thread 0x7f560bc64700 (LWP 3486) 0x000000000042fe31 in nanosleep ()
3 Thread 0x7f560b463700 (LWP 3487) 0x000000000042fe31 in nanosleep ()
2 Thread 0x18b9860 (LWP 3482) 0x000000000042fe31 in nanosleep ()
1 Thread 0x7f560cc66700 (LWP 3484) 0x000000000042fe31 in nanosleep ()
```

Thread #6 is not waiting so we inspect its back trace:

```
(gdb) thread 6
[Switching to thread 6 (Thread 0x7f560d467700 (LWP 3483))]
#0 0x00000000004324a9 in clone ()

(gdb) bt
#0 0x00000000004324a9 in clone ()
#1 0x0000000000401560 in ?? () at pthread_create.c:217
#2 0x00007f560d467700 in ?? ()
#3 0x0000000000000000 in ?? ()

(gdb) x/i 0x4324a9
=> 0x4324a9 : test %rax,%rax
```

Perhaps the core dump was saved at the thread creation time.

[28] https://www.dumpanalysis.org/blog/index.php/2012/11/17/crash-dump-analysis-patterns-part-187-mac-os-x/

[29] https://www.dumpanalysis.org/blog/index.php/2015/10/31/crash-dump-analysis-patterns-part-232/

Lateral Damage

This pattern is a Linux variant of **Lateral Damage** pattern previously described for the Windows[30] platform. It also covers memory dumps where some usual commands may not work, and we have to find a workaround to simulate their output, for example, by using other commands:

```
(gdb) info threads
Cannot find new threads: generic error

(gdb) thread apply all bt
Cannot find new threads: generic error

(gdb) thread 2
[Switching to thread 2 (LWP 12567)]
#0 0x000000000042ff51 in nanosleep ()

(gdb) thread 3
[Switching to thread 3 (LWP 12566)]
#0 0x000000000041482e in _int_malloc ()
```

[30] https://www.dumpanalysis.org/blog/index.php/2006/11/03/crash-dump-analysis-patterns-part-4/

Critical Region

We first introduced **Critical Region** pattern in Accelerated Mac OS X Core Dump Analysis[31] training but didn't submit the pattern itself to the catalog at that time.

A critical region is usually a region of code protected by synchronization objects such as critical sections and mutexes. However, **Critical Region** analysis pattern is about identifying code regions "sandwiched" between contending function calls (which may or may not involve synchronization objects and corresponding synchronization calls such as identified in Contention[32] patterns), and then identifying any possibly shared data referenced by such code regions:

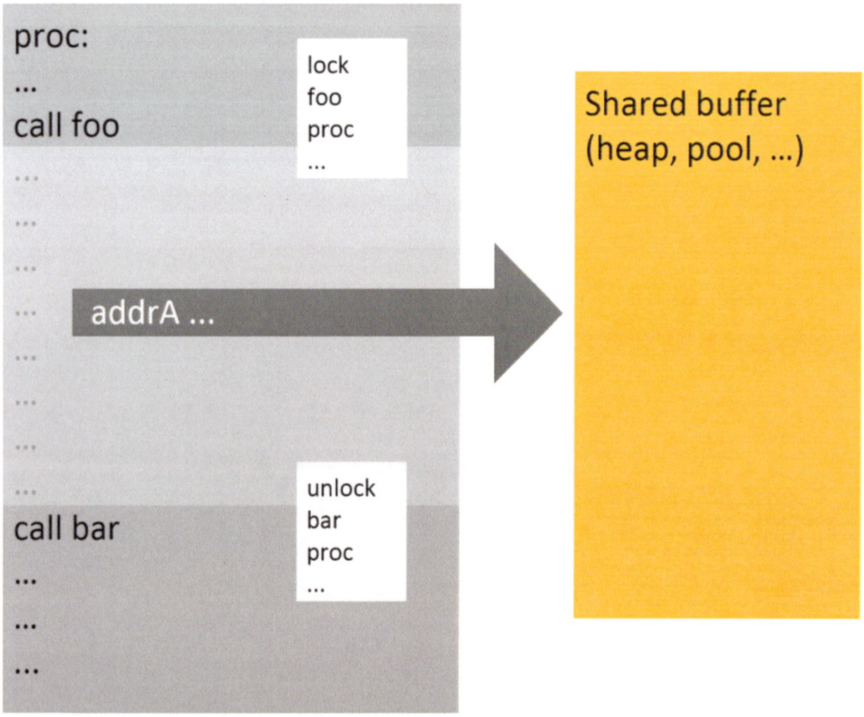


```
(gdb) thread apply all bt

Thread 6 (Thread 0x7f2665377700 (LWP 17000)):
#0  0x00000000004151a1 in _int_malloc ()
#1  0x0000000000416cf8 in malloc ()
#2  0x00000000004005a4 in proc ()
#3  0x0000000000400604 in bar_two ()
#4  0x0000000000400614 in foo_two ()
#5  0x000000000040062c in thread_two ()
#6  0x00000000004016c0 in start_thread (arg=<optimized out>)
at pthread_create.c:304
#7  0x0000000000432589 in clone ()
#8  0x0000000000000000 in ?? ()
```

---

[31] https://www.patterndiagnostics.com/accelerated-macosx-core-dump-analysis-book

[32] https://www.dumpanalysis.org/blog/index.php/2010/09/21/contention-patterns/

```
Thread 5 (Thread 0x7f2664b76700 (LWP 17001)):
#0  __lll_unlock_wake_private ()
at ../nptl/sysdeps/unix/sysv/linux/x86_64/lowlevellock.S:343
#1  0x000000000041886d in _L_unlock_9670 ()
#2  0x0000000000416d22 in malloc ()
#3  0x00000000004005a4 in proc ()
#4  0x0000000000400641 in bar_three ()
#5  0x0000000000400651 in foo_three ()
#6  0x0000000000400669 in thread_three ()
#7  0x00000000004016c0 in start_thread (arg=<optimized out>)
at pthread_create.c:304
#8  0x0000000000432589 in clone ()
#9  0x0000000000000000 in ?? ()

Thread 4 (Thread 0x7f2665b78700 (LWP 16999)):
#0  __lll_lock_wait_private ()
at ../nptl/sysdeps/unix/sysv/linux/x86_64/lowlevellock.S:97
#1  0x0000000000418836 in _L_lock_9558 ()
#2  0x0000000000416c1c in free ()
#3  0x0000000000400586 in proc ()
#4  0x00000000004005c7 in bar_one ()
#5  0x00000000004005d7 in foo_one ()
#6  0x00000000004005ef in thread_one ()
#7  0x00000000004016c0 in start_thread (arg=<optimized out>)
at pthread_create.c:304
#8  0x0000000000432589 in clone ()
#9  0x0000000000000000 in ?? ()

Thread 3 (Thread 0x1ab1860 (LWP 16998)):
#0  0x000000000042fed1 in nanosleep ()
#1  0x000000000042fda0 in sleep ()
#2  0x000000000040078a in main ()

Thread 2 (Thread 0x7f2663b74700 (LWP 17003)):
#0  __lll_lock_wait_private ()
at ../nptl/sysdeps/unix/sysv/linux/x86_64/lowlevellock.S:97
#1  0x0000000000418836 in _L_lock_9558 ()
#2  0x0000000000416c1c in free ()
#3  0x0000000000400586 in proc ()
#4  0x00000000004006bb in bar_five ()
#5  0x00000000004006cb in foo_five ()
#6  0x00000000004006e3 in thread_five ()
#7  0x00000000004016c0 in start_thread (arg=<optimized out>)
at pthread_create.c:304
#8  0x0000000000432589 in clone ()
#9  0x0000000000000000 in ?? ()

Thread 1 (Thread 0x7f2664375700 (LWP 17002)):
#0  0x000000000043ef65 in raise ()
#1  0x0000000000409fc0 in abort ()
#2  0x000000000040bf5b in __libc_message ()
#3  0x0000000000412042 in malloc_printerr ()
#4  0x0000000000416c27 in free ()
#5  0x0000000000400586 in proc ()
#6  0x000000000040067e in bar_four ()
#7  0x000000000040068e in foo_four ()
#8  0x00000000004006a6 in thread_four ()
#9  0x00000000004016c0 in start_thread (arg=<optimized out>)
at pthread_create.c:304
```

```
#10 0x0000000000432589 in clone ()
#11 0x0000000000000000 in ?? ()
```

From threads #4 and #5, we can identify one such a region with a shared buffer 0x6b8fc0, which may further point to heap entries.

```
(gdb) disassemble proc
Dump of assembler code for function proc:
0x00000000004004f0 <+0>: push   %rbp
0x00000000004004f1 <+1>: mov    %rsp,%rbp
0x00000000004004f4 <+4>: push   %rbx
0x00000000004004f5 <+5>: sub    $0x18,%rsp
0x00000000004004f9 <+9>: callq  0x40ac70 <rand>
0x00000000004004fe <+14>: mov    %eax,%ecx
0x0000000000400500 <+16>: mov    $0x68db8bad,%edx
0x0000000000400505 <+21>: mov    %ecx,%eax
0x0000000000400507 <+23>: imul   %edx
0x0000000000400509 <+25>: sar    $0xc,%edx
0x000000000040050c <+28>: mov    %ecx,%eax
0x000000000040050e <+30>: sar    $0x1f,%eax
0x0000000000400511 <+33>: mov    %edx,%ebx
0x0000000000400513 <+35>: sub    %eax,%ebx
0x0000000000400515 <+37>: mov    %ebx,%eax
0x0000000000400517 <+39>: mov    %eax,-0x14(%rbp)
0x000000000040051a <+42>: mov    -0x14(%rbp),%eax
0x000000000040051d <+45>: imul   $0x2710,%eax,%eax
0x0000000000400523 <+51>: mov    %ecx,%edx
0x0000000000400525 <+53>: sub    %eax,%edx
0x0000000000400527 <+55>: mov    %edx,%eax
0x0000000000400529 <+57>: mov    %eax,-0x14(%rbp)
0x000000000040052c <+60>: callq  0x40ac70 <rand>
0x0000000000400531 <+65>: mov    %eax,%ecx
0x0000000000400533 <+67>: mov    $0x68db8bad,%edx
0x0000000000400538 <+72>: mov    %ecx,%eax
0x000000000040053a <+74>: imul   %edx
0x000000000040053c <+76>: sar    $0xc,%edx
0x000000000040053f <+79>: mov    %ecx,%eax
0x0000000000400541 <+81>: sar    $0x1f,%eax
0x0000000000400544 <+84>: mov    %edx,%ebx
0x0000000000400546 <+86>: sub    %eax,%ebx
0x0000000000400548 <+88>: mov    %ebx,%eax
0x000000000040054a <+90>: mov    %eax,-0x18(%rbp)
0x000000000040054d <+93>: mov    -0x18(%rbp),%eax
0x0000000000400550 <+96>: imul   $0x2710,%eax,%eax
0x0000000000400556 <+102>: mov    %ecx,%edx
0x0000000000400558 <+104>: sub    %eax,%edx
0x000000000040055a <+106>: mov    %edx,%eax
0x000000000040055c <+108>: mov    %eax,-0x18(%rbp)
0x000000000040055f <+111>: mov    -0x14(%rbp),%eax
0x0000000000400562 <+114>: cltq
0x0000000000400564 <+116>: mov    0x6b8fc0(,%rax,8),%rax
0x000000000040056c <+124>: test   %rax,%rax
0x000000000040056f <+127>: je     0x400597 <proc+167>
0x0000000000400571 <+129>: mov    -0x14(%rbp),%eax
0x0000000000400574 <+132>: cltq
0x0000000000400576 <+134>: mov    0x6b8fc0(,%rax,8),%rax
0x000000000040057e <+142>: mov    %rax,%rdi
```

```
0x0000000000400581 <+145>: callq  0x416bc0 <free>
0x0000000000400586 <+150>: mov    -0x14(%rbp),%eax
0x0000000000400589 <+153>: cltq
0x000000000040058b <+155>: movq   $0x0,0x6b8fc0(,%rax,8)
0x0000000000400597 <+167>: mov    -0x18(%rbp),%eax
0x000000000040059a <+170>: cltq
0x000000000040059c <+172>: mov    %rax,%rdi
0x000000000040059f <+175>: callq  0x416c90 <malloc>
0x00000000004005a4 <+180>: mov    %rax,%rdx
0x00000000004005a7 <+183>: mov    -0x14(%rbp),%eax
0x00000000004005aa <+186>: cltq
0x00000000004005ac <+188>: mov    %rdx,0x6b8fc0(,%rax,8)
0x00000000004005b4 <+196>: jmpq   0x4004f9 <proc+9>
End of assembler dump.
```

www.ingramcontent.com/pod-product-compliance
Lightning Source LLC
LaVergne TN
LVRC080246220926
848482LV00042B/341